# BARRON'S

# HOW TO PREPARE FOR THE

# GRE

# GRADUATE RECORD EXAMINATION

# 14TH EDITION

**Sharon Weiner Green**
Former Instructor of English

**Ira K. Wolf, Ph.D.**
President, PowerPrep, Inc.
Former Professor of Mathematics
Former Director of University Teacher Preparation Program

## BARRON'S

*All inquiries should be addressed to:*
Barron's Educational Series, Inc.
250 Wireless Boulevard
Hauppauge, New York 11788
**http://www.barronseduc.com**

*Library of Congress Catalog Card Number 00-036085*

International Standard Book Number 0-7641-1592-8
International Standard Book Number 0-7641-7471-1
(with CD-ROM)

**Library of Congress Cataloging-in-Publication Data**
Green, Sharon.
   How to prepare for the GRE, graduate record examination / Sharon Weiner Green, Ira Wolf.—14th ed.
      p.    cm.
   Rev. ed. of: How to prepare for the GRE, graduate record examination / Samuel C. Brownstein, Mitchel Weiner, Sharon Weiner Green. 1999.
   ISBN 0-7641-1592-8
   1. Graduate Record Examination—Study guides.
I. Wolf, Ira K.   II. Weiner, Mitchel, 1907–
III. Brownstein, Samuel C., 1909– How to prepare for the GRE, graduate record examination.   IV. Title.
LB2367.4 .B76 2000
378.1'662—dc21                          00-036085

# Contents

# Acknowledgments

The authors gratefully acknowledge the following for permission to reprint reading passages.

Page 27: Wilcomb E. Washburn, *The Indian in America*. Copyright © 1975. Reprinted with permission of HarperCollins Publishers, Inc.

Page 99: Ladislas Segy, "African Sculpture Speaks," Dover Publications, New York 1958. By permission of Helena Segy.

Page 101: From *The Uses of Enchantment*, by Bruno Bettelheim. Copyright © 1975, 1976 by Bruno Bettelheim. Reprinted by permission of Alfred A. Knopf, Inc.

Page 102: Excerpt from *Geoffrey Chaucer* by John Livingston Lowes. Copyright © 1934, renewed 1955, by John Wilbur Lowes. With permission of Houghton Mifflin Co.

Page 106: From *Black Americans in the Roosevelt Era* by John B. Kirby. Copyright 1980, University of Tennessee Press.

Page 112: From *The Madwoman in the Attic* by Sandra M. Gilbert and Susan Gubar, © 1979 by Yale University Press, publisher.

Page 467: Elaine Showalter, *A Literature of Their Own: British Women Novelists from Brontë to Lessing*. Copyright © 1977 by Princeton University Press. Excerpt, pp. 10–12 reprinted with permission of Princeton University Press.

Page 494: From "W.E.B. Du Bois: Protagonist of the Afro-American Protest" by Elliot Rudwick, in *Black Leaders of the Twentieth Century*, edited by John Hope Franklin and August Meier. Copyright 1982, University of Illinois Press.

Page 548: From *Literary Women: The Great Writers* by Ellen Moers. Copyright © 1976, 1977 by Ellen Moers. Used by permission of Doubleday, a division of Bantam Doubleday Dell Publishing Group Inc.

Page 550: From *Eyes on the Prize: Civil Rights Years*, edited by Clayborne Carson et al. Copyright 1987 by Penguin Books. Blackside, Inc. 1991, with permission.

Page 574: From *The English Novel: Form and Function* by Dorothy Van Ghent. Copyright 1953, Harper & Row Publishers, Inc. By permission of Harcourt Brace & Co.

Page 575: From *Black History and the Historical Profession, 1915–1980* by August Meier and Elliot Rudwick. Copyright 1986, University of Illinois Press.

# Preface

As prospective graduate students concerned with professional advancement, you know the importance of using good tools and drawing on solid research. In this Fourteenth Edition of *Barron's How to Prepare for the GRE*, we offer you both.

This revision contains the fruits of our close study of *all* recent GRE General Tests made public by the Graduate Record Examinations Board. We have scrutinized hundreds of actual GRE questions, traced dozens of GRE reading passages to their sources, analyzed subsets of questions by order of difficulty and question type. In the process, we have come up with the following features, which should make this Fourteenth Edition particularly helpful to you:

## Typical GRE Questions Analyzed

The Fourteenth Edition takes you step by step through dozens of verbal, mathematical, and analytical questions that simulate actual GRE questions, showing you how to solve them and how to avoid going wrong.

## Testing Tactics

The Fourteenth Edition provides you with dozens of proven, highlighted testing tactics that will help you attack the different types of questions on the GRE.

## High-Frequency Word List

The Fourteenth Edition continues to give you an up-to-date 333-word High-Frequency Word List—333 words from *abate* to *zealot* that have been shown by computer analysis to occur and recur on actual published GREs—plus Barron's 3,500-word Master Word List, *the* college-level vocabulary list for over 40 years.

## Comprehensive Mathematics Review

The Fourteenth Edition presents you with extensive mathematical review materials that provide a refresher course for students primarily involved in nonscientific disciplines.

## GRE-Modeled Tests

The Fourteenth Edition offers you a full-length Diagnostic Test geared to the current GRE, a diagnostic test that will enable you to pinpoint your areas of weakness right away and concentrate your review on subjects in which you need the most work, plus five additional Model Tests, all with answers completely explained, that in format, difficulty, and content echo today's GRE.

## Computer GRE Update

The Fourteenth Edition introduces you to the computer-based GRE—and, along with the accompanying CD-ROM (optional—see below), explains everything you need to know about the computer-adaptive GRE.

This Fourteenth Edition once more upgrades what has long been a standard text. It reflects the contributions of numerous teachers, editors, and coaches, and the dedication of the staff at Barron's. We, the authors, are indebted to all these individuals for their ongoing efforts to make this book America's outstanding GRE study guide.

**NOTE:** Because the paper-and-pencil version of the GRE has been phased out, begin with your overview of the GRE with the testing tips and tactics presented in Chapters 1 & 2 of this edition, which will specifically prepare you for the computer-adaptive test you will face. Then proceed to study the review chapters on the various question types.

## CD-ROM

Two versions of this book, *How to Prepare for the GRE Test,* 14th edition, are available: one with a practice CD-ROM attached to the inside back cover, and one (at a somewhat lower price) without the CD-ROM. If you have purchased the latter version, please disregard all references to the CD-ROM.

## TIMETABLE FOR A TYPICAL COMPUTER-BASED GRADUATE RECORD EXAMINATION

*Total Testing Time: 3 to 4 hours*

| Section | Time Allowed | Description |
|---------|--------------|-------------|
| | variable | *Tutorial* |
| 1 | 30 minutes | *Verbal Ability*<br>6 sentence completion questions<br>7 analogy questions<br>8 reading comprehension questions<br>9 antonym questions |
| 2 | 45 minutes | *Quantitative Ability*<br>14 quantitative comparison questions<br>10 discrete quantitative (standard multiple-choice) questions<br>4 data interpretation questions (tables/graphs) |
| | | **10-minute break** |
| 3 | 75 minutes | *Analytical Ability*<br>Replaced by Analytical Writing Ability section |
| 4 | 30, 45, or 75 minutes | *Verbal, Quantitative, or Analytical Ability* |

**NOTE:** On the actual GRE, these sections may appear in any order.

## *FLASH!* GRE GENERAL TEST TO CHANGE IN OCTOBER 2002

As of October 1, 2002, the GRE General Test will consist of 3 sections: verbal, quantitative, and analytical writing. The analytical writing section is brand new. It replaces the current multiple-choice analytical ability section that is described in Chapters 9 and 10. If you plan to take the GRE General Test after October 1, you need to start preparing for the *new* analytical writing test.

What sort of test is this new analytical writing test? First and foremost, it is *not* a multiple-choice test. It is a *performance* test: you have to write 2 analytical essays in an hour and fifteen minutes. In one essay, your task is to give your viewpoint on a particular topic or issue; you have 45 minutes to present your thoughts. In the second essay, your task is to analyze an argument, pointing out its strengths and weaknesses; you have only 30 minutes to complete this task.

For more information on the new analytical writing section, turn to page 598. In addition, be sure to check out the detailed description of the test on the GRE's Website, *www.gre.com*.

# PART ONE

## Introduction/ Diagnostic Test

# 1 What You Need to Know About the GRE

- ■ **An Overview of the GRE General Test**
- ■ **Commonly Asked Questions About the GRE**
- ■ **GRE Test Format**
  **Verbal Ability**
  **Quantitative Ability**
  **Analytical Ability**

## An Overview of the Computer-Based GRE General Test

The GRE General Test is a multiple-choice examination designed to measure the verbal, quantitative, and analytical skills you have developed in the course of your academic career. High GRE scores strongly correlate with the probability of success in graduate school: the higher you score, the more likely you are to complete your graduate degree. For this reason, many graduate and professional schools require applicants to take the GRE General Test, a test now given only on computer. (They may also require you to take the new computer-based GRE Writing Test and/or a pencil-and-paper GRE Subject Test in your particular field. Subject Tests currently are available in 14 fields.)

The computer-based GRE General Test you take will have three, four, or five sections. There will always be

- a 30-question verbal section (30 minutes)
- a 28-question quantitative section (45 minutes)
- a 35-question analytical section (60 minutes)

In addition, there may be

- an unidentified experimental section, which would be a second verbal, quantitative, or analytical section
- an identified optional research section

The verbal section measures your ability to use words as tools in reasoning; you are tested not only on the extent of your vocabulary but on your ability to discern the relationships that exist both within written passages and among individual groups of words. The quantitative section measures your ability to use and reason with numbers or mathematical concepts; you are tested not on advanced mathematical theory but on general concepts expected to be part of everyone's academic background. The analytical section measures your ability to make rational assessments about unfamiliar, fictitious relationships and to think through arguments logically.

There are four very important points you should be aware of:

1. In each section, before you can move from one question to the next, you *must* answer the question currently on screen.

2. Once you have clicked on an answer and confirmed your choice, you *cannot* go back to that question and change your answer choice.

3. Not every question is worth the same number of points; harder questions are worth more than easy ones.

4. The GRE General Test does *not* penalize you for incorrect answers. Therefore, you should leave no question unanswered. When you don't know an answer, try to make an educated guess; if you can't, make a wild guess, and move on.

Keep these points in mind as you learn more about what's on the computer-based test, and, in the next chapter, about the tactics and strategies that will help you maximize your test score.

3

# Commonly Asked Questions About the Computer-Based GRE

## How Does the GRE Differ from Other Tests?

Most tests college students take are straightforward achievement tests. They attempt to find out how much you have learned, usually in a specific subject, and how well you can apply that information. Without emphasizing memorized data, the GRE General Test attempts to measure verbal, quantitative, and analytical reasoning skills that you have acquired over the years both in and out of school.

Although the GRE General Test is claimed to measure skills that you have developed over a long period, even a brief period of intensive study can make a great difference in your eventual GRE scores. By thoroughly familiarizing yourself with the process of computer-based testing, the GRE test format, and the various question types, you can enhance your chances of doing well on the test and of being accepted by the graduate school of your choice.

## How Can I Learn to Handle the Mechanics of Taking a Computer-Based Test?

By using the CD-ROM that may have accompanied this book, you will become familiar with everything you need to know. In addition, at the test site before you get to the actual computer-based GRE, you have to work through four tutorials that train you in the mechanics of taking this particular test. They are

- How to Use a Mouse
- How to Select an Answer
- How to Use the Testing Tools
- How to Scroll

You can't skip these tutorials; they're mandatory, even for computer majors. They're also important—every computer program has its idiosyncrasies, and you need to familiarize yourself with how to handle this particular computer setup.

Plan to take your time on these tutorials, and don't worry about how much time you're taking. The 20 to 30 minutes you spend working through the tutorials *before* you begin testing don't count against your time for taking the test. You can even use this free time to organize your scratch paper before you begin the actual timed test. (More on setting up your scratch paper later.)

## What Is It Like to Take a Computer-Based GRE?

You sit in a carrel in a computer lab or testing center, facing a computer screen. You may be alone in the room, or other test-takers may be taking tests in nearby carrels. With your mouse, you click on an icon to start your test. A question appears on screen. You answer it, clicking on the oval next to your answer choice. Satisfied with your answer, you click on a box marked Confirm, to indicate you have no second thoughts about your choice. Then, ready to move on, you click on the box marked Next. A new question appears on screen, and you go through the process again.

This is what it is like to take a computerized GRE. At the end of the first section, you are given a one-minute break. After finishing the second section, you have a ten-minute break. The third section is followed by another one-minute break, and finally a fourth section. (This is the most likely scenario; it's possible you may be instructed to answer a fifth, research section. It's also possible you may face only three sections on your test.)

## How Does Taking a Computer-Based Test Differ from Taking a Pencil-and-Paper Test?

On a pencil-and-paper standardized test, within any given section of your test booklet you are free to skip from question to question and to answer questions in any order you choose. If you do better on antonyms than on reading comprehension questions, for example, you can temporarily skip the time-consuming reading passages and go straight to the antonyms. Likewise, if you have second thoughts about a particular answer choice, on a pencil-and-paper test you can go back to the question, erase your original pencil mark, and select a different answer choice. You are also free to write in your test booklet, crossing out incorrect answer choices, underlining key words, and highlighting questions you need to reconsider.

On a computer-based test (CBT), there is no test booklet. Your test questions appear, one at a time, on your computer screen. You must answer the question currently on screen and confirm that you are sure of your answer choice before you can move on to the next question. Once you have confirmed your answer choice and moved on, you cannot go back and change it.

In addition, on the CBT, questions are not arranged in groups according to question type: two analogy questions may follow two antonyms; they may in turn be followed by a single sentence completion. You cannot predict what type of question will come up next.

## Why Do Some People Call the Computer-Based General Test a CAT?

CAT stands for Computer-Adaptive Test. What does this mean?

When you take a pencil-and-paper test, the questions in the test booklet you receive are basically the same as the questions printed in every other booklet distributed to test-takers on that day. When you take a computer-based GRE General Test, however, the questions you face on screen are likely to differ markedly from those that come up on the screens of the test-takers in the carrels next to you.

Why will your test be different from someone else's test? Because the CBT GRE is a computer-adaptive test. The test adapts to your skill level: it is customized.

How does this work? The computer program begins by assuming you are the "average" GRE candidate, an imaginary figure whose score would place him or her precisely in the middle of the entire test-taking population. The computer program contains a pool of some 1,000 questions organized by content, question type, and level of difficulty. From this pool the computer selects a math question of medium difficulty, a question the average GRE candidate (someone who would wind up in the 50th percentile of test-takers with a Quantitative score of 550) would be likely to get correct. If you answer this question correctly, the computer revises its estimate of your eventual score upward and proceeds to give you a slightly harder question, one that a student scoring 600 should get correct. However, if you answer that question incorrectly, the computer again revises its estimate of your eventual score—*downward*, and you are presented with an easier question, one that a student scoring 500 might get correct. Thus, as you answer each question, the computer adapts your test, tailoring it to reflect your previous performance. In the process, it fine-tunes its estimate of your skill level, gradually zeroing in on your eventual score.

## Can I Tell How Well I'm Doing on the Test from the Questions the Computer Assigns Me?

Don't even try; it never pays to try to second-guess the computer. There's no point in wasting time and energy wondering whether it's feeding you harder questions or easier ones. Let the computer keep track of how well you're doing—you concentrate on answering questions and pacing yourself.

## Should I Guess?

Yes, you must! You are not going to know the correct answer to every question on the GRE. That's a given. But you can't just skip a question. In order to move on to the next question, you first *must* answer the question currently on screen, even if you haven't a clue as to what the correct answer might be. So if the question on screen has you stumped, eliminate any obviously incorrect answer choices, and then guess and don't worry whether you've guessed right or wrong. Your job is to get to the next question you *can* answer. Just remember to use the process of elimination to improve your guessing odds.

## How Can I Use the Process of Elimination on a Computer-Based GRE?

Even though the current CBT GRE makes no provision for you to cross out incorrect answer choices on screen, you still can eliminate answers you *know* are wrong before guessing which of the remaining answer choices is correct. This is where your scratch paper comes in. During the untimed computer tutorial session, take a few minutes to write out a rough, scratch-paper answer sheet for each section, setting up four columns as shown below. Use this answer sheet as your guessing guide. Before you guess,

| | | | |
|---|---|---|---|
| 1 A B C D E | 1 A B C D E | 1 A B C D E | 1 A B C D E |
| 2 A B C D E | 2 A B C D E | 2 A B C D E | 2 A B C D E |
| 3 A B C D E | 3 A B C D E | 3 A B C D E | 3 A B C D E |
| 4 A B C D E | 4 A B C D E | 4 A B C D E | 4 A B C D E |
| 5 A B C D E | 5 A B C D E | 5 A B C D E | 5 A B C D E |
| 6 A B C D E | 6 A B C D E | 6 A B C D E | 6 A B C D E |
| 7 A B C D E | 7 A B C D E | 7 A B C D E | 7 A B C D E |
| 8 A B C D E | 8 A B C D E | 8 A B C D E | 8 A B C D E |
| 9 A B C D E | 9 A B C D E | 9 A B C D E | 9 A B C D E |
| 10 A B C D E | 10 A B C D E | 10 A B C D E | 10 A B C D E |
| 11 A B C D E | 11 A B C D E | 11 A B C D E | 11 A B C D E |
| 12 A B C D E | 12 A B C D E | 12 A B C D E | 12 A B C D E |
| 13 A B C D E | 13 A B C D E | 13 A B C D E | 13 A B C D E |
| 14 A B C D E | 14 A B C D E | 14 A B C D E | 14 A B C D E |
| 15 A B C D E | 15 A B C D E | 15 A B C D E | 15 A B C D E |
| 16 A B C D E | 16 A B C D E | 16 A B C D E | 16 A B C D E |
| 17 A B C D E | 17 A B C D E | 17 A B C D E | 17 A B C D E |
| 18 A B C D E | 18 A B C D E | 18 A B C D E | 18 A B C D E |
| 19 A B C D E | 19 A B C D E | 19 A B C D E | 19 A B C D E |
| 20 A B C D E | 20 A B C D E | 20 A B C D E | 20 A B C D E |
| 21 A B C D E | 21 A B C D E | 21 A B C D E | 21 A B C D E |
| 22 A B C D E | 22 A B C D E | 22 A B C D E | 22 A B C D E |
| 23 A B C D E | 23 A B C D E | 23 A B C D E | 23 A B C D E |
| 24 A B C D E | 24 A B C D E | 24 A B C D E | 24 A B C D E |
| 25 A B C D E | 25 A B C D E | 25 A B C D E | 25 A B C D E |
| 26 A B C D E | 26 A B C D E | 26 A B C D E | 26 A B C D E |
| 27 A B C D E | 27 A B C D E | 27 A B C D E | 27 A B C D E |
| 28 A B C D E | 28 A B C D E | 28 A B C D E | 28 A B C D E |
| 29 A B C D E | 29 A B C D E | 29 A B C D E | 29 A B C D E |
| 30 A B C D E | 30 A B C D E | 30 A B C D E | 30 A B C D E |
| 31 A B C D E | 31 A B C D E | 31 A B C D E | 31 A B C D E |
| 32 A B C D E | 32 A B C D E | 32 A B C D E | 32 A B C D E |
| 33 A B C D E | 33 A B C D E | 33 A B C D E | 33 A B C D E |
| 34 A B C D E | 34 A B C D E | 34 A B C D E | 34 A B C D E |
| 35 A B C D E | 35 A B C D E | 35 A B C D E | 35 A B C D E |

first cross out any choices on your answer sheet that you are *sure* are wrong. Then choose between the answer choices that are left. You'll increase your chances of coming up with the right answer by making this sort of "educated" guess.

*Make use of your scratch paper throughout the test. In the verbal section, jot down key words or phrases from the reading passages. On the mathematics questions, use your scratch paper to draw diagrams and, of course, to do all of your calculations. On analytical reasoning questions, use your scratch paper to draw diagrams or charts and to represent the given statements in symbolic form.*

## How Can I Determine the Unidentified Experimental Section?

You can't. Do not waste time in the exam room trying to identify the experimental section. If you are presented with four sections, do your best on all four. Some claim that most often the last section is the experimental section. Others claim that the section with unusual questions is the one that does not count. Ignore the claims: you have no sure way to tell. If you encounter a series of questions that seem strange to you, do your best. Either these are experimental and will not count, in which case you have no reason to worry about them, or they will count, in which case they probably will seem just as strange and troublesome to your fellow examinees.

## When and Where Can I Take the Computer-Based GRE?

You can take the computer-based GRE General Test almost any Monday through Saturday all year round. (Testing centers are closed on Christmas and New Year's Day and other major federal holidays.) Because appointments are scheduled on a first-come, first-served basis, you should be sure to register early to get the date you want, especially if that date falls in the highly popular November through January testing period.

The computer-based GRE is administered at a variety of sites: Sylvan Technology Centers, Educational Testing Service (ETS) field offices, university testing centers, and other academic institutions. Test centers are located in all 50 states, in American Samoa, Guam, Puerto Rico, the U.S. Virgin Islands, and eight provinces of Canada. International test centers also exist: a list of them can be found on-line at *www.gre.org* or in the *GRE Registration and Information Bulletin*.

## How Can I Register to Take the GRE?

If you have a credit card or CBT authorization voucher, you can register for the GRE over the phone. This is by far the

fastest way. In the United States, American Samoa, Guam, the U.S. Virgin Islands, Puerto Rico, and Canada, contact the Sylvan Candidate Services Call Center at 1-800-GRE-CALL (1-800-473-2255). You can also register by calling your local test center directly. If you plan to take the GRE when abroad, contact the appropriate international Regional Registration Center, also listed on-line at *www.gre.org* as well as in the *Registration and Information Bulletin*.

You can also register by mail to take the GRE. Simply complete the Computer-Based Test Authorization Voucher request located in the center of the *Registration and Information Bulletin*. Then mail the completed form and a check or money order for the appropriate fee (currently $99; $125 for test locations outside the United States and U.S. territories) to Graduate Record Examinations, Educational Testing Service, P.O. Box 6020, Princeton, NJ 08541-6020. You will receive your authorization voucher in two to three weeks and can then call Sylvan Candidate Services to schedule your test date.

Your college counseling office should be able to provide you with a registration form. If a registration form is not available at your school, download one on-line at *www.gre.org* or request one by mail from Graduate Record Examinations, Educational Testing Service, CN 6000, Princeton, NJ 08541-6000.

## How and When Are GRE Scores Reported?

The General Test raw score, the number of correct answers, is converted to a score on a scale of 200 to 800. With no correct answers at all, a student would still have a score of 200. With one or two incorrectly answered questions, a student could still have a score of 800. You receive separate scores (from 200 to 800) on the verbal, quantitative, and analytical reasoning sections. Your score report will include both your scaled scores and your percentile rank indicating the percent of examinees scoring below your scaled scores on the General Test.

As soon as you have finished taking the test, the computer will calculate your three scaled scores (verbal, quantitative, and analytical reasoning) and display them to you on screen. You should receive your official report confirming these scores in the mail approximately six weeks after the test date.

*NOTE: Every question on the GRE is a multiple-choice question with five choices—except for the quantitative comparisons, which have four choices. In this book, the choices are always labeled A, B, C, D, and E, and these letters are used in the Answer Keys and the explanations. On an actual GRE, these letters never appear on the screen. Rather, each choice is preceded by a blank oval, and you will answer a question by clicking with the mouse on the oval in front of your choice.*

# GRE Test Format
# Verbal Ability

The verbal section consists of 30 questions. These fall into four types: antonyms, analogies, sentence completions, and reading comprehension questions. Your academic success will depend on your verbal abilities, especially your ability to understand scholarly prose and to work with specialized and technical vocabulary.

Here is how the 30-question verbal section generally breaks down:

- 8–10 antonym questions
- 6–8 analogy questions
- 5–7 sentence completion questions
- 6–10 reading comprehension questions (based on two to four passages)

Although the amount of time spent on each type of question varies from person to person, in general, antonyms take the least time, then analogies, then sentence completions, and, finally, reading comprehension questions.

## Antonym Questions

The antonym questions are the most straightforward vocabulary questions on the test. You are given a word and must choose, from the five choices that follow it, the best antonym (opposite). Some of these words may be totally unfamiliar to you.

A typical antonym question looks like this:

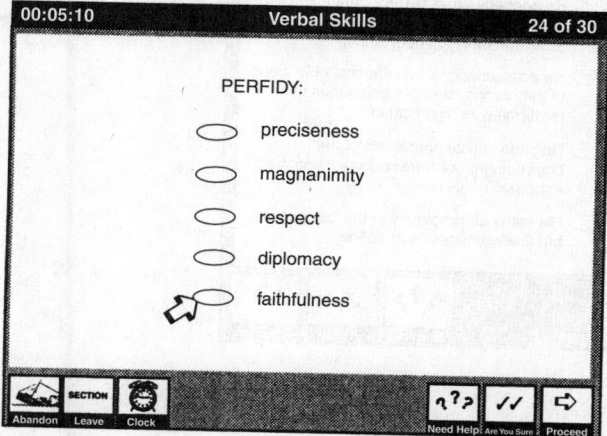

The word *perfidy* contains the root *fid*, meaning faith (as in *fidelity*). *Perfidy* means treachery, the betrayal of faith. Its opposite is *faithfulness*, the last choice given.

Even if you do not know the meaning of *perfidy*, if you know its root, you can guess that its antonym must be either a

word meaning faith or loyalty, or a word opposite in meaning to faith, such as treachery or disloyalty. The only answer containing such a word is the final answer choice.

See Chapter 4 for antonym testing tactics and practice exercises that will help you handle these questions, and Chapter 8 for vocabulary and word-part exercises that will help you throughout the verbal section.

## Analogy Questions

Like antonyms, analogy questions are vocabulary questions. They test your understanding of the relationships among words and ideas. You are given one pair of words and must choose another pair that is related in the same way. Many relationships are possible. The two terms in the pair can be synonyms; one term can be a cause, the other the effect; one can be a tool, the other the worker who uses the tool.

A typical analogy question looks like this:

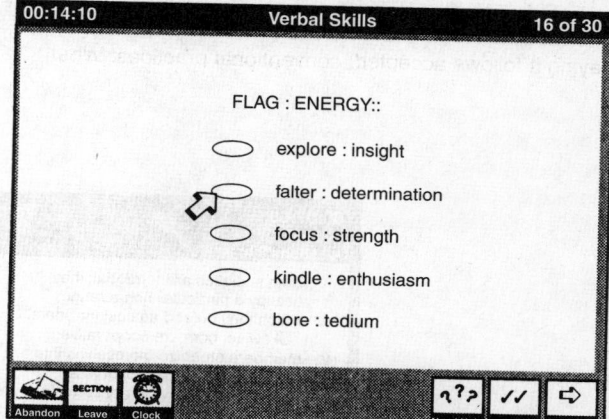

When energy flags, it weakens or grows less. Likewise when determination or resolve falters, it weakens or grows less. The correct answer is the second choice.

See Chapter 5 for analogy question tactics and practice exercises that will help you handle these questions.

## Sentence Completion Questions

In the sentence completion questions you are asked to choose the best way to complete a sentence from which one or two words have been omitted. These questions test a combination of reading comprehension skills and vocabulary. You must be able to recognize the logic, style, and tone of the sentence so that you will be able to choose the answer that makes sense in context. You must also be able to recognize differences in usage. The sentences cover a wide variety of topics from a number of academic fields. They do not, however, test specific academic knowledge. You may feel more comfortable if you are familiar with the topic the sentence is discussing, but you should be able to handle any of the sentences using your knowledge of the English language.

Here is a typical sentence completion question.

The medical researchers defend their new treatment by saying it follows accepted, conventional practices. What,

therefore, must have been the critics' accusation about the treatment? They must have claimed it was unconventional, violating accepted practices. The missing word is the third choice, *unorthodox*.

See Chapter 6 for sentence completion question tactics and practice exercises that will help you handle these questions.

# Reading Comprehension Questions

Reading comprehension questions test your ability to understand and interpret what you read. This is probably the most important ability you will need in graduate school and afterward.

Although the passages may encompass any subject matter, you do not need to know anything about the subject discussed in the passage in order to answer the questions on that passage. The purpose of the questions is to test your reading ability, not your knowledge of history, science, literature, or art.

Here is a typical reading comprehension passage and question.

The key lines here are the passage's final sentences.

The key lines here are the passage's final sentences. Does the author *acknowledge hypothetical objections* to the comparison? Definitely. Does the author conclude by *reaffirming the significance* of the termite/macaque comparison? Clearly he does: he concludes by quoting Wilson (whom he calls an eminent scholar), in doing so giving implicit support to Wilson's assertion that such oversimplified comparisons can provide the basis for an important general theory. The correct answer is the third choice.

See Chapter 7 for reading comprehension tactics and practice exercises that will help you handle these questions.

# Quantitative Ability

The quantitative section consists of 28 questions:

- 14 quantitative comparison questions
- 10 discrete quantitative questions (another name for standard multiple-choice questions)
- 4 data interpretation questions

In order to answer these questions, you need to know arithmetic, some very elementary algebra, and a little geometry. Most of this material you learned in elementary and middle school. You do not need to know any advanced mathematics. The questions are intended to determine if you have a basic knowledge of elementary mathematics, and if you have the ability to reason clearly.

If you haven't done any mathematics in a while, go through the math review in this book before attempting the Model Tests, and certainly before registering to take the GRE. If you feel that your math skills are still pretty good, you can try the Diagnostic Test first, and then read only those sections of the math review relating to those topics that gave you trouble.

## Quantitative Comparison Questions

Of the 28 mathematics questions on the GRE, half of them (14) are what is known as quantitative comparisons. It is very likely that you have not seen such a question since you were in high school preparing for the SAT I; if you didn't have to take the SAT I, it is possible that you have never even seen a quantitative comparison. Therefore, read these instructions *very* carefully.

In these questions there are two quantities, one in Column A and one in Column B, and it is your job to compare them. For these problems there are *only four possible answers*:

The quantity in Column A is greater;

The quantity in Column B is greater;

The two quantities are equal; and

The relationship cannot be determined from the information given.

In this book, these four answer choices will be referred to as A, B, C, and D, respectively. In some of the ques-

tions, information about the quantities being compared is centered above the columns. This information *must* be taken into consideration when comparing the two quantities.

In Chapter 13 you will learn several important strategies for handling quantitative comparisons. For now, let's look at three examples to make sure that you understand the concepts involved.

| Column A | Column B |
|---|---|
| $(3 + 4)^2$ | $3^2 + 4^2$ |

- Evaluate each column: $(3 + 4)^2 = 7^2 = $ **49**, whereas $3^2 + 4^2 = 9 + 16 = $ **25**.
- Since $49 > 25$, the quantity in Column A is greater. The answer is **A**.

| Column A | Column B |
|---|---|
| | $a + b = 16$ |
| The average (arithmetic mean) of $a$ and $b$ | 8 |

The quantity in Column A is the average of $a$ and $b$: $\frac{a + b}{2}$. Since we are told that $a + b = 16$, the quantity in Column A is $\frac{a + b}{2} = \frac{16}{2} = $ **8**. So, the quantities in Columns A and B are equal. The answer is **C**.

**NOTE:** We cannot determine the value of either $a$ or $b$; all we know is that their sum is 16. Perhaps $a = 10$ and $b = 6$, or $a = 0$ and $b = 16$, or $a = -4$ and $b = 20$. *It doesn't matter.* The average of 10 and 6 is 8; the average of 0 and 16 is 8; and the average of $-4$ and 20 is 8. Since $a + b$ is 16, the average of $a$ and $b$ is 8, *all the time, no matter what*. The answer, therefore, is **C**.

| Column A | Column B |
|---|---|
| $a^3$ | $a^2$ |

- If $a = 1$, $a^3 = 1$ and $a^2 = 1$. *In this case*, the quantities in the two columns are equal.
- This means that the answer to this problem *cannot* be A or B. Why?
- The answer can be A (or B) only if the quantity in Column A (or B) is greater *all the time*. But it isn't—not when $a = 1$.
- So, is the answer C? *Maybe*. But for the answer to be C, the quantities would have to be equal *all the time*. Are they?
- No. If $a = 2$, $a^3 = 8$ and $a^2 = 4$, and *in this case* the two quantities are *not equal*.
- The answer, therefore, is **D**.

# Discrete Quantitative Questions

Of the 28 mathematics questions on the GRE, 10 are standard multiple-choice questions, what the ETS calls discrete quantitative questions. The way to answer such a question is to do the necessary work, get the solution, and then look at the five choices to find your answer. In Chapter 12 we will discuss other techniques for answering these questions, but for now let's look at two examples.

> Edison High School has 840 students, and the ratio of the number of students taking Spanish to the number not taking Spanish is 4:3. How many of the students take Spanish?
>
> (A) 280   (B) 360   (C) 480   (D) 560   (E) 630

To solve this problem requires only that you understand what a ratio is. Ignore the fact that this is a multiple-choice question. *Don't even look at the choices.*

- Let $4x$ and $3x$ be the number of students taking and not taking Spanish, respectively.
- Then $4x + 3x = 840 \Rightarrow 7x = 840 \Rightarrow x = 120$.
- The number of students taking Spanish is $4 \times 120 = 480$.
- Having found the answer to be 480, *now look at the five choices*, see 480 listed as Choice C, click on that choice, and confirm your answer.

Another type of multiple-choice question that appears on the GRE is the Roman numeral-type question. These questions consist of three statements labeled I, II, and III. The five answer choices give various possibilities for which of the statements are true. Here is a typical example.

> If $x$ is negative, which of the following *must* be true?
>
> I. $x^3 < x^2$
>
> II. $x + \dfrac{1}{x} < 0$
>
> III. $x = \sqrt{x^2}$
>
> (A) I only   (B) II only   (C) I and II only
> (D) II and III only   (E) I, II, and III

To solve this problem, examine each statement independently, and think of it as a true-false question.

- If $x$ is negative, $x^3$ is negative, and so *must* be less than $x^2$, which is positive. Statement I is true.
- If $x$ is negative, so is $\dfrac{1}{x}$, and the sum of two negative numbers is negative. Statement II is true.
- The square root of a number is *never* negative, and so could *not possibly* equal $x$. Statement III is false.
- Only I and II are true. The answer is **C**.

# Data Interpretation Questions

Four of the questions in the quantitative section are data interpretation questions. There are always two questions based on one set of data, and later in the section, two more questions based on a second set of data. As you might guess from their name, these questions are based on information provided in graphs, tables, or charts. The questions test your ability to interpret the data that have been provided. You will either have to do a calculation or make an inference from the given data. The various types of questions that could arise will be explored in Chapter 14. Here are two questions based on one set of data.

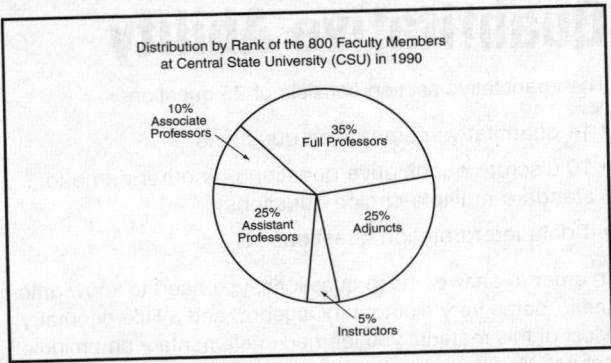

Distribution by Rank of the 800 Faculty Members at Central State University (CSU) in 1990

10% Associate Professors
35% Full Professors
25% Assistant Professors
25% Adjuncts
5% Instructors

> 1. In 1990 how many faculty members did not have a professorial rank?
>
> (A) 200   (B) 240   (C) 320   (D) 400   (E) 520

This is a straightforward question that can easily be answered by looking at the chart and doing a small calculation.

- In 1990, 30% of the faculty were not professors (5% were instructors and 25% were adjunct faculty).
- 30% of 800 = .30 × 800 = **240**.

> 2. From 1990 to 2000 the number of faculty members at CSU increased by 20%. If the total number of assistant, associate, and full professors remained the same, and the number of instructors increased by 50%, how many adjunct faculty were there in 2000?
>
> (A) 240   (B) 340   (C) 384   (D) 480   (E) 516

This question is more complicated and requires several calculations.

- Since the number of faculty members increased by 20%, in 2000 there were 960 people on the faculty (20% of 800 = 160, and 800 + 160 = 960).
- In 1990, there were 560 professors (70% of 800 = 560). So in 2000, there were also 560 professors.
- In 1990, there were 40 instructors (5% of 800 = 40); since that number increased by 50%, there were 60 instructors in 2000.

• Of the 960 faculty members in 2000, 560 were professors and 60 were instructors. The remaining **340** were adjuncts (960 − 560 − 60 = 340).

# Analytical Ability

The analytical ability section consists of 35 questions:

• 26 analytical reasoning questions

• 9 logical reasoning questions

The analytical reasoning questions are always presented in sets of four or five questions based on a single set of conditions that remains on the screen as you answer each of the questions in that set. The logical reasoning questions are usually scattered throughout the section—one or two (occasionally three) separating the sets of analytical reasoning questions. The introduction to Part Three gives a typical distribution of the two types of questions.

## Analytical Reasoning Questions

Answering the four or five analytical reasoning questions based on a set of conditions is similar to trying to solve a logical puzzle. Because few students have ever seen questions such as these, and even fewer have ever tried to solve them, most students find the analytical reasoning questions to be the most difficult part of the GRE. Fortunately, there are many tactics available to help you solve these puzzles. When you read Chapter 9, you will learn all of them. To gain mastery and confidence, try the many sample problems in this book, and carefully study the explanations.

To illustrate what analytical reasoning questions are like, here is a typical set of conditions, followed by two questions. Remember, on the GRE there will always be four or five questions based on each set of conditions.

---

Michel Lubetzki, the personnel director of Computers.com has to interview six applicants—Burns, Cohen, Davis, Eckel, Fox, and Gavalas—for an opening in the data processing department. Each interview will take place on the same day. The interviews will be scheduled at 9:00, 10:00, 11:00, 1:00, 2:00, and 3:00, with a lunch break at noon. In making up the interview schedule, Mr. Lubetzki will be bound by the following conditions:

Fox will have the first interview in the afternoon.

Davis must be interviewed earlier in the day than Eckel.

Burns must be interviewed earlier in the day than both Eckel and Fox.

Cohen and Gavalas must be interviewed consecutively, and in that order.

---

1. If Burns is only available at 10:00, in how many ways can the interviews be scheduled?

(A) 1  (B) 2  (C) 3  (D) 4  (E) 6

In order to keep them straight, write down the conditions on your scratch paper, but to save time, abbreviate as much as possible. For example, write only the first letter of each name, and use symbols, such as D < E to mean that D is interviewed before E.

In conjunction with the given, the added requirement that Burns be interviewed at 10:00 completely determines the schedule. Since Cohen and Gavalas need to be interviewed consecutively, their interviews must be at 2:00 and 3:00, respectively, the only two-hour slot available once Burns is scheduled at 10:00 and Fox at 1:00. Since Burns must interview before Eckel, Eckel has to be scheduled for 11:00, and the first interview of the day will go to Davis. There is only 1 possible schedule:

| D | B | E | F | C | G |
|---|---|---|---|---|---|
| 9 | 10 | 11 | 1 | 2 | 3 |

The answer is Choice A.

2. If Gavalas has the last interview of the day, each of the following could be true EXCEPT

(A) Burns has the first interview of the day.
(B) Davis has the first interview of the day.
(C) Davis has his interview at 10:00.
(D) Eckel has her interview at 10:00.
(E) Cohen has his interview at 2:00.

If Gavalas has the last interview (at 3:00), then Cohen has his interview at 2:00. Since both Burns and Davis have their interviews before Eckel has hers, they must have their interviews at 9:00 and 10:00 (in either order), and Eckel must have hers at 11:00.

| _ | B/D _ | E | F | C | G |
|---|---|---|---|---|---|
| 9 | 10 | 11 | 1 | 2 | 3 |

This shows that Choice E must be true, and that Choices A, B, and C could be true. Only Choice D cannot be true.

## Logical Reasoning Questions

Logical reasoning questions are intended to test your ability to "understand, analyze, and evaluate arguments." This is usually accomplished by having you read a short passage, and answer a question that requires you to analyze the argument in that passage. As a result, logical reasoning questions *look* a lot like short reading comprehension questions, but they are really quite different. This will be explained fully in Chapter 10 where you will learn the various tactics that can be used to answer this type of question. Occasionally, there are two questions that are based on the same passage, but, as in the following example, usually there is just one.

It has long been apparent that the nation's violent crime problem is disproportionately a juvenile crime problem. Those under age 18 constitute a fifth of the population, but account for nearly half of the arrests for the seven major crimes on which the FBI maintains national statistics. The statistical trend lines suggest the problem is growing; the number of juveniles arrested for murder and aggravated assault rose 82 percent and 91 percent respectively from 1967 to 1976. Yet, under the laws of most states, courts are obliged to treat these young hard-core hoodlums as if they were little worse than wayward delinquents.

Each of the following statements is an assumption made by the author EXCEPT

(A) Statistical trend lines are accurate predictors.
(B) 1967 to 1976 were not abnormal years.
(C) The laws of most states are consistent involving juveniles.
(D) The laws governing juvenile criminals are lenient in most states.
(E) The nation's nonviolent crime problem does not involve juveniles.

All of the following except (E) are assumed by the author. He would not rely on statistical trend lines if they were not accurate predictors (A). If the years from 1967 to 1976 were abnormal years, his statistics would be suspect (B). The final sentence of his argument states that the laws in most states handle juveniles in the same manner and leniently (C) and (D). He does not address juveniles and nonviolent crime (E).

# 2 Test-Taking Tactics for the Computer-Based GRE

Before studying the specific tips that will enable you to do your best on this computer-based test or CBT, briefly review the key features of the exam:

- A typical CBT consists of 93 questions in three sections.

- The verbal section contains 30 questions: roughly 9 antonyms, 7 analogies, 6 sentence completions, 8 reading comprehension questions. These appear on screen in no set order: 2 sentence completions may be followed on screen by 2 antonyms.

- The mathematics section contains 28 questions: 14 are quantitative comparisons, 10 are standard multiple-choice questions, and 10 are data interpretation questions based on tables or graphs.

- The analytical section contains 35 questions: 26 analytical reasoning questions (puzzle-solving) and 9 logical reasoning questions (argument analysis).

- Because the CBT you take will be tailored to your skills, it may vary slightly from the typical test described above.

- You receive more credit for getting a hard question right than you do for answering an easy question correctly.

- You cannot skip questions; you must answer the question on screen and confirm that you are satisfied with your answer choice before you can proceed to the next question.

- Once you have confirmed an answer, you cannot go back and change it.

## Starting Right Now
### Begin to Familiarize Yourself with Computer Skills

Use the CD-ROM that accompanies this book to familiarize yourself with computerized testing.

### Using a Mouse

As you probably know, a mouse is a small electronic device that enables you to send signals to your PC. It sits on a mouse pad, its tail (the electric cord that links it to your PC) pointed away from you. As you move the mouse back and forth along the surface of the mouse pad, you see a pointer or arrow moving on the computer screen. There's a "button" on the rear surface of the mouse. Click that button to tell the computer to do something.

Cord

Mouse

Here is an antonym question as it would appear on a computer screen. Right now the arrow is off to one side.

To enter your answer to this question, you must move the mouse until the arrow touches the oval next to your answer choice.

Once the pointer is on the oval, click the button. Note that the oval on which you clicked is now black. This means that the computer has recorded your answer choice.

If you decide that you prefer a different answer, simply move the mouse until the arrow is on the appropriate oval. Click the button. The new oval is now black, while the old oval is once more blank.

Once you're sure of your answer choice, before you can go on to the next question, you have to use the mouse twice more. First, you have to move the pointer until it's on the box labeled "Next" at the bottom of the screen. Click the button. This signals the computer that you want to move on. Before you can do so, however, you have to confirm that you really want to do that. Up to this moment, you can still change your answer. Once you click on the box labeled "Confirm," however, the screen will change to show the next question. You can never go back to change an answer you have confirmed.

There are six icons at the bottom of a CBT screen, three to the left and three to the right. They read, in order from left to right, as follows:

| Quit Test | Exit Section | Time | | Help | Confirm Answer | Next |

Because ETS currently refuses to allow other publishers to duplicate its testing tools, we have had to create alternative icons for the computer screens that appear on the CD-ROM accompanying this book. Thus, in place of the CBT icon "Next," our screen has the icon "Proceed." Where the CBT tells you to "Confirm" your answer, our screen asks, "Are You Sure?"

Our layout thus reads, from left to right:

| Abandon | Leave Section | Clock | Need Help? | Are You Sure? | Proceed |

Do not let these minor differences confuse you. The basic layout of the screen is identical, and the functions of the testing tools are the same. Even if our icons don't match the ones on the CBT exactly, you can depend on what we say about the appearance of the test.

# Scrolling Through a Text

Occasionally, to answer a question you may have to consider more information than can fit conveniently on a single computer screen. A 500-word reading passage, for example, takes up too much room for one screen; so do certain charts and bar and line graphs.

In such cases, a vertical scroll bar will appear along the right side of that reading passage or chart. It enables you to control what part of the text you see on screen. Click on the scroll bar's down arrow, and it will allow you to move down one line to see the next line of text. Keep on clicking on the down arrow and you'll scroll down even more. Click on the up arrow and you'll scroll back up. You can scroll line by

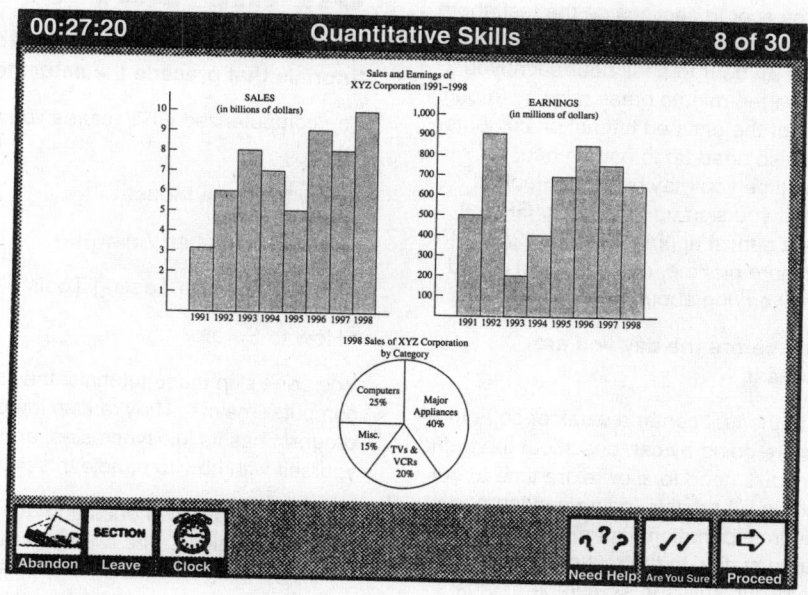

line; you can also scroll a page at a time. If you hold down the mouse button on an arrow, you can scroll through the text quite rapidly.

The small gray status bar at the top of the pane or little window helps you figure out just where you are in the text. When you're at the start of the text, it reads "Begin"; when you're at the end of the text, it reads "End." When you're in the middle and can scroll in either direction, it reads "More Available."

If you're a rapid reader and are unused to word-processing programs and other software programs that incorporate scrolling, you may find the process a bit awkward at first. Practice on the CD-ROM version of this book until you get the hang of it. When you take the CBT, you'll have a chance to work through a tutorial that teaches you how to scroll. However, you'll have an easier time on the test if you come in already comfortable with scrolling techniques.

# Before the Test

**Schedule the test for your best time of day.**

When you sign up to take the test on a specific date, you will be given a choice of time slots. Some people are morning people; others work well in the midafternoon. Consider how your energy and alertness levels vary during the course of a day. Also, consider possible transportation problems, such as rush hour. With these and other relevant factors in mind, select the time slot that works best for you.

**Allow yourself enough time for the test.**

The GRE Bulletin recommends that you allow $4\frac{1}{2}$ hours for the CBT. There are three scored sections on the test; there may also be one or two additional sections. These sections range in length from half an hour to a full hour each; you must also allow time for a ten-minute break midway through the session, as well as for the untimed tutorial on computer-based testing. You will also need up to half an hour for signing in, during which time you may be photographed and even fingerprinted! If you sign up to take the GRE at 8:00 A.M., do not make a dentist appointment for 12:00. You can't possibly get there on time, and you'll just spend the last hour of the test worrying about it.

**Look over the test site before the day you are scheduled to take the test.**

Do a practice run out to the test center a week or so before you take the test. If you're going by car, check out the traffic patterns. See whether you'll need to allow extra time to get to the site, and whether you'll be able to find parking easily. If you'll be using public transportation, figure out how to get from the bus stop or train station to the test center. Some testing centers are located in suites in skyscrapers; others, in storefront locations in the middle of busy malls. Also learn where the restrooms are, and the nearest place to buy a quick snack.

**Set out your test kit the night before the test.**

Avoid sudden panic on the morning of the test. Before you go to bed, set out everything you will need to take with you in the morning. For the CBT GRE, you need two forms of official I.D., at least one of which must include a current photograph; be sure you have these items in your wallet or purse. If you need to wear special glasses when you work at a computer, set them out. Include also your directions to the site, and your CBT authorization voucher, if you have been given one. [If, however, you register by phone for an imminent date and pay via credit card, the Sylvan Candidate Services Call Center will not send you an authorization voucher; instead, the scheduler will assign you a confirmation number by which you can identify yourself to the test center staff. Have that number with you on the day of the test.]

Also set out the clothes you plan to wear. Choose comfortable, casual clothing. Now is not the time to make a fashion statement; simplicity, not elegance, should be the order of the day. Bring along a sweater, however; you can't do your best if you're shivering from the cold.

Don't bother to set out pencils and scratch paper. The test center will supply you with both. You will not be allowed to take any "testing aids"—calculators, watches with calculator functions, pens, rulers, highlighters, books, handheld PCs—into the testing room.

**Get a good night's sleep.**

The way to do your best on any test you ever take is to get a good night's sleep so you are well rested and alert.

# On the Day of the Test

**Take as much time as you need to work through the tutorials that precede the actual test.**

The computerized GRE makes you work through four tutorials:

• How to Use a Mouse

• How to Select an Answer

• How to Use the Testing Tools

• How to Scroll

You can't skip these tutorials; they're mandatory, even for computer majors. They're also important; every computer program has its idiosyncrasies, and you need to familiarize yourself with how to handle this particular computer setup.

Proceed at your own pace and don't worry about how much time you're taking. The twenty to thirty minutes you spend working through the tutorials *before* you begin testing will not count against your time for taking the test.

**As you work through the tutorials, make sure you know all the test directions thoroughly.**

Once the test begins, any time you have to switch screens to look up directions or to get help with scrolling is time you lose from the actual test. The clock keeps on ticking, and, to maximize your score, you've got to keep on thinking and clicking. For this reason, be sure you've memorized the directions for the different question types you'll face on the test.

**Take some time during the tutorials to make yourself a rough answer sheet.**

At the end of the tutorial section, a moment comes when you have to click to indicate either that you're done with reviewing this material and are ready to move on to the actual test, or that you want to review some of the tutorial sections a bit longer. Don't click. This is a good time for you to set up your scratch paper answer sheet as described on page 5. During the actual test, use this rough answer sheet whenever you need to cross out incorrect answer choices before settling on the answer you like best.

**Before you move on from the tutorial section to the actual test, take a break.**

Once you've finished making your rough answer sheet, don't be in a rush to click and start the test. Raise your hand to let the proctor know you need assistance, and, when he or she comes up to your carrel, ask for a restroom break. You'll be escorted out of the computer room and allowed to sign out. You may have spent half an hour or more mastering the material in the tutorials section, and if you're new to working with a mouse, you may be a bit tired or tense. Feel free to wash your face, nibble a quick snack, stretch, or do anything else that will relax you before you move into the test-taking mode. Any time out you take before the test actually starts is "free": it doesn't cost you any of that all important question-answering time.

# Once the Test Has Started

**Avoid clicking on the boxes at the bottom left of the screen.**

As you will learn in the tutorial, there are six boxes at the bottom of the screen, three to the left and three to the right. They read, in order, from left to right: Quit, Exit, Time, Help, Confirm, Next. Avoid the ones to the left, especially the two leftmost ones. If you click on either of those boxes, you're abandoning ship, quitting either the particular section on which you're working or the whole test. There is no point in doing so. Even if you're dissatisfied with your performance and unwilling to have your scores sent to the graduate schools you selected, you still can use this test as a practice session. Don't bail out midway. Wait. After you've completed all four sections of the test, you will get a chance to

indicate whether you want to cancel this test or whether you want to receive a score for your work. Make the decision then. Even if you decide to cancel your test, you'll still benefit from having had the chance to see what specific questions the computer selected for you. After all, you've paid almost $100 to take this test. Get your money's worth from the experience.

Avoid clicking on the third lefthand box as well, the "Time" box. This is the "Time" box. If you click on it, the information line at the top of the computer screen will stop showing the amount of time remaining in the section on which you're working. You won't be able to pace yourself effectively, and you may completely lose track of how much time you have left. Why create problems for yourself? Keep away from those boxes at the bottom left. (If you accidentally click on the "Time" box and hide the time information momentarily, don't panic; just click on the box a second time to turn the time indicator back on again.)

**Keep track of the time.**

Your job is to answer correctly as many questions as you can within the time allowed for that particular section of the test. Because of the computer-adaptive nature of the test, you can't simply skip time-consuming questions or questions that stump you, and hope to return to them if you have time left over. To move on to the next question, you must enter and confirm an answer for the question currently on your screen. Therefore, whenever you decide it's worth your while to spend time working through a complicated question, you've got to keep one eye on the clock to make sure getting this one answer correct isn't costing you too much time.

**Don't get bogged down by any one question.**

Now more than ever it is important for you to avoid getting so caught up in figuring out one question that you lose track of the time. Remember, you can't move on to the next question until you've answered the one on screen. If a question is taking too long, guess at the answer and go on to the next question. This is not the time to prove that you can stick to a job no matter how long it takes.

**On the other hand, don't rush.**

Since your score will depend on how many *correct* answers you give *within a definite period* of time, speed and accuracy both count. Don't fall into the common errors born of haste. Read *all the answer choices*, not just some. Make sure you are answering *the question asked* and not one it may have reminded you of or one you thought was going to be asked. Write down key words like NOT and EXCEPT to make sure that you do not end up trying to answer the exact opposite of the question asked.

**Don't be trigger-happy: Think before you click.**

Once you get into the swing of things, clicking "Next" to indicate you're ready to go on to the next question and "Confirm" to indicate that you're sure of your answer, watch out that you don't start double-clicking automatically. It's all too easy to fall into a game-playing mode and click twice before you've thought things through. The CBT is *not* a computer game; you don't win any points here by zapping the enemy blindly. Take a moment to reconsider each answer choice. Then move on to the next question, sure that you've given this one your best shot.

### Be especially careful answering questions that resemble questions you've seen before.

In the GRE, the test-makers test and retest the same concepts. They follow basic patterns, modifying questions subtly or substantially. Thus, in your CBT, you may come across questions that look very much like ones you have previously seen in published GREs or on *www.gre.org*, the GRE web site. You may even come across some that resemble questions you've just seen on an earlier section of your test. Don't assume that you know the answer to a question because it looks like one you've seen before. Read the question closely. Don't let subtle shifts in wording catch you unaware.

### Never rush through the first questions of a section.

Remember, your answers to these initial questions have a greater impact on your score than your answers to the last few questions of the section do.

### Always eliminate as many wrong answers as you can.

Deciding between two choices is easier than deciding among five. Even if you have to guess, every answer you eliminate improves your chances of guessing correctly.

### Don't waste time second-guessing yourself.

Once you confirm an answer, that's it; you no longer have a chance to change that answer. If, later on in a section, you suddenly realize you got an earlier question wrong, don't sit there kicking yourself. Self-reproach is a waste of time. Remember, the only question you have to worry about is the one now on screen, so concentrate on it.

Similarly, don't try to second-guess the computer. There's no point in wasting time and energy wondering whether it's feeding you harder questions or easier ones. Let the computer keep track of how well you're doing. You concentrate on answering questions and pacing yourself.

### Be alert for the five-minute warning.

Toward the end of each section, a brief flash of the clock will indicate that you have only five minutes left. Even if you have clicked "Time" to hide the remaining time display, the time display will come on automatically at this point. Also, instead of showing just the hours and minutes remaining, the display will change to show seconds as well.

Don't miss your five-minute warning signal. As you work through each section, be aware of the clock. When you are running out of time, eliminate any answer choices you can and then guess. At that point, even random guessing those last questions is better than leaving them unanswered.

# 3 A Diagnostic Test

- ■ **Diagnostic Test**
- ■ **Answer Key**
- ■ **Self-Appraisal**
- ■ **Answer Explanations**

This chapter contains a full-length diagnostic test. The format of the test is identical to the computer-based GRE that you will take, in that it has exactly the same number of verbal, quantitative, and analytical questions that an actual test has. Within each section, there is also exactly the same breakdown of question types. For example, on the verbal section there are the same number of analogies and antonyms as on a real test; in the quantitative section there are four data interpretation questions and 14 quantitative comparisons; and there are nine logical reasoning questions in the analytical ability section. Directions will appear only the first time a given type of question is introduced in each test; after that, only the type of question will appear. What is different, of course, is that this test is not computer adaptive. Later in your preparation, to get a feel for what it is like to take a computerized GRE, do a model test on the CD-ROM that accompanies this book.

After taking the test, score your answers and evaluate your results, using the self-rating guides provided. (Be sure also to read the answer explanations for questions you answered incorrectly and questions you answered correctly but found difficult.)

You should now be in a position to approach your review program realistically and allot your time for study. For example, you should know which topics in mathematics require review and drill. You should also know which of your verbal and analytical skills require concentrated study.

## Simulate Test Conditions

To best simulate actual test conditions, find a quiet place to work. Have a stop watch or a clock handy so that you can keep perfect track of the time. Go through each section by answering the questions in the order in which they appear. If you don't know the answer to a question, guess (making an educated guess, if possible) and move on. Do not return to a question that you were unsure of, and do not go back to check your work if you have some time left over at the end of a section. (It isn't possible to do that on a real GRE.) Knowing how much time you have for each section and how many questions there are, try to pace yourself so that you use all your time and just finish each section in the time allowed. Do not spend too much time on any one question. Again, if you get stuck, just guess and go on to the next question.

# Answer Key—A Diagnostic Test

## Section 1

1. Ⓐ Ⓑ Ⓒ Ⓓ Ⓔ
2. Ⓐ Ⓑ Ⓒ Ⓓ Ⓔ
3. Ⓐ Ⓑ Ⓒ Ⓓ Ⓔ
4. Ⓐ Ⓑ Ⓒ Ⓓ Ⓔ
5. Ⓐ Ⓑ Ⓒ Ⓓ Ⓔ
6. Ⓐ Ⓑ Ⓒ Ⓓ Ⓔ
7. Ⓐ Ⓑ Ⓒ Ⓓ Ⓔ
8. Ⓐ Ⓑ Ⓒ Ⓓ Ⓔ
9. Ⓐ Ⓑ Ⓒ Ⓓ Ⓔ
10. Ⓐ Ⓑ Ⓒ Ⓓ Ⓔ
11. Ⓐ Ⓑ Ⓒ Ⓓ Ⓔ
12. Ⓐ Ⓑ Ⓒ Ⓓ Ⓔ
13. Ⓐ Ⓑ Ⓒ Ⓓ Ⓔ
14. Ⓐ Ⓑ Ⓒ Ⓓ Ⓔ
15. Ⓐ Ⓑ Ⓒ Ⓓ Ⓔ
16. Ⓐ Ⓑ Ⓒ Ⓓ Ⓔ
17. Ⓐ Ⓑ Ⓒ Ⓓ Ⓔ
18. Ⓐ Ⓑ Ⓒ Ⓓ Ⓔ
19. Ⓐ Ⓑ Ⓒ Ⓓ Ⓔ
20. Ⓐ Ⓑ Ⓒ Ⓓ Ⓔ
21. Ⓐ Ⓑ Ⓒ Ⓓ Ⓔ
22. Ⓐ Ⓑ Ⓒ Ⓓ Ⓔ
23. Ⓐ Ⓑ Ⓒ Ⓓ Ⓔ
24. Ⓐ Ⓑ Ⓒ Ⓓ Ⓔ
25. Ⓐ Ⓑ Ⓒ Ⓓ Ⓔ
26. Ⓐ Ⓑ Ⓒ Ⓓ Ⓔ
27. Ⓐ Ⓑ Ⓒ Ⓓ Ⓔ
28. Ⓐ Ⓑ Ⓒ Ⓓ Ⓔ
29. Ⓐ Ⓑ Ⓒ Ⓓ Ⓔ
30. Ⓐ Ⓑ Ⓒ Ⓓ Ⓔ

## Section 2

1. Ⓐ Ⓑ Ⓒ Ⓓ Ⓔ
2. Ⓐ Ⓑ Ⓒ Ⓓ Ⓔ
3. Ⓐ Ⓑ Ⓒ Ⓓ Ⓔ
4. Ⓐ Ⓑ Ⓒ Ⓓ Ⓔ
5. Ⓐ Ⓑ Ⓒ Ⓓ Ⓔ
6. Ⓐ Ⓑ Ⓒ Ⓓ Ⓔ
7. Ⓐ Ⓑ Ⓒ Ⓓ Ⓔ
8. Ⓐ Ⓑ Ⓒ Ⓓ Ⓔ
9. Ⓐ Ⓑ Ⓒ Ⓓ Ⓔ
10. Ⓐ Ⓑ Ⓒ Ⓓ Ⓔ
11. Ⓐ Ⓑ Ⓒ Ⓓ Ⓔ
12. Ⓐ Ⓑ Ⓒ Ⓓ Ⓔ
13. Ⓐ Ⓑ Ⓒ Ⓓ Ⓔ
14. Ⓐ Ⓑ Ⓒ Ⓓ Ⓔ
15. Ⓐ Ⓑ Ⓒ Ⓓ Ⓔ
16. Ⓐ Ⓑ Ⓒ Ⓓ Ⓔ
17. Ⓐ Ⓑ Ⓒ Ⓓ Ⓔ
18. Ⓐ Ⓑ Ⓒ Ⓓ Ⓔ
19. Ⓐ Ⓑ Ⓒ Ⓓ Ⓔ
20. Ⓐ Ⓑ Ⓒ Ⓓ Ⓔ
21. Ⓐ Ⓑ Ⓒ Ⓓ Ⓔ
22. Ⓐ Ⓑ Ⓒ Ⓓ Ⓔ
23. Ⓐ Ⓑ Ⓒ Ⓓ Ⓔ
24. Ⓐ Ⓑ Ⓒ Ⓓ Ⓔ
25. Ⓐ Ⓑ Ⓒ Ⓓ Ⓔ
26. Ⓐ Ⓑ Ⓒ Ⓓ Ⓔ
27. Ⓐ Ⓑ Ⓒ Ⓓ Ⓔ
28. Ⓐ Ⓑ Ⓒ Ⓓ Ⓔ

## Section 3

1. Ⓐ Ⓑ Ⓒ Ⓓ Ⓔ
2. Ⓐ Ⓑ Ⓒ Ⓓ Ⓔ
3. Ⓐ Ⓑ Ⓒ Ⓓ Ⓔ
4. Ⓐ Ⓑ Ⓒ Ⓓ Ⓔ
5. Ⓐ Ⓑ Ⓒ Ⓓ Ⓔ
6. Ⓐ Ⓑ Ⓒ Ⓓ Ⓔ
7. Ⓐ Ⓑ Ⓒ Ⓓ Ⓔ
8. Ⓐ Ⓑ Ⓒ Ⓓ Ⓔ
9. Ⓐ Ⓑ Ⓒ Ⓓ Ⓔ
10. Ⓐ Ⓑ Ⓒ Ⓓ Ⓔ
11. Ⓐ Ⓑ Ⓒ Ⓓ Ⓔ
12. Ⓐ Ⓑ Ⓒ Ⓓ Ⓔ
13. Ⓐ Ⓑ Ⓒ Ⓓ Ⓔ
14. Ⓐ Ⓑ Ⓒ Ⓓ Ⓔ
15. Ⓐ Ⓑ Ⓒ Ⓓ Ⓔ
16. Ⓐ Ⓑ Ⓒ Ⓓ Ⓔ
17. Ⓐ Ⓑ Ⓒ Ⓓ Ⓔ
18. Ⓐ Ⓑ Ⓒ Ⓓ Ⓔ
19. Ⓐ Ⓑ Ⓒ Ⓓ Ⓔ
20. Ⓐ Ⓑ Ⓒ Ⓓ Ⓔ
21. Ⓐ Ⓑ Ⓒ Ⓓ Ⓔ
22. Ⓐ Ⓑ Ⓒ Ⓓ Ⓔ
23. Ⓐ Ⓑ Ⓒ Ⓓ Ⓔ
24. Ⓐ Ⓑ Ⓒ Ⓓ Ⓔ
25. Ⓐ Ⓑ Ⓒ Ⓓ Ⓔ
26. Ⓐ Ⓑ Ⓒ Ⓓ Ⓔ
27. Ⓐ Ⓑ Ⓒ Ⓓ Ⓔ
28. Ⓐ Ⓑ Ⓒ Ⓓ Ⓔ
29. Ⓐ Ⓑ Ⓒ Ⓓ Ⓔ
30. Ⓐ Ⓑ Ⓒ Ⓓ Ⓔ
31. Ⓐ Ⓑ Ⓒ Ⓓ Ⓔ
32. Ⓐ Ⓑ Ⓒ Ⓓ Ⓔ
33. Ⓐ Ⓑ Ⓒ Ⓓ Ⓔ
34. Ⓐ Ⓑ Ⓒ Ⓓ Ⓔ
35. Ⓐ Ⓑ Ⓒ Ⓓ Ⓔ

Remove answer sheet by cutting on dotted line

# DIAGNOSTIC TEST

1

SECTION 1—VERBAL ABILITY

**Time—30 Minutes**
**30 Questions**

**Select the best answer to the following questions, then fill in the appropriate space on your Answer Sheet.**

**Directions:** In each of the following antonym questions, a word printed in capital letters precedes five lettered words or phrases. From these five lettered words or phrases, pick the one most nearly opposite in meaning to the capitalized word.

1. PRODIGAL:
   (A) nomad
   (B) sycophant
   (C) gifted child
   (D) economical person
   (E) antagonist

2. ARTIFICE:
   (A) edifice
   (B) sincerity
   (C) prejudice
   (D) creativity
   (E) affirmation

**Directions:** Each of the following sentence completion questions contains one or two blanks. These blanks signify that a word or set of words has been left out. Below each sentence are five words or sets of words. For each blank, pick the word or set of words that best reflects the sentence's overall meaning.

3. The earth is a planet bathed in light; it is therefore _____ that many of the living organisms that have evolved on the earth have _____ the biologically advantageous capacity to trap light energy.
   (A) anomalous...engendered
   (B) unsurprising...developed
   (C) predictable...forfeited
   (D) problematic...exhibited
   (E) expectable...relinquished

4. Relatively few politicians willingly forsake center stage, although a touch of _____ on their parts now and again might well increase their popularity with the voting public.
   (A) garrulity
   (B) misanthropy
   (C) self-effacement
   (D) self-dramatization
   (E) self-doubt

**Directions:** Each of the following analogy questions presents a related pair of words linked by a colon. Five lettered pairs of words follow the linked pair. Choose the lettered pair of words whose relationship is most like the relationship expressed in the original linked pair.

5. CIRCUITOUS : ROUTE ::
   (A) problematic : solution
   (B) devious : argument
   (C) elliptical : brevity
   (D) judicious : selection
   (E) profound : depth

6. HELPFUL : OFFICIOUS ::
   (A) dutiful : assiduous
   (B) effusive : gushing
   (C) gullible : incredulous
   (D) enigmatic : dumbfounded
   (E) deferential : sycophantic

# 1

**1**

1

---

<u>Directions:</u> Each of the following reading comprehension questions is based on the content of the following passage. Read the passage and then determine the best answer choice for each question. Base your choice on what this passage *states directly* or *implies*, not on any information you may have gained elsewhere.

---

James's first novels used conventional narrative techniques: explicit characterization, action which related events in distinctly phased sequences,
*Line* settings firmly outlined and specifically described.
(5) But this method gradually gave way to a subtler, more deliberate, more diffuse style of accumulation of minutely discriminated details whose total significance the reader can grasp only by constant attention and sensitive inference. His later novels
(10) play down scenes of abrupt and prominent action, and do not so much offer a succession of sharp shocks as slow piecemeal additions of perception. The curtain is not suddenly drawn back from shrouded things, but is slowly moved away.
(15) Such a technique is suited to James's essential subject, which is not human action itself but the states of mind which produce and are produced by human actions and interactions. James was less interested in what characters do, than in the
(20) moral and psychological antecedents, realizations, and consequences which attend their doings. This is why he more often speaks of "cases" than of actions. His stories, therefore, grow more and more lengthy while the actions they relate grow
(25) simpler and less visible; not because they are crammed with adventitious and secondary events, digressive relief, or supernumerary characters, as overstuffed novels of action are; but because he presents in such exhaustive detail every nuance of
(30) his situation. Commonly the interest of a novel is in the variety and excitement of visible actions building up to a climactic event which will settle the outward destinies of characters with storybook promise of permanence. A James novel, however,
(35) possesses its characteristic interest in carrying the reader through a rich analysis of the mental adjustments of characters to the realities of their personal situations as they are slowly revealed to them through exploration and chance discovery.

7. The passage supplies information for answering which of the following questions?
   (A) Did James originate the so-called psychological novel?
   (B) Is conventional narrative technique strictly chronological in recounting action?
   (C) Can novels lacking overtly dramatic incident sustain the reader's interest?
   (D) Were James's later novels more acceptable to the general public than his earlier ones?
   (E) Is James unique in his predilection for exploring psychological nuances of character?

8. According to the passage, James's later novels differ from his earlier ones in their
   (A) preoccupation with specifically described settings
   (B) ever-increasing concision and tautness of plot
   (C) levels of moral and psychological complexity
   (D) development of rising action to a climax
   (E) subordination of psychological exploration to dramatic effect

9. The author's attitude toward the novel of action appears to be one of
   (A) pointed indignation
   (B) detached neutrality
   (C) sharp derision
   (D) strong partisanship
   (E) mild disapprobation

# 1

# 1

## Antonyms

10. EQUIVOCATE:
    (A) yield
    (B) distinguish
    (C) condescend
    (D) pledge
    (E) denounce

11. OPULENCE:
    (A) transience
    (B) penury
    (C) solitude
    (D) generosity
    (E) transparency

## Analogies

12. EPHEMERAL : PERMANENCE ::
    (A) erratic : predictability
    (B) immaculate : cleanliness
    (C) commendable : reputation
    (D) spurious : emulation
    (E) mandatory : obedience

13. NONPLUSSED : BAFFLEMENT ::
    (A) discomfited : embarrassment
    (B) parsimonious : extravagance
    (C) disgruntled : contentment
    (D) despicable : contempt
    (E) surly : harassment

14. OGLE : OBSERVE ::
    (A) haggle : outbid
    (B) clamor : dispute
    (C) discern : perceive
    (D) flaunt : display
    (E) glare : glower

## Sentence Completion

15. It may be useful to think of character in fiction as a function of two _____ impulses: the impulse to individualize and the impulse to _____.
    (A) analogous...humanize
    (B) disparate...aggrandize
    (C) divergent...typify
    (D) comparable...delineate
    (E) related...moralize

16. There are any number of theories to explain these events and, since even the experts disagree, it is _____ the rest of us in our role as responsible scholars to _____ dogmatic statements.
    (A) paradoxical for...abstain from
    (B) arrogant of...compensate with
    (C) incumbent on...refrain from
    (D) opportune for...quarrel over
    (E) appropriate for...issue forth

## Reading Comprehension

According to the theory of plate tectonics, the lithosphere (earth's relatively hard and solid outer layer consisting of the crust and part of the under-
*Line* lying mantle) is divided into a few dozen plates
(5) that vary in size and shape; in general, these plates move in relation to one another. They move away from one another at a mid-ocean ridge, a long chain of sub-oceanic mountains that forms a boundary between plates. At a mid-ocean
(10) ridge, new lithospheric material in the form of hot magma pushes up from the earth's interior. The injection of this new lithospheric material from below causes the phenomenon known as sea-floor spreading.
(15)   Given that the earth is not expanding in size to any appreciable degree, how can "new" litho-sphere be created at a mid-ocean ridge? For new lithosphere to come into being in one region, an equal amount of lithospheric material must be
(20) destroyed somewhere else. This destruction takes place at a boundary between plates called a sub-duction zone. At a subduction zone, one plate is pushed down under another into the red-hot man-tle, where over a span of millions of years it is
(25) absorbed into the mantle.
In the early 1960's, well before scientists had formulated the theory of plate tectonics, Princeton University professor Harry H. Hess proposed the concept of sea-floor spreading. Hess's original
(30) hypothesis described the creation and spread of ocean floor by means of the upwelling and cool-ing of magma from the earth's interior. Hess, however, did not mention rigid lithospheric plates. The subsequent discovery that the oceanic
(35) crust contains evidence of periodic reversals of the earth's magnetic field helped confirm Hess's hypothesis. According to the explanation formu-lated by Princeton's F.J. Vine and D.H. Matthews, whenever magma wells up under a

# 1

# 1

*(40)* mid-ocean ridge, the ferromagnetic minerals within the magma become magnetized in the direction of the geomagnetic field. As the magma cools and hardens into rock, the direction and the polarity of the geometric field are recorded in the magnetized
*(45)* volcanic rock. Thus, when reversals of the earth's magnetic field occur, as they do at intervals of from 10,000 to around a million years, they produce a series of magnetic stripes paralleling the axis of the rift. Thus, the oceanic crust is like a
*(50)* magnetic tape recording, but instead of preserving sounds or visual images, it preserves the history of earth's geomagnetic field. The boundaries between stripes reflect reversals of the magnetic field; these reversals can be dated independently.
*(55)* Given this information, geologists can deduce the rate of sea-floor spreading from the width of the stripes. (Geologists, however, have yet to solve the mystery of exactly how the earth's magnetic field comes to reverse itself periodically.)

17. According to the passage, a mid-ocean ridge differs from a subduction zone in that

    (A) it marks the boundary line between neighboring plates
    (B) only the former is located on the ocean floor
    (C) it is a site for the emergence of new lithospheric material
    (D) the former periodically disrupts the earth's geomagnetic field
    (E) it is involved with lithospheric destruction rather than lithospheric creation

18. It can be inferred from the passage that as new lithospheric material is injected from below

    (A) the plates become immobilized in a kind of gridlock
    (B) it is incorporated into an underwater mountain ridge
    (C) the earth's total mass is altered
    (D) it reverses its magnetic polarity
    (E) the immediately adjacent plates sink

19. According to the passage, lithospheric material at the site of a subduction zone

    (A) rises and is polarized
    (B) sinks and is reincorporated
    (C) slides and is injected
    (D) spreads and is absorbed
    (E) diverges and is consumed

## Antonyms

20. HONE:
    (A) broaden
    (B) twist
    (C) dull
    (D) weld
    (E) break

21. PHLEGMATIC:
    (A) dogmatic
    (B) ardent
    (C) haphazard
    (D) self-assured
    (E) abstracted

22. BANALITY:
    (A) tentative interpretation
    (B) concise summation
    (C) accurate delineation
    (D) laudatory remark
    (E) novel expression

## Analogies

23. THIRST : DRIVE ::
    (A) inebriety : excess
    (B) success : ambition
    (C) indifference : passion
    (D) taste : gusto
    (E) smell : sense

24. SKULDUGGERY : SWINDLER ::
    (A) surgery : quack
    (B) quandary : craven
    (C) chicanery : trickster
    (D) forgery : speculator
    (E) cutlery : butcher

## Sentence Completion

25. According to one optimistic hypothesis, the dense concentration of entrepreneurs and services in the cities would incubate new functions, _____ them, and finally export them to other areas, and so the cities, forever breeding fresh ideas, would _____ themselves repeatedly.

    (A) immunize...perpetuate
    (B) isolate...revitalize
    (C) foster...deplete
    (D) spawn...imitate
    (E) nurture...renew

26. Man is a _____ animal, and much more so in his mind than in his body: he may like to go alone for a walk, but he hates to stand alone in his _____.

    (A) gregarious...opinions
    (B) conceited...vanity
    (C) singular...uniqueness
    (D) solitary...thoughts
    (E) nomadic...footsteps

# 1

# 1

## Antonyms

27. ERUDITE:

    (A) unhealthy
    (B) ignorant
    (C) impolite
    (D) indifferent
    (E) imprecise

28. EFFRONTERY:

    (A) obscurity
    (B) indolence
    (C) separation
    (D) diffidence
    (E) fluctuation

## Reading Comprehension

The stability that had marked the Iroquois
Confederacy's generally pro-British position was
shattered with the overthrow of James II in 1688,
*Line* the colonial uprisings that followed in
(5) Massachusetts, New York, and Maryland, and the
commencement of King William's War against
Louis XIV of France. The increasing French
threat to English hegemony in the interior of
North America was signalized by French-led or
(10) French-inspired attacks on the Iroquois and on
outlying colonial settlements in New York and
New England. The high point of the Iroquois
response was the spectacular raid of August 5,
1689, in which the Iroquois virtually wiped out
(15) the French village of Lachine, just outside
Montreal. A counterraid by the French on the
English village of Schenectady in March, 1690,
instilled an appropriate measure of fear among the
English and their Iroquois allies.
(20) The Iroquois position at the end of the war,
which was formalized by treaties made during the
summer of 1701 with the British and the French,
and which was maintained throughout most of the
(25) eighteenth century, was one of "aggressive neutrality" between the two competing European
powers. Under the new system the Iroquois initiated a peace policy toward the "far Indians,"
tightened their control over the nearby tribes, and
(30) induced both English and French to support their

neutrality toward the European powers by appropriate gifts and concessions.

By holding the balance of power in the sparse-
ly settled borderlands between English and
(35) French settlements, and by their willingness to
use their power against one or the other nation if
not appropriately treated, the Iroquois played the
game of European power politics with effectiveness. The system broke down, however, after the
(40) French became convinced that the Iroquois were
compromising the system in favor of the English
and launched a full-scale attempt to establish
French physical and juridical presence in the
Ohio Valley, the heart of the borderlands long
(45) claimed by the Iroquois. As a consequence of the
ensuing Great War for Empire, in which Iroquois
neutrality was dissolved and European influence
moved closer, the play-off system lost its efficacy
and a system of direct bargaining supplanted it.

29. The author's primary purpose in this passage is to

    (A) denounce the imperialistic policies of the
        French
    (B) disprove the charges of barbarism made
        against the Indian nations
    (C) expose the French government's exploitation
        of the Iroquois balance of power
    (D) describe and assess the effect of European mil-
        itary power on the policy of an Indian nation
    (E) show the inability of the Iroquois to engage in
        European-style diplomacy

30. With which of the following statements would the
    author be LEAST likely to agree?

    (A) The Iroquois were able to respond effectively
        to French acts of aggression.
    (B) James II's removal from the throne caused dis-
        sension to break out among the colonies.
    (C) The French begrudged the British their alleged
        high standing among the Iroquois.
    (D) Iroquois negotiations involved playing one
        side against the other.
    (E) The Iroquois ceased to hold the balance of
        power early in the eighteenth century.

# 2                                                                    2

---

SECTION **2**—QUANTITATIVE ABILITY

**Time—45 Minutes**
**28 Questions**

**In this section solve each problem, using any available space on the page for scratchwork. Then decide which is the best of the choices given and fill in the corresponding oval on the Answer Sheet.**

---

<u>Directions</u>: In the following type of question, two quantities appear, one in Column A and one in Column B. You must compare them. The correct answer to the question is

A if the quantity in Column A is greater
B if the quantity in Column B is greater
C if the two quantities are equal
D it is impossible to determine which quantity is greater

<u>Notes</u>: Sometimes information about one or both of the quantities is centered above the two columns. If the same symbol appears in both columns, it represents the same thing each time.

---

|  | <u>Column A</u> | <u>Column B</u> |  | <u>Column A</u> | <u>Column B</u> |
|---|---|---|---|---|---|

$a > 0$

1. $\quad a^4 a^5 \quad$ | $(a^3)^2$

$0 < a < b < 1$

3. $\quad \sqrt{a+b} \quad$ | $\sqrt{a} + \sqrt{b}$

2. $\quad a + b - c \quad$ | $0$

4. The number of primes between 30 and 40 | The number of primes between 40 and 50

---

<u>Directions</u>: In the following questions, choose the best answer from the five choices listed.

---

5. In the figure at the right, what is the value of $a + b + c$?

(A) 210   (B) 220
(C) 240   (D) 270
(E) 280

$20°$   $60°$   $a°$
$c°$   $b°$

7. Twenty children were sharing equally the cost of a present for their teacher. When 4 of the children decided not to contribute, each of the other children had to pay $1.50 more. How much did the present cost, in dollars?

(A) 50   (B) 80   (C) 100   (D) 120   (E) 150

6. Of the 200 seniors at Monroe High School, exactly 40 are in the band, 60 are in the orchestra, and 10 are in both. How many students are in neither the band nor the orchestra?

(A) 80   (B) 90   (C) 100   (D) 110   (E) 120

**2**                                                                    **2**

| Column A | Column B |
|---|---|
| 8. | $10^{20}$ | $20^{10}$ |

There are 250 people lined up outside a theater. Jack is the 25th person from the front, and Jill is the 125th person from the front.

| Column A | Column B |
|---|---|
| 9. | The number of people between Jack and Jill | 100 |

10.  What is the value of $n$ if $3^{10} \times 27^2 = 9^2 \times 3^n$?

(A) 6    (B) 10    (C) 12    (D) 15    (E) 30

**Column A**                                **Column B**

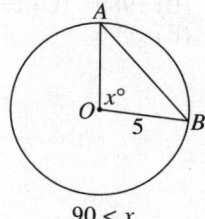

$90 < x$

<u>Note</u>: Figure not drawn to scale

| Column A | Column B |
|---|---|
| 11. | The perimeter of $\triangle AOB$ | 17 |

$$\frac{a-b}{c-a} = 1$$

| Column A | Column B |
|---|---|
| 12. | The average (arithmetic mean) of $b$ and $c$ | $a$ |

| Column A | Column B |
|---|---|
| 13. | The area of a square whose sides are 10 | The area of a square whose diagonals are 15 |

**Questions 14–15 refer to the following graphs.**

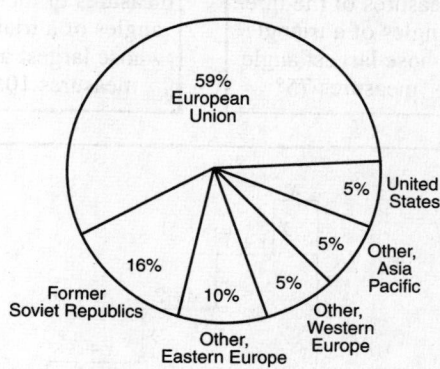

**1993**
Total Exports to Eastern Europe = $98 Billion

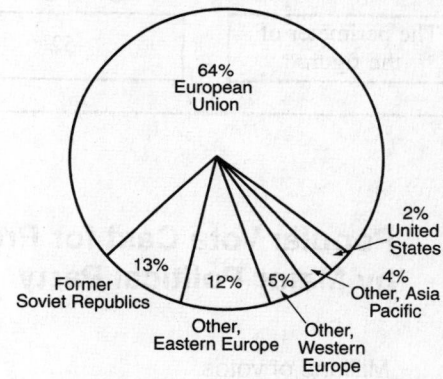

**1996**
Total Exports to Eastern Europe = $174 Billion

14.  Which of the following statements concerning the value of exports to Eastern Europe from other Eastern European countries from 1993 to 1996 is the most accurate?

(A) They increased by 2%.
(B) They increased by 12%.
(C) They increased by 20%.
(D) They increased by 50%.
(E) They increased by 100%.

15.  France is one of the countries in the European Union. If in 1996 France's exports to Eastern Europe were four times those of the United States, then what percent of the European Union's exports to Eastern Europe came from France that year?

(A) 5%    (B) 8%    (C) 12.5%
(D) 20%    (E) 25%

**2**                                                                          **2**

Column B

| The average (arith-metic mean) of the measures of the three angles of a triangle whose largest angle measures 75° | The average (arith-metic mean) of the measures of the three angles of a triangle whose largest angle measures 105° |

16.

In the figure above, all of the line segments meet to form right angles.

| The perimeter of the figure | 52 |

17.

18. Given that $x \neq y$ and that $(x - y)^2 = x^2 - y^2$, which of the following must be true?

    I. $x = 0$
    II. $y = 0$
    III. $x = -y$

(A) I only  (B) II only  (C) III only
(D) I and II  (E) I, II, and III

19. Let the lengths of the sides of a triangle be represented by $x + 3$, $2x - 3$, and $3x - 5$. If the perimeter of the triangle is 25, what is the length of the shortest side?

(A) 5  (B) 6  (C) 7  (D) 8  (E) 10

**Questions 20–21 refer to the graph below.**

20. In which presidential election between 1972 to 1996 inclusive, was the percent of votes received by the winning candidate the lowest?

(A) 1976  (B) 1980  (C) 1988
(D) 1992  (E) 1996

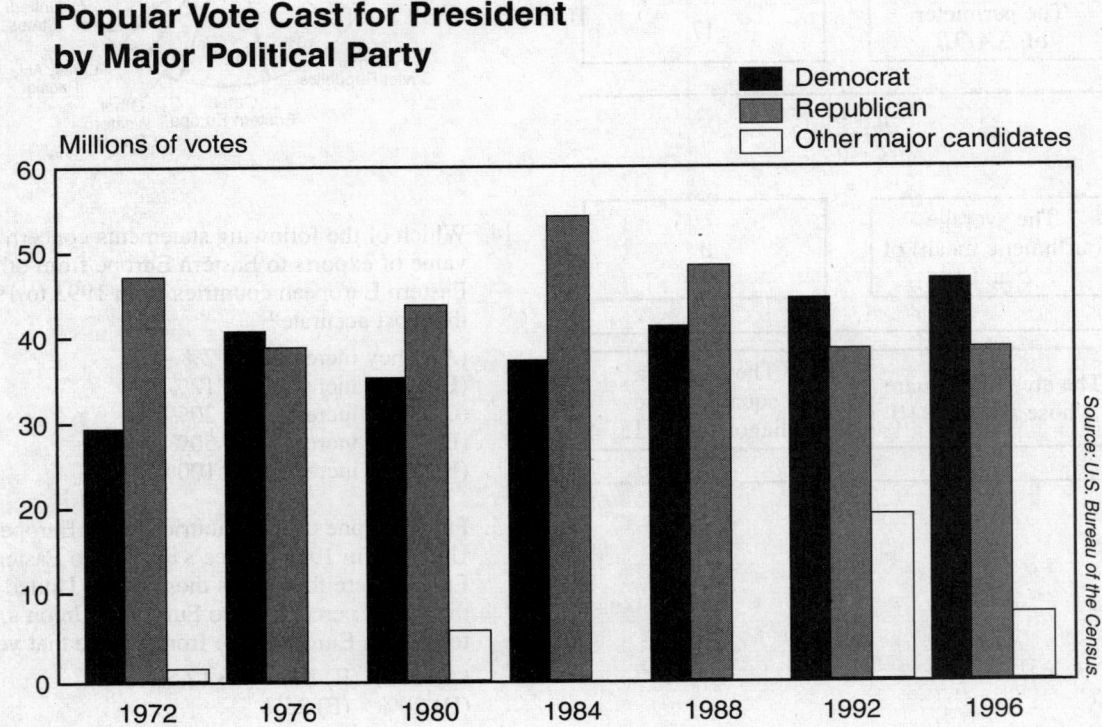

## Popular Vote Cast for President by Major Political Party

# 2

# 2

21. In which year between 1972 and 1996 inclusive were the greatest number of votes cast for president?

    (A) 1980   (B) 1984   (C) 1988
    (D) 1992   (E) 1996

22. In 1990, twice as many boys as girls at Adams High School earned varsity letters. From 1990 to 2000 the number of girls earning varsity letters increased by 25% while the number of boys earning varsity letters decreased by 25%. What was the ratio in 2000 of the number of girls to the number of boys who earned varsity letters?

    (A) $\dfrac{5}{3}$   (B) $\dfrac{6}{5}$   (C) $\dfrac{1}{1}$   (D) $\dfrac{5}{6}$   (E) $\dfrac{3}{5}$

|  <u>Column A</u>  |  <u>Column B</u>  |
|---|---|

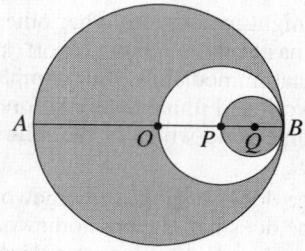

O, P, and Q, which are the centers of the three circles, all lie on diameter AB.

23. 

| The area of the entire shaded region | 4 times the area of the white region |
|---|---|

In 1980, Elaine was 8 times as old as Adam, and Judy was 3 times as old as Adam. Elaine is 20 years older than Judy.

24. 

| Adam's age in 1988 | 12 |
|---|---|

The three circles have the same center. The radii of the circles are 3, 4, and 5.

25. 

| The area of the shaded region | The area of the striped region |
|---|---|

26. A square and an equilateral triangle each have sides of length 5. What is the ratio of the area of the square to the area of the triangle?

    (A) $\dfrac{4}{3}$   (B) $\dfrac{16}{9}$   (C) $\dfrac{\sqrt{3}}{4}$
    (D) $\dfrac{4\sqrt{3}}{3}$   (E) $\dfrac{16\sqrt{3}}{9}$

27. If $x + 2y = a$ and $x - 2y = b$, which of the following expressions is equal to $xy$?

    (A) $ab$   (B) $\dfrac{a+b}{2}$   (C) $\dfrac{a-b}{2}$
    (D) $\dfrac{a^2-b^2}{4}$   (E) $\dfrac{a^2-b^2}{8}$

28. In the figure above, the area of square $ABCD$ is 100, the area of triangle $DEC$ is 10, and $EC = ED$. What is the distance from $A$ to $E$?

    (A) 11   (B) 12   (C) $\sqrt{146}$   (D) 13   (E) $\sqrt{244}$

# 3                                                                3

SECTION **3**—ANALYTICAL ABILITY

Time—60 Minutes
  35 Questions

**Directions**: In this section, each set of questions is based on a short passage or a set of conditions. Sometimes, in answering these questions, you might want to make a table or diagram. For each question, choose the best answer from the five choices listed.

1. The nursing shortage in this country is a phony one, caused by the concentration of nurses in the geographical regions with the highest paid and most generous fringe benefits for nurses. In addition, the League of American Nurses has artificially worsened the shortage by encouraging nursing schools to keep enrollments low in order to boost nurses' salaries to even higher levels.

   All of the following statements, if true, would tend to weaken the argument above except:

   (A) Although nurses are paid less in Texas than in Connecticut, there are 35% more nurses in Texas than in Connecticut.
   (B) Nationwide, the salaries of nurses have risen at a slower rate than inflation over the last ten years.
   (C) The number of students who earned degrees in nursing last year was almost double the number six years ago.
   (D) Those areas of the country with the highest pay for nurses have the highest living costs.
   (E) The League of American Nurses has almost no influence on the policies of American nursing schools.

**Questions 2–5**

Every night Jillian has homework in four subjects: algebra, biology, English, and history. Once she starts an assignment, she always completes it, before beginning another one. She does not do her homework in the same order each night, but she does adhere to the following two rules:

   She always does her algebra before her biology.
   She always does her English before her history.

2. Each of the following is an order in which Jillian could do her assignments EXCEPT

   (A) Algebra, biology, English, history
   (B) Algebra, English, biology, history
   (C) English, algebra, biology, history
   (D) English, history, algebra, biology
   (E) English, biology, algebra, history

3. In how many different orders can Jillian do her homework assignments?

   (A) 2   (B) 3   (C) 6   (D) 12   (E) 24

4. Which of the following, if adopted by Jillian as an additional rule, would mean that she has to do her homework in the exact same order each night?

   (A) She always does her algebra before her history.
   (B) She always does her algebra before her English.
   (C) She always does her biology before her history.
   (D) She always does her history before her algebra.
   (E) She always does her history before her biology.

5. If one night in addition to her other assignments, Jillian has to write a book report, and she decides to do that immediately after completing her algebra homework and immediately before doing her history homework, which of the following CANNOT be true?

   (A) She does her English homework first.
   (B) She does her algebra homework second.
   (C) She does her book report third.
   (D) She does her biology homework last.
   (E) She does her history homework last.

6. Student participation in a voluntary community service program at John Adams High School increased every year, from 20% in 1995 to 40% in 2000.

   If the preceding statement is true, which of the following statements CANNOT be true about the student population at John Adams High School between 1995 and 2000?

   (A) The number of students in the school increased, and the number of students participating in the community service program increased.
   (B) The number of students in the school decreased, and the number of students participating in the community service program increased.

3                                                                         3

(C) The number of students in the school increased, and the number of students participating in the community service program decreased.

(D) The number of students participating in the community service program increased by 40%.

(E) The number of students participating in the community service program remained the same.

## Questions 7–8

The internal combustion engine, which powers all private motorized vehicles, should be banned. It burns up petroleum products that are needed to produce plastics, synthetics, and many medicines. Once all the oil is gone, we will no longer be able to produce these valuable commodities. Yet we do not have to burn gasoline to satisfy our transportation needs. Other kinds of engines could be developed if the oil companies would stop blocking research efforts.

7. The argument above would be most weakened by the development of which of the following?

(A) An internal combustion engine that operated on one-tenth the gasoline used in a normal engine

(B) A car that operated on solar energy stored in special batteries

(C) A method of producing plastic that used no petroleum products

(D) A synthetic oil with all the properties of natural oil

(E) A means of locating numerous undiscovered oil fields

8. The argument above would be most strengthened if which of the following were true?

(A) One of the oil companies has suppressed the discovery of an engine that burns only alcohol.

(B) Some of the medicines that require petroleum for their production help to control and cure several of the world's most deadly diseases.

(C) The world's current oil reserves are about half of what they were 30 years ago.

(D) In high-pollution areas, automobile exhaust fumes have been shown to cause high rates of lung cancer and heart disease.

(E) When gasoline is burned inside an auto engine, less than one-fourth of the energy produced is used to propel the vehicle.

## Questions 9–13

At Bayside High School, each of the seven math teachers—F, G, H, I, J, K, and L—are required to give one extra help class each day. These classes can take place either before school, during lunch period, or after school. In scheduling these classes the chairperson of the math department must follow the following rules:

At least two teachers must hold their classes before school.

At least three teachers must hold their classes after school.

H is not available after school, and J is available only after school.

I always gives extra help during her lunch period.

G will give help before school only if F is also scheduled then.

9. If L gives extra help during lunch, which of the following must be true?

(A) F gives help before school.
(B) H gives help before school.
(C) J gives help before school.
(D) K gives help during lunch.
(E) G gives help after school.

10. Which of the following could be a complete list of the teachers who give help before school?

(A) G
(B) G, H
(C) F, G, I
(D) F, G, K
(E) F, G, H, K

11. All of the following statements could be true EXCEPT

(A) The same number of teachers give help before school as after school.
(B) The same number of teachers give help before school as during lunch.
(C) Twice as many teachers give help after school as before.
(D) Twice as many teachers give help after school as during lunch.
(E) Four times as many teachers give help after school as during lunch.

12. If F is the only teacher not yet scheduled, and without violating any of the given conditions he could be scheduled in any of the three time slots, then which of the following must be true?

   (A) G gives help after school.
   (B) K gives help before school.
   (C) H gives help at lunch.
   (D) K gives help after school.
   (E) L gives help after school.

13. If G and H are both scheduled to give help before school, which of the following CANNOT be true?

   (A) F gives help before school.
   (B) K gives help at lunch.
   (C) Only I gives help at lunch.
   (D) K gives help after school.
   (E) L gives help after school.

14. *Governor*: Compared with children in other states, infants born in California weigh more, survive the first years in greater numbers, and live longer. The hysteria about the danger of pesticides in California has attracted attention simply because a few Hollywood stars have appeared on television talk shows. Pesticides are the responsibility of the California Department of Food and Agriculture, and we can be sure its members are doing their job.

   The governor's argument would be weakened if all of the following were shown to be true EXCEPT

   (A) in California rates of melanoma and some forms of leukemia linked to exposure to pesticides are above national norms
   (B) the three highest positions at the California Department of Food and Agriculture are held by farm owners
   (C) synthetic pesticide residues in food cause more cancer than do "natural pesticides" that the plants themselves produce
   (D) more Californians suffer the consequences of air pollution than do the citizens in any other state
   (E) children of farm workers are three times more likely to suffer childhood cancers than children of urban parents

**Questions 15–18**

Four women—Alice, Bette, Carol, and Diane—and four men—Eric, Frank, George, and Harry—are at a formal dinner party, seated around a rectangular table. The host and hostess are at opposite ends of the table, and there are three guests on each side.

   Each man is sitting next to at least one woman, and each woman is sitting next to at least one man.

Harry is sitting opposite Diane, who is not the hostess.
George is sitting opposite a woman and has a woman on his right.
Alice is at the hostess's right, next to Frank.

15. Which of the following statements could be true?

   I. Eric is the host.
   II. Bette is the hostess.
   III. Each man is sitting opposite his wife.

   (A) I only
   (B) I and II only
   (C) I and III only
   (D) II and III only
   (E) I, II, and III

16. If each man is sitting opposite his wife, which of the following pairs must be married to one another?

   (A) Eric and Bette
   (B) Eric and Carol
   (C) Frank and Carol
   (D) George and Alice
   (E) George and Diane

17. How many people are sitting between two people of the opposite sex? (A man sitting between two women or a woman sitting between two men.)

   (A) 0   (B) 1   (C) 2   (D) 3   (E) 4

18. If during dinner George and Diane exchange seats, which of the following statements must be true of the new seating arrangement?

   I. No one is sitting between two people of the opposite sex.
   II. One side of the table consists entirely of people of the same sex.
   III. A single straight line can be drawn on the table so that all the women are on one side and all the men on the other side.

   (A) I only
   (B) II only
   (C) I and II only
   (D) I and III only
   (E) II and III only

**3**                                    **3**

19. If Rorie wakes up after 7:00 on a school day, she just grabs a granola bar for breakfast. When she wakes up after 7:00 on a day that there is no school, she makes herself an omelette.

    If the preceding statements are true, and if Rorie did not have a granola bar for breakfast today, which of the following statements must be true?

    (A) Today is a school day.
    (B) Today is not a school day.
    (C) Rorie had an omelette today.
    (D) Either today is a school day or Rorie woke up after 7:00.
    (E) Either today is not a school day or Rorie woke up before 7:00.

**Questions 20–23**

The Sociology department at the State University consists of three untenured professors—Q, R, and S—and seven tenured professors—T, U, V, W, X, Y, and Z. At the beginning of a new academic year, Z, the chairperson of the department, decided to reorganize the curriculum and budget committees by assigning each of the other nine professors to exactly one of the two committees. In making her assignments, the chairperson adheres to the following conditions:

> The budget committee will have five members, and the curriculum committee will have four.
> The budget committee will have exactly one untenured professor.
> S and Y cannot be assigned to the same committee.
> U and W cannot be assigned to the same committee.
> V and X must be assigned to the same committee.
> If U and X are on the same committee, then Q must be on the other committee.

20. Which of the following could be the members of the budget committee?

    (A) R, S, U, V, X
    (B) Q, U, V, X, Y
    (C) R, U, V, X, Y
    (D) Q, T, V, X, Y
    (E) S, T, V, X, Y

21. If Q and R are on the same committee, which of the following must be true?

    (A) U is on the curriculum committee.
    (B) V is on the curriculum committee.
    (C) Y is on the curriculum committee.
    (D) U is on the budget committee.
    (E) V is on the budget committee.

22. If Q and X are on the budget committee, which of the following is a pair of professors who must be on different committees?

    (A) U and V
    (B) V and Y
    (C) S and U
    (D) V and W
    (E) R and T

23. Which of the following CANNOT serve on the curriculum committee?

    (A) Q
    (B) R
    (C) U
    (D) W
    (E) X

**Questions 24–28**

On Saturdays, a college admissions office offers five campus tours for prospective students at 10:00, 11:00, 12:00, 1:00, and 2:00. Five students—Adam, Kit, Noah, Pete, and Rebecca—are available to lead the tours. The person in the admissions office who is in charge of scheduling the tours adheres to the following rules and preferences:

> Each tour has exactly two leaders.
> Each student must lead at least one tour.
> No student can lead three consecutive tours.
> Kit must be one of the leaders of the 10:00 tour.
> Rebecca must lead both the 1:00 and 2:00 tours.
> Kit and Pete cannot be assigned to lead the same tour.

24. If Pete leads three tours one Saturday, which of the following is a pair of tours he must lead?

    (A) 10:00 and 12:00
    (B) 11:00 and 12:00
    (C) 11:00 and 1:00
    (D) 11:00 and 2:00
    (E) 12:00 and 2:00

25. If Kit is scheduled to give four tours one Saturday, which of the following could be the leaders of the 12:00 tour that day?

    (A) Adam and Noah
    (B) Adam and Pete
    (C) Pete and Rebecca
    (D) Kit and Rebecca
    (E) Adam and Kit

# 3                                                     3

26. If Pete and Rebecca are scheduled to lead the exact same tours, which of the following could be true?

    (A) Adam and Noah lead two tours together.
    (B) Kit leads a tour at 12:00.
    (C) Pete leads a tour at 12:00.
    (D) Noah leads a tour at 1:00.
    (E) Adam leads a tour at 2:00.

27. In how many ways can an acceptable schedule be completed for a Saturday on which Adam leads four tours?

    (A) 0   (B) 1   (C) 2   (D) 3   (E) 4

28. If on one Saturday, none of the students leads three tours, which of the following must be true?

    (A) Adam and Noah must lead a tour together.
    (B) Some pair of students must lead two tours together.
    (C) Either Kit or Pete must lead a tour with Rebecca.
    (D) Everyone leads two tours in a row.
    (E) No one other than Rebecca leads two tours in a row.

## Questions 29 and 30

In a laboratory study, 160 rabbits in an experimental group were injected with Serum D, while 160 rabbits in a control group were injected with a harmless sugar solution. Within two weeks, 39% of the experimental group rabbits had contracted jungle fever, a highly contagious and usually fatal disease. Therefore, jungle fever must be caused by some substance similar to the substances found in Serum D.

29. The above argument would be most seriously weakened if it were shown that

    (A) none of the substances in Serum D occurs naturally in the habitats of most species of rabbit
    (B) the rabbits in the experimental group had been kept strictly isolated from one another
    (C) jungle fever is usually found only among victims of the bite of the South American Lesser Hooded Viper
    (D) the scientists administering the injections were unaware of the contents of the solutions they were using
    (E) one of the rabbits in the experimental group had had jungle fever prior to the start of the experiment

30. The above argument would be most greatly strengthened if it were shown that

    (A) the normal rate of jungle fever among rabbits is less than 1%
    (B) 40% of the rabbits in the control group had also contracted jungle fever within two weeks

    (C) Serum D contains substances extracted from the root of a certain poisonous jungle wildflower
    (D) the blood of jungle fever victims invariably contains a high level of a certain toxic substance also found in Serum D
    (E) nearly all the rabbits who contracted jungle fever died within two days of the appearance of the first symptoms

## Questions 31–34

In a series of three assemblies for middle school students, six high school varsity athletes—J, K, L, M, N, and P—have been asked to speak about the sports that they play. Exactly four of the athletes will speak at each assembly—two about football and one each about basketball and tennis. J must speak during the first assembly; the other five athletes have no restrictions, except that no athlete will discuss the same sport in two consecutive assemblies. The sports that each of the athletes play is as follows:

    J, K, L, and M all play football.
    L and N play basketball.
    K, M, and P play tennis.

31. If J, K, L, and N speak at assembly 1, which of the following is a list of athletes who could speak at assembly 2?

    (A) J, K, L, P
    (B) J, L, M, P
    (C) K, M, N, P
    (D) L, M, N, P
    (E) K, L, M, P

32. Which of the following is a complete list of the athletes for whom it is possible to create a schedule that would allow them to speak in each of the three assemblies?

    (A) K, L
    (B) K, M
    (C) K, L, M
    (D) J, K, L, M
    (E) K, L, M, N, P

33. If L speaks about basketball in assembly 2, which of the following must be true?

    (A) L does not speak in either assembly 1 or 3.
    (B) J and L never speak in the same assembly.
    (C) K and M speak about football in assembly 1.
    (D) N speaks in exactly two of the three assemblies.
    (E) P speaks about tennis in assembly 3.

**3**

**3**

34. If the high school athletic director needs one of the six students to attend a conference on the day of the assemblies, who could she send and still be able to run all three assemblies under the original conditions?

(A) K   (B) L   (C) M   (D) N   (E) P

35. In recommending to the board of trustees a tuition increase of $500 per year, the president of the university said: "There were no student demonstrations over the previous increases of $300 last year and $200 the year before."

If the president's statement is accurate, which of the following can be validly inferred from the information given?

   I. Most students in previous years felt that the increases were justified because of increased operating costs.

  II. Student apathy was responsible for the failure of students to protest the previous tuition increases.

 III. Students are not likely to demonstrate over the new tuition increases.

(A) None
(B) I only
(C) II only
(D) III only
(E) I and III only

# Answer Key—Diagnostic Test

## Section 1—Verbal Ability

| | | | | | |
|---|---|---|---|---|---|
| 1. **D** | 6. **E** | 11. **B** | 16. **C** | 21. **B** | 26. **A** |
| 2. **B** | 7. **C** | 12. **A** | 17. **C** | 22. **E** | 27. **B** |
| 3. **B** | 8. **C** | 13. **A** | 18. **B** | 23. **E** | 28. **D** |
| 4. **C** | 9. **E** | 14. **D** | 19. **B** | 24. **C** | 29. **D** |
| 5. **B** | 10. **D** | 15. **C** | 20. **C** | 25. **E** | 30. **E** |

## Section 2—Quantitative Ability

*Note*: The letters in brackets following the Quantitative Ability answers refer to the sections of Chapter 15 in which you can find the information you need to answer the questions. For example, 1. **C** [E] means that the answer to question 1 is C, and that the solution requires information found in Section 15-E: Averages. Also, 20. **A** [14] means that the answer to question 20 is based on information in Chapter 14: Data Interpretation.

| | | | | | |
|---|---|---|---|---|---|
| 1. **D** [A] | 6. **D** [O] | 11. **A** [J,L] | 16. **C** [E,J] | 21. **D** [14] | 26. **D** [J,K] |
| 2. **C** [J] | 7. **D** [G] | 12. **C** [E,G] | 17. **C** [K] | 22. **D** [C,D] | 27. **E** [G] |
| 3. **B** [A,B] | 8. **A** [A] | 13. **B** [K] | 18. **B** [F] | 23. **A** [L] | 28. **D** [J,K] |
| 4. **B** [A] | 9. **B** [O] | 14. **E** [14] | 19. **C** [G] | 24. **C** [H] | |
| 5. **B** [I] | 10. **C** [A] | 15. **C** [14] | 20. **D** [14] | 25. **C** [L] | |

## Section 3—Analytical Ability

| | | | | |
|---|---|---|---|---|
| 1. **A** | 8. **B** | 15. **E** | 22. **A** | 29. **E** |
| 2. **E** | 9. **B** | 16. **D** | 23. **E** | 30. **D** |
| 3. **C** | 10. **D** | 17. **E** | 24. **D** | 31. **E** |
| 4. **D** | 11. **D** | 18. **D** | 25. **B** | 32. **C** |
| 5. **E** | 12. **A** | 19. **E** | 26. **B** | 33. **D** |
| 6. **C** | 13. **B** | 20. **C** | 27. **E** | 34. **E** |
| 7. **D** | 14. **D** | 21. **C** | 28. **C** | 35. **A** |

# Self-Appraisal

Now that you have completed the Diagnostic Test, evaluate your performance. Identify your strengths and weaknesses, and then plan a practical study program based on what you have discovered.

Use the Answer Key to check your answers. Your raw score for each section is equal to the number of correct answers you had. Once you have determined your raw score for each ability area, use the conversion chart that follows to get your scaled score. Note that this conversion chart is provided to give you a very rough estimate of the GRE score you would achieve if you took the test now without any further preparation. When you take the computer-based GRE, your scaled score will be determined not only by the number of questions you answer correctly, but also by the difficulty level of those questions. The unofficial conversion chart presented here gives you only an approximate idea of how raw scores convert into scaled scores.

Use this Diagnostic Test to identify areas you may be weak in. You may find that you had trouble with a particular question type (for example, you didn't do well on the analogy questions in the verbal section), or with particular subject matter (for example, you didn't do well on any geometry questions, whether they were quantitative comparisons or discrete quantitative). Determining what you need to concentrate on will help you plan an effective study program.

Remember that, in addition to evaluating your scores and identifying weak areas, you should read all the answer explanations for questions you answered incorrectly, questions you guessed on, and questions you answered correctly but found difficult. Reviewing the answer explanations will help you understand concepts and strategies, and may point out shortcuts.

# Score Conversion Chart

| Raw Score | Scaled Scores | | |
|---|---|---|---|
| | **Verbal Score** | **Quantitative Score** | **Analytical Score** |
| 35 | | | 800 |
| 33 | | | 780 |
| 30 | 800 | | 750 |
| 28 | 760 | 800 | 710 |
| 27 | 720 | 770 | 690 |
| 24 | 650 | 700 | 630 |
| 21 | 590 | 630 | 550 |
| 18 | 500 | 560 | 470 |
| 15 | 450 | 500 | 400 |
| 12 | 390 | 430 | 350 |
| 9 | 310 | 350 | 300 |
| 6 | 240 | 270 | 240 |
| 3 | 200 | 200 | 200 |

# Answer Explanations

## Section 1—Verbal Ability

1. **D.** The opposite of a *prodigal* (spendthrift; extravagant person) is an *economical person*. Beware eye-catchers. Choice C is incorrect. A *prodigal* is not a *prodigy* (wonder; gifted person). Think of "a prodigal squandering his wealth."

2. **B.** The opposite of *artifice* (trickery; guile) is *sincerity*. Think of being "tricked by her skillful artifice."

3. **B.** Given the ubiquity of light, it is *unsurprising* that creatures have *developed* the biologically helpful ability to make use of light energy. Note the use of *therefore* indicating that the omitted portion of the sentence supports or continues a thought developed elsewhere in the sentence.

4. **C.** The politicians do not forsake center stage. However, if they did forsake center stage once in a while, the public might like them better for their *self-effacement* (withdrawal from attention).

5. **B.** By definition, a *route* that is *circuitous* follows an indirect course. Likewise, an *argument* that is *devious* follows an indirect course. (Defining Characteristic)

6. **E.** To be *officious* (meddlesome) is to be *helpful* in an excessive, offensive manner. To be *sycophantic* (fawning, obsequious) is to be *deferential* (respectful) in an excessive, offensive manner. (Manner)

7. **C.** The author states that the later novels of James play down prominent action. Thus they lack *overtly dramatic incident*. However, the author goes on to state that James's novels *do* possess interest; they carry the reader through "a rich analysis of the mental adjustments of the characters to the realities of their personal situations." It is this implicitly dramatic psychological revelation that sustains the reader's interest.
Question A is unanswerable on the basis of the passage. It is evident that James wrote psychological novels; it is nowhere stated that he originated the genre.
Question B is unanswerable on the basis of the passage. Although conventional narrative technique relates "events in distinctly phased sequences," clearly separating them, it does not necessarily recount action in *strictly* chronological order.

Question D is unanswerable on the basis of the passage. The passage does not deal with the general public's reaction to James.
Question E is unanswerable on the basis of the passage. The passage talks of qualities in James as a novelist in terms of their being *characteristic,* not in terms of their making him *unique.*

8. C. While the stories themselves grow simpler, their moral and psychological aspects become increasingly complex. Choice A is incorrect. The passage mentions the specific description of settings as characteristic of James's early, conventional novels, not of his later works.
Choice B is incorrect. In his later novels James grew less concerned with plot and more concerned with psychological revelation.
Choice D is incorrect. The "excitement of visible actions building up to a climactic event" (lines 31–32) is characteristic of the common novel, not of the Jamesian psychological novel.
Choice E is incorrect. The later novels tend instead to subordinate dramatic effect to psychological exploration and revelation.

9. E. The author refers to novels of action as "overstuffed" and describes them as "crammed with *adventitious* events"—events that are not inherent in the situation, but that are added, possibly irrelevantly, to the general story. However, these comments are merely made in passing: the author is not launching an attack against the novel of action. Thus, his attitude is best described as one of *mild disapprobation* or disapproval.
Choice A is incorrect. The author is not *pointedly indignant* or deeply resentful in tone. He is merely making mildly critical remarks in passing.
Choice B is incorrect. The author does make passing comments that disparage the novel of action. He is not wholly *neutral* on the topic.
Choice C is incorrect. While the author does disparage the novel of action, he does not ridicule or *deride* it sharply.
Choice D is incorrect. The author is certainly not a *strong partisan* or advocate of the novel of action.

10. D. The opposite of to *equivocate* (avoid committing oneself in what one says) is to *pledge* (bind or commit oneself solemnly).
Think of politicians "hedging and equivocating."

11. B. The opposite of *opulence* (wealth; affluence) is *penury* or extreme poverty.
Think of "luxurious opulence."

12. A. Something *ephemeral* (fleeting; transient) lacks *permanence.* Something *erratic* (unpredictable) lacks *predictability.*
(Antonym Variant)

13. A. To be *nonplussed* (totally at a loss) is to exhibit *bafflement* (perplexity). To be *discomfited* (abashed; disconcerted) is to exhibit *embarrassment.*
Beware eye-catchers. Choice D is incorrect. To be *despicable* is to be worthy of *contempt*; it is not to *exhibit* contempt.
(Synonym Variant)

14. D. To *ogle* is to *observe* or look at someone provocatively (in an attention-getting manner). To *flaunt* is to *display* or show off something provocatively (in an attention-getting manner).
(Manner)

15. C. You are dealing with either similar or contradictory impulses. If the impulses are similar (that is, *analogous, comparable,* or *related,* the second missing word should be a synonym or near-synonym for *individualize.* If the impulses are contradictory (that is, *disparate* or *divergent*), the second missing word should be an antonym or near-antonym for *individualize.* In this case, the latter holds true. The impulses are *divergent*; they are the impulse to individualize and the contradictory impulse to *typify* (treat characters as representatives of a type).

16. C. In a case in which experts disagree, it is *incumbent on* responsible scholars (that is, falls upon them as a scholarly duty or obligation) to *refrain from* making statements that are dogmatic or excessively assertive and arbitrary about the issue.

17. C. The subduction zone is the site of the destruction or consumption of existing lithospheric material. In contrast, the mid-ocean ridge is the site of the creation or emergence of new lithospheric material.
Choice A is incorrect. Both mid-ocean ridges and subduction zones are boundaries between plates.
Choice B is incorrect. Both are located on the ocean floor.
Choice D is incorrect. It is unsupported by the passage.
Choice E is incorrect. The reverse is true.

18. B. Choice B is correct. You are told that the new lithospheric material is injected into a mid-ocean ridge, a suboceanic mountain range. This new material does not disappear; it is added to the material already there. Thus, it is *incorporated into* the existing mid-ocean ridge.

Choice A is incorrect. "In general the plates are in motion with respect to one another." Nothing suggests that they become immobilized; indeed, they are said to diverge from the ridge, sliding as they diverge.

Choice C is incorrect. The passage specifically denies it. ("The size of the earth is essentially constant.")

Choice D is incorrect. It is the earth itself whose magnetic field reverses. Nothing in the passage suggests the new lithospheric material has any such potential.

Choice E is incorrect. At a mid-ocean ridge, the site at which new lithospheric material is injected from below, the plates diverge; they do not sink. (They sink, one plate diving under another, at a subduction zone.)

19. **B.** Line 23 states that one plate is pushed under another and is reincorporated or *absorbed* into the mantle.

Choice A is incorrect. Lithospheric material rises at mid-ocean ridges, not at subduction zones.

Choice C is incorrect. New lithospheric material is injected at a mid-ocean ridge.

Choice D is incorrect. The injection of new lithospheric material causes sea-floor spreading around the mid-ocean ridge.

Choice E is incorrect. The lithospheric plates are described as diverging from a mid-ocean ridge, not from a subduction zone.

20. **C.** The opposite of to *hone* or sharpen is to *dull* (make blunt).
Think of "honing a razor."

21. **B.** The opposite of *phlegmatic* (stolid; undemonstrative) is *ardent* (passionate; eager).
Think of "phlegmatic and uncaring."

22. **E.** The opposite of a *banality* (commonplace; trite or overused expression) is a *novel expression*.
Think of "the banality of a greeting card rhyme."

23. **E.** *Thirst* is a specific example of a *drive* (state of instinctual need). *Smell* is a specific example of a *sense*. (Class and Member)

24. **C.** *Skulduggery* or dishonest, unscrupulous behavior is the mark of the *swindler. Chicanery* or trickery is the mark of the *trickster.*
(Defining Characteristic)

25. **E.** After incubating the new functions, the next step would be to *nurture* or foster their growth until they were ready to be sent out

into the world. Their departure, however, would not diminish the cities, for by continuing to breed fresh ideas the cities would *renew* themselves.

Note the metaphoric usage of *incubate* and *breed* that influences the writer's choice of words. Cities do not literally incubate businesses or breed ideas; they only do so figuratively.

26. **A.** Man is *gregarious* or sociable. However, he is more in need of mental companionship than of physical companionship. The writer plays on words in his conceit that a man may like to go alone for a walk but hates to stand alone in his *opinions*.

27. **B.** The opposite of *erudite* (scholarly; learned) is *ignorant*. Think of "an erudite scholar."

28. **D.** The opposite of *effrontery* (shameless boldness) is diffidence (tentativeness; timidity). Think of "shocking effrontery."

29. **D.** The opening sentence describes the shattering of the Iroquois leadership's pro-British policy. The remainder of the passage describes how Iroquois policy changed to reflect changes in European military goals.

Choice A is incorrect. The passage is expository, not accusatory.

Choice B is incorrect. Nothing in the passage suggests that such charges were made against the Iroquois.

Choice C is incorrect. It is unsupported by the passage.

Choice E is incorrect. The passage demonstrates the Iroquois were able to play European power politics.

Remember, when asked to find the main idea, be sure to check the opening and summary sentences of each paragraph.

30. **E.** Lines 20–32 indicate that in the early 1700s and through most of the eighteenth century the Iroquois *did* hold the balance of power. Therefore, Choice E is the correct answer.

Choice A is incorrect. The raid on Lachine was an effective response to French aggression, as was the Iroquois-enforced policy of aggressive neutrality.

Choice B is incorrect. James II's overthrow was followed by colonial uprisings.

Choice C is incorrect. In response to the Iroquois leaders' supposed favoring of the British (lines 39–45), the French went to war.

Choice D is incorrect. This sums up the policy of aggressive neutrality.

# Section 2—Quantitative Ability

Two asterisks (**) indicate an alternative method of solving.

1.  **D.**  By the laws of exponents, Column A is $a^4a^5 = a^9$, and Column B is $(a^3)^2 = a^6$. If $a = 1$, the columns are equal; but if $a = 2$, Column A is much greater. Neither column is always greater, and the two columns are not always equal (D).

2.  **C.**  Since the measure of an exterior angle of a triangle is equal to the sum of the measures of the two opposite interior angles [KEY FACT J2], $c = a + b \Rightarrow a + b - c = 0$. The columns are equal (C).
    **Use TACTIC 13-1: plug in easy-to-use numbers. If $a = 60$ and $b = 70$, then $d = 50 \Rightarrow c = 130$, and $60 + 70 - 130 = 0$.

3.  **B.**

    | Column A | Column B |
    |----------|----------|
    | $\sqrt{a + b}$ | $\sqrt{a} + \sqrt{b}$ |

    Since the quantities in each column are positive, we can square them [TACTIC 13-3].

    |   |   |
    |---|---|
    | $a + b$ | $a + 2\sqrt{ab} + b$ |

    Subtract $a + b$ from each column

    |   |   |
    |---|---|
    | $0$ | $2\sqrt{ab}$ |

    Since $a$ and $b$ are positive, $2\sqrt{ab}$ is positive. Column B is greater.

4.  **B.**  There are three primes between 40 and 50: 41, 43, and 47, but only two primes between 30 and 40: 31 and 37. *Note:* remember that other than 2 and 5 *every* prime ends in 1, 3, 7, or 9, so those are the only numbers you need to check.

5.  **B.**  The unmarked angle opposite the 60° angle also measures 60° [KEY FACT I4], and the sum of the measures of all six angles in the diagram is 360° [KEY FACT I3]. So,

    $$360 = a + b + c + 20 + 60 + 60$$
    $$= a + b + c + 140.$$

    Subtracting 140 from each side, we get that $a + b + c = 220$.

6.  **D.**  Draw a Venn diagram. Since 10 seniors are in *both* band and orchestra, 30 are in band only and 50 are in orchestra only. 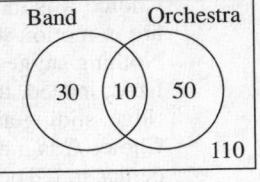 Therefore, $10 + 30 + 50 = 90$ seniors are in at least one group, and the remaining 110 are in neither.

7.  **D**  Let $x$ be the amount in dollars that each of the 20 children were going to contribute; then $20x$ represents the cost of the present. When 4 children dropped out, the remaining 16 each had to pay $(x + 1.50)$ dollars. So, $16(x + 1.5) = 20x \Rightarrow 16x + 24 = 20x \Rightarrow 24 = 4x \Rightarrow x = 6$, and so the cost of the present was $20 \times 6 = 120$ dollars.
    **Since each of the 16 remaining children had to pay an extra \$1.50, the extra payments totaled $16 \times \$1.50 = \$24$. This is the amount that each of the others would have paid, so each one would have paid \$6. The cost of the gift was $20 \times \$6 = \$120$.

8.  **A.**

    |   | Column A | Column B |
    |---|----------|----------|
    | Rewrite $20^{10}$. | $10^{20}$ | $20^{10} = (2 \times 10)^{10}$ |
    | Use a law of exponents. | $10^{20}$ | $2^{10} \times 10^{10}$ |
    | Divide each column by $10^{10}$. | $10^{10}$ | $2^{10}$ |

    Column A is *much* greater.

9.  **B.**  From the 124 people in front of Jill, remove Jack plus the 24 people in front of Jack: $124 - 25 = 99$. Column B is greater.

10. **C.**  $3^{10} \times 27^2 = 3^{10} \times (3^3)^2 = 3^{10} \times 3^6 = 3^{16}$. Also, $9^2 \times 3^n = (3^2)^2 \times 3^n = 3^4 \times 3^n = 3^{4+n}$. So, $3^{16} = 3^{4+n}$ and $16 = 4 + n$. Then $n = 12$.

11. **A.**  Since $OA$ and $OB$ are radii, they are each equal to 5. With no restrictions on $x$, chord $AB$ could be any positive number less than 10 (the length of a diameter), and the bigger $x$ is, the bigger $AB$ is. If $x$ were 90, $AB$ would be $\sqrt{50}$, but you are told that $x > 90$, so $AB > \sqrt{50} > 7$. Therefore, the perimeter of $\triangle AOB$ is greater than $5 + 5 + 7 = 17$. Column A is greater.

12. **C.**  $\dfrac{a - b}{c - a} = 1 \Rightarrow a - b = c - a \Rightarrow 2a = b + c \Rightarrow a = \dfrac{b + c}{2}$. The columns are equal (C).
    **Use TACTIC G2. Since you have an equation with three variables, choose values for two of them and find the third. Let $a = 2$ and $b = 1$. Then $\dfrac{2 - 1}{c - 2} = 1 \Rightarrow c = 3$. The average of $b$ and $c$ is 2, which equals $a$.

13. **B.** If the side of a square is 10, its diagonal is $10\sqrt{2} \approx 14$ [KEY FACTS J8 and J9]. So the square in Column B is larger.
\*\*The area of the square in Column A is $10^2 = 100$. The area of the square in Column B is $\frac{1}{2}(15^2) = \frac{1}{2}(225) = 112.5$.

14. **E.** Exports to Eastern Europe from other Eastern European countries increased from \$9.8 billion (10% of \$98 billion) to \$20.88 billion (12% of \$174 billion)—an increase of slightly more than 100%.

15. **C.** If France's exports to Eastern Europe were four times those of the United States, than France accounted for 8% of the total exports.

Since 8% is $\frac{1}{8}$ of 64%, France accounted for $\frac{1}{8}$ or 12.5% of the exports from the European Union.

16. **C.** The average of the measures of the three angles of *any* triangle is $180° \div 3 = 60°$. The columns are equal (C).

17. **C.** Ignore the $x$'s and the $y$'s. In any "staircase" the perimeter is just twice the sum of the height and the length. So the perimeter is $2(12 + 14) = 2(26) = 52$. The columns are equal (C).

18. **B.** We are given that $x^2 - y^2 = (x - y)^2$
• Expand: $x^2 - y^2 = x^2 - 2xy + y^2$
• Subtract $x^2$ from each side: $-y^2 = -2xy + y^2$
• Add $y^2$ to each side:
$$0 = 2y^2 - 2xy = 2y(y - x)$$
So, either $y = 0$ or $y - x = 0$. But, it is given that $x \neq y$, so $y - x \neq 0$.
Therefore, it *must* be that $y = 0$ (II is true). If we replace $y$ by 0 in the original equation, we get $x^2 = x^2$ which is true for *any* value of $x$. Therefore, it is not true that $x$ must equal 0 (I is false). Also, it is not true that $x = -y$ (III is also false). Then II only is true.
\*\*Look at the choices. *If $x = 0$*, then $-y^2 = (-y)^2 = y^2$ which means that $y = 0$, which is impossible since $x \neq y$. So, I is false. Eliminate Choices A, D, and E. If $y = 0$, then $(x)^2 = x^2$, which is always true *no matter what $x$ is*. So, $y$ could be 0. Don't eliminate B yet. If $x = -y$, $x^2 = y^2 \Rightarrow x^2 - y^2 = 0$; but $(x - y)^2 = (x + x)^2 = (2x)^2 = 4x^2$, which clearly does not have to be 0. Eliminate Choice C. The answer must be B.

19. **C.** Set up the equation:
$$(x + 3) + (2x - 3) + (3x - 5) = 25$$
Collect like terms: $6x - 5 = 25$
Add 5 to each side: $6x = 30$
Divide each side by 6: $x = 5$

Plugging in 5 for $x$, we get that the lengths of the sides are 8, **7**, and 10. The length of the shortest side is **7**.

20. **D.** In each election with only two candidates, the candidate who received the greater number of votes, received more than 50% of them. In 1972 and 1980 the number of votes received by other major candidates was far less than and in 1996 that number was approximately equal to, the difference between the number of votes received by the Republican and the Democrat. Therefore, the percent of votes won by the winner was greater than or approximately equal to 50%. In 1992, however, the sum of the number of votes received by the Republican and the other major candidate greatly exceeded that of the Democratic winner. Consequently, the winner had fewer than 50% of the votes.

21. **D.** It is easy to see that 1992 was the only year in which the total number of votes cast for president exceeded 100 million.

22. **D.** Use TACTIC 12-3: pick easy-to-use numbers. Assume that in 1990 there were 200 boys and 100 girls who earned varsity letters. Then in 2000, there were 150 boys and 125 girls. So, the ratio of girls to boys was 125:150 = 5:6 or $\frac{5}{6}$.

23. **A.** Pick a simple number for the radius of circle $Q$—say, 1. Then the radius of circle $P$ is 2, and the radius of circle $O$ is 4. The area of the large shaded region is the area of circle $O$ minus the area of circle $P$: $16\pi - 4\pi = 12\pi$. The small shaded region is just circle $Q$, whose area is $\pi$. Then, the total shaded area is $12\pi + \pi = 13\pi$.
The white area is the area of circle $P$ minus the area of circle $Q$: $4\pi - \pi = 3\pi$. The area of the shaded region is more than 4 times the area of the white region. Column A is greater.

24. **C.** Let $x$ = Adam's age in 1980. Then, in 1980, Judy's age was $3x$ and Elaine's age was $8x$. Since Elaine is 20 years older than Judy, $8x = 3x + 20 \Rightarrow 5x = 20 \Rightarrow x = 4$. Therefore, in 1988, Adam was $4 + 8 = 12$. The columns are equal (C).

25. **C.** The area of the shaded region is the area of the large circle, $25\pi$, minus the area of the middle circle, $16\pi$: $25\pi - 16\pi = 9\pi$. The striped region is just a circle of radius 3. Its area is also $9\pi$. The columns are equal (C).

26. D. Since you need a ratio, the length of the side is irrelevant. The area of a square is $s^2$ and the area of an equilateral triangle is $\dfrac{s^2\sqrt{3}}{4}$ [KEY FACT J15]. Then the ratio is

$$s^2 \div \frac{s^2\sqrt{3}}{4} = s^2 \times \frac{4}{s^2\sqrt{3}} = \frac{4}{\sqrt{3}} = \frac{4\sqrt{3}}{3}.$$

Of course, you could have used any number instead of $s$, and if you forgot the formula for the area of an equilateral triangle, you could have used $A = \dfrac{1}{2}bh$.

27. E. The easiest way to solve this is to use TAC-TIC 12-2. Let $x = 2$ and $y = 1$. Then $xy = 2$, $a = 4$ and $b = 0$. Now, plug in 4 for $a$ and 0 for $b$ and see which of the five choices is equal to 2. Only E works: $\dfrac{a^2 - b^2}{8} = \dfrac{4^2 - 0^2}{8} = \dfrac{16}{8} = 2.$

**Here is the correct algebraic solution.

Add the two equations:
$$\begin{array}{r} x + 2y = a \\ + \ x - 2y = b \\ \hline 2x = a + b \end{array}$$

Divide by 2: $\quad x = \dfrac{a + b}{2}$

Multiply the second equation by –1 and add it to the first:
$$\begin{array}{r} x + 2y = a \\ + \ -x + 2y = -b \\ \hline 4y = a - b \end{array}$$

Divide by 4: $\quad y = \dfrac{a - b}{4}$

Then $xy = \dfrac{a + b}{2} \cdot \dfrac{a - b}{4} = \dfrac{a^2 - b^2}{8}.$

This is the type of algebra you want to avoid.

28. D. Draw in segment $EXY \perp AB$. Then $XY = 10$ since it is the same length as a side of the

square. $EX$ is the height of $\triangle ECD$, whose base is 10 and whose area is 10, so

$$EX = 2 \left[\frac{1}{2}bh = \frac{1}{2}(10)(2) = 10\right], \text{ and } EY = 12.$$

Since $\triangle ECD$ is isosceles, $DX = 5$, so $AY = 5$. Finally, recognize $\triangle AYE$ as a 5-12-13 right triangle, or use the Pythagorean theorem to find the hypotenuse, $AE$, of the triangle:
$$(AE)^2 = 5^2 + 12^2 = 25 + 144 = 169,$$
so $AE = 13$.

# Section 3—Analytical Ability

1. A. The statement in Choice A may not weaken the argument. Texas is a much bigger, more heavily populated state than Connecticut. Even though there are 35% more nurses in Texas than Connecticut, the lower salary in Texas may still cause fewer nurses to go there than would otherwise go. Each of the other choices does weaken the argument.

**Solutions 2–5**
courses: A, B, E, H     A < B     E < H

2. E. None of Choices A through D violate either condition. Choice E violates the condition that Jillian must do her algebra homework before she does her biology homework.

3. C. When a question asks, "How many?" and the choices are small numbers, often the best approach is just to list the possibilities. There are 3 orders that begin with algebra and 3 that begin with English:

A, B, E, H   A, E, B, H   A, E, H, B
E, H, A, B   E, A, H, B   E, A, B, H

4. D. If Jillian does her history before her algebra, the only acceptable order for doing her homework would be: English, history, algebra, biology. None of the other choices yields a unique order.

5. E. The only possible order for Jillian to do her assignments which conforms to the given conditions is: English, algebra, book report, history, biology. Only Choice E violates this order.

6. C. It is easy to see that each of the choices except C could be true. For example, assume that in 1995 there were 100 students, 20 of whom participated in the community service program. If the number of students increased to 200 and 80 of them participated, then (A) would be true. If the number of students decreased to 90 and 36 of them participated, then (B) would be true. If the number of students decreased to 70 and 28 of them participated, that would be a 40% increase in the number of participants; so Choice D would be

true. If the number of students decreased to 50, and the number of participants remained at 20, then Choice E would be true. If the number of students increased to more than 100, and the number of participants decreased to fewer than 20, then the rate of participation could not be 40% in 2000: Choice C cannot be true.

7. **D.** The author's only basis for advocating the banning of the internal combustion engine is that the oil it burns is needed for other purposes. If a synthetic oil were developed that did everything natural oil does, the author's complaint would lose its force. All the other choices describe events which would ameliorate the problem without eliminating it.

8. **B.** The author claims that the oil we are burning is needed to produce many important commodities. Choice B underscores both the value of some of those items and the necessity of using oil to produce them. Choice A supports the author's secondary point that other methods of transportation could be developed, but does not directly support the main conclusion that the internal combustion engine should be banned. Choice C emphasizes the urgency of the problem, but the original argument makes no claims about time. Choices D and E provide bases of other arguments of gasoline-burning cars, but have no effect on the original argument.

**Solutions 9–13**

teachers: F, G, H, I, J, K, L
times: before, lunch, after

before: at least 2      after: at least 3

I = lunch    J = after    H = before or lunch
G before → F before

9. **B.** Since at least two teachers are scheduled before school and at least three are scheduled after school, there can be at most two who are scheduled during lunch. Since I and L are scheduled during lunch, no one else can be; and since H cannot be scheduled after school, H must give help before school. Choice C is impossible; the other choices could be true, but none need be true.

10. **D.** Only Choice D does not violate any of the given conditions.
Choice A violates the condition that at least two teachers give help before school.
Choice B violates the condition that if G gives help before school, then F must, also.
Choice C violates the condition that I gives help during lunch.
Choice E is impossible: since at least three teachers give help after school, and at least

one gives help during lunch, there can be at most three teachers who give help before school.

11. **D.** Since there are seven teachers at least two of whom must hold their extra help classes before school, at least three of whom must hold theirs after school, and at least one of whom (I) holds hers during lunch, there are only three possibilities for the number of teachers giving help at each time:

| Before School | Lunch | After School |
|:---:|:---:|:---:|
| 3 | 1 | 3 |
| 2 | 2 | 3 |
| 2 | 1 | 4 |

Looking at these possibilities, we see that only Choice D cannot occur.

12. **A.** If F can be scheduled into any of the time slots, the schedule so far must include two teachers before school, one at lunch, and three after school. If G gives help before school, then F must also. Since F is not required to give help before school, G cannot be scheduled then. In fact, G must give help after school, since I is the only one scheduled so far at lunch. Choice A must be true. (NOTE: Choice C is false; Choices B, D, and E could be true, but do not have to be true.)

13. **B.** The given condition completely determines the schedule. Since G is scheduled to give help before school, so is F. Therefore, three teachers—F, G, H—are scheduled before school, I is scheduled at lunch, and J, K, and L must be scheduled after school. Only Choice B is not true.

14. **D.** The issue of the danger of pesticides is addressed by A, C, and E, while B calls into question the objectivity of the Food and Agriculture Department. But Choice D deals with a different issue: air pollution. And if air pollution is a cause of illness, pesticides may be less to blame.

**Solutions 15–18**

women: A, B, C, D      men: E, F, G, H

Draw a rectangle to represent the table and use the given conditions to place as many people as possible. Put the hostess in seat 1 and the host in seat 5. Then place Alice at the hostess's right, in seat 2, and Frank in seat 3.

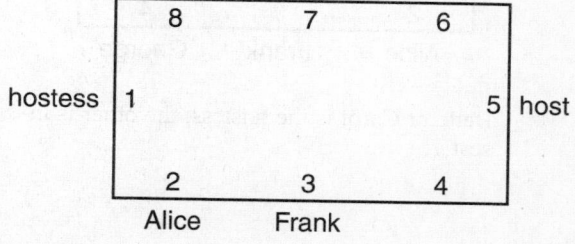

Harry and Diane are sitting opposite one another in seats 4 and 6. If Harry were in seat 4 he would be between two men, which is not allowed, so place Diane in seat 4 and Harry in seat 6. If George were the host, Harry would be at his right, not a woman, so Harry must be in seat 8.

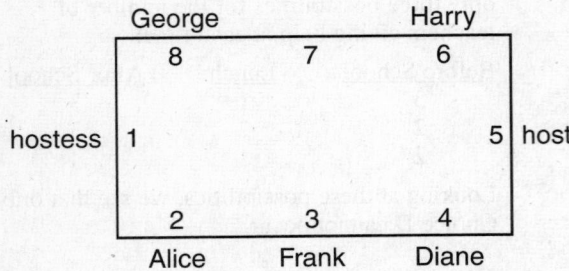

15. E.   Since Eric is the only man not yet in the diagram, he *must* be the host. (I is true.) Either Carol or Bette is the hostess, and the other is in seat 7. Bette *could be* the hostess. (II is true.) Since each man is sitting opposite a woman, it is possible that each man is opposite his wife. (III is true.)

16. D.   From the diagram of the table, we see that George and Alice are sitting opposite one another in seats 2 and 8. Since we are unsure of where Bette and Carol are sitting, some of the other couples listed *could be* married.

17. E.   Frank is sitting between two women: Alice and Diane. Diane is sitting between two men: Frank and Eric, who is the host. The woman in seat 7 is sitting between two men: Harry and George. Finally, George is sitting between Bette and Carol. There are 4 people who are sitting between two people of the opposite sex.

18. D.   Looking at the diagram, below, of the new seating arrangement, it is clear that I and III are true, and that II is not true.

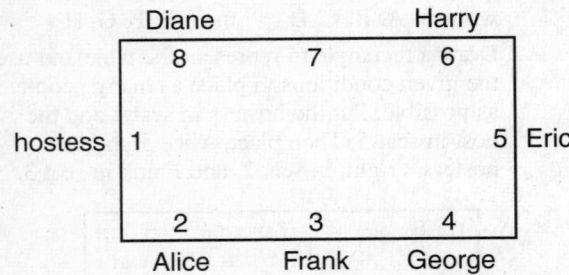

Bette or Carol is the hostess; the other is in seat 7.

19. E.   Represent "Rorie wakes up after 7:00" by W; "today is a school day" by S, and "Rorie has a granola bar for breakfast" by G. Then the logical structure of the first given statement is:

$(W \wedge S) \to G$     which is equivalent to
$\sim G \to \sim(W \wedge S)$     which is equivalent to
$\sim G \to (\sim W \vee \sim S)$.

So if Rorie did not have a granola bar, then either she woke up before 7:00 or today is not a school day (or both). None of the other choices must be true. (Note that we do not know anything about what Rorie eats when she wakes up before 7:00—on school days or otherwise.)

**Solutions 20–23**

untenured: Q, R, S     tenured: T, U, V, W, X, Y

budget: 5   curriculum: 4
of Q, R, S: 1 on budget, 2 on curriculum

$S \neq Y$   $U \neq W$   $V = X$   $(U = X) \to Q \neq X$

20. C.   Only Choice C doesn't violate any of the conditions.
Choice A violates the condition that only one untenured professor can be on the budget committee.
Choice B violates the condition that if U and X are on a committee, then Q is not on that committee.
Choice D is not possible. Since neither U nor W is listed, they must both be on the curriculum committee, violating the condition that they not be on the same committee.
Choice E violates the condition that S and Y are not on the same committee.

21. C.   If the two untenured professors Q and R are on the same committee, the committee must be the curriculum committee, and the third untenured professor, S, must be on the budget committee. Since Y cannot serve with S, Y is on the curriculum committee. None of the other choices must be true, although each of them could be true.

22. A.   The condition that Q and X are on the budget committee completely determines the composition of both committees. V must be on the budget committee with X. R and S must be the two untenured professors on the curriculum committee. U must also be on the curriculum committee, since U, X, and Q cannot be on the same committee. Then, since U and W must be on different committees, W is on the budget committee. Similarly, S and Y must be on different committees, and so Y is on the budget committee. Finally, T is the fourth member of the curriculum committee. The committees are as follows: Budget—Q, V, W,

X, Y—and Curriculum—R, S, T, U. Only Choice A lists two professors on different committees.

23. **E.** Suppose that X was on the curriculum committee. Then V must also be on the committee (V = X). This leaves room for only two more members, both of whom must be untenured. Therefore, U and W must both be on the budget committee, which is impossible (U ≠ W). Each of the other choices is possible.

## Solutions 24–28

students: A, K, N, P, R   times: 10, 11, 12, 1, 2

2 students/tour   each student at least 1 tour

not 3 in a row

K = 10     R = 1 and R = 2     K ≠ P

24. **D.** Since Pete and Kit cannot be assigned to the same tour, and since Kit leads the 10:00 tour, Pete cannot lead the tour at 10:00. Therefore, he must lead three of the four tours between 11:00 and 2:00. To avoid leading three tours in a row, he must lead the tours at 11:00, 12:00, and 2:00 or the tours at 11:00, 1:00, and 2:00. Either way, he must lead tours at both 11:00 and 2:00.

25. **B.** To avoid leading three tours in a row, Kit must be scheduled at 10:00, 11:00, 1:00 and 2:00. Since she cannot give the 12:00 tour, eliminate Choices D and E. Since Pete cannot lead a tour with Kit, and since he must lead at least one tour, he must be scheduled at 12:00; eliminate Choice A. Since Rebecca gives the 1:00 and 2:00 tours, she cannot also give a tour at 12:00; eliminate Choice C.

26. **B.** Since Pete and Rebecca must lead the 1:00 and 2:00 tours, no one else can lead a tour at those times, so eliminate Choices D and E. Also, Pete cannot lead three tours in a row, so eliminate Choice C. The only times available for Adam and Noah to lead tours together would be 11:00 and 12:00 (since Kit leads the tour at 10:00); but if that occurred, no one would be available to lead the 10:00 tour with Kit, so eliminate Choice A. There are several ways to schedule Kit, Adam, and Noah with Kit leading a tour at 12:00.

27. **E.** To avoid leading three tours in a row, Adam must lead the tours at 10:00, 11:00, 1:00, and 2:00. This means that so far the schedule is as follows:

| A/K | A/– | –/– | A/R | A/R |
|-----|-----|-----|-----|-----|
| 10  | 11  | 12  | 1   | 2   |

Since Pete and Kit can't lead the same tour, Noah must be one of the leaders at 12:00 (since neither Adam nor Rebecca is eligible).

- If Noah leads that tour with Kit, then Pete must lead the 11:00 tour with Adam (otherwise Pete wouldn't be on the schedule), and there is only one possible schedule:

| A/K | A/P | N/K | A/R | A/R |
|-----|-----|-----|-----|-----|
| 10  | 11  | 12  | 1   | 2   |

- If Noah leads the 12:00 tour with Pete, then any of Kit, Noah, or Pete could lead the 11:00 tour with Adam; so there are three more possibilities.
- There are a total of 4 possible ways to complete the schedule.

28. **C.** If none of the students leads three tours, then each of them must lead two tours. Since Kit and Pete cannot lead a tour together, they must lead four separate tours; they cannot all be scheduled between 10:00 and 12:00, and so at least one of them must lead a tour with Rebecca at either 1:00 or 2:00. None of the other choices must be true.

29. **E.** Since we are told that jungle fever is a "highly contagious" disease, Choice E suggests an alternative explanation for the high rate of jungle fever in the experimental group. Choice A is irrelevant, since we have no idea whether rabbits in general or any particular species of rabbits are frequent victims of jungle fever in the first place. Choice B would strengthen the argument, not weaken it.

30. **D.** The conclusion that some substance found in Serum D causes jungle fever would be greatly strengthened if the substance and the fever were invariably found together, as stated in Choice D. Choice A does not help to establish the *cause* of the high rate of jungle fever in the experimental group. Choice B would weaken the original argument, not strengthen it. Choices C and E would neither weaken nor strengthen the argument.

## Solutions 31–34

athletes: J, K, L, M, N, P     assemblies: 1, 2, 3

football: J, K, L, M   basketball: L, N   tennis: K, M, P

J = 1   each assembly: 2 football, 1 basketball, 1 tennis

no one speaks about the same sport in assemblies 1 and 2 or 2 and 3

31. **E.** In assembly 1, K must speak about tennis, since he is the only one of the four who plays that sport. Therefore, the athletes who speak about football in assembly 1 are J and L, and since they can't speak about football in two assemblies in a row, K and M must be the football speakers in assembly 2. This leaves P as the only tennis player available for assembly 2. Finally, since N is speaking about

basketball in assembly 1, L must be the basketball speaker in assembly 2.

32. C.   Since no one is allowed to speak about the same sport in two consecutive assemblies, no one who plays only one sport can speak in all three assemblies. This rules out J, N, and P, so eliminate Choices D and E. It is easy to create a schedule in which any of K, L, or M could be scheduled three times.

33. D.   Since L and N are the only basketball players, and since L cannot speak about basketball in either the first or third assembly, N must speak in both of those assemblies. Further, N cannot speak in assembly 2, since his only sport is basketball, and L is speaking about basketball then. None of the other choices must be true.

34. E.   Since two of the athletes have to speak about football during assembly 1, and two different athletes have to speak about football during assembly 2, all four football players must be present. Eliminate Choices A, B, and C. Since L and N are the only basketball players, one of them must speak in assembly 1 and the other in assembly 2, so they both must be present. Eliminate Choice D. It is possible to make a complete schedule without P.

35. A.   Statements I and II are plausible explanations for the students' passivity in previous years, but neither one can be inferred definitely; you cannot conclude that one of them must be true (some third explanation is possible). From the students' previous behavior, *no* valid inferences about their response to a new, larger tuition hike are possible.

# PART TWO

## Verbal Ability: Tactics, Review, and Practice

# 4 Antonym Questions

■ **Testing Tactics**
■ **Practice Exercises**
■ **Answer Key**

These are the antonym directions you will find on the GRE: "Each question below consists of a word printed in capital letters, followed by five lettered words or phrases. Choose the lettered word or phrase that is most nearly *opposite* in meaning to the word in capital letters."

Your task in answering antonym questions is straightforward: You are given a word and must choose, from the five choices that follow it, the best antonym (opposite). Often the first question or two on your verbal section will be an antonym question. Remember, the earliest questions you face on the GRE weigh more heavily than the final ones you answer. Take the time you need to answer these early questions correctly.

# Testing Tactics

## Tactic 1 Think of a Context for the Capitalized Word

Take a quick look at the word in capital letters. If you don't recollect its meaning right away, try to think of a phrase or sentence in which you have heard it used. The context may help you come up with the word's meaning. For example:

MAGNIFY:
(A) forgive
(B) comprehend
(C) extract
(D) diminish
(E) electrify

The term "magnifying glass" should immediately come to mind. A magnifying glass enlarges things. The opposite of enlarging something is to make it smaller or *diminish* it. The answer is Choice D.

Now apply this tactic to a slightly more difficult question.

ABERRANT:
(A) exact
(B) simple
(C) causative
(D) ordinary
(E) pleasant

What phrase comes to your mind? "Aberrant behavior." "Aberrant data." In both cases you should have an impression of something deviating from what is expected, an impression of something unusual or abnormal. Aberrant behavior is odd or extraordinary; *aberrant*, therefore, is an antonym for *ordinary*. The correct answer is Choice D.

# Before You Look at the Choices, Think of Antonyms for the Capitalized Word

Suppose your word is *industrious*, hard-working. What opposites come to your mind? You might come up with *lazy, idle, slothful, inactive*—all words that mean lacking industry and energy.

Now look at the choices:

> INDUSTRIOUS:
> (A) stupid
> (B) harsh
> (C) indolent
> (D) complex
> (E) inexpensive

Lazy, idle, and slothful all are synonyms for *indolent*. Your correct answer is Choice C.

This tactic will help you even when you have to deal with unfamiliar words among your answer choices. Suppose you do not know the meaning of the word *indolent*. You know that one antonym for your key word *industrious* is *lazy*. Therefore, you know that you are looking for a word that means the same as *lazy*. At this point you can go through the answer choices eliminating answers that don't work. Does *stupid* mean the same as *lazy*? No, smart people can

be lazy, too. Does *harsh* mean the same as *lazy*? No, harsh means cruel or rough. Does *indolent* mean the same as *lazy*? You don't know; you should check the other choices and then come back. Does *complex* mean the same as *lazy*? No, *complex* means complicated or intricate. Does *inexpensive* mean the same as *lazy*? No. So what is left? *Indolent*. Once again, your correct answer is Choice C.

See how you do when you apply this tactic to a new question.

> TACITURNITY:
> (A) arrogance
> (B) intolerance
> (C) belligerence
> (D) inconstancy
> (E) loquacity

*Taciturnity* is the quality of being uncommunicative. In thinking of possible antonyms for *taciturnity*, you may have come up with words like *talkativeness, wordiness*, and *garrulity*, words signifying excessiveness of speech. *Talkativeness, wordiness*, and *garrulity* are all synonyms for *loquacity*. The correct answer is Choice E.

# Read All the Choices Before You Decide Which Is Best

On the GRE you are working under time pressure. You may be tempted to mark down the first answer that feels right and ignore the other choices given. Don't do it. Consider each answer. Only in this way can you be sure to distinguish between two possible answers and come up with the best answer for the question.

Words have shades of meaning. In matching a word with its opposite, you must pay attention to these shades of meaning. Try this example to see how this tactic works.

> UNRULY:
> (A) immobile
> (B) engaging
> (C) merciful
> (D) tractable
> (E) indifferent

Suppose you have only a vague sense of the meaning of *unruly*. You associate it with such vaguely negative terms as *wild, disagreeable, bad*. For this reason, you stop short when you come to Choice C. Reasoning that someone wild and disagreeable is *not* compassionate or merciful, you look no further and mark down Choice C.

Choice C, however, is incorrect. True, an unruly person is wild and hard to manage, even rebellious. Someone who lacks rebelliousness, however, is not necessarily merciful. Such a person is easy to manage, compliant, in fact *tractable*. The correct answer is Choice D.

Now try a second example to practice this tactic.

> BANALITY:
> (A) detailed analysis
> (B) unrehearsed statement
> (C) succinct account
> (D) novel expression
> (E) faithful description

A *banality* lacks freshness and originality; something banal is timeworn and trite. Choice B has an immediate appeal: something unrehearsed is by definition spontaneous and at least should seem fresh. However, an unrehearsed statement could be filled with cliches; though spontaneous, it may well be banal or trite. The best antonym for *banality* is Choice D, *novel expression*.

## Look at the Answer Choices to Determine the Word's Part of Speech

Look at the capitalized word. What part of speech is it? Words often exist in several forms. You may think of *run* as a verb, for example, but in the phrases, "a run in her stocking," and "hit a home run," *run* is a noun.

The GRE plays on this confusion in testing your verbal ability. When you look at a particular capitalized word, you may not know whether you are dealing with a noun, a verb, or an adjective. *Harbor*, for example, is a very common noun; in "to harbor a fugitive," to give refuge to a runaway, it is a much less common verb.

If you suspect that a capitalized word may have more than one part of speech, don't worry. Just look at the first couple of answer choices and see what part of speech they are. That part of speech will be the capitalized word's part of speech.

*In GRE Antonym Questions*, **all** *the answer choices have the same part of speech.* You can always tell what that part of speech is by a quick glance at the first answer choice or two.

See how this tactic works in answering a relatively simple question.

> POLISH:
> (A) ruthlessness
> (B) honesty
> (C) indolence
> (D) gaucheness
> (E) complexity

Are you dealing with *polish* the verb or *polish* the noun?

A quick look at the answers assures you that they are all nouns. *Polish* here has nothing to do with rubbing and shining your silverware. The noun *polish* means refinement and culture: The country squire went abroad to acquire polish. Its opposite is *gaucheness* or awkwardness. The correct answer is Choice D.

Now try a second example.

> PRECIPITATE:
> (A) candid
> (B) erratic
> (C) cautious
> (D) generous
> (E) shallow

Is the word in capitals the adjective *precipitate* (hasty, impetuous) or the verb *precipitate* (to expedite or trigger)?

A quick look at the answer choices reveals that it is an adjective. (The *-ic* and *-ous* word endings are common adjective endings.) Thus, its opposite is *cautious* or *deliberate*, Choice C.

## Consider Secondary Meanings of the Capitalized Word As Well as Its Primary Meaning

If none of the answer choices seems right to you, take another look at the capitalized word. It may have more than one meaning. The GRE often constructs questions that make use of secondary, less well-known meanings of deceptively familiar words. Take, for example, this typical question.

> LIST:
> (A) overturn
> (B) be upright
> (C) lie flat
> (D) fall forward
> (E) veer from side to side

*List* here has nothing to do with making lists or enumerating. It has to do with moving. When it *lists* to starboard, a ship simply leans to one side or tilts. The best antonym for this meaning of *list* is Choice B, *be upright*.

Try a second, more difficult question involving a less familiar meaning of a familiar word.

> IMPRECISE:
> (A) direct
> (B) resolute
> (C) voluminous
> (D) nice
> (E) perceptible

Few examinees tested on this question would answer it correctly. Why?

The problem lies not in the capitalized word but in the answer choices. *Imprecise* means inexact, approximate, vague. Thus, its antonym means exact and precise. Not immediately spotting *exact* or *precise* among the answer choices, and looking for a positive term to contrast with *imprecise*, some examinees may settle for Choice A, *direct*.

In doing so, they fail to consider that words have secondary meanings. In this case, *nice* does not mean pleasant or agreeable, as in *enjoying nice weather* or *being nice to your baby brother*. Instead, it means requiring or marked by great accuracy, delicacy, and skill, as in making *a nice distinction* in an argument or hitting *a nice shot* in golf. The correct answer is Choice D.

## Tactic 6 — Break Down Unfamiliar Words into Recognizable Parts

When you come upon a totally unfamiliar word, don't give up. Break it down and see if you recognize any of its parts. Pay particular attention to prefixes—word parts added to the beginning of a word—and to roots, the building blocks of the language.

Look once more at the following question.

ABERRANT:
(A) exact
(B) simple
(C) causative
(D) ordinary
(E) pleasant

Suppose you had never seen *aberrant* before. You have seen dozens of other words beginning with *ab-*: *absent, abnormal, abduct*. Take *abduct*. What do you do when you abduct someone? You kidnap him, or steal him away. *Ab-* means *away*.

What about the root, *err*? To err is to be wrong or to wander, as in wandering from the usual path. Thus, *aberrant* means *wandering away*, straying from what is usual or normal, and its opposite is of course Choice D, *ordinary*.

Now try a second example in which this tactic can prove helpful.

NEOLOGISM:
(A) cordial salutation
(B) brief summary
(C) lengthy diatribe
(D) archaic expression
(E) equivocal remark

*Neo-* means new. *Log-* means word or speech. A *neologism* must have to do with a new sort of word or speech. Logically, therefore, the opposite of *neologism* must have to do with an *old* sort of word or speech. Only one answer seems possible: Choice D, *archaic expression*. *Archaic* means antiquated or obsolete. Choice D is correct.

Here is a final example, with word parts coming from Greek.

SYNCHRONOUS:
(A) not in working order
(B) without problems
(C) out of position
(D) not in phase
(E) without permission

*Syn-* means together. *Chron-* means time. Something *synchronous* must have to do with occurring together in time, like the *synchronous* movements of swimmers keeping time with one another. The antonym for *synchronous* thus is Choice D, *not in phase*.

The word part approach can help you interpret new words you encounter. However, apply it cautiously. In many words the roots, prefixes, and suffixes have lost their original meanings. In others, the same root occurs, but with markedly differing effects. It would not do to call a *philanthropist* a *philanderer*, for instance, though both words contain the root for love.

If you find the word part approach appealing, try to spend some time working with the Basic Word Parts List in Chapter 8. Remember, however, there is no substitute for learning the exact meaning of a word as it is used today.

# Change Unfamiliar Words from One Part of Speech to Another

Sometimes you may be stumped by a word in one form, yet recognize it easily in another. Take, for example, the word *synchronous* in the previous tactic. To most test-takers, the adjective *synchronous* is far less familiar than is the verb *synchronize*, as in "Synchronize your watches!"

When you confront an unfamiliar word, try replacing its suffix with a different word ending and see whether this change jogs your memory. In the case of the noun *assiduity*, for example, cut off the noun suffix *-ity* and replace it with the adjective suffix *-ous*. You now have the word *assiduous*, as in an assiduous worker. Does that ring a bell? *Assiduous* means hardworking; *assiduity*, therefore, is a synonym for industriousness or diligence.

Practice this tactic as you answer the following question:

> DICHOTOMOUS:
> (A) apparent
> (B) undivided
> (C) atypical
> (D) indifferent
> (E) abstract

Remove the *-ous* ending from *dichotomous*. In its place, substitute *-y*. You have the word *dichotomy*, as in the dichotomy between Good and Evil, or the dichotomy between thought and action. A dichotomy is a division or separation in two parts, often mutually exclusive ones. Something dichotomous, therefore, is divided; its opposite is *undivided*, Choice B.

# In Eliminating Answer Choices, Test Words for Their Positive or Negative Connotations

When you are dealing with a partially unfamiliar word, a word that you cannot define or use in a sentence but that you know you have seen previously, try to remember in what sort of context you have seen that word. Did it have positive connotations, or did it have a negative feel? If you are certain the capitalized word has positive connotations, then, since you are looking for its antonym, you *know* the correct answer must have negative ones. Thus, you can eliminate any answer choices that have positive connotations and guess among the answer choices that are negative in tone.

See how this approach applies in the following example.

> CHARY:
> (A) bold
> (B) bright
> (C) unsteady
> (D) unforgiving
> (E) unhappy

You cannot define *chary*. You would hesitate to use it in a sentence of your own. And yet, you are sure the word has a slightly negative feel to it. A person is *chary about* something. You have a sense of someone holding back.

Look at the answer choices. Which of them have negative connotations? *Unsteady? Unforgiving? Unhappy?* Eliminate all three. You have narrowed down your choices to *bold* and *bright*, both words that have a positive feel. You are in an excellent position to guess. As it turns out, *chary* means hesitant or reluctant to proceed. Its opposite is Choice A, *bold*.

## Tactic 9

# Watch Out for Errors Caused by Eye-Catchers

When you look at answer choices, do you find that certain ones seem to leap right off the page? These words are eye-catchers. They look good—but be sure to take a second look.

Try these next antonym questions to see just how an eye-catcher works. First, an easy one.

UNDERMINE:
(A) ensnare
(B) overstrain
(C) mollify
(D) terminate
(E) bolster

What's the opposite of *under? Over*. What's the opposite of *undermine?* No, it's not *overstrain*. Be suspicious of answers that come too easily. To *undermine* means to weaken something or cause it to collapse by removing its underlying supports. The opposite of to *undermine* is Choice E, to *bolster* or support.

Here's a more difficult example. See if you can spot the eye-catcher.

REDOUBTABLE:
(A) unanticipated
(B) unambiguous
(C) unimposing
(D) inescapable
(E) immutable

Few test-takers attempting this question would answer it correctly. Why? Once more an early answer choice has been set up to tempt you. In this case, the presence of the familiar word *doubt* in the unfamiliar word *redoubtable* suggests that the word *redoubtable* has something to do with uncertainty. You know that *ambiguous* means uncertain in meaning. Thus, Choice B, *unambiguous,* is particularly appealing here. It is particularly appealing, and it is wrong.

*Doubt* in *redoubtable* is used in the sense not of uncertainty but of fear. *A redoubtable foe* causes fear; such a person is awesome or imposing. Someone *unimposing* causes no such fear. The correct answer is Choice C.

# Practice Exercises

## Antonym Exercise A

<u>Directions:</u> In each of the following antonym questions, a word printed in capital letters precedes five lettered words or phrases. From these five lettered words or phrases, pick the one most nearly <u>opposite</u> in meaning to the capitalized word.

Because some of the questions require you to distinguish fine shades of meaning, be sure to consider all the choices before deciding which one is best.

1. MOURNFUL: (A) informal (B) sympathetic (C) private (D) appropriate (E) joyous

2. SCAD: (A) parsimony (B) allocation (C) dearth (D) restraint (E) provision

3. GRANDIOSE: (A) docile (B) unlikely to occur (C) simple and unimposing (D) light in weight (E) uncommunicative

4. ENTRENCH: (A) defy (B) oust (C) extinguish (D) squander (E) intercede

5. LACKLUSTER: (A) superficial (B) courteous (C) vibrant (D) complex (E) abundant

6. CENSURE: (A) augment (B) eradicate (C) enthrall (D) commend (E) reform

7. TRANSIENCE: (A) slowness (B) permanence (C) lack of caution (D) desire for perfection (E) original nature

8. DESICCATE: (A) lengthen (B) hallow (C) exonerate (D) saturate (E) anesthetize

9. PROTRUSION: (A) deep recess (B) strong dislike (C) growing scarcity (D) illusion (E) chaos

10. ENTICE: (A) repel (B) authorize (C) baffle (D) misplace (E) diminish

11. ORTHODOXY: (A) renown (B) trepidation (C) unconventionality (D) inquisitiveness (E) remoteness

12. SUMPTUOUS:  (A) dank  (B) frequent
(C) partial  (D) restrained  (E) open

13. DISSOLUTION:  (A) retribution
(B) compliance  (C) futility  (D) persuasion
(E) establishment

14. IRK:  (A) pry  (B) tinge  (C) beguile
(D) convince  (E) soothe

15. LIMBER:  (A) sturdy  (B) orderly
(C) durable  (D) stiff  (E) gloomy

16. OBLIQUITY:  (A) praise
(B) straightforwardness  (C) conformity
(D) self-righteousness  (E) depreciation

17. SLUR:  (A) sensitivity  (B) sacrifice
(C) understatement  (D) challenge
(E) commendation

18. APOTHEOSIS:  (A) departure from tradition
(B) impatience with stupidity
(C) demotion from glory
(D) surrender to impulse
(E) cause for grief

19. ENERVATE:  (A) narrate  (B) enrage
(C) accomplish  (D) invigorate  (E) acquiesce

20. PARSIMONIOUS:  (A) appropriate
(B) generous  (C) complete  (D) radiant
(E) ongoing

# Antonym Exercise B

<u>Directions:</u> In each of the following antonym questions, a word printed in capital letters precedes five lettered words or phrases. From these five lettered words or phrases, pick the one most nearly <u>opposite</u> in meaning to the capitalized word.

Because some of the questions require you to distinguish fine shades of meaning, be sure to consider all the choices before deciding which one is best.

1. HEDGE:
   (A) act on impulse
   (B) refuse to represent
   (C) state without qualification
   (D) make a foolish comment
   (E) establish a connection

2. ABROGATE:  (A) transgress  (B) signify
(C) alleviate  (D) question  (E) ratify

3. INDUSTRY:  (A) cleanliness  (B) pragmatism
(C) sloth  (D) promptness  (E) abasement

4. SPUNK:  (A) success  (B) timidity
(C) growing awareness  (D) lack of intelligence
(E) loss of prestige

5. SAGE:  (A) zealot  (B) miser  (C) braggart
(D) fool  (E) tyrant

6. ADMONITION:  (A) premonition
(B) hallucination  (C) escape  (D) commendation
(E) trepidation

7. CHARY:  (A) lugubrious  (B) brash
(C) indifferent  (D) graceful  (E) scornful

8. STUPEFY:  (A) lie  (B) bend  (C) enliven
(D) talk nonsense  (E) consider thoughtfully

9. COGENT:  (A) contemplative  (B) unpersuasive
(C) expository  (D) stable  (E) inconceivable

10. FICKLE:  (A) spotless  (B) industrious
(C) welcome  (D) urgent  (E) loyal

11. COMPLY:  (A) simplify  (B) strive  (C) rebel
(D) unite  (E) appreciate

12. CREDIT:  (A) believe false  (B) treat as equal
(C) make more difficult  (D) underemphasize
(E) forget

13. STILTED:  (A) informal  (B) verbose
(C) secretive  (D) senseless  (E) tentative

14. UNGAINLY:  (A) slender  (B) graceful
(C) restrained  (D) inaccurate  (E) unnoticed

15. QUIXOTIC:  (A) slow  (B) abstemious
(C) pragmatic  (D) benevolent  (E) grave

16. DISPARITY:  (A) timidity  (B) complacency
(C) bigotry  (D) likeness  (E) influence

17. CRITICAL:  (A) unimportant  (B) uncertain
(C) silent  (D) coherent  (E) destructive

18. SOBRIETY:  (A) influence  (B) nonchalance
(C) holiness  (D) civility  (E) mirth

19. RESTIVENESS:  (A) completeness
(B) conviction  (C) concern  (D) docility
(E) petulance

20. HALLOW:  (A) keep silence  (B) prove incorrect
(C) accuse openly  (D) desecrate  (E) instigate

# Antonym Exercise C

Directions: In each of the following antonym questions, a word printed in capital letters precedes five lettered words or phrases. From these five lettered words or phrases, pick the one most nearly <u>opposite</u> in meaning to the capitalized word.

Because some of the questions require you to distinguish fine shades of meaning, be sure to consider all the choices before deciding which one is best.

1. HARBINGER: (A) ascetic (B) miser
   (C) counselor (D) follower (E) braggart

2. SPUR: (A) embitter (B) discourage
   (C) impress (D) mislead (E) ignore

3. DISJOINTED: (A) responsible (B) connected
   (C) implied (D) useful (E) imprecise

4. MEALYMOUTHED: (A) hungry (B) indefinite
   (C) tightlipped (D) sincere (E) apathetic

5. PREVARICATE: (A) postulate (B) emphasize
   (C) support in theory (D) consider thoughtfully
   (E) state truthfully

6. LUMINARY: (A) impostor (B) nonentity
   (C) pilgrim (D) braggart (E) mutineer

7. TESTY: (A) erroneous (B) uncommunicative
   (C) even-tempered (D) quick-witted
   (E) industrious

8. NEFARIOUS: (A) lackadaisical (B) eccentric
   (C) exemplary (D) corrigible (E) hypocritical

9. BEGRUDGE: (A) mourn silently
   (B) grant freely (C) hunger for
   (D) advance rapidly (E) fight back

10. BILK: (A) reduce in size (B) make famous
    (C) roughen (D) renovate (E) pay in full

11. COMPOSE: (A) disturb (B) reveal
    (C) strengthen (D) isolate (E) prevent

12. OCCLUDE: (A) determine (B) transcend
    (C) surround (D) open (E) regulate

13. AMBIGUITY: (A) extent (B) success
    (C) clarity (D) normality (E) expression

14. AMELIORATION: (A) prevention
    (B) aggravation (C) distraction
    (D) indifference (E) dissuasion

15. CAVIL: (A) discern (B) disclose
    (C) introduce (D) flatter (E) commend

16. SKEPTICAL: (A) theoretical (B) indifferent
    (C) ready to believe (D) eager for change
    (E) lost in thought

17. FLEDGLING: (A) experienced person
    (B) shy onlooker (C) social outcast
    (D) fugitive (E) adversary

18. CRASS: (A) boastful (B) temporary
    (C) cheerful (D) refined (E) extensive

19. RECALCITRANT: (A) tractable (B) erratic
    (C) intuitive (D) vigorous (E) rambling

20. PROTRACT: (A) defy (B) supplement
    (C) postpone (D) shorten (E) design

# Antonym Exercise D

Directions: In each of the following antonym questions, a word printed in capital letters precedes five lettered words or phrases. From these five lettered words or phrases, pick the one most nearly <u>opposite</u> in meaning to the capitalized word.

Because some of the questions require you to distinguish fine shades of meaning, be sure to consider all the choices before deciding which one is best.

1. PRIM: (A) rare (B) careful (C) unnecessary
   (D) improper (E) decisive

2. REPUGNANCE: (A) attraction (B) lethargy
   (C) blame (D) virtue (E) awe

3. NETTLE: (A) disentangle (B) mollify
   (C) magnify (D) muffle (E) recompense

4. REPLETE: (A) unwrinkled (B) devoid
   (C) vulgar (D) matchless (E) unsympathetic

5. UNASSUAGED: (A) presumed (B) deceptive
   (C) singular (D) faulty (E) soothed

6. PALTRY: (A) munificent (B) improvident
   (C) random (D) cautious (E) obsolete

7. CONCLUSIVE: (A) difficult to express
   (B) bringing bad luck (C) easy to solve
   (D) lacking merit (E) open to question

8. RESOURCEFULNESS: (A) wealth
   (B) gratitude (C) melancholy (D) incompetence
   (E) frustration

9. DISSUADE: (A) extol (B) exhort
   (C) intensify (D) complicate (E) precede

10. SPLENETIC: (A) lackluster (B) heartless
    (C) diffident (D) constant (E) cordial

11. VIRULENCE:   (A) pallor   (B) orderliness
    (C) femininity   (D) harmlessness   (E) cowardice

12. ADHERENT:   (A) fugitive   (B) dissembler
    (C) opponent   (D) educator   (E) witness

13. OSCILLATE:   (A) entreat   (B) intensify
    (C) remain fixed   (D) expand gradually
    (E) wither away

14. ASPERITY:   (A) gentility   (B) superiority
    (C) kindness   (D) clarity   (E) vagueness

15. UNSCATHED:   (A) honest   (B) gathered
    (C) injured   (D) cleansed   (E) forgiven

16. FETTER:   (A) diminish   (B) enervate
    (C) liberate   (D) return   (E) cure

17. AUTONOMY:   (A) dependence   (B) animation
    (C) renown   (D) altruism   (E) antipathy

18. SLACK:   (A) rough   (B) active   (C) liberal
    (D) dependent   (E) familiar

19. RECOIL:   (A) plunge forward   (B) cease firing
    (C) skirt an issue   (D) facilitate   (E) surrender

20. ENCUMBER:   (A) disburden   (B) perform easily
    (C) challenge boldly   (D) observe with care
    (E) suppress

# Antonym Exercise E

Directions: In each of the following antonym questions,
a word printed in capital letters precedes five lettered
words or phrases. From these five lettered words or
phrases, pick the one most nearly opposite in meaning
to the capitalized word.

Because some of the questions require you to distinguish fine shades of meaning, be sure to consider all the
choices before deciding which one is best.

1. OPACITY:   (A) iridescence   (B) firmness
   (C) transparence   (D) poverty   (E) slum

2. PREDILECTION:   (A) postponement
   (B) afterthought   (C) lamentation
   (D) reoccurrence   (E) aversion

3. SEEDY:   (A) elegant   (B) intricate   (C) tranquil
   (D) irregular   (E) slow

4. BOGGLE:   (A) disentangle   (B) repudiate
   (C) ascertain   (D) remain unruffled
   (E) lack planning

5. HIDEBOUND:   (A) strong-willed
   (B) open-minded   (C) thin-skinned
   (D) tenderhearted   (E) scatterbrained

6. CASTIGATE:   (A) diminish   (B) imitate
   (C) compare   (D) reward   (E) misjudge

7. GAMBOL:   (A) dodge   (B) masquerade
   (C) digress   (D) plod   (E) vex

8. RAUCOUS:   (A) orderly   (B) absorbent
   (C) mellifluous   (D) contentious   (E) buoyant

9. TAPER:   (A) emphasize   (B) restore
   (C) split   (D) broaden   (E) modify

10. HIGH-HANDED:   (A) dejected   (B) reasonable
    (C) hard-handed   (D) short-handed   (E) dynamic

11. DIMINUTION:   (A) measurement   (B) proximity
    (C) augmentation   (D) orderliness
    (E) inclination

12. DISTEND:   (A) tell the truth
    (B) respond as expected   (C) approximate
    (D) collect   (E) shrink

13. EMBROIL:   (A) disengage   (B) remonstrate
    (C) refute thoroughly   (D) answer hypothetically
    (E) consider genuinely

14. VOUCHSAFE:   (A) postpone   (B) dissemble
    (C) endanger   (D) prohibit   (E) justify

15. JETTISON:   (A) salvage   (B) decelerate
    (C) muffle   (D) distract   (E) anchor

16. STOIC:   (A) savant   (B) herald   (C) whiner
    (D) victor   (E) bystander

17. GAMELY:   (A) fearfully   (B) diligently
    (C) clumsily   (D) gloomily   (E) respectfully

18. CRESTFALLEN:   (A) haughty   (B) impolite
    (C) frivolous   (D) tentative   (E) rough

19. DESULTORY:   (A) apologetic   (B) independent
    (C) laudatory   (D) questionable   (E) methodical

20. PULCHRITUDE:   (A) antipathy
    (B) unsightliness   (C) inexperience   (D) languor
    (E) rancor

# Answer Key

## Antonym Exercise A

| | | | |
|---|---|---|---|
| 1. E | 6. D | 11. C | 16. B |
| 2. C | 7. B | 12. D | 17. E |
| 3. C | 8. D | 13. E | 18. C |
| 4. B | 9. A | 14. E | 19. D |
| 5. C | 10. A | 15. D | 20. B |

## Antonym Exercise B

| | | | |
|---|---|---|---|
| 1. C | 6. D | 11. C | 16. D |
| 2. E | 7. B | 12. A | 17. A |
| 3. C | 8. C | 13. A | 18. E |
| 4. B | 9. B | 14. B | 19. D |
| 5. D | 10. E | 15. C | 20. D |

## Antonym Exercise C

| | | | |
|---|---|---|---|
| 1. D | 6. B | 11. A | 16. C |
| 2. B | 7. C | 12. D | 17. A |
| 3. B | 8. C | 13. C | 18. D |
| 4. D | 9. B | 14. B | 19. A |
| 5. E | 10. E | 15. E | 20. D |

## Antonym Exercise D

| | | | |
|---|---|---|---|
| 1. D | 6. A | 11. D | 16. C |
| 2. A | 7. E | 12. C | 17. A |
| 3. B | 8. D | 13. C | 18. B |
| 4. B | 9. B | 14. C | 19. A |
| 5. E | 10. E | 15. C | 20. A |

## Antonym Exercise E

| | | | |
|---|---|---|---|
| 1. C | 6. D | 11. C | 16. C |
| 2. E | 7. D | 12. E | 17. A |
| 3. A | 8. C | 13. A | 18. A |
| 4. D | 9. D | 14. D | 19. E |
| 5. B | 10. B | 15. A | 20. B |

# 5 Analogy Questions

- ■ **Testing Tactics**
- ■ **Practice Exercises**
- ■ **Answer Key**

Here are the directions for answering analogy questions that you will find on the GRE: "In the following question, a related pair of words or phrases is followed by five lettered pairs of words or phrases. Select the lettered pair that best expresses a relationship similar to that expressed in the original pair."

Analogy questions ask you to determine the relationship between a pair of words and then recognize a similar or parallel relationship between a different pair of words. You are given one pair of words and must choose from the five answer choices another pair that is related in the same way. The relationship between the words in the original pair will always be specific and precise, as will the relationship between the words in the correct answer pair.

Analogies come from a wide variety of fields. You need to know that musicians study in conservatories and ministers in seminaries, that panegyrics praise and elegies lament. You need to be aware of catalysts and conundrums, augers and auguries, and know in which contexts these words are found. You are not, however, dealing with these words in isolation; you are always dealing with them in relationship to other words.

Note how a GRE analogy question is set up. First you have the two capitalized words linked by a symbol. Take a look at a few examples.

### FRESCO : WALL

A fresco is related to a wall. **How?** By *definition*, a fresco or mural painting is painted on a wall.

### STAMMER : TALK

Stammer is related to talk. **How?** To stammer is to talk haltingly, even inarticulately. It is to talk in a defective or faulty *manner*.

### TILE : MOSAIC

Tile is related to mosaic. **How?** A mosaic is made up of tiles. Notice the wording of the last sentence. You could also have said "Tiles are the pieces that make up a mosaic" and maintained the word order of the analogy. Sometimes, however, it is easier to express a relationship if you reverse the order of the words.

Next you come to the five answer choices. See if you can tell which pair best expresses a relationship similar to the relationship of tile to mosaic.

> TILE : MOSAIC ::
> (A) hoop : embroidery
> (B) wick : candle
> (C) whalebone : scrimshaw
> (D) easel : painting
> (E) knot : macrame

The correct answer is Choice E: macrame is made up of knots. Just as the tiles in a mosaic make a pattern, so too the knots in a piece of macrame make a pattern.

Some of the analogy questions on the GRE are as clear-cut as this. Others are more complex. To answer them correctly involves far more than knowing single meanings of individual words: it involves knowing the usual contexts in which they are found, and their connotations as well. Master the tactics that immediately follow. Then proceed to the practice exercises containing both relatively simple and challenging analogies at the chapter's end.

# Testing Tactics

## Before You Look at the Choices, Try to State the Relationship Between the Capitalized Words in a Clear Sentence

In answering an analogy question, your first problem is to determine the exact relationship between the two capitalized words. *Before you look at the answer pairs*, make up a sentence that illustrates how these capitalized words are related. Then test the possible answers by seeing how well they fit in your sentence.

Try this tactic on the following two questions.

> TORRENT : DROPLET ::
> (A) water : eddy
> (B) swamp : desert
> (C) downpour : puddle
> (D) avalanche : pebble
> (E) hurricane : wreckage

A *torrent* (violent downpour or rushing stream) is made up of *droplets*. An *avalanche* or sudden fall of rocks, snow or earth is made up of *pebbles*. Choice D is correct.

Don't let Choice C fool you: while a downpour, like a torrent, is a violent rain, it is not made up of puddles; rather, it leaves puddles in its aftermath.

> PHILATELY : STAMPS ::
> (A) calligraphy : pens
> (B) cartography : maps
> (C) chronology : events
> (D) numismatics : coins
> (E) geriatrics : ailments

*Philately* is the study and collecting of *stamps*. *Numismatics* is the study and collecting of *coins*. Choice D is correct.

Note how difficult this question would be if you did not know that philately involved collecting stamps. You might have guessed that philately primarily involves *working with* stamps (as, for example, calligraphy involves working with pens) or even *making* stamps (as cartography involves making maps). Knowing the primary relationship between the capitalized words, however, you can go through the answer choices eliminating any pairs that do not express the same relationship. Thus, you can eliminate Choice A: someone who practices calligraphy may possibly collect pens, but calligraphy's primary, dictionary-defined role is the art of penmanship, the production of beautiful handwriting. Similarly, you can eliminate Choice E: geriatrics certainly involves studying ailments, but the ailments of the elderly, not ailments in general; furthermore, while it studies the ailments of the elderly, it certainly doesn't *collect* any such ailments. You can eliminate Choice C as well: chronology involves arranging events in the order in which they occur. This process of elimination leaves you with two relatively unfamiliar words—*numismatics* and *cartography*—and a fifty percent chance of guessing the answer correctly.

If you are not sure of the answer, *always* rule out answer choices that you *know* cannot be correct, and then guess among the choices that are left.

Remember, you have to do your best to answer the question on your screen before you can move on to the next.

## If More Than One Answer Fits the Relationship in Your Sentence, Look for a Narrower Approach

When you try to express the relationship between the two capitalized words in sentence form, occasionally you come up with too simple a sentence, one that fails to include enough details to particularize your analogy. In such cases, more than one answer may fit the relationship, and you will have to analyze the original pair again.

Consider this analogy question.

> PSEUDOPOD : AMOEBA ::
> (A) branch : tree
> (B) minnow : fish
> (C) bristle : hedgehog
> (D) tentacle : octopus
> (E) shell : snail

"A pseudopod is part of an amoeba." You have stated a relationship between the capitalized words in a sentence, but you have not stated a relationship that is precise enough. After all, branches are parts of trees, bristles are parts of hedgehogs, tentacles are parts of octopuses, and shells are parts of snails. You need to focus on some aspect of the relationship between the words in the original pair that corresponds to an aspect of only one of the answer pairs. Go back to the original pair of words for more details. How does an amoeba use a pseudopod? What function does it serve? "An amoeba uses a pseudopod for grasping." Try the answer choices in this new test sentence. "A tree uses a branch for grasping." False. "A hedgehog uses a bristle for grasping." False. "A snail uses its shell for grasping." False. "An octopus uses a tentacle for grasping." Choice D clearly is best.

In answering analogy questions on the GRE, pay special attention to how a dictionary would define the words involved. Do not settle for what "may be" a good relationship. Precision is important in analogies: a pseudopod is not just part of an amoeba, it is the part that the amoeba uses for grasping. Strive to identify the relationship that exists "by definition."

# Tactic 3

# Consider Secondary Meanings of Words As Well as Their Primary Meanings

Frequently, the test-makers attempt to mislead you by using familiar words in relatively uncommon ways. When an apparently familiar word seems incongruous in a particular analogy, consider other definitions of that word.

See how this tactic applies to the following examples.

> PAN : CAMERA ::
> (A) ban : book
> (B) tune : radio
> (C) charge : battery
> (D) filter : lens
> (E) rotate : periscope

Before you can answer this question, you have to know the definition of *pan*. You're not dealing with a frying pan or a gold miner's pan or a dish pan; *pan* here is a verb, not a noun. You can tell because the first word of each answer choice is also a verb. The verb ending *-ate* at the end of *rotate* gives that away.

The verb *pan*, however, has several meanings:

> The miner panned for gold. (The miner washed gravel to separate out the gold.)

> The chef panned the carrots. (The chef cooked the carrots in a pan with a small amount of fat or water.)

> The critic panned the comedy. (The critic severely criticized the comedy.)

None of these is the meaning you want.

Think how *pan* relates to *camera*. When someone *pans* a *camera*, what happens? The cameraperson rotates the camera on its axis so that he or she can film a panoramic scene (or a moving person or object). Similarly, a submarine crew member *rotates* or revolves a *periscope* on its axis so that he or she can make a panoramic observation. The correct answer is Choice E.

> NEBULOUSNESS : DEFINITION ::
> (A) apathy : zeal
> (B) impetuosity : intuition
> (C) penetration : depth
> (D) rectitude : somberness
> (E) rigidity : homogeneity

What relationship exists between *nebulousness* and *definition*? *Nebulousness* means haziness or indistinctness; a nebulous idea lacks clarity or sharpness. But what does haziness have to do with *definition*? After all, a definition is a statement of the meaning of a word or phrase.

Look closely at the term *definition*. When you define a word, you distinguish its essential characteristics; you make its features clear. *Definition* in fact possesses a secondary meaning: "sharp demarcation of outlines or limits; distinctness of outline or detail." With this meaning in mind, you can state the essential relationship between the capitalized words: *nebulousness* is a lack of *definition*. Analogously, *apathy* (indifference, lethargy) is a lack of *zeal* or enthusiasm. The correct answer is Choice A.

> EMBROIDER : FABRIC ::
> (A) fret : wood
> (B) spin : yarn
> (C) refine : ore
> (D) sculpt : chisel
> (E) glaze : glass

Ostensibly, this is a simple analogy. One embroiders fabric to ornament it, embellishing it with needlework. The relationship between the capitalized words is clear. However, the bulk of the examinees responding to this question would answer it incorrectly. The problem lies not in the original analogy but in the answer pairs.

Consider the answer choices closely. Choices B, C, D, and E are clear enough: one spins yarn, forming it out of threads (or one spins a yarn, fabricating or inventing a story); one refines ore, purifying it; one sculpts with a chisel; one glazes or fills a window with glass. Several of these straightforward choices have something to do with embell-ishment, but none seems precisely right. But how does one *fret* wood? Certainly not the way one frets a parent! Among the straightforward answer choices, Choice A seems strangely out of place.

When an item in an analogy strikes you as out of place, take a second look. Remember that, if you are a very good test-taker, the computer-adaptive GRE will give you increasingly difficult questions throughout the test. Therefore, if one of the final analogy questions on your screen looks simple, *suspect a trap*. In this case, the trap is a double one. Choice B, *spin : yarn* is an eye-catcher: because embroidery and spinning both are related to cloth, Choice B has an immediate appeal. Choose it and you fall into the test-makers' trap. Choice A, the odd-seeming choice, is the real answer: *fret,* as used here, means to mark decoratively, ornamenting a surface with interlaced designs, as cabinet makers decorate wood with interlaced patterns; fretting wood, thus, is directly analogous to embroidering fabric.

## Tactic 4

# Watch Out for Errors Caused by Eye-Catchers

When you look at answer choices, do you find that certain ones seem to leap right off the screen? For instance, when you were looking for an analogy similar to EMBROIDER : FABRIC, did the terms related to stitchery catch your eye? These words are eye-catchers. They look good—but not if you take a second glance.

In an analogy you have two capitalized words that relate in a particular way. In creating eye-catchers, the test-makers tempt you with pairs of words that are related, but in a grammatically or logically different way. See how eye-catchers work in the following example.

> MENTOR : GUIDE ::
> (A) medium : advise
> (B) mediator : disagree
> (C) mercenary : demand
> (D) mendicant : beg
> (E) merchant : consume

Just as there are many possible relationships linking word pairs, there are many possible ways an eye-catcher may attract your eye. First, an answer choice may somehow remind you in subject matter of one or both of the terms in the original pair. Thus, Choice A is an eye-catcher: *advise* reminds you of *guide;* both words feel as if they belong in the same set of words, the same *semantic field*. Second, the answer choice may masquerade as a clear-cut, precise, dictionary-perfect analogy and yet not be one. Thus, Choice C is an eye-catcher: while there can be a clear relationship between the adjective *mercenary* and the noun *demand*, there is no such clear relationship between the noun *mer-cenary* and the verb *demand*. See how this works:

CLEAR ANALOGY (Adjective/Noun)

MERCENARY : DEMAND :: RAVENOUS : APPETITE

A *mercenary demand* is greedy by definition. A *ravenous appetite* is greedy by definition as well.

VAGUE ANALOGY (Noun/Verb)

A *mercenary demands*.

A mercenary (professional soldier) insists or requires? The sentence makes little sense. Mercenaries work for hire; they may or may not make demands. The relationship is vague. Eliminate vague analogies when you find them; their only function is to catch your eye.

You have ruled out Choice C; you are suspicious of Choice A. How do you determine the correct answer? In this case, ask yourself **who is doing what to whom**. A *mentor* (teacher or counselor) by definition *guides* students or pro-teges. You can eliminate Choices A, B, and E because no necessary, dictionary-supported relationship links the words in these pairs. Mediums represent themselves as channels of communication between the living and the dead; they do not *by definition* advise. Mediators attempt to reconcile dis-agreeing parties; they do not *by definition* disagree. Merchants buy and sell goods that *others* consume; they do not *by definition* consume. The correct answer is Choice D. Just as a *mentor* by definition *guides*, a *mendicant* or beg-gar by definition *begs*.

# Look at the Answer Choices to Determine a Word's Part of Speech

Look at the capitalized words. What parts of speech are they? Words often have several forms. You may think of *flag* as a noun, for example, but in the phrases "to flag a taxi" and "to flag from exhaustion," *flag* is a verb.

If you suspect that a capitalized word may represent more than one part of speech, don't worry. Grammatical information built into the question can help you recognize analogy types and spot the use of unfamiliar or secondary meanings of words. In GRE analogy questions, the relationship between the parts of speech of the capitalized words and the parts of speech of the answer choices is identical. If your capitalized words are a noun and a verb, each of your answer pairs will be a noun and a verb. If they are an adjective and a noun, each of your answer pairs will be an adjective and a noun. If you can recognize the parts of speech in a single answer pair, you know the parts of speech of every other answer pair and of the original pair as well. See how this tactic works in a somewhat difficult question.

> SAP : VITALITY ::
> (A) persevere : fortitude
> (B) bore : tedium
> (C) examine : opinion
> (D) drain : resolve
> (E) enhance : allure

At first glance, you might think that both *sap* and *vigor* were nouns; *sap*, after all, is a common noun (maple syrup comes from the *sap* of the maple tree), and *vitality* ends in *-ity*, a common noun suffix. However, *persevere* is clearly a verb. Simply from looking at the first answer choice, you know *sap* is a verb, not a noun.

What occurs when someone's vitality is sapped? It decreases and becomes weak. When vitality is sapped, it is undermined. Think of a fortress being undermined by military engineers; "sappers," the British army called them. Only one answer choice conveys this sense of something strong weakening: Choice D. If one's resolve (resolution, determination) is drained, it is depleted or undermined.

# Familiarize Yourself with Common Analogy Types

Analogies tend to fall into certain basic types. If you can discover no apparent relationship between the two capitalized words, try establishing a relationship between them based on those types commonly used on this test.

# Common Analogy Types

## Definition

REFUGE : SHELTER
A *refuge* (place of asylum or sanctuary) by definition *shelters*.

TAXONOMIST : CLASSIFY
A *taxonomist*, a person who specializes in classification, by definition *classifies*.

HAGGLER : BARGAIN
A *haggler*, a person who argues over prices, by definition *bargains*.

## Defining Characteristic

TIGER : CARNIVOROUS
A *tiger* is defined as a *carnivorous* or meat-eating animal.

ENTOMOLOGIST : INSECTS
An *entomologist* is defined as a person who studies *insects*.

APIARY : BEE
An *apiary* is defined as a home for *bees*.

## Class and Member

AMPHIBIAN : SALAMANDER
A *salamander* is an example of an *amphibian*.

METAPHYSICS : PHILOSOPHY
*Metaphysics* belongs to (is a branch of) the field of
*philosophy*.

SONNET : POEM
A *sonnet* is a specific kind of *poem*.

## Antonyms

Antonyms are words that are opposite in meaning. Both
words belong to the same part of speech.

CONCERNED : INDIFFERENT
*Concerned* is the opposite of *indifferent*.

WAX : WANE
*Wax*, to grow larger, and *wane*, to dwindle, are opposites.

ANARCHY : ORDER
*Anarchy* is the opposite of *order*.

## Antonym Variants

In an Antonym Variant, the words are not strictly antonyms;
their meanings, however, are opposed. Take the adjective
*nervous*. A strict antonym for the adjective *nervous* would
be the adjective *poised*. However, where an Antonym would
have the adjective *poised*, an Antonym Variant analogy has
the noun *poise*. It looks like this:

NERVOUS : POISE
*Nervous* means lacking in *poise*.

INIQUITOUS : VIRTUE
Something *iniquitous* (wicked) lacks *virtue*. It is the opposite
of virtuous.

ABSTINENT : GORGE
To be *abstinent* or sparing in eating is the opposite of being
inclined to cram or *gorge*.

## Synonyms

Synonyms are words that have the same meaning. Both
words belong to the same part of speech.

MAGNIFICENT : GRANDIOSE
*Grandiose* means *magnificent*.

RATIOCINATE : THINK
To *ratiocinate* is to *think*.

RECIDIVIST : BACKSLIDER
A *recidivist* or habitual offender is a *backslider*.

## Synonym Variants

In a Synonym Variant, the words are not strictly synonyms;
their meanings, however, are opposed. Take the adjective
*willful*. A strict synonym for the adjective *willful* would be the
adjective *unruly*. However, where a Synonym would have
the adjective *unruly,* a Synonym Variant analogy has the
noun *unruliness*. It looks like this:

WILLFUL : UNRULINESS
*Willful* means exhibiting *unruliness*.

VERBOSE : WORDINESS
Someone *verbose* is wordy; he or she exhibits *wordiness*.

SOLICITOUS : CONCERN
Someone *solicitous* is concerned; he or she shows
*concern*.

## Degree of Intensity

FOND : DOTING
*Fond* is less extreme than *doting*.

FLURRY : BLIZZARD
A *flurry* or shower of snow is less extreme than a *blizzard*.

GRASPING : RAPACIOUS
To be *grasping* is less extreme than to be *rapacious*.

## Part to Whole

ISLAND : ARCHIPELAGO
Many *islands* make up an *archipelago*.

SHARD : POTTERY
A *shard* is a fragment of *pottery*.

CANTO : POEM
A *canto* is part of a *poem*.

## Function

ASYLUM : REFUGE
An *asylum* provides *refuge* or protection.

BALLAST : STABILITY
*Ballast* provides *stability*.

LULL : STORM
A *lull* temporarily interrupts a *storm*.

## Manner

MUMBLE : SPEAK
To *mumble* is to *speak* indistinctly.

STRUT : WALK
To *strut* is to *walk* proudly.

STRAINED : WIT
*Wit* that is *strained* is forced in manner.

## Action and Its Significance

WINCE : PAIN
A *wince* is a sign that one feels *pain*.

BLUSH : DISCOMFITURE
A *blush* signifies *discomfiture* or embarrassment.

PROSTRATION : SUBMISSIVENESS
*Prostration* (assuming a prostrate position, face to the
ground) is a sign of *submissiveness* or abasement.

## Worker and Article Created

POET : SONNET
A *poet* creates a *sonnet*.

ARCHITECT : BLUEPRINT
An *architect* designs a *blueprint*.

MASON : WALL
A *mason* builds a *wall*.

## Worker and Tool

PAINTER : BRUSH
A *painter* uses a *brush*.

SICKLE : REAPER
A *reaper* uses a *sickle* to cut the grain.

CARPENTER : VISE
A *carpenter* uses a *vise* to hold the object being worked on.

## Worker and Action

ACROBAT : CARTWHEEL
An *acrobat* performs a *cartwheel*.

FINANCIER : INVEST
A *financier* invests.

TENOR : ARIA
A *tenor* sings an *aria*.

## Worker and Workplace

MUSICIAN : CONSERVATORY
A *musician* studies at a *conservatory*.

SCULPTOR : ATELIER
A *sculptor* works in an *atelier* or studio.

MINER : QUARRY
A *miner* works in a *quarry* or pit.

## Tool and Its Action

DRILL : BORE
A *drill* is a tool used to *bore* holes.

CROWBAR : PRY
A *crowbar* is a tool used to *pry* things apart.

SIEVE : SIFT
A *sieve* is a tool used to strain or *sift*.

## Less Common Analogy Types

### Cause and Effect
SOPORIFIC : SLEEPINESS
A *soporific* (sleep-inducing medicine or drug) causes *sleepiness*.

### Sex
DOE : STAG
A *doe* is a female deer; a *stag*, a male deer.

### Age
COLT : STALLION
A *colt* is a young *stallion*.

### Time Sequence
CORONATION : REIGN
The *coronation* precedes the *reign*.

### Spatial Sequence
ROOF : FOUNDATION
The *roof* is the highest point of a house; the *foundation*, the lowest point.

### Symbol and Quality It Represents
DOVE : PEACE
A *dove* is the symbol of *peace*.

# Practice Exercises

## Analogy Exercise A

<u>Directions:</u> Each of the following analogy questions presents a related pair of words linked by a colon. Five lettered pairs of words follow the linked pair. Choose the lettered pair of words whose relationship is <u>most like</u> the relationship expressed in the original linked pair.

1. MASON : WALL ::   (A) artist : easel
   (B) fisherman : trout   (C) author : book
   (D) congressman : senator   (E) sculptor : mallet

2. FIRE : ASHES ::   (A) accident : delay
   (B) wood : splinters   (C) water : waves
   (D) regret : melancholy   (E) event : memories

3. GOOSE : GANDER ::   (A) duck : drake
   (B) hen : chicken   (C) sheep : flock
   (D) dog : kennel   (E) horse : bridle

4. CARPENTER : SAW ::
   (A) stenographer : typewriter   (B) painter : brush
   (C) lawyer : brief   (D) seamstress : scissors
   (E) runner : sneakers

5. CAPTAIN : SHOAL ::   (A) lawyer : litigation
   (B) pilot : radar   (C) soldier : ambush
   (D) doctor : hospital   (E) corporal : sergeant

6. HORNS : BULL ::   (A) mane : lion
   (B) wattles : turkey   (C) antlers : stag
   (D) hoofs : horse   (E) wings : eagle

7. JUDGE : COURTHOUSE :: (A) carpenter : bench
(B) lawyer : brief (C) architect : blueprint
(D) physician : infirmary (E) landlord : studio

8. HELMET : HEAD :: (A) pedal : foot
(B) gun : hand (C) breastplate : chest
(D) pendant : neck (E) knapsack : back

9. GULLIBLE : DUPED :: (A) credible : cheated
(B) careful : cautioned (C) malleable : molded
(D) myopic : misled (E) articulate : silenced

10. DUNGEON : CONFINEMENT ::
(A) church : chapel (B) school : truancy
(C) asylum : refuge (D) hospital : mercy
(E) courthouse : remorse

11. HERMIT : GREGARIOUS ::
(A) miser : penurious (B) ascetic : hedonistic
(C) coward : pusillanimous (D) scholar : literate
(E) crab : crustacean

12. MENDACITY : HONESTY ::
(A) courage : cravenness
(B) truth : beauty
(C) courage : fortitude
(D) unsophistication : ingenuousness
(E) turpitude : depravity

13. MARATHON : STAMINA ::
(A) relay : independence
(B) hurdle : perseverance (C) sprint : celerity
(D) jog : weariness (E) ramble : directness

14. NAIVE : INGENUE :: (A) ordinary : genius
(B) venerable : celebrity (C) urbane : sophisticate
(D) crafty : artisan (E) modest : braggart

15. RETOUCH : PHOTOGRAPH ::
(A) hang : painting (B) finger : fabric
(C) retract : statement (D) compose : melody
(E) refine : style

16. INDIGENT : WEALTH ::
(A) contented : happiness
(B) aristocratic : stature
(C) smug : complacency
(D) emaciated : nourishment
(E) variegated : variety

17. SHALE : GEOLOGIST ::
(A) catacombs : entomologist (B) aster : botanist
(C) obelisk : fireman (D) love : philologist
(E) reef : astrologer

18. DIDACTIC : TEACH :: (A) sophomoric : learn
(B) satiric : mock (C) reticent : complain
(D) chaotic : rule (E) apologetic : deny

19. HACKNEYED : ORIGINAL ::
(A) mature : juvenile (B) trite : morbid
(C) withdrawn : reserved (D) evasive : elusive
(E) derivative : traditional

20. AUGER : CARPENTER :: (A) studio : sculptor
(B) awl : cobbler (C) seam : seamstress
(D) cement : mason (E) apron : chef

# Analogy Exercise B

Directions: Each of the following analogy questions presents a related pair of words linked by a colon. Five lettered pairs of words follow the linked pair. Choose the lettered pair of words whose relationship is most like the relationship expressed in the original linked pair.

1. MUSTER : CREW :: (A) convene : committee
(B) demobilize : troops (C) dominate : opposition
(D) cheer : team (E) dismiss : jury

2. DWELL : DENIZEN :: (A) shun : outcast
(B) inherit : heir (C) squander : miser
(D) obey : autocrat (E) patronize : protégé

3. MEANDERING : DIRECTNESS ::
(A) menacing : ambition
(B) affable : permissiveness
(C) digressive : conciseness
(D) circuitous : rotation
(E) aboveboard : openness

4. CEMENT : TROWEL :: (A) lawn : rake
(B) conflagration : match (C) paint : brush
(D) floor : polish (E) wallpaper : ladder

5. PIGHEADED : YIELD ::
(A) lionhearted : retreat
(B) lily-livered : flee
(C) dogged : pursue
(D) featherbrained : giggle
(E) eagle-eyed : discern

6. ALARM : TRIGGER :: (A) prison : escape
(B) tunnel : dig (C) criminal : corner
(D) fright : allay (E) trap : spring

7. QUOTATION : QUOTATION MARKS ::
(A) remark : colon (B) sentence : period
(C) aside : parentheses (D) clause : semicolon
(E) interjection : exclamation point

8. SIGNATURE : ILLUSTRATION ::
(A) byline : column (B) alias : charge
(C) credit : purchase (D) note : scale
(E) reference : recommendation

9. SCALES : JUSTICE :: (A) weights : measures
   (B) laws : courts (C) torch : liberty
   (D) laurel : peace (E) balance : equity

10. SURPRISE : EXCLAMATION ::
    (A) insolence : bow (B) dismay : groan
    (C) happiness : grimace (D) deference : nod
    (E) contentment : matter

11. APOSTATE : RELIGION ::
    (A) potentate : kingdom (B) traitor : country
    (C) bureaucrat : government (D) jailer : law
    (E) teacher : education

12. FOX : CUNNING :: (A) dog : playful
    (B) hyena : amusing (C) beaver : industrious
    (D) vixen : cute (E) colt : sturdy

13. PERJURY : OATH :: (A) plagiarism : authority
    (B) embezzlement : trust (C) disrespect : age
    (D) testimony : court (E) jury : vow

14. EULOGY : BLAME :: (A) elegy : loss
    (B) satire : mockery (C) tirade : abuse
    (D) simile : likeness (E) benediction : curse

15. PRIDE : LIONS :: (A) gaggle : geese
    (B) honor : thieves (C) snarl : wolves
    (D) arrogance : kings (E) lair : bears

16. RANGE : MOUNTAINS :: (A) atlas : maps
    (B) plain : prairie (C) string : beads
    (D) novel : short stories (E) sea : rivers

17. EXCESSIVE : MODERATION ::
    (A) extensive : duration
    (B) arbitrary : courage
    (C) impulsive : reflection
    (D) distinguished : reverence
    (E) expensive : cost

18. DEADBEAT : PAY :: (A) killjoy : lament
    (B) spoilsport : refrain (C) daredevil : risk
    (D) diehard : quit (E) turncoat : betray

19. MENDICANT : IMPECUNIOUS ::
    (A) critic : quizzical (B) complainer : petulant
    (C) physician : noble (D) liar : compulsive
    (E) philanthropist : prodigal

20. SNICKER : DISRESPECT ::
    (A) whimper : impatience (B) chortle : glee
    (C) frown : indifference (D) sneer : detachment
    (E) glower : cheerfulness

# Analogy Exercise C

Directions: Each of the following analogy questions presents a related pair of words linked by a colon. Five lettered pairs of words follow the linked pair. Choose the lettered pair of words whose relationship is most like the relationship expressed in the original linked pair.

1. MYTH : LEGENDARY :: (A) sermon : lengthy
   (B) anecdote : witty (C) fable : didactic
   (D) epic : comic (E) allegory : obscure

2. TIRADE : ABUSIVE :: (A) monologue : lengthy
   (B) aphorism : boring (C) prologue : conclusive
   (D) encomium : laudatory (E) critique : insolent

3. EXPEDITIOUS : SPEED ::
   (A) astute : wisdom (B) decorous : impropriety
   (C) thoughtful : inanity (D) haggard : sturdiness
   (E) portable : frailty

4. ANNOTATE : TEXT ::
   (A) enact : law (B) prescribe : medication
   (C) caption : photograph (D) abridge : novel
   (E) censor : film

5. DRUDGERY : IRKSOME ::
   (A) encumbrance : burdensome
   (B) journey : wearisome
   (C) ambivalence : suspicious
   (D) compliance : forced
   (E) dissonance : harmonious

6. IMPROMPTU : REHEARSAL ::
   (A) practiced : technique (B) makeshift : whim
   (C) offhand : premeditation (D) glib : fluency
   (E) numerical : calculation

7. ELISION : SYLLABLES ::
   (A) contraction : letters (B) thesis : ideas
   (C) diagnosis : symptoms (D) almanac : facts
   (E) abacus : numbers

8. STICKLER : INSIST :: (A) mumbler : enunciate
   (B) trickster : risk (C) haggler : concede
   (D) laggard : outlast (E) braggart : boast

9. DETRITUS : GLACIER :: (A) thaw : snowfall
   (B) snow : ice cap (C) silt : river
   (D) range : mountain (E) foliage : tree

10. DESCRY : DISTANT :: (A) mourn : lost
    (B) whisper : muted (C) discern : subtle
    (D) destroy : flagrant (E) entrap : hostile

11. HORSE : CORRAL :: (A) oyster : reef
    (B) dog : muzzle (C) sheep : flock (D) pig : sty
    (E) deer : stag

12. RUBBER : ELASTIC :: (A) paper : brittle
    (B) diamond : hard (C) satin : sheer
    (D) metal : heavy (E) dust : allergic

13. REAM : PAPER :: (A) carton : milk
    (B) statue : marble (C) tablet : clay
    (D) ink : pen (E) cord : wood

14. HOBBLE : WALK :: (A) gallop : run
    (B) stammer : speak (C) stumble : fall
    (D) sniff : smell (E) amble : stroll

15. DETECTIVE : INFORMER ::
    (A) spy : counterspy (B) reporter : source
    (C) author : editor (D) architect : draftsman
    (E) sailor : mutineer

16. SCULPTOR : STONE :: (A) essayist : words
    (B) painter : turpentine (C) composer : symphony
    (D) logger : timber (E) etcher : acid

17. MASTHEAD : NEWSPAPER ::
    (A) footnote : essay (B) credits : film
    (C) spine : book (D) ream : paper
    (E) advertisement : magazine

18. FRAYED : FABRIC :: (A) thawed : ice
    (B) renovated : building (C) frazzled : nerves
    (D) watered : lawn (E) cultivated : manner

19. INDOLENT : WORK :: (A) decisive : act
    (B) gullible : cheat (C) perceptive : observe
    (D) theatrical : perform (E) taciturn : speak

20. INFALLIBLE : ERROR :: (A) irreversible : cure
    (B) invulnerable : emotion (C) impeccable : flaw
    (D) intolerable : defect (E) immovable : choice

# Analogy Exercise D

Directions: Each of the following analogy questions presents a related pair of words linked by a colon. Five lettered pairs of words follow the linked pair. Choose the lettered pair of words whose relationship is most like the relationship expressed in the original linked pair.

1. INFRACTION : LAW ::
   (A) interruption : continuity
   (B) renovation : structure
   (C) establishment : order
   (D) enactment : amendment
   (E) punishment : crime

2. LACHRYMOSE : TEARS ::
   (A) effusive : requests (B) ironic : jests
   (C) morose : speeches (D) profound : sighs
   (E) verbose : words

3. MOISTEN : DRENCH :: (A) enclose : confine
   (B) prick : stab (C) disregard : ignore
   (D) scrub : polish (E) heat : chill

4. WITCH : COVEN :: (A) ogre : castle
   (B) seer : prophecy (C) actor : troupe
   (D) fairy : spell (E) doctor : medicine

5. CONTINENT : ISLAND :: (A) ocean : lake
   (B) isthmus : peninsula (C) cape : cove
   (D) river : canal (E) plateau : plain

6. SKINFLINT : STINGY :: (A) daredevil : alert
   (B) braggart : carefree (C) blackguard : protective
   (D) spendthrift : weak (E) diehard : stubborn

7. STORY : BUILDING :: (A) plot : outline
   (B) rung : ladder (C) cable : elevator
   (D) foundation : skyscraper (E) spire : church

8. CANONIZE : SAINT :: (A) train : athlete
   (B) guard : dignitary (C) deify : sinner
   (D) lionize : celebrity (E) humanize : scholar

9. STARE : GLANCE :: (A) participate : observe
   (B) scorn : admire (C) hunt : stalk
   (D) gulp : sip (E) confide : tell

10. PERFORATE : HOLES :: (A) speckle : spots
    (B) evaporate : perfume (C) decorate : rooms
    (D) filter : water (E) repent : sins

11. PUGNACIOUS : BATTLE :: (A) timorous : beg
    (B) loquacious : drink (C) tenacious : persist
    (D) veracious : lie (E) wicked : survive

12. CLEARSIGHTED : PERSPICACITY ::
    (A) daring : temerity (B) reserved : impulsiveness
    (C) transparent : opacity (D) severe : clemency
    (E) lethargic : energy

13. PLEAD : SUPPLIANT :: (A) disperse : rioter
    (B) shun : outcast (C) revere : elder
    (D) beg : philanthropist (E) translate : interpreter

14. EPIGRAM : PITHY :: (A) allegory : lengthy
    (B) saga : heroic (C) anecdote : humorous
    (D) elegy : satiric (E) proverb : modern

15. BOLT : FABRIC :: (A) lock : key
    (B) book : paper (C) roll : film
    (D) needle : thread (E) light : lamp

16. PROOF : ALCOHOL :: (A) cream : milk
    (B) canteen : water (C) tanker : oil
    (D) octane : gasoline (E) pulp : juice

17. INCUBATOR : INFANT ::
    (A) henhouse : chicken (B) greenhouse : plant
    (C) archives : document (D) cooler : wine
    (E) hive : bee

18. CITADEL : DEFENSE ::   (A) chapel : refreshment
    (B) gazebo : refuge   (C) marina : contemplation
    (D) warehouse : storage   (E) rampart : supervision

19. RANCID : TASTE ::   (A) tepid : temperature
    (B) glossy : look   (C) rank : smell
    (D) dulcet : sound   (E) savory : odor

20. TRYST : CLANDESTINE ::
    (A) reverie : dreamy   (B) acquaintanceship : brief
    (C) expectation : hopeless   (D) glance : resentful
    (E) journey : leisurely

# Analogy Exercise E

<u>Directions:</u> Each of the following analogy questions
presents a related pair of words linked by a colon. Five
lettered pairs of words follow the linked pair. Choose
the lettered pair of words whose relationship is <u>most
like</u> the relationship expressed in the original linked
pair.

1. WHISPER : SPEAK ::   (A) brush : touch
   (B) skip : walk   (C) listen : hear
   (D) request : ask   (E) whimper : whine

2. ELUSIVE : CAPTURE ::
   (A) persuasive : convince   (B) elastic : stretch
   (C) headstrong : control   (D) sensible : decide
   (E) gullible : trick

3. LINEAGE : PERSON ::   (A) foliage : tree
   (B) derivation : word   (C) adolescence : child
   (D) title : book   (E) landscape : portrait

4. IMPANEL : JUROR ::   (A) accuse : defendant
   (B) convict : culprit   (C) testify : witness
   (D) enroll : student   (E) involve : bystander

5. PECCADILLO : TRIFLING ::
   (A) pariah : popular   (B) diagnosis : accurate
   (C) notion : farfetched   (D) squabble : petty
   (E) pursuit : trivial

6. PHYSIQUE : STURDY ::   (A) intellect : noble
   (B) punctuality : tardy   (C) investment : sound
   (D) fabric : worn   (E) technique : inept

7. TRAILER : MOTION PICTURE ::
   (A) truck : cargo   (B) theater : play
   (C) edition : novel   (D) commercial : product
   (E) libretto : opera

8. SIGN : ZODIAC ::   (A) poster : billboard
   (B) letter : alphabet   (C) prediction : prophecy
   (D) signal : beacon   (E) rhyme : almanac

9. LUMINARY : ILLUSTRIOUS ::
   (A) zealot : intense   (B) miser : prodigal
   (C) atheist : devout   (D) dignitary : conceited
   (E) celebrity : wealthy

10. BUFFOON : DIGNITY ::
    (A) braggart : modesty   (B) blackguard : strength
    (C) laughingstock : ridicule
    (D) imposter : identification   (E) gambler : risk

11. ROUT : DEFEAT ::   (A) ovation : applause
    (B) triumph : failure   (C) grief : loss
    (D) pathway : ruin   (E) memory : oblivion

12. METAPHOR : FIGURATIVE ::
    (A) fable : contemporary   (B) adage : paradoxical
    (C) precept : instructive   (D) irony : dramatic
    (E) epic : literal

13. CALUMNY : ASPERSIONS ::
    (A) approbation : praise   (B) slander : mockery
    (C) approval : criticism   (D) expectation : threats
    (E) satire : lamentations

14. LAST : SHOE ::   (A) cuff : trousers
    (B) finale : curtain   (C) pattern : glove
    (D) buckle : belt   (E) strap : slip

15. INDOLENT : SLOTH ::   (A) wrathful : ire
    (B) arrogant : acuity   (C) covetous : enigma
    (D) gluttonous : loyalty   (E) impatient : apathy

16. GROVEL : SERVILITY ::   (A) titter : arrogance
    (B) fume : anger   (C) yawn : civility
    (D) preen : modesty   (E) snivel : hypocrisy

17. DELICATE : FASTIDIOUS ::
    (A) hard-working : diligent
    (B) altruistic : mercenary
    (C) demonstrative : effusive
    (D) deceptive : fallacious
    (E) blithe : melancholy

18. RICOCHET : BULLET ::   (A) soar : falcon
    (B) aim : crossbow   (C) pierce : dart
    (D) carom : ball   (E) catapult : missile

19. JUGGERNAUT : INEXORABLE ::
    (A) cosmonaut : worldly   (B) colossus : gigantic
    (C) demagogue : liberal   (D) philistine : cultivated
    (E) despot : immaculate

20. APOCRYPHAL : AUTHENTICITY ::
    (A) nefarious : wickedness
    (B) dogmatic : assertiveness
    (C) hypocritical : integrity
    (D) perspicacious : discernment
    (E) deceptive : artifice

# Answer Key

## Analogy Exercise A

| | | | |
|---|---|---|---|
| 1. C | 6. C | 11. B | 16. D |
| 2. E | 7. D | 12. A | 17. B |
| 3. A | 8. C | 13. C | 18. B |
| 4. D | 9. C | 14. C | 19. A |
| 5. C | 10. C | 15. E | 20. B |

## Analogy Exercise B

| | | | |
|---|---|---|---|
| 1. A | 6. E | 11. B | 16. C |
| 2. B | 7. C | 12. C | 17. C |
| 3. C | 8. A | 13. B | 18. D |
| 4. C | 9. C | 14. E | 19. B |
| 5. A | 10. B | 15. A | 20. B |

## Analogy Exercise C

| | | | |
|---|---|---|---|
| 1. C | 6. C | 11. D | 16. A |
| 2. D | 7. A | 12. B | 17. B |
| 3. A | 8. E | 13. E | 18. C |
| 4. C | 9. C | 14. B | 19. E |
| 5. A | 10. C | 15. B | 20. C |

## Analogy Exercise D

| | | | |
|---|---|---|---|
| 1. A | 6. E | 11. C | 16. D |
| 2. E | 7. B | 12. A | 17. B |
| 3. B | 8. D | 13. E | 18. D |
| 4. C | 9. D | 14. B | 19. C |
| 5. A | 10. A | 15. C | 20. A |

## Analogy Exercise E

| | | | |
|---|---|---|---|
| 1. A | 6. C | 11. A | 16. B |
| 2. C | 7. D | 12. C | 17. C |
| 3. B | 8. B | 13. A | 18. D |
| 4. D | 9. A | 14. C | 19. B |
| 5. D | 10. A | 15. A | 20. C |

# 6 Sentence Completion Questions

- ■ **Testing Tactics**
- ■ **Practice Exercises**
- ■ **Answer Key**

These are the sentence completion directions you will find on the GRE: "Each sentence below has one or two blanks, each blank indicating that something has been omitted. Beneath the sentence are five lettered words or sets of words. Choose the word or set of words for each blank that best fits the meaning of the sentence as a whole."

GRE sentence completion questions test your ability to use your vocabulary and recognize logical consistency among the elements in a sentence. You need to know more than the dictionary definitions of the words involved. You need to know how the words fit together to make logical and stylistic sense.

Sentence completion questions actually measure one part of reading comprehension. If you can recognize how the different parts of a sentence affect one another, you should do well at choosing the answer that best completes the meaning of the sentence or provides a clear, logical statement of fact. The ability to recognize irony and humor will also stand you in good stead, as will the ability to recognize figurative language and to distinguish between formal and informal levels of speech.

GRE sentence completion questions may come from any of a number of different fields—art, literature, history, philosophy, botany, astronomy, geology, and others. You cannot predict what subject matter the sentences on your test will have. However, even if you are unfamiliar with the subject matter of a particular sentence, you should still be able to analyze that sentence and choose the word that best completes its meaning. It is not the sentence's subject matter that makes hard GRE sentence completion questions hard.

What makes hard sentence completion questions hard?

1. **Vocabulary Level.** Sentences contain words like *intransigence, nonplussed, harbingers.* Answer choices include words like *penchant, abeyance, eclectic.* Questions employ unfamiliar secondary meanings of words—*brook* as a verb, *economy* with the meaning of *restraint.*

2. **Grammatical Complexity.** Sentences combine the entire range of grammatical possibilities—subordinate clauses, relative clauses, prepositional phrases, gerunds, infinitives—in convoluted ways. The more complex the sentence, the more difficult it is for you to spot the key words that can unlock its meaning.

3. **Tone.** Sentences reflect the writer's attitude toward his subject matter. It is simple enough to comprehend material that is presented neutrally. It is far more difficult to comprehend material that is ironic, condescending, playful, somber, or similarly complex in tone.

4. **Style.** Ideas may be expressed in different manners—ornately or sparely, poetically or prosaically, formally or informally, journalistically or academically, originally or imitatively. An author's style depends on such details as word choice, imagery, repetition, rhythm, sentence structure, and length. Many of the most difficult GRE questions hinge on questions of style.

Work through the following tactics and learn the techniques that will help you with vocabulary, grammatical complexity, tone, and style.

# Testing Tactics

## Before You Look at the Choices, Read the Sentence and Think of a Word That Makes Sense

Your problem is to find the word that best completes the sentence in both thought and style. Before you look at the answer choices, see if you can come up with a word that makes logical sense in the context. Then look at all five choices. If the word you thought of is one of your five choices, select that as your answer. If the word you thought of is not one of your five choices, look for a synonym of that word. Select the synonym as your answer.

This tactic is helpful because it enables you to get a sense of the sentence as a whole without being distracted by any misleading answers among the answer choices. You are free to concentrate on spotting key words or phrases in the body of the sentence and to call on your own "writer's intuition" in arriving at a stylistically apt choice of word.

*See how the process works in a typical model question.*

> Because experience had convinced her that he was both self-seeking and avaricious, she rejected the likelihood that his donation had been _____.

> (A) redundant
> (B) frivolous
> (C) inexpensive
> (D) ephemeral
> (E) altruistic

This sentence presents a simple case of cause and effect. The key phrase here is *self-seeking and avaricious*. The woman has found the man to be selfish and greedy. *Therefore*, she refuses to believe he can do something _____. What words immediately come to mind? *Selfless, generous, charitable?* The missing word is, of course, *altruistic*. The woman expects selfishness (*self-seeking*) and greediness (*avaricious*), not altruism (magnanimity). The correct answer is Choice E.

Practice Tactic 1 extensively to develop your intuitive sense of the *mot juste*—the exactly right word. However, do not rely on Tactic 1 alone. On the test, always follow up Tactic 1 with Tactic 2.

## Look at All the Possible Answers Before You Make Your Final Choice

*Never* decide on an answer before you have read all the choices. You are looking for the word that *best* fits the meaning of the sentence as a whole. In order to be sure you have not been hasty in making your decision, substitute all the answer choices for the missing word. Do not spend a lot of time doing so, but do try them all. That way you can satisfy yourself that you have come up with the *best* answer.

See how this tactic helps you deal with another question patterned on examples from the GRE.

> The evil of class and race hatred must be eliminated while it is still in an _____ state; otherwise it may grow to dangerous proportions.

> (A) amorphous
> (B) overt
> (C) uncultivated
> (D) embryonic
> (E) independent

On the basis of a loose sense of this sentence's meaning, you might be tempted to select Choice A. After all, this sentence basically tells you that you should wipe out hatred before it gets too dangerous. Clearly, if hatred is vague or *amorphous*, it is less formidable than if it is well-defined. However, this reading of the sentence is inadequate: it fails to take into account the sentence's key phrase.

The key phrase here is *grow to dangerous proportions*. The writer fears that class and race hatred may grow large enough to endanger society. He wants us to wipe out this hatred before it is fully grown. Examine each answer choice, eliminating those answers that carry no suggestion that something lacks its full growth. Does *overt* suggest that something isn't fully grown? No, it suggests that something is obvious or evident. Does *uncultivated* suggest that something isn't fully grown?

No, it suggests that something is unrefined or growing without proper care or training. Does *independent* suggest that something isn't fully grown? No, it suggests that something is free and unconstrained. Only one word suggests a lack of full growth: *embryonic* (at a rudimentary, early stage of development). The correct answer is Choice D.

## In Double-Blank Sentences, Go Through the Answers, Testing the *First* Word in Each Choice (and Eliminating Those That Don't Fit)

In a sentence completion question with two blanks, read through the entire sentence to get a sense of it as a whole. Then insert the first word of each answer pair in the sentence's first blank. Ask yourself whether this particular word makes sense in this blank. If the initial word of an answer pair makes no sense in the sentence, you can eliminate that answer pair.

(*Note:* Occasionally this tactic will not work. In some questions, for example, the first words of all five answer pairs may be near-synonyms. However, the tactic frequently pays off, as it does in the following example.)

> Critics of the movie version of *The Color Purple* _____ its saccharine, overoptimistic mood as out of keeping with the novel's more _____ tone.
>
> (A) applauded...somber
> (B) condemned...hopeful
> (C) acclaimed...positive
> (D) denounced...sanguine
> (E) decried...acerbic

For a quick, general sense of the opening clause, break it down. What does it say? *Critics _____ the movie's sugary sweet mood.*

How would critics react to something sugary sweet and over-hopeful? They would disapprove. Your first missing word must be a synonym for *disapprove*.

Now eliminate the misfits. Choices A and C fail to meet the test: *applauded* and *acclaimed* signify approval, not disapproval. Choice B, *condemned*, Choice D, *denounced*, and Choice E, *decried*, however, all express disapprobation; they require a second look.

To decide among Choices B, D, and E, consider the second blank. The movie's sugary, overly hopeful mood is out of keeping with the novel's tone: the two moods disagree. Therefore, the novel's tone is *not* hopeful or sickly sweet. It is instead on the bitter or sour side; in a word, *acerbic*. The correct answer is clearly Choice E.

Remember, in double-blank sentences, the right answer must correctly fill **both** blanks. A wrong answer choice often includes one correct and one incorrect answer. ALWAYS test both words.

## Watch for Signal Words That Link One Part of the Sentence to Another

Writers use transitions to link their ideas logically. These transitions or signal words are clues that can help you figure out what the sentence actually means.

GRE sentences often contain several signal words, combining them in complex ways.

### Cause and Effect Signals

Look for words or phrases explicitly indicating that one thing causes another or logically determines another.

**Cause and Effect Signal Words**

| | |
|---|---|
| accordingly | in order to |
| because | so...that |
| consequently | therefore |
| given | thus |
| hence | when...then |
| if...then | |

## Support Signals

Look for words or phrases explicitly indicating that the omitted portion of the sentence **supports** or **continues a thought** developed elsewhere in the sentence. In such cases, a synonym or near-synonym for another word in the sentence may provide the correct answer.

### Support Signal Words

| | |
|---|---|
| additionally | furthermore |
| also | indeed |
| and | likewise |
| as well | moreover |
| besides | too |

## Contrast Signals (Explicit)

Look for function words or phrases (conjunctions, sentence adverbs, etc.) that explicitly indicate a **contrast** between one idea and another, setting up a reversal of a thought. In such cases, an antonym or near-antonym for another word in the sentence may provide the correct answer.

### Explicit Contrast Signal Words

| | |
|---|---|
| albeit | nevertheless |
| although | nonetheless |
| but | notwithstanding |
| despite | on the contrary |
| even though | on the other hand |
| however | rather than |
| in contrast | still |
| in spite of | while |
| instead of | yet |

## Contrast Signals (Implicit)

Look for content words whose meaning inherently indicates a contrast. These words can turn a situation on its head. They indicate that something unexpected, possibly even unwanted, has occurred.

### Implicit Contrast Signal Words

| | | |
|---|---|---|
| anomaly | anomalous | anomalously |
| illogic | illogical | illogically |
| incongruity | incongruous | incongruously |
| irony | ironic | ironically |
| paradox | paradoxical | paradoxically |
| surprise | surprising | surprisingly |
| | unexpected | unexpectedly |

Note the function of such a contrast signal word in the following question.

---

Paradoxically, the more _____ the details this artist chooses, the better able she is to depict her fantastic, other-worldly landscapes.

(A) ethereal
(B) realistic
(C) fanciful
(D) extravagant
(E) sublime

---

The artist creates imaginary landscapes that do not seem to belong to this world. We normally would expect the details comprising these landscapes to be as fantastic and supernatural as the landscapes themselves. But the truth of the matter, however, is paradoxical: it contradicts what we expect. The details she chooses are *realistic*, and the more realistic they are, the more fantastic the paintings become. The correct answer is Choice B.

---

## Use Your Knowledge of Word Parts and Parts of Speech to Get at the Meanings of Unfamiliar Words

If a word used by the author is unfamiliar, or if an answer choice is unknown to you, two approaches are helpful.

1. Break the word down into its component parts—prefixes, suffixes, roots—to see whether they provide a clue to its meaning. For example, in the preceding list of Implicit Contrast Signal Words, the word *incongruous* contains three major word parts. *In-* here

means not; *con-* means together; *gru-* means to move or come. *Incongruous* behavior, therefore, is behavior that does not go together or agree with someone's usual behavior; it is unexpected.

2. Change the unfamiliar word from one part of speech to another. If the adjective *embryonic* is unfamiliar to you, cut off its adjective suffix *-nic* and recognize the familiar word *embryo*. If the noun *precocity* is unfamil-

iar to you, cut off its noun suffix -*ity* and visualize it with different endings. You may come up with the adjective *precocious* (maturing early). If the verb *appropriate* is unfamiliar to you, by adding a word part or two you may come up with the common noun *appropriation* or the still more common noun *misappropriation* (as in the misappropriation of funds).

Note the application of this tactic in the following typical example.

---

This island is a colony; however, in most matters, it is _____ and receives no orders from the mother country.

(A) synoptic
(B) methodical
(C) heretical
(D) autonomous
(E) disinterested

---

First, eliminate any answer choices that are obviously incorrect. If a colony receives no orders from its mother country, it is essentially self-governing. It is not necessarily *methodical* or systematic, nor is it by definition *heretical* (unorthodox) or *disinterested* (impartial). Thus, you may rule out Choices B, C, and E.

The two answer choices remaining may be unfamiliar to you. Analyze them, using what you know of related words. Choice A, *synoptic*, is related to the noun *synopsis*, a summary or abridgment. This has nothing to do with how a colony might govern itself. Choice D, *autonomous*, comes from the prefix *auto-* (self) and the root *nom-* (law). An autonomous nation is independent; it rules itself. Thus, the correct answer is *autonomous*, Choice D.

## Break Down Complex Sentences into Simpler Components

In analyzing long, complex sentence completion items, you may find it useful to simplify the sentences by breaking them down. Rephrase dependent clauses and long participial phrases, turning them into simple sentences.

See how this tactic helps you to analyze the following sentence.

---

Museum director Hoving _____ refers to the smuggled Greek urn as the "hot pot," not because there are doubts about its authenticity or even great reservations as to its price, but because its _____ of acquisition is open to question.

(A) informally...costliness
(B) characteristically...date
(C) colloquially...manner
(D) repeatedly...swiftness
(E) cheerfully...mode

---

What do we know?

1. The urn has been smuggled.

2. Hoving calls it a "hot pot."

3. It is genuine. (There are no doubts about its authenticity.)

4. It did not cost too much. (There are no great reservations as to its price.)

In calling the smuggled urn a "hot pot," Hoving is not necessarily speaking *characteristically* or *repeatedly* or *cheerfully*. He is speaking either *informally* or *colloquially*. (*Hot* here is a slang term meaning stolen or illegally

obtained.) The urn's *costliness* is not being questioned. However, because the urn has been smuggled into the country, there clearly are unresolved questions about how it got here, in other words, about its *manner* of acquisition. The correct answer is Choice C.

Note that in sentence completion questions a choice may be complicated by an *unusual word order*, such as

1. *placing the subject after the verb:*
   To the complaints window *strode* the angry *customer*.

2. *placing the subject after an auxiliary of the verb:*
   Only by unending search *could* some few Havana *cigars* be found.

3. *inverting the subject and verb to give the sense of "if":* Were *defeat* to befall him, today's dear friends would be tomorrow's acquaintances, and next week's strangers.

4. *placing a negative word or phrase first, which usually requires at least part of the verb to follow:*
   Never have I encountered so demanding a test!

In all these instances, rephrase the sentence to make it more straightforward. For example:

The angry customer strode to the complaint window.

Some few Havana cigars could be found only by unending search.

If defeat were to befall him, today's dear friends would be tomorrow's acquaintances, and next week's strangers.

I have never encountered so demanding a test!

## Tactic 7

# If a Sentence Contains a Metaphor, Check to See Whether That Metaphor Controls the Writer's Choice of Words (and Your Answer Choice)

Writers sometimes indulge in extended metaphors, complex analogies that imaginatively identify one object with another.

In the following example, the mind of a prejudiced person is compared to the pupil of an eye in its response to light or illumination.

> The mind of a bigot is like the pupil of the eye: the more light you pour upon it, the more it will
>
> _____.
>
> (A) blink
> (B) veer
> (C) stare
> (D) reflect
> (E) contract

The image of light unifies this sentence. In choosing an answer, it is necessary to complete the sentence in such a way as to develop that metaphor fully and accurately. Exactly what takes place when you shine a light into someone's eye? The person may stare back or blink; you may see the light reflected in the person's eye. But what happens to the pupil of the eye? It neither blinks nor reflects. Instead it shrinks in size; it *contracts*. Likewise, exposed to the light of tolerance, the bigot's mind resists illumination. Choice E completes the metaphor; it is the correct answer choice.

# Practice Exercises

## Sentence Completion Exercise A

Directions: Each of the following sentence completion questions contains one or two blanks. These blanks signify that a word or set of words has been left out. Below each sentence are five words or sets of words. For each blank, pick the word or set of words that <u>best</u> reflects the sentence's overall meaning.

1. Normally an individual thunderstorm lasts about 45 minutes, but under certain conditions the storm may _____, becoming ever more severe, for as long as four hours.

   (A) wane
   (B) moderate
   (C) persist
   (D) vacillate
   (E) disperse

2. Perhaps because something in us instinctively distrusts such displays of natural fluency, some readers approach John Updike's fiction with _____.

   (A) indifference
   (B) suspicion
   (C) veneration
   (D) recklessness
   (E) bewilderment

3. We lost confidence in him because he never _____ the grandiose promises he had made.

   (A) forgot about
   (B) reneged on
   (C) tired of
   (D) delivered on
   (E) retreated from

4. Ms. Sutcliffe's helpful notes on her latest wine discoveries and her no-nonsense warnings to consumers about _____ wines provide _____ guide to the numbing array of wines of Burgundy.

   (A) excellent...a useful
   (B) overrated...an inadequate
   (C) overpriced...a trusty
   (D) unsatisfactory...a spotty
   (E) vintage...an unreliable

5. We were amazed that a man who had been heretofore the most _____ of public speakers could, in a single speech, electrify an audience and bring them cheering to their feet.

   (A) enthralling
   (B) accomplished
   (C) pedestrian
   (D) auspicious
   (E) masterful

6. If you are trying to make a strong impression on your audience, you cannot do so by being understated, tentative, or _____.

   (A) hyperbolic
   (B) restrained
   (C) argumentative
   (D) authoritative
   (E) passionate

7. Despite the mixture's _____ nature, we found that by lowering its temperature in the laboratory we could dramatically reduce its tendency to vaporize.

(A) resilient
(B) volatile
(C) homogeneous
(D) insipid
(E) acerbic

8. No other artist rewards the viewer with more sheer pleasure than Miró; he is one of those blessed artists who combine profundity and _____.

(A) education
(B) wisdom
(C) faith
(D) fun
(E) depth

9. Some Central Intelligence Agency officers have _____ their previous statements denying any involvement on their part with the Contra aid network and are now revising their earlier testimony.

(A) justified
(B) recanted
(C) repeated
(D) protracted
(E) heeded

10. New concerns about growing religious tension in northern India were _____ this week after at least fifty people were killed and hundreds were injured or arrested in rioting between Hindus and Moslems.

(A) lessened
(B) invalidated
(C) restrained
(D) dispersed
(E) fueled

11. In a happy, somewhat boisterous celebration of the European discovery of America, the major phase of the Columbus Cinquecentennial got off to _____ start on Friday.

(A) a slow
(B) a rousing
(C) a reluctant
(D) an indifferent
(E) a quiet

12. In one shocking instance of _____ research, one of the nation's most influential researchers in the field of genetics reported on experiments that were never carried out and published deliberately _____ scientific papers on his nonexistent work.

(A) comprehensive...abstract
(B) theoretical...challenging
(C) fraudulent...deceptive
(D) derivative...authoritative
(E) erroneous...impartial

13. Measurement is, like any other human endeavor, a complex activity, subject to error, not always used _____, and frequently misinterpreted and _____.

(A) mistakenly...derided
(B) erratically...analyzed
(C) systematically...organized
(D) innovatively...refined
(E) properly...misunderstood

14. In a revolutionary development in technology, several manufacturers now make biodegradable forms of plastic; some plastic six-pack rings, for example, gradually _____ when exposed to sunlight.

(A) harden
(B) stagnate
(C) inflate
(D) propagate
(E) decompose

15. To alleviate the problem of contaminated chicken, the study panel recommends that the federal government shift its inspection emphasis from cursory bird-by-bird visual checks to a more _____ random sampling for bacterial and chemical contamination.

(A) rigorous
(B) perfunctory
(C) symbolic
(D) discreet
(E) dubious

16. Her novel published to universal acclaim, her literary gifts acknowledged by the chief figures of the Harlem Renaissance, her reputation as yet _____ by envious slights, Hurston clearly was at the _____ of her career.

(A) undamaged...ebb
(B) untarnished...zenith
(C) untainted...extremity
(D) blackened...mercy
(E) unmarred...brink

17. To the dismay of the student body, the class president was _____ berated by the principal at a school assembly.

(A) ignominiously
(B) privately
(C) magnanimously
(D) fortuitously
(E) inconspicuously

18. Aimed at curbing European attempts to seize territory in the Americas, the Monroe Doctrine was a warning to _____ foreign powers.

(A) pertinacious
(B) credulous
(C) remote
(D) overt
(E) predatory

19. When Frazer's editors at Macmillan tried to _____ his endless augmentations, he insisted on a type size so small and a page so packed as to approach illegibility; and if that proved _____, thinner paper.

    (A) protract...unwarranted
    (B) expurgate...satisfactory
    (C) reprimand...irrelevant
    (D) restrict...insufficient
    (E) revise...idiosyncratic

20. The authority of voice in Frazer's writing strikes many readers today as _____ colonialism; his prose seems as invulnerable and expansive as something on which the sun was presumed never to set.

    (A) consonant with
    (B) independent of
    (C) ambivalent toward
    (D) cognizant of
    (E) detrimental to

# Sentence Completion Exercise B

Directions: Each of the following sentence completion questions contains one or two blanks. These blanks signify that a word or set of words has been left out. Below each sentence are five words or sets of words. For each blank, pick the word or set of words that best reflects the sentence's overall meaning.

1. Baldwin's brilliant *The Fire Next Time* is both so eloquent in its passion and so searching in its _____ that it is bound to _____ any reader.

    (A) bitterness...embarrass
    (B) romanticism...appall
    (C) candor...unsettle
    (D) indifference...disappoint
    (E) conception...bore

2. Unlike other examples of _____ verse, Milton's *Lycidas* does more than merely mourn the death of Edward King; it also denounces corruption in the Church in which King was ordained.

    (A) satiric
    (B) elegiac
    (C) free
    (D) humorous
    (E) didactic

3. Few other plants can grow beneath the canopy of the sycamore tree, whose leaves and pods produce a natural herbicide that leaches into the surrounding soil, _____ other plants that might compete for water and nutrients.

    (A) inhibiting
    (B) distinguishing
    (C) nourishing
    (D) encouraging
    (E) refreshing

4. Although a few years ago the fundamental facts about the Milky Way seemed fairly well _____, now even its mass and its radius have come into _____.

    (A) determined...resolution
    (B) ignored...danger
    (C) problematic...prominence
    (D) diminished...disrepute
    (E) established...question

5. The officers threatened to take _____ if the lives of their men were _____ by the conquered natives.

    (A) liberties...irritated
    (B) measures...enhanced
    (C) pains...destroyed
    (D) reprisals...endangered
    (E) affront...enervated

6. Despite an affected _____ that convinced casual observers that he was indifferent about his painting and enjoyed only frivolity, Warhol cared deeply about his art and labored at it _____.

    (A) nonchalance...diligently
    (B) empathy...methodically
    (C) fervor...secretly
    (D) gloom...intermittently
    (E) hysteria...sporadically

7. Because she had a reputation for _____ we were surprised and pleased when she greeted us so _____.

    (A) insolence...irately
    (B) insouciance...cordially
    (C) graciousness...amiably
    (D) arrogance...disdainfully
    (E) querulousness...affably

8. The child was so spoiled by her indulgent parents that she pouted and became _____ when she did not receive all of their attention.

    (A) discreet
    (B) suspicious
    (C) elated
    (D) sullen
    (E) tranquil

9. Just as disloyalty is the mark of the renegade, _____ is the mark of the _____.

    (A) timorousness...hero
    (B) temerity...coward
    (C) avarice...philanthropist
    (D) cowardice...craven
    (E) vanity...flatterer

10. He became quite overbearing and domineering once he had become accustomed to the _____ shown to soldiers by the natives; he enjoyed his new sense of power and self-importance.

(A) disrespect
(B) apathy
(C) deference
(D) culpability
(E) enmity

11. The _____ of time had left the castle _____; it towered above the village, looking much as it must have done in Richard the Lion-Hearted's time.

(A) repairs...destroyed
(B) remoteness...alone
(C) lack...defended
(D) status...lonely
(E) ravages...untouched

12. One of the most _____ educators in New York, Dr. Shalala ignited a controversy in 1984 by calling the city public schools a "rotten barrel" in need of _____ reform.

(A) disputatious...little
(B) outspoken...systemic
(C) caustic...partial
(D) indifferent...pretentious
(E) sycophantic...superficial

13. The newest fiber-optic cables that carry telephone calls cross-country are made of glass so _____ that a piece 100 miles thick is clearer than a standard windowpane.

(A) fragile
(B) immaculate
(C) tangible
(D) transparent
(E) iridescent

14. The reasoning in this editorial is so _____ that we cannot see how anyone can be deceived by it.

(A) coherent
(B) astute
(C) cogent
(D) specious
(E) dispassionate

15. The _____ of evidence was on the side of the plaintiff since all but one witness testified that his story was correct.

(A) paucity
(B) propensity
(C) accuracy
(D) brunt
(E) preponderance

16. Glendon provides a dark underside to Frederick Jackson Turner's frontier thesis that saw rugged individualism as the essence of American society— an individualism that she sees as _____ atomism.

(A) antithetical toward
(B) skeptical of
(C) degenerating into

(D) aspiring to
(E) renewed by

17. Chatwin has devoted his life to a kind of Grail quest, hoping to prove—by study and direct experience with primitive people—that human nature is gentle and defensive rather than _____, and that man is _____, not a predator.

(A) belligerent...an apostate
(B) martial...a crusader
(C) aggressive...a pilgrim
(D) truculent...a gladiator
(E) pugnacious...a pawn

18. The texts as we have them were written down and edited carefully by Christians proud of their ancestors but unable to bear the thought of their indulging in heathen practices; thus, all references to the ancient religion of the Celts were _____, if not _____.

(A) deleted...expunged
(B) muddied...suppressed
(C) labored...denigrated
(D) aggrieved...overawed
(E) obscure...ironic

19. Because Inspector Morse could not contain his scorn for the police commissioner, he was imprudent enough to make _____ remarks about his superior officer.

(A) ambiguous
(B) dispassionate
(C) unfathomable
(D) interminable
(E) scathing

20. In Japanese art, profound emotion is frequently couched in images of nature, observed with _____ conditioned by life in a land of dramatic seasonal change, where perils of earthquake and typhoon make nature's bounty _____ and its processes awesome and beautiful.

(A) an intimacy...precarious
(B) a fidelity...munificent
(C) a skill...excessive
(D) an indifference...chancy
(E) a sensitivity...distinctive

# Sentence Completion Exercise C

<u>Directions</u>: Each of the following sentence completion questions contains one or two blanks. These blanks signify that a word or set of words has been left out. Below each sentence are five words or sets of words. For each blank, pick the word or set of words that <u>best</u> reflects the sentence's overall meaning.

1. A _____ statement is an _____ comparison: it does not compare things explicitly, but suggests a likeness between them.

(A) sarcastic...unfair
(B) blatant...overt
(C) sanguine...inherent
(D) metaphorical...implied
(E) bellicose...ardent

2. Modern architecture has discarded the_____ trimming on buildings and has concentrated on an almost Greek simplicity of line.

(A) flamboyant
(B) austere
(C) inconspicuous
(D) aesthetic
(E) derivative

3. If you are seeking _____ that will resolve all our ailments, you are undertaking an impossible task.

(A) a precedent
(B) a panacea
(C) an abstraction
(D) a direction
(E) a contrivance

4. I have no _____ motive in offering this advice; I seek no personal advantage or honor.

(A) nominal
(B) altruistic
(C) incongruous
(D) disinterested
(E) ulterior

5. This park has been preserved in all its _____ wildness so that visitors in future years may see how people lived during the eighteenth century.

(A) hedonistic
(B) prospective
(C) esoteric
(D) untrammeled
(E) pristine

6. Though he was theoretically a friend of labor, his voting record in Congress _____ that impression.

(A) implied
(B) created
(C) confirmed
(D) belied
(E) maintained

7. The orator was so _____ that the audience became _____.

(A) soporific...drowsy
(B) inaudible...elated
(C) pompous...bombastic
(D) dramatic...affable
(E) convincing...moribund

8. If you carry this _____ attitude to the conference, you will _____ any supporters you may have at this moment.

(A) belligerent...delight
(B) truculent...alienate
(C) conciliatory...defer
(D) supercilious...attract
(E) ubiquitous...delight

9. The _____ pittance the widow receives from the government cannot keep her from poverty.

(A) magnanimous
(B) indulgent
(C) meticulous
(D) munificent
(E) meager

10. Harriman, Kennan, and Acheson were part of that inner _____ of the American diplomatic establishment whose distinguished legacy _____ U.S. foreign policy.

(A) circle...grieved
(B) sanctum...absorbed
(C) core...dominated
(D) life...biased
(E) coterie...exacerbated

11. The young man was quickly promoted when his employers saw how _____ he was.

(A) indigent
(B) indifferent
(C) assiduous
(D) lethargic
(E) cursory

12. For Miró, art became a _____ ritual; paper and pencils were holy objects to him and he worked as though he were performing a religious rite.

(A) superficial
(B) sacred
(C) banal
(D) cryptic
(E) futile

13. Because it arrives so early in the season, before many other birds, the robin has been called the _____ of spring.

(A) hostage
(B) autocrat
(C) compass
(D) newcomer
(E) harbinger

14. Shy and hypochondriacal, Madison was uncomfortable at public gatherings; his character made him a most _____ lawmaker and practicing politician.

(A) conscientious
(B) unlikely
(C) fervent
(D) gregarious
(E) effective

15. The tapeworm is an example of _____ organism, one that lives within or on another creature, deriving some or all of its nutrients from its host.

   (A) a hospitable
   (B) an exemplary
   (C) a parasitic
   (D) an autonomous
   (E) a protozoan

16. In place of the more general debate about abstract principles of government that most delegates probably expected, the Constitutional Convention put _____ proposals on the table.

   (A) theoretical
   (B) vague
   (C) concrete
   (D) tentative
   (E) redundant

17. Overindulgence _____ character as well as physical stamina.

   (A) strengthens
   (B) stimulates
   (C) debilitates
   (D) maintains
   (E) provides

18. We must try to understand his momentary _____ for he has _____ more strain and anxiety than any among us.

   (A) outcry...described
   (B) senility...understood
   (C) vision...forgotten
   (D) generosity...desired
   (E) aberration...undergone

19. He is _____ opponent; you must respect and fear him at all times.

   (A) a redoubtable
   (B) a disingenuous
   (C) a pugnacious
   (D) an insignificant
   (E) a craven

20. Your _____ tactics may compel me to cancel the contract as the job must be finished on time.

   (A) dilatory
   (B) offensive
   (C) repugnant
   (D) infamous
   (E) confiscatory

# Sentence Completion Exercise D

<u>Directions</u>: Each of the following sentence completion questions contains one or two blanks. These blanks signify that a word or set of words has been left out. Below each sentence are five words or sets of words. For each blank, pick the word or set of words that <u>best</u> reflects the sentence's overall meaning.

1. Truculent in defending their individual rights of sovereignty under the Articles of Confederation, the newly formed states _____ constantly.

   (A) apologized   (B) digressed   (C) conferred
        (D) acquiesced   (E) squabbled

2. If the *Titanic* had hit the iceberg head on, its watertight compartments might have saved it from _____, but it swerved to avoid the iceberg, and in the collision so many compartments were opened to the sea that disaster was _____.

   (A) foundering...inevitable
   (B) sinking...escaped
   (C) damage...limited
   (D) buoyancy...unavoidable
   (E) collapse...averted

3. Written in an amiable style, the book provides a comprehensive overview of European wines that should prove inviting to both the virtual _____ and the experienced connoisseur.

   (A) prodigal
   (B) novice
   (C) zealot
   (D) miser
   (E) glutton

4. The members of the religious sect ostracized the _____ who had abandoned their faith.

   (A) coward
   (B) suppliant
   (C) litigant
   (D) recreant
   (E) proselyte

5. I am not attracted by the _____ life of the _____, always wandering through the countryside, begging for charity.

   (A) proud...almsgiver
   (B) noble...philanthropist
   (C) affluent...mendicant
   (D) natural...philosopher
   (E) peripatetic...vagabond

6. Her true feelings _____ themselves in her sarcastic asides; only then was her _____ revealed.

   (A) concealed...sweetness
   (B) manifested...bitterness
   (C) hid...sarcasm
   (D) developed...anxiety
   (E) grieved...charm

7. They fired upon the enemy from behind trees, walls, and any other _____ point they could find.

   (A) conspicuous
   (B) definitive
   (C) vantage
   (D) exposed
   (E) indefensible

8. Because Pauling stubbornly continued to believe in the power of Vitamin C to cure cancer despite much evidence to the contrary, his colleagues felt he had lost his scientific _____.

   (A) tenacity
   (B) experimentation
   (C) daring
   (D) apparatus
   (E) objectivity

9. We need more men of culture and enlightenment; we have too many _____ among us.

   (A) visionaries
   (B) students
   (C) philistines
   (D) pragmatists
   (E) philosophers

10. The sugar dissolved in water _____; finally all that remained was an almost _____ residue on the bottom of the glass.

    (A) quickly...lumpy
    (B) immediately...fragrant
    (C) gradually...imperceptible
    (D) subsequently...glassy
    (E) spectacularly...opaque

11. Alec Guinness has few equals among English-speaking actors, and in his autobiography he reveals himself to be an uncommonly _____ prose stylist as well.

    (A) ambivalent
    (B) infamous
    (C) supercilious
    (D) felicitous
    (E) pedestrian

12. Traffic speed limits are set at a level that achieves some balance between the danger of _____ speed and the desire of most people to travel as quickly as possible.

    (A) marginal
    (B) normal
    (C) prudent
    (D) inadvertent
    (E) excessive

13. Although the economy suffers downturns, it also has strong _____ and self-correcting tendencies.

    (A) unstable
    (B) recidivist
    (C) inauspicious
    (D) recuperative
    (E) self-destructive

14. It is foolish to vent your spleen on _____ object; still, you make _____ enemies that way.

    (A) an inanimate...fewer
    (B) an immobile...bitter

15. Since Cyrano de Bergerac did not wish to be under an obligation to any man, he refused to be a _____ of Cardinal Richelieu.

    (A) proselytizer
    (B) mentor
    (C) protégé
    (D) benefactor
    (E) predecessor

16. The leader of the group is the passionately committed Crimond, whose _____ politics is inversely proportional to his disciples' _____ political faith.

    (A) retreat from...remote
    (B) penchant for...ardent
    (C) indifference to...jaundiced
    (D) engagement in...lapsed
    (E) disinclination for...problematic

17. After the Japanese attack on Pearl Harbor on December 7, 1941, Japanese-Americans were _____ of being spies for Japan, although there was no _____ to back up this accusation.

    (A) acquitted...buttress
    (B) tired...witness
    (C) reminded...reason
    (D) suspected...evidence
    (E) exonerated...money

18. More than one friendly whale has nudged a boat with such _____ that passengers have been knocked overboard.

    (A) enthusiasm
    (B) lethargy
    (C) hostility
    (D) serenity
    (E) animosity

19. In seeking to rediscover Zora Neale Hurston, it is intriguing to look at the figure she cut in the minds of her contemporaries, the high regard she enjoyed before shifting aesthetic values _____ her to curio status.

    (A) emancipated
    (B) deviated
    (C) exported
    (D) absolved
    (E) relegated

20. We have become so democratic in our habits of thought that we are convinced that truth is determined through _____ of facts.

    (A) a hierarchy
    (B) a transcendance
    (C) a plebiscite
    (D) a repeal
    (E) an ignorance

(C) an interesting...curious
(D) an insipid...dull
(E) a humane...more

# Sentence Completion Exercise E

Directions: Each of the following sentence completion questions contains one or two blanks. These blanks signify that a word or set of words has been left out. Below each sentence are five words or sets of words. For each blank, pick the word or set of words that best reflects the sentence's overall meaning.

1. Studded starfish are well protected from most _____ and parasites by _____ surface whose studs are actually modified spines.

   (A) dangers...a vulnerable
   (B) predators...an armored
   (C) threats...a fragile
   (D) challenges...an obtuse
   (E) exigencies...a brittle

2. Chaotic in conception but not in _____, Kelly's canvases are as neat as the proverbial pin.

   (A) conceit
   (B) theory
   (C) execution
   (D) origin
   (E) intent

3. After having worked in the soup kitchen feeding the hungry, the volunteer began to see her own good fortune as _____ and her difference from the _____ as chance rather than destiny.

   (A) an omen...homeless
   (B) a fluke...impoverished
   (C) a threat...destitute
   (D) a reward...indigent
   (E) a lie...affluent

4. Some students are _____ and want to take only the courses for which they see immediate value.

   (A) theoretical
   (B) impartial
   (C) pragmatic
   (D) idealistic
   (E) opinionated

5. Unlike the Shakespearean plays that lit up the English stage, the "closet dramas" of the nineteenth century were meant to be _____ rather than _____.

   (A) seen...acted
   (B) read...staged
   (C) quiet...raucous
   (D) sophisticated...urbane
   (E) produced...performed

6. Japan's industrial success is _____ in part to its tradition of group effort and _____, as opposed to the emphasis on personal achievement that is a prominent aspect of other industrial nations.

   (A) responsive...independence
   (B) related...introspection
   (C) equivalent...solidarity
   (D) subordinate...individuality
   (E) attributed...cooperation

7. I was so bored with the verbose and redundant style of Victorian novelists that I welcomed the change to the _____ style of Hemingway.

   (A) prolix
   (B) consistent
   (C) terse
   (D) logistical
   (E) florid

8. As _____ head of the organization, he attended social functions and civic meetings but had no _____ in the formulation of company policy.

   (A) titular...voice
   (B) hypothetical...vote
   (C) former...pride
   (D) nominal...competition
   (E) actual...say

9. His listeners enjoyed his _____ wit but his victims often _____ at its satire.

   (A) lugubrious...suffered
   (B) caustic...laughed
   (C) kindly...smarted
   (D) subtle...smiled
   (E) trenchant...winced

10. The first forty years of life give us the text; the next thirty supply the _____.

    (A) abridgement
    (B) bibliography
    (C) commentary
    (D) epitaph
    (E) title

11. The distinctive qualities of African music were not appreciated or even _____ by Westerners until fairly recently.

    (A) deplored
    (B) revered
    (C) ignored
    (D) neglected
    (E) perceived

12. It is only to the vain that all is vanity; and all is _____ only to those who have never been _____ themselves.

    (A) arrogance...proud of
    (B) deception...sincere with
    (C) cowardice...afraid for
    (D) indolence...bored by
    (E) solitude...left to

13. No act of _____ was more pronounced than his refusal of any rewards for his discovery.
    (A) abeyance
    (B) submission
    (C) egoism
    (D) denunciation
    (E) abnegation

14. Tocqueville decided to swear the oath of loyalty to the new Orleanist king in part _____ (he wanted to keep his position as magistrate), and in part pragmatically (he was convinced that the democratization of politics represented by the new regime was _____).
    (A) expediently...calamitous
    (B) opportunistically...inevitable
    (C) imprudently...circumspect
    (D) selflessly...idealistic
    (E) theoretically...negligible

15. Unlike the gregarious Capote, who was never happier than when he was in the center of a crowd of celebrities, Faulkner, in later years, grew somewhat _____ and shunned company.
    (A) congenial
    (B) decorous
    (C) dispassionate
    (D) reclusive
    (E) ambivalent

16. She is a pragmatist, as _____ to base her future on impractical dreams as she would be to build a castle on shifting sand.
    (A) determined
    (B) disinclined
    (C) quick
    (D) apt
    (E) diligent

17. We are _____ the intellects of the past; or, rather, like children we take it for granted that somebody must supply us with our supper and our _____.
    (A) ungrateful to...ideas
    (B) dependent on...repose
    (C) unfaithful to...needs
    (D) fortunate in...allowance
    (E) generous to...wants

18. During the middle of the eighteenth century, the _____ style in furniture and architecture, marked by scrollwork and excessive decoration, flourished.
    (A) austere
    (B) functional
    (C) medieval
    (D) rococo
    (E) abstract

19. Although eighteenth-century English society as a whole did not encourage learning for its own sake in women, nonetheless it illogically _____ women's sad lack of education.
    (A) palliated
    (B) postulated
    (C) decried
    (D) brooked
    (E) vaunted

20. Faced with these massive changes, the government keeps its own counsel; although generally benevolent, it has always been _____ regime.
    (A) an altruistic
    (B) an unpredictable
    (C) a reticent
    (D) a sanguine
    (E) an indifferent

# Answer Key

## Sentence Completion Exercise A
| | | | |
|---|---|---|---|
| 1. C | 6. B | 11. B | 16. B |
| 2. B | 7. B | 12. C | 17. A |
| 3. D | 8. D | 13. E | 18. E |
| 4. C | 9. B | 14. E | 19. D |
| 5. C | 10. E | 15. A | 20. A |

## Sentence Completion Exercise B
| | | | |
|---|---|---|---|
| 1. C | 6. A | 11. E | 16. C |
| 2. B | 7. E | 12. B | 17. C |
| 3. A | 8. D | 13. D | 18. B |
| 4. E | 9. D | 14. D | 19. E |
| 5. D | 10. C | 15. E | 20. A |

## Sentence Completion Exercise C
| | | | |
|---|---|---|---|
| 1. D | 6. D | 11. C | 16. C |
| 2. A | 7. A | 12. B | 17. C |
| 3. B | 8. B | 13. E | 18. E |
| 4. E | 9. E | 14. B | 19. A |
| 5. E | 10. C | 15. C | 20. A |

## Sentence Completion Exercise D
| | | | |
|---|---|---|---|
| 1. E | 6. B | 11. D | 16. E |
| 2. A | 7. C | 12. E | 17. D |
| 3. B | 8. E | 13. D | 18. A |
| 4. D | 9. C | 14. A | 19. E |
| 5. E | 10. C | 15. C | 20. C |

## Sentence Completion Exercise E
| | | | |
|---|---|---|---|
| 1. B | 6. E | 11. E | 16. B |
| 2. C | 7. C | 12. B | 17. A |
| 3. B | 8. A | 13. E | 18. D |
| 4. C | 9. E | 14. B | 19. C |
| 5. B | 10. C | 15. D | 20. C |

# 7 Reading Comprehension Questions

- ■ **Testing Tactics**
- ■ **Practice Exercises**
- ■ **Answer Key**

GRE reading comprehension questions test your ability to understand what you read—both content and technique. Each verbal section on the GRE CAT includes two to four relatively short passages, each passage followed by two to four questions. A passage may deal with the **sciences** (including medicine, botany, zoology, chemistry, physics, geology, astronomy); the **humanities** (including art, literature, music, philosophy, folklore); or the **social sciences** (including history, economics, sociology, government). Some passages are strictly objective, explaining or describing a phenomenon or process neutrally. Others reflect a particular bias or point of view: the author is trying to convince the reader to share his or her opinion about the subject being discussed.

The GRE tends to take its reading passages from *Scientific American*, from prestigious university presses (Harvard, Princeton, Oxford), from scholarly journals. Often the test-makers hit academically "hot" topics— sociobiology, plate tectonics, damage to the ozone layer, Arthurian romance, the status of women's literature—that have aroused controversy over the past sev-

eral decades. Frequently they edit these passages to make them more demanding both in vocabulary level and in grammatical complexity.

Some of the reading comprehension questions on the GRE are factual, asking you about specific details in the passages. Others ask you to interpret the passages, to make judgments about them. Still others ask you to recognize various techniques used by the authors or possible applications of their ideas to other circumstances. Some questions include lengthy and complex statements, as lengthy and complex as any sentences in the passage. Read the questions closely, as closely as you read the text. Be sure, in answering reading comprehension questions, that you read *all* the answer choices before deciding which is correct.

The reading comprehension questions following each passage are not arranged in order of difficulty. They are arranged to reflect the way the passage's content is organized. A question based on information found at the beginning of the passage generally will come before a question based on information at the passage's end.

## Testing Tactics

### Tactic 1
### First Read the Question, Then Read the Passage

In responding to reading comprehension passages on the CAT, you generally will have to consider more material than can fit conveniently on a single screen. You will confront a split screen similar to the one on the next page. On one half of the screen you will see the ques-

tion you must answer; on the other you will see a segment of the passage under consideration. You will have to scroll through the passage in order to read the text in its entirety. (For a more comprehensive explanation of scrolling through passages, see Chapter 2.)

Under these conditions, clearly only one tactic works: first read the question, then read the passage.

1. Read the question carefully, so that you are sure you understand what it is asking. Decide whether it is asking about a specific, readily identifiable detail within the passage, or whether it is asking about the passage as a whole. Note any key words in the question that may help you spot where the answer may be found.

2. Next, turn to the passage. Read as rapidly as you can with understanding, but do not force yourself. Do not worry about the time element. If you worry about not finishing the test, you will begin to take shortcuts and miss the correct answer in your haste.

3. As you read the opening sentences, try to anticipate what the passage will be about. Whom or what is the author talking about? What, in other words, is the *topic* of this passage?

4. As you scroll through the passage, think about what kind of writing this is. What is the author trying to do?

    Is the author trying to *explain* some aspect of the topic?
    Is the author trying to *describe* some aspect of the topic?

    Is the author trying to *argue* or debate some aspect of the topic?

    What does the author feel about this topic? What audience is the author addressing here? Answering these questions will give you a sense of the passage as a whole.

5. Use your scratch paper intelligently. Take brief notes of important words or phrases in different paragraphs so that you can scroll back to them quickly when you want to verify an answer choice. You may also want to note key words in question stems (words like EXCEPT and LEAST, which the test-makers capitalize for emphasis, and that restrict your answer choice).

6. Your first scrolling through the passage should give you a general impression of the scope of the passage and of the location of its major subdivisions. In order to answer the question properly, **you must go back to the passage to verify your answer choice**. Do not rely on your memory. Above all, do not rely on anything you may have learned from your reading or courses about the topic of this passage. Base your answer on what this passage says, not on what you know from other sources.

## Learn to Spot the Major Reading Question Types

Just as it will help you to know the common types of analogies found on the GRE, it will also help you to familiarize yourself with the major types of reading questions on the test.

If you can recognize just what a given question is asking for, you will be better able to tell which reading tactic to apply.

Here are seven categories of reading questions you are likely to face:

1. **Main Idea** Questions that test your ability to find the central thought of a passage or to judge its significance often take one of the following forms:

 The main point of the passage is to...
 The passage is primarily concerned with...
 The author's primary purpose in this passage is to...
 The chief theme of the passage can best be described as...
 Which of the following titles best states the central idea of the passage?
 Which of the following statements best expresses the main idea of the passage?

2. **Finding Specific Details** Questions that test your ability to understand what the author states *explicitly* are often worded:

 According to the author,...
 The author states all of the following EXCEPT...
 According to the passage, which of the following is true of the...
 The passage supplies information that would answer which of the following questions?
 Which of the following statements is (are) best supported by the passage?
 Which of the following is NOT cited in the passage as evidence of...

3. **Drawing Inferences** Questions that test your ability to go beyond the author's explicit statements and see what these statements imply may be worded:

 It can be inferred from the passage that...
 The author implies that...
 The passage suggests that...
 Which of the following statements about...can be inferred from the passage?

4. **Application to Other Situations** Questions that test your ability to recognize how the author's ideas might apply to other situations often are worded:

 With which of the following statements would the author of the passage be most likely to agree?
 With which of the following aphorisms would the author be in strongest agreement?

 The author's argument would be most weakened by the discovery of which of the following?
 The author's contention would be most clearly strengthened if which of the following were found to be true?
 Which of the following examples could best be substituted for the author's example of...
 Which of the following statements would be most likely to begin the paragraph immediately following the passage?
 The author is most probably addressing which of the following audiences?

5. **Tone/Attitude** Questions that test your ability to sense an author's emotional state often take the form:

 The author's attitude toward the problem can best be described as...
 The author regards that idea that...with...
 The author's tone in the passage is that of a person attempting to...
 Which of the following best describes the author's tone in the passage?

6. **Technique** Questions that test your ability to recognize a passage's method of organization or technique often are worded:

 Which of the following best describes the development of this passage?
 In presenting the argument, the author does all of the following EXCEPT...
 The relationship between the second paragraph and the first paragraph can best be described as...
 In the passage, the author makes the central point primarily by...
 The organization of the passage can best be described as...

7. **Determining the Meaning of Words from Their Context** Questions that test your ability to work out the meaning of unfamiliar words from their context often are worded:

 As it is used in the passage, the term...can best be described as...
 The phrase...is used in the passage to mean that...
 As used by the author, the term...refers to...
 The author uses the phrase...to describe...

# When Asked to Find the Main Idea, Be Sure to Check the Opening and Summary Sentences of Each Paragraph

The opening and closing sentences of a paragraph are key sentences for you to read. They can serve as guideposts, pointing out the author's main idea.

When you are asked to determine a passage's main idea, *always* check the opening and summary sen-

tences of each paragraph. Authors typically provide readers with a sentence that expresses a paragraph's main idea succinctly. Although such *topic sentences* may appear anywhere in the paragraph, readers customarily look for them in the opening or closing sentences.

Note that in GRE reading passages topic sentences are sometimes implied rather than stated directly. If you cannot find a topic sentence, ask yourself these questions:

1. Who or what is this passage about?
   (The subject of the passage can be a *person*, *place*, or *thing*. It can be something abstract, such as an *idea*. It can even be a *process*, or something in motion, for which no single-word synonym exists.)

2. What aspect of this subject is the author talking about?

3. What is the author trying to get across about this aspect of the subject?
   (Decide the most important thing that is being said about the subject. Either the subject must be *doing* something, or something is *being done* to it.)

Read the following natural science passage and apply this tactic.

> According to Wilson[1], only when we are able to apply the same parameters and mathematical principles to weighing both troops of rhesus
> *Line* macaques and termite colonies will a unified
> (5) science of sociobiology finally exist. While recognizing that many of his colleagues question such an outcome, Wilson, one of sociobiology's leading proponents, finds himself simultaneously more and more struck by the functional similari-
> (10) ties that characterize both insect and vertebrate societies and less concerned with the structural differences that divide them to such an apparently irreconcilable degree. Thus, he freely compares termites and macaques, pointing out numerous
> (15) likenesses between them. Both societies are territorial: they occupy a particular home range, which they defend against intruders. Likewise, both are cooperative: members organize themselves into working groups that observe a clearly-
> (20) defined division of labor. In addition, members of both groups can convey to each other a range of basic emotions and personal information: animosity, fright, hunger, rank within a particular caste, and ability to reproduce. Wilson readily
> (25) concedes that, from a specialist's perspective, such a likeness may at first appear superficial, even unscientifically glib. Nonetheless, in this eminent scholar's judgment, "it is out of such deliberate oversimplification that the beginnings
> (30) of a general theory are made."

[1]Edwin O. Wilson, Harvard professor and author of *Sociobiology*.

Now look at a typical main idea question on this passage.

> Which of the following best summarizes the author's main point?
> (A) Facile and simplistic comparisons of animal societies could damage the prospects for the establishment of a unified science of sociobiology.

> (B) It is necessary to study both biology and sociology in order to appreciate how animals as different as termites and rhesus macaques can be said to resemble each other.
> (C) The majority of animal species arrange themselves in societies whose patterns of group behavior resemble those of human societies.
> (D) It is worthwhile noting that animals as dissimilar as termites and rhesus monkeys observe certain analogous and predictable behavior patterns.
> (E) An analysis of the ways in which insect and vertebrate societies resemble one another could supply the foundation for a unified science of sociobiology.

Look at the opening and summary sentences of the passage: "only when we are able to apply the same parameters and mathematical principles to weighing both troops of rhesus macaques and termite colonies will a unified science of sociobiology finally exist...it is out of such deliberate oversimplification that the beginnings of a general theory are made." First, is there a person, place, thing, idea, or process that is common to both sentences? Are there any words in the last sentence that repeat something in the first? *A general theory* repeats the idea of *a unified science* of sociobiology. The paragraph's subject seems to be the unified science of sociobiology. Note as well the words pointing to expectations for the future—*will...finally exist, beginnings*. The tone of both sentences appears positive: when certain conditions are met, then, in Wilson's view, a specific result will follow—we will have a unified science or general theory of sociobiology. This result, however, is not guaranteed; it can come about only if the conditions are met.

Now turn to the answer choices. What does Choice A say about a unified science of sociobiology? It states some things could make it less likely, not more likely, to come about. Choice A is incorrect; it contradicts the passage's sense that a unified science of sociobiology is a *likely* outcome. Choices B, C, and D also may be incorrect: not one of them mentions a unified science of sociobiology. On closer inspection, Choice B proves incorrect: it makes an unsupported statement that one needs biological and sociological education to understand the resemblances between insects and vertebrates. Choice C also proves incorrect: it goes far beyond what the passage actually states. Where the passage speaks in terms of termites and rhesus macaques, Choice C speaks in terms of the *majority* of animal species and extends the comparison to include humans as well. Choice D, while factually correct according to the passage, is incorrect because it is too narrow in scope. It ignores the author's main point; it fails to include Wilson's interest in the possibility that a study of such similar patterns of behavior might lead to a general theory of sociobiology. The correct answer is Choice E. It is the only statement that speaks of a unified science of sociobiology as a likely possibility.

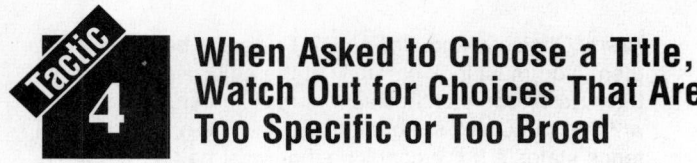

# When Asked to Choose a Title, Watch Out for Choices That Are Too Specific or Too Broad

A paragraph has been defined as a group of sentences revolving around a central theme. An appropriate title for a paragraph, therefore, must express this central theme that each of the sentences in the paragraph develops. It should be neither too broad nor too narrow in scope; it should be specific and yet comprehensive enough to include all the essential ideas presented by the sentences. A good title for a passage of two or more paragraphs should express the thoughts of ALL the paragraphs.

When you are trying to select the best title for a passage, watch out for words that come straight out of the passage. They may not always be your best choice.

This second question on the sociobiology passage is a title question. Note how it resembles questions on the passage's purpose or main idea.

> Which of the following is the best title for the passage?
> (A) Deceptive Comparisons: Oversimplification in Biological Research
> (B) An Uncanny Likeness: Termites and Rhesus Macaques
> (C) Structural Dissimilarities Between Insects and Vertebrates
> (D) Arguments Against a Science of Sociobiology
> (E) Sociobiology: Intimations of a General Theory

Choice A is incorrect: it is at once too narrow and too broad. It is too narrow in that the passage refers to *oversimplification* only in passing; it does not have oversimplification as its subject. It is too broad in that the passage emphasizes sociobiology, not the whole realm of biological research. It is also misleading; the passage never asserts that the deliberate oversimplification of the comparison between termites and macaques is intended to deceive.

Choice B is incorrect: it is too narrow. True, the author discusses the resemblance between termite and macaque societies; however, this likeness is not his subject. He discusses it to provide an example of the sort of comparison that may lay the groundwork for a potential science of sociobiology.

Choice C is also incorrect because it is not inclusive enough. It fails to mention the potential science of sociobiology. In addition, while the passage refers to *structural differences* between insect and vertebrate societies, it stresses structural similarities, not structural dissimilarities.

Choices D and E both mention the theory of sociobiology. Which is the better title for the piece? Clearly, Choice E: the author is not arguing against the potential science of sociobiology; he is reporting Wilson's opinions concerning the likelihood of sociobiology's emergence as a unified science. Thus, he finds in the termite-macaque comparison *intimations* or hints of an incipient general theory.

# When Asked to Determine Questions of Attitude, Mood, or Tone, Look for Words That Convey Emotion, Express Values, or Paint Pictures

In determining the attitude, mood, or tone of an author, examine the specific diction used. Is the author using adjectives to describe the subject? If so, are they words like *fragrant*, *tranquil*, *magnanimous*—words with positive connotations? Or are they words like *fetid*, *ruffled*, *stingy*—words with negative connotations?

When we speak, our tone of voice conveys our mood— frustrated, cheerful, critical, gloomy, angry. When we write, our images and descriptive phrases get our feelings across.

The next model question on the Wilson passage is an attitude question. Note the range of feelings in the answer choices.

> According to the author, Wilson's attitude toward the prospect of a unified theory in sociobiology can best be characterized as which of the following?
> (A) Unconditional enthusiasm
> (B) Cautious optimism
> (C) Unbiased objectivity
> (D) Resigned acquiescence
> (E) Strong displeasure

How does Wilson feel about the possibility of a unified theory of sociobiology? The answer choices range from actively negative (*strong displeasure*) to actively positive (*unconditional enthusiasm*), with passively negative (*resigned acquiescence*), neutral (*unbiased objectivity*), and guardedly positive (*cautious optimism*) in between.

Wilson's attitude toward the possibility of a unified theory of sociobiology is implicit in the author's choice of words. It is clear that Wilson views this possibility positively; the whole thrust of his argument is that the current studies of the similarities between insect and vertebrate societies could mark the beginnings of such a unified theory and that the specialist should not dismiss these studies as glib or simpleminded. Note in the second sentence how the author describes Wilson as a leading proponent or champion of sociobiology, someone whose feelings about the field are by definition positive.

Wilson is certainly not unhappy or *strongly displeased* with this potential unified theory, nor is he merely long-suffering or *resigned* to it. Similarly, he is not *unbiased* and *objective* about it; he actively involves himself in arguing the case for sociobiology. Thus, you can eliminate Choices C, D, and E. But how do you decide between the two positive terms, *enthusiasm* and *opti-*

*mism*, Choice A and Choice B? To decide between them, you must look carefully at the adjectives modifying them. Is Wilson's enthusiasm unqualified or *unconditional?* You may think so, but look again. The opening sentence states a basic condition that must be met before there can be a unified science of sociobiology: the same parameters and mathematical principles must be used to analyze insect and vertebrate societies. Though a proponent of sociobiology, Wilson is first and foremost a scientist, one who tests hypotheses and comes to logical conclusions about them. *Unconditional enthusiasm* seems to overstate his attitude.

Choice A appears incorrect. What of Choice B? Is Wilson's optimism *cautious* or guarded? Yes. According to the passage, Wilson is aware that specialists may well find fault with the sociobiologist's conclusions; the passage uses terms that convey values, first the negative "superficial, even unscientifically glib" to suggest the specialist's negative attitude towards sociobiology, then the positive "deliberate" to convey Wilson's own more positive response. The correct answer is Choice B.

## When Asked About Specific Details in the Passage, Spot Key Words in the Question and Scan the Passage to Find Them (or Their Synonyms)

In developing the main idea of a passage, a writer will make statements to support his or her point. To answer questions about such supporting details, you *must* find a word or group of words in the passage supporting your choice of answer. The words "according to the passage" or "according to the author" should focus your attention on what the passage explicitly states. Do not be misled into choosing an answer (even one that makes good sense) if you cannot find it supported by the text.

Detail questions often ask about a particular phrase or line. In such cases, use the following technique:

1. Look for key words (nouns or verbs) in the answer choices.

2. Scroll through the passage, looking for those key words or their synonyms. (This is *scanning*. It is what you do when you look up someone's number in the phone directory.)

3. When you find a key word or its synonym in a sentence, reread that sentence to make sure the test-makers haven't used the original wording to mislead you.

Read the following brief passage and apply this tactic.

What is involved in the process of visual recognition? First, like computer data, visual memories of an object must be stored; then, a

*Line* mechanism must exist for them to be retrieved.
(5) But how does this process work? The eye triggers the nerves into action. This neural activity constructs a picture in the brain's memory system, an internal image of the object observed. When the eye once again confronts that object, the object is
(10) compared with its internal image; if the two images match, recognition takes place.
     Among psychologists, the question as to whether visual recognition is a parallel, single-step operation or a sequential, step-by-step one is
(15) the subject of much debate. Gestalt psychologists contend that objects are perceived as wholes in a parallel operation: the internal image is matched with the retinal impression in one single step. Psychologists of other schools, however, suggest
(20) the opposite, maintaining that the individual features of an object are matched serially with the features of its internal image. Some experiments have demonstrated that the more well-known an object is, the more holistic its internal image
(25) becomes, and the more parallel the process of recognition tends to be. Nonetheless, the bulk of the evidence appears to uphold the serial hypothesis, at least for simple objects that are relatively unfamiliar to the viewer.

Now look at the following question on a specific detail in the passage.

According to the passage, psychologists of the Gestalt school assume which of the following about the process of visual recognition?

 I. The image an object makes on the retina is exactly the same as its internal image.

 II. The mind recognizes a given object as a whole; it has no need to analyze the object's constituent parts individually.

 III. The process of matching an object with its internal image takes place in a single step.

(A) II only
(B) III only
(C) I and III only
(D) II and III only
(E) I, II, and III

You can arrive at the correct answer to this question by elimination.

First, quickly scan the passage looking for the key word *Gestalt*. The sentence mentioning Gestalt psychologists states they maintain that objects are recognized as wholes in a parallel procedure. The sentence immediately preceding defines a parallel procedure as one that takes only one step.

Now examine the statements. Do Gestalt psychologists maintain that an object's retinal image is exactly the same as its internal image? Statement I is unsupported by the passage. Therefore, you can eliminate Choices C and E.

Statement II is supported by the passage: lines 15–17 indicate that Gestalt psychologists believe objects are recognized as wholes. Therefore, you can eliminate Choice B.

Statement III is supported by the passage: lines 17–18 indicate that Gestalt psychologists believe matching is a parallel process that occurs in one step. Therefore, you can eliminate Choice A.

Only Choice D is left. It is the correct answer.

Note how necessary it is to point to specific lines in the passage when you answer questions on specific details.

# When Asked to Make Inferences, Base Your Answers on What the Passage Implies, Not What It States Directly

In *Language in Thought and Action*, S. I. Hayakawa defines an inference as "a statement about the unknown made on the basis of the known."

Inference questions require you to use your own judgment. You must not take anything directly stated by the author as an inference. Instead, you must look for clues in the passage that you can use in deriving your own conclusion. You should choose as your answer a statement that is a logical development of the information the author has provided.

Try this relatively easy inference question, based on the previous passage about visual recognition.

One can infer from the passage that, in visual recognition, the process of matching

(A) requires neural inactivity
(B) cannot take place if an attribute of a familiar object has been altered in some way
(C) cannot occur when the observer looks at an object for the very first time
(D) has now been proven to necessitate both serial and parallel processes
(E) can only occur when the brain receives a retinal image as a single unit

Go through the answer choices, eliminating any choices that obviously contradict what the passage states or implies. Remember that in answering inference questions you must go beyond the obvious, beyond what the authors explicitly state, to look for logical implications of what they say.

Choice A is incorrect. Nothing in the passage suggests that the matching process requires or demands neural inactivity. Rather, the entire process of visual recognition, including the matching of images, requires neural *activity*.

Choice D is incorrect. It is clear from the passage that the matching process is not fully understood; nothing yet has been absolutely *proven*. The weight of the evidence *seems* to support the serial hypothesis, but controversy still surrounds the entire question.

Choice E is incorrect. It can be eliminated because it directly contradicts information in the passage stating that recognition most likely is a serial or step-by-step process rather than a parallel one receiving an image as a single unit.

Choices B and C are left. Which is a possible inference? Choice C seems a possible inference. Although the author never says so, it seems logical that you could not match an object if you had never seen it before. After all, if you had never seen the object before, you would have no prior internal image of it and would have nothing with which to match it. What of Choice B? Nothing in the passage mentions altering any attributes or features of a familiar object. Therefore, *on the basis of the passage* you have no way to deduce whether matching would or would not be possible if such a change took place. There is not enough information in the passage to justify Choice B as an inference. The correct answer is Choice C.

Another, more difficult inference question is based on the previous excerpt reviewing Wilson's *Sociobiology*. Review the passage briefly and see how you do with a question that very few of the examinees would have answered correctly.

> According to Wilson, only when we are able to apply the same parameters and mathematical principles to weighing both troops of rhesus
> *Line* macaques and termite colonies will a unified
> (5) science of sociobiology finally exist. While recognizing that many of his colleagues question such an outcome, Wilson, one of sociobiology's leading proponents, finds himself simultaneously more and more struck by the functional similari-
> (10) ties that characterize both insect and vertebrate societies and less concerned with the structural differences that divide them to such an apparently irreconcilable degree. Thus, he freely compares termites and macaques, pointing out numerous
> (15) likenesses between them. Both societies are territorial: they occupy a particular home range, which they defend against intruders. Likewise, both are cooperative: members organize themselves into working groups that observe a clearly-
> (20) defined division of labor. In addition, members of both groups can convey to each other a range of basic emotions and personal information: animosity, fright, hunger, rank within a particular caste, and ability to reproduce. Wilson readily
> (25) concedes that, from a specialist's perspective, such a likeness may at first appear superficial, even unscientifically glib. Nonetheless, in this eminent scholar's judgment, "it is out of such deliberate oversimplification that the beginnings
> (30) of a general theory are made."

In analyzing insect and vertebrate societies, the passage suggests which of the following?

(A) A clearly-defined division of labor is a distinguishing feature of most insect and vertebrate societies.

(B) The caste structures of insect and vertebrate societies share certain likenesses.

(C) Most insect and vertebrate societies utilize cooperative groups to hold and defend their home range.

(D) The system of communication employed by members of insect societies resembles the system that members of vertebrate societies follow.

(E) Major structural differences exist between insect and vertebrate societies.

Why would most examinees answer this question incorrectly? The reason is simple: it is easy to confuse statements made about specific insect and vertebrate societies with statements made about insect and vertebrate societies in general. In this passage, in the fourth sentence, the author switches from talking about Wilson's views of insect and vertebrate societies in general and refers to his comments on termites and macaques in specific.

Go through the answer choices one by one. Does the passage suggest that a clearly-defined division of labor distinguishes *most* insect and vertebrate societies? No. It merely states that, according to Wilson, a clearcut division of labor is a characteristic of termite and rhesus macaque societies. Choice A is incorrect: you cannot justify leaping from a single type of insect (*termites*) and a single type of vertebrate (*rhesus macaques*) to most insects and most vertebrates.

Does the passage suggest that the caste structure of insect societies shares certain likenesses with that of their counterparts in vertebrate societies? No. It merely states that, according to Wilson, termites and macaques both can communicate rank within a particular caste. Choice B is incorrect. You cannot assume that the caste structure of insect societies is similar to the caste structure of vertebrate societies just because termites and rhesus macaques both have some way to communicate caste status or rank.

Does the passage suggest that *most* insect and vertebrate societies form cooperative groups in order to hold and defend their home range or territory? No. It merely states that termites and macaques organize themselves into cooperative groups, and that both species occupy and defend territories. Choice C is incorrect: again, you cannot justify leaping from termites and rhesus macaques to *most* insects and *most* vertebrates.

Does the passage suggest that the system of communication employed by members of insect societies resembles that employed by members of vertebrate societies? No. It merely states that communication among termites and macaques serves similar ends; it says nothing about the specific systems of communication they use, nor about those systems of communication used by other insects and vertebrates. Choice D is incorrect.

The correct answer is Choice E. In the passage, the author states that Wilson has grown less impressed "with the structural differences that divide them (i.e., insect and vertebrate societies) to such an apparently irreconcilable degree." This suggests that, even though Wilson may be unimpressed with them, these differences exist and are *major*.

# When Asked to Apply Ideas from the Passage to a New Situation, Put Yourself in the Author's Place

GRE application questions require you to do three things:

1. *Reason*—If X is true, then Y must also be true.

2. *Perceive Feelings*—If the author feels this way about subject A, he probably feels a certain way about subject B.

3. *Sense a Larger Structure*—This passage is part of an argument for a proposal, or part of a description of a process, or part of a critique of a hypothesis.

Like inference questions, application questions require you to go beyond what the author explicitly states. Application questions, however, ask you to go well beyond a simple inference, using clues in the passage to interpret possible reasons for actions and possible outcomes of events. Your concern is to comprehend how the author's ideas might apply to other situations, or be affected by them. To do so, you have to put yourself in the author's place.

Imagine you are the author. What are you arguing for? Given what you have just stated in the passage, what would you want to say next? What might hurt your argument? What might make it stronger? What kind of audience would appreciate what you have to say? Whom are you trying to convince? If you involve yourself personally with the passage, you will be better able to grasp it in its entirety and see its significance.

Answer the following application question based on the previous passage discussing Wilson's *Sociobiology*.

> Which of the following statements would be most likely to begin the paragraph immediately following the passage?
>
> (A) Wilson has raised a problem in ethical philosophy in order to characterize the essence of the discipline of sociobiology.

> (B) It may not be too much to say that sociology and the other social sciences are the last branches of biology waiting to be integrated into neo-Darwinist evolutionary theory.
> (C) Although behavioral biology is traditionally spoken of as if it were a unified subject, it is now emerging as two distinct disciplines centered on neurophysiology and sociobiology, respectively.
> (D) The formulation of a theory of sociobiology constitutes, in Wilson's opinion, one of the great manageable problems of biology for the next twenty or thirty years.
> (E) In the past, the development of sociobiology has been slowed by too close an identification with ethology and behavioral psychology.

As you know from answering the previous main idea and attitude questions, Wilson's point is that students of insect and vertebrate societies may be on the verge of devising a general theory of sociobiology. Like Wilson, the author of the passage appears optimistic about the likelihood of developing this unified science. At the same time, again like Wilson, he is cautious; he too does not wish to overstate the case.

Put yourself in the author's place. What would you be likely to say next? The author has just been describing Wilson's hopeful view of the prospects for putting together a general theory of sociobiology. What would be more natural than for him next to discuss Wilson's opinion of a time frame for formulating this general theory? Choice D, with its confident yet judicious view of the formulation of a theory of sociobiology as "one of the great *manageable* problems of biology for the next twenty or thirty years," seems a logical extension of what the passage has just been saying. While Choices A, B, C, and E all touch on sociobiology in some way, none of them follows as naturally from the passage's immediate argument.

# When Asked to Give the Meaning of an Unfamiliar Word, Look for Nearby Context Clues

When a question in the reading comprehension part of an examination asks for the meaning of a word, that meaning can usually be deduced from the word's con-

text. The purpose of this kind of question is to determine how well you can extract meaning from the text, not how extensive your general vocabulary is.

Sometimes the unknown word is a common word used in one of its special or technical meanings. For example:

He *threw* the pot in an hour. The wheel turned busily and the shape grew quickly as his fingers worked the wet, spinning clay. (*Throw* here means to shape on a potter's wheel.)

At other times, the unknown word may bear a deceptive resemblance to a known word.

He fell *senseless* to the ground. (He was unconscious. He did not fall foolishly or nonsensically to the ground.)

Just because you know *one* meaning of a word, do not assume that you know its meaning as it is used in a particular passage. You must look within the passage for clues. Often authors will use an unfamiliar word and then immediately define it within the same sentence. The two words or groups of words are juxtaposed—set beside one another—to make their relationship clear. Commas, hyphens, and parentheses may signal this relationship.

1. The *rebec*, a medieval stringed instrument played with a bow, has only three strings.

2. *Paleontologists*—students of fossil remains—explore the earth's history.

3. Most mammals are *quadrupeds* (four-footed animals).

Often an unfamiliar word in one clause of a sentence will be defined or clarified in the sentence's other clause.

1. The early morning dew had frozen, and everything was covered with a thin coat of *rime*.

2. Cowards, we use *euphemisms* when we cannot bear the truth, calling our dead "the dear departed," as if they have just left the room.

Refer once more to the passage on visual recognition to answer the following question.

What is involved in the process of visual recognition? First, like computer data, visual memories of an object must be stored; then, a
*Line* mechanism must exist for them to be retrieved.
(5) But how does this process work? The eye triggers the nerves into action. This neural activity constructs a picture in the brain's memory system, an internal image of the object observed. When the eye once again confronts that object, the object is
(10) compared with its internal image; if the two images match, recognition takes place.

Among psychologists, the question as to whether visual recognition is a parallel, single-step operation or a sequential, step-by-step one is
(15) the subject of much debate. Gestalt psychologists contend that objects are perceived as wholes in a parallel operation: the internal image is matched with the retinal impression in one single step. Psychologists of other schools, however, suggest
(20) the opposite, maintaining that the individual features of an object are matched serially with the features of its internal image. Some experiments have demonstrated that the more well-known an object is, the more holistic its internal image
(25) becomes, and the more parallel the process of recognition tends to be. Nonetheless, the bulk of the evidence appears to uphold the serial hypothesis, at least for simple objects that are relatively unfamiliar to the viewer.

---

Which of the following phrases could best replace "the more holistic its internal image becomes" (lines 24–25) without significantly changing the sentence's meaning?

(A) the more its internal image increases in detail
(B) the more integrated its internal image grows
(C) the more its internal image decreases in size
(D) the more it reflects its internal image
(E) the more indistinct its internal image appears

---

What words or phrases in the vicinity of "the more holistic its internal image becomes" give you a clue to the phrase's meaning? The phrase immediately following, "becomes more parallel." If the recognition process becomes more parallel as an object becomes more familiar, then matching takes place in one step in which all the object's features are simultaneously transformed into a single internal representation. Thus, to say that an object's internal image becomes more holistic is to say that it becomes more *integrated* or whole. The correct answer is Choice B.

---

# Familiarize Yourself with the Technical Terms Used to Describe a Passage's Organization

Another aspect of understanding the author's point is understanding how the author organizes what he has to say. You have to understand how the author makes his point, figure out whether he begins with his thesis or main idea or works up to it gradually. Often this means observing how the opening sentence or paragraph relates to the passage as a whole.

Here is a technique question based on the last two sentences of the passage about sociobiology. Those lines are repeated here so that you can easily refer to them.

> Wilson readily concedes that, from a specialist's perspective, such a likeness may at first appear superficial, even unscientifically glib. Nonetheless, in this eminent scholar's judgment, "it is out of such deliberate oversimplification that the beginnings of a general theory are made."

---

Which of the following statements best describes the organization of the author's discussion of the importance of the termite/macaque comparison in the development of a unified science of sociobiology (lines 24–31)?

(A) He provides an example of a comparison and then rejects its implications.

(B) He concedes that current data are insufficient and modifies his initial assertion of their importance.

(C) He acknowledges hypothetical objections to the comparison, but concludes by re-affirming its significance.

(D) He cites critical appraisals of the comparison, but refrains from making an appraisal of his own.

(E) He notes an ambiguity in the comparison, but finally concedes its validity.

---

Consider the first clause of each answer choice.

In his comment on how things may seem from the specialist's point of view, does the author *provide an example* of a comparison? No. He refers to a comparison made earlier. Therefore, you can eliminate Choice A.

Does he *concede the insufficiency* of current data? Not quite. He states that some people may quarrel with the comparison because it seems glib to them; he does not grant that they are right or that the data are inadequate. Therefore, you can eliminate Choice B.

Does he *acknowledge hypothetical objections* to the comparison? Definitely. Make a note to come back later to Choice C.

Does he *cite critical appraisals* of the comparison? Possibly. Again, make a note of Choice D.

Does he *note an ambiguity* in the comparison? No. He notes an objection to the comparison; he mentions no ambiguities within it. Therefore, you can eliminate Choice E.

Now consider the second clause of Choices C and D. Does the author *refrain from making an appraisal* of the comparison? No. He calls it a deliberate oversimplification that may bear fruit. Choice D is incorrect. Does the author conclude by *reaffirming the significance* of the termite/macaque comparison? Clearly he does; he quotes Wilson's conclusion that such oversimplified comparisons can provide the basis for an important general theory. The correct answer is Choice C.

# Practice Exercises

## Reading Comprehension Exercise A

**Directions:** Each of the following reading comprehension questions are based on the content of the following passage. Read the passage and then determine the best answer choice for each question. Base your choice on what this passage <u>states directly</u> or <u>implies</u>, not on any information you may have gained elsewhere.

One phase of the business cycle is the *expansion phase*. This phase is a twofold one, including recovery and prosperity. During the recovery
Line period there is ever-growing expansion of existing
(5) facilities, and new facilities for production are created. More businesses are created and older ones expanded. Improvements of various kinds are made. There is an ever-increasing optimism about the future of economic growth. Much capi-
(10) tal is invested in machinery or "heavy" industry. More labor is employed. More raw materials are required. As one part of the economy develops, other parts are affected. For example, a great expansion in automobiles results in an expansion
(15) of the steel, glass, and rubber industries. Roads are required; thus the cement and machinery industries are stimulated. Demand for labor and materials results in greater prosperity for workers and suppliers of raw materials, including farmers.
(20) This increases purchasing power and the volume of goods bought and sold. Thus prosperity is diffused among the various segments of the population. This prosperity period may continue to rise and rise without an apparent end. However, a
(25) time comes when this phase reaches a peak and stops spiralling upwards. This is the end of the expansion phase.

1. Which of the following statements is the best example of the optimism mentioned in line 8 of the passage as being part of the expansion phase?

(A) Public funds are designated for the construction of new highways designed to stimulate tourism.

(B) Industrial firms allocate monies for the purchase of machine tools.

(C) The prices of agricultural commodities are increased at the producer level.

(D) Full employment is achieved at all levels of the economy.

(E) As technology advances, innovative businesses replace antiquated firms.

2. It can be inferred from the passage that the author believes that

   (A) when consumers lose their confidence in the market, a recession follows
   (B) cyclical ends to business expansion are normal
   (C) luxury goods such as jewelry are unaffected by industrial expansion
   (D) with sound economic policies, prosperity can become a fixed pattern
   (E) the creation of new products is essential for prosperity

3. Which of the following statements would be most likely to begin the paragraph immediately following the passage?

   (A) Union demands may also have an effect on business cycles.
   (B) Some industries are, by their very nature, cyclical, having regular phases of expansion and recession.
   (C) Inflation is a factor that must be taken into consideration in any discussion of the expansion phase.
   (D) The farmer's role during the expansion phase is of vital importance.
   (E) The other phase of the business cycle is called the recession phase.

The history of mammals dates back at least to Triassic time. Development was retarded, however, until the sudden acceleration of evolutional
*Line*  change that occurred in the oldest Paleocene. This
 (5)   led in Eocene time to increase in average size,
larger mental capacity, and special adaptations for
different modes of life. In the Oligocene Epoch,
there was further improvement, with appearance
of some new lines and extinction of others.
(10)  Miocene and Pliocene time was marked by culmination of several groups and continued approach
toward modern characters. The peak of the career
of mammals in variety and average large size was
attained in the Miocene.
(15)    The adaptation of mammals to almost all possible modes of life parallels that of the reptiles in
Mesozoic time, and except for greater intelligence,
the mammals do not seem to have done much better than corresponding reptilian forms. The bat is
(20)  doubtless a better flying animal than the pterosaur,
but the dolphin and whale are hardly more fishlike
than the ichthyosaur. Many swift-running mammals of the plains, like the horse and the antelope,
must excel any of the dinosaurs. The tyrannosaur
(25)  was a more ponderous and powerful carnivore than
any flesh-eating mammal, but the lion or tiger is
probably a more efficient and dangerous beast of
prey because of a superior brain. The significant
point to observe is that different branches of the

(30)  mammals gradually fitted themselves for all sorts
of life, grazing on the plains and able to run swiftly
(horse, deer, bison), living in rivers and swamps
(hippopotamus, beaver), dwelling in trees (sloth,
monkey), digging underground (mole, rodent),
(35)  feeding on flesh in the forest (tiger) and on the plain
(wolf), swimming in the sea (dolphin, whale, seal),
and flying in the air (bat). Man is able by mechanical means to conquer the physical world and to
adapt himself to almost any set of conditions.
(40)    This adaptation produces gradual changes of
form and structure. It is biologically characteristic
of the youthful, plastic stage of a group. Early in its
career, an animal assemblage seems to possess
capacity for change, which, as the unit becomes
(45)  old and fixed, disappears. The generalized types of
organisms retain longest the ability to make adjustments when required, and it is from them that new,
fecund stocks take origin—certainly not from any
specialized end products. So, in the mammals, we
(50)  witness the birth, plastic spread in many directions,
increasing specialization, and in some branches,
the extinction, which we have learned from observation of the geologic record of life is a characteristic of the evolution of life.

4. Which of the following would be the most appropriate title for the passage?

   (A) From Dinosaur to Man
   (B) Adaptation and Extinction
   (C) The Superiority of Mammals
   (D) The Geologic Life Span
   (E) Man, Conqueror of the Physical World

5. It can be inferred from the passage that the chronological order of the geologic periods is

   (A) Paleocene, Miocene, Triassic, Mesozoic
   (B) Paleocene, Triassic, Mesozoic, Miocene
   (C) Miocene, Paleocene, Triassic, Mesozoic
   (D) Mesozoic, Oligocene, Paleocene, Miocene
   (E) Mesozoic, Paleocene, Eocene, Miocene

6. It can be inferred from the passage that the
   pterosaur

   (A) resembled the bat
   (B) was a Mesozoic mammal
   (C) was a flying reptile
   (D) lived in the sea
   (E) evolved during the Miocene period

7. According to the passage, the greatest number of
   forms of mammalian life is found in the

   (A) Triassic period
   (B) Eocene period
   (C) Oligocene period
   (D) Pliocene period
   (E) Miocene period

8. Which of the following statements, if true, would weaken the statement made by the author in lines 15–19?

   (A) Tyrannosaur has been found to have a larger brain than was previously thought.
   (B) Mammals will become extinct within the next thousand years.
   (C) Forms of flying ichthyosaurs have recently been discovered.
   (D) The tiger has now been proved to be more powerful than the carnivorous reptiles.
   (E) Computers have been developed that can double human mental capacity.

9. It can be inferred from the passage that the evidence the author uses in discussing the life of past time periods

   (A) was developed by Charles Darwin
   (B) was uncovered by the author
   (C) has been negated by more recent evidence
   (D) was never definitely established
   (E) is based on fossil remains

10. With which of the following proverbial expressions about human existence would the author be most likely to agree?

   (A) It's a cruel world.
   (B) All the world's a stage.
   (C) The more things change, the more they remain the same.
   (D) Footprints in the sands of time.
   (E) A short life, but a merry one.

---

For me, scientific knowledge is divided into mathematical sciences, natural sciences or sciences dealing with the natural world (physical and
*Line* biological sciences), and sciences dealing with
(5) mankind (psychology, sociology, all the sciences of cultural achievements, every kind of historical knowledge). Apart from these sciences is philosophy, about which we will talk shortly. In the first place, all this is pure or theoretical knowledge,
(10) sought only for the purpose of understanding, in order to fulfill the need to understand that is intrinsic and consubstantial to man. What distinguishes man from animal is that he knows and needs to know. If man did not know that the
(15) world existed, and that the world was of a certain kind, that he was in the world and that he himself was of a certain kind, he wouldn't be man. The technical aspects of applications of knowledge are equally necessary for man and are of the greatest
(20) importance, because they also contribute to defining him as man and permit him to pursue a life increasingly more truly human.
   But even while enjoying the results of technical progress, he must defend the primacy and
(25) autonomy of pure knowledge. Knowledge sought directly for its practical applications will have immediate and foreseeable success, but not the

kind of important result whose revolutionary scope is in large part unforeseen, except by the
(30) imagination of the Utopians. Let me recall a well-known example. If the Greek mathematicians had not applied themselves to the investigation of conic sections, zealously and without the least suspicion that it might someday be useful, it
(35) would not have been possible centuries later to navigate far from shore. The first men to study the nature of electricity could not imagine that their experiments, carried on because of mere intellectual curiosity, would eventually lead to
(40) modern electrical technology, without which we can scarcely conceive of contemporary life. Pure knowledge is valuable for its own sake, because the human spirit cannot resign itself to ignorance. But, in addition, it is the foundation for practical
(45) results that would not have been reached if this knowledge had not been sought disinterestedly.

11. The author points out that the Greeks who studied conic sections

   (A) invented modern mathematical applications
   (B) were interested in navigation
   (C) were unaware of the value of their studies
   (D) worked with electricity
   (E) were forced to resign themselves to failure

12. The title below that best expresses the ideas of this passage is

   (A) Technical Progress
   (B) A Little Learning Is a Dangerous Thing
   (C) Man's Distinguishing Characteristics
   (D) Learning for Its Own Sake
   (E) The Difference Between Science and Philosophy

13. It can be inferred from the passage that to the author man's need to know is chiefly important in that it

   (A) allows the human race to progress technically
   (B) encompasses both the physical and social sciences
   (C) demonstrates human vulnerability
   (D) defines man's essential humanity
   (E) has increased as our knowledge of the world has grown

---

When you first saw a piece of African art, it impressed you as a unit; you did not see it as a collection of shapes or forms. This, of course, means
*Line* that the shapes and volumes within the sculpture
(5) itself were coordinated so successfully that the viewer was affected emotionally.
   It is entirely valid to ask how, from a purely artistic point of view, this unity was achieved. And we must also inquire whether there is a recurrent pat-
(10) tern or rules or a plastic language and vocabulary which is responsible for the powerful communication of emotion which the best African sculpture

achieves. If there is such a pattern or rules, are these
rules applied consciously or instinctively to obtain
(15) so many works of such high artistic quality?

It is obvious from the study of art history that an
intense and unified emotional experience, such as
the Christian credo of the Byzantine or 12th or 13th
century Europe, when expressed in art forms, gave
(20) great unity, coherence, and power to art. But such
an integrated feeling was only the inspirational element for the artist, only the starting point of the creative act. The expression of this emotion and its
realization in the work could be done only with dis-
(25) cipline and thorough knowledge of the craft. And
the African sculptor was a highly trained workman.
He started his apprenticeship with a master when a
child, and he learned the tribal styles and the use of
tools and the nature of woods so thoroughly that his
(30) carving became what Boas calls "motor action." He
carved automatically and instinctively.

The African carver followed his rules without
thinking of them; indeed, they never seem to have
been formulated in words. But such rules existed,
(35) for accident and coincidence cannot explain the
common plastic language of African sculpture.
There is too great a consistency from one work to
another. Yet, although the African, with amazing
insight into art, used these rules, I am certain that
(40) he was not conscious of them. This is the great mystery of such a traditional art: talent, or the ability
certain people have, without conscious effort, to follow the rules which later the analyst can discover
only from the work of art which has already been
(45) created.

14. The author is primarily concerned with

(A) discussing how African sculptors achieved
their effects
(B) listing the rules followed in African art
(C) relating African art to the art of 12th or 13th
century Europe
(D) integrating emotion and realization
(E) expressing the beauty of African art

15. According to the passage, one of the outstanding
features of African sculpture is

(A) its esoteric subject matter
(B) the emotional content of the work
(C) the education or training of the artists
(D) its "foreignness" when compared to Western
art
(E) its high degree of conscious control

16. The author uses the phrase "plastic language" in
lines 10 and 36 to refer to African art's

(A) mass reproduction
(B) unrealistic qualities
(C) modernistic orientation
(D) sculptural symbols
(E) repetitive nature

17. The information in the passage suggests that an
African carver might best be compared to a

(A) chef following a recipe
(B) fluent speaker of English who is just beginning
to study French
(C) batter who hits a home run in his or her first
baseball game
(D) concert pianist performing a well-rehearsed
concerto
(E) writer who is grammatically expert but stylistically uncreative

18. Which of the following does the passage imply
about art?

(A) Content is more important than form.
(B) There is no room for untrained artists.
(C) Form is more important than content.
(D) Western artists are too concerned with
technique.
(E) Great art must be consistent.

19. The author's presentation of the material includes
all of the following EXCEPT

(A) comparison
(B) cause and effect
(C) rhetorical questioning
(D) direct quotation
(E) concrete example

20. Which of the following titles best expresses the
content of the passage?

(A) The Apprenticeship of the African Sculptor
(B) The History of African Sculpture
(C) How African Art Achieves Unity
(D) Analyzing African Art
(E) The Unconscious Rules of African Art

# Reading Comprehension Exercise B

Directions: Each of the following reading comprehension questions are based on the content of the following
passage. Read the passage and then determine the best
answer choice for each question. Base your choice on
what this passage states directly or implies, not on any
information you may have gained elsewhere.

Both plants and animals of many sorts show
remarkable changes in form, structure, growth habits, and even mode of reproduction in becoming
Line adapted to different climatic environment, types of
(5) food supply, or mode of living. This divergence in
response to evolution is commonly expressed by
altering the form and function of some part or parts
of the organism, the original identity of which is
clearly discernible. For example, the creeping foot
(10) of the snail is seen in related marine pteropods to
be modified into a flapping organ useful for swimming, and is changed into prehensile arms that bear

suctorial disks in the squids and other cephalopods. The limbs of various mammals are modified
(15) according to several different modes of life—for swift running (cursorial) as in the horse and antelope, for swinging in trees (arboreal) as in the monkeys, for digging (fossorial) as in the moles and gophers, for flying (volant) as in the bats, for
(20) swimming (aquatic) as in the seals, whales, and dolphins, and for other adaptations. The structures or organs that show main change in connection with this adaptive divergence are commonly identified readily as homologous, in spite of great altera-
(25) tions. Thus, the finger and wristbones of a bat and whale, for instance, have virtually nothing in common except that they are definitely equivalent elements of the mammalian limb.

1. Which of the following is the most appropriate title for the passage, based on its content?

   (A) Adaptive Divergence
   (B) Evolution
   (C) Unusual Structures
   (D) Changes in Organs
   (E) Our Changing Bodies

2. The author provides information that would answer which of the following questions?

   I. What factors cause change in organisms?
   II. What is the theory of evolution?
   III. How are horses' legs related to seals' flippers?

   (A) I only
   (B) II only
   (C) I and II only
   (D) I and III only
   (E) I, II, and III

3. Which of the following words could best be substituted for "homologous" (line 24) without substantially changing the author's meaning?

   (A) altered
   (B) mammalian
   (C) corresponding
   (D) divergent
   (E) tactile

4. The author's style can best be described as

   (A) humorous
   (B) objective
   (C) patronizing
   (D) esoteric
   (E) archaic

---

Plato—who may have understood better what forms the mind of man than do some of our contemporaries who want their children exposed only
Line to "real" people and everyday events—knew
(5) what intellectual experiences make for true humanity. He suggested that the future citizens of his ideal republic begin their literary education with the telling of myths, rather than with mere facts or so-called rational teachings. Even
(10) Aristotle, master of pure reason, said: "The friend of wisdom is also a friend of myth."

Modern thinkers who have studied myths and fairy tales from a philosophical or psychological viewpoint arrive at the same conclusion, regard-
(15) less of their original persuasion. Mircea Eliade, for one, describes these stories as "models for human behavior [that], by that very fact, give meaning and value to life." Drawing on anthropological parallels, he and others suggest that myths
(20) and fairy tales were derived from, or give symbolic expression to, initiation rites or *rites of passage*—such as metaphoric death of an old, inadequate self in order to be reborn on a higher plane of existence. He feels that this is why these tales
(25) meet a strongly felt need and are carriers of such deep meaning.

Other investigators with a depth-psychological orientation emphasize the similarities between the fantastic events in myths and fairy tales and those
(30) in adult dreams and daydreams—the fulfillment of wishes, the winning out over all competitors, the destruction of enemies—and conclude that one attraction of this literature is its expression of that which is normally prevented from coming to
(35) awareness.

There are, of course, very significant differences between fairy tales and dreams. For example, in dreams more often than not the wish fulfillment is disguised, while in fairy tales much of
(40) it is openly expressed. To a considerable degree, dreams are the result of inner pressures which have found no relief, of problems which beset a person to which he knows no solution and to which the dream finds none. The fairy tale does
(45) the opposite: it projects the relief of all pressures and not only offers ways to solve problems but promises that a "happy" solution will be found.

We cannot control what goes on in our dreams. Although our inner censorship influences what we
(50) may dream, such control occurs on an unconscious level. The fairy tale, on the other hand, is very much the result of common conscious and unconscious content having been shaped by the conscious mind, not of one particular person, but
(55) the consensus of many in regard to what they view as universal human problems, and what they accept as desirable solutions. If all these elements were not present in a fairy tale, it would not be retold by generation after generation. Only if a
(60) fairy tale met the conscious and unconscious requirements of many people was it repeatedly retold, and listened to with great interest. No dream of a person could arouse such persistent interest unless it was worked into a myth, as was
(65) the story of the pharaoh's dream as interpreted by Joseph in the Bible.

5. It can be inferred from the passage that the author's interest in fairy tales centers chiefly on their

   (A) literary qualities
   (B) historical background
   (C) factual accuracy
   (D) psychological relevance
   (E) ethical weakness

6. According to the passage, fairy tales differ from dreams in which of the following characteristics?

   I. The communal nature of their creation
   II. Their convention of a happy ending
   III. Their enduring general appeal

   (A) I only
   (B) II only
   (C) I and II only
   (D) II and III only
   (E) I, II, and III

7. It can be inferred from the passage that Mircea Eliade is most likely

   (A) a writer of children's literature
   (B) a student of physical anthropology
   (C) a twentieth-century philosopher
   (D) an advocate of practical education
   (E) a contemporary of Plato

8. Which of the following best describes the author's attitude toward fairy tales?

   (A) Reluctant fascination
   (B) Wary skepticism
   (C) Scornful disapprobation
   (D) Indulgent tolerance
   (E) Open approval

9. The author cites Plato and Aristotle primarily in order to

   (A) define the nature of myth
   (B) contrast their opposing points of view
   (C) support the point that myths are valuable
   (D) prove that myths originated in ancient times
   (E) give an example of depth psychology

10. The author mentions all of the following as reasons for reading fairy tales EXCEPT

    (A) emotional catharsis
    (B) behavioral paradigm
    (C) uniqueness of experience
    (D) sublimation of aggression
    (E) symbolic satisfaction

---

Nothing more unlucky, I sometimes think, could have befallen Chaucer than that he should have been christened "the father of English
*Line* poetry." For "father" in such a context conveys to
(5) most of us, I fear, a faint suggestion of *vicarious* glory—the derivative celebrity of parents, otherwise obscure, who shine, moon-like, in the reflected luster of their sons. What else than progenitors were the fathers of Plato, or Caesar, or
(10) Shakespeare, or Napoleon? And so to call Chaucer the father of English poetry is often tantamount to dismissing him, not unkindly, as the estimable but archaic ancestor of a brilliant line. But Chaucer—if I may risk the paradox—is him-
(15) self the very thing he begat. He *is* English poetry incarnate, and only two, perhaps, of all his sons outshine his fame. It is with Chaucer himself, then, and not save incidentally with his ancestral eminence that we shall be concerned.
(20)     But five hundred and thirty-three years have passed since Chaucer died. And to overleap five centuries is to find ourselves in another world, a world at once familiar and strange. Its determining concepts are implicit in all that Chaucer, who
(25) was of it, thought and wrote. And, woven as they are into his web, they at once lend to it and gain from it fresh significance. To us they are obsolete; in the *Canterbury Tales*, and the *Troilus*, and the *House of Fame* they are current and alive.
(30) And it is in their habit as they lived, and not as mere curious lore, that I mean to deal with them.
    Let me begin with the very tongue which Chaucer spoke—a speech at once our own and not our own. "You know," he wrote—and for the
(35) moment I rudely modernize lines as liquid in their rhythm as smooth-sliding brandy—"you know that in a thousand years there is change in the forms of speech, and words which were then judged apt and choice now seem to us wondrous
(40) quaint and strange, and yet they spoke them so, and managed as well in love with them as men now do." And to us, after only half a thousand years, those very lines are an embodiment of what they state:

(45)     Ye knowe eek, that in forme of speche is chaunge
        With-inne a thousand yeer, and words tho
        That hadden prys, now wonder nyce and straunge
(50)     Us thinketh hem; and yet they spake hem so,
        And spedde as wel in love as men now do.

    But it is not only Chaucer's speech which has undergone transformation. The change in his world is greater still. And the situation which
(55) confronts us is this. In Chaucer's greatest work we have to do with *timeless creations* upon a *time-determined stage*. And it is one of the inescapable ironies of time that creations of the imagination which are at once of no time and for
(60) all time must nevertheless think and speak and act in terms and in ways which are as transient as they themselves are permanent. Their world—the stage on which they play their parts, and in terms of which they think—has become within a few
(65) lifetimes strange and obsolete, and must be deciphered before it can be read. For the immortal puts on mortality when great conceptions are

clothed in the only garment ever possible—in
terms whose import and associations are fixed by
(70) the form and pressure of an inexorably passing
time. And that is the situation which we have to
face.

11. The author of the passage does all of the following
in the discussion of Chaucer and his verse
EXCEPT

(A) pose a rhetorical question
(B) cite specific examples
(C) offer a personal opinion
(D) propose a solution
(E) use figurative language

12. The author's attitude toward "mere curious lore"
(line 31) can best be described as

(A) skeptical but resigned
(B) admiring and intrigued
(C) dismissive
(D) incredulous
(E) completely detached

13. The author uses the Middle English quotation (lines
45–51) to

(A) refute the contention that Chaucer wrote
awkwardly
(B) demonstrate the idiosyncratic spelling common
in Chaucer's time
(C) convey the power of reading poetry in its orig-
inal form
(D) support his hypothesis about the aptness of
Chaucer's choice of words
(E) illustrate the degree of linguistic change that
has occurred

14. How would the author most likely respond to
another critic's use of the term "Father of English
Poetry" to describe Chaucer?

(A) The term "Father of English Poetry" is an
accurate assessment of an exceptionally distinguished literary figure.
(B) The term implies Chaucer is important not as a
great poet in his own right but as the somewhat outdated forerunner of the great poets
of today.
(C) The epithet "Father of English Poetry" has
been applied to so many poets that it has
lost whatever meaning it originally
possessed.
(D) "Father of English Poetry" is a sexist term
that should be replaced by more inclusive
language.
(E) It is appropriate to acknowledge the impact
Chaucer had on posterity by revering him
as the glorious ancestor of all English
poets.

Of the 197 million square miles making up the
surface of the globe, 71 percent is covered by the
interconnecting bodies of marine water; the
Line  Pacific Ocean alone covers half the Earth and
(5)  averages nearly 14,000 feet in depth. The *continents*—Eurasia, Africa, North America, South
America, Australia, and Antarctica—are the portions of the *continental masses* rising above sea
level. The submerged borders of the continental
(10) masses are the *continental shelves*, beyond which
lie the deep-sea basins.

The oceans attain their greatest depths not in
their central parts, but in certain elongated furrows, or long narrow troughs, called *deeps*. These
(15) profound troughs have a peripheral arrangement,
notably around the borders of the Pacific and
Indian oceans. The position of the deeps near the
continental masses suggests that the deeps, like
the highest mountains, are of recent origin, since
(20) otherwise they would have been filled with waste
from the lands. This suggestion is strengthened by
the fact that the deeps are frequently the sites of
world-shaking earthquakes. For example, the
"tidal wave" that in April, 1946, caused wide-
(25) spread destruction along Pacific coasts resulted
from a strong earthquake on the floor of the
Aleutian Deep.

The topography of the ocean floors is none too
well known, since in great areas the available
(30) soundings are hundreds or even thousands of
miles apart. However, the floor of the Atlantic is
becoming fairly well known as a result of special
surveys since 1920. A broad, well-defined
ridge—the Mid-Atlantic ridge—runs north and
(35) south between Africa and the two Americas, and
numerous other major irregularities diversify the
Atlantic floor. Closely spaced soundings show
that many parts of the oceanic floors are as
rugged as mountainous regions of the continents.
(40) Use of the recently perfected method of echo
sounding is rapidly enlarging our knowledge of
submarine topography. During World War II
great strides were made in mapping submarine
surfaces, particularly in many parts of the vast
(45) Pacific basin.

The continents stand on the average 2870
feet—slightly more than half a mile—above sea
level. North America averages 2300 feet; Europe
averages only 1150 feet; and Asia, the highest of
(50) the larger continental subdivisions, averages 3200
feet. The highest point on the globe, Mount
Everest in the Himalayas, is 29,000 feet above the
sea; and as the greatest known depth in the sea is
over 35,000 feet, the maximum *relief* (that is, the
(55) difference in altitude between the lowest and
highest points) exceeds 64,000 feet, or exceeds 12
miles. The continental masses and the deep-sea
basins are relief features of the first order; the
deeps, ridges, and volcanic cones that diversify
(60) the sea floor, as well as the plains, plateaus, and
mountains of the continents, are relief features of

the second order. The lands are unendingly subject to a complex of activities summarized in the term *erosion*, which first sculptures them in great
(65) detail and then tends to reduce them ultimately to sea level. The modeling of the landscape by weather, running water, and other agents is apparent to the keenly observant eye and causes thinking people to speculate on what must be the final
(70) result of the ceaseless wearing down of the lands. Long before there was a science of geology, Shakespeare wrote "the revolution of the times makes mountains level."

15. Which of the following would be the most appropriate title for the passage?

(A) Features of the Earth's Surface
(B) Marine Topography
(C) The Causes of Earthquakes
(D) Primary Geologic Considerations
(E) How to Prevent Erosion

16. It can be inferred from the passage that the largest ocean is the

(A) Atlantic
(B) Pacific
(C) Indian
(D) Antarctic
(E) Arctic

17. The "revolution of the times" as used in the final sentence means

(A) the passage of years
(B) the current rebellion
(C) the science of geology
(D) the action of the ocean floor
(E) the overthrow of natural forces

18. According to the passage, the peripheral furrows or *deeps* are found

(A) only in the Pacific and Indian oceans
(B) near earthquakes
(C) near the shore
(D) in the center of the ocean
(E) to be 14,000 feet in depth in the Pacific

19. The passage contains information that would answer which of the following questions?

   I. What is the highest point on North America?
   II. Which continental subdivision is, on the average, 1150 feet above sea level?
   III. How deep is the deepest part of the ocean?

(A) I only
(B) II only
(C) III only
(D) I and II only
(E) II and III only

20. From this passage, it can be inferred that earthquakes

(A) occur only in the peripheral furrows
(B) occur more frequently in newly formed land or sea formations
(C) are a prime cause of soil erosion
(D) will ultimately "make mountains level"
(E) are caused by the weight of the water

# Reading Comprehension Exercise C

Directions: Each of the following reading comprehension questions are based on the content of the following passage. Read the passage and then determine the best answer choice for each question. Base your choice on what this passage states directly or implies, not on any information you may have gained elsewhere.

An essay which appeals chiefly to the intellect is Francis Bacon's "Of Studies." His careful tripartite division of studies expressed succinctly in aphoris-
Line tic prose demands the complete attention of the
(5) mind of the reader. He considers studies as they should be: for pleasure, for self-improvement, for business. He considers the evils of excess study: laziness, affectation, and preciosity. Bacon divides books into three categories: those to be read in part,
(10) those to be read cursorily, and those to be read with care. Studies should include reading, which gives depth; speaking, which adds readiness of thought; and writing, which trains in preciseness. Somewhat mistakenly, the author ascribes certain virtues to
(15) individual fields of study: wisdom to history, wit to poetry, subtlety to mathematics, and depth to natural philosophy. Bacon's four-hundred-word essay, studded with Latin phrases and highly compressed in thought, has intellectual appeal indeed.

1. Which of the following is the most appropriate title for the passage, based on its content?

(A) Francis Bacon and the Appeal of the Essay
(B) "Of Studies": A Tripartite Division
(C) An Intellectual Exercise: Francis Bacon's "Of Studies"
(D) The Categorization of Books According to Bacon
(E) A Method for Reading Books

2. Which of the following words could best be substituted for "aphoristic" (lines 3–4) without substantially changing the author's meaning?

(A) abstruse
(B) pithy
(C) tripartite
(D) proverbial
(E) realistic

3. The passage suggests that the author would be most likely to agree with which of the following statements?

(A) "Of Studies" belongs in the category of works that demand to be read with care.

(B) Scholars' personalities are shaped by the academic discipline in which they are engaged.

(C) It is an affectation to use foreign words in one's writing.

(D) An author can be more persuasive in a long work than in a shorter one.

(E) Studies should be undertaken without thought of personal gain.

---

Rocks which have solidified directly from molten materials are called igneous rocks. Igneous rocks are commonly referred to as
Line primary rocks because they are the original
(5) source of material found in sedimentaries and metamorphics. Igneous rocks compose the greater part of the earth's crust, but they are generally covered at the surface by a relatively thin layer of sedimentary or metamorphic rocks. Igneous rocks
(10) are distinguished by the following characteristics: (1) they contain no fossils; (2) they have no regular arrangement of layers; and (3) they are nearly always made up of crystals.

Sedimentary rocks are composed largely of
(15) minute fragments derived from the disintegration of existing rocks and in some instances from the remains of animals. As sediments are transported, individual fragments are assorted according to size. Distinct layers of such sediments as gravels,
(20) sand, and clay build up, as they are deposited by water and occasionally wind. These sediments vary in size with the material and the power of the eroding agent. Sedimentary materials are laid down in layers called strata.

(25)     When sediments harden into sedimentary rocks, the names applied to them change to indicate the change in physical state. Thus, small stones and gravel cemented together are known as conglomerates; cemented sand becomes sand-
(30) stone; and hardened clay becomes shale. In addition to these, other sedimentary rocks such as limestone frequently result from the deposition of dissolved material. The ingredient parts are normally precipitated by organic substances, such as
(35) shells of clams or hard skeletons of other marine life.

Both igneous and sedimentary rocks may be changed by pressure, heat, solution, or cementing action. When individual grains from existing
(40) rocks tend to deform and interlock, they are called metamorphic rocks. For example, granite, an igneous rock, may be metamorphosed into a gneiss or a schist. Limestone, a sedimentary rock, when subjected to heat and pressure may become
(45) marble, a metamorphic rock. Shale under pressure becomes slate.

4. The primary purpose of the passage is to

(A) differentiate between and characterize igneous and sedimentary rocks

(B) explain the factors that may cause rocks to change in form

(C) show how the scientific names of rocks reflect the rocks' composition

(D) define and describe several diverse kinds of rocks

(E) explain why rocks are basic parts of the earth's structure

5. All of the following are sedimentary rocks EXCEPT

(A) shale
(B) gravel
(C) sand
(D) limestone
(E) schist

6. The passage would be most likely to appear in a

(A) technical article for geologists

(B) teaching manual accompanying an earth science text

(C) pamphlet promoting conservation of natural resources

(D) newspaper feature explaining how oil is found

(E) nonfiction book explaining where to find the results of sedimentation

7. The relationship between igneous and sedimentary rocks may best be compared to the relationship between

(A) leaves and compost
(B) water and land
(C) DNA and heredity
(D) nucleus and cell wall
(E) sand and clay

8. The passage contains information that would answer which of the following questions?

   I. Which elements form igneous rocks?
   II. What produces sufficient pressure to alter a rock?
   III. Why is marble called a metamorphic rock?

(A) I only
(B) III only
(C) I and II only
(D) II and III only
(E) I, II, and III

9. Which of the following methods is NOT used by the author?

(A) inclusion of concrete examples
(B) classification and discussion
(C) comparison and contrast
(D) observation and hypothesis
(E) cause and effect

10. The author's tone in the passage can best be described as

(A) meditative
(B) objective
(C) ironic
(D) concerned
(E) bombastic

Although vocal cords are lacking in cetaceans, phonation is undoubtedly centered in the larynx.

The toothed whales or odontocetes (sperm whale
*Line* and porpoises) are much more vociferous than the
(5) whalebone whales, or mysticetes. In this country observers have recorded only occasional sounds from two species of mysticetes (the humpback and right whale). A Russian cetologist reports hearing sounds from at least five species of whalebone
(10) whales but gives no details of the circumstances or descriptions of the sounds themselves. Although comparison of the sound-producing apparatus in the two whale groups cannot yet be made, it is interesting to note that the auditory centers of the
(15) brain are much more highly developed in the odontocetes than in the mysticetes, in fact, to a degree unsurpassed by any other mammalian group.

11. The passage contains information that would answer which of the following questions?

    I. What are odontocetes and mysticetes?
    II. In which part of the body do whales produce sounds?
    III. In which animals is the auditory center of the brain most developed?

(A) I only
(B) II only
(C) I and II only
(D) II and III only
(E) I, II, and III

12. The author's attitude toward the observations reported by the Russian cetologist mentioned in lines 8-11 is best described as one of

(A) admiration
(B) indignation
(C) surprise
(D) skepticism
(E) pessimism

13. It can be inferred from the passage that

(A) animals with more highly developed auditory apparatuses tend to produce more sounds
(B) animals without vocal cords tend to produce as much sound as those with vocal cords
(C) highly intelligent animals tend to produce more sound than less intelligent species
(D) the absence of vocal cords has hindered the adaptation of cetaceans
(E) sound is an important means of communication among whales

---

\*Like her white friends Eleanor Roosevelt and Aubrey Williams, Mary Bethune believed in the fundamental commitment of the New Deal to
*Line* assist the black American's struggle and in the
(5) need for blacks to assume responsibilities to help win that struggle. Unlike those of her white

liberal associates, however, Bethune's ideas had evolved out of a long experience as a "race leader." Founder of a small black college in
(10) Florida, she had become widely known by 1935 as an organizer of black women's groups and as a civil and political rights activist. Deeply religious, certain of her own capabilities, she held a relatively uncluttered view of what she felt were the
(15) New Deal's and her own people's obligations to the cause of racial justice. Unafraid to speak her mind to powerful whites, including the President, or to differing black factions, she combined faith in the ultimate willingness of whites to discard
(20) their prejudice and bigotry with a strong sense of racial pride and commitment to Negro self-help.

More than her liberal white friends, Bethune argued for a strong and direct black voice in initiating and shaping government policy. She pur-
(25) sued this in her conversations with President Roosevelt, in numerous memoranda to Aubrey Williams, and in her administrative work as head of the National Youth Administration's Office of Negro Affairs. With the assistance of Williams,
(30) she was successful in having blacks selected to NYA posts at the national, state, and local levels. But she also wanted a black presence throughout the federal government. At the beginning of the war she joined other black leaders in demanding
(35) appointments to the Selective Service Board and to the Department of the Army; and she was instrumental in 1941 in securing Earl Dickerson's membership on the Fair Employment Practices Committee. By 1944, she was still making
(40) appeals for black representation in "all public programs, federal, state, and local," and "in policymaking posts as well as rank and file jobs."

Though recognizing the weakness in the Roosevelt administration's response to Negro
(45) needs, Mary Bethune remained in essence a black partisan champion of the New Deal during the 1930s and 1940s. Her strong advocacy of administration policies and programs was predicated on a number of factors: her assessment of the low
(50) status of black Americans during the Depression; her faith in the willingness of some liberal whites to work for the inclusion of blacks in the government's reform and recovery measures; her conviction that only massive federal aid could elevate
(55) the Negro economically; and her belief that the thirties and forties were producing a more selfaware and self-assured black population. Like a number of her white friends in government, Bethune assumed that the preservation of democ-
(60) racy and black people's "full integration into the benefits and the responsibilities" of American life were inextricably tied together. She was convinced that, with the help of a friendly government, a militant, aggressive "New Negro" would
(65) emerge out of the devastation of depression and war, a "New Negro" who would "save America from itself," who would lead America toward the full realization of its democratic ideas.

---

\*Note that this passage is representative of the time it discusses, and therefore uses the terminology commonly accepted in that period.

14. The author's main purpose in this passage is to

    (A) criticize Mary Bethune for adhering too closely to New Deal policies
    (B) argue that Mary Bethune was too optimistic in her assessment of race relations
    (C) demonstrate Mary Bethune's influence on black progress during the Roosevelt years
    (D) point out the weaknesses of the white liberal approach to black needs
    (E) summarize the attainments of blacks under the auspices of Roosevelt's New Deal

15. It can be inferred from the passage that Aubrey Williams was which of the following?

    I. A man with influence in the National Youth Administration
    II. A white liberal
    III. A man of strong religious convictions

    (A) I only
    (B) II only
    (C) I and II only
    (D) II and III only
    (E) I, II, and III

16. The author mentions Earl Dickerson (line 37) primarily in order to

    (A) cite an instance of Bethune's political impact
    (B) contrast his career with that of Bethune
    (C) introduce the subject of a subsequent paragraph
    (D) provide an example of Bethune's "New Negro"
    (E) show that Dickerson was a leader of his fellow blacks

17. It can be inferred from the passage that Bethune believed the "New Negro" would "save America from itself" (lines 66–67) by

    (A) joining the army and helping America overthrow its Fascist enemies
    (B) helping America accomplish its egalitarian ideals
    (C) voting for administration antipoverty programs
    (D) electing other blacks to government office
    (E) expressing a belief in racial pride

18. The tone of the author's discussion of Bethune is best described as

    (A) deprecatory
    (B) sentimental
    (C) ironic
    (D) objective
    (E) recriminatory

19. The author uses all the following techniques in the passage EXCEPT

    (A) comparison and contrast
    (B) development of an extended analogy
    (C) direct quotation
    (D) general statement and concrete examples
    (E) reiteration of central ideas

20. Which of the following statements about the New Deal does the passage best support?

    (A) It was strongly committed to justice for all races.
    (B) It encouraged black participation in making policy decisions.
    (C) It was actively involved in military strategy.
    (D) It was primarily the province of Eleanor Roosevelt.
    (E) It shaped programs for economic aid and growth.

# Reading Comprehension Exercise D

<u>Directions:</u> Each of the following reading comprehension questions are based on the content of the following passage. Read the passage and then determine the best answer choice for each question. Base your choice on what this passage <u>states directly</u> or <u>implies</u>, not on any information you may have gained elsewhere.

"The emancipation of women," James Joyce told one of his friends, "has caused the greatest revolution in our time in the most important rela-
*Line* tionship there is—that between men and women."
(5) Other modernists agreed: Virginia Woolf, claiming that in about 1910 "human character changed," and, illustrating the new balance between the sexes, urged, "Read the 'Agamemnon,' and see whether...your sympathies
(10) are not almost entirely with Clytemnestra." D.H. Lawrence wrote, "perhaps the deepest fight for 2000 years and more, has been the fight for women's independence."
     But if modernist writers considered women's
(15) revolt against men's domination one of their "greatest" and "deepest" themes, only recently—in perhaps the past 15 years—has literary criticism begun to catch up with it. Not that the images of sexual antagonism that abound in modern litera-
(20) ture have gone unremarked; far from it. But what we are able to see in literary works depends on the perspectives we bring to them, and now that women—enough to make a difference—are reforming canons and interpreting literature, the
(25) landscapes of literary history and the features of individual books have begun to change.

1. According to the passage, women are changing literary criticism by

    (A) noting instances of hostility between men and women
    (B) seeing literature from fresh points of view
    (C) studying the works of early twentieth-century writers
    (D) reviewing books written by feminists
    (E) resisting masculine influence

2. The author quotes James Joyce, Virginia Woolf, and D.H. Lawrence primarily in order to show that

(A) these were feminist writers
(B) although well-meaning, they were ineffectual
(C) before the twentieth century, there was little interest in women's literature
(D) modern literature is dependent on the women's movement
(E) the interest in feminist issues is not new

3. The author's attitude toward women's reformation of literary canons can best be described as one of

(A) ambivalence
(B) antagonism
(C) indifference
(D) endorsement
(E) skepticism

4. Which of the following titles best describes the content of the passage?

(A) Modernist Writers and the Search for Equality
(B) The Meaning of Literary Works
(C) Toward a New Criticism
(D) Women in Literature, from 1910 On
(E) Transforming Literature

---

Ocean water plays an indispensable role in supporting life. The great ocean basins hold about 300 million cubic miles of water. From this vast
*Line* amount, about 80,000 cubic miles of water are
(5) sucked into the atmosphere each year by evaporation and returned by precipitation and drainage to the ocean. More than 24,000 cubic miles of rain descend annually upon the continents. This vast amount is required to replenish the lakes and
(10) streams, springs and water tables on which all flora and fauna are dependent. Thus, the hydrosphere permits organic existence.

The hydrosphere has strange characteristics because water has properties unlike those of any
(15) other liquid. One anomaly is that water upon freezing expands by about 9 percent, whereas most liquids contract on cooling. For this reason, ice floats on water bodies instead of sinking to the bottom. If the ice sank, the hydrosphere would
(20) soon be frozen solidly, except for a thin layer of surface melt water during the summer season. Thus, all aquatic life would be destroyed and the interchange of warm and cold currents, which moderates climate, would be notably absent.
(25) Another outstanding characteristic of water is that water has a heat capacity which is the highest of all liquids and solids except ammonia. This characteristic enables the oceans to absorb and store vast quantities of heat, thereby often pre-
(30) venting climatic extremes. In addition, water dissolves more substances than any other liquid. It is this characteristic which helps make oceans a great storehouse for minerals which have been washed down from the continents. In several

(35) areas of the world these minerals are being commercially exploited. Solar evaporation of salt is widely practiced, potash is extracted from the Dead Sea, and magnesium is produced from sea water along the American Gulf Coast.

5. The author's main purpose in this passage is to

(A) describe the properties and uses of water
(B) illustrate the importance of conserving water
(C) explain how water is used in commerce and industry
(D) reveal the extent of the earth's ocean masses
(E) compare water with other liquids

6. According to the passage, fish can survive in the oceans because

(A) they do not need oxygen
(B) ice floats
(C) evaporation and condensation create a water cycle
(D) there are currents in the oceans
(E) water absorbs heat

7. Which of the following characteristics of water does the author mention in the passage?

    I. Water expands when it is frozen.
   II. Water is a good solvent.
  III. Water can absorb heat.

(A) I only
(B) II only
(C) I and II only
(D) II and III only
(E) I, II, and III

8. According to the passage, the hydrosphere is NOT

(A) responsible for all forms of life
(B) able to modify weather
(C) a source of natural resources
(D) in danger of freezing over
(E) the part of the earth covered by water

9. The author's tone in the passage can best be described as

(A) dogmatic
(B) dispassionate
(C) speculative
(D) biased
(E) hortatory

10. The author organizes the passage by

(A) comparison and contrast
(B) juxtaposition of true and untrue ideas
(C) general statements followed by examples
(D) hypothesis and proof
(E) definition of key terms

11. Which of the following statements would be most likely to begin the paragraph immediately following the passage?

(A) Water has the ability to erode the land.

(B) Magnesium is widely used in metallurgical processes.

(C) No let us consider the great land masses.

(D) Another remarkable property of ice is its strength.

(E) Droughts and flooding are two types of disasters associated with water.

---

The opposite of adaptive divergence is an interesting and fairly common expression of evolution. Whereas related groups of organisms take
Line on widely different characters in becoming adapt-
(5) ed to unlike environments in the case of adaptive divergence, we find that unrelated groups of organisms exhibit adaptive convergence when they adopt similar modes of life or become suited for special sorts of environments. For example,
(10) invertebrate marine animals living firmly attached to the sea bottom or to some foreign object tend to develop a subcylindrical or conical form. This is illustrated by coral individuals, by many sponges, and even by the diminutive tubes of bry-
(15) ozoans. Adaptive convergence in taking this coral-like form is shown by some brachiopods and pelecypods that grew in fixed position. More readily appreciated is the streamlined fitness of most fishes for moving swiftly through water;
(20) they have no neck, the contour of the body is smoothly curved so as to give minimum resistance, and the chief propelling organ is a powerful tail fin. The fact that some fossil reptiles (ichthyosaurs) and modern mammals (whales,
(25) dolphins) are wholly fishlike in form is an expression of adaptive convergence, for these air-breathing reptiles and mammals, which are highly efficient swimmers, are not closely related to fishes. Unrelated or distantly related organisms that
(30) develop similarity of form are sometimes designated as homeomorphs (having the same form).

12. The author mentions ichthyosaurs and dolphins (lines 24 and 25) as examples of

(A) modern mammalian life forms that are aquatic

(B) species of slightly greater mobility than brachiopods

(C) air-breathing reptiles closely related to fish

(D) organisms that have evolved into fishlike forms

(E) invertebrate and vertebrate marine animals

13. According to the passage, adaptive convergence and adaptive divergence are

(A) manifestations of evolutionary patterns

(B) hypotheses unsupported by biological phenomena

(C) ways in which plants and animals adjust to a common environment

(D) demonstrated by brachiopods and pelecypods

(E) compensatory adjustments made in response to unlike environments

14. It can be inferred that in the paragraph immediately preceding this passage the author discussed

(A) marine intelligence

(B) adaptive divergence

(C) air-breathing reptiles

(D) environmental impacts

(E) organisms with similar forms

---

Nearly two thousand years have passed since a census decreed by Caesar Augustus became part of the greatest story every told. Many things have
Line changed in the intervening years. The hotel indus-
(5) try worries more about overbuilding than overcrowding, and if they had to meet an unexpected influx, few inns would have a manger to accommodate the weary guests. Now it is the census taker that does the traveling in the fond hope that
(10) a highly mobile population will stay put long enough to get a good sampling. Methods of gathering, recording, and evaluating information have presumably been improved a great deal. And where then it was the modest purpose of Rome to
(15) obtain a simple head count as an adequate basis for levying taxes, now batteries of complicated statistical series furnished by governmental agencies and private organizations are eagerly scanned and interpreted by sages and seers to get a clue to
(20) future events. The Bible does not tell us how the Roman census takers made out, and as regards our more immediate concern, the reliability of present-day economic forecasting, there are considerable differences of opinion. They were aired
(25) at the celebration of the 125th anniversary of the American Statistical Association. There was the thought that business forecasting might well be on its way from an art to a science, and some speakers talked about newfangled computers and high-
(30) falutin mathematical systems in terms of excitement and endearment which we, at least in our younger years when these things matter, would have associated more readily with the description of a fair maiden. But others pointed to the
(35) deplorable record of highly esteemed forecasts and forecasters with a batting average below that of the Mets, and the president-elect of the Association cautioned that "high powered statistical methods are usually in order where the facts
(40) are crude and inadequate, the exact contrary of what crude and inadequate statisticians assume." We left this birthday party somewhere between hope and despair and with the conviction, not really newly acquired, that proper statistical
(45) methods applied to ascertainable facts have their merits in economic forecasting as long as neither forecaster nor public is deluded into mistaking the delineation of probabilities and trends for a prediction of certainties of mathematical exactitude.

15. The passage would be most likely to appear in

    (A) a journal of biblical studies
    (B) an introductory college textbook on statistics
    (C) the annual report of the American Statistical Association
    (D) a newspaper review of a recent professional festivity
    (E) the current bulletin of the census bureau

16. According to the passage, taxation in Roman times was based on

    (A) mobility
    (B) wealth
    (C) population
    (D) census takers
    (E) economic predictions

17. The author refers to the Romans primarily in order to

    (A) prove the superiority of modern sampling methods to ancient ones
    (B) provide a historical framework for the passage
    (C) relate an unfamiliar concept to a familiar one
    (D) show that statistical forecasts have not significantly deteriorated
    (E) cite an authority to support the thesis of the passage

18. The author refers to the Mets primarily in order to

    (A) show that sports do not depend on statistics
    (B) provide an example of an unreliable statistic
    (C) contrast verifiable and unverifiable methods of record keeping
    (D) indicate the changes in attitudes from Roman days to the present
    (E) illustrate the failure of statistical predictions

19. On the basis of the passage, it can be inferred that the author would agree with which of the following statements?

    (A) Computers have significantly improved the application of statistics in business.
    (B) Statistics is not, at the present time, a science.
    (C) It is useless to try to predict the economy.
    (D) Most mathematical systems are inexact.
    (E) Statisticians should devote themselves to the study of probability.

20. The author's tone can best be described as

    (A) jocular
    (B) scornful
    (C) pessimistic
    (D) objective
    (E) humanistic

# Reading Comprehension Exercise E

<u>Directions:</u> Each of the following reading comprehension questions are based on the content of the following passage. Read the passage and then determine the best answer choice for each question. Base your choice on what this passage <u>states directly</u> or <u>implies</u>, not on any information you may have gained elsewhere.

Observe the dilemma of the fungus: it is a plant, but it possesses no chlorophyll. While all other plants put the sun's energy to work for them combining the nutrients of ground and air into the
(5) body structure, the chlorophylless fungus must look elsewhere for an energy supply. It finds it in those other plants which, having received their energy free from the sun, relinquish it at some point in their cycle either to animals (like us
(10) humans) or to fungi.

In this search for energy the fungus has become the earth's major source of rot and decay. Wherever you see mold forming on a piece of bread, or a pile of leaves turning to compost, or a
(15) blown-down tree becoming pulp on the ground, you are watching a fungus eating. Without fungus action the earth would be piled high with the dead plant life of past centuries. In fact, certain plants which contain resins that are toxic to fungi will
(20) last indefinitely; specimens of the redwood, for instance, can still be found resting on the forest floor centuries after having been blown down.

1. Which of the following words best describes the fungus as depicted in the passage?

    (A) Unevolved
    (B) Sporadic
    (C) Enigmatic
    (D) Parasitic
    (E) Toxic

2. The passage states all the following about fungi EXCEPT:

    (A) They are responsible for the decomposition of much plant life.
    (B) They cannot live completely apart from other plants.
    (C) They are vastly different from other plants.
    (D) They are poisonous to resin-producing plants.
    (E) They cannot produce their own store of energy.

3. The author's statement that "you are watching a fungus eating" (line 16) is best described as

    (A) figurative
    (B) ironical
    (C) parenthetical
    (D) erroneous
    (E) contradictory

4. The author is primarily concerned with

    (A) warning people of the dangers of fungi
    (B) writing a humorous essay on fungi
    (C) relating how most plants use solar energy
    (D) describing the actions of fungi
    (E) explaining the long life of some redwoods

The establishment of the Third Reich influenced events in American history by starting a chain of events which culminated in war between *Line* Germany and the United States. The complete
(5) destruction of democracy, the persecution of Jews, the war on religion, the cruelty and barbarism of the Nazis, and especially the plans of Germany and her allies, Italy and Japan, for world conquest caused great indignation in this country
(10) and brought on fear of another world war. While speaking out against Hitler's atrocities, the American people generally favored isolationist policies and neutrality. The Neutrality Acts of 1935 and 1936 prohibited trade with any belliger-
(15) ents or loans to them. In 1937 the President was empowered to declare an arms embargo in wars between nations at his discretion.

American opinion began to change somewhat after President Roosevelt's "quarantine the
(20) aggressor" speech at Chicago (1937), in which he severely criticized Hitler's policies. Germany's seizure of Austria and the Munich Pact for the partition of Czechoslovakia (1938) also aroused the American people. The conquest of
(25) Czechoslovakia in March 1939 was another rude awakening to the menace of the Third Reich. In August 1939 came the shock of the Nazi-Soviet Pact and in September the attack on Poland and the outbreak of European war. The United States
(30) attempted to maintain neutrality in spite of sympathy for the democracies arrayed against the Third Reich. The Neutrality Act of 1939 repealed the arms embargo and permitted "cash and carry" exports of arms to belligerent nations. A strong
(35) national defense program was begun. A draft act was passed (1940) to strengthen the military services. A Lend-Lease Act (1941) authorized the President to sell, exchange, or lend materials to any country deemed necessary by him for the
(40) defense of the United States. Help was given to Britain by exchanging certain overage destroyers for the right to establish American bases in British territory in the Western Hemisphere. In August 1941 President Roosevelt and Prime
(45) Minister Churchill met and issued the Atlantic Charter, which proclaimed the kind of a world that should be established after the war. In December 1941 Japan launched an unprovoked attack on the United States at Pearl Harbor.
(50) Immediately thereafter, Germany declared war on the United States.

5. The author is primarily concerned with
(A) evaluating various legislative efforts to strengthen national defense
(B) summarizing the events that led up to America's involvement in the war
(C) criticizing the atrocities perpetrated by the Third Reich
(D) explaining a basic distinction between American and German policy
(E) describing the social and psychological effects of war

6. During the years 1933–36, American foreign policy may best be described as being one of
(A) overt belligerence
(B) deliberate uninvolvement
(C) moral indignation
(D) veiled contempt
(E) reluctant admiration

7. According to the passage, the United States, while maintaining neutrality, showed its sympathy for the democracies by which of the following actions?
   I. It came to the defense of Poland.
   II. It conscripted recruits for the armed forces.
   III. It supplied weapons to friendly countries.
(A) I only
(B) III only
(C) I and II only
(D) II and III only
(E) I, II, and III

8. According to the passage, all of the following events occurred in 1939 EXCEPT
(A) the invasion of Poland
(B) the invasion of Czechoslovakia
(C) the annexation of Austria
(D) passage of the Neutrality Act
(E) the beginning of the war in Europe

9. With which of the following statements would the author of the passage be most likely to agree?
(A) American neutrality during the 1930s was a natural consequence of the course of world events.
(B) Every nation should be free to determine its own internal policy without interference.
(C) The United States, through its aggressive actions, invited an attack on its territory.
(D) Americans were slow to realize the full danger posed by Nazi Germany.
(E) President Roosevelt showed undue sympathy for Britain.

10. Which of the following best describes the organization of the passage?
(A) The author presents a thesis and then lists events that support that thesis in chronological order.
(B) The author presents a thesis and then cites examples that support the thesis as well as evidence that tends to negate it.
(C) The author summarizes a historical study and then discusses an aspect of the study in detail.
(D) The author describes historical events and then gives a personal interpretation of them.
(E) The author cites noted authorities as a means of supporting his or her own opinion.

Not a few of Jane Austen's personal acquaintances might have echoed Sir Samuel Egerton Brydges, who noticed that "she was fair and
*Line* handsome, slight and elegant, but with cheeks a
(5) little too full," while "never suspect[ing] she was an authoress." For this novelist whose personal obscurity was more complete than that of any other famous writer was always quick to insist either on complete anonymity or on the propriety
(10) of her limited craft, her delight in delineating just "3 or 4 Families in a Country Village." With her self-deprecatory remarks about her inability to join "strong manly, spirited sketches, full of Variety and Glow" with her "little bit (two Inches
(15) wide) of Ivory," Jane Austen perpetuated the belief among her friends that her art was just an accomplishment "by a lady," if anything "rather too light and bright and sparkling." In this respect she resembled one of her favorite contemporaries,
(20) Mary Brunton, who would rather have "glid[ed] through the world unknown" than been "suspected of literary airs—to be shunned, as literary women are, by the more pretending of their own sex, and abhorred, as literary women are, by the
(25) more pretending of the other!—my dear, I would sooner exhibit as a ropedancer."

Yet, decorous though they might first seem, Austen's self-effacing anonymity and her modest description of her miniaturist art also imply a crit-
(30) icism, even a rejection, of the world at large. For, as Gaston Bachelard explains, the miniature "allows us to be world conscious at slight risk." While the creators of satirically conceived diminutive landscapes seem to see everything as
(35) small because they are themselves so grand, Austen's analogy for her art—her "little bit (two Inches wide) of Ivory"—suggests a fragility that reminds us of the risk and instability outside the fictional space. Besides seeing her art metaphori-
(40) cally, as her critics would too, in relation to female arts severely devalued until quite recently (for painting on ivory was traditionally a "lady-like" occupation), Austen attempted through self-imposed novelistic limitations to define a secure
(45) place, even as she seemed to admit the impossibility of actually inhabiting such a small space with any degree of comfort. And always, for Austen, it is women—because they are too vulnerable in the world at large—who must
(50) acquiesce in their own confinement, no matter how stifling it may be.

11. The passage focuses primarily on
   (A) Jane Austen's place in English literature
   (B) the literary denigration of female novelists
   (C) the implications of Austen's attitude to her work
   (D) critical evaluations of the novels of Jane Austen
   (E) social rejection of professional women in the 18th and 19th centuries

12. According to the passage, Austen concentrated on a limited range of subjects because
   (A) she had a limited degree of experience of fiction
   (B) her imagination was incapable of creating other worlds
   (C) women in her time were prohibited from writing about significant topics
   (D) she wanted to create a safe niche for the exercise of her talents
   (E) she did not wish to be acknowledged as an author

13. Which of the following best expresses the relationship of the first sentence to the rest of the passage?
   (A) Specific instance followed by generalizations
   (B) Assertion followed by analysis
   (C) Objective statement followed by personal opinion
   (D) Quotation from an authority followed by conflicting views
   (E) Challenge followed by debate

The atmosphere is a mixture of several gases. There are about ten chemical elements which remain permanently in gaseous form in the atmo-
*Line* sphere under all natural conditions. Of these per-
(5) manent gases, oxygen makes up about 21 percent and nitrogen about 78 percent. Several other gases, such as argon, carbon dioxide, hydrogen, neon, krypton, and xenon, comprise the remaining 1 percent of the volume of dry air. The amount of
(10) water vapor, and its variations in amount and distribution, are of extraordinary importance in weather changes. Atmospheric gases hold in suspension great quantities of dust, pollen, smoke, and other impurities which are always present in
(15) considerable, but variable amounts.

The atmosphere has no definite upper limits but gradually thins until it becomes imperceptible. Until recently it was assumed that the air above the first few miles gradually grew thinner and
(20) colder at a constant rate. It was also assumed that upper air had little influence on weather changes. Recent studies of the upper atmosphere, currently being conducted by earth satellites and missile probings, have shown these assumptions to be
(25) incorrect. The atmosphere has three well-defined strata.

The layer of the air next to the earth, which extends upward for about 10 miles, is known as the *troposphere*. On the whole, it makes up about
(30) 75 percent of all the weight of the atmosphere. It is the warmest part of the atmosphere because most of the solar radiation is absorbed by the earth's surface, which warms the air immediately surrounding it. A steady decrease of temperature
(35) with increasing elevation is a most striking characteristic. The upper layers are colder because of their greater distance from the earth's surface

and rapid radiation of heat into space. The temperatures within the troposphere decrease about
(40) 3.5 degrees per 1,000-foot increase in altitude. Within the troposphere, winds and air currents distribute heat and moisture. Strong winds, called jet streams, are located at the upper levels of the troposphere. These jet streams are both complex
(45) and widespread in occurrence. They normally show a waveshaped pattern and move from west to east at velocities of 150 mph, but velocities as high as 400 mph have been noted. The influences of changing locations and
(50) strengths of jet streams upon weather conditions and patterns are no doubt considerable. Current intensive research may eventually reveal their true significance.

Above the troposphere to a height of about
(55) 50 miles is a zone called the *stratosphere*. The stratosphere is separated from the troposphere by a zone of uniform temperatures called the tropopause. Within the lower portions of the stratosphere is a layer of ozone gases which filters
(60) out most of the ultraviolet rays from the sun. The ozone layer varies with air pressure. If this zone were not there, the full blast of the sun's ultraviolet light would burn our skins, blind our eyes, and eventually result in our destruction. Within
(65) the stratosphere, the temperature and atmospheric composition are relatively uniform.

The layer upward of about 50 miles is the most fascinating but the least known of these three strata. It is called the *ionosphere* because it
(70) consists of electrically charged particles called ions, thrown from the sun. The northern lights (*aurora borealis*) originate within this highly charged portion of the atmosphere. Its effect upon weather conditions, if any, is as yet unknown.

14. Which of the following titles best summarizes the content of the passage?

(A) New Methods for Calculating the Composition of the Atmosphere
(B) New Evidence Concerning the Stratification of the Atmosphere
(C) The Atmosphere: Its Nature and Importance to Our Weather
(D) The Underlying Causes of Atmospheric Turbulence
(E) Stratosphere, Troposphere, Ionosphere: Three Similar Zones

15. The passage supplies information that would answer which of the following question?

I. How do the troposphere and the stratosphere differ?
II. How does the ionosphere affect the weather?
III. How do earth satellites study the atmosphere?

(A) I only
(B) III only
(C) I and II only
(D) I and III only
(E) I, II, and III

16. According to the passage, life as we know it exists on earth because the atmosphere

(A) contains a layer of ozone gases
(B) contains electrically charged particles
(C) is warmest at the bottom
(D) carries the ultraviolet rays of the sun
(E) provides the changes in weather

17. It can be inferred from the passage that a jet plane will usually have its best average rate of speed on its run from

(A) New York to San Francisco
(B) Los Angeles to New York
(C) Boston to Miami
(D) Bermuda to New York
(E) London to Washington, D.C.

18. It can be inferred from the passage that at the top of Jungfrau, which is 12,000 feet above the town of Interlaken in Switzerland, the temperature is usually

(A) below freezing
(B) about 42 degrees colder than on the ground
(C) warmer than in Interlaken
(D) affected by the ionosphere
(E) about 75 degrees colder than in Interlaken

19. The passage states that the troposphere is the warmest part of the atmosphere because it

(A) is closest to the sun
(B) contains electrically charged particles
(C) radiates heat into space
(D) has winds and air current that distribute the heat
(E) is warmed by the earth's heat

20. According to the passage, the atmosphere consists of all of the following EXCEPT

(A) 21 percent oxygen
(B) a definite amount of water vapor
(C) ten permanent elements
(D) less than 1 percent xenon
(E) considerable waste products

# Answer Key

## *Reading Comprehension Exercise A*

| | | | |
|---|---|---|---|
| 1. B | 6. C | 11. C | 16. D |
| 2. B | 7. E | 12. D | 17. D |
| 3. E | 8. A | 13. D | 18. C |
| 4. B | 9. E | 14. A | 19. E |
| 5. E | 10. D | 15. B | 20. E |

## *Reading Comprehension Exercise B*

| | | | |
|---|---|---|---|
| 1. A | 6. E | 11. D | 16. B |
| 2. D | 7. C | 12. C | 17. A |
| 3. C | 8. E | 13. E | 18. C |
| 4. B | 9. C | 14. B | 19. E |
| 5. D | 10. C | 15. A | 20. B |

## *Reading Comprehension Exercise C*

| | | | |
|---|---|---|---|
| 1. C | 6. B | 11. C | 16. A |
| 2. B | 7. A | 12. D | 17. B |
| 3. A | 8. B | 13. A | 18. D |
| 4. D | 9. D | 14. C | 19. B |
| 5. E | 10. B | 15. C | 20. E |

## *Reading Comprehension Exercise D*

| | | | |
|---|---|---|---|
| 1. B | 6. B | 11. A | 16. C |
| 2. E | 7. E | 12. D | 17. B |
| 3. D | 8. D | 13. A | 18. E |
| 4. C | 9. B | 14. B | 19. B |
| 5. A | 10. C | 15. D | 20. A |

## *Reading Comprehension Exercise E*

| | | | |
|---|---|---|---|
| 1. D | 6. B | 11. C | 16. A |
| 2. D | 7. D | 12. D | 17. B |
| 3. A | 8. C | 13. B | 18. B |
| 4. D | 9. D | 14. C | 19. E |
| 5. B | 10. A | 15. A | 20. B |

# 8 Reviewing Vocabulary

- ■ **GRE High-Frequency Words**
- ■ **Master Word List**
- ■ **Basic Word Parts**

Now that you have mastered the appropriate strategies for dealing with the four basic types of questions on the Graduate Record Examination that test your verbal ability, you have the opportunity to spend some time refining your vocabulary and acquainting yourself with the fine shades of meaning that words possess. Studies show that, where the average high school graduate recognizes around 50,000 words, the average college graduate recognizes around 70,000. The increase indicates that during your four years of college you have rapidly acquired about 20,000 new words (many of them technical terms from a variety of disciplines), some of which may have connotations and nuances that still escape you.

The best way to develop a powerful vocabulary is to read extensively and well. However, it is possible to fine-tune your vocabulary by exploring unabridged dictionaries, in which usage notes make clear the fine distinctions between related words, and by studying high-level vocabulary lists, such as our 3,500-word Master Word List.

This chapter presents the Master Word List and a Basic Word Parts List, a chart of prefixes, roots, and suffixes that may provide you with clues to the meanings of unfamiliar words. The chapter begins with the GRE High-Frequency Word List, 333 words that have occurred and reoccurred on GREs published in the 1980s and 1990s.

# The GRE High-Frequency Word List

How many of the following words do you think you know? Half? Even more? First, check off those words that you recognize. Then, look up all 333 words and their definitions in our Master Word List. Pay particular attention to the following:

1. Words you recognize but cannot use in a sentence or define. You have a feel for these words—you are on the brink of knowing them. Effort you put into mastering these "borderline" words will pay off soon.

2. Words you thought you knew—but didn't. See whether any of them are defined in an unexpected way. If they are, make a special note of them. As you know from the preceding chapters, the GRE often stumps students with questions based on unfamiliar meanings of familiar-looking words.

In the course of your undergraduate career, you have undoubtedly developed your own techniques for building your vocabulary. One familiar technique—flash cards—often is used less than effectively. Students either try to cram too much information onto a flash card or try to cram too many flash cards into a practice session. If you wish to work with flash cards, try following these suggestions.

*Writing the Flash Card*   Be brief—but include all the information you need. On one side write the word. On the other side write a *concise* definition—two or three words at most—for each major meaning of the word you want to learn. Include an antonym, too: the synonym-antonym associations can help you remember both words. To fix the word in your mind, use it in a short phrase. Then write that phrase down.

*Memorizing the Flash Card*   Carry a few of your flash cards with you every day. Look them over whenever you have a spare moment or two. Work in short bursts. Try going through five flash cards at a time, shuffling through them quickly so that you can build up your rapid sight recognition of the words for the test. You want these words and their antonyms to spring to your mind instantaneously.

Test your memory: don't look at the back of the card unless you must. Go through your five cards several times a day. Then, when you have mastered two or three of the cards and have them down pat, set those cards aside and add a couple of new ones to your working pile. That way you will always be working with a limited group, but you won't be wasting time reviewing words you already recognize on sight.

*Never* try to master a whole stack of flash cards in one long cram session. It won't work.

# GRE High-Frequency Words

abate
aberrant
abeyance
abscond
abstemious
admonish
adulterate
aesthetic
aggregate
alacrity
alleviate
amalgamate
ambiguous
ambivalence
ameliorate
anachronism
analogous
anarchy
anomalous
antipathy
apathy
appease
apprise
approbation
appropriate [v.]
arduous
artless
ascetic
assiduous
assuage
attenuate
audacious
austere
autonomous
aver
banal
belie
beneficent
bolster
bombastic
boorish
burgeon
burnish
buttress
cacophonous
capricious
castigation
catalyst
caustic

chicanery
coagulate
coda
cogent
commensurate
compendium
complaisant
compliant
conciliatory
condone
confound
connoisseur
contention
contentious
contrite
conundrum
converge
convoluted
craven
daunt
decorum
default
deference
delineate
denigrate
deride
derivative
desiccate
desultory
deterrent
diatribe
dichotomy
diffidence
diffuse
digression
dirge
disabuse
discerning
discordant
discredit
discrepancy
discrete
disingenuous
disinterested
disjointed
dismiss
disparage
disparate
dissemble

disseminate
dissolution
dissonance
distend
distill
diverge
divest
document [v.]
dogmatic
dormant
dupe
ebullient
eclectic
efficacy
effrontery
elegy
elicit
embellish
empirical
emulate
endemic
enervate
engender
enhance
ephemeral
equanimity
equivocate
erudite
esoteric
eulogy
euphemism
exacerbate
exculpate
exigency
extrapolation
facetious
facilitate
fallacious
fatuous
fawning
felicitous
fervor
flag [v.]
fledgling
flout
foment
forestall
frugality
futile

gainsay
garrulous
goad
gouge
grandiloquent
gregarious
guileless
gullible
harangue
homogeneous
hyperbole
iconoclastic
idolatry
immutable
impair
impassive
impede
impermeable
imperturbable
impervious
implacable
implicit
implode
inadvertently
inchoate
incongruity
inconsequential
incorporate
indeterminate
indigence
indolent
inert
ingenuous
inherent
innocuous
insensible
insinuate
insipid
insularity
intractable
intransigence
inundate
inured
invective
irascible
irresolute
itinerary
laconic
lassitude

latent
laud
lethargic
levee
levity
log
loquacious
lucid
luminous
magnanimity
malingerer
malleable
maverick
mendacious
metamorphosis
meticulous
misanthrope
mitigate
mollify
morose
mundane
negate
neophyte
obdurate
obsequious
obviate
occlude
officious
onerous
opprobrium
oscillate
ostentatious
paragon
partisan
pathological
paucity
pedantic
penchant
penury
perennial
perfidious
perfunctory
permeable
pervasive
phlegmatic
piety
placate
plasticity
platitude

| | | | | |
|---|---|---|---|---|
| plethora | propitiate | rescind | sporadic | tractable |
| plummet | propriety | resolution | stigma | transgression |
| porous | proscribe | resolve | stint [v.] | truculence |
| pragmatic | pungent | reticent | stipulate | vacillate |
| preamble | qualified | reverent | stolid | venerate |
| precarious | quibble | sage [N.] | striated | veracious |
| precipitate (ADJ.) | quiescent | salubrious | strut [N.] | verbose |
| precursor | rarefied | sanction | subpoena | viable |
| presumptuous | recalcitrant | satiate | subside | viscous |
| prevaricate | recant | saturate | substantiate | vituperative |
| pristine | recluse | savor | supersede | volatile |
| probity | recondite | secrete | supposition | warranted |
| problematic | refractory | shard | tacit | wary |
| prodigal | refute | skeptic | tangential | welter |
| profound | relegate | solicitous | tenuous | whimsical |
| prohibitive | reproach | soporific | tirade | zealot |
| proliferate | reprobate | specious | torpor | |
| propensity | repudiate | spectrum | tortuous | |

# The 3,500-word Master Word List

The 3,500-word Master Word List begins on the following page. As a graduate student you should be familiar with the majority of these words. You do not, however, need to memorize every word.

The best way to enlarge your vocabulary is to read extensively in a variety of fields. You can, however, assess the extent of your vocabulary by exploring specialized word lists such as this one.

For those of you who wish to work your way through the word list and feel the need for a plan, we recommend that you follow the procedure described below in order to use the lists and the exercises most profitably:

1. Allot a definite time each day for the study of a list.

2. Devote at least one hour to each list.

3. First go through the list looking at the short, simple-looking words (seven letters at most). Mark those you don't know. In studying, pay particular attention to them.

4. Go through the list again looking at the longer words. Pay particular attention to words with more than one meaning and familiar-looking words with unusual definitions that come as a surprise to you. Many tests make use of these secondary definitions.

5. List unusual words on index cards, which you can shuffle and review from time to time. (Use the flash card technique described earlier in this chapter.)

6. Using the illustrative sentences in the list as models, make up new sentences on your own.

7. Take the test that follows each list at least one day after studying the words. In this way, you will check your ability to remember what you have studied.

8. If you can answer correctly 12 of the 15 questions in the test, you may proceed to the next list; if you cannot answer this number, restudy the list.

9. Keep a record of your guesses and of your success as a guesser.

For each word, the following is provided:

1. The word (printed in heavy type).

2. Its part of speech (abbreviated).

3. A brief definition.

4. A sentence or sentences illustrating the word's use.

5. Whenever appropriate, related words together with their parts of speech.

The word lists are arranged in strict alphabetical order. In each list, words that appear also on the High-Frequency GRE Word List are marked with a square bullet (■).

# Master Word List

## Word List 1    abase-adroit

**abase** v. lower; degrade; humiliate. Anna expected to have to curtsy to the King of Siam; when told to cast herself down on the ground before him, however, she refused to *abase* herself. abasement, N.

**abash** v. embarrass. He was not at all *abashed* by her open admiration.

■ **abate** v. subside or moderate. Rather than leaving immediately, they waited for the storm to *abate*.

**abbreviate** v. shorten. Because we were running out of time, the lecturer had to *abbreviate* her speech.

**abdicate** v. renounce; give up. When Edward VIII *abdicated* the British throne, he surprised the entire world.

■ **aberrant** ADJ. abnormal or deviant. Given the *aberrant* nature of the data, we came to doubt the validity of the entire experiment.

**aberration** N. deviation from the expected or the normal; mental irregularity or disorder. Survivors of a major catastrophe are likely to exhibit *aberrations* of behavior because of the trauma they have experienced.

**abet** v. assist, usually in doing something wrong; encourage. She was unwilling to *abet* him in the swindle he had planned.

■ **abeyance** N. suspended action. The deal was held in *abeyance* until her arrival.

**abhor** v. detest; hate. She *abhorred* all forms of bigotry. abhorrence, N.

**abject** ADJ. wretched; lacking pride. On the streets of New York the homeless live in *abject* poverty, huddling in doorways to find shelter from the wind.

**abjure** v. renounce upon oath. He *abjured* his allegiance to the king. abjuration, N.

**ablution** N. washing. His daily *ablutions* were accompanied by loud noises that he humorously labeled "Opera in the Bath."

**abnegation** N. renunciation; self-sacrifice. Though Rudolph and Duchess Flavia loved one another, their love was doomed, for she had to wed the king; their act of *abnegation* was necessary to preserve the kingdom.

**abolish** v. cancel; put an end to. The president of the college refused to *abolish* the physical education requirement. abolition, N.

**abominable** ADJ. detestable; extremely unpleasant; very bad. Mary liked John until she learned he was also dating Susan; then she called him an *abominable* young man, with *abominable* taste in women.

**abominate** v. loathe; hate. Moses scolded the idol worshippers in the tribe because he *abominated* the custom.

**aboriginal** ADJ., N. being the first of its kind in a region; primitive; native. Her studies of the primitive art forms of the *aboriginal* Indians were widely reported in the scientific journals. aborigine, N.

**abortive** ADJ. unsuccessful; fruitless. Attacked by armed troops, the Chinese students had to abandon their *abortive* attempt to democratize Beijing peacefully. abort, v.

**abrasive** ADJ. rubbing away; tending to grind down. Just as *abrasive* cleaning powders can wear away a shiny finish, *abrasive* remarks can wear away a listener's patience. abrade, v.

**abridge** v. condense or shorten. Because the publishers felt the public wanted a shorter version of *War and Peace*, they proceeded to *abridge* the novel.

**abrogate** v. abolish. The king intended to *abrogate* the decree issued by his predecessor.

**abscission** N. cutting off; separation. When a flower or leaf separates naturally from the parent plant, this process is called *abscission*.

■ **abscond** v. depart secretly and hide. The teller who *absconded* with the bonds went uncaptured until someone recognized him from his photograph on *America's Most Wanted*.

**absolute** ADJ. complete; totally unlimited; certain. Although the King of Siam was an *absolute* monarch, he did not want to behead his unfaithful wife without *absolute* evidence of her infidelity.

**absolve** v. pardon (an offense). The father confessor *absolved* him of his sins. absolution, N.

**abstain** v. refrain; withhold from participation. After considering the effect of alcohol on his athletic performance, he decided to *abstain* from drinking while he trained for the race.

■ **abstemious** ADJ. sparing in eating and drinking; temperate. Concerned whether her vegetarian son's *abstemious* diet provided him with sufficient protein, the worried mother pressed food on him.

**abstinence** N. restraint from eating or drinking. The doctor recommended total *abstinence* from salted foods. abstain, v.

**abstract** ADJ. theoretical; not concrete; nonrepresentational. To him, hunger was an *abstract* concept; he had never missed a meal.

**abstruse** ADJ. obscure; profound; difficult to understand. Baffled by the *abstruse* philosophical texts assigned in class, Dave asked Lexy to explain Kant's *Critique of Pure Reason*.

**abusive** ADJ. coarsely insulting; physically harmful. An *abusive* parent damages a child both mentally and physically.

**abut** v. border upon; adjoin. Where our estates *abut*, we must build a fence.

**abysmal** ADJ. bottomless. His arrogance is exceeded only by his *abysmal* ignorance.

**abyss** N. enormous chasm; vast, bottomless pit. Darth Vader seized the evil emperor and hurled him into the *abyss*.

**academic** ADJ. related to a school; not practical or directly useful. The dean's talk about reforming *academic* policies was only an *academic* discussion: we knew little, if anything, would change.

**accede** v. agree. If I *accede* to this demand for blackmail, I am afraid that I will be the victim of future demands.

**accelerate** v. move faster. In our science class, we learn how falling bodies *accelerate*.

**accessible** ADJ. easy to approach; obtainable. We asked our guide whether the ruins were *accessible* on foot.

**accessory** N. additional object; useful but not essential thing. She bought an attractive handbag as an *accessory* for her dress. also ADJ.

**acclaim** v. applaud; announce with great approval. The sportscasters *acclaimed* every American victory in the Olympics and decried every American defeat. acclamation, N.

**acclimate** v. adjust to climate or environment; adapt. One of the difficulties of our present air age is the need of travelers to *acclimate* themselves to their new and often strange environments.

**acclivity** N. sharp upslope of a hill. The car could not go up the *acclivity* in high gear.

**accolade** N. award of merit. In Hollywood, an "Oscar" is the highest *accolade*.

**accommodate** v. oblige or help someone; adjust or bring into harmony; adapt. Mitch always did everything possible to *accommodate* his elderly relatives, from driving them to medical appointments to helping them with paperwork. (secondary meaning)

**accomplice** N. partner in crime. Because he had provided the criminal with the lethal weapon, he was arrested as an *accomplice* in the murder.

**accord** N. agreement. She was in complete *accord* with the verdict.

**accost** v. approach and speak first to a person. When the two young men *accosted* me, I was frightened because I thought they were going to attack me.

**accoutre** v. equip. The fisherman was *accoutred* with the best that the sporting goods store could supply. accoutrement, N.

**accretion** N. growth; increase. Over the years Bob put on weight; because of this *accretion* of flesh, he went from size M to size XL. accrete, v.

**accrue** v. come about by addition. You must pay the interest that has *accrued* on your debt as well as the principal sum. accrual, N.

**acerbity** N. bitterness of speech and temper. The meeting of the United Nations Assembly was marked with such *acerbity* that observers held little hope of reaching any useful settlement of the problem. acerbic, ADJ.

**acetic** ADJ. vinegary. The salad had an exceedingly *acetic* flavor.

**acidulous** ADJ. slightly sour; sharp; caustic. James was unpopular because of his sarcastic and *acidulous* remarks.

**acknowledge** v. recognize; admit. Although I *acknowledge* that the Beatles' tunes sound pretty dated nowadays, I still prefer them to the gangsta rap songs my brothers play.

**acme** N. peak; pinnacle; highest point. Welles's success in *Citizen Kane* marked the *acme* of his career as an actor; never again did he achieve such popular acclaim.

**acoustics** N. science of sound; quality that makes a room easy or hard to hear in. Carnegie Hall is liked by music lovers because of its fine *acoustics*.

**acquiesce** v. assent; agree passively. Although she appeared to *acquiesce* to her employer's suggestions, I could tell she had reservations about the changes he wanted made. acquiescence, N.; acquiescent, ADJ.

**acquittal** N. deliverance from a charge. His *acquittal* by the jury surprised those who had thought him guilty. acquit, v.

**acrid** ADJ. sharp; bitterly pungent. The *acrid* odor of burnt gunpowder filled the room after the pistol had been fired.

**acrimonious** ADJ. bitter in words or manner. The candidate attacked his opponent in highly *acrimonious* terms. acrimony, N.

**acrophobia** N. fear of heights. A born salesman, he could convince someone with a bad case of *acrophobia* to sign up for a life membership in a sky-diving club.

**actuarial** ADJ. calculating; pertaining to insurance statistics. According to recent *actuarial* tables, life expectancy is greater today than it was a century ago.

**actuate** v. motivate. I fail to understand what *actuated* you to reply to this letter so nastily.

**acuity** N. sharpness. In time his youthful *acuity* of vision failed him, and he needed glasses.

**acumen** N. mental keenness. Her business *acumen* helped her to succeed where others had failed.

**acute** ADJ. quickly perceptive; keen; brief and severe. The *acute* young doctor realized immediately that the gradual deterioration of her patient's once-*acute* hearing was due to a chronic illness, not an *acute* one.

**adage** N. wise saying; proverb. There is much truth in the old *adage* about fools and their money.

**adamant** ADJ. hard; inflexible. In this movie Bronson played the part of a revenge-driven man, *adamant* in his determination to punish the criminals who destroyed his family. adamancy, N.

**adapt** v. alter; modify. Some species of animals have become extinct because they could not *adapt* to a changing environment.

**addendum**   N. addition; appendix to book. Jane's editor approved her new comparative literature text but thought it would be even better with an *addendum* on recent developments in literary criticism.

✗**addiction**   N. compulsive, habitual need. His *addiction* to drugs caused his friends much grief.

**addle**   V. muddle; drive crazy; become rotten. This idiotic plan is confusing enough to *addle* anyone. addled, ADJ.

✗**address**   V. direct a speech to; deal with or discuss. Due to *address* the convention in July, Brown planned to *address* the issue of low-income housing in his speech.

**adept**   ADJ. expert at. She was *adept* at the fine art of irritating people. also N.

**adhere**   V. stick fast. I will *adhere* to this opinion until proof that I am wrong is presented. adhesion, N.; adherence, N.

**adherent**   N. supporter; follower. In the wake of the scandal, the senator's one-time *adherents* quietly deserted him.

✗**adjacent**   ADJ. adjoining; neighboring; close by. Philip's best friend Jason lived only four houses down the block, near but not immediately *adjacent*.

**adjunct**   N. something (generally nonessential or inferior) added on or attached. Although I don't absolutely need a second computer, I plan to buy a laptop to serve as an *adjunct* to my desktop model. also ADJ.

**adjuration**   N. solemn urging. Her *adjuration* to tell the truth did not change the witnesses' testimony. adjure, v.

**adjutant**   N. staff officer assisting the commander; assistant. Though Wellington delegated many tasks to his chief *adjutant*, Lord Fitzroy Somerset, Somerset was in no doubt as to who made all major decisions.

■**admonish**   V. warn; reprove. He *admonished* his listeners to change their wicked ways. admonition, N.

**adorn**   V. decorate. Wall paintings and carved statues *adorned* the temple. adornment, N.

**adroit**   ADJ. skillful. Her *adroit* handling of the delicate situation pleased her employers.

# Test

## Word List 1    *Synonyms*

Each of the questions below consists of a word in capital letters, followed by five lettered words or phrases. Choose the lettered word or phrase that is most nearly similar in meaning to the word in capital letters and write the letter of your choice on your answer paper.

1.  ABASE (A) incur (B) tax (C) estimate (D) elope (E) humiliate
2.  ABERRATION (A) deviation (B) abhorrence (C) dislike (D) absence (E) anecdote
3.  ABET (A) conceive (B) wager (C) encourage (D) evade (E) protect
4.  ABEYANCE (A) obedience (B) discussion (C) excitement (D) suspended action (E) editorial
5.  ABJURE (A) discuss (B) renounce (C) run off secretly (D) perjure (E) project
6.  ABLUTION (A) censure (B) forgiveness (C) mutiny (D) survival (E) washing
7.  ABNEGATION (A) blackness (B) self-denial (C) selfishness (D) cause (E) effectiveness
8.  ABORIGINE (A) first design (B) absolution (C) finale (D) concept (E) primitive inhabitant
9.  ABORTIVE (A) unsuccessful (B) consuming (C) financing (D) familiar (E) fruitful
10. ABSTINENCE (A) restrained eating or drinking (B) vulgar display (C) deportment (D) reluctance (E) population
11. ABSTRUSE (A) profound (B) irrespective (C) suspended (D) protesting (E) not thorough
12. ABUT (A) stimulate (B) grasp (C) oppose (D) widen (E) adjoin
13. ABYSMAL (A) bottomless (B) eternal (C) meteoric (D) diabolic (E) internal
14. ACCEDE (A) fail (B) compromise (C) correct (D) consent (E) mollify
15. ACCLIVITY (A) index (B) report (C) upslope of a hill (D) character (E) negotiator

## Word List 2    adulation-amend

**adulation**   N. flattery; admiration. The rock star thrived on the *adulation* of his groupies and yes-men. adulate, v.

■**adulterate**   V. make impure by adding inferior or tainted substances. It is a crime to *adulterate* foods without informing the buyer; when consumers learned that Beechnut had *adulterated* its apple juice by mixing the juice with water, they protested vigorously. adulteration, N.

**advent**   N. arrival. Most Americans were unaware of the *advent* of the Nuclear Age until the news of Hiroshima reached them.

**adventitious**   ADJ. accidental; casual. She found this *adventitious* meeting with her friend extremely fortunate.

**adversary**   N. opponent; enemy. Batman struggled to save Gotham City from the machinations of his wicked *adversary*, the Joker.

**adverse**   ADJ. unfavorable; hostile. The recession had a highly *adverse* effect on Father's investment portfolio: he lost so much money that he could no longer afford the butler and the upstairs maid.

**adversity**   N. poverty; misfortune. We must learn to meet *adversity* gracefully.

**advert**   V. refer (to). Since you *advert* to this matter so frequently, you must regard it as important.

**advocacy** N. support; active pleading on behalf of someone or something. No threats could dissuade Bishop Desmond Tutu from his *advocacy* of the human rights of black South Africans.

**advocate** V. urge; plead for. The abolitionists *advocated* freedom for the slaves. also N.

**aegis** N. shield; defense. Under the *aegis* of the Bill of Rights, we enjoy our most treasured freedoms.

**aerie** N. nest of a large bird of prey (eagle, hawk). The mother eagle swooped down on the rabbit and bore it off to her *aerie* high in the Rocky Mountains.

■ **aesthetic** ADJ. artistic; dealing with or capable of appreciating the beautiful. The beauty of Tiffany's stained glass appealed to Alice's *aesthetic* sense. aesthete, N.

**affable** ADJ. easily approachable; warmly friendly. Accustomed to cold, aloof supervisors, Nicholas was amazed at how *affable* his new employer was. affability, N.

**affected** ADJ. artificial; pretended; assumed in order to impress. His *affected* mannerisms—his "Harvard" accent, his air of boredom, his use of obscure foreign words—bugged us: he acted as if he thought he was too good for his old high school friends. affectation, N.

**affidavit** N. written statement made under oath. The court refused to accept her statement unless she presented it in the form of an *affidavit*.

**affiliation** N. joining; associating with. His *affiliation* with the political party was of short duration for he soon disagreed with his colleagues.

**affinity** N. kinship. She felt an *affinity* with all who suffered; their pains were her pains.

**affirmation** N. positive assertion; confirmation; solemn pledge by one who refuses to take an oath. Despite Tom's *affirmations* of innocence, Aunt Polly still suspected he had eaten the pie.

**affix** V. attach or add on; fasten. First the registrar had to *affix* his signature to the license; then he had to *affix* his official seal.

**affliction** N. state of distress; cause of suffering. Even in the midst of her *affliction*, Elizabeth tried to keep up the spirits of those around her.

**affluence** N. abundance; wealth. Foreigners are amazed by the *affluence* and luxury of the American way of life.

**affront** N. insult; offense; intentional act of disrespect. When Mrs. Proudie was not seated beside the Archdeacon at the head table, she took it as a personal *affront* and refused to speak to her hosts for a week. also V.

**agape** ADJ. openmouthed. She stared, *agape*, at the many strange animals in the zoo.

**agenda** N. items of business at a meeting. We had so much difficulty agreeing upon an *agenda* that there was very little time for the meeting.

**agglomeration** N. collection; heap. It took weeks to assort the *agglomeration* of miscellaneous items she had collected on her trip.

**aggrandize** V. increase or intensify; raise in power, wealth, rank or honor. The history of the past quarter century illustrates how a President may *aggrandize* his power to act aggressively in international affairs without considering the wishes of Congress.

■ **aggregate** V. gather; accumulate. Before the Wall Street scandals, dealers in so-called junk bonds managed to *aggregate* great wealth in short periods of time. also ADJ. aggregation, N.

**aggressor** N. attacker. Before you punish both boys for fighting, see whether you can determine which one was the *aggressor*.

**aghast** ADJ. horrified; dumbfounded. Miss Manners was *aghast* at the crude behavior of the fraternity brothers at the annual toga party.

**agility** N. nimbleness. The *agility* of the acrobat amazed and thrilled the audience.

**agitate** V. stir up; disturb. Her fiery remarks *agitated* the already angry mob.

**agnostic** N. one who is skeptical of the existence of a god or any ultimate reality. *Agnostics* say we can neither prove nor disprove the existence of God; we simply have no way to know. also ADJ.

**agog** ADJ. highly excited; intensely curious. We were all *agog* at the news that the celebrated movie star was giving up his career in order to enter a monastery.

**agrarian** ADJ. pertaining to land or its cultivation. As a result of its recent industrialization, the country is gradually losing its *agrarian* traditions.

■ **alacrity** N. cheerful promptness; eagerness. Phil and Dave were raring to get off to the mountains; they packed up their ski gear and climbed into the van with *alacrity*.

**alchemy** N. medieval chemistry. The changing of baser metals into gold was the goal of the students of *alchemy*. alchemist, N.

**alcove** N. nook; recess. Though their apartment lacked a full-scale dining room, an *alcove* adjacent to the living room made an adequate breakfast nook for the young couple.

**alias** N. an assumed name. John Smith's *alias* was Bob Jones. also ADV.

**alienate** V. make hostile; separate. Her attempts to *alienate* the two friends failed because they had complete faith in each other.

**alimentary** ADJ. supplying nourishment. The *alimentary* canal in our bodies is so named because digestion of foods occurs there. When asked for the name of the digestive tract, Sherlock Holmes replied, "*Alimentary*, my dear Watson."

**alimony** N. payments made to an ex-spouse after divorce. Because Tony had supported Tina through medical school, on their divorce he asked the court to award him $500 a month in *alimony*.

**allay** v. calm; pacify. The crew tried to *allay* the fears of the passengers by announcing that the fire had been controlled.

**allege** v. state without proof. Although it is *alleged* that she has worked for the enemy, she denies the *allegation* and, legally, we can take no action against her without proof. allegation, N.

**allegiance** N. loyalty. Not even a term in prison could shake Lech Walesa's *allegiance* to Solidarity, the Polish trade union he had helped to found.

**allegory** N. story in which characters are used as symbols; fable. *Pilgrim's Progress* is an *allegory* of the temptations and victories of the human soul. allegorical, ADJ.

■ **alleviate** v. relieve. This should *alleviate* the pain; if it does not, we shall have to use stronger drugs.

**alliteration** N. repetition of beginning sound in poetry. "The furrow followed free" is an example of *alliteration*.

**allocate** v. assign. Even though the Red Cross had *allocated* a large sum for the relief of the sufferers of the disaster, many people perished.

**alloy** N. a mixture as of metals. *Alloys* of gold are used more frequently than the pure metal.

**alloy** v. mix; make less pure; lessen or moderate. Our delight at the Mets' victory was *alloyed* by our concern for Al Laites, who injured his pitching arm in the game.

**allude** v. refer indirectly. Try not to mention divorce in Jack's presence because he will think you are *alluding* to his marital problems with Jill.

**allure** v. entice; attract. *Allured* by the song of the sirens, the helmsman steered the ship toward the reef. also N.

**allusion** N. indirect reference. When Amanda said to the ticket scalper, "One hundred bucks? What do you want, a pound of flesh?" she was making an *allusion* to Shakespeare's *Merchant of Venice*.

**alluvial** ADJ. pertaining to soil deposits left by running water. The farmers found the *alluvial* deposits at the mouth of the river very fertile.

**aloof** ADJ. apart; reserved. Shy by nature, she remained *aloof* while all the rest conversed.

**aloft** ADV. upward. The sailor climbed *aloft* into the rigging.

**altercation** N. noisy quarrel; heated dispute. In that hot-tempered household, no meal ever came to a peaceful conclusion; the inevitable *altercation* sometimes even ended in blows.

**altruistic** ADJ. unselfishly generous; concerned for others. In providing tutorial assistance and college scholarships for hundreds of economically disadvantaged youths, Eugene Lang performed a truly *altruistic* deed. altruism, N.

■ **amalgamate** v. combine; unite in one body. The unions will attempt to *amalgamate* their groups into one national body.

**amass** v. collect. The miser's aim is to *amass* and hoard as much gold as possible.

**amazon** N. female warrior. Ever since the days of Greek mythology we refer to strong and aggressive women as *amazons*.

**ambidextrous** ADJ. capable of using either hand with equal ease. A switch-hitter in baseball should be naturally *ambidextrous*.

**ambience** N. environment; atmosphere. She went to the restaurant not for the food but for the *ambience*.

■ **ambiguous** ADJ. unclear or doubtful in meaning. His *ambiguous* instructions misled us; we did not know which road to take. ambiguity, N.

■ **ambivalence** N. the state of having contradictory or conflicting emotional attitudes. Torn between loving her parents one minute and hating them the next, she was confused by the *ambivalence* of her feelings. ambivalent, ADJ.

**amble** N. moving at an easy pace. When she first mounted the horse, she was afraid to urge the animal to go faster than a gentle *amble*. also v.

**ambrosia** N. food of the gods. *Ambrosia* was supposed to give immortality to any human who ate it.

**ambulatory** ADJ. able to walk; not bedridden. Calvin was a highly *ambulatory* patient; not only did he refuse to be confined to bed, but also he insisted on riding his skateboard up and down the halls.

■ **ameliorate** v. improve. Many social workers have attempted to *ameliorate* the conditions of people living in the slums.

**amenable** ADJ. readily managed or willing to be led; answerable or accountable legally. Although the ambassador was usually *amenable* to friendly suggestions, he balked when we hinted he should pay his parking tickets. As a foreign diplomat, he claimed he was not *amenable* to minor local laws.

**amend** v. correct; change, generally for the better. Hoping to *amend* his condition, he left Vietnam for the United States.

# Test

## Word List 2   *Antonyms*

Each of the following questions consists of a word in capital letters, followed by five lettered words or phrases. Choose the lettered word or phrase that is most nearly opposite in meaning to the word in capital letters and write the letter of your choice on your answer paper.

16. ADULATION (A) youth (B) purity (C) brightness (D) defense (E) criticism
17. ADVOCATE (A) define (B) oppose (C) remove (D) inspect (E) discern
18. AFFABLE (A) rude (B) ruddy (C) needy (D) useless (E) conscious

19. AFFECTED (A) weary (B) unfriendly (C) divine (D) unfeigned (E) slow
20. AFFLUENCE (A) poverty (B) fear (C) persuasion (D) consideration (E) neglect
21. AGILITY (A) awkwardness (B) solidity (C) temper (D) harmony (E) warmth
22. ALACRITY (A) slowness (B) plenty (C) filth (D) courtesy (E) despair
23. ALLEVIATE (A) endure (B) worsen (C) enlighten (D) maneuver (E) humiliate
24. ALLURE (A) hinder (B) repel (C) ignore (D) leave (E) wallow
25. ALOOF (A) triangular (B) gregarious (C) comparable (D) honorable (E) savory
26. AMALGAMATE (A) equip (B) separate (C) generate (D) materialize (E) repress
27. AMBIGUOUS (A) salvageable (B) corresponding (C) responsible (D) clear (E) auxiliary
28. AMBLE (A) befriend (B) hasten (C) steal (D) browse (E) prattle
29. AMBULATORY (A) convalescent (B) valedictory (C) bedridden (D) emergency (E) congenital
30. AMELIORATE (A) make slow (B) make sure (C) make young (D) make worse (E) make able

# Word List 3    amenities–apothecary

**amenities** N. convenient features; courtesies. In addition to the customary *amenities* for the business traveler—fax machines, modems, a health club—the hotel offers the services of a butler versed in the social *amenities*.

**amiable** ADJ. agreeable; lovable; warmly friendly. In *Little Women*, Beth is the *amiable* daughter whose loving disposition endears her to all who know her.

**amicable** ADJ. politely friendly; not quarrelsome. Beth's sister Jo is the hot-tempered tomboy who has a hard time maintaining *amicable* relationships with those around her. Jo's quarrel with her friend Laurie finally reaches an *amicable* settlement, but not because Jo turns amiable overnight.

**amiss** ADJ. wrong; faulty. Seeing her frown, he wondered if anything were *amiss*. also ADV.

**amity** N. friendship. Student exchange programs such as the Experiment in International Living were established to promote international *amity*.

**amnesia** N. loss of memory. Because she was suffering from *amnesia*, the police could not get the young girl to identify herself.

**amnesty** N. pardon. When his first child was born, the king granted *amnesty* to all in prison.

**amoral** ADJ. nonmoral. The *amoral* individual lacks a code of ethics; he cannot tell right from wrong. The immoral person can tell right from wrong; he chooses to do something he knows is wrong.

**amorous** ADJ. moved by sexual love; loving. "Love them and leave them" was the motto of the *amorous* Don Juan.

**amorphous** ADJ. formless; lacking shape or definition. As soon as we have decided on our itinerary, we shall send you a copy; right now, our plans are still *amorphous*.

**amphibian** ADJ. able to live both on land and in water. Frogs are classified as *amphibian*. also N.

**amphitheater** N. oval building with tiers of seats. The spectators in the *amphitheater* cheered the gladiators.

**ample** ADJ. abundant. Bond had *ample* opportunity to escape. Why, then, did he let us capture him?

**amplify** V. broaden or clarify by expanding; intensify; make stronger. Charlie Brown tried to *amplify* his remarks, but he was drowned out by jeers from the audience. Lucy was smarter: she used a loudspeaker to *amplify* her voice.

**amputate** V. cut off part of body; prune. When the doctors had to *amputate* Ted Kennedy's leg to prevent the spread of cancer, he did not let the loss of his leg keep him from participating in sports.

**amok (also amuck)** ADV. in a state of rage. The police had to be called in to restrain him after he ran *amok* in the department store.

**amulet** N. charm; talisman. Around her neck she wore the *amulet* that the witch doctor had given her.

■ **anachronism** N. something or someone misplaced in time. Shakespeare's reference to clocks in *Julius Caesar* is an *anachronism*; no clocks existed in Caesar's time. anachronistic, ADJ.

**analgesic** ADJ. causing insensitivity to pain. The *analgesic* qualities of this lotion will provide temporary relief.

■ **analogous** ADJ. comparable. She called our attention to the things that had been done in an *analogous* situation and recommended that we do the same.

**analogy** N. similarity; parallelism. A well-known *analogy* compares the body's immune system with an army whose defending troops are the lymphocytes or white blood cells.

**anarchist** N. person who seeks to overturn the established government; advocate of abolishing authority. Denying she was an *anarchist*, Katya maintained she wished only to make changes in our government, not to destroy it entirely.

■ **anarchy** N. absence of governing body; state of disorder. The assassination of the leaders led to a period of *anarchy*.

**anathema** N. solemn curse; someone or something regarded as a curse. The Ayatolla Khomeini heaped *anathema* upon "the Great Satan," that is, the United States. To the Ayatolla, America and the West were *anathema*; he loathed the democratic nations, cursing them in his dying words. anathematize, v.

**ancestry** N. family descent. David can trace his *ancestry* as far back as the seventeenth century, when one of his *ancestors* was a court trumpeter somewhere in Germany. ancestral, ADJ.

**anchor** V. secure or fasten firmly; be fixed in place. We set the post in concrete to *anchor* it in place. anchorage, N.

**ancillary** ADJ. serving as an aid or accessory; auxiliary. In an *ancillary* capacity Doctor Watson was helpful; however, Holmes could not trust the good doctor to solve a perplexing case on his own. also N.

**anecdote** N. short account of an amusing or interesting event. Rather than make concrete proposals for welfare reform, President Reagan told *anecdotes* about poor people who became wealthy despite their impoverished backgrounds.

**anemia** N. condition in which blood lacks red corpuscles. The doctor ascribes her tiredness to *anemia*. anemic, ADJ.

**anesthetic** N. substance that removes sensation with or without loss of consciousness. His monotonous voice acted like an *anesthetic*; his audience was soon asleep. anesthesia, N.

**anguish** N. acute pain; extreme suffering. Visiting the site of the explosion, the president wept to see the *anguish* of the victims and their families.

**angular** ADJ. sharp-cornered; stiff in manner. Mr. Spock's features, though *angular*, were curiously attractive, in a Vulcan way.

**animadversion** N. critical remark. He resented the *animadversions* of his critics, particularly because he realized they were true.

**animated** ADJ. lively; spirited. Jim Carrey's facial expressions are highly *animated*: when he played Ace Ventura, he was practically rubber-faced.

**animosity** N. active enmity. He incurred the *animosity* of the ruling class because he advocated limitations of their power.

**animus** N. hostile feeling or intent. The *animus* of the speaker became obvious to all when he began to indulge in sarcastic and insulting remarks.

**annals** N. records; history. In the *annals* of this period, we find no mention of democratic movements.

**anneal** V. reduce brittleness and improve toughness by heating and cooling. After the glass is *annealed*, it will be less subject to chipping and cracking.

**annex** V. attach; take possession of. Mexico objected to the United States' attempts to *annex* the territory that later became the state of Texas.

**annihilate** V. destroy. The enemy in its revenge tried to *annihilate* the entire population.

**annotate** V. comment; make explanatory notes. In the appendix to the novel, the critic sought to *annotate* many of the more esoteric references.

**annuity** N. yearly allowance. The *annuity* she set up with the insurance company supplements her social security benefits so that she can live very comfortably without working.

**annul** V. make void. The parents of the eloped couple tried to *annul* the marriage.

**anodyne** N. drug that relieves pain; opiate. His pain was so great that no *anodyne* could relieve it.

**anoint** V. consecrate. The prophet Samuel *anointed* David with oil, crowning him king of Israel.

■ **anomalous** ADJ. abnormal; irregular. She was placed in the *anomalous* position of seeming to approve procedures that she despised.

**anomaly** N. irregularity. A bird that cannot fly is an *anomaly*.

**anonymity** N. state of being nameless; anonymousness. The donor of the gift asked the college not to mention her by name; the dean readily agreed to respect her *anonymity*. anonymous, ADJ.

**antagonism** N. hostility; active resistance. Barry showed his *antagonism* toward his new stepmother by ignoring her whenever she tried talking to him. antagonistic, ADJ.

**antecede** V. precede. The invention of the radiotelegraph *anteceded* the development of television by a quarter of a century.

**antecedents** N. preceding events or circumstances that influence what comes later; ancestors or early background. Susi Bechhofer's ignorance of her Jewish background had its *antecedents* in the chaos of World War II. Smuggled out of Germany and adopted by a Christian family, she knew nothing of her birth and *antecedents* until she was reunited with her Jewish family in 1989.

**antediluvian** ADJ. antiquated; extremely ancient. Looking at his great-aunt's antique furniture, which must have been cluttering up her attic since before Noah's flood, the young heir exclaimed, "Heavens! How positively *antediluvian*!"

**anthem** N. song of praise or patriotism. Let us now all join in singing the national *anthem*.

**anthology** N. book of literary selections by various authors. This *anthology* of science fiction was compiled by the late Isaac Asimov. anthologize, V.

**anthropoid** ADJ. manlike. The gorilla is the strongest of the *anthropoid* animals. also N.

**anthropologist** N. student of the history and science of humankind. *Anthropologists* have discovered several relics of prehistoric humans in this area.

**anthropomorphic** ADJ. having human form or characteristics. Primitive religions often have deities with *anthropomorphic* characteristics.

**anticlimax** N. letdown in thought or emotion. After the fine performance in the first act, the rest of the play was an *anticlimax*. anticlimactic, ADJ.

**antidote** N. remedy to counteract a poison or disease. When Marge's child accidentally swallowed some cleaning fluid, the local poison control hotline instructed Marge how to administer the *antidote*.

■ **antipathy** N. aversion; dislike. Tom's extreme *antipathy* for disputes keeps him from getting into arguments with his temperamental wife. Noise in any form is *antipathetic* to him. Among his other *antipathies* are honking cars, boom boxes, and heavy metal rock.

**antiquated** ADJ. obsolete; outdated. Accustomed to editing his papers on word processors, Philip thought typewriters were too *antiquated* for him to use.

**antiseptic** N. substance that prevents infection. It is advisable to apply an *antiseptic* to any wound, no matter how slight or insignificant. also ADJ.

**antithesis** N. contrast; direct opposite of or to. This tyranny was the *antithesis* of all that he had hoped for, and he fought it with all his strength. antithetical or antithetic, ADJ.

**anvil** N. iron block used in hammering out metals. After heating the iron horseshoe in the forge, the blacksmith picked it up with his tongs and set it on the *anvil*.

■ **apathy** N. lack of caring; indifference. A firm believer in democratic government, she could not understand the *apathy* of people who never bothered to vote. apathetic, ADJ.

**ape** V. imitate or mimic. In the comedy *Young Frankenstein*, when the servant Igor limps off, saying, "Walk this way," the hero *apes* him, hobbling after Igor in an imitation of his walk.

**aperture** N. opening; hole. She discovered a small *aperture* in the wall, through which the insects had entered the room.

**apex** N. tip; summit; climax. At the *apex* of his career, the star received offers of leading roles daily; two years later, he was reduced to taking bit parts in B-movies.

**aphasia** N. loss of speech due to injury or illness. After the automobile accident, the victim had periods of *aphasia* when he could not speak at all or could only mumble incoherently.

**aphorism** N. pithy maxim or saying. An *aphorism* is usually philosophic or scientific, as compared to an adage, which is usually more homely and concrete. "Absolute power corrupts absolutely" is an *aphorism*. "You can lead a horse to water, but you can't make him drink" is an adage. aphoristic, ADJ.

**apiary** N. a place where bees are kept. Although he spent many hours daily in the *apiary*, he was very seldom stung by a bee.

**aplomb** N. poise; assurance. Gwen's *aplomb* in handling potentially embarrassing moments was legendary around the office; when one of her clients broke a piece of her best crystal, she coolly picked up her own goblet and hurled it into the fireplace.

**apocalyptic** ADJ. prophetic; pertaining to revelations. The crowd jeered at the street preacher's *apocalyptic* predictions of doom. The *Apocalypse* or *Book of Revelations* of Saint John prophesies the end of the world as we know it and foretells marvels and prodigies that signal the coming doom. apocalypse, N.

**apocryphal** ADJ. untrue; made up. To impress his friends, Tom invented *apocryphal* tales of his adventures in the big city.

**apogee** N. highest point. When the moon in its orbit is furthest away from the earth, it is at its *apogee*.

**apolitical** ADJ. having an aversion or lack of concern for political affairs. It was hard to remain *apolitical* during the Vietnam War; even people who generally ignored public issues felt they had to take political stands.

**apologist** N. one who writes in defense of a cause or institution. Rather than act as an *apologist* for the current regime in Beijing and defend its brutal actions, the young diplomat decided to defect to the West.

**apostate** N. one who abandons his religious faith or political beliefs. Because he switched from one party to another, his former friends shunned him as an *apostate*. apostasy, N.

**apothecary** N. druggist. In Holland, *apothecaries* still sell spices as well as ointments and pills.

# Test

## Word List 3 *Antonyms*

Each of the questions below consists of a word in capital letters, followed by five lettered words or phrases. Choose the lettered word or phrase that is most nearly opposite in meaning to the word in capital letters and write the letter of your choice on your answer paper.

31. AMICABLE (A) penetrating (B) compensating (C) unfriendly (D) zigzag (E) inescapable
32. AMORAL (A) unusual (B) unfriendly (C) ethical (D) suave (E) firm
33. AMORPHOUS (A) nauseous (B) obscene (C) providential (D) definite (E) happy
34. AMPLIFY (A) distract (B) infer (C) publicize (D) decrease (E) pioneer
35. ANALOGOUS (A) not comparable (B) not capable (C) not culpable (D) not corporeal (E) not congenial
36. ANATHEMATIZE (A) locate (B) deceive (C) regulate (D) radiate (E) bless

37. ANEMIC (A) pallid (B) cruel (C) red-blooded (D) ventilating (E) hazardous
38. ANIMATED (A) worthy (B) dull (C) humorous (D) lengthy (E) realistic
39. ANIMUS (A) pterodactyl (B) bastion (C) giraffe (D) grimace (E) favor
40. ANOMALY (A) desperation (B) requisition (C) registry (D) regularity (E) radiation
41. ANONYMOUS (A) desperate (B) signed (C) defined (D) expert (E) written
42. ANTEDILUVIAN (A) transported (B) subtle (C) isolated (D) celebrated (E) modern
43. ANTIPATHY (A) profundity (B) objection (C) willingness (D) abstention (E) fondness
44. ANTITHESIS (A) velocity (B) maxim (C) similarity (D) acceleration (E) reaction
45. APHASIA (A) volubility (B) necessity (C) pain (D) crack (E) prayer

# Word List 4    apothegm-astigmatism

**apothegm** N. pithy, compact saying. Proverbs are *apothegms* that have become familiar sayings.

**apotheosis** N. elevation to godhood; an ideal example of something. The *apotheosis* of a Roman emperor was designed to ensure his eternal greatness: people would worship at his altar forever. The hero of the novel *Generation X* was the *apotheosis* of a slacker, the quintessential example of a member of his generation.

**appall** V. dismay; shock. We were *appalled* by the horrifying conditions in the city's jails.

**apparition** N. ghost; phantom. On the castle battlements, an *apparition* materialized and spoke to Hamlet, warning him of his uncle's treachery. In *Ghostbusters*, hordes of *apparitions* materialized, only to be dematerialized by the specialized apparatus wielded by Bill Murray.

■ **appease** V. pacify or soothe; relieve. Tom and Jody tried to *appease* the crying baby by offering him one toy after another. However, he would not calm down until they *appeased* his hunger by giving him a bottle. appeasement, N.

**appellation** N. name; title. Macbeth was startled when the witches greeted him with an incorrect *appellation*. Why did they call him Thane of Cawdor, he wondered, when the holder of that title still lived?

**append** V. attach. When you *append* a bibliography to a text, you have created an *appendix*.

**application** N. diligent attention. Pleased with how well Tom had whitewashed the fence, Aunt Polly praised him for his *application*. (secondary meaning) apply, V.

**apposite** ADJ. appropriate; fitting. She was always able to find the *apposite* phrase, the correct expression for every occasion.

**appraise** V. estimate value of. It is difficult to *appraise* old paintings; it is easier to call them priceless. appraisal, N.

**appreciate** V. be thankful for; increase in worth; be thoroughly conscious of. Little Orphan Annie truly *appreciated* the stocks Daddy Warbucks gave her, whose value *appreciated* considerably over the years.

**apprehend** V. arrest (a criminal); dread; perceive. The police will *apprehend* the culprit and convict him before long.

**apprehensive** ADJ. fearful; discerning. His *apprehensive* glances at the people who were walking in the street revealed his nervousness.

■ **apprise** V. inform. When she was *apprised* of the dangerous weather conditions, she decided to postpone her trip.

■ **approbation** N. approval. Wanting her parents' regard, she looked for some sign of their *approbation*.

■ **appropriate** V. acquire; take possession of for one's own use. The ranch owners *appropriated* the lands that had originally been set aside for the Indians' use.

**appurtenances** N. subordinate possessions. He bought the estate and all its *appurtenances*.

**apropos** PREP. with reference to; regarding. I find your remarks *apropos* of the present situation timely and pertinent. also ADJ. and ADV.

**aptitude** N. fitness; talent. The counselor evaluated his *aptitudes* before advising him about the career he should follow.

**aquiline** ADJ. curved, hooked. He can be recognized by his *aquiline* nose, curved like the beak of the eagle.

**arable** ADJ. fit for growing crops. The first settlers wrote home glowing reports of the New World, praising its vast acres of *arable* land ready for the plow.

**arbiter** N. person with power to decide a matter in dispute; judge. As an *arbiter* in labor disputes, she has won the confidence of the workers and the employers.

**arbitrary** ADJ. unreasonable or capricious; tyrannical. The coach claimed the team lost because the umpire made some *arbitrary* calls.

**arbitrate** V. act as judge. She was called upon to *arbitrate* the dispute between the union and the management.

**arboretum** N. place where different varieties of trees and shrubs are studied and exhibited. Walking along the treelined paths of the *arboretum*, Rita noted poplars, firs, and some particularly fine sycamores.

**arcade** N. a covered passageway, usually lined with shops. The *arcade* was popular with shoppers because it gave them protection from the summer sun and the winter rain.

**arcane** ADJ. secret; mysterious; known only to the initiated. Secret brotherhoods surround themselves with *arcane* rituals and trappings to mystify outsiders. So do doctors. Consider the *arcane* terminology they use and the impression they try to give that what is *arcane* to us is obvious to them.

**archaeology** N. study of artifacts and relics of early mankind. The professor of *archaeology* headed an expedition to the Gobi Desert in search of ancient ruins.

**archaic** ADJ. antiquated. "Methinks," "thee," and "thou" are *archaic* words that are no longer part of our normal vocabulary.

**archetype** N. prototype; primitive pattern. The Brooklyn Bridge was the *archetype* of the many spans that now connect Manhattan with Long Island and New Jersey.

**archipelago** N. group of closely located islands. When he looked at the map and saw the *archipelagoes* in the South Seas, he longed to visit them.

**archives** N. public records; place where public records are kept. These documents should be part of the *archives* so that historians may be able to evaluate them in the future.

**ardor** N. heat; passion; zeal. Katya's *ardor* was contagious; soon all her fellow demonstrators were busily making posters and handing out flyers, inspired by her *ardent* enthusiasm for the cause. ardent, ADJ.

■ **arduous** ADJ. hard; strenuous. Her *arduous* efforts had sapped her energy.

**argot** N. slang. In the *argot* of the underworld, she "was taken for a ride."

**aria** N. operatic solo. At her Metropolitan Opera audition, Marian Anderson sang an *aria* from *Norma*.

**arid** ADJ. dry; barren. The cactus has adapted to survive in an *arid* environment.

**aristocracy** N. hereditary nobility; privileged class. Americans have mixed feelings about hereditary *aristocracy*: we say all men are created equal, but we describe particularly outstanding people as natural *aristocrats*.

**armada** N. fleet of warships. Queen Elizabeth's navy was able to defeat the mighty *armada* that threatened the English coast.

**aromatic** ADJ. fragrant. Medieval sailing vessels brought *aromatic* herbs from China to Europe.

**arraign** V. charge in court; indict. After his indictment by the Grand Jury, the accused man was *arraigned* in the County Criminal Court.

**array** V. marshal; draw up in order. His actions were bound to *array* public sentiment against him. also N.

**array** V. clothe; adorn. She liked to watch her mother *array* herself in her finest clothes before going out for the evening. also N.

**arrears** N. being in debt. He was in *arrears* with his payments on the car.

**arrhythmic** ADJ. lacking rhythm or regularity. The doctors feared his *arrhythmic* heartbeat might be the first symptom of an imminent heart attack. arrhythmia, N.

**arrogance** N. pride; haughtiness. Convinced that Emma thought she was better than anyone else in the class, Ed rebuked her for her *arrogance*.

**arroyo** N. gully. Until the heavy rains of the past spring, this *arroyo* had been a dry bed.

**arsenal** N. storage place for military equipment. People are forbidden to smoke in the *arsenal* lest a stray spark set off the munitions stored there.

**articulate** ADJ. effective; distinct. Her *articulate* presentation of the advertising campaign impressed her employers. also V.

**artifact** N. object made by human beings, either handmade or mass-produced. Archaeologists debated the significance of the *artifacts* discovered in the ruins of Asia Minor but came to no conclusion about the culture they represented.

**artifice** N. deception; trickery. The Trojan War proved to the Greeks that cunning and *artifice* were often more effective than military might.

**artisan** N. a manually skilled worker. Artists and *artisans* alike are necessary to the development of a culture.

■ **artless** ADJ. without guile; open and honest. Red Riding Hood's *artless* comment, "Grandma, what big eyes you have!" indicates the child's innocent surprise at her "grandmother's" changed appearance.

**ascendancy** N. controlling influence. President Marcos failed to maintain his *ascendancy* over the Philippines.

**ascertain** V. find out for certain. Please *ascertain* her present address.

■ **ascetic** ADJ. practicing self-denial; austere. The wealthy, self-indulgent young man felt oddly drawn to the strict, *ascetic* life led by members of some monastic orders. also N. asceticism, N.

**ascribe** V. refer; attribute; assign. I can *ascribe* no motive for her acts.

**aseptic** ADJ. preventing infection; having a cleansing effect. Hospitals succeeded in lowering the mortality rate as soon as they introduced *aseptic* conditions.

**ashen** ADJ. ash-colored; deadly pale. Her face was *ashen* with fear.

**asinine** ADJ. stupid. Your *asinine* remarks prove that you have not given this problem any serious consideration.

**askance** ADV. with a sideways or indirect look. Looking *askance* at her questioner, she displayed her scorn.

**askew** ADV. crookedly; slanted; at an angle. When the clown placed his hat *askew* upon his head, the children in the audience laughed.

**asperity** N. sharpness (of temper). These remarks, spoken with *asperity*, stung the boys to whom they had been directed.

**aspersion** N. slanderous remark. Do not cast *aspersions* on her character.

**aspirant** N. seeker after position or status. Although I am an *aspirant* for public office, I am not willing to accept the dictates of the party bosses. also ADJ.

**aspire** V. seek to attain; long for. Because he *aspired* to a career in professional sports, Philip enrolled in a graduate program in sports management. aspiration, N.

**assail** V. assault. He was *assailed* with questions after his lecture.

**assay** V. analyze; evaluate. When they *assayed* the ore, they found that they had discovered a very rich vein. also N.

**assent** V. agree; accept. It gives me great pleasure to *assent* to your request. also N.

**assert** V. state strongly or positively; insist on or demand recognition of (rights, claims, etc.). When Jill *asserted* that nobody else in the junior class had such an early curfew, her parents *asserted* themselves, telling her that if she didn't get home by nine o'clock she would be grounded for the week. assertion, N.

**assessment** N. estimation; appraisal. I would like to have your *assessment* of the situation in South Africa.

■ **assiduous** ADJ. diligent. It took Rembrandt weeks of *assiduous* labor before he was satisfied with his portrait of his son.

**assimilate** V. absorb; cause to become homogenous. The manner in which the United States was able to *assimilate* the hordes of immigrants during the nineteenth and early part of the twentieth centuries will always be a source of pride.

■ **assuage** V. ease or lessen (pain); satisfy (hunger); soothe (anger). Jilted by Jane, Dick tried to *assuage* his heartache by indulging in ice cream. One gallon later, he had *assuaged* his appetite but not his grief. assuagement, N.

**assumption**   N. something taken for granted; the taking over or taking possession of. The young princess made the foolish *assumption* that the regent would not object to her *assumption* of power. assume, v.

**assurance**   N. promise or pledge; certainty; self-confidence. When Guthrie gave Guinness his *assurance* that rehearsals were going well, he spoke with such *assurance* that Guinness was convinced. assure, v. assured, ADJ.

**asteroid**   N. small planet. *Asteroids* have become commonplace to the readers of interstellar travel stories in science fiction magazines.

**astigmatism**   N. eye defect that prevents proper focus. As soon as his parents discovered that the boy suffered from *astigmatism*, they took him to the optometrist for corrective glasses.

# Test

## Word List 4    *Synonyms and Antonyms*

Each of the questions below consists of a word in capital letters, followed by five lettered words or phrases. Choose the lettered word or phrase that is most nearly similar or opposite in meaning to the word in capital letters and write the letter of your choice on your answer paper.

46. APPEASE (A) agitate (B) qualify (C) display (D) predestine (E) interrupt
47. APPOSITE (A) inappropriate (B) diagonal (C) exponential (D) unobtrusive (E) discouraging
48. APPREHEND (A) obviate (B) set free (C) shiver (D) understand (E) contrast
49. APTITUDE (A) sarcasm (B) inversion (C) adulation (D) lack of talent (E) gluttony
50. AQUILINE (A) watery (B) hooked (C) refined (D) antique (E) rodentlike
51. ARCHAIC (A) youthful (B) cautious (C) antiquated (D) placated (E) buttressed

52. ARDOR (A) zeal (B) paint (C) proof (D) group (E) excitement
53. ARRAY (A) swindle (B) lighten (C) strip bare (D) set free (E) cleanse
54. ARROYO (A) crevice (B) gully (C) value (D) food (E) fabric
55. ARTIFICE (A) spite (B) exception (C) anger (D) candor (E) loyalty
56. ARTISAN (A) educator (B) decider (C) sculptor (D) discourser (E) unskilled laborer
57. ASCERTAIN (A) amplify (B) master (C) discover (D) retain (E) explode
58. ASPERITY (A) anguish (B) absence (C) innuendo (D) good temper (E) snake
59. ASSUAGE (A) stuff (B) describe (C) wince (D) worsen (E) introduce
60. ASTEROID (A) Milky Way (B) radiance (C) large planet (D) rising moon (E) setting moon

## Word List 5    astral-barb

**astral**   ADJ. relating to the stars. She was amazed at the number of *astral* bodies the new telescope revealed.

**astringent**   ADJ. binding; causing contraction; harsh or severe. The *astringent* quality of the unsweetened lemon juice made swallowing difficult. also N.

**astronomical**   ADJ. enormously large or extensive. The government seemed willing to spend *astronomical* sums on weapons development.

**astute**   ADJ. wise; shrewd; keen. The painter was an *astute* observer, noticing every tiny detail of her model's appearance and knowing exactly how important each one was.

**asunder**   ADV. into parts; apart. A fierce quarrel split the partnership *asunder*; the two partners finally sundered their connections because their points of view were poles *asunder*.

**asylum**   N. place of refuge or shelter; protection. The refugees sought *asylum* from religious persecution in a new land.

**asymmetric**   ADJ. not identical on both sides of a dividing central line. Because one eyebrow was set markedly higher than the other, William's face had a particularly *asymmetric* appearance. asymmetry, N.

**atavism**   N. resemblance to remote ancestors rather than to parents; reversion to an earlier type; throwback. In his love for gardening, Martin seemed an *atavism* to his Tuscan ancestors who lavished great care on their small plots of soil. atavistic, ADJ.

**atheistic**   ADJ. denying the existence of God. His *atheistic* remarks shocked the religious worshippers.

**atone**   V. make amends for; pay for. He knew no way in which he could *atone* for his brutal crime.

**atrocity**   N. brutal deed. In time of war, many *atrocities* are committed by invading armies.

**atrophy**   N. wasting away. Polio victims need physiotherapy to prevent the *atrophy* of affected limbs. also v.

**attentive**   ADJ. alert and watchful; considerate; thoughtful. Spellbound, the *attentive* audience watched the final game of the tennis match, never taking their eyes from the ball. A cold wind sprang up; Stan's *attentive* daughter slipped a sweater over his shoulders without distracting his attention from the game.

■ **attenuate**   V. make thin; weaken. By withdrawing their forces, the generals hoped to *attenuate* the enemy lines.

**attest** V. testify; bear witness. Having served as a member of a grand jury, I can *attest* that our system of indicting individuals is in need of improvement.

**attribute** N. essential quality. His outstanding *attribute* was his kindness.

**attribute** V. ascribe; explain. I *attribute* her success in science to the encouragement she received from her parents.

**attrition** N. gradual decrease in numbers; reduction in the work force without firing employees; wearing away of opposition by means of harassment. In the 1960s urban churches suffered from *attrition* as members moved from the cities to the suburbs. Rather than fire staff members, church leaders followed a policy of *attrition*, allowing elderly workers to retire without replacing them.

**atypical** ADJ. not normal. The child psychiatrist reassured Mrs. Keaton that playing doctor was not *atypical* behavior for a child of young Alex's age. "Perhaps not," she replied, "but charging for house calls is!"

■ **audacious** ADJ. daring; bold. Audiences cheered as Luke Skywalker and Princess Leia made their *audacious*, death-defying leap to freedom and escaped Darth Vader's troops. audacity, N.

**audit** N. examination of accounts. When the bank examiners arrived to hold their annual *audit*, they discovered the embezzlements of the chief cashier. also v.

**augment** V. increase; add to. Armies *augment* their forces by calling up reinforcements; teachers *augment* their salaries by taking odd jobs.

**augury** N. omen; prophecy. He interpreted the departure of the birds as an *augury* of evil. augur, v.

**august** ADJ. impressive; majestic. Visiting the palace at Versailles, she was impressed by the *august* surroundings in which she found herself.

**aureole** N. sun's corona; halo. Many medieval paintings depict saintly characters with *aureoles* around their heads.

**auroral** ADJ. pertaining to the aurora borealis. The *auroral* display was particularly spectacular that evening.

**auspicious** ADJ. favoring success. With favorable weather conditions, it was an *auspicious* moment to set sail. Thomas, however, had doubts about sailing: a paranoid, he became suspicious whenever conditions seemed *auspicious*.

■ **austere** ADJ. forbiddingly stern; severely simple and unornamented. The headmaster's *austere* demeanor tended to scare off the more timid students, who never visited his study willingly. The room reflected the man, *austere* and bare, like a monk's cell, with no touches of luxury to moderate its *austerity*.

**authenticate** V. prove genuine. An expert was needed to *authenticate* the original Van Gogh painting, distinguishing it from its imitation.

**authoritarian** ADJ. subordinating the individual to the state; completely dominating another's will. The leaders of the *authoritarian* regime ordered the suppression of the democratic protest movement. After years of submitting to the will of her *authoritarian* father, Elizabeth Barrett ran away from home with the poet Robert Browning.

**authoritative** ADJ. having the weight of authority; peremptory and dictatorial. Impressed by the young researcher's well-documented presentation, we accepted her analysis of the experiment as *authoritative*.

**autocratic** ADJ. having absolute, unchecked power; dictatorial. A person accustomed to exercising authority may become *autocratic* if his or her power is unchecked. Dictators by definition are *autocrats*. Bosses who dictate behavior as well as letters can be *autocrats* too. autocracy, N.

**automaton** N. mechanism that imitates actions of humans. Long before science fiction readers became aware of robots, writers were creating stories of *automatons* who could outperform humans.

■ **autonomous** ADJ. self-governing. Although the University of California at Berkeley is just one part of the state university system, in many ways Cal Berkeley is *autonomous*, for it runs several programs that are not subject to outside control. autonomy, N.

**autopsy** N. examination of a dead body; postmortem. The medical examiner ordered an *autopsy* to determine the cause of death. also v.

**auxiliary** ADJ. offering or providing help; additional or subsidiary. To prepare for the emergency, they built an *auxiliary* power station. also N.

**avalanche** N. great mass of falling snow and ice. The park ranger warned the skiers to stay on the main trails, where they would be in no danger of being buried beneath a sudden *avalanche*.

**avarice** N. greediness for wealth. King Midas is a perfect example of *avarice*; he was so greedy that he wished everything he touched would turn to gold.

**avenge** V. take vengeance for something (or on behalf of someone). Hamlet vowed he would *avenge* his father's murder and punish Claudius for his horrible crime.

■ **aver** V. state confidently. I wish to *aver* that I am certain of success.

**averse** ADJ. reluctant; disinclined. The reporter was *averse* to revealing the sources of his information.

**aversion** N. firm dislike. Bert had an *aversion* to yuppies; Alex had an *aversion* to punks. Their mutal *aversion* was so great that they refused to speak to one another.

**avert** V. prevent; turn away. She *averted* her eyes from the dead cat on the highway.

**aviary** N. enclosure for birds. The *aviary* at the zoo held nearly 300 birds.

**avid** ADJ. greedy; eager for. He was *avid* for learning and read everything he could get. avidity, N.

**avocation** N. secondary or minor occupation. His hobby proved to be so fascinating and profitable that gradually he abandoned his regular occupation and concentrated on his *avocation*.

**avow** V. declare openly. Lana *avowed* that she never meant to steal Debbie's boyfriend, but no one believed her *avowal* of innocence.

**avuncular** ADJ. like an uncle. *Avuncular* pride did not prevent him from noticing his nephew's shortcomings.

**awe** N. solemn wonder. The tourists gazed with *awe* at the tremendous expanse of the Grand Canyon.

**awl** N. pointed tool used for piercing. She used an *awl* to punch additional holes in the leather belt she had bought.

**awry** ADV. distorted; crooked. He held his head *awry*, giving the impression that he had caught cold in his neck during the night. also ADJ.

**axiom** N. self-evident truth requiring no proof. Before a student can begin to think along the lines of Euclidean geometry, he must accept certain principles or *axioms*. axiomatic, ADJ.

**azure** ADJ. sky blue. *Azure* skies are indicative of good weather.

**babble** V. chatter idly. The little girl *babbled* about her doll. also N.

**bacchanalian** ADJ. drunken. Emperor Nero attended the *bacchanalian* orgy.

**badger** V. pester; annoy. She was forced to change her telephone number because she was *badgered* by obscene phone calls.

**badinage** N. teasing conversation. Her friends at work greeted the news of her engagement with cheerful *badinage*.

**baffle** V. frustrate; perplex. The new code *baffled* the enemy agents.

**bait** V. harass; tease. The school bully *baited* the smaller children, terrorizing them.

**baleful** ADJ. deadly; having a malign influence; ominous. The fortune teller made *baleful* predictions of terrible things to come.

**balk** V. stop short, as if faced with an obstacle, and refuse to continue. The chief of police *balked* at sending his officers into the riot-torn area.

**balk** V. foil. When the warden learned that several inmates were planning to escape, he took steps to *balk* their attempt.

**ballast** N. heavy substance used to add stability or weight. The ship was listing badly to one side; it was necessary to shift the *ballast* in the hold to get her back on an even keel. also v.

**balm** N. something that relieves pain. Friendship is the finest *balm* for the pangs of disappointed love.

**balmy** ADJ. mild; fragrant. A *balmy* breeze refreshed us after the sultry blast.

■ **banal** ADJ. hackneyed; commonplace; trite; lacking originality. The hack writer's worn-out clichés made his comic sketch seem *banal*. He even resorted to the *banality* of having someone slip on a banana peel!

**bandy** V. discuss lightly or glibly; exchange (words) heatedly. While the president was happy to *bandy* patriotic generalizations with anyone who would listen to him, he refused to *bandy* words with unfriendly reporters at the press conference.

**bane** N. cause of ruin; curse. Lucy's little brother was the *bane* of her existence: his attempts to make her life miserable worked so well that she could have poisoned him with ratsbane for having such a *baneful* effect.

**bantering** ADJ. good-naturedly ridiculing. They resented his *bantering* remarks because they misinterpreted his teasing as sarcasm.

**barb** N. sharp projection from fishhook or other object; openly cutting remark. If you were a politician, which would you prefer, being caught on the *barb* of a fishhook or being subjected to malicious verbal *barbs*? Who can blame the president if he's happier fishing than he is listening to his critics' *barbed* remarks?

# Test

## Word List 5  *Synonyms*

Each of the questions below consists of a word in capital letters, followed by five lettered words or phrases. Choose the lettered word or phrase that is most nearly similar in meaning to the word in capital letters and write the letter of your choice on your answer paper.

61. ASTUTE (A) sheer (B) noisy (C) astral (D) unusual (E) clever
62. ATROCITY (A) endurance (B) fortitude (C) session (D) heinous act (E) hatred
63. ATROPHY (A) capture (B) waste away (C) govern (D) award prize (E) defeat
64. ATTENUATE (A) appear (B) be absent (C) weaken (D) testify (E) soothe
65. ATYPICAL (A) superfluous (B) fortitude (C) unusual (D) clashing (E) lovely
66. AUDACITY (A) boldness (B) asperity (C) strength (D) stature (E) anchorage

67. AUGMENT (A) make noble (B) anoint (C) increase (D) harvest (E) reach
68. AUXILIARY (A) righteous (B) prospective (C) assistant (D) archaic (E) mandatory
69. AVARICE (A) easiness (B) greed (C) statement (D) invoice (E) power
70. AVERT (A) entertain (B) transform (C) turn away (D) lead toward (E) displease
71. AWRY (A) recommended (B) commiserating (C) startled (D) crooked (E) psychological
72. BALEFUL (A) doubtful (B) virtual (C) deadly (D) conventional (E) virtuous
73. BALMY (A) venturesome (B) dedicated (C) mild (D) fanatic (E) memorable
74. BANAL (A) philosophical (B) trite (C) dramatic (D) heedless (E) discussed
75. BANEFUL (A) intellectual (B) thankful (C) decisive (D) poisonous (E) remorseful

# Word List 6    bard-bluff

**bard** N. poet. The ancient *bard* Homer sang of the fall of Troy.

**barefaced** ADJ. shameless; bold; unconcealed. Shocked by Huck Finn's *barefaced* lies, Miss Watson prayed the good Lord would give him a sense of his unregenerate wickedness.

**baroque** ADJ. highly ornate. Accustomed to the severe, angular lines of modern skyscrapers, they found the flamboyance of *baroque* architecture amusing.

**barrage** N. barrier laid down by artillery fire; overwhelming profusion. The company was forced to retreat through the *barrage* of heavy cannons.

**barrister** N. counselor-at-law. Galsworthy started as a *barrister*, but, when he found the practice of law boring, turned to writing.

**barterer** N. trader. The *barterer* exchanged trinkets for the natives' furs.

**bask** V. luxuriate; take pleasure in warmth. *Basking* on the beach, she relaxed so completely that she fell asleep.

**bastion** N. stronghold; something seen as a source of protection. The villagers fortified the town hall, hoping this improvised *bastion* could protect them from the guerrilla raids.

**bate** V. let down; restrain. Until it was time to open the presents, the children had to *bate* their curiosity. bated, ADJ.

**bauble** N. trinket; trifle. The child was delighted with the *bauble* she had won in the grab bag.

**bawdy** ADJ. indecent; obscene. Jack took offense at Jill's *bawdy* remarks. What kind of young man did she think he was?

**beatific** ADJ. giving bliss; blissful. The *beatific* smile on the child's face made us very happy.

**beatitude** N. blessedness; state of bliss. Growing closer to God each day, the mystic achieved a state of indescribable *beatitude*.

**bedizen** V. dress with vulgar finery. The witch doctors were *bedizened* in their gaudiest costumes.

**bedraggle** V. wet thoroughly. We were so *bedraggled* by the severe storm that we had to change into dry clothing. bedraggled, ADJ.

**beeline** N. direct, quick route. As soon as the movie was over, Jim made a *beeline* for the exit.

**befuddle** V. confuse thoroughly. His attempts to clarify the situation succeeded only in *befuddling* her further.

**beget** V. father; produce; give rise to. One good turn may deserve another; it does not necessarily *beget* another.

**begrudge** V. resent. I *begrudge* every minute I have to spend attending meetings.

**beguile** V. mislead or delude; cheat; pass time. With flattery and big talk of easy money, the con men *beguiled* Kyle into betting his allowance on the shell game. The men quickly *beguiled* poor Kyle of his money. Broke, he *beguiled* himself during the long hours by playing solitaire.

**behemoth** N. huge creature; something of monstrous size or power. Sportscasters nicknamed the linebacker "The *Behemoth*."

**beholden** ADJ. obligated; indebted. Since I do not wish to be *beholden* to anyone, I cannot accept this favor.

**behoove** V. be suited to; be incumbent upon. In this time of crisis, it *behooves* all of us to remain calm and await the instructions of our superiors.

**belabor** V. explain or go over excessively or to a ridiculous degree; assail verbally. The debate coach warned her student not to bore the audience by *belaboring* his point.

**belated** ADJ. delayed. He apologized for his *belated* note of condolence to the widow of his friend and explained that he had just learned of her husband's untimely death.

**beleaguer** V. besiege or attack; harass. The babysitter was surrounded by a crowd of unmanageable brats who relentlessly *beleaguered* her.

■ **belie** V. contradict; give a false impression. His coarse, hard-bitten exterior *belied* his innate sensitivity.

**belittle** V. disparage; deprecate. Parents should not *belittle* their children's early attempts at drawing, but should encourage their efforts.

**bellicose** ADJ. warlike. His *bellicose* disposition alienated his friends. bellicosity, N.

**belligerent** ADJ. quarrelsome. Whenever he had too much to drink, he became *belligerent* and tried to pick fights with strangers. belligerence, N.

**bemoan** V. lament; express disapproval of. The widow *bemoaned* the death of her beloved husband. Although critics *bemoaned* the serious flaws in the author's novels, each year his latest book topped the best-seller list.

**bemused** ADJ. confused; lost in thought; preoccupied. Jill studied the garbled instructions with a *bemused* look on her face.

**benediction** N. blessing. The appearance of the sun after the many rainy days was like a *benediction*.

**benefactor** N. gift giver; patron. Scrooge later became Tiny Tim's *benefactor* and gave him gifts.

■ **beneficent** ADJ. kindly; doing good. The overgenerous philanthropist had to curb his *beneficent* impulses before he gave away all his money and left himself with nothing.

**beneficial** ADJ. helpful; useful. Tiny Tim's cheerful good nature had a *beneficial* influence on Scrooge's once-uncharitable disposition.

**beneficiary** N. person entitled to benefits or proceeds of an insurance policy or will. In Scrooge's will, he made Tiny Tim his *beneficiary*: everything he left would go to young Tim.

**benevolent** ADJ. generous; charitable. Mr. Fezziwig was a *benevolent* employer who wished to make Christmas merrier for young Scrooge and his other employees. benevolence, N.

**benign** ADJ. kindly; favorable; not malignant. Though her *benign* smile and gentle bearing made Miss Marple seem a sweet little old lady, in reality she was a tough-minded, shrewd observer of human nature. benignity, N.

**benison** N. blessing. Let us pray that the *benison* of peace once more shall prevail among the nations of the world.

**bent** ADJ.; N. determined; natural talent or inclination. *Bent* on advancing in the business world, the secretary-heroine of *Working Girl* had a true *bent* for high finance.

**bequeath** V. leave to someone by means of a will; hand down. In his will, Father *bequeathed* his watch to Philip; the *bequest* meant a great deal to the boy. bequest, N.

**berate** V. scold strongly. He feared she would *berate* him for his forgetfulness.

**bereavement** N. state of being deprived of something valuable or beloved. His friends gathered to console him upon his sudden *bereavement*.

**bereft** ADJ. deprived of; lacking. The foolish gambler soon found himself *bereft* of funds.

**berserk** ADV. frenzied. Angered, he went *berserk* and began to wreck the room.

**beseech** V. beg; plead with. The workaholic executive's wife *beseeched* him to spend more time with their son.

**beset** V. harass or trouble; hem in. Many vexing problems *beset* the American public school system. Sleeping Beauty's castle was *beset* on all sides by dense thickets that hid it from view.

**besiege** V. surround with armed forces; harass (with requests). When the bandits *besieged* the village, the villagers holed up in the town hall and prepared to withstand a long siege. Members of the new administration were *besieged* with job applications from people who had worked on the campaign.

**besmirch** V. soil, defile. The scandalous remarks in the newspaper *besmirch* the reputations of every member of the society.

**bestial** ADJ. beastlike; brutal; inhuman. According to legend, the werewolf was able to abandon its human shape and assume a *bestial* form. The Red Cross sought to put an end to the *bestial* treatment of prisoners of war.

**bestow** V. confer. He wished to *bestow* great honors upon the hero.

**betoken** V. signify; indicate. The well-equipped docks, tall piles of cargo containers, and numerous vessels being loaded all *betoken* Oakland's importance as a port.

**betray** V. be unfaithful; reveal (unconsciously or unwillingly). The spy *betrayed* his country by selling military secrets to the enemy. When he was taken in for questioning, the tightness of his lips *betrayed* his fear of incriminating himself. betrayal, N.

**betroth** V. become engaged to marry. The announcement that they had become *betrothed* surprised their friends who had not suspected any romance. betrothal, N.

**bevy** N. large group. The movie actor was surrounded by a *bevy* of starlets.

**bicameral** ADJ. two-chambered, as a legislative body. The United States Congress is a *bicameral* body.

**bicker** V. quarrel. The children *bickered* morning, noon and night, exasperating their parents.

**biennial** ADJ. every two years. Seeing no need to meet more frequently, the group held *biennial* meetings instead of annual ones. Plants that bear flowers *biennially* are known as *biennials*.

**bifurcated** ADJ. divided into two branches; forked. With a *bifurcated* branch and a piece of elastic rubber, he made a crude but effective slingshot.

**bigotry** N. stubborn intolerance. Brought up in a democratic atmosphere, the student was shocked by the *bigotry* and narrowness expressed by several of his classmates.

**bilious** ADJ. suffering from indigestion; irritable. His *bilious* temperament was apparent to all who heard him rant about his difficulties.

**bilk** V. swindle; cheat. The con man specialized in *bilking* insurance companies.

**billowing** ADJ. swelling out in waves; surging. Standing over the air vent, Marilyn Monroe tried vainly to control her *billowing* skirts.

**bivouac** N. temporary encampment. While in *bivouac*, we spent the night in our sleeping bags under the stars. also v.

**bizarre** ADJ. fantastic; violently contrasting. The plot of the novel was too *bizarre* to be believed.

**blanch** V. bleach; whiten. Although age had *blanched* his hair, he was still vigorous and energetic.

**bland** ADJ. soothing or mild; agreeable. Jill tried a *bland* ointment for her sunburn. However, when Jack absent-mindedly patted her on the sunburned shoulder, she couldn't maintain her *bland* persona. blandness, N.

**blandishment** N. flattery. Despite the salesperson's *blandishments*, the customer did not buy the outfit.

**blare** N. loud, harsh roar or screech; dazzling blaze of light. I don't know which is worse: the steady *blare* of a boom box deafening your ears or a sudden *blare* of flashbulbs dazzling your eyes. also v.

**blasé** ADJ. bored with pleasure or dissipation. Although Beth was as thrilled with the idea of a trip to Paris as her classmates were, she tried to act supercool and *blasé*, as if she'd been abroad hundreds of times.

**blasphemy** N. irreverence; sacrilege; cursing. In my father's house, the Dodgers were the holiest of holies; to cheer for another team was to utter words of *blasphemy*. blasphemous, ADJ.

**blatant** ADJ. extremely obvious; loudly offensive. Caught in a *blatant* lie, the scoundrel had only one regret: he wished that he had lied more subtly. blatancy, N.

**bleak** ADJ. cold or cheerless; unlikely to be favorable. The frigid, inhospitable Aleutian Islands are *bleak* military outposts. It's no wonder that soldiers assigned there have a *bleak* attitude toward their posting.

**blighted** ADJ. suffering from a disease; destroyed. The extent of the *blighted* areas could be seen only when viewed from the air.

**blithe** ADJ. gay; joyous. Shelley called the skylark a "*blithe* spirit" because of its happy song.

**bloated** ADJ. swollen or puffed as with water or air. Her *bloated* stomach came from drinking so much water.

**blowhard** N. talkative boaster. After all Sol's talk about his big show business connections led nowhere, Sally decided he was just another *blowhard*.

**bludgeon** N. club; heavy-headed weapon. Attacked by Dr. Moriarty, Holmes used his walking stick as a *bludgeon* to defend himself. "Watson," he said. "I fear I may have *bludgeoned* Moriarty to death."

**bluff** ADJ. rough but good-natured. Jack had a *bluff* and hearty manner that belied his actual sensitivity; he never let people know how thin-skinned he really was.

**bluff** N. pretense (of strength); deception; high cliff. Claire thought Lord Byron's boast that he would swim the Hellespont was just a *bluff*; she was astounded when he dove from the high *bluff* into the waters below.

# Test

## Word List 6    *Antonyms*

Each of the questions below consists of a word in capital letters, followed by five lettered words or phrases. Choose the lettered word or phrase that is most nearly opposite in meaning to the word in capital letters and write the letter of your choice on your answer paper.

76. BAROQUE (A) polished (B) constant (C) transformed (D) simple (E) aglow
77. BEATIFIC (A) glorious (B) dreadful (C) theatrical (D) crooked (E) handsome
78. BELITTLE (A) disobey (B) forget (C) magnify (D) extol (E) envy
79. BELLICOSE (A) peaceful (B) naval (C) amusing (D) piecemeal (E) errant
80. BENIGN (A) tenfold (B) peaceful (C) blessed (D) wavering (E) malignant
81. BENISON (A) curse (B) bachelor (C) wedding (D) orgy (E) tragedy
82. BERATE (A) grant (B) praise (C) refer (D) purchase (E) deny
83. BESTIAL (A) animated (B) noble (C) zoological (D) clear (E) dusky
84. BIGOTRY (A) arrogance (B) approval (C) mourning (D) promptness (E) tolerance
85. BIZARRE (A) roomy (B) veiled (C) subdued (D) triumphant (E) normal
86. BLANCH (A) bleach (B) scatter (C) darken (D) analyze (E) subdivide
87. BLAND (A) caustic (B) meager (C) soft (D) uncooked (E) helpless
88. BLASÉ (A) fiery (B) clever (C) intriguing (D) slim (E) ardent
89. BLEAK (A) pale (B) sudden (C) dry (D) narrow (E) cheerful
90. BLITHE (A) spiritual (B) profuse (C) cheerless (D) hybrid (E) comfortable

## Word List 7    blunder-canter

**blunder** N. error. The criminal's fatal *blunder* led to his capture. also v.

**blurt** V. utter impulsively. Before she could stop him, he *blurted* out the news.

**bluster** V. blow in heavy gusts; threaten emptily; bully. "Let the stormy winds *bluster*," cried Jack, "we'll set sail tonight." Jill let Jack *bluster*: she wasn't going anywhere, no matter what he said. also N.

**bode** V. foreshadow; portend. The gloomy skies and the sulfurous odors from the mineral springs seemed to *bode* evil to those who settled in the area.

**bogus** ADJ. counterfiet; not authentic. The police quickly found the distributors of the *bogus* twenty-dollar bills.

**bohemian** ADJ. unconventional (in an artistic way). Gertrude Stein ran off to Paris to live an eccentric, *bohemian* life with her writer friends. Oakland was not *bohemian*: it was too bourgeois, too middle-class.

**boisterous** ADJ. violent; rough; noisy. The unruly crowd became even more *boisterous* when he tried to quiet them.

■ **bolster** V. support; reinforce. The debaters amassed file boxes full of evidence to *bolster* their arguments.

**bolt** N. door bar; fastening pin or screw; length of fabric. The carpenter shut the workshop door, sliding the heavy metal *bolt* into place. He sorted through his toolbox for the nuts and *bolts* and nails required for the job. Before he cut into the *bolt* of canvas, he measured how much fabric he would need.

**bolt** V. dash or dart off; fasten (a door); gobble down. Jack was set to *bolt* out the front door, but Jill *bolted* the door. "Eat your breakfast," she said, "don't *bolt* your food."

**bombardment** N. attack (as with missiles). The enemy *bombardment* demolished the town. Members of the opposition party *bombarded* the prime minister with questions about the enemy attack.

■ **bombastic** ADJ. pompous; using inflated language. Puffed up with conceit, the orator spoke in such a *bombastic* manner that we longed to deflate him. bombast, N.

**boon** N. blessing; benefit. The recent rains that filled our empty reservoirs were a *boon* to the whole community.

■ **boorish** ADJ. rude; insensitive. Though Mr. Potts constantly interrupted his wife, she ignored his *boorish* behavior, for she had lost hope of teaching him courtesy.

**bouillon** N. clear beef soup. The cup of *bouillon* served by the stewards was welcomed by those who had been chilled by the cold ocean breezes.

**bountiful** ADJ. abundant; graciously generous. Thanks to the good harvest, we had a *bountiful* supply of food and we could be as *bountiful* as we liked in distributing food to the needy.

**bourgeois** ADJ. middle class; selfishly materialistic; dully conventional. Technically, anyone who belongs to the middle class is *bourgeois*, but, given the word's connotations, most people resent it if you call them that.

**bovine** ADJ. cowlike; placid and dull. Nothing excites Esther; even when she won the state lottery, she still preserved her air of *bovine* calm.

**bowdlerize** V. expurgate. After the film editors had *bowdlerized* the language in the script, the motion picture's rating was changed from "R" to "PG."

**boycott** V. refrain from buying or using. To put pressure on grape growers to stop using pesticides that harmed the farm workers' health, Cesar Chavez called for consumers to *boycott* grapes. also N.

**brackish** ADJ. somewhat saline. He found the only wells in the area were *brackish*; drinking the water made him nauseous.

**braggadocio** N. boasting. He was disliked because his manner was always full of *braggadocio*.

**braggart** N. boaster. Modest by nature, she was no *braggart*, preferring to let her accomplishments speak for themselves.

**brandish** V. wave around; flourish. Alarmed, Doctor Watson wildly *brandished* his gun until Holmes told him to put the thing away before he shot himself.

**bravado** N. swagger; assumed air of defiance. The *bravado* of the young criminal disappeared when he was confronted by the victims of his brutal attack.

**brawn** N. muscular strength; sturdiness. It takes *brawn* to become a champion weight-lifter. brawny, ADJ.

**brazen** ADJ. insolent. Her *brazen* contempt for authority angered the officials.

**breach** N. breaking of contract or duty; fissure or gap. Jill sued Jack for *breach* of promise, claiming he had broken their engagement. The attackers found a *breach* in the enemy's fortifications and penetrated their lines. also V.

**breadth** N. width; extent. We were impressed by the *breadth* of her knowledge.

**brevity** N. conciseness. *Brevity* is essential when you send a telegram or cablegram; you are charged for every word.

**brindled** ADJ. tawny or grayish with streaks or spots. He was disappointed in the litter because the puppies were *brindled*; he had hoped for animals of a uniform color.

**bristling** ADJ. rising like bristles; showing irritation. The dog stood there, *bristling* with anger.

**brittle** ADJ. easily broken; difficult. My employer's *brittle* personality made it difficult for me to get along with her.

**broach** V. introduce; open up. Jack did not even try to *broach* the subject of religion with his in-laws. If you *broach* a touchy subject, the result may be a *breach*.

**brocade** N. rich, figured fabric. The sofa was covered with expensive *brocade*.

**brochure** N. pamphlet. This *brochure* of farming was issued by the Department of Agriculture.

**brooch** N. ornamental clasp. She treasured the *brooch* because it was an heirloom.

**brook** V. tolerate; endure. The dean would *brook* no interference with his disciplinary actions. (secondary meaning)

**browbeat** V. bully; intimidate. Billy resisted Ted's attempts to *browbeat* him into handing over his lunch money.

**browse** V. graze; skim or glance at casually. "How now, brown cow, *browsing* in the green, green grass." I remember lines of verse that I came across while *browsing* through the poetry section of the local bookstore.

**brunt** N. main impact or shock. Tom Sawyer claimed credit for painting the fence, but the *brunt* of the work fell on others. However, Tom bore the *brunt* of Aunt Polly's complaints when the paint began to peel.

**brusque** ADJ. blunt; abrupt. She was offended by his *brusque* reply.

**buccaneer** N. pirate. At Disneyland the Pirates of the Caribbean sing a song about their lives as bloody *buccaneers*.

**bucolic** ADJ. rustic; pastoral. Filled with browsing cows and bleating sheep, the meadow was a charmingly *bucolic* sight.

**buffet** N. table with food set out for people to serve themselves; meal at which people help themselves to food that's been set out. (*Buffet* rhymes with *tray*.) Please convey the soufflé on the tray to the *buffet*.

**buffet** V. slap; batter; knock about. To *buffet* something is to rough it up. (*Buffet* rhymes with *Muffett*.) Was Miss Muffett *buffeted* by the crowd on the way to the buffet tray?

**buffoonery** N. clowning. In the Ace Ventura movies, Jim Carrey's *buffoonery* was hilarious: like Bozo the Clown, he's a natural *buffoon*.

**bugaboo** N. bugbear; object of baseless terror. If we become frightened by such *bugaboos*, we are no wiser than the birds who fear scarecrows.

**bullion** N. gold and silver in the form of bars. Much *bullion* is stored in the vaults at Fort Knox.

**bulwark** N. earthwork or other strong defense; person who defends. The navy is our principal *bulwark* against invasion.

**bungle** V. mismanage; blunder. Don't botch this assignment, Bumstead; if you *bungle* the job, you're fired!

**buoyant** ADJ. able to float; cheerful and optimistic. When the boat capsized, her *buoyant* life jacket kept Jody afloat. Scrambling back on board, she was still in a *buoyant* mood, certain that despite the delay she'd win the race. buoyancy, N.

**bureaucracy** N. overregulated administrative system marked by red tape. The Internal Revenue Service is the ultimate *bureaucracy*: taxpayers wasted so much paper filling out IRS forms that the IRS *bureaucrats* printed up a new set of rules requiring taxpayers to comply with the Paperwork Reduction Act. bureaucratic, ADJ.

■ **burgeon** V. grow forth; send out buds. In the spring, the plants that *burgeon* are a promise of the beauty that is to come.

**burlesque** V. give an imitation that ridicules. In *Galaxy Quest*, Alan Rickman *burlesques* Mr. Spock of *Star Trek*, outrageously parodying Spock's unemotional manner and stiff bearing. also N.

■ **burnish** V. make shiny by rubbing; polish. The maid *burnished* the brass fixtures until they reflected the lamp-light.

■ **buttress** V. support; prop up. Just as architects *buttress* the walls of cathedrals with flying *buttresses*, debaters *buttress* their arguments with facts. also N.

**buxom** ADJ. full-bosomed; plump; jolly. High-fashion models usually are slender rather than *buxom*.

**cabal** N. small group of persons secretly united to promote their own interests. The *cabal* was defeated when its scheme was discovered.

**cache** N. hiding place. The detectives followed the suspect until he led them to the *cache* where he had stored his loot. also v.

■ **cacophonous** ADJ. discordant; inharmonious. Do the students in the orchestra enjoy the *cacophonous* sounds they make when they're tuning up? I don't know how they can stand the racket. cacophony, N.

**cadaver** N. corpse. In some states, it is illegal to dissect *cadavers*.

**cadaverous** ADJ. like a corpse; pale. From his *cadaverous* appearance, we could see how the disease had ravaged him.

**cadence** N. rhythmic rise and fall (of words or sounds); beat. Marching down the road, the troops sang out, following the *cadence* set by the sergeant.

**cajole** V. coax; wheedle. Cher tried to *cajole* her father into letting her drive the family car. cajolery, N.

**calamity** N. disaster; misery. As news of the *calamity* spread, offers of relief poured in to the stricken community.

**calculated** ADJ. deliberately planned; likely. Lexy's choice of clothes to wear to the debate tournament was carefully *calculated*. Her conventional suit was *calculated* to appeal to the conservative judges.

**caldron** N. large kettle. "Why, Mr. Crusoe," said the savage heating the giant *caldron*, "we'd love to have you for dinner!"

**caliber** N. ability; quality. Einstein's cleaning the blackboards again? Albert, quit it! A man of your *caliber* shouldn't have to do such menial tasks.

**calligraphy** N. beautiful writing; excellent penmanship. As we examine ancient manuscripts, we become impressed with the *calligraphy* of the scribes.

**callous** ADJ. hardened; unfeeling. He had worked in the hospital for so many years that he was *callous* to the suffering in the wards. callus, N.

**callow** ADJ. youthful; immature; inexperienced. As a freshman, Jack was sure he was a man of the world; as a sophomore, he made fun of freshmen as *callow* youths. In both cases, his judgment showed just how *callow* he was.

**calorific** ADJ. heat-producing. Coal is much more *calorific* than green wood.

**calumny** N. malicious misrepresentation; slander. He could endure his financial failure, but he could not bear the *calumny* that his foes heaped upon him.

**camaraderie** N. good-fellowship. What he loved best about his job was the sense of *camaraderie* he and his coworkers shared.

**cameo** N. shell or jewel carved in relief; star's special appearance in a minor role in a film. Don't bother buying *cameos* from the street peddlers in Rome: the carvings they sell are clumsy jobs. Did you enjoy Bill Murray's *cameo* in *Little Shop of Horrors*? He was onscreen for only a minute, but he cracked me up.

**camouflage** V. disguise; conceal. In order to rescue Han Solo, Princess Leia *camouflaged* herself in the helmet and cloak of a space bandit. also N.

**canard** N. unfounded rumor; exaggerated report. It is almost impossible to protect oneself from such a base *canard*.

**candor** N. frankness; open honesty. Jack can carry *candor* too far: when he told Jill his honest opinion of her, she nearly slapped his face. candid, ADJ.

**canine** ADJ. related to dogs; doglike. Some days the *canine* population of Berkeley seems almost to outnumber the human population.

**canker** N. any ulcerous sore; any evil. Poverty is a *canker* in the body politic; it must be cured.

**canny** ADJ. shrewd; thrifty. The *canny* Scotsman was more than a match for the swindlers.

**canon** N. collection or authoritative list of books (e.g., by an author, or accepted as scripture); rule or standard set by ecclesiastical authority. Scholars hotly debated whether the newly discovered sonnet should be accepted as part of the Shakespearean *canon*.

**cant** N. insincere expressions of piety; jargon of thieves. Shocked by news of the minister's extramarital love affairs, the worshippers dismissed his talk about the sacredness of marriage as mere *cant*. *Cant* is a form of hypocrisy: those who can, pray; those who *cant*, pretend.

**cantankerous** ADJ. ill-humored; irritable. Constantly complaining about his treatment and refusing to cooperate with the hospital staff, he was a *cantankerous* patient.

**cantata** N. story set to music, to be sung by a chorus. The choral society sang the new *cantata* composed by its leader.

**canter** N. slow gallop. Because the racehorse had outdistanced its competition so easily, the reporter wrote that the race was won in a *canter*. also v.

# Test

## Word List 7    *Synonyms*

Each of the questions below consists of a word in capital letters, followed by five lettered words or phrases. Choose the lettered word or phrase that is most nearly similar in meaning to the word in capital letters and write the letter of your choice on your answer paper.

91. BOISTEROUS (A) conflicting (B) noisy (C) testimonial (D) grateful (E) adolescent
92. BOMBASTIC (A) sensitive (B) pompous (C) rapid (D) sufficient (E) expensive
93. BOORISH (A) brave (B) oafish (C) romantic (D) speedy (E) dry
94. BOUILLON (A) insight (B) chowder (C) gold (D) clear soup (E) stew
95. BRACKISH (A) careful (B) salty (C) chosen (D) tough (E) wet
96. BRAGGADOCIO (A) weaponry (B) boasting (C) skirmish (D) encounter (E) position
97. BRAZEN (A) shameless (B) quick (C) modest (D) pleasant (E) melodramatic
98. BRINDLED (A) equine (B) pathetic (C) hasty (D) spotted (E) mild tasting
99. BROCHURE (A) opening (B) pamphlet (C) censor (D) bureau (E) pin
100. BUCOLIC (A) diseased (B) repulsive (C) rustic (D) twinkling (E) cold
101. BUXOM (A) voluminous (B) indecisive (C) convincing (D) plump (E) bookish
102. CACHE (A) lock (B) hiding place (C) tide (D) automobile (E) grappling hook
103. CACOPHONY (A) discord (B) dance (C) applause (D) type of telephone (E) rooster
104. CALLOW (A) youthful (B) holy (C) mild (D) colored (E) seated
105. CANDID (A) vague (B) outspoken (C) experienced (D) anxious (E) sallow

## Word List 8    canto-chameleon

**canto** N. division of a long poem. Dante's poetic masterpiece *The Divine Comedy* is divided into *cantos*.

**canvass** V. determine or seek opinions, votes, etc. After *canvassing* the sentiments of his constituents, the congressman was confident that he represented the majority opinion of his district. also N.

**capacious** ADJ. spacious. In the *capacious* areas of the railroad terminal, thousands of travelers lingered while waiting for their trains.

**capacity** N. mental or physical ability; role; ability to accommodate. Mike had the *capacity* to handle several jobs at once. In his *capacity* as president of SelecTronics he marketed an electronic dictionary with a *capacity* of 200,000 words.

**capillary** ADJ. having a very fine bore. The changes in surface tension of liquids in *capillary* vessels is of special interest to physicists. also N.

**capitulate** V. surrender. The enemy was warned to *capitulate* or face annihilation.

**caprice** N. whim. She was an unpredictable creature, acting on *caprice*, never taking thought of the consequences.

■ **capricious** ADJ. unpreditable; fickle. The storm was *capricious*: it changed course constantly. Jill was *capricious*, too: she changed boyfriends almost as often as she changed clothes.

**caption** N. title; chapter heading; text under illustration. The *captions* that accompany *The Far Side* cartoons are almost as funny as the pictures. also v.

**captious** ADJ. faultfinding. His criticisms were always *captious* and frivolous, never offering constructive suggestions.

**carafe** N. glass water bottle; decanter. With each dinner, the patron receives a *carafe* of red or white wine.

**carapace** N. shell covering the back (of a turtle, crab, etc.). At the children's zoo, Richard perched on top of the giant turtle's hard *carapace* as the creature slowly made its way around the enclosure.

**carat** N. unit of weight for precious stones; measure of fineness of gold. He gave her a diamond that weighed three *carats* and was mounted in an eighteen-*carat* gold band.

**carcinogenic** ADJ. causing cancer. Many supposedly harmless substances have been revealed to be *carcinogenic*.

**cardinal** ADJ. chief. If you want to increase your word power, the *cardinal* rule of vocabulary-building is to read.

**cardiologist** N. doctor specializing in ailments of the heart. When the pediatrician noticed Philip had a slight heart murmur, she referred him to a *cardiologist* for further tests.

**careen** V. lurch; sway from side to side. The taxicab *careened* wildly as it rounded the corner.

**caricature** N. distortion; burlesque. The *caricatures* he drew always emphasized personal weaknesses of the people he burlesqued. also v.

**carillon** N. a set of bells capable of being played. The *carillon* in the bell tower of the Coca-Cola pavilion at the New York World's Fair provided musical entertainment every hour.

**carnage** N. destruction of life. The film *The Killing Fields* vividly depicts the *carnage* wreaked by Pol Pot's followers in Cambodia.

**carnal** ADJ. fleshly. Is the public more interested in *carnal* pleasures than in spiritual matters? Compare the number of people who read *Playboy* daily to the number of those who read the Bible every day.

**carnivorous** ADJ. meat-eating. The lion's a *carnivorous* beast; a hunk of meat makes up his feast. A cow is not a *carnivore*; she likes the taste of grain, not gore.

**carousal** N. drunken revel. The party degenerated into an ugly *carousal*.

**carping** N. petty criticism; fault-finding. Welcoming constructive criticism, Lexy appreciated her editor's comments, finding them free of *carping*. also ADJ.

**carrion** N. rotting flesh of a dead body. Buzzards are nature's scavengers; they eat the *carrion* left behind by other predators.

**cartographer** N. map-maker. Though not a professional *cartographer*, Tolkien was able to construct a map of his fictional world.

**cascade** N. small waterfall. We were too tired to appreciate the beauty of the many *cascades* because we had to detour around them to avoid being drenched by the torrents *cascading* down.

**caste** N. one of the hereditary classes in Hindu society, social stratification; prestige. The differences created by *caste* in India must be wiped out if true democracy is to prevail in that country.

■ **castigation** N. punishment; severe criticism. Sensitive even to mild criticism, Woolf could not bear the *castigation* that she found in certain reviews. castigate, v.

**casualty** N. serious or fatal accident. The number of automotive *casualties* on this holiday weekend was high.

**cataclysm** N. deluge; upheaval. A *cataclysm* such as the French Revolution affects all countries. cataclysmic, ADJ.

■ **catalyst** N. agent that brings about a chemical change while it remains unaffected and unchanged. Many chemical reactions cannot take place without the presence of a *catalyst*.

**catapult** N. slingshot; hurling machine. Airplanes are sometimes launched from battleships by *catapults*. also V.

**cataract** N. great waterfall; eye abnormality. She gazed with awe at the mighty *cataract* known as Niagara Falls.

**catastrophe** N. calamity; disaster. The 1906 San Francisco earthquake was a *catastrophe* that destroyed most of the city. A similar earthquake striking today could have even more *catastrophic* results.

**catcall** N. shout of disapproval; boo. Every major league pitcher has off days during which he must learn to ignore *catcalls* and angry hisses from the crowd.

**catechism** N. book for religious instruction; instruction by question and answer. He taught by engaging his pupils in a *catechism* until they gave him the correct answer.

**categorical** ADJ. without exceptions; unqualified; absolute. Though the captain claimed he was never, never sick at sea, he finally qualified his *categorical* denial: he was "hardly ever" sick at sea.

**catharsis** N. purging or cleansing of any passage of the body. Aristotle maintained that tragedy created a *catharsis* by purging the soul of base concepts.

**cathartic** N. purgative. Some drugs act as laxatives when taken in small doses but act as *cathartics* when taken in much larger doses. also ADJ.

**catholic** ADJ. universal; wide-ranging liberal. He was extremely *catholic* in his taste and read everything he could find in the library.

**caucus** N. private meeting of members of a party to select officers or determine policy. At the opening of Congress the members of the Democratic Party held a *caucus* to elect the majority leader of the House and the party whip.

**caulk** V. to make watertight (by plugging seams). When water from the shower leaked into the basement, we knew it was time to *caulk* the tiles at the edges of the shower stall.

**causal** ADJ. implying a cause-and-effect relationship. The psychologist maintained there was a *causal* relationship between the nature of one's early childhood experiences and one's adult personality. causality, N.

■ **caustic** ADJ. burning; sarcastically biting. The critic's *caustic* remarks angered the hapless actors who were the subjects of his sarcasm.

**cauterize** V. burn with hot iron or caustic. In order to prevent infection, the doctor *cauterized* the wound.

**cavalcade** N. procession; parade. As described by Chaucer, the *cavalcade* of Canterbury pilgrims was a motley group.

**cavalier** ADJ. casual and offhand; arrogant. Sensitive about having her ideas taken lightly, Marcia felt insulted by Mark's *cavalier* dismissal of her suggestion.

**cavil** V. make frivolous objections. I respect your sensible criticisms, but I dislike the way you *cavil* about unimportant details. also N.

**cede** V. yield (title, territory) to; surrender formally. Eventually the descendants of England's Henry II were forced to *cede* their French territories to the King of France. cession, N.

**celerity** N. speed; rapidity. Hamlet resented his mother's *celerity* in remarrying within a month after his father's death.

**celestial** ADJ. heavenly. She spoke of the *celestial* joys that awaited virtuous souls in the hereafter.

**celibate** ADJ. abstaining from sexual intercourse; unmarried. Though the late Havelock Ellis wrote extensively about sexual customs and was considered an expert in such matters, recent studies maintain he was *celibate* throughout his life. celibacy, N.

**censor** N. overseer of morals; person who eliminates inappropriate matter. Soldiers dislike having their mail read by a *censor* but understand the need for this precaution. also v.

**censorious** ADJ. critical. *Censorious* people delight in casting blame.

**censure** v. blame; criticize. The senator was *censured* for behavior inappropriate to a member of Congress. also N.

**centaur** N. mythical figure, half man and half horse. I was particularly impressed by the statue of the *centaur* in the Roman Hall of the museum.

**centigrade** ADJ. denoting a widely used temperature scale (basically same as Celsius). On the *centigrade* thermometer, the freezing point of water is zero degrees.

**centrifugal** ADJ. radiating; departing from the center. Many automatic drying machines remove excess moisture from clothing by *centrifugal* force.

**centrifuge** N. machine that separates substances by whirling them. At the dairy, we employ a *centrifuge* to separate cream from milk. also v.

**centripetal** ADJ. tending toward the center. Does *centripetal* force or the force of gravity bring orbiting bodies to the earth's surface?

**centurion** N. Roman army officer. Because he was in command of a company of one hundred soldiers, he was called a *centurion*.

**cerebral** ADJ. pertaining to the brain or intellect. The content of philosophical works is *cerebral* in nature and requires much thought.

**cerebration** N. thought. Mathematics problems sometimes require much *cerebration*.

**ceremonious** ADJ. marked by formality. Ordinary dress would be inappropriate at so *ceremonious* an affair.

**certitude** N. certainty. Though there was no *certitude* of his getting the job, Lou thought he had a good chance of being hired.

**cessation** N. stoppage. The airline's employees threatened a *cessation* of all work if management failed to meet their demands. cease, v.

**cession** N. yielding to another; ceding. The *cession* of Alaska to the United States is discussed in this chapter.

**chafe** v. warm by rubbing; make sore (by rubbing). Chilled, he *chafed* his hands before the fire. The collar of his school uniform *chafed* Tom's neck, but not as much the school's strict rules *chafed* his spirit. also N.

**chaff** N. worthless products of an endeavor. When you separate the wheat from the *chaff*, be sure you throw out the *chaff*.

**chaffing** ADJ. bantering; joking. Sometimes Chad's flippant, *chaffing* remarks annoy us. Still, Chad's *chaffing* keeps us laughing.

**chagrin** N. vexation (caused by humiliation or injured pride); disappointment. Embarrassed by his parents' shabby, working-class appearance, Doug felt their visit to his school would bring him nothing but *chagrin*. A person filled with *chagrin* doesn't grin: he's too mortified.

**chalice** N. goblet; consecrated cup. In a small room adjoining the cathedral, many ornately decorated *chalices* made by the most famous European goldsmiths were on display.

**chameleon** N. lizard that changes color in different situations. Like the *chameleon*, he assumed the political coloration of every group he met.

# Test

## Word List 8 *Antonyms*

Each of the questions below consists of a word in capital letters, followed by five lettered words or phrases. Choose the lettered word or phrase that is most nearly opposite in meaning to the word in capital letters and write the letter of your choice on your answer paper.

106. CAPACIOUS (A) warlike (B) cordial (C) curious (D) not spacious (E) not capable

107. CAPRICIOUS (A) satisfied (B) insured (C) photographic (D) scattered (E) steadfast

108. CAPTIOUS (A) tolerant (B) capable (C) frivolous (D) winning (E) recollected

109. CARNAL (A) impressive (B) minute (C) spiritual (D) actual (E) private

110. CARNIVOROUS (A) gloomy (B) tangential (C) productive (D) weak (E) vegetarian

111. CARPING (A) rapid (B) uncritical (C) unintellectual (D) illegal (E) terse

112. CASTIGATION (A) commendation (B) patience (C) generosity (D) understatement (E) honesty

113. CATEGORICAL (A) negative (B) ironic (C) impartial (D) qualified (E) permanent

114. CATHOLIC (A) religious (B) pacific (C) narrow (D) weighty (E) funny

115. CELERITY (A) assurance (B) state (C) acerbity (D) delay (E) infamy

116. CELIBATE (A) investing (B) married (C) retired (D) commodious (E) dubious

117. CENSURE (A) process (B) enclose (C) interest (D) praise (E) penetrate

118. CENTRIFUGAL (A) centripetal (B) ephemeral (C) lasting (D) barometric (E) algebraic

119. CESSATION (A) premium (B) gravity (C) beginning (D) composition (E) apathy

120. CHAFFING (A) achieving (B) serious (C) capitalistic (D) sneezing (E) expensive

# Word List 9　　champion-colander

**champion** V. support militantly. Martin Luther King, Jr., won the Nobel Peace Prize because he *championed* the oppressed in their struggle for equality. also N.

**chaotic** ADJ. in utter disorder. He tried to bring order into the *chaotic* state of affairs. chaos, N.

**charisma** N. divine gift; great popular charm or appeal. Political commentators have deplored the importance of a candidate's *charisma* in these days of television campaigning.

**charlatan** N. quack; pretender to knowledge. When they realized that the Wizard didn't know how to get them back to Kansas, Dorothy and her friends were sure they'd been duped by a *charlatan*.

**chary** ADJ. cautious; sparing or restrained about giving. A prudent, thrifty New Englander, DeWitt was as *chary* of investing money in junk bonds as he was *chary* of paying people unnecessary compliments.

**chase** V. ornament a metal surface by indenting. With his hammer, he carefully *chased* an intricate design onto the surface of the chalice. (secondary meaning)

**chasm** N. abyss. They could not see the bottom of the *chasm*.

**chassis** N. framework and working parts of an automobile. Examining the car after the accident, the owner discovered that the body had been ruined but that the *chassis* was unharmed.

**chaste** ADJ. pure; virginal; modest. To ensure that his bride would stay *chaste* while he was off to the wars, the crusader had her fitted out with a *chastity* belt. chastity, N.

**chasten** V. discipline; punish in order to correct. Whom God loves, God *chastens*.

**chastise** V. punish. I must *chastise* you for this offense.

**chauvinist** N. blindly devoted patriot; zealous adherent of a group or cause. A *chauvinist* cannot recognize any faults in his country, no matter how flagrant they may be. Likewise, a male *chauvinist* cannot recognize how biased he is in favor of his own sex, no matter how flagrant that bias may be. chauvinistic, ADJ.

**check** V. stop motion; curb or restrain. Thrusting out her arm, Grandma *checked* Bobby's lunge at his sister. "Young man," she said, "you'd better *check* your temper." (secondary meaning)

**checkered** ADJ. marked by changes in fortune. During his *checkered* career he had lived in palatial mansions and in dreary boardinghouses.

**cherubic** ADJ. angelic; innocent-looking. With her cheerful smile and rosy cheeks, she was a particularly *cherubic* child.

■ **chicanery** N. trickery; deception. Those sneaky lawyers misrepresented what occurred, made up all sorts of implausible alternative scenarios to confuse the jurors, and in general depended on *chicanery* to win the case.

**chide** V. scold. Grandma began to *chide* Steven for his lying.

**chimerical** ADJ. fantastically improbable; highly unrealistic; imaginative. As everyone expected, Ted's *chimerical* scheme to make a fortune by raising ermines in his backyard proved a dismal failure. chimera, N.

**chisel** N. wedgelike tool for cutting. With his hammer and *chisel*, the sculptor chipped away at the block of marble.

**chisel** V. swindle or cheat; cut with a chisel. That crook *chiseled* me out of a hundred dollars when he sold me that "marble" statue he'd *chiseled* out of some cheap hunk of rock.

**chivalrous** ADJ. courteous; faithful; brave. *Chivalrous* behavior involves noble words and good deeds.

**choleric** ADJ. hot-tempered. His flushed, angry face indicated a *choleric* nature.

**choreography** N. art of representing dances in written symbols; arrangement of dances. Merce Cunningham uses a computer in designing *choreography*: a software program allows him to compose arrangements of possible moves and immediately view them onscreen.

**chortle** V. chuckle with delight. When she heard that her rival had just been jailed for embezzlement, she *chortled* with joy. She was *not* a nice lady.

**chronic** ADJ. long established, as a disease. The doctors were finally able to attribute his *chronic* headaches and nausea to traces of formaldehyde gas in his apartment.

**chronicle** V. report; record (in chronological order). The gossip columnist was paid to *chronicle* the latest escapades of the socially prominent celebrities. also N.

**churlish** ADJ. boorish; rude. Dismayed by his *churlish* manners at the party, the girls vowed never to invite him again.

**ciliated** ADJ. having minute hairs. The paramecium is a *ciliated*, one-celled animal.

**cipher** N. nonentity; worthless person or thing. She claimed her ex-husband was a total *cipher* and wondered why she had ever married him.

**cipher** N. secret code. Lacking his code book, the spy was unable to decode the message sent to him in *cipher*.

**circlet** N. small ring; band. This tiny *circlet* is very costly because it is set with precious stones.

**circuitous** ADJ. roundabout. Because of the traffic congestion on the main highways, she took a *circuitous* route. circuit, N.

**circumlocution** N. indirect or roundabout expression. He was afraid to call a spade a spade and resorted to *circumlocutions* to avoid direct reference to his subject.

**circumscribe** V. limit; confine. Although I do not wish to *circumscribe* your activities, I must insist that you complete this assignment before you start anything else.

**circumspect**  ADJ. prudent; cautious. Investigating before acting, she tried always to be *circumspect*.

**circumvent**  V. outwit; baffle. In order to *circumvent* the enemy, we will make two preliminary attacks in other sections before starting our major campaign.

**cistern**  N. reservoir or water tank. The farmers were able to withstand the dry season by using rainwater they had stored in an underground *cistern*.

**citadel**  N. fortress. The *citadel* overlooked the city like a protecting angel.

**cite**  V. quote; commend. She could *cite* passages in the Bible from memory. citation, N.

**civil**  ADJ. having to do with citizens or the state; courteous and polite. Although Internal Revenue Service agents are *civil* servants, they are not always *civil* to suspected tax evaders.

**clairvoyant**  ADJ., N. having foresight; fortuneteller. Cassandra's *clairvoyant* warning was not heeded by the Trojans. clairvoyance, N.

**clamber**  V. climb by crawling. She *clambered* over the wall.

**clamor**  N. noise. The *clamor* of the children at play outside made it impossible for her to take a nap. also V.

**clandestine**  ADJ. secret. After avoiding their chaperon, the lovers had a *clandestine* meeting.

**clangor**  N. loud, resounding noise. The blacksmith was accustomed to the *clangor* of hammers on steel.

**clapper**  N. striker (tongue) of a bell. Wishing to be undisturbed by the bell, Dale wound his scarf around the *clapper* to muffle its striking.

**clarion**  ADJ. shrill, trumpetlike sound. We woke to the *clarion* call of the bugle.

**claustrophobia**  N. fear of being locked in. His fellow classmates laughed at his *claustrophobia* and often threatened to lock him in his room.

**clavicle**  N. collarbone. Even though he wore shoulder pads, the football player broke his *clavicle* during a practice scrimmage.

**cleave**  V. split or sever; cling to; remain faithful to. With her heavy *cleaver*, Julia Child can *cleave* a whole roast duck in two. Soaked through, the soldier tugged at the uniform that *cleaved* annoyingly to his body. He would *cleave* to his post, come rain or shine. cleavage, N. cloven, ADJ.

**cleft**  N. split. Trying for a fresh handhold, the mountain climber grasped the edge of a *cleft* in the sheer rockface. also ADJ.

**clemency**  N. disposition to be lenient; mildness, as of the weather. The lawyer was pleased when the case was sent to Judge Smith's chambers because Smith was noted for her *clemency* toward first offenders.

**cliché**  N. phrase dulled in meaning by repetition. High school compositions are often marred by such *clichés* as "strong as an ox."

**clientele**  N. body of customers. The rock club attracted a young, stylish *clientele*.

**climactic**  ADJ. relating to the highest point. When he reached the *climactic* portions of the book, he could not stop reading. climax, N.

**clime**  N. region; climate. His doctor advised him to move to a milder *clime*.

**clique**  N. small, exclusive group. Fitzgerald wished that he belonged to the *clique* of popular athletes and big men on campus who seemed to run Princeton's social life.

**cloister**  N. monastery or convent. The nuns lived in the *cloister*.

**clout**  N. great influence (especially political or social). Gatsby wondered whether he had enough *clout* to be admitted to the exclusive club.

**cloying**  ADJ. distasteful (because excessive); excessively sweet or sentimental. Disliking the *cloying* sweetness of standard wedding cakes, Jody and Tom chose a homemade carrot cake for their reception. cloy, V.

■ **coagulate**  V. thicken; congeal; clot. Even after you remove the pudding from the burner, it will continue to *coagulate* as it stands. coagulant, N.

**coalesce**  V. combine; fuse. The brooks *coalesce* into one large river. When minor political parties *coalesce*, their *coalescence* may create a major coalition.

**coalition**  N. partnership; league; union. The Rainbow *Coalition* united people of all races in a common cause.

■ **coda**  N. concluding section of a musical or literary composition. The piece concluded with a distinctive *coda* that strikingly brought together various motifs.

**coddle**  V. treat gently; pamper. Don't *coddle* the children so much; they need a taste of discipline.

**codicil**  N. supplement to the body of a will. Miss Havisham kept her lawyers busy drawing up *codicils* to her already complicated will.

**codify**  V. arrange (laws, rules) as a code; classify. We need to take the varying rules and regulations of the different health agencies and *codify* them into a national health code.

**coercion**  N. use of force to get someone to obey. The inquisitors used both physical and psychological *coercion* to force Joan of Arc to recant her assertions that her visions were sent by God. coerce, V.

**coeval**  ADJ. living at the same time as; contemporary. *Coeval* with the dinosaur, the pterodactyl flourished during the Mesozoic era.

**cog**  N. tooth projecting from a wheel. A bicycle chain moves through a series of *cogs* in order to propel the bike.

■ **cogent**  ADJ. convincing. It was inevitable that David chose to go to Harvard: he had several *cogent* reasons for doing so, including a full-tuition scholarship. Katya argued her case with such *cogency* that the jury had to decide in favor of her client.

**cogitate**  V. think over. *Cogitate* on this problem; the solution will come.

cognate ADJ. related linguistically; allied by blood; similar or akin in nature. The English word "mother" is *cognate* to the Latin word "mater," whose influence is visible in the words "maternal" and "maternity." also N.

cognitive ADJ. having to do with knowing or perceiving related to the mental processes. Though Jack was emotionally immature, his *cognitive* development was admirable; he was very advanced intellectually.

cognizance N. knowledge. During the election campaign, the two candidates were kept in full *cognizance* of the international situation.

cohabit V. live together. Many unwed couples who *cohabit* peacefully for years wind up fighting night and day once they marry.

cohere V. stick together. Solids have a greater tendency to *cohere* than liquids.

cohesion N. tendency to keep together. A firm believer in the maxim "Divide and conquer," the emperor, by lies and trickery, sought to disrupt the *cohesion* of the free nations.

cohorts N. armed band. Caesar and his Roman *cohorts* conquered almost all of the known world.

coiffure N. hairstyle. You can make a statement with your choice of *coiffure*: in the '60's many African-Americans affirmed their racial heritage by wearing their hair in Afros.

coin V. make coins; invent or fabricate. Mints *coin* good money; counterfeiters *coin* fakes. Slanderers *coin* nasty rumors; writers *coin* words. A neologism is a newly *coined* expression.

coincidence N. the chance occurrence, at the same time, of two or more seemingly connected events. Was it just a *coincidence* that John and she had met at the market for three days running, or was he deliberately trying to seek her out? coincidental, ADJ.

colander N. utensil with perforated bottom used for straining. Before serving the spaghetti, place it in a *colander* to drain it.

## Test

## Word List 9    *Synonyms*

Each of the questions below consists of a word in capital letters, followed by five lettered words or phrases. Choose the lettered word or phrase that is most nearly similar in meaning to the word in capital letters and write the letter of your choice on your answer paper.

121. CHASTE (A) loyal (B) timid (C) curt (D) pure (E) outspoken
122. CHIDE (A) unite (B) fear (C) record (D) skid (E) scold
123. CHIMERICAL (A) developing (B) brief (C) distant (D) economical (E) fantastic
124. CHOLERIC (A) musical (B) episodic (C) hotheaded (D) global (E) seasonal
125. CHURLISH (A) marine (B) economical (C) impolite (D) compact (E) young
126. CILIATED (A) foolish (B) swift (C) early (D) constructed (E) hairy
127. CIRCUITOUS (A) indirect (B) complete (C) obvious (D) aware (E) tortured

128. CITE (A) galvanize (B) visualize (C) locate (D) quote (E) signal
129. CLANDESTINE (A) abortive (B) secret (C) tangible (D) doomed (E) approved
130. CLAUSTROPHOBIA (A) lack of confidence (B) fear of spiders (C) love of books (D) fear of grammar (E) fear of closed places
131. CLEFT (A) split (B) waterfall (C) assembly (D) adherence (E) surplus
132. CLICHÉ (A) increase (B) vehicle (C) morale (D) platitude (E) pique
133. COERCE (A) recover (B) begin (C) force (D) license (E) ignore
134. COGNIZANCE (A) policy (B) knowledge (C) advance (D) omission (E) examination
135. COHERE (A) hold together (B) occur simultaneously (C) recollect (D) materialize (E) understand

## Word List 10    collaborate-congenital

collaborate V. work together. Two writers *collaborated* in preparing this book.

collage N. work of art put together from fragments. Scraps of cloth, paper doilies, and old photographs all went into her *collage*.

collate V. examine in order to verify authenticity; arrange in order. They *collated* the newly found manuscripts to determine their age.

collateral N. security given for loan. The sum you wish to borrow is so large that it must be secured by *collateral*.

collation N. a light meal. Tea sandwiches and cookies were offered at the *collation*.

colloquial ADJ. pertaining to conversational or common speech; informal. Some of the new *colloquial* reading passages on standardized tests have a conversational tone intended to make them more appealing to test-takers.

colloquy N. informal discussion. I enjoy our *colloquies*, but I sometimes wish that they could be made more formal and more searching.

collusion N. conspiring in a fraudulent scheme. The swindlers were found guilty of *collusion*.

colossal ADJ. huge. Radio City Music Hall has a *colossal* stage.

**colossus** N. gigantic statue. The legendary *Colossus* of Rhodes, a bronze statue of the sun god that dominated the harbor of the Greek seaport, was one of the Seven Wonders of the World.

**comatose** ADJ. in a coma; extremely sleepy. The long-winded orator soon had his audience in a *comatose* state.

**combustible** ADJ. easily burned. After the recent outbreak of fires in private homes, the fire commissioner ordered that all *combustible* materials be kept in safe containers. also N.

**comely** ADJ. attractive; agreeable. I would rather have a poor and *comely* wife than a rich and homely one.

**comestible** N. something fit to be eaten. The roast turkey and other *comestibles*, the wines, and the excellent service made this Thanksgiving dinner particularly memorable.

**comeuppance** N. rebuke; deserts. After his earlier rudeness, we were delighted to see him get his *comeuppance*.

**comity** N. courtesy; civility. A spirit of *comity* should exist among nations.

**commandeer** V. to draft for military purposes; to take for public use. The policeman *commandeered* the first car that approached and ordered the driver to go to the nearest hospital.

**commemorative** ADJ. remembering; honoring. The new *commemorative* stamp honors the late Martin Luther King, Jr.

■ **commensurate** ADJ. equal in extent. Your reward will be *commensurate* with your effort.

**commiserate** V. feel or express pity or sympathy for. Her friends *commiserated* with the widow.

**commodious** ADJ. spacious and comfortable. After sleeping in small roadside cabins, they found their hotel suite *commodious*.

**communal** ADJ. held in common; a group of people. When they were divorced, they had trouble dividing their *communal* property.

**compact** N. agreement; contract. The signers of the Mayflower *Compact* were establishing a form of government.

**compact** ADJ. tightly packed; firm; brief. His short, *compact* body was better suited to wrestling than to basketball.

**compatible** ADJ. harmonious; in harmony with. They were *compatible* neighbors, never quarreling over unimportant matters. compatibility, N.

**compelling** ADJ. overpowering; irresistible in effect. The prosecutor presented a well-reasoned case, but the defense attorney's *compelling* arguments for leniency won over the jury.

■ **compendium** V. brief, comprehensive summary. This text can serve as a *compendium* of the tremendous amount of new material being developed in this field.

**compensatory** ADJ. making up for; repaying. Can a *compensatory* education program make up for the inadequate schooling he received in earlier years?

**compilation** N. listing of statistical information in tabular or book form. The *compilation* of available scholarships serves a very valuable purpose.

**compile** V. assemble; gather; accumulate. We planned to *compile* a list of the words most frequently used on the GRE.

**complacency** N. self-satisfaction; smugness. Full of *complacency* about his latest victories, he looked smugly at the row of trophies on his mantelpiece. complacent, ADJ.

■ **complaisant** ADJ. trying to please; obliging. The courtier obeyed the king's orders in a *complaisant* manner.

**complement** V. complete; consummate; make perfect. The waiter recommended a glass of port to *complement* the cheese. also N.

**complementary** ADJ. serving to complete something. John's and Lexy's skills are *complementary*: he's good at following a daily routine, while she's great at improvising and handling emergencies. Together they make a great team.

**compliance** N. readiness to yield; conformity in fulfilling requirements. Bullheaded Bill was not noted for his easy *compliance* to the demands of others. As an architect, however, Bill recognized that his design for the new school had to be in *compliance* with the local building code.

■ **compliant** ADJ. yielding; conforming to requirements. Because Joel usually gave in and went along with whatever his friends desired, his mother worried that he might be too *compliant*.

**complicity** N. participation; involvement. You cannot keep your *complicity* in this affair secret very long; you would be wise to admit your involvement immediately.

**component** N. element; ingredient. I wish all the *components* of my stereo system were working at the same time.

**comport** V. bear one's self; behave. He *comported* himself with great dignity.

**composure** N. mental calmness. Even the latest work crisis failed to shake her *composure*.

**compound** V. combine; constitute; pay interest; increase. The makers of the popular cold remedy *compounded* a nasal decongestant with an antihistamine. also N.

**comprehensive** ADJ. thorough; inclusive. This book provides a *comprehensive* review of verbal and math skills for the GRE.

**compress** V. close; squeeze; contract. She *compressed* the package under her arm.

**comprise** V. include; consist of. If the District of Columbia were to be granted statehood, the United States of America would *comprise* fifty-one states, not just fifty.

**compromise** V. adjust or settle by making mutual concessions; endanger the interests or reputation of. Sometimes the presence of a neutral third party can help adversaries *compromise* their differences. Unfortunately, you're not neutral. Therefore, your presence here *compromises* our chances of reaching an agreement. also N.

**compunction** N. remorse. The judge was especially severe in his sentencing because he felt that the criminal had shown no *compunction* for his heinous crime.

**compute** V. reckon; calculate. He failed to *compute* the interest, so his bank balance was not accurate.

**concatenate** V. link as in a chain. It is difficult to understand how these events could *concatenate* as they did without outside assistance.

**concave** ADJ. hollow. The back-packers found partial shelter from the storm by huddling against the *concave* wall of the cliff.

**concede** V. admit; yield. Despite all the evidence Monica had assembled, Mark refused to *concede* that she was right.

**conceit** N. vanity or self-love; whimsical idea; extravagant metaphor. Although Jack was smug and puffed up with *conceit*, he was an entertaining companion, always expressing himself in amusing *conceits* and witty turns of phrase.

**concentric** ADJ. having a common center. The target was made of *concentric* circles.

**conception** N. beginning; forming of an idea. At the first *conception* of the work, he was consulted. conceive, V.

**concerted** ADJ. mutually agreed on; done together. All the Girl Scouts made a *concerted* effort to raise funds for their annual outing. When the movie star appeared, his fans let out a *concerted* sigh.

**concession** N. an act of yielding. Before they could reach an agreement, both sides had to make certain *concessions*.

■ **conciliatory** ADJ. reconciling; soothing. She was still angry despite his *conciliatory* words. conciliate, V.

**concise** ADJ. brief and compact. When you define a new word, be *concise*: the shorter the definition, the easier it is to remember.

**conclave** N. private meeting. He was present at all their *conclaves* as an unofficial observer.

**conclusive** ADJ. decisive; ending all debate. When the stolen books turned up in John's locker, we finally had *conclusive* evidence of the identity of the mysterious thief.

**concoct** V. prepare by combining; make up in concert. How did the inventive chef ever *concoct* such a strange dish? concoction, N.

**concomitant** N. that which accompanies. Culture is not always a *concomitant* of wealth. also ADJ.

**concord** N. harmony. Watching Tweedledum and Tweedledee battle, Alice wondered why the two brothers could not manage to live in *concord*.

**concur** V. agree. Did you *concur* with the decision of the court or did you find it unfair?

**concurrent** ADJ. happening at the same time. In America, the colonists were resisting the demands of the mother country; at the *concurrent* moment in France, the middle class was sowing the seeds of rebellion.

**condescend** V. bestow courtesies with a superior air. The king *condescended* to grant an audience to the friends of the condemned man. condescension, N.

**condign** ADJ. adequate; deservedly severe. The public approved the *condign* punishment for the crime.

**condiments** N. seasonings; spices. Spanish food is full of *condiments*.

**condole** V. express sympathetic sorrow. His friends gathered to *condole* with him over his loss. condolence, N.

■ **condone** V. overlook; forgive; give tacit approval; excuse. Unlike Widow Douglass, who *condoned* Huck's minor offenses, Miss Watson did nothing but scold.

**conducive** ADJ. helpful; contributive. Rest and proper diet are *conducive* to good health.

**conduit** N. aqueduct; passageway for fluids. Water was brought to the army in the desert by an improvised *conduit* from the adjoining mountain.

**confidant** N. trusted friend. He had no *confidants* with whom he could discuss his problems at home.

**confine** V. shut in; restrict. The terrorists had *confined* their prisoner in a small room. However, they had not chained him to the wall or done anything else to *confine* his movements. confinement, N.

**confiscate** V. seize; commandeer. The army *confiscated* all available supplies of uranium.

**conflagration** N. great fire. In the *conflagration* that followed the 1906 earthquake, much of San Francisco was destroyed.

**confluence** N. flowing together; crowd. They built the city at the *confluence* of two rivers.

**conformity** N. harmony; agreement. In *conformity* with our rules and regulations, I am calling a meeting of our organization.

■ **confound** V. confuse; puzzle. No mystery could *confound* Sherlock Holmes for long.

**congeal** V. freeze; coagulate. His blood *congealed* in his veins as he saw the dread monster rush toward him.

**congenial** ADJ. pleasant; friendly. My father loved to go out for a meal with *congenial* companions.

**congenital** ADJ. existing at birth. Doctors are able to cure some *congenital* deformities such as cleft palates by performing operations on infants.

# Test

# Word List 10    *Synonyms and Antonyms*

Each of the following questions consists of a word in capital letters, followed by five lettered words or phrases. Choose the lettered word or phrase that is most nearly similar or opposite in meaning to the word in capital letters and write the letter of your choice on your answer paper.

136. COLLATION (A) furor (B) emphasis (C) distillery (D) spree (E) lunch
137. COLLOQUIAL (A) burnt (B) polished (C) political (D) gifted (E) problematic
138. COLLOQUY (A) dialect (B) diversion (C) announcement (D) discussion (E) expansion

139. COMATOSE (A) cozy (B) restrained (C) alert (D) dumb (E) grim
140. COMBUSTIBLE (A) flammable (B) industrious (C) waterproof (D) specific (E) plastic
141. COMELY (A) yielding (B) unattractive (C) extremely sleepy (D) equal in extent (E) roving
142. COMMISERATE (A) communicate (B) expand (C) repay (D) diminish (E) sympathize
143. COMMODIOUS (A) numerous (B) yielding (C) leisurely (D) limited (E) expensive
144. COMPLIANT (A) numerous (B) veracious (C) soft (D) adamant (E) livid
145. CONCILIATE (A) defend (B) activate (C) integrate (D) quarrel (E) react
146. CONCOCT (A) thrive (B) wonder (C) intrude (D) drink (E) invent
147. CONDONE (A) build (B) evaluate (C) pierce (D) infuriate (E) overlook
148. CONFISCATE (A) discuss (B) discover (C) seize (D) exist (E) convey
149. CONFORMITY (A) agreement (B) ambition (C) confinement (D) pride (E) restraint
150. CONGENITAL (A) slight (B) obscure (C) thorough (D) existing at birth (E) classified

# Word List 11    conglomeration–countermand

**conglomeration** N. mass of material sticking together. In such a *conglomeration* of miscellaneous statistics, it was impossible to find a single area of analysis.

**congruence** N. correspondence of parts; harmonious relationship. The student demonstrated the *congruence* of the two triangles by using the hypotenuse-leg theorem.

**congruent** ADJ. in agreement; corresponding. In formulating a hypothesis, we must keep it *congruent* with what we know of the real world; it cannot disagree with our experience.

**conifer** N. pine tree; cone-bearing tree. According to geologists, the *conifers* were the first plants to bear flowers.

**conjecture** N. surmise; guess. I will end all your *conjectures*; I admit I am guilty as charged. also v.

**conjugal** ADJ. pertaining to marriage. Their dreams of *conjugal* bliss were shattered as soon as their temperaments clashed.

**conjure** V. summon a devil; practice magic; imagine or invent. Sorcerers *conjure* devils to appear. Magicians *conjure* white rabbits out of hats. Political candidates *conjure* up images of reformed cities and a world at peace.

**connivance** N. pretense of ignorance of something wrong; assistance; permission to offend. With the *connivance* of his friends, he plotted to embarrass the teacher. connive, v.

■ **connoisseur** N. person competent to act as a judge of art, etc.; a lover of an art. She had developed into a *connoisseur* of fine china.

**connotation** N. suggested or implied meaning of an expression. Foreigners frequently are unaware of the *connotations* of the words they use.

**connubial** ADJ. pertaining to marriage or the matrimonial state. In his telegram, he wished the newlyweds a lifetime of *connubial* bliss.

**consanguinity** N. kinship. The lawsuit developed into a test of the *consanguinity* of the claimant to the estate.

**conscientious** ADJ. scrupulous; careful. A *conscientious* editor, she checked every definition for its accuracy.

**conscript** N. draftee; person forced into military service. Did Rambo volunteer to fight in Vietnam, or was he a *conscript*, drafted against his will? also v.

**consecrate** V. dedicate; sanctify. We shall *consecrate* our lives to this noble purpose.

**consensus** N. general agreement. The *consensus* indicates that we are opposed to entering into this pact.

**consequential** ADJ. pompous; self-important. Convinced of his own importance, the actor strutted about the dressing room with a *consequential* air.

**conservatory** N. school of the fine arts (especially music or drama). A gifted violinist, Marya was selected to study at the *conservatory*.

**consign** V. deliver officially; entrust; set apart. The court *consigned* the child to her paternal grandmother's care. consignment, N.

**consistency** N. absence of contradictions; dependability; uniformity; degree of thickness. Holmes judged puddings and explanations on their *consistency*: he liked his puddings without lumps and his explanations without improbabilities.

**console** V. lessen sadness or disappointment; give comfort. When her father died, Marius did his best to *console* Cosette. consolation, N.

**consolidation** N. unification; process of becoming firmer or stronger. The recent *consolidation* of several small airlines into one major company has left observers of the industry wondering whether room still exists for the "little guy" in aviation. consolidate, v.

**consonance** N. harmony; agreement. Her agitation seemed out of *consonance* with her usual calm.

**consort** V. associate with. We frequently judge people by the company with whom they *consort*.

**consort** N. husband or wife. The search for a *consort* for the young Queen Victoria ended happily.

**conspiracy** N. treacherous plot. Brutus and Cassius joined in the *conspiracy* to kill Julius Caesar.

**constituent** N. supporter. The congressman received hundreds of letters from angry *constituents* after the Equal Rights Amendment failed to pass.

**constraint** N. compulsion; repression of feelings. There was a feeling of *constraint* in the room because no one dared to criticize the speaker. constrain, v.

**construe** v. explain; interpret. If I *construe* your remarks correctly, you disagree with the theory already advanced.

**consummate** ADJ. complete. I have never seen anyone who makes as many stupid errors as you do; you must be a *consummate* idiot. also v.

**contagion** N. infection. Fearing *contagion*, they took drastic steps to prevent the spread of the disease.

**contaminate** v. pollute. The sewage system of the city so *contaminated* the water that swimming was forbidden.

**contempt** N. scorn; disdain. The heavyweight boxer looked on ordinary people with *contempt*, scorning them as weaklings who couldn't hurt a fly. We thought it was *contemptible* of him to be *contemptuous* of people for being weak.

**contend** v. struggle; compete; assert earnestly. In *Revolt of the Black Athlete*, sociologist Harry Edwards *contends* that young black athletes have been exploited by some college recruiters. contention, N.

■ **contention** N. claim; thesis. It is our *contention* that, if you follow our tactics, you will boost your score on the GRE. contend, v.

■ **contentious** ADJ. quarrelsome. Disagreeing violently with the referees' ruling, the coach became so *contentious* that the referees threw him out of the game.

**contest** v. dispute. The defeated candidate attempted to *contest* the election results.

**context** N. writings preceding and following the passage quoted. Because these lines are taken out of *context*, they do not convey the message the author intended.

**contiguous** ADJ. adjacent to; touching upon. The two countries are *contiguous* for a few miles; then they are separated by the gulf.

**continence** N. self-restraint; sexual chastity. At the convent, Connie vowed to lead a life of *continence*. The question was, could Connie be content with always being *continent*?

**contingent** ADJ. dependent on; conditional. Cher's father informed her that any increase in her allowance was *contingent* on the quality of her final grades. contingency, N.

**contingent** N. group that makes up part of a gathering. The New York *contingent* of delegates at the Democratic National Convention was a boisterous, sometimes rowdy lot.

**contortions** N. twistings; distortions. As the effects of the opiate wore away, the *contortions* of the patient became more violent and demonstrated how much pain she was enduring.

**contraband** N. illegal trade; smuggling; smuggled goods. The Coast Guard tries to prevent *contraband* in U.S. waters. also ADJ.

**contravene** v. contradict; oppose: infringe on or transgress. Mr. Barrett did not expect his frail daughter Elizabeth to *contravene* his will by eloping with Robert Browning.

■ **contrite** ADJ. penitent. Her *contrite* tears did not influence the judge when he imposed sentence. contrition, N.

**contrived** ADJ. forced; artificial; not spontaneous. Feeling ill at ease with his new in-laws, James made a few *contrived* attempts at conversation and then retreated into silence.

**controvert** v. oppose with arguments; attempt to refute; contradict. The witness's testimony was so clear and her reputation for honesty so well established that the defense attorney decided it was wiser to make no attempt to *controvert* what she said.

**contumacious** ADJ. disobedient; resisting authority. The *contumacious* mob shouted defiantly at the police. contumacy, N.

**contusion** N. bruise. Black and blue after her fall, Sue was treated for *contusions* and abrasions.

■ **conundrum** N. riddle; difficult problem. During the long car ride, she invented *conundrums* to entertain the children.

**convene** v. assemble. Because much needed legislation had to be enacted, the governor ordered the legislature to *convene* in special session by January 15.

**convention** N. social or moral custom; established practice. Flying in the face of *convention*, George Sand (Amandine Dudevant) shocked her contemporaries by taking lovers and wearing men's clothes.

**conventional** ADJ. ordinary; typical. His *conventional* upbringing left him wholly unprepared for his wife's eccentric family.

■ **converge** v. approach; tend to meet; come together. African-American men from all over the United States *converged* on Washington to take part in the historic Million Man March. convergence, N.

**conversant** ADJ. familiar with. The lawyer is *conversant* with all the evidence.

**converse** N. opposite. The inevitable *converse* of peace is not war but annihilation.

**convert** N. one who has adopted a different religion or opinion. On his trip to Japan, though the president spoke at length about the merits of American automobiles, he made few *converts* to his beliefs. also v.

**convex** ADJ. curving outward. She polished the *convex* lens of her telescope.

**conveyance** N. vehicle; transfer. During the transit strike, commuters used various kinds of *conveyances*.

**conviction** N. judgment that someone is guilty of a crime; strongly held belief. Even her *conviction* for murder did not shake Lord Peter's *conviction* that Harriet was innocent of the crime.

**convivial** ADJ. festive; gay; characterized by joviality. The *convivial* celebrators of the victory sang their college songs.

**convoke** v. call together. Congress was *convoked* at the outbreak of the emergency. convocation, N.

■ **convoluted** ADJ. coiled around; involved; intricate. His argument was so *convoluted* that few of us could follow it intelligently.

**copious** ADJ. plentiful. She had *copious* reasons for rejecting the proposal.

**coquette** N. flirt. Because she refused to give him an answer to his proposal of marriage, he called her a *coquette*. also v.

**cordial** ADJ. gracious; heartfelt. Our hosts greeted us at the airport with a *cordial* welcome and a hearty hug.

**cordon** N. extended line of men or fortifications to prevent access or egress. The police *cordon* was so tight that the criminals could not leave the area. also v.

**cornice** N. projecting molding on building (usually above columns). Because the stones forming the *cornice* had been loosened by the storms, the police closed the building until repairs could be made.

**cornucopia** N. horn overflowing with fruit and grain; symbol of abundance. The encyclopedia salesman claimed the new edition was a veritable *cornucopia* of information, an inexhaustible source of knowledge for the entire family.

**corollary** N. consequence; accompaniment. Brotherly love is a complex emotion, with sibling rivalry its natural *corollary*.

**corporeal** ADJ. bodily; material. The doctor had no patience with spiritual matters: his job was to attend to his patients' *corporeal* problems, not to minister to their souls.

**corpulent** ADJ. very fat. The *corpulent* man resolved to reduce. corpulence, N.

**correlation** N. mutual relationship. He sought to determine the *correlation* that existed between ability in algebra and ability to interpret reading exercises. correlate, v., N.

**corroborate** V. confirm; support. Though Huck was quite willing to *corroborate* Tom's story, Aunt Polly knew better than to believe either of them.

**corrode** V. destroy by chemical action. The girders supporting the bridge *corroded* so gradually that no one suspected any danger until the bridge suddenly collapsed. corrosion, N.

**corrosive** ADJ. eating away by chemicals or disease. Stainless steel is able to withstand the effects of *corrosive* chemicals.

**corrugated** ADJ. wrinkled; ridged. She wished she could smooth away the wrinkles from his *corrugated* brow.

**cosmic** ADJ. pertaining to the universe; vast. *Cosmic* rays derive their name from the fact that they bombard the earth's atmosphere from outer space. cosmos, N.

**coterie** N. group that meets socially; select circle. After his book had been published, he was invited to join the literary *coterie* that lunched daily at the hotel.

**countenance** V. approve; tolerate. Miss Manners refused to *countenance* such rude behavior on their part.

**countenance** N. face. When José saw his newborn daughter, a proud smile spread across his *countenance*.

**countermand** V. cancel; revoke. The general *countermanded* the orders issued in his absence.

# Test

## Word List 11    *Synonyms*

Each of the questions below consists of a word in capital letters, followed by five lettered words or phrases. Choose the lettered word or phrase that is most nearly similar in meaning to the word in capital letters and write the letter of your choice on your answer paper.

151. CONJECTURE (A) magic (B) guess (C) position (D) form (E) place
152. CONNOISSEUR (A) gourmand (B) lover of art (C) humidor (D) delinquent (E) interpreter
153. CONSANGUINITY (A) kinship (B) friendship (C) bloodletting (D) relief (E) understanding
154. CONSENSUS (A) general agreement (B) project (C) insignificance (D) sheaf (E) crevice
155. CONSTRUE (A) explain (B) promote (C) reserve (D) erect (E) block
156. CONTAMINATE (A) arrest (B) prepare (C) pollute (D) beam (E) inform

157. CONTENTIOUS (A) squealing (B) surprising (C) quarrelsome (D) smug (E) creative
158. CONTINENCE (A) humanity (B) research (C) embryology (D) bodies of land (E) self-restraint
159. CONTRABAND (A) purpose (B) rogue (C) rascality (D) difficulty (E) smuggling
160. CONTRITE (A) smart (B) penitent (C) restful (D) recognized (E) perspiring
161. CONTROVERT (A) turn over (B) contradict (C) mind (D) explain (E) swing
162. CONVENE (A) propose (B) restore (C) question (D) gather (E) motivate
163. CONVERSANT (A) ignorant (B) speaking (C) incorporated (D) familiar (E) pedantic
164. COPIOUS (A) plentiful (B) cheating (C) dishonorable (D) adventurous (E) inspired
165. CORPULENT (A) regenerate (B) obese (C) different (D) hungry (E) bloody

# Word List 12    counterpart-decelerate

**counterpart** N. a thing that completes another; things very much alike. Night and day are *counterparts*.

**coup** N. highly successful action or sudden attack. As the news of his *coup* spread throughout Wall Street, his fellow brokers dropped by to congratulate him.

**couple** V. join; unite. The Flying Karamazovs *couple* expert juggling and amateur joking in their nightclub act.

**courier** N. messenger. The publisher sent a special *courier* to pick up the manuscript.

**covenant** N. agreement. We must comply with the terms of the *covenant*.

**covert** ADJ. secret; hidden; implied. Investigations of the Central Intelligence Agency and other secret service networks reveal that such *covert* operations can get out of control.

**covetous** ADJ. avaricious; eagerly desirous of. The child was *covetous* by nature and wanted to take the toys belonging to his classmates. covet, V.

**cow** V. terrorize; intimidate. The little boy was so *cowed* by the hulking bully that he gave up his lunch money without a word of protest.

**cower** V. shrink quivering, as from fear. The frightened child *cowered* in the corner of the room.

**coy** ADJ. shy; modest; coquettish. Reluctant to commit herself so early in the game, Kay was *coy* in her answers to Ken's offer.

**cozen** V. cheat; hoodwink; swindle. He was the kind of individual who would *cozen* his friends in a cheap card game but remain eminently ethical in all his business dealings.

**crabbed** ADJ. sour; peevish. The children avoided the *crabbed* old man because he scolded them when they made noise.

**crass** ADJ. very unrefined; grossly insensible. The film critic deplored the *crass* commercialism of movie-makers who abandon artistic standards in order to make a quick buck.

■ **craven** ADJ. cowardly. Lillian's *craven* refusal to join the protest was criticized by her comrades, who had expected her to be brave enough to stand up for her beliefs.

**credence** N. belief. Do not place any *credence* in his promises.

**credo** N. creed. I believe we may best describe her *credo* by saying that it approximates the Golden Rule.

**credulity** N. belief on slight evidence; gullibility; naiveté. Con artists take advantage of the *credulity* of inexperienced investors to swindle them out of their savings. credulous, ADJ.

**creed** N. system of religious or ethical belief. Any loyal American's *creed* must emphasize love of democracy.

**crescendo** N. increase in the volume or intensity, as in a musical passage; climax. The overture suddenly changed from a quiet pastoral theme to a *crescendo* featuring blaring trumpets and clashing cymbals.

**crestfallen** ADJ. dejected; dispirited. We were surprised at his reaction to the failure of his project; instead of being *crestfallen*, he was busily engaged in planning new activities.

**crevice** N. crack; fissure. The mountain climbers found footholds in the tiny *crevices* in the mountainside.

**cringe** V. shrink back, as if in fear. The dog *cringed*, expecting a blow.

**criteria** N. PL. standards used in judging. What *criteria* did you use when you selected this essay as the prize winner? criterion, SING.

**crone** N. hag. The toothless *crone* frightened us when she smiled.

**crotchety** ADJ. eccentric; whimsical. Although he was reputed to be a *crotchety* old gentleman, I found his ideas substantially sound and sensible.

**crux** N. essential or main point. This is the *crux* of the entire problem: everything centers on its being resolved. crucial, ADJ.

**crypt** N. secret recess or vault usually used for burial. Until recently only bodies of rulers and leading statesmen were interred in this *crypt*.

**cryptic** ADJ. mysterious; hidden; secret. Thoroughly baffled by Holmes's *cryptic* remarks, Watson wondered whether Holmes was intentionally concealing his thoughts about the crime.

**cubicle** N. small chamber used for sleeping. After her many hours of intensive study in the library, she retired to her *cubicle*.

**cuisine** N. style of cooking. French *cuisine* is noted for its use of sauces and wines.

**culinary** ADJ. relating to cooking. Many chefs attribute their *culinary* success to the wise use of spices.

**cull** V. pick out; reject. Every month the farmer *culls* the nonlaying hens from his flock and sells them to the local butcher. also N.

**culmination** N. attainment of highest point. His inauguration as President of the United States marked the *culmination* of his political career.

**culpable** ADJ. deserving blame. Corrupt politicians who condone the activities of the gamblers are equally *culpable*.

**culvert** N. artificial channel for water. If we build a *culvert* under the road at this point, we will reduce the possibility of the road's being flooded during the rainy season.

**cumbersome** ADJ. heavy; hard to manage. She was burdened with *cumbersome* parcels.

**cumulative** ADJ. growing by addition. Vocabulary-building is a *cumulative* process: as you go through your flash cards, you will add new words to your vocabulary, one by one.

**cupidity** N. greed. The defeated people could not satisfy the *cupidity* of the conquerors, who demanded excessive tribute.

**curator** N. superintendent; manager. The members of the board of trustees of the museum expected the new *curator* to plan events and exhibits that would make the museum more popular.

**curmudgeon** N. churlish, miserly individual. Although many regarded him as a *curmudgeon*, a few of us were aware of the many kindnesses and acts of charity that he secretly performed.

**cursive** ADJ. flowing, running. In normal writing we run our letters together in *cursive* form; in printing, we separate the letters.

**cursory** ADJ. casual; hastily done. Because a *cursory* examination of the ruins indicates the possibility of arson, we believe the insurance agency should undertake a more extensive investigation of the fire's cause.

**curtail** V. shorten; reduce. When Elton asked Cher for a date, she said she was really sorry she couldn't go out with him, but her dad had ordered her to *curtail* her social life.

**cynical** ADJ. skeptical or distrustful of human motives. *Cynical* from birth, Sidney was suspicious whenever anyone gave him a gift "with no strings attached." cynic, N. cynicism, N.

**cynosure** N. object of general attention. As soon as the movie star entered the room, she became the *cynosure* of all eyes.

**dabble** V. work at in a nonserious fashion; splash around. The amateur painter *dabbled* at art, but seldom produced a finished piece. The children *dabbled* their hands in the bird bath, splashing one another gleefully.

**dais** N. raised platform for guests of honor. When she approached the *dais*, she was greeted by cheers from the people who had come to honor her.

**dally** V. trifle with; procrastinate. Laertes told Ophelia that Hamlet would only *dally* with her affections.

**dank** ADJ. damp. The walls of the dungeon were *dank* and slimy.

**dapper** ADJ. neat and trim. In *The Odd Couple*, Tony Randall played Felix Unger, an excessively *dapper* soul who could not stand to have a hair out of place.

**dappled** ADJ. spotted. The sunlight filtering through the screens created a *dappled* effect on the wall.

**daub** V. smear (as with paint). From the way he *daubed* his paint on the canvas, I could tell he knew nothing of oils. also N.

■ **daunt** V. intimidate; frighten. "Boast all you like of your prowess. Mere words cannot *daunt* me," the hero answered the villain.

**dauntless** ADJ. bold. Despite the dangerous nature of the undertaking, the *dauntless* soldier volunteered for the assignment.

**dawdle** V. loiter; waste time. We have to meet a deadline. Don't *dawdle*; just get down to work.

**deadlock** N. standstill; stalemate. Because negotiations had reached a *deadlock*, some of the delegates had begun to mutter about breaking off the talks. also V.

**deadpan** ADJ. wooden; impassive. We wanted to see how long he could maintain his *deadpan* expression.

**dearth** N. scarcity. The *dearth* of skilled labor compelled the employers to open trade schools.

**debacle** N. sudden downfall; complete disaster. In the *Airplane* movies, every flight turns into a *debacle*, with passengers and crew members collapsing, engines falling apart, and carry-on baggage popping out of the overhead bins.

**debase** V. reduce the quality or value; lower in esteem; degrade. In *The King and I*, Anna refuses to kneel down and prostrate herself before the king; she feels that to do so would *debase* her position, and she will not submit to such *debasement*.

**debauch** V. corrupt; seduce from virtue. Did Socrates' teachings lead the young men of Athens to be virtuous citizens, or did they *debauch* the young men, causing them to question the customs of their fathers? Clearly, Socrates' philosophical talks were nothing like the wild *debauchery* of the toga parties in *Animal House*.

**debilitate** V. weaken; enfeeble. Michael's severe bout of the flu *debilitated* him so much that he was too tired to go to work for a week.

**debonair** ADJ. friendly; aiming to please. The *debonair* youth was liked by all who met him, because of his cheerful and obliging manner.

**debris** N. rubble. A full year after the earthquake in Mexico City, workers were still carting away the *debris*.

**debunk** V. expose as false, exaggerated, worthless, etc.; ridicule. Pointing out that he consistently had voted against strengthening antipollution legislation, reporters *debunked* the candidate's claim that he was a fervent environmentalist.

**debutante** N. young woman making formal entrance into society. As a *debutante*, she was often mentioned in the society columns of the newspapers.

**decadence** N. decay. The moral *decadence* of the people was reflected in the lewd literature of the period.

**decant** V. pour off gently. Be sure to *decant* this wine before serving it.

**decapitate** V. behead. They did not hang Lady Jane Grey; they *decapitated* her. "Off with her head!" cried the Duchess, eager to *decapitate* poor Alice.

**decelerate** V. slow down. Seeing the emergency blinkers in the road ahead, he *decelerated* quickly.

# Test

## Word List 12    *Antonyms*

Each of the questions below consists of a word in capital letters, followed by five lettered words or phrases. Choose the lettered word or phrase that is most nearly opposite in meaning to the word in capital letters and write the letter of your choice on your answer paper.

166. COY (A) weak (B) airy (C) brazen (D) old (E) tiresome
167. COZEN (A) amuse (B) treat honestly (C) prate (D) shackle (E) vilify
168. CRAVEN (A) desirous (B) direct (C) bold (D) civilized (E) controlled
169. CRUX (A) affliction (B) spark (C) events (D) trivial point (E) belief
170. CRYPTIC (A) tomblike (B) futile (C) famous (D) candid (E) indifferent
171. CUPIDITY (A) anxiety (B) tragedy (C) generosity (D) entertainment (E) love

172. CURTAIL (A) mutter (B) lengthen (C) express (D) burden (E) shore up
173. CYNICAL (A) trusting (B) effortless (C) conclusive (D) gallant (E) vertical
174. DANK (A) dry (B) guiltless (C) warm (D) babbling (E) reserved
175. DAPPER (A) unintelligent (B) untidy (C) uncertain (D) ungrateful (E) unhealthy
176. DAUNTLESS (A) stolid (B) cowardly (C) irrelevant (D) peculiar (E) particular
177. DEARTH (A) life (B) abundance (C) brightness (D) terror (E) width
178. DEBACLE (A) progress (B) refusal (C) masque (D) cowardice (E) traffic
179. DEBILITATE (A) bedevil (B) repress (C) strengthen (D) animate (E) deaden
180. DEBONAIR (A) awkward (B) windy (C) balmy (D) strong (E) stormy

## Word List 13    deciduous-dermatologist

**deciduous**   ADJ. falling off, as of leaves. The oak is a *deciduous* tree.

**decimate**   V. kill, usually one out of ten. We do more to *decimate* our population in automobile accidents than we do in war.

**decipher**   V. decode. I could not *decipher* the doctor's handwriting.

**declivity**   N. downward slope. The children loved to ski down the *declivity*.

**décolleté**   ADJ. having a low-cut neckline. Fashion decrees that evening gowns be *décolleté* this season; bare shoulders are again the vogue.

**decomposition**   N. decay. Despite the body's advanced state of *decomposition*, the police were able to identify the murdered man.

■ **decorum**   N. propriety; orderliness and good taste in manners. Even the best-mannered students have trouble behaving with *decorum* on the last day of school. decorous, ADJ.

**decoy**   N. lure or bait. The wild ducks were not fooled by the *decoy*. also V.

**decrepitude**   N. state of collapse caused by illness or old age. I was unprepared for the state of *decrepitude* in which I had found my old friend; he seemed to have aged twenty years in six months.

**decry**   V. express strong disapproval of; disparage. The founder of the Children's Defense Fund, Marian Wright Edelman, strongly *decries* the lack of financial and moral support for children in America today.

**deducible**   ADJ. derived by reasoning. If we accept your premise, your conclusions are easily *deducible*.

**deface**   V. mar; disfigure. If you *deface* a library book you will have to pay a hefty fine.

**defame**   V. harm someone's reputation; malign; slander. If you try to *defame* my good name, my lawyers will see you in court. If rival candidates persist in *defaming* one another, the voters may conclude that all politicians are crooks. defamation, N.

■ **default**   N. failure to act. When the visiting team failed to show up for the big game, they lost the game by *default*. When Jack failed to make the payments on his Jaguar, the dealership took back the car because he had *defaulted* on his debt.

**defeatist**   ADJ. resigned to defeat; accepting defeat as a natural outcome. If you maintain your *defeatist* attitude, you will never succeed. also N.

**defection**   N. desertion. The children, who had made him an idol, were hurt most by his *defection* from our cause.

**defer**   V. delay till later; exempt temporarily. In wartime, some young men immediately volunteer to serve; others *defer* making plans until they hear from their draft boards. During the Vietnam War, many young men, hoping to be *deferred*, requested student *deferments*.

**defer**   V. give in respectfully; submit. When it comes to making decisions about purchasing software, we must *defer* to Michael, our computer guru; he has the final word. Michael, however, can *defer* these questions to no one; only he can decide.

■ **deference**   N. courteous regard for another's wish. In *deference* to the minister's request, please do not take photographs during the wedding service.

**defiance**   N. refusal to yield; resistance. When John reached the "terrible two's," he responded to every parental request with howls of *defiance*. defy, V. defiant, ADJ.

**defile**   V. pollute; profane. The hoodlums *defiled* the church with their scurrilous writing.

**definitive** ADJ. most reliable or complete. Carl Sandburg's *Abraham Lincoln* may be regarded as the *definitive* work on the life of the Great Emancipator.

**deflect** V. turn aside. His life was saved when his cigarette case *deflected* the bullet.

**defoliate** V. destroy leaves. In Vietnam the army made extensive use of chemical agents to *defoliate* the woodlands.

**defray** V. provide for the payment of. Her employer offered to *defray* the costs of her postgraduate education.

**defrock** V. to strip a priest or minister of church authority. We knew the minister had violated church regulations, but we had not realized his offense was serious enough to cause him to be *defrocked*.

**deft** ADJ. neat; skillful. The *deft* waiter uncorked the champagne without spilling a drop.

**defunct** ADJ. dead; no longer in use or existence. The lawyers sought to examine the books of the *defunct* corporation.

**degenerate** V. become worse; deteriorate. As the fight dragged on, the champion's style *degenerated* until he could barely keep on his feet.

**degradation** N. humiliation; debasement; degeneration. Some secretaries object to fetching the boss a cup of coffee because they resent the *degradation* of being made to perform such lowly tasks. degrade, V.

**dehydrate** V. remove water from; dry out. Running under a hot sun quickly *dehydrates* the body; joggers avoid *dehydration* by carrying water bottles and drinking from them frequently.

**deify** V. turn into a god; idolize. Admire the rock star all you want; just don't *deify* him.

**deign** V. condescend; stoop. The celebrated fashion designer would not *deign* to speak to a mere seamstress; his overburdened assistant had to convey the master's wishes to the lowly workers assembling his great designs.

**delete** V. erase; strike out. If you *delete* this paragraph, the composition will have more appeal.

**deleterious** ADJ. harmful. If you believe that smoking is *deleterious* to your health (and the Surgeon General surely does), then quit!

**deliberate** V. consider; ponder. Offered the new job, she asked for time to *deliberate* before she made her decision.

■ **delineate** V. portray; depict; sketch. Using only a few descriptive phrases, Austen *delineates* the character of Mr. Collins so well that we can predict his every move. delineation, N.

**delirium** N. mental disorder marked by confusion. In his *delirium*, the drunkard saw pink panthers and talking pigs. Perhaps he wasn't *delirious*: he might just have wandered into a movie house.

**delta** N. flat plain of mud or sand between branches of a river. His dissertation discussed the effect of intermittent flooding on the fertility of the Nile *delta*.

**delude** V. deceive. The mistress *deludes* herself into believing that her lover will leave his wife and marry her.

**deluge** N. flood; rush. When we advertised the position we received a *deluge* of applications. also V.

**delusion** N. false belief; hallucination. Don suffers from *delusions* of grandeur: he thinks he's a world-famous author when he's published just one paperback book.

**delusive** ADJ. deceptive; raising vain hopes. Do not raise your hopes on the basis of his *delusive* promises.

**delve** V. dig; investigate. *Delving* into old books and manuscripts is part of a researcher's job.

**demagogue** N. person who appeals to people's prejudice; false leader. He was accused of being a *demagogue* because he made promises that aroused futile hopes in his listeners.

**demean** V. degrade; humiliate. Standing on his dignity, he refused to *demean* himself by replying to the offensive letter. If you truly believed in the dignity of labor, you would not think it would *demean* you to work as a janitor.

**demeanor** N. behavior; bearing. His sober *demeanor* quieted the noisy revelers.

**demented** ADJ. insane. Doctor Demento was a radio personality who liked to act as if he were truly *demented*. If you're *demented*, your mental state is out of whack; in other words, you're wacky.

**demise** N. death. Upon the *demise* of the dictator, a bitter dispute about succession to power developed.

**demographic** ADJ. related to population balance. In conducting a survey, one should take into account *demographic* trends in the region. demography, N.

**demolition** N. destruction. One of the major aims of the air force was the complete *demolition* of all means of transportation by the bombing of rail lines and terminals. demolish, V.

**demoniac** ADJ. fiendish. The Spanish Inquisition devised many *demoniac* means of torture. demon, N.

**demotic** ADJ. pertaining to the people. He lamented the passing of aristocratic society and maintained that a *demotic* society would lower the nation's standards.

**demur** V. object (because of doubts, scruples); hesitate. When offered a post on the board of directors, David *demurred*: he had scruples about taking on the job because he was unsure he could handle it in addition to his other responsibilities.

**demure** ADJ. grave; serious; coy. She was *demure* and reserved, a nice modest girl whom any young man would be proud to take home to his mother.

■ **denigrate** V. blacken. All attempts to *denigrate* the character of our late president have failed; the people still love him and cherish his memory.

**denizen** N. inhabitant or resident; regular visitor. In *The Untouchables*, Eliot Ness fights Al Capone and the other *denizens* of Chicago's underworld. Ness's fight against corruption was the talk of all the *denizens* of the local bars.

**denotation** N. meaning; distinguishing by name. A dictionary will always give us the *denotation* of a word; frequently, it will also give us its connotation.

**denouement** N. outcome; final development of the plot of a play or other literary work. The play was childishly written; the *denouement* was obvious to sophisticated theatergoers as early as the middle of the first act.

**denounce** v. condemn; criticize. The reform candidate *denounced* the corrupt city officers for having betrayed the public's trust. denunciation, N.

**depict** v. portray. In this sensational exposé, the author *depicts* Beatle John Lennon as a drug-crazed neurotic. Do you question the accuracy of this *depiction* of Lennon?

**deplete** v. reduce; exhaust. We must wait until we *deplete* our present inventory before we order replacements.

**deplore** v. regret. Although I *deplore* the vulgarity of your language, I defend your right to express yourself freely.

**deploy** v. spread out [troops] in an extended though shallow battle line. The general ordered the battalion to *deploy* in order to meet the enemy offensive.

**depose** v. dethrone; remove from office. The army attempted to *depose* the king and set up a military government.

**deposition** N. testimony under oath. She made her *deposition* in the judge's chamber.

**depravity** N. extreme corruption; wickedness. The *depravity* of Caligula's behavior eventually sickened even those who had willingly participated in his earlier, comparatively innocent orgies. deprave, v.

**deprecate** v. express disapproval of; protest against; belittle. A firm believer in old-fashioned courtesy, Miss Post *deprecated* the modern tendency to address new acquaintances by their first names. deprecatory, ADJ.

**depreciate** v. lessen in value. If you neglect this property, it will *depreciate*.

**depredation** N. plundering. After the *depredations* of the invaders, the people were penniless.

**deranged** ADJ. insane. He had to be institutionalized because he was *deranged*.

**derelict** ADJ. abandoned; negligent. The *derelict* craft was a menace to navigation. Whoever abandoned it in the middle of the harbor was *derelict* in living up to his responsibilities as a boat owner. also N.

■ **deride** v. ridicule; make fun of. The critics *derided* his pretentious dialogue and refused to consider his play seriously. Despite the critics' *derision*, however, audiences were moved by the play, cheering its unabashedly sentimental conclusion. derisive, ADJ.

■ **derivative** ADJ. unoriginal; obtained from another source. Although her early poetry was clearly *derivative* in nature, the critics thought she had promise and eventually would find her own voice.

**dermatologist** N. one who studies the skin and its diseases. I advise you to consult a *dermatologist* about your acne.

# Test

## Word List 13    *Synonyms*

Each of the questions below consists of a word in capital letters, followed by five lettered words or phrases. Choose the lettered word or phrase that is most nearly similar in meaning to the word in capital letters and write the letter of your choice on your answer paper.

181. DECIMATE (A) kill (B) disgrace (C) search (D) collide (E) deride
182. DECLIVITY (A) trap (B) quadrangle (C) quarter (D) activity (E) downward slope
183. DÉCOLLETÉ (A) flavored (B) demure (C) flowery (D) low-necked (E) sweet
184. DECOROUS (A) momentary (B) emotional (C) suppressed (D) proper (E) unexpected
185. DECREPITUDE (A) feebleness (B) disease (C) coolness (D) melee (E) crowd
186. DEFAULT (A) failure to act (B) tendency to err (C) desire to remedy (D) debt (E) misunderstanding
187. DEFECTION (A) determination (B) desertion (C) invitation (D) affection (E) reservation
188. DEFILE (A) manicure (B) ride (C) pollute (D) assemble (E) order
189. DEGRADED (A) surprised (B) lowered (C) ascended (D) learned (E) prejudged
190. DELETERIOUS (A) delaying (B) experimental (C) harmful (D) graduating (E) glorious
191. DELUGE (A) confusion (B) deception (C) flood (D) mountain (E) weapon
192. DENIGRATE (A) refuse (B) blacken (C) terrify (D) admit (E) review
193. DENOUEMENT (A) action (B) scenery (C) resort (D) character (E) solution
194. DEPRAVITY (A) wickedness (B) sadness (C) heaviness (D) tidiness (E) seriousness
195. DERANGED (A) insane (B) systematic (C) neighborly (D) alphabetical (E) surrounded

## Word List 14    derogatory-disgruntle

**derogatory** ADJ. expressing a low opinion. I resent your *derogatory* remarks.

**descry** v. catch sight of. In the distance, we could barely *descry* the enemy vessels.

**desecrate** v. profane; violate the sanctity of. Shattering the altar and trampling the holy objects underfoot, the invaders *desecrated* the sanctuary.

■ **desiccate** v. dry up. A tour of this smokehouse will give you an idea of how the pioneers used to *desiccate* food in order to preserve it.

**desolate** ADJ. unpopulated; joyless. After six months in the crowded, bustling metropolis, David was so sick of people that he was ready to head for the most *desolate* patch of wilderness he could find.

**desolate**  V. rob of joy; lay waste to; forsake. The bandits *desolated* the countryside, burning farms and carrying off the harvest.

**desperado**  N. reckless outlaw. Butch Cassidy was a bold *desperado* with a price on his head.

**despise**  V. look on with scorn; regard as worthless or distasteful. Mr. Bond, I *despise* spies; I look down on them as mean, *despicable*, honorless men, whom I would wipe from the face of the earth with as little concern as I would scrape dog droppings from the bottom of my shoe.

**despoil**  V. plunder. If you do not yield, I am afraid the enemy will *despoil* the countryside.

**despondent**  ADJ. depressed; gloomy. To the distress of his parents, William became seriously *despondent* after he broke up with Jan. despondency, N.

**despot**  N. tyrant; harsh, authoritarian ruler. How could a benevolent king turn overnight into a *despot*? despotism, N.

**destitute**  ADJ. extremely poor. Because they had no health insurance, the father's costly illness left the family *destitute*. destitution, N.

■ **desultory**  ADJ. aimless; haphazard; digressing at random. In prison Malcolm X set himself the task of reading straight through the dictionary; to him, reading was purposeful, not *desultory*.

**detached**  ADJ. emotionally removed; calm and objective; physically separate. A psychoanalyst must maintain a *detached* point of view and stay uninvolved with her patients' personal lives. To a child growing up in an apartment or a row house, to live in a *detached* house was an unattainable dream. (secondary meaning) detachment, N.

**determinate**  ADJ. having a fixed order of procedure; invariable. At the royal wedding, the procession of the nobles followed a *determinate* order of precedence.

**determination**  N. resolve; measurement or calculation; decision. Nothing could shake his *determination* that his children would get the best education that money could buy. Thanks to my pocket calculator, my *determination* of the answer to the problem took only seconds of my time.

■ **deterrent**  N. something that discourages; hindrance. Does the threat of capital punishment serve as a *deterrent* to potential killers? also ADJ.

**detonation**  N. explosion. The *detonation* of the bomb could be heard miles away.

**detraction**  N. slandering; aspersion. He is offended by your frequent *detractions* of his ability as a leader.

**detrimental**  ADJ. harmful; damaging. The candidate's acceptance of major financial contributions from a well-known racist ultimately proved *detrimental* to his campaign, for he lost the backing of many of his early grassroots supporters. detriment, N.

**deviate**  V. turn away from (a principle, norm); depart; diverge. Richard never *deviated* from his daily routine: every day he set off for work at eight o'clock, had his sack lunch at noon, and headed home at the stroke of five.

**devious**  ADJ. roundabout; erratic; not straightforward. The Joker's plan was so *devious* that it was only with great difficulty we could follow its shifts and dodges.

**devise**  V. think up; invent; plan. How clever he must be to have *devised* such a devious plan! What ingenious inventions might he have *devised* if he had turned his mind to science rather than crime.

**devoid**  ADJ. lacking. You may think Cher's mind is a total void, but she's actually not *devoid* of intelligence. She just sounds like an airhead.

**devolve**  V. deputize; pass to others. It *devolved* upon us, the survivors, to arrange peace terms with the enemy.

**devotee**  N. enthusiastic follower. A *devotee* of the opera, she bought season tickets every year.

**devout**  ADJ. pious. The *devout* man prayed daily.

**dexterous**  ADJ. skillful. The magician was so *dexterous* that we could not follow his movements as he performed his tricks.

**diabolical**  ADJ. devilish. "What a fiend I am, to devise such a *diabolical* scheme to destroy Gotham City," chortled the Joker.

**diadem**  N. crown. The king's *diadem* was on display at the museum.

**dialectical**  ADJ. relating to the art of debate; mutual or reciprocal. The debate coach's students grew to develop great forensic and *dialectical* skill. Teaching, however, is inherently a *dialectical* situation: the coach learned at least as much from her students as they learned from her. dialectics, N.

**diaphanous**  ADJ. sheer; transparent. They saw the burglar clearly through the *diaphanous* curtain.

■ **diatribe**  N. bitter scolding; invective. During the lengthy *diatribe* delivered by his opponent he remained calm and self-controlled.

■ **dichotomy**  N. split; branching into two parts (especially contradictory ones). Willie didn't know how to resolve the *dichotomy* between his ambition to go to college and his childhood longing to run away and join the circus. Then he heard about Ringling Brothers Circus College, and he knew he'd found his school.

**dictum**  N. authoritative and weighty statement; saying; maxim. University administrations still follow the old *dictum* "Publish or perish." They don't care how good a teacher you are; if you don't publish enough papers, you're out of a job.

**didactic**  ADJ. teaching; instructional. Pope's lengthy poem *An Essay on Man* is too *didactic* for my taste: I dislike it when poets turn preachy and moralize. didacticism, N.

**die**  N. device for stamping or impressing; mold. In coining pennies, workers at the old mint squeezed sheets of softened copper between two *dies*.

■ **diffidence**  N. shyness. You must overcome your *diffidence* if you intend to become a salesperson.

■ **diffuse**  ADJ. wordy; rambling; spread out (like a gas). If you pay authors by the word, you tempt them to produce *diffuse* manuscripts rather than brief ones. also V. diffusion, N.

■ **digression** N. wandering away from the subject. Nobody minded when Professor Renoir's lectures wandered away from their official theme; his *digressions* were always more fascinating than the topic of the day. digress, V.

**dilapidated** ADJ. ruined because of neglect. The *dilapidated* old building needed far more work than just a new coat of paint. dilapidation, N.

**dilate** V. expand. In the dark, the pupils of your eyes *dilate*.

**dilatory** ADJ. delaying. Your *dilatory* tactics may compel me to cancel the contract.

**dilemma** N. problem; choice of two unsatisfactory alternatives. In this *dilemma*, he knew no one to whom he could turn for advice.

**dilettante** N. aimless follower of the arts; amateur; dabbler. He was not serious in his painting; he was rather a *dilettante*.

**diligence** N. steadiness of effort; persistent hard work. Her employers were greatly impressed by her *diligence* and offered her a partnership in the firm.

**dilute** V. make less concentrated; reduce in strength. She preferred her coffee *diluted* with milk.

**diminution** N. lessening; reduction in size. Old Jack was as sharp at eighty as he had been at fifty; increasing age led to no *diminution* of his mental acuity.

**din** N. continued loud noise. The *din* of the jackhammers outside the classroom window drowned out the lecturer's voice. also v.

**dinghy** N. small boat (often ship's boat). In the film *Lifeboat*, an ill-assorted group of passengers from a sunken ocean liner are marooned at sea in a *dinghy*.

**dingy** ADJ. dull; not fresh; cheerless. Refusing to be depressed by her *dingy* studio apartment, Bea spent the weekend polishing the floors and windows and hanging bright posters on the walls.

**dint** N. means; effort. By *dint* of much hard work, the volunteers were able to control the raging forest fire.

**diorama** N. life-size, three-dimensional scene from nature or history. Because they dramatically pose actual stuffed animals against realistic painted landscapes, the *dioramas* at the Museum of Natural History particularly impress high school biology students.

**dire** ADJ. disastrous. People ignored her *dire* predictions of an approaching depression.

■ **dirge** N. lament with music. The funeral *dirge* stirred us to tears.

■ **disabuse** V. correct a false impression; undeceive. I will attempt to *disabuse* you of your impression of my client's guilt; I know he is innocent.

**disaffected** ADJ. disloyal. Once the most loyal of Bradley's supporters, Senator Moynihan found himself becoming increasingly *disaffected*.

**disapprobation** N. disapproval; condemnation. The conservative father viewed his daughter's radical boyfriend with *disapprobation*.

**disarray** N. a disorderly or untidy state. After the New Year's party, the once orderly house was in total *disarray*.

**disavowal** N. denial; disclaiming. His *disavowal* of his part in the conspiracy was not believed by the jury. disavow, V.

**disband** V. dissolve; disperse. The chess club *disbanded* after its disastrous initial season.

**disburse** V. pay out. When you *disburse* money on the company's behalf, be sure to get a receipt.

**discernible** ADJ. distinguishable; perceivable. The ships in the harbor were not *discernible* in the fog.

■ **discerning** ADJ. mentally quick and observant; having insight. Though no genius, the star was sufficiently *discerning* to distinguish her true friends from the countless phonies who flattered her. discern, V. discernment, N.

**disclaim** V. disown; renounce claim to. If I grant you this privilege, will you *disclaim* all other rights?

**disclose** V. reveal. Although competitors offered him bribes, he refused to *disclose* any information about his company's forthcoming product. disclosure, N.

**discombobulated** ADJ. confused; discomposed. The novice square dancer became so *discombobulated* that he wandered into the wrong set.

**discomfit** V. put to rout; defeat; disconcert. This ruse will *discomfit* the enemy. discomfiture, N. discomfited, ADJ.

**disconcert** V. confuse; upset; embarrass. The lawyer was *disconcerted* by the evidence produced by her adversary.

**disconsolate** ADJ. sad. The death of his wife left him *disconsolate*.

**discord** N. conflict; lack of harmony. Watching Tweedledum battle Tweedledee, Alice wondered what had caused this pointless *discord*.

■ **discordant** ADJ. not harmonious; conflicting. Nothing is quite so *discordant* as the sound of a junior high school orchestra tuning up.

**discount** V. disregard. Be prepared to *discount* what he has to say about his ex-wife.

**discourse** N. formal discussion; conversation. The young Plato was drawn to the Agora to hear the philosophical *discourse* of Socrates and his followers. also v.

■ **discredit** V. defame; destroy confidence in; disbelieve. The campaign was highly negative in tone; each candidate tried to *discredit* the other.

■ **discrepancy** N. lack of consistency; difference. The police noticed some *discrepancies* in his description of the crime and did not believe him.

■ **discrete** ADJ. separate; unconnected. The universe is composed of *discrete* bodies.

**discretion** N. prudence; ability to adjust actions to circumstances. Use your *discretion* in this matter and do not discuss it with anyone. discreet, ADJ.

**discriminating** ADJ. able to see differences; prejudiced. A superb interpreter of Picasso, she was sufficiently *discriminating* to judge the most complex works of modern art. discrimination, N.

**discursive** ADJ. digressing; rambling. As the lecturer wandered from topic to topic, we wondered what if any point there was to his *discursive* remarks.

**disdain** V. view with scorn or contempt. In the film *Funny Face*, the bookish heroine *disdained* fashion models for their lack of intellectual interests. also N.

**disembark** V. go ashore; unload cargo from a ship. Before the passengers could *disembark*, they had to pick up their passports from the ship's purser.

**disenfranchise** V. deprive of a civil right. The imposition of the poll tax effectively *disenfranchised* poor Southern blacks, who lost their right to vote.

**disengage** V. uncouple; separate; disconnect. A standard movie routine involves the hero's desperate attempt to *disengage* a railroad car from a moving train.

**disfigure** V. mar the appearance of; spoil. An ugly frown *disfigured* her normally pleasant face.

**disgorge** V. surrender something; eject; vomit. Unwilling to *disgorge* the cash he had stolen from the pension fund, the embezzler tried to run away.

**disgruntle** V. make discontented. The passengers were *disgruntled* by the numerous delays.

## Test

## Word List 14    *Antonyms*

Each of the questions below consists of a word in capital letters, followed by five lettered words or phrases. Choose the lettered word or phrase that is most nearly opposite in meaning to the word in capital letters and write the letter of your choice on your answer paper.

196. DEROGATORY (A) roguish (B) immediate (C) opinionated (D) praising (E) conferred
197. DESECRATE (A) desist (B) integrate (C) confuse (D) intensify (E) consecrate
198. DESPICABLE (A) steering (B) worthy of esteem (C) inevitable (D) featureless (E) incapable
199. DESTITUTE (A) affluent (B) dazzling (C) stationary (D) characteristic (E) explanatory
200. DEVOID (A) latent (B) eschewed (C) full of (D) suspecting (E) evident
201. DEVOUT (A) quiet (B) dual (C) impious (D) straightforward (E) wrong

202. DIABOLICAL (A) mischievous (B) lavish (C) seraphic (D) azure (E) redolent
203. DIATRIBE (A) mass (B) range (C) eulogy (D) elegy (E) starvation
204. DIFFIDENCE (A) sharpness (B) boldness (C) malcontent (D) dialogue (E) catalog
205. DILATE (A) procrastinate (B) contract (C) conclude (D) participate (E) divert
206. DILATORY (A) narrowing (B) prompt (C) enlarging (D) portentous (E) sour
207. DIMINUTION (A) expectation (B) context (C) validity (D) appreciation (E) difficulty
208. DIN (A) lightness (B) safety (C) silence (D) hunger (E) promptness
209. DISABUSE (A) crash (B) violate (C) renege (D) control (E) deceive
210. DISCONSOLATE (A) unprejudiced (B) thankful (C) theatrical (D) joyous (E) prominent

## Word List 15    dishearten–duplicity

**dishearten** V. discourage. His failure to pass the bar exam *disheartened* him.

**disheveled** ADJ. untidy. Your *disheveled* appearance will hurt your chances in this interview.

**disinclination** N. unwillingness. Some mornings I feel a great *disinclination* to get out of bed.

■ **disingenuous** ADJ. not naive; sophisticated. Although he was young, his remarks indicated that he was *disingenuous*.

**disinter** V. dig up; unearth. They *disinterred* the body and held an autopsy.

■ **disinterested** ADJ. unprejudiced. Given the judge's political ambitions and the lawyers' financial interest in the case, the only *disinterested* person in the courtroom may have been the court reporter.

■ **disjointed** ADJ. disconnected. His remarks were so *disjointed* that we could not follow his reasoning.

**disjunction** N. act or state of separation; disunity. Believing the mind could greatly affect the body's health, the holistic doctor rejected the notion of a necessary *disjunction* of mind and body.

**dislodge** V. remove (forcibly). Thrusting her fist up under the choking man's lower ribs, Margaret used the Heimlich maneuver to *dislodge* the food caught in his throat.

**dismantle** V. take apart. When the show closed, they *dismantled* the scenery before storing it.

**dismember** V. cut into small parts. When the Austrian Empire was *dismembered*, several new countries were established.

■ **dismiss** V. eliminate from consideration; reject. Believing in John's love for her, she *dismissed* the notion that he might be unfaithful. (secondary meaning)

■ **disparage** V. belittle. A doting mother, Emma was more likely to praise her son's crude attempts at art than to *disparage* them.

■ **disparate** ADJ. basically different; unrelated. Unfortunately Tony and Tina have *disparate* notions of marriage: Tony sees it as a carefree extended love affair, while Tina sees it as a solemn commitment to build a family and a home.

**disparity** N. difference; condition of inequality. Their *disparity* in rank made no difference at all to the prince and Cinderella.

**dispassionate** ADJ. calm; impartial. Known in the company for his cool judgment, Bill could impartially examine the causes of a problem, giving a *dispassionate* analysis of what had gone wrong, and go on to suggest how to correct the mess.

**dispatch** N. speediness; prompt execution; message sent with all due speed. Young Napoleon defeated the enemy with all possible *dispatch*; he then sent a *dispatch* to headquarters, informing his commander of the great victory. also V.

**dispel** V. scatter; drive away; cause to vanish. The bright sunlight eventually *dispelled* the morning mist.

**disperse** V. scatter. The police fired tear gas into the crowd to *disperse* the protesters. dispersion, N.

**dispirited** ADJ. lacking in spirit. The coach used all the tricks at his command to buoy up the enthusiasm of his team, which had become *dispirited* at the loss of the star player.

**disport** V. amuse. The popularity of Florida as a winter resort is constantly increasing; each year, thousands more *disport* themselves at Miami and Palm Beach.

**disputatious** ADJ. argumentative; fond of arguing. Convinced he knew more than his lawyers, Tony was a *disputatious* client, ready to argue about the best way to conduct the case.

**disquietude** N. uneasiness; anxiety. When Holmes had been gone for a day, Watson felt only a slight sense of *disquietude*, but after a week with no word, Watson's uneasiness about his missing friend had grown into a deep fear for Holmes's safety. disquiet, V., N.

**disquisition** N. a formal systematic inquiry; an explanation of the results of a formal inquiry. In his *disquisition*, he outlined the steps he had taken in reaching his conclusions.

**dissection** N. analysis; cutting apart in order to examine. The *dissection* of frogs in the laboratory is particularly unpleasant to some students.

■ **dissemble** V. disguise; pretend. Even though John tried to *dissemble* his motive for taking modern dance, we all knew he was there not to dance but to meet girls.

■ **disseminate** V. distribute; spread; scatter (like seeds). By their use of the Internet, propagandists have been able to *disseminate* their pet doctrines to new audiences around the globe.

**dissent** V. disagree. In the recent Supreme Court decision, Justice O'Connor *dissented* from the majority opinion. also N.

**dissertation** N. formal essay. In order to earn a graduate degree from many of our universities, a candidate is frequently required to prepare a *dissertation* on some scholarly subject.

**dissident** ADJ. dissenting; rebellious. In the purge that followed the student demonstrations at Tianamen Square, the government hunted down the *dissident* students and their supporters. also N.

**dissimulate** V. pretend; conceal by feigning. She tried to *dissimulate* her grief by her exuberant attitude.

**dissipate** V. squander; waste; scatter. He is a fine artist, but I fear he may *dissipate* his gifts if he keeps wasting his time playing Trivial Pursuit.

■ **dissolution** N. disintegration; looseness in morals. The profligacy and *dissolution* of life in Caligula's Rome appall some historians. dissolute, ADJ.

■ **dissonance** N. discord; opposite of harmony. Composer Charles Ives often used *dissonance*—clashing or unresolved chords—for special effects in his musical works. dissonant, ADJ.

**dissuade** V. persuade not to do; discourage. Since Tom could not *dissuade* Huck from running away from home, he decided to run away with his friend. dissuasion, N.

**distant** ADJ. reserved or aloof; cold in manner. Her *distant* greeting made me feel unwelcome from the start. (secondary meaning)

■ **distend** V. expand; swell out. I can tell when he is under stress by the way the veins *distend* on his forehead.

■ **distill** V. purify; refine; concentrate. A moonshiner *distills* mash into whiskey; an epigrammatist *distills* thoughts into quips.

**distinction** N. honor; contrast; discrimination. A holder of the Medal of Honor, George served with great *distinction* in World War II. He made a *distinction*, however, between World War II and Vietnam, which he considered an immoral conflict.

**distort** V. twist out of shape. It is difficult to believe the newspaper accounts of the riots because of the way some reporters *distort* and exaggerate the actual events. distortion, N.

**distrait** ADJ. absentminded. Because of his concentration on the problem, the professor often appeared *distrait* and unconcerned about routine.

**distraught** ADJ. upset; distracted by anxiety. The *distraught* parents frantically searched the ravine for their lost child.

**diurnal** ADJ. daily. A farmer cannot neglect his *diurnal* tasks at any time; cows, for example, must be milked regularly.

**diva** N. operatic singer; prima donna. Although world famous as a *diva*, she did not indulge in fits of temperament.

■ **diverge** V. vary; go in different directions from the same point. The spokes of the wheel *diverge* from the hub.

**divergent** ADJ. differing; deviating. Since graduating from medical school, the two doctors have followed *divergent* paths, the one going on to become a nationally prominent surgeon, the other dedicating himself to a small family practice in his hometown. divergence, N.

**diverse** ADJ. differing in some characteristics; various. The professor suggested *diverse* ways of approaching the assignment and recommended that we choose one of them.

**diversion** N. act of turning aside; pastime. After studying for several hours, he needed a *diversion* from work. divert, V.

**diversity** N. variety; dissimilitude. The *diversity* of colleges in this country indicates that many levels of ability are being served.

■ **divest** V. strip; deprive. He was *divested* of his power to act and could no longer govern. divestiture, N.

**divine** V. perceive intuitively; foresee the future. Nothing infuriated Tom more than Aunt Polly's ability to *divine* when he was not telling the truth.

**divulge** V. reveal. No lover of gossip, Charlotte would never *divulge* anything that a friend told her in confidence.

**docile** ADJ. obedient; easily managed. As *docile* as he seems today, that old lion was once a ferocious, snarling beast. docility, N.

**docket** N. program as for trial; book where such entries are made. The case of *Smith v. Jones* was entered in the *docket* for July 15. also v.

**doctrinaire** ADJ. unable to compromise about points of doctrine; dogmatic; unyielding. Weng had hoped that the student-led democracy movement might bring about change in China, but the repressive response of the *doctrinaire* hard-liners crushed his dreams of democracy.

**doctrine** N. teachings in general; particular principle (religious, legal, etc.) taught. He was so committed to the *doctrines* of his faith that he was unable to evaluate them impartially.

■ **document** V. provide written evidence. She kept all the receipts from her business trip in order to *document* her expenses for the firm. also N.

**doddering** ADJ. shaky; infirm from old age. Although he is not as yet a *doddering* and senile old man, his ideas and opinions no longer can merit the respect we gave them years ago.

**doff** V. take off. A gentleman used to *doff* his hat to a lady.

**dogged** ADJ. determined; stubborn. *Les Miserables* tells of Inspector Javert's long, *dogged* pursuit of the criminal Jean Valjean.

**doggerel** N. poor verse. Although we find occasional snatches of genuine poetry in her work, most of her writing is mere *doggerel*.

■ **dogmatic** ADJ. opinionated; arbitrary; doctrinal. We tried to discourage Doug from being so *dogmatic*, but never could convince him that his opinions might be wrong.

**doldrums** N. blues; listlessness; slack period. Once the excitement of meeting her deadline was over, she found herself in the *doldrums*.

**dolorous** ADJ. sorrowful. He found the *dolorous* lamentations of the bereaved family emotionally disturbing and he left as quickly as he could.

**dolt** N. stupid person. I thought I was talking to a mature audience; instead, I find myself addressing a pack of *dolts*.

**domicile** N. home. Although his legal *domicile* was in New York City, his work kept him away from his residence for many years. also v.

**domineer** V. rule over tyrannically. Students prefer teachers who guide, not ones who *domineer*.

**don** V. put on. When Clark Kent had to *don* his Superman outfit, he changed clothes in a convenient phone booth.

■ **dormant** ADJ. sleeping; lethargic; latent. At fifty her long-*dormant* ambition to write flared up once more; within a year she had completed the first of her great historical novels. dormancy, N.

**dormer** N. window projecting from roof. In remodeling the attic into a bedroom, we decided that we needed to put in *dormers* to provide sufficient ventilation for the new room.

**dorsal** ADJ. relating to the back of an animal. A shark may be identified by its *dorsal* fin, which projects above the surface of the ocean.

**dossier** N. file of documents on a subject. Ordered by J. Edgar Hoover to investigate the senator, the FBI compiled a complete *dossier* on him.

**dotage** N. senility. In his *dotage*, the old man bored us with long tales of events in his childhood.

**dote** V. be excessively fond of; show signs of mental decline. Not only grandmothers bore you with stories about their brilliant grandchildren; grandfathers *dote* on the little rascals, too.

**dour** ADJ. sullen; stubborn. The man was *dour* and taciturn.

**douse** V. plunge into water; drench; extinguish. They *doused* each other with hoses and water balloons.

**dowdy** ADJ. slovenly; untidy. She tried to change her *dowdy* image by buying a fashionable new wardrobe.

**downcast** ADJ. disheartened; sad. Cheerful and optimistic by nature, Beth was never *downcast* despite the difficulties she faced.

**drab** ADJ. dull; lacking color; cheerless. The Dutch woman's *drab* winter coat contrasted with the distinctive, colorful native costume she wore beneath it.

**draconian** ADJ. extremely severe. When the principal canceled the senior prom because some seniors had been late to school that week, we thought the *draconian* punishment was far too harsh for such a minor violation of the rules.

**dregs** N. sediment; worthless residue. David poured the wine carefully to avoid stirring up the *dregs*.

**drivel** N. nonsense; foolishness. Why do I have to spend my days listening to such idiotic *drivel*? Drivel is related to dribble: think of a dribbling, *driveling* idiot.

**droll** ADJ. queer and amusing. He was a popular guest because his *droll* anecdotes were always entertaining.

**drone** N. idle person; male bee. Content to let his wife support him, the would-be writer was in reality nothing but a *drone*.

**drone** V. talk dully; buzz or murmur like a bee. On a gorgeous day, who wants to be stuck in a classroom listening to the teacher *drone*?

**dross** N. waste matter; worthless impurities. Many methods have been devised to separate the valuable metal from the *dross*.

**drudgery** N. menial work. Cinderella's fairy godmother rescued her from a life of *drudgery*.

**dubious** ADJ. questionable; filled with doubt. Some critics of the GRE contend the test is of *dubious* worth. Tony claimed he could get a perfect score on the test, but Tina was *dubious*: she knew he hadn't cracked a book in three years. dubiety, N.

**ductile** ADJ. malleable; flexible; pliable. Copper is an extremely *ductile* material: you can stretch it into the thinnest of wires, bend it, even wind it into loops. ductility, N.

**dulcet** ADJ. sweet sounding. The *dulcet* sounds of the birds at dawn were soon drowned out by the roar of traffic passing our motel.

**dumbfound** V. astonish. Egbert's perfect score on the GRE *dumbfounded* his classmates, who had always considered him to be utterly dumb.

■ **dupe** N. someone easily fooled. While the gullible Watson often was made a *dupe* by unscrupulous parties, Sherlock Holmes was far more difficult to fool.

**duplicity** N. double-dealing; hypocrisy. When Tanya learned that Mark had been two-timing her, she was furious at his *duplicity*. duplicitous, ADJ.

# Test

## Word List 15 *Synonyms and Antonyms*

Each of the questions below consists of a word in capital letters, followed by five lettered words or phrases. Choose the lettered word or phrase that is most nearly similar or opposite in meaning to the word in capital letters and write the letter of your choice on your answer paper.

211. DISINGENUOUS (A) uncomfortable (B) eventual (C) naive (D) complex (E) enthusiastic

212. DISINTERESTED (A) prejudiced (B) horrendous (C) affected (D) arbitrary (E) bored

213. DISJOINTED (A) satisfied (B) carved (C) understood (D) connected (E) evicted

214. DISPARITY (A) resonance (B) elocution (C) relief (D) difference (E) symbolism

215. DISPASSIONATE (A) sensual (B) immoral (C) inhibited (D) impartial (E) scientific

216. DISPIRITED (A) current (B) dented (C) drooping (D) alcoholic (E) dallying

217. DISSIPATE (A) economize (B) clean (C) accept (D) anticipate (E) withdraw

218. DISTEND (A) bloat (B) adjust (C) exist (D) materialize (E) finish

219. DISTRAIT (A) clever (B) industrial (C) absentminded (D) narrow (E) crooked

220. DIVULGE (A) look (B) refuse (C) deride (D) reveal (E) harm

221. DOFF (A) withdraw (B) take off (C) remain (D) control (E) start

222. DOGMATIC (A) benign (B) canine (C) impatient (D) petulant (E) arbitrary

223. DOTAGE (A) senility (B) silence (C) sensitivity (D) interest (E) generosity

224. DOUR (A) sullen (B) ornamental (C) grizzled (D) lacking speech (E) international

225. DROLL (A) rotund (B) amusing (C) fearsome (D) tiny (E) strange

## Word List 16 duration–encroachment

**duration** N. length of time something lasts. Because she wanted the children to make a good impression on the dinner guests, Mother promised them a treat if they'd behave well for the *duration* of the meal.

**duress** N. forcible restraint, especially unlawfully. The hostages were held under *duress* until the prisoners' demands were met.

**dutiful** ADJ. respectful; obedient. When Mother told Billy to kiss Great-Aunt Hattie, the boy obediently gave the old woman a *dutiful* peck on her cheek.

**dwindle** V. shrink; reduce. The food in the lifeboat gradually *dwindled* away to nothing.

**dynamic** ADJ. energetic; vigorously active. The *dynamic* aerobics instructor kept her students on the run; she was a little *dynamo*.

**dyspeptic** ADJ. suffering from indigestion. All the talk about rich food made him feel *dyspeptic*. dyspepsia, N.

**earthy** ADJ. unrefined; coarse. His *earthy* remarks often embarrassed the women in his audience.

**ebb**  V. recede; lessen. Sitting on the beach, Mrs. Dalloway watched the tide *ebb:* the waters receded, drawing away from her as she sat there all alone. also N.

■ **ebullient**  ADJ. showing excitement; overflowing with enthusiasm. Amy's *ebullient* nature could not be repressed; she was always bubbling over with excitement. ebullience, N.

**eccentric**  ADJ. irregular; odd; whimsical; bizarre. The comet veered dangerously close to the earth in its *eccentric* orbit.  People came up with some *eccentric* ideas for dealing with the emergency: one kook suggested tying a knot in the comet's tail!

**eccentricity**  N. oddity; idiosyncrasy. Some of his friends tried to account for his rudeness to strangers as the *eccentricity* of genius.

**ecclesiastic**  ADJ. pertaining to the church. The minister donned his *ecclesiastic* garb and walked to the pulpit. also N.

■ **eclectic**  ADJ. selective; composed of elements drawn from disparate sources. His style of interior decoration was *eclectic:* bits and pieces of furnishings from widely divergent periods, strikingly juxtaposed to create a unique decor. eclecticism, N.

**eclipse**  V. darken; extinguish; surpass. The new stock market high *eclipsed* the previous record set in 1985.

**ecologist**  N. person concerned with the interrelationship between living organisms and their environment. The *ecologist* was concerned that the new dam would upset the natural balance of the creatures living in Glen Canyon.

**economy**  N. efficiency or conciseness in using something. Reading the epigrams of Pope, I admire the *economy* of his verse: in few words he conveys worlds of meaning. (secondary meaning)

**ecstasy**  N. rapture; joy; any overpowering emotion. When Allison received her long-hoped-for letter of acceptance from Harvard, she was in *ecstasy*. ecstatic, ADJ.

**eddy**  N. swirling current of water, air, etc. The water in the tide pool was still, except for an occasional *eddy*. also V.

**edict**  N. decree (especially one issued by a sovereign); official command. The emperor issued an *edict* decreeing that everyone should come see him model his magnificent new clothes.

**edify**  V. instruct; correct morally. Although his purpose was to *edify* and not to entertain his audience, many of his listeners were amused and not enlightened.

**eerie**  ADJ. weird. In that *eerie* setting, it was easy to believe in ghosts and other supernatural beings

**efface**  V. rub out. The coin had been handled so many times that its date had been *effaced*.

**effectual**  ADJ. able to produce a desired effect; valid. Medical researchers are concerned because of the development of drug-resistant strains of bacteria; many once-useful antibiotics are no longer *effectual* in curing bacterial infections.

**effeminate**  ADJ. having womanly traits. His voice was high-pitched and *effeminate*.

**effervescence**  N. inner excitement or exuberance; bubbling from fermentation or carbonation. Nothing depressed Sue for long; her natural *effervescence* soon reasserted itself.  Soda that loses its *effervescence* goes flat. effervescent, ADJ. effervesce, V.

**effete**  ADJ. worn out; exhausted; barren. The literature of the age reflected the *effete* condition of the writers; no new ideas were forthcoming.

■ **efficacy**  N. power to produce desired effect. The *efficacy* of this drug depends on the regularity of the dosage. efficacious, ADJ.

**effigy**  N. dummy. The mob showed its irritation by hanging the judge in *effigy*.

**effluvium**  N. noxious smell. Air pollution has become a serious problem in our major cities; the *effluvium* and the poisons in the air are hazards to life. effluvia, PL.

■ **effrontery**  N. shameless boldness. She had the *effrontery* to insult the guest.

**effusion**  N. pouring forth. The critics objected to her literary *effusion* because it was too flowery.

**effusive**  ADJ. pouring forth; gushing. Her *effusive* manner of greeting her friends finally began to irritate them.

**egoism**  N. excessive interest in one's self; belief that one should be interested in one's self rather than in others. His *egoism* prevented him from seeing the needs of his colleagues.

**egotistical**  ADJ. excessively self-centered; self-important; conceited. Typical *egotistical* remark: "But enough of this chitchat about you and your little problems. Let's talk about what's really important: me!" egotistic, ADJ. egotism, N.

**egregious**  ADJ. notorious; conspicuously bad or shocking. She was an *egregious* liar; we all knew better than to believe a word she said. Ed's housekeeping was *egregious:* he let his dirty dishes pile up so long that they were stuck together with last week's food.

**egress**  N. exit. Barnum's sign "To the *Egress*" fooled many people who thought they were going to see an animal and instead found themselves in the street.

**ejaculation**  N. exclamation. He could not repress an *ejaculation* of surprise when he heard the news.

**elaboration**  N. addition of details; intricacy. Tell what happened simply, without any *elaboration*. elaborate, V.

**elated**  ADJ. overjoyed; in high spirits. Grinning from ear to ear, Bonnie Blair was clearly *elated* by her fifth Olympic gold medal. elation, N.

■ **elegy**  N. poem or song expressing lamentation. On the death of Edward King, Milton composed the *elegy* "Lycidas." elegiacal, ADJ.

■ **elicit**  V. draw out by discussion. The detectives tried to *elicit* where he had hidden his loot.

**elixir**  N. cure-all; something invigorating. The news of her chance to go abroad acted on her like an *elixir*.

**ellipsis**  N. omission of words from a text. Sometimes an *ellipsis* can lead to a dangling modifier, as in the sentence "Once dressed, ... you should refrigerate the pota-to salad."

**elliptical** ADJ. oval; ambiguous, either purposely or because key words have been left out. An *elliptical* billiard ball wobbles because it is not perfectly round; an *elliptical* remark baffles because it is not perfectly clear.

**eloquence** N. expressiveness; persuasive speech. The crowds were stirred by Martin Luther King's *eloquence*.

**elucidate** V. explain; enlighten. He was called upon to *elucidate* the disputed points in his article.

**elusive** ADJ. evasive; baffling; hard to grasp. Trying to pin down exactly when the contractors would be done remodeling the house, Nancy was frustrated by their *elusive* replies. elude, V.

**elysian** ADJ. relating to paradise; blissful. An afternoon sail on the bay was for her an *elysian* journey.

**emaciated** ADJ. thin and wasted. His long period of starvation had left him *emaciated*.

**emanate** V. issue forth. A strong odor of sulfur *emanated* from the spring.

**emancipate** V. set free. At first, the attempts of the Abolitionists to *emancipate* the slaves were unpopular in New England as well as in the South.

**embargo** N. ban on commerce or other activity. As a result of the *embargo*, trade with the colonies was at a standstill.

**embark** V. commence; go on board a boat; begin a journey. In devoting herself to the study of gorillas, Dian Fossey *embarked* on a course of action that was to cost her her life.

**embed** V. enclose; place in something. Tales of actual historical figures like King Alfred have become *embedded* in legends.

■ **embellish** V. adorn; ornament; enhance, as a story. The costume designer *embellished* the leading lady's ball gown with yards and yards of ribbon and lace.

**embezzlement** N. stealing. The bank teller confessed his *embezzlement* of the funds.

**emboss** V. produce a design in raised relief. The secretary of the corporation uses a special stamp to *emboss* the corporate seal on all official documents.

**embrace** V. hug; adopt or espouse; accept readily; encircle; include. Clasping Maid Marian in his arms, Robin Hood *embraced* her lovingly. In joining the outlaws in Sherwood Forest, she had openly *embraced* their cause. also N.

**embroider** V. decorate with needlework; ornament with fancy or fictitious details. For her mother's birthday, Beth *embroidered* a lovely design on a handkerchief. When asked what made her late getting home, Jo *embroidered* her account with tales of runaway horses and rescuing people from a ditch. embroidery, N.

**embroil** V. throw into confusion; involve in strife; entangle. He became *embroiled* in the heated discussion when he tried to arbitrate the dispute.

**embryonic** ADJ. undeveloped; rudimentary. The evil of class and race hatred must be eliminated while it is still in an *embryonic* state; otherwise, it may grow to dangerous proportions.

**emend** V. correct, usually a text. The critic *emended* the book by retranslating several passages.

**emendation** N. correction of errors; improvement. Please initial all the *emendations* you have made in this contract.

**emetic** N. substance causing vomiting. Ingesting an *emetic* like mustard is useful in some cases of poisoning.

**eminent** ADJ. high; lofty. After her appointment to this *eminent* position, she seldom had time for her former friends.

**emissary** N. agent; messenger. The Secretary of State was sent as the president's special *emissary* to the conference on disarmament.

**emollient** N. soothing or softening remedy. He applied an *emollient* to the inflamed area. also ADJ.

**emolument** N. salary; compensation. In addition to the *emolument* this position offers, you must consider the social prestige it carries with it.

**empathy** N. ability to identify with another's feelings, ideas, etc. What made Ann such a fine counselor was her *empathy*, her ability to put herself in her client's place and feel his emotions as if they were her own. empathize, V.

■ **empirical** ADJ. based on experience. He distrusted hunches and intuitive flashes; he placed his reliance entirely on *empirical* data.

■ **emulate** V. imitate; rival. In a brief essay, describe a person you admire, someone whose virtues you would like to *emulate*.

**enamored** ADJ. in love. Narcissus became *enamored* of his own beauty.

**encipher** V. encode; convert a message into code. In one of Bond's first lessons he learned how to *encipher* the messages he sent to Miss Moneypenny so that none of his other lady friends could read them.

**enclave** N. territory enclosed within an alien land. The Vatican is an independent *enclave* in Italy.

**encomiastic** ADJ. praising; eulogistic. Some critics believe that his *encomiastic* statements about Napoleon were inspired by his desire for material advancement rather than by an honest belief in the Emperor's genius.

**encomium** N. high praise; eulogy. Uneasy with the *encomiums* expressed by his supporters, Tolkien felt unworthy of such high praise.

**encompass** V. surround. Although we were *encompassed* by enemy forces, we were cheerful for we were well stocked and could withstand a siege until our allies joined us.

**encroachment** N. gradual intrusion. The *encroachment* of the factories upon the neighborhood lowered the value of the real estate.

# Test

## Word List 16    *Synonyms*

Each of the questions below consists of a word in capital letters, followed by five lettered words or phrases. Choose the lettered word or phrase that is most nearly similar in meaning to the word in capital letters and write the letter of your choice on your answer paper.

226. DWINDLE (A) blow (B) inhabit (C) spin (D) lessen (E) combine

227. ECSTASY (A) joy (B) speed (C) treasure (D) warmth (E) lack

228. EDIFY (A) mystify (B) suffice (C) improve (D) erect (E) entertain

229. EFFACE (A) countenance (B) encourage (C) recognize (D) blackball (E) rub out

230. EFFIGY (A) requisition (B) organ (C) charge (D) accordion (E) dummy

231. EGREGIOUS (A) pious (B) shocking (C) anxious (D) sociable (E) gloomy

232. EGRESS (A) entrance (B) bird (C) exit (D) double (E) progress

233. ELATED (A) debased (B) respectful (C) drooping (D) gay (E) charitable

234. ELUSIVE (A) deadly (B) eloping (C) evasive (D) simple (E) petrified

235. EMACIATED (A) garrulous (B) primeval (C) vigorous (D) disparate (E) thin

236. EMANCIPATE (A) set free (B) take back (C) make worse (D) embolden (E) run away

237. EMBELLISH (A) doff (B) don (C) abscond (D) adorn (E) equalize

238. EMBROIL (A) cherish (B) overheat (C) entangle (D) assure (E) worry

239. EMENDATION (A) correction (B) interpretation (C) exhumation (D) inquiry (E) fault

240. EMINENT (A) purposeful (B) high (C) delectable (D) curious (E) urgent

## Word List 17    encumber–eulogistic

**encumber** v. burden. Some people *encumber* themselves with too much luggage when they take short trips.

**endearment** N. fond word or act. Your gifts and *endearments* cannot make me forget your earlier insolence.

■ **endemic** ADJ. prevailing among a specific group of people or in a specific area or country. This disease is *endemic* in this part of the world; more than 80 percent of the population are at one time or another affected by it.

**endorse** v. approve; support. Everyone waited to see which one of the rival candidates for the city council the mayor would *endorse*. (secondary meaning) endorsement, N.

**endue** v. provide with some quality; endow. He was *endued* with a lion's courage.

**enduring** ADJ. lasting; surviving. Keats believed in the *enduring* power of great art, which would outlast its creators' brief lives.

**energize** v. invigorate; make forceful and active. Rather than exhausting Maggie, dancing *energized* her.

■ **enervate** v. weaken. She was slow to recover from her illness; even a short walk to the window *enervated* her. enervation, N.

**enfranchise** v. admit to the rights of citizenship (especially the right to vote). Although blacks were *enfranchised* shortly after the Civil War, women did not receive the right to vote until 1920.

**engage** v. attract; hire; pledge oneself; confront. "Your case has *engaged* my interest, my lord," said Holmes. "You may *engage* my services."

**engaging** ADJ. charming; attractive. Everyone liked Nancy's pleasant manners and *engaging* personality.

■ **engender** v. cause; produce. To receive praise for real accomplishments *engenders* self-confidence in a child.

**engross** v. occupy fully. John was so *engrossed* in his studies that he did not hear his mother call.

■ **enhance** v. increase; improve. You can *enhance* your chances of being admitted to the college of your choice by learning to write well; an excellent essay will *enhance* any application.

**enigma** N. puzzle; mystery. "What do women want?" asked Dr. Sigmund Freud. Their behavior was an *enigma* to him.

**enigmatic** ADJ. obscure; puzzling. Many have sought to fathom the *enigmatic* smile of the *Mona Lisa*.

**enjoin** v. command; order; forbid. The owners of the company asked the court to *enjoin* the union from picketing the plant.

**enmity** N. ill will; hatred. At Camp David President Carter labored to bring an end to the *enmity* that prevented Egypt and Israel from living in peace.

**ennui** N. boredom. The monotonous routine of hospital life induced a feeling of *ennui* that made her moody and irritable.

**enormity** N. hugeness (in a bad sense). He did not realize the *enormity* of his crime until he saw what suffering he had caused.

**enrapture** v. please intensely. The audience was *enraptured* by the freshness of the voices and the excellent orchestration.

**ensconce** V. settle comfortably. Now that their children were *ensconced* safely in the private school, the jet-setting parents decided to leave for Europe.

**ensue** V. follow. The evils that *ensued* were the direct result of the miscalculations of the leaders.

**entail** V. require; necessitate; involve. Building a college-level vocabulary will *entail* some work on your part.

**enterprising** ADJ. full of initiative. By coming up with fresh ways to market the company's products, Mike proved himself to be an *enterprising* businessman.

**enthrall** V. capture; enslave. From the moment he saw her picture, he was *enthralled* by her beauty.

**entice** V. lure; attract; tempt. She always tried to *entice* her baby brother into mischief.

**entity** N. real being. As soon as the charter was adopted, the United Nations became an *entity* and had to be considered as a factor in world diplomacy.

**entomology** N. study of insects. Kent found *entomology* the most annoying part of his biology course; studying insects bugged him.

**entrance** V. put under a spell; carry away with emotion. Shafts of sunlight on a wall could *entrance* her and leave her spellbound.

**entreat** V. plead; ask earnestly. She *entreated* her father to let her stay out till midnight.

**entree** N. entrance; a way in. Because of his wealth and social position, he had *entree* into the most exclusive circles.

**entrepreneur** N. businessperson; contractor. Opponents of our present tax program argue that it discourages *entrepreneurs* from trying new fields of business activity.

**enumerate** V. list; mention one by one. Huck hung his head in shame as Miss Watson *enumerated* his many flaws.

**enunciate** V. utter or speak, especially distinctly. Stop mumbling! How will people understand you if you do not *enunciate* clearly?

**environ** V. enclose; surround. In medieval days, Paris was *environed* by a wall. environs, N.

**eon** N. long period of time; an age. It has taken *eons* for our civilization to develop.

**epaulet** N. ornament worn on the shoulder (of a uniform, etc.). The shoulder loops on Sam Spade's trench coat are the nonmilitary counterparts of the fringed *epaulets* on George Washington's uniform.

■ **ephemeral** ADJ. short-lived; fleeting. The mayfly is an *ephemeral* creature: its adult life lasts little more than a day.

**epic** N. long heroic poem, novel, or similar work of art. Kurosawa's film *Seven Samurai* is an *epic* portraying the struggle of seven warriors to destroy a band of robbers. also ADJ.

**epicure** N. connoisseur of food and drink. *Epicures* frequent this restaurant because it features exotic wines and dishes. epicurean, ADJ.

**epigram** N. witty thought or saying, usually short. Poor

Richard's *epigrams* made Benjamin Franklin famous.

**epilogue** N. short speech at conclusion of dramatic work. The audience was so disappointed in the play that many did not remain to hear the *epilogue*.

**episodic** ADJ. loosely connected. Though he tried to follow the plot of *Gravity's Rainbow*, John found the novel too *episodic*.

**epistemologist** N. philosopher who studies the nature of knowledge. "What is more important, a knowledge of nature or the nature of knowledge?" the *epistemologist* asked the naturalist.

**epitaph** N. inscription in memory of a dead person. In his will, he dictated the *epitaph* he wanted placed on his tombstone.

**epithet** N. word or phrase characteristically used to describe a person or thing. So many kings of France were named Charles that modern students need *epithets* to tell them apart: Charles the Wise, for example, was someone far different from Charles the Fat.

**epitome** N. perfect example or embodiment. Singing "I am the very model of a modern Major-General" in *The Pirates of Penzance*, Major-General Stanley proclaimed himself the *epitome* of an officer and a gentleman. epitomize, V.

**epoch** N. period of time. The glacial *epoch* lasted for thousands of years.

**equable** ADJ. tranquil; steady; uniform. After the hot summers and cold winters of New England, she found the climate of the West Indies *equable* and pleasant.

■ **equanimity** N. calmness of temperament; composure. Even the inevitable strains of caring for an ailing mother did not disturb Bea's *equanimity*.

**equestrian** N. rider on horseback. These paths in the park are reserved for *equestrians* and their steeds. also ADJ.

**equilibrium** N. balance. After the divorce, he needed some time to regain his *equilibrium*.

**equine** ADJ. resembling a horse. Her long, bony face had an *equine* look to it.

**equinox** N. period of equal days and nights; the beginning of spring and autumn. The vernal *equinox* is usually marked by heavy rainstorms.

**equipoise** N. balance; balancing force; equilibrium. The high-wire acrobat used his pole as an *equipoise* to overcome the swaying caused by the wind.

**equitable** ADJ. fair; impartial. I am seeking an *equitable* solution to this dispute, one that will be fair and acceptable to both sides.

**equity** N. fairness; justice. Our courts guarantee *equity* to all.

**equivocal** ADJ. ambiguous; intentionally misleading. Rejecting the candidate's *equivocal* comments on tax reform, the reporters pressed him to state clearly where he stood on the issue. equivocate, V. equivocation, N.

■ **equivocate** V. lie; mislead; attempt to conceal the truth. The audience saw through his attempts to *equivocate* on the subject under discussion and ridiculed his remarks.

**erode** v. eat away. The limestone was *eroded* by the dripping water until only a thin shell remained. erosion, N.

**erotic** ADJ. pertaining to passionate love. The *erotic* passages in this novel should be removed as they are merely pornographic.

**errant** ADJ. wandering. Many a charming tale has been written about the knights-*errant* who helped the weak and punished the guilty during the Age of Chivalry.

**erratic** ADJ. odd; unpredictable. Investors become anxious when the stock market appears *erratic*.

**erroneous** ADJ. mistaken; wrong. I thought my answer was correct, but it was *erroneous*.

■ **erudite** ADJ. learned; scholarly. Though his fellow students thought him *erudite*, Paul knew he would have to spend many years in serious study before he could consider himself a scholar. erudition, N.

**escapade** N. prank; flighty conduct. The headmaster could not regard this latest *escapade* as a boyish joke and expelled the young man.

**eschew** v. avoid. Hoping to present himself to his girlfriend as a totally reformed character, he tried to *eschew* all the vices, especially chewing tobacco and drinking bathtub gin.

■ **esoteric** ADJ. hard to understand; known only to the chosen few. *New Yorker* short stories often include *esoteric* allusions to obscure people and events. The implication is, if you are in the in-crowd, you'll get the reference; if you come from Cleveland, you won't. esoterica, N.

**espionage** N. spying. In order to maintain its power, the government developed a system of *espionage* that penetrated every household.

**espouse** v. adopt; support. She was always ready to *espouse* a worthy cause.

**esteem** v. respect; value. Jill *esteemed* Jack's taste in music, but she deplored his taste in clothes. also N.

**estranged** ADJ. separated; alienated. The *estranged* wife sought a divorce. estrangement, N.

**ethereal** ADJ. light; heavenly; unusually refined. In Shakespeare's *The Tempest*, the spirit Ariel is an *ethereal* creature, too airy and unearthly for our mortal world.

**ethnic** ADJ. relating to races. Intolerance between *ethnic* groups is deplorable and usually is based on lack of information.

**ethnology** N. study of humankind. Sociology is one aspect of the science of *ethnology*.

**ethos** N. underlying character of a culture, group, etc. Seeing how tenderly Spaniards treated her small daughter made author Barbara Kingsolver aware of how greatly children were valued in the Spanish *ethos*.

**etymology** N. study of word parts. A knowledge of *etymology* can help you on many English tests: if you know what the roots and prefixes mean, you can determine the meanings of unfamiliar words.

**eugenic** ADJ. pertaining to the improvement of race. It is easier to apply *eugenic* principles to the raising of racehorses or prize cattle than to the development of human beings.

**eulogistic** ADJ. praising. To everyone's surprise, the speech was *eulogistic* rather than critical in tone.

**Test**

# Word List 17    *Antonyms*

Each of the questions below consists of a word in capital letters, followed by five lettered words or phrases. Choose the lettered word or phrase that is most nearly opposite in meaning to the word in capital letters and write the letter of your choice on your answer paper.

241. ENERVATE (A) strengthen (B) sputter (C) arrange (D) scrutinize (E) agree

242. ENHANCE (A) degrade (B) doubt (C) scuff (D) gasp (E) avoid

243. ENNUI (A) hate (B) excitement (C) seriousness (D) humility (E) kindness

244. ENUNCIATE (A) pray (B) request (C) deliver (D) wait (E) mumble

245. EPHEMERAL (A) sensuous (B) passing (C) popular (D) distasteful (E) eternal

246. EQUABLE (A) flat (B) decisive (C) stormy (D) dishonest (E) scanty

247. EQUANIMITY (A) agitation (B) stirring (C) volume (D) identity (E) luster

248. EQUILIBRIUM (A) imbalance (B) peace (C) inequity (D) directness (E) urgency

249. EQUITABLE (A) able to leave (B) able to learn (C) unfair (D) preferable (E) rough

250. EQUIVOCAL (A) mistaken (B) quaint (C) azure (D) clear (E) universal

251. ERRATIC (A) unromantic (B) free (C) popular (D) steady (E) unknown

252. ERRONEOUS (A) accurate (B) dignified (C) curious (D) abrupt (E) round

253. ERUDITE (A) professorial (B) stately (C) short (D) unknown (E) ignorant

254. ETHEREAL (A) long-lasting (B) earthy (C) ill (D) critical (E) false

255. EULOGISTIC (A) pretty (B) critical (C) brief (D) stern (E) free

# Word List 18     eulogy-faculty

■ **eulogy**  N. expression of praise, often on the occasion of someone's death. Instead of delivering a spoken *eulogy* at Genny's memorial service, Jeff sang a song he had written in her honor. eulogize, V.

■ **euphemism**  N. mild expression in place of an unpleasant one. The expression "he passed away" is a *euphemism* for "he died."

**euphony**  N. sweet sound. Noted for its *euphony* even when it is spoken, the Italian language is particularly pleasing to the ear when sung. euphonious, ADJ.

**euphoria**  N. feeling of exaggerated (or unfounded) well-being. "Jill's been on cloud nine ever since Jack asked her out," said Betty, dismissing her friend's *euphoria.*

**euthanasia**  N. mercy killing. Many people support *euthanasia* for terminally ill patients who wish to die.

**evanescent**  ADJ. fleeting; vanishing. For a brief moment, the entire skyline was bathed in an orange-red hue in the *evanescent* rays of the sunset.

**evasive**  ADJ. not frank; eluding. Your *evasive* answers convinced the judge that you were withholding important evidence. evade, V.

**evince**  V. show clearly. When he tried to answer the questions, he *evinced* his ignorance of the subject matter.

**evenhanded**  ADJ. impartial; fair. Do men and women receive *evenhanded* treatment from their teachers, or, as recent studies suggest, do teachers pay more attention to male students than to females?

**evocative**  ADJ. tending to call up (emotions, memories). Scent can be remarkably *evocative*. The aroma of pipe tobacco *evokes* the memory of my father; a whiff of talcum powder calls up images of my daughter as a child.

**evoke**  V. call forth. He *evoked* much criticism by his hostile manner. evocation, N.

**ewe**  N. female sheep. The flock of sheep was made up of dozens of *ewes,* together with only a handful of rams.

■ **exacerbate**  V. worsen; embitter. The latest bombing *exacerbated* England's already existing bitterness against the IRA, causing the Prime Minister to break off the peace talks abruptly. exacerbation, N.

**exacting**  ADJ. extremely demanding. Cleaning the ceiling of the Sistine Chapel was an *exacting* task, one that demanded extremely meticulous care on the part of the restorers. exaction, N.

**exalt**  V. raise in rank or dignity; praise. The actor Alec Guinness was *exalted* to the rank of knighthood by the Queen; he now is known as Sir Alec Guinness.

**exasperate**  V. vex. Johnny often *exasperates* his mother with his pranks.

**exceptionable**  ADJ. objectionable. Do you find the punk rock band Green Day a highly *exceptionable,* thoroughly distasteful group, or do you think they are exceptionally talented performers?

**excerpt**  N. selected passage (written or musical). The cinematic equivalent of an *excerpt* from a novel is a clip from a film. also V.

**exchequer**  N. treasury. He had been Chancellor of the *Exchequer* before his promotion to the office he now holds.

**excise**  V. cut away; cut out. When you *excise* the dead and dying limbs of a tree, you not only improve its appearance but also enhance its chances of bearing fruit. excision, N.

**exclaim**  V. cry out suddenly. "Watson!  Behind you!" Holmes *exclaimed,* seeing the assassin hurl himself on his friend. exclamation, N. exclamatory, ADJ.

**excoriate**  V. scold with biting harshness; strip the skin off. Seeing the rips in Bill's new pants, his mother furiously *excoriated* him for ruining his good clothes. The tight, starched collar chafed and *excoriated* his neck, rubbing it raw.

■ **exculpate**  V. clear from blame. She was *exculpated* of the crime when the real criminal confessed.

**execrable**  ADJ. very bad. The anecdote was in such *execrable* taste that the audience was revolted.

**execrate**  V. curse; express abhorrence for. The world *execrates* the memory of Hitler and hopes that genocide will never again be the policy of any nation.

**execute**  V. put into effect; carry out. The choreographer wanted to see how well she could *execute* a pirouette. (secondary meaning) execution, N.

**exegesis**  N. explanation, especially of biblical passages. I can follow your *exegesis* of this passage to a limited degree; some of your reasoning eludes me.

**exemplary**  ADJ. serving as a model; outstanding. At commencement the dean praised Ellen for her *exemplary* behavior as class president.

**exemplify**  V. show by example; furnish an example. Three-time winner of the Super Bowl, Joe Montana *exemplifies* the ideal quarterback.

**exempt**  ADJ. not subject to a duty or obligation. Because of his flat feet, Foster was *exempt* from serving in the armed forces. also V.

**exertion**  N. effort; expenditure of much physical work. The *exertion* involved in unscrewing the rusty bolt left her exhausted.

**exhilarating**  ADJ. invigorating and refreshing; cheering. Though some of the hikers found tramping through the snow tiring, Jeffrey found the walk on the cold, crisp day *exhilarating.* His *exhilaration* was so great that, at the hike's end, he wanted to walk another five miles.

**exhort**  V. urge. The evangelist *exhorted* all the sinners in the audience to reform. exhortation, N.

**exhume**  V. dig out of the ground; remove from the grave. Could evidence that might identify the serial killer have been buried with his victim? To answer this question, the police asked the authorities for permission to *exhume* the victim's body.

■ **exigency** N. urgent situation. In this *exigency*, we must look for aid from our allies. exigent, ADJ.

**exiguous** ADJ. small; minute. Grass grew here and there, an *exiguous* outcropping among the rocks.

**existential** ADJ. pertaining to existence; pertaining to the philosophy of existentialism. To the *existential* philosopher, human reason is inadequate to explain an irrational, meaningless universe.

**exodus** N. departure. The *exodus* from the hot and stuffy city was particularly noticeable on Friday evenings.

**exonerate** V. acquit; exculpate. The defense team feverishly sought fresh evidence that might *exonerate* their client.

**exorbitant** ADJ. excessive. The people grumbled at his *exorbitant* prices but paid them because he had a monopoly.

**exorcise** V. drive out evil spirits. By incantation and prayer, the medicine man sought to *exorcise* the evil spirits that had taken possession of the young warrior.

**exotic** ADJ. not native; strange. Because of his *exotic* headdress, he was followed in the streets by small children who laughed at his strange appearance.

**expansive** ADJ. outgoing and sociable; broad and extensive; able to increase in size. Mr. Fezziwig was in an *expansive* humor, cheerfully urging his guests to join in the Christmas feast. Looking down on his *expansive* paunch, he sighed: if his belly expanded any further, he'd need an *expansive* waistline for his pants.

**expatiate** V. talk at length. At this time, please give us a brief résumé of your work; we shall permit you to *expatiate* later.

**expatriate** N. exile; someone who has withdrawn from his native land. Henry James was an American *expatriate* who settled in England.

**expedient** ADJ. suitable; practical; politic. A pragmatic politician, she was guided by what was *expedient* rather than by what was ethical. expediency, N.

**expedite** V. hasten. Because we are on a tight schedule, we hope you will be able to *expedite* the delivery of our order. The more *expeditious* your response is, the happier we'll be.

**expenditure** N. payment or expense; output. When you are operating on an expense account, you must keep receipts for all your *expenditures*. If you don't save your receipts, you won't get repaid without the *expenditure* of a lot of energy arguing with the firm's accountants.

**expertise** N. specialized knowledge; expert skill. Although she was knowledgeable in a number of fields, she was hired for her particular *expertise* in computer programming.

**expiate** V. make amends for (a sin). He tried to *expiate* his crimes by a full confession to the authorities.

**expletive** N. interjection; profane oath. The sergeant's remarks were filled with *expletives* that offended the new recruits.

**explicate** V. explain; interpret; clarify. Harry Levin *explicated* James Joyce's novels with such clarity that even *Finnegan's Wake* seemed comprehensible to his students.

**explicit** ADJ. totally clear; definite; outspoken. Don't just hint around that you're dissatisfied: be *explicit* about what's bugging you.

**exploit** N. deed or action, particularly a brave deed. Raoul Wallenberg was noted for his *exploits* in rescuing Jews from Hitler's forces.

**exploit** V. make use of, sometimes unjustly. Cesar Chavez fought attempts to *exploit* migrant farmworkers in California. exploitation, N.

**expository** ADJ. explanatory; serving to explain. The manual that came with my VCR was no masterpiece of *expository* prose: its explanations were so garbled that I couldn't even figure out how to rewind a tape.

**expostulation** N. protest; remonstrance. Despite the teacher's scoldings and *expostulations*, the class remained unruly.

**exposure** N. risk, particularly of being exposed to disease or to the elements; unmasking; act of laying something open. *Exposure* to sun and wind had dried out her hair and weathered her face. She looked so changed that she no longer feared *exposure* as the notorious Irene Adler, one-time antagonist of Sherlock Holmes.

**expropriate** V. take possession of. He questioned the government's right to *expropriate* his land to create a wildlife preserve.

**expunge** V. cancel; remove. If you behave, I will *expunge* this notation from your record.

**expurgate** V. clean; remove offensive parts of a book. The editors felt that certain passages in the book had to be *expurgated* before it could be used in the classroom.

**extant** ADJ. still in existence. Although the book is out of print, some copies are still *extant*. Unfortunately, all of them are in libraries or private collections; none is for sale.

**extemporaneous** ADJ. not planned; impromptu. Because her *extemporaneous* remarks were misinterpreted, she decided to write all her speeches in advance.

**extenuate** V. weaken; mitigate. It is easier for us to *extenuate* our own shortcomings than those of others.

**extirpate** V. root up. The Salem witch trials were a misguided attempt to *extirpate* superstition and heresy.

**extol** V. praise; glorify. The president *extolled* the astronauts, calling them the pioneers of the Space Age.

**extort** V. wring from; get money by threats, etc. The blackmailer *extorted* money from his victim.

**extradition** N. surrender of prisoner by one state to another. The lawyers opposed the *extradition* of their client on the grounds that for more than five years he had been a model citizen.

**extraneous** ADJ. not essential; superfluous. No wonder Ted can't think straight! His mind is so cluttered up with *extraneous* details, he can't concentrate on the essentials.

■ **extrapolation** N. projection; conjecture. Based on their *extrapolation* from the results of the primaries on Super Tuesday, the networks predicted that George W. Bush would be the Republican candidate for the presidency. extrapolate, V.

**extricate** V. free; disentangle. Icebreakers were needed to *extricate* the trapped whales from the icy floes that closed them in.

**extrinsic** ADJ. external; not essential; extraneous. A critically acclaimed *extrinsic* feature of the Chrysler Building is its ornate spire. The judge would not admit the testimony, ruling that it was *extrinsic* to the matter at hand.

**extrovert** N. person interested mostly in external objects and actions. A good salesperson is usually an *extrovert* who likes to mingle with people.

**extrude** V. force or push out. Much pressure is required to *extrude* these plastics.

**exuberance** N. overflowing abundance; joyful enthusiasm; flamboyance; lavishness. I was bowled over by the *exuberance* of Amy's welcome. Cheeks glowing, she was the picture of *exuberant* good health.

**exude** V. discharge; give forth. The maple syrup is obtained from the sap that the trees *exude* in early spring. exudation, N.

**exult** V. rejoice. We *exulted* when our team won the victory.

**fabricate** V. build; lie. If we *fabricate* the buildings in this project out of standardized sections, we can reduce construction costs considerably. Because of Jack's tendency to *fabricate,* Jill had trouble believing a word he said.

**facade** N. front (of building); superficial or false appearance. The ornate *facade* of the church was often photographed by tourists, who never bothered to walk around the building to view its other sides. Cher's outward show of confidence was just a *facade* she assumed to hide her insecurity.

**facet** N. small plane surface (of a gem); a side. The stonecutter decided to improve the rough diamond by providing it with several *facets.*

■ **facetious** ADJ. joking (often inappropriately); humorous. I'm serious about this project; I don't need any *facetious,* smart-alecky cracks about do-good little rich girls.

**facile** ADJ. easily accomplished; ready or fluent; superficial. Words came easily to Jonathan: he was a *facile* speaker and prided himself on being ready to make a speech at a moment's notice. facility, N.

■ **facilitate** V. help bring about; make less difficult. Rest and proper nourishment should *facilitate* the patient's recovery.

**facsimile** N. copy. Many museums sell *facsimiles* of the works of art on display.

**faction** N. party; clique; dissension. The quarrels and bickering of the two small *factions* within the club disturbed the majority of the members.

**factious** ADJ. inclined to form factions; causing dissension. Your statement is *factious* and will upset the harmony that now exists.

**factitious** ADJ. artificial; sham. Hollywood actresses often create *factitious* tears by using glycerine.

**factotum** N. handyman; person who does all kinds of work. Although we had hired him as a messenger, we soon began to use him as a general *factotum* around the office.

**faculty** N. mental or bodily powers; teaching staff. As he grew old, Professor Twiggly feared he might lose his *faculties* and become unfit to teach. However, while he was in full possession of his *faculties,* the school couldn't kick him off the *faculty.*

# Test

## Word List 18    *Antonyms*

Each of the questions below consists of a word in capital letters, followed by five lettered words or phrases. Choose the lettered word or phrase that is most nearly opposite in meaning to the word in capital letters and write the letter of your choice on your answer paper.

256. EUPHONIOUS (A) strident (B) lethargic (C) literary (D) significant (E) merry

257. EVASIVE (A) frank (B) correct (C) empty (D) fertile (E) watchful

258. EXASPERATE (A) confide (B) formalize (C) placate (D) betray (E) bargain

259. EXCORIATE (A) scandalize (B) encourage (C) avoid (D) praise (E) vanquish

260. EXCULPATE (A) blame (B) prevail (C) acquire (D) ravish (E) accumulate

261. EXECRABLE (A) innumerable (B) philosophic (C) physical (D) excellent (E) meditative

262. EXECRATE (A) disobey (B) enact (C) perform (D) acclaim (E) fidget

263. EXHUME (A) decipher (B) sadden (C) integrate (D) admit (E) inter

264. EXODUS (A) neglect (B) consent (C) entry (D) gain (E) rebuke

265. EXONERATE (A) forge (B) accuse (C) record (D) doctor (E) reimburse

266. EXORBITANT (A) moderate (B) partisan (C) military (D) barbaric (E) counterfeit

267. EXTEMPORANEOUS (A) rehearsed (B) hybrid (C) humiliating (D) statesmanlike (E) picturesque

268. EXTRANEOUS (A) modern (B) decisive (C) essential (D) effective (E) expressive

269. EXTRINSIC (A) reputable (B) inherent (C) swift (D) ambitious (E) cursory

270. EXTROVERT (A) clown (B) hero (C) ectomorph (D) neurotic (E) introvert

## Word List 19   fallacious–flinch

■ **fallacious**   ADJ. false; misleading. Paradoxically, *fallacious* reasoning does not always yield erroneous results: even though your logic may be faulty, the answer you get may be correct. fallacy, N.

**fallible**   ADJ. liable to err. I know I am *fallible*, but I feel confident that I am right this time.

**fallow**   ADJ. plowed but not sowed; uncultivated. Farmers have learned that it is advisable to permit land to lie *fallow* every few years.

**falter**   V. hesitate. When told to dive off the high board, she did not *falter*, but proceeded at once.

**fanaticism**   N. excessive zeal; extreme devotion to a belief or cause. When Islamic fundamentalists demanded the death of Salman Rushdie because his novel questioned their faith, world opinion condemned them for their *fanaticism*. fanatic, ADJ., N.

**fancied**   ADJ. imagined; unreal. You are resenting *fancied* insults. No one has ever said such things about you.

**fancier**   N. breeder or dealer of animals. The dog *fancier* exhibited her prize collie at the annual Kennel Club show.

**fanciful**   ADJ. whimsical; visionary. This is a *fanciful* scheme because it does not consider the facts.

**fanfare**   N. call by bugles or trumpets; showy display. The exposition was opened with a *fanfare* of trumpets and the firing of cannon.

**farce**   N. broad comedy; mockery. Nothing went right; the entire interview degenerated into a *farce*. farcical, ADJ.

**fastidious**   ADJ. difficult to please; squeamish. Bobby was such a *fastidious* eater that he would eat a sandwich only if his mother first cut off every scrap of crust.

**fatalism**   N. belief that events are determined by forces beyond one's control. With *fatalism*, he accepted the hardships that beset him. fatalistic, ADJ.

**fathom**   V. comprehend; investigate. I find his motives impossible to *fathom*; in fact, I'm totally clueless about what goes on in his mind.

■ **fatuous**   ADJ. foolish; inane. She is far too intelligent to utter such *fatuous* remarks.

**fauna**   N. animals of a period or region. The scientist could visualize the *fauna* of the period by examining the skeletal remains and the fossils.

■ **fawning**   ADJ. courting favor by cringing and flattering. She was constantly surrounded by a group of *fawning* admirers who hoped to win some favor. fawn, V.

**faze**   V. disconcert; dismay. No crisis could *faze* the resourceful hotel manager.

**feasible**   ADJ. practical. Is it *feasible* to build a new stadium for the Yankees on New York's West Side? Without additional funding, the project is clearly unrealistic.

**febrile**   ADJ. feverish. In his *febrile* condition, he was subject to nightmares and hallucinations.

**fecundity**   N. fertility; fruitfulness. The *fecundity* of her mind is illustrated by the many vivid images in her poems.

**feign**   V. pretend. Lady Macbeth *feigned* illness in the courtyard although she was actually healthy.

**feint**   N. trick; shift; sham blow. The boxer was fooled by his opponent's *feint* and dropped his guard. also V.

■ **felicitous**   ADJ. apt; suitably expressed; well chosen. He was famous for his *felicitous* remarks and was called upon to serve as master-of-ceremonies at many a banquet.

**felicity**   N. happiness; appropriateness (of a remark, choice, etc.). She wrote a note to the newlyweds wishing them great *felicity* in their wedded life.

**fell**   ADJ. cruel; deadly. The newspapers told of the tragic spread of the *fell* disease.

**fell**   V. cut or knock down; bring down (with a missile). Crying "Timber!" Paul Bunyan *felled* the mighty redwood tree. Robin Hood loosed his arrow and *felled* the king's deer.

**felon**   N. person convicted of a grave crime. A convicted *felon* loses the right to vote.

**feral**   ADJ. not domestic; wild. Abandoned by their owners, dogs may revert to their *feral* state, roaming the woods in packs.

**ferment**   N. agitation; commotion. With the breakup of the Soviet Union, much of Eastern Europe was in a state of *ferment*. also V.

**ferret**   V. drive or hunt out of hiding. She *ferreted* out their secret.

**fervent**   ADJ. ardent; hot. She felt that the *fervent* praise was excessive and somewhat undeserved.

**fervid**   ADJ. ardent. Her *fervid* enthusiasm inspired all of us to undertake the dangerous mission.

■ **fervor**   N. glowing ardor; intensity of feeling. At the protest rally, the students cheered the strikers and booed the dean with equal *fervor*.

**fester**   V. rankle; produce irritation or resentment. Joe's insult *festered* in Anne's mind for days, and made her too angry to speak to him.

**festive**   ADJ. joyous; celebratory. Their wedding in the park was a *festive* occasion.

**fete**   V. honor at a festival. The returning hero was *feted* at a community supper and dance. also N.

**fetid**   ADJ. malodorous. The neglected wound became *fetid*.

**fetter** V. shackle. The prisoner was *fettered* to the wall.

**fiasco** N. total failure. Our ambitious venture ended in a *fiasco* and we were forced to flee.

**fiat** N. command. I cannot accept government by *fiat;* I feel that the wishes of the citizens must be consulted.

**fickle** ADJ. changeable; faithless. As soon as Romeo saw Juliet, he forgot all about his old girlfriend Rosaline. Was Romeo *fickle*?

**fictitious** ADJ. imaginary. Although this book purports to be a biography of George Washington, many of the incidents are *fictitious*.

**fidelity** N. loyalty. A dog's *fidelity* to its owner is one of the reasons why that animal is a favorite household pet.

**figment** N. invention; imaginary thing. That incident never took place; it is a *figment* of your imagination.

**figurative** ADJ. not literal, but metaphorical; using a figure of speech. "To lose one's marbles" is a *figurative* expression; if you're told Jack has lost his marbles, no one expects you to rush out to buy him a replacement set.

**figurine** N. small ornamental statuette. In *The Maltese Falcon*, Sam Spade was hired to trace the missing *figurine* of a black bird.

**filch** V. steal. The boys *filched* apples from the fruit stand.

**filial** ADJ. pertaining to a son or daughter. Many children forget their *filial* obligations and disregard the wishes of their parents.

**filibuster** V. block legislation by making long speeches. Even though we disapproved of Senator Foghorn's political goals, we were impressed by his ability to *filibuster* endlessly to keep an issue from coming to a vote.

**filigree** N. delicate, lacelike metalwork. The pendant with gold *filigree* that she wore round her neck trembled with each breath she took.

**filing** N. particle removed by a file. As the prisoner *filed* away at the iron bar on the cell window, a small heap of *filings* accumulated on the window sill.

**finale** N. conclusion. It is not until we reach the *finale* of this play that we can understand the author's message.

**finesse** N. delicate skill. The *finesse* and adroitness of the surgeon impressed the observers in the operating room.

**finicky** ADJ. too particular; fussy. The little girl was *finicky* about her food, leaving anything that wasn't to her taste.

**finite** ADJ. limited. It is difficult for humanity with its *finite* existence to grasp the infinite.

**firebrand** N. hothead; troublemaker. The police tried to keep track of all the local *firebrands* when the president came to town.

**fissure** N. crevice. The mountain climbers secured footholds in tiny *fissures* in the rock.

**fitful** ADJ. spasmodic; intermittent. After several *fitful* attempts, he decided to postpone the start of the project until he felt more energetic.

**flaccid** ADJ. flabby. His sedentary life had left him with *flaccid* muscles.

■ **flag** V. droop; grow feeble. When the opposing hockey team scored its third goal only minutes into the first period, the home team's spirits *flagged.* flagging, ADJ.

**flagrant** ADJ. conspicuously wicked; blatant; outrageous. The governor's appointment of his brother-in-law to the state Supreme Court was a *flagrant* violation of the state laws against nepotism (favoritism based on kinship).

**flail** V. thresh grain by hand; strike or slap; toss about. In medieval times, warriors *flailed* their foe with a metal ball attached to a handle.

**flair** N. talent. She has an uncanny *flair* for discovering new artists before the public has become aware of their existence.

**flamboyant** ADJ. ornate. Modern architecture has discarded the *flamboyant* trimming on buildings and emphasizes simplicity of line.

**flaunt** V. display ostentatiously. Mae West saw nothing wrong with showing off her considerable physical charms, saying, "Honey, if you've got it, *flaunt* it!"

**flay** V. strip off skin; plunder. The criminal was condemned to be *flayed* alive.

**fleck** V. spot. Her cheeks, *flecked* with tears, were testimony to the hours of weeping.

■ **fledgling** ADJ. inexperienced. While it is necessary to provide these *fledgling* poets with an opportunity to present their work, it is not essential that we admire everything they write. also N.

**fleece** N. wool coat of a sheep. They shear sheep of their *fleece,* which they then comb into separate strands of wool.

**fleece** V. rob; plunder. The tricksters *fleeced* him of his inheritance.

**flick** N. light stroke as with a whip. The horse needed no encouragement; only one *flick* of the whip was all the jockey had to apply to get the animal to run at top speed.

**flinch** V. hesitate; shrink. She did not *flinch* in the face of danger but fought back bravely.

# Test

## Word List 19    *Synonyms and Antonyms*

Each of the following questions consists of a word in capital letters, followed by five lettered words or phrases. Choose the lettered word or phrase that is most nearly similar or opposite in meaning to the word in capital letters and write the letter of your choice on your answer paper.

271. FANCIFUL (A) imaginative (B) knowing (C) elaborate (D) quick (E) lusty

272. FATUOUS (A) fatal (B) natal (C) terrible (D) sensible (E) tolerable

273. FEASIBLE (A) theoretical (B) impatient (C) constant (D) present (E) impractical

274. FECUNDITY (A) prophecy (B) futility (C) fruitfulness (D) need (E) dormancy

275. FEIGN (A) deserve (B) condemn (C) condone (D) attend (E) pretend

276. FELL (A) propitious (B) illiterate (C) uppermost (D) futile (E) inherent

277. FERMENT (A) stir up (B) fill (C) ferret (D) mutilate (E) banish

278. FIASCO (A) cameo (B) mansion (C) pollution (D) success (E) gamble

279. FICKLE (A) fallacious (B) tolerant (C) loyal (D) hungry (E) stupid

280. FILCH (A) milk (B) purloin (C) itch (D) cancel (E) resent

281. FINITE (A) bounded (B) established (C) affirmative (D) massive (E) finicky

282. FLAIL (A) succeed (B) harvest (C) mend (D) strike (E) resent

283. FLAIR (A) conflagration (B) inspiration (C) bent (D) egregiousness (E) magnitude

284. FLAMBOYANT (A) old-fashioned (B) restrained (C) impulsive (D) cognizant (E) eloquent

285. FLEDGLING (A) weaving (B) bobbing (C) beginning (D) studying (E) flaying

---

# Word List 20    flippant-gaffe

**flippant** ADJ. lacking proper seriousness. When Mark told Mona he loved her, she dismissed his earnest declaration with a *flippant* "Oh, you say that to all the girls!" flippancy, N.

**flit** V. fly; dart lightly; pass swiftly by. Like a bee *flitting* from flower to flower, Rose *flitted* from one boyfriend to the next.

**floe** N. mass of floating ice. The ship made slow progress as it battered its way through the ice *floes*.

**flora** N. plants of a region or era. Because she was a botanist, she spent most of her time studying the *flora* of the desert.

**florid** ADJ. ruddy; reddish; flowery. If you go to Florida and get a sunburn, your complexion will look *florid*. If your postcards about your trip praise it in flowery words, your prose will be *florid*, too.

**flotsam** N. drifting wreckage. Beachcombers eke out a living by salvaging the *flotsam* and jetsam of the sea.

**flounder** V. struggle and thrash about; proceed clumsily or falter. Up to his knees in the bog, Floyd *floundered* about, trying to regain his footing. Bewildered by the new software, Flo *floundered* until Jan showed her how to get started.

**flourish** V. grow well; prosper; make sweeping gestures. The orange trees *flourished* in the sun.

■ **flout** V. reject; mock. The headstrong youth *flouted* all authority; he refused to be curbed.

**fluctuate** V. waver; shift. The water pressure in our shower *fluctuates* wildly; you start rinsing yourself off with a trickle, and two minutes later a blast of water nearly knocks you off your feet. I'll never get used to these *fluctuations*.

**fluency** N. smoothness of speech. She spoke French with *fluency* and ease.

**fluke** N. unlikely occurrence; stroke of fortune. When Douglas defeated Tyson for the heavyweight championship, some sportscasters dismissed his victory as a *fluke*.

**fluster** V. confuse. The teacher's sudden question *flustered* him and he stammered his reply.

**fluted** ADJ. having vertical parallel grooves (as in a pillar). All that remained of the ancient building were the *fluted* columns.

**flux** N. flowing; series of changes. While conditions are in such a state of *flux*, I do not wish to commit myself too deeply in this affair.

**fodder** N. coarse food for cattle, horses, etc. One of Nancy's chores at the ranch was to put fresh supplies of *fodder* in the horses' stalls.

**foible** N. weakness; slight fault. We can overlook the *foibles* of our friends; no one is perfect.

**foil** N. contrast. In *Star Wars*, dark, evil Darth Vader is a perfect *foil* for fair-haired, naive Luke Skywalker.

**foil** V. defeat; frustrate. In the end, Skywalker is able to *foil* Vader's diabolical schemes.

**foist** V. insert improperly; palm off. I will not permit you to *foist* such ridiculous ideas upon the membership of this group.

**foliage** N. masses of leaves. Every autumn before the leaves fell he promised himself he would drive through New England to admire the colorful fall *foliage*.

■ **foment** V. stir up; instigate. Cher's archenemy Heather spread some nasty rumors that *fomented* trouble in the club. Do you think Cher's foe meant to *foment* such discord?

**foolhardy** ADJ. rash. Don't be *foolhardy*. Get the advice of experienced people before undertaking this venture.

**foppish** ADJ. vain about dress and appearance. He tried to imitate the *foppish* manner of the young men of the court.

**foray** N. raid. The company staged a midnight *foray* against the enemy outpost.

**forbearance** N. patience. We must use *forbearance* in dealing with him because he is still weak from his illness.

**ford** N. place where a river can be crossed on foot. Rather than risk using the shaky rope bridge, David walked a half-mile downstream until he came to the nearest *ford*. also V.

**forebears** N. ancestors. Reverence for one's *forebears* (sometimes referred to as ancestor worship) plays an important part in many Oriental cultures.

**foreboding** N. premonition of evil. Suspecting no conspiracies against him, Caesar gently ridiculed his wife's *forebodings* about the Ides of March.

**forensic** ADJ. suitable to debate or courts of law. In her best *forensic* manner, the lawyer addressed the jury.

**foreshadow** V. give an indication beforehand; portend; prefigure. In retrospect, political analysts realized that Yeltsin's defiance of the attempted coup *foreshadowed* his emergence as the dominant figure of the new Russian republic.

**foresight** N. ability to foresee future happenings; prudence. A wise investor, she had the *foresight* to buy land just before the current real estate boom.

■ **forestall** V. prevent by taking action in advance. By setting up a prenuptial agreement, the prospective bride and groom hoped to *forestall* any potential arguments about money in the event of a divorce.

**forgo** V. give up; do without. Determined to lose weight for the summer, Ida decided to *forgo* dessert until she could fit into a size eight again.

**forlorn** ADJ. sad and lonely; wretched. Deserted by her big sisters and her friends, the *forlorn* child sat sadly on the steps awaiting their return.

**formality** N. ceremonious quality; something done just for form's sake. The president received the visiting heads of state with due *formality*: flags waving, honor guards standing at attention, bands playing anthems at full blast. Signing this petition is a mere *formality*; it does not obligate you in any way.

**formidable** ADJ. menacing; threatening. We must not treat the battle lightly for we are facing a *formidable* foe.

**forsake** V. desert; abandon; renounce. No one expected Foster to *forsake* his wife and children and run off with another woman.

**forswear** V. renounce; abandon. The captured knight could escape death only if he agreed to *forswear* Christianity and embrace Islam as the one true faith.

**forte** N. strong point or special talent. I am not eager to play this rather serious role, for my *forte* is comedy.

**forthright** ADJ. straightforward; direct; frank. I prefer Jill's *forthright* approach to Jack's tendency to beat around the bush.

**fortitude** N. bravery; courage. He was awarded the medal for his *fortitude* in the battle.

**fortuitous** ADJ. accidental; by chance. Though he pretended their encounter was *fortuitous*, he'd actually been hanging around her usual haunts for the past two weeks, hoping she'd turn up.

**foster** V. rear; encourage. According to the legend, Romulus and Remus were *fostered* by a she-wolf that raised the abandoned infants as her own. also ADJ.

**founder** V. fail completely; sink. After hitting the submerged iceberg, the *Titanic* started taking in water rapidly and soon *foundered*.

**founder** N. person who establishes (an organization, business). Among those drowned when the *Titanic* sank was the *founder* of the Abraham & Straus chain.

**fracas** N. brawl, melee. The military police stopped the *fracas* in the bar and arrested the belligerents.

**fractious** ADJ. unruly. The *fractious* horse unseated its rider.

**frail** ADJ. weak. The delicate child seemed too *frail* to lift the heavy carton. frailty, N.

**franchise** N. right granted by authority; right to vote; license to sell a product in a particular territory. The city issued a *franchise* to the company to operate surface transit lines on the streets for 99 years. For most of American history women lacked the right to vote: not until the early twentieth century was the *franchise* granted to women. Stan owns a Carvel's ice cream *franchise* in Chinatown.

**frantic** ADJ. wild. At the time of the collision, many people became *frantic* with fear.

**fraudulent** ADJ. cheating; deceitful. The government seeks to prevent *fraudulent* and misleading advertising.

**fraught** ADJ. filled. Since this enterprise is *fraught* with danger, I will ask for volunteers who are willing to assume the risks.

**fray** N. brawl. The three musketeers were in the thick of the *fray*.

**frenetic** ADJ. frenzied; frantic. His *frenetic* activities convinced us that he had no organized plan of operation.

**frenzied** ADJ. madly excited. As soon as they smelled smoke, the *frenzied* animals milled about in their cages.

**fresco** N. painting on plaster (usually fresh). The cathedral is visited by many tourists who wish to admire the *frescoes* by Giotto.

**fret** V. be annoyed or vexed. To *fret* over your poor grades is foolish; instead, decide to work harder in the future.

**friction** N. clash in opinion; rubbing against. At this time when harmony is essential, we cannot afford to have any *friction* in our group.

**frieze** N. ornamental band on a wall. The *frieze* of the church was adorned with sculpture.

**frigid** ADJ. intensely cold. Alaska is in the *frigid* zone.

**fritter** V. waste. He could not apply himself to any task and *frittered* away his time in idle conversation.

**frivolous** ADJ. lacking in seriousness; self-indulgently carefree; relatively unimportant. Though Nancy enjoyed Bill's *frivolous*, lighthearted companionship, she sometimes wondered whether he could ever be serious. frivolity, N.

**frolicsome** ADJ. prankish; gay. The *frolicsome* puppy tried to lick the face of its master.

**frond** N. fern leaf; palm or banana leaf. After the storm the beach was littered with the *fronds* of palm trees.

**fructify** V. bear fruit. This peach tree should *fructify* in three years.

■ **frugality** N. thrift; economy. In these economically difficult days businesses must practice *frugality* or risk bankruptcy. frugal, ADJ.

**fruition** N. bearing of fruit; fulfillment; realization. This building marks the *fruition* of all our aspirations and years of hard work.

**frustrate** V. thwart; defeat. We must *frustrate* this dictator's plan to seize control of the government.

**fugitive** ADJ. fleeting or transitory; roving. The film brought a few *fugitive* images to her mind, but on the whole it made no lasting impression upon her.

**fulcrum** N. support on which a lever rests. If we use this stone as a *fulcrum* and the crowbar as a lever, we may be able to move this boulder.

**fulminate** V. thunder; explode. The people against whom she *fulminated* were innocent of any wrongdoing.

**fulsome** ADJ. disgustingly excessive. His *fulsome* praise of the dictator annoyed his listeners.

**functionary** N. official. As his case was transferred from one *functionary* to another, he began to despair of ever reaching a settlement.

**fundamental** V. basic; primary; essential. The committee discussed all sorts of side issues without ever getting down to addressing the *fundamental* problem.

**funereal** ADJ. sad; solemn. I fail to understand why there is such a *funereal* atmosphere; we have lost a battle, not a war.

**furor** N. frenzy; great excitement. The story of her embezzlement of the funds created a *furor* on the stock exchange.

**furtive** ADJ. stealthy; sneaky. Noticing the *furtive* glance the customer gave the diamond bracelet on the counter, the jeweler wondered whether he had a potential shoplifter on his hands.

**fusillade** N. simultaneous firing or outburst (of missiles, questions, etc.). Tchaikovsky's 1812 *Overture* concludes with a thunderous *fusillade* of cannon fire.

**fusion** N. union; coalition. The opponents of the political party in power organized a *fusion* of disgruntled groups and became an important element in the election.

■ **futile** ADJ. useless; hopeless; ineffectual. It is *futile* for me to try to get any work done around here while the telephone is ringing every 30 seconds. futility, N.

**gadfly** N. animal-biting fly; an irritating person. Like a *gadfly*, he irritated all the guests at the hotel; within forty-eight hours, everyone regarded him as an annoying busybody.

**gaffe** N. social blunder. According to Miss Manners, to call your husband by your lover's name is worse than a mere *gaffe;* it is a tactical mistake.

# Test

## Word List 20    *Synonyms*

Each of the questions below consists of a word in capital letters, followed by five lettered words or phrases. Choose the lettered word or phrase that is most nearly similar in meaning to the word in capital letters and write the letter of your choice on your answer paper.

286. FLORID (A) ruddy (B) rusty (C) ruined (D) patient (E) poetic

287. FOIL (A) bury (B) frustrate (C) shield (D) desire (E) gain

288. FOMENT (A) spoil (B) instigate (C) interrogate (D) spray (E) maintain

289. FOOLHARDY (A) strong (B) unwise (C) brave (D) futile (E) erudite

290. FOPPISH (A) scanty (B) radical (C) orthodox (D) dandyish (E) magnificent

291. FORAY (A) excursion (B) contest (C) ranger (D) intuition (E) fish

292. FORMIDABLE (A) dangerous (B) outlandish (C) grandiloquent (D) impenetrable (E) venerable

293. FOSTER (A) accelerate (B) fondle (C) become infected (D) raise (E) roll

294. FRANCHISE (A) subway (B) discount (C) license (D) reason (E) fashion

295. FRITTER (A) sour (B) chafe (C) dissipate (D) cancel (E) abuse

296. FRUGALITY (A) foolishness (B) extremity (C) indifference (D) enthusiasm (E) economy

297. FULMINATE (A) fulfill (B) contemplate (C) talk nonsense (D) protest loudly (E) meander

298. FUROR (A) excitement (B) worry (C) flux (D) anteroom (E) lover

299. FURTIVE (A) underhanded (B) coy (C) brilliant (D) quick (E) abortive

300. GADFLY (A) humorist (B) nuisance (C) scholar (D) bum (E) thief

## Word List 21    gainsay-gossamer

■ **gainsay** V. deny. She was too honest to *gainsay* the truth of the report.

**gait** N. manner of walking or running; speed. The lame man walked with an uneven *gait*.

**galaxy** N. large, isolated system of stars, such as the Milky Way; a collection of brilliant personalities. Science fiction speculates about the possible existence of life in other *galaxies*. The deaths of such famous actors as John Candy and George Burns tells us that the *galaxy* of Hollywood superstars is rapidly disappearing.

**gale** N. windstorm; gust of wind; emotional outburst (laughter, tears). The Weather Channel warned viewers about a rising *gale*, with winds of up to 60 miles per hour.

**gall** N. bitterness; nerve. The knowledge of his failure filled him with *gall*.

**gall** V. annoy; chafe. Their taunts *galled* him.

**galleon** N. large sailing ship. The Spaniards pinned their hopes on the *galleon*, the large warship; the British, on the smaller and faster pinnace.

**galvanize** V. stimulate by shock; stir up; revitalize. News that the prince was almost at their door *galvanized* the ugly stepsisters into a frenzy of combing and primping.

**gambit** N. opening in chess in which a piece is sacrificed. The player was afraid to accept his opponent's *gambit* because he feared a trap that as yet he could not see.

**gambol** V. romp; skip about; leap playfully. Watching the children *gambol* in the park, Betty marveled at their youthful energy and zest. also N.

**gamely** ADV. in a spirited manner; with courage. Because he had fought *gamely* against a much superior boxer, the crowd gave him a standing ovation when he left the arena.

**gamut** N. entire range. In this performance, the leading lady was able to demonstrate the complete *gamut* of her acting ability.

**gape** V. open widely. The huge pit *gaped* before him; if he stumbled, he would fall in. Slack-jawed in wonder, Huck *gaped* at the huge stalactites hanging from the ceiling of the limestone cavern.

**garbled** ADJ. mixed up; jumbled; distorted. A favorite party game involves passing a whispered message from one person to another; by the time it reaches the last player, the message has become totally *garbled*. garble, V.

**gargantuan** ADJ. huge; enormous. The *gargantuan* wrestler was terrified of mice.

**gargoyle** N. waterspout carved in grotesque figures on a building. The *gargoyles* adorning the Cathedral of Notre Dame in Paris are amusing in their grotesqueness.

**garish** ADJ. overbright in color; gaudy. She wore a rhinestone necklace with a *garish* red and gold dress trimmed with sequins.

**garner** V. gather; store up. She hoped to *garner* the world's literature in one library.

**garnish** V. decorate. Parsley was used to *garnish* the boiled potato. also N.

■ **garrulous** ADJ. loquacious; wordy; talkative. My Uncle Henry can out-talk any other three people I know. He is the most *garrulous* person in Cayuga County. garrulity, N.

**gastronomy** N. science of preparing and serving good food. One of the by-products of his trip to Europe was his interest in *gastronomy*; he enjoyed preparing and serving foreign dishes to his friends.

**gauche** ADJ. clumsy; coarse and uncouth. Compared to the sophisticated young ladies in their elegant gowns, tomboyish Jo felt *gauche* and out of place.

**gaudy** ADJ. flashy; showy. The newest Trump skyscraper is typically *gaudy*, covered in gilded panels that gleam in the sun.

**gaunt** ADJ. lean and angular; barren. His once-round face looked surprisingly *gaunt* after he had lost weight.

**gavel** N. hammerlike tool; mallet. "Sold!" cried the auctioneer, banging her *gavel* on the table to indicate she'd accepted the final bid. also V.

**gawk** V. stare foolishly; look in open-mouthed awe. The country boy *gawked* at the skyscrapers and neon lights of the big city.

**gazette** N. official periodical publication. He read the *gazettes* regularly for the announcement of his promotion.

**genealogy** N. record of descent; lineage. He was proud of his *genealogy* and constantly referred to the achievements of his ancestors.

**generality** N. vague statement. This report is filled with *generalities*; you must be more specific in your statements.

**generate** V. cause; produce; create. In his first days in office, President Clinton managed to *generate* a new mood of optimism; we hoped he could also *generate* a few new jobs.

**generic** ADJ. characteristic of an entire class or species. Sue knew so many computer programmers who spent their spare time playing fantasy games that she began to think that playing Dungeons & Dragons was a *generic* trait.

**genesis** N. beginning; origin. Tracing the *genesis* of a family is the theme of "Roots."

**geniality** N. cheerfulness; kindliness; sympathy. This restaurant is famous and popular because of the *geniality* of the proprietor, who tries to make everyone happy. genial, ADJ.

**genre** N. particular variety of art or literature. Both a short story writer and a poet, Langston Hughes proved himself equally skilled in either *genre*.

**genteel** ADJ. well-bred; elegant. We are looking for a man with a *genteel* appearance who can inspire confidence by his cultivated manner.

**gentility** N. those of gentle birth; refinement. Her family was proud of its *gentility* and elegance.

**gentry**   N. people of standing; class of people just below nobility. The local *gentry* did not welcome the visits of the summer tourists and tried to ignore their presence in the community.

**genuflect**   V. bend the knee as in worship. A proud democrat, he refused to *genuflect* to any man.

**germane**   ADJ. pertinent; bearing upon the case at hand. The lawyer objected that the testimony being offered was not *germane* to the case at hand.

**germinal**   ADJ. pertaining to a germ; creative. Such an idea is *germinal*; I am certain that it will influence thinkers and philosophers for many generations.

**germinate**   V. cause to sprout; sprout. After the seeds *germinate* and develop their permanent leaves, the plants may be removed from the cold frames and transplanted to the garden.

**gerontocracy**   N. government ruled by old people. Gulliver visited a *gerontocracy* in which the young people acted as servants to their elders, all the while dreaming of the day they would be old enough to have servants of their own.

**gerrymander**   V. change voting district lines in order to favor a political party. The illogical pattern of the map of this congressional district is proof that the state legislature *gerrymandered* this area in order to favor the majority party. also N.

**gestate**   V. evolve, as in prenatal growth. While this scheme was being *gestated* by the conspirators, they maintained complete silence about their intentions.

**gesticulation**   N. motion; gesture. Operatic performers are trained to make exaggerated *gesticulations* because of the large auditoriums in which they appear.

**ghastly**   ADJ. horrible. The murdered man was a *ghastly* sight.

**gibberish**   N. nonsense; babbling. Did you hear that foolish boy spouting *gibberish* about monsters from outer space?

**gibe**   V. mock. As you *gibe* at their superstitious beliefs, do you realize that you, too, are guilty of similarly foolish thoughts?

**giddy**   ADJ. light-hearted; dizzy. He felt his *giddy* youth was past.

**gingerly**   ADV. very carefully. To separate egg whites, first crack the egg *gingerly*. also ADJ.

**girth**   N. distance around something; circumference. It took an extra-large cummerbund to fit around Andrew Carnegie's considerable *girth*.

**gist**   N. essence. She was asked to give the *gist* of the essay in two sentences.

**glacial**   ADJ. like a glacier; extremely cold. Never a warm person, when offended Hugo could seem positively *glacial*.

**glaring**   ADJ. highly conspicuous; harshly bright. *Glaring* spelling or grammatical errors in your résumé will unfavorably impress potential employers.

**glaze**   V. cover with a thin and shiny surface. The freezing rain *glazed* the streets and made driving hazardous. also N.

**glean**   V. gather leavings. After the crops had been harvested by the machines, the peasants were permitted to *glean* the wheat left in the fields.

**glib**   ADJ. fluent; facile; slick. Keeping up a steady patter to entertain his customers, the kitchen gadget salesman was a *glib* speaker, never at a loss for a word.

**glimmer**   V. shine erratically; twinkle. In the darkness of the cavern, the glowworms hanging from the cavern roof *glimmered* like distant stars.

**gloat**   V. express evil satisfaction; view malevolently. As you *gloat* over your ill-gotten wealth, do you think of the many victims you have defrauded?

**gloss over**   V. explain away. No matter how hard he tried to talk around the issue, President Bush could not *gloss over* the fact that he had raised taxes after all.

**glossary**   N. brief explanation of words used in the text. I have found the *glossary* in this book very useful; it has eliminated many trips to the dictionary.

**glossy**   ADJ. smooth and shining. I want this photograph printed on *glossy* paper, not matte.

**glower**   V. scowl. The angry boy *glowered* at his father.

**glut**   V. overstock; fill to excess. The many manufacturers *glutted* the market and could not find purchasers for the many articles they had produced. also N.

**glutinous**   ADJ. sticky; viscous. Molasses is a *glutinous* substance.

**glutton**   N. someone who eats too much. When Mother saw that Bobby had eaten all the cookies, she called him a little *glutton*. gluttonous, ADJ.

**gnarled**   ADJ. twisted. The *gnarled* oak tree had been a landmark for years and was mentioned in several deeds.

**gnome**   N. dwarf; underground spirit. In medieval mythology, *gnomes* were the special guardians and inhabitants of subterranean mines.

■ **goad**   V. urge on. She was *goaded* by her friends until she yielded to their wishes. also N.

**gorge**   N. narrow canyon; steep, rocky cleft. Terrified of heights, George could not bring himself to peer down into the *gorge* to see the rapids below.

**gorge**   V. stuff oneself. The gluttonous guest *gorged* himself with food as though he had not eaten for days.

**gory**   ADJ. bloody. The audience shuddered as they listened to the details of the *gory* massacre. gore, N.

**gossamer**   ADJ. sheer; like cobwebs. Nylon can be woven into *gossamer* or thick fabrics. also N.

# Test

## Word List 21    *Synonyms*

Each of the questions below consists of a word in capital letters, followed by five lettered words or phrases. Choose the lettered word or phrase that is most nearly similar in meaning to the word in capital letters and write the letter of your choice on your answer paper.

301. GALLEON (A) liquid measure (B) ship (C) armada (D) company (E) printer's proof

302. GARISH (A) sordid (B) flashy (C) prominent (D) lusty (E) thoughtful

303. GARNER (A) prevent (B) assist (C) collect (D) compute (E) consult

304. GARNISH (A) paint (B) garner (C) adorn (D) abuse (E) banish

305. GARRULITY (A) credulity (B) senility (C) loquaciousness (D) speciousness (E) artistry

306. GARRULOUS (A) arid (B) hasty (C) sociable (D) quaint (E) talkative

307. GAUCHE (A) rigid (B) swift (C) awkward (D) taciturn (E) needy

308. GAUDY (A) holy (B) showy (C) sentimental (D) mild (E) whimsical

309. GAUNT (A) victorious (B) tiny (C) stylish (D) haggard (E) nervous

310. GENUFLECT (A) falsify (B) trick (C) project (D) bend the knee (E) pronounce correctly

311. GERMANE (A) bacteriological (B) Middle European (C) prominent (D) warlike (E) relevant

312. GERMINAL (A) creative (B) excused (C) sterilized (D) primitive (E) strategic

313. GIST (A) chaff (B) summary (C) expostulation (D) expiation (E) chore

314. GLIB (A) slippery (B) fashionable (C) antiquated (D) articulate (E) anticlimactic

315. GNOME (A) fury (B) giant (C) dwarf (D) native (E) alien

## Word List 22    gouge-hiatus

**gouge** v. tear out. In that fight, all the rules were forgotten; the adversaries bit, kicked, and tried to *gouge* each other's eyes out.

■ **gouge** v. overcharge. During the World Series, ticket scalpers tried to *gouge* the public, asking astronomical prices even for bleacher seats.

**gourmand** N. epicure; person who takes excessive pleasure in food and drink. *Gourmands* lack self-restraint; if they enjoy a particular cuisine, they eat far too much of it.

**gourmet** N. connoisseur of food and drink. The *gourmet* stated that this was the best onion soup she had ever tasted.

**graduated** ADJ. arranged by degrees (of height, difficulty, etc.). Margaret loved her *graduated* set of Russian hollow wooden dolls; she spent hours happily putting the smaller dolls into their larger counterparts.

**granary** N. storehouse for grain. We have reason to be thankful, for our crops were good and our *granaries* are full.

**grandeur** N. impressiveness; stateliness; majesty. No matter how often he hiked through the mountains, David never failed to be struck by the *grandeur* of the Sierra Nevada range.

■ **grandiloquent** ADJ. pompous; bombastic; using high-sounding language. The politician could never speak simply; she was always *grandiloquent*.

**grandiose** ADJ. pretentious; high-flown; ridiculously exaggerated; impressive. The aged matinee idol still had *grandiose* notions of his supposed importance in the theatrical world.

**granulate** v. form into grains. Sugar that has been *granulated* dissolves more readily than lump sugar. granule, N.

**graphic** ADJ. pertaining to the art of delineating; vividly described. I was particularly impressed by the *graphic* presentation of the storm.

**grapple** v. wrestle; come to grips with. He *grappled* with the burglar and overpowered him.

**grate** v. make a harsh noise; have an unpleasant effect; shred. The screams of the quarreling children *grated* on her nerves.

**gratify** v. please. Lori's parents were *gratified* by her successful performance on the GRE.

**gratis** ADV. free. The company offered to give one package *gratis* to every purchaser of one of their products. also ADJ.

**gratuitous** ADJ. given freely; unwarranted; uncalled for. Quit making *gratuitous* comments about my driving; no one asked you for your opinion.

**gratuity** N. tip. Many service employees rely more on *gratuities* than on salaries for their livelihood.

**gravity** N. seriousness. We could tell we were in serious trouble from the *gravity* of her expression. grave, ADJ.

■ **gregarious** ADJ. sociable. Typically, party-throwers are *gregarious*; hermits are not.

**grievance** N. cause of complaint. When her supervisor ignored her complaint, she took her *grievance* to the union.

**grill** V. question severely. In violation of the Miranda law, the police *grilled* the suspect for several hours before reading him his rights. (secondary meaning)

**grimace** N. a facial distortion to show feeling such as pain, disgust, etc. Even though he remained silent, his *grimace* indicated his displeasure. also V.

**grisly** ADJ. ghastly. She shuddered at the *grisly* sight.

**grotesque** ADJ. fantastic; comically hideous. On Halloween people enjoy wearing *grotesque* costumes.

**grotto** N. small cavern. The Blue *Grotto* in Capri can be entered only by small boats rowed by natives through a natural opening in the rocks.

**grouse** V. complain; fuss. Students traditionally *grouse* about the abysmal quality of "mystery meat" and similar dormitory food.

**grovel** V. crawl or creep on ground; remain prostrate. Even though we have been defeated, we do not have to *grovel* before our conquerors.

**grudging** ADJ. unwilling; reluctant; stingy. We received only *grudging* support from the mayor despite his earlier promises of aid.

**gruel** N. thin, liquid porridge. Our daily allotment of *gruel* made the meal not only monotonous but also unpalatable.

**grueling** ADJ. exhausting. The marathon is a *grueling* race.

**gruesome** ADJ. grisly; horrible. His face was the stuff of nightmares: all the children in the audience screamed when Freddy Kruger's *gruesome* countenance was flashed on the screen.

**gruff** ADJ. rough-mannered. Although he was blunt and *gruff* with most people, he was always gentle with children.

**guffaw** N. boisterous laughter. The loud *guffaws* that came from the closed room indicated that the members of the committee had not yet settled down to serious business. also V.

**guile** N. deceit; duplicity; wiliness; cunning. Iago uses considerable *guile* to trick Othello into believing that Desdemona has been unfaithful.

■ **guileless** ADJ. without deceit. He is naive, simple, and *guileless*; he cannot be guilty of fraud.

**guise** N. appearance; costume. In the *guise* of a plumber, the detective investigated the murder case.

**gull** V. trick; hoodwink. Confident no one could *gull* him, Paul prided himself on his skeptical disposition.

■ **gullible** ADJ. easily deceived. *Gullible* people have only themselves to blame if they fall for con artists repeatedly. As the saying goes, "Fool me once, shame on you. Fool me twice, shame on me."

**gustatory** ADJ. affecting the sense of taste. The Thai restaurant offered an unusual *gustatory* experience for those used to a bland cuisine.

**gusto** N. enjoyment; enthusiasm. He accepted the assignment with such *gusto* that I feel he would have been satisfied with a smaller salary.

**gusty** ADJ. windy. The *gusty* weather made sailing precarious.

**guy** N. cable or chain attached to something that needs to be braced or steadied. If the *guys* holding up the mast on that derrick snap, the mast will topple.

**gyroscope** N. apparatus used to maintain balance, ascertain direction, etc. By using a rotating *gyroscope*, they were able to stabilize the vessel, counteracting the rolling movements of the sea.

**habituate** V. accustom or familiarize; addict. Macbeth gradually *habituated* himself to murder, shedding his scruples as he grew accustomed to his bloody deeds.

**hackles** N. hairs on back and neck, especially of a dog. The dog's *hackles* rose and he began to growl as the sound of footsteps grew louder.

**hackneyed** ADJ. commonplace; trite. When the reviewer criticized the movie for its *hackneyed* plot, we agreed; we had seen similar stories hundreds of times before.

**haggard** ADJ. wasted away; gaunt. After his long illness, he was pale and *haggard*.

**haggle** V. argue about prices. I prefer to shop in a store that has a one-price policy because, whenever I *haggle* with a shopkeeper, I am never certain that I paid a fair price for the articles I purchased.

**halcyon** ADJ. calm; peaceful. In those *halcyon* days, people were not worried about sneak attacks and bombings.

**hale** ADJ. healthy. After a brief illness, he was soon *hale*.

**hallowed** ADJ. blessed; consecrated. Although the dead girl's parents had never been active churchgoers, they insisted that their daughter be buried in *hallowed* ground.

**hallucination** N. delusion. I think you were frightened by a *hallucination* that you created in your own mind.

**halting** ADJ. hesitant; faltering. Novice extemporaneous speakers often talk in a *halting* fashion as they grope for the right words.

**hamper** V. obstruct. The new mother hadn't realized how much the effort of caring for an infant would *hamper* her ability to keep an immaculate house.

**hap** N. chance; luck. In his poem *Hap*, Thomas Hardy objects to the part chance plays in our lives. also V.

**haphazard** ADJ. random; by chance. His *haphazard* reading left him unacquainted with many classic books.

**hapless** ADJ. unfortunate. This *hapless* creature had never known a moment's pleasure.

■ **harangue** N. long, passionate, and vehement speech. In her lengthy *harangue*, the principal berated the offenders. also V.

**harass** V. annoy by repeated attacks. When he could not pay his bills as quickly as he had promised, he was *harassed* by his creditors.

**harbinger** N. forerunner. The crocus is an early *harbinger* of spring.

**harbor** v. provide a refuge for; hide. The church *harbored* illegal aliens who were political refugees. also N.

**hardy** ADJ. sturdy; robust; able to stand inclement weather. We asked the gardening expert to recommend particularly *hardy* plants that could withstand our harsh New England winters.

**harping** N. tiresome dwelling on a subject. After he had reminded me several times about what he had done for me I told him to stop his *harping* on my indebtedness to him. harp, v.

**harrowing** ADJ. agonizing; distressing; traumatic. At first Terry Anderson did not wish to discuss his *harrowing* months of captivity as a political hostage. harrow, v.

**harry** v. harass, annoy, torment; raid. The guerrilla band *harried* the enemy nightly.

**hatch** N. deck opening; lid covering a deck opening. The latch on the *hatch* failed to catch, so the *hatch* remained unlatched.

**haughtiness** N. pride; arrogance. When she realized that Darcy believed himself too good to dance with his inferiors, Elizabeth took great offense at his *haughtiness*.

**haven** N. place of safety; refuge. For Ricardo, the school library became his *haven*, a place to which he could retreat during chaotic times.

**hazardous** ADJ. dangerous. Your occupation is too *hazardous* for insurance companies to consider your application.

**hazy** ADJ. slightly obscure. In *hazy* weather, you cannot see the top of this mountain.

**headlong** ADJ. hasty; rash. The slave seized the unexpected chance to make a *headlong* dash across the border to freedom.

**headstrong** ADJ. stubborn; willful; unyielding. Because she refused to marry the man her parents had chosen for her, everyone scolded Minna and called her a foolish, *headstrong* girl.

**heckler** N. person who verbally harasses others. The *heckler* kept interrupting the speaker with rude remarks. heckle, v.

**hedonist** N. one who believes that pleasure is the sole aim in life. A thoroughgoing *hedonist*, he considered only his own pleasure and ignored any claims others had on his money or time. hedonism, N.

**heedless** ADJ. not noticing; disregarding. She drove on, *heedless* of the warnings that the road was dangerous. heed, v.

**hegemony** N. dominance, especially of one nation over others. As one Eastern European nation after another declared its independence, commentators marveled at the sudden breakdown of the once monolithic Soviet *hegemony*.

**heinous** ADJ. atrocious; hatefully bad. Hitler's *heinous* crimes will never be forgotten.

**herbivorous** ADJ. grain-eating. Some *herbivorous* animals have two stomachs for digesting their food.

**heresy** N. opinion contrary to popular belief; opinion contrary to accepted religion. Galileo's assertion that the earth moved around the sun directly contradicted the religious teachings of his day; as a result, he was tried for *heresy*. heretic, N. heretical, ADJ.

**hermetic** ADJ. sealed by fusion so as to be airtight. After you sterilize the bandages, place them in a container and seal it with a *hermetic* seal to protect them from contamination by airborne bacteria.

**hermetic** ADJ. obscure and mysterious; occult. It is strange to consider that modern chemistry originated in the *hermetic* teachings of the ancient alchemists. (secondary meaning)

**hermitage** N. home of a hermit. Even in his remote *hermitage* he could not escape completely from the world.

**herpetologist** N. one who studies reptiles. As a boy, Indiana Jones had a traumatic experience involving snakes; sensibly enough, he studied to be an archaeologist, not a *herpetologist*.

**heterodox** ADJ. unorthodox; unconventional. To those who upheld the belief that the earth did not move, Galileo's theory that the earth circled the sun was disturbingly *heterodox*.

**heterogeneous** ADJ. dissimilar; mixed. This year's entering class is a remarkably *heterogeneous* body: it includes students from 40 different states and 26 foreign countries, some the children of billionaires, others the offspring of welfare families. heterogeneity, N.

**hew** v. cut to pieces with ax or sword. The cavalry rushed into the melee and *hewed* the enemy with their swords, N.

**heyday** N. time of greatest success; prime. In their *heyday*, the San Francisco Forty-Niners won the Super Bowl two years running.

**hiatus** N. gap; pause. Except for a brief two-year *hiatus*, during which she enrolled in the Peace Corps, Ms. Clements has devoted herself to her medical career.

# Test

## Word List 22 *Antonyms*

Each of the following questions consists of a word in capital letters, followed by five lettered words or phrases. Choose the lettered word or phrase that is most nearly opposite in meaning to the word in capital letters and write the letter of your choice on your answer paper.

316. GRANDIOSE (A) false (B) ideal (C) proud (D) simple (E) functional

317. GRATUITOUS (A) warranted (B) frank (C) ingenuous (D) frugal (E) pithy

318. GREGARIOUS (A) antisocial (B) anticipatory (C) glorious (D) horrendous (E) similar

319. GRISLY (A) suggestive (B) doubtful (C) untidy (D) pleasant (E) bearish

320. GULLIBLE (A) incredulous (B) fickle (C) tantamount (D) easy (E) stylish

321. GUSTO (A) noise (B) panic (C) atmosphere (D) gloom (E) distaste

322. GUSTY (A) calm (B) noisy (C) fragrant (D) routine (E) gloomy

323. HACKNEYED (A) carried (B) original (C) banned (D) timely (E) oratorical

324. HAGGARD (A) shrewish (B) inspired (C) plump (D) maidenly (E) vast

325. HALCYON (A) wasteful (B) prior (C) subsequent (D) puerile (E) martial

326. HAPHAZARD (A) safe (B) indifferent (C) deliberate (D) tense (E) conspiring

327. HAPLESS (A) cheerful (B) consistent (C) fortunate (D) considerate (E) shapely

328. HEED (A) ignore (B) hope (C) overtake (D) nurture (E) depart

329. HERETIC (A) sophist (B) believer (C) interpreter (D) pacifist (E) owner

330. HETEROGENEOUS (A) orthodox (B) pagan (C) unlikely (D) similar (E) banished

---

# Word List 23    hibernal-imbue

**hibernal**   ADJ. wintry. Bears prepare for their long *hibernal* sleep by overeating.

**hibernate**   V. sleep throughout the winter. Bears are one of the many species of animals that *hibernate*. hibernation, N.

**hierarchy**   N. arrangement by rank or standing; authoritarian body divided into ranks. To be low man on the totem pole is to have an inferior place in the *hierarchy*. hierarchical, ADJ.

**hieroglyphic**   N. picture writing. The discovery of the Rosetta Stone enabled scholars to read the ancient Egyptian *hieroglyphics*.

**hilarity**   N. boisterous mirth. This *hilarity* is improper on this solemn day of mourning. hilarious, ADJ.

**hindmost**   ADJ. furthest behind. The coward could always be found in the *hindmost* lines whenever a battle was being waged.

**hindrance**   N. block; obstacle. Stalled cars along the highway are a *hindrance* to traffic that tow trucks should remove without delay. hinder, V.

**hinterlands**   N. back country. They seldom had visitors, living as they did way out in the *hinterlands*.

**hireling**   N. one who serves for hire (usually used contemptuously). In a matter of such importance, I do not wish to deal with *hirelings;* I must meet with the chief.

**hirsute**   ADJ. hairy. He was a *hirsute* individual with a heavy black beard.

**histrionic**   ADJ. theatrical. He was proud of his *histrionic* ability and wanted to play the role of Hamlet. histrionics, N.

**hoard**   V. stockpile; accumulate for future use. Whenever there are rumors of a food shortage, people are tempted to *hoard* food. also N.

**hoary**   ADJ. white with age. The man was *hoary* and wrinkled when he was 70.

**hoax**   N. trick; practical joke. Embarrassed by the *hoax*, she reddened and left the room. also V.

**holocaust**   N. destruction by fire. Citizens of San Francisco remember that the destruction of the city was caused not by the earthquake but by the *holocaust* that followed.

**holster**   N. pistol case. Even when he was not in uniform, he carried a *holster* and pistol under his arm.

**homage**   N. honor; tribute. In her speech she tried to pay *homage* to a great man.

**homeostasis**   N. tendency of a system to maintain relative stability. A breakdown of the body's immune system severely undermines the body's ability to maintain *homeostasis*.

**homespun**   ADJ. domestic; made at home. *Homespun* wit, like *homespun* cloth, was often coarse and plain.

**homily**   N. sermon; serious warning. His speeches were always *homilies,* advising his listeners to repent and reform. homiletic, ADJ.

■ **homogeneous**   ADJ. of the same kind. Because the student body at Elite Prep was so *homogeneous*, Sara and James decided to send their daughter to a school that offered greater cultural diversity. homogeneity, N.

**hone**   V. sharpen. To make shaving easier, he *honed* his razor with great care.

**hoodwink**   V. deceive; delude. Having been *hoodwinked* once by the fast-talking salesman, he was extremely cautious when he went to purchase a used car.

**horde**   N. crowd. Just before Christmas the stores are filled with *hordes* of shoppers.

**hortatory**   ADJ. encouraging; exhortive. The crowd listened to his *hortatory* statements with ever-growing excitement; finally they rushed from the hall to carry out his suggestions.

**horticultural**   ADJ. pertaining to cultivation of gardens. When he bought his house, he began to look for flowers and decorative shrubs, and began to read books dealing with *horticultural* matters.

**hostility**   N. unfriendliness; hatred. A child who has been the sole object of his parents' affection often feels *hostility* toward a new baby in the family, resenting the newcomer who has taken his place. hostile, ADJ.

**hovel** N. shack; small, wretched house. She wondered how poor people could stand living in such a *hovel*.

**hover** V. hang about; wait nearby. The police helicopter *hovered* above the accident.

**hubbub** N. confused uproar. The marketplace was a scene of *hubbub* and excitement; in all the noise, we could not distinguish particular voices.

**hubris** N. arrogance; excessive self-conceit. Filled with *hubris*, Lear refused to heed his friends' warnings.

**hue** N. color; aspect. The aviary contained birds of every possible *hue*.

**hue and cry** N. outcry. When her purse was snatched, she raised such a *hue and cry* that the thief was captured.

**humane** ADJ. marked by kindness or consideration. It is ironic that the *Humane* Society sometimes must show its compassion toward mistreated animals by killing them to end their misery.

**humdrum** ADJ. dull; monotonous. After her years of adventure, she could not settle down to a *humdrum* existence.

**humid** ADJ. damp. She could not stand the *humid* climate and moved to a drier area.

**humility** N. humbleness of spirit. He spoke with a *humility* and lack of pride that impressed his listeners.

**hummock** N. small hill. The ascent of the *hummock* is not difficult and the view from the hilltop is ample reward for the effort.

**humus** N. substance formed by decaying vegetable matter. In order to improve his garden, he spread *humus* over his lawn and flower beds.

**hurtle** V. crash; rush. The runaway train *hurtled* toward disaster.

**husband** V. use sparingly; conserve; save. Marathon runners must *husband* their energy so that they can keep going for the entire distance.

**husbandry** N. frugality; thrift; agriculture. He accumulated his small fortune by diligence and *husbandry*. husband, V.

**hybrid** N. mongrel; mixed breed. Mendel's formula explains the appearance of *hybrids* and pure species in breeding. also ADJ.

**hydrophobia** N. fear of water; rabies. A dog that bites a human being must be observed for symptoms of *hydrophobia*.

■ **hyperbole** N. exaggeration; overstatement. As far as I'm concerned, Apple's claims about the new computer are pure *hyperbole*: no machine is that good! hyperbolic, ADJ.

**hypercritical** ADJ. excessively exacting. You are *hypercritical* in your demands for perfection; we all make mistakes.

**hypochondriac** N. person unduly worried about his health; worrier without cause about illness. The doctor prescribed chocolate pills for her patient who was a *hypochondriac*.

**hypocritical** ADJ. pretending to be virtuous; deceiving. Because he believed Eddie to be interested only in his own advancement, Greg resented Eddie's *hypocritical* protestations of friendship. hypocrisy, N.

**hypothetical** ADJ. based on assumptions or hypotheses; supposed. Suppose you are accepted by Harvard, Stanford, and Yale. Which graduate school will you choose to attend? Remember, this is only a *hypothetical* situation. hypothesis, N.

**ichthyology** N. study of fish. Jacques Cousteau's programs about sea life have advanced the cause of *ichthyology*.

**icon** N. religious image; idol. The *icons* on the walls of the church were painted in the 13th century.

■ **iconoclastic** ADJ. attacking cherished traditions. Deeply *iconoclastic*, Jean Genet deliberately set out to shock conventional theatergoers with his radical plays. iconoclasm, N.

**ideology** N. system of ideas characteristic of a group or culture. For people who had grown up believing in the Communist *ideology*, it was hard to adjust to capitalism.

**idiom** N. expression whose meaning as a whole differs from the meanings of its individual words; distinctive style. The phrase "to lose one's marbles" is an *idiom*: if I say that Joe has lost his marbles, I'm not asking you to find them for him. I'm telling you *idiomatically* that he's crazy.

**idiosyncrasy** N. individual trait, usually odd in nature; eccentricity. One of Richard Nixon's little *idiosyncrasies* was his liking for ketchup on cottage cheese. One of Hannibal Lecter's little *idiosyncrasies* was his liking for human flesh. idiosyncratic, ADJ.

■ **idolatry** N. worship of idols; excessive admiration. Such *idolatry* of singers of country music is typical of the excessive enthusiasm of youth.

**idyllic** ADJ. charmingly carefree; simple. Far from the city, she led an *idyllic* existence in her rural retreat.

**igneous** ADJ. produced by fire; volcanic. Lava, pumice, and other *igneous* rocks are found in great abundance around Mount Vesuvius near Naples.

**ignite** V. kindle; light. When Desi crooned, "Baby, light my fire," literal-minded Lucy looked around for some paper to *ignite*.

**ignoble** ADJ. unworthy; not noble. A true knight, Sir Galahad never stooped to perform an *ignoble* deed.

**ignominy** N. deep disgrace; shame or dishonor. To lose the Ping-Pong match to a trained chimpanzee! How could Rollo endure the *ignominy* of his defeat? ignominious, ADJ.

**illicit** ADJ. illegal. The defense attorney claimed that the police had entrapped his client; that is, they had elicited the *illicit* action of which they now accused him.

**illimitable** ADJ. infinite. Human beings, having explored the far corners of the earth, are now reaching out into *illimitable* space.

**illuminate**   V. brighten; clear up or make understandable; enlighten. Just as a lamp can *illuminate* a dark room, a perceptive comment can *illuminate* a knotty problem.

**illusion**   N. misleading vision. It is easy to create an optical *illusion* in which lines of equal length appear different.

**illusive**   ADJ. deceiving. This is only a mirage; let us not be fooled by its *illusive* effect.

**illusory**   ADJ. deceptive; not real. Unfortunately, the costs of running the lemonade stand were so high that Tom's profits proved *illusory*.

**imbalance**   N. lack of balance or symmetry; disproportion. To correct racial *imbalance* in the schools, school boards have bused black children into white neighborhoods and white children into black ones.

**imbecility**   N. weakness of mind. I am amazed at the *imbecility* of the readers of these trashy magazines.

**imbibe**   V. drink in. The dry soil *imbibed* the rain quickly.

**imbroglio**   N. complicated situation; painful or complex misunderstanding; entanglement; confused mass (as of papers). The humor of Shakespearean comedies often depends on cases of mistaken identity that involve the perplexed protagonists in one comic *imbroglio* after another. embroil, V.

**imbue**   V. saturate, fill. His visits to the famous Gothic cathedrals *imbued* him with feelings of awe and reverence.

**Test**

# Word List 23    *Antonyms*

Each of the questions below consists of a word in capital letters, followed by five lettered words or phrases. Choose the lettered word or phrase that is most nearly opposite in meaning to the word in capital letters and write the letter of your choice on your answer paper.

331. HIBERNAL (A) musical (B) summerlike (C) local (D) seasonal (E) discordant

332. HILARITY (A) gloom (B) heartiness (C) weakness (D) casualty (E) paucity

333. HIRSUTE (A) scaly (B) bald (C) erudite (D) quiet (E) long

334. HORTATORY (A) inquiring (B) denying (C) killing (D) frantic (E) dissuading

335. HOVER (A) commence (B) soothe (C) leave (D) transform (E) solidify

336. HUBBUB (A) calm (B) fury (C) capital (D) axle (E) wax

337. HUMMOCK (A) unmusical (B) scorn (C) wakefulness (D) vale (E) vestment

338. HUSBANDRY (A) sportsmanship (B) dishonesty (C) wastefulness (D) friction (E) cowardice

339. HYBRID (A) productive (B) special (C) purebred (D) oafish (E) genial

340. HYPERBOLE (A) velocity (B) climax (C) curve (D) understatement (E) expansion

341. HYPERCRITICAL (A) tolerant (B) false (C) extreme (D) inarticulate (E) cautious

342. HYPOCRITICAL (A) sincere (B) narrow-minded (C) shameful (D) amiable (E) modest

343. HYPOTHETICAL (A) rational (B) fantastic (C) wizened (D) opposed (E) axiomatic

344. IGNOBLE (A) produced by fire (B) worthy (C) given to questioning (D) huge (E) known

345. ILLUSIVE (A) not deceptive (B) not certain (C) not obvious (D) not coherent (E) not brilliant

# Word List 24    immaculate-incessant

**immaculate**   ADJ. spotless; flawless; absolutely clean. Ken and Jessica were wonderful tenants who left the apartment in *immaculate* condition when they moved out.

**imminent**   ADJ. near at hand; impending. Rosa was such a last-minute worker that she could never start writing a paper till the deadline was *imminent*.

**immobility**   N. state of being immovable. Modern armies cannot afford the luxury of *immobility,* as they are vulnerable to attack while standing still.

**immolate**   V. offer as a sacrifice. The tribal king offered to *immolate* his daughter to quiet the angry gods.

**immune**   ADJ. resistant to; free or exempt from. Fortunately, Florence had contracted chicken pox as a child and was *immune* to it when her baby came down

with spots. immunity, N.

**immure**   V. imprison; shut up in confinement. For the two weeks before the examination, the student *immured* himself in his room and concentrated upon his studies.

■ **immutable**   ADJ. unchangeable. All things change over time; nothing is *immutable.*

■ **impair**   V. injure; hurt. Drinking alcohol can *impair* your ability to drive safely; if you're going to drink, don't drive.

**impale**   V. pierce. He was *impaled* by the spear hurled by his adversary.

**impalpable**   ADJ. imperceptible; intangible. The ash is so fine that it is *impalpable* to the touch but it can be seen as a fine layer covering the window ledge.

**impartial** ADJ. not biased; fair. Knowing she could not be *impartial* about her own child, Jo refused to judge any match in which Billy was competing. impartiality, N.

**impassable** ADJ. not able to be traveled or crossed. A giant redwood had fallen across the highway, blocking all four lanes: the road was *impassable*.

**impasse** N. predicament from which there is no escape. In this *impasse,* all turned to prayer as their last hope.

■ **impassive** ADJ. without feeling; imperturbable; stoical. Refusing to let the enemy see how deeply shaken he was by his capture, the prisoner kept his face *impassive*.

**impeach** V. charge with crime in office; indict. The angry congressman wanted to *impeach* the president for his misdeeds.

**impeccable** ADJ. faultless. The uncrowned queen of the fashion industry, Diana was acclaimed for her *impeccable* taste.

**impecunious** ADJ. without money. Though Scrooge claimed he was too *impecunious* to give alms, he easily could have afforded to be charitable.

■ **impede** V. hinder; block. The special prosecutor determined that the Attorney General, though inept, had not intentionally set out to *impede* the progress of the investigation.

**impediment** N. hindrance; stumbling-block. She had a speech *impediment* that prevented her from speaking clearly.

**impel** V. drive or force onward. A strong feeling of urgency *impelled* her; if she failed to finish the project right then, she knew that she would never get it done.

**impending** ADJ. nearing; approaching. The entire country was saddened by the news of his *impending* death.

**impenetrable** ADJ. not able to be pierced or entered; beyond understanding. How could the murderer have gotten into the locked room? To Watson, the mystery, like the room, was *impenetrable*.

**impenitent** ADJ. not repentant. We could see by his brazen attitude that he was *impenitent*.

**imperative** ADJ. absolutely necessary; critically important. It is *imperative* that you be extremely agreeable to Great-Aunt Maud when she comes to tea: otherwise she may not leave you that million dollars in her will. also N.

**imperceptible** ADJ. unnoticeable; undetectable. Fortunately, the stain on the blouse was *imperceptible* after the garment had gone through the wash.

**imperial** ADJ. like an emperor; related to an empire. When hotel owner Leona Helmsley appeared in ads as Queen Leona standing guard over the Palace Hotel, her critics mocked her *imperial* fancies.

**imperious** ADJ. domineering; haughty. Jane rather liked a man to be masterful, but Mr. Rochester seemed so bent on getting his own way that he was actually *imperious*! imperiousness, N.

■ **impermeable** ADJ. impervious; not permitting passage through its substance. This new material is *impermeable* to liquids.

**impertinent** ADJ. insolent; rude. His neighbors' *impertinent* curiosity about his lack of dates angered Ted. It was downright rude of them to ask him such personal questions. impertinence, N.

■ **imperturbable** ADJ. calm; placid. Wellington remained *imperturbable* and in full command of the situation in spite of the hysteria and panic all around him. imperturbability, N.

■ **impervious** ADJ. impenetrable; incapable of being damaged or distressed. The carpet salesman told Simone that his most expensive brand of floor covering was warranted to be *impervious* to ordinary wear and tear. Having read so many negative reviews of his acting, the movie star had learned to ignore them, and was now *impervious* to criticism.

**impetuous** ADJ. violent; hasty; rash. "Leap before you look" was the motto suggested by one particularly *impetuous* young man.

**impetus** N. moving force; incentive; stimulus. A new federal highway program would create jobs and give added *impetus* to our economic recovery.

**impiety** N. irreverence; lack of respect for God. When members of the youth group draped the church in toilet paper one Halloween, the minister reprimanded them for their *impiety*. impious, ADJ.

**impinge** V. infringe; touch; collide with. How could they be married without *impinging* on one another's freedom?

**impious** ADJ. irreverent. The congregation was offended by her *impious* remarks.

■ **implacable** ADJ. incapable of being pacified. Madame Defarge was the *implacable* enemy of the Evremonde family.

**implausible** ADJ. unlikely; unbelievable. Though her alibi seemed *implausible,* it in fact turned out to be true.

**implement** V. put into effect; supply with tools. The mayor was unwilling to *implement* the plan until she was sure it had the governor's backing. also N.

**implicate** V. incriminate; show to be involved. Here's the deal: if you agree to take the witness stand and *implicate* your partners in crime, the prosecution will recommend that the judge go easy in sentencing you.

**implication** N. something hinted at or suggested. When Miss Watson said she hadn't seen her purse since the last time Jim was in the house, the *implication* was that she suspected Jim had taken it.

■ **implicit** ADJ. understood but not stated. Jack never told Jill he adored her; he believed his love was *implicit* in his deeds.

■ **implode** V. burst inward. If you break a vacuum tube, the glass tube *implodes*. implosion, N.

**implore** V. beg. He *implored* her to give him a second chance.

**imply** V. suggest a meaning not expressed; signify. When Aunt Millie said, "My! That's a big piece of pie, young man!" was she *implying* that Bobby was being a glutton in helping himself to such a huge piece?

**impolitic** ADJ. not wise. I think it is *impolitic* to raise this issue at the present time because the public is too angry.

**imponderable** ADJ. weightless. I can evaluate the data gathered in this study; the *imponderable* items are not so easily analyzed.

**import** N. significance. I feel that you have not grasped the full *import* of the message sent to us by the enemy.

**importunate** ADJ. urging; demanding. He tried to hide from his *importunate* creditors until his allowance arrived.

**importune** V. beg persistently. Democratic and Republican phone solicitors *importuned* her for contributions so frequently that she decided to give nothing to either party.

**imposture** N. assuming a false identity; masquerade. She was imprisoned for her *imposture* of a doctor.

**impotent** ADJ. weak; ineffective. Although he wished to break the nicotine habit, he found himself *impotent* in resisting the craving for a cigarette.

**imprecation** N. curse. Roused from bed at what he considered an ungodly hour, Roy muttered *imprecations* under his breath.

**impregnable** ADJ. invulnerable. Until the development of the airplane as a military weapon, the fort was considered *impregnable*.

**impromptu** ADJ. without previous preparation; off the cuff; on the spur of the moment. The judges were amazed that she could make such a thorough, well-supported presentation in an *impromptu* speech.

**impropriety** N. improperness; unsuitableness. Because of the *impropriety* of the punk rocker's slashed T-shirt and jeans, the management refused to admit him to the hotel's very formal dining room.

**improvident** ADJ. thriftless. He was constantly being warned to mend his *improvident* ways and begin to "save for a rainy day." improvidence, N.

**improvise** V. compose on the spur of the moment. She would sit at the piano and *improvise* for hours on themes from Bach and Handel.

**imprudent** ADJ. lacking caution; injudicious. It is *imprudent* to exercise vigorously and become overheated when you are unwell.

**impudence** N. impertinence; insolence. Kissed on the cheek by a perfect stranger, Lady Catherine exclaimed, "Of all the nerve! Young man, I should have you horsewhipped for your *impudence*."

**impugn** V. dispute or contradict (often in an insulting way); challenge; gainsay. Our treasurer was furious when the finance committee's report *impugned* the accuracy of his financial records and recommended that he take bonehead math.

**impuissance** N. powerlessness; feebleness. The lame duck president was frustrated by his shift from enormous power to relative *impuissance*.

**impunity** N. freedom from punishment or harm. A 98-pound weakling can't attack a beachfront bully with *impunity:* the poor, puny guy is sure to get mashed.

**impute** V. attribute; ascribe. If I wished to *impute* blame to the officers in charge of this program, I would state my feelings definitely and immediately.

■ **inadvertently** ADV. unintentionally; by oversight; carelessly. Judy's great fear was that she might *inadvertently* omit a question on the exam and mismark her whole answer sheet.

**inalienable** ADJ. not to be taken away; nontransferable. The Declaration of Independence mentions the *inalienable* rights that all of us possess.

**inane** ADJ. silly; senseless. There's no point in what you're saying. Why are you bothering to make such *inane* remarks? inanity, N.

**inanimate** ADJ. lifeless. She was asked to identify the still and *inanimate* body.

**inarticulate** ADJ. speechless; producing indistinct speech. She became *inarticulate* with rage and uttered sounds without meaning.

**inaugurate** V. begin formally; install in office. The candidate promised that he would *inaugurate* a new nationwide health care plan as soon as he was *inaugurated* as president. inauguration, N.

**incandescent** ADJ. strikingly bright; shining with intense heat. If you leave on an *incandescent* light bulb, it quickly grows too hot to touch.

**incantation** N. singing or chanting of magic spells; magical formula. Uttering *incantations* to make the brew more potent, the witch doctor stirred the liquid in the caldron.

**incapacitate** V. disable. During the winter, many people were *incapacitated* by respiratory ailments.

**incarcerate** V. imprison. The civil rights workers were willing to be arrested and even *incarcerated* if by their imprisonment they could serve the cause.

**incarnate** ADJ. endowed with flesh; personified. Your attitude is so fiendish that you must be a devil *incarnate*.

**incarnation** N. act of assuming a human body and human nature. The *incarnation* of Jesus Christ is a basic tenet of Christian theology.

**incendiary** N. arsonist. The fire spread in such an unusual manner that the fire department chiefs were certain that it had been set by an *incendiary*. also ADJ.

**incense** V. enrage; infuriate. Cruelty to defenseless animals *incensed* Kit: the very idea brought tears of anger to her eyes.

**incentive** N. spur; motive. Mike's strong desire to outshine his big sister was all the *incentive* he needed to do well in school.

**inception** N. start; beginning. She was involved with the project from its *inception*.

**incessant** ADJ. uninterrupted; unceasing. In a famous TV commercial, the frogs' *incessant* croaking goes on and on until eventually it turns into a single word: "Budweis-er."

# Test

## Word List 24    *Synonyms and Antonyms*

Each of the questions below consists of a word in capital letters, followed by five lettered words or phrases. Choose the lettered word or phrase that is most nearly similar or opposite in meaning to the word in capital letters and write the letter of your choice on your answer paper.

346. IMMOLATE (A) debate (B) scour (C) sacrifice (D) sanctify (E) ratify

347. IMMUTABLE (A) silent (B) changeable (C) articulate (D) loyal (E) varied

348. IMPAIR (A) separate (B) make amends (C) make worse (D) falsify (E) cancel

349. IMPALPABLE (A) obvious (B) combined (C) high (D) connecting (E) lost

350. IMPASSIVE (A) active (B) demonstrative (C) perfect (D) anxious (E) irritated

351. IMPECCABLE (A) unmentionable (B) quotable (C) blinding (D) faulty (E) hampering

352. IMPECUNIOUS (A) affluent (B) afflicted (C) affectionate (D) affable (E) afraid

353. IMPERVIOUS (A) impenetrable (B) perplexing (C) chaotic (D) cool (E) perfect

354. IMPETUOUS (A) rash (B) inane (C) just (D) flagrant (E) redolent

355. IMPOLITIC (A) campaigning (B) advisable (C) aggressive (D) legal (E) fortunate

356. IMPORTUNE (A) export (B) plead (C) exhibit (D) account (E) visit

357. IMPROMPTU (A) prompted (B) appropriate (C) rehearsed (D) foolish (E) vast

358. INALIENABLE (A) inherent (B) repugnant (C) closed to immigration (D) full (E) accountable

359. INANE (A) passive (B) wise (C) intoxicated (D) mellow (E) silent

360. INCARCERATE (A) inhibit (B) acquit (C) account (D) imprison (E) force

## Word List 25    inchoate-infraction

■ **inchoate** ADJ. recently begun; rudimentary; elementary. Before the Creation, the world was an *inchoate* mass.

**incidence** N. rate of occurrence; particular occurrence. Health professionals expressed great concern over the high *incidence* of infant mortality in major urban areas.

**incidental** ADJ. not essential; minor. The scholarship covered his major expenses at college and some of his *incidental* expenses as well.

**incipient** ADJ. beginning; in an early stage. I will go to sleep early for I want to break an *incipient* cold.

**incisive** ADJ. cutting; sharp. Her *incisive* remarks made us see the fallacy in our plans. incision, N.

**incite** V. arouse to action; goad; motivate; induce to exist. In a fiery speech, Mario *incited* his fellow students to go out on strike to protest the university's anti-affirmative-action stand.

**inclement** ADJ. stormy; unkind. In *inclement* weather, I like to curl up on the sofa with a good book and listen to the storm blowing outside.

**incline** N. slope; slant. The architect recommended that the nursing home's ramp be rebuilt because its *incline* was too steep for wheelchairs.

**inclined** ADJ. tending or leaning toward; bent. Though I am *inclined* to be skeptical, the witness's manner *inclines* me to believe his story. incline, V.

**inclusive** ADJ. tending to include all. The comedian turned down the invitation to join the Players' Club, saying any club that would let him in was too *inclusive* for him.

**incognito** ADV. with identity concealed; using an assumed name. The monarch enjoyed traveling through the town *incognito* and mingling with the populace. also ADJ.

**incoherent** ADJ. unintelligible; muddled; illogical. The excited fan blushed and stammered, her words becoming almost *incoherent* in the thrill of meeting her favorite rock star face to face. incoherence, N.

**incommodious** ADJ. not spacious; inconvenient. In their *incommodious* quarters, they had to improvise for closet space.

**incompatible** ADJ. inharmonious. The married couple argued incessantly and finally decided to separate because they were *incompatible*. incompatibility, N.

■ **incongruity** N. lack of harmony; absurdity. The *incongruity* of his wearing sneakers with formal attire amused the observers. incongruous, ADJ.

■ **inconsequential** ADJ. insignificant; unimportant. Brushing off Ali's apologies for having broken the wine glass, Tamara said, "Don't worry about it; it's *inconsequential.*"

**inconsistency** N. state of being self-contradictory; lack of uniformity or steadiness. How are lawyers different from agricultural inspectors? Where lawyers check *inconsistencies* in witnesses' statements, agricultural inspectors check *inconsistencies* in Grade A eggs. inconsistent, ADJ.

**incontinent** ADJ. lacking self-restraint; licentious. His *incontinent* behavior off stage so shocked many people that they refused to attend the plays and movies in which he appeared.

**incontrovertible** ADJ. indisputable; not open to question. Unless you find the evidence against my client absolutely *incontrovertible,* you must declare her not guilty of this charge.

■ **incorporate** V. introduce something into a larger whole; combine; unite. Breaking with precedent, President Truman ordered the military to *incorporate* blacks into every branch of the armed services. also ADJ.

**incorporeal** ADJ. lacking a material body; insubstantial. Although Casper the friendly ghost is an *incorporeal* being, he and his fellow ghosts make quite an impact on the physical world.

**incorrigible** ADJ. uncorrectable. Though Widow Douglass hoped to reform Huck, Miss Watson pronounced him *incorrigible* and said he would come to no good end.

**incredulity** N. tendency to disbelief. Your *incredulity* in the face of all the evidence is hard to understand.

**incredulous** ADJ. withholding belief; skeptical. When Jack claimed he hadn't eaten the jelly doughnut, Jill took an *incredulous* look at his smeared face and laughed.

**increment** N. increase. The new contract calls for a ten percent *increment* in salary for each employee for the next two years.

**incriminate** V. accuse; serve as evidence against. The witness's testimony against the racketeers *incriminates* some high public officials as well.

**incrustation** N. hard coating or crust. In dry dock, we scraped off the *incrustation* of dirt and barnacles that covered the hull of the ship.

**incubate** V. hatch. Inasmuch as our supply of electricity is cut off, we shall have to rely on the hens to *incubate* these eggs.

**incubus** N. burden; mental care; nightmare. The *incubus* of financial worry helped bring on her nervous breakdown.

**inculcate** V. teach. In an effort to *inculcate* religious devotion, the officials ordered that the school day begin with the singing of a hymn.

**incumbent** ADJ. obligatory; currently holding an office. It is *incumbent* upon all *incumbent* elected officials to keep accurate records of expenses incurred in office. also N.

**incur** V. bring upon oneself. His parents refused to pay any future debts he might *incur.*

**incursion** N. temporary invasion. The nightly *incursions* and hit-and-run raids of our neighbors across the border tried the patience of the country to the point where we decided to retaliate in force.

**indefatigable** ADJ. tireless. Although the effort of taking out the garbage exhausted Wayne for the entire morning, when it came to partying, he was *indefatigable.*

**indelible** ADJ. not able to be erased. The *indelible* ink left a permanent mark on my shirt. Young Bill Clinton's meeting with President Kennedy made an *indelible* impression on the youth.

**indemnify** V. make secure against loss; compensate for loss. The city will *indemnify* all home owners whose property is spoiled by this project.

**indentation** N. notch; deep recess. You can tell one tree from another by noting the differences in the *indentations* along the edges of the leaves. indent, V.

**indenture** V. bind as servant or apprentice to master. Many immigrants could come to America only after they had *indentured* themselves for several years. also N.

■ **indeterminate** ADJ. uncertain; not clearly fixed; indefinite. That interest rates shall rise appears certain; when they will do so, however, remains *indeterminate.*

**indicative** ADJ. suggestive; implying. A lack of appetite may be *indicative* of a major mental or physical disorder.

**indices** N. PL. signs; indications. Many college admissions officers believe that SAT scores and high school grades are the best *indices* of a student's potential to succeed in college. index, N. SING.

**indict** V. charge. The district attorney didn't want to *indict* the suspect until she was sure she had a strong enough case to convince a jury. indictment, N.

**indifferent** ADJ. unmoved or unconcerned by; mediocre. Because Ann felt no desire to marry, she was *indifferent* to Carl's constant proposals. Not only was she *indifferent* to him personally, but she felt that, given his general inanity, he would make an *indifferent* husband.

■ **indigence** N. poverty. Neither the economists nor the political scientists have found a way to wipe out the inequities of wealth and eliminate *indigence* from our society. indigent, ADJ., N.

**indigenous** ADJ. native. Cigarettes are made of tobacco, a plant *indigenous* to the New World.

**indigent** ADJ. poor; destitute. Someone who is truly *indigent* can't even afford to buy a pack of cigarettes. [Don't mix up *indigent* and *indigenous.* See preceding entry.] also N.

**indignation** N. anger at an injustice. She felt *indignation* at the ill-treatment of the helpless animals.

**indignity** N. offensive or insulting treatment. Although he seemed to accept cheerfully the *indignities* heaped upon him, he was inwardly very angry.

**indiscriminate** ADJ. choosing at random; confused. She disapproved of her son's *indiscriminate* television viewing and decided to restrict him to educational programs.

**indisputable** ADJ. too certain to be disputed. In the face of these *indisputable* statements, I withdraw my complaint.

**indissoluble** ADJ. permanent. The *indissoluble* bonds of marriage are all too often being dissolved.

**indite** V. write; compose. Cyrano *indited* many letters for Christian.

■ **indolent** ADJ. lazy. Couch potatoes lead an *indolent* life lying back in their Lazyboy recliners watching TV. indolence, N.

**indomitable** ADJ. unconquerable; unyielding. Focusing on her game despite all her personal problems, tennis champion Steffi Graf displayed an *indomitable* will to win.

**indubitable** ADJ. unable to be doubted; unquestionable. Auditioning for the chorus line, Molly was an *indubitable* hit: the director fired the leading lady and hired Molly in her place!

**induce**  v. persuade; bring about. After the quarrel, Tina said nothing could *induce* her to talk to Tony again. inducement, N.

**inductive**  ADJ. pertaining to induction or proceeding from the specific to the general. The discovery of the planet Pluto is an excellent example of the results that can be obtained from *inductive* reasoning.

**indulgent**  ADJ. humoring; yielding; lenient. Jay's mom was excessively *indulgent*: she bought him every computer game on the market. In fact, she *indulged* Jay so much, she spoiled him rotten.

**industrious**  ADJ. diligent; hard-working. Look busy when the boss walks by your desk; it never hurts to appear *industrious*. industry, N.

**inebriated**  ADJ. habitually intoxicated; drunk. Abe was *inebriated* more often than he was sober. Because of his *inebriety*, he was discharged from his job as a bus driver.

**ineffable**  ADJ. unutterable; cannot be expressed in speech. Such *ineffable* joy must be experienced; it cannot be described.

**ineffectual**  ADJ. not effective; weak. Because the candidate failed to get across her message to the public, her campaign was *ineffectual*.

**ineluctable**  ADJ. irresistible; not to be escaped. He felt that his fate was *ineluctable* and refused to make any attempt to improve his lot.

**inept**  ADJ. lacking skill; unsuited; incompetent. The *inept* glovemaker was all thumbs. ineptness, N.

**inequity**  N. unfairness. In demanding equal pay for equal work, women protest the basic *inequity* of a system that allots greater financial rewards to men. inequitable, ADJ.

**inerrancy**  N. infallibility. Jane refused to believe in the pope's *inerrancy*, reasoning: "All human beings are capable of error. The pope is a human being. Therefore, the pope is capable of error."

■ **inert**  ADJ. inactive; lacking power to move. "Get up, you lazybones," Tina cried to Tony, who lay in bed *inert*. inertia, N.

**inevitable**  ADJ. unavoidable. Though death and taxes are both supposedly *inevitable*, some people avoid paying taxes for years.

**inexorable**  ADJ. relentless; unyielding; implacable. After listening to the pleas for clemency, the judge was *inexorable* and gave the convicted man the maximum punishment allowed by law.

**infallible**  ADJ. unerring. We must remember that none of us is *infallible*; we all make mistakes.

**infamous**  ADJ. notoriously bad. Charles Manson and Jeffrey Dahmer are two examples of *infamous* killers.

**infantile**  ADJ. childish; infantlike. When will he outgrow such *infantile* behavior?

**infer**  v. deduce; conclude. From the students' glazed looks, it was easy for me to *infer* that they were bored out of their minds. inference, N.

**infernal**  ADJ. pertaining to hell; devilish. Batman was baffled: he could think of no way to hinder the Joker's *infernal* scheme to destroy the city.

**infidel**  N. unbeliever. The Saracens made war against the *infidels*.

**infiltrate**  v. pass into or through; penetrate (an organization) sneakily. In order to *infiltrate* enemy lines at night without being seen, the scouts darkened their faces and wore black coveralls. infiltrator, N.

**infinitesimal**  ADJ. very small. In the twentieth century, physicists have made their greatest discoveries about the characteristics of *infinitesimal* objects like the atom and its parts.

**infirmity**  N. weakness. Her greatest *infirmity* was lack of willpower.

**inflated**  ADJ. exaggerated; pompous; enlarged (with air or gas). His claims about the new product were *inflated*; it did not work as well as he had promised.

**influx**  N. flowing into. The *influx* of refugees into the country has taxed the relief agencies severely.

**infraction**  N. violation (of a rule or regulation); breach. When basketball star Dennis Rodman butted heads with the referee, he committed a clear *infraction* of NBA rules.

# Test

## Word List 25 *Synonyms*

Each of the questions below consists of a word in capital letters, followed by five lettered words or phrases. Choose the lettered word or phrase that is most nearly similar in meaning to the word in capital letters and write the letter of your choice on your answer paper.

361. INCLEMENT (A) unfavorable (B) abandoned (C) kindly (D) selfish (E) active

362. INCOMPATIBLE (A) capable (B) reasonable (C) faulty (D) indifferent (E) alienated

363. INCONSEQUENTIAL (A) disorderly (B) insignificant (C) subsequent (D) insufficient (E) preceding

364. INCONTINENT (A) insular (B) complaisant (C) crass (D) wanton (E) false

365. INCORRIGIBLE (A) narrow (B) straight (C) inconceivable (D) unreliable (E) unreformable

366. INCRIMINATE (A) exacerbate (B) involve (C) intimidate (D) lacerate (E) prevaricate

367. INCULCATE (A) exculpate (B) educate (C) exonerate (D) prepare (E) embarrass

368. INDIGENT (A) lazy (B) pusillanimous (C) penurious (D) affluent (E) contrary

369. INDIGNITY (A) pomposity (B) bombast (C) obeisance (D) insult (E) message

370. INDOLENCE (A) sloth (B) poverty (C) latitude (D) aptitude (E) anger

371. INDUBITABLY (A) flagrantly (B) doubtfully (C) carefully (D) carelessly (E) certainly

372. INEBRIETY (A) revelation (B) drunkenness (C) felony (D) starvation (E) gluttony

373. INEPT (A) outward (B) spiritual (C) foolish (D) clumsy (E) abundant

374. INFALLIBLE (A) final (B) unbelievable (C) perfect (D) inaccurate (E) inquisitive

375. INFIRMITY (A) disability (B) age (C) inoculation (D) hospital (E) unity

## Word List 26 infringe-invert

**infringe** V. violate; encroach. I think your machine *infringes* on my patent and I intend to sue.

**ingenious** ADJ. clever; resourceful. Kit admired the *ingenious* way that her computer keyboard opened up to reveal the built-in CD-ROM below. ingenuity, N.

■ **ingenuous** ADJ. naive and trusting; young; unsophisticated. The woodsman did not realize how *ingenuous* Little Red Riding Hood was until he heard that she had gone off for a walk in the woods with the Big Bad Wolf. ingenue, N.

**ingrained** ADJ. deeply established; firmly rooted. Try as they would, the missionaries were unable to uproot the *ingrained* superstitions of the natives.

**ingrate** N. ungrateful person. That *ingrate* Bob sneered at the tie I gave him.

**ingratiate** V. become popular with. He tried to *ingratiate* himself into her parents' good graces.

■ **inherent** ADJ. firmly established by nature or habit. Katya's *inherent* love of justice caused her to champion anyone she considered to be treated unfairly by society.

**inhibit** V. restrain; retard or prevent. Only two things *inhibited* him from taking a punch at Mike Tyson: Tyson's left hook, and Tyson's right jab. The protective undercoating on my car *inhibits* the formation of rust. inhibition, N.

**inimical** ADJ. unfriendly; hostile; harmful; detrimental. I've always been friendly to Martha. Why is she so *inimical* to me?

**inimitable** ADJ. matchless; not able to be imitated. We admire Auden for his *inimitable* use of language; he is one of a kind.

**iniquitous** ADJ. wicked; immoral; unrighteous. Whether or not King Richard III was responsible for the murder of the two young princes in the Tower, it was an *iniquitous* deed. iniquity, N.

**initiate** V. begin; originate; receive into a group. The college is about to *initiate* a program for reducing math anxiety among students.

**injurious** ADJ. harmful. Smoking cigarettes can be *injurious* to your health.

**inkling** N. hint. This came as a complete surprise to me as I did not have the slightest *inkling* of your plans.

**innate** ADJ. inborn. Mozart's parents soon recognized young Wolfgang's *innate* talent for music.

■ **innocuous** ADJ. harmless. An occasional glass of wine with dinner is relatively *innocuous* and should have no ill effect on most people.

**innovation** N. change; introduction of something new. Although Richard liked to keep up with all the latest technological *innovations*, he didn't always abandon tried and true techniques in favor of something new. innovate, V. innovative, ADJ.

**innuendo** N. hint; insinuation. I can defend myself against direct accusations; *innuendos* and oblique attacks on my character are what trouble me.

**inopportune**  ADJ. untimely; poorly chosen. A rock concert is an *inopportune* setting for a quiet conversation.

**inordinate**  ADJ. unrestrained; excessive. She had an *inordinate* fondness for candy, eating two or three boxes in a single day.

**inquisitor**  N. questioner (especially harsh); investigator. Fearing being grilled ruthlessly by the secret police, Marsha faced her *inquisitors* with trepidation.

**insalubrious**  ADJ. unwholesome; not healthful. The mosquito-ridden swamp was an *insalubrious* place, a breeding ground for malarial contagion.

**insatiable**  ADJ. not easily satisfied; unquenchable; greedy. The young writer's thirst for knowledge was *insatiable;* she was always in the library.

**inscrutable**  ADJ. impenetrable; not readily understood; mysterious. Experienced poker players try to keep their expressions *inscrutable,* hiding their reactions to the cards behind a so-called poker face.

**insensate**  ADJ. without feeling. She lay there as *insensate* as a log.

■ **insensible**  ADJ. unconscious; unresponsive. Sherry and I are very different; at times when I would be covered with embarrassment, she seems *insensible* to shame.

**insidious**  ADJ. treacherous; stealthy; sly. The fifth column is *insidious* because it works secretly within our territory for our defeat.

**insightful**  ADJ. discerning; perceptive. Sol thought he was very *insightful* about human behavior, but actually he was clueless as to why people acted the way they did.

■ **insinuate**  V. hint; imply; creep in. When you said I looked robust, did you mean to *insinuate* that I'm getting fat?

■ **insipid**  ADJ. lacking in flavor; dull. Flat prose and flat ginger ale are equally *insipid:* both lack sparkle.

**insolence**  N. impudent disrespect; haughtiness. How dare you treat me so rudely! The manager will hear of your *insolence*. insolent, ADJ.

**insolvent**  ADJ. bankrupt; lacking money to pay. When rumors that he was *insolvent* reached his creditors, they began to press him for payment of the money due them. insolvency, N.

**insomnia**  N. wakefulness; inability to sleep. She refused to join us in a midnight cup of coffee because she claimed it gave her *insomnia*.

**insouciant**  ADJ. indifferent; without concern or care. Your *insouciant* attitude at such a critical moment indicates that you do not understand the gravity of the situation.

**instigate**  V. urge; start; provoke. Delighting in making mischief, Sir Toby sets out to *instigate* a quarrel between Sir Andrew and Cesario.

**insubordination**  N. disobedience; rebelliousness. At the slightest hint of *insubordination* from the sailors on the *Bounty,* Captain Bligh had them flogged; finally, they mutinied. insubordinate, ADJ.

**insubstantial**  ADJ. lacking substance; insignificant; frail. His hopes for a career in acting proved *insubstantial;* no one would cast him, even in an *insubstantial* role.

■ **insularity**  N. narrow-mindedness; isolation. The *insularity* of the islanders manifested itself in their suspicion of anything foreign. insular, ADJ.

**insuperable**  ADJ. insurmountable; unbeatable. Though the odds against their survival seemed *insuperable,* the Apollo 13 astronauts reached earth safely.

**insurgent**  ADJ. rebellious. Because the *insurgent* forces had occupied the capital and had gained control of the railway lines, several of the war correspondents covering the uprising predicted a rebel victory. also N. insurgency, N.

**insurmountable**  ADJ. overwhelming; unbeatable; insuperable. Facing almost *insurmountable* obstacles, the members of the underground maintained their courage and will to resist.

**insurrection**  N. rebellion; uprising. In retrospect, given how badly the British treated the American colonists, the eventual *insurrection* seems inevitable.

**intangible**  ADJ. not able to be perceived by touch; vague. Though the financial benefits of his Oxford post were meager, Lewis was drawn to it by its *intangible* rewards: prestige, intellectual freedom, the fellowship of his peers.

**integral**  ADJ. complete; necessary for completeness. Physical education is an *integral* part of our curriculum; a sound mind and a sound body are complementary.

**integrate**  V. make whole; combine; make into one unit. She tried to *integrate* all their activities into one program.

**integrity**  N. uprightness; wholeness. Lincoln, whose personal *integrity* has inspired millions, fought a civil war to maintain the *integrity* of the republic, that these United States might remain undivided for all time.

**intellect**  N. higher mental powers. He thought college would develop his *intellect*.

**intelligentsia**  N. intellectuals; members of the educated elite [often used derogatorily]. She preferred discussions about sports and politics to the literary conversations of the *intelligentsia*.

**inter**  V. bury. They are going to *inter* the body tomorrow at Broadlawn Cemetry. interment, N.

**interdict**  V. prohibit; forbid. Civilized nations must *interdict* the use of nuclear weapons if we expect our society to live.

**interim**  N. meantime. The company will not consider our proposal until next week; in the *interim,* let us proceed as we have in the past.

**interloper**  N. intruder. The merchant thought of his competitors as *interlopers* who were stealing away his trade.

**interminable**  ADJ. endless. Although his speech lasted for only twenty minutes, it seemed *interminable* to his bored audience.

**intermittent**  ADJ. periodic; on and off. The outdoor wedding reception had to be moved indoors to avoid the *intermittent* showers that fell on and off all afternoon.

**internecine**  ADJ. mutually destructive. The rising death toll on both sides indicates the *internecine* nature of this conflict.

**interpolate**  V. insert between. She talked so much that I could not *interpolate* a single remark.

**interregnum** N. period between two reigns. Henry VIII desperately sought a male heir because he feared the civil strife that might occur if any prolonged *interregnum* succeeded his death.

**interrogate** V. question closely; cross-examine. Knowing that the Nazis would *interrogate* him about his background, the secret agent invented a cover story that would help him meet their questions.

**intervene** V. come between. When two close friends get into a fight, be careful if you try to *intervene;* they may join forces and gang up on you. intervention, N.

**intimate** V. hint. She *intimated* rather than stated her preferences.

**intimidate** V. frighten. I'll learn karate and then those big bullies won't be able to *intimidate* me anymore. intimidation, N.

■ **intractable** ADJ. unruly; stubborn; unyielding. Charlie Brown's friend Pigpen was *intractable:* he absolutely refused to take a bath.

■ **intransigence** N. refusal of any compromise; stubbornness. The negotiating team had not expected such *intransigence* from the striking workers, who rejected any hint of a compromise. intransigent, ADJ.

**intrepid** ADJ. fearless. For her *intrepid* conduct nursing the wounded during the war, Florence Nightingale was honored by Queen Victoria.

**intrinsic** ADJ. essential; inherent; built-in. Although my grandmother's china has little *intrinsic* value, I shall always cherish it for the memories it evokes.

**introspective** ADJ. looking within oneself. Though young Francis of Assisi led a wild and worldly life, even he had *introspective* moments during which he examined his soul. introspection, N.

**introvert** N. one who is introspective; inclined to think more about oneself. In his poetry, he reveals that he is an *introvert* by his intense interest in his own problems.

**intrude** V. trespass; enter as an uninvited person. She hesitated to *intrude* on their conversation.

**intuition** N. immediate insight; power of knowing without reasoning. Even though Tony denied that anything was wrong, Tina trusted her *intuition* that something was bothering him. intuitive, ADJ. intuit, V.

■ **inundate** V. overwhelm; flood; submerge. This semester I am *inundated* with work: you should see the piles of paperwork flooding my desk. Until the great dam was built, the waters of the Nile used to *inundate* the river valley every year.

■ **inured** ADJ. accustomed; hardened. She became *inured* to the Alaskan cold.

**invalidate** V. weaken; destroy. The relatives who received little or nothing sought to *invalidate* the will by claiming that the deceased had not been in his right mind when he signed the document.

■ **invective** N. abuse. He had expected criticism but not the *invective* that greeted his proposal.

**inveigh** V. denounce; utter censure or invective. He *inveighed* against the demagoguery of the previous speaker and urged that the audience reject his philosophy as dangerous.

**inveigle** V. lead astray; wheedle. She was *inveigled* into joining the club after an initial reluctance.

**inverse** ADJ. opposite. There is an *inverse* ratio between the strength of light and its distance.

**invert** V. turn upside down or inside out. When he *inverted* his body in a hand stand, he felt the blood rush to his head.

# Test

## Word List 26    *Synonyms*

Each of the questions below consists of a word in capital letters, followed by five lettered words or phrases. Choose the lettered word or phrase that is most nearly similar in meaning to the word in capital letters and write the letter of your choice on your answer paper.

376. INGENUOUS (A) clever (B) stimulating (C) naive (D) worried (E) cautious

377. INIMICAL (A) antagonistic (B) anonymous (C) fanciful (D) accurate (E) atypical

378. INNOCUOUS (A) not capable (B) not dangerous (C) not eager (D) not frank (E) not peaceful

379. INSINUATE (A) resist (B) suggest (C) report (D) rectify (E) lecture

380. INSIPID (A) witty (B) flat (C) wily (D) talkative (E) lucid

381. INTEGRATE (A) tolerate (B) unite (C) flow (D) copy (E) assume

382. INTER (A) bury (B) amuse (C) relate (D) frequent (E) abandon

383. INTERDICT (A) acclaim (B) dispute (C) prohibit (D) decide (E) fret

384. INTERMITTENT (A) heavy (B) fleet (C) occasional (D) fearless (E) responding

385. INTRACTABLE (A) culpable (B) flexible (C) unruly (D) efficient (E) base

386. INTRANSIGENCE (A) lack of training (B) stubbornness (C) novelty (D) timidity (E) cupidity

387. INTREPID (A) cold (B) hot (C) understood (D) callow (E) courageous

388. INTRINSIC (A) extrinsic (B) abnormal (C) above (D) abandoned (E) basic

389. INUNDATE (A) abuse (B) deny (C) swallow (D) treat (E) flood

390. INVEIGH (A) speak violently (B) orate (C) disturb (D) apply (E) whisper

---

# Word List 27    inveterate-laggard

**inveterate** ADJ. deep-rooted; habitual. She is an *inveterate* smoker and cannot break the habit.

**invidious** ADJ. designed to create ill will or envy. We disregarded her *invidious* remarks because we realized how jealous she was.

**invincible** ADJ. unconquerable. Superman is *invincible*.

**inviolable** ADJ. secure from corruption, attack, or violation; unassailable. Batman considered his oath to keep the people of Gotham City safe *inviolable*: nothing on earth could make him break this promise. inviolability, N.

**invocation** N. prayer for help; calling upon as a reference or support. The service of Morning Prayer opens with an *invocation* during which we ask God to hear our prayers.

**invoke** V. call upon; ask for. She *invoked* her advisor's aid in filling out her financial aid forms.

**invulnerable** ADJ. incapable of injury. Achilles was *invulnerable* except in his heel.

**iota** N. very small quantity. She hadn't an *iota* of common sense.

■ **irascible** ADJ. irritable; easily angered. Miss Minchin's *irascible* temper intimidated the younger schoolgirls, who feared she'd burst into a rage at any moment.

**irate** ADJ. angry. When John's mother found out that he had overdrawn his checking account for the third month in a row, she was so *irate* that she could scarcely speak to him.

**iridescent** ADJ. exhibiting rainbowlike colors. She admired the *iridescent* hues of the oil that floated on the surface of the water. iridescence, N.

**irksome** ADJ. annoying; tedious. He found working on the assembly line *irksome* because of the monotony of the operation he had to perform. irk, V.

**ironic** ADJ. occurring in an unexpected and contrary manner. It is *ironic* that his success came when he least wanted it.

**irony** N. hidden sarcasm or satire; use of words that seem to mean the opposite of what they actually mean. Gradually his listeners began to realize that the excessive praise he was lavishing on his opponent was actually *irony*; he was, in fact, ridiculing the poor fool.

**irreconcilable** ADJ. incompatible; not able to be resolved. Because the separated couple were *irreconcilable*, the marriage counselor recommended a divorce.

**irrefutable** ADJ. indisputable; incontrovertible; undeniable. No matter how hard I tried to find a good comeback for her argument, I couldn't think of one: her logic was *irrefutable*.

**irrelevant** ADJ. not applicable; unrelated. No matter how *irrelevant* the patient's mumblings may seem, they give us some indications of what is on his mind. irrelevancy, N.

**irremediable** ADJ. incurable; uncorrectable. The error she made was *irremediable*; she could see no way to repair it.

**irreparable** ADJ. not able to be corrected or repaired. Your apology cannot atone for the *irreparable* damage you have done to her reputation.

**irrepressible** ADJ. unable to be restrained or held back. My friend Kitty's curiosity was *irrepressible*: she poked her nose into everybody's business and just laughed when I warned her that curiosity killed the cat.

**irreproachable** ADJ. blameless; impeccable. Homer's conduct at the office party was *irreproachable*; even Marge had nothing bad to say about how he behaved.

■ **irresolute** ADJ. uncertain how to act; weak. Once you have made your decision, don't waver; a leader should never appear *irresolute*.

**irretrievable** ADJ. impossible to recover or regain; irreparable. The left fielder tried to retrieve the ball, but it flew over the fence, bounced off a wall, and fell into the sewer: it was *irretrievable*.

**irreverence** N. lack of proper respect. Some people in the audience were amused by the *irreverence* of the comedian's jokes about the Pope; others felt offended by his lack of respect for their faith. irreverent, ADJ.

**irrevocable** ADJ. unalterable; irreversible. As Sue dropped the "Dear John" letter into the mailbox, she suddenly had second thoughts and wanted to take it back, but she could not: her action was *irrevocable*.

**isotope** N. varying form of an element. The study of the *isotopes* of uranium led to the development of the nuclear bomb.

**isthmus** N. narrow neck of land connecting two larger bodies of land. In a magnificent feat of engineering, Goethals and his men cut through the *isthmus* of Panama in constructing the Panama Canal.

**itinerant** ADJ. wandering; traveling. He was an *itinerant* peddler and traveled through Pennsylvania and Virginia selling his wares. also N.

■ **itinerary** N. plan of a trip. Disliking sudden changes in plans when she traveled abroad, Ethel refused to make any alterations in her *itinerary*.

**jabber** V. chatter rapidly or unintelligibly. Why does the fellow insist on *jabbering* away in French when I can't understand a word he says?

**jaded** ADJ. fatigued; surfeited. He looked for exotic foods to stimulate his *jaded* appetite.

**jargon** N. language used by a special group; technical terminology; gibberish. The computer salesmen at the store used a *jargon* of their own that we simply couldn't follow; we had no idea what they were jabbering about.

**jaundiced** ADJ. prejudiced (envious, hostile, or resentful); yellowed. Because Sue disliked Carolyn, she looked at Carolyn's paintings with a *jaundiced* eye, calling them formless smears. Newborn infants afflicted with *jaundice* look slightly yellow: they have *jaundiced* skin.

**jaunt** N. trip; short journey. He took a quick *jaunt* to Atlantic City.

**jaunty** ADJ. lighthearted; animated; easy and carefree. In *Singing in the Rain,* Gene Kelly sang and danced his way through the lighthearted title number in a properly *jaunty* style.

**jeopardize** V. endanger; imperil; put at risk. You can't give me a D in chemistry: you'll *jeopardize* my chances of being admitted to M.I.T. jeopardy, N.

**jettison** V. throw overboard. In order to enable the ship to ride safely through the storm, the captain had to *jettison* much of his cargo.

**jibe** V. agree; be in harmony with. Moe says Curly started the fight; Curly insists it was Moe. Their stories just don't *jibe*.

**jingoist** N. extremely aggressive and militant patriot; war-like chauvinist. Always bellowing "America first!" the congressman was such a *jingoist* you could almost hear the sabers rattling as he marched down the halls. jingoism, N.

**jocose** ADJ. given to joking. The salesman was so *jocose* that many of his customers suggested that he become a stand-up comic.

**jocular** ADJ. said or done in jest. Although Bill knew the boss hated jokes, he couldn't resist making one *jocular* remark; his *jocularity* cost him the job.

**jocund** ADJ. merry. Santa Claus is always cheerful and *jocund*.

**jollity** N. gaiety; cheerfulness. The festive Christmas dinner was a merry one, and old and young alike joined in the general *jollity*.

**jostle** V. shove; bump. In the subway he was *jostled* by the crowds.

**jovial** ADJ. good-natured; merry. A frown seemed out of place on his invariably *jovial* face.

**jubilation** N. rejoicing. There was great *jubilation* when the armistice was announced.

**judicious** ADJ. sound in judgment; wise. At a key moment in his life, he made a *judicious* investment that was the foundation of his later wealth.

**juggernaut** N. irresistible crushing force. Nothing could survive in the path of the *juggernaut*.

**juncture** N. crisis; joining point. At this critical *juncture,* let us think carefully before determining the course we shall follow.

**junket** N. trip, especially one taken for pleasure by an official at public expense. Though she maintained she had gone abroad to collect firsthand data on the Common Market, the opposition claimed that her trip was merely a political *junket*.

**junta** N. group of persons joined in political intrigue; cabal. As soon as he learned of its existence, the dictator ordered the execution of all of the members of the *junta*.

**jurisprudence** N. science of law. She was more a student of *jurisprudence* than a practitioner of the law.

**justification** N. good or just reason; defense; excuse. The jury found him guilty of the more serious charge because they could see no possible *justification* for his actions.

**juxtapose** V. place side by side. Comparison will be easier if you *juxtapose* the two objects.

**kaleidoscope** N. tube in which patterns made by the reflection in mirrors of colored pieces of glass, etc., produce interesting symmetrical effects. People found a new source of entertainment while peering through the *kaleidoscope;* they found the ever-changing patterns fascinating.

**ken** N. range of knowledge. I cannot answer your question since this matter is beyond my *ken*.

**kernel** N. central or vital part; whole seed (as of corn). "Watson, buried within this tissue of lies there is a *kernel* of truth; when I find it, the mystery will be solved."

**killjoy** N. grouch; spoilsport. At breakfast we had all been enjoying our bacon and eggs until that *killjoy* John started talking about how bad animal fats and cholesterol were for our health.

**kindle** V. start a fire; inspire. One of the first things Ben learned in the Boy Scouts was how to *kindle* a fire by rubbing two dry sticks together. Her teacher's praise for her poetry *kindled* a spark of hope inside Maya.

**kindred** ADJ. related; similar in nature or character. Tom Sawyer and Huck Finn were two *kindred* spirits. also N.

**kinetic** ADJ. producing motion. Designers of the electric automobile find that their greatest obstacle lies in the development of light and efficient storage batteries, the source of the *kinetic* energy needed to propel the vehicle.

**kismet** N. fate. *Kismet* is the Arabic word for "fate."

**kleptomaniac** N. person who has a compulsive desire to steal. They discovered that the wealthy customer was a *kleptomaniac* when they caught her stealing some cheap trinkets.

**knave** N. untrustworthy person; rogue; scoundrel. Any politician nicknamed Tricky Dick clearly has the reputation of a *knave*. knavery, N.

**knead** V. mix; work dough. Her hands grew strong from *kneading* bread.

**knell** N. tolling of a bell, especially to indicate a funeral, disaster, etc.; sound of the funeral bell. "The curfew tolls the *knell* of parting day." also V.

**knit** V. contract into wrinkles; grow together. Whenever David worries, his brow *knits* in a frown. When he broke his leg, he sat around the house all day waiting for the bones to *knit*.

**knoll** N. little, round hill. Robert Louis Stevenson's grave is on a *knoll* in Samoa; to reach the grave site, you must climb uphill and walk a short distance along a marked path.

**knotty**  ADJ. intricate; difficult; tangled. What to Watson had been a *knotty* problem to Sherlock Holmes was simplicity itself.

**kudos**  N. honor; glory; praise. The singer complacently received *kudos* on his performance from his entourage.

**labile**  ADJ. likely to change; unstable. Because the hormonal changes they undergo affect their spirits, adolescents may become emotionally *labile* and experience sudden shifts of mood. lability, N.

**laborious**  ADJ. demanding much work or care; tedious. In putting together his dictionary of the English language, Doctor Johnson undertook a *laborious* task.

**labyrinth**  N. maze. Hiding from Indian Joe, Tom and Becky soon lost themselves in the *labyrinth* of secret underground caves.

**laceration**  N. torn, ragged wound. The stock-car driver needed stitches to close the *lacerations* he received in the car crash. lacerate, V.

**lachrymose**  ADJ. producing tears. His voice has a *lachrymose* quality that is more appropriate at a funeral than a class reunion.

**lackadaisical**  ADJ. lacking purpose or zest; halfhearted; languid. Because Gatsby had his mind more on his love life than on his finances, he did a very *lackadaisical* job of managing his money.

**lackluster**  ADJ. dull. We were disappointed by the *lackluster* performance.

■ **laconic**  ADJ. brief and to the point. Many of the characters portrayed by Clint Eastwood are *laconic* types: strong men of few words.

**laggard**  ADJ. slow; sluggish. The sailor had been taught not to be *laggard* in carrying out orders. lag, N., V.

# Test

## Word List 27    *Antonyms*

Each of the questions below consists of a word in capital letters, followed by five lettered words or phrases. Choose the lettered word or phrase that is most nearly opposite in meaning to the word in capital letters and write the letter of your choice on your answer paper.

391. IRKSOME (A) interesting (B) lazy (C) tireless (D) devious (E) excessive

392. IRRELEVANT (A) lacking piety (B) fragile (C) congruent (D) pertinent (E) varied

393. IRREPARABLE (A) legible (B) correctable (C) proverbial (D) concise (E) legal

394. IRREVERENT (A) related (B) mischievous (C) respective (D) pious (E) violent

395. JADED (A) upright (B) stimulated (C) aspiring (D) applied (E) void

396. JAUNDICED (A) whitened (B) inflamed (C) quickened (D) aged (E) unbiased

397. JAUNTY (A) youthful (B) ruddy (C) strong (D) untraveled (E) sedate

398. JEOPARDY (A) patience (B) courage (C) safety (D) willingness (E) liberty

399. JETTISON (A) salvage (B) submerge (C) descend (D) decelerate (E) repent

400. JOCULAR (A) arterial (B) bloodless (C) verbose (D) serious (E) blind

401. JUDICIOUS (A) punitive (B) unwise (C) criminal (D) licit (E) temporary

402. KINDLE (A) dislike (B) quench (C) gather (D) sparkle (E) estrange

403. LACHRYMOSE (A) cheering (B) smooth (C) passionate (D) curt (E) tense

404. LACKADAISICAL (A) monthly (B) possessing time (C) ambitious (D) pusillanimous (E) intelligent

405. LACONIC (A) milky (B) verbose (C) wicked (D) flagrant (E) derelict

## Word List 28    lagoon-loquacious

**lagoon**  N. shallow body of water near a sea; lake. They enjoyed their swim in the calm *lagoon*.

**laity**  N. laypersons; persons not connected with the clergy. The *laity* does not always understand the clergy's problems.

**lambaste**  V. beat; thrash verbally or physically. It was painful to watch the champion *lambaste* his opponent, tearing into him mercilessly.

**lament**  V. grieve; express sorrow. Even advocates of the war *lamented* the loss of so many lives in combat. lamentation, N.

**lampoon**  V. ridicule. This article *lampoons* the pretensions of some movie moguls. also N.

**lancet**  N. small surgical tool for making incisions. With the sharp tip of her *lancet*, Doctor Wheeler cut into the abscess, opening it to let it drain.

**languid** ADJ. weary; sluggish; listless. Her siege of illness left her *languid* and pallid.

**languish** V. lose animation or strength. Left at Miss Minchin's school for girls while her father went off to war, Sarah Crewe refused to *languish;* instead, she hid her grief and actively befriended her less fortunate classmates.

**languor** N. lassitude; depression. His friends tried to overcome the *languor* into which he had fallen by taking him to parties and to the theater.

**lank** ADJ. long and thin. *Lank,* gaunt, Abraham Lincoln was a striking figure.

**lap** V. take in food or drink with one's tongue; splash gently. The kitten neatly *lapped* up her milk. The waves softly *lapped* against the pier.

**larceny** N. theft. Because of the prisoner's record, the district attorney refused to reduce the charge from grand *larceny* to petty *larceny.*

**larder** N. pantry; place where food is kept. The first thing Bill did on returning home from school was to check what snacks his mother had in the *larder.*

**largess** N. generous gift. Lady Bountiful distributed *largess* to the poor.

**lascivious** ADJ. lustful. Because they might arouse *lascivious* impulses in their readers, the lewd books were banned by the clergy.

■ **lassitude** N. languor; weariness. After a massage and a long soak in the hot tub, I surrendered to my growing *lassitude* and lay down for a nap.

■ **latent** ADJ. potential but undeveloped; dormant; hidden. Polaroid pictures are popular at parties because you can see the *latent* photographic image gradually appear before your eyes. latency, N.

**lateral** ADJ. coming from the side. In order to get good plant growth, the gardener must pinch off all *lateral* shoots.

**latitude** N. freedom from narrow limitations. I think you have permitted your son too much *latitude* in this matter.

■ **laud** V. praise. The NFL *lauded* Boomer Esiason's efforts to raise money to combat cystic fibrosis. also N. laudable, laudatory, ADJ.

**lavish** ADJ. liberal; wasteful. The actor's *lavish* gifts pleased her. also V.

**lax** ADJ. careless. We dislike restaurants where the service is *lax* and inattentive.

**leaven** V. cause to rise or grow lighter; enliven. As bread dough is *leavened,* it puffs up, expanding in volume.

**lechery** N. gross lewdness; lustfulness. In his youth he led a life of *lechery* and debauchery; he did not mend his ways until middle age. lecherous, ADJ.

**lectern** N. reading desk. The chaplain delivered his sermon from a hastily improvised *lectern.*

**leery** ADJ. suspicious; cautious. Don't eat the sushi at this restaurant; I'm a bit *leery* about how fresh it is.

**leeway** N. room to move; margin. When you set a deadline, allow a little *leeway.*

**legacy** N. a gift made by a will. Part of my *legacy* from my parents is an album of family photographs.

**legend** N. explanatory list of symbols on a map. The *legend* at the bottom of the map made it clear which symbols stood for rest areas along the highway and which stood for public camp sites. (secondary meaning)

**legerdemain** N. sleight of hand. The magician demonstrated his renowned *legerdemain.*

**leniency** N. mildness; permissiveness. Considering the gravity of the offense, we were surprised by the *leniency* of the sentence. lenient, ADJ.

**leonine** ADJ. like a lion. He was *leonine* in his rage.

**lethal** ADJ. deadly. It is unwise to leave *lethal* weapons where children may find them.

■ **lethargic** ADJ. drowsy; dull. The stuffy room made her *lethargic:* she felt as if she was about to nod off. lethargy, N.

■ **levee** N. earthen or stone embankment to prevent flooding. As the river rose and threatened to overflow the *levee,* emergency workers rushed to reinforce the walls with sandbags.

**levitate** V. float in the air (especially by magical means). As the magician passed his hands over the recumbent body of his assistant, she appeared to rise and *levitate* about three feet above the table.

■ **levity** N. lack of seriousness or steadiness; frivolity. Stop giggling and wriggling around in the pew: such *levity* is improper in church.

**levy** V. impose (a fine); collect (a payment). Crying "No taxation without representation!" the colonists demonstrated against England's power to *levy* taxes. also N.

**lewd** ADJ. lustful. They found his *lewd* stories objectionable.

**lexicographer** N. compiler of a dictionary. The new dictionary is the work of many *lexicographers* who spent years compiling and editing the work.

**lexicon** N. dictionary. I cannot find this word in any *lexicon* in the library.

**liability** N. drawback; debts. Her lack of an extensive vocabulary was a *liability* that she was able to overcome.

**liaison** N. contact that keeps parties in communication; go-between; secret love affair. As the *liaison* between the American and British forces during World War II, the colonel had to ease tensions between the leaders of the two armies. Romeo's romantic *liaison* with Juliet ended in tragedy. also ADJ.

**libel** N. defamatory statement; act of writing something that smears a person's character. If Batman wrote that the Joker was a dirty, rotten, mass-murdering criminal, could the Joker sue Batman for *libel?* libelous, ADJ.

**libertine** N. debauched person, roué. Although she was aware of his reputation as a *libertine,* she felt she could reform him and help him abandon his dissolute way of life.

**libidinous** ADJ. lustful. They objected to his *libidinous* behavior.

**libido** N. emotional urges behind human activity. The psychiatrist maintained that suppression of the *libido* often resulted in maladjustment and neuroses.

**libretto** N. text of an opera. The composer of an opera's music is remembered more frequently than the author of its *libretto*.

**licentious** ADJ. amoral; lewd and lascivious; unrestrained. Unscrupulously seducing the daughter of his host, Don Juan felt no qualms about the immorality of his *licentious* behavior.

**lien** N. legal claim on a property. There was a delay before Ralph could take possession of his late uncle's home; apparently, another claimant had a *lien* upon the estate.

**ligneous** ADJ. like wood. Petrified wood may be *ligneous* in appearance, but it is stonelike in composition.

**lilliputian** ADJ. extremely small. Tiny and delicate, the model was built on a *lilliputian* scale. also N.

**limber** ADJ. flexible. Hours of ballet classes kept him *limber*.

**limbo** N. region near heaven or hell where certain souls are kept; a prison (slang). Among the divisions of Hell are Purgatory and *Limbo*.

**limn** V. draw; outline; describe. Paradoxically, the more realistic the details this artist chooses, the better able she is to *limn* her fantastic, other-worldly landscapes.

**limpid** ADJ. clear. A *limpid* stream ran through his property.

**lineage** N. descent; ancestry. He traced his *lineage* back to *Mayflower* days.

**lineaments** N. features, especially of the face. She quickly sketched the *lineaments* of his face.

**linger** V. loiter or dawdle; continue or persist. Hoping to see Juliet pass by, Romeo *lingered* outside the Capulet house for hours. Though Mother made stuffed cabbage on Monday, the smell *lingered* around the house for days.

**linguistic** ADJ. pertaining to language. The modern tourist will encounter very little *linguistic* difficulty as English has become an almost universal language.

**lionize** V. treat as a celebrity. She enjoyed being *lionized* and adored by the public.

**liquidate** V. settle accounts; clear up. He was able to *liquidate* all his debts in a short period of time.

**list** V. tilt; lean over. That flagpole should be absolutely vertical; instead, it *lists* to one side. (secondary meaning) also N.

**listless** ADJ. lacking in spirit or energy. We had expected her to be full of enthusiasm and were surprised by her *listless* attitude.

**litany** N. supplicatory prayer. On this solemn day, the congregation responded to the prayers of the priest during the *litany* with fervor and intensity.

**lithe** ADJ. flexible; supple. Her figure was *lithe* and willowy.

**litigation** N. lawsuit. Try to settle this amicably; I do not want to start *litigation*. litigant, N.

**litotes** N. understatement for emphasis. To say, "He little realizes," when we mean that he does not realize at all, is an example of the kind of understatement we call *litotes*.

**livid** ADJ. lead-colored; black and blue; ashen; enraged. His face was so *livid* with rage that we were afraid that he might have an attack of apoplexy.

**loath** ADJ. reluctant; disinclined. Romeo and Juliet were both *loath* for him to go.

**loathe** V. detest. Booing and hissing, the audience showed how much they *loathed* the villain. loathsome, ADJ.

**lode** N. metal-bearing vein. If this *lode* that we have discovered extends for any distance, we have found a fortune.

**lofty** ADJ. very high. Though Barbara Jordan's fellow students used to tease her about her *lofty* ambitions, she rose to hold one of the highest positions in the land.

■ **log** N. record of a voyage or flight; record of day-to-day activities. "Flogged two seamen today for insubordination," wrote Captain Bligh in the *Bounty's log*. To see how much work I've accomplished recently, just take a look at the number of new files listed on my computer *log*. also V.

**loiter** V. hang around; linger. The policeman told him not to *loiter* in the alley.

**loll** V. lounge about. They *lolled* around in their chairs watching television.

**longevity** N. long life. When he reached ninety, the old man was proud of his *longevity*.

**loom** V. appear or take shape (usually in an enlarged or distorted form). The shadow of the gallows *loomed* threateningly above the small boy.

**lope** V. gallop slowly. As the horses *loped* along, we had an opportunity to admire the ever-changing scenery.

■ **loquacious** ADJ. talkative. Though our daughter barely says a word to us these days, put a phone in her hand and see how *loquacious* she can be: our phone bills are out of sight! loquacity, N.

# Test

# Word List 28 *Antonyms*

Each of the following questions consists of a word in capital letters, followed by five lettered words or phrases. Choose the lettered word or phrase that is most nearly opposite in meaning to the word in capital letters and write the letter of your choice on your answer paper.

406. LAMPOON (A) darken (B) praise (C) abandon (D) sail (E) fly

407. LANGUOR (A) vitality (B) length (C) embarrassment (D) wine (E) avarice

408. LATENT (A) trim (B) forbidding (C) execrable (D) early (E) obvious

409. LAVISH (A) hostile (B) unwashed (C) timely (D) decent (E) frugal

410. LAUDATORY (A) dirtying (B) disclaiming (C) defamatory (D) inflammatory (E) debased

411. LAX (A) salty (B) strict (C) shrill (D) boring (E) cowardly

412. LECHERY (A) trust (B) compulsion (C) zeal (D) addiction (E) purity

413. LETHARGIC (A) convalescent (B) beautiful (C) enervating (D) invigorating (E) interrogating

414. LEVITY (A) bridge (B) dam (C) praise (D) blame (E) solemnity

415. LILLIPUTIAN (A) destructive (B) proper (C) gigantic (D) elegant (E) barren

416. LIMPID (A) erect (B) turbid (C) tangential (D) timid (E) weary

417. LITHE (A) stiff (B) limpid (C) facetious (D) insipid (E) vast

418. LIVID (A) alive (B) mundane (C) positive (D) undiscolored (E) vast

419. LOATH (A) loose (B) evident (C) deliberate (D) eager (E) tiny

420. LOQUACIOUS (A) taciturn (B) sentimental (C) soporific (D) soothing (E) sedate

---

# Word List 29    lout-maul

**lout** N. clumsy person. The delivery boy is an awkward *lout*. loutish, ADJ.

**low** V. moo. From the hilltop, they could see the herd like ants in the distance; they could barely hear the cattle *low*.

■ **lucid** ADJ. easily understood; clear; intelligible. Lexy makes an excellent teacher: her explanations of technical points are *lucid* enough for a child to grasp. lucidity, N.

**lucrative** ADJ. profitable. He turned his hobby into a *lucrative* profession.

**lucre** N. money. Preferring *lucre* to undying fame, he wrote stories of popular appeal.

**ludicrous** ADJ. laughable; trifling. Let us be serious; this is not a *ludicrous* issue.

**lugubrious** ADJ. mournful. The *lugubrious* howling of the dogs added to our sadness.

**lull** N. moment of calm. Not wanting to get wet, they waited under the awning for a *lull* in the rain.

**lumber** V. move heavily or clumsily. Still somewhat torpid after its long hibernation, the bear *lumbered* through the woods.

**lumen** N. unit of light energy (one candle's worth). In buying light bulbs, she checked not only their power, as measured in watts, but their brightness, as measured in *lumens*.

**luminary** N. celebrity; dignitary. A leading light of the American stage, Ethel Barrymore was a theatrical *luminary* whose name lives on.

■ **luminous** ADJ. shining; issuing light. The sun is a *luminous* body.

**lunar** ADJ. pertaining to the moon. *Lunar* craters can be plainly seen with the aid of a small telescope.

**lunge** V. make a quick forward dive or reach; thrust. The wide receiver *lunged* forward to grab the football. With his sword, Dartagnan *lunged* at his adversary. also N.

**lurid** ADJ. wild; sensational; graphic; gruesome. Do the *lurid* cover stories in the *Enquirer* actually influence people to buy that trashy tabloid?

**lurk** V. stealthily lie in waiting; slink; exist unperceived. "Who knows what evils *lurk* in the hearts of men? The Shadow knows."

**luscious** ADJ. pleasing to taste or smell. The ripe peach was *luscious*.

**luster** N. shine; gloss. The soft *luster* of the silk in the dim light was pleasing.

**lustrous** ADJ. shining. Her large and *lustrous* eyes gave a touch of beauty to an otherwise drab face.

**luxuriant** ADJ. abundant; rich and splendid; fertile. Lady Godiva was completely covered by her *luxuriant* hair.

**macabre** ADJ. gruesome; grisly. The city morgue is a *macabre* spot for the uninitiated.

**mace** N. ceremonial staff; clublike medieval weapon. The Grand Marshal of the parade raised his *mace* to signal that it was time for the procession to begin.

**macerate** V. soften by soaking in liquid; waste away. The strawberries had been soaking in the champagne for so long that they had begun to *macerate*: they literally fell apart at the touch of a spoon.

**Machiavellian** ADJ. crafty; double-dealing. I do not think he will be a good ambassador because he is not accustomed to the *Machiavellian* maneuverings of foreign diplomats.

**machinations** N. evil schemes or plots. Fortunately, Batman saw through the wily *machinations* of the Riddler and saved Gotham City from destruction by the forces of evil.

**maculated** ADJ. spotted; stained. Instead of writing that Gorbachev had a birthmark on his forehead, the pompous young poet sang of the former premier's *maculated* brow.

**madrigal** N. pastoral song. Her program of folk songs included several *madrigals* that she sang to the accompaniment of a lute.

**maelstrom** N. whirlpool. The canoe was tossed about in the *maelstrom*.

**magisterial** ADJ. authoritative; imperious. The learned doctor laid down the law to his patient in a *magisterial* tone of voice.

■ **magnanimity** N. generosity. Noted for his *magnanimity*, philanthropist Eugene Lang donated millions to charity. magnanimous, ADJ.

**magnate** N. person of prominence or influence. Growing up in Pittsburgh, Annie Dillard was surrounded by the mansions of the great steel and coal *magnates* who set their mark on that city.

**magniloquent** ADJ. boastful, pompous. In their stories of the trial, the reporters ridiculed the *magniloquent* speeches of the defense attorney.

**magnitude** N. greatness; extent. It is difficult to comprehend the *magnitude* of his crime.

**maim** V. mutilate; injure. The hospital could not take care of all who had been mangled or *maimed* in the railroad accident.

**maladroit** ADJ. clumsy; bungling. "Oh! My stupid tongue!" exclaimed Jane, embarrassed at having said anything so *maladroit*.

**malady** N. illness. A mysterious *malady* swept the country, filling doctors' offices with feverish, purple-spotted patients.

**malaise** N. uneasiness; vague feeling of ill health. Feeling slightly queasy before going onstage, Carol realized that this touch of *malaise* was merely stage fright.

**malapropism** N. comic misuse of a word. When Mrs. Malaprop criticizes Lydia for being "as headstrong as an allegory on the banks of the Nile," she confuses "allegory" and "alligator" in a typical *malapropism*.

**malcontent** N. person dissatisfied with existing state of affairs. He was one of the few *malcontents* in Congress; he constantly voiced his objections to the presidential program. also ADJ.

**malediction** N. curse. When the magic mirror revealed that Snow White was still alive, the wicked queen cried out in rage and uttered dreadful *maledictions*.

**malefactor** N. evildoer; criminal. Mighty Mouse will save the day, hunting down *malefactors* and rescuing innocent mice from peril.

**malevolent** ADJ. wishing evil. Iago is a *malevolent* villain who takes pleasure in ruining Othello. malevolence, N.

**malfeasance** N. wrongdoing. The authorities did not discover the campaign manager's *malfeasance* until after he had spent most of the money he had embezzled.

**malicious** ADJ. hateful; spiteful. Jealous of Cinderella's beauty, her *malicious* stepsisters expressed their spite by forcing her to do menial tasks. malice, N.

**malign** V. speak evil of; bad-mouth; defame. Putting her hands over her ears, Rose refused to listen to Betty *malign* her friend Susan.

**malignant** ADJ. injurious; tending to cause death; aggressively malevolent. Though many tumors are benign, some are *malignant*, growing out of control and endangering the life of the patient. malignancy, N.

■ **malingerer** N. one who feigns illness to escape duty. The captain ordered the sergeant to punish all *malingerers* and force them to work. malinger, V.

■ **malleable** ADJ. capable of being shaped by pounding; impressionable. Gold is a *malleable* metal, easily shaped into bracelets and rings. Fagin hoped Oliver was a *malleable* lad, easily shaped into a thief.

**malodorous** ADJ. foul-smelling. The compost heap was most *malodorous* in summer.

**mammal** N. vertebrate animal whose female suckles its young. Many people regard the whale as a fish and do not realize that it is a *mammal*.

**mammoth** ADJ. gigantic; enormous. To try to memorize every word on this vocabulary list would be a *mammoth* undertaking; take on projects that are more manageable in size.

**manacle** V. restrain; handcuff. The police immediately *manacled* the prisoner so he could not escape. also N.

**mandate** N. order; charge. In his inaugural address, the president stated that he had a *mandate* from the people to seek an end to social evils such as poverty and poor housing. also V.

**mandatory** ADJ. obligatory. These instructions are *mandatory*; any violation will be severely punished.

**mangy** ADJ. shabby; wretched. We finally threw out the *mangy* rug that the dog had destroyed.

**maniacal** ADJ. raging mad; insane. Though Mr. Rochester had locked his mad wife in the attic, he could still hear her *maniacal* laughter echoing throughout the house. maniac, N.

**manifest** ADJ. evident; visible; obvious. Digby's embarrassment when he met Madonna was *manifest*: his ears turned bright pink, he kept scuffing one shoe in the dirt, and he couldn't look her in the eye.

**manifestation** N. outward demonstration; indication. Mozart's early attraction to the harpsichord was the first *manifestation* of his pronounced musical bent.

**manifesto** N. declaration; statement of policy. The *Communist Manifesto* by Marx and Engels proclaimed the principles of modern communism.

**manifold** ADJ. numerous; varied. I cannot begin to tell you how much I appreciate your *manifold* kindnesses.

**manipulate** V. operate with one's hands; control or play upon (people, forces, etc.) artfully. Jim Henson understood how to *manipulate* the Muppets. Madonna understands how to *manipulate* publicity (and men).

**mannered** ADJ. affected; not natural. Attempting to copy the style of his wealthy neighbors, Gatsby adopted a *mannered*, artificial way of speech.

**manumit** V. emancipate; free from bondage. Enlightened slave owners were willing to *manumit* their slaves and thus put an end to the evil of slavery in the country.

**marital** ADJ. pertaining to marriage. After the publication of his book on *marital* affairs, he was often consulted by married people on the verge of divorce.

**maritime** ADJ. bordering on the sea; nautical. The *Maritime* Provinces depend on the sea for their wealth.

**marked** ADJ. noticeable; targeted for vengeance. He walked with a *marked* limp, a souvenir of an old IRA attack. As British ambassador, he knew he was a *marked* man.

**marred** ADJ. damaged; disfigured. She had to refinish the *marred* surface of the table. mar, V.

**marshal** V. put in order. At a debate tournament, extemporaneous speakers have only a minute or two to *marshal* their thoughts before addressing their audience.

**marsupial** N. one of a family of mammals that nurse their offspring in a pouch. The most common *marsupial* in North America is the opossum.

**martial** ADJ. warlike. The sound of *martial* music inspired the young cadet with dreams of military glory.

**martinet** N. No talking at meals! No mingling with the servants! Miss Minchin was a *martinet* who insisted that the schoolgirls in her charge observe each regulation to the letter.

**martyr** N. one who voluntarily suffers death for his or her religion or cause; great sufferer. By burning her at the stake, the English made Joan of Arc a *martyr* for her faith. Mother played the *martyr* by staying home to clean the house while the rest of the family went off to the beach.

**masochist** N. person who enjoys his own pain. The *masochist* begs, "Hit me." The sadist smiles and says, "I won't."

**masticate** V. chew. We must *masticate* our food carefully and slowly in order to avoid digestive disorders.

**materialism** N. preoccupation with physical comforts and things. By its nature, *materialism* is opposed to idealism, for where the *materialist* emphasizes the needs of the body, the idealist emphasizes the needs of the soul.

**maternal** ADJ. motherly. Many animals display *maternal* instincts only while their offspring are young and helpless. maternity, N.

**matriarch** N. woman who rules a family or larger social group. The *matriarch* ruled her gypsy tribe with a firm hand.

**matriculate** V. enroll (in college or graduate school). Incoming students formally *matriculate* at our college in a special ceremony during which they sign the official register of students.

**matrix** N. point of origin; array of numbers or algebraic symbols; mold or die. Some historians claim the Nile Valley was the *matrix* of Western civilization.

**maudlin** ADJ. effusively sentimental. Whenever a particularly *maudlin* tearjerker was playing at the movies, Marvin would embarrass himself by weeping copiously.

**maul** V. handle roughly. The rock star was *mauled* by his overexcited fans.

# Test

# Word List 29 *Synonyms and Antonyms*

Each of the questions below consists of a word in capital letters, followed by five lettered words or phrases. Choose the lettered word or phrase that is most nearly similar to or opposite of the word in capital letters and write the letter of your choice on your answer paper.

421. LUGUBRIOUS (A) frantic (B) cheerful (C) burdensome (D) oily (E) militant

422. LURID (A) dull (B) duplicate (C) heavy (D) painstaking (E) intelligent

423. MACABRE (A) musical (B) frightening (C) chewed (D) wicked (E) exceptional

424. MAGNILOQUENT (A) loquacious (B) bombastic (C) rudimentary (D) qualitative (E) minimizing

425. MAGNITUDE (A) realization (B) fascination (C) enormity (D) gratitude (E) interference

426. MALADROIT (A) malicious (B) starving (C) thirsty (D) tactless (E) artistic

427. MALEDICTION (A) misfortune (B) hap (C) fruition (D) correct pronunciation (E) benediction

428. MALEFACTOR (A) quail (B) lawbreaker (C) beneficiary (D) banker (E) female agent

429. MALEVOLENT (A) kindly (B) vacuous (C) ambivalent (D) volatile (E) primitive

430. MALIGN (A) intersperse (B) vary (C) emphasize (D) frighten (E) eulogize

431. MALLEABLE (A) brittle (B) blatant (C) brilliant (D) brownish (E) basking

432. MANIACAL (A) demoniac (B) saturated (C) sane (D) sanitary (E) handcuffed

433. MANIFEST (A) limited (B) obscure (C) faulty (D) varied (E) vital

434. MANUMIT (A) print (B) impress (C) enslave (D) endeavor (E) fail

435. MARTIAL (A) bellicose (B) celibate (C) divorced (D) quiescent (E) planetary

# Word List 30    mausoleum-misnomer

**mausoleum**  N. monumental tomb. His body was placed in the family *mausoleum.*

**mauve**  ADJ. pale purple. The *mauve* tint in the lilac bush was another indication that spring had finally arrived.

■ **maverick**  N. rebel; nonconformist. To the masculine literary establishment, George Sand with her insistence on wearing trousers and smoking cigars was clearly a *maverick* who fought her proper womanly role.

**mawkish**  ADJ. mushy and gushy; icky-sticky sentimental; maudlin. Whenever Gigi and her boyfriend would sigh and get all lovey-dovey, her little brother would shout, "Yuck!" protesting their *mawkish* behavior.

**maxim**  N. proverb; a truth pithily stated. Aesop's fables illustrate moral *maxims.*

**mayhem**  N. injury to body. The riot was marked not only by *mayhem,* with its attendant loss of life and limb, but also by arson and pillage.

**meager**  ADJ. scanty; inadequate. Still hungry after his *meager* serving of porridge, Oliver Twist asked for a second helping.

**mealymouthed**  ADJ. indirect in speech; hypocritical; evasive. Rather than tell Jill directly what he disliked, Jack made a few *mealymouthed* comments and tried to change the subject.

**meander**  V. wind or turn in its course. Needing to stay close to a source of water, he followed every twist and turn of the stream as it *meandered* through the countryside.

**meddlesome**  ADJ. interfering. He felt his marriage was suffering because of his *meddlesome* mother-in-law.

**mediate**  V. settle a dispute through the services of an outsider. King Solomon was asked to *mediate* a dispute between two women, each of whom claimed to be the mother of the same child.

**mediocre**  ADJ. ordinary; commonplace. We were disappointed because he gave a rather *mediocre* performance in this role.

**meditation**  N. reflection; thought. She reached her decision only after much *meditation.*

**medium**  N. element that is a creature's natural environment; nutrient setting in which microorganisms are cultivated. We watched the dolphins sporting in the sea and marveled at their grace in their proper *medium.* The bacteriologist carefully observed the microorganisms' rapid growth in the culture *medium.*

**medium**  N. appropriate occupation or means of expression; channel of communication; compromise. Film was Anna's *medium:* she expressed herself through her cinematography. However, she never watched television, claiming she despised the *medium.* For Anna, it was all or nothing: she could never strike a happy *medium.*

**medley**  N. mixture. To avoid boring dancers by playing any one tune for too long, bands may combine three or four tunes into a *medley.*

**meek**  ADJ. submissive; patient and long-suffering. Mr. Barrett never expected his *meek* daughter would dare to defy him by eloping with her suitor.

**megalomania**  N. mania for doing grandiose things. Developers who spend millions trying to build the world's tallest skyscraper suffer from *megalomania.*

**melancholy**  ADJ. gloomy; morose; blue. To Eugene, stuck in his small town, a train whistle was a *melancholy* sound, for it made him think of all the places he would never get to see.

**melee**  N. fight. The captain tried to ascertain the cause of the *melee* that had broken out among the crew members.

**mellifluous**  ADJ. sweetly or smoothly flowing; melodious. Italian is a *mellifluous* language, especially suited to being sung.

**memento**  N. token; reminder. Take this book as a *memento* of your visit.

**memorialize**  V. commemorate. Let us *memorialize* his great contribution by dedicating this library in his honor.

**menagerie**  N. collection of wild animals. Whenever the children run wild around the house, Mom shouts, "Calm down! I'm not running a *menagerie!*"

■ **mendacious**  ADJ. lying; habitually dishonest. Distrusting Huck from the start, Miss Watson assumed he was *mendacious* and refused to believe a word he said. mendacity, N.

**mendicant**  N. beggar. "O noble sir, give alms to the poor," cried Aladdin, playing the *mendicant.* mendicancy, N.

**menial**  ADJ. suitable for servants; lowly; mean. Her wicked stepmother forced Cinderella to do *menial* tasks around the house while her ugly stepsisters lolled around painting their toenails. also N.

**mentor**  N. counselor; teacher. During this very trying period, she could not have had a better *mentor,* for the teacher was sympathetic and understanding.

**mercantile**  ADJ. concerning trade. I am more interested in the opportunities available in the *mercantile* field than I am in those in the legal profession.

**mercenary**  ADJ. motivated solely by money or gain. "I'm not in this war because I get my kicks waving flags," said the *mercenary* soldier. "I'm in it for the dough." also N.

**mercurial**  ADJ. capricious; changing; fickle. Quick as quicksilver to change, he was *mercurial* in nature and therefore unreliable.

**meretricious**  ADJ. flashy; tawdry. Her jewels were inexpensive but not *meretricious.*

**merger**  N. combination (of two business corporations). When the firm's president married the director of financial planning, the office joke was that it wasn't a marriage, it was a *merger.*

**mesmerize**  V. hypnotize. The incessant drone seemed to *mesmerize* him and place him in a trance.

**metallurgical**  ADJ. pertaining to the art of removing metals from ores. During the course of his *metallurgical* research, the scientist developed a steel alloy of tremendous strength.

■ **metamorphosis**  N. change of form. The *metamorphosis* of caterpillar to butterfly is typical of many such changes in animal life. metamorphose, V.

**metaphor**  N. implied comparison. "He soared like an eagle" is an example of a simile; "He is an eagle in flight," a *metaphor.*

**metaphysical**  ADJ. pertaining to speculative philosophy. The modern poets have gone back to the fanciful poems of the *metaphysical* poets of the seventeenth century for many of their images. metaphysics, N.

**mete**  V. measure; distribute. He tried to be impartial in his efforts to *mete* out justice.

**meteoric**  ADJ. swift; momentarily brilliant. We all wondered at his *meteoric* rise to fame.

**methodical**  ADJ. systematic. An accountant must be *methodical* and maintain order among his financial records.

■ **meticulous**  ADJ. excessively careful; painstaking; scrupulous. Martha Stewart was a *meticulous* housekeeper, fussing about each and every detail that went into making up her perfect home.

**metropolis**  N. large city. Every evening this terminal is filled with the thousands of commuters who are going from this *metropolis* to their homes in the suburbs.

**mettle**  N. courage; spirit. When challenged by the other horses in the race, the thoroughbred proved its *mettle* by its determination to hold the lead. mettlesome, ADJ.

**miasma**  N. swamp gas; heavy, vaporous atmosphere, often emanating from decaying matter; pervasive corrupting influence. The smog hung over Victorian London like a dark cloud; noisome, reeking of decay, it was a visible *miasma.*

**microcosm**  N. small world; the world in miniature. The village community that Jane Austen depicts serves as a *microcosm* of English society in her time, for in this small world we see all the social classes meeting and mingling.

**migrant**  ADJ. changing its habitat; wandering. These *migrant* birds return every spring. also N.

**migratory**  ADJ. wandering. The return of the *migratory* birds to the northern sections of this country is a harbinger of spring.

**milieu**  N. environment; means of expression. Surrounded by smooth preppies and arty bohemians, the country boy from Smalltown, USA, felt out of his *milieu.* Although he has produced excellent oil paintings and lithographs, his proper *milieu* is watercolor.

**militant**  ADJ. combative; bellicose. Although at this time he was advocating a policy of neutrality, one could usually find him adopting a more *militant* attitude. also N.

**militate**  V. work against. Your record of lateness and absence will *militate* against your chances of promotion.

**millennium**  N. thousand-year period; period of happiness and prosperity. I do not expect the *millennium* to come during my lifetime.

**mimicry**  N. imitation. Her gift for *mimicry* was so great that her friends said that she should be in the theater.

**minatory**  ADJ. menacing; threatening. Jabbing a *minatory* forefinger at Dorothy, the Wicked Witch cried, "I'll get you, and your little dog, too!"

**mincing**  ADJ. affectedly dainty. Yum-Yum walked across the stage with *mincing* steps.

**minion**  N. a servile dependent. He was always accompanied by several of his *minions* because he enjoyed their subservience and flattery.

**minuscule**  ADJ. extremely small. Why should I involve myself with a project with so *minuscule* a chance for success?

**minute**  ADJ. extremely small. The twins resembled one another closely; only *minute* differences set them apart.

**minutiae**  N. petty details. She would have liked to ignore the *minutiae* of daily living.

**mirage**  N. unreal reflection; optical illusion. The lost prospector was fooled by a *mirage* in the desert.

**mire**  V. entangle; stick in swampy ground. Their rear wheels became *mired* in mud. also N.

**mirth**  N. merriment; laughter. Sober Malvolio found Sir Toby's *mirth* improper.

**misadventure**  N. mischance; ill luck. The young explorer met death by *misadventure.*

■ **misanthrope**  N. one who hates mankind. In *Gulliver's Travels*, Swift portrays human beings as vile, degraded beasts; for this reason, various critics consider him a *misanthrope.* misanthropic, ADJ.

**misapprehension**  N. error; misunderstanding. To avoid *misapprehension,* I am going to ask all of you to repeat the instructions I have given.

**miscellany**  N. mixture of writings on various subjects. This is an interesting *miscellany* of nineteenth-century prose and poetry.

**mischance**  N. ill luck. By *mischance,* he lost his week's salary.

**misconstrue**  V. interpret incorrectly; misjudge. She took the passage seriously rather than humorously because she *misconstrued* the author's ironic tone.

**miscreant**  N. wretch; villain. His kindness to the *miscreant* amazed all of us who had expected to hear severe punishment pronounced.

**misdemeanor**  N. minor crime. The culprit pleaded guilty to a *misdemeanor* rather than face trial for a felony.

**miserly**  ADJ. stingy; mean. Transformed by his vision on Christmas Eve, mean old Scrooge ceased being *miserly* and became a generous, kind old man. miser, N.

**misgivings**  N. doubts. Hamlet described his *misgivings* to Horatio but decided to fence with Laertes despite his foreboding of evil.

**mishap**  N. accident. With a little care you could have avoided this *mishap.*

**misnomer**  N. wrong name; incorrect designation. His tyrannical conduct proved to all that his nickname, King Eric the Just, was a *misnomer.*

# Test

## Word List 30  *Synonyms*

Each of the questions below consists of a word in capital letters, followed by five lettered words or phrases. Choose the lettered word or phrase that is most nearly similar in meaning to the word in capital letters and write the letter of your choice on your answer paper.

436. MAWKISH (A) sentimental (B) true (C) certain (D) devious (E) carefree

437. MEDIOCRE (A) average (B) bitter (C) medieval (D) industrial (E) agricultural

438. MELEE (A) heat (B) brawl (C) attempt (D) weapon (E) choice

439. MELLIFLUOUS (A) porous (B) honeycombed (C) strong (D) smooth (E) viscous

440. MENIAL (A) intellectual (B) clairvoyant (C) servile (D) arrogant (E) laudatory

441. MENTOR (A) guide (B) genius (C) talker (D) philosopher (E) stylist

442. MESMERIZE (A) remember (B) hypnotize (C) delay (D) bore (E) analyze

443. METICULOUS (A) steadfast (B) recent (C) quaint (D) painstaking (E) overt

444. MIASMA (A) dream (B) noxious fumes (C) scenario (D) quantity (E) total

445. MILITANT (A) combative (B) dramatic (C) religious (D) quaint (E) paternal

446. MINION (A) monster (B) quorum (C) majority (D) host (E) dependent

447. MIRAGE (A) dessert (B) illusion (C) water (D) mirror (E) statement

448. MISANTHROPE (A) benefactor (B) philanderer (C) man-hater (D) aesthete (E) epicure

449. MISCHANCE (A) gamble (B) ordinance (C) aperture (D) anecdote (E) adversity

450. MISDEMEANOR (A) felony (B) peccadillo (C) indignity (D) fiat (E) illiteracy

## Word List 31  misogamy-nascent

**misogamy**  N. hatred of marriage. He remained a bachelor not because of *misogamy* but because of ill fate: his fiancee died before the wedding.

**misogynist**  N. hater of women. She accused him of being a *misogynist* because he had been a bachelor all his life.

**missile**  N. object to be thrown or projected. After carefully folding his book report into a paper airplane, Beavis threw the *missile* across the classroom at Butthead. Rocket scientists are building guided *missiles;* Beavis and Butthead can barely make unguided ones.

**missive**  N. letter. The ambassador received a *missive* from the Secretary of State.

**mite**  N. very small object or creature; small coin. Gnats are annoying *mites* that sting.

■ **mitigate**  V. appease; moderate. Nothing Jason did could *mitigate* Medea's anger; she refused to forgive him for betraying her.

**mnemonic**  ADJ. pertaining to memory. She used *mnemonic* tricks to master new words.

**mobile**  ADJ. movable; not fixed. The *mobile* blood bank operated by the Red Cross visited our neighborhood today. mobility, N.

**mock**  V. ridicule; imitate, often in derision. It is unkind to *mock* anyone; it is stupid to *mock* anyone significantly bigger than you. mockery, N.

**mode**  N. prevailing style; manner; way of doing something. The rock star had to have her hair done in the latest *mode:* frizzed, with occasional moussed spikes for variety. Henry plans to adopt a simpler *mode* of life: he is going to become a mushroom hunter and live off the land.

**modicum**  N. limited quantity. Although his story is based on a *modicum* of truth, most of the events he describes are fictitious.

**modish**  ADJ. fashionable. She always discarded all garments that were no longer *modish.*

**modulate**  V. tone down in intensity; regulate; change from one key to another. Always singing at the top of her lungs, the budding Brunhilde never learned to *modulate* her voice. modulation, N.

**mogul**  N. powerful person. The oil *moguls* made great profits when the price of gasoline rose.

**molecule**  N. the smallest particle (one or more atoms) of a substance that has all the properties of that substance. In chemistry, we study how atoms and *molecules* react to form new substances.

■ **mollify**  V. soothe. The airline customer service representative tried to *mollify* the angry passenger by offering her a seat in first class.

**mollycoddle**  V. pamper; indulge excessively. Don't *mollycoddle* the boy, Maud! You'll spoil him.

**molt**  V. shed or cast off hair or feathers. When Molly's canary *molted,* he shed feathers all over the house.

**molten**  ADJ. melted. The city of Pompeii was destroyed

by volcanic ash rather than by *molten* lava flowing from Mount Vesuvius.

**momentous** ADJ. very important. When Marie and Pierre Curie discovered radium, they had no idea of the *momentous* impact their discovery would have upon society.

**momentum** N. quantity of motion of a moving body; impetus. The car lost *momentum* as it tried to ascend the steep hill.

**monarchy** N. government under a single ruler. Though England today is a *monarchy*, there is some question whether it will be one in 20 years, given the present discontent at the prospect of Prince Charles as king.

**monastic** ADJ. related to monks or monasteries; removed from worldly concerns. Withdrawing from the world, Thomas Merton joined a contemplative religious order and adopted the *monastic* life.

**monetary** ADJ. pertaining to money. Jane held the family purse strings: she made all *monetary* decisions affecting the household.

**monochromatic** ADJ. having only one color. Most people who are color blind actually can distinguish several colors; some, however, have a truly *monochromatic* view of a world all in shades of gray.

**monolithic** ADJ. solidly uniform; unyielding. Knowing the importance of appearing resolute, the patriots sought to present a *monolithic* front.

**monotheism** N. belief in one God. Abraham was the first to proclaim his belief in *monotheism*.

**monotony** N. sameness leading to boredom. What could be more deadly dull than the *monotony* of punching numbers into a computer hour after hour? monotonous, ADJ.

**monumental** ADJ. massive. Writing a dictionary is a *monumental* task.

**moodiness** N. fits of depression or gloom. We could not discover the cause of her recurrent *moodiness*.

**moratorium** N. legal delay of payment. If we declare a *moratorium* and delay collection of debts for six months, I am sure the farmers will be able to meet their bills.

**morbid** ADJ. given to unwholesome thought; moody; characteristic of disease. People who come to disaster sites just to peer at the grisly wreckage are indulging their *morbid* curiosity. morbidity, N.

**mordant** ADJ. biting; sarcastic; stinging. Actors feared the critic's *mordant* pen.

**mores** N. conventions; moral standards; customs. In America, Benazir Bhutto dressed as Western women did; in Pakistan, however, she followed the *mores* of her people, dressing in traditional veil and robes.

**moribund** ADJ. dying. Hearst took a *moribund*, failing weekly newspaper and transformed it into one of the liveliest, most profitable daily papers around.

■ **morose** ADJ. ill-humored; sullen; melancholy. Forced to take early retirement, Bill acted *morose* for months; then, all of a sudden, he shook off his gloom and was his usual cheerful self.

**mortician** N. undertaker. The *mortician* prepared the corpse for burial.

**mortify** V. humiliate; punish the flesh. She was so *mortified* by her blunder that she ran to her room in tears.

**mosaic** N. picture made of small, colorful inlaid tiles. The mayor compared the city to a beautiful *mosaic* made up of people of every race and religion on earth. also ADJ.

**mote** N. small speck. The tiniest *mote* in the eye is very painful.

**motif** N. theme. This simple *motif* runs throughout the score.

**motility** N. ability to move spontaneously. Certain organisms exhibit remarkable *motility*; *motile* spores, for example, may travel for miles before coming to rest. motile, ADJ.

**motley** ADJ. multicolored; mixed. The jester wore a *motley* tunic, red and green and blue and gold all patched together haphazardly. Captain Ahab had gathered a *motley* crew to sail the vessel: old sea dogs and runaway boys, pillars of the church and drunkards, even a tattooed islander who terrified the rest of the crew.

**mottled** ADJ. blotched in coloring; spotted. When old Falstaff blushed, his face became *mottled*, all pink and purple and red.

**mountebank** N. charlatan; boastful pretender. The patent medicine man was a *mountebank*.

**muddle** V. confuse; mix up. Her thoughts were *muddled* and chaotic. also N.

**muggy** ADJ. warm and damp. August in New York City is often *muggy*.

**mulct** V. defraud a person of something. The lawyer was accused of trying to *mulct* the boy of his legacy.

**multifarious** ADJ. varied; greatly diversified. A career woman and mother, she was constantly busy with the *multifarious* activities of her daily life.

**multiform** ADJ. having many forms. Snowflakes are *multiform* but always hexagonal.

**multilingual** ADJ. having many languages. Because they are bordered by so many countries, the Swiss people are *multilingual*.

**multiplicity** N. state of being numerous. She was appalled by the *multiplicity* of details she had to complete before setting out on her mission.

■ **mundane** ADJ. worldly as opposed to spiritual; everyday. Uninterested in philosophical or spiritual discussions, Tom talked only of *mundane* matters such as the daily weather forecast or the latest basketball results.

**munificent** ADJ. very generous. Shamelessly fawning over a particularly generous donor, the dean kept referring to her as "our *munificent* benefactor." munificence, N.

**mural** N. wall painting. The walls of the Chicano Community Center are covered with *murals* painted in the style of Diego Rivera, the great Mexican artist.

**murky** ADJ. dark and gloomy; thick with fog; vague. The *murky* depths of the swamp were so dark that you couldn't tell the vines and branches from the snakes. murkiness, N.

**muse** V. ponder. For a moment he *mused* about the beauty of the scene, but his thoughts soon changed as he recalled his own personal problems. also N.

**musky** ADJ. having the odor of musk. She left a trace of *musky* perfume behind her.

**muster** V. gather; assemble. Washington *mustered* his forces at Trenton.

**musty** ADJ. stale; spoiled by age. The attic was dark and *musty*.

**mutability** N. ability to change in form; fickleness. Going from rags to riches, and then back to rags again, the bankrupt financier was a victim of the *mutability* of fortune. mutable, ADJ.

**muted** ADJ. silent; muffled; toned down. Thanks to the thick, sound-absorbing walls of the cathedral, only *muted* traffic noise reached the worshippers within. mute, V., N.

**mutilate** V. maim. The torturer threatened to *mutilate* his victim.

**mutinous** ADJ. unruly; rebellious. The captain had to use force to quiet his *mutinous* crew. mutiny, N.

**myopic** ADJ. nearsighted; lacking foresight. Stumbling into doors despite the coke-bottle lenses on his glasses, the nearsighted Mr. Magoo is markedly *myopic*. In play-

ing all summer long and failing to store up food for winter, the grasshopper in Aesop's fable was *myopic* as well. myopia, N.

**myriad** N. very large number. *Myriads* of mosquitoes from the swamps invaded our village every twilight. also ADJ.

**nadir** N. lowest point. Although few people realized it, the Dow-Jones averages had reached their *nadir* and would soon begin an upward surge.

**naiveté** N. quality of being unsophisticated; simplicity; artlessness; gullibility. Touched by the *naiveté* of sweet, convent-trained Cosette, Marius pledges himself to protect her innocence. naive, ADJ.

**narcissist** N. conceited person. A *narcissist* is his own best friend.

**narrative** ADJ. related to telling a story. A born teller of tales, Olsen used her impressive *narrative* skills to advantage in her story "I Stand Here Ironing." also N. narration, N.

**nascent** ADJ. incipient; coming into being. If we could identify these revolutionary movements in their *nascent* state, we would be able to eliminate serious trouble in later years.

# Test

## Word List 31    *Synonyms*

Each of the questions below consists of a word in capital letters, followed by five lettered words or phrases. Choose the lettered word or phrase that is most nearly similar in meaning to the word in capital letters and write the letter of your choice on your answer paper.

451. MODISH (A) sentimental (B) stylish (C) vacillating (D) contrary (E) adorned

452. MOLLIFY (A) avenge (B) attenuate (C) attribute (D) mortify (E) appease

453. MONETARY (A) boring (B) fascinating (C) fiscal (D) stationary (E) scrupulous

454. MORATORIUM (A) burial (B) gathering (C) delay (D) refusal (E) suspicion

455. MORDANT (A) dying (B) trenchant (C) fabricating (D) controlling (E) avenging

456. MORIBUND (A) dying (B) appropriate (C) leather bound (D) answering (E) undertaking

457. MOTLEY (A) active (B) disguised (C) variegated (D) somber (E) sick

458. MUGGY (A) attacking (B) fascinating (C) humid (D) characteristic (E) gelid

459. MULCT (A) swindle (B) hold (C) record (D) print (E) fertilize

460. MULTILINGUAL (A) variegated (B) polyglot (C) multilateral (D) polyandrous (E) multiplied

461. MUNDANE (A) global (B) futile (C) spatial (D) heretic (E) worldly

462. MUNIFICENT (A) grandiose (B) puny (C) philanthropic (D) poor (E) gracious

463. MUSTY (A) flat (B) necessary (C) indifferent (D) nonchalant (E) vivid

464. MYOPIC (A) visionary (B) nearsighted (C) moral (D) glassy (E) blind

465. NASCENT (A) incipient (B) ignorant (C) loyal (D) treacherous (E) unnamed

## Word List 32    natation-obsidian

**natation** N. swimming. The Red Cross emphasizes the need for courses in *natation*.

**natty** ADJ. neatly or smartly dressed. Priding himself on

being a *natty* dresser, the gangster Bugsy Siegel collected a wardrobe of imported suits and ties.

**nauseate** V. cause to become sick; fill with disgust. The foul smells began to *nauseate* her.

**nautical**  ADJ. pertaining to ships or navigation. The Maritime Museum contains models of clipper ships, log-books, anchors, and many other items of a *nautical* nature.

**navigable**  ADJ. wide and deep enough to allow ships to pass through; able to be steered. So much sand had built up at the bottom of the canal that the waterway was barely *navigable*.

**nebulous**  ADJ. vague; hazy; cloudy. Phil and Dave tried to come up with a clear, intelligible business plan, not some hazy, *nebulous* proposal.

**necromancy**  N. black magic; dealings with the dead. The evil sorcerer performed feats of *necromancy*, calling on the spirits of the dead to tell the future. necromancer, N.

**nefarious**  ADJ. very wicked. The villain's crimes, though various, were one and all *nefarious*.

■ **negate**  V. cancel out; nullify; deny. A sudden surge of adrenalin can *negate* the effects of fatigue: there's nothing like a good shock to wake you up. negation, N.

**negligence**  N. neglect; failure to take reasonable care. Tommy failed to put back the cover on the well after he fetched his pail of water; because of his *negligence*, Kitty fell in. negligent, ADJ.

**negligible**  ADJ. so small, trifling, or unimportant as to be easily disregarded. Because the damage to his car had been *negligible*, Michael decided he wouldn't bother to report the matter to his insurance company.

**nemesis**  N. someone seeking revenge. Abandoned at sea in a small boat, the vengeful Captain Bligh vowed to be the *nemesis* of Fletcher Christian and his fellow mutineers.

**neologism**  N. new or newly coined word or phrase. As we invent new techniques and professions, we must also invent *neologisms* such as "microcomputer" and "astronaut" to describe them.

■ **neophyte**  N. recent convert; beginner. This mountain slope contains slides that will challenge experts as well as *neophytes*.

**nepotism**  N. favoritism (to a relative). John left his position with the company because he felt that advancement was based on *nepotism* rather than ability.

**nether**  ADJ. lower. Tradition locates hell in the *nether* regions.

**nettle**  V. annoy; vex. Do not let her *nettle* you with her sarcastic remarks.

**nexus**  N. connection. I fail to see the *nexus* that binds these two widely separated events.

**nib**  N. beak; pen point. The *nibs* of fountain pens often become clotted and corroded.

**nicety**  N. precision; minute distinction. I cannot distinguish between such *niceties* of reasoning. nice, ADJ. (secondary meaning)

**niggardly**  ADJ. meanly stingy; parsimonious. The *niggardly* pittance the widow receives from the government cannot keep her from poverty.

**niggle**  V. spend too much time on minor points; carp.

Let's not *niggle* over details. niggling, ADJ.

**nihilist**  N. one who considers traditional beliefs to be groundless and existence meaningless; absolute skeptic; revolutionary terrorist. In his final days, Hitler revealed himself a power-mad *nihilist*, ready to annihilate all of Western Europe, even to destroy Germany itself, in order that his will might prevail. The root of the word *nihilist* is *nihil*, Latin for "nothing." nihilism, N.

**nip**  V. stop something's growth or development; snip off; bite; make numb with cold. The twins were plotting mischief, but Mother intervened and *nipped* their plan in the bud. The gardener *nipped* off a lovely rose and gave it to me. Last week a guard dog *nipped* the postman in the leg; this week the extreme chill *nipped* his fingers till he could barely hold the mail.

**nirvana**  N. in Buddhist teachings, the ideal state in which the individual loses himself in the attainment of an impersonal beatitude. Despite his desire to achieve *nirvana*, the young Buddhist found that even the buzzing of a fly could distract him from his meditation.

**nocturnal**  ADJ. done at night. Mr. Jones obtained a watchdog to prevent the *nocturnal* raids on his chicken coops.

**noisome**  ADJ. foul-smelling; unwholesome. The *noisome* atmosphere downwind of the oil refinery not only stank but also damaged the lungs of everyone living in the area.

**nomadic**  ADJ. wandering. Several *nomadic* tribes of Indians would hunt in this area each year. nomad, N.

**nomenclature**  N. terminology; system of names. Sharon found Latin word parts useful in translating medical *nomenclature*: when her son had to have a bilateral myringotomy, she figured out that he needed a hole in each of his eardrums to end his earaches.

**nominal**  ADJ. in name only; trifling. He offered to drive her to the airport for only a *nominal* fee.

**nonchalance**  N. indifference; lack of concern; composure. Cool, calm, and collected under fire, James Bond shows remarkable *nonchalance* in the face of danger. nonchalant, ADJ.

**noncommittal**  ADJ. neutral; unpledged; undecided. We were annoyed by his *noncommittal* reply for we had been led to expect definite assurances of his approval.

**nondescript**  ADJ. undistinctive; ordinary. The private detective was a short, *nondescript* fellow with no outstanding features, the sort of person one would never notice in a crowd.

**nonentity**  N. person of no importance; nonexistence. Because the two older princes dismissed their youngest brother as a *nonentity*, they did not realize that he was quietly plotting to seize the throne.

**nonplus**  V. bring to a halt by confusion; perplex. Jack's uncharacteristic rudeness *nonplussed* Jill, leaving her uncertain how to react.

**nostalgia**  N. homesickness; longing for the past. My grandfather seldom spoke of life in the old country; he had little patience with *nostalgia*. nostalgic, ADJ.

**nostrum** N. questionable medicine. No quack selling *nostrums* is going to cheat me.

**notable** ADJ. conspicuous; important; distinguished. Normally *notable* for his calm in the kitchen, today the head cook was shaking, for the *notable* chef Julia Child was coming to dinner. also N.

**notoriety** N. disrepute; ill fame. To the starlet, any publicity was good publicity: if she couldn't have a good reputation, she'd settle for *notoriety.* notorious, ADJ.

**novelty** N. something new; newness. The computer is no longer a *novelty* around the office. novel, ADJ.

**novice** N. beginner. Even a *novice* at working with computers can install *Barron's Computer Study Program for the GRE* by following the easy steps outlined in the user's manual.

**noxious** ADJ. harmful. We must trace the source of these *noxious* gases before they asphyxiate us.

**nuance** N. shade of difference in meaning or color; subtle distinction. Jody gazed at the Monet landscape for an hour, appreciating every subtle *nuance* of color in the painting.

**nubile** ADJ. marriageable. Mrs. Bennet, in *Pride and Prejudice* by Jane Austen, was worried about finding suitable husbands for her five *nubile* daughters.

**nugatory** ADJ. futile; worthless. This agreement is *nugatory* for no court will enforce it.

**nullify** V. to make invalid. Once the contract was *nullified,* it no longer had any legal force.

**numismatist** N. person who collects coins. The *numismatist* had a splendid collection of antique coins.

**nuptial** ADJ. related to marriage. Reluctant to be married in a traditional setting, they decided to hold their *nuptial* ceremony at the carousel in Golden Gate Park. nuptials, N. PL.

**nurture** V. nourish; educate; foster. The Head Start program attempts to *nurture* prekindergarten children so that they will do well when they enter public school. also N.

**nutrient** N. nourishing substance. As a budding nutritionist, Kim has learned to design diets that contain foods rich in important basic *nutrients.* also ADJ.

**oaf** N. stupid, awkward person. "Watch what you're doing, you clumsy *oaf!*" Bill shouted at the waiter who had drenched him with iced coffee.

■ **obdurate** ADJ. stubborn. He was *obdurate* in his refusal to listen to our complaints.

**obeisance** N. bow. She made an *obeisance* as the king and queen entered the room.

**obelisk** N. tall column tapering and ending in a pyramid. Cleopatra's Needle is an *obelisk* in New York City's Central Park.

**obese** ADJ. excessively fat. It is advisable that *obese* people try to lose weight. obesity, N.

**obfuscate** V. confuse; muddle; cause confusion; make needlessly complex. Was the president's spokesman trying to clarify the Whitewater mystery, or was he trying to *obfuscate* the issue so the voters would never figure out what went on?

**obituary** N. death notice. I first learned of her death when I read the *obituary* in the newspaper. also ADJ.

**objective** ADJ. not influenced by emotions; fair. Even though he was her son, she tried to be *objective* about his behavior.

**objective** N. goal; aim. A degree in medicine was her ultimate *objective.*

**obligatory** ADJ. binding; required. It is *obligatory* that books borrowed from the library be returned within two weeks.

**oblique** ADJ. indirect; slanting (deviating from the perpendicular or from a straight line). Casting a quick, *oblique* glance at the reviewing stand, the sergeant ordered the company to march "*Oblique* Right."

**obliterate** V. destroy completely. The tidal wave *obliterated* several island villages.

**oblivion** N. obscurity; forgetfulness. After a decade of popularity, Hurston's works had fallen into *oblivion;* no one bothered to read them any more.

**oblivious** ADJ. inattentive or unmindful; wholly absorbed. Deep in her book, Nancy was *oblivious* to the noisy squabbles of her brother and his friends.

**obloquy** N. slander; disgrace; infamy. I resent the *obloquy* that you are casting upon my reputation.

**obnoxious** ADJ. offensive. I find your behavior *obnoxious;* please mend your ways.

**obscure** ADJ. dark; vague; unclear. Even after I read the poem a fourth time, its meaning was still *obscure.* obscurity, N.

**obscure** V. darken; make unclear. At times he seemed purposely to *obscure* his meaning, preferring mystery to clarity.

■ **obsequious** ADJ. slavishly attentive; servile; sycophantic. Helen valued people who behaved as if they respected themselves; nothing irritated her more than an excessively *obsequious* waiter or a fawning salesclerk.

**obsequy** N. funeral ceremony. Hundreds paid their last respects at his *obsequies.*

**obsessive** ADJ. related to thinking about something constantly; preoccupying. Ballet, which had been a hobby, began to dominate his life: his love of dancing became *obsessive.* obsession, N.

**obsidian** N. black volcanic rock. The deposits of *obsidian* on the mountain slopes were an indication that the volcano had erupted in ancient times.

# Test

## Word List 32   *Antonyms*

Each of the questions below consists of a word in capital letters, followed by five lettered words or phrases. Choose the lettered word or phrase that is most nearly opposite in meaning to the word in capital letters and write the letter of your choice on your answer paper.

466. NEBULOUS (A) starry (B) clear (C) cold (D) fundamental (E) porous

467. NEFARIOUS (A) various (B) lacking (C) benign (D) pompous (E) futile

468. NEGATION (A) postulation (B) hypothecation (C) affirmation (D) violation (E) anticipation

469. NEOPHYTE (A) veteran (B) satellite (C) desperado (D) handwriting (E) violence

470. NIGGARDLY (A) protected (B) biased (C) prodigal (D) bankrupt (E) placated

471. NOCTURNAL (A) harsh (B) marauding (C) patrolling (D) daily (E) fallow

472. NOISOME (A) quiet (B) dismayed (C) fragrant (D) sleepy (E) inquisitive

473. NOTORIOUS (A) fashionable (B) renowned (C) inactive (D) intrepid (E) invincible

474. OBDURATE (A) yielding (B) fleeting (C) finite (D) fascinating (E) permanent

475. OBESE (A) skillful (B) cadaverous (C) clever (D) unpredictable (E) lucid

476. OBJECTIVE (A) indecisive (B) apathetic (C) markedly inferior (D) emotionally involved (E) authoritative

477. OBLIGATORY (A) demanding (B) optional (C) facile (D) friendly (E) divorced

478. OBLOQUY (A) praise (B) rectangle (C) circle (D) dialogue (E) cure

479. OBSEQUIOUS (A) successful (B) democratic (C) supercilious (D) ambitious (E) lamentable

480. OBSESSION (A) whim (B) loss (C) phobia (D) delusion (E) feud

## Word List 33   obsolete–overweening

**obsolete**   ADJ. outmoded. "Hip" is an *obsolete* expression; it went out with love beads and tie-dye shirts.

**obstetrician**   N. physician specializing in delivery of babies. Unlike midwives, who care for women giving birth at home, *obstetricians* generally work in a hospital setting.

**obstinate**   ADJ. stubborn; hard to control or treat. We tried to persuade him to give up smoking, but he was *obstinate* and refused to change. Blackberry stickers are the most *obstinate* weeds I know: once established in a yard, they're extremely hard to root out. obstinacy, N.

**obstreperous**   ADJ. boisterous; noisy. What do you do when an *obstreperous* horde of drunken policemen carouses through your hotel, crashing into potted plants and singing vulgar songs?

**obtrude**   V. push (oneself or one's ideas) forward or intrude; butt in; stick out or extrude. Because Fanny was reluctant to *obtrude* her opinions about child-raising upon her daughter-in-law, she kept a close watch on her tongue. obtrusive, ADJ. obtrusion, N.

**obtuse**   ADJ. blunt; stupid. What can you do with somebody who's so *obtuse* that he can't even tell that you're insulting him?

■ **obviate**   V. make unnecessary; get rid of. I hope this contribution will *obviate* any need for further collections of funds.

**Occident**   N. the West. It will take time for the *Occident* to understand the ways and customs of the Orient.

■ **occlude**   V. shut; close. A blood clot *occluded* an artery to the heart. occlusion, N.

**occult**   ADJ. mysterious; secret; supernatural. The *occult* rites of the organization were revealed only to members. also N.

**oculist**   N. physician who specializes in treatment of the eyes. In many states, an *oculist* is the only one who may apply medicinal drops to the eyes for the purpose of examining them.

**odious**   ADJ. hateful; vile. Cinderella's ugly stepsisters had the *odious* habit of popping their zits in public.

**odium**   N. detestation; hatefulness; disrepute. Prince Charming could not express the *odium* he felt toward Cinderella's stepsisters because of their mistreatment of poor Cinderella.

**odoriferous**   ADJ. giving off an odor. The *odoriferous* spices stimulated her jaded appetite.

**odorous**   ADJ. having an odor. This variety of hybrid tea rose is more *odorous* than the one you have in your garden.

**odyssey**   N. long, eventful journey. The refugee's journey from Cambodia was a terrifying *odyssey*.

**offensive**   ADJ. attacking; insulting; distasteful. Getting into street brawls is no minor offense for professional boxers, who are required by law to restrict their *offensive* impulses to the ring.

**offhand**   ADJ. casual; done without prior thought. Expecting to be treated with due propriety by her hosts, Great-Aunt Maud was offended by their *offhand* manner.

■ **officious** ADJ. meddlesome; excessively pushy in offering one's services. After her long flight, Jill just wanted to nap, but the *officious* bellboy was intent on showing her all the special features of the deluxe suite.

**ogle** V. look at amorously; make eyes at. At the coffee house, Walter was too shy to *ogle* the pretty girls openly; instead, he peeked out at them from behind a rubber plant.

**olfactory** ADJ. concerning the sense of smell. A wine taster must have a discriminating palate and a keen *olfactory* sense, for a good wine appeals both to the taste buds and to the nose.

**oligarchy** N. government by a privileged few. One small clique ran the student council: what had been intended as a democratic governing body had turned into an *oligarchy*.

**ominous** ADJ. threatening. Those clouds are *ominous;* they suggest that a severe storm is on the way.

**omnipotent** ADJ. all-powerful. The monarch regarded himself as *omnipotent* and responsible to no one for his acts.

**omnipresent** ADJ. universally present; ubiquitous. On Christmas Eve, Santa Claus is *omnipresent*.

**omniscient** ADJ. all-knowing. I do not pretend to be *omniscient,* but I am positive about this fact.

**omnivorous** ADJ. eating both plant and animal food; devouring everything. Some animals, including humans, are *omnivorous* and eat both meat and vegetables; others are either carnivorous or herbivorous.

■ **onerous** ADJ. burdensome. She asked for an assistant because her work load was too *onerous*.

**onomatopoeia** N. words formed in imitation of natural sounds. Words like "rustle" and "gargle" are illustrations of *onomatopoeia*.

**onslaught** N. vicious assault. We suffered many casualties during the unexpected *onslaught* of the enemy troops.

**onus** N. burden; responsibility. The emperor was spared the *onus* of signing the surrender papers; instead, he relegated the assignment to his generals.

**opalescent** ADJ. iridescent; lustrous. The oil slick on the water had an *opalescent,* rainbowlike sheen. opalescence, N.

**opaque** ADJ. dark; not transparent. The *opaque* window kept the sunlight out of the room. opacity, N.

**opiate** N. medicine to induce sleep or deaden pain; something that relieves emotions or causes inaction. To say that religion is the *opiate* of the people is to condemn religion as a drug that keeps the people quiet and submissive to those in power.

**opportune** ADJ. timely; well-chosen. Cher looked at her father struggling to balance his checkbook; clearly this would not be an *opportune* moment to ask him for an increase in her allowance.

**opportunist** N. individual who sacrifices principles for expediency by taking advantage of circumstances. Forget about ethics! He's such an *opportunist* that he'll vote in favor of any deal that will give him a break.

■ **opprobrium** N. infamy; vilification. He refused to defend himself against the slander and *opprobrium* hurled against him by the newspapers; he preferred to rely on his record.

**optician** N. maker and seller of eyeglasses. The patient took the prescription given him by his oculist to the *optician*.

**optimist** N. person who looks on the bright side. The pessimist says the glass is half-empty; the *optimist* says it is half-full.

**optimum** ADJ. most favorable. If you wait for the *optimum* moment to act, you may never begin your project. also N.

**optional** ADJ. not compulsory; left to one's choice. I was impressed by the range of *optional* accessories for my microcomputer that were available. option, N.

**optometrist** N. one who fits glasses to remedy visual defects. Although an *optometrist* is qualified to treat many eye disorders, she may not use medicines or surgery in her examinations.

**opulence** N. extreme wealth; luxuriousness; abundance. The glitter and *opulence* of the ballroom took Cinderella's breath away. opulent, ADJ.

**opus** N. work. Although many critics hailed his Fifth Symphony, he did not regard it as his major *opus*.

**oracular** ADJ. prophetic; uttered as if with divine authority; mysterious or ambiguous. Like many others who sought divine guidance from the *oracle* at Delphi, Oedipus could not understand the enigmatic *oracular* warning he received. oracle, N.

**orator** N. public speaker. The abolitionist Frederick Douglass was a brilliant *orator* whose speeches brought home to his audience the evils of slavery.

**oratorio** N. dramatic poem set to music. The Glee Club decided to present an *oratorio* during their recital.

**ordain** V. decree or command; grant holy orders; predestine. The king *ordained* that no foreigner should be allowed to enter the city. The Bishop of Michigan *ordained* David a deacon in the Episcopal Church. The young lovers felt that fate had *ordained* their meeting.

**ordeal** N. severe trial or affliction. June was so painfully shy that it was an *ordeal* for her to speak up when the teacher called on her in class.

**ordinance** N. decree. Passing a red light is a violation of a city *ordinance*.

**ordination** N. ceremony conferring holy orders. The candidate for *ordination* had to meet with the bishop and the diocesan officers before being judged ready to be *ordained* a deacon. ordain, V.

**orgy** N. wild, drunken revelry; unrestrained indulgence. The Roman emperor's *orgies* were far wilder than the toga party in the movie *Animal House*. When her income tax refund check finally arrived, Sally indulged in an *orgy* of shopping.

**orient** V. get one's bearings; adjust. Philip spent his first day in Denver *orienting* himself to the city.

**orientation** N. act of finding oneself in society. Freshman *orientation* provides the incoming students with an opportunity to learn about their new environment and their place in it.

**orifice** N. mouthlike opening; small opening. The Howe Caverns were discovered when someone observed that a cold wind was issuing from an *orifice* in the hillside.

**ornate** ADJ. excessively or elaborately decorated. With its elaborately carved, convoluted lines, furniture of the Baroque period was highly *ornate*.

**ornithologist** N. scientific student of birds. Audubon's drawings of American bird life have been of interest not only to the *ornithologists* but also to the general public.

**orthodox** ADJ. traditional; conservative in belief. Faced with a problem, she preferred to take an *orthodox* approach rather than shock anyone. orthodoxy, N.

**orthography** N. correct spelling. Many of us find English *orthography* difficult to master because so many of our words are not written phonetically.

■ **oscillate** V. vibrate pendulumlike; waver. It is interesting to note how public opinion *oscillates* between the extremes of optimism and pessimism.

**osseous** ADJ. made of bone; bony. The hollow "soft spot" found at the top of the infant's skull gradually closes as new *osseous* tissue fills in the gap.

**ossify** V. change or harden into bone. When he called his opponent a "bonehead," he implied that his adversary's brain had *ossified* and that he was not capable of clear thinking.

**ostensible** ADJ. apparent; professed; pretended. Although the ostensible purpose of this expedition is to discover new lands, we are really interested in finding new markets for our products.

■ **ostentatious** ADJ. showy; pretentious; trying to attract attention. Trump's latest casino in Atlantic City is the most *ostentatious* gambling palace in the East: it easily out-glitters its competitors. ostentation, N.

**ostracize** V. exclude from public favor; ban. As soon as the newspapers carried the story of his connection with the criminals, his friends began to *ostracize* him. ostracism, N.

**oust** V. expel; drive out. The world wondered if Aquino would be able to *oust* Marcos from office.

**outlandish** ADJ. bizarre; peculiar; unconventional. The eccentric professor who engages in markedly *outlandish* behavior is a stock figure in novels with an academic setting.

**outmoded** ADJ. no longer stylish; old-fashioned. Unconcerned about keeping in style, Lenore was perfectly happy to wear *outmoded* clothes as long as they were clean and unfrayed.

**outskirts** N. fringes; outer borders. Living on the *outskirts* of Boston, Sarah sometimes felt as if she were cut off from the cultural heart of the city.

**outspoken** ADJ. candid; blunt. The candidate was too *outspoken* to be a successful politician; he had not yet learned to weigh his words carefully.

**outstrip** V. surpass; outdo. Jesse Owens easily *outstripped* his competitors to win the gold medal at the Olympic Games.

**outwit** V. outsmart; trick. By disguising himself as an old woman, Holmes was able to *outwit* his pursuers and escape capture.

**ovation** N. enthusiastic applause. When Placido Domingo came on stage in the first act of *La Bohème*, he was greeted by a tremendous *ovation*.

**overbearing** ADJ. bossy; arrogant; decisively important. Certain of her own importance and of the unimportance of everyone else, Lady Bracknell was intolerably *overbearing* in manner. "In choosing a husband," she said, "good birth is of *overbearing* importance; compared to that, neither wealth nor talent signifies."

**overt** ADJ. open to view. According to the United States Constitution, a person must commit an *overt* act before he may be tried for treason.

**overweening** ADJ. presumptuous; arrogant. His *overweening* pride in his accomplishments was not justified.

# Test

## Word List 33   *Antonyms*

Each of the questions below consists of a word in capital letters, followed by five lettered words or phrases. Choose the lettered word or phrase that is most nearly opposite in meaning to the word in capital letters and write the letter of your choice on your answer paper.

481. OBSOLETE (A) heated (B) desolate (C) renovated (D) frightful (E) automatic

482. OBSTREPEROUS (A) turbid (B) quiet (C) remote (D) lucid (E) active

483. OBTUSE (A) sheer (B) transparent (C) tranquil (D) timid (E) shrewd

484. ODIOUS (A) fragrant (B) redolent (C) fetid (D) delightful (E) puny

485. ODIUM (A) noise (B) liking (C) dominant (D) hasty (E) atrium

486. OMNIPOTENT (A) weak (B) democratic (C) despotic (D) passionate (E) late

487. OMNISCIENT (A) sophisticated (B) ignorant (C) essential (D) trivial (E) isolated

488. OPIATE (A) distress (B) sleep (C) stimulant (D) laziness (E) despair

489. OPPORTUNE (A) occasional (B) fragrant (C) fragile (D) awkward (E) neglected

490. OPPORTUNIST (A) man of destiny (B) man of principle (C) changeling (D) adversary (E) colleague

491. OPPROBRIUM (A) delineation (B) aptitude (C) majesty (D) freedom (E) praise

492. OPTIMUM (A) pessimistic (B) knowledgeable (C) worst (D) minimum (E) chosen

493. OPULENCE (A) pessimism (B) patriotism (C) potency (D) passion (E) poverty

494. OSTENTATIOUS (A) inactive (B) unassuming (C) impolite (D) illicit (E) irrational

495. OVERWEENING (A) humble (B) impotent (C) avid (D) acrimonious (E) exaggerated

---

# Word List 34   overwrought-peccadillo

**overwrought** ADJ. extremely agitated; hysterical. When Kate heard the news of the sudden tragedy, she became too *overwrought* to work and had to leave the office early.

**ovoid** ADJ. egg-shaped. At Easter she had to cut out hundreds of brightly colored *ovoid* shapes.

**pachyderm** N. thick-skinned animal. The elephant is probably the best-known *pachyderm*.

**pacifist** N. one opposed to force; antimilitarist. During the war, *pacifists*, though they refused to bear arms, served in the front lines as ambulance drivers and medical corpsmen. also ADJ. pacifism, N.

**pacify** V. soothe; make calm or quiet; subdue. Dentists criticize the practice of giving fussy children sweets to *pacify* them.

**paean** N. song of praise or joy. *Paeans* celebrating the victory filled the air.

**painstaking** ADJ. showing hard work; taking great care. The new high-frequency word list is the result of *painstaking* efforts on the part of our research staff.

**palatable** ADJ. agreeable; pleasing to the taste. Neither Jack's underbaked opinions nor his overcooked casseroles were *palatable* to me.

**palate** N. roof of the mouth; sense of taste. When you sound out the letter "d," your tongue curves up to touch the edge of your *palate*. When Alice was sick, her mother made special meals to tempt her *palate*.

**palatial** ADJ. magnificent. He proudly showed us through his *palatial* home.

**paleontology** N. study of prehistoric life. The professor of *paleontology* had a superb collection of fossils.

**palette** N. board on which a painter mixes pigments. At the present time, art supply stores are selling a paper *palette* that may be discarded after use.

**palimpsest** N. parchment used for second time after original writing has been erased. Using chemical reagents, scientists have been able to restore the original writings on many *palimpsests*.

**pall** V. grow tiresome. The study of word lists can eventually *pall* and put one to sleep.

**pallet** N. small, poor bed. The weary traveler went to sleep on his straw *pallet*.

**palliate** V. ease pain; make less severe or offensive. If we cannot cure this disease at present, we can, at least, try to *palliate* the symptoms. palliation, N.

**pallid** ADJ. pale; wan. Because his occupation required that he work at night and sleep during the day, he had an exceptionally *pallid* complexion.

**palpable** ADJ. tangible; easily perceptible. I cannot understand how you could overlook such a *palpable* blunder.

**palpitate** V. throb; flutter. As she became excited, her heart began to *palpitate* more and more erratically.

**paltry** ADJ. insignificant; petty; trifling. "One hundred dollars for a genuine imitation Rolex watch! Lady, this is a *paltry* sum to pay for such a high-class piece of jewelry."

**pan** V. criticize harshly. Hoping for a rave review of his new show, the playwright was miserable when the critics *panned* it unanimously.

**panacea** N. cure-all; remedy for all diseases. There is no easy *panacea* that will solve our complicated international situation.

**panache** N. flair; flamboyance. Many performers imitate Noel Coward, but few have his *panache* and sense of style.

**pandemic** ADJ. widespread; affecting the majority of people. They feared the AIDS epidemic would soon reach *pandemic* proportions.

**pandemonium** N. wild tumult. When the ships collided in the harbor, *pandemonium* broke out among the passengers.

**pander** V. cater to the low desires of others. The reviewer accused the makers of *Lethal Weapon* of *pandering* to the masses' taste for violence.

**panegyric** N. formal praise. Blushing at all the praise heaped upon him by the speakers, the modest hero said, "I don't deserve such *panegyrics*."

**panoramic** ADJ. denoting an unobstructed and comprehensive view. On a clear day, from the top of the World Trade Center you can get a *panoramic* view of New York City and neighboring stretches of New Jersey and Long Island. panorama, N.

**pantomime** N. acting without dialogue. Because he worked in *pantomime*, the clown could be understood wherever he appeared. also V.

**papyrus** N. ancient paper made from stem of papyrus plant. The ancient Egyptians were among the first to write on *papyrus*.

**parable** N. short, simple story teaching a moral. Let us apply to our own conduct the lesson that this *parable* teaches.

**paradigm** N. model; example; pattern. Pavlov's experiment in which he trains a dog to salivate on hearing a bell is a *paradigm* of the conditioned-response experiment in behavioral psychology. paradigmatic, ADJ.

**paradox** N. something apparently contradictory in nature; statement that looks false but is actually correct. Richard presents a bit of a *paradox*, for he is a card-carrying member of both the National Rifle Association and the relatively pacifist American Civil Liberties Union. paradoxical, ADJ.

■ **paragon** N. model of perfection. Her fellow students disliked Lavinia because Miss Minchin always pointed her out as a *paragon* of virtue.

**parallelism** N. state of being parallel; similarity. Although the twins were separated at birth and grew up in different adoptive families, a striking *parallelism* exists between their lives.

**parameter** N. limit; independent variable. We need to define the *parameters* of the problem.

**paramount** ADJ. foremost in importance; supreme. Proper nutrition and hygiene are of *paramount* importance in adolescent development and growth.

**paramour** N. illicit lover. She sought a divorce on the grounds that her husband had a *paramour* in another town.

**paranoia** N. psychosis marked by delusions of grandeur or persecution. Suffering from *paranoia*, he claimed everyone was out to get him. Ironically, his claim was accurate; even *paranoids* have enemies. paranoid, paranoiac, N. and ADJ.

**paraphernalia** N. equipment; odds and ends. Her desk was cluttered with paper, pen, ink, dictionary and other *paraphernalia* of the writing craft.

**paraphrase** V. restate a passage in one's own words while retaining thought of author. In 250 words or less, *paraphrase* this article. also N.

**parasite** N. animal or plant living on another; toady; sycophant. The tapeworm is an example of the kind of *parasite* that may infest the human body.

**parched** ADJ. extremely dry; very thirsty. The *parched* desert landscape seemed hostile to life.

**pariah** N. social outcast. If everyone ostracized singer Mariah Carey, would she then be Mariah the *pariah*?

**parity** N. equality; close resemblance. I find your analogy inaccurate because I do not see the *parity* between the two illustrations.

**parlance** N. language; idiom. All this legal *parlance* confuses me; I need an interpreter.

**parley** N. conference. The peace *parley* has not produced the anticipated truce. also V.

**parochial** ADJ. narrow in outlook; provincial; related to parishes. Although Jane Austen writes novels set in small rural communities, her concerns are universal, not *parochial*.

**parody** N. humorous imitation; spoof; takeoff; travesty. The show *Forbidden Broadway* presents *parodies* spoofing the year's new productions playing on Broadway. also V.

**paroxysm** N. fit or attack of pain, laughter, rage. When he heard of his son's misdeeds, he was seized by a *paroxysm* of rage.

**parquet** N. floor made of wood strips inlaid in a mosaic-like pattern. In laying the floor, the carpenters combined redwood and oak in an elegant *parquet*.

**parry** V. ward off a blow; deflect. Unwilling to injure his opponent in such a pointless clash, Dartagnan simply tried to *parry* his rival's thrusts. What fun it was to watch Katherine Hepburn and Spencer Tracy *parry* each other's verbal thrusts in their classic screwball comedies! also N.

**parsimony** N. stinginess; excessive frugality. Silas Marner's *parsimony* did not allow him to indulge in any luxuries. parsimonious, ADJ.

**partial** ADJ. incomplete; having a liking for something. In this issue we have published only a *partial* list of contributors because we lack space to acknowledge everyone. I am extremely *partial* to chocolate eclairs. partiality, N.

**partiality** N. inclination; bias. As a judge, not only must I be unbiased, but I must also avoid any evidence of *partiality* when I award the prize.

■ **partisan** ADJ. one-sided; prejudiced; committed to a party. Rather than joining forces to solve our nation's problems, the Democrats and Republicans spend their time on *partisan* struggles. also N.

**partition** V. divide into parts. Before their second daughter was born, Jason and Lizzie decided each child needed a room of her own, and so they *partitioned* a large bedroom into two small but separate rooms. also N.

**passé** ADJ. old-fashioned; past the prime. Her style is *passé* and reminiscent of the Victorian era.

**passive** ADJ. not active; acted upon. Mahatma Gandhi urged his followers to pursue a program of *passive* resistance as he felt that it was more effective than violence and acts of terrorism.

**pastiche** N. imitation of another's style in musical composition or in writing. We cannot even say that her music is a *pastiche* of this or that composer; it is, rather, reminiscent of many musicians.

**pastoral** ADJ. rural. In these stories of *pastoral* life, we find an understanding of the daily tasks of country folk.

**patent** ADJ. open for the public to read; obvious. It was *patent* to everyone that the witness spoke the truth.

**pathetic** ADJ. causing sadness, compassion, pity; touching. Everyone in the auditorium was weeping by the time she finished her *pathetic* tale about the orphaned boy.

■ **pathological** ADJ. pertaining to disease. As we study the *pathological* aspects of this disease, we must not overlook the psychological elements.

**pathos** N. tender sorrow; pity; quality in art or literature that produces these feelings. The quiet tone of *pathos* that ran through the novel never degenerated into the maudlin or the overly sentimental.

**patina** N. green crust on old bronze works; tone slowly taken by varnished painting. Judging by the *patina* on this bronze statue, we can conclude that this is the work of a medieval artist.

**patois**  N. local or provincial dialect. His years of study of the language at the university did not enable him to understand the *patois* of the natives.

**patriarch**  N. father and ruler of a family or tribe. In many primitive tribes, the leader and lawmaker was the *patriarch*.

**patrician**  ADJ. noble; aristocratic. We greatly admired her well-bred, *patrician* elegance. also N.

**patronize**  V. support; act superior toward; be a customer of. Penniless artists hope to find some wealthy art lover who will *patronize* them. If some condescending wine steward *patronized* me because he saw I knew nothing about fine wine, I'd refuse to *patronize* his restaurant.

■ **paucity**  N. scarcity. They closed the restaurant because the *paucity* of customers made it uneconomical to operate.

**pauper**  N. very poor person. Though Widow Brown was living on a reduced income, she was by no means a *pauper*.

**peccadillo**  N. slight offense. Whenever Huck swiped a cookie from the jar, Miss Watson reacted as if he were guilty of armed robbery, not of some mere *peccadillo*.

## Test

## Word List 34    *Synonyms and Antonyms*

Each of the following questions consists of a word in capital letters, followed by five lettered words or phrases. Choose the lettered word or phrase that is most nearly similar or opposite in meaning to the word in capital letters and write the letter of your choice on your answer paper.

496. PAEAN (A) serf (B) pealing (C) lien (D) lament (E) folly

497. PALLET (A) bed (B) pigment board (C) bench (D) spectrum (E) quality

498. PALLIATE (A) smoke (B) quicken (C) substitute (D) alleviate (E) sadden

499. PANDEMONIUM (A) calm (B) frustration (C) efficiency (D) impishness (E) sophistication

500. PANEGYRIC (A) medication (B) panacea (C) rotation (D) vacillation (E) praise

501. PARABLE (A) equality (B) allegory (C) frenzy (D) folly (E) cuticle

502. PARADOX (A) exaggeration (B) contradiction (C) hyperbole (D) invective (E) poetic device

503. PARAMOUR (A) illicit lover (B) majority (C) importance (D) hatred (E) clandestine affair

504. PARANOIA (A) fracture (B) statement (C) quantity (D) benefaction (E) sanity

505. PARIAH (A) village (B) suburb (C) outcast (D) disease (E) benefactor

506. PARITY (A) duplicate (B) miniature (C) golf tee (D) similarity (E) event

507. PARSIMONIOUS (A) grammatical (B) syntactical (C) effective (D) extravagant (E) esoteric

508. PARTIALITY (A) completion (B) equality (C) bias (D) divorce (E) reflection

509. PASSÉ (A) scornful (B) rural (C) out-of-date (D) silly (E) barbaric

510. PASTICHE (A) imitation (B) glue (C) present (D) greeting (E) family

## Word List 35    pecuniary-philanderer

**pecuniary**  ADJ. pertaining to money. Seldom earning enough to cover their expenses, folk-dance teachers work because they love dancing, not because they expect any *pecuniary* reward.

**pedagogue**  N. teacher. He could never be a stuffy *pedagogue*; his classes were always lively and filled with humor.

**pedagogy**  N. teaching; art of education. Though Maria Montessori gained fame for her innovations in *pedagogy*, it took years before her teaching techniques became common practice in American schools.

**pedant**  N. scholar who overemphasizes book learning or technicalities. Her insistence that the book be memorized marked the teacher as a *pedant* rather than a scholar.

■ **pedantic**  ADJ. showing off learning; bookish. Leavening her decisions with humorous, down-to-earth anecdotes, Judge Judy was not at all the *pedantic* legal scholar. pedantry, N.

**pedestrian**  ADJ. ordinary; unimaginative. Unintentionally boring, he wrote page after page of *pedestrian* prose.

**pediatrician**  N. physician specializing in children's diseases. The family doctor advised the parents to consult a *pediatrician* about their child's ailment.

**peerless**  ADJ. having no equal; incomparable. The reigning operatic tenor of his generation, to his admirers Luciano Pavarotti was *peerless*: no one could compare with him.

**pejorative**  ADJ. negative in connotation; having a belittling effect. Instead of criticizing Clinton's policies, the Republicans made *pejorative* remarks about his character.

**pell-mell**  ADV. in confusion; disorderly. The excited students dashed *pell-mell* into the stadium to celebrate the victory.

**pellucid**   ADJ.   transparent; limpid; easy to understand. After reading these stodgy philosophers, I find his *pellucid* style very enjoyable.

**penance**   N.   self-imposed punishment for sin. The Ancient Mariner said, "I have *penance* done and *penance* more will do," to atone for the sin of killing the albatross.

■ **penchant**   N.   strong inclination; liking. Dave has a *penchant* for taking risks: one semester he went steady with three girls, two of whom were stars on the school karate team.

**pendant**   ADJ.   hanging down from something. Her *pendant* earrings glistened in the light.

**pendant**   N.   ornament (hanging from a necklace, etc.). The grateful team presented the coach with a silver chain and *pendant* engraved with the school's motto.

**pendulous**   ADJ.   hanging; suspended. The *pendulous* chandeliers swayed in the breeze as if they were about to fall from the ceiling.

**penitent**   ADJ.   repentant. When he realized the enormity of his crime, he became remorseful and *penitent*. also N.

**pensive**   ADJ.   dreamily thoughtful; thoughtful with a hint of sadness; contemplative. The *pensive* lover gazed at the portrait of his beloved and sighed deeply.

**penumbra**   N.   partial shadow (in an eclipse). During an eclipse, we can see an area of total darkness and a lighter area, which is the *penumbra*.

■ **penury**   N.   severe poverty; stinginess. When his pension fund failed, George feared he would end his days in *penury*. He became such a penny-pincher that he turned into a closefisted, *penurious* miser.

**peon**   N.   landless agricultural worker; bond servant. The land reformers sought to liberate the *peons* and establish them as independent farmers. peonage, N.

**perceptive**   ADJ.   insightful; aware; wise. Although Maud was a generally *perceptive* critic, she had her blind spots: she could never see flaws in the work of her friends.

**percussion**   ADJ.   striking one object against another sharply. The drum is a *percussion* instrument. also N.

**perdition**   N.   damnation; complete ruin. Praying for salvation, young Daedalus feared he was damned to eternal *perdition*.

**peregrination**   N.   journey. Auntie Mame was a world traveler whose *peregrinations* took her from Tijuana to Timbuktu.

**peremptory**   ADJ.   demanding and leaving no choice. From Jack's *peremptory* knock on the door, Jill could tell he would not give up until she let him in.

■ **perennial**   N.   something long-lasting. These plants are hardy *perennials* and will bloom for many years. also ADJ.

■ **perfidious**   ADJ.   treacherous; disloyal. When Caesar realized that Brutus had betrayed him, he reproached his *perfidious* friend. perfidy, N.

**perforate**   V.   pierce; put a hole through. Before you can open the aspirin bottle, you must first *perforate* the plastic safety seal that covers the cap.

■ **perfunctory**   ADJ.   superficial; not thorough; lacking interest, care, or enthusiasm. The auditor's *perfunctory* inspection of the books overlooked many errors.

**perigee**   N.   point of moon's orbit when it is nearest the earth. The rocket which was designed to take photographs of the moon was launched as the moon approached its *perigee*.

**perimeter**   N.   outer boundary. To find the *perimeter* of any quadrilateral, we add the lengths of the four sides.

**peripatetic**   ADJ.   walking about; moving. The *peripatetic* school of philosophy derives its name from the fact that Aristotle walked with his pupils while discussing philosophy with them.

**peripheral**   ADJ.   marginal; outer. We lived, not in central London, but in one of those *peripheral* suburbs that spring up on the outskirts of a great city.

**periphery**   N.   edge, especially of a round surface. He sensed that there was something just beyond the *periphery* of his vision.

**perjury**   N.   false testimony while under oath. Rather than lie under oath and perhaps be indicted for *perjury*, the witness chose to take the Fifth Amendment, refusing to answer any questions on the grounds that he might incriminate himself.

■ **permeable**   ADJ.   penetrable; porous; allowing liquids or gas to pass through. If your jogging clothes weren't made out of *permeable* fabric, you'd drown in your own sweat (figuratively speaking). permeate, V.

**pernicious**   ADJ.   very destructive. The Athenians argued that Socrates's teachings had a *pernicious* effect on young and susceptible minds; therefore, they condemned him to death.

**peroration**   N.   conclusion of an oration. The *peroration* was largely hortatory and brought the audience to its feet clamoring for action at its close.

**perpetrate**   V.   commit an offense. Only an insane person could *perpetrate* such a horrible crime.

**perpetual**   ADJ.   everlasting. Ponce de Leon hoped to find the legendary fountain of *perpetual* youth.

**perpetuate**   V.   make something last; preserve from extinction. Some critics attack *The Adventures of Huckleberry Finn* because they believe Twain's book *perpetuates* a false image of blacks in this country. perpetuity, N.

**perquisite**   N.   any gain above stipulated salary. The *perquisites* attached to this job make it even more attractive than the salary indicates.

**personable**   ADJ.   attractive. The individual I am seeking to fill this position must be *personable* since he or she will be representing us before the public.

**perspicacious**   ADJ.   having insight; penetrating; astute. The brilliant lawyer was known for his *perspicacious* deductions.

**perspicuity**   N.   clearness of expression; freedom from ambiguity. One of the outstanding features of this book is the *perspicuity* of its author; her meaning is always clear.

**perspicuous** ADJ. plainly expressed. Her *perspicuous* comments eliminated all possibility of misinterpretation.

**pert** ADJ. impertinent; forward. I think your *pert* and impudent remarks call for an apology.

**pertinacious** ADJ. stubborn; persistent. She is bound to succeed because her *pertinacious* nature will not permit her to quit.

**pertinent** ADJ. suitable; to the point. The lawyer wanted to know all the *pertinent* details.

**perturb** V. disturb greatly. The thought that electricity might be leaking out of the empty light-bulb sockets *perturbed* my aunt so much that at night she crept about the house screwing fresh bulbs in the vacant spots. perturbation, N.

**peruse** V. read with care. After the conflagration that burned down her house, Joan closely *perused* her home insurance policy to discover exactly what benefits her coverage provided. perusal, N.

■ **pervasive** ADJ. spread throughout. Despite airing them for several hours, she could not rid her clothes of the *pervasive* odor of mothballs that clung to them. pervade, V.

**perverse** ADJ. stubbornly wrongheaded; wicked and unacceptable. When Jack was in a *perverse* mood, he would do the opposite of whatever Jill asked him. When Hannibal Lecter was in a *perverse* mood, he ate the flesh of his victims. perversity, N.

**perversion** N. corruption; turning from right to wrong. Inasmuch as he had no motive for his crimes, we could not understand his *perversion*.

**pessimism** N. belief that life is basically bad or evil; gloominess. Considering how well you have done in the course so far, you have no real reason for such *pessimism* about your final grade. pessimistic, ADJ.

**pestilential** ADJ. causing plague; baneful. People were afraid to explore the *pestilential* swamp. pestilence, N.

**pestle** N. tool for mashing or grinding substances in a hard bowl. From the way in which the elderly pharmacist pounded the drug with his *pestle,* young George could tell that his employer was agitated about something.

**petrify** V. turn to stone. His sudden and unexpected appearance seemed to *petrify* her.

**petty** ADJ. trivial; unimportant; very small. She had no major complaints to make about his work, only a few *petty* quibbles that were almost too minor to state.

**petulant** ADJ. touchy; peevish. If you'd had hardly any sleep for three nights and people kept on phoning and waking you up, you'd sound *petulant*, too. petulance, N.

**pharisaical** ADJ. pertaining to the Pharisees, who paid scrupulous attention to tradition; self-righteous; hypocritical. Walter Lippmann has pointed out that moralists who do not attempt to explain the moral code they advocate are often regarded as *pharisaical* and ignored.

**phenomena** N, PL. observable facts; subjects of scientific investigation. We kept careful records of the *phenomena* we noted in the course of these experiments. phenomenon, SING.

**philanderer** N. faithless lover; flirt. Swearing he had never so much as looked at another woman, Jack assured Jill he was no *philanderer*.

# Test

## Word List 35  *Antonyms*

Each of the questions below consists of a word in capital letters, followed by five lettered words or phrases. Choose the lettered word or phrase that is most nearly opposite in meaning to the word in capital letters and write the letter of your choice on your answer paper.

511. PEJORATIVE (A) positive (B) legal (C) determining (D) delighting (E) declaiming

512. PELLUCID (A) logistical (B) philandering (C) incomprehensible (D) vagrant (E) warranted

513. PENCHANT (A) distance (B) imminence (C) dislike (D) attitude (E) void

514. PENURIOUS (A) imprisoned (B) captivated (C) generous (D) vacant (E) abolished

515. PERFUNCTORY (A) official (B) thorough (C) insipid (D) vicarious (E) distinctive

516. PERIGEE (A) eclipse (B) planet (C) apogee (D) refugee (E) danger

517. PERIPATETIC (A) worldly (B) stationary (C) disarming (D) seeking (E) inherent

518. PERMEABLE (A) perishable (B) effective (C) plodding (D) impenetrable (E) lasting

519. PERNICIOUS (A) practical (B) comparative (C) harmless (D) tangible (E) detailed

520. PERPETUAL (A) momentary (B) standard (C) serious (D) industrial (E) interpretive

521. PERSPICUITY (A) grace (B) feature (C) review (D) difficulty (E) vagueness

522. PERT (A) polite (B) perishable (C) moral (D) deliberate (E) stubborn

523. PERTINACIOUS (A) vengeful (B) consumptive (C) superficial (D) skilled (E) advertised

524. PERTINENT (A) understood (B) living (C) discontented (D) puzzling (E) irrelevant

525. PETULANT (A) angry (B) moral (C) declining (D) underhanded (E) uncomplaining

# Word List 36    philanthropist-precedent

**philanthropist**   N. lover of mankind; doer of good. In his role as *philanthropist* and public benefactor, John D. Rockefeller, Sr., donated millions to charity; as an individual, however, he was a tight-fisted old man.

**philatelist**   N. stamp-collector. When she heard the value of the Penny Black stamp, Phyllis was inspired to become a *philatelist*.

**philistine**   N. narrow-minded person, uncultured and exclusively interested in material gain. We need more men and women of culture and enlightenment; we have too many *philistines* among us.

**philology**   N. study of language. The professor of *philology* advocated the use of Esperanto as an international language.

■ **phlegmatic**   ADJ. calm; not easily disturbed. The nurse was a cheerful but *phlegmatic* person, unexcited in the face of sudden emergencies.

**phobia**   N. morbid fear. Her fear of flying was more than mere nervousness; it was a real *phobia*.

**phoenix**   N. symbol of immortality or rebirth. Like the legendary *phoenix* rising from its ashes, the city of San Francisco rose again after its destruction during the 1906 earthquake.

**phylum**   N. major classification, second to kingdom, of plants and animals; division. In sorting out her hundreds of packets of seeds, Katya decided to file them by *phylum*.

**physiognomy**   N. face. He prided himself on his ability to analyze a person's character by studying his *physiognomy*.

**physiological**   ADJ. pertaining to the science of the function of living organisms. To understand this disease fully, we must examine not only its *physiological* aspects but also its psychological elements.

**piebald**   ADJ. of different colors; mottled; spotted. You should be able to identify Polka Dot in this race; he is the only *piebald* horse running.

**piecemeal**   ADV. one part at a time; gradually. Tolstoy's *War and Peace* is too huge to finish in one sitting; I'll have to read it *piecemeal*.

**pied**   ADJ. variegated; multicolored. The *Pied* Piper of Hamelin got his name from the multicolored clothing he wore.

■ **piety**   N. devoutness; reverence for God. Living her life in prayer and good works, Mother Teresa exemplified the true spirit of *piety*. pious, ADJ.

**pigment**   N. coloring matter. Van Gogh mixed various *pigments* with linseed oil to create his paints.

**pillage**   V. plunder. The enemy *pillaged* the quiet village and left it in ruins. also N.

**pillory**   V. punish by placing in a wooden frame; subject to criticism and ridicule. Even though he was mocked and *pilloried*, he maintained that he was correct in his beliefs. also N.

**pine**   V. languish, decline; long for; yearn. Though she tried to be happy living with Clara in the city, Heidi *pined* for the mountains and for her gruff but loving grandfather.

**pinion**   V. restrain. They *pinioned* his arms against his body but left his legs free so that he could move about. also N.

**pinnacle**   N. peak. We could see the morning sunlight illuminate the *pinnacle* while the rest of the mountain lay in shadow.

**pious**   ADJ. devout; religious. The challenge for church people today is how to be *pious* in the best sense, that is, to be devout without becoming hypocritical or sanctimonious. piety, N.

**piquant**   ADJ. pleasantly tart-tasting; stimulating. The *piquant* sauce added to our enjoyment of the meal. piquancy, N.

**pique**   N. irritation; resentment. She showed her *pique* at her loss by refusing to appear with the other contestants at the end of the competition.

**pique**   V. provoke or arouse; annoy. "I know something *you* don't know," said Lucy, trying to *pique* Ethel's interest.

**piscatorial**   ADJ. pertaining to fishing. He spent many happy hours at the lake in his *piscatorial* activities.

**pitfall**   N. hidden danger; concealed trap. The preacher warned his flock to beware the *pitfall* of excessive pride, for pride brought on the angels' fall.

**pith**   N. core or marrow; essence; substance. In preparing a pineapple for the table, first slice it in half and remove the woody central *pith*.

**pithy**   ADJ. concise; meaningful; substantial; meaty. While other girls might have gone on and on about how uncool Elton was, Cher summed it up in one *pithy* remark: "He's bogus!"

**pittance**   N. a small allowance or wage. He could not live on the *pittance* he received as a pension and had to look for an additional source of revenue.

**pivotal**   ADJ. central; critical. De Klerk's decision to set Nelson Mandela free was *pivotal;* without Mandela's release, there was no possibility that the African National Congress would entertain talks with the South African government.

■ **placate**   V. pacify; conciliate. The store manager tried to *placate* the angry customer, offering to replace the damaged merchandise or to give back her money.

**placebo**   N. harmless substance prescribed as a dummy pill. In a controlled experiment, fifty volunteers were given erythromycin tablets; the control group received only *placebos*.

**placid**   ADJ. peaceful; calm. After his vacation in this *placid* section, he felt soothed and rested.

**plagiarize**   V. steal another's ideas and pass them off as one's own. The teacher could tell that the student had *plagiarized* parts of his essay; she recognized whole paragraphs straight from *Barron's Book Notes*. plagiarism, N.

**plaintive**   ADJ. mournful. The dove has a *plaintive* and melancholy call.

**plait** V. braid; intertwine. The maypole dancers *plaited* bright green ribbons in their hair. also N.

■ **plasticity** N. ability to be molded. When clay dries out, it loses its *plasticity* and becomes less malleable.

■ **platitude** N. trite remark; commonplace statement. In giving advice to his son, old Polonius expressed himself only in *platitudes*; every word out of his mouth was a truism.

**platonic** ADJ. purely spiritual; theoretical; without sensual desire. Accused of impropriety in his dealings with female students, the professor maintained he had only a *platonic* interest in the women involved.

**plaudit** N. enthusiastic approval; round of applause. The theatrical company reprinted the *plaudits* of the critics in its advertisements. plauditory, ADJ.

**plausible** ADJ. having a show of truth but open to doubt; specious. Your mother made you stay home from school because she needed you to program the VCR? I'm sorry, you'll have to come up with a more *plausible* excuse than that.

**plebeian** ADJ. common; pertaining to the common people. His speeches were aimed at the *plebeian* minds and emotions; they disgusted the more refined.

**plenary** ADJ. complete; full. The union leader was given *plenary* power to negotiate a new contract with the employers.

**plenitude** N. abundance; completeness. Looking in the pantry, we admired the *plenitude* of fruits and pickles we had preserved during the summer.

■ **plethora** N. excess; overabundance. She offered a *plethora* of excuses for her shortcomings.

**pliable** ADJ. flexible; yielding; adaptable. In remodeling the bathroom, we replaced all the old, rigid lead pipes with new, *pliable* copper tubing.

**pliant** ADJ. flexible; easily influenced. Pinocchio's disposition was *pliant*; he was like putty in his tempters' hands.

**plight** N. condition, state (especially a bad state or condition); predicament. Loggers, unmoved by the *plight* of the spotted owl, plan to keep on felling trees whether or not they ruin the bird's habitat.

**pluck** N. courage. Even the adversaries of young Indiana Jones were impressed by the boy's *pluck* in trying to rescue the archeological treasure they had stolen.

**plumage** N. feathers of a bird. Bird watchers identify different species of birds by their characteristic songs and distinctive *plumage*.

**plumb** V. examine critically in order to understand; measure depth (by sounding). Try as he would, Watson could never fully *plumb* the depths of Holmes's thought processes.

**plumb** ADJ. vertical. Before hanging wallpaper it is advisable to drop a *plumb* line from the ceiling as a guide. also N.

■ **plummet** V. fall sharply. Stock prices *plummeted* as Wall Street reacted to the rise in interest rates.

**plutocracy** N. society ruled by the wealthy. From the way the government caters to the rich, you might think our society is a *plutocracy* rather than a democracy.

**podiatrist** N. doctor who treats ailments of the feet. He consulted a *podiatrist* about his fallen arches.

**podium** N. pedestal; raised platform. The audience applauded as the conductor made her way to the *podium*.

**poignancy** N. quality of being deeply moving; keenness of emotion. Watching the tearful reunion of the long-separated mother and child, the social worker was touched by the *poignancy* of the scene. poignant, ADJ.

**polarize** V. split into opposite extremes or camps. The abortion issue has *polarized* the country into pro-choice and anti-abortion camps.

**polemic** N. controversy; argument in support of point of view. Her essays were, for the main part, *polemics* for the party's policy.

**polemical** ADJ. aggressive in verbal attack; disputatious. Lexy was a master of *polemical* rhetoric; she should have worn a T-shirt with the slogan "Born to Debate."

**politic** ADJ. expedient; prudent; well devised. Even though he was disappointed, he did not think it *politic* to refuse this offer.

**polity** N. form of government of nation or state. Our *polity* should be devoted to the concept that the government should strive for the good of all citizens.

**polygamist** N. one who has more than one spouse at a time. He was arrested as a *polygamist* when his two wives filed complaints about him.

**polyglot** ADJ. speaking several languages. New York City is a *polyglot* community because of the thousands of immigrants who settle there.

**pomposity** N. self-important behavior; acting like a stuffed shirt. Although the commencement speaker had some good things to say, we had to laugh at his *pomposity* and general air of parading his own dignity. pompous, ADJ.

**ponderous** ADJ. weighty; unwieldy. His humor lacked the light touch; his jokes were always *ponderous*.

**pontifical** ADJ. pertaining to a bishop or pope; pompous or pretentious. From the very beginning of his ministry it was clear from his *pontifical* pronouncements that John was destined for a high *pontifical* office.

**pore** V. study industriously; ponder; scrutinize. Determined to become a physician, Beth spends hours *poring* over her anatomy text.

■ **porous** ADJ. full of pores; like a sieve. Dancers like to wear *porous* clothing because it allows the ready passage of water and air.

**portend** V. foretell; presage. The king did not know what these omens might *portend* and asked his soothsayers to interpret them.

**portent** N. sign; omen; forewarning. He regarded the black cloud as a *portent* of evil.

**portly** ADJ. stout; corpulent. The salesclerk tactfully referred to the overweight customer as *portly* rather than fat.

**poseur** N. person who pretends to be sophisticated, elegant, etc., to impress others. Some thought Dali was a brilliant painter; others dismissed him as a *poseur.*

**posterity** N. descendants; future generations. We hope to leave a better world to *posterity.*

**posthumous** ADJ. after death (as of child born after father's death or book published after author's death). The critics ignored his works during his lifetime; it was only after the *posthumous* publication of his last novel that they recognized his great talent.

**postulate** N. self-evident truth. We must accept these statements as *postulates* before pursuing our discussions any further. also V.

**posture** V. assume an affected pose; act artificially. No matter how much Arnold boasted or *postured,* I could not believe he was as important as he pretended to be.

**potable** ADJ. suitable for drinking. The recent drought in the Middle Atlantic States has emphasized the need for extensive research in ways of making sea water *potable.* also N.

**potent** ADJ. powerful; persuasive; greatly influential. Looking at the expiration date on the cough syrup bottle, we wondered whether the medication would still be *potent.* potency, N.

**potentate** N. monarch; sovereign. The *potentate* spent more time at Monte Carlo than he did at home on his throne.

**potential** ADJ. expressing possibility; latent. This juvenile delinquent is a *potential* murderer. also N.

**potion** N. dose (of liquid). Tristan and Isolde drink a love *potion* in the first act of the opera.

**potpourri** N. heterogeneous mixture; medley. The folk singer offered a *potpourri* of songs from many lands.

**poultice** N. soothing application applied to sore and inflamed portions of the body. She was advised to apply a flaxseed *poultice* to the inflammation.

**practicable** ADJ. feasible. The board of directors decided that the plan was *practicable* and agreed to undertake the project.

**practical** ADJ. based on experience; useful. He was a *practical* man, opposed to theory.

■ **pragmatic** ADJ. practical (as opposed to idealistic); concerned with the practical worth or impact of something. This coming trip to France should provide me with a *pragmatic* test of the value of my conversational French class.

**pragmatist** N. practical person. No *pragmatist* enjoys becoming involved in a game that he can never win.

**prate** V. speak foolishly; boast idly. Let us not *prate* about our qualities; rather, let our virtues speak for themselves.

**prattle** V. babble. Baby John *prattled* on and on about the cats and his ball and the Cookie Monster. also N.

■ **preamble** N. introductory statement. In the *Preamble* to the Constitution, the purpose of the document is set forth.

■ **precarious** ADJ. uncertain; risky. Saying the stock was currently overpriced and would be a *precarious* investment, the broker advised her client against purchasing it.

**precedent** N. something preceding in time that may be used as an authority or guide for future action; an earlier occurrence. The law professor asked Jill to state which famous case served as a *precedent* for the court's decision in *Brown II.* precede, V.

**precedent** ADJ. preceding in time, rank, etc. Our discussions, *precedent* to this event, certainly did not give you any reason to believe that we would adopt your proposal.

# Test

## Word List 36    *Synonyms*

Each of the questions below consists of a word in capital letters, followed by five lettered words or phrases. Choose the lettered word or phrase that is most nearly similar in meaning to the word in capital letters and write the letter of your choice on your answer paper.

526. PHLEGMATIC (A) calm (B) cryptic (C) practical
(D) salivary (E) dishonest

527. PHYSIOGNOMY (A) posture (B) head
(C) physique (D) face (E) size

528. PIEBALD (A) motley (B) coltish (C) hairless
(D) thoroughbred (E) delicious

529. PILLAGE (A) hoard (B) plunder (C) versify
(D) denigrate (E) confide

530. PINION (A) express (B) report (C) reveal
(D) submit (E) restrain

531. PINNACLE (A) foothills (B) card game (C) pass
(D) taunt (E) peak

532. PIOUS (A) historic (B) devout (C) multiple
(D) fortunate (E) authoritative

533. PIQUE (A) pyramid (B) revolt (C) resentment
(D) struggle (E) inventory

534. PLACATE (A) determine (B) transmit (C) pacify
(D) allow (E) define

535. PLAGIARISM (A) theft of funds (B) theft of ideas
(C) belief in God (D) arson (E) ethical theory

536. PLAINTIVE (A) mournful (B) senseless
(C) persistent (D) rural (E) evasive

537. PLATITUDE (A) fatness (B) bravery (C) dimension
(D) trite remark (E) strong belief

538. POLEMIC (A) blackness (B) lighting (C) magnetism (D) controversy (E) grimace

539. PONDEROUS (A) contemplative (B) moist (C) rambling (D) bulky (E) erect

540. PRECARIOUS (A) priceless (B) premature (C) primitive (D) hazardous (E) unwelcome

---

# Word List 37    precept-propitiate

**precept** N. practical rule guiding conduct. "Love thy neighbor as thyself" is a worthwhile *precept*.

**precipice** N. cliff; dangerous position. Suddenly Indiana Jones found himself dangling from the edge of a *precipice*.

**precipitant** N. something that causes a substance in a chemical solution to separate out in solid form. Solvents by definition dissolve; *precipitants*, however, cause solids to *precipitate* or form. precipitate, V.

■ **precipitate** ADJ. rash; premature; hasty; sudden. Though I was angry enough to resign on the spot, I had enough sense to keep myself from quitting a job in such a *precipitate* fashion.

**precipitate** V. throw headlong; hasten. The removal of American political support appeared to have *precipitated* the downfall of the Marcos regime.

**precipitous** ADJ. steep; overhasty. This hill is difficult to climb because it is so *precipitous;* one slip, and our descent will be *precipitous* as well.

**précis** N. concise summing up of main points. Before making her presentation at the conference, Ellen wrote a neat *précis* of the major elements she would cover.

**precise** ADJ. exact. If you don't give me *precise* directions and a map, I'll never find your place.

**preclude** V. make impossible; eliminate. The fact that the band was already booked to play in Hollywood on New Year's Eve *precluded* their accepting the offer of a New Year's Eve gig in London.

**precocious** ADJ. advanced in development. Listening to the grown-up way the child discussed serious topics, we couldn't help remarking how *precocious* she was. precocity, N.

■ **precursor** N. forerunner. Though Gray and Burns share many traits with the Romantic poets who followed them, most critics consider them *precursors* of the Romantic Movement, not true Romantics.

**predator** N. creature that seizes and devours another animal; person who robs or exploits others. Not just cats, but a wide variety of *predators*—owls, hawks, weasels, foxes—catch mice for dinner. A carnivore is by definition *predatory*, for he *preys* on weaker creatures. predation, N.

**predecessor** N. former occupant of a post. I hope I can live up to the fine example set by my late *predecessor* in this office.

**predetermine** V. predestine; settle or decide beforehand; influence markedly. Romeo and Juliet believed that Fate had *predetermined* their meeting. Bea gathered estimates from caterers, florists, and stationers so that she could *predetermine* the costs of holding a catered buffet. Philip's love of athletics *predetermined* his choice of a career in sports marketing.

**predicament** N. tricky or dangerous situation; dilemma. Tied to the railroad tracks by the villain, Pauline strained against her bonds. How would she escape from this terrible *predicament*?

**predilection** N. partiality; preference. Although the artist used various media from time to time, she had a *predilection* for watercolors.

**predispose** V. give an inclination toward; make susceptible to. Oleg's love of dressing up his big sister's Barbie doll may have *predisposed* him to become a fashion designer. Genetic influences apparently *predispose* people to certain forms of cancer. predisposition, N.

**preeminent** ADJ. outstanding; superior. The king traveled to Boston because he wanted the *preeminent* surgeon in the field to perform the operation.

**preempt** V. head off; forestall by acting first; appropriate for oneself; supplant. Hoping to *preempt* any attempts by the opposition to make educational reform a hot political issue, the candidate set out her own plan to revitalize the public schools. preemptive, ADJ.

**preen** V. make oneself tidy in appearance; feel self-satisfaction. As Kitty *preened* before the mirror, carefully smoothing her shining hair, she couldn't help *preening* herself on her good looks.

**prefatory** ADJ. introductory. The chairman made a few *prefatory* remarks before he called on the first speaker.

**prehensile** ADJ. capable of grasping or holding. Monkeys use not only their arms and legs but also their *prehensile* tails in traveling through the trees.

**prelate** N. church dignitary. The archbishop of Moscow and other high-ranking *prelates* visited the Russian Orthodox seminary.

**prelude** N. introduction; forerunner. I am afraid that this border raid is the *prelude* to more serious attacks.

**premeditate** V. plan in advance. She had *premeditated* the murder for months, reading about common poisons and buying weed killer that contained arsenic.

**premise** N. assumption; postulate. On the *premise* that there's no fool like an old fool, P. T. Barnum hired a 90-year-old clown for his circus.

**premonition** N. forewarning. We ignored these *premonitions* of disaster because they appeared to be based on childish fears.

**premonitory** ADJ. serving to warn. You should have visited a doctor as soon as you felt these *premonitory* chest pains.

**preponderance** N. superiority of power, quantity, etc. The rebels sought to overcome the *preponderance* of strength of the government forces by engaging in guerrilla tactics. preponderate, V. preponderant, ADJ.

**preposterous** ADJ. absurd; ridiculous. When the candidate tried to downplay his youthful experiments with marijuana by saying he hadn't inhaled, we all thought, "What a *preposterous* excuse!"

**prerogative** N. privilege; unquestionable right. The President cannot levy taxes; that is the *prerogative* of the legislative branch of government.

**presage** V. foretell. The vultures flying overhead *presaged* the discovery of the corpse in the desert.

**prescience** N. ability to foretell the future. Given the current wave of Japan-bashing, it does not take *prescience* for me to foresee problems in our future trade relations with Japan.

**presentiment** N. feeling something will happen; anticipatory fear; premonition. Saying goodbye at the airport, Jack had a sudden *presentiment* that this was the last time he would see Jill.

**prestige** N. impression produced by achievements or reputation. Many students want to go to Harvard University, not for the education offered, but for the *prestige* of Harvard's name. prestigious, ADJ.

■ **presumptuous** ADJ. arrogant; taking liberties. It seems *presumptuous* for one so relatively new to the field to challenge the conclusions of its leading experts. presumption, N.

**pretentious** ADJ. ostentatious; pompous; making unjustified claims; overambitious. The other prize winner isn't wearing her medal; isn't it a bit *pretentious* of you to wear yours?

**preternatural** ADJ. beyond that which is normal in nature. John's mother's total ability to tell when he was lying struck him as almost *preternatural*.

**pretext** N. excuse. She looked for a good *pretext* to get out of paying a visit to her aunt.

**prevail** V. induce; triumph over. He tried to *prevail* on her to type his essay for him.

**prevalent** ADJ. widespread; generally accepted. A radical committed to social change, Reed had no patience with the conservative views *prevalent* in the America of his day.

■ **prevaricate** V. lie. Some people believe that to *prevaricate* in a good cause is justifiable and regard the statement as a "white lie."

**prey** N. target of a hunt; victim. In *Stalking the Wild Asparagus*, Euell Gibbons has as his *prey* not wild beasts but wild plants. also V.

**prim** ADJ. very precise and formal; exceedingly proper. Many people commented on the contrast between the *prim* attire of the young lady and the inappropriate clothing worn by her escort.

**primogeniture** N. seniority by birth. By virtue of *primogeniture*, in some cultures the first-born child has many privileges denied his brothers and sisters.

**primordial** ADJ. existing at the beginning (of time); rudimentary. The Neanderthal Man is one of our *primordial* ancestors.

**primp** V. groom oneself with care; adorn oneself. The groom stood by idly while his nervous bride-to-be *primped* one last time before the mirror.

■ **pristine** ADJ. characteristic of earlier times; primitive, unspoiled. This area has been preserved in all its *pristine* wildness.

**privation** N. hardship; want. In his youth, he knew hunger and *privation*.

**privy** ADJ. secret; hidden; not public. We do not care for *privy* chamber government.

**probe** V. explore with tools. The surgeon *probed* the wound for foreign matter before suturing it. also N.

■ **probity** N. uprightness; incorruptibility. Everyone took his *probity* for granted; his defalcations, therefore, shocked us all.

■ **problematic** ADJ. doubtful; unsettled; questionable; perplexing. Given the way building costs have exceeded estimates for the job, whether the arena will ever be completed is *problematic*.

**proclivity** N. inclination; natural tendency. Watching the two-year-old voluntarily put away his toys, I was amazed by his *proclivity* for neatness.

**procrastinate** V. postpone; delay or put off. Looking at four years of receipts and checks he still had to sort through, Bob was truly sorry he had *procrastinated* for so long and had not finished filing his taxes long ago.

**procurement** N. obtaining. The personnel department handles the *procurement* of new employees.

**prod** V. poke; stir up; urge. If you *prod* him hard enough, he'll eventually clean his room.

■ **prodigal** ADJ. wasteful; reckless with money. Don't be so *prodigal* spending my money; when you've earned some money, you can waste as much of it as you want! also N.

**prodigious** ADJ. marvelous; enormous. Watching the champion weight lifter heave the weighty barbell to shoulder height and then boost it overhead, we marveled at his *prodigious* strength.

**prodigy** N. highly gifted child; marvel. Menuhin was a *prodigy*, performing wonders on his violin when he was barely eight years old.

**profane** V. violate; desecrate; treat unworthily. The members of the mysterious Far Eastern cult sought to kill the British explorer because he had *profaned* the sanctity of their holy goblet by using it as an ashtray. also ADJ.

**profligate** ADJ. dissipated; wasteful; wildly immoral. Although surrounded by wild and *profligate* companions, she managed to retain some sense of decency. also N. profligacy, N.

■ **profound** ADJ. deep; not superficial; complete. Freud's remarkable insights into human behavior caused his fellow scientists to honor him as a *profound* thinker. profundity, N.

**profusion** N. overabundance; lavish expenditure; excess. Freddy was so overwhelmed by the *profusion* of choices on the menu that he knocked over his wine glass and soaked his host. He made *profuse* apologies to his host, the waiter, the busboy, the people at the next table, and the man in the men's room giving out paper towels.

**progenitor** N. ancestor. The Roth family, whose *progenitors* emigrated from Germany early in the nineteenth century, settled in Peru, Illinois.

**progeny** N. children; offspring. He was proud of his *progeny* but regarded George as the most promising of all his children.

**prognosis** N. forecasted course of a disease; prediction. If the doctor's *prognosis* is correct, the patient will be in a coma for at least twenty-four hours.

**prognosticate** V. predict. I *prognosticate* disaster unless we change our wasteful ways.

■ **prohibitive** ADJ. tending to prevent the purchase or use of something; inclined to prevent or forbid. Susie wanted to buy a new Volvo but had to settle for a used Dodge because the new car's price was *prohibitive*. prohibition, N.

**projectile** N. missile. Man has always hurled *projectiles* at his enemy whether in the form of stones or of highly explosive shells.

**proletarian** N. member of the working class; blue collar guy. "Workers of the world, unite! You have nothing to lose but your chains" is addressed to *proletarians*, not preppies. also ADJ. proletariat, N.

■ **proliferate** V. grow rapidly; spread; multiply. Times of economic hardship inevitably encourage countless get-rich-quick schemes to *proliferate*. proliferation, N.

**prolific** ADJ. abundantly fruitful. She was a *prolific* writer who produced as many as three books a year.

**prolixity** N. tedious wordiness; verbosity. A writer who suffers from *prolixity* tells his readers everything they *never* wanted to know about his subject (or were too bored to ask). prolix, ADJ.

**prologue** N. introduction (to a poem or play). In the *prologue* to *Romeo and Juliet*, Shakespeare introduces the audience to the feud between the Montagues and the Capulets.

**prolong** V. extend; draw out; lengthen. In their determination to discover ways to *prolong* human life, doctors fail to take into account that longer lives are not always happier ones.

**prominent** ADJ. conspicuous; notable; protruding. Have you ever noticed that Prince Charles's *prominent* ears make him resemble the big-eared character in *Mad* comics?

**promiscuous** ADJ. mixed indiscriminately; haphazard; irregular, particularly sexually. In the opera *La Bohème*, we get a picture of the *promiscuous* life led by the young artists of Paris. promiscuity, N.

**promontory** N. headland. They erected a lighthouse on the *promontory* to warn approaching ships of their nearness to the shore.

**promote** V. help to flourish; advance in rank; publicize. Founder of the Children's Defense Fund, Marian Wright Edelman ceaselessly *promotes* the welfare of young people everywhere.

**prompt** V. cause; provoke; provide a cue for an actor. Whatever *prompted* you to ask for such a big piece of cake when you're on a diet?

**promulgate** V. proclaim a doctrine or law; make known by official publication. When Moses came down from the mountaintop prepared to *promulgate* God's commandments, he was appalled to discover his followers worshipping a golden calf.

**prone** ADJ. inclined to; prostrate. She was *prone* to sudden fits of anger during which she would lie *prone* on the floor, screaming and kicking her heels.

**propagate** V. multiply; spread. Since bacteria *propagate* more quickly in unsanitary environments, it is important to keep hospital rooms clean.

**propellant** N. substance that propels or drives forward. The development of our missile program has forced our scientists to seek more powerful *propellants*. also ADJ.

■ **propensity** N. natural inclination. Convinced of his own talent, Sol has an unfortunate *propensity* to belittle the talents of others.

**prophetic** ADJ. having to do with predicting the future. In interpreting Pharaoh's *prophetic* dream, Joseph said that the seven fat cows eaten by the seven lean cows represented seven years of plenty followed by seven years of famine. prophecy, N.

**prophylactic** ADJ. used to prevent disease. Despite all *prophylactic* measures introduced by the authorities, the epidemic raged until cool weather set in. prophylaxis, N.

**propinquity** N. nearness; kinship. Their relationship could not be explained as being based on mere *propinquity*. They were more than relatives; they were true friends.

■ **propitiate** V. appease. The natives offered sacrifices to *propitiate* the gods.

# Test

# Word List 37 *Antonyms*

Each of the following questions consists of a word in capital letters, followed by five lettered words or phrases. Choose the lettered word or phrase that is most nearly opposite in meaning to the word in capital letters and write the letter of your choice on your answer paper.

541. PRECIPITATE (A) dull (B) anticipatory (C) cautious (D) considerate (E) welcome

542. PREFATORY (A) outstanding (B) magnificent (C) conclusive (D) intelligent (E) predatory

543. PRELUDE (A) intermezzo (B) diva (C) aria (D) aftermath (E) duplication

544. PRESUMPTION (A) assertion (B) activation (C) motivation (D) proposition (E) humility

545. PRETENTIOUS (A) ominous (B) calm (C) unassuming (D) futile (E) volatile

546. PRIM (A) informal (B) prior (C) exterior (D) private (E) cautious

547. PRISTINE (A) cultivated (B) condemned (C) irreligious (D) cautious (E) critical

548. PROBITY (A) regret (B) assumption (C) corruptibility (D) extent (E) upswing

549. PRODIGAL (A) large (B) thrifty (C) consistent (D) compatible (E) remote

550. PRODIGIOUS (A) infinitesimal (B) indignant (C) indifferent (D) indisposed (E) insufficient

551. PROFANE (A) sanctify (B) desecrate (C) define (D) manifest (E) urge

552. PROLIFIC (A) unworkable (B) backward (C) barren (D) controversial (E) unfocused

553. PROLIX (A) stupid (B) indifferent (C) redundant (D) livid (E) pithy

554. PROPHYLACTIC (A) causing growth (B) causing disease (C) antagonistic (D) brushing (E) favorable

555. PROPINQUITY (A) remoteness (B) uniqueness (C) health (D) virtue (E) simplicity

# Word List 38    propitious-quarry

**propitious** ADJ. favorable; fortunate; advantageous. Chloe consulted her horoscope to see whether Tuesday would be a *propitious* day to dump her boyfriend.

**proponent** N. supporter; backer; opposite of *opponent*. In the Senate, *proponents* of the universal health care measure lobbied to gain additional support for the controversial legislation.

**propound** V. put forth for analysis. In your discussion, you have *propounded* several questions; let us consider each one separately.

■ **propriety** N. fitness; correct conduct. Miss Manners counsels her readers so that they may behave with *propriety* in any social situation and not embarrass themselves.

**propulsive** ADJ. driving forward. The jet plane has a greater *propulsive* power than the engine-driven plane.

**prosaic** ADJ. dull and unimaginative; matter-of-fact; factual. Though the ad writers had come up with a highly creative campaign to publicize the company's newest product, the head office rejected it for a more *prosaic*, down-to-earth approach.

**proscenium** N. part of stage in front of curtain. In the theater-in-the-round there can be no *proscenium* or *proscenium* arch. also ADJ.

■ **proscribe** V. ostracize; banish; outlaw. Antony, Octavius, and Lepidus *proscribed* all those who had conspired against Julius Caesar.

**proselytize** V. induce someone to convert to a religion or belief. In these interfaith meetings, there must be no attempt to *proselytize;* we must respect all points of view.

**prosody** N. the art of versification. This book on *prosody* contains a rhyming dictionary as well as samples of the various verse forms.

**prosperity** N. good fortune; financial success; physical well-being. Promising to stay together "for richer, for poorer," the newlyweds vowed to be true to one another in *prosperity* and hardship alike.

**prostrate** V. stretch out full on ground. He *prostrated* himself before the idol. also ADJ.

**protean** ADJ. versatile; able to take on many forms. A remarkably *protean* actor, Alec Guinness could take on any role.

**protégé** N. person receiving protection and support from a patron. Born with an independent spirit, Cyrano de Bergerac refused to be a *protégé* of Cardinal Richelieu.

**protocol** N. diplomatic etiquette. We must run this state dinner according to *protocol* if we are to avoid offending any of our guests.

**prototype** N. original work used as a model by others. The crude typewriter on display in this museum is the *prototype* of the elaborate machines in use today.

**protract** V. prolong. Seeking to delay the union members' vote, the management team tried to *protract* the negotiations endlessly, but the union representatives saw through their strategy.

**protrude** V. stick out. His fingers *protruded* from the holes in his gloves.

**protuberance** N. protrusion; bulge. A ganglionic cyst is a fluid-filled tumor (generally benign) that develops near a joint membrane or tendon sheath, and that bulges beneath the skin, forming a *protuberance*.

**provenance** N. origin or source of something. I am not interested in its *provenance;* I am more concerned with its usefulness than with its source.

**provender** N. dry food; fodder. I am not afraid of a severe winter because I have stored a large quantity of *provender* for the cattle.

**provident** ADJ. displaying foresight; thrifty; preparing for emergencies. In his usual *provident* manner, he had insured himself against this type of loss.

**provincial** ADJ. pertaining to a province; limited in outlook; unsophisticated. As *provincial* governor, Sir Henry administered the Queen's law in his remote corner of Canada. Caught up in local problems, out of touch with London news, he became sadly *provincial.*

**provisional** ADJ. tentative. Kim's acceptance as an American Express cardholder was *provisional*: before issuing her a card, American Express wanted to check her employment record and credit history.

**proviso** N. stipulation. I am ready to accept your proposal with the *proviso* that you meet your obligations within the next two weeks.

**provocative** ADJ. arousing anger or interest; annoying. In a typically *provocative* act, the bully kicked sand into the weaker man's face. provoke, V. provocation, N.

**prowess** N. extraordinary ability; military bravery. Performing triple axels and double lutzes at the age of six, the young figure skater was world famous for her *prowess* on the ice.

**proximity** N. nearness. Blind people sometimes develop a compensatory ability to sense the *proximity* of objects around them.

**proxy** N. authorized agent. Please act as my *proxy* and vote for this slate of candidates in my absence.

**prude** N. excessively modest or proper person. The X-rated film was definitely not for *prudes.*

**prudent** ADJ. cautious; careful. A miser hoards money not because he is *prudent* but because he is greedy. prudence, N.

**prune** V. cut away; trim. With the help of her editor, she was able to *prune* her manuscript into publishable form.

**prurient** ADJ. having or causing lustful thoughts and desires. Aroused by his *prurient* impulses, the dirty old man leered at the sweet young thing and offered to give her a sample of his "prowess"; his *prurience* appalled her.

**pry** V. inquire impertinently; use leverage to raise or open something. Though Nora claimed she didn't mean to *pry,* everyone knew she was just plain nosy. With a crowbar Long John Silver *pried* up the lid of the treasure chest.

**pseudonym** N. pen name. Samuel Clemens' *pseudonym* was Mark Twain.

**psyche** N. soul; mind. It is difficult to delve into the *psyche* of a human being.

**psychiatrist** N. a doctor who treats mental diseases. A *psychiatrist* often needs long conferences with his patient before a diagnosis can be made.

**psychopathic** ADJ. pertaining to mental derangement. The *psychopathic* patient suffers more frequently from a disorder of the nervous system than from a diseased brain.

**psychosis** N. mental disorder. We must endeavor to find an outlet for the patient's repressed desires if we hope to combat this *psychosis*. psychotic, ADJ.

**pterodactyl** N. extinct flying reptile. The remains of *pterodactyls* indicate that these flying reptiles had a wingspan of as much as twenty feet.

**puerile** ADJ. childish. His *puerile* pranks sometimes offended his more mature friends.

**pugilist** N. boxer. The famous *pugilist* Cassius Clay changed his name to Muhammed Ali.

**pugnacity** N. combativeness; disposition to fight. "Put up your dukes!" he cried, making a fist to show his *pugnacity*. pugnacious, ADJ.

**puissant** ADJ. powerful; strong; potent. We must keep his friendship for he will make a *puissant* ally.

**pulchritude** N. beauty; comeliness. I do not envy the judges who have to select this year's Miss America from this collection of female *pulchritude.*

**pulmonary** ADJ. pertaining to the lungs. In his researches on *pulmonary* diseases, he discovered many facts about the lungs of animals and human beings.

**pulsate** V. throb. We could see the blood vessels in his temple *pulsate* as he became more angry.

**pulverize** V. crush or grind into very small particles. Before sprinkling the dried herbs into the stew, Michael first *pulverized* them into a fine powder.

**pummel** V. beat or pound with fists. Swinging wildly, Pammy *pummeled* her brother around the head and shoulders.

**punctilious** ADJ. stressing niceties of conduct or form; minutely attentive (perhaps too much so) to fine points. Percy is *punctilious* about observing the rules of etiquette whenever Miss Manners invites him to stay. punctiliousness, N.

**pundit** N. authority on a subject; learned person; expert. Some authors who write about the GRE as if they are *pundits* actually know very little about the test.

■ **pungent** ADJ. stinging; sharp in taste or smell; caustic. The *pungent* odor of ripe Limburger cheese appealed to Simone but made Stanley gag. pungency, N.

**punitive** ADJ. punishing. He asked for *punitive* measures against the offender.

**puny** ADJ. insignificant; tiny; weak. Our *puny* efforts to stop the flood were futile.

**purchase** N. firm grasp or footing. The mountaineer struggled to get a proper *purchase* on the slippery rock.

**purgatory** N. place of spiritual expiation. In this *purgatory,* he could expect no help from his comrades.

**purge** V. remove or get rid of something unwanted; free from blame or guilt; cleanse or purify. The Communist government *purged* the party to get rid of members suspected of capitalist sympathies, sending those believed to be disloyal to labor camps in Siberia. also N.

**purport** N. intention; meaning. If the *purport* of your speech was to arouse the rabble, you succeeded admirably. also V.

**purported** ADJ. alleged; claimed; reputed or rumored. The *purported* Satanists sacrificing live roosters in the park turned out to be a party of Shriners holding a chicken barbecue.

**purse** V. pucker; contract into wrinkles. Miss Watson *pursed* her lips to show her disapproval of Huck's bedraggled appearance.

**purveyor** N. furnisher of foodstuffs; caterer. As *purveyor* of rare wines and viands, he traveled through France and Italy every year in search of new products to sell.

**pusillanimous** ADJ. cowardly; fainthearted. You should be ashamed of your *pusillanimous* conduct during this dispute. pusillanimity, N.

**putative** ADJ. supposed; reputed. Although there are some doubts, the *putative* author of this work is Massinger.

**putrid** ADJ. foul; rotten; decayed. When the doctor removed the bandages, the *putrid* smell indicated that the wound had turned gangrenous. putrescence, putrefaction, N.

**pylon** N. marking post to guide aviators; steel tower supporting cables or telephone lines. Amelia Earhart carefully banked her airplane as she followed the line of *pylons* set up to mark the course of the Great Plane Race.

**pyromaniac** N. person with an insane desire to set things on fire. The detectives searched the area for the *pyromaniac* who had set these costly fires.

**quack** N. charlatan; impostor. Do not be misled by the exorbitant claims of this *quack;* he cannot cure you.

**quadruped** N. four-footed animal. Most mammals are *quadrupeds*.

**quaff** V. drink with relish. As we *quaffed* our ale, we listened to the gay songs of the students in the tavern.

**quagmire** N. soft, wet, boggy land; complex or dangerous situation from which it is difficult to free oneself. Up to her knees in mud, Myra wondered how on earth she was going to extricate herself from this *quagmire*.

**quail** V. cower; lose heart. He was afraid that he would *quail* in the face of danger.

**quaint** ADJ. odd; old-fashioned; picturesque. Her *quaint* clothes and old-fashioned language marked her as an eccentric.

■ **qualified** ADJ. limited; restricted. Unable to give the candidate full support, the mayor gave him only a *qualified* endorsement. (secondary meaning)

**qualms** N. misgivings; uneasy fears, especially about matters of conscience. I have no *qualms* about giving this assignment to Helen; I know she will handle it admirably.

**quandary** N. dilemma. When both Harvard and Stanford accepted Laura, she was in a *quandary* as to which school she should attend.

**quarantine** N. isolation of a person, place, or ship to prevent spread of infection. We will have to place this house under *quarantine* until we determine the exact nature of the disease. also V.

**quarry** N. victim; object of a hunt. The police closed in on their *quarry*.

**quarry** V. dig into. They *quarried* blocks of marble out of the hillside.

# Test

## Word List 38    *Antonyms*

Each of the questions below consists of a word in capital letters, followed by five lettered words or phrases. Choose the lettered word or phrase that is most nearly opposite in meaning to the word in capital letters and write the letter of your choice on your answer paper.

556. PROPITIOUS (A) rich (B) induced (C) promoted (D) indicative (E) unfavorable

557. PROSAIC (A) pacified (B) reprieved (C) pensive (D) imaginative (E) rhetorical

558. PROTEAN (A) amateur (B) catholic (C) unchanging (D) rapid (E) unfavorable

559. PROTRACT (A) make circular (B) shorten (C) further (D) retrace (E) involve

560. PROVIDENT (A) unholy (B) rash (C) miserable (D) disabled (E) remote

561. PROVINCIAL (A) wealthy (B) crass (C) literary (D) aural (E) sophisticated

562. PSYCHOTIC (A) dangerous (B) clairvoyant (C) criminal (D) soulful (E) sane

563. PUERILE (A) fragrant (B) adult (C) lonely (D) feminine (E) masterly

564. PUGNACIOUS (A) pacific (B) feline (C) mature (D) angular (E) inactive

565. PUISSANT (A) pouring (B) fashionable (C) articulate (D) healthy (E) weak

566. PULCHRITUDE (A) ugliness (B) notoriety (C) bestiality (D) masculinity (E) servitude

567. PUNCTILIOUS (A) happy (B) active (C) vivid (D) careless (E) futile

568. PUNITIVE (A) large (B) humorous (C) rewarding (D) restive (E) languishing

569. PUSILLANIMOUS (A) poverty-stricken (B) chained (C) posthumous (D) courageous (E) strident

570. PUTATIVE (A) colonial (B) quarrelsome (C) undisputed (D) powerful (E) unremarkable

# Word List 39    quash-recurrent

**quash** v. subdue; crush; squash. The authorities acted quickly to *quash* the student rebellion, sending in tanks to cow the demonstrators.

**quay** N. dock; landing place. Because of the captain's carelessness, the ship crashed into the *quay*.

**queasy** ADJ. easily nauseated; squeamish. Remember that great chase movie, the one with the carsick passenger? That's right: *Queasy Rider*!

**quell** v. extinguish; put down; quiet. Miss Minchin's demeanor was so stern and forbidding that she could *quell* any unrest among her students with one intimidating glance.

**quench** v. douse or extinguish; assuage or satisfy. What's the favorite song of the Fire Department? "Baby, *Quench* My Fire!" After Bob ate the heavily salted popcorn, he had to drink a pitcherful of water to *quench* his thirst.

**querulous** ADJ. fretful; whining. Even the most agreeable toddlers can begin to act *querulous* if they miss their nap.

**query** N. inquiry; question. In her column "Ask Beth," the columnist invites young readers to send their *queries* about life and love to her. also v.

**queue** N. line. They stood patiently in the *queue* outside the movie theatre.

■ **quibble** N. minor objection or complaint. Aside from a few hundred teensy-weensy *quibbles* about the set, the script, the actors, the director, the costumes, the lighting, and the props, the hypercritical critic loved the play. also v.

■ **quiescent** ADJ. at rest; dormant; temporarily inactive. After the devastating eruption, fear of Mount Etna was great; people did not return to cultivate its rich hillside lands until the volcano had been *quiescent* for a full two years. quiescence, N.

**quietude** N. tranquillity. He was impressed by the air of *quietude* and peace that pervaded the valley.

**quintessence** N. purest and highest embodiment. Noel Coward displayed the *quintessence* of wit.

**quip** N. taunt. You are unpopular because you are too free with your *quips* and sarcastic comments. also v.

**quirk** N. startling twist; caprice, By a *quirk* of fate, he found himself working for the man whom he had discharged years before.

**quisling** N. traitor who aids invaders. In his conquest of Europe, Hitler was aided by the *quislings* who betrayed their own people and served in the puppet governments established by the Nazis.

**quiver** N. case for arrows. Robin Hood reached back and plucked one last arrow from his *quiver*. (secondary meaning)

**quiver** v. tremble; shake. The bird dog's nose twitched and his whiskers *quivered* as he strained eagerly against the leash. also N.

**quixotic** ADJ. idealistic but impractical. Constantly coming up with *quixotic*, unworkable schemes to save the world, Simon has his heart in the right place, but his head is somewhere off in the clouds.

**quizzical** ADJ. teasing; bantering; mocking; curious. When the skinny teenager tripped over his own feet stepping into the bullpen, Coach raised one *quizzical* eyebrow, shook his head, and said, "Okay, kid. You're here; let's see what you've got."

**quorum** N. number of members necessary to conduct a meeting. The senator asked for a roll call to determine whether a *quorum* was present.

**quotidian** ADJ. daily; commonplace; customary. To Philip, each new day of his internship was filled with excitement; he could not dismiss his rounds as merely *quotidian* routine.

**rabid** ADJ. like a fanatic; furious. He was a *rabid* follower of the Dodgers and watched them play whenever he could go to the ballpark.

**raconteur** N. story-teller. My father was a gifted *raconteur* with an unlimited supply of anecdotes.

**ragamuffin** N. person wearing tattered clothes. He felt sorry for the *ragamuffin* who was begging for food and gave him money to buy a meal.

**rail** v. scold; rant. You may *rail* at him all you want; you will never change him.

**raiment** N. clothing. "How can I go to the ball?" asked Cinderella. "I have no *raiment* fit to wear."

**rakish** ADJ. stylish; sporty. He wore his hat at a *rakish* and jaunty angle.

**rally** v. call up or summon (forces, vital powers, etc.); revive or recuperate. Washington quickly *rallied* his troops to fight off the British attack. The patient had been sinking throughout the night, but at dawn she *rallied* and made a complete recovery. also N.

**ramble** v. wander aimlessly (physically or mentally). Listening to the teacher *ramble*, Judy wondered whether he'd ever get to his point. also N.

**ramification** N. branching out; subdivision. We must examine all the *ramifications* of this problem.

**ramify** v. divide into branches or subdivisions. When the plant begins to *ramify*, it is advisable to nip off most of the new branches.

**ramp** N. slope; inclined plane. The house was built with *ramps* instead of stairs in order to enable the man in the wheelchair to move easily from room to room and floor to floor.

**rampant** ADJ. growing in profusion; unrestrained. The *rampant* weeds in the garden choked the asters and marigolds until the flowers died. rampancy, N.

**rampart** N. defensive mound of earth. "From the *ramparts* we watched" as the fighting continued.

**ramshackle** ADJ. rickety; falling apart. The boys propped up the *ramshackle* clubhouse with a couple of boards.

**rancid** ADJ. having the odor of stale fat. A *rancid* odor filled the ship's galley and nauseated the crew.

**rancor** N. bitterness; hatred. Thirty years after the war, she could not let go of the past but was still consumed with *rancor* against the foe. rancorous, ADJ.

**random** ADJ. without definite purpose, plan, or aim; haphazard. Although the sponsor of the raffle claimed all winners were chosen at *random,* people had their suspicions when the grand prize went to the sponsor's brother-in-law.

**rankle** V. irritate; fester. The memory of having been jilted *rankled* him for years.

**rant** V. rave; talk excitedly; scold; make a grandiloquent speech. When he heard that I'd totaled the family car, Dad began to *rant* at me like a complete madman.

**rapacious** ADJ. excessively grasping; plundering. Hawks and other *rapacious* birds prey on a variety of small animals.

**rapport** N. emotional closeness; harmony. In team teaching, it is important that all teachers in the group have good *rapport* with one another.

**rapt** ADJ. absorbed; enchanted. Caught up in the wonder of the storyteller's tale, the *rapt* listeners sat motionless, hanging on his every word.

■ **rarefied** ADJ. made less dense [of a gas]. The mountain climbers had difficulty breathing in the *rarefied* atmosphere. rarefy, V. rarefaction, N.

**raspy** ADJ. grating; harsh. The sergeant's *raspy* voice grated on the recruits' ears.

**ratify** V. approve formally; confirm; verify. Party leaders doubted that they had enough votes in both houses of Congress to *ratify* the constitutional amendment.

**ratiocination** N. reasoning; act of drawing conclusions from premises. While Watson was a man of average intelligence, Holmes was a genius, whose gift for *ratiocination* made him a superb detective.

**rationale** N. fundamental reason or justification; grounds for an action. Her need for a vehicle large enough to accommodate five children and a Saint Bernard was Judy's *rationale* for buying a minivan.

**rationalize** V. give a plausible reason for an action in place of a true, less admirable one; offer an excuse. When David refused gabby Gabrielle a ride to the dance because, he said, he had no room in the car, he was *rationalizing*; actually, he couldn't stand being cooped up in a car with anyone who talked as much as she did. rationalization, N.

**raucous** ADJ. harsh and shrill; disorderly and boisterous. The *raucous* crowd of New Year's Eve revelers grew progressively noisier as midnight drew near.

**ravage** V. plunder; despoil. The marauding army *ravaged* the countryside.

**rave** N. overwhelmingly favorable review. Though critic John Simon seldom has a good word to say about contemporary plays, his review of *All in the Timing* was a total *rave.*

**ravel** V. fall apart into tangles; unravel or untwist; entangle. A single thread pulled loose, and the entire scarf started to *ravel.*

**ravenous** ADJ. extremely hungry. The *ravenous* dog upset several garbage pails in its search for food.

**ravine** N. narrow valley with steep sides. Steeper than a gully, less precipitous than a canyon, a *ravine* is, like them, the product of years of erosion.

**raze** V. destroy completely. Spelling matters: to raise a building is to put it up; to *raze* a building is to tear it down.

**reactionary** ADJ. opposing progress; politically ultraconservative. Opposing the use of English in worship services, *reactionary* forces in the church fought to reinstate the mass in Latin. also N.

**realm** N. kingdom; field or sphere. In the animal *realm,* the lion is the king of beasts.

**reaper** N. one who harvests grain. Death, the Grim *Reaper,* cuts down mortal men and women, just as a farmer cuts down the ripened grain.

**rebate** N. discount. We offer a *rebate* of ten percent to those who pay cash.

**rebuff** V. snub; beat back. She *rebuffed* his invitation so smoothly that he did not realize he had been snubbed. also N.

**rebuke** V. scold harshly; criticize severely. No matter how sharply Miss Watson *rebuked* Huck for his misconduct, he never talked back but just stood there like a stump. also N.

**rebus** N. puzzle in which pictures stand for words. A coven of witches beside a tree is a possible *rebus* for the town Coventry.

**rebuttal** N. refutation; response with contrary evidence. The defense lawyer confidently listened to the prosecutor sum up his case, sure that she could answer his arguments in her *rebuttal.*

■ **recalcitrant** ADJ. obstinately stubborn; determined to resist authority; unruly. Which animal do you think is more *recalcitrant*, a pig or a mule?

■ **recant** V. disclaim or disavow; retract a previous statement; openly confess error. Hoping to make Joan of Arc *recant* her sworn testimony, her English captors tried to convince her that her visions had been sent to her by the Devil.

**recapitulate** V. summarize. Let us *recapitulate* what has been said thus far before going ahead.

**recast** V. reconstruct (a sentence, story, etc.); fashion again. Let me *recast* this sentence in terms your feeble brain can grasp: in words of one syllable, you are a fool.

**receptive** ADJ. quick or willing to receive ideas, suggestions, etc. Adventure-loving Huck Finn proved a *receptive* audience for Tom's tales of buried treasure and piracy.

**recession** N. withdrawal; retreat; time of low economic activity. The slow *recession* of the flood waters created problems for the crews working to restore power to the area.

**recidivism** N. habitual return to crime. Prison reformers in the United States are disturbed by the high rate of *recidivism;* the number of persons serving second and third terms indicates the failure of the prisons to rehabilitate the inmates.

**recipient** N. receiver. Although he had been the *recipient* of many favors, he was not grateful to his benefactor.

**reciprocal** ADJ. mutual; exchangeable; interacting. The two nations signed a *reciprocal* trade agreement.

**reciprocate** V. repay in kind. If they attack us, we shall be compelled to *reciprocate* and bomb their territory. reciprocity, N.

■ **recluse** N. hermit; loner. Disappointed in love, Miss Emily became a *recluse*; she shut herself away in her empty mansion and refused to see another living soul. reclusive, ADJ.

**reconcile** V. correct inconsistencies; become friendly after a quarrel. Every time we try to *reconcile* our checkbook with the bank statement, we quarrel. However, despite these monthly lovers' quarrels, we always manage to *reconcile*.

■ **recondite** ADJ. abstruse; profound; secret. He read many *recondite* books in order to obtain the material for his scholarly thesis.

**reconnaissance** N. survey of enemy by soldiers; reconnoitering. If you encounter any enemy soldiers during your *reconnaissance,* capture them for questioning.

**recount** V. narrate or tell; count over again. About to *recount* the latest adventure of Sherlock Holmes, Watson lost track of exactly how many cases Holmes had solved and refused to begin his tale until he'd *recounted* them one by one.

**recourse** N. resorting to help when in trouble. The boy's only *recourse* was to appeal to his father for aid.

**recrimination** N. countercharges. Loud and angry *recriminations* were her answer to his accusations.

**rectify** V. set right; correct. You had better send a check to *rectify* your account before American Express cancels your credit card.

**rectitude** N. uprightness; moral virtue; correctness of judgment. The Eagle Scout was a model of *rectitude*; smugness was the only flaw he needed to correct.

**recumbent** ADJ. reclining; lying down completely or in part. The command "AT EASE" does not permit you to take a *recumbent* position.

**recuperate** V. recover. The doctors were worried because the patient did not *recuperate* as rapidly as they had expected.

**recurrent** ADJ. occurring again and again. These *recurrent* attacks disturbed us and we consulted a physician.

# Test

## Word List 39    *Synonyms and Antonyms*

Each of the questions below consists of a word in capital letters, followed by five lettered words or phrases. Choose the lettered word or phrase that is most nearly similar or opposite in meaning to the word in capital letters and write the letter of your choice on your answer paper.

571. QUEASY (A) toxic (B) easily upset (C) chronic
     (D) choleric (E) false

572. QUELL (A) boast (B) incite (C) reverse (D) wet
     (E) answer

573. QUIXOTIC (A) rapid (B) exotic (C) longing
     (D) timid (E) idealistic

574. RAGAMUFFIN (A) dandy (B) miser
     (C) exotic dance (D) light snack (E) baker

575. RAUCOUS (A) mellifluous (B) uncooked
     (C) realistic (D) veracious (E) anticipating

576. RAVAGE (A) rankle (B) revive (C) plunder
     (D) pillory (E) age

577. RAZE (A) shave (B) heckle (C) finish
     (D) tear down (E) write

578. REACTIONARY (A) conservative (B) retrograde
     (C) dramatist (D) militant (E) chemical

579. REBATE (A) relinquish (B) settle (C) discount
     (D) cancel (E) elicit

580. RECALCITRANT (A) grievous (B) secretive
     (C) cowardly (D) thoughtful (E) cooperative

581. RECLUSE (A) learned scholar (B) mocker
     (C) social person (D) careful worker (E) daredevil

582. RECONDITE (A) unfriendly (B) easily
     comprehensible (C) closely juxtaposed
     (D) broadminded (E) sardonic

583. RECTIFY (A) remedy (B) avenge (C) create
     (D) assemble (E) attribute

584. RECUPERATE (A) reenact (B) engage
     (C) recapitulate (D) recover (E) encounter

585. RECURRENT (A) happening repeatedly
     (B) flowing backward (C) healing quickly
     (D) eventful (E) timely

# Word List 40    redolent-requite

**redolent** ADJ. fragrant; odorous; suggestive of an odor. Even though it is February, the air is *redolent* of spring.

**redoubtable** ADJ. formidable; causing fear. During the Cold War period, neighboring countries tried not to offend the Russians because they could be *redoubtable* foes.

**redress** N. remedy; compensation. Do you mean to tell me that I can get no *redress* for my injuries? also V.

**redundant** ADJ. superfluous; repetitious; excessively wordy. The bottle of wine I brought to Bob's party was certainly *redundant*: how was I to know Bob owned a winery? In your essay, you repeat several points unnecessarily; try to avoid *redundancy* in the future.

**reek** V. emit (odor). The room *reeked* with stale tobacco smoke. also N.

**refectory** N. dining hall. In this huge *refectory,* we can feed the entire student body at one sitting.

**refraction** N. bending of a ray of light. When you look at a stick inserted in water, it looks bent because of the *refraction* of the light by the water.

■ **refractory** ADJ. stubborn; unmanageable. The *refractory* horse was eliminated from the race when he refused to obey the jockey.

**refrain** V. abstain from; resist. N. chorus. Whenever he heard a song with a lively chorus, Sol could never *refrain* from joining in on the *refrain.*

**refulgent** ADJ. brightly shining; gleaming. The squire polished the knight's armor until it gleamed in the light like the *refulgent* moon.

**refurbish** V. renovate; make bright by polishing. The flood left a deposit of mud on everything; it was necessary to *refurbish* our belongings.

■ **refute** V. disprove. The defense called several respectable witnesses who were able to *refute* the false testimony of the prosecution's only witness. refutation, N.

**regal** ADJ. royal. Prince Albert had a *regal* manner.

**regale** V. entertain. John *regaled* us with tales of his adventures in Africa.

**regatta** N. boat or yacht race. Many boating enthusiasts followed the *regatta* in their own yachts.

**regeneration** N. spiritual rebirth. Modern penologists strive for the *regeneration* of the prisoners.

**regicide** N. murder of a king or queen. The beheading of Mary Queen of Scots was an act of *regicide.*

**regime** N. method or system of government. When a Frenchman mentions the Old *Regime,* he refers to the government existing before the revolution.

**regimen** N. prescribed diet and habits. I doubt whether the results warrant our living under such a strict *regimen.*

**rehabilitate** V. restore to proper condition. We must *rehabilitate* those whom we send to prison.

**reimburse** V. repay. Let me know what you have spent and I will *reimburse* you.

**reiterate** V. repeat. She *reiterated* the warning to make sure everyone understood it.

**rejoinder** N. retort; comeback; reply. When someone has been rude to me, I find it particularly satisfying to come up with a quick *rejoinder.*

**rejuvenate** V. make young again. The charlatan claimed that his elixir would *rejuvenate* the aged and weary.

■ **relegate** V. banish to an inferior position; delegate; assign. After Ralph dropped his second tray of drinks that week, the manager swiftly *relegated* him to a minor post cleaning up behind the bar.

**relent** V. give in. When her stern father would not *relent* and allow her to marry Robert Browning, Elizabeth Barrett eloped with her suitor. relentless, ADJ.

**relevant** ADJ. pertinent; referring to the case in hand. Teri was impressed by how *relevant* Virginia Woolf's remarks were to her as a woman writer; it was as if Woolf had been writing with Teri's situation in mind. relevance, N. relevancy, N.

**relic** N. surviving remnant; memento. Egypt's Department of Antiquities prohibits tourists from taking mummies and other ancient *relics* out of the country. Mike keeps his photos of his trip to Egypt in a box with other *relics* of his travels.

**relinquish** V. give up something with reluctance; yield. Once you get used to fringe benefits like expense-account meals and a company car, it's very hard to *relinquish* them.

**relish** V. savor; enjoy. Watching Peter enthusiastically chow down, I thought, "Now there's a man who *relishes* a good dinner!" also N.

**remediable** ADJ. reparable. Let us be grateful that the damage is *remediable.*

**reminiscence** N. recollection. Her *reminiscences* of her experiences are so fascinating that she ought to write a book.

**remiss** ADJ. negligent. When the prisoner escaped, the guard was accused of being *remiss* in his duty.

**remission** N. temporary moderation of disease symptoms; cancellation of a debt; forgiveness or pardon. Though Senator Tsongas had been treated for cancer, his symptoms were in *remission,* and he was considered fit to handle the strains of a presidential race.

**remnant** N. remainder. I suggest that you wait until the store places the *remnants* of these goods on sale.

**remonstrance** N. protest; objection. The authorities were deaf to the pastor's *remonstrances* about the lack of police protection in the area. remonstrate, V.

**remorse** N. guilt; self-reproach. The murderer felt no *remorse* for his crime.

**remunerative** ADJ. compensating; rewarding. I find my new work so *remunerative* that I may not return to my previous employment. remuneration, N.

**rend** V. split; tear apart. In his grief, he tried to *rend* his garments. rent, N.

**render** V. deliver; provide; represent. He *rendered* aid to the needy and indigent.

**rendezvous** N. meeting place. The two fleets met at the *rendezvous* at the appointed time. also V.

**rendition** N. translation; artistic interpretation of a song, etc. The audience cheered enthusiastically as she completed her *rendition* of the aria.

**renegade** N. deserter; traitor. Because he had abandoned his post and joined forces with the Indians, his fellow officers considered the hero of *Dances with Wolves* a *renegade*. also ADJ.

**renege** V. deny; go back on. He *reneged* on paying off his debt.

**renounce** V. abandon; disown; repudiate. Even though she knew she would be burned at the stake as a witch, Joan of Arc refused to *renounce* her belief that her voices came from God. renunciation, N.

**renovate** V. restore to good condition; renew. They claim that they can *renovate* worn shoes so that they look like new ones.

**renown** N. fame. For many years an unheralded researcher, Barbara McClintock gained international *renown* when she won the Nobel Prize in Physiology and Medicine. renowned, ADJ.

**rent** N. rip; split. Kit did an excellent job of mending the *rent* in the lining of her coat. rend, V.

**reparable** ADJ. capable of being repaired. Fortunately, the damages we suffered in the accident were *reparable* and our car looks brand new.

**reparation** N. amends; compensation. At the peace conference, the defeated country promised to pay *reparations* to the victors.

**repartee** N. clever reply. He was famous for his witty *repartee* and his sarcasm.

**repast** N. meal; feast; banquet. The caterers prepared a delicious *repast* for Fred and Judy's wedding day.

**repeal** V. revoke; annul. What would the effect on our society be if we decriminalized drug use by *repealing* the laws against the possession and sale of narcotics?

**repel** V. drive away; disgust. At first, the Beast's ferocious appearance *repelled* Beauty, but she came to love the tender heart hidden behind that beastly exterior.

**repellent** ADJ. driving away; unattractive. Mosquitoes find the odor so *repellent* that they leave any spot where this liquid has been sprayed. also N.

**repercussion** N. rebound; reverberation; reaction. I am afraid that this event will have serious *repercussions*.

**repertoire** N. list of works of music, drama, etc., a performer is prepared to present. The opera company decided to include *Madame Butterfly* in its *repertoire* for the following season.

**repine** V. fret; complain. There is no sense *repining* over the work you have left undone.

**replenish** V. fill up again. Before she could take another backpacking trip, Carla had to *replenish* her stock of freeze-dried foods.

**replete** ADJ. filled to the brim or to the point of being stuffed; abundantly supplied. The movie star's memoir was *replete* with juicy details about the love life of half of Hollywood.

**replica** N. copy. Are you going to hang this *replica* of the Declaration of Independence in the classroom or in the auditorium?

**replicate** V. reproduce; duplicate. Because he had always wanted a palace, Donald decided to *replicate* the Taj Mahal in miniature on his estate.

**repository** N. storehouse. Libraries are *repositories* of the world's best thoughts.

**reprehensible** ADJ. deserving blame. Shocked by the viciousness of the bombing, politicians of every party uniformly condemned the terrorists' *reprehensible* deed.

**repress** V. restrain; crush; oppress. Anne's parents tried to curb her impetuosity without *repressing* her boundless high spirits.

**reprieve** N. temporary stay. During the twenty-four-hour *reprieve*, the lawyers sought to make the stay of execution permanent. also V.

**reprimand** V. reprove severely; rebuke. Every time Ermengarde made a mistake in class, she was afraid that Miss Minchin would *reprimand* her and tell her father how badly she was doing in school. also N.

**reprisal** N. retaliation. I am confident that we are ready for any *reprisals* the enemy may undertake.

**reprise** N. musical repetition; repeat performance; recurrent action. We enjoyed the soprano's solo in Act I so much that we were delighted by its *reprise* in the finale. At Waterloo, it was not the effect of any one skirmish that exhausted Colonel Audley; rather, it was the cumulative effect of the constant *reprises* that left him spent.

■ **reproach** V. express disapproval or disappointment. He never could do anything wrong without imagining how the look on his mother's face would *reproach* him afterwards. also N. reproachful, ADJ.

■ **reprobate** N. person hardened in sin, devoid of a sense of decency. I cannot understand why he has so many admirers if he is the *reprobate* you say he is.

**reprobation** N. severe disapproval. The students showed their *reprobation* of his act by refusing to talk with him.

**reprove** V. censure; rebuke. Though Aunt Bea at times would *reprove* Opie for inattention in church, she believed he was at heart a God-fearing lad. reproof, N.

■ **repudiate** V. disown; disavow. On separating from Tony, Tina announced that she would *repudiate* all debts incurred by her soon-to-be ex-husband.

**repugnance** N. loathing. She looked at the snake with *repugnance*.

**repulsion** N. distaste; act of driving back. Hating bloodshed, she viewed war with *repulsion*. Even defensive battles distressed her, for the *repulsion* of enemy forces is never accomplished bloodlessly. repulse, V.

**reputable** ADJ. respectable. If you want to buy antiques, look for a *reputable* dealer; far too many dealers today pass off fakes as genuine antiques.

**reputed** ADJ. supposed. He is the *reputed* father of the child. repute, V. repute, N.

**requiem** N. mass for the dead; dirge. They played Mozart's *Requiem* at the funeral.

**requisite** N. necessary requirement. Many colleges state that a student must offer three years of a language as a *requisite* for admission.

**requite** V. repay; revenge. The wretch *requited* his benefactors by betraying them.

# Test

## Word List 40    *Synonyms*

Each of the questions below consists of a word in capital letters, followed by five lettered words or phrases. Choose the lettered word or phrase that is most nearly similar in meaning to the word in capital letters and write the letter of your choice on your answer paper.

586. REFRACTORY (A) articulate (B) sinkable
(C) vaunted (D) useless (E) unmanageable

587. REGAL (A) oppressive (B) royal (C) major
(D) basic (E) entertaining

588. REITERATE (A) gainsay (B) revive (C) revenge
(D) repeat (E) return

589. RELISH (A) desire (B) nibble (C) savor
(D) vindicate (E) avail

590. REMISS (A) lax (B) lost (C) foolish (D) violating
(E) ambitious

591. REMONSTRATE (A) display (B) restate (C) protest
(D) resign (E) reiterate

592. REPARTEE (A) witty retort (B) willful departure
(C) spectator (D) monologue (E) sacrifice

593. REPELLENT (A) propulsive (B) unattractive
(C) porous (D) stiff (E) elastic

594. REPERCUSSION (A) reaction (B) restitution
(C) resistance (D) magnificence (E) acceptance

595. REPLENISH (A) polish (B) repeat (C) reinstate
(D) refill (E) refuse

596. REPLICA (A) museum piece (B) famous site
(C) battle emblem (D) facsimile (E) replacement

597. REPRISAL (A) reevaluation (B) assessment
(C) loss (D) retaliation (E) nonsense

598. REPROVE (A) prevail (B) rebuke (C) ascertain
(D) prove false (E) draw back

599. REPUDIATE (A) besmirch (B) appropriate
(C) annoy (D) reject (E) avow

600. REPUGNANCE (A) belligerence (B) tenacity
(C) renewal (D) pity (E) loathing

## Word List 41    rescind-sacrosanct

■ **rescind** V. cancel. Because of the public outcry against the new taxes, the senator proposed a bill to *rescind* the unpopular financial measure.

**resentment** N. indignation; bitterness; displeasure. Not wanting to appear a sore loser, Bill tried to hide his *resentment* of Barry's success.

**reserve** N. self-control; formal but distant manner. Although some girls were attracted by Mark's *reserve*, Judy was put off by it, for she felt his aloofness indicated a lack of openness. reserved, ADJ.

**residue** N. remainder; balance. In his will, he requested that after payment of debts, taxes, and funeral expenses, the *residue* be given to his wife.

**resignation** N. patient submissiveness; statement that one is quitting a job. If Bob Cratchit had not accepted Scrooge's bullying with timid *resignation,* he might have gotten up the nerve to hand in his *resignation*. resigned, ADJ.

**resilient** ADJ. elastic; having the power of springing back. Highly *resilient,* steel makes excellent bedsprings. resilience, N.

■ **resolution** N. determination. Nothing could shake his *resolution* to succeed despite all difficulties. resolute, ADJ.

■ **resolve** N. determination; firmness of purpose. How dare you question my *resolve* to take up sky-diving! Of course I haven't changed my mind! also V.

**resolve** V. decide; settle; solve. Holmes *resolved* to travel to Bohemia to resolve the dispute between Irene Adler and the King.

**resonant** ADJ. echoing; resounding; deep and full in sound. The deep, *resonant* voice of the actor James Earl Jones makes him particularly effective when he appears on stage.

**respiration** N. breathing; exhalation. The doctor found that the patient's years of smoking had adversely affected both his lung capacity and his rate of *respiration*.

**respite** N. interval of relief; time for rest; delay in punishment. For David, the two weeks vacationing in New Zealand were a delightful *respite* from the pressures of his job.

**resplendent** ADJ. dazzling; glorious; brilliant. While all the adults were commenting how glorious the emperor looked in his *resplendent* new clothes, one little boy was heard to say, "But he's naked!"

**responsiveness** N. state of reacting readily to appeals, orders, etc. The audience cheered and applauded, delighting the performers by its *responsiveness.*

**restitution** N. reparation; indemnification. He offered to make *restitution* for the window broken by his son.

**restive** ADJ. restlessly impatient; obstinately resisting control. Waiting impatiently in line to see Santa Claus, even the best-behaved children grow *restive* and start to fidget.

**restraint** N. moderation or self-control; controlling force; restriction. Show some *restraint,* young lady! Three desserts is quite enough!

**resumption** N. taking up again; recommencement. During the summer break, Don had not realized how much he missed university life: at the *resumption* of classes, however, he felt marked excitement and pleasure. resume, V.

**resurge** V. rise again; flow to and fro. It was startling to see the spirit of nationalism *resurge* as the Soviet Union disintegrated into a loose federation of ethnic and national groups. resurgence, N. resurgent, ADJ.

**resuscitate** V. revive. The lifeguard tried to *resuscitate* the drowned child by applying artificial respiration.

**retain** V. keep; employ. Fighting to *retain* his seat in Congress, Senator Foghorn *retained* a new manager to head his reelection campaign.

**retaliation** V. repayment in kind (usually for bad treatment). Because everyone knew the Princeton band had stolen Brown's mascot, the whole Princeton student body expected some sort of *retaliation* from Brown. retaliate, V.

**retentive** ADJ. holding; having a good memory. The pupil did not need to spend much time in study as he had a *retentive* mind.

■ **reticent** ADJ. reserved; uncommunicative; inclined to silence. Fearing his competitors might get advance word about his plans from talkative staff members, Hughes preferred *reticent* employees to loquacious ones. reticence, N.

**retinue** N. following; attendants. The queen's *retinue* followed her down the aisle.

**retiring** ADJ. modest; shy. Given Susan's *retiring* personality, no one expected her to take up public speaking; surprisingly enough, she became a star of the school debate team.

**retort** N. quick, sharp reply. Even when it was advisable for her to keep her mouth shut, she was always ready with a *retort.* also V.

**retract** V. withdraw; take back. When I saw how Fred and his fraternity brothers had trashed the frat house, I decided to *retract* my offer to let them use our summer cottage for the weekend. retraction, N.

**retrench** V. cut down; economize. If they were to be able to send their children to college, they would have to *retrench.*

**retribution** N. vengeance; compensation; punishment for offenses. The evangelist maintained that an angry deity would exact *retribution* from the sinners.

**retrieve** V. recover; find and bring in. The dog was intelligent and quickly learned to *retrieve* the game killed by the hunter. retrieval, N.

**retroactive** ADJ. taking effect before its enactment (as a law) or imposition (as a tax). Because the new pension law was *retroactive* to the first of the year, even though Martha had retired in February she was eligible for the pension.

**retrograde** V. go backwards; degenerate. Instead of advancing, our civilization seems to have *retrograded* in ethics and culture. also ADJ.

**retrospective** ADJ. looking back on the past. The Museum of Graphic Arts is holding a *retrospective* showing of the paintings of Michael Whelan over the past two decades. also N. retrospection, N.

**revelry** N. boisterous merrymaking. New Year's Eve is a night of *revelry.*

**reverberate** V. echo; resound. The entire valley *reverberated* with the sound of the church bells.

■ **reverent** ADJ. respectful; worshipful. Though I bow my head in church and recite the prayers, sometimes I don't feel properly *reverent.* revere, V. reverence, N.

**reverie** N. daydream; musing. She was awakened from her *reverie* by the teacher's question.

**revert** V. relapse; backslide; turn back to. Most of the time Andy seemed sensitive and mature, but occasionally he would *revert* to his smart-alecky, macho, adolescent self. reversion, N.

**revile** V. attack with abusive language; vilify. Though most of his contemporaries *reviled* Captain Kidd as a notorious, bloody-handed pirate, some of his fellow merchant-captains believed him innocent of his alleged crimes.

**revoke** V. cancel; retract. Repeat offenders who continue to drive under the influence of alcohol face having their driver's licenses permanently *revoked.* revocation, N.

**revulsion** N. sudden violent change of feeling; negative reaction. Many people in this country who admired dictatorships underwent a *revulsion* when they realized what Hitler and Mussolini were trying to do.

**rhapsodize** V. to speak or write in an exaggeratedly enthusiastic manner. She greatly enjoyed her Hawaiian vacation and *rhapsodized* about it for weeks.

**rhetoric** N. art of effective communication; insincere or grandiloquent language. All writers, by necessity, must be skilled in *rhetoric.* rhetorical, ADJ.

**ribald** ADJ. wanton; profane. He sang a *ribald* song that offended many of the more prudish listeners. ribaldry, N.

**riddle** V. pierce with holes; permeate or spread throughout. With his machine gun, Tracy *riddled* the car with bullets till it looked like a slice of Swiss cheese. During the proofreaders' strike, the newspaper was *riddled* with typos.

**rider** N. amendment or clause added to a legislative bill. Senator Foghorn said he would support Senator Filibuster's tax reform bill only if Filibuster agreed to add an antipollution *rider* to the bill.

**rife** ADJ. abundant; current. In the face of the many rumors of scandal, which are *rife* at the moment, it is best to remain silent.

**rift** N. opening; break. The plane was lost in the stormy sky until the pilot saw the city through a *rift* in the clouds.

**rig** V. fix or manipulate. The ward boss was able to *rig* the election by bribing people to stuff the ballot boxes with ballots marked in his candidate's favor.

**rigid** ADJ. stiff and unyielding; strict; hard and unbending. By living with a man to whom she was not married, George Eliot broke Victorian society's most *rigid* rule of respectable behavior.

**rigor** N. severity. Many settlers could not stand the *rigors* of the New England winters.

**rile** V. vex; irritate; muddy. Red had a hair-trigger temper: he was an easy man to *rile*.

**riveting** ADJ. absorbing; engrossing. The reviewer described Byatt's novel *Possession* as a *riveting* tale: absorbed in the story, she had finished it in a single evening.

**rivulet** N. small stream. As the rains continued, the trickle of water running down the hillside grew into a *rivulet* that threatened to wash away a portion of the slope.

**robust** ADJ. vigorous; strong. After pumping iron and taking karate for six months, the little old lady was far more *robust* in health and could break a plank with her fist.

**rococo** ADJ. ornate; highly decorated. The *rococo* style in furniture and architecture, marked by scrollwork and excessive decoration, flourished during the middle of the eighteenth century.

**roil** V. to make liquids murky by stirring up sediment; to disturb. Be careful when you pour not to *roil* the wine; if you stir up the sediment you'll destroy the flavor.

**roseate** ADJ. rosy; optimistic. I am afraid you will have to alter your *roseate* views in the light of the distressing news that has just arrived.

**roster** N. list. They print the *roster* of players in the season's program.

**rostrum** N. platform for speech-making; pulpit. The crowd murmured angrily and indicated that they did not care to listen to the speaker who was approaching the *rostrum*.

**rote** N. repetition. He recited the passage by *rote* and gave no indication he understood what he was saying. also ADJ.

**rotunda** N. circular building or hall covered with a dome. His body lay in state in the *rotunda* of the Capitol.

**rotundity** N. roundness; sonorousness of speech. Washington Irving emphasized the *rotundity* of the governor by describing his height and circumference.

**rousing** ADJ. lively; stirring. "And now, let's have a *rousing* welcome for TV's own Rosie O'Donnell, who'll lead us in a *rousing* rendition of 'The Star-Spangled Banner.'"

**rout** V. stampede; drive out. The reinforcements were able to *rout* the enemy. also N.

**rubble** N. fragments. Ten years after World War II, some of the *rubble* left by enemy bombings could still be seen.

**rubric** N. title or heading (in red print); directions for religious ceremony; protocol. In ordaining the new priests, the bishop carefully observed all the *rubrics* for the ordination service.

**ruddy** ADJ. reddish; healthy-looking. Santa Claus's *ruddy* cheeks nicely complement Rudolph the Reindeer's bright red nose.

**rudimentary** ADJ. not developed; elementary; crude. Although my grandmother's English vocabulary was limited to a few *rudimentary* phrases, she always could make herself understood.

**rue** V. regret; lament; mourn. Tina *rued* the night she met Tony and wondered how she ever fell for such a jerk. also N. rueful, ADJ.

**ruffian** N. bully; scoundrel. The *ruffians* threw stones at the police.

**ruminate** V. chew over and over (mentally or, like cows, physically); mull over; ponder. Unable to digest quickly the baffling events of the day, Reuben *ruminated* about them till four in the morning.

**rummage** V. ransack; thoroughly search. When we *rummaged* through the trunks in the attic, we found many souvenirs of our childhood days. also N.

**runic** ADJ. mysterious; set down in an ancient alphabet. Tolkien's use of Old English words and inscriptions in the *runic* alphabet give *The Lord of the Rings* its atmosphere of antiquity.

**ruse** N. trick; stratagem. You will not be able to fool your friends with such an obvious *ruse*.

**rustic** ADJ. pertaining to country people; uncouth. The backwoodsman looked out of place in his *rustic* attire.

**rusticate** V. banish to the country; dwell in the country. I like city life so much that I can never understand how people can *rusticate* in the suburbs.

**ruthless** ADJ. pitiless; cruel. Captain Hook was a dangerous, *ruthless* villain who would stop at nothing to destroy Peter Pan.

**saboteur** N. one who commits sabotage; destroyer of property. Members of the Resistance acted as *saboteurs*, blowing up train lines to prevent supplies from reaching the Nazi army.

**saccharine** ADJ. cloyingly sweet. She tried to ingratiate herself, speaking sweetly and smiling a *saccharine* smile.

**sacrilegious** ADJ. desecrating; profane. His stealing of the altar cloth was a very *sacrilegious* act.

**sacrosanct** ADJ. most sacred; inviolable. The brash insurance salesman invaded the *sacrosanct* privacy of the office of the president of the company.

# Test

## Word List 41    *Antonyms*

Each of the questions below consists of a word in capital letters, followed by five lettered words or phrases. Choose the lettered word or phrase that is most nearly opposite in meaning to the word in capital letters and write the letter of your choice on your answer paper.

601. RESILIENT (A) pungent (B) foolish (C) worthy (D) insolent (E) unyielding

602. RESTIVE (A) buoyant (B) placid (C) remorseful (D) resistant (E) retiring

603. RETENTIVE (A) forgetful (B) accepting (C) repetitive (D) avoiding (E) fascinating

604. RETICENCE (A) fatigue (B) fashion (C) treachery (D) loquaciousness (E) magnanimity

605. RETROGRADE (A) progressing (B) inclining (C) evaluating (D) concentrating (E) directing

606. REVERE (A) advance (B) dishonor (C) age (D) precede (E) wake

607. RIFE (A) direct (B) scant (C) peaceful (D) grim (E) mature

608. ROBUST (A) weak (B) violent (C) vicious (D) villainous (E) hungry

609. ROTUNDITY (A) promenade (B) nave (C) grotesqueness (D) slimness (E) impropriety

610. RUBBLE (A) artificial facade (B) unbroken stone (C) pale complexion (D) strong defense (E) glib answer

611. RUDDY (A) robust (B) witty (C) wan (D) exotic (E) creative

612. RUDIMENTARY (A) pale (B) polite (C) asinine (D) developed (E) quiescent

613. RUEFUL (A) trite (B) content (C) capable (D) capital (E) zealous

614. RUSTIC (A) urban (B) slow (C) corroded (D) mercenary (E) civilian

615. RUTHLESS (A) merciful (B) majestic (C) mighty (D) militant (E) maximum

## Word List 42    sadistic–sepulcher

**sadistic** ADJ. inclined to cruelty. If we are to improve conditions in this prison, we must first get rid of the *sadistic* warden. sadism, N.

**saga** N. Scandinavian myth; any legend. This is a *saga* of the sea and the men who risk their lives on it.

**sagacious** ADJ. perceptive; shrewd; having insight. My father was a *sagacious* judge of character: he could spot a phony a mile away. sagacity, N.

■ **sage** N. person celebrated for wisdom. Hearing tales of a mysterious Master of All Knowledge who lived in the hills of Tibet, Sandy was possessed with a burning desire to consult the legendary *sage*. also ADJ.

**salacious** ADJ. lascivious; lustful. Chaucer's monk is not pious but *salacious*, a teller of lewd tales and ribald jests.

**salient** ADJ. prominent. One of the *salient* features of that newspaper is its excellent editorial page.

**saline** ADJ. salty. The slightly *saline* taste of this mineral water is pleasant.

**sallow** ADJ. yellowish; sickly in color. We were disturbed by her *sallow* complexion, which was due to jaundice.

■ **salubrious** ADJ. healthful. Many people with hay fever move to more *salubrious* sections of the country during the months of August and September.

**salutary** ADJ. tending to improve; beneficial; wholesome. The punishment had a *salutary* effect on the boy, as he became a model student.

**salvage** V. rescue from loss. All attempts to *salvage* the wrecked ship failed. also N.

**sanctimonious** ADJ. displaying ostentatious or hypocritical devoutness. You do not have to be so *sanctimonious* to prove that you are devout.

■ **sanction** V. approve; ratify. Nothing will convince me to *sanction* the engagement of my daughter to such a worthless young man.

**sanctuary** N. refuge; shelter; shrine; holy place. The tiny attic was Helen's *sanctuary* to which she fled when she had to get away from her bickering parents and brothers.

**sanguinary** ADJ. bloody. The battle of Iwo Jima was unexpectedly *sanguinary,* with many casualties.

**sanguine** ADJ. cheerful; hopeful. Let us not be too *sanguine* about the outcome; something could go wrong.

**sap** V. diminish; undermine. The element kryptonite had an unhealthy effect on Superman: it *sapped* his strength.

**sarcasm** N. scornful remark; stinging rebuke. Though Ralph pretended to ignore the mocking comments of his supposed friends, their *sarcasm* wounded him deeply. sarcastic, ADJ.

**sardonic** ADJ. disdainful; sarcastic; cynical. The *sardonic* humor of nightclub comedians who satirize or ridicule patrons in the audience strikes some people as amusing and others as rude.

**sartorial** ADJ. pertaining to tailors. He was as famous for the *sartorial* splendor of his attire as he was for his acting.

**sate** V. satisfy to the full; cloy. Its hunger *sated*, the lion dozed.

**satellite** N. small body revolving around a larger one. During the first few years of the Space Age, hundreds of *satellites* were launched by Russia and the United States.

■ **satiate** V. satisfy fully. Having stuffed themselves with goodies until they were *satiated*, the guests were so full they were ready for a nap. satiety, N.

**satire** N. form of literature in which irony, sarcasm, and ridicule are employed to attack vice and folly. *Gulliver's Travels,* which is regarded by many as a tale for children, is actually a bitter *satire* attacking human folly.

**satirical** ADJ. mocking. The humor of cartoonist Gary Trudeau often is *satirical;* through the comments of the Doonesbury characters, Trudeau ridicules political corruption and folly.

■ **saturate** V. soak thoroughly. Thorough watering is the key to lawn care: you must *saturate* your new lawn well to encourage its growth.

**saturnine** ADJ. gloomy. Do not be misled by his *saturnine* countenance; he is not as gloomy as he looks.

**satyr** N. half-human, half-bestial being in the court of Dionysus, portrayed as wanton and cunning. He was like a *satyr* in his lustful conduct.

**saunter** V. stroll slowly. As we *sauntered* through the park, we stopped frequently to admire the spring flowers.

**savant** N. scholar. Our faculty includes many world-famous *savants.*

■ **savor** V. enjoy; have a distinctive flavor, smell, or quality. Relishing his triumph, Costner especially *savored* the chagrin of the critics who had predicted his failure.

**savory** ADJ. tasty; pleasing, attractive, or agreeable. Julia Child's recipes enable amateur chefs to create *savory* delicacies for their guests.

**scabbard** N. case for a sword blade; sheath. The drill master told the recruit to wipe the blood from his sword before slipping it back into the *scabbard.*

**scad** N. a great quantity. Refusing Dave's offer to lend him a shirt, Phil replied, "No, thanks; I've got *scads* of clothes."

**scaffold** N. temporary platform for workers; bracing framework; platform for execution. Before painting the house, the workers put up a *scaffold* to allow them to work on the second story.

**scale** V. climb up; ascend. To locate a book on the top shelf of the stacks, Lee had to *scale* an exceptionally rickety ladder.

**scanty** ADJ. meager; insufficient. Thinking his helping of food was *scanty,* Oliver Twist asked for more.

**scapegoat** N. someone who bears the blame for others. After the Challenger disaster, NASA searched for *scapegoats* on whom they could cast the blame.

**scavenge** V. hunt through discarded materials for usable items; search, especially for food. If you need car parts that the dealers no longer stock, try *scavenging* for odd bits and pieces at the auto wreckers' yards. scavenger, N.

**scenario** N. plot outline; screenplay; opera libretto. Scaramouche startled the other actors in the commedia troupe when he suddenly departed from their customary *scenario* and began to improvise.

**schematic** ADJ. relating to an outline or diagram; using a system of symbols. In working out the solution to an analytical logic question, you may find it helpful to construct a simple *schematic* diagram illustrating the relationships between the items of information given in the question. schema, N.

**schism** N. division; split. Let us not widen the *schism* by further bickering.

**scintilla** N. shred; least bit. You have not produced a *scintilla* of evidence to support your argument.

**scintillate** V. sparkle; flash. I enjoy her dinner parties because the food is excellent and the conversation *scintillates.*

**scoff** V. mock; ridicule. He *scoffed* at dentists until he had his first toothache.

**scotch** V. stamp out; thwart; hinder. Heather tried to *scotch* the rumor that she had stolen her best friend's fiancé.

**scourge** N. lash; whip; severe punishment. They feared the plague and regarded it as a deadly *scourge.* also V.

**scruple** V. fret about; hesitate, for ethical reasons. Fearing that her husband had become involved in an affair, she did not *scruple* to read his diary. also N.

**scrupulous** ADJ. conscientious; extremely thorough. Though Alfred is *scrupulous* in fulfilling his duties at work, he is less conscientious about his obligations to his family and friends.

**scrutinize** V. examine closely and critically. Searching for flaws, the sergeant *scrutinized* every detail of the private's uniform.

**scuffle** V. struggle confusedly; move off in a confused hurry. The twins briefly *scuffled,* wrestling to see which of them would get the toy. When their big brother yelled, "Let go of my Gameboy!" they *scuffled* off down the hall.

**scurrilous** ADJ. obscene; indecent. Your *scurrilous* remarks are especially offensive because they are untrue.

**scurry** V. move briskly. The White Rabbit had to *scurry* to get to his appointment on time.

**scurvy** ADJ. despicable; contemptible. Peter Pan sneered at Captain Hook and his *scurvy* crew.

**scuttle** V. sink. The sailors decided to *scuttle* their vessel rather than surrender it to the enemy.

**seamy** ADJ. sordid; unwholesome. In *The Godfather,* Michael Corleone is unwilling to expose his wife and children to the *seamy* side of his life as the son of a Mafia don.

**sear** V. char or burn; brand. Accidentally brushing against the hot grill, she *seared* her hand badly.

**seasoned** ADJ. experienced. Though pleased with her new batch of rookies, the basketball coach wished she had a few more *seasoned* players on the team.

**secession** N. withdrawal. The *secession* of the Southern states provided Lincoln with his first major problem after his inauguration. secede, V.

**seclusion** N. isolation; solitude. One moment she loved crowds; the next, she sought *seclusion*.

■ **secrete** V. hide away or cache; produce and release a substance into an organism. The pack rat *secretes* odds and ends in its nest; the pancreas *secretes* insulin in the islets of Langerhans.

**sect** N. separate religious body; faction. As university chaplain, she sought to address universal religious issues and not limit herself to the concerns of any one *sect*. sectarian, ADJ.

**secular** ADJ. worldly; not pertaining to church matters; temporal. The church leaders decided not to interfere in *secular* matters.

**sedate** ADJ. composed; grave. The parents were worried because they felt their son was too quiet and *sedate*.

**sedentary** ADJ. requiring sitting. Sitting all day at the computer, Sharon grew to resent the *sedentary* nature of her job.

**sedition** N. resistance to authority; insubordination. Her words, though not treasonous in themselves, were calculated to arouse thoughts of *sedition*.

**sedulous** ADJ. diligent. The young woman was so *sedulous* that she received a commendation for her hard work. sedulity, N.

**seedy** ADJ. run-down; decrepit; disreputable. I would rather stay in dormitory lodgings in a decent youth hostel than have a room of my own in a *seedy* downtown hotel.

**seemly** ADJ. proper; appropriate. Lady Bracknell did not think it was *seemly* for Ernest to lack a proper family: no baby abandoned on a doorstep could grow up to marry *her* daughter.

**seep** V. ooze; trickle. During the rainstorm, water *seeped* through the crack in the basement wall and damaged the floor boards. seepage, N.

**seethe** V. be disturbed; boil. The nation was *seething* with discontent as the noblemen continued their arrogant ways.

**seine** N. net for catching fish. When the shad run during the spring, you may see fishermen with *seines* along the banks of our coastal rivers.

**seismic** ADJ. pertaining to earthquakes. The Richter scale is a measurement of *seismic* disturbances.

**semblance** N. outward appearance; guise. Although this book has a *semblance* of wisdom and scholarship, a careful examination will reveal many errors and omissions.

**seminal** ADJ. germinal; influencing future developments; related to seed or semen. Although Freud has generally been regarded as a *seminal* thinker who shaped the course of psychology, his psychoanalytic methods have come under attack recently.

**seminary** N. school for training future ministers; secondary school, especially for young women. Sure of his priestly vocation, Terrence planned to pursue his theological training at the local Roman Catholic *seminary*.

**senility** N. old age; feeblemindedness of old age. Most of the decisions are being made by the junior members of the company because of the *senility* of the president. senile, ADJ.

**sensitization** N. process of being made sensitive or acutely responsive to an external agent or substance. The paint fumes triggered a bad allergic response in Vicky; even now, her extreme *sensitization* to these chemicals causes her to faint whenever she is around wet paint.

**sensual** ADJ. devoted to the pleasures of the senses; carnal; voluptuous. I cannot understand what caused him to drop his *sensual* way of life and become so ascetic.

**sensuous** ADJ. pertaining to the physical senses; operating through the senses. She was stimulated by the sights, sounds, and smells about her; she was enjoying her *sensuous* experience.

**sententious** ADJ. terse; concise; aphoristic. After reading so many redundant speeches, I find his *sententious* style particularly pleasing.

**sentient** ADJ. capable of sensation; aware; sensitive. In the science fiction story, the hero had to discover a way to prove that the rocklike extraterrestrial creature was actually a *sentient*, intelligent creature. sentience, N.

**sentinel** N. sentry; lookout. Though camped in enemy territory, Bledsoe ignored the elementary precaution of posting *sentinels* around the encampment.

**septic** ADJ. putrid; producing putrefaction. The hospital was in such a filthy state that we were afraid that many of the patients would suffer from *septic* poisoning. sepsis, N.

**sepulcher** N. tomb. Annabel Lee was buried in a *sepulcher* by the sea.

# Test

# Word List 42 *Antonyms*

Each of the following questions consists of a word in capital letters, followed by five lettered words or phrases. Choose the lettered word or phrase that is most nearly opposite in meaning to the word in capital letters and write the letter of your choice on your answer paper.

616. SADISTIC (A) happy (B) quaint (C) kindhearted (D) vacant (E) fortunate

617. SAGACIOUS (A) foolish (B) bitter (C) voracious (D) veracious (E) fallacious

618. SALLOW (A) salacious (B) ruddy (C) colorless (D) permitted (E) minimum

619. SALUBRIOUS (A) salty (B) bloody (C) miasmic (D) maudlin (E) wanted

620. SALVAGE (A) remove (B) outfit (C) burn (D) lose (E) confuse

621. SANCTIMONIOUS (A) hypothetical (B) paltry (C) mercenary (D) pious (E) grateful

622. SANGUINE (A) choleric (B) sickening (C) warranted (D) irritated (E) pessimistic

623. SATIETY (A) emptiness (B) warmth (C) erectness (D) ignorance (E) straightness

624. SCANTY (A) collected (B) remote (C) invisible (D) plentiful (E) straight

625. SCURRILOUS (A) savage (B) scabby (C) decent (D) volatile (E) major

626. SECULAR (A) vivid (B) clerical (C) punitive (D) positive (E) varying

627. SEDENTARY (A) vicarious (B) loyal (C) accidental (D) active (E) afraid

628. SEDULOUS (A) indolent (B) guileless (C) vindictive (D) upright (E) incorrect

629. SENILITY (A) virility (B) loquaciousness (C) forgetfulness (D) youth (E) majority

630. SENTENTIOUS (A) paragraphed (B) positive (C) posthumous (D) pacific (E) wordy

---

# Word List 43    sequester-somatic

**sequester** v. isolate; retire from public life; segregate; seclude. To prevent the jurors from hearing news broadcasts about the case, the judge decided to *sequester* the jury.

**sere** ADJ. parched; dry. After the unseasonably dry winter the Berkeley hills looked dusty and *sere*.

**serendipity** N. gift for finding valuable or desirable things by accident; accidental good fortune or luck. Many scientific discoveries are a matter of *serendipity:* Newton was not sitting there thinking about gravity when the apple dropped on his head.

**serenity** N. calmness, placidity. The *serenity* of the sleepy town was shattered by a tremendous explosion.

**serpentine** ADJ. winding; twisting. The car swerved at every curve in the *serpentine* road.

**serrated** ADJ. having a sawtoothed edge. The beech tree is one of many plants that have *serrated* leaves.

**servile** ADJ. slavish; cringing. Constantly fawning on his employer, humble Uriah Heep was a *servile* creature. servility, N.

**servitude** N. slavery; compulsory labor. Born a slave, Douglass resented his life of *servitude* and plotted to escape to the North.

**sever** v. cut; separate. Dr. Guillotin invented a machine that could neatly *sever* an aristocratic head from its equally aristocratic body. Unfortunately, he couldn't collect any *severance* pay.

**severity** N. harshness; intensity; sternness; austerity. The *severity* of Jane's migraine attack was so great that she took to her bed for a week. severe, ADJ.

**sextant** N. navigation tool used to determine a ship's latitude and longitude. Given a clear night, with the aid of his *sextant* and compass he could keep the ship safely on course.

**shackle** v. chain; fetter. The criminal's ankles were *shackled* to prevent his escape. also N.

**sham** v. pretend. She *shammed* sickness to get out of going to school. also N.

**shambles** N. wreck; mess. After the hurricane, the Carolina coast was a *shambles*. After the New Year's Eve party, the host's apartment was a *shambles*.

■ **shard** N. fragment, generally of pottery. The archaeologist assigned several students the task of reassembling earthenware vessels from the *shards* he had brought back from the expedition.

**shaving** N. very thin piece, usually of wood. As the carpenter pared away the edge of the board with his plane, a small pile of *shavings* began to accumulate on the floor.

**sheaf** N. bundle of stalks of grain; any bundle of things tied together. The lawyer picked up a *sheaf* of papers as she rose to question the witness.

**sheathe** v. place into a case. As soon as he recognized the approaching men, he *sheathed* his dagger and hailed them as friends.

**sherbet** N. flavored dessert ice. I prefer raspberry *sherbet* to ice cream since it is less fattening.

**shimmer** v. glimmer intermittently. The moonlight *shimmered* on the water as the moon broke through the clouds for a moment. also N.

**shirk** v. avoid (responsibility, work, etc.); malinger. Brian has a strong sense of duty; he would never *shirk* any responsibility.

**shoddy** ADJ. sham; not genuine; inferior. You will never get the public to buy such *shoddy* material.

**shrew** N. scolding woman. No one wanted to marry Shakespeare's Kate because she was a *shrew*.

**shrewd** ADJ. clever; astute. A *shrewd* investor, she took clever advantage of the fluctuations of the stock market.

**shun** v. keep away from. Cherishing his solitude, the recluse *shunned* the company of other human beings.

**shunt**  v. turn aside; divert; sidetrack. If the switchman failed to *shunt* the Silver Streak onto a side track, the train would plow right into Union Station.

**shyster**  N. lawyer using questionable methods. On *L.A. Law,* respectable attorney Brackman was horrified to learn that his newly discovered half brother was a cheap *shyster.*

**sibling**  N. brother or sister. We may not enjoy being *siblings,* but we cannot forget that we still belong to the same family.

**sibylline**  ADJ. prophetic; oracular. Until their destruction by fire in 83 B.C., the *sibylline* books were often consulted by the Romans.

**sidereal**  ADJ. relating to the stars. Although hampered by optical and mechanical flaws, the orbiting *Hubble* space telescope has relayed extraordinary images of distant *sidereal* bodies.

**silt**  N. sediment deposited by running water. The harbor channel must be dredged annually to remove the *silt.*

**simian**  ADJ. monkeylike. Lemurs are nocturnal mammals and have many *simian* characteristics, although they are less intelligent than monkeys.

**simile**  N. comparison of one thing with another, using the word *like* or *as.* "My love is like a red, red rose" is a *simile.*

**simper**  v. smirk; smile affectedly. Complimented on her appearance, Stella self-consciously *simpered.*

**simplistic**  ADJ. oversimplified. Though Jack's solution dealt adequately with one aspect of the problem, it was *simplistic* in failing to consider various complicating factors that might arise.

**simulate**  v. feign. She *simulated* insanity in order to avoid punishment for her crime.

**sinecure**  N. well-paid position with little responsibility. My job is no *sinecure;* I work long hours and have much responsibility.

**sinewy**  ADJ. tough; strong and firm. The steak was too *sinewy* to chew.

**singular**  ADJ. unique; extraordinary; odd. Though the young man tried to understand Father William's *singular* behavior, he still found it odd that the old man incessantly stood on his head.

**sinister**  ADJ. evil. We must defeat the *sinister* forces that seek our downfall.

**sinuous**  ADJ. winding; bending in and out; not morally honest. The snake moved in a *sinuous* manner.

■ **skeptic**  N. doubter; person who suspends judgment until having examined the evidence supporting a point of view. I am a *skeptic* about the new health plan; I want some proof that it can work. skeptical, ADJ. skepticism, N.

**skiff**  N. small, light sailboat or rowboat. Tom dreamed of owning an ocean-going yacht but had to settle for a *skiff* he could sail in the bay.

**skimp**  v. provide scantily; live very economically. They were forced to *skimp* on necessities in order to make their limited supplies last the winter.

**skinflint**  N. stingy person; miser. Scrooge was an ungenerous old *skinflint* until he reformed his ways and became a notable philanthropist.

**skirmish**  N. minor fight. Custer's troops expected they might run into a *skirmish* or two on maneuvers; they did not expect to face a major battle. also v.

**skittish**  ADJ. lively; frisky. She is as *skittish* as a kitten playing with a piece of string.

**skulduggery**  N. dishonest behavior. The investigation into municipal corruption turned up new instances of *skulduggery* daily.

**skulk**  v. move furtively and secretly. He *skulked* through the less fashionable sections of the city in order to avoid meeting any of his former friends.

**slacken**  v. slow up; loosen. As they passed the finish line, the runners *slackened* their pace.

**slag**  N. residue from smelting metal; dross; waste matter. The blast furnace had a special opening at the bottom to allow the workers to remove the worthless *slag.*

**slake**  v. quench; sate. When we reached the oasis, we were able to *slake* our thirst.

**slander**  N. defamation; utterance of false and malicious statements. Considering the negative comments politicians make about each other, it's a wonder that more of them aren't sued for *slander.* also v. slanderous, ADJ.

**slapdash**  ADJ. haphazard; careless; sloppy. From the number of typos and misspellings I've found in it, it's clear that Mario proofread the report in a remarkably *slapdash* fashion.

**sleazy**  ADJ. flimsy; unsubstantial. This is a *sleazy* fabric; it will not wear well.

**sleeper**  N. something originally of little value or importance that in time becomes very valuable. Unnoticed by the critics at its publication, the eventual Pulitzer Prize winner was a classic *sleeper.*

**sleight**  N. dexterity. The magician amazed the audience with his *sleight* of hand.

**slew**  N. large quantity or number. Although Ellen had checked off a number of items on her "To Do" list, she still had a whole *slew* of errands left.

**slight**  N. insult to one's dignity; snub. Hypersensitive and ready to take offense at any discourtesy, Bertha was always on the lookout for real or imaginary *slights.* also v.

**slipshod**  ADJ. untidy or slovenly; shabby. As a master craftsman, the carpenter prided himself on never doing *slipshod* work.

**slither**  v. slip or slide. During the recent ice storm, many people *slithered* down this hill as they walked to the station.

**sloth**  N. slow-moving tree-dwelling mammal. Note how well the somewhat greenish coat of the *sloth* enables it to blend in with its arboreal surroundings. (secondary meaning)

**slothful**  ADJ. lazy. The British word "layabout" is a splendid descriptive term for someone *slothful*: What did the lazy bum do? He lay about the house all day. sloth, N.

**slough**  v. cast off. Each spring, the snake *sloughs* off its skin. also N.

**slovenly** ADJ. untidy; careless in work habits. Unshaven, sitting around in his bathrobe all afternoon, Gus didn't care about the *slovenly* appearance he presented. sloven, N.

**sluggard** N. lazy person. "You are a *sluggard,* a drone, a parasite," the angry father shouted at his lazy son.

**sluggish** ADJ. slow; lazy; lethargic. After two nights without sleep, she felt *sluggish* and incapable of exertion.

**sluice** N. artificial channel for directing or controlling the flow of water. In times of drought, this *sluice* enables farmers to obtain water for irrigation.

**slur** N. insult to one's character or reputation; slander. Polls revealed that the front-runner's standing had been damaged by the *slurs* and innuendoes circulated by his opponent's staff. (secondary meaning) also V.

**slur** V. speak indistinctly; mumble. When Sol has too much to drink, he starts to *slur* his words: "Washamatter? Cansh you undershtand what I shay?"

**smattering** N. slight knowledge. I don't know whether it is better to be ignorant of a subject or to have a mere *smattering* of information about it.

**smelt** V. melt or blend ores, changing their chemical composition. The furnaceman *smelts* tin with copper to create a special alloy used in making bells.

**smirk** N. conceited smile. Wipe that *smirk* off your face! also V.

**smolder** V. burn without flame; be liable to break out at any moment. The rags *smoldered* for hours before they burst into flame.

**snicker** N. half-stifled laugh. The boy could not suppress a *snicker* when the teacher sat on the tack. also V.

**snivel** V. run at the nose; snuffle; whine. Don't you come *sniveling* to me complaining about your big brother.

**sobriety** N. moderation (especially regarding indulgence in alcohol); seriousness. Neither falling-down drunks nor stand-up comics are noted for *sobriety.* sober, ADJ.

**sodden** ADJ. soaked; dull, as if from drink. He set his *sodden* overcoat near the radiator to dry.

**sojourn** N. temporary stay. After his *sojourn* in Florida, he began to long for the colder climate of his native New England home.

**solace** N. comfort in trouble. I hope you will find *solace* in the thought that all of us share your loss.

**solder** V. repair or make whole by using a metal alloy. The plumber fixed the leak in the pipes by *soldering* a couple of joints from which water had been oozing.

**solecism** N. construction that is flagrantly incorrect grammatically. I must give this paper a failing mark because it contains many *solecisms.*

**solemnity** N. seriousness; gravity. The minister was concerned that nothing should disturb the *solemnity* of the marriage service.

**solicit** V. request earnestly; seek. Knowing she needed to have a solid majority for the budget to pass, the mayor telephoned all the members of the city council to *solicit* their votes.

■ **solicitous** ADJ. worried, concerned. The employer was very *solicitous* about the health of her employees as replacements were difficult to get. solicitude, N.

**soliloquy** N. talking to oneself. The *soliloquy* is a device used by the dramatist to reveal a character's innermost thoughts and emotions.

**solitude** N. state of being alone; seclusion. Much depends on how much you like your own company. What to one person seems fearful isolation to another is blessed *solitude.* solitary, ADJ.

**solstice** N. point at which the sun is farthest from the equator. The winter *solstice* usually occurs on December 21.

**soluble** ADJ. able to be dissolved; able to be worked out. Sugar is *soluble* in water; put a sugar cube in water and it will quickly dissolve. Because the test-maker had left out some necessary data, the problem was not *soluble.*

**solvent** ADJ. able to pay all debts. By dint of very frugal living, he was finally able to become *solvent* and avoid bankruptcy proceedings. solvency, N.

**solvent** N. substance that dissolves another. Dip a cube of sugar into a cup of water; note how the water acts as a *solvent,* causing the cube to break down.

**somatic** ADJ. pertaining to the body; physical. Why do you ignore the spiritual aspects and emphasize only the corporeal and the *somatic* ones?

## Test

---

# Word List 43    *Synonyms and Antonyms*

Each of the following questions consists of a word in capital letters, followed by five lettered words or phrases. Choose the lettered word or phrase that is most nearly similar or opposite in meaning to the word in capital letters and write the letter of your choice on your answer paper.

631. SEQUESTER (A) request (B) preclude (C) seclude (D) witness (E) evolve

632. SERRATED (A) riddled (B) diagonal (C) sawtoothed (D) grooved (E) linear

633. SERVILE (A) moral (B) puerile (C) futile (D) foul (E) haughty

634. SHODDY (A) superior (B) barefoot (C) sunlit (D) querulous (E) garrulous

635. SINGULAR (A) silent (B) angular (C) ordinary (D) desirable (E) garrulous

636. SINISTER (A) unwed (B) ministerial (C) good (D) returned (E) splintered

637. SKITTISH (A) tractable (B) inquiring (C) dramatic (D) vain (E) frisky

638. SLEAZY (A) fanciful (B) creeping (C) substantial (D) uneasy (E) warranted

639. SLOTH (A) penitence (B) filth (C) futility (D) poverty (E) industry

640. SLOUGH (A) toughen (B) trap (C) violate (D) cast off (E) depart quickly

641. SLOVENLY (A) half-baked (B) loved (C) inappropriate (D) tidy (E) rapid

642. SOBRIETY (A) inebriety (B) aptitude (C) scholasticism (D) monotony (E) aversion

643. SOLECISM (A) praise (B) embarrassment (C) concise phrase (D) inaccurate count (E) correct expression

644. SOLSTICE (A) equinox (B) sunrise (C) pigsty (D) interstices (E) iniquity

645. SOLVENT (A) enigmatic (B) bankrupt (C) fiducial (D) puzzling (E) gilded

# Word List 44   somber-sublime

**somber**   ADJ. gloomy; depressing. From the doctor's grim expression, I could tell he had *somber* news.

**somnambulist**   N. sleepwalker. The most famous *somnambulist* in literature is Lady Macbeth; her monologue in the sleepwalking scene is one of the highlights of Shakespeare's play.

**somnolent**   ADJ. half asleep. The heavy meal and the overheated room made us all *somnolent* and indifferent to the speaker. somnolence, N.

**sonorous**   ADJ. resonant. His *sonorous* voice resounded through the hall.

**sophist**   N. teacher of philosophy; quibbler; employer of fallacious reasoning. You are using all the devices of a *sophist* in trying to prove your case; your argument is specious.

**sophisticated**   ADJ. worldly wise and urbane; complex. When Sophy makes wisecracks, she thinks she sounds *sophisticated*, but instead she sounds sophomoric. The IBM laptop with the butterfly keyboard and the built-in FAX modem is a pretty *sophisticated* machine. sophistication, N.

**sophistry**   N. seemingly plausible but fallacious reasoning. Instead of advancing valid arguments, he tried to overwhelm his audience with a flood of *sophistries*.

**sophomoric**   ADJ. immature; half-baked, like a sophomore. Even if you're only a freshman, it's no compliment to be told your humor is *sophomoric*. The humor in *Dumb and Dumber* is *sophomoric* at best.

■ **soporific**   ADJ. sleep-causing; marked by sleepiness. Professor Pringle's lectures were so *soporific* that even he fell asleep in class. also N.

**sordid**   ADJ. filthy; base; vile. The social worker was angered by the *sordid* housing provided for the homeless.

**spangle**   N. small metallic piece sewn to clothing for ornamentation. The thousands of *spangles* on her dress sparkled in the glare of the stage lights.

**sparse**   ADJ. not thick; thinly scattered; scanty. No matter how carefully Albert combed his hair to make it appear as full as possible, it still looked *sparse*.

**spartan**   ADJ. lacking luxury and comfort; sternly disciplined. Looking over the bare, unheated room with its hard cot, he wondered what he was doing in such *spartan* quarters. Only his *spartan* sense of duty kept him at his post.

**spasmodic**   ADJ. fitful; periodic. The *spasmodic* coughing in the auditorium annoyed the performers.

**spat**   N. squabble; minor dispute. What had started out as a mere *spat* escalated into a full-blown argument.

**spate**   N. sudden flood. I am worried about the possibility of a *spate* if the rains do not diminish soon.

**spatial**   ADJ. relating to space. Certain exercises test your sense of *spatial* relations by asking you to identify two views of an object seen from different points in space.

**spatula**   N. broad-bladed instrument used for spreading or mixing. The manufacturers of this frying pan recommend the use of a rubber *spatula* to avoid scratching the specially treated surface.

**spawn**   V. lay eggs. Fish ladders had to be built in the dams to assist the salmon returning to *spawn* in their native streams. also N.

■ **specious**   ADJ. seemingly reasonable but incorrect; misleading (often intentionally). To claim that, because houses and birds both have wings, both can fly is extremely *specious* reasoning.

**spectral**   ADJ. ghostly. We were frightened by the *spectral* glow that filled the room.

■ **spectrum**   N. colored band produced when a beam of light passes through a prism. The visible portion of the *spectrum* includes red at one end and violet at the other.

**spendthrift**   N. someone who wastes money. Easy access to credit encourages people to turn into *spendthrifts* who shop till they drop.

**sphinx-like**   ADJ. enigmatic; mysterious. The Mona Lisa's *sphinx-like* expression has puzzled art lovers for centuries.

**splice**   V. fasten together; unite. Before you *splice* two strips of tape together, be sure to line them up evenly. also N.

**spontaneity**   N. lack of premeditation; naturalness; freedom from constraint. The cast overrehearsed the play so much that the eventual performance lacked any *spontaneity*. spontaneous, ADJ.

**spoonerism**   N. accidental transposition of sounds in successive words. When the radio announcer introduced the President as Hoobert Herver, he was guilty of a *spoonerism*.

■ **sporadic** ADJ. occurring irregularly. Although you can still hear *sporadic* outbursts of laughter and singing outside, the big Halloween parade has passed; the party's over till next year.

**sportive** ADJ. playful. Such a *sportive* attitude is surprising in a person as serious as you usually are.

**spruce** ADJ. neat and trim. Every button buttoned, tie firmly in place, young Alex Keaton looked *spruce* and tidy for his job interview at the bank. also V.

**spry** ADJ. vigorously active; nimble. She was eighty years old, yet still *spry* and alert.

**spurious** ADJ. false; counterfeit; forged; illogical. The hero of Jonathan Gash's mystery novels is an antique dealer who gives the reader advice on how to tell *spurious* antiques from the real thing.

**spurn** V. reject; scorn. The heroine *spurned* the villain's advances.

**squabble** N. minor quarrel; bickering. Children invariably get involved in petty *squabbles;* wise parents know when to interfere and when to let the children work things out on their own.

**squalor** N. filth; degradation; dirty, neglected state. Rusted, broken-down cars in the yard, trash piled on the porch, tar paper peeling from the roof—the shack was the picture of *squalor*. squalid, ADJ.

**squander** V. waste. If you *squander* your allowance on candy and comic books, you won't have any money left to buy the new box of crayons you want.

**squat** ADJ. stocky; short and thick. Tolkien's hobbits are somewhat *squat*, sturdy little creatures, fond of good ale, good music, and good food.

**staccato** ADJ. played in an abrupt manner; marked by abrupt, sharp sound. His *staccato* speech reminded one of the sound of a machine gun.

**stagnant** ADJ. motionless; stale; dull. Mosquitoes commonly breed in ponds of *stagnant* water. Mike's career was *stagnant*; it wasn't going anywhere, and neither was he! stagnate, V.

**staid** ADJ. sober; sedate. Her conduct during the funeral ceremony was *staid* and solemn.

**stalemate** N. deadlock. Negotiations between the union and the employers have reached a *stalemate;* neither side is willing to budge from previously stated positions.

**stalwart** ADJ. strong, brawny; steadfast. His consistent support of the party has proved that he is a *stalwart* and loyal member. also N.

**stamina** N. strength; staying power. I doubt that she has the *stamina* to run the full distance of the marathon race.

**stanch** V. check flow of blood. It is imperative that we *stanch* the gushing wound before we attend to the other injuries.

**stanza** N. division of a poem. Do you know the last *stanza* of "The Star-Spangled Banner"?

**static** ADJ. unchanging; lacking development. Why do you watch chess on TV? I like watching a game with action, not something *static* where nothing seems to be going on. stasis, N.

**statute** N. law enacted by the legislature. The *statute* of limitations sets limits on how long you have to take legal action in specific cases.

**statutory** ADJ. created by statute or legislative action. The judicial courts review and try *statutory* crimes.

**steadfast** ADJ. loyal; unswerving. Penelope was *steadfast* in her affections, faithfully waiting for Ulysses to return from his wanderings.

**stealth** N. slyness; sneakiness; secretiveness. Fearing detection by the sentries on duty, the scout inched his way toward the enemy camp with great *stealth*.

**steep** V. soak; saturate. Be sure to *steep* the fabric in the dye bath for the full time prescribed.

**stellar** ADJ. pertaining to the stars. He was the *stellar* attraction of the entire performance.

**stem** V. check the flow. The paramedic used a tourniquet to *stem* the bleeding from the slashed artery.

**stem from** V. arise from. Milton's problems in school *stemmed from* his poor study habits.

**stentorian** ADJ. extremely loud. The town crier had a *stentorian* voice.

**stereotype** N. fixed and unvarying representation; standardized mental picture, often reflecting prejudice. Critics object to the character of Jim in *The Adventures of Huckleberry Finn* because he seems to reflect the *stereotype* of the happy, ignorant slave. also V.

**stickler** N. perfectionist; person who insists things be exactly right. The Internal Revenue Service agent was a *stickler* for accuracy; no approximations or rough estimates would satisfy him.

**stifle** V. suppress; extinguish; inhibit. Halfway through the boring lecture, Laura gave up trying to *stifle* her yawns.

■ **stigma** N. token of disgrace; brand. I do not attach any *stigma* to the fact that you were accused of this crime; the fact that you were acquitted clears you completely. stigmatize, N.

**stilted** ADJ. bombastic; stiffly pompous. His *stilted* rhetoric did not impress the college audience; they were immune to bombastic utterances.

■ **stint** V. be thrifty; set limits. "Spare no expense," the bride's father said, refusing to *stint* on the wedding arrangements.

**stint** N. supply; allotted amount; assigned portion of work. She performed her daily *stint* cheerfully and willingly.

**stipend** N. pay for services. There is a nominal *stipend* for this position.

**stipple** V. paint or draw with dots. Seurat carefully *stippled* dabs of pure color on the canvas, juxtaposing dots of blue and yellow that the viewer's eye would interpret as green.

■ **stipulate** V. make express conditions, specify. Before agreeing to reduce American military forces in Europe, the president *stipulated* that NATO teams be allowed to inspect Russian bases.

**stock** ADJ. typical; standard; kept regularly in supply. Victorian melodramas portrayed *stock* characters—the rich but wicked villain, the sweet young ingenue, the poor but honest young man—in exaggerated situations. Although the stationery store kept only *stock* sizes of paper on hand, the staff would special-order any items not regularly in *stock*.

**stockade** N. wooden enclosure or pen; fixed line of posts used as defensive barrier. The Indians are coming! Quick! Round up the horses and drive them into the *stockade*.

**stodgy** ADJ. stuffy; boringly conservative. For a young person, Winston seems remarkably *stodgy*: you'd expect someone his age to have a little more life.

**stoic** ADJ. impassive; unmoved by joy or grief. I wasn't particularly *stoic* when I had my flu shot; I squealed like a stuck pig. also N. stoicism, N.

**stoke** V. stir up a fire; feed plentifully. As a Scout, Marisa learned how to light a fire, how to *stoke* it if it started to die down, and how to extinguish it completely.

■ **stolid** ADJ. dull; impassive. The earthquake shattered Stuart's usual *stolid* demeanor; trembling, he crouched on the no longer stable ground. stolidity, N.

**stratagem** N. clever trick; deceptive scheme. What a gem of a *stratagem*! Watson, I have the perfect plan to trick Moriarty into revealing himself.

**stratified** ADJ. divided into classes; arranged into strata. As the economic gap between the rich and the poor increased, Roman society grew increasingly *stratified*. stratify, V.

**stratum** N. layer of earth's surface; layer of society. Unless we alleviate conditions in the lowest *stratum* of our society, we may expect grumbling and revolt. strata, PL.

**strew** V. spread randomly; sprinkle; scatter. Preceding the bride to the altar, the flower girl will *strew* rose petals along the aisle.

■ **striated** ADJ. marked with parallel bands; grooved. The glacier left many *striated* rocks. striate, V.

**stricture** N. critical comments; severe and adverse criticism. His *strictures* on the author's style are prejudiced and unwarranted.

**strident** ADJ. loud and harsh; insistent. We could barely hear the speaker over the *strident* cries of the hecklers. stridency, N.

**stringent** ADJ. binding; rigid. I think these regulations are too *stringent*.

■ **strut** N. pompous walk. His *strut* as he marched about the parade ground revealed him for what he was: a pompous buffoon. also V.

■ **strut** N. supporting bar. The engineer calculated that the *strut* supporting the rafter needed to be reinforced.

**studied** ADJ. unspontaneous; deliberate; thoughtful. Given Jill's previous slights, Jack felt that the omission of his name from the guest list was a *studied* insult.

**stultify** V. cause to appear or become stupid or inconsistent; frustrate or hinder. His long hours in the blacking factory left young Dickens numb and incurious, as if the menial labor had *stultified* his mind.

**stupefy** V. make numb; stun; amaze. Disapproving of drugs in general, Laura refused to take sleeping pills or any other medicine that might *stupefy* her.

**stupor** N. state of apathy; daze; lack of awareness. In his *stupor*, the addict was unaware of the events taking place around him.

**stygian** ADJ. gloomy; hellish; deathly. Shielding the flickering candle from any threatening draft, Tom and Becky descended into the *stygian* darkness of the underground cavern. *Stygian* derives from *Styx*, the chief river in the subterranean land of the dead.

**stymie** V. present an obstacle; stump. The detective was *stymied* by the contradictory evidence in the robbery investigation.

**suavity** N. urbanity; polish. He is particularly good in roles that require *suavity* and sophistication. suave, ADJ.

**subaltern** N. subordinate. The captain treated his *subalterns* as though they were children rather than commissioned officers.

**subdued** ADJ. less intense; quieter. Bob liked the *subdued* lighting at the restaurant because he thought it was romantic. I just thought the place was dimly lit.

**subjective** ADJ. occurring or taking place within the mind; unreal. Your analysis is highly *subjective*; you have permitted your emotions and your opinions to color your thinking.

**subjugate** V. conquer; bring under control. It is not our aim to *subjugate* our foe; we are interested only in establishing peaceful relations.

**sublimate** V. refine; purify. We must strive to *sublimate* these desires and emotions into worthwhile activities.

**sublime** ADJ. exalted; noble and uplifting; utter. Lucy was in awe of Desi's *sublime* musicianship, while he was in awe of her *sublime* naiveté.

# Test

## Word List 44    *Synonyms and Antonyms*

Each of the following questions consists of a word in capital letters, followed by five lettered words or phrases. Choose the lettered word or phrase that is most nearly similar or opposite in meaning to the word in capital letters and write the letter of your choice on your answer paper.

646. SONOROUS (A) resonant (B) reassuring (C) repetitive (D) resinous (E) sisterly

647. SOPHOMORIC (A) unprecedented (B) mature (C) insipid (D) intellectual (E) illusionary

648. SOPORIFIC (A) dining (B) caustic (C) memorial (D) awakening (E) springing

649. SPASMODIC (A) intermittent (B) fit (C) inaccurate (D) violent (E) physical

650. SPORADIC (A) seedy (B) latent (C) vivid (D) inconsequential (E) occasional

651. SPORTIVE (A) competing (B) playful (C) indignant (D) foppish (E) fundamental

652. SPURIOUS (A) genuine (B) angry (C) mitigated (D) interrogated (E) glorious

653. SQUANDER (A) fortify (B) depart (C) roam (D) preserve (E) forfeit

654. STACCATO (A) musical (B) long (C) legato (D) sneezing (E) pounded

655. STAMINA (A) patience (B) pistils (C) weakness (D) fascination (E) patina

656. STEREOTYPED (A) original (B) antique (C) modeled (D) repetitious (E) continued

657. STILTED (A) candid (B) pompous (C) modish (D) acute (E) inarticulate

658. STRINGENT (A) binding (B) reserved (C) utilized (D) lambent (E) indigent

659. SUAVITY (A) ingeniousness (B) indifference (C) urbanity (D) constancy (E) paucity

660. SUBLIME (A) unconscious (B) respected (C) exalted (D) sneaky (E) replaced

---

# Word List 45   subliminal-tantamount

**subliminal**   ADJ. below the threshold. We may not be aware of the *subliminal* influences that affect our thinking.

**submissive**   ADJ. yielding; timid. When he refused to permit Elizabeth to marry her poet, Mr. Barrett expected her to be properly *submissive*; instead, she eloped with the guy!

**subordinate**   ADJ. occupying a lower rank; inferior; submissive. Bishop Proudie's wife expected the *subordinate* clergy to behave with great deference to the wife of their superior. also N.

**suborn**   V. persuade to act unlawfully (especially to commit perjury). In *The Godfather,* the mobsters used bribery and threats to *suborn* the witnesses against Don Michael Corleone.

■ **subpoena**   N. writ summoning a witness to appear. The prosecutor's office was ready to serve a *subpoena* on the reluctant witness. also V.

**subsequent**   ADJ. following; later. In *subsequent* lessons, we shall take up more difficult problems.

**subservient**   ADJ. behaving like a slave; servile; obsequious. She was proud and dignified; she refused to be *subservient* to anyone. subservience, N.

■ **subside**   V. settle down; descend; grow quiet. The doctor assured us that the fever would eventually *subside*.

**subsidiary**   ADJ. subordinate; secondary. This information may be used as *subsidiary* evidence but is not sufficient by itself to prove your argument. also N.

**subsidy**   N. direct financial aid by government, etc. Without this *subsidy,* American ship operators would not be able to compete in world markets.

**subsistence**   N. existence; means of support; livelihood. In those days of inflated prices, my salary provided a mere *subsistence*.

**substantial**   ADJ. ample; solid; essential or fundamental. The generous scholarship represented a *substantial* sum of money. If you don't eat a more *substantial* dinner, you'll be hungry later on.

■ **substantiate**   V. establish by evidence; verify; support. These endorsements from satisfied customers *substantiate* our claim that Barron's *How to Prepare for the GRE* is the best GRE-prep book on the market.

**substantive**   ADJ. essential; pertaining to the substance. Although the delegates were aware of the importance of the problem, they could not agree on the *substantive* issues.

**subsume**   V. include; encompass. Does the general theory of relativity contradict Newtonian physics, or is Newton's law of gravity *subsumed* into Einstein's larger scheme?

**subterfuge**   N. pretense; evasion. As soon as we realized that you had won our support by a *subterfuge,* we withdrew our endorsement of your candidacy.

**subtlety**   N. perceptiveness; ingenuity; delicacy. Never obvious, she expressed herself with such *subtlety* that her remarks went right over the heads of most of her audience. subtle, ADJ.

**subversive**   ADJ. tending to overthrow; destructive. At first glance, the notion that Styrofoam cups may actually be more ecologically sound than paper cups strikes most environmentalists as *subversive*.

**succinct**   ADJ. brief; terse; compact. Don't bore your audience with excess verbiage: be *succinct*.

**succor**   V. aid; assist; comfort. If you believe that con man has come here to *succor* you in your hour of need, you're even a bigger sucker than I thought. also N.

**succulent**   ADJ. juicy; full of richness. To some people, Florida citrus fruits are more *succulent* than those from California. also N.

**succumb** v. yield; give in; die. I *succumb* to temptation whenever it comes my way.

**suffragist** N. advocate of voting rights (for women). In recognition of her efforts to win the vote for women, Congress authorized coining a silver dollar honoring the *suffragist* Susan B. Anthony.

**suffuse** v. spread over. A blush *suffused* her cheeks when we teased her about her love affair.

**sully** v. tarnish; soil. He felt that it was beneath his dignity to *sully* his hands in such menial labor.

**sultry** ADJ. sweltering. He could not adjust himself to the *sultry* climate of the tropics.

**summation** N. act of finding the total; summary. In his *summation*, the lawyer emphasized the testimony given by the two witnesses.

**sumptuous** ADJ. lavish; rich. I cannot recall when I have had such a *sumptuous* Thanksgiving feast.

**sunder** v. separate; part. Northern and southern Ireland are politically and religiously *sundered*.

**sundry** ADJ. various; several. My suspicions were aroused when I read *sundry* items in the newspapers about your behavior.

**superannuated** ADJ. retired or disqualified because of age. Don't call me *superannuated*; I can still perform a good day's work!

**supercilious** ADJ. arrogant; condescending; patronizing. The *supercilious* headwaiter sneered at customers who he thought did not fit the image of a restaurant catering to an ultrafashionable crowd.

**supererogatory** ADJ. superfluous; more than needed or demanded. We have more than enough witnesses to corroborate your statement; to present any more would be *supererogatory*.

**superficial** ADJ. trivial; shallow. Since your report gave only a *superficial* analysis of the problem, I cannot give you more than a passing grade.

**superfluous** ADJ. excessive; overabundant, unnecessary. Please try not to include so many *superfluous* details in your report; just give me the bare facts. superfluity, N.

**superimpose** v. place over something else. Your attempt to *superimpose* another agency in this field will merely increase the bureaucratic nature of our government.

**supernumerary** N. person or thing in excess of what is necessary; extra. His first appearance on the stage was as a *supernumerary* in a Shakespearean tragedy.

■ **supersede** v. cause to be set aside; replace; make obsolete. Bulk mailing postal regulation 326D *supersedes* bulk mailing postal regulation 326C. If, in bundling your bulk mailing, you follow regulation 326C, your bulk mailing will be returned. supersession, N.

**supine** ADJ. lying on back. The defeated pugilist lay *supine* on the canvas.

**supplant** v. replace; usurp. Did the other woman actually *supplant* Princess Diana in Prince Charles's affections, or did Charles never love Diana at all? Bolingbroke, later to be known as King Henry IV, fought to *supplant* his

cousin, Richard III, as King of England.

**supple** ADJ. flexible; pliant. Years of yoga exercises made Grace's body *supple*.

**suppliant** ADJ. entreating; beseeching. Unable to resist the dog's *suppliant* whimpering, he gave it some food. also N.

**supplicate** v. petition humbly; pray to grant a favor. We *supplicate* Your Majesty to grant him amnesty.

■ **supposition** N. hypothesis; surmise. I based my decision to confide in him on the *supposition* that he would be discreet. suppose, v.

**supposititious** ADJ. assumed; counterfeit; hypothetical. I find no similarity between your *supposititious* illustration and the problem we are facing.

**suppress** v. stifle; overwhelm; subdue; inhibit. Too polite to laugh in anyone's face, Roy did his best to *suppress* his amusement at Ed's inane remark.

**surfeit** v. satiate; stuff; indulge to excess in anything. Every Thanksgiving we are *surfeited* with an overabundance of holiday treats. also N.

**surly** ADJ. rude; cross. Because of his *surly* attitude, many people avoided his company.

**surmise** v. guess. I *surmise* that he will be late for this meeting. also N.

**surmount** v. overcome. I know you can *surmount* any difficulties that may stand in the way of your getting an education.

**surpass** v. exceed. Her SAT scores *surpassed* our expectations.

**surreptitious** ADJ. secret; furtive; sneaky; hidden. Hoping to discover where his mom had hidden the Christmas presents, Timmy took a *surreptitious* peek into the master bedroom closet.

**surrogate** N. substitute. For a fatherless child, a male teacher may become a father *surrogate*.

**surveillance** N. watching; guarding. The FBI kept the house under constant *surveillance* in the hope of capturing all the criminals at one time.

**susceptible** ADJ. impressionable; easily influenced; having little resistance, as to a disease; receptive to. Said the patent medicine man to his very *susceptible* customer: "Buy this new miracle drug, and you will no longer be *susceptible* to the common cold." susceptibility, N.

**sustain** v. experience; support; nourish. He *sustained* such a severe injury that the doctors feared he would be unable to work to *sustain* his growing family.

**sustenance** N. means of support, food, nourishment. In the tropics, the natives find *sustenance* easy to obtain because of all the fruit trees.

**suture** N. stitches sewn to hold the cut edges of a wound or incision; material used in sewing. We will remove the *sutures* as soon as the wound heals. also v.

**swarthy** ADJ. dark; dusky. Despite the stereotype, not all Italians are *swarthy*; many are fair and blond.

**swathe** v. wrap around; bandage. When I visited him in

the hospital, I found him *swathed* in bandages.

**swelter** v. be oppressed by heat. I am going to buy an air conditioning unit for my apartment as I do not intend to *swelter* through another hot and humid summer.

**swerve** v. deviate; turn aside sharply. The car *swerved* wildly as the driver struggled to regain control of the wheel.

**swill** v. drink greedily. Singing "Yo, ho, ho, and a bottle of rum," Long John Silver and his fellow pirates *swilled* their grog.

**swindler** N. cheat. She was gullible and trusting, an easy victim for the first *swindler* who came along.

**sybarite** N. lover of luxury. Rich people are not always *sybarites;* some of them have little taste for a life of luxury.

**sycophant** N. servile flatterer; bootlicker; yes man. Fed up with the toadies and brownnosers who made up his entourage, the star cried, "Get out, all of you! I'm sick of *sycophants*!" sycophantic, ADJ.

**syllogism** N. logical formula consisting of a major premise, a minor premise and a conclusion; deceptive or specious argument. There must be a fallacy in this *syllogism*; I cannot accept its conclusion.

**sylvan** ADJ. pertaining to the woods; rustic. His paintings of nymphs in *sylvan* backgrounds were criticized as oversentimental.

**symbiosis** N. interdependent relationship (between groups, species), often mutually beneficial. Both the crocodile bird and the crocodile derive benefit from their *symbiosis;* pecking away at food particles embedded in the crocodile's teeth, the bird derives nourishment; the crocodile, meanwhile, derives proper dental hygiene. symbiotic, ADJ.

**symmetry** N. arrangement of parts so that balance is obtained; congruity. By definition, something lopsided lacks *symmetry*. symmetrical, ADJ.

**synchronous** ADJ. similarly timed; simultaneous with. We have many examples of scientists in different parts of the world who have made *synchronous* discoveries.

**synoptic** ADJ. providing a general overview; summary. The professor turned to the latest issue of *Dissertation Abstracts* for a *synoptic* account of what was new in the field. synopsis, N.

**synthesis** N. combining parts into a whole. Now that we have succeeded in isolating this drug, our next problem is to plan its *synthesis* in the laboratory. syntheses, PL., synthesize, V.

**synthetic** ADJ. artificial; resulting from synthesis. During the twentieth century, many *synthetic* products have replaced their natural counterparts. also N.

■ **tacit** ADJ. understood; not put into words. We have a *tacit* agreement based on only a handshake.

**taciturn** ADJ. habitually silent; talking little. The stereotypical cowboy is a *taciturn* soul, answering lengthy questions with a "Yep" or "Nope."

**tactile** ADJ. pertaining to the organs or sense of touch. His callused hands had lost their *tactile* sensitivity.

**taint** v. contaminate; cause to lose purity; modify with a trace of something bad. One speck of dirt on your utensils may contain enough germs to *taint* an entire batch of preserves. also N.

**talisman** N. charm. She wore the *talisman* to ward off evil.

**talon** N. claw of bird. The falconer wore a leather gauntlet to avoid being clawed by the hawk's *talons*.

■ **tangential** ADJ. peripheral; only slightly connected; digressing. Despite Clark's attempts to distract her with *tangential* remarks, Lois kept on coming back to her main question: Why couldn't he come out to dinner with Superman and her?

**tangible** ADJ. able to be touched; real; palpable. Although Tom did not own a house, he had several *tangible* assets—a car, a television, a PC—that he could sell if he needed cash.

**tanner** N. person who turns animal hides into leather. Using a solution of tanbark, the *tanner* treated the cowhide, transforming it into supple leather.

**tantalize** v. tease; torture with disappointment. Tom loved to *tantalize* his younger brother with candy; he knew the boy was forbidden to have it.

**tantamount** ADJ. equivalent in effect or value. Because so few Southern blacks could afford to pay the poll tax, the imposition of this tax on prospective voters was *tantamount* to disenfranchisement for black voters.

# Test

## Word List 45    *Synonyms and Antonyms*

Each of the following questions consists of a word in capital letters, followed by five lettered words or phrases. Choose the lettered word or phrase that is most nearly similar or opposite in meaning to the word in capital letters and write the letter of your choice on your answer paper.

661. SUBLIMINAL (A) radiant (B) indifferent (C) obvious (D) domestic (E) horizontal

662. SUPERANNUATED (A) senile (B) experienced (C) retired (D) attenuated (E) accepted

663. SUPERCILIOUS (A) haughty (B) highbrow (C) angry (D) inane (E) philosophic

664. SUPERFICIAL (A) abnormal (B) portentous (C) shallow (D) angry (E) tiny

665. SUPERNUMERARY (A) miser (B) extra (C) associate (D) astronomer (E) inferiority

666. SUPPLIANT (A) intolerant (B) swallowing (C) beseeching (D) finishing (E) flexible

667. SURFEIT (A) belittle (B) cloy (C) drop (D) estimate (E) claim

668. SURREPTITIOUS (A) secret (B) snakelike (C) nightly (D) abstract (E) furnished

669. SUTURE (A) stitch (B) reflection (C) knitting (D) tailor (E) past

670. SWATHED (A) wrapped around (B) waved (C) gambled (D) rapt (E) mystified

671. SYCOPHANTIC (A) quiet (B) reclusive (C) servilely flattering (D) frolicsome (E) eagerly awaiting

672. SYNTHETIC (A) simplified (B) doubled (C) tuneful (D) artificial (E) fiscal

673. TACIT (A) spoken (B) allowed (C) neutral (D) impertinent (E) unwanted

674. TALISMAN (A) chief (B) juror (C) medicine man (D) amulet (E) gift

675. TANTALIZE (A) tease (B) wax (C) warrant (D) authorize (E) summarize

---

# Word List 46   tantrum-tome

**tantrum** N. fit of petulance; caprice. The child learned that he could have almost anything if he went into *tantrums*.

**taper** N. candle. She lit the *taper* on the windowsill.

**tarantula** N. venomous spider. We need an antitoxin to counteract the bite of the *tarantula*.

**tarry** V. delay; dawdle. We can't *tarry* if we want to get to the airport on time.

**taut** ADJ. tight; ready. The captain maintained that he ran a *taut* ship.

**tautological** ADJ. needlessly repetitious. In the sentence "It was visible to the eye," the phrase "to the eye" is *tautological*. tautology, N.

**tawdry** ADJ. cheap and gaudy. He won a few *tawdry* trinkets at Coney Island.

**taxonomist** N. specialist in classifying (animals, etc.). Dental patterns often enable the *taxonomist* to distinguish members of one rodent species from those of another.

**tedium** N. boredom; weariness. We hope this radio will help overcome the *tedium* of your stay in the hospital. tedious, ADJ.

**teetotalism** N. practice of abstaining totally from alcoholic drinks. Though the doctor warned Bert to cut down his booze intake, she didn't insist that he practice *teetotalism*. teetotaler, N.

**temerity** N. boldness; rashness. Do you have the *temerity* to argue with me?

**temper** V. moderate; tone down or restrain; toughen (steel). Not even her supervisor's grumpiness could *temper* Nancy's enthusiasm for her new job.

**temperament** N. characteristic frame of mind; disposition; emotional excess. Although the twins look alike, they differ markedly in *temperament*: Tod is calm, but Rod is excitable.

**temperate** ADJ. restrained; self-controlled; moderate in respect to temperature. Try to be *temperate* in your eating this holiday season; if you control your appetite, you won't gain too much weight. Goldilocks found San Francisco's *temperate* climate neither too hot nor too cold but just right.

**tempestuous** ADJ. stormy; impassioned; violent. Racket-throwing tennis star John McEnroe was famed for his displays of *tempestuous* temperament.

**tempo** N. speed of music. I find the conductor's *tempo* too slow for such a brilliant piece of music.

**temporal** ADJ. not lasting forever; limited by time; secular. At one time in our history, *temporal* rulers assumed that they had been given their thrones by divine right.

**temporize** V. avoid committing oneself; gain time. I cannot permit you to *temporize* any longer; I must have a definite answer today.

**tenacious** ADJ. holding fast. I had to struggle to break his *tenacious* hold on my arm.

**tenacity** N. firmness; persistence. Jean Valjean could not believe the *tenacity* of Inspector Javert. Here all Valjean had done was to steal a loaf of bread, and the inspector had pursued him doggedly for 20 years!

**tendentious** ADJ. having an aim; biased; designed to further a cause. The editorials in this periodical are *tendentious* rather than truth-seeking.

**tender** V. offer; extend. Although no formal charges had been made against him, in the wake of the recent scandal the mayor felt he should *tender* his resignation.

**tenet** N. doctrine; dogma. The agnostic did not accept the *tenets* of their faith.

**tensile** ADJ. capable of being stretched. Mountain climbers must know the *tensile* strength of their ropes.

**tentative** ADJ. hesitant; not fully worked out or developed; experimental; not definite or positive. Unsure of his welcome at the Christmas party, Scrooge took a *tentative* step into his nephew's drawing room.

■ **tenuous** ADJ. thin; rare; slim. The allegiance of our allies is held by rather *tenuous* ties; let us hope they will remain loyal.

**tenure** N. holding of an office; time during which such an office is held. She has permanent *tenure* in this position and cannot be fired.

**tepid** ADJ. lukewarm. During the summer, I like to take a *tepid* bath, not a hot one.

**termination** N. end. Though the time for *termination* of the project was near, we still had a lot of work to finish before we shut up shop. terminate, V.

**terminology** N. terms used in a science or art. The special *terminology* developed by some authorities in the field has done more to confuse laypersons than to enlighten them.

**terminus** N. last stop of railroad. After we reached the railroad *terminus,* we continued our journey into the wilderness on saddle horses.

**terrestrial** ADJ. on or relating to the earth. We have been able to explore the *terrestrial* regions much more thoroughly than the aquatic or celestial regions.

**terse** ADJ. concise; abrupt; pithy. There is a fine line between speech that is *terse* and to the point and speech that is too abrupt.

**tertiary** ADJ. third. He is so thorough that he analyzes *tertiary* causes where other writers are content with primary and secondary reasons.

**tesselated** ADJ. inlaid; mosaic. I recall seeing a table with a *tesselated* top of bits of stone and glass in a very interesting pattern.

**testator** N. maker of a will. The attorney called in his secretary and his partner to witness the signature of the *testator.*

**testy** ADJ. irritable; short-tempered. My advice is to avoid discussing this problem with her today as she is rather *testy* and may shout at you. testiness, N.

**tether** V. tie with a rope. Before we went to sleep, we *tethered* the horses to prevent their wandering off during the night.

**thematic** ADJ. relating to a unifying motif or idea. Those who think of *Moby Dick* as a simple adventure story about whaling miss its underlying *thematic* import.

**theocracy** N. government run by religious leaders. Though some Pilgrims aboard the Mayflower favored the establishment of a *theocracy* in New England, many of their fellow voyagers preferred a nonreligious form of government.

**theoretical** ADJ. not practical or applied; hypothetical. Bob was better at applied engineering and computer programming than he was at *theoretical* physics and math. While I can still think of some *theoretical* objections to your plan, you've convinced me of its basic soundness.

**therapeutic** ADJ. curative. Now better known for its racetrack, Saratoga Springs first gained attention for the *therapeutic* qualities of its famous "healing waters."

**thermal** ADJ. pertaining to heat. The natives discovered that the hot springs gave excellent *thermal* baths and began to develop their community as a health resort. also N.

**thespian** ADJ. pertaining to drama. Her success in the school play convinced her she was destined for a *thespian* career. also N.

**thrall** N. slave; bondage. The captured soldier was held in *thrall* by the conquering army.

**threadbare** ADJ. worn through till the threads show; shabby and poor. The poorly paid adjunct professor hid the *threadbare* spots on his jacket by sewing leather patches on his sleeves.

**thrifty** ADJ. careful about money; economical. A *thrifty* shopper compares prices before making major purchases.

**thrive** V. prosper; flourish. Despite the impact of the recession on the restaurant trade, Philip's cafe *thrived.*

**throes** N. violent anguish. The *throes* of despair can be as devastating as the spasms accompanying physical pain.

**throng** N. crowd. *Throngs* of shoppers jammed the aisles. also V.

**throttle** V. strangle. The criminal tried to *throttle* the old man with his bare hands.

**thwart** V. baffle; frustrate. He felt that everyone was trying to *thwart* his plans and prevent his success.

**tightwad** N. excessively frugal person; miser. Jill called Jack a *tightwad* because he never picked up the check.

**tiller** N. handle used to move boat's rudder (to steer). Fearing the wind might shift suddenly and capsize the skiff, Tom kept one hand on the *tiller* at all times.

**timbre** N. quality of a musical tone produced by a musical instrument. We identify the instrument producing a musical sound by its *timbre.*

**timidity** N. lack of self-confidence or courage. If you are to succeed as a salesperson, you must first lose your *timidity* and fear of failure.

**timorous** ADJ. fearful; demonstrating fear. Her *timorous* manner betrayed the anxiety she felt at the moment.

**tipple** V. drink (alcoholic beverages) frequently. He found that his most enjoyable evenings occurred when he *tippled* with his friends at the local pub. N.

■ **tirade** N. extended scolding; denunciation; harangue. Every time the boss holds a meeting, he goes into a lengthy *tirade,* scolding us for everything from tardiness to padding our expenses.

**titanic** ADJ. gigantic. *Titanic* waves beat against the majestic S.S. *Titanic,* driving it against the concealed iceberg. titan, N.

**tithe** N. tax of one-tenth. Because he was an agnostic, he refused to pay his *tithes* to the clergy. also V.

**titillate** V. tickle. I am here not to *titillate* my audience but to enlighten it.

**title** N. right or claim to possession; mark of rank; name (of a book, film, etc.). Though the penniless Duke of Ragwort no longer held *title* to the family estate, he still retained his *title* as head of one of England's oldest families.

**titter** N. nervous laugh. Her aunt's constant *titter* nearly drove her mad. also V.

**titular** ADJ. having the title of an office without the obligations. Although he was the *titular* head of the company, the real decisions were made by his general manager.

**toady** N. servile flatterer; yes man. Never tell the boss anything he doesn't wish to hear: he doesn't want an independent adviser, he just wants a *toady.* also V.

toga   N. Roman outer robe. Marc Antony pointed to the slashes in Caesar's *toga.*

tome   N. large volume. She spent much time in the libraries poring over ancient *tomes.*

## Test

## Word List 46   *Synonyms*

Each of the questions below consists of a word in capital letters, followed by five lettered words or phrases. Choose the lettered word or phrase that is most nearly similar in meaning to the word in capital letters and write the letter of your choice on your answer paper.

676. TARRY (A) polish (B) restrain (C) surpass (D) linger (E) disturb

677. TAUTOLOGY (A) memory (B) repetition (C) tension (D) simile (E) lack of logic

678. TAWDRY (A) orderly (B) meretricious (C) reclaimed (D) filtered (E) proper

679. TEMERITY (A) timidity (B) resourcefulness (C) boldness (D) tremulousness (E) caution

680. TEMPORAL (A) priestly (B) scholarly (C) secular (D) sleepy (E) sporadic

681. TENACIOUS (A) fast running (B) intentional (C) obnoxious (D) holding fast (E) collecting

682. TENACITY (A) splendor (B) perseverance (C) tendency (D) ingratitude (E) decimation

683. TENDENTIOUS (A) biased (B) likely (C) absurd (D) festive (E) literary

684. TENTATIVE (A) prevalent (B) portable (C) mocking (D) wry (E) experimental

685. TENUOUS (A) vital (B) thin (C) careful (D) dangerous (E) necessary

686. TEPID (A) boiling (B) lukewarm (C) freezing (D) gaseous (E) cold

687. TERSE (A) brief in speech (B) bold in manner (C) under strain (D) without honor (E) beyond fear

688. TESSELATED (A) striped (B) made of mosaics (C) piebald (D) uniform (E) trimmed

689. THESPIAN (A) foreigner (B) skeptic (C) daydreamer (D) magician (E) actor

690. TITILLATE (A) hasten (B) fasten (C) stimulate (D) incorporate (E) enlarge

## Word List 47   tonsure-ubiquitous

tonsure   N. shaving of the head, especially by person entering religious orders. His *tonsure,* even more than his monastic garb, indicated that he was a member of the religious order.

topography   N. physical features of a region. Before the generals gave the order to attack, they ordered a complete study of the *topography* of the region.

■ torpor   N. lethargy; sluggishness; dormancy. Throughout the winter, nothing aroused the bear from his *torpor:* he would not emerge from hibernation until spring. torpid, ADJ.

torque   N. twisting force; force producing rotation. With her wrench she applied sufficient *torque* to the nut to loosen it.

torrent   N. rushing stream; flood. Day after day of heavy rain saturated the hillside until the water ran downhill in *torrents.* torrential, ADJ.

torrid   ADJ. passionate; hot or scorching. The novels published by Harlequin Romances feature *torrid* love affairs, some set in *torrid* climates.

torso   N. trunk of statue with head and limbs missing; human trunk. This *torso,* found in the ruins of Pompeii, is now on exhibition in the museum in Naples.

■ tortuous   ADJ. winding; full of curves. Because this

road is so *tortuous,* it is unwise to go faster than twenty miles an hour on it.

totter   V. move unsteadily; sway, as if about to fall. On unsteady feet, the drunk *tottered* down the hill to the nearest bar.

touchstone   N. stone used to test the fineness of gold alloys; criterion. What *touchstone* can be used to measure the character of a person?

touchy   ADJ. sensitive; irascible. Do not discuss his acne with Archy; he is very *touchy* about it.

tout   V. publicize; praise excessively. I lost confidence in my broker after he *touted* some junk bonds that turned out to be a bad investment.

toxic   ADJ. poisonous. We must seek an antidote for whatever *toxic* substance he has eaten. toxicity, N.

tract   N. pamphlet; a region of indefinite size. The King granted William Penn a *tract* of land in the New World.

■ tractable   ADJ. docile; easily managed. Although Susan seemed a *tractable* young woman, she had a stubborn streak of independence that occasionally led her to defy the powers-that-be when she felt they were in the wrong. tractability, N.

traduce   V. expose to slander. His opponents tried to *traduce* the candidate's reputation by spreading rumors about his past.

**trajectory** N. path taken by a projectile. The police tried to locate the spot from which the assassin had fired the fatal shot by tracing the *trajectory* of the bullet.

**tranquillity** N. calmness; peace. After the commotion and excitement of the city, I appreciate the *tranquillity* of these fields and forests.

**transcendent** ADJ. surpassing; exceeding ordinary limits; superior. Standing on the hillside watching the sunset through the Golden Gate was a *transcendent* experience for Lise: the sight was so beautiful it surpassed her wildest dreams. transcend, V. transcendency, N.

**transcribe** V. copy. When you *transcribe* your notes, please send a copy to Mr. Smith and keep the original for our files. transcription, N.

■ **transgression** N. violation of a law; sin. Forgive us our *transgressions;* we know not what we do.

**transient** ADJ. momentary; temporary; staying for a short time. Lexy's joy at finding the perfect Christmas gift for Phil was *transient;* she still had to find presents for the cousins and Uncle Bob. Located near the airport, this hotel caters to the largely *transient* trade. also N.

**transition** N. going from one state of action to another. During the period of *transition* from oil heat to gas heat, the furnace will have to be shut off.

**transitory** ADJ. impermanent; fleeting. Fame is *transitory*: today's rising star is all too soon tomorrow's washed-up has-been. transitoriness, N.

**translucent** ADJ. partly transparent. We could not recognize the people in the next room because of the *translucent* curtains that separated us.

**transmute** V. change; convert to something different. He was unable to *transmute* his dreams into actualities.

**transparent** ADJ. easily detected; permitting light to pass through freely. John's pride in his son is *transparent*; no one who sees the two of them together can miss it. transparency, N.

**transpire** V. be revealed; happen. When Austen writes the sentence "It had just *transpired* that he had left gaming debts behind him," her meaning is not that the debts had just been incurred, but that the shocking news had just leaked out.

**transport** N. strong emotion. Margo was a creature of extremes, at one moment in *transports* of joy over a vivid sunset, at another moment in *transports* of grief over a dying bird. also V.

**trappings** N. outward decorations; ornaments. He loved the *trappings* of success: the limousines, the stock options, the company jet.

**traumatic** ADJ. pertaining to an injury caused by violence. In his nightmares, he kept on recalling the *traumatic* experience of being wounded in battle. trauma, N.

**travail** N. painful labor. How long do you think a man can endure such *travail* and degradation without rebelling?

**traverse** V. go through or across. When you *traverse* this field, be careful of the bull.

**travesty** N. comical parody; treatment aimed at making something appear ridiculous. The ridiculous decision the jury has arrived at is a *travesty* of justice.

**treatise** N. article treating a subject systematically and thoroughly. He is preparing a *treatise* on the Elizabethan playwrights for his graduate degree.

**trek** N. travel; journey. The tribe made their *trek* further north that summer in search of game. also V.

**tremor** N. trembling; slight quiver. She had a nervous *tremor* in her right hand.

**tremulous** ADJ. trembling; wavering. She was *tremulous* more from excitement than from fear.

**trenchant** ADJ. cutting; keen. I am afraid of his *trenchant* wit for it is so often sarcastic.

**trepidation** N. fear; nervous apprehension. As she entered the office of the dean of admissions, Sharon felt some *trepidation* about how she would do in her interview.

**tribulation** N. distress; suffering. After all the trials and *tribulations* we have gone through, we need this rest.

**tribunal** N. court of justice. The decision of the *tribunal* was final and the prisoner was sentenced to death.

**tribute** N. tax levied by a ruler; mark of respect. The colonists refused to pay *tribute* to a foreign despot.

**trident** N. three-pronged spear. Neptune is usually depicted as rising from the sea, carrying his *trident* on his shoulder.

**trifling** ADJ. trivial; unimportant. Why bother going to see a doctor for such a *trifling*, everyday cold? trifle, N.

**trigger** V. set off. John is touchy today; say one word wrong and you'll *trigger* an explosion.

**trilogy** N. group of three works. Romain Rolland's novel *Jean Christophe* was first published as a *trilogy*.

**trinket** N. knickknack; bauble. Whenever she traveled abroad, Ethel would pick up costume jewelry and other *trinkets* as souvenirs.

**trite** ADJ. hackneyed; commonplace. The *trite* and predictable situations in many television programs turn off many viewers, who, in turn, turn off their sets.

**trivia** N. trifles; unimportant matters. Too many magazines ignore newsworthy subjects and feature *trivia*.

**troth** N. pledge of good faith especially in betrothal. He gave her his *troth* and vowed to cherish her always.

**trough** N. container for feeding farm animals; lowest point (of a wave, business cycle, etc.). The hungry pigs struggled to get at the fresh swill in the *trough*. The surfer rode her board, coasting along in the *trough* between two waves.

■ **truculence** N. aggressiveness; ferocity. Tynan's reviews were noted for their caustic attacks and general tone of *truculence*. truculent, ADJ.

**truism** N. self-evident truth. Many a *truism* is summed up in a proverb; for example, "Marry in haste, repent at leisure."

**truncate** V. cut the top off. The top of the cone that has been *truncated* in a plane parallel to its base is a circle.

**tryst** N. meeting. The lovers kept their *tryst* even though they realized their danger. also V.

**tumid** ADJ. swollen; pompous; bombastic. I especially dislike his *tumid* style; I prefer writing that is less swollen and bombastic.

**tumult** N. commotion; riot; noise. She could not make herself heard over the *tumult* of the mob.

**tundra** N. rolling, treeless plain in Siberia and arctic North America. Despite the cold, many geologists are trying to discover valuable mineral deposits in the *tundra*.

**turbid** ADJ. muddy; having the sediment disturbed. The water was *turbid* after the children had waded through it.

**turbulence** N. state of violent agitation. Warned of approaching *turbulence* in the atmosphere, the pilot told the passengers to fasten their seat belts.

**tureen** N. deep dish for serving soup. The waiters brought the soup to the tables in silver *tureens*.

**turgid** ADJ. swollen; distended. The *turgid* river threatened to overflow the levees and flood the countryside.

**turmoil** N. great commotion and confusion. Lydia running off with a soldier! Mother fainting at the news! The Bennet household was in *turmoil*.

**turncoat** N. traitor. The British considered Benedict Arnold a loyalist; the Americans considered him a *turncoat*.

**turpitude** N. depravity. A visitor may be denied admittance to this country if she has been guilty of moral *turpitude*.

**tutelage** N. guardianship; training. Under the *tutelage* of such masters of the instrument, she made rapid progress as a virtuoso.

**tutelary** ADJ. protective; pertaining to a guardianship. I am acting in my *tutelary* capacity when I refuse to grant you permission to leave the campus.

**tycoon** N. wealthy leader. John D. Rockefeller was a prominent *tycoon*.

**typhoon** N. tropical hurricane or cyclone. If you liked *Twister*, you'll love *Typhoon*!

**tyranny** N. oppression; cruel government. Frederick Douglass fought against the *tyranny* of slavery throughout his entire life.

**tyro** N. beginner; novice. For a mere *tyro*, you have produced some marvelous results.

**ubiquitous** ADJ. being everywhere; omnipresent. That Christmas "The Little Drummer Boy" seemed *ubiquitous*: Justin heard the tune everywhere he went. ubiquity, N.

# Test

## Word List 47  *Antonyms*

Each of the questions below consists of a word in capital letters, followed by five lettered words or phrases. Choose the lettered word or phrase that is most nearly opposite in meaning to the word in capital letters and write the letter of your choice on your answer paper.

691. TRACTABLE (A) unmanageable (B) irreligious (C) mortal (D) incapable (E) unreal

692. TRADUCE (A) exhume (B) increase (C) purchase (D) extol (E) donate

693. TRANQUILLITY (A) lack of sleep (B) lack of calm (C) emptiness (D) renewal (E) closeness

694. TRANSIENT (A) carried (B) close (C) permanent (D) removed (E) certain

695. TREMULOUS (A) steady (B) obese (C) young (D) healthy (E) unkempt

696. TRENCHANT (A) lacking bite (B) imperious (C) inessential (D) unafraid (E) narrow-minded

697. TREPIDATION (A) slowness (B) amputation (C) fearlessness (D) adroitness (E) death

698. TRITE (A) correct (B) original (C) distinguished (D) premature (E) certain

699. TRUCULENT (A) juicy (B) overflowing (C) peaceful (D) determined (E) false

700. TUMULT (A) scarcity (B) defeat (C) coolness (D) density (E) serenity

701. TURBID (A) clear (B) improbable (C) invariable (D) honest (E) turgid

702. TURBULENCE (A) reaction (B) approach (C) impropriety (D) calm (E) hostility

703. TURGID (A) rancid (B) shrunken (C) cool (D) explosive (E) painful

704. TURPITUDE (A) amplitude (B) heat (C) wealth (D) virtue (E) quiet

705. TYRO (A) infant (B) rubber (C) personnel (D) idiot (E) expert

# Word List 48    ulterior-vehement

**ulterior** ADJ. situated beyond; unstated and often questionable. You must have an *ulterior* motive for your behavior, since there is no obvious reason for it.

**ultimate** ADJ. final; not susceptible to further analysis. Scientists are searching for the *ultimate* truths.

**ultimatum** N. last demand; warning. Since they have ignored our *ultimatum,* our only recourse is to declare war.

**umbrage** N. resentment; anger; sense of injury or insult. She took *umbrage* at his remarks and stormed away in a huff.

**unaccountable** ADJ. inexplicable; unreasonable or mysterious. I have taken an *unaccountable* dislike to my doctor: "I do not love thee, Doctor Fell. The reason why, I cannot tell."

**unanimity** N. complete agreement. We were surprised by the *unanimity* with which our proposals were accepted by the different groups. unanimous, ADJ.

**unassailable** ADJ. not subject to question; not open to attack. Penelope's virtue was *unassailable*; while she waited for her husband to come back from the war, no other guy had a chance.

**unassuaged** ADJ. unsatisfied; not soothed. Her anger is *unassuaged* by your apology.

**unassuming** ADJ. modest. He is so *unassuming* that some people fail to realize how great a man he really is.

**unbridled** ADJ. violent. She had a sudden fit of *unbridled* rage.

**uncanny** ADJ. strange; mysterious. You have the *uncanny* knack of reading my innermost thoughts.

**unconscionable** ADJ. unscrupulous; excessive. She found the loan shark's demands *unconscionable* and impossible to meet.

**uncouth** ADJ. outlandish; clumsy; boorish. Most biographers portray Lincoln as an *uncouth* and ungainly young man.

**unction** N. the act of anointing with oil. The anointing with oil of a person near death is called extreme *unction.*

**unctuous** ADJ. oily; bland; insincerely suave. Uriah Heep disguised his nefarious actions by *unctuous* protestations of his "'umility."

**underlying** ADJ. fundamental; lying below. The *underlying* cause of the student riot was not the strict curfew rule but the moldy cafeteria food. Miss Marple seems a sweet little old lady at first, but an iron will *underlies* that soft and fluffy facade.

**undermine** V. weaken; sap. The recent corruption scandals have *undermined* many people's faith in the city government.

**underscore** V. emphasize. Addressing the jogging class, Kim *underscored* the importance to runners of good nutrition.

**undulating** ADJ. moving with a wavelike motion. The Hilo Hula Festival featured an *undulating* sea of grass skirts.

**unearth** V. dig up. When they *unearthed* the city, the archeologists found many relics of an ancient civilization.

**unearthly** ADJ. not earthly; weird. There is an *unearthly* atmosphere in her work that amazes the casual observer.

**unequivocal** ADJ. plain; obvious. My answer to your proposal is an *unequivocal* and absolute "No."

**unerringly** ADV. infallibly. My teacher *unerringly* pounced on the one typographical error in my essay.

**unexceptionable** ADJ. not offering any basis for criticism; entirely acceptable. Objecting to Jack's lack of a respectable family background, Lady Bracknell declared that Cecily could marry only a man of *unexceptionable* lineage and character.

**unfaltering** ADJ. steadfast. She approached the guillotine with *unfaltering* steps.

**unfeigned** ADJ. genuine; real. She turned so pale that I am sure her surprise was *unfeigned.*

**unfettered** ADJ. liberated; freed from chains. Chained to the wall for months on end, the hostage despaired that he would ever be *unfettered.* unfetter, V.

**unfledged** ADJ. immature. It is hard for an *unfledged* writer to find a sympathetic publisher.

**unfrock** V. to strip a priest or minister of church authority. To disbar a lawyer, to *unfrock* a priest, to suspend a doctor's license to practice—these are extreme steps that the authorities should take only after careful consideration.

**ungainly** ADJ. awkward; clumsy; unwieldy. "If you want to know whether Nick's an *ungainly* dancer, check out my bruised feet," said Nora. Anyone who has ever tried to carry a bass fiddle knows it's an *ungainly* instrument.

**unguent** N. ointment. Apply this *unguent* to the sore muscles before retiring.

**uniformity** N. sameness; monotony. At *Persons* magazine, we strive for *uniformity* of style; as a result, all our writers wind up sounding exactly alike. uniform, ADJ.

**unilateral** ADJ. one-sided. This legislation is *unilateral* since it binds only one party in the controversy.

**unimpeachable** ADJ. blameless and exemplary. Her conduct in office was *unimpeachable* and her record is spotless.

**uninhibited** ADJ. unrepressed. The congregation was shocked by her *uninhibited* laughter during the sermon.

**unintimidating** ADJ. unfrightening. Though Phil had expected to feel overawed when he met Joe Montana, he found the world-famous quarterback friendly and *unintimidating.*

**unique** ADJ. without an equal; single in kind. You have the *unique* distinction of being the first student whom I have had to fail in this course.

**unison** N. unity of pitch; complete accord. The choir sang in *unison.*

**universal** ADJ. characterizing or affecting all; present everywhere. At first, no one shared Christopher's opinions; his theory that the world was round was met with *universal* disdain.

**unkempt** ADJ. disheveled; uncared for in appearance. Jeremy hated his neighbor's *unkempt* lawn: he thought its neglected appearance had a detrimental effect on neighborhood property values.

**unmitigated** ADJ. unrelieved or immoderate; absolute. After four days of *unmitigated* heat, I was ready to collapse from heat prostration. The congresswoman's husband was an *unmitigated* jerk: not only did he abandon her, but also he took her campaign funds!

**unobtrusive** ADJ. inconspicuous; not blatant. Reluctant to attract notice, the governess took a chair in a far corner of the room and tried to be as *unobtrusive* as possible.

**unprecedented** ADJ. novel; unparalleled. Margaret Mitchell's book *Gone with the Wind* was an *unprecedented* success.

**unprepossessing** ADJ. unattractive. During adolescence many attractive young people somehow acquire the false notion that their appearance is *unprepossessing*.

**unravel** V. disentangle; solve. With equal ease Miss Marple *unraveled* tangled balls of yarn and baffling murder mysteries.

**unrequited** ADJ. not reciprocated. Suffering the pangs of *unrequited* love, Olivia rebukes Cesario for his hard-heartedness.

**unruly** ADJ. disobedient; lawless. The only way to curb this *unruly* mob is to use tear gas.

**unsavory** ADJ. distasteful; morally offensive. People with *unsavory* reputations should not be allowed to work with young children.

**unscathed** ADJ. unharmed. They prayed he would come back from the war *unscathed.*

**unseemly** ADJ. unbecoming; indecent; in poor taste. When Seymour put whoopee cushions on all the seats in the funeral parlor, his conduct was most *unseemly.*

**unsightly** ADJ. ugly. Although James was an experienced emergency room nurse, he occasionally became queasy when faced with a particularly *unsightly* injury.

**unsullied** ADJ. untarnished. I am happy that my reputation is *unsullied.*

**untenable** ADJ. indefensible; not able to be maintained. Wayne is so contrary that, the more *untenable* a position is, the harder he'll try to defend it.

**untoward** ADJ. unfortunate or unlucky; adverse; unexpected. Trying to sneak out of the house, Huck had a most *untoward* encounter with Miss Watson, who thwarted his escape.

**unwarranted** ADJ. unjustified; groundless; undeserved. We could not understand Martin's *unwarranted* rudeness to his mother's guests.

**unwieldy** ADJ. awkward; cumbersome; unmanageable. The large carton was so *unwieldy* that the movers had trouble getting it up the stairs.

**unwitting** ADJ. unintentional; not knowing. She was the *unwitting* tool of the swindlers.

**unwonted** ADJ. unaccustomed. He hesitated to assume the *unwonted* role of master of ceremonies at the dinner.

**upbraid** V. severely scold; reprimand. Not only did Miss Minchin *upbraid* Ermengarde for her disobedience, but also she hung her up by her braids from a coatrack in the classroom.

**uproarious** ADJ. marked by commotion; extremely funny; very noisy. The *uproarious* comedy hit *Ace Ventura: Pet Detective* starred Jim Carrey, whose comic mugging provoked gales of *uproarious* laughter from audiences coast to coast.

**upshot** N. outcome. The *upshot* of the rematch was that the former champion proved that he still possessed all the skills of his youth.

**urbane** ADJ. suave; refined; elegant. The courtier was *urbane* and sophisticated. urbanity, N.

**urchin** N. mischievous child (usually a boy). Get out! This store is no place for grubby *urchins!*

**ursine** ADJ. bearlike; pertaining to a bear. Because of its *ursine* appearance, the great panda has been identified with the bears; actually, it is closely related to the raccoon.

**usurp** V. seize another's power or rank. The revolution ended when the victorious rebel general succeeded in his attempt to *usurp* the throne. usurpation, N.

**usury** N. lending money at illegal rates of interest. The loan shark was found guilty of *usury.*

**utopia** N. ideal place, state, or society. Fed up with this imperfect universe, Don would have liked to run off to Shangri-la or some other imaginary *utopia.* utopian, ADJ.

**uxorious** ADJ. excessively devoted to one's wife. His friends laughed at him because he was so *uxorious* and submissive to his wife's desires.

■ **vacillate** V. waver; fluctuate. Uncertain which suitor she ought to marry, the princess *vacillated,* saying now one, now the other. vacillation, N.

**vacuous** ADJ. empty; lacking in ideas; stupid. The candidate's *vacuous* remarks annoyed the audience, who had hoped to hear more than empty platitudes. vacuity, N.

**vagabond** N. wanderer; tramp. In summer, college students wander the roads of Europe like carefree *vagabonds.* also ADJ.

**vagary** N. caprice; whim. She followed every *vagary* of fashion.

**vagrant** ADJ. stray; random. He tried to study, but could not collect his *vagrant* thoughts.

**vagrant** N. homeless wanderer. Because he was a stranger in town with no visible means of support, Martin feared he would be jailed as a *vagrant.* vagrancy, N.

**vainglorious** ADJ. boastful; excessively conceited. She was a *vainglorious* and arrogant individual.

**valedictory** ADJ. pertaining to farewell. I found the *valedictory* address too long; leave-taking should be brief. also N.

**valid** ADJ. logically convincing; sound; legally acceptable. You're going to have to come up with a better argument if you want to convince me that your reasoning is *valid*.

**validate** V. confirm; ratify. I will not publish my findings until I *validate* my results.

**valor** N. bravery. He received the Medal of Honor for his *valor* in battle.

**vampire** N. ghostly being that sucks the blood of the living. Children were afraid to go to sleep at night because of the many legends of *vampires*.

**vanguard** N. forerunners; advance forces. We are the *vanguard* of a tremendous army that is following us.

**vantage** N. position giving an advantage. They fired upon the enemy from behind trees, walls and any other point of *vantage* they could find.

**vapid** ADJ. dull and unimaginative; insipid and flavorless. "*Bor*-ing!" said Cher, as she suffered through yet another *vapid* lecture about Dead White Male Poets.

**vaporize** V. turn into vapor (steam, gas, fog, etc.). "Zap!" went Super Mario's atomic ray gun as he *vaporized* another deadly foe.

**variegated** ADJ. many-colored. Without her glasses, Gretchen saw the fields of tulips as a *variegated* blur.

**vassal** N. in feudalism, one who held land of a superior lord. The lord demanded that his *vassals* contribute more to his military campaign.

**vaunted** ADJ. boasted; bragged; highly publicized. This much *vaunted* project proved a disappointment when it collapsed.

**veer** V. change in direction. After what seemed an eternity, the wind *veered* to the east and the storm abated.

**vegetate** V. live in a monotonous way. I do not understand how you can *vegetate* in this quiet village after the adventurous life you have led.

**vehement** ADJ. forceful; intensely emotional; with marked vigor. Alfred became so *vehement* in describing what was wrong with the Internal Revenue Service that he began jumping up and down and gesticulating wildly. vehemence, N.

# Test

## Word List 48 *Antonyms*

Each of the questions below consists of a word in capital letters, followed by five lettered words or phrases. Choose the lettered word or phrase that is most nearly opposite in meaning to the word in capital letters and write the letter of your choice on your answer paper.

706. UNEARTH (A) conceal (B) gnaw (C) clean (D) fling (E) react

707. UNFEIGNED (A) pretended (B) fashionable (C) wary (D) switched (E) colonial

708. UNGAINLY (A) ignorant (B) graceful (C) detailed (D) dancing (E) pedantic

709. UNIMPEACHABLE (A) fruitful (B) rampaging (C) faulty (D) pensive (E) thorough

710. UNKEMPT (A) bombed (B) washed (C) neat (D) showy (E) tawdry

711. UNRULY (A) chatting (B) obedient (C) definite (D) lined (E) curious

712. UNSEEMLY (A) effortless (B) proper (C) conducive (D) pointed (E) informative

713. UNSULLIED (A) tarnished (B) countless (C) soggy (D) papered (E) homicidal

714. UNTENABLE (A) supportable (B) tender (C) sheepish (D) tremulous (E) adequate

715. UNWITTING (A) clever (B) intense (C) sensitive (D) freezing (E) intentional

716. VACILLATION (A) remorse (B) relief (C) respect (D) steadfastness (E) inoculation

717. VALEDICTORY (A) sad (B) collegiate (C) derivative (D) salutatory (E) promising

718. VALOR (A) admonition (B) injustice (C) cowardice (D) generosity (E) repression

719. VANGUARD (A) regiment (B) rear (C) echelon (D) protection (E) loyalty

720. VAUNTED (A) unvanquished (B) fell (C) belittled (D) exacting (E) believed

## Word List 49 velocity–vogue

**velocity** N. speed. The train went by at considerable *velocity*.

**venal** ADJ. capable of being bribed. The *venal* policeman accepted the bribe offered him by the speeding motorist whom he had stopped.

**vendetta** N. blood feud. The rival mobs engaged in a bitter *vendetta*.

**vendor** N. seller. The fruit *vendor* sold her wares from a stall on the sidewalk.

**veneer** N. thin layer; cover. Casual acquaintances were deceived by his *veneer* of sophistication and failed to recognize his fundamental shallowness.

**venerable** ADJ. deserving high respect. We do not mean to be disrespectful when we refuse to follow the advice of our *venerable* leader.

■ **venerate** V. revere. In Tibet today, the common people still *venerate* their traditional spiritual leader, the Dalai Lama.

**venial** ADJ. forgivable; trivial. When Jean Valjean stole a loaf of bread to feed his starving sister, he committed a *venial* offense.

**venison** N. the meat of a deer. The hunters dined on *venison*.

**venom** N. poison; hatred. Bitten on his ankle by a *venomous* snake, the cowboy contortionist curled up like a pretzel and sucked the *venom* out of the wound.

**vent** N. small opening; outlet. The wine did not flow because the air *vent* in the barrel was clogged.

**vent** V. express; utter. He *vented* his wrath on his class.

**ventral** V. abdominal. We shall now examine the *ventral* plates of this serpent, not the dorsal side.

**ventriloquist** N. someone who can make his or her voice seem to come from another person or thing. This *ventriloquist* does an act in which she has a conversation with a wooden dummy.

**venture** V. risk; dare; undertake a risk. Fearing to distress the actors, the timorous reviewer never *ventured* to criticize a performance in harsh terms. also N.

**venturesome** ADJ. bold. A group of *venturesome* women were the first to scale Mt. Annapurna.

**venue** N. location. The attorney asked for a change of *venue;* he thought his client would do better if the trial were held in a less conservative county.

■ **veracious** ADJ. truthful. I can recommend him for this position because I have always found him *veracious* and reliable. veracity, N.

**veracity** N. truthfulness. Trying to prove Hill a liar, Senator Spector repeatedly questioned her *veracity*. veracious, ADJ.

**verbalize** V. put into words. I know you don't like to talk about these things, but please try to *verbalize* your feelings.

**verbatim** ADV. word for word. He repeated the message *verbatim*. also ADJ.

**verbiage** N. pompous array of words. After we had waded through all the *verbiage*, we discovered that the writer had said very little.

■ **verbose** ADJ. wordy. We had to make some major cuts in Senator Foghorn's speech because it was far too *verbose*. verbosity, N.

**verdant** ADJ. green; lush in vegetation. Monet's paintings of the *verdant* meadows were symphonies in green.

**verdigris** N. green coating on copper that has been exposed to the weather. Despite all attempts to protect the statue from the elements, it became coated with *verdigris*.

**verge** N. border; edge. Madame Curie knew she was on the *verge* of discovering the secrets of radioactive elements. also V.

**verisimilar** ADJ. probable or likely; having the appearance of truth. Something *verisimilar* is very similar to the truth, or at least seems to be.

**verisimilitude** N. appearance of truth; likelihood. Critics praised her for the *verisimilitude* of her performance as Lady Macbeth. She was completely believable.

**veritable** ADJ. actual; being truly so; not false or imaginary. At his computer, Pavel is a *veritable* wizard, creating graphic effects that seem magical to programmers less skilled than he.

**verity** N. quality of being true; lasting truth or principle. Do you question the *verity* of Kato Kaelin's testimony about what he heard the night Nicole Brown Simpson was slain? To the skeptic, everything was relative: there were no eternal *verities* in which one could believe.

**vernacular** N. living language; natural style. Cut out those old-fashioned "thee's" and "thou's" and write in the *vernacular*. also ADJ.

**vernal** ADJ. pertaining to spring. We may expect *vernal* showers all during the month of April.

**versatile** ADJ. having many talents; capable of working in many fields. She was a *versatile* athlete, earning varsity letters in basketball, hockey, and track. versatility, N.

**vertex** N. summit. Let us drop a perpendicular line from the *vertex* of the triangle to the base. vertices, PL.

**vertigo** N. severe dizziness. When you test potential plane pilots for susceptibility to spells of *vertigo*, be sure to hand out airsick bags.

**verve** N. enthusiasm; liveliness. She approached her studies with such *verve* that it was impossible for her to do poorly.

**vestige** N. trace; remains. We discovered *vestiges* of early Indian life in the cave.

**vex** N. annoy; distress. Please try not to *vex* your mother; she is doing the best she can.

■ **viable** ADJ. practical or workable; capable of maintaining life. The plan to build a new baseball stadium, though missing a few details, is *viable* and stands a good chance of winning popular support.

**viand** N. food. There was a variety of *viands* at the feast.

**vicarious** ADJ. acting as a substitute; done by a deputy. Many people get a *vicarious* thrill at the movies by imagining they are the characters on the screen.

**vicissitude** N. change of fortune. Humbled by life's *vicissitudes,* the last emperor of China worked as a lowly gardener in the palace over which he had once ruled.

**victuals** N. food. I am very happy to be able to provide you with these *victuals;* I know you are hungry.

**vie** V. contend; compete. Politicians *vie* with one another, competing for donations and votes.

**vigilant**  ADJ. watchfully awake; alert to spot danger. From the battlement, the *vigilant* sentry kept his eyes open for any sign of enemy troops approaching. vigilance, N.

**vigor**  N. active strength. Although he was over seventy years old, Jack had the *vigor* of a man in his prime. vigorous, ADJ.

**vignette**  N. picture; short literary sketch. The *New Yorker* published her latest *vignette*.

**vilify**  V. slander. Waging a highly negative campaign, the candidate attempted to *vilify* his opponent's reputation. vilification, N.

**vindicate**  V. clear from blame; exonerate; justify or support. The lawyer's goal was to *vindicate* her client and prove him innocent on all charges. The critics' extremely favorable reviews *vindicate* my opinion that *The Madness of King George* is a brilliant movie.

**vindictive**  ADJ. out for revenge; malicious. Divorce sometimes brings out a *vindictive* streak in people; when Tony told Tina he was getting a divorce, she poured green Jell-O into his aquarium and turned his tropical fish into dessert.

**vintner**  N. winemaker; seller of wine. The poet wondered what the *vintners* could buy that would be half as precious as the wine they sold.

**viper**  N. poisonous snake. The habitat of the horned *viper*, a particularly venomous snake, is in sandy regions like the Sahara or the Sinai peninsula.

**virile**  ADJ. manly. I do not accept the premise that a man is *virile* only when he is belligerent.

**virtual**  ADJ. in essence; for practical purposes. She is a *virtual* financial wizard when it comes to money matters.

**virtue**  N. goodness; moral excellence; good quality. A *virtue* carried to extremes can turn into something resembling vice; humility, for example, can degenerate into servility and spinelessness.

**virtuoso**  N. highly skilled artist. The child prodigy Yehudi Menuhin grew into a *virtuoso* whose *virtuosity* on the violin thrilled millions. virtuosity, N.

**virulent**  ADJ. extremely poisonous; hostile; bitter. Laid up with a *virulent* case of measles, Vera blamed her doctors because her recovery took so long. In fact, she became quite *virulent* on the subject of the quality of modern medical care. virulence, N.

**virus**  N. disease communicator. The doctors are looking for a specific medicine to control this *virus*.

**visage**  N. face; appearance. The stern *visage* of the judge indicated that she had decided to impose a severe penalty.

**visceral**  ADJ. felt in one's inner organs. She disliked the *visceral* sensations she had whenever she rode the roller coaster.

**viscid**  ADJ. adhesive; gluey. The trunk of the maple tree was *viscid* with sap.

■ **viscous**  ADJ. sticky, gluey. Melted tar is a *viscous* substance. viscosity, N.

**vise**  N. tool for holding work in place. Before filing its edges, the keysmith took the blank key and fixed it firmly between the jaws of a *vise*.

**visionary**  ADJ. produced by imagination; fanciful; mystical. She was given to *visionary* schemes that never materialized. also N.

**vital**  ADJ. vibrant and lively; critical; living; breathing. The *vital*, highly energetic first aid instructor stressed that it was *vital* in examining accident victims to note their *vital* signs.

**vitiate**  V. spoil the effect of; make inoperative. Fraud will *vitiate* the contract.

**vitreous**  ADJ. pertaining to or resembling glass. Although this plastic has many *vitreous* qualities such as transparency, it is unbreakable.

**vitriolic**  ADJ. corrosive; sarcastic. Such *vitriolic* criticism is uncalled for.

■ **vituperative**  ADJ. abusive; scolding. He became more *vituperative* as he realized that we were not going to grant him his wish.

**vivacious**  ADJ. lively or animated; sprightly. She had always been *vivacious* and sparkling.

**vivisection**  N. act of dissecting living animals. The Society for the Prevention of Cruelty to Animals opposed *vivisection* and deplored the practice of using animals in scientific experiments.

**vixen**  N. female fox; ill-tempered woman. Aware that she was right once again, he lost his temper and called her a shrew and a *vixen*.

**vociferous**  ADJ. clamorous; noisy. The crowd grew *vociferous* in its anger and threatened to take the law into its own hands.

**vogue**  N. popular fashion. Jeans became the *vogue* on many college campuses.

# Test

## Word List 49    *Synonyms and Antonyms*

Each of the questions below consists of a word in capital letters, followed by five lettered words or phrases. Choose the lettered word or phrase that is most nearly similar or opposite in meaning to the word in capital letters and write the letter of your choice on your answer paper.

721. VENAL (A) springlike (B) honest (C) angry (D) indifferent (E) going

722. VENERATE (A) revere (B) age (C) reject (D) reverberate (E) degenerate

723. VENIAL (A) unforgivable (B) unforgettable (C) unmistaken (D) fearful (E) fragrant

724. VERACIOUS (A) worried (B) slight (C) alert (D) truthful (E) instrumental

725. VERDANT (A) poetic (B) green (C) red (D) autumnal (E) frequent

726. VERITY (A) sanctity (B) reverence (C) falsehood (D) rarity (E) household

727. VESTIGE (A) trek (B) trail (C) trace (D) trial (E) tract

728. VIABLE (A) moribund (B) salable (C) useful (D) foolish (E) inadequate

729. VIAND (A) wand (B) gown (C) food (D) orchestra (E) frock

730. VICARIOUS (A) substitutional (B) aggressive (C) sporadic (D) reverent (E) internal

731. VIGILANCE (A) bivouac (B) guide (C) watchfulness (D) mob rule (E) posse

732. VILIFY (A) erect (B) eulogize (C) better (D) magnify (E) horrify

733. VINDICTIVE (A) revengeful (B) fearful (C) divided (D) literal (E) convincing

734. VIRULENT (A) sensuous (B) malignant (C) masculine (D) conforming (E) approaching

735. VISAGE (A) doubt (B) personality (C) hermitage (D) face (E) armor

## Word List 50    volatile-zephyr

■ **volatile** ADJ. changeable; explosive; evaporating rapidly. The political climate today is extremely *volatile*: no one can predict what the electorate will do next. Maria Callas's temper was extremely *volatile*: the only thing you could predict was that she would blow up. Acetone is an extremely *volatile* liquid: it evaporates instantly. volatility, N.

**volition** N. act of making a conscious choice. She selected this dress of her own *volition*.

**voluble** ADJ. fluent; glib; talkative. An excessively *voluble* speaker suffers from logorrhea: he continually runs off at the mouth! volubility, N.

**voluminous** ADJ. bulky; large. A caftan is a *voluminous* garment; the average person wearing one looks as if he or she is draped in a small tent.

**voracious** ADJ. ravenous. The wolf is a *voracious* animal, its hunger never satisfied.

**vortex** N. whirlwind; whirlpool; center of turbulence; predicament into which one is inexorably plunged. Sucked into the *vortex* of the tornado, Dorothy and Toto were carried from Kansas to Oz.

**vouchsafe** V. grant condescendingly; guarantee. I can safely *vouchsafe* you fair return on your investment.

**voyeur** N. Peeping Tom. Jill called Jack a *voyeur* when she caught him aiming his binoculars at a bedroom window of the house next door.

**vulnerable** ADJ. susceptible to wounds. His opponents could not harm Achilles, who was *vulnerable* only in his heel. vulnerability, N.

**vulpine** ADJ. like a fox; crafty. She disliked his sly ways, but granted him a certain *vulpine* intelligence.

**waffle** V. speak equivocally about an issue. When asked directly about the governor's involvement in the savings and loan scandal, the press secretary *waffled*, talking all around the issue.

**waft** V. moved gently by wind or waves. Daydreaming, he gazed at the leaves that *wafted* past his window.

**waggish** ADJ. mischievous; humorous; tricky. He was a prankster who, unfortunately, often overlooked the damage he could cause with his *waggish* tricks. wag, N.

**waif** N. homeless child or animal. Although he already had eight cats, he could not resist adopting yet another feline *waif*.

**waive** V. give up temporarily; yield. I will *waive* my rights in this matter in order to expedite our reaching a proper decision.

**wake** N. trail of ship or other object through water; path of something that has gone before. The *wake* of the swan gliding through the water glistened in the moonlight. Reporters and photographers converged on South Carolina in the *wake* of the hurricane that devastated much of the eastern seaboard.

**wallow** V. roll in; indulge in; become helpless. The hippopotamus loves to *wallow* in the mud.

**wan** ADJ. having a pale or sickly color; pallid. Suckling asked, "Why so pale and *wan*, fond lover?"

**wanderlust** N. strong longing to travel. Don't set your heart on a traveling man. He's got too much *wanderlust* to settle down.

**wane** V. decrease in size or strength; draw gradually to an end. To *wane* is the opposite of to wax or increase in size. When lit, does a wax candle *wane*?

**wangle** V. wiggle out; fake. She tried to *wangle* an invitation to the party.

**wanton** ADJ. unrestrained; willfully malicious; unchaste. Pointing to the stack of bills, Sheldon criticized Sarah for her *wanton* expenditures. In response, Sara accused Sheldon of making an unfounded, *wanton* attack.

**warble** V. sing; babble. Every morning the birds *warbled* outside her window. also N.

■ **warranted** ADJ. justified; authorized. Before the judge issues the injunction, you must convince her this action is *warranted*.

**warranty** N. guarantee; assurance by seller. The purchaser of this automobile is protected by the manufacturer's *warranty* that he will replace any defective part for five years or 50,000 miles.

**warren** N. tunnels in which rabbits live; crowded conditions in which people live. The tenement was a veritable *warren*, packed with people too poor to live elsewhere.

■ **wary** ADJ. very cautious. The spies grew *wary* as they approached the sentry.

**wastrel** N. profligate. He was denounced as a *wastrel* who had dissipated his inheritance.

**wax** V. increase; grow. With proper handling, her fortunes *waxed* and she became rich.

**waylay** V. ambush; lie in wait. They agreed to *waylay* their victim as he passed through the dark alley going home.

**wean** V. accustom a baby not to nurse; give up a cherished activity. He decided he would *wean* himself away from eating junk food and stick to fruits and vegetables.

**weather** V. endure the effects of weather or other forces. He *weathered* the changes in his personal life with difficulty, as he had no one in whom to confide.

**welt** N. mark from a beating or whipping. The evidence of child abuse was very clear; Jennifer's small body was covered with *welts* and bruises.

■ **welter** N. turmoil; bewildering jumble. The existing *welter* of overlapping federal and state proclaims cries out for immediate reform.

**welter** V. wallow. At the height of the battle, the casualties were so numerous that the victims *weltered* in their blood while waiting for medical attention.

**wheedle** V. cajole; coax; deceive by flattery. She knows she can *wheedle* almost anything she wants from her father.

**whelp** N. young wolf, dog, tiger, etc. This collie *whelp* won't do for breeding, but he'd make a fine pet.

**whet** V. sharpen; stimulate. The odors from the kitchen are *whetting* my appetite; I will be ravenous by the time the meal is served.

**whiff** N. puff or gust (of air, scent, etc.); hint. The slightest *whiff* of Old Spice cologne brought memories of George to her mind.

■ **whimsical** N. capricious; fanciful. In *Mrs. Doubtfire*, the hero is a playful, *whimsical* man who takes a notion to dress up as a woman so that he can look after his children, who are in the custody of his ex-wife. whimsy, N.

**whinny** V. neigh like a horse. When he laughed through his nose, it sounded as if he *whinnied*.

**whit** N. smallest speck. There is not a *whit* of intelligence or understanding in your observations.

**whittle** V. pare; cut off bits. As a present for Aunt Polly, Tom *whittled* some clothespins out of a chunk of wood.

**whorl** N. ring of leaves around stem; ring. Identification by fingerprints is based on the difference in shape and number of the *whorls* on the fingers.

**willful** ADJ. intentional; headstrong. Donald had planned to kill his wife for months; clearly, her death was a case of deliberate, *willful* murder, not a crime of passion committed by a hasty, *willful* youth unable to foresee the consequences of his deeds.

**wily** ADJ. cunning; artful. She is as *wily* as a fox in avoiding trouble.

**wince** V. shrink back; flinch. The screech of the chalk on the blackboard made her *wince*.

**windfall** N. fallen fruit; unexpected lucky event. This huge tax refund is quite a *windfall*.

**winnow** V. sift; separate good parts from bad. This test will *winnow* out the students who study from those who don't bother.

**winsome** ADJ. agreeable; gracious; engaging. By her *winsome* manner, she made herself liked by everyone who met her.

**wispy** ADJ. thin; slight; barely discernible. Worried about preserving his few *wispy* tufts of hair, Walter carefully massaged his scalp and applied hair restorer every night.

**wistful** ADJ. vaguely longing; sadly pensive. With a last *wistful* glance at the happy couples dancing in the hall, Sue headed back to her room to study for her exam.

**withdrawn** ADJ. introverted; remote. Rebuffed by his colleagues, the initially outgoing young researcher became increasingly *withdrawn*.

**wither** V. shrivel; decay. Cut flowers are beautiful for a day, but all too soon they *wither*.

**withhold** V. refuse to give; hold back. The tenants decided to *withhold* a portion of the rent until the landlord kept his promise to renovate the building.

**withstand** V. stand up against; successfully resist. If you can *withstand* all the peer pressure in high school to cut classes and goof off, you should survive college in fine shape.

**witless** ADJ. foolish; idiotic. If Beavis is a half-wit, then Butthead is totally *witless*.

**witticism** N. witty saying; wisecrack. I don't mean any criticism, but your last supposed *witticism* really hurt my feelings.

**wizardry**  N. sorcery; magic. Merlin amazed the knights with his *wizardry*.

**wizened**  ADJ. withered; shriveled. The *wizened* old man in the home for the aged was still active and energetic.

**woe**  N. deep, inconsolable grief; affliction; suffering. Pale and wan with grief, Wanda was bowed down beneath the burden of her *woes*.

**wont**  N. custom; habitual procedure. As was her *wont*, she jogged two miles every morning before going to work.

**worldly**  ADJ. engrossed in matters of this earth; not spiritual. You must leave your *worldly* goods behind you when you go to meet your Maker.

**wrangle**  V. quarrel; obtain through arguing; herd cattle. They *wrangled* over their inheritance.

**wrath**  N. anger; fury. She turned to him, full of *wrath*, and said, "What makes you think I'll accept lower pay for this job than you get?"

**wreak**  V. inflict. I am afraid he will *wreak* his vengeance on the innocent as well as the guilty.

**wrench**  V. pull; strain; twist. She *wrenched* free of her attacker and landed a powerful kick to his kneecap.

**wrest**  V. pull away; take by violence. With only ten seconds left to play, our team *wrested* victory from their grasp.

**writ**  N. written command issued by a court. The hero of Leonard's novel is a process server who invents unorthodox ways of serving *writs* on reluctant parties.

**writhe**  V. twist in coils; contort in pain. In *Dances with Snakes*, the snake dancer wriggled sinuously as her boa constrictor *writhed* around her torso.

**wry**  ADJ. twisted; with a humorous twist. We enjoy Dorothy Parker's verse for its *wry* wit.

**xenophobia**  N. fear or hatred of foreigners. When the refugee arrived in America, he was unprepared for the *xenophobia* he found there.

**yen**  N. longing; urge. She had a *yen* to get away and live on her own for a while.

**yeoman**  N. man owning small estate; middle-class farmer. It was not the aristocrat but the *yeoman* who determined the nation's policies.

**yield**  N. amount produced; crop; income on investment. An experienced farmer can estimate the annual *yield* of his acres with surprising accuracy. also V.

**yield**  V. give in; surrender. The wounded knight refused to *yield to* his foe.

**yoke**  V. join together, unite. I don't wish to be *yoked* to him in marriage, as if we were cattle pulling a plow. also N.

**yokel**  N. country bumpkin. At school, his classmates regarded him as a *yokel* and laughed at his rustic mannerisms.

**yore**  N. time past. She dreamed of the elegant homes of *yore*, but gave no thought to their inelegant plumbing.

**zany**  ADJ. crazy; comic. I can watch the Marx brothers' *zany* antics for hours.

**zeal**  N. eager enthusiasm. Wang's *zeal* was contagious; soon all his fellow students were busily making posters, inspired by his ardent enthusiasm for the cause. zealous, ADJ.

■ **zealot**  N. fanatic; person who shows excessive zeal. Though Glenn was devout, he was no *zealot*; he never tried to force his religious beliefs on his friends.

**zenith**  N. point directly overhead in the sky; summit. When the sun was at its *zenith*, the glare was not as strong as at sunrise and sunset.

**zephyr**  N. gentle breeze; west wind. When these *zephyrs* blow, it is good to be in an open boat under a full sail.

# Test

## Word List 50    *Synonyms*

Each of the following questions consists of a word in capital letters, followed by five lettered words or phrases. Choose the lettered word or phrase that is most nearly similar in meaning to the word in capital letters and write the letter of your choice on your answer paper.

736. VOLUBLE (A) worthwhile (B) serious (C) terminal (D) loquacious (E) circular

737. VORACIOUS (A) ravenous (B) spacious (C) truthful (D) pacific (E) tenacious

738. VOUCHSAFE (A) borrow (B) grant (C) punish (D) desire (E) qualify

739. WAIF (A) soldier (B) urchin (C) surrender (D) breeze (E) spouse

740. WANTON (A) needy (B) passive (C) rumored (D) oriental (E) unchaste

741. WARRANTY (A) threat (B) guarantee (C) order for arrest (D) issue (E) fund

742. WASTREL (A) refuse (B) spendthrift (C) mortal (D) tolerance (E) song

743. WAYLAY (A) ambush (B) journey (C) rest (D) road map (E) song

744. WELTER (A) heat (B) greeting (C) recovery (D) universe (E) tumult

745. WHINNY (A) complain (B) hurry (C) request
(D) neigh (E) gallop

746. WINDFALL (A) unexpected gain
(B) widespread destruction (C) calm (D) autumn
(E) wait

747. WINSOME (A) victorious (B) gracious (C) married
(D) permanent (E) pained

748. WIZENED (A) magical (B) clever (C) shriveled
(D) swift (E) active

749. YEOMAN (A) masses (B) middle-class farmer
(C) proletarian (D) indigent person (E) man of rank

750. ZEALOT (A) beginner (B) patron (C) fanatic
(D) murderer (E) leper

# Answer Key

**Test—Word List 1**
1. E   6. E   11. A
2. A   7. B   12. E
3. C   8. E   13. A
4. D   9. A   14. D
5. B   10. A   15. C

**Test—Word List 2**
16. E   21. A   26. B
17. B   22. A   27. D
18. A   23. B   28. B
19. D   24. B   29. C
20. A   25. B   30. D

**Test—Word List 3**
31. C   36. E   41. B
32. C   37. C   42. E
33. D   38. B   43. E
34. D   39. E   44. C
35. A   40. D   45. A

**Test—Word List 4**
46. A   51. C   56. E
47. A   52. A   57. C
48. B   53. C   58. D
49. D   54. B   59. D
50. B   55. D   60. C

**Test—Word List 5**
61. E   66. A   71. D
62. D   67. C   72. C
63. B   68. C   73. C
64. C   69. B   74. B
65. C   70. C   75. D

**Test—Word List 6**
76. D   81. A   86. C
77. B   82. B   87. A
78. D   83. B   88. E
79. A   84. E   89. E
80. E   85. E   90. C

**Test—Word List 7**
91. B   96. B   101. D
92. B   97. A   102. B
93. B   98. D   103. A
94. D   99. B   104. A
95. B   100. C   105. B

**Test—Word List 8**
106. D   111. B   116. B
107. E   112. A   117. D
108. A   113. D   118. A
109. C   114. C   119. C
110. E   115. D   120. B

**Test—Word List 9**
121. D   126. E   131. A
122. E   127. A   132. D
123. E   128. D   133. C
124. C   129. B   134. B
125. C   130. E   135. A

**Test—Word List 10**
136. E   141. B   146. E
137. B   142. E   147. E
138. D   143. D   148. C
139. C   144. D   149. A
140. A   145. D   150. D

**Test—Word List 11**
151. B   156. C   161. B
152. B   157. C   162. D
153. A   158. E   163. D
154. A   159. E   164. A
155. A   160. B   165. A

**Test—Word List 12**
166. C   171. C   176. B
167. B   172. C   177. B
168. C   173. A   178. A
169. D   174. A   179. C
170. D   175. B   180. A

**Test—Word List 13**
181. A   186. A   191. C
182. E   187. B   192. B
183. D   188. C   193. E
184. D   189. B   194. A
185. A   190. C   195. A

**Test—Word List 14**
196. D   201. C   206. B
197. E   202. C   207. D
198. B   203. C   208. C
199. A   204. B   209. E
200. C   205. B   210. D

**Test—Word List 15**
211. C   216. C   221. B
212. A   217. E   222. E
213. D   218. A   223. A
214. D   219. C   224. A
215. D   220. D   225. B

**Test—Word List 16**
226. D   231. B   236. A
227. A   232. C   237. D
228. C   233. D   238. C
229. E   234. C   239. A
230. E   235. E   240. B

**Test—Word List 17**
241. A   246. C   251. D
242. A   247. A   252. E
243. B   248. A   253. E
244. E   249. C   254. B
245. E   250. D   255. B

**Test—Word List 18**
256. A   261. D   266. A
257. A   262. D   267. A
258. C   263. E   268. C
259. D   264. C   269. B
260. A   265. B   270. E

**Test—Word List 19**
271. A   276. A   281. A
272. D   277. A   282. D
273. E   278. D   283. C
274. C   279. C   284. B
275. E   280. B   285. C

**Test—Word List 20**
286. A   291. A   296. E
287. B   292. A   297. D
288. B   293. D   298. A
289. B   294. C   299. A
290. D   295. C   300. B

**Test—Word List 21**
301. B   306. E   311. E
302. B   307. C   312. A
303. C   308. B   313. B
304. C   309. D   314. D
305. C   310. D   315. C

**Test—Word List 22**
316. D   321. E   326. C
317. A   322. A   327. C
318. A   323. B   328. A
319. D   324. C   329. B
320. A   325. E   330. D

**Test—Word List 23**
331. B   336. A   341. A
332. A   337. D   342. A
333. B   338. C   343. E
334. E   339. C   344. B
335. C   340. D   345. A

**Test—Word List 24**
346. C   351. D   356. B
347. B   352. B   357. C
348. C   353. A   358. A
349. A   354. A   359. B
350. B   355. B   360. D

**Test—Word List 25**
361. A   366. B   371. E
362. E   367. B   372. B
363. B   368. C   373. D
364. D   369. D   374. C
365. E   370. A   375. A

**Test—Word List 26**
376. C   381. B   386. B
377. A   382. A   387. E
378. B   383. C   388. E
379. B   384. C   389. E
380. B   385. C   390. A

**Test—Word List 27**
391. A   396. E   401. B
392. D   397. E   402. B
393. B   398. C   403. A
394. D   399. A   404. C
395. B   400. D   405. B

## Test—Word List 28

| | | |
|---|---|---|
| 406. B | 411. B | 416. B |
| 407. A | 412. E | 417. A |
| 408. E | 413. D | 418. D |
| 409. E | 414. E | 419. D |
| 410. C | 415. C | 420. A |

## Test—Word List 29

| | | |
|---|---|---|
| 421. B | 426. D | 431. A |
| 422. A | 427. E | 432. C |
| 423. B | 428. B | 433. B |
| 424. B | 429. A | 434. C |
| 425. C | 430. E | 435. A |

## Test—Word List 30

| | | |
|---|---|---|
| 436. A | 441. A | 446. E |
| 437. A | 442. B | 447. B |
| 438. B | 443. D | 448. C |
| 439. D | 444. B | 449. E |
| 440. C | 445. A | 450. B |

## Test—Word List 31

| | | |
|---|---|---|
| 451. B | 456. A | 461. E |
| 452. E | 457. C | 462. C |
| 453. C | 458. C | 463. A |
| 454. C | 459. A | 464. B |
| 455. B | 460. B | 465. A |

## Test—Word List 32

| | | |
|---|---|---|
| 466. B | 471. D | 476. D |
| 467. C | 472. C | 477. B |
| 468. C | 473. B | 478. A |
| 469. A | 474. A | 479. C |
| 470. C | 475. B | 480. A |

## Test—Word List 33

| | | |
|---|---|---|
| 481. C | 486. A | 491. E |
| 482. B | 487. B | 492. C |
| 483. E | 488. C | 493. E |
| 484. D | 489. D | 494. B |
| 485. B | 490. B | 495. A |

## Test—Word List 34

| | | |
|---|---|---|
| 496. D | 501. B | 506. D |
| 497. A | 502. B | 507. D |
| 498. D | 503. A | 508. C |
| 499. A | 504. E | 509. C |
| 500. E | 505. C | 510. A |

## Test—Word List 35

| | | |
|---|---|---|
| 511. A | 516. C | 521. E |
| 512. C | 517. B | 522. A |
| 513. C | 518. D | 523. C |
| 514. C | 519. C | 524. E |
| 515. B | 520. A | 525. E |

## Test—Word List 36

| | | |
|---|---|---|
| 526. A | 531. E | 536. A |
| 527. D | 532. B | 537. D |
| 528. A | 533. C | 538. D |
| 529. B | 534. C | 539. D |
| 530. E | 535. B | 540. D |

## Test—Word List 37

| | | |
|---|---|---|
| 541. C | 546. A | 551. A |
| 542. C | 547. A | 552. C |
| 543. D | 548. C | 553. E |
| 544. E | 549. B | 554. B |
| 545. C | 550. A | 555. A |

## Test—Word List 38

| | | |
|---|---|---|
| 556. E | 561. E | 566. A |
| 557. D | 562. E | 567. D |
| 558. C | 563. B | 568. C |
| 559. B | 564. A | 569. D |
| 560. B | 565. E | 570. C |

## Test—Word List 39

| | | |
|---|---|---|
| 571. B | 576. C | 581. C |
| 572. B | 577. D | 582. B |
| 573. E | 578. B | 583. A |
| 574. A | 579. C | 584. D |
| 575. A | 580. E | 585. A |

## Test—Word List 40

| | | |
|---|---|---|
| 586. E | 591. C | 596. D |
| 587. B | 592. A | 597. D |
| 588. D | 593. B | 598. B |
| 589. C | 594. A | 599. D |
| 590. A | 595. D | 600. E |

## Test—Word List 41

| | | |
|---|---|---|
| 601. E | 606. B | 611. C |
| 602. B | 607. B | 612. D |
| 603. A | 608. A | 613. B |
| 604. D | 609. D | 614. A |
| 605. A | 610. B | 615. A |

## Test—Word List 42

| | | |
|---|---|---|
| 616. C | 621. D | 626. B |
| 617. A | 622. E | 627. D |
| 618. B | 623. A | 628. A |
| 619. C | 624. D | 629. D |
| 620. D | 625. C | 630. E |

## Test—Word List 43

| | | |
|---|---|---|
| 631. C | 636. C | 641. D |
| 632. C | 637. E | 642. A |
| 633. E | 638. C | 643. E |
| 634. A | 639. E | 644. A |
| 635. C | 640. D | 645. B |

## Test—Word List 44

| | | |
|---|---|---|
| 646. A | 651. B | 656. A |
| 647. B | 652. A | 657. B |
| 648. D | 653. D | 658. A |
| 649. A | 654. C | 659. C |
| 650. E | 655. C | 660. C |

## Test—Word List 45

| | | |
|---|---|---|
| 661. C | 666. C | 671. C |
| 662. C | 667. B | 672. D |
| 663. A | 668. A | 673. A |
| 664. C | 669. A | 674. D |
| 665. B | 670. A | 675. A |

## Test—Word List 46

| | | |
|---|---|---|
| 676. D | 681. D | 686. B |
| 677. B | 682. B | 687. A |
| 678. B | 683. A | 688. B |
| 679. C | 684. E | 689. E |
| 680. C | 685. B | 690. C |

## Test—Word List 47

| | | |
|---|---|---|
| 691. A | 696. A | 701. A |
| 692. D | 697. C | 702. D |
| 693. B | 698. B | 703. B |
| 694. C | 699. C | 704. D |
| 695. A | 700. E | 705. E |

## Test—Word List 48

| | | |
|---|---|---|
| 706. A | 711. B | 716. D |
| 707. A | 712. B | 717. D |
| 708. B | 713. A | 718. C |
| 709. C | 714. A | 719. B |
| 710. C | 715. E | 720. C |

## Test—Word List 49

| | | |
|---|---|---|
| 721. B | 726. C | 731. C |
| 722. A | 727. C | 732. B |
| 723. A | 728. A | 733. A |
| 724. D | 729. C | 734. B |
| 725. B | 730. A | 735. D |

## Test—Word List 50

| | | |
|---|---|---|
| 736. D | 741. B | 746. A |
| 737. A | 742. B | 747. B |
| 738. B | 743. A | 748. C |
| 739. B | 744. E | 749. B |
| 740. E | 745. D | 750. C |

# Basic Word Parts

Words are made up of word parts: prefixes, suffixes and roots. A knowledge of these word parts and their meanings can help you determine the meanings of unfamiliar words.

# Common Prefixes

A *prefix* is a syllable that precedes the root or stem and changes or refines its meaning.

| Prefix | Meaning | Illustration |
|---|---|---|
| ab, abs | from, away from | *abduct* lead away, kidnap<br>*abjure* renounce |
| ad, ac, af, ag, an, ap, ar, as, at | to, forward | *adit* entrance<br>*accord* agreement, harmony<br>*affliction* cause of distress<br>*aggregation* collection<br>*annexation* addition<br>*appease* bring toward peace<br>*arraignment* indictment<br>*assumption* arrogance, taking for granted<br>*attendance* presence, the persons present |
| ambi | both | *ambiguous* of double meaning<br>*ambivalent* having two conflicting emotions |
| an, a | without | *anarchy* lack of government<br>*amoral* without moral sense |
| ante | before | *antecedent* preceding event or word<br>*antediluvian* ancient (before the flood) |
| anti | against, opposite | *antipathy* hatred<br>*antithetical* exactly opposite |
| arch | chief, first | *archetype* original<br>*archbishop* chief bishop |
| be | over, thoroughly | *bedaub* smear over<br>*befuddle* confuse thoroughly |
| bi | two | *bicameral* composed of two houses (Congress)<br>*biennial* every two years |
| cata | down | *catastrophe* disaster<br>*cataract* waterfall<br>*catapult* hurl (throw down) |
| circum | around | *circumnavigate* sail around (the globe)<br>*circumspect* cautious (looking around)<br>*circumscribe* limit (place a circle around) |
| com, co, col, con, cor | with, together | *combine* merge with<br>*coeditor* joint editor<br>*collateral* subordinate, connected<br>*conference* meeting<br>*corroborate* confirm |

| Prefix | Meaning | Illustration |
|---|---|---|
| **contra, contro** | against | *contravene* conflict with<br>*controversy* dispute |
| **de** | down, away | *debase* lower in value<br>*decadence* deterioration |
| **demi** | partly, half | *demigod* partly divine being |
| **di** | two | *dichotomy* division into two parts<br>*dilemma* choice between two bad alternatives |
| **dia** | across | *diagonal* across a figure<br>*diameter* distance across a circle |
| **dis, dif** | not, apart | *discord* lack of harmony<br>*differ* disagree (carry apart) |
| **dys** | faulty, bad | *dyslexia* faulty ability to read<br>*dyspepsia* indigestion |
| **ex, e** | out | *expel* drive out<br>*eject* throw out |
| **extra, extro** | beyond, outside | *extracurricular* beyond the curriculum<br>*extraterritorial* beyond a nation's bounds<br>*extrovert* person interested chiefly in external objects and actions |
| **hyper** | above; excessively | *hyperbole* exaggeration<br>*hyperventilate* breathe at an excessive rate |
| **hypo** | beneath; lower | *hypoglycemia* low blood sugar |
| **in, il, im, ir** | not | *inefficient* not efficient<br>*inarticulate* not clear or distinct<br>*illegible* not readable<br>*impeccable* not capable of sinning; flawless<br>*irrevocable* not able to be called back |
| **in, il, im, ir** | in, on, upon | *invite* call in<br>*illustration* something that makes clear<br>*impression* effect upon mind or feelings<br>*irradiate* shine upon |
| **inter** | between, among | *intervene* come between<br>*international* between nations<br>*interjection* a statement thrown in |
| **intra, intro** | within | *intramural* within a school<br>*introvert* person who turns within himself |
| **macro** | large, long | *macrobiotic* tending to prolong life<br>*macrocosm* the great world (the entire universe) |
| **mega** | great, million | *megalomania* delusions of grandeur<br>*megaton* explosive force of a million tons of TNT |
| **meta** | involving change | *metamorphosis* change of form |
| **micro** | small | *microcosm* miniature universe<br>*microscopic* extremely small |

| Prefix | Meaning | Illustration |
|---|---|---|
| mis | bad, improper | *misdemeanor* minor crime; bad conduct<br>*mischance* unfortunate accident |
| mis | hatred | *misanthrope* person who hates mankind<br>*misogynist* woman-hater |
| mono | one | *monarchy* government by one ruler<br>*monotheism* belief in one god |
| multi | many | *multifarious* having many parts<br>*multitudinous* numerous |
| neo | new | *neologism* newly coined word<br>*neophyte* beginner; novice |
| non | not | *noncommittal* undecided |
| ob, oc, of, op | against | *obloquy* infamy; disgrace<br>*occlude* close; block out<br>*offend* insult<br>*opponent* someone who struggles against; foe |
| olig | few | *oligarchy* government by a few |
| pan | all, every | *panacea* cure-all<br>*panorama* unobstructed view in all directions |
| para | beyond, related | *parallel* similar<br>*paraphrase* restate; translate |
| per | through, completely | *permeable* allowing passage through<br>*pervade* spread throughout |
| peri | around, near | *perimeter* outer boundary<br>*periphery* edge |
| poly | many | *polyglot* speaking several languages |
| post | after | *posthumous* after death |
| pre | before | *preamble* introductory statement<br>*premonition* forewarning |
| prim | first | *primordial* existing at the dawn of time<br>*primogeniture* state of being the first born |
| pro | forward, in favor of | *propulsive* driving forward<br>*proponent* supporter |
| proto | first | *prototype* first of its kind |
| pseudo | false | *pseudonym* pen name |
| re | again, back | *reiterate* repeat<br>*reimburse* pay back |
| retro | backward | *retrospect* looking back<br>*retroactive* effective as of a past date |
| se | away, aside | *secede* withdraw<br>*seclude* shut away |
| semi | half, partly | *semiconscious* partly conscious |

| Prefix | Meaning | Illustration |
|---|---|---|
| sub, suc, suf, sug, sup, sus | under, less | *subjugate* bring under control<br>*succumb* yield; cease to resist<br>*suffuse* spread through<br>*suggest* hint<br>*suppress* put down by force<br>*suspend* delay; temporarily cease |
| super, sur | over, above | *supernatural* above natural things<br>*surtax* additional tax |
| syn, sym, syl, sys | with, together | *synchronize* time together<br>*sympathize* pity; identify with<br>*syllogism* explanation of how ideas relate<br>*system* network |
| tele | far | *telegraphic* communicated over a distance |
| trans | across | *transport* carry across |
| ultra | beyond, excessive | *ultracritical* exceedingly critical |
| un | not | *unkempt* not combed; disheveled |
| under | below | *underling* someone inferior |
| uni | one | *unison* oneness of pitch; complete accord |
| vice | in place of | *viceroy* governor acting in place of a king |
| with | away, against | *withstand* stand up against; resist |

# Common Roots and Stems

*Roots* are basic words which have been carried over into English. *Stems* are variations of roots brought about by changes in declension or conjugation.

| Root or Stem | Meaning | Illustration |
|---|---|---|
| ac, acr | sharp | *acrimonious* bitter; caustic<br>*acerbity* bitterness of temper<br>*acidulate* make somewhat acid or sour |
| aev, ev | age, era | *primeval* of the age<br>*coeval* of the same age or era<br>*medieval* or *mediaeval* of the Middle Ages |
| ag, act | to do | *act* deed<br>*agent* doer |
| agog | leader | *demagogue* false leader of people<br>*pedagogue* teacher (leader of children) |
| agri, agrari | field | *agrarian* one who works in the field<br>*agriculture* cultivation of fields<br>*peregrination* wandering (through fields) |

| Root or Stem | Meaning | Illustration |
|---|---|---|
| ali | another | *alias* assumed (another) name<br>*alienate* estrange (turn away from another) |
| alt | high | *altitude* height<br>*altimeter* instrument for measuring height |
| alter | other | *altruistic* unselfish, considering others<br>*alter ego* a second self |
| am | love | *amorous* loving, especially sexually<br>*amity* friendship<br>*amicable* friendly |
| anim | mind, soul | *animadvert* cast criticism upon<br>*unanimous* of one mind<br>*magnanimity* greatness of mind or spirit |
| ann, enn | year | *annuity* yearly remittance<br>*biennial* every two years<br>*perennial* present all year; persisting for several years |
| anthrop | human beings | *anthropology* study of human beings<br>*misanthrope* hater of humankind<br>*philanthropy* love of humankind; charity |
| apt | fit | *aptitude* skill<br>*adapt* make suitable or fit |
| aqua | water | *aqueduct* passageway for conducting water<br>*aquatic* living in water<br>*aqua fortis* nitric acid (strong water) |
| arch | ruler, first | *archaeology* study of antiquities (study of first things)<br>*monarch* sole ruler<br>*anarchy* lack of government |
| aster | star | *astronomy* study of the stars<br>*asterisk* starlike type character (*)<br>*disaster* catastrophe (contrary star) |
| aud, audit | to hear | *audible* able to be heard<br>*auditorium* place where people may be heard<br>*audience* hearers |
| auto | self | *autocracy* rule by one person (self)<br>*automobile* vehicle that moves by itself<br>*autobiography* story of one's own life |
| belli | war | *bellicose* inclined to fight<br>*belligerent* inclined to wage war<br>*rebellious* resisting authority |
| ben, bon | good | *benefactor* one who does good deeds<br>*benevolence* charity (wishing good)<br>*bonus* something extra above regular pay |
| biblio | book | *bibliography* list of books<br>*bibliophile* lover of books<br>*Bible* The Book |

| Root or Stem | Meaning | Illustration |
|---|---|---|
| bio | life | *biography* writing about a person's life<br>*biology* study of living things<br>*biochemist* student of the chemistry of living things |
| breve | short | *brevity* briefness<br>*abbreviate* shorten<br>*breviloquent* marked by brevity of speech |
| cad, cas | to fall | *decadent* deteriorating<br>*cadence* intonation, musical movement<br>*cascade* waterfall |
| cap, capt, cept, cip | to take | *capture* seize<br>*participate* take part<br>*precept* wise saying (originally a command) |
| capit, capt | head | *decapitate* remove (cut off) someone's head<br>*captain* chief |
| carn | flesh | *carnivorous* flesh-eating<br>*carnage* destruction of life<br>*carnal* fleshly |
| ced, cess | to yield, to go | *recede* go back, withdraw<br>*antecedent* that which goes before<br>*process* go forward |
| celer | swift | *celerity* swiftness<br>*decelerate* reduce swiftness<br>*accelerate* increase swiftness |
| cent | one hundred | *century* one hundred years<br>*centennial* one-hundredth anniversary<br>*centipede* many-footed, wingless animal |
| chron | time | *chronology* timetable of events<br>*anachronism* a thing out of time sequence<br>*chronicle* register events in order of time |
| cid, cis | to cut, to kill | *incision* a cut (surgical)<br>*homicide* killing of a human being<br>*fratricide* killing of a brother |
| cit, citat | to call, to start | *incite* stir up, start up<br>*excite* stir up<br>*recitation* a recalling (or repeating) aloud |
| civi | citizen | *civilization* society of citizens, culture<br>*civilian* member of community<br>*civil* courteous |
| clam, clamat | to cry out | *clamorous* loud<br>*declamation* speech<br>*acclamation* shouted approval |
| claud, claus, clos, clud | to close | *claustrophobia* fear of close places<br>*enclose* close in<br>*conclude* finish |

| Root or Stem | Meaning | Illustration |
|---|---|---|
| cognosc, cognit | to learn | *agnostic* lacking knowledge, skeptical<br>*incognito* traveling under assumed name<br>*cognition* knowledge |
| compl | to fill | *complete* filled out<br>*complement* that which completes something<br>*comply* fulfill |
| cord | heart | *accord* agreement (from the heart)<br>*cordial* friendly<br>*discord* lack of harmony |
| corpor | body | *incorporate* organize into a body<br>*corporeal* pertaining to the body, fleshly<br>*corpse* dead body |
| cred, credit | to believe | *incredulous* not believing, skeptical<br>*credulity* gullibility<br>*credence* belief |
| cur | to care | *curator* person who has the care of something<br>*sinecure* position without responsibility<br>*secure* safe |
| curr, curs | to run | *excursion* journey<br>*cursory* brief<br>*precursor* forerunner |
| da, dat | to give | *data* facts, statistics<br>*mandate* command<br>*date* given time |
| deb, debit | to owe | *debt* something owed<br>*indebtedness* debt<br>*debenture* bond |
| dem | people | *democracy* rule of the people<br>*demagogue* (false) leader of the people<br>*epidemic* widespread (among the people) |
| derm | skin | *epidermis* skin<br>*pachyderm* thick-skinned quadruped<br>*dermatology* study of skin and its disorders |
| di, diurn | day | *diary* a daily record of activities, feelings, etc.<br>*diurnal* pertaining to daytime |
| dic, dict | to say | *abdicate* renounce<br>*diction* speech<br>*verdict* statement of jury |
| doc, doct | to teach | *docile* obedient; easily taught<br>*document* something that provides evidence<br>*doctor* learned person (originally, teacher) |
| domin | to rule | *dominate* have power over<br>*domain* land under rule<br>*dominant* prevailing |

| Root or Stem | Meaning | Illustration |
| --- | --- | --- |
| **duc, duct** | to lead | *viaduct* arched roadway<br>*aqueduct* artificial waterway |
| **dynam** | power, strength | *dynamic* powerful<br>*dynamite* powerful explosive<br>*dynamo* engine making electric power |
| **ego** | I | *egoist* person who is self-centered<br>*egotist* selfish person<br>*egocentric* revolving about self |
| **erg, urg** | work | *energy* power<br>*ergatocracy* rule of the workers<br>*metallurgy* science and technology of metals |
| **err** | to wander | *error* mistake<br>*erratic* not reliable, wandering<br>*knight-errant* wandering knight |
| **eu** | good, well, beautiful | *eupeptic* having good digestion<br>*eulogize* praise<br>*euphemism* pleasant way of saying something blunt |
| **fac, fic, fec, fect** | to make, to do | *factory* place where things are made<br>*fiction* manufactured story<br>*affect* cause to change |
| **fall, fals** | to deceive | *fallacious* misleading<br>*infallible* not prone to error, perfect<br>*falsify* lie |
| **fer, lat** | to bring, to bear | *transfer* bring from one place to another<br>*translate* bring from one language to another<br>*conifer* bearing cones, as pine trees |
| **fid** | belief, faith | *infidel* nonbeliever, heathen<br>*confidence* assurance, belief |
| **fin** | end, limit | *confine* keep within limits<br>*finite* having definite limits |
| **flect, flex** | to bend | *flexible* able to bend<br>*deflect* bend away, turn aside |
| **fort** | luck, chance | *fortuitous* accidental, occurring by chance<br>*fortunate* lucky |
| **fort** | strong | *fortitude* strength, firmness of mind<br>*fortification* strengthening<br>*fortress* stronghold |
| **frag, fract** | to break | *fragile* easily broken<br>*infraction* breaking of a rule<br>*fractious* unruly, tending to break rules |
| **fug** | to flee | *fugitive* someone who flees<br>*refuge* shelter, home for someone fleeing |
| **fus** | to pour | *effusive* gushing, pouring out<br>*diffuse* widespread (poured in many directions) |

| Root or Stem | Meaning | Illustration |
|---|---|---|
| gam | marriage | *monogamy* marriage to one person<br>*bigamy* marriage to two people at the same time<br>*polygamy* having many wives or husbands at the same time |
| gen, gener | class, race | *genus* group of animals or plants with similar traits<br>*generic* characteristic of a class<br>*gender* class organized by sex |
| grad, gress | to go, to step | *digress* go astray (from the main point)<br>*regress* go backward<br>*gradual* step by step, by degrees |
| graph, gram | writing | *epigram* pithy statement<br>*telegram* instantaneous message over great distance<br>*stenography* shorthand (writing narrowly) |
| greg | flock, herd | *gregarious* tending to group together as in a herd<br>*aggregate* group, total<br>*egregious* conspicuously bad; shocking |
| helio | sun | *heliotrope* flower that faces the sun<br>*heliograph* instrument that uses the sun's rays to send signals |
| it, itiner | journey, road | *exit* way out<br>*itinerary* plan of journey |
| jac, jact, jec | to throw | *projectile* missile; something thrown forward<br>*trajectory* path taken by thrown object<br>*ejaculatory* casting or throwing out |
| jur, jurat | to swear | *perjure* testify falsely<br>*jury* group of men and women sworn to seek the truth<br>*adjuration* solemn urging |
| labor, laborat | to work | *laboratory* place where work is done<br>*collaborate* work together with others<br>*laborious* difficult |
| leg, lect, lig | to choose, to read | *election* choice<br>*legible* able to be read<br>*eligible* able to be selected |
| leg | law | *legislature* law-making body<br>*legitimate* lawful<br>*legal* lawful |
| liber, libr | book | *library* collection of books<br>*libretto* the "book" of a musical play<br>*libel* slander (originally found in a little book) |
| liber | free | *liberation* the fact of setting free<br>*liberal* generous (giving freely); tolerant |
| log | word, study | *entomology* study of insects<br>*etymology* study of word parts and derivations<br>*monologue* speech by one person |

| Root or Stem | Meaning | Illustration |
| --- | --- | --- |
| loqu, locut | to talk | *soliloquy* speech by one individual<br>*loquacious* talkative<br>*elocution* speech |
| luc | light | *elucidate* enlighten<br>*lucid* clear<br>*translucent* allowing some light to pass through |
| magn | great | *magnify* enlarge<br>*magnanimity* generosity, greatness of soul<br>*magnitude* greatness, extent |
| mal | bad | *malevolent* wishing evil<br>*malediction* curse<br>*malefactor* evil-doer |
| man | hand | *manufacture* create (make by hand)<br>*manuscript* written by hand<br>*emancipate* free (let go from the hand) |
| mar | sea | *maritime* connected with seafaring<br>*submarine* undersea craft<br>*mariner* seafarer |
| mater, matr | mother | *maternal* pertaining to motherhood<br>*matriarch* female ruler of a family, group, or state<br>*matrilineal* descended on the mother's side |
| mit, miss | to send | *missile* projectile<br>*dismiss* send away<br>*transmit* send across |
| mob, mot, mov | to move | *mobilize* cause to move<br>*motility* ability to move<br>*immovable* not able to be moved |
| mon, monit | to warn | *admonish* warn<br>*premonition* foreboding<br>*monitor* watcher (warner) |
| mori, mort | to die | *mortuary* funeral parlor<br>*moribund* dying<br>*immortal* not dying |
| morph | shape, form | *amorphous* formless, lacking shape<br>*metamorphosis* change of shape<br>*anthropomorphic* in human shape |
| mut | to change | *immutable* not able to be changed<br>*mutate* undergo a great change<br>*mutability* changeableness, inconstancy |
| nat | born | *innate* from birth<br>*prenatal* before birth<br>*nativity* birth |
| nav | ship | *navigate* sail a ship<br>*circumnavigate* sail around the world<br>*naval* pertaining to ships |

| Root or Stem | Meaning | Illustration |
| --- | --- | --- |
| neg | to deny | *negation* denial<br>*renege* deny, go back on one's word<br>*renegade* turncoat, traitor |
| nomen | name | *nomenclature* act of naming, terminology<br>*nominal* in name only (as opposed to actual)<br>*cognomen* surname, distinguishing nickname |
| nov | new | *novice* beginner<br>*renovate* make new again<br>*novelty* newness |
| omni | all | *omniscient* all knowing<br>*omnipotent* all powerful<br>*omnivorous* eating everything |
| oper | to work | *operate* work<br>*cooperation* working together |
| pac | peace | *pacify* make peaceful<br>*pacific* peaceful<br>*pacifist* person opposed to war |
| pass | to feel | *dispassionate* free of emotion<br>*impassioned* emotion-filled<br>*impassive* showing no feeling |
| pater, patr | father | *patriotism* love of one's country (fatherland)<br>*patriarch* male ruler of a family, group, or state<br>*paternity* fatherhood |
| path | disease, feeling | *pathology* study of diseased tissue<br>*apathetic* lacking feeling; indifferent<br>*antipathy* hostile feeling |
| ped, pod | foot | *impediment* stumbling-block; hindrance<br>*tripod* three-footed stand<br>*quadruped* four-footed animal |
| ped | child | *pedagogue* teacher of children<br>*pediatrician* children's doctor |
| pel, puls | to drive | *compulsion* a forcing to do<br>*repel* drive back<br>*expel* drive out, banish |
| pet, petit | to seek | *petition* request<br>*appetite* craving, desire<br>*compete* vie with others |
| phil | love | *philanthropist* benefactor, lover of humanity<br>*Anglophile* lover of everything English<br>*philanderer* one involved in brief love affairs |
| pon, posit | to place | *postpone* place after<br>*positive* definite, unquestioned (definitely placed) |
| port, portat | to carry | *portable* able to be carried<br>*transport* carry across |

| Root or Stem | Meaning | Illustration |
|---|---|---|
| poten | able, powerful | *omnipotent* all-powerful |
| psych | mind | *psychology* study of the mind |
| put, putat | to trim, to calculate | *computation* calculation<br>*amputate* cut off |
| quer, ques, quir, quis | to ask | *inquiry* investigation<br>*inquisitive* questioning<br>*query* question |
| reg, rect | to rule | *regent* ruler<br>*insurrection* rebellion; overthrow of a ruler |
| rid, ris | to laugh | *derision* scorn<br>*ridiculous* deserving to be laughed at |
| rog, rogat | to ask | *interrogate* question |
| rupt | to break | *interrupt* break into<br>*rupture* a break |
| sacr | holy | *sacrilegious* impious, violating something holy<br>*sacrament* religious act |
| sci | to know | *omniscient* knowing all<br>*conscious* aware |
| scop | to watch, to see | *periscope* device for seeing around corners<br>*microscope* device for seeing small objects |
| scrib, script | to write | *transcribe* make a written copy<br>*script* written text |
| sect | cut | *dissect* cut apart<br>*bisect* cut into two pieces |
| sed, sess | to sit | *sedentary* inactive (sitting) |
| sent, sens | to think, to feel | *resent* show indignation<br>*sensitive* showing feeling |
| sequi, secut, seque | to follow | *consecutive* following in order<br>*sequence* arrangement<br>*sequel* that which follows<br>*nonsequitur* something that does not follow logically |
| solv, solut | to loosen | *absolve* free from blame<br>*dissolute* morally lax |
| somn | sleep | *insomnia* inability to sleep |
| soph | wisdom | *philosopher* lover of wisdom |
| spec, spect, spic | to look at | *spectator* observer<br>*circumspect* cautious (looking around)<br>*despicable* detestable (deserving to be looked down on)<br>*perspicacity* clearsightedness |
| spir | to breathe | *respiratory* pertaining to breathing<br>*spirited* full of life (breathe) |
| string, strict | bind | *stringent* strict<br>*stricture* limit, something that restrains |

| Root or Stem | Meaning | Illustration |
|---|---|---|
| stru, struct | to build | *constructive* helping to build<br>*construe* analyze (how something is built) |
| tang, tact, ting | to touch | *tangent* touching<br>*contact* touching with, meeting<br>*contingent* depending upon |
| tempor | time | *contemporary* at same time |
| ten, tent | to hold | *tenable* able to be held<br>*retentive* holding; having a good memory |
| term | end | *interminable* endless<br>*terminate* end |
| terr | land | *terrestrial* pertaining to earth<br>*subterranean* underground |
| therm | heat | *thermostat* instrument that regulates heat |
| tors, tort | to twist | *distort* twist out of true shape or meaning<br>*torsion* act of twisting |
| tract | to drag, to pull | *distract* pull (one's attention) away<br>*intractable* stubborn, unable to be dragged |
| trud, trus | to push, to shove | *intrude* push one's way in<br>*protrusion* something sticking out |
| urb | city | *urban* pertaining to a city |
| vac | empty | *vacuous* lacking content, empty-headed<br>*evacuate* compel to empty an area |
| vad, vas | to go | *invade* enter in a hostile fashion<br>*evasive* not frank; eluding |
| veni, vent, ven | to come | *intervene* come between<br>*prevent* stop<br>*convention* meeting |
| ver | true | *veracious* truthful<br>*verisimilitude* appearance of truth |
| verb | word | *verbose* wordy |
| vers, vert | to turn | *vertigo* turning dizzy<br>*revert* turn back (to an earlier state)<br>*diversion* something causing one to turn aside |
| via | way | *deviation* departure from the way<br>*viaduct* roadway (arched) |
| vid, vis | to see | *vision* sight<br>*evidence* things seen |
| vinc, vict, vanq | to conquer | *invincible* unconquerable<br>*victory* winning<br>*vanquish* defeat |
| viv, vit | alive | *vivacious* full of life<br>*vitality* liveliness |

| Root or Stem | Meaning | Illustration |
|---|---|---|
| **voc, vocat** | to call | *avocation* calling, minor occupation<br>*provocation* calling or rousing the anger of |
| **vol** | wish | *malevolent* wishing someone ill<br>*voluntary* of one's own will |
| **volv, volut** | to roll | *revolve* roll around<br>*convolution* coiled state |

# Common Suffixes

A *suffix* is a syllable that is added to a word. Occasionally, it changes the meaning of the word; more frequently, it serves to change the grammatical form of the word (noun to adjective, adjective to noun, noun to verb).

| Suffix | Meaning | Illustration |
|---|---|---|
| **able, ible** | capable of (adjective suffix) | *portable* able to be carried<br>*legible* able to be read |
| **ac, ic** | like, pertaining to (adjective suffix) | *cardiac* pertaining to the heart<br>*aquatic* pertaining to the water |
| **acious, icious** | full of (adjective suffix) | *audacious* full of daring<br>*avaricious* full of greed |
| **al** | pertaining to (adjective or noun suffix) | *maniacal* insane<br>*portal* doorway<br>*logical* pertaining to logic |
| **ant, ent** | full of (adjective or noun suffix) | *eloquent* pertaining to fluid, effective speech<br>*suppliant* pleader (person full of requests)<br>*verdant* green |
| **ary** | like, connected with (adjective or noun suffix) | *dictionary* book connected with words<br>*honorary* with honor<br>*luminary* celestial body |
| **ate** | to make (verb suffix) | *consecrate* to make holy<br>*enervate* to make weary<br>*mitigate* to make less severe |
| **ation** | that which is (noun suffix) | *exasperation* irritation<br>*irritation* annoyance |
| **cy** | state of being (noun suffix) | *democracy* government ruled by the people<br>*obstinacy* stubbornness |
| **eer, er, or** | person who (noun suffix) | *mutineer* person who rebels<br>*lecher* person who lusts<br>*censor* person who deletes improper remarks |
| **escent** | becoming (adjective suffix) | *evanescent* tending to vanish<br>*pubescent* arriving at puberty |

| Suffix | Meaning | Illustration |
|--------|---------|--------------|
| fic | making, doing (adjective suffix) | *terrific* arousing great fear <br> *soporific* causing sleep |
| fy | to make (verb suffix) | *magnify* enlarge <br> *petrify* turn to stone |
| iferous | producing, bearing (adjective suffix) | *pestiferous* carrying disease <br> *vociferous* bearing a loud voice |
| il, ile | pertaining to, capable of (adjective suffix) | *puerile* pertaining to a boy or child <br> *civil* polite |
| ism | doctrine, belief (noun suffix) | *monotheism* belief in one god <br> *fanaticism* excessive zeal; extreme belief |
| ist | dealer, doer (noun suffix) | *realist* one who is realistic <br> *artist* one who deals with art |
| ity | state of being (noun suffix) | *credulity* state of being unduly willing to believe <br> *sagacity* wisdom |
| ive | like (adjective suffix) | *quantitative* concerned with quantity <br> *effusive* gushing |
| ize, ise | to make (verb suffix) | *harmonize* make harmonious <br> *enfranchise* make free or set free |
| oid | resembling, like (adjective suffix) | *ovoid* like an egg <br> *anthropoid* resembling a human being <br> *spheroid* resembling a sphere |
| ose | full of (adjective suffix) | *verbose* full of words |
| osis | condition (noun suffix) | *psychosis* diseased mental condition <br> *hypnosis* condition of induced sleep |
| ous | full of (adjective suffix) | *nauseous* full of nausea <br> *ludicrous* foolish |
| tude | state of (noun suffix) | *fortitude* state of strength <br> *certitude* state of sureness |

# PART THREE

## ANALYTICAL ABILITY: TACTICS, STRATEGIES, AND PRACTICE

# Introduction to Part Three

The analytical ability section of the GRE is the longest of the three sections, both in terms of time allotted (60 minutes) and the number of questions (35). This section has two types of questions: 26 analytical reasoning questions and nine logical reasoning questions. The analytical reasoning questions, which will be discussed in Chapter 9, are presented in groups of four or five questions, each group based on a single set of conditions. The logical reasoning questions, which will be discussed in Chapter 10, are interspersed throughout the section. The groups of analytical reasoning questions could be separated by one, two, or three logical reasoning questions. Occasionally, there are two logical reasoning questions based on the same passage, but most often there is just one. A typical analytical ability section might be broken up as follows:

| | |
|---|---|
| Question 1 | a logical reasoning question |
| Questions 2–5 | four analytical reasoning questions |
| Questions 6–8 | three logical reasoning questions |
| Questions 9–13 | five analytical reasoning questions |
| Question 14 | a logical reasoning question |
| Questions 15–18 | four analytical reasoning questions |
| Question 19 | a logical reasoning question |
| Questions 20–23 | four analytical reasoning questions |
| Questions 24–28 | five analytical reasoning questions |
| Questions 29–30 | two logical reasoning questions |
| Questions 31–34 | four analytical reasoning questions |
| Question 35 | a logical reasoning question |

Each analytical reasoning question is a logical puzzle based on a given set of conditions. Most students have never seen questions like this and have no idea how to even begin solving such puzzles; consequently, they find this section to be the most difficult part of the GRE. Fortunately, there are several easy-to-learn strategies that can help you solve these puzzles. Going through Chapter 9, you will learn all of them. The most valuable thing you can do to master analytical reasoning questions is to practice. Therefore, Chapter 9 has several sample questions, all of which have complete solutions.

Each logical reasoning question requires you to analyze an argument presented in a short passage. Often you are asked either to find a conclusion which is a logical consequence of the passage, or to choose a statement which, if true, would strengthen or weaken the argument presented in the passage. The various tactics for handling this type of question are presented in Chapter 10, along with several practice questions. For each sample question, not only will you be given an explanation for the correct choice, you will be told why each of the other choices is incorrect. As you go through the sample questions in Chapter 10, be sure to read the full explanations; don't just check the answers.

If you study the tactics and do all of the problems in Chapters 9 and 10, you will be well prepared for the analytical ability section of the GRE, and should have the confidence you need to earn a high score.

# 9 Analytical Reasoning Questions

- ■ **Logic Facts**
- ■ **Tactics**
- ■ **Practice Exercises**
- ■ **Answer Key and Explanations**

Before beginning their preparation for the GRE, the vast majority of college students have never even seen an analytical reasoning question. As we stated in Chapter 1, on first reading, these questions seem mind-boggling and hopelessly complicated. It is likely that when you took the diagnostic test you felt overwhelmed and intimidated by them. Don't panic! On the next several pages we will explain all of the techniques needed for correctly answering analytical reasoning questions, and by the time you finish reading this chapter you should feel completely at ease with them.

When you take the test, the only directions for answering analytical reasoning questions are the following three sentences, which will appear on the screen at the beginning of the section:

<u>Directions</u>: Each group of questions is based on a passage, graph, table, or set of conditions. In answering some of the questions, it might be useful to draw a rough diagram. For each question, select the best answer choice given.

As always, you should immediately click on "Dismiss the Instructions," not only to save the time it takes to read them, but because they are useless. They give you absolutely no insight into how to answer these questions. The first sentence is misleading, because, in fact, almost all questions are based on a short introductory passage, followed by a list of several conditions—very few questions, if any, are based on graphs or tables. The second sentence is correct; drawing a diagram, chart, table, or other pictorial representation of the situation is often helpful. In this chapter you will learn when and how you should do this. Finally, these questions don't have two or three reasonable answers, of which one is *best;* like math questions, they have *exactly one correct answer*, which is what you are to select.

Once you have dismissed the instructions, the first analytical reasoning question will appear on a split screen. The given set of statements will appear on the left-hand side of the screen and the first question will appear on the right-hand side. Often it will be necessary to scroll down to read all of the conditions listed. Until all of the questions based on a particular set of conditions are answered, the list of conditions remains on the left-hand side of the screen for you to consult. As soon as you answer a question, the next question in that set will replace it on the right-hand side of the screen. When all of the questions based on that set of conditions have been answered, the list of conditions is removed and is replaced by either a new set of conditions or a logical reasoning question. Note: Occasionally, the screen splits horizontally, in which case, the list of conditions will be on the top half of the screen, and the questions will be on the bottom.)

Before you learn the various tactics for answering analytical reasoning questions, it will be very helpful for you to learn (or review) some basic logic. Don't worry: this will *not* be a mini-course in symbolic logic, and you definitely don't need one to do well on these questions. But you must be able to analyze the underlying logic of the statements in the given sets of conditions. As you will soon see, it will be much easier to replace the words of the statements with letters and symbols. For example, if the conditions involve the herbs parsley, sage, rosemary, and thyme, we would abbreviate them P, S, R, and T, respectively; and if they involve Senators Adams, Blair, Clay, Donahue, and Ellsworth, we would simply write A, B, C, D, and E. To symbolize "Adams is shorter (or younger, or lighter) than Blair," we might write "A < B." Often the letters will represent complete sentences rather than just words or names. For example, if some of the senators are going to a conference, A could represent the sentence, "Adams is going," and B could represent the sentence "Blair is going." To handle analytical reasoning questions adequately, we need symbols to represent statements such as "Adams is not going," "Adams and Blair are both going," and "Adams will go, only if Blair goes too."

There is another important reason to use letters and symbols when working on analytical reasoning questions. There are always four or five analytical reasoning questions based on a given set of conditions. The conditions remain fixed on the left side of the screen as the questions come up one at a time on the right. It is not easy to answer these questions if you have to keep looking up at the screen to reread the conditions. It is particularly annoying when there are so many conditions that you can't see them all at the same time and you have to scroll up and down. It is much more convenient to have the statements on your scrap paper. However, it is too time consuming to copy them completely, and besides, they are much easier to use if you can eliminate the excess verbiage and just write down the essence of each statement.

Although you can use any symbols you like, we recommend the following logical symbols, which are easy to remember and have proved to be very useful to students taking the GRE.

| SYMBOL | MEANING | | EXAMPLES |
|--------|---------|---------|----------|
| ~ | not | ~A | Al is not going. |
| ∧ | and | A ∧ B | Al and Bob are going. |
| | | A ∧ ~B | Al is going and Bob is not going. |
| ∨ | or | A ∨ B | Al or Bob is going. |
| | | A ∨ ~B | Al is going or Bob is not going. |
| → | if, then | A → B | If Al is going, then Bob is going. |
| | | (A ∧ B) → ~C | If Al and Bob are going, then Carol is not going. |
| ↔ | if and only if | A ↔ B: | Al is going if and only if Bob is going. |

Let's examine each of these five symbols to make sure their meanings are clear.

~A is called the negation of A and is equivalent to "it is not true that A." For any statement A, either A or ~A is true, and the other is false. Do not make the common mistake of assuming that ~A is a false statement. It is perfectly possible that A (Al is going) is false, and ~A (Al is not going) is true.

## Logic Fact 1

**A is true means ~A is false.**

## Logic Fact 2

**~A is true means A is false.**

CAUTION: The negation of "Al is taller than Bob" is not "Al is shorter than Bob," both of which would be false if Al and Bob were the same height. The negation of "Al is taller than Bob" is "Al is *not* taller than Bob."

A ∧ B presents no difficulties. Just as in normal English, *and* means *both*.

If "Al and Bob are going" is a *true* statement, then

"Al is going" and "Bob is going" are *both true* statements.

## Logic Fact 3

**(A ∧ B) is true means A is true and B is true.**

If the statement "Al and Bob are going" is *false*, then *either* "Al is not going" or "Bob is not going." As we shall see in a moment, this includes the possibility that *neither* Al *nor* Bob is going.

## Logic Fact 4

**~(A ∧ B) is true means A is false or B is false.**

Another way to express LOGIC FACT 4 is as follows:

**~(A ∧ B) is equivalent to ~A ∨ ~B.**

A ∨ B requires a little more care. Sometimes in English, *or* means *one or the other, but* not *both*. If a waiter tells you, "The dinner special includes soup or salad," you would not expect to get both soup and salad. In mathematics and logic (including all GRE analytical reasoning questions), however, *or* always means *one or the other, possibly both*.

If "Al or Bob is going" is a true statement, then *at least one* of the two statements "Al is going" and "Bob is going" is true (*possibly both are true*).

## Logic Fact 5

**(A ∨ B) is true means at least one of A and B is true.**

If "Al or Bob is going" is not true then neither are going; that is, Al is not going *and* Bob is not going.

## Logic Fact 6

**~(A ∨ B) is true means A is false and B is false.**

Another way to express LOGIC FACT 6 is as follows:

**~( A ∨ B) is equivalent to ~A ∧ ~B.**

NOTE: Even though the condition "Al is going or Bob is going," allows for the possibility that Al and Bob are both going, often on the GRE, to avoid any confusion, the condition will be written "Either Al or Bob or both are going." But whether or not the words *or both* appear in the stated condition, the meaning is the same.

Assume that the statement "Al is going or Bob is going" (A ∨ B) is true, and consider the following four possibilities:

1. Al is not going. (~A is true).
   - Since either Al is going or Bob is going, and Al is not going, we can conclude that Bob is going.

## Logic Fact 7

| If | A ∨ B | is true, and |
|----|-------|--------------|
| if | ~A | is true (i.e., A is false), |
| then | B is true | |

2. Bob is not going. (~B is true)
   - Since either Al is going or Bob is going, and Bob is not going, we can conclude that Al is going.

## Logic Fact 8

| If | A ∨ B | is true, and |
|----|-------|--------------|
| if | ~B | is true (i.e., B is false), |
| then | A is true | |

3. Al is going. (A is true)
   - "Al is going or Bob is going" means that at least one of them is going, but it is possible that both of them are going. Knowing that Al is going gives us no additional information about Bob. Bob could go (in which case, they are both going), or Bob could not go (in which case, only Al is going).

## Logic Fact 9

| If | A ∨ B | is true, and |
|----|-------|--------------|
| if | A | is true, |
| then | no conclusion about **B** is possible | |

4. Bob is going. (B is true)
   - Just as in 3, above, "Al is going or Bob is going" means that at least one and possibly both of them are going. Al could go (in which case, they are both going) or Al could not go (in which case, only Bob is going).

## Logic Fact 10

| If | A ∨ B | is true, and |
|----|-------|--------------|
| if | B | is true, |
| then | no conclusion about **A** is possible | |

Here are a few analytical reasoning questions that test your understanding of these concepts. Remember that the conditions listed in an analytical reasoning question are always assumed to be true. The questions will ask you to deduce what is true or false, based on those conditions. Note that these examples are shorter than actual GRE questions because they involve fewer conditions, but the required level of logical reasoning is equivalent.

---

> For Question 1
> A committee will be formed consisting of exactly three of A, B, C, D, and E.
> A or B must be on the committee.

> 1. Of ACD, BC, BCD, ABC, ABCE, ADE, and CDE, how many are *not* acceptable committees?
>    (A) 1   (B) 2   (C) 3   (D) 4   (E) 5

SOLUTION. On your scrap paper, write
ABCDE: <u>exactly 3</u>        A ∨ B

Now do not look back at the conditions—refer only to what you just wrote. Neither BC nor ABCE is acceptable since they violate the first condition (exactly 3). Since the second condition (A ∨ B) requires A or B to be on the committee, CDE is not acceptable. Each of the other choices includes one or both of A and B, and so is acceptable. (In particular, ABC is acceptable; the condition that A *or* B serve does not preclude them both from serving.) The answer is C: 3 are unacceptable.

---

> For Questions 2–3
> A committee will be formed consisting of exactly three of A, B, C, D, and E.
>    Jen: A and B will be on the committee.
>    Ken: E will not be on the committee.

> 2. If the statements made by Jen and Ken are both true, how many different committees can be formed?
>    (A) 1   (B) 2   (C) 3   (D) 4   (E) 5

SOLUTION. On your scrap paper, write
ABCDE: <u>exactly 3</u>        A ∧ B        ~E

From Jen's statement (A ∧ B), we know that A and B must be on the committee, and the third member could be any of C, D, and E. Ken's statement (~E) eliminates E. So there are 2 possibilities: ABC and ABD. The answer is B.

---

> 3. If the statements made by Jen and Ken are both false, how many different committees can be formed?
>    (A) 1   (B) 2   (C) 3   (D) 4   (E) 5

SOLUTION. On your scrap paper, write
ABCDE: <u>exactly 3</u>        ~(A ∧ B)        E

Use LOGIC FACT 4: cross out
and replace it by its equivalent:        ~(A ∧ B)
                                          ~ A ∨ ~B

List all 3-letter combinations which include A and E, but not B: ACE, ADE

List all 3-letter combinations which include B and E, but not A: BCE, BDE

List all 3-letter combinations which include E, but neither A nor B: CDE

There are a total of 5 possibilities. The answer is E.

---

**For Questions 4-5**

A committee will be formed consisting of exactly three of A, B, C, D, and E.

Jen: A or B will be on the committee.

Ken: E will not be on the committee.

---

4. If the statements made by Jen and Ken are both true, how many different committees can be formed?

(A) 1 (B) 2 (C) 3 (D) 4 (E) 5

---

SOLUTION. On your scrap paper, write
ABCDE: exactly 3      A ∨ B      ~E

From Ken's statement (~E), we know that E is not on the committee. So of A, B, C, and D, three must be on the committee and one not on it. So there are 4 possibilities, depending on which of the four is excluded: ABC, ABD, ACD, and BCD. Each of these satisfies Jen's statement (A ∨ B), so there are 4 possible committees. The answer is D.

---

5. If the statements made by Jen and Ken are both false, how many different committees can be formed?

(A) 1 (B) 2 (C) 3 (D) 4 (E) 5

---

SOLUTION. On your scrap paper, write
ABCDE: exactly 3      ~(A ∨ B)      E

Use LOGIC FACT 6: cross out ~(A ∨ B) and replace it by its equivalent:      ~ A ∧ ~B

Now, looking at the symbolic statements, this question is really easy to answer. Since neither A nor B can be on the committee, there is only 1 possibility: CDE. The answer is A.

---

**For Question 6**

A committee will be formed consisting of exactly three of A, B, C, D, E, and F.

B or D will be on the committee.

C or D will be on the committee.

C or E will be on the committee.

Neither A nor C will be on the committee.

---

6. Which of the following must be on the committee?
   I. D
   II. E
   III. F

(A) I only    (B) II only    (C) I and II only
(D) I and III    (E) I, II, and III

---

SOLUTION. On your scrap paper, write
ABCDEF: exactly 3      B ∨ D   C ∨ D   C ∨ E   ~A ∧ ~C

• Since ~A ∧ ~C is true, cross out A and C.

A̶ B C̶ D E F

• Since C or D is on the committee, but C isn't, D must be on the committee. Similarly, E must be on the committee. Circle both D and E.

A̶ B C̶ Ⓓ Ⓔ F

• Since D is on the committee, the condition B ∨ D adds no new information. B may be on the committee, but does not have to be. The possible committees are BDE and DEF.

• D and E must be on the committee; F could be on the committee, but does not have to be. I and II only are true. The answer is C.

Many students are confused about what conclusions they can draw from a conditional statement, such as "If Al is going, then Bob is going," and what such a statement really means. As a result, they often make errors on analytical reasoning questions. If you carefully read the following explanations, and do the next few examples, you will be able to avoid those pitfalls.

Assume that the statement "If Al is going, then Bob is going" (A → B) is true, and consider the following four possibilities:

1. "Al is going" is true. (A is true)
   • This is easy. Since Al is going, and if Al is going, then Bob is going, we can conclude that Bob is going.

**Logic Fact 9**

| If | A → B | is true, and |
|---|---|---|
| if | A | is true, |
| then | **B** | is true |

2. "Al is going" is false; so, "Al is not going" is true. (~A is true)
   • "If Al is going, then Bob is going" tells us what must be true about Bob if Al *is* going; it tells us nothing about what must be true about Bob if Al *is not* going. Bob may go anyway, or he may not go.

## Logic Fact 10

If    A → B    is true, and
if    ~A    is true (i.e., A is false),
then   no conclusion about **B** is possible

3. "Bob is going" is true. (B is true)
   - "If Al is going, then Bob is going" tells us what must be true about Bob if Al is going; it tells us nothing about what must be true about Al if Bob is going. Al may go, or he may not go.

## Logic Fact 11

If    A → B    is true, and
if    B    is true,
then   no conclusion about **A** is possible

4. "Bob is going" is false; i.e., "Bob is not going" is true. (~B is true)
   - Since Bob is not going, Al is not going; because if Al were to go, then the true conditional "If Al is going, then Bob is going" would guarantee that Bob is going (and we know he isn't).

## Logic Fact 12

If    A → B    is true, and
if    ~B    is true (i.e., B is false),
then   ~A    is true (i.e., A is false)

The following examples will test your understanding of the conditional.

### For Question 7

A committee will be formed consisting of exactly two of A, B, C, and D.

   If A serves, then B will too.

7. How many different committees could be formed?

   (A) 1   (B) 2   (C) 3   (D) 4   (E) 5

SOLUTION. On your scrap paper, write
ABCD: <u>exactly 2</u>    A → B

There are two possibilities: A serves or A does not serve:

- If A serves on the committee, then A → B allows us to conclude that B must also serve (LOGIC FACT 9); so the only possible committee is AB.

- If A does not serve on the committee, then A → B does not allow us to make any conclusion about B (LOGIC FACT 10). The committee can consist of *any* two of B, C, and D. So there are three possibilities: BC, BD, and CD.

- In all there are 4 possible committees. The answer is D.

### For Question 8

A three-person committee will be chosen from A, B, C, D, E, and F.

   If A serves, then B will too.

   If C serves, then D will too.

   D is on the committee, but B is not.

8. Which of the following are acceptable committees?
   - I. CDE
   - II. CDF
   - III. CEF

   (A) I only   (B) I and II only   (C) I and III only
   (D) II and III only   (E) I, II, and III

SOLUTION. On your scrap paper, write
ABCDEF: <u>exactly 3</u>    A → B   C → D   D   ~B

Cross out B (to indicate B cannot serve), and circle D (to indicate D must serve):

A B̶ C Ⓓ E F

- From the conditions A → B and ~B, we can conclude ~A (LOGIC FACT 12). Therefore, A cannot serve. Cross out A:

A̶ B̶ C Ⓓ E F

- From the conditions C → D and D, we can make no conclusion about C (LOGIC FACT 11): C can be on the committee, but does not have to be.

- From our list, (A̶ B̶ C Ⓓ E F), we see that an acceptable committee must include D and two of C, E, and F.

- Of the committees listed, CDE and CDF are acceptable, whereas CEF is not. Only I and II are true. The correct answer is B.

Some of the confusion that students have with the conditional statement "If A, then B" and the biconditional statement "A if and only if B" can be eliminated by properly representing these statements symbolically. There is no problem when the English sentence exactly follows the *if . . . then* format. However, the wording of conditional statements in analytical reasoning questions often uses a different word order, or other words. Consider the following sentences:

1. A will serve on the committee if B does.
2. A will serve on the committee only if B does.
3. A will not serve on the committee unless B does.
4. A will serve on the committee if and only if B does.

Let's examine each of these statements. For each one, we will determine its correct meaning, and show how to write it symbolically.

1. "A will serve if B does" means "If B serves, then A serves." Writing "if B" in the middle of the sentence instead of at the beginning doesn't change the meaning. If B serves, then A *must* serve, too; but A can serve without B.

$$B \to A$$

2. "A will serve on the committee only if B does." The *only* way that A can serve is if B does. This means that if A is on the committee, then B must be, too.

$$A \to B$$

3. "A will not serve on the committee unless B does." So if B doesn't serve on the committee, then A won't serve either.

$$\sim\!B \to \sim\!A$$

4. "A serves if and only if B serves" means "If A serves, then B serves; *and* if B serves, then A serves." Therefore, neither A nor B can serve without the other; either both are on the committee or neither is.

$$A \leftrightarrow B$$

NOTE: Statements 2 and 3, above, convey the exact same meaning. Statement 2 says that the *only* way that A can serve is if B does, which means that if B does not serve, then A will not serve; but that is exactly what Statement 3 says. It is a very important and useful fact that they are equivalent.

**Logic Fact 13**

**A → B  is equivalent to  ~B → ~A**

NOTE:  If A ↔ B is true, then if either A or B is true, so is the other; and if either A or B is false, so is the other.

**Logic Fact 14**

**A ↔ B is equivalent to  [(A → B) ∧ (B → A)]**

Let's apply what you have just learned to a typical group of five analytical reasoning questions based on a single set of conditions. We will start by translating each condition into logical symbols. We will then explain the correct answer to each question and, equally important, indicate why the other choices are incorrect.

For Questions 9–13

The principal of a school is forming a committee. There are to be five members: three teachers, chosen from Mr. Jones, Ms. Kaplan, Ms. Lane, Mr. Moss, and Mr. Nichols; and two students, chosen from Oscar, Peter, Quincy, and Ruth. The composition of the committee must conform to the following conditions:

Mr. Jones will serve only if Ruth is also on the committee.

Ms. Lane will not serve unless Ms. Kaplan and Oscar also serve.

Neither Mr. Moss nor Mr. Nichols will serve without the other.

If Peter serves, neither Quincy nor Ruth can serve.

Before even reading the first question, let's collect all of the information in the simplest form possible. On your scrap paper replace all the names with letters, and write each of the four conditions symbolically.

teachers: J K L M N      students: O P Q R
                3                        2

$$J \to R \quad L \to (K \wedge O) \quad M \leftrightarrow N \quad P \to (\sim\!Q \wedge \sim\!R)$$

We will now answer all the questions, without having to constantly reread the wordy set of conditions which would be on the screen. Rather, we will refer only to these concise symbolic statements that we have written down.

9. Which of the following is an acceptable committee?

   (A) Jones, Lane, Moss, Nichols, Oscar
   (B) Kaplan, Lane, Nichols, Oscar, Peter
   (C) Kaplan, Moss, Nichols, Oscar, Ruth
   (D) Lane, Moss, Nichols, Oscar, Ruth
   (E) Moss, Nichols, Oscar, Peter, Quincy

SOLUTION.
Only choice (C) does not violate any of the given conditions.

(A) is unacceptable because it contains four teachers (J, L, M, N).

(B) violates the condition M ↔ N, which states that if either of M and N serve, so does the other.

(D) violates the condition L → (K ∧ O), which states that if L serves, K must too.

(E) violates the condition P → (~Q ∧ ~R), which states that if P serves, Q cannot.

10. How many different committees could include Mr. Jones and Quincy?
    (A) 1    (B) 2    (C) 3    (D) 4    (E) 5

SOLUTION.

• Since J and Q are on the committee, circle J and Q.

    Ⓙ K  L  M  N  O  P  Ⓠ R

• Since J → R, and J is included, R is too. Circle R.

    Ⓙ K  L  M  N  O  P  Ⓠ Ⓡ

- Since R and Q are the two students, cross out O and P.

$$Ⓙ \ K \ L \ M \ N \ \cancel{Ø} \ \cancel{P} \ Ⓠ \ Ⓡ$$

- Since L → (K ∧ O), if L were on a committee, O would be too; but this is impossible. So cross out L.

$$Ⓙ \ K \ \cancel{L} \ M \ N \ \cancel{Ø} \ \cancel{P} \ Ⓠ \ Ⓡ$$

- If K serves, the third teacher would have to be M or N, but M ↔ N means it is impossible for only one of them to serve; so K cannot serve. Cross out K.

$$Ⓙ \ \cancel{K} \ \cancel{L} \ M \ N \ \cancel{Ø} \ \cancel{P} \ Ⓠ \ Ⓡ$$

- Since there must be three teachers, circle M and N.

$$Ⓙ \ \cancel{K} \ \cancel{L} \ Ⓜ \ Ⓝ \ \cancel{Ø} \ \cancel{P} \ Ⓠ \ Ⓡ$$

- There is only 1 acceptable committee: JMNQR.

- The answer is A.

---

11. If Quincy and Ruth are both on the committee, who else *must* be on the committee?

(A) J  (B) K  (C) L  (D) M  (E) O

---

SOLUTION.

- Since Q and R are on the committee, and the committee has only two student members, O is not on the committee. Eliminate choice E.

- Since L → (K ∧ O), and we know that O is not on the committee, neither is L. Eliminate C.

- J, M, N, Q, R and K, M, N, Q, R are each acceptable committees, so J *could* be on the committee and K *could* be on the committee, but neither one *must* be on the committee. Eliminate A and B.

- The committee *must* include M. (It must also contain N, but that wasn't one of the choices.) The answer is D.

---

12. If M is not on the committee, each of the following must be on the committee EXCEPT

(A) J  (B) L  (C) O  (D) Q  (E) R

---

SOLUTION.

- Since M is not on the committee, neither is N, and so the three teachers must be J, K, and L. Cross out M and N, and circle J, K , and L. Eliminate choices A and B.

$$Ⓙ Ⓚ Ⓛ \ \cancel{M} \ \cancel{N} \ O \ P \ Q \ R$$

- Since L is on the committee and L → (K ∧ O), then O is on the committee. Circle O and eliminate choice C.

$$Ⓙ Ⓚ Ⓛ \ \cancel{M} \ \cancel{N} \ Ⓞ \ P \ Q \ R$$

- Since J is on the committee, and J → R, R must be too. Circle R, and eliminate choice E.

$$Ⓙ Ⓚ Ⓛ \ \cancel{M} \ \cancel{N} \ Ⓞ \ P \ Q \ Ⓡ$$

- The only acceptable committee is J, K, L, O, R. So Q is not on the committee. The answer is D.

---

13. In how many different ways can the principal select an acceptable committee?

(A) Fewer than 3   (B) 3   (C) 5   (D) 7
(E) More than 7

---

SOLUTION. In the solution to question 12, we saw that if M is not on the committee, there is only 1 way the committee can be formed. What if M is on the committee? Then, of course, N must be on the committee, and the third teacher must be J, K, or L. Let's examine each of those possibilities.

- The teachers are M, N, and J.

Since J is on the committee, and J → R, then R must be, too. Since P →(~Q ∧ ~R), the other student can't be P. Therefore, the second student must be either O or Q, neither of which violates any condition. So there are 2 possibilities: M, N, J, R, O and M, N, J, R, Q.

- The teachers are M, N, and K.

If O is on the committee, there are no restrictions on the second student, so there are 3 possibilities: M, N, K, O, P; M, N, K, O, Q; and M, N, K, O, R.

Since P cannot serve with either Q or R, if O is not on the committee, P cannot be on the committee. So, if O is not on the committee, the two students must be Q and R. Therefore, there is 1 additional possibility: M, N, K, Q, R.

- The teachers are M, N, and L.

Since L → (K ∧ O), K must also be on the committee. There would then be four teachers on the committee, which is not permitted. So M, N, and L cannot serve together.

Adding up the underlined numbers, we see that there are a total of 7 ways that the principal can select the committee. The answer is D.

It is now time to discuss eight essential test-taking tactics for handling the analytical reasoning questions on the GRE.

# Testing Tactics

## Be Familiar with the Most Common Types of Analytical Reasoning Questions

As you will see, there is a great variety of types of analytical reasoning questions that can be asked on the GRE. However, there are four types that occur much more frequently than the others, and when you see them, you should immediately know what you need to do to answer them. Each of Questions 9–13 (pp. 280–281) illustrate one of these question types. We will now list each of the four types, state the strategy for answering it, and give an example.

- **Which of the following *could* be true?**

  If only one of the answer choices *could* be true, then each of the other four choices *must be false;* that is, each one must violate at least one of the given conditions.

  Question 9 asks, "Which of the following is an acceptable committee?" In other words, "Which of the following lists of people *could be* the committee that the principal picked?" In answering that question, we showed that four of the choices contradicted at least one of the given conditions.

- **Which of the following *must* be true?**

  Since only one of the answer choices *must* be true, then for each of the other choices, either it is false or it is possibly (but not definitely) true.

  Question 11 asks, "If Quincy and Ruth are both on the committee, who else *must be* on the committee?" In answering this question, we eliminated two of the incorrect choices by showing that they *could not possibly* be on the committee (they were false) and two of them by showing that although they *could be* on the

committee, they did not have to be on the committee (they were possibly, but not definitely, true).

- **Which of the following *cannot* be true?**

  Since only one of the answer choices *cannot* be true, then each of the other choices could be or must be true. The correct answer is the only choice which violates at least one of the given conditions or is otherwise inconsistent with what we know must be true.

  Question 12 states, "If M is not on the committee, each of the following *must be* on the committee EXCEPT..." In other words, *only one* of the five choices given *cannot* be on the committee. In this case, we were able to determine the exact membership of the committee, so anyone who could be on the committee, was on the committee. The correct answer was the only choice that violated one or more of the given conditions.

- **How many possibilities are there?**

  This question asks, "How many different ways are there to satisfy all of the given conditions?" Here, you must systematically count or list all of the possibilities that do not violate the conditions.

  Question 13 asks, "In how many different ways can the principal select an acceptable committee?" To arrive at the correct answer of 7, we counted all of the ways of taking three teachers and two students that did not violate any of the conditions. In question 10, we examined the consequences of having both J and Q on the committee, and concluded that only one possible committee could be formed.

## Simplify the Information by Using Abbreviations and Symbols

The analytical reasoning questions are not intended to be ambiguous or deceptive. In fact, the testmakers take great pains to use language precisely and to word the set of conditions describing a particular relationship so carefully that only one interpretation is possible. In doing so, however, they use so many words that it is easy to get lost. To see the situation clearly, you need to replace those words with symbols. There are two reasons for this. First, it is very difficult to keep looking at the list of conditions on the screen, especially when you

have to scroll down to see them all. So you can't solve most analytical reasoning questions until you write the conditions on your scrap paper, and writing full sentences would be far too time-consuming. Second, it is much easier to work with a few symbols than with lengthy sentences.

The first step is to strip away all of the excess verbiage and then to abbreviate the remaining key words with single letters. GRE questions sometimes help in this process by using letters rather than words; for example, "six floats—C, D, E, F, G, and H are lined up for a parade," or "five singers—P, Q, R, S, and T are auditioning for a part in an opera." Other times, words are used. When this occurs, you must immediately replace each word with an uppercase letter. For example, if a question states that "five musicians—a bassist, a drummer, a guitarist, a pianist, and a trumpeter—are performing in a talent show," you should immediately abbreviate them B, D, G, P, and T; and if a question refers to "three girls—Amanda, Brianne, and Cindy, and four boys—Dave, Ed, Frank, and George," immediately write: "girls: A B C   boys: D E F G" on your scrap paper.

You have already seen how the use of logical symbols can make it easier to deal with the conditions given in a particular set of analytical reasoning questions. We now introduce other symbols that many students find useful. You do not have to use all of them and are certainly free to use others if you prefer. However, you must symbolize and abbreviate the conditions to avoid getting lost.

| MEANING | SYMBOL |
|---|---|
| is equal to; is the same (weight, height, age, etc.) as | = |
| is not equal to; is not the same (weight, height, age, etc.) as | ≠ |
| is less than; is (lighter, shorter, younger, etc.) than; is to the left of; is in front of; precedes; etc. | < |
| is immediately (to the left of, in front of, etc.); immediately precedes | << |
| is greater than; is (heavier, taller, older, etc.) than; is to the right of; is behind; follows; etc. | > |
| is immediately (to the right of, behind, etc.); immediately follows; etc. | >> |
| is going to; is connected to (by a one-way street); etc. | → |
| is connected to (by a two-way street); etc. | ↔ |

Observe how we reduce the following set of conditions to a few manageable symbolic statements.

> A college is sponsoring a variety show. Auditions were held for eight students: Alan, Beth, Carol, Diane, Ellen, Frank, George, and Hank. The director will choose six of them to perform in the show. So far, the following decisions have been made:
>
> > Alan will perform immediately after Diane does.

> The show must open with Ellen's comedy routine.
>
> Since Frank and Hank both play the piano, at most one of them will be permitted to perform.
>
> Carol will not perform unless Beth performs earlier in the program.
>
> If Beth is chosen to do her ballet, she will perform after Diane does her dance number, with only one intervening act.

First, replace the name of each student by its initial letter.

| | | | |
|---|---|---|---|
| Alan | = A | Ellen | = E |
| Beth | = B | Frank | = F |
| Carol | = C | George | = G |
| Diane | = D | Hank | = H |

Second, using logical symbols, on your scrap paper write down what you know about the students who have auditioned for the show.

Let X < Y signify that X will perform before Y, and X << Y signify that X will perform *immediately* before Y.

| | |
|---|---|
| D << A | Diane performs immediately before Alan. |
| E = 1 | Ellen performs first. |
| F → ~H | If Frank performs, then Hank doesn't. |
| H → ~F | If Hank performs, then Frank doesn't. |
| C → (B < C) | If Carol performs, then Beth performs before Carol does. |
| B → (D << x << B) | If Beth performs, then someone (x) performs immediately after Diane and before Beth. |

Consider the last condition in conjunction with the first. Since Diane immediately precedes Alan, x = A, and the last condition can be written B → (D << A << B).

So, if Beth is selected, you know the exact order of three of the performers.

Having translated each of the given conditions into symbols, you should *never* look at the conditions on the computer screen again. You should answer every question based on this set of conditions by referring to the symbolic statements on your scrap paper.

## Tactic 3

# Pay Careful Attention to the Key Words that Serve to Limit the Situation

Look at the set of conditions presented in the discussion of TACTIC 2. Note the words that limit the situations presented. The show *must* open with Ellen's comedy routine; ... *at most one* of Frank and Hank will be permitted to perform; Alan will perform *immediately* after Diane; ... there will be *only one* intervening act between Diane and Beth.

Certain words are critical to your understanding of the situation. Take particular note of them, and be sure to incorporate them in your symbols.

### FREQUENTLY USED KEY WORDS

| | |
|---|---|
| after | entire |
| all | every |
| always | exactly |
| at least *n* (*n*, *n* + 1, *n* + 2, ...) | except |
| | fewer |
| at most *n* (0, 1, 2, ... , *n*) | first |
| before | if |
| but | if and only if |
| can be | immediately |
| cannot be | impossible |
| consecutive | last |
| different | less, least |
| directly | more, most |
| each | must be |

| | |
|---|---|
| no | same |
| no fewer than *n* (= at least *n*) | some |
| | the least (smallest, shortest, youngest, etc.) |
| no more than *n* (= at most *n*) | the most (greatest, tallest, oldest, etc.) |
| only | |
| possible | unless |

Note that certain of these key words have only one function—to rule out a potential ambiguity. These words so precisely define the situation that only one interpretation is possible. Take, for example, *immediately*. What does the statement "Alan will perform after Diane does" tell you? It tells you that Diane will perform sometime earlier in the program than Alan. What does the statement "Alan will perform immediately after Diane does" tell you? It tells you the exact relationship between Alan and Diane, letting you know that Diane is the person who performs right before Alan with nobody else coming between them.

## Tactic 4

# First, Eliminate Answer Choices Ruled Out by Individual Conditions; Then, Work Through the Remaining Choices

Pay special attention to any conditions phrased in unambiguous terms—*always, never, all, none*. Because they allow only one interpretation of the situation, you may be able to use them to instantly rule out several answer choices.

See how each of the given conditions concerning the variety show can be used to eliminate one or more of the choices in Question 1. Remember to refer only to the symbolic statements we wrote down; do not refer back to the original list of conditions.

> 14. Which of the following program listings satisfies each of the director's requirements?
>
> (A) Diane, Alan, Beth, Carol, Hank, George
> (B) Ellen, Diane, Alan, Hank, Beth, George
> (C) Beth, Diane, Frank, George, Alan, Ellen
> (D) Ellen, Diane, Alan, Beth, Frank, Hank
> (E) Ellen, Frank, Diane, Alan, Beth, George

NOTE: Remember that on an actual GRE, the five choices appear on the screen, one under the other, with an oval in front of each choice, and you record your answer by clicking on the appropriate oval with your mouse. As we have been doing throughout this book, we will label the five choices A, B, C, D, and E.

SOLUTION.

- The first condition is: D << A. So eliminate Choice C, in which Diane does not *immediately* precede Alan.

- The next condition is: E = 1. Therefore, we can eliminate Choice A, in which Ellen is not the first performer. (Note that Ellen is not first in Choice C either, but C has already been eliminated, and so we never have to consider it again).

- The third condition states that F → ~H; so eliminate Choice D, in which both Frank and Hank appear.

- The next condition, C → (B < C), doesn't apply. This condition says what must be true *if Carol is selected;* but Carol is not listed in either of the two remaining choices—B and E.

- Finally, recall from our discussion in TACTIC 2 that we determined that if Beth is selected to perform, we must have the sequence D << A << B somewhere in the program. Hence we can eliminate Choice B.

By the process of elimination, we now know that the answer is Choice E. In fact, the program

E, F, D, A, B, G

does *not* violate any of the given conditions, and so *is* acceptable.

## Study Conditions Not Merely for What They State But Also for What They Imply

Certain analytical reasoning questions resemble the inference questions you find in the reading comprehension section of the GRE. To answer them correctly, you must understand not only what the conditions state explicitly, but what they imply.

Consider the following question based on the same set of conditions given in the discussion of TACTIC 2.

---

15. Which of the following students could *not* be the last person to perform in the program?

    (A) Alan   (B) Beth   (C) Carol
    (D) Diane   (E) Frank

---

SOLUTION. Note that none of the conditions discusses who will be the last to perform. However, the correct *implication* can easily be made by referring to the first condition: D << A. This tells us that Alan must perform immediately after Diane does, and so Diane cannot be the last performer on the program. The answer is D.

## Organize Information in a List or Table

Often the key to answering analytical reasoning questions is to organize the given information in a list or table. Notice that we did not do this in the questions about the students auditioning for the variety show. As you go through lots of different types of analytical reasoning questions, you will begin to sense intuitively when making a list or a table will be helpful.

Consider the following set of conditions. Before attempting to answer any of the questions based on it, we will enter as much information as possible into a table.

---

At a high school science fair, the four top winners were a freshman, a sophomore, a junior, and a senior. Each of the winners did a project in a different field: astronomy, biology, chemistry, and geology. The names of the four winners were: Ken, Larry, Mary, and Nancy.

Through discussions with various students, the following facts were ascertained.

The geology project won neither first nor second prize.

Mary won second prize.

The junior won first prize.

The chemistry project, which was done by the senior, won fourth prize.

Ken did the astronomy project.

---

First use TACTIC 2 to abbreviate all of the words. Clearly, we will let K, L, M, and N represent the four names, and A, B, C, and G represent the four subject areas. Since both *sophomore* and *senior* begin with S, we could use So. for *sophomore* and Sr. for *senior,* or we could just use 9, 10, 11, and 12 to represent the four grades.

The most convenient way to display the given information is in a table. You should set up a blank table, and use each of the given conditions to enter information.

Start with a blank grid, and read each condition in order.

| Prize | Grade | Subject | Name |
|-------|-------|---------|------|
| 1st   |       |         |      |
| 2nd   |       |         |      |
| 3rd   |       |         |      |
| 4th   |       |         |      |

Since the geology project won neither first nor second prize, the G must go in the third or fourth row.

| Prize | Grade | Subject | Name |
|-------|-------|---------|------|
| 1st   |       |         |      |
| 2nd   |       |         |      |
| 3rd   |       | G       |      |
| 4th   |       | G       |      |

Since Mary won second prize, put an M in the second row.

| Prize | Grade | Subject | Name |
|-------|-------|---------|------|
| 1st   |       |         |      |
| 2nd   |       |         | M    |
| 3rd   |       | G       |      |
| 4th   |       | G       |      |

Since the junior won first prize, put an 11 in the first row.

| Prize | Grade | Subject | Name |
|-------|-------|---------|------|
| 1st   | 11    |         |      |
| 2nd   |       |         | M    |
| 3rd   |       | G       |      |
| 4th   |       | G       |      |

The chemistry project, which was done by the senior, won fourth prize. Therefore, in the fourth row we can replace the G with a C and enter a 12.

| Prize | Grade | Subject | Name |
|-------|-------|---------|------|
| 1st   | 11    |         |      |
| 2nd   |       |         | M    |
| 3rd   |       | G       |      |
| 4th   | 12    | C       |      |

Since Ken did the astronomy project, Ken didn't win third or fourth prize (they went to the geology and chemistry projects), and Mary won second prize; so Ken's astronomy project won first prize.

| Prize | Grade | Subject | Name |
|-------|-------|---------|------|
| 1st   | 11    | A       | K    |
| 2nd   |       |         | M    |
| 3rd   |       | G       |      |
| 4th   | 12    | C       |      |

We do not have complete information, but this is all we can deduce from the given conditions, and so we will have to use it in answering the questions.

16. Which of the following statements *must* be true?

(A) The freshman won second prize.
(B) Larry is a sophomore.
(C) Mary did the biology report.
(D) Nancy is a senior.
(E) Ken won fourth prize.

SOLUTION. Looking at our final table, we see that Choice E is definitely wrong (Ken won first prize, not fourth). Choices A, B, and D are all possible; they do not violate the entries in the table, and so *could* be true, but none of them *must* be true. Choice C, on the other hand, *must* be true. The only science not listed is biology, so it *must* go in the second row, next to Mary.

| Prize | Grade | Subject | Name |
|-------|-------|---------|------|
| 1st   | 11    | A       | K    |
| 2nd   |       | B       | M    |
| 3rd   |       | G       |      |
| 4th   | 12    | C       |      |

## Do Not Use Information Specific to One Question in a Subsequent Question

We will now answer two more questions based on the set of conditions discussed in TACTIC 6.

17. If Nancy is a sophomore, which of the following is the correct order of the winners, from first place to fourth place?

(A) Ken, Mary, Larry, Nancy
(B) Mary, Ken, Nancy, Larry
(C) Larry, Ken, Nancy, Mary
(D) Ken, Mary, Nancy, Larry
(E) Ken, Larry, Nancy, Mary

SOLUTION. Question 17 adds another condition which we must now take into account, namely that Nancy is a sophomore. Start with the last table we used in TACTIC 6, and put in this additional information.

Rows 1 and 2 are already taken by Ken and Mary, and row 4 is reserved for a senior. Therefore, Nancy must go in row 3.

| Prize | Grade | Subject | Name |
|-------|-------|---------|------|
| 1st | 11 | A | K |
| 2nd | | B | M |
| 3rd | 10 | G | N |
| 4th | 12 | C | |

We can now complete the table.

The freshman must go in row 2, and Larry must go in row 4.

| Prize | Grade | Subject | Name |
|-------|-------|---------|------|
| 1st | 11 | A | K |
| 2nd | 9 | B | M |
| 3rd | 10 | G | N |
| 4th | 12 | C | L |

It is now an easy task to answer question 4. Choice D is the correct order:

Ken, Mary, Nancy, Larry.

We have now answered two questions on this set of conditions. Suppose the third question is question 18, below.

18. Which of the following statements must be true?
   I. Mary is a freshman.
   II. Larry won fourth prize.

III. Both the freshman and the sophomore placed higher than the senior.
(A) None   (B) I only   (C) III only
(D) I and III only   (E) I, II, and III

Be careful! Looking at the complete table that we created in answering question 17, it appears that all of the statements are true, and that the answer is E. However, our final table was based on a condition stated in question 17 that was not one of the original conditions—namely, that Nancy is a sophomore. That condition applied to question 17 *only*. We may not rely on it in answering question 18. We must go back to the table we had after question 16—the table that was created based only on the original set of conditions:

SOLUTION.

| Prize | Grade | Subject | Name |
|-------|-------|---------|------|
| 1st | 11 | A | K |
| 2nd | | B | M |
| 3rd | | G | |
| 4th | 12 | C | |

From this table it is clear that although statements I and II *could* be true, they are not necessarily true. Statement III, on the other hand, *must* be true. (Both the freshman and sophomore placed higher than the senior, who, we know, won fourth prize.) The correct answer is Choice C: III only.

# Draw a Simple Picture or Diagram That Correctly Illustrates the Given Set of Conditions

On some analytical reasoning questions, an excellent way to deal with the information is to draw a simple diagram, picture, or map. This is particularly helpful when you are dealing with the physical or temporal order of things. It is much easier to tell whether person A can be seated opposite person B if you have sketched a diagram of the table; it is easier to know whether person C is older or younger than person D if you have entered all of the given information on a time line; and it is easier to determine whether town E is east of town W if you have drawn a simple map.

Questions 19–22 are based on the following set of conditions.

The chairperson and vice-chairperson of a congressional committee are seated opposite one another at the ends of a rectangular conference table. The other six members of the committee are seated around the table, three on each side.

The chairperson is a senator; the vice-chairperson a representative.

Each senator must be seated next to at least one representative, and vice versa.

Rep. Adams is seated at the vice-chairperson's right, next to Sen. Byrd.

Rep. Cohen, who is not the vice-chairperson, is sitting opposite Sen. Davis.

Sen. Evans is sitting between two representatives.

Only one person is sitting between Rep. Frank and Rep. Gold.

Remember that on the GRE, the preceding set of conditions would appear on the left-hand side of a split screen, and the first question would be on the right-hand side. However, you should not even read that question until you have drawn a rectangle to represent the table. Then reread each of the given conditions, in order, filling in the new information on your drawing as you proceed. Use a dash (—) to represent a seat at the table, and let *r* = representative, and *s* = senator.

The chairperson and vice-chairperson are seated opposite one another at the ends of the table.

The chairperson is a senator; the vice-chairperson a representative.

Each senator must be seated next to at least one representative, and vice versa.

> This condition does not help us here, but we will use it as we proceed.

Rep. Adams is seated at the vice-chairperson's right, next to Sen. Byrd.

> We now know a senator is to the vice-chairperson's left.

|  | Byrd | Adams |  |
|---|---|---|---|
|  | *s* | *r* |  |
| C *s* |  |  | *r* V-C |
|  | — | *s* |  |

*(row: — / s / r ; — / — / s)*

Rep. Cohen, who is not the vice-chairperson, is sitting opposite Sen. Davis.

> Cohen is not the vice-chairperson, and cannot be the chairperson, since the chairperson is a senator. Since he is sitting opposite Davis, he cannot sit opposite Byrd or Adams. So he must be on either side of the chairperson. If he were to the right of the chairperson, Sen. Davis would be between two senators, which is not allowed. So Cohen is to the left of the chairperson. Also, a representative is to the right of Davis.

|  | Cohen | Byrd | Adams |  |
|---|---|---|---|---|
|  | *r* | *s* | *r* |  |
| C *s* |  |  |  | *r* V-C |
|  | *s* | *r* | *s* |  |
|  | Davis |  |  |  |

Sen. Evans is sitting between two representatives.

> The only place for Evans to sit is opposite Adams. He is then between the vice-chairperson, a representative, and another representative, who is still unknown.

|  | Cohen | Byrd | Adams |  |
|---|---|---|---|---|
|  | *r* | *s* | *r* |  |
| C *s* |  |  |  | *r* V-C |
|  | *s* | *r* | *s* |  |
|  | Davis |  | Evans |  |

Only one person is sitting between Rep. Frank and Rep. Gold.

> Representatives Frank and Gold are the only representatives missing in the previous diagram. It is clear that they are to sit on either side of Sen. Evans; but there is no way to determine which one is the vice-chairman and which one is seated opposite Sen. Byrd. Therefore, there are <u>two</u> possible seating arrangements.

|  | Cohen | Byrd | Adams |  |
|---|---|---|---|---|
|  | *r* | *s* | *r* |  |
| C *s* |  |  |  | *r* V-C Gold |
|  | *s* | *r* | *s* |  |
|  | Davis | Frank | Evans |  |

or

|  | Cohen | Byrd | Adams |  |
|---|---|---|---|---|
|  | *r* | *s* | *r* |  |
| C *s* |  |  |  | *r* V-C Frank |
|  | *s* | *r* | *s* |  |
|  | Davis | Gold | Evans |  |

> Note that the chairperson is a senator whose name is not mentioned in the set of conditions.

Having created an accurate picture of the situation, you can now easily answer *any* question based on this set of conditions. Without this diagram, you would have to constantly refer back to the original statements, and the solutions would be much less obvious. Now refer to the final diagrams to answer each of questions 19–22.

---

19.  How many senators are not sitting next to another senator?

(A) 0   (B) 1   (C) 2   (D) 3   (E) 4

---

SOLUTION. Only two senators—Byrd and Evans—are not sitting next to a senator. They are each between two representatives. The answer is Choice C.

---

20.  Which of the following statements concerning Sen. Harris, the eighth member of the committee, must be true?

　　I. He is the chairperson.
　　II. He is sitting opposite Rep. Frank.
　　III. A senator is sitting on his right.

(A) I only   (B) II only   (C) I and II only
(D) I and III only   (E) I, II, and III

SOLUTION. The only place for Sen. Harris is in the chairperson's seat. I is true. Rep. Frank *could* be the vice-chairperson, in which case he would be opposite Sen. Harris; but the vice-chairperson could also be Rep. Gold, so it is not true that Sen. Harris *must* be sitting opposite Rep. Frank. II is false. From the diagram, we see that Sen. Davis is sitting to the right of the chairperson. III is true. The answer is Choice D: I and III only.

---

21. Which committee member is the vice-chairperson?

    (A) Adams  (B) Cohen  (C) Frank
    (D) Gold  (E) It cannot be determined from the information given.

---

SOLUTION. We have seen that the vice-chairperson could be either Frank or Gold, so the answer is Choice E: It cannot be determined from the information given.

---

22. If Sen. Jones is added to the committee, where could she be seated without violating any of the given conditions?

    (A) Immediately to the right of Sen. Evans
    (B) Immediately to the left of Sen. Evans
    (C) Immediately to the right of Sen. Davis
    (D) Immediately to the left of Sen. Davis
    (E) Immediately to the right of Sen. Byrd

---

SOLUTION. If Sen. Jones is seated on either side of Sen. Evans, there would be two people between Representatives Frank and Gold. So neither Choice A nor B is correct. If Sen. Jones is seated to the right of Sen. Davis, then Sen. Davis would be between two senators, whereas if she is seated to the left of Sen. Davis, she would be between two senators. Eliminate Choices C and D. The answer is Choice E: sitting to the right of Sen. Byrd would not violate any condition.

It was probably obvious that in order to tackle the preceding set of questions, it would be helpful to draw a rectangle to represent the table. However, there are many other types of analytical reasoning questions on which you should draw some sort of diagram. Consider Questions 23–26, which are based on the following set of conditions.

---

Six people are ranked from 1 to 6 in height (1 being the shortest and 6 being the tallest) and from 1 to 6 in weight (1 being the lightest and 6 being the heaviest). Each person's score is the sum of his or her two rankings.

   Gary is taller than Mary and lighter than Barry.

   Harry is taller than Gary and lighter than Larry.

   Carrie is shorter and heavier than Gary.

   Mary is taller than Larry and heavier than Carrie.

---

Larry is taller than Carrie and lighter than **Gary**.

Barry is shorter than Larry and lighter than Carrie.

---

On the GRE, these statements would appear on the left-hand side of the screen, and question 23 would appear on the right-hand side of the screen. Questions 24–26, of course, would not be visible, and would only appear after the previous questions had been answered. Before even *reading* question 23, make a diagram which will, hopefully, enable you to answer *any* question based on the given information.

Draw two horizontal lines: one will represent height and will go from *short* to *tall*; the other will represent weight and will go from *light* to *heavy*.

Gary is taller than Mary and lighter than Barry.

> On the top line, write a G to the right of an M, to represent the fact that Gary is taller than Mary. Similarly, on the bottom line, write a G to the left of a B.

Short ——————————— M    G ——————— Tall

Light ——————————— G    B ——————— Heavy

Harry is taller than Gary and lighter than Larry.

> Note that on the lower line we don't know yet whether the H and L should be to the left or right of the G and B.

Short ——————————— M   G   H ——————— Tall

Light ——————————— G    B ——————— Heavy
                    H    L

Carrie is shorter and heavier than Gary.

> On the top line, C has to be to the left of G, but we don't yet know whether it is to the left or right of M. On the bottom line, we still have a lot of uncertainty.

Short ——————————— M   G   H ——————— Tall
              ←—— C ——→

                        ——— C —→
Light ——————————— G    B ——————— Heavy
              ←—— H ——— L —→

Mary is taller than Larry and heavier than Carrie.

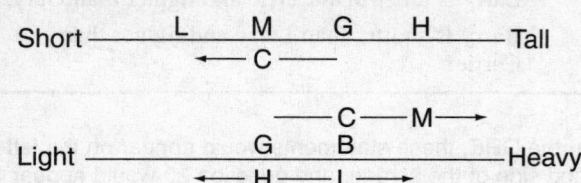

Larry is taller than Carrie and lighter than Gary.

> On the top line, we can now move the C to the left of the L. On the bottom line, we can move the H—L to the left of the G.

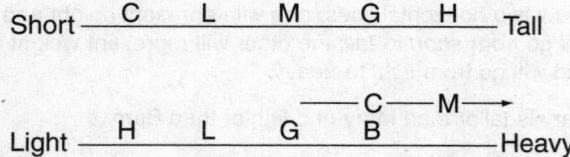

Barry is shorter than Larry and lighter than Carrie.

> The B goes to the left of the L, but we don't know whether it is to the left or right of the C. On the bottom line, we can now move the C—M to the right of the B.

Short ——— C  L  M  G  H ——— Tall
                 ←—B—

Light ——— H  L  G  B  C  M ——— Heavy

With practice you will find that you will usually be able to create a diagram to represent the data in an analytical reasoning question in far less time than it took us to explain it here. Now use the information in your diagram to answer the following questions.

---

23. How many people are both shorter and lighter than at least one other person?

    (A) 1   (B) 2   (C) 3   (D) 4   (E) 5

---

SOLUTION. Harry and Mary are out, since he is the tallest and she is the heaviest. Gary is shorter, but heavier, than Harry. Barry, Carrie, and Larry are all shorter and lighter than Mary. The answer is 3, Choice C.

---

24. Who among the following are both taller and heavier than Larry?

    I. Gary
    II. Harry
    III. Mary

    (A) I only   (B) III only   (C) I and II only
    (D) I and III only   (E) I, II, and III

---

SOLUTION. From the diagram it is clear that all three of them are taller than Larry, but Harry is lighter than Larry. Only Gary and Mary are also heavier than Larry. The answer is Choice D.

---

25. Who has the highest score?

    (A) Barry   (B) Gary   (C) Harry
    (D) Larry   (E) Mary

---

SOLUTION. Mary's score of 10 (4 for height and 6 for weight) is the highest, E.

---

26. Which of the following statements if true would resolve any ambiguity about the relative heights and weights of the six people?

    I. Barry and Carrie have the same score.
    II. Barry and Larry have the same score.
    III. The same number of people are taller than Carrie as are lighter than she is.

    (A) I only   (B) II only   (C) III only
    (D) I and III only   (E) I, II, and III

---

SOLUTION. The only ambiguity that exists is that we do not know who is taller: Barry or Carrie. Any statement that allows us to determine who is the taller will resolve this ambiguity.

• Since Carrie's weight ranking is 1 more than Barry's, if they have the same score, her height ranking would have to be 1 less than Barry's; that is, Carrie would be shorter. I is true.

• Larry's score is 5 (3 + 2). If Barry has the same score, his height ranking would have to be 1 (since his weight ranking is 4), and so Barry would be the shortest. II is true.

• Four people are lighter than Carrie. If four people are also taller, her height ranking would be 2, and she would be taller than Barry. III is true.

• The answer is E.

# Practice Exercises

## Analytical Reasoning Questions

### Questions 1–5

Six actors—Bob, Carol, Dave, Ed, Frank, and Grace—are auditioning for a part in an off-Broadway play. The auditions will take place over four consecutive days, starting on a Thursday. Each actor will have one audition. The days on which the different actors will audition must conform to the following conditions:

> At least one audition will take place each day.
>
> No more than two auditions will take place on any day.
>
> No more than three auditions will take place on any two consecutive days.
>
> Bob's audition must take place on Saturday.
>
> Carol's audition must take place on the same day as another audition.
>
> Frank's audition must take place on a day before Grace's audition.
>
> Dave's audition must take place on a day after Ed's audition.

1.  If only one audition takes place on Thursday, which actor could have that audition?

    (A) Bob   (B) Carol   (C) Dave   (D) Frank
        (E) Grace

2.  If Bob's and Frank's auditions are on the same day, which of the following must be true?

    (A) Dave's audition will take place on Thursday.
    (B) Dave's audition will take place on Friday.
    (C) Grace's audition will take place on Thursday.
    (D) Carol's audition will take place on Sunday.
    (E) Ed's audition will take place on Sunday.

3.  If the director decides to hold two auditions on Thursday and two on Sunday, how many actors would be eligible to audition on Friday?

    (A) 1   (B) 2   (C) 3   (D) 4   (E) 5

4.  If Ed and Grace have their auditions on the same day, which of the following must be true?

    (A) Ed's audition will take place on Thursday.
    (B) Frank's audition will take place on Friday.
    (C) Carol's audition will take place on Saturday.
    (D) Grace's audition will take place on Saturday.
    (E) Carol's audition will take place on Sunday.

5.  If Ed's audition is on Saturday, which of the following actors cannot audition on the same day as any other actor?

    (A) Bob   (B) Carol   (C) Ed   (D) Frank
        (E) Grace

### Questions 6–9

As part of their sports physicals, seven collegiate athletes—F, G, H, I, J, K, and L—are being weighed. In announcing the results of the physical exams, the coach has given the following information:

> None of the athletes is exactly the same weight as another athlete.
>
> K is heavier than L, but lighter than H.
>
> I is heavier than J.
>
> Both F and G are heavier than H.

6.  Each of the following could be true EXCEPT

    (A) F is the heaviest.
    (B) G is the heaviest.
    (C) I is the heaviest.
    (D) More than three athletes are heavier than K.
    (E) More than three athletes are lighter than K.

7.  Which of the following, if true, would be sufficient to determine which athlete is the lightest?

    (A) I is the heaviest.
    (B) I is lighter than K.
    (C) K is heavier than J.
    (D) J is heavier than K.
    (E) Exactly five students are lighter than F.

8.  If J is heavier than F, how many different rankings, by weight, of the athletes are possible?

    (A) 1   (B) 2   (C) 4   (D) 6   (E) 8

9.  If H is heavier than I, which of the following CANNOT be true?

    (A) I's weight is equal to the average of F's weight and G's weight.
    (B) I's weight is equal to the average of K's weight and L's weight.
    (C) J's weight is equal to the average of K's weight and L's weight.
    (D) J is the second lightest.
    (E) J is the lightest.

### Questions 10–13

Jacqueline placed nine books—two biographies, two computer books, two dictionaries, two novels, and a thesaurus—in a row on a shelf over her desk. The positions of the books are numbered from 1 to 9, with the leftmost book being book 1 and the rightmost book being book 9. The following facts are known about the order in which the books were placed:

> The two biographies are next to each other.
>
> The fourth book is a novel.
>
> The two computer books are not next to each other.
>
> Both the first and last book are dictionaries.
>
> The thesaurus is not next to either novel.

10. If one of the biographies is book number 3, in what position is the other biography?

    (A) 2   (B) 4   (C) 5   (D) 6   (E) 7

11. If a novel is in position 5, each of the following could be true EXCEPT

    (A) The thesaurus is next to one of the dictionaries.
    (B) The thesaurus is in position 6.
    (C) The two computer books and the thesaurus are in three consecutive positions.
    (D) A biography is in position 2.
    (E) A biography is in position 8.

12. If a novel is in position 6, which of the following could be true?

    (A) A computer book is in position 2.
    (B) The thesaurus is in position 3.
    (C) A biography is in position 5.
    (D) The thesaurus is in position 5.
    (E) A computer book is in position 7.

13. Which of the following, if true, would enable you to determine the position of every type of book?

    (A) A computer book is in position 2.
    (B) A computer book is in position 3.
    (C) A biography is in position 5.
    (D) A computer book is in position 7.
    (E) A novel is in position 7.

## Questions 14–17

A nine-member parent-teacher planning committee consists of five teachers—A, B, C, D, and E—and four parents—F, G, H, and I. Five members of this committee are to be chosen to meet with the superintendent concerning some issues on the budget. The committee will be chosen in accordance with the following requirements:

Exactly two parents will be chosen.

If B is chosen, both D and G must also be chosen.

A cannot be chosen unless F is chosen.

If either C or E is chosen, so must the other.

If I is chosen, neither F nor H may be chosen.

14. Which of the following could be a list of the five people chosen?

    (A) D, E, F, G, H
    (B) A, B, D, F, H
    (C) B, C, D, F, G
    (D) A, C, E, F, I
    (E) A, B, D, F, G

15. If both F and H are chosen, who among the following must also be chosen?

    (A) A   (B) B   (C) C   (D) D   (E) G

16. If E is not chosen, then all of the following must be chosen EXCEPT

    (A) A   (B) D   (C) F   (D) G   (E) H

17. If the committee decides to choose only four people—two teachers and two parents—but adhere to all the other conditions, in how many different ways can the choice be made?

    (A) 2   (B) 3   (C) 6   (D) 9   (E) 12

## Questions 18–22

During the first half of the year, from January through June, the chairperson of the Mathematics Department will be on sabbatical. The dean of the college has asked each of six professors in the department—Arkes, Borofsky, Chang, Dexter, Hobbes, and Lee—to serve as acting chairperson during one of those months. The mathematicians can decide the order themselves subject only to the following criteria established by the dean:

Chang will serve as chairperson in February.

Arkes will serve as chairperson before Hobbes does.

Borofsky and Dexter will serve as chairpersons in consecutive months.

18. Which of the following professors could serve as chairperson in January?

    (A) Borofsky   (B) Chang   (C) Dexter
        (D) Hobbes   (E) Lee

19. In how many ways can the schedule be made up if Lee has to serve as chairperson in May?

    (A) 1   (B) 2   (C) 3   (D) 4   (E) 6

20. If Lee serves in April, all of the following could be true EXCEPT

    (A) Arkes serves in January.
    (B) Hobbes serves in March.
    (C) Borofsky serves in May.
    (D) Borofsky serves in June.
    (E) Hobbes serves in June.

21. If Borofsky serves in May, what is the latest month in which Arkes could serve?

    (A) January
    (B) February
    (C) March
    (D) April
    (E) June

22. Which of the following CANNOT be true?

    (A) Arkes and Lee serve in consecutive months.
    (B) Lee and Hobbes serve in consecutive months.
    (C) Hobbes and Dexter serve in consecutive months.
    (D) Arkes and Chang serve in consecutive months.
    (E) Borofsky and Chang serve in consecutive months.

## Answer Key

| | | | |
|---|---|---|---|
| 1. **D** | 7. **D** | 13. **E** | 19. **B** |
| 2. **B** | 8. **C** | 14. **E** | 20. **E** |
| 3. **D** | 9. **A** | 15. **C** | 21. **C** |
| 4. **E** | 10. **A** | 16. **E** | 22. **A** |
| 5. **E** | 11. **B** | 17. **D** | |
| 6. **E** | 12. **E** | 18. **E** | |

## Answer Explanations

### Questions 1–5

First express each of the conditions symbolically:

B, C, D, E, F, G: 1 audition each

Days: Thu, Fri, Sat, Sun

Each day: 1 or 2 auditions

2 consecutive days: 2 or 3 auditions

B = Sat.    C—x    F < G    E < D

1. **D.**   Only Choice D does not violate any of the given conditions.
    A violates the condition that Bob's audition will take place on Saturday (B = Sat.).
    B violates the condition that Carol's audition cannot be the only audition on a particular day (C—x).
    Choices C and E are impossible. Since Dave's audition must take place on a day *after* Ed's audition (E < D) and Grace's audition must take place on a day *after* Frank's audition (F < G), neither can take place on Thursday.

2. **B.**   The condition that Bob's and Frank's auditions are on the same day completely determines the schedule. They must take place on Saturday (B = Sat.). To avoid having more than three auditions on two consecutive days, there can be only one audition on Friday and one on Sunday, which means there will be two on Thursday. Since (F < G), Grace's audition will take place on Sunday. Since (E < D), Ed's audition will take place on Thursday and Dave's audition on Friday. Finally, Carol's audition will be the second audition on Thursday.

    | C/E | D | B/F | G |
    |---|---|---|---|
    | Th. | Fri. | Sat. | Sun. |

    Only Choice B is consistent with this schedule.

3. **D.**   Since only one audition can take place on Friday, it cannot be Carol's (C—x); and, of course, it cannot be Bob's (B = Sat.). Any of the other four actors could audition on Friday as indicated on the following schedules:

    | E/F | D | B | C/G |
    |---|---|---|---|
    | Th. | Fri. | Sat. | Sun. |

    | C/F | E | B | D/G |
    |---|---|---|---|
    | Th. | Fri. | Sat. | Sun. |

    | C/E | F | B | D/G |
    |---|---|---|---|
    | Th. | Fri. | Sat. | Sun. |

    | E/F | G | B | C/D |
    |---|---|---|---|
    | Th. | Fri. | Sat. | Sun. |

4. **E.**   The condition that Ed and Grace have their auditions on the same day completely determines the schedule. They cannot take place on Saturday (B = Sat.); they cannot take place on Sunday since Dave's audition must take place after Ed's (E < D); and they cannot take place on Thursday since Frank's audition must precede Grace's (F < G). So Ed's and Grace's auditions must take place on Friday. To avoid having more than three auditions on two consecutive days, there can be only one audition on Thursday and one on Saturday, which means there will be two on Sunday. The complete schedule is as follows:

    | F | E/G | B | C/D |
    |---|---|---|---|
    | Th. | Fri. | Sat. | Sun. |

    Only Choice E is consistent with this schedule.

5. **E.**   Since Ed and Bob's auditions are both taking place on Saturday, eliminate Choices A and C. Since Carol must audition on the same day as another actor, eliminate B. Finally, since Dave's audition must take place on Sunday (E < D), Frank's audition must take place on Thursday and Grace's audition on Friday (F < G). Eliminate Choice D. The complete schedule is:

    | C/F | G | B/E | D |
    |---|---|---|---|
    | Th. | Fri. | Sat. | Sun. |

### Solutions 6–9

Symbolically, the given conditions can be expressed as follows:

L < K < H    F > H    G > H    I > J

Exhibiting this information on a line, we see:

**B407**

6. **E.**   From the line we drew based on the given conditions, we see that any of F, G, or I could be the heaviest, so any one of Choices A, B, and C could be true. F, G, and H are all heavier than K, and I (and even J) could be heavier, so D could be true. At most there are three students (L, J, and I) who could be lighter than K, so Choice E cannot be true.

7. **D.**   From the line we drew based on the given conditions, we know that either J or L is the lightest. Clearly, if J is heavier than K (Choice

D), then J cannot be the lightest; so L is. None of the other choices permits us to distinguish definitively between J and L.

8. C. From the line we drew based on the given conditions, we know that the correct order of F, G, H, K, L is either:

L K H G F    or    L K H F G

Since we are told that J > F and in an original condition it is given that I > J, in the first case, there is only one possibility: L K H G F J I. In the second case, there are three possibilities: J and I could both be between F and G; they could both be greater than G; or J could be between F and G, and I greater than G. In all, there are four possible rankings.

9. A. Since both F and G are heavier than H, the average of their weights is greater than H's weight, which is greater than I's weight. Choice A cannot be true. None of the other choices must be true, but each of them *could be* true.

**Solutions 10–13**

Symbolically, the given conditions can be expressed as follows:

| D | | | | N | | | | D |
|---|---|---|---|---|---|---|---|---|
| 1 | 2 | 3 | 4 | 5 | 6 | 7 | 8 | 9 |
| B—B | | C—C | | T↗̸N | | N↗̸T | | |

10. A. Since the biographies are next to each other, the other biography must be in the second or fourth position. However, it is given that a novel is in the fourth position, so the other biography must be in position 2.

11. B. If the thesaurus were in position 6, it would be next to the novel in position 5, which is explicitly prohibited. It is easy to show that each of the other choices is possible.

12. E. Only Choice E does not violate any of the given conditions.
Choice A is impossible because if a computer book is in position 2, then the biographies must be in positions 7 and 8, and then the thesaurus would be next to one of the novels:

| D | C | | N | | N | B | B | D |
|---|---|---|---|---|---|---|---|---|
| 1 | 2 | 3 | 4 | 5 | 6 | 7 | 8 | 9 |

Choices B and D are impossible because the thesaurus cannot be next to a novel.
Choice C violates the condition that the two biographies are next to each other.

13. E. Only Choice E completely determines the positions of each book. If a novel is in position 7, then since the thesaurus cannot be next to either novel, the thesaurus must be in position 2. Then the biographies must be in posi-

tions 5 and 6 (the only consecutive numbers not accounted for), and the computer books must be in positions 3 and 8.

| D | T | C | N | B | B | N | C | D |
|---|---|---|---|---|---|---|---|---|
| 1 | 2 | 3 | 4 | 5 | 6 | 7 | 8 | 9 |

None of the other choices completely determines the position of each type of book.

**Solutions 14–17**

exactly 2 of F, G, H, I    exactly 3 of A, B, C, D, E

B → (D ∧ G)    A → F    C ↔ E    I → ~F    I → ~H

14. E. Only Choice E doesn't violate any of the conditions.
Choice A violates the condition that there be exactly two parents.
Choice B violates the condition that if B is chosen, both D and G must be chosen: B → (D ∧ G).
Choice C violates the condition that if C is chosen then E must also be chosen: C ↔ E.
Choice D violates the condition that if I is chosen, F cannot be chosen: I → ~F.

15. C. Since another parent cannot be chosen, eliminate Choice E; also since if B is chosen, G must be too; eliminate Choice B. Therefore, the other people who will attend the meeting must be three of the four teachers A, C, D, and E. If C is not chosen, then E cannot be chosen either (C ↔ E), and then there would be only two teachers. So C must be chosen.

16. E. If E is not chosen, then neither is C (C ↔ E), so the three teachers chosen are A, B, and D. Since A → F and B → G, F and G must be the parents who are chosen; H cannot be chosen.

17. D. • If A is chosen, B cannot be chosen (since that requires D to be chosen); and neither C nor E can be chosen (since if either one is chosen, both must be). Therefore, the other teacher must be D. Since A → F, F must be chosen, which implies that I is not chosen. There are 2 possibilities: A, D, F, G and A, D, F, H.
• If A is not chosen, but B is chosen, then D and G must also be chosen. The fourth person could be any of the other three parents, so there are 3 possibilities.
• If neither A nor B is chosen, C and E must be. There are then 4 possibilities for the two parents: F–G; F–H; G–H; G–I.
• There are a total of 2 + 3 + 4 = 9 different ways to make the choice.

**Solutions 18–22**

A, B, C, D, H, M    January–June
C = February    A < H    B << D or D << B

18. E. Only Choice E doesn't violate any of the conditions. Since Chang serves in February, eliminate Choice B. Also, since Borofsky and Dexter must serve in consecutive months, and neither can serve in February, then neither can serve in January. Eliminate Choices A and C. Finally, Hobbes must serve sometime after Arkes does, so Hobbes cannot serve during the first month; eliminate Choice D.

19. B. With Chang serving in February and Lee in May, the only consecutive months available for Borofsky and Dexter are March and April. Then since Arkes must serve before Hobbes, Arkes has to serve in January and Hobbes in June. There are two possible schedules, depending on the order of Borofsky and Dexter.

20. E. If Lee serves in April, the consecutive months available for Borofsky and Dexter are May

and June; so Choices C and D *could* be true. Since Arkes must serve before Hobbes, Choices A and B *must* be true. Only Choice E *cannot* be true.

21. C. Since Arkes must serve before Hobbes does, Arkes cannot serve in June. Can Arkes serve in April? No, because then Dexter would serve in June (Borofsky and Dexter need to serve consecutively), and again Arkes would not precede Hobbes. The latest that Arkes could serve is March, which could occur if the final order was: Lee, Chang, Arkes, Dexter, Borofsky, Hobbes.

22. A. The only professors that are eligible to serve in January are Arkes and Lee (see the solution to Question 18). So one of them must serve in January, and neither serves in February (Chang does). The other choices are all possible.

# 10 Logical Reasoning Questions

- ■ **Tactics**
- ■ **Practice Exercises**
- ■ **Answer Key and Explanations**

According to the ETS, logical reasoning questions are designed to test your ability to "understand, analyze, and evaluate arguments." This is usually accomplished by having you read a short passage, called an *argument,* and answering a question based on it. Consequently, logical reasoning questions *look* a lot like reading comprehension questions. However, there are some fundamental differences.

- The passages are much shorter—occasionally, only a single sentence, but usually a short paragraph consisting of two to five sentences.

- Most often there is only one question based on a passage, and there are never more than two.

- You are never asked for information that appears in the passage or for the main idea of the passage; rather you are asked to analyze the passage for its logical structure.

On the GRE, the only directions for answering logical reasoning questions are the three sentences that appear at the beginning of the analytical ability section.

- Each group of questions is based on a passage, graph, table, or set of conditions.

- In answering some of the questions, it might be useful to draw a rough diagram.

- For each question, select the best answer choice given.

As explained on the first page of Chapter 9, these instructions are useless; so, of course, you should dismiss them immediately. To understand how to attack

logical reasoning questions, study this chapter very carefully. If you do, you will be well-prepared for any logical reasoning question you might encounter on the GRE.

For each logical reasoning question, the five answer choices are statements. Typically, they begin with (or contain) the phrase, "Which of the following statements." Here are a few examples.

- Which of the following statements is an assumption on which the conclusion of this argument is based?

- Which of the following statements identifies a flaw in the reasoning in this argument?

- Which of the following statements can be most reasonably inferred from the statements in the given passage?

- Which of the following statements, if true, would most seriously weaken the argument offered?

- Which of the following statements, if true, would strengthen the conclusion in the preceding argument?

- Which of the following statements would be the most important to know to evaluate the argument given in the preceding paragraph?

Not every logical reasoning question fits this mold, but most do. In this chapter, in addition to giving several worked-out examples of this type of question, we will also provide examples of the other question types. In doing this, we will present several tactics for handling these types of questions.

# Testing Tactics

## Look at the Question Before You Look at the Argument

We have seen that in analytical reasoning questions we always analyze the set of conditions completely, before even looking at the first question. With logical reasoning questions, however, the situation is different. Rather than jumping in blindly and analyzing each and every aspect of the argument—assumptions, central point, evidence, conclusions, logical flaws—do no more work than necessary. Look at the question stem. Then examine the argument. Know what aspect of the argument you are to concentrate on, and focus on it. You will save time and effort.

The logical reasoning question that follows consists of a short passage, followed by the question, "Which of the following best serves as an assumption that would make the argument above logically correct?" If you read the question before you read the passage, you will know that, as presented, the argument is faulty. As a result, you will be looking for the flaw as you read the passage, and may already realize what's wrong before reading through the five choices. If you read the passage first, you may not catch the subtle flaw, and you may find the conclusion perfectly reasonable. Then when you read the question, and learn that the argument was not logically correct, you will be forced to go back and reread the passage, wasting valuable time.

CAUTION: Read only the question itself—*do not read the choices* before reading the passage. Doing so will confuse you and waste time.

In order to save $500,000 in this year's budget, the city council voted to freeze the salaries of its school building inspectors. This short-sighted decision is yet another example of the council being penny wise and pound foolish. The cursory inspections that will result from this action will cause many structural defects to go undetected, resulting in millions more dollars being spent on repairs in the future.

In order for his argument to be logically correct, the author of the above argument used which of the following statements as an unstated underlying assumption?

(A) City inspectors are already overpaid and so the wage freeze is warranted.

(B) The city council cares less about the safety of the school children than it does about saving money.

(C) If they do not receive an increase in their wages, school inspectors will become lax in performing their jobs.

(D) The council does not feel that cursory inspections will necessarily result in defects going undetected.

(E) The council will not authorize repairs in the future, so it will never have to incur the extra costs.

The passage attempts to justify the conclusion that the city will eventually have to pay much more than it is now saving. Alerted to the fact that the logic is faulty (by having first read the question), you probably picked up the subtle shift from "freeze the salaries" in the first sentence to perform "cursory inspections" in the third sentence. If you did, you might have said to yourself, "the fact that the wages of the inspectors are not being raised does not necessarily mean that they will retaliate by rendering poorer service." This then is the gap in the logic. To justify the conclusion presented, we need to *assume* that freezing salaries *will* result in cursory or slipshod inspections; and this is precisely what Choice C says.

In this example, none of the other choices is an assumption upon which the argument depends. You can read and analyze each of the other choices before eliminating it, but that takes time. It is always better if you can anticipate the correct choice.

You have just seen how reading a question before reading the argument to which it refers can save you valuable time. Here are a few more typical questions followed by explanations of how you should critically read the argument in order to make the most efficient use of your time.

• Which of the following statements identifies a flaw in the reasoning in the argument above?

    If you have read the question first, you will be looking for flaws as you read the passage, whereas you might otherwise be taken in by the faulty logic presented.

• Which of the following statements, if true, best supports the conclusion of the argument?

    Now, as you read the passage, you know that the facts as stated are not sufficient to justify the conclusion, and you can actually be thinking about what else you would need to know to have more confidence in the truth of what is being claimed.

• Which of the following statements is best supported by the facts presented in the passage above?

> Having read the question first, you know that the passage does *not* reach a conclusion. Rather, you

are being asked to form a conclusion based on the given statements (facts), which you are to accept as true.

# Learn to Spot the Major Logical Reasoning Question Types

## Tactic 2

Just as it will help you to know the major types of reading questions on the GRE, it will also help you to familiarize yourself with the major types of logical reasoning questions on the test.

If you can recognize just what a given question is asking for, you'll be better able to tell which particular approach to take to the argument at hand.

Here are six categories of logical reasoning questions you are sure to face.

1. **Assumption**    Questions that test your ability to recognize the premises on which an argument is based often take the following forms:

   • The conclusion above depends on which of the following assumptions?
   • The author of the passage above makes which of the following assumptions?
   • The author of the passage above presupposes that...
   • In the passage above, the author assumes which of the following statements to be true?

2. **Inference**    Questions that test your ability to go beyond the author's explicit statements and see what these statements imply may be worded like these.

   • It can be inferred from the passage above that the author believes that...
   • Which of the following is implied by the passage above?
   • From the information above, which of the following is the most reasonable inference?

3. **Conclusion**    Questions that test your ability to determine what claim can logically be made on the basis of the evidence in the passage often take these forms.

   • If the statements above are true, which of the following is a conclusion that can be properly drawn?
   • Which of the following would provide the most logical conclusion for the preceding paragraph?
   • The statements in the passage, if true, best support which of the following conclusions?

4. **Central Point**    Questions that test your ability to understand the thrust of an argument are often worded like these.

   • The statement cited above conveys which of the following propositions?
   • The passage above emphasizes which of the following points?
   • The author in the passage above argues that...
   • Which of the following expresses the point the author of the passage above makes?

5. **Support**    Questions that test your ability to recognize whether an assertion supports or undermines an argument are often worded like these.

   • Which of the following, if true, best supports the author's conclusion?
   • Which of the following, if true, most weakens the author's conclusion?
   • Which of the following, if true, would constitute the strongest evidence in support of the claim made above?
   • Which of the following, if true, would most weaken the persuasiveness of the claim made above?

NOTE: Implicit in the question, "Which of the following best supports (or most weakens) the conclusion?" is the fact that at least a few of the choices support (or weaken) the conclusion. Your job is to find the one that <u>best</u> supports (or <u>most</u> weakens) it.

6. **Argument Evaluation**    Questions that test your ability to judge an argument often take these forms.

   • Which of the following would be most important to know in evaluating the accuracy of the argument above?
   • Which of the following hypotheses, if true, would help resolve the apparent paradox introduced above?
   • If all of the statements above are correct, an explanation of their apparent contradiction is provided by...
   • Which of the following identifies a flaw in the speaker's reasoning?
   • Knowledge of which of the following would be least useful in evaluating the claims made in the passage above?

# Read Each Argument Very Carefully

Some students, who find that they can answer many reading comprehension questions correctly by skimming the passage, without reading every word, attack logical reasoning questions in the same way. *This is a very poor strategy.*

First of all, the temptation to skim logical arguments should not be as strong since these passages are much shorter, and less time will be saved. More important, it is

not enough to have a general idea about the argument; you must be able to analyze it very carefully.

A cursory reading is not sufficient to pick up a subtle flaw in the logic or to ascertain what unstated premise the author is assuming to be true. The importance of reading the passage carefully is underscored later in this chapter in the analysis of the sample logical reasoning question used to illustrate TACTIC 5.

# Find the Conclusion of the Argument

It is imperative that you are absolutely clear about what conclusion the author of the argument claims to have reached. The three most common situations are as follows:

• The conclusion is the last sentence of the passage, often introduced by a word such as *therefore, so, thus, hence,* or *consequently.* Here is a simple example of this type of argument:

> Joan Smith has those qualities that we seek in our congressional leaders. She is honest, hard-working, intelligent, and dedicated. Having served for ten years in the House of Representatives, she has the requisite experience to be an effective United States Senator. Therefore, you should enthusiastically vote for Ms. Smith in this year's election.

• The conclusion is the first sentence of the passage, followed by the supporting evidence. In this case, there is no word such as *therefore* signaling the conclusion, but it is still very easy to spot. For example,

the preceding argument could have been presented as follows:

> Joan Smith deserves your vote for United States Senator. She has those qualities that we seek in our congressional leaders. She is honest, hard-working, intelligent, and dedicated. In addition, having served for ten years in the House of Representatives, she has the requisite congressional experience to be an effective United States Senator.

• The conclusion is not in the passage. In this case, the question usually asks you to identify the conclusion that is implicit in the argument. For example, if in the two preceding arguments the last or first sentences, respectively, had been omitted, you would have no difficulty determining that the author of the passage wanted you to vote for Joan Smith. The question might have asked, "Which of the following five statements can most reasonably be inferred from the statements in the given passage?"

# Pay Particular Attention to Signal Words in the Question (and in the Argument as Well)

In answering logical reasoning questions, you must read closely both the argument and the question or questions based on it. When you do so, be on the lookout for certain signal words that can clarify the situation. In particular, be alert for:

*Cause and Effect Signal Words*

The following words often signal the conclusion of an argument.

accordingly
consequently

for this reason
hence
so
therefore
thus

*Contrast Signal Words*

The following words often signal a reversal of thought within an argument or a question stem.

although
but
despite
even though
except
however
in contrast
instead
nevertheless
not
on the contrary
on the other hand
rather than
unlike

Notice that in the following logical reasoning problem several of these words are present: the argument contains the words *despite*, *not*, and *consequently*, and the question stem has the word *except*. Each of these words plays a role in your reasoning.

> Despite the fact that River City increased the average class size by more than 15% in all grades two years ago, this year's average SAT scores for the junior class were the highest ever. This shows that class size is not a good determinant of student performance. Consequently, other school districts should follow River City's lead and save money by increasing the size of their classes.
>
> Each of the following statements, if true, is a valid objection to this argument EXCEPT
>
> (A) The advantages of smaller classes are more pronounced in elementary school than in high school.
> (B) The number of classroom discipline problems reported by teachers is directly proportional to the number of students in the classroom.
> (C) Japanese schools have a lower teacher to student ratio than American schools, and have generally better results on international standardized tests.
> (D) Three years ago, the eighth graders in River City Middle School had very high scores on their standardized tests.
> (E) The effects on students of learning in larger classes takes at least three or four years to manifest itself completely.

It is implicit in the question stem that the argument is not very persuasive, and that there are several possible objections that could be raised. In fact, you are told that four of the five statements given raise valid objections to the argument presented. Your job is to determine the only one which does not.

The conclusion that larger class sizes are not detrimental to student learning is based on a single piece of data concerning high school juniors.

Choice A raises the objection that looking at the results of high school students on the SAT does not tell the whole story and that elementary school students will suffer from the larger classes.

Choice E raises an even stronger objection. It suggests that all students may suffer the consequences of increased class sizes; it will just take more time until the results are clearly discernible.

Choice B raises a completely different objection. Even if student academic performance is not adversely affected, there are behavioral disadvantages to having large classes.

Choice D raises still another objection to the argument, the support for which is based on the performance of this year's junior class. Since three years ago, as eighth graders, they had very high scores, it is possible that this group of students is brighter than the average. It is likely that they would excel regardless of class size, whereas other students might suffer more.

Choice C is slightly harder to analyze. If the word *lower* makes you think *smaller,* Choice C seems to say that smaller classes, at least in Japan, result in higher test scores, and are thus beneficial; this then would be yet another valid objection to the given argument. If, however, you are confident in your analysis to this point, TACTIC 6 that follows tells you that by the process of elimination, Choice C must be the correct answer. So look at Choice C again. In fact, it refers to a *lower teacher to student ratio,* which means more students per teacher, which translates as *larger* class sizes. Choice C then is not an objection; it supports the argument by showing that good results can occur in larger classes.

As this example shows, logical reasoning questions must be read very carefully. Do not attempt to analyze them too quickly.

# Always Use the Process of Elimination to Reject Incorrect Choices

**Tactic 6**

From TACTIC 1, you know that in logical reasoning questions you should *always* read the question first. This, of course, does not guarantee that you will know the correct answer before reading the choices; in fact, more often than not, you won't. What do you do then? Use the process of elimination. In the best case scenario, this will allow you to zoom in on the correct answer; at worst, it eliminates some obvious wrong choices and allows you to make an educated guess and move on.

Let's see how the process of elimination works on the next logical reasoning question.

---

In the United States between 1993 and 1998, the number of people on death row continued to increase, but at a rate lower than that of the general prison population.

Which of the following statements directly contradicts this claim?

(A) The number of death row inmates increased slightly from 1993 to 1998.

(B) Among people convicted of murder, the proportion who were sentenced to death decreased from 1993 to 1998.

(C) Each year from 1993 to 1998, more death row inmates were executed than in the previous year.

(D) Each year from 1993 to 1998, fewer people were sentenced to death than in the previous year.

(E) The proportion of death row inmates among the general prison population rose from 0.6% in 1993 to 0.8% in 1998.

---

Even though the passage is only one sentence long, you should have read the question "Which of the following statements directly contradicts this claim?" first. Unfortunately, there are many ways to contradict the claim made in that sentence. So there is no point in trying to think of one, and then looking to see if it is one of the five choices. You simply must read each choice, and then, by process of elimination, find the correct one.

CAUTION: Do not spend even one second deciding whether or not you think the claim in the passage or any of the choices is true. That is completely irrelevant. We are examining only the logic of the argument. We are

looking for a statement that, *if true*, would mean that the claim is false. [See Tactic 7]

- The passage states that the death row population increased; Choice A confirms this (and says nothing about the general prison population). Choice A is incorrect.

- Choice B compares the proportion of new death row inmates to the number of people convicted of murder, not to the general prison population. Choice B is incorrect.

- If the number of people executed each year went up, the death row population *might* have decreased (thereby contradicting the first part of the claim), but not necessarily (not if they were replaced by many more people being sentenced to death). Choice C is incorrect.

- Choice D doesn't guarantee that the claim is true, but it comes closer to confirming it than contradicting it. Even if fewer people were sentenced to death each year, some still were, so the number of people on death row might have increased. Again, no reference is made to the general prison population. Choice D is incorrect.

Choice E is a little harder to analyze, but because it refers to an increase, many students would not choose it, thinking it confirms rather than refutes the claim. But you must. Having definitively rejected Choices A, B, C, and D, you know, by the process of elimination, that Choice E *must* be the correct answer. Let's examine why, in fact, it is.

- The passage claims that the death row population increased at a slower rate than the prison population. This means that the *proportion* of death row inmates in the prison population actually *decreased*. Choice E, which states that the proportion increased, is a direct contradiction of that claim.

NOTE:
(1) Although any of Choices A, B, C, and D could be true without the claim being true, none of them is inconsistent with the truth of the claim.

(2) Choices B, C, and D each introduce an extraneous issue. Neither the number of murder convictions nor the number of executions nor the number of people sentenced to death is directly relevant to the claim.

# Tactic 7

## In Questions About Weakening or Strengthening an Argument, Examine the Argument for Any Unstated Assumptions It Makes

An argument is based upon certain assumptions made by its author. If an argument's basic premises are sound, the argument is strengthened. If the argument's basic premises are flawed, the argument is weakened.

Pinpoint what the argument assumes. Then compare that assumption with the answer choices. If the question asks you to choose an answer that most strengthens the argument, look for the answer choice that is most in keeping with the argument's basic assumption. If the question asks you to choose an answer that most weakens the argument, look for the answer choice that casts the most doubt on that assumption.

Apply this tactic to the following question.

> In a recent speech, the president of a major college said, "It is extremely valuable for college-educated adults entering the workplace to be able to speak at least one foreign language fluently. I am, therefore, proposing that all of our students be encouraged to spend their junior year abroad."
>
> Which of the following, if true, most weakens the president's argument?
>
> (A) Most students who study abroad for a full year return home with a good working knowledge of the language spoken in the country.
> (B) Only students who already know a language well will choose to study in a country where that language is spoken.
> (C) Some colleges do a much better job than others in teaching foreign languages.
> (D) Some students learn to speak foreign languages fluently by taking intensive immersion courses in the United States.
> (E) Many students who spend their junior year abroad learn to speak the language fluently, but cannot read and write with ease.

The argument claims that, in order for students to learn to speak foreign languages well, they should study abroad. It clearly assumes a high correlation between studying in a foreign country and learning to speak the language well. It assumes, at the least, that students who have studied abroad can speak a foreign language well, and, possibly, that students who have not studied abroad cannot.

Choice A is in keeping with the assumption inherent in the president's argument. If true, it would strengthen the argument, not weaken it. Choice E, by stating that many students who study abroad do not learn to read and write the language well, seems to cast doubt on the value of the junior year abroad program. However, since the president talked only about the value of being able to speak a foreign language well, Choice E also strengthens his argument.

Choices B and C are also incorrect. They neither strengthen nor weaken the president's argument. At worst, Choice B suggests that it may be difficult to convince some students to study abroad, but it doesn't state that they shouldn't be encouraged to do so. In order to weaken the president's argument, Choice C would have to go much further than it does; it would have to state that some colleges do such a good job, that their students actually learn to speak foreign languages fluently.

The correct answer is Choice D. It states that it is possible for American students to learn to speak foreign languages fluently without studying abroad. Choice D weakens the president's argument by suggesting an alternative method by which college students could achieve the president's goal of speaking a foreign language.

# Tactic 8

## Be Familiar with All of the Important Logic Facts

In Chapter 9 we presented 14 Logic Facts that are indispensable in answering analytical reasoning questions. Some logical reasoning questions are essentially mini-analytical reasoning questions, and as such, their solutions also depend on a careful application of these same facts. The following example illustrates this type of logical reasoning question.

> On any day when Dori has both a morning and an afternoon meeting scheduled, she skips lunch. If she has a morning meeting, but no afternoon meeting, she has lunch at a diner near her office.

If the preceding statements are true, and if Dori did not skip lunch today, which of the following statements must be true?

(A) Dori had an afternoon meeting today.
(B) Dori did not have an afternoon meeting today.
(C) Dori had lunch in a diner today.
(D) Dori had either a morning or afternoon meeting today.
(E) Either Dori did not have a morning meeting or she did not have an afternoon meeting today.

To answer this logical reasoning question, you need to apply a couple of Logical Facts from Chapter 9. First, let M represent "Dori had a morning meeting;" let A represent "Dori had an afternoon meeting;" let S represent "Dori skipped lunch;" and let D represent "Dori ate in a diner." Then the first sentence in the passage can be translated as

$$(M \wedge A) \to S$$

which (by Logical Fact 12) is equivalent to

$$\sim S \to \sim(M \wedge A)$$

which in turn (by Logical Fact 4) is equivalent to

$$\sim S \to (\sim M \vee \sim A).$$

In the question, we are told that Dori did not skip lunch, so ~S is true. Finally, from ~S → (~M ∨ ~A) and ~S, we can use Logic Fact 9 to conclude that ~M ∨ ~A is true; this is exactly what Choice E states.

# Practice Exercises

## Logical Reasoning Questions

### Questions 1–2

The microwave oven has become a standard appliance in many kitchens, mainly because it offers a fast way of cooking food. Yet, some homeowners believe that the ovens are still not completely safe. Microwaves, therefore, should not be standard appliances until they are more carefully researched and tested.

1. Which one of the following, if true, would most weaken the conclusion of the passage above?

(A) Homeowners often purchase items despite knowing they may be unsafe.
(B) Those homeowners in doubt about microwave safety ought not to purchase microwaves.
(C) Research and testing of home appliances seldom reveal safety hazards.
(D) Microwaves are not as dangerous as steam irons, which are used in almost every home.
(E) Homeowners often purchase items that they do not need.

2. Which one of the following, if true, would most strengthen the conclusion of the passage above?

(A) Homeowners often doubt the advertised safety of all new appliances.
(B) Speed of food preparation is not the only concern of today's homeowner.
(C) Modern homeowners have more free time than ever before.
(D) Food preparation has become almost a science, with more complicated and involved recipes.
(E) Many microwave ovens have been found to leak radioactive elements.

3. Ms. Weissman teaches five French classes—three beginning classes and two advanced classes. From the first marking period to the second, although the number of students earning A's in all of her classes increased by 8%, the number of students earning A's in her three beginning classes actually decreased.

Which of the following statements can definitely be inferred from the information above?

(A) Ms. Weissman has more students in her advanced classes than in her beginning classes.
(B) Ms. Weissman has fewer students in her advanced classes than in her beginning classes.
(C) The number of students earning A's in each of Ms. Weissman's advanced classes increased by more than 8%.
(D) In at least one of Ms. Weissman's advanced classes, the number of students earning A's increased by more than 8%.
(E) More advanced students than beginning students earned A's during the second marking period.

4. The likelihood of America's exhausting her natural resources is growing less. All kinds of waste are being reworked and new uses are constantly being found for almost everything. We are getting more use out of our goods and are making many new by-products out of what was formerly thrown away. It is, therefore, unnecessary to continue to ban logging in national parks, nature reserves, or areas inhabited by endangered species of animals.

Which one of the following most seriously undermines the conclusion of this argument?

(A) The increasing amount of recycled material made available each year is equal to one-tenth of the increasing amount of natural material consumed annually.

(B) Recent studies have shown that the number of endangered animals throughout the world fluctuates sharply and is chiefly determined by changes in weather conditions.

(C) The logging industry contributes huge sums of money to the political campaigns in states where it has a financial interest.

(D) The techniques that make recycling possible are constantly improved so that more is reclaimed for lower costs each year.

(E) Political contributions by the recycling industry are now greater than those of the logging or animal protection interests.

5. In order to increase the number of riders and improve its financial position, the Central Transit Company has purchased new air-conditioned buses for its routes from the west side and the east side to the city center. The routes from the north side and the south side continue to use the older buses, which are not air-conditioned. In the six spring and summer months since the new buses were put into service, the ridership on the west side and east side routes has increased. Therefore, the purchase of the new buses was a wise expenditure.

Which one of the following, if true, most calls into question the conclusion of this passage?

(A) The ridership on the bus routes from the north and south has increased more than that on the east and west routes in the spring and summer.

(B) The increased ridership on the north and south routes normally falls off in the fall and winter.

(C) The price of fares on all the city bus routes was increased early in the spring, though the increase was a very small one.

(D) There are more buses on the north and south routes to the city center than on the east and west routes.

(E) If more commuters in the city take the buses to work than drive their own cars, the traffic congestion problem in the downtown area will be solved.

6. Al's GPA is higher than Bob's. Carol's GPA is lower than Bob's, but it is higher than Dan's.

If the preceding statements are true, which of the following statements would have to be true in order to conclude that Ellen has a higher GPA than Carol?

(A) Ellen's GPA is higher than Dan's.

(B) Bob's GPA is lower than Ellen's.

(C) Ellen's GPA is equal to the average of Al's GPA and Dan's GPA.

(D) Al's GPA is higher than Ellen's.

(E) Bob or Dan has a lower GPA than Ellen's.

7. A recent study of Hodgkin's disease in young adults has examined a large number of sets of twins, half of them identical and half nonidentical. Identical twins have the same genetic makeup, but like any other siblings, nonidentical twins share only about 50 percent of their genetic material. In the study of twins with Hodgkin's disease, the researchers found that the chances of the second of a set of identical twins also developing the disease was 100 times higher than in the case of the sibling of a nonidentical twin, or of any other average individual. The number of cases where both identical twins were affected was, however, not a very large proportion of the identical twin pairs.

Based on the information in this passage, we can infer all of the following EXCEPT

(A) genetic inheritance is one factor in determining the susceptibility to Hodgkin's disease

(B) if one twin of a set of nonidentical twins develops Hodgkin's disease, the chances of the second twin developing Hodgkin's disease are no greater than that of a person who is not a twin

(C) Hodgkin's disease is more likely to appear first in a twin who is one of a pair of identical twins than one of a pair of nonidentical twins

(D) genetics alone is not sufficient to cause Hodgkin's disease

(E) the chances of the second of a pair of identical twins whose twin has developed Hodgkin's disease also developing the disease are not very high

8. Years ago, a nationwide poll concluded that there are more televisions than there are bathtubs in American homes. No doubt that fact remains today, especially in light of the growing popularity of home computers. Now, in addition to owning televisions for entertainment, more and more families are purchasing TV monitors for use with a personal computer. We can safely guess that there are still many more people staring at a picture tube than singing in the shower.

Which one of the following statements can be deduced from this passage?

(A) Personal computers probably cost less than installing a shower or a bathtub.

(B) People can wash themselves without a tub or shower, but they cannot watch television unless they own a television set.

(C) TV monitors will work with personal computers in place of regular computer monitors.

(D) As many computers are sold today as television sets a few years ago.

(E) More television monitors are now used with personal computers than are used to watch commercial television broadcasts.

9. Jeremy: Since Prof. Sanchez is a brilliant teacher whose students excel, she should be granted tenure.

Alberto: Since Prof. Sanchez has not published any research, she is not widely respected in the academic community. Therefore, she should not be granted tenure.

Which of the following is an underlying assumption that Alberto has used in reaching his conclusion?

(A) Prof. Sanchez has applied for tenure.
(B) Brilliant teachers usually publish their research.
(C) Good teaching should not be considered in making tenure decisions.
(D) All professors who are respected in the academic community should be granted tenure.
(E) Being widely respected in the academic community should be a prerequisite for being granted tenure.

10. Some scientists have proposed that, over two hundred million years ago, one giant land mass—rather than various continents and islands—covered one-third of the earth. Long before there was any human life, and over vast periods of time, islands and continents drifted apart. Australia was the first to separate, while South America and Africa were late in splitting apart. Some islands, of course, were formed by volcanoes and were never part of the great land mass.

All the following would support the author's claim EXCEPT

(A) Many of the plants of the South American rain forests are markedly similar to those of the African rain forest.
(B) Australia has more animals that are not found on any other continent than have several of the much larger continents.
(C) Volcanic islands like Hawaii have ecosystems very different from those of continental lands with the same average temperature.
(D) The plants of similar conditions in South America have less in common with those of Australia than with those of Asia, Africa, or Europe.
(E) The primitive languages of Australia are unlike those of Africa, which resemble those of South America.

11. A recent study of children between 2 and 4 years old has shown that in this period of their lives, they show no preference for cereals that have been sweetened either naturally or artificially. But almost all of the same group four years later preferred sweetened cereals. This change shows that the preference for sweetened foods is acquired rather than natural, and that without the example of others using sweeteners, whether in television advertisements or in the home, children would avoid the chief causes of obesity and cavities.

Which one of the following, if true, would provide the best support for this argument?

(A) A second study showed that children who had eaten sweetened food between the ages of 2 and 4 showed no greater preference for sweetened foods at the ages of 6 to 8 than children who had not eaten sweetened foods at the younger age.
(B) A second study showed that children between 4 and 6 who had been sequestered from advertising for sweeteners preferred sugar-free cereals when they were 6 to 8 years old.
(C) Studies of children 6 to 8 who ate sweetened foods show those who live in areas where the water is fluoridated had fewer cavities than children who ate unsweetened foods and lived in areas where the water was not fluoridated.
(D) Studies have shown that the influence of parents upon their children's behavior at early ages is measurably greater than the influence of peer groups or school teachers.
(E) Contrary to what advertisers claim, both adults and children have no difficulty in distinguishing between naturally and artificially sweetened foods or beverages.

12. Every Saturday, Maria has pizza for lunch and then goes to the movies.

If the sentence above is true, which of the following statements must also be true?

  I. If it is not Saturday, then Maria is not having pizza for lunch and is not going to the movies.
  II. If Maria has pizza for lunch and then goes to the movies, it is Saturday.
  III. If Maria has pizza for lunch, but does not go to the movies, then it is not Saturday.

(A) I only
(B) II only
(C) III only
(D) I and III only
(E) II and III only

13. In America, a baseball game should be described as a series of solo performances: at any given moment, attention is focused on one player and one play. On the other hand, soccer involves all of the team most of the time: each player interacts with others constantly, so that no single individual seems responsible for success or failure. It is because spectators prefer concentrating on individual personalities that baseball remains a much more popular spectator sport than soccer.

Which one of the following, if true, can best be used to undermine the conclusion of this argument?

(A) Soccer is more popular with spectators in France than baseball.
(B) Among the ten most televised sports in America, by far the most watched is football, and the least watched are tennis and bowling.
(C) Many people watch only the baseball teams of the city in which they live and for whom they root.

(D) Compared to football and basketball, baseball games are much cheaper to attend.

(E) In some sections of the United States, soccer leagues for children under fifteen are more popular than Little League baseball.

14. The average number of fatal cases of influenza in the winter months in the Boston area is likely to decline noticeably if 50 percent of the population over the age of fifty is inoculated in October or November. Since the government program that supplies information about influenza and makes free shots widely available is being discontinued to save money, the number of men and women over age fifty who will have been inoculated before the flu season begins this year will sharply decrease.

Which one of the following is the conclusion most likely to follow from the statements above?

(A) Programs that contribute to the health of the community should not be dependent on public funding.

(B) The severity and frequency of influenza outbreaks in the winter months can vary widely from year to year.

(C) The number of influenza fatalities this winter will probably increase.

(D) The number of fatal cases of influenza will sharply increase this year.

(E) The number of fatal cases in men and women less than fifty years old is likely to remain unchanged.

15. Antifreeze lowers the melting point of any liquid to which it is added so that the liquid will not freeze in cold weather. It is commonly used to maintain the cooling system in automobile radiators. Of course, the weather may become so cold that even antifreeze is not effective, but such a severe climatic condition rarely occurs in well-traveled places.

Which one of the following can be deduced from the passage?

(A) Well-traveled places have means of transportation other than automobiles.

(B) Antifreeze does not lower the melting point of certain liquids in extreme conditions.

(C) Severe climatic conditions rarely occur.

(D) It is not often that many travelers who use antifreeze have their cooling systems freeze.

(E) Antifreeze raises the melting point of some liquids.

# Answer Key

| | | | | |
|---|---|---|---|---|
| 1. **C** | 4. **A** | 7. **C** | 10. **E** | 13. **B** |
| 2. **E** | 5. **A** | 8. **C** | 11. **B** | 14. **C** |
| 3. **D** | 6. **B** | 9. **E** | 12. **C** | 15. **D** |

# Answer Explanations

1. **C.** The conclusion of the passage is that, because of safety concerns, more research and testing ought to be done before microwaves become standard household appliances. If, however, research and testing are ineffective means of discerning safety problems, then research and testing would be irrelevant. This criticism seriously weakens the conclusion.

2. **E.** If many microwave ovens have been found to leak radioactive elements, then the conclusion—that microwaves should not be standard appliances until they are more carefully researched and tested—is further strengthened because more safety concerns needed to be addressed.

3. **D.** If the number of students earning A's in all of Ms. Weissman's classes increased by 8%, then to compensate for the decline in the beginning classes, the number of students earning A's in the advanced classes must have gone up by more than 8%. It is possible, however, that the entire increase came from the students in just one of the advanced classes. For example, if

Ms. Weissman has a total of 100 students in her five classes, the number of students earning A's increased by 8. It is possible that in each of the beginning classes and one of the advanced classes the number of students earning A's decreased by one, and that in the other advanced class the number of students earning A's increased by 12. Therefore, whereas Choice C could be true, Choice D must be true. None of the given information supports Choices A or B. Although at first glance, Choice E might seem reasonable, it is possible that every beginning and no advanced student earned an A during the first marking period; then even if the number of advanced students earning A's increased dramatically, if the number of beginning students earning A's decreased only slightly, far more beginning students than advanced ones would have A's.

4. **A.** Choice D would support rather than undermine the conclusion. Choices B, C, and E neither support nor weaken the argument, though with more information C and E might be relevant. If the recycled materials are equal

to only one-tenth of the natural materials lost each year, the argument is seriously injured.

5. **A.** Because the ridership on the route served by the older buses that are not air-conditioned increased, the larger number of commuters on the other routes may not be due to the new vehicles.

6. **B.** From the given statements we see that:

$$D < C < B < A$$

If Bob's GPA is lower than Ellen's, then $C < B < E$. Choice B, therefore, allows us to conclude that $C < E$. In each of the other choices, it is possible that Ellen has a lower GPA than Carol.

7. **C.** If the chances of a person with the same genetic makeup as someone who has developed the disease are 100 times higher than someone with different genes, genetic material must play some role. But if the proportion of people who do develop the disease is very small, genetics cannot be the only cause. The study supports Choices B and E, but gives no information on whether the disease is more likely to affect one identical twin than one nonidentical twin.

8. **C.** Though Choices A and B may well be true, they are not deductions that we can make from the information in the passage. But Choice C can be deduced since, "more and more families are purchasing TV monitors for use with a personal computer." TV monitors must work with these computers. Otherwise, people would not buy them for that purpose. Choices D and E may or may not be true, but they are not deductions from the passage, simply additional information.

9. **E.** Alberto explicitly states that because Prof. Sanchez is not widely respected in the academic community, she should not be granted tenure. This is precisely the statement in Choice E. Choice D is incorrect: Alberto states that the lack of respect should mean no tenure [$\sim R \rightarrow \sim T$]; this is not equivalent to, nor does it imply, that respect should necessarily lead to tenure [$R \rightarrow T$]. None of the other choices make any sense.

10. **E.** If Australia was the first continent to separate, it would follow that its flora and fauna would develop in isolation over a longer period of time. Similarly, we may expect the plants and animals of South America and Africa that separated later to be more alike. Choices A, B, and D support these ideas. That the separately developed islands are different is also in accord with the passage. However, the languages of all the continents would have developed in isolation, since man did not evolve until after the break-up of the land mass, and it is surprising that African and South American languages are similar. Human likeness or difference are irrelevant to the claims of the passage.

11. **B.** The trouble with the conclusion in the original paragraph is there is no demonstration of the cause of the change of taste. But if children who had not been exposed to advertising did not prefer sweetened foods, support for the claim that the preference is acquired would be strengthened.

12. **C.** This logical reasoning question is very easy as soon as you express the given statement symbolically. "If it is <u>S</u>aturday, then Maria has <u>P</u>izza and goes to the <u>M</u>ovies" translates as $S \rightarrow (P \wedge M)$. By Logic Fact 13 this is equivalent to $\sim(P \wedge M) \rightarrow \sim S$, which by Logic Fact 4 is equivalent to $(\sim P \vee \sim M) \rightarrow \sim S$. So if either P or M is false, then S is false. Therefore, III is true. Neither I nor II is true: (I) knowing what happens when it is Saturday doesn't tell us anything about what happens when it is not Saturday (Logic Fact 10); and (II) the converse of a true conditional is not necessarily true (Logic Fact 11). Only III is true.

13. **B.** The weakness of this argument is not its claim that baseball is more popular than soccer with spectators in America. This is true from the passage. The weakness is its claim that the reason for baseball's greater popularity is that it is an individual performance rather than a team sport. Choice B cites a team sport that is more watched than baseball and two solo performance sports that are not very popular. Choice A makes a good point, but the passage is concerned with spectators "in America." Even if C is true, it may be that these people watch the teams to see individual performances. Choice D is true, but not as powerful a criticism as Choice B. Choice E does not necessarily deal with spectators; popularity could refer to the number of participants.

14. **C.** Although the writer would probably agree with the ideas of Choices A, B, and C, the most logical conclusion from the information in the passage is Choice C. If the number of fatalities increases when less than 50 percent of the older population has been inoculated, and the number of those inoculated declines, the number of fatalities should increase. Because we do not know how many (50 percent or more?) were inoculated last year and only that fewer will be inoculated this year, we cannot be sure that "fatalities will increase sharply," Choice D.

15. D.  Since severe climatic conditions rarely occur in well-traveled places, it is necessarily true that "It is not often that many travelers who use antifreeze have their cooling systems freeze." Choice A mentions other means of transportation, which is not addressed in the passage. Choice B refers to "certain" liquids, which again are not addressed. You cannot deduce that "severe climatic conditions rarely occur"—Choice C—because the passage alludes to only well-traveled places. Choice E discusses raising the melting point, which is irrelevant to the passage.

# PART FOUR

## QUANTITATIVE ABILITY: TACTICS, STRATEGIES, PRACTICE, AND REVIEW

# Introduction to Part Four

PART FOUR consists of five chapters. Chapter 11 presents several important strategies that can be used on any mathematics questions that appear on the GRE. In Chapters 12, 13, and 14 you will find tactics that are specific to one of the three different types of questions: discrete quantitative questions, quantitative comparison questions, and data interpretation questions, respectively. Chapter 15 contains a complete review of all the mathematics you need to know in order to do well on the GRE, as well as hundreds of sample problems patterned on actual test questions.

# Five Types of Tactics

Five different types of tactics are discussed in this book.

1. In Chapters 1 and 2, you learned many basic tactics used by all good test-takers, such as read each question carefully, pace yourself, don't get bogged down on any one question, and never waste time reading the directions. You also learned the specific tactics required to excel on a computer-adaptive test. These tactics apply to all of the sections of the GRE: verbal, quantitative, and analytical.

2. In Chapters 4, 5, 6, and 7 you learned the important tactics needed for handling each of the four types of verbal questions.

3. In Chapters 9 and 10 you learned the special tactics that are unique to analytical reasoning and logical reasoning questions.

4. In Chapters 11–14 you will find all of the tactics that apply to the quantitative sections of the GRE. Chapter 11 contains those techniques that can be applied to all types of mathematics questions; Chapters 12, 13, and 14 present specific strategies to deal with each of the three kinds of quantitative questions found on the GRE: discrete quantitative questions, quantitative comparison questions, and data interpretation questions.

5. In Chapter 15 you will learn or review all of the mathematics that is needed for the GRE, and you will master the specific tactics and key facts that apply to each of the different mathematical topics.

Using these tactics will enable you to answer more quickly many questions that you already know how to do. But the greatest value of these tactics is that they will allow you to correctly answer or make educated guesses on problems that *you do not know how to do.*

# An Important Symbol

Throughout the rest of this book, the symbol "$\Rightarrow$" is used to indicate that one step in the solution of a problem follows *immediately* from the preceding one, and no explanation is necessary. You should read

$$3x = 12 \Rightarrow x = 4$$

as $3x = 12$ *implies that* $x = 4$ or $3x = 12$, *which implies that* $x = 4$

or                since $3x = 12$, *then* $x = 4$.

Here is a sample solution to the following problem using $\Rightarrow$:

What is the value of $2x^2 - 5$ when $x = -4$?

$$x = -4 \Rightarrow x^2 = (-4)^2 = 16 \Rightarrow$$

$$2x^2 = 2(16) = 32 \Rightarrow$$

$$2x^2 - 5 = 32 - 5 = \textbf{27}$$

When the reason for a step is not obvious, $\Rightarrow$ is not used: rather, an explanation is given, often including a reference to a KEY FACT from Chapter 15. In many solutions, some steps are explained, while others are linked by the $\Rightarrow$ symbol, as in the following example.

In the diagram at the right, if $w = 10$, what is the value of $z$?

• By KEY FACT J1, $w + x + y = 180$.

• Since $\triangle ABC$ is isosceles, $x = y$ (KEY FACT J5).

• Therefore, $w + 2y = 180 \Rightarrow 10 + 2y = 180 \Rightarrow$ $2y = 170 \Rightarrow y = 85$.

• Finally, since $y + z = 180$ (KEY FACT I3), $85 + z = 180 \Rightarrow z = \textbf{95}$.

# 11 General Math Strategies

- ■ **Tactics**
- ■ **Practice Exercises**
- ■ **Answer Key and Explanations**

---

In Chapters 12 and 13, you will learn tactics that are specifically applicable to multiple-choice questions and quantitative comparison questions, respectively. In this chapter you will learn several important general math strategies that can be used on both of these types of questions.

The directions that appear on the screen at the beginning of the quantitative section include the following cautionary information:

> Figures that accompany questions are intended to provide information useful in answering the questions.

> However, unless a note states that a figure is drawn to scale, you should solve these problems NOT by estimating sizes by sight or measurement, but by using your knowledge of mathematics.

Despite the fact that they are telling you that you cannot totally rely on *their* diagrams, if you learn how to draw diagrams accurately, *you can trust the ones you draw*. Knowing the best ways of handling diagrams on the GRE is critically important. Consequently, the first five tactics all deal with diagrams.

**TACTIC 1.**   **Draw a diagram.**

**TACTIC 2.**   **Trust a diagram that has been drawn to scale.**

**TACTIC 3.**   **Exaggerate or change a diagram.**

**TACTIC 4.**   **Add a line to a diagram.**

**TACTIC 5.**   **Subtract to find shaded regions.**

To implement these tactics, you need to be able to draw line segments and angles accurately, and you need to be able to look at segments and angles and accurately estimate their measures. Let's look at three variations of the same problem.

1. If the diagonal of a rectangle is twice as long as the shorter side, what is the degree measure of the angle it makes with the longer side?

2. In the rectangle at the right, what is the value of *x*?

3. In the rectangle at the right, what is the value of *x*?

For the moment, let's ignore the correct mathematical way of solving this problem. In the diagram in (3), the side labeled 2 appears to be half as long as the diagonal, which is labeled 4; consequently, you should assume that the diagram has been drawn to scale, and you should see that *x* is about 30, *certainly* between 25 and 35. In (1) you aren't given a diagram, and in (2) the diagram is useless because you can see that it has not been drawn to scale (the side labeled 2 is nearly as long as the diagonal, which is labeled 4). However, if while taking the GRE, you see a question such as (1) or (2), you should be able to quickly draw on your scrap paper a diagram that looks just like the one in (3), and then look at *your* diagram and see that the measure of *x* is just about 30. If the answer choices for these questions were

    (A) 15   (B) 30   (C) 45   (D) 60   (E) 75

you would, of course, choose **30, B**. If the choices were

    (A) 20   (B) 25   (C) 30   (D) 35   (E) 40

you might not be quite as confident, but you should still choose **30**, here **C**.

When you take the GRE, even though you are not allowed to have rulers or protractors, you should be able to draw your diagrams very accurately. For example, in (1) above, you should draw a horizontal line, and then, either freehand or by tracing the corner of a piece of scrap paper, draw a right angle on the line. The vertical line segment will be the width of the rectangle; label it 2.

Mark off that distance twice on a piece of scrap paper and use that to draw the diagonal.

You should now have a diagram that is similar to that in (3), and you should be able to see that *x* is about 30.

By the way, *x* is *exactly* 30. A right triangle in which one leg is half the hypotenuse must be a 30-60-90 triangle, and that leg is opposite the 30° angle [see KEY FACT J11].

Having drawn an accurate diagram, are you still unsure as to how you should know that the value of *x* is 30 just by looking at the diagram? You will now learn not only how to look at *any* angle and know its measure within 5 or 10 degrees, but how to draw any angle that accurately.

You should easily recognize a 90° angle and can probably draw one freehand; but you can always just trace the corner of a piece of scrap paper. To draw a 45° angle, just bisect a 90° angle. Again, you can probably do this freehand. If not, or to be even more accurate, draw a right angle, mark off the same distance on each side, draw a square, and then draw in the diagonal.

To draw other acute angles, just divide the two 45° angles in the above diagram with as many lines as necessary.

Finally, to draw an obtuse angle, add an acute angle to a right angle.

Now, to estimate the measure of a given angle, just draw in some lines.

To test yourself, find the measure of each angle shown. The answers are found below.

Answers: (a) 80° (b) 20° (c) 115° (d) 160°. Did you come within 10° on each one?

# Testing Tactics

## Draw a Diagram

On *any* geometry question for which a figure is not provided, draw one (as accurately as possible) on your scrap paper—*never attempt a geometry problem without first drawing a diagram.*

### Example 1.
What is the area of a rectangle whose length is twice its width and whose perimeter is equal to that of a square whose area is 1?

(A) 1   (B) 6   (C) $\dfrac{2}{3}$   (D) $\dfrac{4}{3}$   (E) $\dfrac{8}{9}$

SOLUTION. Don't even think of answering this question until you have drawn a square and a rectangle and labeled each of them: each side of the square is 1, and if the width of the rectangle is $w$, its length ($\ell$) is $2w$.

*Now*, write the required equation and solve it:

$$6w = 4 \Rightarrow w = \frac{4}{6} = \frac{2}{3} \Rightarrow 2w = \frac{4}{3}$$

The area of the rectangle = $\ell w = \left(\dfrac{4}{3}\right)\left(\dfrac{2}{3}\right) = \dfrac{8}{9}$, **E**.

### Example 2.
Betty drove 8 miles west, 6 miles north, 3 miles east, and 6 more miles north. How many miles was Betty from her starting place?

(A) 13   (B) 17   (C) 19   (D) 21   (E) 23

SOLUTION. Draw a diagram. Now, extend line segment *ED* until it intersects *AB* at *F*. Then, *AFE* is a right triangle, whose legs are 5 and 12 and, therefore, whose hypotenuse is **13, A**.

### Example 3.
What is the difference in the degree measures of the angles formed by the hour hand and the minute hand of a clock at 12:35 and 12:36?

(A) 1°   (B) 5°   (C) 5.5°   (D) 6°   (E) 30°

SOLUTION. Draw a simple picture of a clock. The hour hand makes a complete revolution, 360°, once every 12 hours. So, in 1 hour it goes through 360° ÷ 12 = 30°, and in one minute it advances through 30° ÷ 60 = 0.5°. The minute hand moves through 30° every 5 minutes or 6° per minute. So, in the minute from 12:35 to 12:36 (or any other minute), the *difference* between the hands increased by 6° − 0.5° = **5.5°, C**.

30° in 1 hr.
0.5° in 1 min.

30° in 5 min.
6° in 1 min.

NOTE: It was not necessary, and would have been more time-consuming, to determine the angle between the hands at either 12:35 or 12:36. (See TACTIC 6: Don't do more than you have to.)

Drawings should not be limited to geometry questions; there are many other questions on which drawings will help.

### Example 4.
A jar contains 10 red marbles and 30 green ones. How many red marbles must be added to the jar so that 60% of the marbles will be red?

(A) 25   (B) 30   (C) 35   (D) 40   (E) 60

SOLUTION. First, draw a diagram and label it. From the diagram it is clear that there are now 40 + $x$ marbles in the jar, of which 10 + $x$ are red. Since we want the fraction of red marbles to be 60%, we have

$$\frac{10 + x}{40 + x} = 60\% = \frac{3}{5}.$$

| $x$ | Red |
| --- | --- |
| 30 | Green |
| 10 | Red |

Cross-multiplying, we get:

$$50 + 5x = 120 + 3x \Rightarrow 2x = 70 \Rightarrow x = \textbf{35, C.}$$

Of course, you could have set up the equation and solved it without the diagram, but the diagram makes the solution easier and you are less likely to make a careless mistake.

# Tactic 2
# Trust a Diagram That Has Been Drawn to Scale

Whenever diagrams have been drawn to scale, they can be trusted. This means that you can look at the diagram and use your eyes to accurately estimate the sizes of angles and line segments. For example, in the first problem discussed at the beginning of this chapter, you could "see" that the measure of the angle was about 30°.

To take advantage of this situation:

• If a diagram is given that appears to be drawn to scale, trust it.

• If a diagram is given that has not been drawn to scale, try to draw it to scale on your scrap paper, and then trust it.

• When no diagram is provided, and you draw one on your scrap paper, try to draw it to scale.

In Example 5, below, we are told that *ABCD* is a square and that diagonal *BD* is 3. In the diagram provided, quadrilateral *ABCD* does indeed look like a square, and *BD* = 3 does not contradict any other information. We can, therefore, assume that the diagram has been drawn to scale.

**Example 5.**

In the figure at the right, diagonal *BD* of square *ABCD* is 3. What is the perimeter of the square?

(A) 4.5  (B) 12  (C) $3\sqrt{2}$
(D) $6\sqrt{2}$  (E) $12\sqrt{2}$

SOLUTION. Since this diagram has been drawn to scale, you can trust it. The sides of the square appear to be about two thirds as long as the diagonal, so assume that each side is 2. Then the perimeter is 8. Which of the choices is approximately 8? Certainly not A or B. Since $\sqrt{2} \approx 1.4$, Choices C, D, and E are approximately 4.2, 8.4, and 12.6, respectively. Clearly, the answer must be **D**.

**Direct mathematical solution**. Let *s* be a side of the square. Then since $\triangle BCD$ is a 45-45-90 right triangle,

$s = \dfrac{3}{\sqrt{2}} = \dfrac{3\sqrt{2}}{2}$, and the perimeter of the square is

$4s = 4\left(\dfrac{3\sqrt{2}}{2}\right) = 6\sqrt{2}$.

Remember the goal of this book is to help you get credit for *all* the problems you know how to do, and, by using the

TACTICS, to get credit for *many* that you don't know how to do. Example 5 is typical. Many students would miss this question. *You*, however, can now answer it correctly, even though you may not remember how to solve it directly.

**Example 6.**

In $\triangle ABC$, what is the value of *x*?

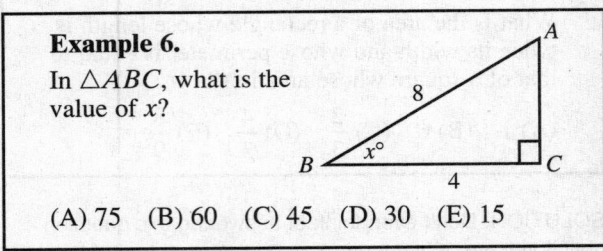

(A) 75  (B) 60  (C) 45  (D) 30  (E) 15

SOLUTION. If you don't see the correct mathematical solution, you should use TACTIC 2 and trust the diagram; but to do that you must be careful that when you copy it onto your scrap paper you *fix it*. What's wrong with the way it is drawn now? *AB* = 8 and *BC* = 4, but in the figure, *AB* and *BC* are almost the same length. Redraw it so that *AB* is *twice* as long as *BC*. Now, just look: *x* is about **60, B**.

In fact, *x* is exactly 60. If the hypotenuse of a right triangle is twice the length of one of the legs, then it's a 30-60-90 triangle, and the angle formed by the hypotenuse and that leg is 60° (see Section 15-J).

TACTIC 2 is equally effective on quantitative comparison questions that have diagrams.

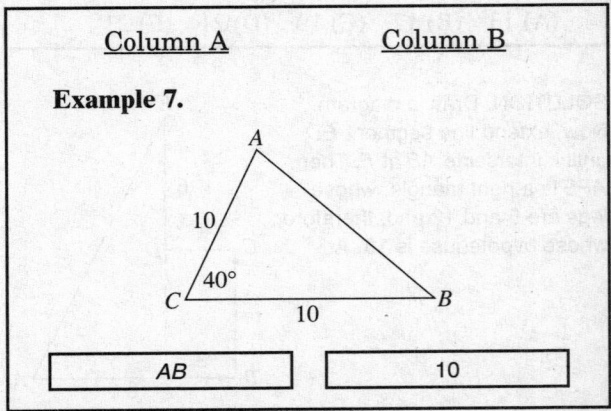

| Column A | Column B |
|----------|----------|
| **Example 7.** | |
| *AB* | 10 |

SOLUTION. There are two things wrong with the given diagram: ∠C is labeled 40°, but looks much more like 60° or 70°, and AC and BC are each labeled 10, but BC is drawn much longer. When you copy the diagram onto your scrap paper, be sure to correct these two mistakes: draw a triangle that has a 40° angle and two sides of the same length.

Now, it's clear: AB < 10. The answer is **B**.

| Column A | Column B |
|---|---|
| **Example 8.** | |
| | O is the center of the circle |
| | PQ = 6 |
| | OR = 12 |
| x | 45 |

SOLUTION. In the diagram at the left, the value of x is at least 60, so if the diagram has been drawn to scale, the answer must be **A**. If, on the other hand, the diagram has not been drawn to scale, we can't trust it. Which is it? The diagram is *not* OK—PQ is drawn almost as long as OR, even though OR is twice as long. Correct the diagram:

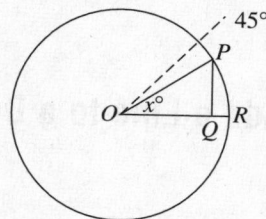

Now you can see that x is less than 45. The answer is **B**.

## Tactic 3

# Exaggerate or Otherwise Change a Diagram

Sometimes it is appropriate to take a diagram that appears to be drawn to scale and intentionally exaggerate it. Why would we do this? Consider the following example.

| Column A | Column B |
|---|---|
| **Example 9.** | |
| Line ℓ is parallel to line k. | |
| AB | CD |

SOLUTION. In the diagram, which appears to be drawn correctly, AB and CD look as though they are the same length. However, there *might* be an imperceptible difference due to the fact that one of the angles measures 61° and the other measures only 60°. So exaggerate the diagram:

redraw it, making one angle *much* smaller than the other. Now, it's clear: CD is longer. The answer is **B**.

When you copy a diagram onto your scrap paper, you can change anything you like as long as your diagram is consistent with all the given data.

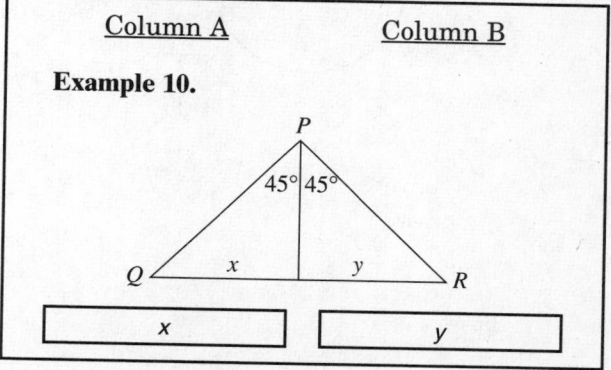

| Column A | Column B |
|---|---|
| **Example 10.** | |
| x | y |

SOLUTION. You may redraw this diagram any way you like, as long as the two angles that are marked 45° remain 45°. If *PQ* and *PR* are equal, as they appear to be in the given diagram, then *x* would equal *y*. In the diagram at the right, however, *PR* is longer than *PQ*, and *x* and *y* are clearly unequal. The answer is **D**.

## Add a Line to a Diagram

Occasionally, after staring at a diagram, you still have no idea how to solve the problem to which it applies. It looks as though not enough information has been given. When this happens, it often helps to draw another line in the diagram.

### Example 11.

In the figure at the right, *Q* is a point on the circle whose center is *O* and whose radius is *r*, and *OPQR* is a rectangle. What is the length of diagonal *PR*?

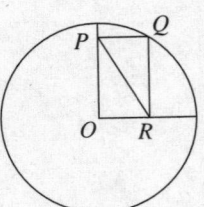

(A) $r$   (B) $r^2$   (C) $\dfrac{r^2}{\pi}$   (D) $\dfrac{r\sqrt{2}}{\pi}$

(E) It cannot be determined from the information given.

SOLUTION. If after staring at the diagram and thinking about rectangles, circles, and the Pythagorean theorem, you're still lost, don't give up. Ask yourself, "Can I add another line to this diagram?" As soon as you think to draw in *OQ*, the other diagonal, the problem becomes easy: the two diagonals are equal and, since *OQ* is a radius, it is equal to *r*, **A**.

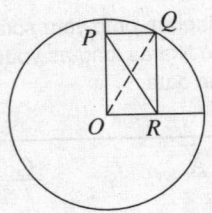

### Example 12.

What is the area of quadrilateral *ABCD*?

(A) 24   (B) 28   (C) 30   (D) 38   (E) 60

SOLUTION. Since the quadrilateral is irregular, there isn't a formula to find the area. However, if you draw in *AC*, you will divide *ABCD* into two triangles, each of whose areas can be determined. If you then draw in the height of each triangle, you see that the area of △*ACD* is $\frac{1}{2}$(4)(4) = 8, and the area of △*BAC* is $\frac{1}{2}$(6)(10) = 30, so the area of *ABCD* is 30 + 8 = **38**, **D**.

Note that this problem could also have been solved by drawing in lines to create rectangle *ABEF*, and subtracting the areas of △*BEC* and △*CFD* from the area of the rectangle.

## Tactic 5

# Subtract to Find Shaded Regions

Whenever part of a figure is shaded, the straightforward way to find the area of the shaded portion is to find the area of the entire figure and subtract from it the area of the unshaded region. Of course, if you are asked for the area of the unshaded region, you can, instead, subtract the shaded area from the total area. Occasionally, you may see an easy way to calculate the shaded area directly, but usually you should subtract.

---

**Example 13.**

In the figure below, $ABCD$ is a rectangle, and $BE$ and $CF$ are arcs of circles centered at $A$ and $D$. What is the area of the striped region?

(A) $10 - \pi$   (B) $2(5 - \pi)$   (C) $2(5 - 2\pi)$
(D) $6 + 2\pi$   (E) $5(2 - \pi)$

---

SOLUTION. The entire region is a $2 \times 5$ rectangle whose area is 10. Since the white region consists of two quarter-circles of radius 2, the total white area is that of a semicircle of radius 2: $\frac{1}{2}\pi(2)^2 = 2\pi$. Therefore, the area of the striped region is $10 - 2\pi = \mathbf{2(5 - \pi)}$, **B**.

---

**Example 14.**

In the figure at the right, square $ABCD$ is inscribed in circle $O$. If the perimeter of $ABCD$ is 24, what is the area of the shaded region?

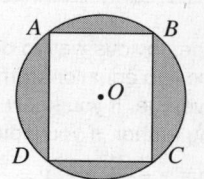

(A) $18\pi - 36$   (B) $18\pi - 24$   (C) $12\pi - 36$
(D) $9\pi - 36$   (E) $9\pi - 24$

---

SOLUTION. Since the perimeter of square $ABCD$ is 24, each of its sides is 6, and its area is $6^2 = 36$. Since diagonal $AC$ is the hypotenuse of isosceles right triangle $ABC$, $AC = 6\sqrt{2}$. But $AC$ is also a diameter of circle $O$, so the radius of the circle is $3\sqrt{2}$, and its area is $\pi(3\sqrt{2})^2 = 18\pi$. Finally, the area of the shaded region is $\mathbf{18\pi - 36}$, **A**.

---

## Tactic 6

# Don't Do More Than You Have To

Very often a problem can be solved in more than one way. You should always try to do it in the easiest way possible. Consider the following examples.

---

**Example 15.**

If $5(3x - 7) = 20$, what is $3x - 8$?

(A) $\dfrac{11}{3}$   (B) 0   (C) 3   (D) 14   (E) 19

---

It is not difficult to solve for $x$:

$$5(3x - 7) = 20 \Rightarrow 15x - 35 = 20 \Rightarrow 15x = 55 \Rightarrow$$
$$x = \frac{55}{15} = \frac{11}{3}.$$

But it's too much work. Besides, once you find that $x = \dfrac{11}{3}$, you still have to multiply to get $3x$: $3\left(\dfrac{11}{3}\right) = 11$, and then subtract to get $3x - 8$: $11 - 8 = 3$.

SOLUTION. The key is to recognize that you don't need to find $x$. Finding $3x - 7$ is easy (just divide the original equation by 5), and $3x - 8$ is just 1 less:

$$5(3x - 7) = 20 \Rightarrow 3x - 7 = 4 \Rightarrow 3x - 8 = \mathbf{3}, \mathbf{C}.$$

**Example 16.**

If $7x + 3y = 17$ and $3x + 7y = 19$, what is the average (arithmetic mean) of $x$ and $y$?

(A) $\dfrac{31}{30}$   (B) $\dfrac{41}{20}$   (C) 1.8   (D) 3.6   (E) 36

The obvious way to do this is to first find $x$ and $y$ by solving the two equations simultaneously and then to take their average. If you know how to do this, try it now, before reading further. If you worked carefully, you should have found that $x = \dfrac{31}{20}$ and $y = \dfrac{41}{20}$, and their average is

$\dfrac{\frac{31}{20} + \frac{41}{20}}{2} = \dfrac{9}{5}$. This is not too difficult, but it is quite

time-consuming, and questions on the GRE never require you to do that much work. Look for a shortcut. Is there a way to find the average without first finding $x$ and $y$? Absolutely! Here's the best way to do this.

SOLUTION. Add the two equations:

$$\begin{array}{r} 7x + 3y = 17 \\ + \; 3x + 7y = 19 \\ \hline 10x + 10y = 36 \end{array}$$

Divide each side by 10:    $x + y = 3.6$

Calculate the average:    $\dfrac{x + y}{2} = \dfrac{3.6}{2} = \mathbf{1.8}$

The answer is **C**.

| Column A | Column B |
|---|---|
| **Example 17.** | |

Benjamin worked from 9:47 A.M. until 12:11 P.M.
Jeremy worked from 9:11 A.M. until 12:47 P.M.

| The number of minutes Benjamin worked | The number of minutes Jeremy worked |
|---|---|

Do not spend any time calculating how many minutes either of them worked. You only need to know which column is greater, and since Jeremy started earlier and finished later, he clearly worked longer. The answer is **B**.

## Pay Attention to Units

Often the answer to a question must be in units different from the data given in the question. As you read the question, write on your scratch paper exactly what you are being asked and circle it or put an asterisk next to it. Do they want hours or minutes or seconds, dollars or cents, feet or inches, meters or centimeters? On multiple-choice questions, an answer using the wrong units is almost always one of the choices.

**Example 18.**

Driving at 48 miles per hour, how many minutes will it take to drive 32 miles?

(A) $\dfrac{2}{3}$   (B) $\dfrac{3}{2}$   (C) 40   (D) 45   (E) 2400

SOLUTION. This is a relatively easy question. Just be attentive. Since $\dfrac{32}{48} = \dfrac{2}{3}$, it will take $\dfrac{2}{3}$ of an *hour* to drive

32 miles. Choice A is $\dfrac{2}{3}$, but that is not the correct answer, because you are asked how many *minutes* it will take. The

correct answer is $\dfrac{2}{3}(60) = \mathbf{40}$, **C**.

Note that you could have been asked how many *seconds* it would take, in which case the answer would be 40(60) = 2400, Choice E.

**Example 19.**

At Nat's Nuts a $2\dfrac{1}{4}$-pound bag of pistachio nuts costs \$6.00. At this rate, what is the cost in cents of a bag weighing 9 ounces?

(A) 1.5   (B) 24   (C) 150   (D) 1350   (E) 2400

SOLUTION. This is a relatively simple ratio, but make sure you get the units right. To do this you need to know that there are 100 cents in a dollar and 16 ounces in a pound.

$\dfrac{\text{price}}{\text{weight}} : \dfrac{6 \text{ dollars}}{2.25 \text{ pounds}} = \dfrac{600 \text{ cents}}{36 \text{ ounces}} = \dfrac{x \text{ cents}}{9 \text{ ounces}}$. Now

cross-multiply and solve: $36x = 5400 \Rightarrow x = \mathbf{150}$, **C**.

# Systematically Make Lists

When a question asks "how many," often the best strategy is to make a list of all the possibilities. If you do this it is important that you make the list in a *systematic* fashion so that you don't inadvertently leave something out. Often, shortly after starting the list, you can see a pattern developing and you can figure out how many more entries there will be without writing them all down. Even if the question does not specifically ask "how many," you may need to count something to answer it; in this case, as well, the best plan may be to write out a list.

By now you should see the pattern: there are 10 numbers beginning with 1, 10 beginning with 2, and there will be 10 beginning with 3, 4, ..., 9 for a total of 9 × 10 = **90** palindromes, **C**.

---

### Example 20.

A palindrome is a number, such as 93539, that reads the same forward and backward. How many palindromes are there between 100 and 1,000?

(A) 10   (B) 81   (C) 90   (D) 100   (E) 200

---

SOLUTION. First, write down the numbers that begin and end in 1:

   101, 111, 121, 131, 141, 151, 161, 171, 181, 191

Next write the numbers that begin and end in a 2:

   202, 212, 222, 232, 242, 252, 262, 272, 282, 292

---

### Example 21.

The product of three positive integers is 300. If one of them is 5, what is the least possible value of the sum of the other two?

(A) 16   (B) 17   (C) 19   (D) 23   (E) 32

---

SOLUTION. Since one of the integers is 5, the product of the other two is 60. Systematically, list all possible pairs, (a, b), of positive integers whose product is 60 and check their sums. First let a = 1, then 2, and so on.

| a | b | a + b |
|---|---|-------|
| 1 | 60 | 61 |
| 2 | 30 | 32 |
| 3 | 20 | 23 |
| 4 | 15 | 19 |
| 5 | 12 | 17 |
| 6 | 10 | 16 |

The answer is **16**, **A**.

---

# Practice Exercises

## General Math Strategies

1. At Leo's Lumberyard, an 8-foot long wooden pole costs $3.00. At this rate, what is the cost, in cents, of a pole that is 16 inches long?

   (A) 0.5   (B) 48   (C) 50   (D) 64   (E) 96

2. In the figure below, vertex Q of square OPQR is on a circle with center O. If the area of the square is 8, what is the area of the circle?

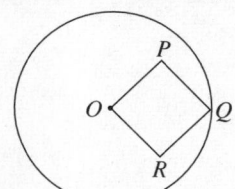

   (A) 8π   (B) 8π √2   (C) 16π   (D) 32π   (E) 64π

3. In 1999, Diana read 10 English books and 7 French books. In 2000, she read twice as many French books as English books. If 60% of the books that she read during the two years were French, how many books did she read in 2000?

   (A) 16   (B) 26   (C) 32   (D) 39   (E) 48

4. In the figure below, if the radius of circle O is 10, what is the length of diagonal AC of rectangle OABC?

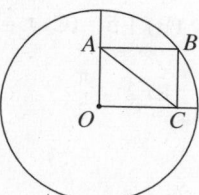

   (A) √2   (B) √10   (C) 5 √2   (D) 10   (E) 10 √2

5. In writing all of the integers from 1 to 300, how many times is the digit 1 used?

   (A) 60   (B) 120   (C) 150   (D) 160   (E) 180

6. In the figure at the right, *ABCD* is a square and *AED* is an equilateral triangle. If *AB* = 2, what is the area of the shaded region?

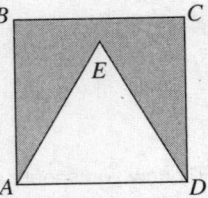

(A) $\sqrt{3}$ (B) 2 (C) 3 (D) $4 - 2\sqrt{3}$ (E) $4 - \sqrt{3}$

7. If $5x + 13 = 31$, what is the value of $\sqrt{5x + 31}$ ?

(A) $\sqrt{13}$ (B) $\sqrt{\dfrac{173}{5}}$ (C) 7 (D) 13 (E) 169

8. If $a + 2b = 14$ and $5a + 4b = 16$, what is the average (arithmetic mean) of *a* and *b*?

(A) 1.5 (B) 2 (C) 2.5 (D) 3 (E) 3.5

9. In the figure below, equilateral triangle *ABC* is inscribed in circle *O*, whose radius is 4. Altitude *BD* is extended until it intersects the circle at *E*. What is the length of *DE*?

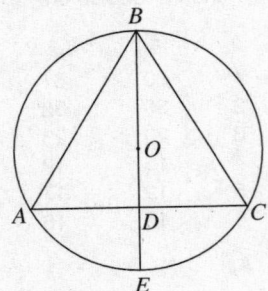

(A) 1 (B) $\sqrt{3}$ (C) 2 (D) $2\sqrt{3}$ (E) $4\sqrt{3}$

10. In the figure below, three circles of radius 1 are tangent to one another. What is the area of the shaded region between them?

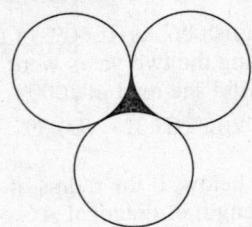

(A) $\dfrac{\pi}{2} - \sqrt{3}$ (B) 1.5 (C) $\pi - \sqrt{3}$

(D) $\sqrt{3} - \dfrac{\pi}{2}$ (E) $2 - \dfrac{\pi}{2}$

| Column A | Column B |
|---|---|

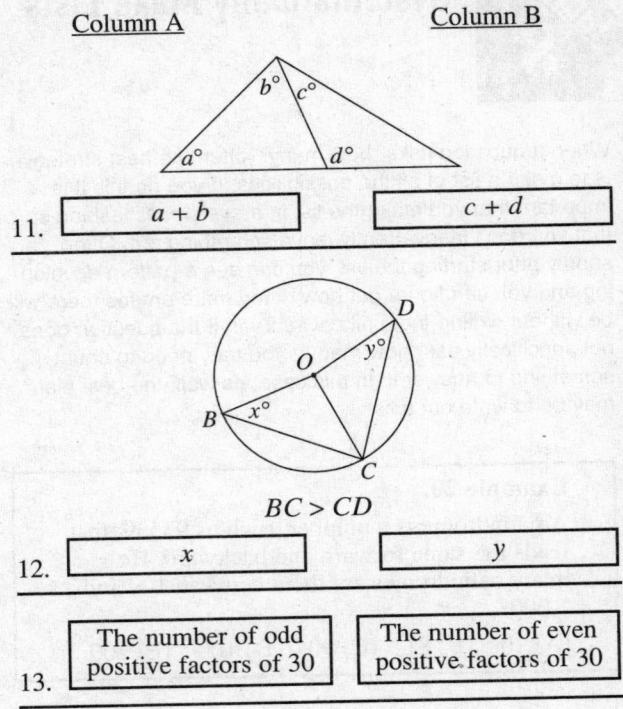

11. | $a + b$ | $c + d$ |

$BC > CD$

12. | $x$ | $y$ |

13. | The number of odd positive factors of 30 | The number of even positive factors of 30 |

Questions 14–15 refer to the following definition.

$\{a, b\}$ represents the remainder when *a* is divided by *b*.

14. | $\{10^3, 3\}$ | $\{10^5, 5\}$ |

*c* and *d* are positive integers with $c < d$.

15. | $\{c, d\}$ | $\{d, c\}$ |

## Answer Key

| 1. **C** | 3. **E** | 5. **D** | 7. **C** | 9. **C** | 11. **B** | 13. **C** | 15. **A** |
|---|---|---|---|---|---|---|---|
| 2. **C** | 4. **D** | 6. **E** | 8. **C** | 10. **D** | 12. **B** | 14. **A** | |

# Answer Explanations

Two asterisks (**) indicate an alternative method of solving.

1. **C.** This is a relatively simple ratio problem, but use TACTIC 7 and make sure you get the units right. To do this you need to know that there are 100 cents in a dollar and 12 inches in a foot.

$$\frac{price}{weight} : \frac{3 \text{ dollars}}{8 \text{ feet}} = \frac{300 \text{ cents}}{96 \text{ inches}} = \frac{x \text{ cents}}{16 \text{ inches}}.$$

Now cross-multiply and solve: $96x = 4800 \Rightarrow$ $x = 50$.

2. **C.** Use TACTICS 2 and 4. On your scrap paper, extend line segments $OP$ and $OR$. Square $OPQR$, whose area is 8, takes up most of the quarter-circle. So the area of the quarter-circle is certainly between 11 and 13. The area of the whole circle is 4 times as great: between 44 and 52. Check the five choices: they are approximately 25, 36, 50, 100, 200. The answer is clearly C.

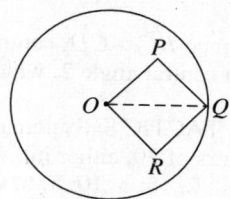

**Another way to use TACTIC 4 is to draw in line segment $OQ$. Since the area of the square is 8, each side is $\sqrt{8}$, and diagonal $OQ$ is $\sqrt{8} \times \sqrt{2} = \sqrt{16} = 4$. But $OQ$ is also a radius, so the area of the circle is $16\pi$.

3. **E.** Use TACTIC 1: draw a picture representing a pile of books or a bookshelf.

|  | | |
|---|---|---|
| 2000 | $2x$ | French |
| | $x$ | English |
| 1999 | 10 | English |
| | 7 | French |

| Eng. | Fr. | Eng. | Fr. |
|---|---|---|---|
| 10 | 7 | $x$ | $2x$ |
| 1999 | | 2000 | |

In the two years the number of French books Diana read was $7 + 2x$ and the total number of books was $17 + 3x$. Then 60% or $\frac{3}{5} = \frac{7+2x}{17+3x}$. To solve, cross-multiply:

$$35 + 10x = 51 + 9x \Rightarrow x = 16.$$

In 2000, Diana read 16 English books and 32 French books, a total of 48 books.

4. **D.** Use TACTIC 2. Trust the diagram: $AC$, which is clearly longer than $OC$, is approximately as long as radius $OE$. Therefore, $AC$ must be about 10. Check the choices. They are approximately 1.4, 3.1, 7, 10, and 14. The answer must be 10.
   **The answer *is* 10. Use TACTIC 4: copy the diagram on your scrap paper and draw in diagonal $OB$.

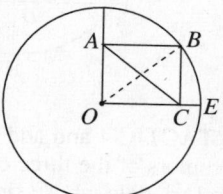

The two diagonals of a rectangle are equal, and diagonal $OB$ is a radius.

5. **D.** Use TACTIC 8. Systematically list the numbers that contain the digit 1, writing as many as you need to see the pattern. Between 1 and 99 the digit 1 is used 10 times as the units digit (1, 11, 21, ... , 91) and 10 times as the tens digit (10, 11, 12, ... , 19) for a total of 20 times. From 200 to 299, there are 20 more (the same 20 preceded by a 2). From 100 to 199 there are 20 more plus 100 numbers where the digit 1 is used in the hundreds place. So the total is $20 + 20 + 20 + 100 = 160$.

6. **E.** Use TACTIC 5: subtract to find the shaded area. The area of the square is 4. The area of the equilateral triangle (see Section 15-J) is $\frac{2^2\sqrt{3}}{4} = \frac{4\sqrt{3}}{4} = \sqrt{3}$. So the area of the shaded region is $4 - \sqrt{3}$.

7. **C.** Use TACTIC 6: don't do more than you have to. In particular, don't solve for $x$.
   $5x + 13 = 31 \Rightarrow 5x = 18 \Rightarrow 5x + 31 = 18 + 31 = 49 \Rightarrow \sqrt{5x+31} = \sqrt{49} = 7$.

8. **C.** Use TACTIC 6: don't do more than is necessary. You do not need to solve this system of equations; we don't need to know the values of $a$ and $b$, only their average. Adding the two equations, we get $6a + 6b = 30 \Rightarrow a + b = 5 \Rightarrow \frac{a+b}{2} = \frac{5}{2} = 2.5$.

9. C. Use TACTIC 5: to get *DE*, subtract *OD* from radius *OE*, which is 4. Draw *AO* (TACTIC 4). Since △*AOD* is a 30-60-90 right triangle, *OD* is 2 (one half of *OA*). So, *DE* = 4 − 2 = 2.

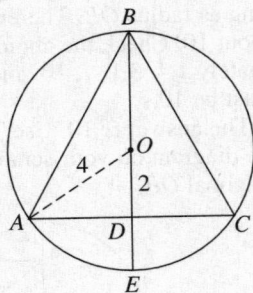

10. D. Use TACTIC 4 and add some lines: connect the centers of the three circles to form an equilateral triangle whose sides are 2.

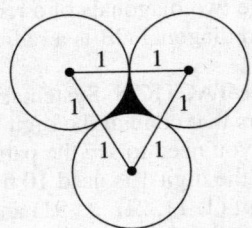

Now use TACTIC 5 and find the shaded area by subtracting the area of the three sectors from the area of the triangle. The area of the triangle is $\dfrac{2^2\sqrt{3}}{4} = \sqrt{3}$ (see Section 15-J).

Each sector is one sixth of a circle of radius 1. Together they form one half of such a circle, so their total area is $\dfrac{1}{2}\pi(1)^2 = \dfrac{\pi}{2}$. Finally, subtract: the shaded area is $\sqrt{3} - \dfrac{\pi}{2}$.

11. B. If you don't see how to do this, use TACTIC 2: trust the diagram. Estimate the measure of each angle: for example, *a* = 45, *b* = 70, *c* = 30, and *d* = 120. So *c* + *d* (150) is considerably greater than *a* + *b* (115). Choose B.

**In fact, *d* by itself is equal to *a* + *b* (an exterior angle of a triangle is equal to the sum of the opposite two interior angles). So *c* + *d* > *a* + *b*.

12. B. From the figure, it appears that *x* and *y* are equal, or nearly so. Use TACTIC 3: when you draw the figure on your scrap paper, exaggerate the figure. Draw it with *BC* much greater than *CD*. Now it is clear that *y* is greater.

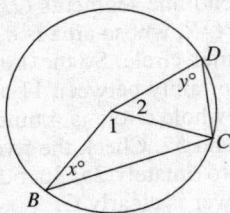

**Since *BC* > *CD*, central angle 1 is greater than central angle 2, which means that *x* < *y*.

13. C. Use TACTIC 8. Systematically list all the factors of 30, either individually or in pairs: 1, 30; 2, 15; 3, 10; 5, 6. Of the 8 factors, 4 are even and 4 are odd.

14. A. Column A: When $10^3$ (1000) is divided by 3, the quotient is 333 and the remainder is 1. Column B: $10^5$ is divisible by 5, so the remainder is 0.

15. A. Column A: since *c* < *d*, the quotient when *c* is divided by *d* is 0, and the remainder is *c*. Column B: when *d* is divided by *c* the remainder must be less than *c*. So Column A is greater.

# 12 Discrete Quantitative Questions

- ■ Tactics
- ■ Practice Exercises
- ■ Answer Key and Explanations

---

Of the 28 questions in the quantitative section, 10 are called discrete quantitative questions, which is just a fancy name for standard multiple-choice questions, similar to those that you have encountered on many other standardized tests, such as the PSAT and SAT I.

In this chapter you will learn all of the important strategies to help you answer multiple-choice questions on the GRE. However, as invaluable as these tactics are, use them only when you need them. *If you know how to do a problem and are confident that you can do it accurately and reasonably quickly, JUST DO IT!*

Before the first discrete quantitative question appears on the screen, you will see the following instructions:

> Select the best of the answer choices given.

This one-sentence set of directions is quite simple. Unfortunately, it is also quite useless. First of all, it is misleading. It is never the case that two of the answers are bad and three are good, and you then need to choose the *best* answer from among the three good ones. Every quantitative multiple-choice question has exactly one correct answer and four incorrect ones. Second, the implication is that you should just *solve each problem* and *then* look at the five choices to see which one is best (i.e., correct). As you will learn in this chapter, that is not always the best strategy.

---

**Helpful Hint**

*When you take the GRE, dismiss the instructions for these questions instantly — do not spend even one second reading them — and certainly never accept their offer of clicking on "HELP" to return to them during the test.*

---

As we have done throughout this book, we will continue to label the five answer choices A, B, C, D, and E and to refer to them as such. Of course, when you take the the GRE, these letters will not appear—there will simply be a blank oval in front of each of the answer choices. When we refer to Choice C—as we do, for example, in TACTIC 1 below—we are simply referring to the third answer choice among the five presented.

---

# Testing Tactics

## Test the Choices, Starting with C

TACTIC 1, often called **backsolving**, is useful when you are asked to solve for an unknown and you understand what needs to be done to answer the question, but you want to avoid doing the algebra. The idea is simple: test the various choices to see which one is correct.

NOTE: On the GRE the answers to virtually all numerical multiple-choice questions are listed in either increasing or decreasing order. Consequently, C is the middle value, and *in applying TACTIC 1, you should always start with C.* For example, assume that choices A, B, C,

D, and E are given in increasing order. Try C. If it works, you've found the answer. If C doesn't work, you should know whether you need to test a larger number or a smaller one, and that permits you to eliminate two more choices. If C is too small, you need a larger number, and so A and B are out; if C is too large, eliminate D and E, which are even larger.

Examples 1 and 2 illustrate the proper use of TACTIC 1.

---

**Example 1.**

If the average (arithmetic mean) of 5, 6, 7, and $w$ is 10, what is the value of $w$?

(A) 8   (B) 13   (C) 18   (D) 22   (E) 28

---

SOLUTION. Use TACTIC 1. Test Choice C: $w = 18$.

• Is the average of 5, 6, 7, and 18 equal to 10?

• No: $\dfrac{5 + 6 + 7 + 18}{4} = \dfrac{36}{4} = 9$, which is *too small*.

• Eliminate C, and, since for the average to be 10, $w$ must be *greater* than 18, eliminate A and B, as well.

• Try D: $w = 22$. Is the average of 5, 6, 7, and 22 equal to 10?

• Yes: $\dfrac{5 + 6 + 7 + 22}{4} = \dfrac{40}{4} = 10$. The answer is **D**.

Every problem that can be solved using TACTIC 1 can be solved directly, usually in less time. So we stress: *if you are confident that you can solve a problem quickly and accurately, just do so.*

Here are two direct methods for solving Example 1, each of which is faster than backsolving. (See Section 15-E on averages.) If you know either method you should use it, and save TACTIC 1 for those problems which you can't easily solve directly.

**Direct Solution 1.** If the average of four numbers is 10, their sum is 40. So, $5 + 6 + 7 + w = 40 \Rightarrow 18 + w = 40 \Rightarrow w = $ **22.**

**Direct Solution 2.** Since 5 is *5 less than* 10, 6 is *4 less than* 10, and 7 is *3 less than* 10, to compensate, $w$ must be $5 + 4 + 3 = 12$ *more* than 10. So, $w = 10 + 12 = $ **22.**

---

**Example 2.**

Judy is now twice as old as Adam, but 6 years ago, she was 5 times as old as he was. How old is Judy now?

(A) 10   (B) 16   (C) 20   (D) 24   (E) 32

---

SOLUTION. Use TACTIC 1: backsolve starting with C. If Judy is now 20, Adam is 10, and 6 years ago, they

would have been 14 and 4. Since Judy would have been less than 5 times as old as Adam, eliminate C, D, and E, and try a smaller value. If Judy is now 16, Adam is 8; 6 years ago, they would have been 10 and 2. That's it; 10 *is* 5 times 2. The answer is **B**.

(See Section 15-H on word problems for the correct algebraic solution.)

Some tactics allow you to eliminate a few choices so you can make an educated guess. On those problems where it can be used, TACTIC 1 *always* gets you the right answer. The only reason not to use it on a particular problem is that you can *easily* solve the problem directly.

---

**Helpful Hint**

Don't start with C if some of the other choices are much easier to work with. If you start with B and it is too small, you may only get to eliminate two choices (A and B), instead of three, but it will save time if plugging in Choice C would be messy.

---

**Example 3.**

If $3x = 2(5 - 2x)$, then $x = $

(A) $-\dfrac{10}{7}$   (B) 0   (C) $\dfrac{3}{7}$   (D) 1   (E) $\dfrac{10}{7}$

---

SOLUTION. Since plugging in 0 is so much easier than plugging in $\dfrac{3}{7}$, start with B: then the left-hand side of the equation is 0 and the right-hand side is 10. The left-hand side is much too small. Eliminate A and B and try something bigger—D, of course; it will be much easier to deal with 1 than with $\dfrac{3}{7}$ or $\dfrac{10}{7}$. Now the left-hand side is 3 and the right-hand side is 6. We're closer, but not there. The answer must be **E**. Notice that we got the right answer without ever plugging in one of those unpleasant fractions. Are you uncomfortable choosing E without checking it? Don't be. If you *know* that the answer is greater than 1, and only one choice is greater than 1, that choice has to be right.

Again, we emphasize that, no matter what the choices are, you backsolve *only* if you can't easily do the algebra. Most students would probably do this problem directly:

$$3x = 2(5 - 2x) \Rightarrow 3x = 10 - 4x \Rightarrow 7x = 10 \Rightarrow x = \dfrac{10}{7}$$

and save backsolving for a harder problem. You have to determine which method is best for you.

# Replace Variables with Numbers

Mastery of TACTIC 2 is critical for anyone developing good test-taking skills. This tactic can be used whenever the five choices involve the variables in the question. There are three steps:

1. Replace each letter with an easy-to-use number.

2. Solve the problem using those numbers.

3. Evaluate each of the five choices with the numbers you picked to see which choice is equal to the answer you obtained.

Examples 4 and 5 illustrate the proper use of TACTIC 2.

---

**Example 4.**

If $a$ is equal to the sum of $b$ and $c$, which of the following is equal to the difference of $b$ and $c$?

(A) $a - b - c$   (B) $a - b + c$   (C) $a - c$
(D) $a - 2c$   (E) $a - b - 2c$

---

SOLUTION.

- Pick three easy-to-use numbers which satisfy $a = b + c$: for example, $a = 5$, $b = 3$, $c = 2$.

- Then, solve the problem with these numbers: the difference of $b$ and $c$ is $3 - 2 = 1$.

- Finally, check each of the five choices to see which one is equal to 1:

(A) Does $a - b - c = 1$?   NO. $5 - 3 - 2 = 0$

(B) Does $a - b + c = 1$?   NO. $5 - 3 + 2 = 4$

(C) Does $a - c = 1$?      NO. $5 - 2 = 3$

(D) Does $a - 2c = 1$?     YES! $5 - 2(2) = 5 - 4 = 1$

(E) Does $a - b - 2c = 1$? NO. $5 - 3 - 2(2) = 2 - 4 = -2$

- The answer is **D**.

---

**Example 5.**

If the sum of five consecutive even integers is $t$, then, in terms of $t$, what is the greatest of these integers?

(A) $\dfrac{t - 20}{5}$   (B) $\dfrac{t - 10}{5}$   (C) $\dfrac{t}{5}$   (D) $\dfrac{t + 10}{5}$
(E) $\dfrac{t + 20}{5}$

---

SOLUTION.

- Pick five easy-to-use consecutive even integers: say, 2, 4, 6, 8, 10. Then $t$, their sum, is 30.

- Solve the problem with these numbers: the greatest of these integers is 10.

- When $t = 30$, the five choices are $\dfrac{10}{5}, \dfrac{20}{5}, \dfrac{30}{5}, \dfrac{40}{5}, \dfrac{50}{5}$.

- Only $\dfrac{50}{5}$, Choice **E**, is equal to 10.

Of course, Examples 4 and 5 can be solved without using TACTIC 3 *if your algebra skills are good.* Here are the solutions.

**Solution 4.** $a = b + c \Rightarrow b = a - c \Rightarrow$
$b - c = (a - c) - c = a - 2c.$

**Solution 5.** Let $n$, $n + 2$, $n + 4$, $n + 6$, and $n + 8$ be five consecutive even integers, and let $t$ be their sum. Then,

$$t = n + (n + 2) + (n + 4) + (n + 6) + (n + 8) = 5n + 20$$

So, $n = \dfrac{t - 20}{5} \Rightarrow n + 8 = \dfrac{t - 20}{5} + 8 =$

$$\dfrac{t - 20}{5} + \dfrac{40}{5} = \dfrac{t + 20}{5}.$$

The important point is that if you can't do the algebra, you can still use TACTIC 2 and *always* get the right answer. Of course, you should use TACTIC 2 even if you can do the algebra, if you think that by using this tactic you will solve the problem faster or will be less likely to make a mistake. This is a good example of what we mean when we say that with the proper use of these tactics, you can correctly answer many questions for which you may not know the correct mathematical solution.

Examples 6 and 7 are somewhat different. You are asked to reason through word problems involving only variables. Most students find problems like these mind-boggling. Here, the use of TACTIC 2 is essential. Without it, Example 6 is difficult and Example 7 is nearly impossible. This is not an easy tactic to master, but with practice you will catch on.

---

**Helpful Hint**

Replace the letters with numbers that are easy to use, not necessarily ones that make sense. *It is perfectly OK to ignore reality.* A school can have 5 students, apples can cost 10 dollars each, trains can go 5 miles per hour or 1000 miles per hour—it doesn't matter.

## Example 6.

If a school cafeteria needs $c$ cans of soup each week for each student, and if there are $s$ students in the school, for how many weeks will $x$ cans of soup last?

(A) $csx$   (B) $\dfrac{xs}{c}$   (C) $\dfrac{s}{cx}$   (D) $\dfrac{x}{cs}$   (E) $\dfrac{cx}{s}$

SOLUTION.

• Replace $c$, $s$, and $x$ with three easy-to-use numbers. If a school cafeteria needs 2 cans of soup each week for each student, and if there are 5 students in the school, how many weeks will 20 cans of soup last?

• Since the cafeteria needs $2 \times 5 = 10$ cans of soup per week, 20 cans will last 2 weeks.

• Which of the choices equals 2 when $c = 2$, $s = 5$, and $x = 20$?

• $csx = 200$; $\dfrac{xs}{c} = 50$; $\dfrac{s}{cx} = \dfrac{1}{8}$; $\dfrac{x}{cs} = 2$; and $\dfrac{cx}{s} = 8$. The answer is $\dfrac{x}{cs}$, **D**.

NOTE: You do not need to get the exact value of each choice. As soon as you see that a choice does not equal the value you are looking for, stop—eliminate that choice and move on. For example, in the preceding problem, it is clear that $csx$ is much greater than 2, so eliminate it immediately; you do not need to multiply it out to determine that the value is 200.

CAUTION: In this type of problem it is *not* a good idea to replace any of the variables by 1. Since multiplying and dividing by 1 give the same result, you would not be able to distinguish between $\dfrac{cx}{s}$ and $\dfrac{x}{s}$, both of which are equal to 4 when $c = 1$, $s = 5$, and $x = 20$. It is also not a good idea to use the same number for different variables: $\dfrac{cx}{s}$ and $\dfrac{xs}{c}$ are each equal to $x$ when $c$ and $s$ are equal.

## Example 7.

A vendor sell $h$ hot dogs and $s$ sodas. If a hot dog costs twice as much as a soda, and if the vendor takes in a total of $d$ dollars, how many cents does a soda cost?

(A) $\dfrac{100d}{s + 2h}$   (B) $\dfrac{s + 2h}{100d}$   (C) $\dfrac{d(s + 2h)}{100}$

(D) $100d(s + 2h)$   (E) $\dfrac{d}{100(s + 2h)}$

SOLUTION.

• Replace $h$, $s$, and $d$ with three easy-to-use numbers. Suppose a soda costs 50¢ and a hot dog $1.00. Then, if he sold 2 sodas and 3 hot dogs, he took in 4 dollars.

• Which of the choices equals 50 when $s = 2$, $h = 3$, and $d = 4$?

• Only $\dfrac{100d}{s + 2h}$ (**A**): $\dfrac{100(4)}{2 + 2(3)} = \dfrac{400}{8} = 50$.

Now, practice TACTIC 2 on the following problems.

## Example 8.

Yann will be $x$ years old $y$ years from now. How old was he $z$ years ago?

(A) $x + y + z$   (B) $x + y - z$   (C) $x - y - z$
(D) $y - x - z$   (E) $z - y - x$

## Example 9.

Stan drove for $h$ hours at a constant rate of $r$ miles per hour. How many miles did he go during the final 20 minutes of his drive?

(A) $20r$   (B) $\dfrac{hr}{3}$   (C) $3rh$   (D) $\dfrac{hr}{20}$   (E) $\dfrac{r}{3}$

**Solution 8.** Assume that Yann will be 10 in 2 years. How old was he 3 years ago? If he will be 10 in 2 years, he is 8 now and 3 years ago he was 5. Which of the choices equals 5 when $x = 10$, $y = 2$, and $z = 3$? Only $x - y - z$, **C**.

**Solution 9.** If Stan drove at 60 miles per hour for 2 hours, how far did he go in the last 20 minutes? Since 20 minutes is $\dfrac{1}{3}$ of an hour, he went 20 ($\dfrac{1}{3}$ of 60) miles. Only $\dfrac{r}{3}$ is 20 when $r = 60$ and $h = 2$. Notice that $h$ is irrelevant. Whether he had been driving for 2 hours or 20 hours, the distance he covered in the last 20 minutes would be the same.

## Choose an Appropriate Number

TACTIC 3 is similar to TACTIC 2, in that we pick convenient numbers. However, here no variable is given in the problem. TACTIC 3 is especially useful in problems involving fractions, ratios, and percents.

---

**Helpful Hint**

In problems involving fractions, the best number to use is the least common denominator of all the fractions. In problems involving percents, the easiest number to use is 100. (See Sections 15-B and 15-C.)

---

**Example 10.**

At Madison High School each student studies exactly one foreign language. Three-fifths of the students take Spanish, and one-fourth of the remaining students take German. If all of the others take French, what <u>percent</u> of the students take French?

(A) 10   (B) 15   (C) 20   (D) 25   (E) 30

SOLUTION. The least common denominator of $\frac{3}{5}$ and $\frac{1}{4}$ is 20, so assume that there are 20 students at

Madison High. (Remember the numbers don't have to be realistic.) The number of students taking Spanish is $12\left(\frac{3}{5}\text{ of }20\right)$. Of the remaining 8 students, 2 of them $\left(\frac{1}{4}\text{ of }8\right)$ take German. The other 6 take French. Finally, 6 is **30%** of 20. The answer is **E**.

**Example 11.**

From 1994 to 1995 the sales of a book decreased by 80%. If the sales in 1996 were the same as in 1994, by what percent did they increase from 1995 to 1996?

(A) 80%   (B) 100%   (C) 120%
    (D) 400%   (E) 500%

SOLUTION. Since this problem involves percents, assume that 100 copies of the book were sold in 1994 (and 1996). Sales dropped by 80 (80% of 100) to 20 in 1995 and then increased by 80, from 20 back to 100, in 1996. The percent increase was

$$\frac{\text{the actual increase}}{\text{the original amount}} \times 100\% = \frac{80}{20} \times 100\% = \textbf{400\%, D.}$$

## Eliminate Absurd Choices and Guess

When you have no idea how to solve a problem, you have to guess in order to move on; but first eliminate all the absurd choices. Then guess from among the remaining ones.

During the course of a GRE, you will probably find at least a few multiple-choice questions that you have no idea how to solve. Since you can't omit them, you have to guess. But take a moment to look at the answer choices. Often two or three of them are absurd. Eliminate those and then guess one of the others. Occasionally, four of the choices are absurd. When this occurs, your answer is no longer a guess.

What makes a choice absurd? Lots of things. Here are a few. Even if you don't know how to solve a problem you may realize that

• the answer must be positive, but some of the choices are negative;

• the answer must be even, but some of the choices are odd;

• the answer must be less than 100, but some choices exceed 100;

• a ratio must be less than 1, but some choices are greater than 1.

Let's look at several examples. In a few of them the information given is intentionally insufficient to solve the problem; but you will still be able to determine that some of the answers are absurd. In each case the "solution" will indicate which choices you should have eliminated. At that point you would simply guess. Remember, on the GRE when you have to guess, don't agonize. Just guess and move on.

---

**Example 12.**

A region inside a semicircle of radius $r$ is shaded and you are asked for its area.

(A) $\frac{1}{4}\pi r^2$    (B) $\frac{1}{3}\pi r^2$    (C) $\frac{1}{2}\pi r^2$

     (D) $\frac{2}{3}\pi r^2$    (E) $\pi r^2$

---

SOLUTION. You may have no idea how to find the area of the shaded region, but you should know that since the area of a circle is $\pi r^2$, the area of a semicircle is $\frac{1}{2}\pi r^2$. Therefore, the area of the shaded region must be *less* than $\frac{1}{2}\pi r^2$, so eliminate C, D, and E. On an actual GRE problem, you may be able to make an educated guess between A and B. If so, terrific; if not, just choose one or the other.

---

**Example 13.**

The average (arithmetic mean) of 5, 10, 15, and $z$ is 20. What is $z$?

(A) 0    (B) 20    (C) 25    (D) 45    (E) 50

---

SOLUTION. If the average of four numbers is 20, and three of them are less than 20, the other one must be greater than 20. Eliminate A and B and guess. If you further realize that since 5 and 10 are a *lot less* than 20, $z$ will probably be a *lot more* than 20; eliminate C, as well.

---

**Example 14.**

If 25% of 260 equals 6.5% of $a$, what is $a$?

(A) 10    (B) 65    (C) 100    (D) 130    (E) 1000

---

SOLUTION. Since 6.5% of $a$ equals 25% of 260, which is surely greater than 6.5% of 260, $a$ must be greater than 260. Eliminate A, B, C, and D. The answer *must* be **E**!

Example 14 illustrates an important point. *Even if you know how to solve a problem*, if you immediately see that four of the five choices are absurd, just pick the fifth choice and move on.

---

**Example 15.**

A jackpot of $39,000 is to be divided in some ratio among three people. What is the value of the largest share?

(A) $23,400    (B) $19,500    (C) $11,700

     (D) $7800    (E) $3900

---

SOLUTION. If the prize were divided equally, each of the three shares would be worth $13,000. If it is divided unequally, the largest share is surely worth *more than*

$13,000. Eliminate C, D, and E. In an actual question, you would be told what the ratio is, and that might enable you to eliminate A or B. If not, you just guess.

---

**Example 16.**

In a certain club, the ratio of the number of boys to girls is 5:3. What percent of the members of the club are girls?

(A) 37.5%    (B) 50%    (C) 60%    (D) 62.5%

     (E) 80%

---

SOLUTION. Since there are 5 boys for every 3 girls, there are fewer girls than boys. Therefore, *fewer than half* (50%) of the members are girls. Eliminate B, C, D, and E. The answer is **A**.

---

**Example 17.**

In the figure at the right, four semicircles are drawn, each one centered at the midpoint of one of the sides of square *ABCD*. Each of the four shaded "petals" is the intersection of two of the semicircles. If $AB = 4$, what is the total area of the shaded region?

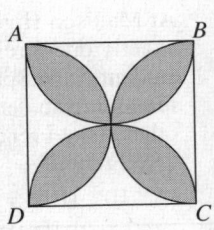

(A) $8\pi$    (B) $32 - 8\pi$    (C) $16 - 8\pi$    (D) $8\pi - 32$

     (E) $8\pi - 16$

---

SOLUTION. Since the diagram is drawn to scale, you may trust it in making your estimate (TACTIC 2, chapter 11).

• Since the shaded area *appears* to take up a little more than half of the square, it does.

• The area of the square is 16, and so the area of the shaded region must be *about* 9.

• Check each choice. Since $\pi$ is slightly more than 3 ($\pi \approx 3.14$), $8\pi$ is somewhat greater than 24, approximately 25.

• (A) $8\pi \approx 25$. More than the area of the whole square: *way* too big.

• (B) $32 - 8\pi \approx 32 - 25 = 7$. Too small (but close enough to consider if nothing is closer).

• (C) $16 - 8\pi$ is negative. Clearly impossible!

• (D) $8\pi - 32$ is also negative.

• (E) $\mathbf{8\pi - 16} \approx 25 - 16 = 9$. Finally! The answer is **E**.

NOTE: Three of the choices are absurd: A is more than the area of the entire square and C and D are negative; they can be eliminated immediately. No matter what your estimate was, at worst you had to guess between two choices.

Now use TACTIC 5 on each of the following problems. Even if you know how to solve them, don't. Practice this technique and see how many choices you can eliminate *without* actually solving.

---

**Example 18.**

In the figure at the right, diagonal $EG$ of square $EFGH$ is $\frac{1}{2}$ of diagonal $AC$ of the square $ABCD$. What is the ratio of the area of the shaded region to the area of $ABCD$?

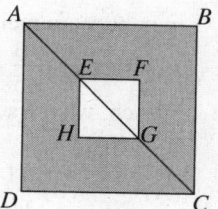

(A) $\sqrt{2}$:1    (B) 3:4    (C) $\sqrt{2}$:2

   (D) 1:2    (E) 1:$2\sqrt{2}$

---

**Example 19.**

Shari receives a commission of 25¢ for every $20.00 worth of merchandise she sells. What percent is her commission?

(A) $1\frac{1}{4}$%    (B) $2\frac{1}{2}$%    (C) 5%

   (D) 25%    (E) 125%

---

**Example 20.**

From 1980 to 1990, Lior's weight increased by 25%. If his weight was $k$ kilograms in 1990, what was it in 1980?

(A) 1.75$k$    (B) 1.25$k$    (C) 1.20$k$

   (D) .80$k$    (E) .75$k$

---

**Example 21.**

The average of 10 numbers is −10. If the sum of 6 of them is 100, what is the average of the other 4?

(A) −100    (B) −50    (C) 0    (D) 50    (E) 100

---

**Solution 18.** Obviously, the shaded region is smaller than square $ABCD$, so the ratio must be less than 1. Eliminate A. Also, from the diagram, it is clear that the shaded region is more than half of square $ABCD$, so the ratio is greater than 0.5. Eliminate D and E. Since 3:4 = .75 and $\sqrt{2}$:2 ≈ .71, B and C are too close to tell which is correct just by looking; so guess. The answer is **B**.

**Solution 19.** Clearly, a commission of 25¢ on $20 is quite small. Eliminate D and E and guess one of the small percents. If you realize that 1% of $20 is 20¢, then you know the answer is a little more than 1%, and you should guess A (maybe B, but definitely not C). The answer is **A**.

**Solution 20.** Since Lior's weight increased, his weight in 1980 was *less than k*. Eliminate A, B, and C and guess. The answer is **D**.

**Solution 21.** Since the average of all 10 numbers is negative, so is their sum. But the sum of the first 6 is positive, so the sum (and the average) of the others must be negative. Eliminate C, D, and E. **B** is correct.

---

# Practice Exercises

## Discrete Quantitative Questions

1. Evan has 4 times as many books as David and 5 times as many as Jason. If Jason has more than 40 books, what is the least number of books that Evan could have?

   (A) 200    (B) 205    (C) 210    (D) 220    (E) 240

2. Judy plans to visit the National Gallery once each month in 2001 except in July and August when she plans to go three times each. A single admission costs $3.50, a pass valid for unlimited visits in any 3-month period can be purchased for $18, and an annual pass costs $60.00. What is the least amount, in dollars, that Judy can spend for her intended number of visits?

   (A) 72    (B) 60    (C) 56    (D) 49.5    (E) 48

3. Alison is now three times as old as Jeremy, but 5 years ago, she was 5 times as old as he was. How old is Alison now?

   (A) 10    (B) 12    (C) 24    (D) 30    (E) 36

4. What is the largest prime factor of 255?

   (A) 5    (B) 15    (C) 17    (D) 51    (E) 255

5. If $c$ is the product of $a$ and $b$, which of the following is the quotient of $a$ and $b$?

   (A) $\dfrac{b^2}{c}$    (B) $\dfrac{c}{b^2}$    (C) $\dfrac{b}{c^2}$    (D) $\dfrac{c^2}{b}$    (E) $b^2c$

6. If $w$ widgets cost $c$ cents, how many widgets can you get for $d$ dollars?

   (A) $\dfrac{100dw}{c}$    (B) $\dfrac{dw}{100c}$    (C) 100$cdw$

   (D) $\dfrac{dw}{c}$    (E) $cdw$

7. If 120% of $a$ is equal to 80% of $b$, which of the following is equal to $a + b$?

(A) $1.5a$    (B) $2a$    (C) $2.5a$    (D) $3a$    (E) $5a$

8. In the figure at the right, $WXYZ$ is a square whose sides are 12. $AB$, $CD$, $EF$, and $GH$ are each 8, and are the diameters of the four semicircles. What is the area of the shaded region?

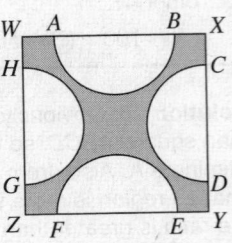

(A) $144 - 128\pi$    (B) $144 - 64\pi$    (C) $144 - 32\pi$
(D) $144 - 16\pi$    (E) $16\pi$

9. If $x$ and $y$ are integers such that $x^3 = y^2$, which of the following could <u>not</u> be the value of $y$?

(A) $-1$    (B) 1    (C) 8    (D) 16    (E) 27

10. What is $a$ divided by $a$% of $a$?

(A) $\dfrac{a}{100}$    (B) $\dfrac{100}{a}$    (C) $\dfrac{a^2}{100}$    (D) $\dfrac{100}{a^2}$
(E) $100a$

11. If an object is moving at a speed of 36 kilometers per hour, how many meters does it travel in one second?

(A) 10    (B) 36    (C) 100    (D) 360    (E) 1000

12. On a certain French-American committee, $\dfrac{2}{3}$ of the members are men, and $\dfrac{3}{8}$ of the men are Americans. If $\dfrac{3}{5}$ of the committee members are French, what fraction of the members are American women?

(A) $\dfrac{3}{20}$    (B) $\dfrac{11}{60}$    (C) $\dfrac{1}{4}$    (D) $\dfrac{2}{5}$    (E) $\dfrac{5}{12}$

13. For what value of $c$ is $8^{2x-4} = 16^{xc}$?

(A) 2    (B) 3    (C) 4    (D) 6    (E) 8

14. If $12a + 3b = 1$ and $7b - 2a = 9$, what is the average (arithmetic mean) of $a$ and $b$?

(A) 0.1    (B) 0.5    (C) 1    (D) 2.5    (E) 5

15. If $x$% of $y$ is 10, what is $y$?

(A) $\dfrac{10}{x}$    (B) $\dfrac{100}{x}$    (C) $\dfrac{1000}{x}$    (D) $\dfrac{x}{100}$    (E) $\dfrac{x}{10}$

## Answer Key

| | | |
|---|---|---|
| 1. **D** | 6. **A** | 11. **A** |
| 2. **D** | 7. **C** | 12. **A** |
| 3. **D** | 8. **C** | 13. **D** |
| 4. **C** | 9. **D** | 14. **B** |
| 5. **B** | 10. **B** | 15. **C** |

## Answer Explanations

Two asterisks (**) indicate an alternative method of solving.

1. **D.** Test the answer choices starting with the smallest value. If Evan had 200 books, Jason would have 40. But Jason has more than 40, so 200 is too small. Trying 205 and 210, we see that neither is a multiple of 4, so David wouldn't have a whole number of books. Finally, 220 works. (So does 240, but we shouldn't even test it since we want the least value.)
   **Since Jason has at least 41 books, Evan has at least 205. But Evan's total must be a multiple of 4 and 5, hence of 20. The smallest multiple of 20 greater than 205 is 220.

2. **D.** Judy intends to go to the Gallery 16 times during the year. Buying a single admission each time would cost $16 \times \$3.50 = \$56$, which is less than the annual pass. If she bought a 3-month pass for June, July, and August, she would pay $18 plus $31.50 for 9 single admissions ($9 \times \$3.50$), for a total expense of $49.50, which is the least expensive option.

3. **D.** Use TACTIC 1: backsolve starting with C. If Alison is now 24, Jeremy is 8, and 5 years ago, they would have been 19 and 3, which is more than 5 times as much. Eliminate A, B, and C, and try a bigger value. If Alison is now 30, Jeremy is 10, and 5 years ago, they would have been 25 and 5. That's it; 25 is 5 times 5.
   **If Jeremy is now $x$, Alison is $3x$, and 5 years ago they were $x - 5$ and $3x - 5$, respectively. Now, solve:
   $$3x - 5 = 5(x - 5) \Rightarrow 3x - 5 = 5x - 25 \Rightarrow$$
   $$2x = 20 \Rightarrow x = 10 \Rightarrow 3x = 30.$$

4. **C.** Test the choices starting with C: 255 *is* divisible by 17 ($255 = 17 \times 15$), so this is a possible answer. Does 255 have a larger prime factor? Neither Choice D nor E is prime, so the answer must be Choice C.

5. **B.** Use TACTIC 2. Pick simple values for $a$, $b$, and $c$. Let $a = 3$, $b = 2$, and $c = 6$. Then $a \div b = 3/2$. Without these values of $a$, $b$, and $c$, only B is equal to 3/2.
   ** $c - ab \Rightarrow a = c/b \Rightarrow a \div b = c/b \div b = c/b \cdot 1/b = c/b^2$.

6. **A.** Use TACTIC 2. If 2 widgets cost 10 cents, then widgets cost 5 cents each, and for 3 dollars, you can get 60. Which of the choices equals 60 when $w = 2$, $c = 10$, and $d = 3$? Only A.
   ** $\dfrac{\text{widgets}}{\text{cents}} = \dfrac{w}{c} = \dfrac{x}{100d} \Rightarrow x = \dfrac{100dw}{c}$.

7. **C.** Since 120% of 80 = 80% of 120, let $a = 80$ and $b = 120$. Then $a + b = 200$, and $200 \div 80 = 2.5$.

8. **C.** If you don't know how to solve this, you must use TACTIC 4 and guess after eliminating the absurd choices. Which choices are absurd? Certainly, A and B, both of which are negative. Also, since Choice D is about 94, which is much more than half the area of the square, it is much too big. Guess between Choice C (about 43) and Choice E (about 50). If you remember that the way to find shaded areas is to subtract, guess C.
   **The area of the square is $12^2 = 144$. The area of each semicircle is $8\pi$, one-half the area of a circle of radius 4. So together the areas of the semicircles is $32\pi$.

9. **D.** Test each choice until you find the correct answer. Could $y = -1$? Is there an integer $x$ such that $x^3 = (-1)^2 = 1$? Yes, $x = 1$. Similarly, if $y = 1$, $x = 1$. Could $y = 8$? Is there an integer $x$ such that $x^3 = (8)^2 = 64$? Yes, $x = 4$. Could $y = 16$? Is there an integer $x$ such that $x^3 = 16^2 = 256$? No, $6^3 = 216$, which is too small; and $7^3 = 343$, which is too big. The answer is D.

10. **B.** $a \div (a\% \text{ of } a) = a \div \left(\dfrac{a}{100} \times a\right) =$
    $$a \div \left(\dfrac{a^2}{100}\right) = a \times \dfrac{100}{a^2} = \dfrac{100}{a}.$$
    **Use TACTICS 2 and 3: replace $a$ by a number, and use 100 since the problem involves percents. $100 \div (100\% \text{ of } 100) = 100 \div 100 = 1$. Test each choice; which one equals 1 when $a = 100$. Both A and B: $\dfrac{100}{100} = 1$. Eliminate Choices C, D, and E, and

test A and B with another value for $a$. $50 \div (50\% \text{ of } 50) = 50 \div (25) = 2$. Now, only B works $\left(\dfrac{100}{50} = 2, \text{whereas } \dfrac{50}{100} = \dfrac{1}{2}\right)$.

11. **A.** Set up a ratio:
    $$\dfrac{\text{distance}}{\text{time}} = \dfrac{36 \text{ kilometers}}{1 \text{ hour}} = \dfrac{36,000 \text{ meters}}{60 \text{ minutes}} =$$
    $$\dfrac{36,000 \text{ meters}}{3600 \text{ seconds}} = 10 \text{ meters/second}.$$
    **Use TACTIC 1: Test choices starting with C:

    100 meters/second = 6000 meters/minute = 360,000 meters/hour = 360 kilometers/hour.

    Not only is that too big, it is too big by a factor of 10. The answer is 10.

12. **A.** Use TACTIC 3. The LCM of all the denominators is 120, so assume that the committee has 120 members. Then there are $\dfrac{2}{3} \times 120 = 80$ men and 40 women. Of the 80 men 30 $\left(\dfrac{3}{8} \times 80\right)$ are American. Since there are 72 $\left(\dfrac{3}{5} \times 120\right)$ French members, there are $120 - 72 = 48$ Americans, of whom 30 are men, so the other 18 are women. Finally, the fraction of American women is $\dfrac{18}{120} = \dfrac{3}{20}$. This is illustrated in the Venn diagram below.

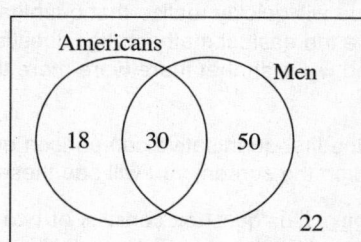

13. **D.** Use the laws of exponents to simplify the equation, and then solve it: $8^{2x-4} = 16^x \Rightarrow (2^3)^{2x-4} = (2^4)^x \Rightarrow 3(2x - 4) = 4x \Rightarrow 6x - 12 = 4x \Rightarrow 2x = 12 \Rightarrow x = 6$.

14. **B.** Add the two equations: $10a + 10b = 10 \Rightarrow a + b = 1 \Rightarrow \dfrac{a+b}{2} = \dfrac{1}{2}$. (Do not waste time solving for $a$ and $b$.)

15. **C.** Pick easy-to-use numbers. Since 100% of 10 is 10, let $x = 100$ and $y = 10$. When $x = 100$, Choices C and E are each 10. Eliminate Choices A, B, and D, and try some other numbers: 50% of 20 is 10. Of Choices C and E, only C = 20 when $x = 50$.

# 13 Quantitative Comparison Questions

- ■ **Tactics**
- ■ **Practice Exercises**
- ■ **Answer Key and Explanations**

---

One half of the 28 questions on the quantitative section of the GRE are quantitative comparisons. It is very likely that the only time you ever encountered questions of this type before was when you were preparing for the PSAT or SAT I, in your junior or senior year of high school. Therefore, it may be at least four years since you last answered a quantitative comparison question. Even if you knew all the various strategies for answering them at the time, and it is likely that you didn't, you are probably no longer familiar with them. In this chapter you will learn all of the necessary tactics. If you master them, you will quickly realize that quantitative comparisons are the easiest mathematics questions on the GRE and will wish that there were more than 14 of them.

Before the first quantitative comparison question appears on the screen, you will see these instructions.

<u>Directions:</u> This question consists of two quantities, one in Column A and one in Column B. You are to compare the two quantities and decide whether

> the quantity in Column A is greater;
> the quantity in Column B is greater;
> the two quantities are equal;
> the relationship cannot be determined from the information given.

<u>Common information:</u> Information concerning one or both of the quantities to be compared is centered above the two columns. A symbol that appears in both columns represents the same thing in Column A as it does in Column B.

Before learning the different strategies for solving this type of question, let's clarify these instructions. In quantitative comparison questions there are two quantities, one in Column A and one in Column B, and it is your job to compare them.

| You should click on the oval in front of | if |
|---|---|
| The quantity in Column A is greater. | The quantity in Column A is greater *all the time, no matter what.* |
| The quantity in Column B is greater. | The quantity in Column B is greater *all the time, no matter what.* |
| The two quantities are equal. | The two quantities are equal *all the time, no matter what.* |
| The relationship cannot be determined from the information given. | *The answer is not one of the first three choices.* |

This means, for example, that *if you can find a single instance* when the quantity in Column A is greater than the quantity in Column B, then you can immediately eliminate two choices: the answer cannot be "The quantity in Column B is greater," and the answer cannot be "The two quantities are equal." In order for the answer to be "The quantity in Column B is greater," the quantity in Column B would have to be greater *all the time*; but you know of one instance when it isn't. Similarly, since the quantities are not equal *all the time*, the answer can't be "The two quantities are equal." The correct answer, therefore, is either "The quantity in Column A is greater" or "The relationship cannot be determined from the information given." If it turns out that the quantity in Column A *is* greater all the time, then that is the answer; if, however, you can find a single instance where the quantity in Column A is not greater, the answer is "The relationship cannot be determined from the information given."

By applying the tactics that you will learn in this chapter, you will probably be able to determine which of the choices is correct; if, however, after eliminating two of the choices, you still cannot determine which answer is correct, quickly guess between the two remaining choices and move on.

---

### Helpful Hint

Right now, memorize the instructions for answering quantitative comparison questions. *When you take the GRE, dismiss the instructions for these questions immediately— do not spend even one second reading the directions (or looking at the sample problems.)*

---

Before learning the most important tactics for handling quantitative comparison questions, let's look at two examples to illustrate the preceding instructions.

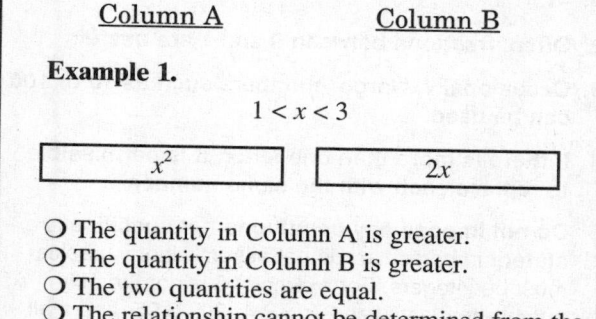

SOLUTION. In each column, $x$ represents the same thing—a number between 1 and 3. If $x$ is 2, then $x^2$ and $2x$ are each 4, and *in this case* the two quantities are equal. We can, therefore, eliminate the first two choices: neither Column A nor Column B is greater *all the time*. However, in order for the correct answer to be "The two quantities are equal," the columns would have to be

equal *all the time*. Are they? Note that although 2 is the only *integer* between 1 and 3, it is not the only *number* between 2 and 3: $x$ could be 1.1 or 2.5 or any of infinitely many other numbers. And in those cases the quantities are not equal (For example, $2.5^2 = 6.25$, whereas $2(2.5) = 5$). The columns are *not* always equal, and so the correct answer is the fourth choice: "The relationship cannot be determined from the information given."

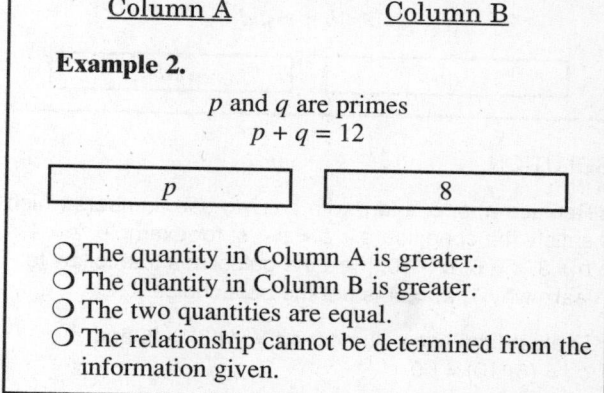

SOLUTION. Since 5 and 7 are the only primes whose sum is 12, $p$ could be 5 or 7. In either case, $p$ is less than 8, and so the quantity in Column B is greater, *all the time*. Note that although $1 + 11 = 12$, p cannot be 11, because 1 is not a prime [See Section 15-A].

NOTE: To simplify the discussion, throughout the rest of this chapter, in the explanations of the answers to all sample questions and the Model Tests, the four answer choices will be referred to as A, B, C, and D, respectively. For example, we will write

The correct answer is **B**.

rather than

The correct answer is "The quantity in Column B is greater."

# Testing Tactics

## Replace Variables with Numbers

Many problems that are hard to analyze because they contain variables become easy to solve when the variables are replaced by simple numbers.

TACTIC 1 is the most important tactic in this chapter. Using it properly will earn you more points on the quantitative comparison questions of the GRE than you can gain by applying any of the others. *Be sure to master it!*

Most quantitative comparison questions contain variables. When those variables are replaced by simple numbers such as 0 or 1, the quantities in the two columns become much easier to compare.

The reason that TACTIC 1 is so important is that it *guarantees* that on any quantitative comparison question that involve variables, you will be able to immediately eliminate two of the four choices, and very often a third choice as well, leaving you with at least a 50% chance of guessing correctly, and often a certainty. Try the following example, and then read the explanation very carefully.

| Column A | Column B |
|---|---|

**Example 3.**

$$a < b < c < d$$

| $ab$ | $cd$ |
|---|---|

SOLUTION.

• Replace $a$, $b$, $c$, and $d$ with easy-to-use numbers which satisfy the condition $a < b < c < d$: for example, $a = 1$, $b = 3$, $c = 6$, $d = 10$. [See the guidelines that follow to learn why 1, 2, 3, 4 is not the best choice.]

• Evaluate the two columns: $ab = (1)(3) = 3$, and $cd = (6)(10) = 60$.

• So *in this case*, the quantity in Column B is greater.

• Does that mean that B is the correct answer? Not necessarily. The quantity in Column B *is* greater this time, but will it be greater **every single time, no matter what**?

• What it does mean is that neither A nor C could possibly be the correct answer: Column A can't be greater **every single time, no matter what** because it isn't greater *this* time; and the quantities aren't equal **every single time, no matter what** because they aren't equal *this* time.

So in the few seconds that it took you to plug in 1, 3, 6, and 10 for $a$, $b$, $c$, and $d$, you were able to eliminate two of the four choices. You now know that the correct answer is either B or D, and if you could do nothing else, you would now guess with a 50% chance of being correct.

But, of course, *you will do something else*. You will try some other numbers. But *which* numbers? Since the first numbers you chose were positive, try some negative numbers this time.

• Let $a = -5$, $b = -3$, $c = -2$, and $d = -1$.

• Evaluate: $ab = (-5)(-3) = 15$ and $cd = (-2)(-1) = 2$.

• So *in this case*, the quantity in Column A is greater.

• Column B is *not* greater all the time. B is *not* the correct answer.

• The correct answer is **D**: The relationship cannot be determined from the information given.

NOTES:

1. If for your second substitution you had chosen 3, 7, 8, 10 or 2, 10, 20, 35 or *any* four positive numbers, Column B would have been bigger. No matter how many substitutions you made, Column B would have been bigger each time, and you would have incorrectly concluded that B was the answer. In fact, if the given condition had been $0 < a < b < c < d$, then B *would have been* the correct answer.

2. Therefore, knowing which numbers to plug in when you are using TACTIC 1 is critical. As long as you comply with the conditions written above the columns, you have complete freedom in choosing the numbers. Some choices, however, are much better than others.

Here are some guidelines for deciding which numbers to use when applying TACTIC 1.

1. **The very best numbers to use first are: 1, 0, and −1.**

2. **Often, fractions between 0 and 1 are useful.**

3. **Occasionally, "large" numbers such as 10 or 100 can be used.**

4. **If there is more than one letter, it is permissible to replace each with the same number.**

5. **Do not impose any conditions not specifically stated.** In particular, do not assume that variables must be integers. For example, 3 is not the only number that satisfies $2 < x < 4$ (2.1, 3.95, and $\pi$ all work). The expression $a < b < c < d$ does not mean that $a$, $b$, $c$, $d$ are *integers*, let alone *consecutive* integers (which is why we didn't choose 1, 2, 3, and 4 in Example 3), nor does it mean that any or all of them are *positive*.

When you replace the variables in a quantitative comparison question with numbers, remember:

| If the value in Column A is ever greater: | eliminate B and C — the answer must be A or D. |
|---|---|
| If the value in Column B is ever greater: | eliminate A and C — the answer must be B or D. |
| If the two columns are ever equal: | eliminate A and B — the answer must be C or D. |

You have learned that, no matter how hard a quantitative comparison is, as soon as you replace the variables, two choices can *immediately* be eliminated; and if you can't decide between the other two, just guess. This guarantees that in addition to correctly answering all the questions that you know how to solve, you will be able to answer correctly at least half, and probably many more, of the questions that you don't know how to do.

Practice applying TACTIC 1 on these examples.

| | Column A | Column B |
|---|---|---|
| | **Example 4.** | |

$m > 0$ and $m \neq 1$

| $m^2$ | $m^3$ |
|---|---|

**Example 5.**

| $13y$ | $15y$ |
|---|---|

**Example 6.**

| $w + 11$ | $w - 11$ |
|---|---|

**Example 7.**

| The perimeter of a rectangle whose area is 18 | The perimeter of a rectangle whose area is 28 |
|---|---|

**Example 8.**

$$a = \frac{2}{3}t \quad b = \frac{5}{6}t \quad c = \frac{3}{5}b$$

| $3a$ | $4c$ |
|---|---|

**SOLUTION 4.** Use TACTIC 1. Replace $m$ with numbers satisfying $m > 0$ and $m \neq 1$.

| | Column A | Column B | Compare | Eliminate |
|---|---|---|---|---|
| Let $m = 2$ | $2^2 = 4$ | $2^3 = 8$ | B is greater | A and C |
| Let $m = \frac{1}{2}$ | $\left(\frac{1}{2}\right)^2 = \frac{1}{4}$ | $\left(\frac{1}{2}\right)^3 = \frac{1}{8}$ | A is greater | B |

The answer is **D**.

**SOLUTION 5.** Use TACTIC 1. There are no restrictions on $y$, so use the best numbers: 1, 0, −1.

| | Column A | Column B | Compare | Eliminate |
|---|---|---|---|---|
| Let $y = 1$ | $13(1) = 13$ | $15(1) = 15$ | B is greater | A and C |
| Let $y = 0$ | $13(0) = 0$ | $15(0) = 0$ | They're equal | B |

The answer is **D**.

**SOLUTION 6.** Use TACTIC 1. There are no restrictions on $w$, so use the best numbers: 1, 0, −1.

| | Column A | Column B | Compare | Eliminate |
|---|---|---|---|---|
| Let $w = 1$ | $1 + 11 = 12$ | $1 - 11 = -10$ | A is greater | B and C |
| Let $w = 0$ | $0 + 11 = 11$ | $0 - 11 = -11$ | A is greater | |
| Let $w = -1$ | $-1 + 11 = 10$ | $-1 - 11 = -12$ | A is greater | |

Guess **A**. We let $w$ be a positive number, a negative number, and 0. Each time, Column A was greater. That's not proof, but it justifies an educated guess. [The answer is A. Clearly, $11 > -11$ and if we add $w$ to each side, we get: $w + 11 > w - 11$.]

**SOLUTION 7.** What's this question doing here? How can we use TACTIC 1? Where are the variables that we're supposed to replace? Well, in each column there are rectangles, and the variables are their lengths and widths.

| Column A | Column B | Compare | Eliminate |
|---|---|---|---|
| Choose a rectangle whose area is 18: | Choose a rectangle whose area is 28: | | |
| The perimeter here is $9 + 2 + 9 + 2$ = **22** | The perimeter here is $7 + 4 + 7 + 4$ = **22** | Columns A and B are equal | A and B |

Keep Column B, but take a different rectangle of area 18 in Column A:

| | | | |
|---|---|---|---|
| Perimeter = $3 + 6 + 3 + 6$ = **18** | Perimeter = **22** | B is greater | C |

The answer is **D**.

**SOLUTION 8.** Use TACTIC 1. First, try the easiest number: let $t = 0$. Then $a$, $b$, and $c$ are each 0, and *in this case*, the columns are equal—they're both 0. Eliminate A and B. Now, try another number for $t$. The obvious choice is 1, but then $a$, $b$, and $c$ will all be fractions. To avoid this, let $t = 6$. Then, $a = \frac{2}{3}(6) = 4$, $b = \frac{5}{6}(6) = 5$, and $c = \frac{3}{5}(5) = 3$. This time, $3a = 3(4) =$ **12** and $4b = 4(3) =$ **12**. *Again, the two columns are equal.* Choose **C**.

NOTE: You should consider answering this question directly (i.e., without plugging in numbers), *only if you* are very comfortable with <u>both</u> *fractions and elementary algebra*. Here's the solution:

$$c = \frac{3}{5}b = \frac{3}{5}\left(\frac{5}{6}t\right) = \frac{1}{2}t$$

Therefore, $2c = t$, and $4c = 2t$. Since $a = \frac{2}{3}t$, $3a = 2t$. So, $4c = 3a$. The answer is **C**.

## Choose an Appropriate Number

This is just like TACTIC 1. We are replacing a variable with a number, but the variable isn't mentioned in the problem.

| Column A | Column B |
|---|---|

**Example 9.**

Every band member is either 15, 16, or 17 years old. One third of the band members are 16, and twice as many band members are 16 as 15.

| The number of 17-year-old band members | The total number of 15- and 16-year-old band members |
|---|---|

If the first sentence of Example 9 had been "There are *n* students in the school band, all of whom are 15, 16, or 17 years old," the problem would have been identical to this one. Using TACTIC 1, you could have replaced *n* with an easy-to-use number, such as 6, and solved: $\frac{1}{3}(6) = 2$ are 16 years old; 1 is 15, and the remaining 3 are 17. The answer is **C**.

The point of TACTIC 2 is that you can plug in numbers even if there are no variables. As discussed in TACTIC 3, chapter 12, this is especially useful on problems involving percents, in which case 100 is a good number, and problems involving fractions, in which case the LCD of the fractions is a good choice. However, the use of TACTIC 2 is not limited to these situations. Try using TACTIC 2 on the following three problems.

| Column A | Column B |
|---|---|

**Example 10.**

The perimeter of a square and the circumference of a circle are equal.

| The area of the circle | The area of the square |
|---|---|

**Example 11.**

Jen, Ken, and Len divided a cash prize.

Jen took 50% of the money and spent $\frac{3}{5}$ of what she took.

Ken took 40% of the money and spent $\frac{3}{4}$ of what he took.

| The amount that Jen spent | The amount that Ken spent |
|---|---|

**Example 12.**

Eliane types twice as fast as Delphine. Delphine charges 50% more per page than Eliane.

| Amount Eliane earns in 9 hours | Amount Delphine earns in 12 hours |
|---|---|

SOLUTION 10. First use TACTIC 1, chapter 11: draw a diagram.

$$C = 2\pi(1) = 2\pi$$
$$A = \pi(1)^2 = \pi \approx 3.14$$

Then use TACTIC 2: choose an easy-to-use number. Let the radius of the circle be 1. Then its area is $\pi$. If $s$ is the side of the square:

$$4s = 2\pi \approx 6 \Rightarrow s \approx 1.5 \Rightarrow$$
$$\text{area of the square} \approx (1.5)^2 = 2.25$$

$$P = 4s$$
$$A = s^2$$

The answer is **A**.

SOLUTION 11. Use TACTIC 2. Assume the prize was $100. Then Jen took $50 and spent $\frac{3}{5}$($50) = $30. Ken took $40 and spent $\frac{3}{4}$($40) = $30. The answer is **C**.

SOLUTION 12. Use TACTIC 2. Choose appropriate numbers. Assume Delphine can type 1 page per hour

and Eliane can type 2. Assume Eliane charges $1.00 per page and Delphine charges $1.50. Then in 9 hours, Eliane types 18 pages, earning **$18.00**. In 12 hours, Delphine types 12 pages, earning 12 × $1.50 = **$18.00**. The answer is **C**.

## Make the Problem Easier: Do the Same Thing to Each Column

A quantitative comparison question can be treated as an equation or an inequality. Either:

Column A < Column B, or
Column A = Column B, or
Column A > Column B

In solving an equation or an inequality, you can always add the same quantity to each side or subtract the same quantity from each side. Similarly, in solving a quantitative comparison, you can always add the same quantity to each column or subtract the same quantity from each column. You can also multiply or divide each side of an equation or inequality by the same quantity, *but in the case of __inequalities__ you can do this only if the quantity is positive*. Since you don't know whether the columns are equal or unequal, you cannot multiply or divide by a variable *unless you know that it is positive*. If the quantities in each column are positive you may square them or take their square roots.

To illustrate the proper use of TACTIC 3, we will give alternate solutions to three of the examples which we already solved using TACTIC 1.

|  | Column A | Column B |
|---|---|---|
| SOLUTION 4. Divide each column by $m^2$ (that's OK—$m^2$ is positive]): | $\dfrac{m^2}{m^2} = 1$ | $\dfrac{m^3}{m^2} = m$ |

This is a much easier comparison. Which is greater, $m$ or 1? We don't know. We know $m > 0$ and $m \neq 1$, but it could be greater than 1 or less than 1. The answer is **D**.

SOLUTION 5. Subtract $13y$ from each column:   $13y - 13y = 0$   $15y - 13y = 2y$

Since there are no restrictions on $y$, $2y$ could be greater than, less than, or equal to 0. The answer is **D**.

SOLUTION 6. Subtract $w$ from each column:

$$\begin{array}{r} w + 11 \\ -\ w \\ \hline 11 \end{array} \qquad \begin{array}{r} w - 11 \\ -\ w \\ \hline -11 \end{array}$$

Clearly, 11 is greater than −11. Column **A** is greater.

Here are five more examples on which to practice TACTIC 3.

| Column A | Column B |
|---|---|
| **Example 4.** | |
| $m > 0$ and $m \neq 1$ | |
| $m^2$ | $m^3$ |
| **Example 5.** | |
| $13y$ | $15y$ |
| **Example 6.** | |
| $w + 11$ | $w - 11$ |

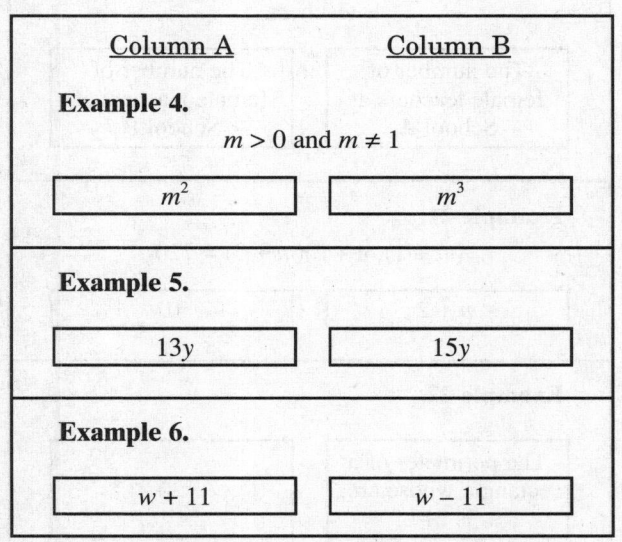

| Column A | Column B |
|---|---|
| **Example 13.** | |
| $\dfrac{1}{3} + \dfrac{1}{4} + \dfrac{1}{9}$ | $\dfrac{1}{9} + \dfrac{1}{3} + \dfrac{1}{5}$ |
| **Example 14.** | |
| $(43 + 59)(17 - 6)$ | $(43 + 59)(17 + 6)$ |
| **Example 15.** | |
| $(43 - 59)(43 - 49)$ | $(43 - 59)(43 + 49)$ |

| Column A | Column B |
|----------|----------|

**Example 16.**

*a* is a negative number

| $a^2$ | $-a^2$ |
|-------|--------|

**Example 17.**

| $\dfrac{\sqrt{20}}{2}$ | $\dfrac{5}{\sqrt{5}}$ |
|-----------------------|------------------------|

| Column A | Column B |
|----------|----------|

SOLUTION 13.
Subtract $\dfrac{1}{3}$ and $\dfrac{1}{9}$
from each column:

$$\cancel{\dfrac{1}{3}} + \dfrac{1}{4} + \cancel{\dfrac{1}{9}} \qquad \cancel{\dfrac{1}{9}} + \cancel{\dfrac{1}{3}} + \dfrac{1}{5}$$

Since $\dfrac{1}{4} > \dfrac{1}{5}$, the answer is **A**.

SOLUTION 14.　　$\cancel{(43 + 59)}(17 - 6)$　$\cancel{(43 + 59)}(17 + 6)$
Divide each
column by
$(43 + 59)$:

Clearly, $(17 + 6) > (17 - 6)$. The answer is **B**.

SOLUTION 15. CAUTION: $(43 - 59)$ is negative, and you *may not* divide the columns by a negative number. The easiest alternative: Column A, being the product of 2 negative numbers, is positive, whereas Column B is negative. Column **A** is greater.

SOLUTION 16.　　$a^2 + a^2 = 2a^2$　　　$-a^2 + a^2 = 0$
Add $a^2$ to each
column:

Since *a* is negative, $2a^2$ is positive. The answer is **A**.

SOLUTION 17.　　$\left(\dfrac{\sqrt{20}}{2}\right)^2 = \dfrac{20}{4} = 5$　$\left(\dfrac{5}{\sqrt{5}}\right)^2 = \dfrac{25}{5} = 5$
Square each
column:

The answer is **C**.

## Tactic 4 — Ask "Could They Be Equal?" and "Must They Be Equal?"

TACTIC 4 has many applications, but is most useful when one of the columns contains a variable and the other contains a number. In this situation ask yourself, "Could they be equal?" If the answer is "yes," eliminate A and B, and then ask, "Must they be equal?" If the second answer is "yes," then C is correct; if the second answer is "no," then choose D. When the answer to "Could they be equal?" is "no," we usually know right away what the correct answer is. In both questions, "Could they be equal" and "Must they be equal," the word *they* refers, of course, to the quantities in Columns A and B.

Let's look at a few examples.

| Column A | Column B |
|----------|----------|

**Example 18.**

The sides of a triangle are 3, 4, and *x*

| *x* | 5 |
|-----|---|

**Example 19.**

$$56 < 5c < 64$$

| *c* | 12 |
|-----|----|

| Column A | Column B |
|----------|----------|

**Example 20.**

School A has 100 teachers and School B has 200 teachers.

Each school has more female teachers than male teachers.

| The number of female teachers at School A | The number of female teachers at School B |
|-------------------------------------------|-------------------------------------------|

**Example 21.**

$$(m + 1)(m + 2)(m + 3) = 720$$

| *m* + 2 | 10 |
|---------|----|

**Example 22.**

| The perimeter of a rectangle whose area is 21 | 20 |
|-----------------------------------------------|----|

SOLUTION 18. Could they be equal? Could $x = 5$? Of course. That's the all-important 3-4-5 right triangle. Eliminate A and B. Must they be equal? Must $x = 5$? If you're not sure, try drawing an acute or an obtuse triangle. The answer is No. Actually, $x$ can be any number satisfying: $1 < x < 7$. (See KEY FACT J12, the triangle inequality, and the figure below.) The answer is **D**.

SOLUTION 19. Could they be equal? Could $c = 12$? If $c = 12$, then $5c = 60$, so, yes, they could be equal. Eliminate A and B. Must they be equal? Must $c = 12$? Could $c$ be more or less than 12? BE CAREFUL: $5 \times 11 = 55$, which is too small; and $5 \times 13 = 65$, which is too big. Therefore, the only *integer* that $c$ could be is 12; but $c$ *doesn't have to be an integer*. The *only* restriction is that $56 < 5c < 64$. If $5c$ were 58 or 61.6 or 63, then $c$ would not be 12. The answer is **D**.

SOLUTION 20. Could they be equal? Could the number of female teachers be the same in both schools? No. More than half (i.e., more than 100) of School B's 200 teachers are female, but School A has only 100 teachers in all. The answer is **B**.

SOLUTION 21. Could they be equal? Could $m + 2 = 10$? No, if $m + 2 = 10$, then $m + 1 = 9$ and $m + 3 = 11$, and $9 \times 10 \times 11 = 990$, which is too big. The answer is *not* C, and since $m + 2$ clearly has to be smaller than 10, the answer is **B**.

SOLUTION 22. Could they be equal? Could a rectangle whose area is 21 have a perimeter of 20? Yes, if its length is 7 and its width is 3: $7 + 3 + 7 + 3 = 20$. Eliminate A and B. Must they be equal? If you're *sure* that there is no other rectangle with an area of 21, then choose C; if you're *not* sure, guess between C and D; if you *know* there are other rectangles of area 21, choose D.

There are other possibilities—lots of them; here are a $7 \times 3$ rectangle and a few others:

## Don't Calculate: Compare

Avoid unnecessary calculations. You don't have to determine the exact values of the quantities in Columns A and B; you just have to compare them.

TACTIC 5 is the special application of TACTIC 7, chapter 11 (Don't do more than you have to) to quantitative comparison questions. The proper use of TACTIC 5 allows you to solve many quantitative comparisons without doing tedious calculations, thereby saving you valuable test time that you can use on other questions. *Before you start calculating,* stop, look at the columns, and ask yourself, "Can I easily and quickly determine which quantity is greater without doing *any* arithmetic?" Consider Examples 23 and 24, which look very similar, but really aren't.

| Column A | Column B |
|---|---|
| **Example 23.** | |
| $37 \times 43$ | $30 \times 53$ |

| Column A | Column B |
|---|---|
| **Example 24.** | |
| $37 \times 43$ | $39 \times 47$ |

Example 23 is very easy. Just multiply: $37 \times 43 = 1591$ and $30 \times 53 = 1590$. The answer is **A**.

Example 24 is even easier. *Don't* multiply. In far less time than it takes to do the multiplications, you can see that $37 < 39$ and $43 < 47$, so clearly $37 \times 43 < 39 \times 47$. The answer is **B**. *You don't get any extra credit for taking the time to determine the value of each product!*

Remember: do not start calculating immediately. Always take a second or two to glance at each column. In Example 23 it's not at all clear which product is larger, so you have to multiply. In Example 24, however, no calculations are necessary.

These are problems on which poor test-takers do a lot of arithmetic and good test-takers think! Practicing TACTIC 5 will help you become a good test-taker.

Now, test your understanding of TACTIC 5 by solving these problems.

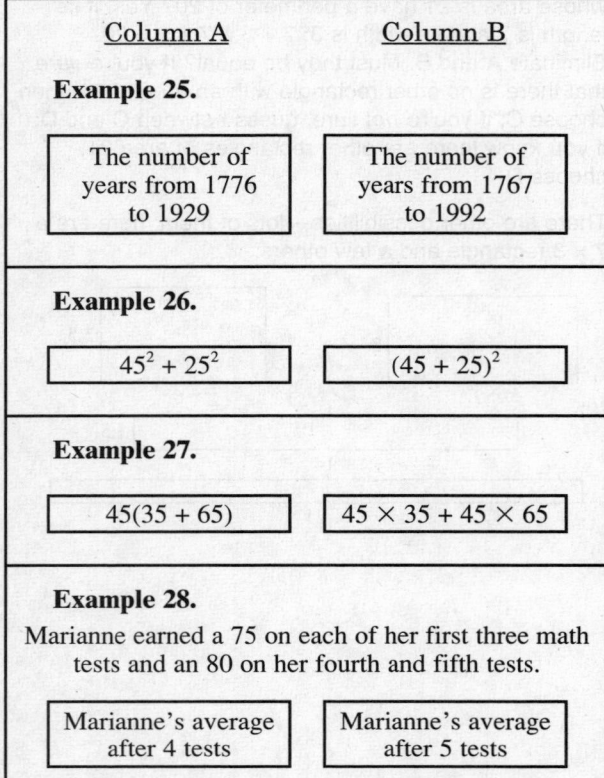

| Column A | Column B |
|---|---|
| **Example 25.** | |
| The number of years from 1776 to 1929 | The number of years from 1767 to 1992 |
| **Example 26.** | |
| $45^2 + 25^2$ | $(45 + 25)^2$ |
| **Example 27.** | |
| $45(35 + 65)$ | $45 \times 35 + 45 \times 65$ |

**Example 28.**
Marianne earned a 75 on each of her first three math tests and an 80 on her fourth and fifth tests.

| Column A | Column B |
|---|---|
| Marianne's average after 4 tests | Marianne's average after 5 tests |

SOLUTIONS 25–28

| Performing the Indicated Calculations | Using TACTIC 5 to Avoid Doing the Calculations |
|---|---|
| 25. Column A: $1929 - 1776 = 153$ Column B: $1992 - 1767 = 225$ The answer is **B**. | 25. The subtraction is easy enough, but why do it? The dates in Column **B** start earlier and end later. Clearly, they span more years. You don't need to know how many years. The answer is **B**. |
| 26. Column A: $45^2 + 25^2 =$ $2025 + 625 = 2650$ Column B: $(45 + 25)^2$ $= 70^2 = 4900$ The answer is **B**. | 26. For *any* positive numbers *a* and *b*: $(a + b)^2 > a^2 + b^2$. You should do the calculations only if you don't know this fact. The answer is **B**. |
| 27. Column A: $45(35 + 65) =$ $45(100) = 4500$ Column B: $45 \times 35 + 45 \times 65 =$ $1575 + 2925 = 4500$ The answer is **C**. | 27. This is just the distributive property (KEY FACT A20), which states that, for *any* numbers *a, b, c*: $a(b + c) = ab + ac$. The answer is **C**. |
| 28. Column A: $\dfrac{75 + 75 + 75 + 80}{4} =$ $\dfrac{305}{4} = 76.25$ Column B: $\dfrac{75 + 75 + 75 + 80 + 80}{5} =$ $\dfrac{385}{5} = 77$ The answer is **B**. | 26. Remember, you want to know which average is higher, *not* what the averages are. After 4 tests Marianne's average is clearly less than 80, so an 80 on the fifth test had to *raise* her average (KEY FACT E4). The answer is **B**. |

CAUTION: TACTIC 5 is important, but *don't spend a lot of time looking for ways to avoid a simple calculation.*

## Know When to Avoid Choice D

If the quantities in Columns A and B are both fixed numbers, the answer cannot be D.

Notice that D was not the correct answer to any of the six examples discussed under TACTIC 5. Those problems had no variables. The quantities in each column were all specific numbers. In each of the next four examples, the quantities in Columns A and B are also fixed numbers. In each case, either the two numbers are equal or one is greater than the other. It can *always* be determined, and so D *cannot* be the correct answer to *any of these problems*. If, while taking the GRE, you find a problem of this type that you can't solve, just guess: A, B, or C. Now try these four examples.

| Column A | Column B |
|---|---|

**Example 29.**

| The number of seconds in one day | The number of days in one century |
|---|---|

**Example 30.**

| The area of a square whose sides are 4 | Twice the area of an equilateral triangle whose sides are 4 |
|---|---|

**Example 31.**

Three fair coins are flipped.

| The probability of getting one head | The probability of getting two heads |
|---|---|

**Example 32.**

| The time it takes to drive 40 miles at 35 mph | The time it takes to drive 35 miles at 40 mph |
|---|---|

Here's the important point to remember: don't choose D because *you* can't determine which quantity is bigger; choose D only if *nobody* could determine it. *You* may or may not know how to compute the number of seconds in a day, the area of an equilateral triangle, or a certain probability, but *these calculations can be made*.

SOLUTIONS 29–32

| Direct Calculation | Solution Using Various TACTICS |
|---|---|
| 29. Recall the facts you need and calculate. 60 seconds = 1 minute, 60 minutes = 1 hour, 24 hours = 1 day, 365 days = 1 year, and 100 years = 1 century. Column A: $60 \times 60 \times 24 = 86,400$ Column B: $365 \times 100 = 36,500$ Even if we throw in some days for leap years, the answer is clearly **A**. | 29. The point of TACTIC 6 is that even if you have no idea how to calculate the number of seconds in a day, you can eliminate two choices. The answer *cannot* be D, and it would be an incredible coincidence if these two quantities were actually equal, so don't choose C. *Guess* between A and B. |

| Direct Calculation | Solution Using Various TACTICS |
|---|---|
| 30. Calculate both areas. (See KEY FACT J15 for the easy way to find the area of an equilateral triangle.) Column A: $A = s^2 = 4^2 = 16$ Column B: $A = \frac{s^2\sqrt{3}}{4} = \frac{4^2\sqrt{3}}{4} = 4\sqrt{3}$; and *twice* A is $8\sqrt{3}$. Since $\sqrt{3} \approx 1.7$, $8\sqrt{3} \approx 13.6$. The answer is **A**. | 30. Use TACTIC 5: don't calculate—compare. Since the height of the triangle is less than 4, its area is less than $\frac{1}{2}(4)(4) = 8$, and twice its area is less than 16, the area of the square.  The answer is **A**. (If you don't see that, and just have to guess in order to move on, be sure not to guess D.) |
| 31. When a coin is flipped 3 times, there are 8 possible outcomes: HHH, HHT, HTH, HTT, THH, THT, TTH, and TTT. Of these, 3 have one head and 3 have two heads. Each probability is $\frac{3}{8}$. The answer is **C**. | 31. Don't forget TACTIC 5. Even if you know how, you don't *have to* calculate the probabilities. When 3 coins are flipped, getting two heads means getting one tail. Therefore, the probability of two heads equals the probability of one tail, which by symmetry equals the probability of one head. The answer is **C**. (If you don't remember anything about probability, TACTIC 6 at least allows you to eliminate D before you guess.) |
| 32. Since $d = rt$, $t = \frac{d}{r}$ [see Sect. 12-H]. Column A: $\frac{40}{35}$ hours—more than 1 hour. Column B: $\frac{35}{40}$ hours—less than 1 hour. The answer is **A**. | 32. You *do* need to know these formulas, but *not* for this problem. At 35 mph it takes *more than an hour* to drive 40 miles. At 40 mph it takes *less than an hour* to drive 35 miles. Choose **A**. |

# Practice Exercises

## Quantitative Comparison Questions

| Column A | Column B |
|---|---|
| **1.** $197 + 398 + 586$ | $203 + 405 + 607$ |

$x > 0$

| Column A | Column B |
|---|---|
| **2.** $10x$ | $\dfrac{10}{x}$ |

| Column A | Column B |
|---|---|
| **3.** The time that it takes to type 7 pages at a rate of 6 pages per hour | The time that it takes to type 6 pages at a rate of 7 pages per hour |

$cd < 0$

| Column A | Column B |
|---|---|
| **4.** $(c + d)^2$ | $c^2 + d^2$ |

$a$, $b$, and $c$ are the measures of the angles of isosceles triangle $ABC$
$x$, $y$, and $z$ are the measures of the angles of right triangle $XYZ$

| Column A | Column B |
|---|---|
| **5.** The average of $a$, $b$, and $c$ | The average of $x$, $y$, and $z$ |

$b < 0$

| Column A | Column B |
|---|---|
| **6.** $6b$ | $b^6$ |

| Column A | Column B |
|---|---|
| **7.** The area of a circle whose radius is 17 | The area of a circle whose diameter is 35 |

Line $k$ goes through $(1,1)$ and $(5,2)$.
Line $m$ is perpendicular to $k$.

| Column A | Column B |
|---|---|
| **8.** The slope of line $k$ | The slope of line $m$ |

$x$ is a positive integer

| Column A | Column B |
|---|---|
| **9.** The number of multiples of 6 between 100 and $x + 100$ | The number of multiples of 9 between 100 and $x + 100$ |

**Column A**        **Column B**

$x + y = 5$
$y - x = -5$

| Column A | Column B |
|---|---|
| **10.** $y$ | $0$ |

| Column A | Column B |
|---|---|
| **11.** $\dfrac{7}{8}$ | $\left(\dfrac{7}{8}\right)^5$ |

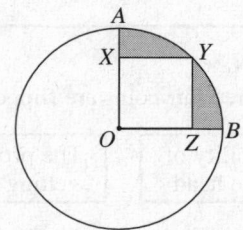

$O$ is the center of the circle of radius 6.
$OXYZ$ is a square.

| Column A | Column B |
|---|---|
| **12.** The area of the shaded region | $12$ |

The number of square inches in the surface area of a cube is equal to the number of cubic inches in its volume.

| Column A | Column B |
|---|---|
| **13.** The length of an edge of the cube | 6 inches |

$1 < x < 4$

| Column A | Column B |
|---|---|
| **14.** $\pi x$ | $x^2$ |

$AB = AC$

| Column A | Column B |
|---|---|
| **15.** The area of $\triangle ABC$ | $3$ |

# Answer Key

| | | |
|---|---|---|
| 1. **B** | 6. **B** | 11. **A** |
| 2. **D** | 7. **B** | 12. **B** |
| 3. **A** | 8. **A** | 13. **C** |
| 4. **B** | 9. **D** | 14. **D** |
| 5. **C** | 10. **C** | 15. **D** |

# Answer Explanations

The direct mathematical solution to a problem is almost always the preferable one, so it is given first. It is often followed by one or more alternate solutions, indicated by a double asterisk, based on the various tactics discussed in this chapter. Occasionally, a solution based on one of the tactics is much easier than the straightforward one. In that case, it is given first.

1. **B.** This can easily be solved in less than a minute by adding, but in only 5 seconds by thinking! Use TACTIC 5: don't calculate; compare. Each of the three numbers in Column B is greater than the corresponding number in Column A.

2. **D.** Use TACTIC 1. When $x = 1$, the columns are equal; when $x = 2$, they aren't.
   **Use TACTIC 3

   | | Column A | Column B |
   |---|---|---|
   | | $10x$ | $\dfrac{10}{x}$ |

   Multiply each column by $x$ (this is OK since $x > 0$):    $10x^2$    $10$

   Divide each column by 10:    $x^2$    $1$

   This is a much easier comparison. $x^2$ *could* equal 1, but doesn't have to. The answer is Choice D.

3. **A.** You can easily calculate each of the times—by dividing 7 by 6 in Column A, and 6 by 7 in Column B. However, it is easier to just observe that the time in Column A is more than one hour, whereas the time in Column B is less than one hour.

4. **B.** Use TACTIC 3

   | | Column A | Column B |
   |---|---|---|
   | Expand Column A: | $(c + d)^2 =$ | |
   | | $c^2 + 2cd + d^2$ | $c^2 + d^2$ |
   | Subtract $c^2 + d^2$ from each column: | $2cd$ | $0$ |

   Since it is given that $cd < 0$, so is $2cd$.
   **If you can't expand $(c + d)^2$, use TACTIC 1. Replace $c$ and $d$ with numbers satisfying $cd < 0$.

| | Column A | Column B | Compare | Eliminate |
|---|---|---|---|---|
| Let $c = 1$ and $d = -1$ | $(1 + -1)^2 =$ $0$ | $1^2 + (-1)^2 =$ $1 + 1 = 2$ | B is greater | A and C |
| Let $c = 3$ and $d = -5$ | $(3 + -5)^2 =$ $(-2)^2 = 4$ | $3^2 + (-5)^2 =$ $9 + 25 = 34$ | B is greater | |

Both times Column B was greater: choose B.

5. **C.** The average of 3 numbers is their sum divided by 3. Since in *any* triangle the sum of the measures of the 3 angles is 180° [KEY FACT J1], the average in each column is equal to $180 \div 3 = 60$.
   **Use TACTIC 1. Pick values for the measures of the angles. For example, in isosceles $\triangle ABC$ choose 70, 70, 40; in right $\triangle XYZ$, choose 30, 60, 90. Each average is 60. Choose C.

6. **B.** Since $b < 0$, $6b$ is negative, whereas $b^6$ is positive.
   **Use TACTIC 1. Replace $b$ with numbers satisfying $b < 0$.

| | Column A | Column B | Compare | Eliminate |
|---|---|---|---|---|
| Let $b = -1$ | $6(-1) = -6$ | $(-1)^6 = 1$ | B is greater | B and C |
| Let $b = -2$ | $6(-2) = -12$ | $(-2)^6 = 64$ | B is greater | |

Both times Column B was greater: choose B.

7. **B.** Again, use TACTIC 5: don't calculate the two areas; compare them. The circle in Column A has a radius of 17, and so its diameter is 34. Since the circle in Column B has a larger diameter, its area is greater.

8. **A.** Again, use TACTIC 5: don't calculate either slope. Quickly, make a rough sketch of line $k$, going through $(1,1)$ and $(5,2)$, and draw line $m$ perpendicular to it. Line $k$ has a positive slope (it slopes upward), whereas line $m$ has a negative slope. [Note: the slope of $k$ is $\dfrac{1}{4}$ and the slope of $m$ is $-4$. See Section 15-N for all the facts you need to know about slopes.]

**If you don't know this fact about slopes, use TACTIC 6. The answer cannot be Choice D, and if two lines intersect, their slopes cannot be equal, so eliminate Choice C. Guess Choices A or B.

9. D. Every sixth integer is a multiple of 6 and every ninth integer is a multiple of 9, so in a large interval there will be many more multiples of 6. But in a very small interval, there might be none or possibly just one of each. **Use TACTIC 1. Let $x = 1$. Between 100 and 101 there are *no* multiples of 6 and *no* multiples of 9. Eliminate Choices A and B. Choose a large number for $x$: 100, for example. Between 100 and 200 there are many more multiples of 6 than there are of 9. Eliminate Choice C.

10. C. add the equations.

$$\begin{array}{r} x + y = 5 \\ + \; y - x = -5 \\ \hline 2y = 0 \end{array}$$

Since $2y = 0$, $y = 0$.
**Use TACTIC 4. Could $y = 0$? In each equation, if $y = 0$, then $x = -5$. So, $y$ can equal 0. Eliminate Choices A and B, and either guess between Choices C and D or try to continue. Must $y = 0$? Yes, when you have two equations in two variables, there is only one solution, so nothing else is possible.

11. A. The arithmetic is annoying and time-consuming, but not difficult. However, you can avoid the arithmetic, if you know KEY FACT A24:
If $0 < x < 1$ and $n > 1$, then $x^n < x$. $\frac{7}{8}$ *is less*
than 1, so $\left(\frac{7}{8}\right)^5 < \frac{7}{8}$.

12. B. The area of the shaded region is the area of quarter-circle *AOB* minus the area of the square. Since $r = OA = 6$, the area of the quarter-circle is $\frac{1}{4}\pi r^2 = \frac{1}{4} 36\pi = 9\pi$. *OY*, the diagonal of the square, is 6 (since it is a radius of the circle), so *OZ*, the side of the square, is $\frac{6}{\sqrt{2}}$ [KEY FACT J8]. So the area of the square is $\left(\frac{6}{\sqrt{2}}\right)^2 = \frac{36}{2} = 18$. Finally, the area of the shaded region is $9\pi - 18$, which is approximately 10.
**The solution above requires several steps. [See Sections 12-J, K, L to review any of the facts used.] If you can't reason through this, you still should be able to answer this question correctly. Use TACTIC 8 in chapter 2. The shaded region has a definite area, which is either 12, more than 12, or less than 12. Eliminate D. Also, the area of a curved region almost always involves $\pi$, so assume the area isn't exactly 12. Eliminate Choice C. You can now *guess* between Choices A and B, but if you trust the diagram and know a little bit you can improve your guess. If you know that the

area of the circle is $36\pi$, so that the quarter-circle is $9\pi$ or about 28, you can estimate the shaded region. It's well less than half of the quarter-circle, so less than 14 and probably less than 12. Guess Choice B.

13. C. Use TACTIC 4. Could the edge be 6? Test it. If each edge is 6, the area of each face is $6 \times 6 = 36$, and since a cube has 6 faces, the total surface area is $6 \times 36 = 216$. The volume is $6^3 = 216$. So the columns could be equal. Eliminate Choices A and B. If you have a sense that this is the only cube with this property, choose C. In fact, if you had no idea how to do this, you might use TACTIC 6, assume that there is only one way, eliminate Choice D, and then guess C. The direct solution is simple enough if you know the formulas. The area is $6e^2$ and the volume is $e^3$: $6e^2 = e^3 \Rightarrow 6 = e$.

14. D. There are several ways to do this. Use TACTIC 1: plug in a number for $x$. If $x = 2$, Column A is $2\pi$, which is slightly more than 6, and Column B is $2^2 = 4$. Column A is greater: eliminate Choices B and C. Must Column A be greater? If the only other number you try is $x = 3$, you'll think so, because $3^2 = 9$, but $3\pi > 9$. But remember, $x$ does not have to be an integer: $3.9^2 > 15$, whereas $3.9\pi < 4\pi$, which is a little over 12. **Use TACTIC 4. Could $\pi x = x^2$? Yes, if $x = \pi$. Must $x = \pi$? No.
**Use TACTIC 3. Divide each side by $x$: Now Column A is $\pi$ and Column B is $x$. Which is bigger, $\pi$ or $x$? We cannot tell.

15. D. Use TACTIC 4. Could the area of $\triangle ABC = 3$? Since the height is 6, the area would be 3 only if the base were 1: $\frac{1}{2}(1)(6) = 3$. Could $BC = 1$? Sure (see the figure). Must the base be 1? Of course not.

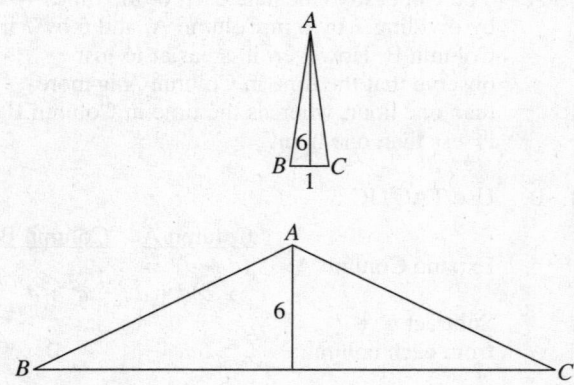

# 14 Data Interpretation Questions

- ■ **Tactics**
- ■ **Practice Exercises**
- ■ **Answer Key and Explanations**

Four of the 28 questions in the quantitative section are data interpretation questions. As their name suggests, these questions are always based on the information that is presented in some form of a graph or a chart. Occasionally, the data are presented in a chart or table, but much more often, they are presented graphically. The most common types of graphs are

- line graphs    • bar graphs    • circle graphs

Data interpretation questions always appear in two sets of two questions each. For example, questions 14 and 15 might refer to a particular set of graphs or charts, and then later there will be two more questions, say numbers 22 and 23, which refer to a completely different set of graphs and charts.

When the first data interpretation question appears, one or more graphs will be on the left-hand side of the screen, and the question will be on the right-hand side. It is possible that you will have to scroll down in order to see all of the data. After you confirm your answer to the

first question, the second question will replace it on the right-hand side of the screen; the graphs, of course, will still be on the left-hand side for you to refer to.

The tactics discussed in this chapter can be applied to any type of data, no matter how they are displayed. In the practice exercises at the end of the chapter, there are data interpretation questions based on every type of graph that could appear on the GRE. Carefully, read through the answer explanations for each exercise, so that you learn the best way to handle each type of graph.

Infrequently, an easy data interpretation question will require only that you read the graph and find a numerical fact that is displayed. Usually, however, you will have to do some calculation on the data that you are analyzing. In harder questions, you may be given hypothetical situations and asked to make inferences based on the information provided in the given graphs.

## Testing Tactics

The four questions that follow will be used to illustrate the tactics that you should use in answering data interpretation questions. Remember, however, that on the

GRE there will always be exactly two questions that refer to a particular graph or set of graphs.

<u>Questions 1–4</u> refer to the following graphs.

Sales and Earnings of
XYZ Corporation 1991–1998

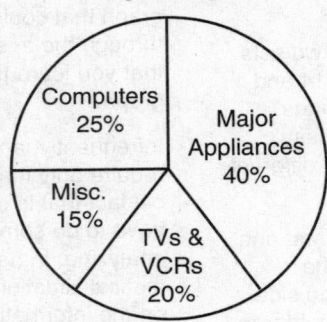

1998 Sales of XYZ Corporation
by Category

1. What is the average (arithmetic mean) in billions of dollars of the sales of XYZ Corporation for the period 1991–1998?

   (A) 5.5   (B) 6.0   (C) 7.0   (D) 8.0   (E) 8.5

2. For which year was the percentage increase in earnings from the previous year the greatest?

   (A) 1992   (B) 1993   (C) 1994
       (D) 1995   (E) 1996

3. Which of the following statements can be deduced from the data in the given charts and circle graph?

   I. Sales of major appliances in 1998 exceeded total sales in 1991.
   II. Earnings for the year in which earnings were greatest were more than sales for the year in which sales were lowest.
   III. If in 1998, the sales of major appliances had been 10% less, and the sales of computers had been 10% greater, the sales of major appliances would have been less than the sales of computers.

   (A) None   (B) I only   (C) III only
       (D) I and III only   (E) I, II, and III

4. What was the ratio of earnings to sales in 1993?

   (A) $\frac{1}{40}$   (B) $\frac{1}{25}$   (C) $\frac{1}{4}$   (D) $\frac{25}{1}$   (E) $\frac{40}{1}$

# First Read the Titles

When the first data interpretation question appears on the screen, do not even read it! Before you attempt to answer a data interpretation question, take 15 or 30 seconds to study the graphs. Try to get a general idea about the information that is being displayed.

Observe that the bar graphs on which questions 1–4 are based present two different sets of data. The bar graph

on the left-hand side provides information about the sales of XYZ Corporation, and the right-hand graph provides information about the corporation's earnings. Also, note that whereas sales are given in billions of dollars, earnings are given in millions of dollars. Finally, the circle graph gives a breakdown by category of the sales of XYZ Corporation for one particular year.

# Don't Confuse Percents and Numbers

Many students make mistakes on data interpretation questions because they don't distinguish between absolute numbers and percents. Although few students would look at the circle graph shown and think that XYZ Corporation sold 25 computers in 1998, many would mistakenly think that it sold 15% more major appliances than computers.

The problem is particularly serious when the questions involve percent increases or percent decreases. In question 2 you are not asked for the year in which the increase in earnings from the previous year was the greatest. You are asked for the year in which the per-

cent increase in earnings was the greatest. A quick glance at the right-hand graph reveals that the greatest increase occurred from 1991 to 1992 when earnings jumped by $400 million. However, when we solve this problem in the discussion of TACTIC 3, you will see that Choice A is not the correct answer.

NOTE: Since many data interpretation questions involve percents, you should carefully study Section 15-C, and be sure that you know all of the tactics for solving percent problems. In particular, always try to use the number 100 or 1000, since it is so easy to mentally calculate percents of powers of 10.

# Whenever Possible, Estimate

Since you are not allowed to have a calculator when you take the GRE, you will not be expected to do complicated or lengthy calculations. Often, thinking and using some common sense can save you considerable time. For example, it may seem that in order to get the correct answer to question 2, you have to calculate five different percents. In fact, you only need to do one calculation, and that one you can do in your head!

Just looking at the Earnings bar graph, it is clear that the only possible answers are 1992, 1994, and 1995,

the three years in which there was a significant increase in earnings from the year before. From 1993 to 1994 expenditures doubled, from $200 million to $400 million—an increase of 100%. From 1991 to 1992 expenditures increased by $400 million (from $500 million to $900 million), but that is less than a 100% increase (we don't care how much less). From 1994 to 1995 expenditures increased by $300 million (from $400 million to $700 million); but again, this is less than a 100% increase. The answer is C.

## Do Each Calculation Separately

As in all Roman numeral questions, question 3 requires you to determine which of three separate statements is true. The key is to work with the statements individually.

To determine whether or not statement I is true, look at both the Sales bar graph and the circle graph. In 1998, total sales were $10 billion, and sales of major appliances accounted for 40% of the total: 40% of $10 billion = $4 billion. This exceeds the $3 billion total sales figure for 1991, so statement I is true.

In 1992, the year in which earnings were greatest, earnings were $900 million. In 1991, the year in which sales

were lowest, sales were $3 billion, which is much greater than $900 million. Statement II is false.

In 1998, sales of major appliances were $4 billion. If they had been 10% less, they would have been $3.6 billion. That year, sales of computers were $2.5 billion (25% of $10 billion). If computer sales had increased by 10%, sales would have been $2.75 billion. Statement III is false.

The answer is **B**: only statement I is true.

## Use Only the Information Given

You must base your answer to each question only on the information in the given charts and graphs. It is unlikely that you have any preconceived notion as to the sales of XYZ Corporation, but you might think that you know the population of the United States for a particular year or the percent of women currently in the workplace.

If your knowledge contradicts any of the data presented in the graphs, ignore what you know. First of all, you may be mistaken; but more important, the data may refer to a different, unspecified location or year. In any event, *always* base your answers on the given data.

## Always Use the Proper Units

In answering question 4, observe that earnings are given in millions, while sales are in billions. If you answer too quickly, you might say that in 1993 earnings were 200 and sales were 8, and conclude that the desired ratio is $\frac{200}{8} = \frac{25}{1}$. You will avoid this mistake if you keep track

of units: earnings were 200 *million* dollars, whereas sales were 8 *billion* dollars. The correct ratio is

$$\frac{200,000,000}{8,000,000,000} = \frac{2}{80} = \frac{1}{40}.$$

The answer is **A**.

## Be Sure That Your Answer Is Reasonable

Before confirming your answer, take a second to be sure that it is reasonable. For example, in question 4,

Choices D and E are unreasonable. From the logic of the situation, you should realize that earnings can't exceed sales. The desired ratio, therefore, must be less than 1. If you use the wrong units (see TACTIC 6, above), your initial thought would be to choose D. By testing your answer for reasonableness, you will realize that you made a mistake.

Remember that if you don't know how to solve a problem, you must guess in order to move on. Before guess-

ing, however, check to see if one or more of the choices are unreasonable. If so, eliminate them. For example, if you forget how to calculate a percent increase, you would have to guess at question 2. But before guessing wildly, you should at least eliminate Choice B, since from 1992 to 1993 earnings decreased.

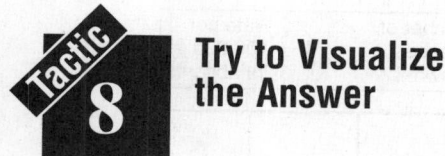

## Try to Visualize the Answer

Because graphs and tables present data in a form that enables you to readily see relationships and to make quick comparisons, you can often avoid doing any calculations. Whenever possible, use your eye instead of your computational skills.

For example, to answer question 1, rather than reading the sales figures in the bar graph on the left for each of the eight years, adding them, and then dividing by 8,

visualize the situation. Where could you draw a horizontal line across the graph so that there would be the same amount of gray area above the line as white area below it? Imagine a horizontal line drawn through the 7 on the vertical axis. The portions of the bars above the line for 1993 and 1996–1998 are just about exactly the same size as the white areas below the line for 1991, 1992, and 1994. The answer is **C**.

# Practice Exercises

## Data Interpretation Questions

On the GRE there will always be exactly two questions based on any set of graphs. Accordingly, in all the model tests in this book, there are two pairs of data

interpretation questions, each pair referring to a different set of graphs. However, to illustrate the variety of questions that can be asked, in this exercise set, for some of the graphs there is only one question and for some there are three questions.

**Questions 1–2** refer to the following graphs.

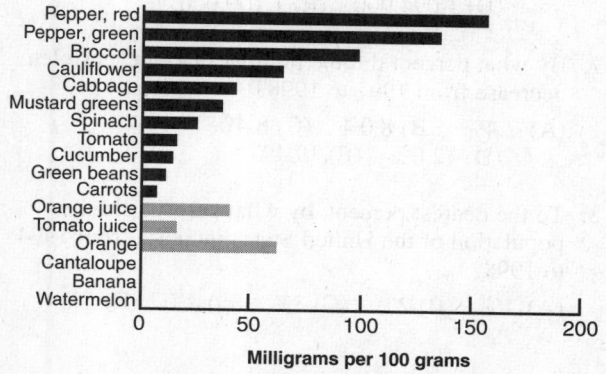

*Source: U.S. Department of Agriculture.*

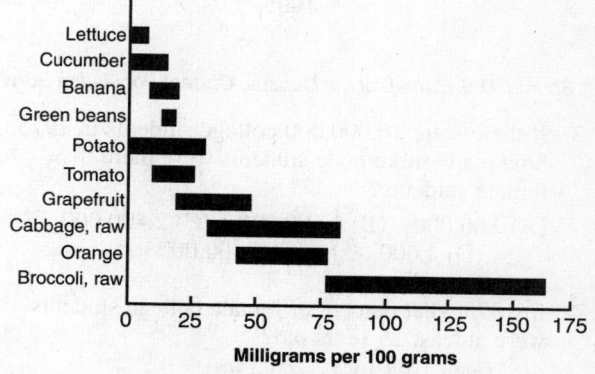

*Source: U.S. Department of Agriculture.*

1. What is the ratio of the amount of Vitamin C in 500 grams of orange to the amount of Vitamin C in 500 grams of orange juice?

   (A) 4:7   (B) 1:1   (C) 7:4   (D) 2:1   (E) 4:1

2. How many grams of tomato would you have to eat to be certain of getting more vitamin C than you would get by eating 100 grams of raw broccoli?

   (A) 300   (B) 500   (C) 750   (D) 1200   (E) 1650

**Questions 3–5 refer to the following graphs.**

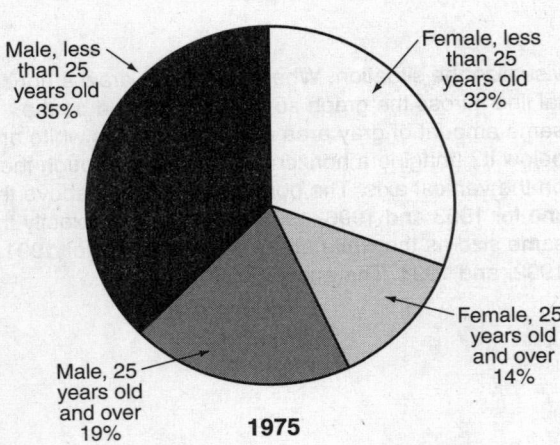

### College Enrollment, by Age and Sex: 1975 and 1995

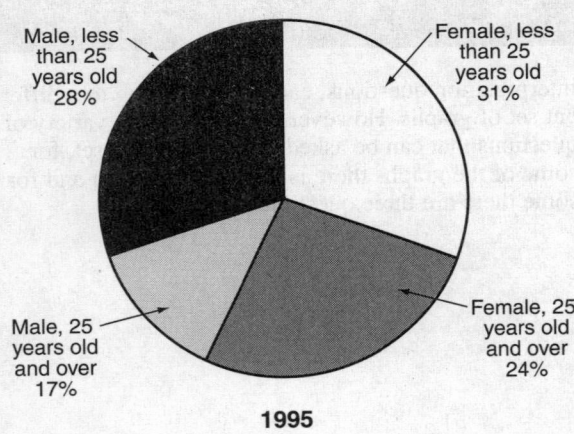

Source: U.S. Bureau of the Census, Current Population Surve

3. If there were 10,000,000 college students in 1975, how many more male students were there than female students?

   (A) 800,000   (B) 1,600,000   (C) 2,400,000
   (D) 4,600,000   (E) 5,400,000

4. In 1975 what percent of female college students were at least 25 years old?

   (A) 14%   (B) 30%   (C) 45%
   (D) 69%   (E) 76%

5. If the total number of students enrolled in college was 40% higher in 1995 than in 1975, what is the ratio of the number of male students in 1995 to the number of male students in 1975?

   (A) 5:6   (B) 6:7   (C) 7:6   (D) 6:5   (E) 7:5

**Questions 6–8 refer to the following graph.**

### Motor Vehicle Theft in the U.S. Percent Change from 1994 to 1998

Source: U.S. Department of Justice, Federal Bureau of Investigation.

6. If 1,000,000 vehicles were stolen in 1994, how many were stolen in 1996?

   (A) 889,000   (B) 906,000   (C) 940,000
   (D) 1,094,000   (E) 1,100,000

7. By what percent did the number of vehicles stolen decrease from 1997 to 1998?

   (A) 7.4%   (B) 8.0%   (C) 8.4%
   (D) 12.0%   (E) 19.4%

8. To the nearest percent, by what percent did the population of the United States increase from 1994 to 1998?

   (A) 1%   (B) 2%   (C) 3%   (D) 4%   (E) 5%

**Questions 9–10** refer to the following graph.

**Perceptions of Body Weight Status**

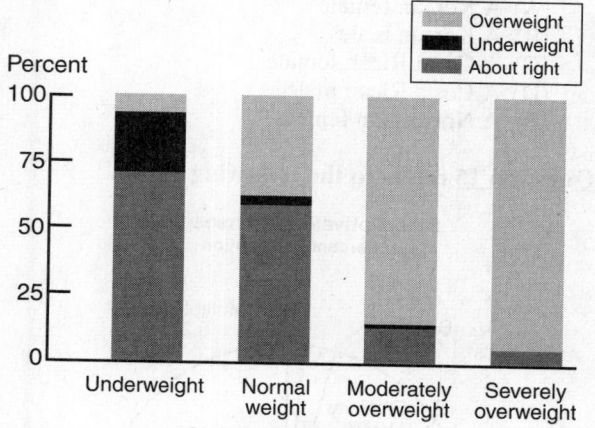

Legend: Overweight / Underweight / About right

Percent axis: 100, 75, 50, 25, 0

Actual weight status: Underweight, Normal weight, Moderately overweight, Severely overweight

**Actual weight status**

Perceived compared with actual weight status of adult females.

*Source: U.S. Department of Agriculture.*

9. What percent of underweight adult females perceive themselves to be underweight?

(A) 5%  (B) 22%  (C) 38%  (D) 50%  (E) 70%

10. The members of which of the four groups had the least accurate perception of their body weight?

(A) Underweight

(B) Normal weight
(C) Moderately overweight
(D) Severely overweight
(E) It cannot be determined from the information given in the graph.

**Questions 11–12** refer to the tables at the bottom of the page.

Residents of New York City pay both New York State and New York City tax.

Residents of New York State who live and work outside of New York City pay only New York State tax.

11. In 1979 how much tax would a resident of New York State who lived and worked outside New York City have paid on a taxable income of $16,100?

(A) $34  (B) $110  (C) $352  (D) $970  (E) $1322

12. In 1979, how much more total tax would a resident of New York City who had a taxable income of $36,500 pay, compared to a resident of New York City who had a taxable income of $36,000?

(A) $21.50  (B) $43  (C) $70  (D) $91.50  (E) $183

## Tax Rate Schedules for 1979

### New York State

| Taxable Income over | but not over | Amount of Tax | | | |
|---|---|---|---|---|---|
| $ 0 | $1,000 | | 2% | of taxable income | |
| 1,000 | 3,000 | $20 | plus | 3% of excess over | $1,000 |
| 3,000 | 5,000 | 80 | plus | 4% of excess over | 3,000 |
| 5,000 | 7,000 | 160 | plus | 5% of excess over | 5,000 |
| 7,000 | 9,000 | 260 | plus | 6% of excess over | 7,000 |
| 9,000 | 11,000 | 380 | plus | 7% of excess over | 9,000 |
| 11,000 | 13,000 | 520 | plus | 8% of excess over | 11,000 |
| 13,000 | 15,000 | 680 | plus | 9% of excess over | 13,000 |
| 15,000 | 17,000 | 860 | plus | 10% of excess over | 15,000 |
| 17,000 | 19,000 | 1,060 | plus | 11% of excess over | 17,000 |
| 19,000 | 21,000 | 1,280 | plus | 12% of excess over | 19,000 |
| 21,000 | 23,000 | 1,520 | plus | 13% of excess over | 21,000 |
| 23,000 | | 1,780 | plus | 14% of excess over | 23,000 |

### City of New York

| Taxable Income over | but not over | Amount of Tax | | | |
|---|---|---|---|---|---|
| $ 0 | $1,000 | | 0.9% | of taxable income | |
| 1,000 | 3,000 | $ 9 | plus | 1.4% of excess over | $1,000 |
| 3,000 | 5,000 | 37 | plus | 1.8% of excess over | 3,000 |
| 5,000 | 7,000 | 73 | plus | 2.0% of excess over | 5,000 |
| 7,000 | 9,000 | 113 | plus | 2.3% of excess over | 7,000 |
| 9,000 | 11,000 | 159 | plus | 2.5% of excess over | 9,000 |
| 11,000 | 13,000 | 209 | plus | 2.7% of excess over | 11,000 |
| 13,000 | 15,000 | 263 | plus | 2.9% of excess over | 13,000 |
| 15,000 | 17,000 | 321 | plus | 3.1% of excess over | 15,000 |
| 17,000 | 19,000 | 383 | plus | 3.3% of excess over | 17,000 |
| 19,000 | 21,000 | 449 | plus | 3.5% of excess over | 19,000 |
| 21,000 | 23,000 | 519 | plus | 3.8% of excess over | 21,000 |
| 23,000 | 25,000 | 595 | plus | 4.0% of excess over | 23,000 |
| 25,000 | | 675 | plus | 4.3% of excess over | 25,000 |

**Questions 13–14** refer to the following tables.

**Years of Life Expectancy at Birth**
**(Life expectancy in years)**

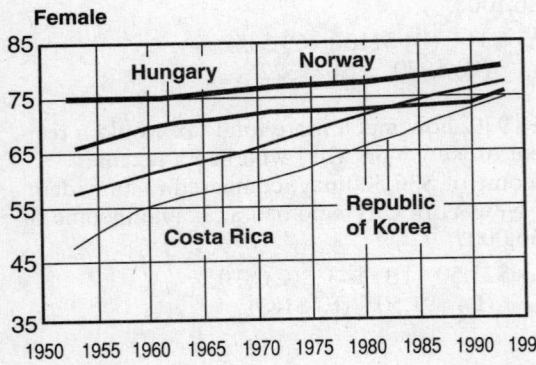

*Source: U.S. Bureau of the Census,*
*Center for International Research.*

13. For how many of the countries listed in the graphs is it true that the life expectancy of a female born in 1955 was higher than the life expectancy of a male born in 1990?

(A) None   (B) 1   (C) 2   (D) 3   (E) 4

14. By sex and nationality, who had the greatest increase in life expectancy between 1955 and 1990?

(A) A Korean female
(B) A Korean male
(C) A Costa Rican female
(D) A Costa Rican male
(E) A Norwegian female

**Question 15** refers to the following graph.

**Bias-Motivated Offenses 1998**
**Percent Distribution**

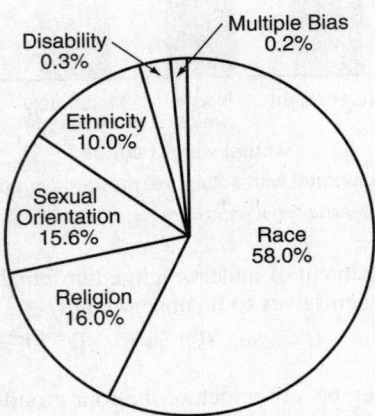

*Source: U.S. Department of Justice,*
*Federal Bureau of Investigation.*

15. If in 1998 there were 10,000 bias-motivated offenses based on ethnicity, how many more offenses were based on religion than on sexual orientation?

(A) 4   (B) 40   (C) 400   (D) 4000   (E) 40,000

# Answer Key

| | | |
|---|---|---|
| 1. C | 6. B | 11. D |
| 2. E | 7. C | 12. D |
| 3. A | 8. D | 13. B |
| 4. B | 9. B | 14. A |
| 5. C | 10. A | 15. C |

# Answer Explanations

1. **C.** According to the graph on the left, there are approximately 70 milligrams of vitamin C in 100 grams of orange and 40 milligrams in the same amount of orange juice. This is a ratio of 70:40 = 7:4. Since the question refers to the same amount of orange and orange juice (500 grams), the ratio is unchanged.

2. **E.** From the graph on the right, you can see that by eating 100 grams of raw broccoli, you could receive as much as 165 milligrams of vitamin C. Since 100 grams of tomato could have as little as 10 milligrams of vitamin C, you would have to eat 1650 grams of tomato to be sure of getting 165 milligrams of vitamin C.

3. **A.** From the top graph, we see that in 1975, 54% (35% + 19%) of all college students were male, and the other 46% were female. So there

were 5,400,000 males and 4,600,000 females—a difference of 800,000.

4. B. In 1975, of every 100 college students, 46 were female—32 of whom were less than 25 years old, and 14 of whom were 25 years old and over. So, 14 of every 46 female students were at least 25 years old. Finally, $\frac{14}{46} = .30 = 30\%$.

5. C. From the two graphs, we see that in 1975 54% (35% + 19%) of all college students were male, whereas in 1995 the corresponding figure was 45% (28% + 17%). For simplicity, assume that there were 100 college students in 1975, 54 of whom were male. Then in 1995, there were 140 college students, 63 of whom were male (45% of 140 = 63). So the ratio of the number of male students in 1995 to the number of male students in 1975 is 63:54 = 7:6.

6. B. From 1994 to 1996 there was a 9.4% decrease in the number of vehicles stolen. Since 9.4% of 1,000,000 = 94,000, the number of vehicles stolen in 1996 was 1,000,000 – 94,000 = 906,000. If you can't solve problems such as this, you have to guess. But since the number of stolen vehicles is clearly decreasing, be sure to eliminate Choices D and E first.

7. C. For simplicity, assume that 1000 vehicles were stolen in 1994. By 1997, the number had decreased by 12.0% to 880 (12% of 1000 = 120, and 1000 – 120 = 880); by 1998, the number had decreased 19.4% to 806 (19.4% of 1000 = 194 and 1000 – 194 = 806). So from 1997 to 1998, the number of vehicles stolen decreased by 74 from 880 to 806. This represents a decrease of $\frac{74}{880} = .084 = 8.4\%$.

8. D. Simplify the situation by assuming that in 1994 the population was 100,000 and there were 1000 vehicles stolen. As in the solution to question 7, in 1998 the number of stolen vehicles was 806. At the same time, the number of thefts per 100,000 inhabitants decreased 22.4% from 1000 to 776. So if there were 776 vehicles stolen for every 100,000 inhabitants, and 806 cars were stolen, the number of inhabitants must have increased. To know by how much, solve the proportion: $\frac{776}{100,000} = \frac{806}{x}$. Cross-multiply: $776x = 80,600,000$.

Divide by 776: $x = 103,800$. So for every 100,000 inhabitants in 1994, there were 103,800 in 1998, an increase of 3.8%.

9. B. The bar representing underweight adult females who perceive themselves to be underweight extends from about 70% to about 95%, a range of approximately 25%. Choice B is closest.

10. A. Almost all overweight females correctly considered themselves to be overweight; and more than half of all females of normal weight correctly considered themselves "about right." But nearly 70% of underweight adult females inaccurately considered themselves "about right."

11. D. Referring only to the New York State table, we see that the amount of tax on a taxable income between $15,000 and $17,000 was $860 plus 10% of the excess over $15,000. Therefore, the tax on $16,100 is $860 plus 10% of $1,100 = $860 + $110 = $970.

12. D. According to the tables, each additional dollar of taxable income over $25,000 was subject to a New York State tax of 14% and a New York City tax of 4.3%, for a total tax of 18.3%. Therefore, an additional $500 in taxable income would have incurred an additional tax of $0.183 \times 500 = $91.50$.

13. B. In Norway, the life expectancy of a female born in 1955 was 75 years, which is greater than the life expectancy of a male born in 1990. In Hungary, the life expectancy of a female born in 1955 was 66 years, whereas the life expectancy of a male born in 1990 was greater than 67. In the other two countries, the life expectancy of a female born in 1955 was less than 65 years, and the life expectancy of a male born in 1990 was greater than 65.

14. A. The life expectancy of a Korean female born in 1955 was about 51 and in 1990 it was about 74, an increase of 23 years. This is greater than any other nationality and sex.

15. C. Since there were 10,000 bias-motivated offenses based on ethnicity, and that represents 10% of the total, there were 100,000 bias-motivated offenses in total. Of these, 16,000 (16% of 100,000) were based on religion, and 15,600 (15.6% of 100,000) were based on sexual orientation. The difference is 400.

# 15 Mathematics Review

- Arithmetic
- Algebra
- Geometry
- Counting and Probability

The mathematics questions on the GRE General Test require a working knowledge of mathematical principles, including an understanding of the fundamentals of algebra, plane geometry, and arithmetic, as well as the ability to translate problems into formulas and to interpret graphs. The following review covers these areas thoroughly and will prove helpful.

This chapter is divided into 15 sections, labeled 15-A through 15-O. For each question on the Diagnostic Test and the five Model Tests, the Answer Key indicates which section of Chapter 15 you should consult if you need help on a particular topic.

How much time you initially devote to reviewing mathematics should depend on your math skills. If you have always been a good math student and you have taken some math in college and remember most of your high school math, you can skip the instructional parts of this chapter for now. If while doing the model tests in PART FIVE or on the accompanying CD-ROM, you find that you keep making mistakes on certain types of problems (averages, percents, circles, solid geometry, word problems, for example), or they take you too long, you should then study the appropriate sections here. Even if your math skills are excellent, and you don't need the review, you should complete the sample questions in those sections; they are an excellent source of additional GRE questions. If you know that your math skills are not very good and you have not done much math since high school, then it is advisable to review all of this material, including working out the problems, *before* tackling the model tests.

No matter how good you are in math, *you should carefully read and do the problems* in Chapters 11, 12, 13, and 14. For many of these problems, two solutions are given: the most direct mathematical solution and a second solution using one or more of the special tactics taught in these chapters.

Review the tactics in Chapter 2 for test-taking help.

# ARITHMETIC

To do well on the GRE, you need to feel comfortable with most topics of basic arithmetic. In the first five sections of Chapter 15, we will review the basic arithmetic operations, signed numbers, fractions, decimals, ratios, percents, and averages. Since the GRE uses these concepts to test your reasoning skills, not your ability to perform tedious calculations, we will concentrate on the concepts and not on arithmetic drill. The solutions to more than one-third of the mathematics questions on the GRE depend on your knowing the key facts in these sections. Be sure to review them all.

## 15-A. BASIC ARITHMETIC CONCEPTS

Let's start by reviewing the most important sets of numbers and their properties. On the GRE the word *number* always means *real number*, a number that can be represented by a point on the number line.

### Signed Numbers

The numbers to the right of 0 on the number line are called **positive** and those to the left of 0 are called **negative**. Negative numbers must be written with a *negative sign* (–2); positive numbers can be written with a *plus sign* (+2) but are usually written without a sign (2). All numbers can be called **signed numbers**.

## KEY FACT A1:

**For any number $a$, exactly one of the following is true:**

| | | |
|---|---|---|
| • $a$ is negative | • $a = 0$ | • $a$ is positive |

The **absolute value** of a number $a$, denoted $|a|$, is the distance between $a$ and 0 on the number line. Since 3 is 3 units to the right of 0 on the number line and –3 is 3 units to the left of 0, both have an absolute value of 3:

> • $|3| = 3$      • $|-3| = 3$

Two unequal numbers that have the same absolute value are called **opposites**. So, 3 is the opposite of –3 and –3 is the opposite of 3.

## KEY FACT A2:

**The only number that is equal to its opposite is 0.**

| Column A | Column B |
|---|---|

**Example 1.**

$$a - b = -(a - b)$$

| $a$ | $b$ |
|---|---|

SOLUTION. Since $-(a - b)$ is the opposite of $a - b$, $a - b = 0$, and so $a = b$. The answer is **C**.

In arithmetic we are basically concerned with the addition, subtraction, multiplication, and division of numbers. The third column of the following table gives the terms for the results of these operations.

| Operation | Symbol | Result | Example | |
|---|---|---|---|---|
| Addition | + | **Sum** | 16 is the sum of 12 and 4 | $16 = 12 + 4$ |
| Subtraction | – | **Difference** | 8 is the difference of 12 and 4 | $8 = 12 - 4$ |
| Multiplication* | × | **Product** | 48 is the product of 12 and 4 | $48 = 12 \times 4$ |
| Division | ÷ | **Quotient** | 3 is the quotient of 12 and 4 | $3 = 12 \div 4$ |

*Multiplication can be indicated also by a dot, parentheses, or the juxtaposition of symbols without any sign: $2^2 \cdot 2^4$, 3(4), $3(x + 2)$, $3a$, $4abc$.

Given any two numbers $a$ and $b$, we can *always* find their sum, difference, product, and quotient, except that we may *never divide by zero*.

> • $0 \div 7 = 0$      • $7 \div 0$ is meaningless

## Example 2.

What is the sum of the product and quotient of 8 and 8?

(A) 16   (B) 17   (C) 63   (D) 64   (E) 65

SOLUTION: Product: $8 \times 8 = 64$. Quotient: $8 \div 8 = 1$. Sum: $64 + 1 = $ **65 (E)**.

## KEY FACT A3:

• **The product of 0 and any number is 0. For any number $a$: $a \times 0 = 0$.**

• **Conversely, if the product of two numbers is 0, *at least one* of them must be 0: $ab = 0 \Rightarrow a = 0$ or $b = 0$.**

| Column A | Column B |
|---|---|

**Example 3.**

| The product of the integers from –7 to 2 | The product of the integers from –2 to 7 |
|---|---|

SOLUTION. *Do not multiply.* Each column is the product of 10 numbers, one of which is 0. So, by KEY FACT A3, each product is 0. The columns are equal (**C**).

## KEY FACT A4:

**The product and quotient of two positive numbers or two negative numbers are positive; the product and quotient of a positive number and a negative number are negative.**

| × | + | – |   | ÷ | + | – |
|---|---|---|---|---|---|---|
| + | + | – |   | + | + | – |
| – | – | + |   | – | – | + |

$6 \times 3 = 18$   $6 \times (-3) = -18$   $(-6) \times 3 = -18$   $(-6) \times (-3) = 18$
$6 \div 3 = 2$   $6 \div (-3) = -2$   $(-6) \div 3 = -2$   $(-6) \div (-3) = 2$

To determine whether a product of more than two numbers is positive or negative, count the number of negative factors.

## KEY FACT A5:

• **The product of an *even* number of negative factors is positive.**

• **The product of an *odd* number of negative factors is negative.**

|  Column A | Column B |
| --- | --- |

**Example 4.**

| $(-1)(2)(-3)(4)(-5)$ | $(1)(-2)(3)(-4)(5)$ |
| --- | --- |

SOLUTION. *Don't waste time multiplying.* The product in Column A is negative since it has 3 negative factors, whereas the product in Column B is positive since it has 2 negative factors. The answer is **B**.

## KEY FACT A6:

- The *reciprocal* of any nonzero number $a$ is $\dfrac{1}{a}$.

- The product of any number and its reciprocal is 1:

$$a \times \left(\dfrac{1}{a}\right) = 1.$$

## KEY FACT A7:

- **The sum of two positive numbers is positive.**

- **The sum of two negative numbers is negative.**

- **To find the sum of a positive and a negative number, find the difference of their absolute values and use the sign of the number with the larger absolute value.**

$$6 + 2 = 8 \qquad (-6) + (-2) = -8$$

To calculate either $6 + (-2)$ or $(-6) + 2$, take the *difference*, $6 - 2 = 4$, and use the sign of the number whose absolute value is 6. So,

$$6 + (-2) = 4 \qquad (-6) + 2 = -4$$

## KEY FACT A8:

**The sum of any number and its opposite is 0:**
$a + (-a) = 0.$

Many of the properties of arithmetic depend on the relationship between subtraction and addition and between division and multiplication.

## KEY FACT A9:

- **Subtracting a number is the same as adding its opposite.**

- **Dividing by a number is the same as multiplying by its reciprocal.**

$$a - b = a + (-b) \qquad a \div b = a \times \left(\dfrac{1}{b}\right)$$

Many problems involving subtraction and division can be simplified by changing them to addition and multiplication problems, respectively.

## KEY FACT A10:

**To subtract signed numbers, change the problem to an addition problem, by changing the sign of what is being subtracted, and use KEY FACT A7.**

$$2 - 6 = 2 + (-6) = -4 \qquad 2 - (-6) = 2 + (6) = 8$$

$$(-2) - (-6) = (-2) + (6) = 4 \qquad (-2) - 6 = (-2) + (-6) = -8$$

In each case, the minus sign was changed to a plus sign, and either the 6 was changed to –6 or the –6 was changed to 6.

## Integers

The **integers** are $\{..., -4, -3, -2, -1, 0, 1, 2, 3, 4, ...\}$.

The **positive integers** are $\{1, 2, 3, 4, 5, ...\}$.

The **negative integers** are $\{..., -5, -4, -3, -2, -1\}$.

NOTE: The integer 0 is neither positive nor negative. Therefore, if a question on the GRE asks how many positive numbers have a certain property, and the only numbers with that property are –2, –1, 0, 1, and 2, the answer is **2**.

**Consecutive integers** are two or more integers written in sequence in which each integer is 1 more than the preceding integer. For example:

$$22, 23 \quad 6, 7, 8, 9 \quad -2, -1, 0, 1 \quad n, n+1, n+2, n+3$$

**Example 5.**

If the sum of three consecutive integers is less than 75, what is the greatest possible value of the smallest one?

(A) 23   (B) 24   (C) 25   (D) 26   (E) 27

SOLUTION. Let the numbers be $n$, $n + 1$, and $n + 2$. Then,

$$n + (n + 1) + (n + 2) = 3n + 3 \Rightarrow$$
$$3n + 3 < 75 \Rightarrow 3n < 72 \Rightarrow n < 24.$$

So, the most $n$ can be is **23** (**A**).

CAUTION: Never assume that *number* means *integer*: 3 is not the only number between 2 and 4; there are infinitely many, including 2.5, 3.99, $\dfrac{10}{3}$, $\pi$, and $\sqrt{10}$.

**Example 6.**

If $2 < x < 4$ and $3 < y < 7$, what is the largest integer value of $x + y$?

(A) 7   (B) 8   (C) 9   (D) 10   (E) 11

SOLUTION. If $x$ and $y$ are integers, the largest value is $3 + 6 = 9$. However, although $x + y$ is to be an integer, neither $x$ nor $y$ must be. If $x = 3.8$ and $y = 6.2$, then $x + y = 10$ **(D)**.

The sum, difference, and product of two integers are *always* integers; the quotient of two integers may be an integer, but it is not necessarily one. The quotient $23 \div 10$ can be expressed as $\frac{23}{10}$ or $2\frac{3}{10}$ or 2.3. If the quotient is to be an integer, we can also say that the quotient is 2 and there is a *remainder* of 3. It depends upon our point of view. For example, if 23 dollars is to be divided among 10 people, each one will get $2.30 (2.3 dollars); but if 23 books are to be divided among 10 people, each one will get 2 books and there will be 3 left over (the remainder).

---

**Example 7.**

How many positive integers less than 100 have a remainder of 3 when divided by 7?

---

SOLUTION. To leave a remainder of 3 when divided by 7, an integer must be 3 more than a multiple of 7. For example, when 73 is divided by 7, the quotient is 10 and the remainder is 3: $73 = 10 \times 7 + 3$. So, just take the multiples of 7 and add 3. (*Don't forget that 0 is a multiple of 7.*)

$\underline{0} \times 7 + 3 = 3;$     $\underline{1} \times 7 + 3 = 10;$     $\underline{2} \times 7 + 3 = 17;$
 ... ;     $\underline{13} \times 7 + 3 = 94$

A total of **14** numbers.

If $a$ and $b$ are integers, the following four terms are synonymous:

$a$ is a *divisor* of $b$     $a$ is a *factor* of $b$
$b$ is *divisible* by $a$     $b$ is a *multiple* of $a$

They all mean that when $b$ is divided by $a$ there is no remainder (or, more precisely, the remainder is 0). For example:

3 is a divisor of 12     3 is a factor of 12
12 is divisible by 3     12 is a multiple of 3

**KEY FACT A11:**

**Every integer has a finite set of factors (or divisors) and an infinite set of multiples.**

The factors of 12:     $-12, -6, -4, -3, -2, -1, 1, 2, 3, 4,$
                        $6, 12$

The multiples of 12:   $... , -48, -36, -24, -12, 0, 12, 24,$
                        $36, 48, ...$

The only positive divisor of 1 is 1. All other positive integers have at least 2 positive divisors: 1 and itself, and possibly many more. For example, 6 is divisible by 1 and 6, as well as 2 and 3, whereas 7 is divisible only by 1 and 7. Positive integers, such as 7, that have exactly

2 positive divisors are called *prime numbers* or *primes*. The first few primes are

$$2, 3, 5, 7, 11, 13, 17, 19, 23.$$

Memorize this list—it will come in handy. Note that 1 is not a prime.

**KEY FACT A12:**

**Every integer greater than 1 that is not a prime can be written as a product of primes.**

To find the prime factorization of any integer, find any two factors; if they're both primes, you are done; if not, factor them. Continue until each factor has been written in terms of primes. A useful method is to make a *factor tree*.

For example, here are the prime factorizations of 108 and 240:

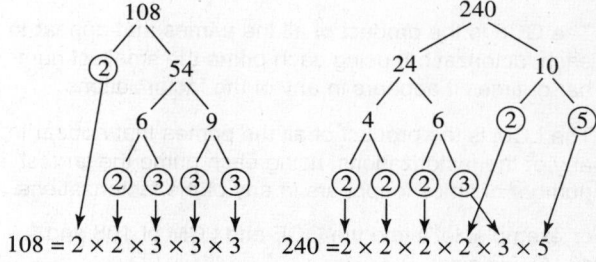

$$108 = 2 \times 2 \times 3 \times 3 \times 3 \qquad 240 = 2 \times 2 \times 2 \times 2 \times 3 \times 5$$

---

**Example 8.**

For any positive integer $a$, let $\lceil a \rfloor$ denote the smallest prime factor of $a$. Which of the following is equal to $\lceil 35 \rfloor$?
(A) $\lceil 10 \rfloor$   (B) $\lceil 15 \rfloor$   (C) $\lceil 45 \rfloor$   (D) $\lceil 55 \rfloor$
     (E) $\lceil 75 \rfloor$

---

SOLUTION. Check the first few primes; 35 is not divisible by 2 or 3, but is divisible by 5, so 5 is the *smallest* prime factor of 35: $\lceil 35 \rfloor = 5$. Now check the five choices: $\lceil 10 \rfloor = 2$, and $\lceil 15 \rfloor$, $\lceil 45 \rfloor$, and $\lceil 75 \rfloor$ are all equal to 3. Only $\lceil 55 \rfloor = 5$. The answer is **D**.

The *least common multiple* **(LCM)** of two or more integers is the smallest positive integer that is a multiple of each of them. For example, the LCM of 6 and 10 is 30. Infinitely many positive integers are multiples of both 6 and 10, including 60, 90, 180, 600, 6000, and 66,000,000, but 30 is the smallest one. The *greatest common factor* **(GCF)** or *greatest common divisor* **(GCD)** of two or more integers is the largest integer that is a factor of each of them. For example, the only positive integers that are factors of both 6 and 10 are 1 and 2, so the GCF of 6 and 10 is 2. For small numbers, you can often find their GCF and LCM by inspection. For larger numbers, KEY FACTS A13 and A14 are useful.

**KEY FACT A13:**

The product of the GCF and LCM of two numbers is equal to the product of the two numbers.

---

**Helpful Hint**

It is usually easier to find the GCF than the LCM. For example, you might see immediately that the GCF of 36 and 48 is 12. You could then use KEY FACT A12 to find the LCM: since $GCF \times LCM = 36 \times 48$, then

$$LCM = \frac{\overset{3}{\cancel{36}} \times 48}{\underset{1}{\cancel{12}}} = 3 \times 48 = 144.$$

---

**KEY FACT A14:**

To find the GCF or LCM of two or more integers, first get their prime factorizations.

- The GCF is the product of all the primes that appear in each factorization, using each prime the smallest number of times it appears in any of the factorizations.

- The LCM is the product of all the primes that appear in any of the factorizations, using each prime the largest number of times it appears in any of the factorizations.

For example, let's find the GCF and LCM of 108 and 240. As we saw:

$108 = 2 \times 2 \times 3 \times 3 \times 3$ and $240 = 2 \times 2 \times 2 \times 2 \times 3 \times 5$.

- **GCF.** The primes that appear in both factorizations are 2 and 3: 2 appears twice in the factorization of 108 and 4 times in the factorization of 240, so we take it twice; 3 appears 3 times in the factorization of 108, but only once in the factorization of 240, so we take it just once. The GCF = $2 \times 2 \times 3 =$ **12**.

- **LCM.** Take one of the factorizations and add to it any primes from the other that are not yet listed. So, start with $2 \times 2 \times 3 \times 3 \times 3$ (108) and look at the primes from 240: there are four 2s; we already wrote two 2s, so we need two more; there is a 3 but we already have that; there is a 5, which we need. So, the LCM = $(2 \times 2 \times 3 \times 3 \times 3) \times (2 \times 2 \times 5) = 108 \times 20 =$ **2160**.

---

> **Example 9.**
> What is the smallest number that is divisible by both 34 and 35?

---

SOLUTION. We are being asked for the LCM of 34 and 35. By KEY FACT A12, $LCM = \dfrac{34 \times 35}{GCF}$. But the GCF is 1 since no number greater than 1 divides evenly into both 34 and 35. So, the LCM is $34 \times 35 =$ **1190**.

The **even numbers** are all the multiples of 2:
$$\{..., -4, -2, 0, 2, 4, 6, ...\}$$

The **odd numbers** are the integers not divisible by 2:
$$\{..., -5, -3, -1, 1, 3, 5, ...\}$$

NOTE: • The terms *odd* and *even* apply only to integers.
- Every integer (positive, negative, or 0) is either odd or even.
- 0 is an even integer; it is a multiple of 2. $(0 = 0 \times 2)$
- 0 is a multiple of *every* integer. $(0 = 0 \times n)$
- 2 is the only even prime number.

**KEY FACT A15:**

The tables below summarize three important facts:

1. If two integers are both even or both odd, their sum and difference are even.

2. If one integer is even and the other odd, their sum and difference are odd.

3. The product of two integers is even unless both of them are odd.

| + and − | even | odd |
|---------|------|-----|
| even | even | odd |
| odd | odd | even |

| × | even | odd |
|---|------|-----|
| even | even | even |
| odd | even | odd |

## Exponents and Roots

Repeated addition of the same number is indicated by multiplication:

$$17 + 17 + 17 + 17 + 17 + 17 + 17 = 7 \times 17$$

Repeated multiplication of the same number is indicated by an exponent:

$$17 \times 17 \times 17 \times 17 \times 17 \times 17 \times 17 = 17^7$$

In the expression $17^7$, 17 is called the **base** and 7 is the **exponent**.

At some time, you may have seen expressions such as $2^{-4}$, $2^{\frac{1}{2}}$, or even $2^{\sqrt{2}}$. On the GRE, although the base, $b$, can be any number, the only exponents you will see will be positive integers.

**KEY FACT A16:**

For any number $b$: $b^1 = b$, and $b^n = b \times b \times ... \times b$, where $b$ is used as a factor $n$ times.

(i) $2^5 \times 2^3 = (2 \times 2 \times 2 \times 2 \times 2) \times (2 \times 2 \times 2) = 2^8 = 2^{5+3}$

(ii) $\dfrac{2^5}{2^3} = \dfrac{2 \times 2 \times 2 \times 2 \times 2}{2 \times 2 \times 2} = 2 \times 2 = 2^2 = 2^{5-3}$

(iii) $(2^2)^3 = (2 \times 2)^3 = (2 \times 2) \times (2 \times 2) \times (2 \times 2) = 2^6 = 2^{2 \times 3}$

(iv) $2^3 \times 7^3 = (2 \times 2 \times 2) \times (7 \times 7 \times 7) = (2 \times 7)(2 \times 7)(2 \times 7) = (2 \times 7)^3$

These four examples illustrate the following important laws of exponents given in KEY FACT A17.

### KEY FACT A17:

For any numbers $b$ and $c$ and positive integers $m$ and $n$:

(i) $b^m b^n = b^{m+n}$  (ii) $\dfrac{b^m}{b^n} = b^{m-n}$  (iii) $(b^m)^n = b^{mn}$

(iv) $b^m c^m = (bc)^m$

CAUTION: In (i) and (ii) the bases are the same and in (iv) the exponents are the same. None of these rules applies to expressions such as $7^5 \times 5^7$, in which both the bases and the exponents are different.

**Example 10.**

If $2^x = 32$, what is $x^2$?

(A) 5  (B) 10  (C) 25  (D) 100  (E) 1024

SOLUTION. To solve $2^x = 32$, just count (and keep track of) how many 2s you need to multiply to get 32: $2 \times 2 \times 2 \times 2 \times 2 = 32$, so $x = 5$ and $x^2 = $ **25 (C)**.

**Example 11.**

If $3^a \times 3^b = 3^{100}$, what is the average (arithmetic mean) of $a$ and $b$?

SOLUTION. Since $3^a \times 3^b = 3^{a+b}$, we see that $a + b = 100 \Rightarrow \dfrac{a+b}{2} = $ **50**.

The next KEY FACT is an immediate consequence of KEY FACTS A4 and A5.

### KEY FACT A18:

For any positive integer $n$:

• $0^n = 0$                    • if $a$ is positive, $a^n$ is positive

• if $a$ is negative, $a^n$ is positive if $n$ is even, and negative if $n$ is odd.

| Column A | Column B |
|---|---|
| **Example 12.** | |
| $(-13)^{10}$ | $(-13)^{25}$ |

SOLUTION. Column A is positive and Column B is negative. So Column **A** is greater.

## Squares and Square Roots

The exponent that appears most often on the GRE is 2. It is used to form the square of a number, as in $\pi r^2$ (the area of a circle), $a^2 + b^2 = c^2$ (the Pythagorean theorem), or $x^2 - y^2$ (the difference of two squares). Therefore, it is helpful to recognize the **perfect squares**, numbers that are the squares of integers. The squares of the integers from 0 to 15 are as follows:

| $x$ | 0 | 1 | 2 | 3 | 4 | 5 | 6 | 7 |
|---|---|---|---|---|---|---|---|---|
| $x^2$ | 0 | 1 | 4 | 9 | 16 | 25 | 36 | 49 |

| $x$ | 8 | 9 | 10 | 11 | 12 | 13 | 14 | 15 |
|---|---|---|---|---|---|---|---|---|
| $x^2$ | 64 | 81 | 100 | 121 | 144 | 169 | 196 | 225 |

There are two numbers that satisfy the equation $x^2 = 9$: $x = 3$ and $x = -3$. The positive one, 3, is called the (**principal**) **square root** of 9 and is denoted by the symbol $\sqrt{9}$. Clearly, each perfect square has a square root: $\sqrt{0} = 0$, $\sqrt{36} = 6$, $\sqrt{81} = 9$, and $\sqrt{144} = 12$. But, it is an important fact that *every* positive number has a square root.

### KEY FACT A19:

For any positive number $a$, there is a positive number $b$ that satisfies the equation $b^2 = a$. That number is called the square root of $a$: $b = \sqrt{a}$. So, for any positive number $a$: $(\sqrt{a})^2 = \sqrt{a} \times \sqrt{a} = a$.

The only difference between $\sqrt{9}$ and $\sqrt{10}$ is that the first square root is an integer, while the second one isn't. Since 10 is a little more than 9, we should expect that $\sqrt{10}$ is a little more than $\sqrt{9} = 3$. In fact, $(3.1)^2 = 9.61$, which is close to 10, and $(3.16)^2 = 9.9856$, which is very close to 10. So, $\sqrt{10} \approx 3.16$. On the GRE you will *never* have to evaluate such a square root; if the solution to a problem involves a square root, that square root will be among the answer choices.

**Example 13.**

What is the circumference of a circle whose area is $10\pi$?

(A) $5\pi$  (B) $10\pi$  (C) $\pi\sqrt{10}$  (D) $2\pi\sqrt{10}$
(E) $\pi\sqrt{20}$

SOLUTION. Since the area of a circle is given by the formula $A = \pi r^2$, we have
$$\pi r^2 = 10\pi \Rightarrow r^2 = 10 \Rightarrow r = \sqrt{10}.$$
The circumference is given by the formula $C = 2\pi r$, so $C = 2\pi\sqrt{10}$ **(D)**. (See Section 12-L on circles.)

### KEY FACT A20:

For any positive numbers $a$ and $b$:

$$\sqrt{ab} = \sqrt{a} \times \sqrt{b} \qquad \sqrt{\frac{a}{b}} = \frac{\sqrt{a}}{\sqrt{b}}$$

**CAUTION:** $\sqrt{a+b} \neq \sqrt{a} + \sqrt{b}$. For example:
$5 = \sqrt{25} = \sqrt{9+16} \neq \sqrt{9} + \sqrt{16} = 3 + 4 = 7$.

**CAUTION:** Although it is always true that $(\sqrt{a})^2 = a$, $\sqrt{a^2} = a$ is true only if $a$ is positive: $\sqrt{(-5)^2} = \sqrt{25} = 5$, *not* $-5$.

| Column A | Column B |
| --- | --- |
| **Example 14.** | |

SOLUTION. Column A: Since $x^{10}x^{10} = x^{20}$, $\sqrt{x^{20}} = x^{10}$.

Column B: $(x^5)^2 = x^{10}$. The columns are equal **(C)**.

## PEMDAS

When a calculation requires performing more than one operation, it is important to carry them out in the correct order. For decades students have memorized the sentence "<u>P</u>lease <u>E</u>xcuse <u>M</u>y <u>D</u>ear <u>A</u>unt <u>S</u>ally," or just the first letters, PEMDAS, to remember the proper order of operations. The letters stand for:

* <u>P</u>arentheses: first do whatever appears in parentheses, following PEMDAS within the parentheses if necessary.

* <u>E</u>xponents: next evaluate all terms with exponents.

* <u>M</u>ultiplication and <u>D</u>ivision: then do all multiplications and divisions *in order from left to right—do not* multiply first and then divide.

* <u>A</u>ddition and <u>S</u>ubtraction: finally, do all additions and subtractions *in order from left to right—do not add* first and then subtract.

Here are some worked-out examples.

1. $12 + 3 \times 2 = 12 + 6 = 18$   [Multiply before you add.]
   $(12 + 3) \times 2 = 15 \times 2 = 30$   [First add in the parentheses.]

2. $12 \div 3 \times 2 = 4 \times 2 = 8$   [Just go from left to right.]
   $12 \div (3 \times 2) = 12 \div 6 = 2$   [First multiply inside the parentheses.]

3. $5 \times 2^3 = 5 \times 8 = 40$   [Do exponents first.]
   $(5 \times 2)^3 = 10^3 = 1000$   [First multiply inside the parentheses.]

4. $4 + 4 \div (2 + 6) = 4 + 4 \div 8 = 4 + .5 = 4.5$
   [First add in the parentheses, then divide, and finally add.]

5. $100 - 2^2(3 + 4 \times 5) = 100 - 2^2(23) = 100 - 4(23) = 100 - 92 = 8$
   [First evaluate what's inside the parentheses (using PEMDAS); then take the exponent; then multiply; and finally subtract.]

There is an important situation when you shouldn't start with what's in the parentheses. Consider the following two examples.

(i) What is the value of $7(100 - 1)$ ?

Using PEMDAS, you would write $7(100 - 1) = 7(99)$, and then multiply: $7 \times 99 = 693$. But you can do this even quicker in your head if you think of it this way: $7(100 - 1) = 700 - 7 = 693$.

(ii) What is the value of $(77 + 49) \div 7$?

If you followed the rules of PEMDAS, you would first add, $77 + 49 = 126$, and then divide, $126 \div 7 = 18$. This is definitely more difficult and time-consuming than mentally doing $\frac{77}{7} + \frac{49}{7} = 11 + 7 = 18$.

Both of these examples illustrate the very important distributive law.

### KEY FACT A21:

**The distributive law**

For any real numbers $a$, $b$, and $c$:

$$a(b + c) = ab + ac \qquad a(b - c) = ab - ac$$

and if $a \neq 0$

$$\frac{b + c}{a} = \frac{b}{a} + \frac{c}{a} \qquad \frac{b - c}{a} = \frac{b}{a} - \frac{c}{a}$$

**Helpful Hint**

Many students who use the distributive law with multiplication forget about it with division. Don't you do that.

SOLUTION 15. By the distributive law, Column $A = 5a - 35$. The result of subtracting 35 from a number is *always less* than the result of subtracting 7 from that number. Column **B** is greater.

SOLUTION 16.

| | Column A | Column B |
|---|---|---|
| By the distributive law: | $10 + \dfrac{x}{5}$ | $10 + x$ |
| Subtract 10 from each column: | $\dfrac{x}{5}$ | $x$ |

The columns are equal if $x = 0$, but not if $x = 1$.

The answer is **D**.

---

**Example 17.**
If $a = 9 \times 8321$ and $b = 9 \times 7321$, what is the value of $a - b$?

---

SOLUTION. Remember, you will *never* have to do tedious multiplications on the GRE, so there must be an easier way to solve this. If you think, you can do it in your head. Remember the distributive law—in far less time than it takes to write the equation on your scrap paper, you should realize that $a - b = 9(8321) - 9(7321) = 9(8321 - 7321) = 9(1000) = $ **9000**.

## Inequalities

The number $a$ is **greater than** the number $b$, denoted $a > b$, if $a$ is to the right of $b$ on the number line. Similarly, $a$ is **less than** $b$, denoted $a < b$, if $a$ is to the left of $b$ on the number line. Therefore, if $a$ is positive, $a > 0$, and if $a$ is negative, $a < 0$. Clearly, if $a > b$, then $b < a$.

The following KEY FACT gives an important alternate way to describe greater than and less than.

### KEY FACT A22:

- For any numbers $a$ and $b$: $a > b$ means that $a - b$ is positive.

- For any numbers $a$ and $b$: $a < b$ means that $a - b$ is negative.

### KEY FACT A23:

- For any numbers $a$ and $b$, exactly one of the following is true:

$$a > b \quad \text{or} \quad a = b \quad \text{or} \quad a < b.$$

The symbol $\geq$ means **greater than or equal to** and the symbol $\leq$ means **less than or equal to**. The statement "$x \geq 5$" means that $x$ can be 5 or any number greater than 5; the statement "$x \leq 5$" means that $x$ can be 5 or any number less than 5. The statement "$2 < x < 5$" is an abbreviation for the statement "$2 < x$ and $x < 5$." It means that $x$ is a number between 2 and 5 (greater than 2 and less than 5).

Inequalities are very important on the GRE, especially on the quantitative comparison questions where you have to determine which of two quantities is the greater one. KEY FACTS A24 and A25 give some important facts about inequalities.

If the result of performing an arithmetic operation on an inequality is a new inequality in the same direction, we say that the inequality has been **preserved**. If the result of performing an arithmetic operation on an inequality is a new inequality in the opposite direction, we say that the inequality has been **reversed**.

### KEY FACT A24:

- **Adding a number to an inequality or subtracting a number from an inequality preserves it.**

If $a < b$, then $a + c < b + c$ and $a - c < b - c$.
$3 < 7 \Rightarrow 3 + 100 < 7 + 100 \quad (103 < 107)$
$3 < 7 \Rightarrow 3 - 100 < 7 - 100 \quad (-97 < -93)$

- **Adding inequalities in the same direction preserves them.**

If $a < b$ and $c < d$, then $a + c < b + d$.
$3 < 7$ and $5 < 10 \Rightarrow 3 + 5 < 7 + 10 \quad (8 < 17)$

- **Multiplying or dividing an inequality by a positive number preserves it.**

If $a < b$, and $c$ is positive, then $ac < bc$ and $\dfrac{a}{c} < \dfrac{b}{c}$.
$3 < 7 \Rightarrow 3 \times 100 < 7 \times 100 \quad (300 < 700)$
$3 < 7 \Rightarrow 3 \div 100 < 7 \div 100 \quad \left(\dfrac{3}{100} < \dfrac{7}{100}\right)$

- **Multiplying or dividing an inequality by a negative number reverses it.**

If $a < b$, and $c$ is negative, then $ac > bc$ and $\dfrac{a}{c} > \dfrac{b}{c}$.
$3 < 7 \Rightarrow 3 \times (-100) > 7 \times (-100) \quad (-300 > -700)$
$3 < 7 \Rightarrow 3 \div (-100) > 7 \div (-100) \quad \left(-\dfrac{3}{100} > -\dfrac{7}{100}\right)$

- **Taking negatives reverses an inequality.**

If $a < b$, then $-a > -b$ and if $a > b$, then $-a < -b$.
$3 < 7 \Rightarrow -3 > -7$ and $7 > 3 \Rightarrow -7 < -3$

- **If two numbers are each positive or negative, then taking reciprocals reverses an inequality.**

If $a$ and $b$ are both positive or both negative and $a < b$, then $\dfrac{1}{a} > \dfrac{1}{b}$.
$3 < 7 \Rightarrow \dfrac{1}{3} > \dfrac{1}{7}$

---

**Helpful Hint**

Be sure you understand KEY FACT A24; it is very useful. Also, review the important properties listed in KEY FACTS A25 and A26. These properties come up often on the GRE.

**KEY FACT A25:**

**Important inequalities for numbers between 0 and 1.**

- If $0 < x < 1$, and $a$ is positive, then $xa < a$. For example: $.85 \times 19 < 19$.

- If $0 < x < 1$, and $m$ and $n$ are integers with $m > n$, then $x^m < x^n < x$.

    For example, $\left(\frac{1}{2}\right)^5 < \left(\frac{1}{2}\right)^2 < \frac{1}{2}$.

- If $0 < x < 1$, then $\sqrt{x} > x$. For example, $\sqrt{\frac{3}{4}} > \frac{3}{4}$.

- If $0 < x < 1$, then $\frac{1}{x} > x$. In fact, $\frac{1}{x} > 1$.

    For example, $\frac{1}{0.2} > 1 > 0.2$.

**KEY FACT A26:**

**Properties of Zero**

- 0 is the only number that is neither positive nor negative.

- 0 is smaller than every positive number and greater than every negative number.

- 0 is an even integer.

- 0 is a multiple of every integer.

- For every number $a$: $a + 0 = a$ and $a - 0 = a$.

- For every number $a$: $a \times 0 = 0$.

- For every positive integer $n$: $0^n = 0$.

- For every number $a$ (including 0): $a \div 0$ and $\frac{a}{0}$ are *meaningless symbols*. (They are *undefined*.)

- For every number $a$ other than 0: $0 \div a = \frac{0}{a} = 0$.

- 0 is the only number that is equal to its opposite: $0 = -0$.

- If the product of two or more numbers is 0, at least one of them is 0.

**KEY FACT A27:**

**Properties of 1**

- For any number $a$: $1 \times a = a$ and $\frac{a}{1} = a$.

- For any integer $n$: $1^n = 1$.

- 1 is a divisor of every integer.

- 1 is the smallest positive integer.

- 1 is an odd integer.

- 1 is *not* a prime.

# PRACTICE EXERCISES—BASIC ARITHMETIC

## Multiple-Choice Questions

1. For how many positive integers, $a$, is it true that $a^2 \le 2a$?
   (A) None   (B) 1   (C) 2   (D) 4   (E) More than 4

2. If $0 < a < b < 1$, which of the following are true?
   I. $a - b$ is negative
   II. $\frac{1}{ab}$ is positive
   III. $\frac{1}{b} - \frac{1}{a}$ is positive
   (A) I only   (B) II only   (C) III only
   (D) I and II only   (E) I, II, and III

3. If the product of 4 consecutive integers is equal to one of them, what is the largest possible value of one of the integers?
   (A) 0   (B) 3   (C) 4   (D) 6   (E) 24

4. At 3:00 A.M. the temperature was 13° below zero. By noon it had risen to 32°. What was the average hourly increase in temperature?
   (A) $\left(\frac{19}{9}\right)^\circ$   (B) $\left(\frac{19}{6}\right)^\circ$   (C) 5°   (D) 7.5°
   (E) 45°

5. If $a$ and $b$ are negative, and $c$ is positive, which of the following statements are true?
   I. $a - b < a - c$
   II. If $a < b$, then $\frac{a}{c} < \frac{b}{c}$
   III. $\frac{1}{b} < \frac{1}{c}$
   (A) I only   (B) II only   (C) III only
   (D) II and III only   (E) I, II, and III

6. If $-7 \le x \le 7$ and $0 \le y \le 12$, what is the greatest possible value of $y - x$?
   (A) –19   (B) 5   (C) 7   (D) 17   (E) 19

7. If $(7^a)(7^b) = \dfrac{7^c}{7^d}$, what is $d$ in terms of $a$, $b$, and $c$?

   (A) $\dfrac{c}{ab}$   (B) $c - a - b$   (C) $a + b - c$   (D) $c - ab$

   (E) $\dfrac{c}{a + b}$

8. If each of ★ and ❖ can be replaced by $+$, $-$, or $\times$, how many different values are there for the expression $2 ★ 2 ❖ 2$?

   (A) 4   (B) 5   (C) 6   (D) 7   (E) 9

9. A number is "terrific" if it is a multiple of 2 or 3. How many terrific numbers are there between $-11$ and 11?

   (A) 6   (B) 7   (C) 11   (D) 15   (E) 17

Questions 10 and 11 refer to the following definition. For any positive integer $n$, $\tau(n)$ represents the number of positive divisors of $n$.

10. Which of the following are true?

    I. $\tau(5) = \tau(7)$
    II. $\tau(5) \cdot \tau(7) = \tau(35)$
    III. $\tau(5) + \tau(7) = \tau(12)$

    (A) I only   (B) II only   (C) I and II only
    (D) I and III only   (E) I, II, and III

11. What is the value of $\tau(\tau(\tau(12)))$?

    (A) 1   (B) 2   (C) 3   (D) 4   (E) 6

12. If $p$ and $q$ are primes greater than 2, which of the following must be true?

    I. $p + q$ is even
    II. $pq$ is odd
    III. $p^2 - q^2$ is even

    (A) I only   (B) II only   (C) I and II only
    (D) I and III only   (E) I, II, and III

13. If $0 < x < 1$, which of the following lists the numbers in increasing order?

    (A) $\sqrt{x}, x, x^2$   (B) $x^2, x, \sqrt{x}$   (C) $x^2, \sqrt{x}, x$
    (D) $x, x^2, \sqrt{x}$   (E) $x, \sqrt{x}, x^2$

14. Which of the following is equal to $(7^8 \times 7^9)^{10}$?

    (A) $7^{27}$   (B) $7^{82}$   (C) $7^{170}$   (D) $49^{170}$   (E) $49^{720}$

15. If $x \, ⊗ \, y$ represents the number of integers greater than $x$ and less than $y$, what is the value of $-\pi \, ⊗ \, \sqrt{2}$?

    (A) 2   (B) 3   (C) 4   (D) 5   (E) 6

## Quantitative Comparison Questions

| Column A | Column B |
|---|---|
| 16. The product of the odd integers between $-8$ and 8 | The product of the even integers between $-9$ and 9 |

*a* and *b* are nonzero integers

| Column A | Column B |
|---|---|
| 17. $a + b$ | $ab$ |

| Column A | Column B |
|---|---|
| 18. The remainder when a positive integer is divided by 7 | 7 |

| Column A | Column B |
|---|---|
| 19. $24 \div 6 \times 4$ | 12 |

| Column A | Column B |
|---|---|
| 20. $\dfrac{2x - 17}{2}$ | $x - 17$ |

$n$ is an integer greater than 1 that leaves a remainder of 1 when it is divided by 2, 3, 4, 5, and 6

| Column A | Column B |
|---|---|
| 21. $n$ | 60 |

| Column A | Column B |
|---|---|
| 22. The number of primes that are divisible by 2 | The number of primes that are divisible by 3 |

$n$ is a positive integer

| Column A | Column B |
|---|---|
| 23. The number of different prime factors of $n$ | The number of different prime factors of $n^2$ |

| Column A | Column B |
|---|---|
| 24. The number of even positive factors of 30 | The number of odd positive factors of 30 |

$n$ is a positive integer

| Column A | Column B |
|---|---|
| 25. $(-10)^n$ | $(-10)^{n+1}$ |

GO ON TO THE NEXT

# Answer Key

| | | | | |
|---|---|---|---|---|
| 1. C | 6. E | 11. C | 16. A | 21. A |
| 2. D | 7. B | 12. E | 17. D | 22. C |
| 3. B | 8. A | 13. B | 18. B | 23. C |
| 4. C | 9. D | 14. C | 19. A | 24. C |
| 5. D | 10. C | 15. D | 20. A | 25. D |

# Answer Explanations

1. **C.** Since $a$ is positive, we can divide both sides of the given inequality by $a$:
$$a^2 \le 2a \Rightarrow a \le 2 \Rightarrow a = 1 \text{ or } 2.$$

2. **D.** Since $a < b$, $a - b$ is negative (I is true). Since $a$ and $b$ are positive, so is their product, $ab$; and the reciprocal of a positive number is positive (II is true). $\dfrac{1}{b} - \dfrac{1}{a} = \dfrac{a-b}{ab}$. We have just seen that the numerator is negative and the denominator positive, so the value of the fraction is negative (III is false).

3. **B.** If all four integers were negative, their product would be positive, and so could not equal one of them. If all of the integers were positive, their product would be much greater than any of them (even $1 \times 2 \times 3 \times 4 = 24$). So, the integers must include 0, in which case their product *is* 0. The largest set of four consecutive integers that includes 0 is 0, 1, 2, 3.

4. **C.** In the 9 hours from 3:00 to 12:00, the temperature rose $32 - (-13) = 32 + 13 = 45$ degrees. So, the average hourly increase was $45° \div 9 = 5°$.

5. **D.** Since $b$ is negative and $c$ is positive,
$$b < c \Rightarrow -b > -c \Rightarrow a - b > a - c$$
(I is false). Since $c$ is positive, dividing by $c$ preserves the inequality. (II is true.) Since $b$ is negative, $\dfrac{1}{b}$ is negative, and so is less than $\dfrac{1}{c}$, which is positive (III is true).

6. **E.** To make $y - x$ as large as possible, let $y$ be as big as possible (12), and subtract the smallest amount possible ($x = -7$): $12 - (-7) = 19$.

7. **B.** $(7^a)(7^b) = 7^{a+b}$, and $\dfrac{7^c}{7^d} = 7^{c-d}$. Therefore,
$$a + b = c - d \Rightarrow a + b + d = c \Rightarrow d = c - a - b$$

8. **A.** Just list the 9 possible outcomes of replacing ★ and ❖ by $+$, $-$, and $\times$, and see that there are 4 different values: $-2, 2, 6, 8$.

| | | |
|---|---|---|
| $2 + 2 + 2 = 6$ | $2 - 2 - 2 = -2$ | $2 \times 2 \times 2 = 8$ |
| $2 + 2 - 2 = 2$ | $2 - 2 \times 2 = -2$ | $2 \times 2 + 2 = 6$ |
| $2 + 2 \times 2 = 6$ | $2 - 2 + 2 = 2$ | $2 \times 2 - 2 = 2$ |

9. **D.** There are 15 "terrific" numbers: 2, 3, 4, 6, 8, 9, 10, their opposites, and 0.

10. **C.** Since 5 and 7 have two positive factors each, $\tau(5) = \tau(7)$. I is true. Since 35 has 4 divisors (1, 5, 7, and 35) and $\tau(5) \cdot \tau(7) = 2 \times 2 = 4$, II is true. $\tau(12)$ is 6, which is *not* equal to $2 + 2$; III is false.

11. **C.** $\tau(\tau(\tau(12))) = \tau(\tau(6)) = \tau(4) = 3$

12. **E.** All primes greater than 2 are odd, so $p$ and $q$ are odd, and $p + q$ is even (I is true). The product of two odd numbers is odd (II is true). Since $p$ and $q$ are odd, so are their squares, and so the difference of the squares is even (III is true).

13. **B.** For any number, $x$, between 0 and 1:
$$x^2 < x \text{ and } x < \sqrt{x}.$$

14. **C.** First, multiply inside the parentheses: $7^8 \times 7^9 = 7^{17}$; then, raise to the 10th power: $(7^{17})^{10} = 7^{170}$.

15. **D.** There are 5 integers $(1, 0, -1, -2, -3)$ that are greater than $-3.14$ $(-\pi)$ and less than $1.41$ $(\sqrt{2})$.

16. **A.** Since the product in Column A has 4 negative factors $(-7, -5, -3, -1)$, it is positive. The product in Column B also has 4 negative factors, but be careful—it also has the factor 0, and so Column B is 0.

17. **D.** If $a$ and $b$ are each 1, then $a + b = 2$, and $ab = 1$; so, Column A is greater. But, if $a$ and $b$ are each 3, $a + b = 6$, and $ab = 9$, and Column B is greater.

18. **B.** The remainder is *always* less than the divisor.

19. **A.** According to PEMDAS, you divide and multiply from left to right (do *not* do the multiplication first): $24 \div 6 \times 4 = 4 \times 4 = 16$.

20. **A.** By the distributive law,
$$\frac{2x - 17}{2} = \frac{2x}{2} - \frac{17}{2} = x - 8.5,$$ which is greater than $x - 17$ (the larger the number you subtract, the smaller the difference.)

21. **A.** The LCM of 2, 3, 4, 5, 6 is 60; and all multiples of 60 are divisible by each of them. So, *n* could be 61 or 1 more than any multiple of 60.

22. **C.** The only prime divisible by 2 is 2, and the only prime divisible by 3 is 3. The number in each column is 1.

23. **C.** If you make a factor tree for $n^2$, the first branches would be *n* and *n*. Now, when you factor each of the *n*s, you get exactly the same prime factors. (See the example below.)

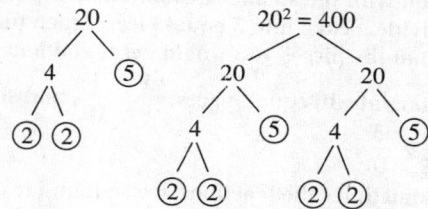

24. **C.** Just list the factors of 30: 1, 2, 3, 5, 6, 10, 15, 30. Four of them are odd and four are even.

25. **D.** If *n* is even, then *n* + 1 is odd, and consequently $(-10)^n$ is positive, whereas $(-10)^{n+1}$ is negative. If *n* is odd, exactly the opposite is true.

# 15-B. FRACTIONS AND DECIMALS

Several questions on the GRE involve fractions or decimals. The 23 KEY FACTS in this section cover all of the important facts you need to know for the GRE.

When a whole is *divided* into *n* equal parts, each part is called *one nth* of the whole, written $\frac{1}{n}$. For example, if a pizza is cut (*divided*) into 8 equal slices, each slice is one eighth $\left(\frac{1}{8}\right)$ of the pizza; a day is *divided* into 24 equal hours, so an hour is one twenty-fourth $\left(\frac{1}{24}\right)$ of a day; and an inch is one twelfth $\left(\frac{1}{12}\right)$ of a foot.

• If Donna slept for 5 hours, she slept for five twenty-fourths $\left(\frac{5}{24}\right)$ of a day.

• If Taryn bought 8 slices of pizza, she bought eight eighths $\left(\frac{8}{8}\right)$ of a pie.

• If Aviva's shelf is 30 inches long, it measures thirty twelfths $\left(\frac{30}{12}\right)$ of a foot.

Numbers such as $\frac{5}{24}$, $\frac{8}{8}$, and $\frac{30}{12}$, in which one integer is written over a second integer, are called

*fractions*. The center line is called the fraction bar. The number above the bar is called the **numerator,** and the number below the bar is called the **denominator.**

> CAUTION: The denominator of a fraction can *never* be 0.

• A fraction, such as $\frac{5}{24}$, in which the numerator is less than the denominator, is called a **proper fraction**. Its value is less than 1.

• A fraction, such as $\frac{30}{12}$, in which the numerator is more than the denominator, is called an **improper fraction**. Its value is greater than 1.

• A fraction, such as $\frac{8}{8}$, in which the numerator and denominator are the same, is also **improper**, but it is equal to 1.

It is useful to think of the fraction bar as a symbol for division. If three pizzas are divided equally among eight people, each person gets $\frac{3}{8}$ of a pizza. If you actually divide 3 by 8, you get that $\frac{3}{8}$ = .375.

**KEY FACT B1:**

**Every fraction, proper or improper, can be expressed in decimal form (or as a whole number) by dividing the numerator by the denominator.**

$$\frac{3}{10} = 0.3 \qquad \frac{3}{4} = 0.75 \qquad \frac{5}{8} = 0.625 \qquad \frac{3}{16} = 0.1875$$

$$\frac{8}{8} = 1 \qquad \frac{11}{8} = 1.375 \qquad \frac{48}{16} = 3 \qquad \frac{100}{8} = 12.5$$

Note that any number beginning with a decimal point can be written with a 0 to the left of the decimal point. In fact, some calculators will express 3 ÷ 8 as .375, whereas others will print 0.375.

Unlike the examples above, when most fractions are converted to decimals, the division does not terminate after 2 or 3 or 4 decimal places; rather it goes on forever with some set of digits repeating itself.

$$\frac{2}{3} = 0.666666... \qquad \frac{3}{11} = 0.272727... \qquad \frac{5}{12} = 0.416666...$$

$$\frac{17}{15} = 1.133333...$$

However, *on the GRE, you do not need to be concerned with this.* On both multiple-choice and quantitative comparison questions, all numbers written as decimals terminate.

## Comparing Fractions and Decimals

### KEY FACT B2:

To compare two decimals, follow these rules.

• Whichever number has the greater number to the left of the decimal point is greater: since 11 > 9, 11.001 > 9.896 and since 1 > 0, 1.234 > 0.8. (Recall that if a decimal is written without a number to the left of the decimal point, you may assume that a 0 is there. So, 1.234 > .8.)

• If the numbers to the left of the decimal point are equal (or if there are no numbers to the left of the decimal point), proceed as follows:

(1) If the numbers do not have the same number of digits to the right of the decimal point, add zeros to the end of the shorter one.

(2) Now, compare the numbers *ignoring* the decimal point.

For example, to compare 1.83 and 1.823, add a 0 to the end of 1.83, forming 1.830. Now compare them, *thinking of them as whole numbers*: since, 1830 > 1823, then 1.830 > 1.823.

| Column A | Column B |
|----------|----------|
| **Example 1.** | |
| .2139 | .239 |

SOLUTION. Do not think that Column A is greater because 2139 > 239. Be sure to add a 0 to the end of .239 (forming .2390) before comparing. Now, since 2390 > 2139, Column **B** is greater.

### KEY FACT B3:

There are two methods of comparing fractions:

1. Convert them to decimals (by dividing), and use KEY FACT B2.

2. Cross-multiply.

For example, to compare $\frac{1}{3}$ and $\frac{3}{8}$, we have two choices.

1. Write $\frac{1}{3}$ = .3333... and $\frac{3}{8}$ = .375. Since .375 > .333, then $\frac{3}{8} > \frac{1}{3}$.

2. Cross-multiply:

$\frac{1}{3} \diagdown\diagup \frac{3}{8}$    Since $3 \times 3 > 8 \times 1$, then $\frac{3}{8} > \frac{1}{3}$.

### KEY FACT B4:

When comparing fractions, there are three situations in which it is easier just to look at the fractions, and not use either method in KEY FACT B3.

1. If the fractions have the same denominator, the fraction with the larger numerator is greater. Just as $9 is more than $7, and 9 books are more than 7 books, 9 tenths are more than 7 tenths: $\frac{9}{10} > \frac{7}{10}$.

2. If the fractions have the same numerator, the fraction with the smaller denominator is greater. If you divide a cake into 5 equal pieces, each piece is larger than the pieces you would get if you had divided the cake into 10 equal pieces: $\frac{1}{5} > \frac{1}{10}$, and similarly $\frac{3}{5} > \frac{3}{10}$.

3. Sometimes the fractions are so familiar or easy to work with, you just know the answer. For example, $\frac{3}{4} > \frac{1}{5}$ and $\frac{11}{20} > \frac{1}{2}$ $\left(\text{since } \frac{10}{20} = \frac{1}{2}\right)$.

### KEY FACT B5:

KEY FACTS B2, B3, and B4 apply to *positive* decimals and fractions.

• Clearly, any positive number is greater than any negative number:

$$\frac{1}{2} > -\frac{1}{5} \quad \text{and} \quad 0.123 > -2.56$$

• For negative decimals and fractions, use KEY FACT A24, which states that if $a > b$, then $-a < -b$:

$$\frac{1}{2} > \frac{1}{5} \Rightarrow -\frac{1}{2} < -\frac{1}{5} \quad \text{and} \quad .83 > .829 \Rightarrow -.83 < -.829$$

**Example 2.**

Which of the following lists the fractions $\frac{2}{3}$, $\frac{5}{8}$, and $\frac{13}{20}$ in order from least to greatest?

(A) $\frac{2}{3}, \frac{5}{8}, \frac{13}{20}$    (B) $\frac{5}{8}, \frac{2}{3}, \frac{13}{20}$

(C) $\frac{5}{8}, \frac{13}{20}, \frac{2}{3}$    (D) $\frac{13}{20}, \frac{5}{8}, \frac{2}{3}$

(E) $\frac{13}{20}, \frac{2}{3}, \frac{5}{8}$

SOLUTION. Quickly, convert each to a decimal, writing down the first few decimal places: $\frac{2}{3}$ = .666,

$\frac{5}{8}$ = .625, and $\frac{13}{20}$ = .65. It is now easy to order the decimals: .625 < .650 < .666. The answer is **C**.

**Alternative solution.** Cross-multiply.

- Since $8 \times 2 > 3 \times 5$, then $\frac{2}{3} > \frac{5}{8}$.

- Since $8 \times 13 > 20 \times 5$, then $\frac{13}{20} > \frac{5}{8}$.

- Since $20 \times 2 > 3 \times 13$, then $\frac{2}{3} > \frac{13}{20}$.

| Column A | Column B |
|---|---|
| **Example 3.** | |
| $0 < x < y$ | |
| $\frac{1}{x} - \frac{1}{y}$ | $0$ |

SOLUTION. By KEY FACT B4, $x < y \Rightarrow \frac{1}{x} > \frac{1}{y}$, and so by KEY FACT A22, $\frac{1}{x} - \frac{1}{y}$ is positive. Column **A** is greater.

## Equivalent Fractions

If Bill and Al shared a pizza, and Bill ate $\frac{1}{2}$ the pizza and Al ate $\frac{4}{8}$ of it, they had exactly the same amount.

We express this idea by saying that $\frac{1}{2}$ and $\frac{4}{8}$ are **equivalent fractions**: they have the exact same value.

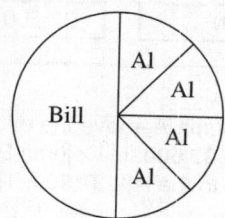

NOTE: If you multiply both the numerator and denominator of $\frac{1}{2}$ by 4 you get $\frac{4}{8}$; and if you divide both the numerator and denominator of $\frac{4}{8}$ by 4 you get $\frac{1}{2}$. This illustrates the next KEY FACT.

### KEY FACT B6:

**Two fractions are equivalent if multiplying or dividing both the numerator and denominator of the first one *by the same number* gives the second one.**

Consider the following two cases.

1. When the numerator and denominator of $\frac{3}{8}$ are each multiplied by 15, the products are $3 \times 15 = 45$ and $8 \times 15 = 120$. Therefore, $\frac{3}{8}$ and $\frac{45}{120}$ and are equivalent fractions.

2. Since 2 must be multiplied by 14 to get 28, but 3 must be multiplied by 15 to get 45, then $\frac{2}{3}$ and $\frac{28}{45}$ are not equivalent fractions.

### KEY FACT B7:

**To determine if two fractions are equivalent , cross-multiply. The fractions are equivalent if and only if the two products are equal.**

For example, since $120 \times 3 = 8 \times 45$, then $\frac{3}{8}$ and $\frac{45}{120}$ are equivalent.

Since $45 \times 2 \neq 3 \times 28$, then $\frac{2}{3}$ and $\frac{28}{45}$ are not equivalent fractions.

A fraction is in ***lowest terms*** if no positive integer greater than 1 is a factor of both the numerator and denominator. For example, $\frac{9}{20}$ is in lowest terms, since no integer greater than 1 is a factor of both 9 and 20; but $\frac{9}{24}$ is not in lowest terms, since 3 is a factor of both 9 and 24.

### KEY FACT B8:

**Every fraction can be *reduced* to lowest terms by dividing the numerator and the denominator by their greatest common factor (GCF). If the GCF is 1, the fraction is already in lowest terms.**

**Example 4.**

For any positive integer $n$: $n!$ means the product of all the integers from 1 to $n$. What is the value of $\frac{6!}{8!}$?

(A) $\frac{1}{56}$  (B) $\frac{1}{48}$  (C) $\frac{1}{8}$  (D) $\frac{1}{4}$  (E) $\frac{3}{4}$

SOLUTION. Clearly, you do not want to calculate 6! ($1 \cdot 2 \cdot 3 \cdot 4 \cdot 5 \cdot 6 = 720$) and 8! ($1 \cdot 2 \cdot 3 \cdot 4 \cdot 5 \cdot 6 \cdot 7 \cdot 8 = 40,320$) and then have to reduce $\frac{720}{40,320}$. Here's the easy solution:

$$\frac{6!}{8!} = \frac{\overset{1}{\cancel{6 \times 5 \times 4 \times 3 \times 2 \times 1}}}{8 \times 7 \times \underset{1}{\cancel{6 \times 5 \times 4 \times 3 \times 2 \times 1}}} = \frac{1}{8 \times 7} = \frac{1}{56}$$

## Arithmetic Operations with Decimals

### KEY FACT B9:

To add or subtract decimal numbers, make sure that the decimal points are lined up, and then add or subtract normally, ignoring the decimal points. Finally, place a decimal point in the answer immediately below the other decimal points.

For example, 3.2 + 7 + 1.125 = 11.325 and 3.456 − 1.28 = 2.176

$$
\begin{array}{r}
3.2 \\
7. \\
+\,1.1\,2\,5 \\
\hline
11.3\,2\,5
\end{array}
\qquad
\begin{array}{r}
3.4\,5\,6 \\
-\,1.2\,8 \\
\hline
2.1\,7\,6
\end{array}
$$

### KEY FACT B10:

To multiply decimal numbers, multiply normally, ignoring the decimal points. Then count the total number of digits to the right of the decimal points in both factors, and place a decimal point in the product that many places from the right.

For example, 2.6 × 3.14 = 8.164

$$
\begin{array}{r}
3.14 \text{ (two decimal places)} \\
\times\,2.6 \text{ (one decimal place)} \\
\hline
1884 \\
628\phantom{0} \\
\hline
8.164 \text{ (three decimal places)}
\end{array}
$$

### KEY FACT B11:

To divide decimal numbers, count the number of digits to the right of the decimal point in the divisor, and move the decimal point in both the divisor and the dividend that many places to the right (adding zeros if necessary). Now, divide normally and if there is a decimal point in the dividend, place a decimal place in the quotient directly above the one in the dividend.

For example, 35 ÷ 1.25 = 28 and .035 ÷ 1.25 = .028

$$
1.25\overline{)35} \qquad\qquad 1.25\overline{).035}
$$

$$
\begin{array}{r}
28 \\
=125\overline{)3500} \\
250\!\downarrow \\
\hline
1000 \\
1000 \\
\hline
0
\end{array}
\qquad
\begin{array}{r}
.028 \\
=125\overline{)03.500} \\
2\,50\!\downarrow \\
\hline
1\,000 \\
1\,000 \\
\hline
0
\end{array}
$$

Multiplying and dividing by powers of 10 is particularly easy and can be accomplished just by moving the decimal point.

### KEY FACT B12:

To multiply any decimal or whole number by a power of 10, move the decimal point as many places to the right as there are 0s in the power of 10, filling in with 0s, if necessary.

$$
1.35 \times 10 = 13.5 \qquad 1.35 \times 100 = 135
$$
$$
1.35 \times 1000 = 1350
$$

$$
23 \times 10 = 230 \qquad 23 \times 100 = 2300
$$
$$
23 \times 1,000,000 = 23,000,000
$$

### KEY FACT B13:

To divide any decimal or whole number by a power of 10, move the decimal point as many places to the left as there are 0s in the power of 10, filling in with 0s, if necessary.

$$
67.8 \div 10 = 6.78 \qquad 67.8 \div 100 = 0.678
$$
$$
67.8 \div 1000 = 0.0678
$$

$$
14 \div 10 = 1.4 \qquad 14 \div 100 = 0.14
$$
$$
14 \div 1,000,000 = 0.000014
$$

| Column A | Column B |
|----------|----------|
| **Example 5.** | |
| $3.75 \times 10^4$ | $37,500,000 \div 10^3$ |

SOLUTION. In Column A, move the decimal point 4 places to the right: **37,500**. In Column B, move the decimal point 3 places to the left: **37,500**. The answer is **C**.

## Arithmetic Operations with Fractions

### KEY FACT B14:

To multiply two fractions, multiply their numerators and multiply their denominators: $\dfrac{3}{5} \times \dfrac{4}{7} = \dfrac{3 \times 4}{5 \times 7} = \dfrac{12}{35}$

**KEY FACT B15:**

To multiply a fraction by any other number, write that number as a fraction whose denominator is 1:

$$\frac{3}{5} \times 7 = \frac{3}{5} \times \frac{7}{1} = \frac{21}{5} \qquad \frac{3}{4} \times \pi = \frac{3}{4} \times \frac{\pi}{1} = \frac{3\pi}{4}$$

**B1**

Before multiplying fractions, reduce. You may reduce by dividing any numerator and any denominator by a common factor.

> **Example 6.**
> Express the product, $\frac{3}{4} \times \frac{8}{9} \times \frac{15}{16}$, in lowest terms.

SOLUTION. If you multiply the numerators and denominators you get $\frac{360}{576}$, which is a nuisance to reduce. It is better to use TACTIC B1 and reduce first:

$$\frac{\overset{1}{\cancel{3}}}{4} \times \frac{\overset{1}{\cancel{8}}}{\underset{3}{\cancel{9}}} \times \frac{\overset{5}{\cancel{15}}}{\underset{2}{\cancel{16}}} = \frac{1 \times 1 \times 5}{4 \times 1 \times 2} = \frac{5}{8}$$

**B2**

When a problem requires you to find a fraction of a number, multiply.

> **Example 7.**
> If $\frac{4}{7}$ of the 350 sophomores at Monroe High
> School are girls, and $\frac{7}{8}$ of them play on a team,
> how many sophomore girls do <u>not</u> play on a team?

SOLUTION. There are $\frac{4}{7} \times 350 = 200$ sophomore girls.

Of these, $\frac{7}{8} \times 200 = 175$ play on a team. So,

$200 - 175 = \mathbf{25}$ do not play on a team.

The *reciprocal* of any nonzero number $x$ is that number $y$ such that $xy = 1$. Since $x\left(\frac{1}{x}\right) = 1$, then $\frac{1}{x}$ is the reciprocal of $x$. Similarly, the reciprocal of the fraction $\frac{a}{b}$ is the fraction $\frac{b}{a}$, since $\frac{a}{b} \cdot \frac{b}{a} = 1$.

**KEY FACT B16:**

To divide any number by a fraction, multiply that number by the reciprocal of the fraction.

$$20 \div \frac{2}{3} = \frac{20}{1} \times \frac{3}{2} = 30 \qquad \frac{3}{5} \div \frac{2}{3} = \frac{3}{5} \times \frac{3}{2} = \frac{9}{10}$$

$$\sqrt{2} \div \frac{2}{3} = \frac{\sqrt{2}}{1} \times \frac{3}{2} = \frac{3\sqrt{2}}{2}$$

> **Example 8.**
> In the meat department of a supermarket, 100 pounds of chopped meat was divided into packages, each of which weighed $\frac{4}{7}$ of a pound. How many packages were there?

SOLUTION. $100 \div \frac{4}{7} = \frac{100}{1} \times \frac{7}{4} = \mathbf{175}$

**KEY FACT B17:**

- To add or subtract fractions with the same denominator, add or subtract the numerators and keep the denominator:

$$\frac{4}{9} + \frac{1}{9} = \frac{5}{9} \quad \text{and} \quad \frac{4}{9} - \frac{1}{9} = \frac{3}{9} = \frac{1}{3}$$

- To add or subtract fractions with different denominators, first rewrite the fractions as equivalent fractions with the same denominators:

$$\frac{1}{6} + \frac{3}{4} = \frac{2}{12} + \frac{9}{12} = \frac{11}{12}$$

NOTE: The *easiest* common denominator to find is the product of the denominators ($6 \times 4 = 24$, in this example), but the best denominator to use is the **least common denominator**, which is the least common multiple (LCM) of the denominators (12, in this case). Using the least common denominator minimizes the amount of reducing that is necessary to express the answer in lowest terms.

**KEY FACT B18:**

If $\frac{a}{b}$ is the fraction of the whole that satisfies some

property, then $1 - \frac{a}{b}$ is the fraction of the whole that does not satisfy it.

**Example 9.**

In a jar, $\dfrac{1}{2}$ of the marbles are red, $\dfrac{1}{4}$ are white, and $\dfrac{1}{5}$ are blue. What fraction of the marbles are neither red, white, nor blue?

SOLUTION. The red, white, and blue marbles constitute

$$\frac{1}{2} + \frac{1}{4} + \frac{1}{5} = \frac{10}{20} + \frac{5}{20} + \frac{4}{20} = \frac{19}{20}$$

of the total, so

$$1 - \frac{19}{20} = \frac{20}{20} - \frac{19}{20} = \frac{1}{\mathbf{20}}$$

of the marbles are neither red, white, nor blue.

**Example 10.**

Lindsay ate $\dfrac{1}{3}$ of a cake and Emily ate $\dfrac{1}{4}$ of it. What fraction of the cake was still uneaten?

**Example 11.**

Lindsay ate $\dfrac{1}{3}$ of a cake and Emily ate $\dfrac{1}{4}$ of what was left. What fraction of the cake was still uneaten?

CAUTION: Be sure to read questions carefully. In Example 10, Emily ate $\dfrac{1}{4}$ of the cake. In Example 11, however, she only ate $\dfrac{1}{4}$ of the $\dfrac{2}{3}$ that was left after Lindsay had her piece: she ate $\dfrac{1}{4} \times \dfrac{2}{3} = \dfrac{1}{6}$ of the cake.

SOLUTION 10: $\dfrac{1}{3} + \dfrac{1}{4} = \dfrac{4}{12} + \dfrac{3}{12} = \dfrac{7}{12}$ of the cake was eaten, and $1 - \dfrac{7}{12} = \dfrac{5}{\mathbf{12}}$ was uneaten.

SOLUTION 11: $\dfrac{1}{3} + \dfrac{1}{6} = \dfrac{2}{6} + \dfrac{1}{6} = \dfrac{1}{2}$ of the cake was eaten, and the other $\dfrac{1}{\mathbf{2}}$ was uneaten.

## Arithmetic Operations with Mixed Numbers

A **mixed number** is a number such as $3\dfrac{1}{2}$, which consists of an integer followed by a fraction. It is an abbreviation for the *sum* of the number and the fraction; so, $3\dfrac{1}{2}$ is an abbreviation for $3 + \dfrac{1}{2}$. Every mixed number can be written as an improper fraction, and every improper fraction can be written as a mixed number:

$$3\frac{1}{2} = 3 + \frac{1}{2} = \frac{3}{1} + \frac{1}{2} = \frac{6}{2} + \frac{1}{2} = \frac{7}{2}$$

and $\quad \dfrac{7}{2} = \dfrac{6}{2} + \dfrac{1}{2} = 3 + \dfrac{1}{2} = 3\dfrac{1}{2}$

**KEY FACT B19:**

1. To write a mixed number $\left(3\dfrac{1}{2}\right)$ as an improper fraction, multiply the whole number (3) by the denominator (2), add the numerator (1), and write the sum over the denominator (2): $\dfrac{3 \times 2 + 1}{2} = \dfrac{7}{2}$.

2. To write an improper fraction $\left(\dfrac{7}{2}\right)$ as a mixed number, divide the numerator by the denominator; the quotient (3) is the whole number and the remainder (1) is placed over the denominator to form the fractional part $\left(\dfrac{1}{2}\right)$: $3\dfrac{1}{2}$.

**KEY FACT B20:**

To add mixed numbers, add the integers and add the fractions:

$$5\frac{1}{4} + 3\frac{2}{3} = (5 + 3) + \left(\frac{1}{4} + \frac{2}{3}\right) = 8 + \left(\frac{3}{12} + \frac{8}{12}\right) =$$

$$8 + \frac{11}{12} = 8\frac{11}{12}$$

**KEY FACT B21:**

To subtract mixed numbers, subtract the integers and the fractions. However, if the fraction in the second number is greater than the fraction in the first number, you first have to borrow 1 from the integer part. For example, since $\dfrac{2}{3} > \dfrac{1}{4}$, we can't subtract $5\dfrac{1}{4} - 3\dfrac{2}{3}$ until we borrow 1 from the 5:

$$5\frac{1}{4} = 5 + \frac{1}{4} = (4 + 1) + \frac{1}{4} = 4 + \left(1 + \frac{1}{4}\right) = 4 + \frac{5}{4}$$

Now, you have

$$5\frac{1}{4} - 3\frac{2}{3} = 4\frac{5}{4} - 3\frac{2}{3} = (4 - 3) + \left(\frac{5}{4} - \frac{2}{3}\right) =$$

$$1 + \left(\frac{15}{12} - \frac{8}{12}\right) = 1\frac{7}{12}.$$

### KEY FACT B22:

To multiply or divide mixed numbers, change them to improper fractions:

$$1\frac{2}{3} \times 3\frac{1}{4} = \frac{5}{3} \times \frac{13}{4} = \frac{65}{12} = 5\frac{5}{12}.$$

**CAUTION:** Be aware that $3 \times 5\frac{1}{2}$ is *not* $15\frac{1}{2}$; rather:

$$3 \times 5\frac{1}{2} = 3\left(5 + \frac{1}{2}\right) = 15 + \frac{3}{2} =$$

$$15 + 1\frac{1}{2} = 16\frac{1}{2}.$$

### Complex Fractions

A *complex fraction* is a fraction, such as $\dfrac{1+\frac{1}{6}}{2-\frac{3}{4}}$, which

has one or more fractions in its numerator or denominator or both.

### KEY FACT B23:

There are two ways to simplify a complex fraction:

- Multiply *every* term in the numerator and denominator by the least common multiple of all the denominators that appear in the fraction.

- Simplify the numerator and the denominator, and then divide.

To simplify $\dfrac{1+\frac{1}{6}}{2-\frac{3}{4}}$, multiply each term by 12, the LCM of

6 and 4:

$$\frac{12(1) + 12\left(\frac{1}{6}\right)}{12(2) - 12\left(\frac{3}{4}\right)} = \frac{12 + 2}{24 - 9} = \frac{14}{15},$$

or write

$$\frac{1+\frac{1}{6}}{2-\frac{3}{4}} = \frac{\frac{7}{6}}{\frac{5}{4}} = \frac{7}{6} \times \frac{4}{5} = \frac{14}{15}.$$

# PRACTICE EXERCISES—FRACTIONS AND DECIMALS

## Multiple-Choice Questions

1. A biology class has 12 boys and 18 girls. What fraction of the class are boys?

   (A) $\dfrac{2}{5}$   (B) $\dfrac{3}{5}$   (C) $\dfrac{2}{3}$   (D) $\dfrac{3}{4}$   (E) $\dfrac{3}{2}$

2. For how many integers, $a$, between 30 and 40 is it true that $\dfrac{5}{a}$, $\dfrac{8}{a}$, and $\dfrac{13}{a}$ are all in lowest terms?

   (A) 1   (B) 2   (C) 3   (D) 4   (E) 5

3. What fractional part of a week is 98 hours?

   (A) $\dfrac{7}{24}$   (B) $\dfrac{24}{98}$   (C) $\dfrac{1}{2}$   (D) $\dfrac{4}{7}$   (E) $\dfrac{7}{12}$

4. What is the value of the product $\dfrac{5}{5} \times \dfrac{5}{10} \times \dfrac{5}{15} \times \dfrac{5}{20} \times \dfrac{5}{25}$?

   (A) $\dfrac{1}{120}$   (B) $\dfrac{1}{60}$   (C) $\dfrac{1}{30}$   (D) $\dfrac{5}{30}$   (E) $\dfrac{1}{2}$

5. If $\dfrac{3}{11}$ of a number is 22, what is $\dfrac{6}{11}$ of that number?

   (A) 6   (B) 11   (C) 12   (D) 33   (E) 44

6. Jason won some goldfish at the state fair. During the first week, $\dfrac{1}{5}$ of them died, and during the second week, $\dfrac{3}{8}$ of those still alive at the end of the first week died. What fraction of the original goldfish were still alive after two weeks?

   (A) $\dfrac{3}{10}$   (B) $\dfrac{17}{40}$   (C) $\dfrac{1}{2}$   (D) $\dfrac{23}{40}$   (E) $\dfrac{7}{10}$

7. $\dfrac{5}{8}$ of 24 is equal to $\dfrac{15}{7}$ of what number?

   (A) 7   (B) 8   (C) 15   (D) $\dfrac{7}{225}$   (E) $\dfrac{225}{7}$

8. If $7a = 3$ and $3b = 7$, what is the value of $\dfrac{a}{b}$?

   (A) $\dfrac{9}{49}$   (B) $\dfrac{3}{7}$   (C) 1   (D) $\dfrac{7}{3}$   (E) $\dfrac{49}{9}$

9. What is the value of $\dfrac{\frac{7}{9} \times \frac{7}{9}}{\frac{7}{9} + \frac{7}{9} + \frac{7}{9}}$ ?

   (A) $\dfrac{7}{27}$   (B) $\dfrac{2}{3}$   (C) $\dfrac{7}{9}$   (D) $\dfrac{9}{7}$   (E) $\dfrac{3}{2}$

10. Which of the following are greater than $x$ when $x = \dfrac{9}{11}$?

   I. $\dfrac{1}{x}$

   II. $\dfrac{x+1}{x}$

   III. $\dfrac{x+1}{x-1}$

   (A) I only   (B) I and II only   (C) I and III only
   (D) II and III only   (E) I, II, and III

11. One day at Lincoln High School, $\dfrac{1}{12}$ of the students were absent, and $\dfrac{1}{5}$ of those present went on a field trip. If the number of students staying in school that day was 704, how many students are enrolled at Lincoln High?

   (A) 840   (B) 960   (C) 1080   (D) 1600
   (E) 3520

12. If $a = 0.87$, which of the following are less than $a$?

   I. $\sqrt{a}$

   II. $a^2$

   III. $\dfrac{1}{a}$

   (A) None   (B) I only   (C) II only   (D) III only
   (E) II and III only

13. For what value of $x$ is
   $\dfrac{(34.56)(7.89)}{x} = (.3456)(78.9)$?

   (A) .001   (B) .01   (C) .1   (D) 10   (E) 100

14. If $A = \{1, 2, 3\}$, $B = \{2, 3, 4\}$, and $C$ is the set consisting of all the fractions whose numerators are in $A$ and whose denominators are in $B$, what is the product of all of the numbers in $C$?

   (A) $\dfrac{1}{64}$   (B) $\dfrac{1}{48}$   (C) $\dfrac{1}{24}$   (D) $\dfrac{1}{12}$   (E) $\dfrac{1}{2}$

15. For the final step in a calculation, Ezra accidentally divided by 1000 instead of multiplying by 1000. What should he do to his incorrect answer to correct it?

   (A) Multiply it by 1000.
   (B) Multiply it by 100,000.
   (C) Multiply it by 1,000,000.
   (D) Square it.
   (E) Double it.

## Quantitative Comparison Questions

| Column A | Column B |
|---|---|
| 16. $\dfrac{5}{13}$ of 47 | $\dfrac{47}{13}$ of 5 |

$x = -\dfrac{2}{3}$ and $y = \dfrac{3}{5}$

| Column A | Column B |
|---|---|
| 17. $xy$ | $\dfrac{x}{y}$ |
| 18. $\dfrac{15}{\frac{1}{15}}$ | 1 |

Judy needed 8 pounds of chopped meat. At the supermarket, the only packages available weighed $\dfrac{3}{4}$ of a pound each.

| Column A | Column B |
|---|---|
| 19. The number of packages Judy needed to buy | 11 |
| 20. $\dfrac{11}{12}$ of $\dfrac{13}{14}$ | $\dfrac{14}{15}$ |

$a \nabla b = \dfrac{a}{b} + \dfrac{b}{a}$

| Column A | Column B |
|---|---|
| 21. $3 \nabla 4$ | $\dfrac{1}{2} \nabla \dfrac{2}{3}$ |
| 22. $\dfrac{100}{2^{100}}$ | $\dfrac{100}{3^{100}}$ |
| 23. $\left(-\dfrac{1}{2}\right)\left(-\dfrac{3}{4}\right)\left(-\dfrac{5}{6}\right)\left(-\dfrac{7}{8}\right)$ | $\left(-\dfrac{3}{7}\right)\left(-\dfrac{5}{9}\right)\left(-\dfrac{7}{11}\right)$ |

$a = \dfrac{1}{2}$ and $b = \dfrac{1}{3}$

| Column A | Column B |
|---|---|
| 24. $\dfrac{a}{b}$ | $\dfrac{b}{a}$ |
| 25. $\left(\dfrac{3}{11}\right)^2$ | $\sqrt{\dfrac{3}{11}}$ |

# Answer Key

| | | | | |
|---|---|---|---|---|
| 1. **A** | 6. **C** | 11. **B** | 16. **C** | 21. **C** |
| 2. **C** | 7. **A** | 12. **C** | 17. **A** | 22. **A** |
| 3. **E** | 8. **A** | 13. **D** | 18. **A** | 23. **A** |
| 4. **A** | 9. **A** | 14. **A** | 19. **C** | 24. **A** |
| 5. **E** | 10. **B** | 15. **C** | 20. **B** | 25. **B** |

# Answer Explanations

1. **A.** The class has 30 students, of whom 12 are boys. So, the boys make up $\frac{12}{30} = \frac{2}{5}$ of the class.

2. **C.** If $a$ is even, then $\frac{8}{a}$ is *not* in lowest terms, since both $a$ and 8 are divisible by 2. Therefore, the only possibilities are 31, 33, 35, 37, and 39; but $\frac{5}{35} = \frac{1}{7}$ and $\frac{13}{39} = \frac{1}{3}$, so only 3 integers—31, 33, and 37—satisfy the given condition.

3. **E.** There are 24 hours in a day and 7 days in a week, so there are $24 \times 7 = 168$ hours in a week: $\frac{98}{168} = \frac{7}{12}$.

4. **A.** Reduce each fraction and multiply:
$1 \times \frac{1}{2} \times \frac{1}{3} \times \frac{1}{4} \times \frac{1}{5} = \frac{1}{120}$.

5. **E.** Don't bother writing an equation for this one; just think. We know that $\frac{3}{11}$ of the number is 22, and $\frac{6}{11}$ of a number is twice as much as $\frac{3}{11}$ of it: $2 \times 22 = 44$.

6. **C.** The *algebra* way is to let $x =$ the number of goldfish Jason won. During the first week $\frac{1}{5}x$ died, so $\frac{4}{5}x$ were still alive. During week two, $\frac{3}{8}$ of them died and $\frac{5}{8}$ of them survived: $\left(\frac{5}{8}\right)\left(\frac{4}{5}x\right) = \frac{1}{2}x$.

On the GRE, the best way is to assume that the original number of goldfish was 40, the LCM of the denominators (see TACTIC 3, Chapter 12).

Then, 8 died the first week $\left(\frac{1}{5} \text{ of } 40\right)$, and 12

of the 32 survivors $\left(\frac{3}{8} \text{ of } 32\right)$ died the second week. In all, $8 + 12 = 20$ died; the other 20 $\left(\frac{1}{2} \text{ the original number}\right)$ were still alive.

7. **A.** If $x$ is the number, then $\frac{15}{7}x = \frac{5}{8} \times 24 = 15$. So, $\frac{15}{7}x = 15$, which means (dividing by 15) that $\frac{1}{7}x = 1$, and so $x = 7$.

8. **A.** $7a = 3$ and $3b = 7 \Rightarrow a = \frac{3}{7}$ and $b = \frac{7}{3} \Rightarrow$
$\frac{a}{b} = \frac{3}{7} \div \frac{7}{3} = \frac{3}{7} \times \frac{3}{7} = \frac{9}{49}$.

9. **A.** Don't start by doing the arithmetic. This is just
$$\frac{(a)(a)}{a + a + a} = \frac{(a)(a)}{3a} = \frac{a}{3}.$$
*Now*, replacing $a$ with $\frac{7}{9}$ gives $\frac{7}{9} \div 3 = \frac{7}{27}$.

10. **B.** The reciprocal of a positive number less than 1 is greater than 1 (I is true); $\frac{x+1}{x} = 1 + \frac{1}{x}$, which is greater than 1 (II is true); since $\frac{9}{11} + 1$ is positive and $\frac{9}{11} - 1$ is negative, when $x = \frac{9}{11}$, $\frac{x+1}{x-1} < 0$ and, therefore, less than $x$.

11. **B.** If $s$ is the number of students enrolled, $\frac{1}{12}s$ is the number who were absent, and $\frac{11}{12}s$ is the number who were present. Since $\frac{1}{5}$ of them went on a field trip, $\frac{4}{5}$ of them stayed in school. Therefore,
$$704 = \frac{4}{5} \times \frac{11}{12}s = \frac{11}{15}s \Rightarrow s = 704 \div \frac{11}{15} =$$
$$704 \times \frac{15}{11} = 960.$$

12. **C.** Since $a < 1$, $\sqrt{a} > a$ (I is false). Since $a < 1$,

GO ON TO THE NEXT P

$a^2 < a$ (II is true). The reciprocal of a positive number less than 1 is greater than 1 (III is false).

13. **D.** There are two easy ways to do this. The faster way is to see that (34.56)(7.89) has 4 decimal places, whereas (.3456)(78.9) has 5, so the numerator has to be divided by 10. The second way is to round off and calculate mentally: since $30 \times 8 = 240$, and $.3 \times 80 = 24$, we must divide by 10.

14. **A.** Nine fractions are formed:

$$\frac{1}{2}, \frac{1}{3}, \frac{1}{4}, \frac{2}{2}, \frac{2}{3}, \frac{2}{4}, \frac{3}{2}, \frac{3}{3}, \frac{3}{4}.$$

When you multiply, the three 2s and the three 3s in the numerators cancel with the three 2s and three 3s in the denominators. So, the numerator is 1 and the denominator is $4 \times 4 \times 4 = 64$.

15. **C.** Multiplying his incorrect answer by 1000 would undo the final division he made. At that point he should have multiplied by 1000. So, to correct his error, we have to multiply again by 1000. In all, we have to multiply $1000 \times 1000 = 1,000,000$.

16. **C.** Each column equals $\dfrac{5 \times 47}{13}$.

17. **A.** Column A: $-\dfrac{2}{3} \times \dfrac{3}{5} = -\dfrac{2}{5}$.

Column B: $-\dfrac{2}{3} \div \dfrac{3}{5} = -\dfrac{2}{3} \times \dfrac{5}{3} = -\dfrac{10}{9}$.

Finally, $\dfrac{10}{9} > \dfrac{2}{5} \Rightarrow -\dfrac{10}{9} < -\dfrac{2}{5}$.

18. **A.** Column A: $\dfrac{15}{\frac{1}{15}} = 15 \times 15 = 225$.

19. **C.** $8 \div \dfrac{3}{4} = 8 \times \dfrac{4}{3} = \dfrac{32}{3} = 10\dfrac{2}{3}$. Since 10 packages wouldn't be enough, she had to buy 11. (10 packages would weigh only $7\dfrac{1}{2}$ pounds.)

20. **B.** You don't need to multiply on this one: since $\dfrac{11}{12} < 1$, $\dfrac{11}{12}$ of $\dfrac{13}{14}$ is less than $\dfrac{13}{14}$, which is already less than $\dfrac{14}{15}$.

21. **C.** Column B is the sum of 2 complex fractions:

$$\frac{\frac{1}{2}}{\frac{2}{3}} + \frac{\frac{2}{3}}{\frac{1}{2}}.$$

Simplifying each complex fraction, by multiplying numerator and denominator by 6, or treating these as the quotient of 2 fractions, we get $\dfrac{3}{4} + \dfrac{4}{3}$, which is exactly the value of Column A.

22. **A.** When two fractions have the same numerator, the one with the smaller denominator is bigger, and $2^{100} < 3^{100}$.

23. **A.** Since Column A is the product of 4 negative numbers, it is positive, and so is greater than Column B, which, being the product of 3 negative numbers, is negative.

24. **A.** Column A: $\dfrac{1}{2} \div \dfrac{1}{3} = \dfrac{1}{2} \times \dfrac{3}{1} = \dfrac{3}{2}$. Since Column B is the reciprocal of Column A, Column B $= \dfrac{2}{3}$.

25. **B.** If $0 < x < 1$, then $x^2 < x < \sqrt{x}$. In this question, $x = \dfrac{3}{11}$.

# 15-C. PERCENTS

The word **percent** means hundredth. We use the symbol "%" to express the word "percent." For example, "17 percent" means "17 hundredths," and can be written with a % symbol, as a fraction, or as a decimal:

$$17\% = \frac{17}{100} = 0.17.$$

**KEY FACT C1:**

- **To convert a percent to a decimal, drop the % symbol and move the decimal point two places to the left, adding 0s if necessary. (Remember that we assume that there is a decimal point to the right of any whole number.)**

- **To convert a percent to a fraction, drop the % symbol, write the number over 100, and reduce.**

$$25\% = 0.25 = \frac{25}{100} = \frac{1}{4} \qquad 100\% = 1.00 = \frac{100}{100}$$

$$12.5\% = 0.125 = \frac{12.5}{100} = \frac{125}{1000} = \frac{1}{8}$$

$$1\% = 0.01 = \frac{1}{100} \qquad \frac{1}{2}\% = 0.5\% = 0.005 = \frac{.5}{100} = \frac{1}{200}$$

$$250\% = 2.50 = \frac{250}{100} = \frac{5}{2}$$

## KEY FACT C2:

- **To convert a decimal to a percent, move the decimal point two places to the right, adding 0s if necessary, and add the % symbol.**

- **To convert a fraction to a percent, first convert the fraction to a decimal, then convert the decimal to a percent, as indicated above.**

$$0.375 = 37.5\% \qquad 0.3 = 30\% \qquad 1.25 = 125\% \qquad 10 = 1000\%$$

$$\frac{3}{4} = 0.75 = 75\% \qquad \frac{1}{3} = 0.33333\ldots = 33.333\ldots\% = 33\frac{1}{3}\%$$

$$\frac{1}{5} = 0.2 = 20\%$$

You should be familiar with the following basic conversions:

$$\frac{1}{2} = 50\% \qquad \frac{1}{10} = 10\% \qquad \frac{6}{10} = \frac{3}{5} = 60\%$$

$$\frac{1}{3} = 33\frac{1}{3}\% \qquad \frac{2}{10} = \frac{1}{5} = 20\% \qquad \frac{7}{10} = 70\%$$

$$\frac{2}{3} = 66\frac{2}{3}\% \qquad \frac{3}{10} = 30\% \qquad \frac{8}{10} = \frac{4}{5} = 80\%$$

$$\frac{1}{4} = 25\% \qquad \frac{4}{10} = \frac{2}{5} = 40\% \qquad \frac{9}{10} = 90\%$$

$$\frac{3}{4} = 75\% \qquad \frac{5}{10} = \frac{1}{2} = 50\% \qquad \frac{10}{10} = 1 = 100\%$$

Knowing the above conversions can help solve many problems more quickly. For example, the fastest way to find 25% of 32 is not to multiply 32 by 0.25; rather, it is to know that $25\% = \frac{1}{4}$, and that $\frac{1}{4}$ of 32 is 8.

Many questions involving percents can actually be answered more quickly in your head than by using paper and pencil. Since $10\% = \frac{1}{10}$, to take 10% of a number, just divide by 10 by moving the decimal point one place to the left: 10% of 60 is 6. Also, since 5% is half of 10%, then 5% of 60 is 3 (half of 6); and since 30% is 3 times 10%, then 30% of 60 is 18 (3 × 6).

Practice doing this, because improving your ability to do mental math will add valuable points to your score on the GRE.

## Solving Percent Problems

Consider the following three questions:

(i) What is 45% of 200?
(ii) 90 is 45% of what number?
(iii) 90 is what percent of 200?

The arithmetic needed to answer each of these questions is very easy, but unless you set a question up properly, you won't know whether you should multiply or divide. In each case, there is one unknown, which we will call x. Now just translate each sentence, replacing "is" by "=" and the unknown by x.

(i) $x = 45\%$ of $200 \Rightarrow x = .45 \times 200 = 90$
(ii) $90 = 45\%$ of $x \Rightarrow 90 = .45x \Rightarrow x = 90 \div .45 = 200$
(iii) $90 = x\%$ of $200 \Rightarrow 90 = \frac{x}{100}(200) \Rightarrow 90 = 2x \Rightarrow x = 45$

---

**Example 1.**

Charlie gave 20% of his baseball cards to Kenne and 15% to Paulie. If he still had 520 cards, how many did he have originally?

(A) 555   (B) 700   (C) 800   (D) 888   (E) 1000

---

SOLUTION. Originally, Charlie had 100% of the cards (all of them). Since he gave away 35% of them, he has 100% − 35% = 65% of them left. So, 520 is 65% of what number?

$$520 = .65x \Rightarrow x = 520 \div .65 = \mathbf{800 \ (C)}.$$

---

**Example 2.**

After Ruth gave 110 baseball cards to Alison and 75 to Susanna, she still had 315 left. What percent of her cards did Ruth give away?

(A) 25%   (B) $33\frac{1}{3}\%$   (C) 37%   (D) 40%
(E) 50%

---

SOLUTION. Ruth gave away a total of 185 cards and had 315 left. Therefore, she started with 185 + 315 = 500 cards. So, 185 is what percent of 500?

$$185 = \frac{x}{100}\overset{5}{\underset{1}{(500)}} \Rightarrow 5x = 185 \Rightarrow x = 185 \div 5 = \mathbf{37}$$

Ruth gave away 37% of her cards, (**C**).

Since percent means hundredth, the easiest number to use in any percent problem is 100:

$$a\% \text{ of } 100 = \frac{a}{100} \times 100 = a.$$

## KEY FACT C3:

**For any positive number $a$: $a\%$ of 100 is $a$.**

For example: 91.2% of 100 is 91.2; 300% of 100 is 300; and $\frac{1}{2}\%$ of 100 is $\frac{1}{2}$.

**Tactic C1**

In any problem involving percents, use the number 100 (It doesn't matter whether or not 100 is a realistic number—a country can have a population of 100; an apple can cost $100; a man can run 100 miles per hour.)

---

**Example 3.**

In 1985 the populations of town A and town B were the same. From 1985 to 1995 the population of town A increased by 60% while the population of town B decreased by 60%. In 1995, the population of town B was what percent of the population of town A?

(A) 25%    (B) 36%    (C) 40%    (D) 60%
        (E) 120%

---

SOLUTION. *On the GRE, do not waste time with a nice algebraic solution.* Simply, assume that in 1985 the population of each town was 100. Then, since 60% of 100 is 60, in 1995, the populations were 100 + 60 = 160 and 100 − 60 = 40. So, in 1995, town B's population was

$$\frac{40}{160} = \frac{1}{4} = \mathbf{25\%} \text{ of town A's (A)}.$$

Since $a\%$ of $b$ is $\frac{a}{100} \times b = \frac{ab}{100}$, and $b\%$ of $a$ is

$\frac{b}{100} \times a = \frac{ba}{100}$, we have the result shown in KEY FACT C4.

**KEY FACT C4:**

For any positive numbers $a$ and $b$: $a\%$ of $b = b\%$ of $a$.

KEY FACT C4 often comes up on the GRE in quantitative comparison questions: Which is greater, 13% of 87 or 87% of 13? Don't multiply—they're equal.

## Percent Increase and Decrease

**KEY FACT C5:**

• The *percent increase* of a quantity is

$\dfrac{\text{actual increase}}{\text{original amount}} \times 100\%.$

• The *percent decrease* of a quantity is

$\dfrac{\text{actual decrease}}{\text{original amount}} \times 100\%.$

For example:

• If the price of a lamp goes from $80 to $100, the actual increase is $20, and the percent increase is

$\dfrac{20}{80} \times 100\% = \dfrac{1}{4} \times 100\% = 25\%.$

• If a $100 lamp is on sale for $80, the actual decrease in price is $20, and the percent decrease is

$\dfrac{20}{100} \times 100\% = 20\%.$

Notice that the percent increase in going from 80 to 100 is not the same as the percent decrease in going from 100 to 80.

**KEY FACT C6:**

If $a < b$, the percent increase in going from $a$ to $b$ is *always* greater than the percent decrease in going from $b$ to $a$.

**KEY FACT C7:**

• To increase a number by $k\%$, multiply it by $(1 + k\%)$.

• To decrease a number by $k\%$, multiply it by $(1 - k\%)$.

For example:

• The value of a $1600 investment after a 25% increase is $1600(1 + 25%) = $1600(1.25) = $2000.

• If the investment then loses 25% of its value, it is worth $2000(1 − 25%) = $2000(.75) = $1500.

Note that, after a 25% increase followed by a 25% decrease, the value is $1500, $100 *less* than the original amount.

**KEY FACT C8:**

An increase of $k\%$ followed by a decrease of $k\%$ is equal to a decrease of $k\%$ followed by an increase of $k\%$, and is *always* less than the original value. The original value is never regained.

---

| Column A | Column B |
|---|---|

**Example 4.**

Store B always sells CDs at 60% off the list price. Store A sells its CDs at 40% off the list price, but often runs a special sale during which it reduces its prices by 20%.

| The price of a CD when it is on sale at store A | The price of the same CD at store B |
|---|---|

---

SOLUTION. Assume the list price of the CD is $100. Store B always sells the CD for $40 ($60 off the list price). Store A normally sells the CD for $60 ($40 off the list price), but on sale reduces its price by 20%. Since 20% of 60 is 12, the sale price is $48 ($60 − $12). The price is greater at Store A.

Notice that a decrease of 40% followed by a decrease of 20% is not the same as a single decrease of 60%; it is less. In fact, a decrease of 40% followed by a decrease of 30% wouldn't even be as much as a single decrease of 60%.

## KEY FACT C9:

- A decrease of $a\%$ followed by a decrease of $b\%$ *always* results in a smaller decrease than a single decrease of $(a + b)\%$.

- An increase of $a\%$ followed by an increase of $b\%$ *always* results in a larger increase than a single increase of $(a + b)\%$.

- An increase (or decrease) of $a\%$ followed by another increase (or decrease) of $a\%$ is *never* the same as a single increase (or decrease) of $2a\%$.

| Column A | Column B |
| --- | --- |

**Example 5.**

Sally and Heidi were both hired in January at the same salary. Sally got two 40% raises, one in July and another in November. Heidi got one 90% raise in October.

| Sally's salary at the end of the year | Heidi's salary at the end of the year |
| --- | --- |

SOLUTION. Since this is a percent problem, assume their salaries were $100. Column A: Sally's salary rose to 100(1.40) = 140, and then to 140(1.40) = $196. Column B: Heidi's salary rose to 100(1.90) = $190. Column **A** is greater.

**Example 6.**

In January, the value of a stock increased by 25%, and in February, it decreased by 20%. How did the value of the stock at the end of February compare with its value at the beginning of January?

(A) It was less.
(B) It was the same.
(C) It was 5% greater.
(D) It was more than 5% greater.
(E) It cannot be determined from the information given.

SOLUTION. Assume that at the beginning of January the stock was worth $100. Then at the end of January it was worth $125. Since 20% of 125 is 25, during February its value decreased from $125 to $100. The answer is **B**.

## KEY FACT C10:

- If a number is the result of increasing another number by $k\%$, to find the original number, divide by $(1 + k\%)$.

- If a number is the result of decreasing another number by $k\%$, to find the original number, divide it by $(1 - k\%)$.

For example, if the population of a town in 1990 was 3000, and this represents an increase of 20% since 1980, to find the population in 1980, divide 3000 by $(1 + 20\%)$: 3000 ÷ 1.20 = 2500.

**Example 7.**

From 1989 to 1990, the number of applicants to a college increased 15% to 5060. How many applicants were there in 1989?

(A) 759　(B) 4301　(C) 4400　(D) 5819
  (E) 5953

SOLUTION. The number of applicants in 1989 was 5060 ÷ 1.15 = **4400 (C)**.

CAUTION. Percents over 100%, which come up most often on questions involving percent increases, are often confusing for students. First of all, be sure you understand that 100% of a number is that number, 200% of a number is 2 times the number, and 1000% of a number is 10 times the number. If the value of an investment goes from $1000 to $5000, it is now worth 5 times, or 500%, as much as it was originally; but there has only been a *400%* increase in value:

$$\frac{\text{actual increase}}{\text{original amount}} \times 100\% = \frac{4000}{1000} \times 100\% =$$
$$4 \times 100\% = 400\%.$$

**Example 8.**

The population of a country doubled every 10 years from 1960 to 1990. What was the percent increase in population during this time?

(A) 200%　(B) 300%　(C) 700%　(D) 800%
  (E) 1000%

SOLUTION. The population doubled three times (once from 1960 to 1970, again from 1970 to 1980, and a third time from 1980 to 1990). Assume that the population was originally 100. Then it increased from 100 to 200 to 400 to 800. So the population in 1990 was 8 times the population in 1960, but this was an increase of 700 people, or **700% (C)**.

# PRACTICE EXERCISES—PERCENTS

## Multiple-Choice Questions

1. If 25 students took an exam and 4 of them failed, what percent of them passed?
   (A) 4%   (B) 21%   (C) 42%   (D) 84%   (E) 96%

2. Amanda bought a $60 sweater on sale at 5% off. How much did she pay, including 5% sales tax?
   (A) $54.15   (B) $57.00   (C) $57.75   (D) $59.85
   (E) $60.00

3. What is 10% of 20% of 30%?
   (A) 0.006%   (B) 0.6%   (C) 6%   (D) 60%
   (E) 6000%

4. If $c$ is a positive number, 500% of $c$ is what percent of $500c$?
   (A) 0.01   (B) 0.1   (C) 1   (D) 10   (E) 100

5. What percent of 50 is $b$?
   (A) $\dfrac{b}{50}$   (B) $\dfrac{b}{2}$   (C) $\dfrac{50}{b}$   (D) $\dfrac{2}{b}$   (E) $2b$

6. 8 is $\dfrac{1}{3}$% of what number?
   (A) .24   (B) 2.4   (C) 24   (D) 240   (E) 2400

7. During his second week on the job, Mario earned $110. This represented a 25% increase over his earnings of the previous week. How much did he earn during his first week of work?
   (A) $82.50   (B) $85.00   (C) $88.00
   (D) $137.50   (E) $146.67

8. At Bernie's Bargain Basement everything is sold for 20% less than the price marked. If Bernie buys radios for $80, what price should he mark them if he wants to make a 20% profit on his cost?
   (A) $96   (B) $100   (C) $112   (D) $120
   (E) $125

9. Mrs. Fisher was planning on depositing a certain amount of money each month into a vacation fund. She then decided not to make any contributions during June and July. To make the same annual contribution that she had originally planned, by what percent should she increase her monthly deposits?
   (A) $16\dfrac{2}{3}$%   (B) 20%   (C) 25%   (D) $33\dfrac{1}{3}$%
   (E) It cannot be determined from the information given.

10. If 1 micron = 10,000 angstroms, then 100 angstroms is what percent of 10 microns?
    (A) 0.0001%   (B) 0.001%   (C) 0.01%   (D) 0.1%
    (E) 1%

11. The price of a loaf of bread was increased by 20%. How many loaves can be purchased for the amount of money that used to buy 300 loaves?
    (A) 240   (B) 250   (C) 280   (D) 320   (E) 360

12. There are twice as many girls as boys in an English class. If 30% of the girls and 45% of the boys have already handed in their book reports, what percent of the students have not yet handed in their reports?
    (A) 25%   (B) 35%   (C) 50%   (D) 65%   (E) 75%

13. An art dealer bought a Ming vase for $1000 and later sold it for $10,000. By what percent did the value of the vase increase?
    (A) 10%   (B) 90%   (C) 100%   (D) 900%
    (E) 1000%

14. During a sale a clerk was putting a new price tag on each item. On one jacket, he accidentally raised the price by 15% instead of lowering the price by 15%. As a result the price on the tag was $45 too high. What was the original price of the jacket?
    (A) $60   (B) $75   (C) $90   (D) $105   (E) $150

15. On a test consisting of 80 questions, Eve answered 75% of the first 60 questions correctly. What percent of the other 20 questions does she need to answer correctly for her grade on the entire exam to be 80%?
    (A) 85%   (B) 87.5%   (C) 90%   (D) 95%
    (E) 100%

## Quantitative Comparison Questions

| Column A | Column B |
| --- | --- |

16. 
| 400% of 3 | 300% of 4 |
| --- | --- |

17. $n$% of 25 is 50
| 50% of $n$ | 75 |
| --- | --- |

18. 
| The price of a television when it is on sale at 25% off | The price of that television when it's on sale at $25 off |
| --- | --- |

| Column A | Column B |
|---|---|

The price of cellular phone 1 is 20% more than the price of cellular phone 2.

19.

| The price of cellular phone 1 when it is on sale at 20% off | The price of cellular phone 2 |
|---|---|

20.

| $\frac{2}{3}\%$ of $\frac{3}{4}$ | $\frac{3}{4}\%$ of $\frac{2}{3}$ |
|---|---|

21.

| $a\%$ of $\frac{1}{b}$ | $b\%$ of $\frac{1}{a}$ |
|---|---|

Bank A pays 5% interest on its savings accounts. Bank B pays 4% interest on its savings accounts.

22.

| Percent by which bank B would have to raise its interest rate to match bank A | 20% |
|---|---|

| Column A | Column B |
|---|---|

A solution that is 20% sugar is made sweeter by doubling the amount of sugar.

23.

| The percent of sugar in the new solution | 40% |
|---|---|

$b$ is an integer greater than 1, and $b$ equals $n\%$ of $b^2$

24.

| $n$ | 50 |
|---|---|

After Ali gave Lior 50% of her money, she had 20% as much as he did.

25.

| 75% of the amount Lior had originally | 150% of the amount Ali had originally |
|---|---|

# Answer Key

| | | | | |
|---|---|---|---|---|
| 1. D | 6. E | 11. B | 16. C | 21. D |
| 2. D | 7. C | 12. D | 17. A | 22. A |
| 3. B | 8. D | 13. D | 18. D | 23. B |
| 4. C | 9. B | 14. E | 19. B | 24. D |
| 5. E | 10. D | 15. D | 20. C | 25. C |

# Answer Explanations

1. **D.** If 4 students failed, then the other $25 - 4 = 21$ students passed, and $\frac{21}{25} = \frac{84}{100} = .84 = 84\%$.

2. **D.** Since 5% of 60 is 3, Amanda saved $3, and thus paid $57 for the sweater. She then had to pay 5% sales tax on the $57: $.05 \times 57 = 2.85$, so the total cost was $57 + \$2.85 = \$59.85$.

3. **B.** 10% of 20% of 30% = $.10 \times .20 \times .30 = .006 = .6\%$.

4. **C.** 500% of $c = 5c$, which is 1% of $500c$.

5. **E.** $b = \frac{x}{100}(50) \Rightarrow b = \frac{x}{2} \Rightarrow x = 2b$.

6. **E.** $8 = \frac{\frac{1}{3}}{100}x = \frac{1}{300}x \Rightarrow x = 8 \times 300 = 2400$.

7. **C.** To find Mario's earnings during his first week, divide his earnings from the second week by 1.25: $110 \div 1.25 = 88$.

8. **D.** Since 20% of 80 is 16, Bernie wants to get $96 for each radio he sells. What price should the radios be marked so that after a 20% discount, the customer will pay $96? If $x$ represents the marked price, then
$.80x = 96 \Rightarrow x = 96 \div .80 = 120$.

9. **B.** Assume that Mrs. Fisher was going to contribute $100 each month, for an annual total of

$1200. Having decided not to contribute for 2 months, the $1200 will have to be paid in 10 monthly deposits of $120 each. This is an increase of $20, and a percent increase of

$$\frac{\text{actual increase}}{\text{original amount}} = \frac{20}{100} = 20\%.$$

10.  D.  1 micron = 10,000 angstroms $\Rightarrow$ 10 microns = 100,000 angstroms; dividing both sides by 1000, we get

100 angstroms = $\frac{1}{1000}$ (10 microns);

and $\frac{1}{1000} = .001 = 0.1\%$.

11.  B.  Assume that a loaf of bread used to cost $1 and that now it costs $1.20 (20% more). Then 300 loaves of bread used to cost $300. How many loaves costing $1.20 each can be bought for $300? 300 ÷ 1.20 = 250.

12.  D.  Assume that there are 100 boys and 200 girls in the class. Then, 45 boys (45% of 100) and 60 girls (30% of 200), have handed in their reports. So 105 of the 300 students have handed them in, and 300 − 105 = 195 have not handed them in. What percent of 300 is 195? $\frac{195}{300} = .65 = 65\%.$

13.  D.  The increase in the value of the vase was $9,000, and the percent increase = 
$$\frac{\text{the actual increase in value}}{\text{the original cost}} = \frac{9000}{1000} = 9 =$$
900%.

14.  E.  If $p$ represents the original price, the jacket was priced at 1.15$p$ instead of .85$p$. Since this was a $45 difference,
$$45 = 1.15p - .85p = .30p \Rightarrow$$
$$p = 45 \div .30 = \$150.$$

15.  D.  To earn a grade of 80% on the entire exam, Eve needs to correctly answer 64 questions (80% of 80). So far, she has answered 45 questions correctly (75% of 60). Therefore, on the last 20 questions she needs 64 − 45 = 19 correct answers; and $\frac{19}{20} = 95\%.$

16.  C.  Column A: 400% of 3 = 4 × 3 = 12.
Column B: 300% of 4 = 3 × 4 = 12.

17.  A.  Since $n\%$ of 25 is 50, then 25% of $n$ is also 50, and 50% of $n$ is twice as much: 100. If you don't see that, just solve for $n$:

$$\frac{n}{100} \times 25 = 50 \Rightarrow \frac{n}{4} = 50 \Rightarrow n = 200 \Rightarrow$$
50% of $n$ = 100.

18.  D.  A 25% discount on a $10 television is much less than $25, whereas a 25% discount on a $1000 television is much more than $25. (They would be equal only if the regular price of the television were $100.)

19.  B.  Assume that the price of cellular phone 2 is $100; then the price of cellular phone 1 is $120, and on sale at 20% off it costs $24 less: $96.

20.  C.  For *any* numbers $a$ and $b$: $a\%$ of $b$ is equal to $b\%$ of $a$.

21.  D.  

| Column A | Column B |
| --- | --- |
| $a\%$ of $\dfrac{1}{b}$ | $b\%$ of $\dfrac{1}{a}$ |
| $\dfrac{a}{100} \times \dfrac{1}{b} = \dfrac{a}{100b}$ | $\dfrac{b}{100} \times \dfrac{1}{a} = \dfrac{b}{100a}$ |

Multiply by 100: $\dfrac{a}{b}$  $\dfrac{b}{a}$

The columns are equal if $a$ and $b$ are equal, and unequal otherwise.

22.  A.  Bank B would have to increase its rate from 4% to 5%, an actual increase of 1%. This represents a percent increase of
$$\frac{1\%}{4\%} \times 100\% = 25\%.$$

23.  B.  Assume a vat contains 100 ounces of a solution, of which 20% or 20 ounces is sugar (the remaining 80 ounces being water). If the amount of sugar is doubled, there would be 40 ounces of sugar and 80 ounces of water. The sugar will then comprise
$$\frac{40}{120} = \frac{1}{3} = 33\frac{1}{3}\% \text{ of the solution.}$$

24.  D.  If $b = 2$, $b^2 = 4$, and 2 = 50% of 4, the columns could be equal. If $b = 4$, $b^2 = 16$, and 4 is not 50% of 16, the columns don't have to be equal.

25.  C.  Avoid the algebra and just assume Ali started with $100. After giving Lior $50, she had $50 left, which was 20% or one-fifth of what he had. So, Lior had 5 × $50 = $250, which means that originally he had $200.

Column A: 75% of $200 = $150.

Column B: 150% of $100 = $150.

The columns are equal.

# 15-D. RATIOS AND PROPORTIONS

A *ratio* is a fraction that compares two quantities that are measured in the same units. The first quantity is the numerator and the second quantity is the denominator.

For example, if there are 4 boys and 16 girls on the debate team, we say that the ratio of the number of boys to the number of girls on the team is 4 to 16, or $\frac{4}{16}$. This is often written 4:16. Since a ratio is just a fraction, it can be reduced or converted to a decimal or a percent. The following are all different ways to express the same ratio:

$$4 \text{ to } 16 \quad 4:16 \quad \frac{4}{16} \qquad 2 \text{ to } 8 \quad 2:8 \quad \frac{2}{8}$$
$$1 \text{ to } 4 \quad 1:4 \quad \frac{1}{4} \qquad\qquad 0.25 \quad 25\%$$

> CAUTION: Saying that the ratio of boys to girls on the team is 1:4 does *not* mean that $\frac{1}{4}$ of the team members are boys. It means that for each boy on the team there are 4 girls; so for every 5 members of the team, there are 4 girls and 1 boy. Boys, therefore, make up $\frac{1}{5}$ of the team, and girls $\frac{4}{5}$.

### KEY FACT D1:

If a set of objects is divided into two groups in the ratio of *a*:*b*, then the first group contains $\frac{a}{a+b}$ of the objects and the second group contains $\frac{b}{a+b}$ of the objects.

> **Example 1.**
>
> Last year, the ratio of the number of tennis matches that Central College's women's team won to the number of matches they lost was 7:3. What percent of their matches did the team win?

SOLUTION. The team won $\frac{7}{7+3} = \frac{7}{10} = \mathbf{70\%}$ of their matches.

> **Example 2.**
>
> If 45% of the students at a college are male, what is the ratio of male students to female students?

Reminder: In problems involving percents the best number to use is 100.

SOLUTION. Assume that there are 100 students. Then 45 of them are male, and $100 - 45 = 55$ of them are female. So, the ratio of males to females is $= \frac{45}{55} = \mathbf{\frac{9}{11}}$.

If we know how many boys and girls there are in a club, then, clearly, we know not only the ratio of boys to girls, but several other ratios too. For example, if the club has 7 boys and 3 girls: the ratio of boys to girls is $\frac{7}{3}$, the ratio of girls to boys is $\frac{3}{7}$, the ratio of boys to members is $\frac{7}{10}$, the ratio of members to girls is $\frac{10}{3}$, and so on.

However, if we know a ratio, we *cannot* determine how many objects there are. For example, if a jar contains only red and blue marbles, and if the ratio of red marbles to blue marbles is 3:5, there *may* be 3 red marbles and 5 blue marbles, but *not necessarily*. There may be 300 red marbles and 500 blue ones, since the ratio 300:500 reduces to 3:5. In the same way, all of the following are possibilities for the distribution of marbles.

| Red | 6 | 12 | 33 | 51 | 150 | 3000 | *3x* |
|------|----|----|----|----|-----|------|------|
| Blue | 10 | 20 | 55 | 85 | 250 | 5000 | *5x* |

The important thing to observe is that the number of red marbles can be *any* multiple of 3, as long as the number of blue marbles is the *same* multiple of 5.

### KEY FACT D2:

If two numbers are in the ratio of *a*:*b*, then for some number *x*, the first number is *ax* and the second number is *bx*. If the ratio is in lowest terms, and if the quantities must be integers, then *x* is also an integer.

**Tactic D1**

In any ratio problem, write the letter *x* after each number and use some given information to solve for *x*.

> **Example 3.**
>
> If the ratio of men to women in a particular dormitory is 5:3, which of the following could not be the number of residents in the dormitory?
> (A) 24   (B) 40   (C) 96   (D) 150   (E) 224

SOLUTION. If 5*x* and 3*x* are the number of men and women in the dormitory, respectively, then the number of residents in the dormitory is $5x + 3x = 8x$. So, the number of students must be a multiple of 8. Of the five choices, only **150 (D)** is not divisible by 8.

Note: Assume that the ratio of the number of pounds of cole slaw to the number of pounds of potato salad consumed in the dormitory's cafeteria was 5:3. Then, it is possible that a total of exactly 150 pounds was eaten:

93.75 pounds of cole slaw and 56.25 pounds of potato salad. In Example 3, 150 wasn't possible because there had to be a *whole* number of men and women.

---

**Example 4.**

The measures of the two acute angles in a right triangle are in the ratio of 5:13. What is the measure of the larger angle?

(A) 25°    (B) 45°    (C) 60°    (D) 65°    (E) 75°

---

SOLUTION: Let the measure of the smaller angle be $5x$ and the measure of the larger angle be $13x$. Since the sum of the measures of the 2 acute angles of a right triangle is 90° (KEY FACT J3),

$$5x + 13x = 90 \Rightarrow 18x = 90 \Rightarrow x = 5.$$

Therefore, the measure of the larger angle is $13 \times 5 =$ **65° (D)**.

Ratios can be extended to 3 or 4 or more terms. For example, we can say that the ratio of freshmen to sophomores to juniors to seniors in a college marching band is 6:8:5:8, which means that for every 6 freshmen in the band there are 8 sophomores, 5 juniors, and 8 seniors.

NOTE: TACTIC D1 applies to extended ratios, as well.

---

**Example 5.**

The concession stand at Cinema City sells popcorn in three sizes: large, super, and jumbo. One day, Cinema City sold 240 bags of popcorn, and the ratio of large to super to jumbo was 8:17:15. How many super bags of popcorn were sold that day?

(A) 48    (B) 90    (C) 102    (D) 108    (E) 120

---

SOLUTION: Let $8x$, $17x$, and $15x$ be the number of large, super, and jumbo bags of popcorn sold, respectively. Then

$$8x + 17x + 15x = 240 \Rightarrow 40x = 240 \Rightarrow x = 6.$$

The number of super bags sold was $17 \times 6 =$ **102 (D)**.

**KEY FACT D3:**

**KEY FACT D1 applies to extended ratios, as well. If a set of objects is divided into 3 groups in the ratio $a:b:c$, then the first group contains $\dfrac{a}{a+b+c}$ of the objects, the second $\dfrac{b}{a+b+c}$, and the third $\dfrac{c}{a+b+c}$.**

---

**Example 6.**

If the ratio of large to super to jumbo bags of popcorn sold at Cinema City was 8:17:15, what percent of the bags sold were super?

(A) 20%    (B) 25%    (C) $33\frac{1}{3}$%    (D) 37.5%

(E) 42.5%

---

SOLUTION. Super bags made up $\dfrac{17}{8+17+15} = \dfrac{17}{40} =$ **42.5%** of the total (**E**).

A jar contains a number of red (R), white (W), and blue (B) marbles. Suppose that R:W = 2:3 and W:B = 3:5. Then, for every 2 red marbles, there are 3 white ones, and for those 3 white ones, there are 5 blue ones. So, R:B = 2:5, and we can form the extended ratio R:W:B = 2:3:5.

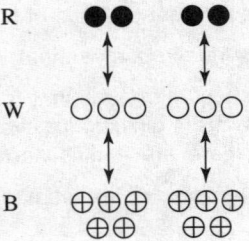

If the ratios were R:W = 2:3 and W:B = 4:5, however, we wouldn't be able to combine them as easily. From the diagram below, you see that for every 8 reds there are 15 blues, so R:B = 8:15.

To see this without drawing a picture, we write the ratios as fractions: $\dfrac{R}{W} = \dfrac{2}{3}$ and $\dfrac{W}{B} = \dfrac{4}{5}$. Then, we multiply the fractions:

$$\frac{R}{\cancel{W}} \times \frac{\cancel{W}}{B} = \frac{2}{3} \times \frac{4}{5} = \frac{8}{15}, \quad \text{so} \quad \frac{R}{B} = \frac{8}{15}.$$

Not only does this give us R:B = 8:15, but also, if we multiply both W numbers, $3 \times 4 = 12$, we can write the extended ratio: R:W:B = 8:12:15.

## Column A          Column B

**Example 7.**

Jar A and jar B each have 70 marbles, all of which are red, white, or blue.
In jar A: R:W = 2:3 and W:B = 3:5.
In jar B: R:W = 2:3 and W:B = 4:5.

| The number of white marbles in jar A | The number of white marbles in jar B |

**SOLUTION.** From the discussion immediately preceding this example, in jar A the extended ratio R:W:B is 2:3:5, which implies that the white marbles constitute $\frac{3}{2+3+5} = \frac{3}{10}$ of the total: $\frac{3}{10} \times 70 = \mathbf{21.}$
In jar B the extended ratio R:W:B is 8:12:15, so the white marbles are $\frac{12}{8+12+15} = \frac{12}{35}$ of the total: $\frac{12}{35} \times 70 = \mathbf{24.}$ The answer is **B**.

A **proportion** is an equation that states that two ratios are equivalent. Since ratios are just fractions, any equation such as $\frac{4}{6} = \frac{10}{15}$ in which each side is a single fraction is a proportion. Usually the proportions you encounter on the GRE involve one or more variables.

Solve proportions by cross-multiplying: if $\frac{a}{b} = \frac{c}{d}$, then $ad = bc$.

Setting up a proportion is a common way of solving a problem on the GRE.

**Example 8.**

If $\frac{3}{7} = \frac{x}{84}$, what is the value of $x$?

(A) 12   (B) 24   (C) 36   (D) 42   (E) 48

**SOLUTION.** Cross-multiply:
$$3(84) = 7x \Rightarrow 252 = 7x \Rightarrow x = \mathbf{36\ (C)}.$$

**Example 9.**

If $\frac{x+2}{17} = \frac{x}{16}$, what is the value of $\frac{x+6}{19}$?

(A) $\frac{1}{2}$   (B) 1   (C) $\frac{3}{2}$   (D) 2   (E) 3

**SOLUTION.** Cross-multiply:
$$16(x + 2) = 17x \Rightarrow 16x + 32 = 17x \Rightarrow x = 32.$$
So, $\frac{x+6}{19} = \frac{32+6}{19} = \frac{38}{19} = \mathbf{2\ (D)}.$

**Example 10.**

A state law requires that on any field trip the ratio of the number of chaperones to the number of students must be at least 1:12. If 100 students are going on a field trip, what is the minimum number of chaperones required?

(A) 6   (B) 8   (C) $8\frac{1}{3}$   (D) 9   (E) 12

**SOLUTION:** Let $x$ represent the number of chaperones required, and set up a proportion:
$$\frac{\text{number of chaperones}}{\text{number of students}} = \frac{1}{12} = \frac{x}{100}.$$ Cross-multiply:
$100 = 12x \Rightarrow x = 8\frac{1}{3}.$ This, of course, is *not* the answer since, clearly, the number of chaperones must be a whole number. Since $x$ is greater than 8, 8 chaperones would not be enough. The answer is **9 (D)**.

A **rate** is a fraction that compares two quantities measured in different units. The word "per" often appears in rate problems: miles per hour, dollars per week, cents per ounce, students per classroom, and so on.

Set up rate problems just like ratio problems. Solve the proportions by cross-multiplying.

**Example 11.**

Brigitte solved 24 math problems in 15 minutes. At this rate, how many problems can she solve in 40 minutes?

(A) 25   (B) 40   (C) 48   (D) 60   (E) 64

**SOLUTION.** Handle this rate problem exactly like a ratio problem. Set up a proportion and cross-multiply:
$$\frac{\text{problems}}{\text{minutes}} = \frac{24}{15} = \frac{x}{40} \Rightarrow 15x = 40 \times 24 = 960 \Rightarrow x = \mathbf{64\ (E)}.$$

When the denominator in the given rate is 1 unit (1 minute, 1 mile, 1 dollar), the problem can be solved by a single division or multiplication. Consider Examples 12 and 13.

**Example 12.**

If Stefano types at the rate of 35 words per minute, how long will it take him to type 987 words?

**Example 13.**

If Mario types at the rate of 35 words per minute, how many words can he type in 85 minutes?

SOLUTION 12. Set up a proportion and cross-multiply:

$$\frac{\text{words typed}}{\text{minutes}} = \frac{35}{1} = \frac{987}{x} \Rightarrow 35x = 987 \Rightarrow$$

$$x = \frac{987}{35} = \textbf{28.2 minutes.}$$

SOLUTION 13. Set up a proportion and cross-multiply:

$$\frac{\text{words typed}}{\text{minutes}} = \frac{35}{1} = \frac{x}{85} \Rightarrow x = 35 \times 85 = \textbf{2975 words.}$$

Notice that in Example 12, all we did was divide 987 by 35, and in Example 13, we multiplied 35 by 85. If you realize that, you don't have to introduce $x$ and set up a proportion. You must know, however, whether to multiply or divide. If you're not absolutely positive which is correct, write the proportion; then you can't go wrong.

CAUTION: In rate problems it is essential that the units in both fractions be the same.

**Example 14.**

If 3 apples cost 50¢, how many apples can you buy for $20?
(A) 20   (B) 60   (C) 120   (D) 600   (E) 2000

SOLUTION. We have to set up a proportion, but it is *not* $\frac{3}{50} = \frac{x}{20}$. In the first fraction, the denominator represents *cents*, whereas in the second fraction, the denominator represents *dollars*. The units must be the same. We can change 50 cents to 0.5 dollar or we can change 20 dollars to 2000 cents:

$$\frac{3}{50} = \frac{x}{2000} \Rightarrow 50x = 6000 \Rightarrow x = \textbf{120 apples (C).}$$

On the GRE, some rate problems involve only variables. They are handled in exactly the same way.

**Example 15.**

If $a$ apples cost $c$ cents, how many apples can be bought for $d$ dollars?

(A) $100acd$   (B) $\frac{100d}{ac}$   (C) $\frac{ad}{100c}$   (D) $\frac{c}{100ad}$

(E) $\frac{100ad}{c}$

SOLUTION. First change $d$ dollars to $100d$ cents, and set up a proportion: $\frac{\text{apples}}{\text{cents}} = \frac{a}{c} = \frac{x}{100d}$. Now cross-multiply:

$$100ad = cx \Rightarrow x = \frac{100ad}{c} \textbf{ (E).}$$

Most students find problems such as Example 15 very difficult. If you get stuck on such a problem, use TACTIC 3, Chapter 12, which gives another strategy for handling these problems.

Notice that in rate problems, as one quantity increases or decreases, so does the other. If you are driving at 45 miles per hour, the more hours you drive, the further you go; if you drive fewer miles, it takes less time. If chopped meat cost $3.00 per pound, the less you spend, the fewer pounds you get; the more meat you buy, the more it costs.

In some problems, however, as one quantity increases, the other decreases. These *cannot* be solved by setting up a proportion. Consider the following two examples, which look similar but must be handled differently.

**Example 16.**

A hospital needs 150 pills to treat 6 patients for a week. How many pills does it need to treat 10 patients for a week?

**Example 17.**

A hospital has enough pills on hand to treat 10 patients for 14 days. How long will the pills last if there are 35 patients?

SOLUTION 16. Example 16 is a standard rate problem. The more patients there are, the more pills are needed. The *ratio* or *quotient* remains constant:

$$\frac{150}{6} = \frac{x}{10} \Rightarrow 6x = 1500 \Rightarrow x = \textbf{250.}$$

SOLUTION 17. In Example 17, the situation is different. With more patients, the supply of pills will last for a shorter period of time; if there were fewer patients, the supply would last longer. It is not the ratio that remains constant, it is the *product*.

There are enough pills to last for $10 \times 14 = 140$ patient-days:

$$\frac{140 \text{ patient-days}}{10 \text{ patients}} = \textbf{14 days}$$

$$\frac{140 \text{ patient-days}}{35 \text{ patients}} = \textbf{4 days}$$

$$\frac{140 \text{ patient-days}}{70 \text{ patients}} = \textbf{2 days}$$

$$\frac{140 \text{ patient-days}}{1 \text{ patient}} = \textbf{140 days}$$

There are many mathematical situations in which one quantity increases as another decreases, but their product is not constant. Those types of problems, however, do not appear on the GRE.

**D4**

If one quantity increases as a second quantity decreases, multiply them; their product will be a constant.

> **Example 18.**
>
> If 15 workers can pave a certain number of driveways in 24 days, how many days will 40 workers take, working at the same rate, to do the same job?
>
> (A) 6   (B) 9   (C) 15   (D) 24   (E) 40

**SOLUTION.** Clearly, the more workers there are, the less time it will take, so use TACTIC D4: multiply. The job takes $15 \times 24 = 360$ worker-days:

$$\frac{360 \text{ worker-days}}{40 \text{ workers}} = \textbf{9 days (B)}.$$

Note that it doesn't matter how many driveways have to be paved, as long as the 15 workers and the 40 workers are doing the same job. Even if the question had said, "15 workers can paint 18 houses in 24 days," the number 18 would not have entered into the solution. This number would be important only if the second group of workers was going to pave a different number of driveways.

> **Example 19.**
>
> If 15 workers can pave 18 driveways in 24 days, how many days would it take 40 workers to pave 22 driveways?
>
> (A) 6   (B) 9   (C) 11   (D) 15   (E) 18

**SOLUTION.** This question is similar to Example 18, except that now the jobs that the two groups of workers are doing is different. The solution, however, starts out exactly the same way. Just as in Example 18, 40 workers can do in 9 days the *same* job that 15 workers can do in 24 days. Since that job is to pave 18 driveways, 40 workers can pave $18 \div 9 = 2$ driveways every day. So, it will take **11** days to pave 22 driveways (**C**).

# PRACTICE EXERCISES—RATIOS AND PROPORTIONS

## Multiple-Choice Questions

1. If $\frac{3}{4}$ of the employees in a supermarket are not college graduates, what is the ratio of the number of college graduates to those who are not college graduates?

   (A) 1:3   (B) 3:7   (C) 3:4   (D) 4:3   (E) 3:1

2. If $\frac{a}{9} = \frac{10}{2a}$, what is the value of $a^2$?

   (A) $3\sqrt{6}$   (B) $3\sqrt{5}$   (C) $9\sqrt{6}$   (D) 45   (E) 90

3. If the ratio of juniors to seniors on the team is 3:5, what percent of the team members are seniors?

   (A) 37.5%   (B) 40%   (C) 60%   (D) 62.5%
   (E) It cannot be determined from the information given.

4. Scott can read 50 pages per hour. At this rate, how many pages can he read in 50 minutes?

   (A) 25   (B) $41\frac{2}{3}$   (C) $45\frac{1}{2}$   (D) 48   (E) 60

5. If 80% of the applicants to a program were rejected, what is the ratio of the number accepted to the number rejected?

   (A) $\frac{1}{5}$   (B) $\frac{1}{4}$   (C) $\frac{2}{5}$   (D) $\frac{4}{5}$   (E) $\frac{4}{1}$

6. The measures of the three angles in a triangle are in the ratio of 1:1:2. Which of the following must be true?

   I.   The triangle is isosceles.
   II.  The triangle is a right triangle.
   III. The triangle is equilateral.

   (A) None   (B) I only   (C) II only
       (D) I and II only   (E) I and III only

7. What is the ratio of the circumference of a circle to its radius?

   (A) 1   (B) $\frac{\pi}{2}$   (C) $\sqrt{\pi}$   (D) $\pi$   (E) $2\pi$

8. The ratio of the number of freshmen to sophomores to juniors to seniors on a college basketball team is 4:7:6:8. What percent of the team are sophomores?

   (A) 16%   (B) 24%   (C) 25%   (D) 28%
   (E) 32%

9. At Central State College the ratio of the number of students taking Spanish to the number taking French is 7:2. If 140 students are taking French, how many are taking Spanish?

   (A) 40   (B) 140   (C) 360   (D) 490   (E) 630

10. If $a:b = 3:5$ and $a:c = 5:7$, what is the value of $b:c$?

    (A) 3:7   (B) 21:35   (C) 21:25   (D) 25:21
    (E) 7:3

11. If $x$ is a positive number and $\dfrac{x}{3} = \dfrac{12}{x}$, then $x =$

    (A) 3   (B) 4   (C) 6   (D) 12   (E) 36

12. In the diagram below, $b:a = 7:2$. What is $b - a$?

    (A) 20   (B) 70   (C) 100   (D) 110   (E) 160

13. A snail can move $i$ inches in $m$ minutes. At this rate, how many feet can it move in $h$ hours?

    (A) $\dfrac{5hi}{m}$   (B) $\dfrac{60hi}{m}$   (C) $\dfrac{hi}{12m}$   (D) $\dfrac{5m}{hi}$
    (E) $5him$

14. Gilda can grade $t$ tests in $\dfrac{1}{x}$ hours. At this rate, how many tests can she grade in $x$ hours?

    (A) $tx$   (B) $tx^2$   (C) $\dfrac{1}{t}$   (D) $\dfrac{x}{t}$   (E) $\dfrac{1}{tx}$

15. A club had 3 boys and 5 girls. During a membership drive the same number of boys and girls joined the club. How many members does the club have now if the ratio of boys to girls is 3:4?

    (A) 12   (B) 14   (C) 16   (D) 21   (E) 28

16. If $\dfrac{3x-1}{25} = \dfrac{x+5}{11}$, what is the value of $x$?

    (A) $\dfrac{3}{4}$   (B) 3   (C) 7   (D) 17   (E) 136

17. If 4 boys can shovel a driveway in 2 hours, how many minutes will it take 5 boys to do the job?

    (A) 60   (B) 72   (C) 96   (D) 120   (E) 150

18. If 500 pounds of mush will feed 20 pigs for a week, for how many days will 200 pounds of mush feed 14 pigs?

    (A) 4   (B) 5   (C) 6   (D) 7   (E) 8

## Quantitative Comparison Questions

| Column A | Column B |
| --- | --- |

The ratio of red to blue marbles in a jar was 3:5. The same number of red and blue marbles were added to the jar.

19.

| The ratio of red to blue marbles now | 3:5 |
| --- | --- |

Three associates agreed to split the $3000 profit of an investment in the ratio of 2:5:8.

20.

| The difference between the largest and the smallest share | $1200 |
| --- | --- |

The ratio of the number of boys to girls in the chess club is 5:2.
The ratio of the number of boys to girls in the glee club is 11:4.

21.

| The number of boys in the chess club | The number of boys in the glee club |
| --- | --- |

Sally invited the same number of boys and girls to her party. Everyone who was invited came, but 5 additional boys showed up. This caused the ratio of girls to boys at the party to be 4:5.

22.

| The number of people she invited to her party | 40 |
| --- | --- |

A large jar is full of marbles. When a single marble is drawn at random from the jar, the probability that it is red is $\dfrac{3}{7}$.

23.

| The ratio of the number of red marbles to non-red marbles in the jar | $\dfrac{1}{2}$ |
| --- | --- |

$3a = 2b$ and $3b = 5c$

24.

| The ratio of $a$ to $c$ | 1 |
| --- | --- |

The radius of circle II is 3 times the radius of circle I

25.

| area of circle II / area of circle I | $3\pi$ |
| --- | --- |

# Answer Key

| | | | | |
|---|---|---|---|---|
| 1. A | 6. D | 11. C | 16. D | 21. D |
| 2. D | 7. E | 12. C | 17. C | 22. C |
| 3. D | 8. D | 13. A | 18. A | 23. A |
| 4. B | 9. D | 14. B | 19. A | 24. A |
| 5. B | 10. D | 15. B | 20. C | 25. B |

# Answer Explanations

1. **A.** Of every 4 employees, 3 are not college graduates, and 1 is a college graduate. So the ratio of graduates to nongraduates is 1:3.

2. **D.** Cross-multiplying, we get:
$$2a^2 = 90 \Rightarrow a^2 = 45.$$

3. **D.** Out of every 8 team members, 3 are juniors and 5 are seniors. Seniors, therefore, make up $\frac{5}{8} = 62.5\%$ of the team.

4. **B.** Set up a proportion:
$$\frac{50 \text{ pages}}{1 \text{ hour}} = \frac{50 \text{ pages}}{60 \text{ minutes}} = \frac{x \text{ pages}}{50 \text{ minutes}}, \text{ and}$$
cross-multiply: $50 \times 50 = 60x \Rightarrow$
$2500 = 60x \Rightarrow x = 41\frac{2}{3}.$

5. **B.** If 80% were rejected, 20% were accepted, and the ratio of accepted to rejected is $20:80 = 1:4$.

6. **D.** It is worth remembering that if the ratio of the measures of the angles of a triangle is 1:1:2, the angles are 45-45-90 (see Section 12-J). Otherwise, the first step is to write $x + x + 2x = 180 \Rightarrow 4x = 180 \Rightarrow x = 45$. Since two of the angles have the same measure, the triangle is isosceles, and since one of the angles measures 90°, it is a right triangle. I and II are true, and, of course, III is false.

7. **E.** By definition, $\pi$ is the ratio of the circumference to the diameter of a circle (see Section 12-L). Therefore, $\pi = \frac{C}{d} = \frac{C}{2r} \Rightarrow 2\pi = \frac{C}{r}$.

8. **D.** The *fraction* of the team that is sophomores is
$\frac{7}{4 + 7 + 6 + 8} = \frac{7}{25}$, and $\frac{7}{25} \times 100\% = 28\%$.

9. **D.** Let the number of students taking Spanish be $7x$, and the number taking French be $2x$. Then,
$$2x = 140 \Rightarrow x = 70 \Rightarrow 7x = 490.$$

10. **D.** Since $\frac{a}{b} = \frac{3}{5}$, $\frac{b}{a} = \frac{5}{3}$. So,
$$\frac{b}{\cancel{a}} \times \frac{\cancel{a}}{c} = \frac{5}{3} \times \frac{5}{7} \Rightarrow \frac{b}{c} = \frac{25}{21}.$$

Alternatively, we could write equivalent ratios with the same value for $a$:

$$a{:}b = 3{:}5 = 15{:}25 \text{ and } a{:}c = 5{:}7 = 15{:}21.$$

So, when $a = 15$, $b = 25$, and $c = 21$.

11. **C.** To solve a proportion, cross-multiply:
$$\frac{x}{3} = \frac{12}{x} \Rightarrow x^2 = 36 \Rightarrow x = 6.$$

12. **C.** Let $b = 7x$ and $a = 2x$. Then,
$$7x + 2x = 180 \Rightarrow 9x = 180 \Rightarrow x = 20 \Rightarrow$$
$b = 140$ and $a = 40 \Rightarrow b - a = 140 - 40 = 100$.

13. **A.** Set up the proportion, keeping track of units:
$$\frac{x \text{ feet}}{h \text{ hours}} = \frac{12x \text{ inches}}{60h \text{ minutes}} = \frac{i \text{ inches}}{m \text{ minutes}} \Rightarrow$$
$$\frac{x}{5h} = \frac{i}{m} \Rightarrow x = \frac{5hi}{m}.$$

14. **B.** Gilda grades at the rate of $\frac{\frac{t}{x} \text{ tests}}{\text{hours}} = \frac{tx \text{ tests}}{1 \text{ hour}}$.

Since she can grade $tx$ tests each hour, in $x$ hours she can grade $x(tx) = tx^2$ tests.

15. **B.** Suppose that $x$ boys and $x$ girls joined the club. Then, the new ratio of boys to girls would be $(3 + x){:}(5 + x)$, which we are told is 3:4. So, $\frac{3 + x}{5 + x} = \frac{3}{4} \Rightarrow 4(3 + x) = 3(5 + x) \Rightarrow$
$12 + 4x = 15 + 3x \Rightarrow x = 3$. Therefore, 3 boys and 3 girls joined the other 3 boys and 5 girls: a total of 14.

16. **D.** Cross-multiplying, we get:
$$11(3x - 1) = 25(x + 5) \Rightarrow$$
$$33x - 11 = 25x + 125 \Rightarrow 8x = 136 \Rightarrow x = 17.$$

17. **C.** Since 4 boys can shovel the driveway in 2 hours, or $2 \times 60 = 120$ minutes, the job takes $4 \times 120 = 480$ boy-minutes; and so 5 boys would need $\frac{480 \text{ boy-minutes}}{5 \text{ boys}} = 96$ minutes.

18. **A.** Since 500 pounds will last for 20 pig-weeks = 140 pig-days, 200 pounds will last for

$\dfrac{2}{5} \times 140$ pig-days = 56 pig-days, and

$\dfrac{56 \text{ pig-days}}{14 \text{ pigs}} = 4$ days.

19. A.   Assume that to start there were $3x$ red marbles and $5x$ blue ones and that $y$ of each color were added.

| | Column A | Column B |
|---|---|---|
| | $\dfrac{3x+y}{5x+y}$ | $\dfrac{3}{5}$ |
| Cross-multiply: | $5(3x+y)$ | $3(5x+y)$ |
| Distribute: | $15x + 5y$ | $15x + 3y$ |
| Subtract $15x$: | $5y$ | $3y$ |

Since $y$ is positive, Column A is greater.

20. C.   The shares are $2x$, $5x$, and $8x$, and their sum is 3000:

$$2x + 5x + 8x = 3000 \Rightarrow 15x = 3000 \Rightarrow$$
$$x = 200, \text{ and so } 8x - 2x = 6x = 1200.$$

21. D.   Ratios alone can't answer the question, "How many?" There could be 5 boys in the chess club or 500. We can't tell.

22. C.   Assume that Sally invited $x$ boys and $x$ girls. When she wound up with $x$ girls and $x + 5$ boys, the girl:boy ratio was 4:5. So,

$$\frac{x}{x+5} = \frac{4}{5} \Rightarrow 5x = 4x + 20 \Rightarrow x = 20$$

Sally invited 40 people (20 boys and 20 girls).

23. A.   If the probability of drawing a red marble is $\dfrac{3}{7}$, 3 out of every 7 marbles are red, and 4 out of every 7 are non-red. So the ratio red:non-red = 3:4, which is greater than $\dfrac{1}{2}$.

24. A.   Multiplying the first equation by 3 and the second by 2 to get the same coefficient of $b$, we have:

$$9a = 6b \text{ and } 6b = 10c \Rightarrow 9a = 10c \Rightarrow \frac{a}{c} = \frac{10}{9}.$$

25. B.   Assume the radius of circle I is 1 and the radius of circle II is 3. Then the areas are $\pi$ and $9\pi$, respectively. So, the area of circle II is 9 times the area of circle I, and $3\pi > 9$.

## 15-E. AVERAGES

The **average** of a set of $n$ numbers is the sum of those numbers divided by $n$.

$$\text{average} = \frac{\text{sum of the } n \text{ numbers}}{n} \text{ or simply}$$

$$A = \frac{\text{sum}}{n}.$$

If the weights of three children are 80, 90, and 76 pounds, respectively, to calculate the average weight of the children, you would add the three weights and divide by 3:

$$\frac{80 + 90 + 76}{3} = \frac{246}{3} = 82$$

The technical name for this type of average is "arithmetic mean," and on the GRE those words always appear in parentheses—for example, "What is the average (arithmetic mean) of 80, 90, and 76?"

Usually, on the GRE, you are not asked to find an average; rather, you are given the average of a set of numbers and asked for some other information. The key to solving all of these problems is to first find the sum of the numbers. Since $A = \dfrac{\text{sum}}{n}$, multiplying both sides by $n$ yields the equation: sum = $nA$.

Tactic **E1**

If you know the average, $A$, of a set of $n$ numbers, multiply $A$ by $n$ to get their sum.

---

**Example 1.**

One day a supermarket received a delivery of 25 frozen turkeys. If the average (arithmetic mean) weight of a turkey was 14.2 pounds, what was the total weight, in pounds, of all the turkeys?

---

SOLUTION. Use TACTIC E1: $25 \times 14.2 =$ **355**.

NOTE: We do not know how much any individual turkey weighed nor how many turkeys weighed more or less than 14.2 pounds. All we know is their total weight.

---

**Example 2.**

Sheila took five chemistry tests during the semester and the average (arithmetic mean) of her test scores was 85. If her average after the first three tests was 83, what was the average of her fourth and fifth tests?

(A) 83   (B) 85   (C) 87   (D) 88   (E) 90

SOLUTION.

- Use TACTIC E1: On her five tests, Sheila earned $5 \times 85 = 425$ points.

- Use TACTIC E1 again: On her first three tests she earned $3 \times 83 = 249$ points.

- Subtract: On her last two tests Sheila earned $425 - 249 = 176$ points.

- Calculate her average on her last two tests: $\dfrac{176}{2} = 88$ **(D)**.

NOTE: *We cannot determine Sheila's grade on even one of the tests.*

### KEY FACT E1:

- **If all the numbers in a set are the same, then that number is the average.**

- **If the numbers in a set are not all the same, then the average must be greater than the smallest number and less than the largest number. Equivalently, at least one of the numbers is less than the average and at least one is greater.**

If Jessica's test grades are 85, 85, 85, and 85, her average is 85. If Gary's test grades are 76, 83, 88, and 88, his average must be greater than 76 and less than 88. What can we conclude if, after taking five tests, Kristen's average is 90? We know that she earned exactly $5 \times 90 = 450$ points, and that either she got a 90 on every test or at least one grade was less than 90 and at least one was over 90. Here are a few of the thousands of possibilities for Kristen's grades:

- (a) 90, 90, 90, 90, 90    (b) 80, 90, 90, 90, 100
- (c) 83, 84, 87, 97, 99    (d) 77, 88, 93, 95, 97
- (e) 50, 100, 100, 100, 100

In (b), 80, the one grade below 90, is *10 points below*, and 100, the one grade above 90, is *10 points above*. In (c), 83 is 7 points below 90, 84 is 6 points below 90, and 87 is 3 points below 90, for a total of $7 + 6 + 3 = 16$ *points below 90*; 97 is 7 points above 90, and 99 is 9 points above 90, for a total of $7 + 9 = 16$ *points above 90*.

These differences from the average are called *deviations*, and the situation in these examples is not a coincidence.

### KEY FACT E2:

**The total deviation below the average is equal to the total deviation above the average.**

---

**Example 3.**

If the average (arithmetic mean) of 25, 31, and $x$ is 37, what is the value of $x$?

(A) 31   (B) 37   (C) 43   (D) 55   (E) 56

---

SOLUTION 1. Use KEY FACT E2. Since 25 is 12 less than 37 and 31 is 6 less than 37, the total deviation below the average is $12 + 6 = 18$. Therefore, the total deviation above must also be 18. So, $x = 37 + 18 = 55$ **(D)**.

SOLUTION 2. Use TACTIC E1. Since the average of the three numbers is 37, the sum of the 3 numbers is $3 \times 37 = 111$. Then,

$$25 + 31 + x = 111 \Rightarrow 56 + x = 111 \Rightarrow x = 55.$$

### KEY FACT E3:

**Assume that the average of a set of numbers is $A$. If a number $x$ is added to the set and a new average is calculated, then the new average will be less than, equal to, or greater than $A$, depending on whether $x$ is less than, equal to, or greater than $A$, respectively.**

| Column A | Column B |
|---|---|
| **Example 4.** | |
| The average (arithmetic mean) of the integers from 0 to 12 | The average (arithmetic mean) of the integers from 1 to 12 |

---

**Helpful Hint**

Remember TACTIC 5 from Chapter 13. We don't have to *calculate* the averages, we just have to *compare* them.

---

SOLUTION 1. Column B is the average of the integers from 1 to 12, which is surely greater than 1. In Column A we are taking the average of those same 12 numbers and 0. Since the extra number, 0, is less than the Column B average, the Column A average must be *lower* [KEY FACT E3]. The answer is **B**.

SOLUTION 2. Clearly the sum of the 13 integers from 0 to 12 is the same as the sum of the 12 integers from 1 to 12. Since that sum is positive, dividing by 13 yields a smaller quotient than dividing by 12 [KEY FACT B4].

Although in solving Example 4 we didn't calculate the averages, we could have:

$$0 + 1 + 2 + 3 + 4 + 5 + 6 + 7 + 8 + 9 + 10 + 11 + 12 = 78$$
$$\text{and } \frac{78}{13} = 6.$$

$$1 + 2 + 3 + 4 + 5 + 6 + 7 + 8 + 9 + 10 + 11 + 12 = 78$$
$$\text{and } \frac{78}{12} = 6.5.$$

Notice that the average of the 13 *consecutive* integers 0, 1,...,12 is the *middle integer*, **6**, and the average of the 12 *consecutive* integers 1, 2,...,12 is the *average of the two middle integers*, **6** and **7**. This is a special case of KEY FACT E4.

### KEY FACT E4:

**Whenever $n$ numbers form an arithmetic sequence (one in which the difference between any two consecutive terms is the same): (i) if $n$ is odd, the average of the numbers is the middle term in the sequence and (ii) if $n$ is even, the average of the numbers is the average of the two middle terms.**

For example, in the arithmetic sequence 6, 9, 12, 15, 18, the average is the middle number, **12**; in the sequence 10, 20, 30, 40, 50, 60, the average is **35**, the average of the two middle numbers—30 and 40.

---

**Example 5.**

On Thursday, 20 of the 25 students in a chemistry class took a test and their average was 80. On Friday, the other 5 students took the test, and their average was 90. What was the average (arithmetic mean) for the entire class?

(A) 80    (B) 82    (C) 84    (D) 85    (E) 88

---

SOLUTION. The class average is calculated by dividing the sum of all 25 test grades by 25.

- The first 20 students
  earned a total of:          $20 \times 80 = 1600$ points
- The other 5 students
  earned a total of:          $5 \times 90 = 450$ points
- Add: altogether the
  class earned:               $1600 + 450 = 2050$ points
- Calculate the class
  average:                    $\frac{2050}{25} = 82$ **(B)**.

Notice that the answer to Example 5 is *not* 85, which is the average of 80 and 90. This is because the averages of 80 and 90 were earned by different numbers of students, and so the two averages had to be given different weights in the calculation. For this reason, this is called a *weighted average*.

### KEY FACT E5:

**To calculate the weighted average of a set of numbers, multiply each number in the set by the number of times it appears, add all the products, and divide by the total number of numbers in the set.**

So, the solution to Example 5 should look like this:

$$\frac{20(80) + 5(90)}{25} = \frac{1600 + 450}{25} = \frac{2050}{25} = 82$$

---

**Helpful Hint**

Without doing any calculations, you should immediately realize that since the grade of 80 is being given more weight than the grade of 90, the average will be closer to 80 than to 90—certainly *less than 85*.

---

Problems involving *average speed* will be discussed in Section 15-H, but we mention them briefly here because they are closely related to problems on weighted averages.

---

**Example 6.**

For the first 3 hours of his trip, Justin drove at 50 miles per hour. Then, due to construction delays, he drove at only 40 miles per hour for the next 2 hours. What was his average speed, in miles per hour, for the entire trip?

(A) 40    (B) 43    (C) 46    (D) 48    (E) 50

---

SOLUTION. This is just a weighted average:

$$\frac{3(50) + 2(40)}{5} = \frac{150 + 80}{5} = \frac{230}{5} = 46.$$

Note that in the fractions above, the numerator is the total distance traveled and the denominator the total time the trip took. This is *always* the way to find an average speed. Consider the following slight variation on Example 6.

---

**Example 6a.**

For the first 100 miles of his trip, Justin drove at 50 miles per hour, and then due to construction delays, he drove at only 40 miles per hour for the next 120 miles. What was his average speed, in miles per hour, for the entire trip?

---

SOLUTION. This is not a *weighted* average. Here we immediately know the total distance traveled, 220 miles. To get the total time the trip took, we find the time for each portion and add: the first 100 miles took $100 \div 50 = 2$ hours, and the next 120 miles took $120 \div 40 = 3$ hours. So the average speed was $\frac{220}{5} = $ **44** miles per hour.

Notice that in Example 6 since Justin spent more time traveling at 50 miles per hour than at 40 miles per hour, his average speed was closer to 50; in Example 6a, he spent more time driving at 40 miles per hour than at 50 miles per hour, so his average speed was closer to 40.

Two other terms that are associated with averages are *median* and *mode*. In a set of $n$ numbers that are arranged in increasing order, the *median* is the middle number (if $n$ is odd), or the average of the two middle numbers (if $n$ is even). The **mode** is the number in the set that occurs most often.

---

**Example 7.**

During a 10-day period, Jorge received the following number of phone calls each day: 2, 3, 9, 3, 5, 7, 7, 10, 7, 6. What is the average (arithmetic mean) of the median and mode of this set of data?

(A) 6   (B) 6.25   (C) 6.5   (D) 6.75   (E) 7

---

SOLUTION. The first step is to write the data in increasing order: 2, 3, 3, 5, 6, 7, 7, 7, 9, 10.

• The median is 6.5, the average of the middle two numbers.

• The mode is 7, the number that appears more times than any other.

• The average of the median and the mode is $\frac{6.5 + 7}{2}$ = **6.75 (D)**.

# PRACTICE EXERCISES—AVERAGES

## Multiple-Choice Questions

1. Michael's average (arithmetic mean) on 4 tests is 80. What does he need on his fifth test to raise his average to 84?

   (A) 82   (B) 84   (C) 92   (D) 96   (E) 100

2. Maryline's average (arithmetic mean) on 4 tests is 80. Assuming she can earn no more than 100 on any test, what is the least she can earn on her fifth test and still have a chance for an 85 average after seven tests?

   (A) 60   (B) 70   (C) 75   (D) 80   (E) 85

3. Sandrine's average (arithmetic mean) on 4 tests is 80. Which of the following <u>cannot</u> be the number of tests on which she earned exactly 80 points?

   (A) 0   (B) 1   (C) 2   (D) 3   (E) 4

4. What is the average (arithmetic mean) of the positive integers from 1 to 100, inclusive?

   (A) 49   (B) 49.5   (C) 50   (D) 50.5   (E) 51

5. If $10a + 10b = 35$, what is the average (arithmetic mean) of $a$ and $b$?

   (A) 1.75   (B) 3.5   (C) 7   (D) 10   (E) 17.5

6. If $x + y = 6$, $y + z = 7$, and $z + x = 9$, what is the average (arithmetic mean) of $x$, $y$, and $z$?

   (A) $\frac{11}{3}$   (B) $\frac{11}{2}$   (C) $\frac{22}{3}$   (D) 11   (E) 22

7. If $a + b = 3(c + d)$, which of the following is the average (arithmetic mean) of $a$, $b$, $c$, and $d$?

   (A) $\frac{c+d}{4}$   (B) $\frac{3(c+d)}{8}$   (C) $\frac{c+d}{2}$   (D) $\frac{3(c+d)}{4}$
   (E) $c + d$

8. If the average (arithmetic mean) of 5, 6, 7, and $w$ is 8, what is the value of $w$?

   (A) 8   (B) 12   (C) 14   (D) 16   (E) 24

9. What is the average (arithmetic mean) of the measures of the five angles in a pentagon?

   (A) 36°   (B) 72°   (C) 90°   (D) 108°   (E) 144°

10. In the diagram below, lines $\ell$ and $m$ are *not* parallel.

   If $A$ represents the average (arithmetic mean) of the degree measures of all eight angles, which of the following is true?

   (A) $A = 45$   (B) $45 < A < 90$   (C) $A = 90$
   (D) $90 < A < 180$   (E) $A = 180$

11. What is the average (arithmetic mean) of $2^{10}$ and $2^{20}$?

   (A) $2^{15}$   (B) $2^5 + 2^{10}$   (C) $2^9 + 2^{19}$   (D) $2^{29}$   (E) 30

12. Let $M$ be the median and $m$ the mode of the following set of numbers: 10, 70, 20, 40, 70, 90. What is the average (arithmetic mean) of $M$ and $m$?

   (A) 50   (B) 55   (C) 60   (D) 62.5   (E) 65

## Quantitative Comparison Questions

| Column A | Column B |
|---|---|

**13.** The average (arithmetic mean) of the measures of the three angles of an equilateral triangle | The average (arithmetic mean) of the measures of the three angles of a right triangle

10 students took a test and the average grade was 80. No one scored exactly 80.

**14.** The number of grades over 80 | 5

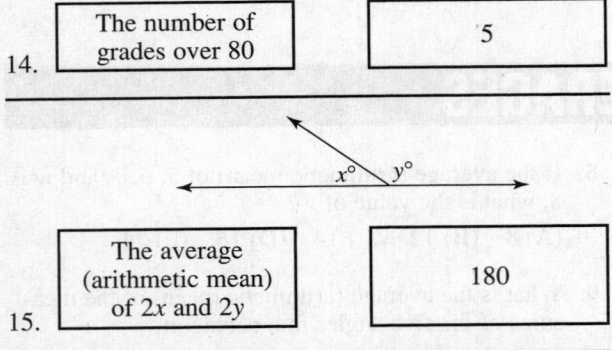

**15.** The average (arithmetic mean) of 2x and 2y | 180

There are the same number of boys and girls in a club. The average weight of the boys is 150 pounds. The average weight of the girls is 110 pounds.

**16.** The number of boys weighing over 150 | The number of girls weighing over 110

| Column A | Column B |
|---|---|

The average (arithmetic mean) of 22, 38, $x$, and $y$ is 15.

$x > 0$

**17.** $y$ | 0

**18.** The average (arithmetic mean) of the even numbers between 1 and 11 | The average (arithmetic mean) of the odd numbers between 2 and 12

**19.** The average (arithmetic mean) of 17, 217, 417 | The average (arithmetic mean) of 0, 17, 217, 417

$y > 0$

**20.** The average (arithmetic mean) of $x$ and $y$ | The average (arithmetic mean) of $x$, $y$, and $2y$

## Answer Key

| | | | |
|---|---|---|---|
| 1. **E** | 6. **A** | 11. **C** | 16. **D** |
| 2. **C** | 7. **E** | 12. **D** | 17. **B** |
| 3. **D** | 8. **C** | 13. **C** | 18. **B** |
| 4. **D** | 9. **D** | 14. **D** | 19. **A** |
| 5. **A** | 10. **C** | 15. **C** | 20. **D** |

## Answer Explanations

1. **E.** Use TACTIC E1. For Michael's average on five tests to be an 84, he needs a total of $5 \times 84 = 420$ points. So far, he has earned $4 \times 80 = 320$ points. Therefore, he needs 100 points more.
*Alternative solution.* Use KEY FACT E2. Assume Michael's first 4 tests were all 80s. His total deviation below 84 is $4 \times 4 = 16$. So, his total deviation above 84 must also be 16. He needs $84 + 16 = 100$.

2. **C.** Use TACTIC E1. So far, Maryline has earned 320 points. She can survive a low grade on

test five if she gets the maximum possible on both the sixth and seventh tests. So, assume she gets two 100s. Then her total for tests 1, 2, 3, 4, 6, and 7 would be 520. For her seven-test average to be 85, she needs a total of $7 \times 85 = 595$ points. Therefore, she needs at least $595 - 520 = 75$ points.
*Alternative solution.* Use KEY FACT E2. Assume Maryline's first four tests were all 80s. Then her total deviation below 85 would be $4 \times 5 = 20$. Her maximum possible deviation above 85 (assuming 100s on tests 6 and 7) is $15 + 15 = 30$. So, on test 5 she can devi-

ate at most 10 more points below 85: $85 - 10 = 75$.

3. **D.** To determine which choice is *not* possible, test the choices starting with E: Could Sandrine have earned an 80 on all four tests? Of course, she could have; that's the easiest way to have an 80 average. Test Choice D: Could she have earned an 80 on exactly three tests? Well, if she did, her average for those three tests would clearly be 80, and since adding the fourth score didn't change her average, KEY FACT E3 tells us that her fourth score must also be 80. So, it is *not* possible for her to have had exactly three 80s. *Alternative solution.* Could Sandrine have earned a total of 320 points with:

| | |
|---|---|
| 0 grades of 80? | Easily; for example, 20, 100, 100, 100 or 60, 70, 90, 100. |
| 1 grade of 80? | Lots of ways; 80, 40, 100, 100, for instance. |
| 2 grades of 80? | Yes; 80, 80, 60, 100. |
| 4 grades of 80? | Sure: 80, 80, 80, 80. |
| 3 grades of 80? | NO! $80 + 80 + 80 + x = 320 \Rightarrow x = 80$, as well. |

4. **D.** Clearly, the sequence of integers from 1 to 100 has 100 terms, and so by KEY FACT E4, we know that the average of all the numbers is the average of the two middle ones: 50 and 51. The average, therefore, is 50.5.

5. **A.** Since $10a + 10b = 35$, dividing both sides of the equation by 10, we get that $a + b = 3.5$. Therefore, the average of $a$ and $b$ is $3.5 \div 2 = 1.75$.

6. **A.** Whenever a question involves three equations, add them:

$$\begin{array}{r} x + y = 6 \\ y + z = 7 \\ + \quad z + x = 9 \\ \hline 2x + 2y + 2z = 22 \end{array}$$

Divide by 2:     $x + y + z = 11$

The average of $x$, $y$, and $z$ is $\dfrac{x+y+z}{3} = \dfrac{11}{3}$.

7. **E.** Calculate the average:

$$\frac{a+b+c+d}{4} = \frac{3(c+d)+c+d}{4} =$$

$$\frac{3c+3d+c+d}{4} = \frac{4c+4d}{4} = c+d$$

8. **C.** Use TACTIC E1: the sum of the 4 numbers is 4 times their average:

$$5 + 6 + 7 + w = 4 \times 8 = 32 \Rightarrow$$
$$18 + w = 32 \Rightarrow w = 14.$$

*Alternative solution.* Use KEY FACT E2: 5 is 3 below 8, 6 is 2 below 8, and 7 is 1 below 8,

for a total deviation of $3 + 2 + 1 = 6$ below the average of 8. To compensate, $w$ must be 6 more than 8: $6 + 8 = 14$.

9. **D.** The average of the measures of the five angles is the sum of their measures divided by 5. The sum is $(5 - 2) \times 180 = 3 \times 180 = 540$ (see Section 15-K). So, the average is $540 \div 5 = 108$.

10. **C.** Since $a + b + c + d = 360$, and $w + x + y + z = 360$ (see Section 15-I), the sum of the measures of all 8 angles is $360 + 360 = 720$, and their average is $720 \div 8 = 90$.

11. **C.** The average of $2^{10}$ and $2^{20}$ is

$$\frac{2^{10} + 2^{20}}{2} = \frac{2^{10}}{2} + \frac{2^{20}}{2} = 2^9 + 2^{19}.$$

12. **D.** Arrange the numbers in increasing order: 10, 20, 40, 70, 70, 90. $M$, the median, is the average of the middle two numbers: $\dfrac{40+70}{2} = 55$; the mode, $m$, is 70, the number that appears most frequently. The average of $M$ and $m$, therefore, is the average of 55 and 70, which is 62.5.

13. **C.** In *any* triangle, the sum of the measures of the three angles is 180°, and the average of their measures is $180 \div 3 = 60$.

14. **D.** From KEY FACT E1, we know only that *at least one grade was above 80*. In fact, there may have been only one (9 grades of 79 and 1 grade of 89, for example). But there could have been five or even nine (for example, 9 grades of 85 and 1 grade of 35). *Alternative solution.* The ten students scored exactly 800 points. Ask, "Could they be equal?" Could there be exactly five grades above 80? Sure, five grades of 100 for 500 points and five grades of 60 for 300 points. Must they be equal? No, eight grades of 100 and two grades of 0 also total 800.

15. **C.** The average of $2x$ and $2y$ is $\dfrac{2x+2y}{2} = x + y$, which equals 180.

16. **D.** It is possible that no boy weighs over 150 (if every single boy weighs exactly 150); on the other hand, it is possible that almost every boy weighs over 150. The same is true for the girls.

17. **B.** Use TACTIC E1:

$$22 + 38 + x + y = 4(15 = 60 \Rightarrow$$
$$60 + x + y = 60 \Rightarrow x + y = 0.$$

Since it is given that $x$ is positive, $y$ must be negative.

18. B.  Don't calculate the averages. Each number in Column A (2, 4, 6, 8, 10) is less than the corresponding number in Column B (3, 5, 7, 9, 11), and so the Column A average must be less than the Column B average.
*Alternative solution.* Observe that the numbers in each column form an arithmetic sequence, so by KEY FACT E4 the averages are just the middle numbers (6 and 7).

19. A.  You don't have to calculate the averages. The average of the set of numbers in Column A is clearly positive, and by KEY FACT E3, adding 0 to that set must lower the average.

20. D.  Use KEY FACT E3: if $x < y$, then the average of $x$ and $y$ is less than $y$, and surely less than $2y$. So, $2y$ has to raise the average. On the other hand, if $x$ is much larger than $y$, then $2y$ would lower the average.

# ALGEBRA

For the GRE you need to know only a small portion of the algebra normally taught in a high school elementary algebra course and none of the material taught in an intermediate or advanced algebra course. Sections 15-F, 15-G, and 15-H review only those topics that you absolutely need for the GRE.

## 15-F. POLYNOMIALS

Even though the terms *monomial*, *binomial*, *trinomial*, and *polynomial* are not used on the GRE, you must be able to work with simple polynomials, and the use of these terms will make it easier for us to discuss the important concepts.

A *monomial* is any number or variable or product of numbers and variables. Each of the following is a monomial:

$$3 \quad -4 \quad x \quad y \quad 3x \quad -4xyz \quad 5x^3 \quad 1.5xy^2 \quad a^3b^4$$

The number that appears in front of the variables in a monomial is called the *coefficient*. The coefficient of $5x^3$ is 5. If there is no number, the coefficient is 1 or –1, because $x$ means $1x$ and $-ab^2$ means $-1ab^2$.

On the GRE, you could be asked to evaluate a monomial for specific values of the variables.

---

**Example 1.**
What is the value of $-3a^2b$ when $a = -4$ and $b = 0.5$?
(A) –72   (B) –24   (C) 24   (D) 48   (E) 72

---

SOLUTION. Rewrite the expression, replacing the letters $a$ and $b$ with the numbers –4 and 0.5, respectively. Make sure to write each number in parentheses. Then evaluate: $-3(-4)^2(0.5) = -3(16)(0.5) = $ **–24 (B)**.

CAUTION: Be sure you follow PEMDAS (see Section 15-A): handle exponents before the other operations. In Example 1, you *cannot* multiply –4 by –3, get 12, and then square the 12; you must first square –4.

A *polynomial* is a monomial or the sum of two or more monomials. Each monomial that makes up the polynomial is called a *term* of the polynomial. Each of the following is a polynomial:

$$2x^2 \quad 2x^2 + 3 \quad 3x^2 - 7 \quad x^2 + 5x - 1$$
$$a^2b + b^2a \quad x^2 - y^2 \quad w^2 - 2w + 1$$

The first polynomial in the above list is a monomial; the second, third, fifth, and sixth polynomials are called *binomials*, because each has two terms; the fourth and seventh polynomials are called *trinomials*, because each has three terms. Two terms are called *like terms* if they have exactly the same variables and exponents; they can differ only in their coefficients: $5a^2b$ and $-3a^2b$ are like terms, whereas $a^2b$ and $b^2a$ are not.

The polynomial $3x^2 + 4x + 5x + 2x^2 + x - 7$ has 6 terms, but some of them are like terms and can be combined:

$$3x^2 + 2x^2 = 5x^2 \quad \text{and} \quad 4x + 5x + x = 10x.$$

So, the original polynomial is equivalent to the trinomial $5x^2 + 10x - 7$.

**KEY FACT F1:**

**The only terms of a polynomial that can be combined are like terms.**

---

**Helpful Hint**
To add, subtract, multiply, and divide polynomials, use the usual laws of arithmetic. To avoid careless errors, before performing any arithmetic operations, write each polynomial in parentheses.

---

**KEY FACT F2:**

**To add two polynomials, put a plus sign between them, erase the parentheses, and combine like terms.**

---

**Example 2.**
What is the sum of $5x^2 + 10x - 7$ and $3x^2 - 4x + 2$?

---

SOLUTION. $(5x^2 + 10x - 7) + (3x^2 - 4x + 2)$
$= 5x^2 + 10x - 7 + 3x^2 - 4x + 2$
$= (5x^2 + 3x^2) + (10x - 4x) + (-7 + 2)$
$= \mathbf{8x^2 + 6x - 5}$.

## KEY FACT F3:

To subtract two polynomials, change the minus sign between them to a plus sign and change the sign of every term in the second parentheses. Then just use KEY FACT F2 to add them: erase the parentheses and then combine like terms.

CAUTION: Make sure you get the order right in a subtraction problem.

**Example 3.**
Subtract $3x^2 - 4x + 2$ from $5x^2 + 10x - 7$.

SOLUTION. Be careful. Start with the second polynomial and subtract the first:

$(5x^2 + 10x - 7) - (3x^2 - 4x + 2)$
$= (5x^2 + 10x - 7) + (-3x^2 + 4x - 2)$
$= \mathbf{2x^2 + 14x - 9}$.

**Example 4.**
What is the average (arithmetic mean) of $5x^2 + 10x - 7$, $3x^2 - 4x + 2$, and $4x^2 + 2$?

SOLUTION. As in any average problem, add and divide:

$(5x^2 + 10x - 7) + (3x^2 - 4x + 2) + (4x^2 + 2) =$
$12x^2 + 6x - 3$,

and by the distributive law (KEY FACT A21),
$\dfrac{12x^2 + 6x - 3}{3} = \mathbf{4x^2 + 2x - 1}$.

## KEY FACT F4:

To multiply monomials, first multiply their coefficients, and then multiply their variables (letter by letter), by adding the exponents (see Section 12A).

**Example 5.**
What is the product of $3xy^2z^3$ and $-2x^2y^2$?

SOLUTION. $(3xy^2z^3)(-2x^2y^2) =$
$3(-2)(x)(x^2)(y^2)(y^2)(z^3) = \mathbf{-6x^3y^4z^3}$.

All other polynomials are multiplied by using the distributive law.

## KEY FACT F5:

To multiply a monomial by a polynomial, just multiply each term of the polynomial by the monomial.

**Example 6.**
What is the product of $2a$ and $3a^2 - 6ab + b^2$?

SOLUTION. $2a(3a^2 - 6ab + b^2) = \mathbf{6a^3 - 12a^2b + 2ab^2}$.

On the GRE, the only other polynomials that you could be asked to multiply are two binomials.

## KEY FACT F6:

To multiply two binomials, use the so-called FOIL method, which is really nothing more than the distributive law: Multiply each term in the first parentheses by each term in the second parentheses and simplify by combining terms, if possible.

$(2x - 7)(3x + 2) = (2x)(3x) + (2x)(2) + (-7)(3x) + (-7)(2) =$
First terms   Outer terms  Inner terms   Last terms
$6x^2 + 4x - 21x - 14 = 6x^2 - 17x - 14$

**Example 7.**
What is the value of $(x - 2)(x + 3) - (x - 4)(x + 5)$?

SOLUTION. First, multiply both pairs of binomials:

$(x - 2)(x + 3) = x^2 + 3x - 2x - 6 = x^2 + x - 6$

$(x - 4)(x + 5) = x^2 + 5x - 4x - 20 = x^2 + x - 20$

Now, subtract:
$(x^2 + x - 6) - (x^2 + x - 20) =$

$x^2 + x - 6 - x^2 - x + 20 = \mathbf{14}$.

## KEY FACT F7:

The three most important binomial products on the GRE are these:

• $(x - y)(x + y) = x^2 + xy - yx - y^2 = x^2 - y^2$

• $(x - y)^2 = (x - y)(x - y) = x^2 - xy - yx + y^2 =$
  $x^2 - 2xy + y^2$

• $(x + y)^2 = (x + y)(x + y) = x^2 + xy + yx + y^2 =$
  $x^2 + 2xy + y^2$

---

**Helpful Hint**
If you memorize these, you won't have to multiply them out each time you need them.

---

**Example 8.**

If $a - b = 7$ and $a + b = 13$, what is the value of $a^2 - b^2$?

(A) –120   (B) 20   (C) 91   (D) 120   (E) 218

SOLUTION. In Section 15-G, we will review how to solve such a pair of equations; but even if you know how, *you should not do it here*. You do not need to know the values of *a* and *b* to answer this question. The moment you see $a^2 - b^2$, you should think $(a - b)(a + b)$. Then:

$$a^2 - b^2 = (a - b)(a + b) = (7)(13) = \mathbf{91 \ (C)}.$$

**Example 9.**

If $x^2 + y^2 = 36$ and $(x + y)^2 = 64$, what is the value of $xy$?

(A) 14   (B) 28   (C) 100   (D) 128   (E) 2304

SOLUTION.

$$64 = (x + y)^2 = x^2 + 2xy + y^2 = x^2 + y^2 + 2xy = 36 + 2xy.$$

Therefore, $2xy = 64 - 36 = 28 \Rightarrow xy = \mathbf{14 \ (A)}.$

On the GRE, the only division of polynomials you might have to do is to divide a polynomial by a monomial. You will *not* have to do long division of polynomials.

**KEY FACT F8:**

**To divide a polynomial by a monomial, use the distributive law. Then simplify each term by reducing the fraction formed by the coefficients to lowest terms and applying the laws of exponents.**

**Example 10.**

What is the quotient when $32a^2b + 12ab^3c$ is divided by $8ab$ ?

SOLUTION. By the distributive law,

$$\frac{32a^2b + 12ab^3c}{8ab} = \frac{32a^2b}{8ab} + \frac{12ab^3c}{8ab}.$$

Now reduce each fraction: $\mathbf{4a + \dfrac{3}{2}b^2c}.$

On the GRE, the most important way to use the three formulas in KEY FACT F7 is to recognize them in reverse. In other words, whenever you see $x^2 - y^2$, you should realize that it can be rewritten as $(x - y)(x + y)$. This process, which is the reverse of multiplication, is called *factoring*.

| Column A | Column B |
|---|---|

**Example 11.**

| The value of $x^2 + 4x + 4$ when $x = 95.9$ | The value of $x^2 - 4x + 4$ when $x = 99.5$ |
|---|---|

SOLUTION. Obviously, you don't want to plug in 95.9 and 99.5 (remember that the GRE *never* requires you to do tedious arithmetic). Recognize that $x^2 + 4x + 4$ is equal to $(x + 2)^2$ and that $x^2 - 4x + 4$ is equal to $(x - 2)^2$. So, Column A is just $(95.9 + 2)^2 = 97.9^2$, whereas Column B is $(99.5 - 2)^2 = 97.5^2$. Column **A** is greater.

**Example 12.**

What is the value of $(1,000,001)^2 - (999,999)^2$?

SOLUTION. Do not even consider squaring 999,999. You know that there has to be an easier way to do this. In fact, if you stop to think, you can get the right answer in a few seconds. This is just $a^2 - b^2$ where $a = 1,000,001$ and $b = 999,999$, so change it to $(a - b)(a + b)$:

$$(1,000,001)^2 - (999,999)^2$$
$$= (1,000,001 - 999,999)(1,000,001 + 999,999)$$
$$= (2)(2,000,000) = \mathbf{4,000,000}.$$

Although the coefficients of any of the terms in a polynomial can be in fractions, as in $\dfrac{2}{3}x^2 - \dfrac{1}{2}x$, the variable itself cannot be in the denominator. An expression such as $\dfrac{3 + x}{x^2}$, which does have a variable in the denominator is called an *algebraic fraction*. Fortunately, you should have no trouble with algebraic fractions, since they are handled just like regular fractions. The rules that you reviewed in Section 15-B for adding, subtracting, multiplying, and dividing fractions apply to algebraic fractions, as well.

**Example 13.**

What is the sum of the reciprocals of $x^2$ and $y^2$?

SOLUTION. To add $\dfrac{1}{x^2} + \dfrac{1}{y^2}$, you need a common denominator, which is $x^2y^2$.

Multiply the numerator and denominator of $\dfrac{1}{x^2}$ by $y^2$ and the numerator and denominator of $\dfrac{1}{y^2}$ by $x^2$, and then add:

$$\frac{1}{x^2} + \frac{1}{y^2} = \frac{y^2}{x^2y^2} + \frac{x^2}{x^2y^2} = \frac{x^2 + y^2}{x^2y^2}.$$

Often, the way to simplify algebraic fractions is to factor the numerator or the denominator or both. Consider the following example, which is harder than anything you will see on the GRE, but still quite manageable.

---

**Example 14.**

What is the value of $\dfrac{4x^3 - x}{(2x+1)(6x-3)}$ when $x = 9999$?

---

SOLUTION. Don't use FOIL to multiply the denominator. That's going the wrong way. We want to simplify this fraction by factoring everything we can. First factor an $x$ out of the numerator and notice that what's left is the difference of two squares, which can be factored. Then factor out the 3 in the second factor in the denominator:

$$\frac{4x^3 - x}{(2x+1)(6x-3)} = \frac{x(4x^2 - 1)}{(2x+1)3(2x-1)} =$$

$$\frac{x\cancel{(2x-1)}\cancel{(2x+1)}}{3\cancel{(2x+1)}\cancel{(2x-1)}} = \frac{x}{3}.$$

So, instead of plugging 9999 into the original expression, plug it into $\dfrac{x}{3}$: $9999 \div 3 = \mathbf{3333}$.

# PRACTICE EXERCISES—POLYNOMIALS

## Multiple-Choice Questions

1. What is the value of $\dfrac{a^2 - b^2}{a - b}$ when $a = 117$ and $b = 118$?

   (A) –1    (B) 1    (C) 117.5    (D) 175    (E) 235

2. If $a^2 - b^2 = 21$ and $a^2 + b^2 = 29$, which of the following could be the value of $ab$?

   I. –10
   II. $5\sqrt{2}$
   III. 10

   (A) I only    (B) II only    (C) III only
   (D) I and III only    (E) II and III only

3. What is the average (arithmetic mean) of $x^2 + 2x - 3$, $3x^2 - 2x - 3$, and $30 - 4x^2$?

   (A) $\dfrac{8x^2 + 4x + 24}{3}$    (B) $\dfrac{8x^2 + 24}{3}$    (C) $\dfrac{24 - 4x}{3}$

   (D) –12    (E) 8

4. What is the value of $x^2 + 12x + 36$ when $x = 994$?

   (A) 11,928    (B) 98,836    (C) 100,000
   (D) 988,036    (E) 1,000,000

5. If $c^2 + d^2 = 4$ and $(c - d)^2 = 2$, what is the value of $cd$?

   (A) 1    (B) $\sqrt{2}$    (C) 2    (D) 3    (E) 4

6. What is the value of
   $(2x + 3)(x + 6) - (2x - 5)(x + 10)$?

   (A) 32    (B) 16    (C) 68
   (D) $4x^2 + 30x + 68$    (E) $4x^2 + 30x - 32$

7. If $\dfrac{1}{a} + \dfrac{1}{b} = \dfrac{1}{c}$ and $ab = c$, what is the average of $a$ and $b$?

   (A) 0    (B) $\dfrac{1}{2}$    (C) 1    (D) $\dfrac{c}{2}$    (E) $\dfrac{a+b}{2c}$

8. If $x^2 - y^2 = 28$ and $x - y = 8$, what is the average of $x$ and $y$?

   (A) 1.75    (B) 3.5    (C) 7    (D) 8    (E) 10

9. Which of the following is equal to

   $\left(\dfrac{1}{a} + a\right)^2 - \left(\dfrac{1}{a} - a\right)^2$?

   (A) 0    (B) 4    (C) $\dfrac{1}{a^2} - a^2$    (D) $\dfrac{2}{a^2} - 2a^2$

   (E) $\dfrac{1}{a^2} - 4 - a^2$

10. If $\left(\dfrac{1}{a} + a\right)^2 = 100$, what is the value of $\dfrac{1}{a^2} + a^2$?

    (A) 10    (B) 64    (C) 98    (D) 100    (E) 102

## Quantitative Comparison Questions

| Column A | Column B |
|---|---|
| $n < 0$ || |
| 11. $-2n^2$ | $(-2n)^2$ |
| $d < c$ || |
| 12. $(c - d)(c + d)$ | $(c - d)(c - d)$ |
| $x = -3$ and $y = 2$ || |
| 13. $-x^2y^3$ | 0 |
| 14. $(r + s)(r - s)$ | $r(s + r) - s(r + s)$ |
| 15. $\dfrac{5x^2 - 20}{x - 2}$ | $4x + 8$ |

# Answer Key

| | | |
|---|---|---|
| 1. E | 6. C | 11. B |
| 2. D | 7. B | 12. D |
| 3. E | 8. A | 13. B |
| 4. E | 9. B | 14. C |
| 5. A | 10. C | 15. D |

# Answer Explanations

1. E. $\dfrac{a^2 - b^2}{a - b} = \dfrac{(a-b)(a+b)}{a-b} = a + b =$
   $117 + 118 = 235$.

2. D. Adding the two equations, we get that $2a^2 = 50 \Rightarrow a^2 = 25 \Rightarrow b^2 = 4$. So, $a = 5$ or $-5$ and $b = 2$ or $-2$. The only possibilities for their product are 10 and $-10$. (Only I and III are true.)

3. E. To find the average, take the sum of the three polynomials and then divide by 3. Their sum is $(x^2 + 2x - 3) + (3x^2 - 2x - 3) + (30 - 4x^2) = 24$, and $24 \div 3 = 8$.

4. E. You can avoid messy, time-consuming arithmetic if you recognize that $x^2 + 12x + 36 = (x + 6)^2$. The value is $(994 + 6)^2 = 1000^2 = 1,000,000$.

5. A. Start by squaring $c - d$:
   $2 = (c - d)^2 = c^2 - 2cd + d^2 = c^2 + d^2 - 2cd = 4 - 2cd$.
   So, $2 = 4 - 2cd \Rightarrow 2cd = 2 \Rightarrow cd = 1$.

6. C. First multiply out both pairs of binomials:
   $(2x + 3)(x + 6) = 2x^2 + 15x + 18$
   and $(2x - 5)(x + 10) = 2x^2 + 15x - 50$.

   Now subtract:
   $(2x^2 + 15x + 18) - (2x^2 + 15x - 50) = 18 - (-50) = 68$.

7. B. $\dfrac{1}{c} = \dfrac{1}{a} + \dfrac{1}{b} = \dfrac{a+b}{ab} = \dfrac{a+b}{c} \Rightarrow$
   $1 = a + b \Rightarrow \dfrac{a+b}{2} = \dfrac{1}{2}$.

8. A. $x^2 - y^2 = (x - y)(x + y) \Rightarrow 28 = 8(x + y) \Rightarrow x + y = 28 \div 8 = 3.5$. Finally, the average of $x$ and $y$ is $\dfrac{x+y}{2} = \dfrac{3.5}{2} = 1.75$.

9. B. Expand each square: $\left(\dfrac{1}{a} + a\right)^2 =$
   $\dfrac{1}{a^2} + 2\left(\dfrac{1}{a}\right)(a) + a^2 = \dfrac{1}{a^2} + 2 + a^2$.

   Similarly, $\left(\dfrac{1}{a} - a\right)^2 = \dfrac{1}{a^2} - 2 + a^2$.

   Subtract: $\left(\dfrac{1}{a^2} + 2 + a^2\right) - \left(\dfrac{1}{a^2} - 2 + a^2\right) = 4$.

10. C. $100 = \left(\dfrac{1}{a} + a\right)^2 = \dfrac{1}{a^2} + 2 + a^2 \Rightarrow \dfrac{1}{a^2} + a^2 = 98$.

11. B. Since $n$ is negative, $n^2$ is positive, and so $-2n^2$ is negative. Therefore, Column A is negative, whereas Column B is positive.

|  | Column A | Column B |
|---|---|---|

12. D. $c > d \Rightarrow c - d$ is positive, so divide each side by $c - d$:     $c + d$     $c - d$
    Subtract $c$ from each column:     $d$     $-d$
    If $d = 0$ the columns are equal; if $d = 1$, they aren't.

13. B. Column A: $-(-3)^2 2^3 = -(9)(8) = -72$.

14. C. Column B: $r(s + r) - s(r + s) = rs + r^2 - sr - s^2 = r^2 - s^2$
    Column A: $(r + s)(r - s) = r^2 - s^2$.

15. D. Column A: $\dfrac{5x^2 - 20}{x - 2} = \dfrac{5(x^2 - 4)}{x - 2} = \dfrac{5(x-2)(x+2)}{x-2} = 5(x + 2)$.
    Column B: $4x + 8 = 4(x + 2)$. If $x = -2$, both columns are 0; for any other value of $x$ the columns are unequal.

# 15-G. SOLVING EQUATIONS AND INEQUALITIES

The basic principle that you must adhere to in solving any *equation* is that you can manipulate it in any way, as long as *you do the same thing to both sides*. For example, you may always add the same number to each side; subtract the same number from each side; multiply or divide each side by the same number (except 0); square each side; take the square root of each side (if the quantities are positive); or take the reciprocal of each side. These comments apply to inequalities, as well, except you must be very careful, because some procedures, such as multiplying or dividing by a negative number and taking reciprocals, reverse inequalities (see Section 15-A).

Most of the equations and inequalities that you will have to solve on the GRE have only one variable and no exponents. The following simple six-step method can be used on all of them.

---

**Example 1.**

If $\frac{1}{2}x + 3(x - 2) = 2(x + 1) + 1$, what is the value of $x$?

---

SOLUTION. Follow the steps outlined in the following table.

| Step | What to Do | Example 1 |
|---|---|---|
| 1 | Get rid of fractions and decimals by multiplying both sides by the Lowest Common Denominator (LCD). | Multiply each term by 2: $x + 6(x - 2) = 4(x + 1) + 2.$ |
| 2 | Get rid of all parentheses by using the distributive law. | $x + 6x - 12 = 4x + 4 + 2.$ |
| 3 | Combine like terms on each side. | $7x - 12 = 4x + 6.$ |
| 4 | By adding or subtracting, get all the variables on one side. | Subtract $4x$ from each side: $3x - 12 = 6.$ |
| 5 | By adding or subtracting, get all the plain numbers on the other side. | Add 12 to each side: $3x = 18.$ |
| 6 | Divide both sides by the coefficient of the variable.* | Divide both sides by 3: $x = 6.$ |

*Note: If you start with an inequality and in Step 6 you divide by a negative number, remember to reverse the inequality (see KEY FACT A24).

*Example 1 is actually harder than any equation on the GRE*, because it required all six steps. On the GRE that

never happens. Think of the six steps as a list of questions that must be answered. Ask if each step is necessary. If it isn't, move on to the next one; if it is, do it.

Let's look at Example 2, which does not require all six steps.

---

**Example 2.**

For what real number $n$ is it true that $3(n - 20) = n$?

(A) –10   (B) 0   (C) 10   (D) 20   (E) 30

---

SOLUTION. Do whichever of the six steps are necessary.

| Step | Question | Yes/No | What to Do |
|---|---|---|---|
| 1 | Are there any fractions or decimals? | No | |
| 2 | Are there any parentheses? | Yes | Get rid of them: $3n - 60 = n.$ |
| 3 | Are there any like terms to combine? | No | |
| 4 | Are there variables on both sides? | Yes | Subtract $n$ from each side: $2n - 60 = 0.$ |
| 5 | Is there a plain number on the same side as the variable? | Yes | Add 60 to each side: $2n = 60.$ |
| 6 | Does the variable have a coefficient? | Yes | Divide both sides by 2: $n = \mathbf{30}.$ |

Tactic
**G1**

Memorize the six steps *in order* and use this method whenever you have to solve this type of equation or inequality.

---

**Example 3.**

Three brothers divided a prize as follows. The oldest received $\frac{2}{5}$ of it, the middle brother received $\frac{1}{3}$ of it, and the youngest received the remaining \$120. What was the value of the prize?

---

SOLUTION: If $x$ represents the value of the prize, then

$$\frac{2}{5}x + \frac{1}{3}x + 120 = x.$$

Solve this equation using the six-step method.

| Step | Question | Yes/No | What to Do |
|------|----------|--------|------------|
| 1 | Are there any fractions or decimals? | Yes | To get rid of them, multiply by 15. $15\left(\frac{2}{5}x\right)+15\left(\frac{1}{3}x\right)+$ $15(120) = 15(x)$ $6x + 5x + 1800 = 15x$ |
| 2 | Are there any parentheses? | No | |
| 3 | Are there any like terms to combine? | Yes | Combine them: $11x + 1800 = 15x$. |
| 4 | Are there variables on both sides? | Yes | Subtract $11x$ from each side: $1800 = 4x$. |
| 5 | Is there a plain number on the same side as the variable? | No | |
| 6 | Does the variable have a coefficient? | Yes | Divide both sides by 4: $x = \mathbf{450}$. |

Sometimes on the GRE, you are given an equation with several variables and asked to solve for one of them in terms of the others.

**G2**

When you have to solve for one variable in terms of the others, treat all of the others as if they were numbers, and apply the six-step method.

> **Example 4.**
> If $a = 3b - c$, what is the value of $b$ in terms of $a$ and $c$?

SOLUTION. To solve for $b$, treat $a$ and $c$ as numbers and use the six-step method with $b$ as the variable.

| Step | Question | Yes/No | What to Do |
|------|----------|--------|------------|
| 1 | Are there any fractions or decimals? | No | |
| 2 | Are there any parentheses? | No | |
| 3 | Are there any like terms to combine? | No | |
| 4 | Are there variables on both sides? | No | Remember: the only variable is $b$. |
| 5 | Is there a plain number on the same side as the variable? | Yes | Remember: we're considering $c$ as a number, and it is on the same side as $b$, the variable. Add $c$ to both sides: $a + c = 3b$. |
| 6 | Does the variable have a coefficient? | Yes | Divide both sides by 3: $b = \dfrac{a+c}{3}$. |

Sometimes when solving equations, you may see a shortcut. For example, to solve $7(w - 3) = 42$, it saves time to start by dividing both sides by 7, getting $w - 3 = 6$, rather than by using the distributive law to eliminate the parentheses. Similarly, if you have to solve a proportion such as $\dfrac{x}{7} = \dfrac{3}{5}$, it is easier to cross-multiply, getting $5x = 21$, than to multiply both sides by 35 to get rid of the fractions (although that's exactly what cross-multiplying accomplishes). Other shortcuts will be illustrated in the problems at the end of the section. If you spot such a shortcut, use it; but if you don't, be assured that the six-step method *always* works.

---

**Helpful Hint**

In applying the six-step method, you shouldn't actually write out the table, as we did in Examples 1–4, since it would be too time consuming. Instead, use the method as a guideline and mentally go through each step, doing whichever ones are required.

---

> **Example 5.**
> If $x - 4 = 11$, what is the value of $x - 8$?
> (A) –15  (B) –7  (C) –1  (D) 7  (E) 15

SOLUTION. Going immediately to Step 5, add 4 to each side: $x = 15$. But this is *not* the answer. You need the value not of $x$, but of $x - 8$: $15 - 8 = \mathbf{7}$ **(D)**.

As in Example 5, on the GRE you are often asked to solve for something other than the simple variable. In

Example 5, we could have been asked for the value of $x^2$ or $x + 4$ or $(x - 4)^2$, and so on.

**G3**

As you read each question on the GRE, on your scrap paper write down whatever you are looking for, and circle it. This way you will always be sure that you are answering the question that is asked.

---

### Helpful Hint

Very often, solving the equation is *not* the quickest way to answer the question. Consider the following example.

---

**Example 6.**

If $2x - 5 = 98$, what is the value of $2x + 5$?

SOLUTION. The first thing you should do is write $2x + 5$ on your paper and circle it. The fact that you are asked for the value of something other than $x$ should alert you to look at the question carefully to see if there is a shortcut.

• The best approach here is to observe that $2x + 5$ is 10 more than $2x - 5$, so the answer is **108** (10 more than 98).

• Next best would be to do only one step of the six-step method, add 5 to both sides: $2x = 103$. Now, add 5 to both sides: $2x + 5 = 103 + 5 = 108$.

• The *worst* method would be to divide $2x = 103$ by 2, get $x = 51.5$, and then use that to calculate $2x + 5$.

**Example 7.**

If $w$ is an integer, and the average (arithmetic mean) of 3, 4, and $w$ is less than 10, what is the greatest possible value of $w$ ?

(A) 9    (B) 10    (C) 17    (D) 22    (E) 23

SOLUTION. Set up the inequality: $\frac{3 + 4 + w}{3} < 10$. Do Step 1 (get rid of fractions by multiplying by 3): $3 + 4 + w < 30$. Do Step 3 (combine like terms): $7 + w < 30$. Finally, do Step 5 (subtract 7 from each side): $w < 23$. Since $w$ is an integer, the most it can be is **22**.

The six-step method also works when there are variables in denominators.

**Example 8.**

For what value of $x$ is $\frac{4}{x} + \frac{3}{5} = \frac{10}{x}$?

(A) 5    (B) 10    (C) 20    (D) 30    (E) 50

SOLUTION. Multiply each side by the LCD, $5x$:

$$5x\left(\frac{4}{x}\right) + 5x\left(\frac{3}{5}\right) = 5x\left(\frac{10}{x}\right) \Rightarrow 20 + 3x = 50.$$

Now solve normally: $20 + 3x = 50 \Rightarrow 3x = 30 \Rightarrow x = 10$ **(B)**.

**Example 9.** If $x$ is positive, and $y = 5x^2 + 3$, which of the following is an expression for $x$ in terms of $y$?

(A) $\sqrt{\dfrac{y}{5} - 3}$    (B) $\sqrt{\dfrac{y - 3}{5}}$    (C) $\dfrac{\sqrt{y - 3}}{5}$

(D) $\dfrac{\sqrt{y} - 3}{5}$    (E) $\dfrac{\sqrt{y} - \sqrt{3}}{5}$

SOLUTION. The six-step method works when there are no exponents. However, we can treat $x^2$ as a single variable, and use the method as far as possible:

$$y = 5x^2 + 3 \Rightarrow y - 3 = 5x^2 \Rightarrow \frac{y - 3}{5} = x^2.$$

Now take the square root of each side; since $x$ is positive, the only solution is $x = \sqrt{\dfrac{y - 3}{5}}$ **(B)**.

CAUTION: Doing the same thing to each *side* of an equation does *not* mean doing the same thing to each *term* of the equation. Study Examples 10 and 11 carefully.

**Example 10.**

If $\dfrac{1}{a} = \dfrac{1}{b} + \dfrac{1}{c}$, what is $a$ in terms of $b$ and $c$?

NOTE: You *cannot* just take the reciprocal of each term; the answer is *not* $a = b + c$. Here are two solutions.

SOLUTION 1. First add the fractions on the right hand side: $\dfrac{1}{a} = \dfrac{1}{b} + \dfrac{1}{c} = \dfrac{b + c}{bc}$.

Now, take the reciprocal of each *side*: $a = \dfrac{bc}{b + c}$.

SOLUTION 2. Use the six-step method. Multiply each term by $abc$, the LCD: $abc\left(\dfrac{1}{a}\right) = abc\left(\dfrac{1}{b}\right) + abc\left(\dfrac{1}{c}\right) \Rightarrow$ $bc = ac + ab = a(c + b) \Rightarrow a = \dfrac{bc}{c + b}$.

**Example 11.**

If $a > 0$ and $a^2 + b^2 = c^2$, what is $a$ in terms of $b$ and $c$?

SOLUTION. $a^2 + b^2 = c^2 \Rightarrow a^2 = c^2 - b^2$. Be careful: you *cannot* now take the square root of each *term* and write, $a = c - b$. Rather, you must take the square root of each side: $a = \sqrt{a^2} = \sqrt{c^2 - b^2}$.

There are a few other types of equations that you could have to solve on the GRE. Fortunately, they are quite easy. You probably will not have to solve a quadratic equation. However, if you do, you will *not* need the quadratic formula, and you will not have to factor a trinomial. Here are two examples.

**Example 12.**

If $x$ is a positive number and $x^2 + 64 = 100$, what is the value of $x$?

(A) 6   (B) 12   (C) 13   (D) 14   (E) 36

SOLUTION. When there is an $x^2$-term, but no $x$-term, we just have to take the square root:

$$x^2 + 64 = 100 \Rightarrow x^2 = 36 \Rightarrow x = \sqrt{36} = \textbf{6 (A)}.$$

**Example 13.**

What is the largest value of $x$ that satisfies the equation $2x^2 - 3x = 0$?

(A) 0   (B) 1.5   (C) 2   (D) 2.5   (E) 3

SOLUTION: When an equation has an $x^2$-term and an $x$-term but no constant term, the way to solve it is to factor out the $x$ and to use the fact that if the product of two numbers is 0, one of them must be 0 (KEY FACT A3):

$$2x^2 - 3x = 0 \Rightarrow x(2x - 3) = 0$$
$$x = 0 \text{ or } 2x - 3 = 0$$
$$x = 0 \text{ or } 2x = 3$$
$$x = 0 \text{ or } x = 1.5.$$

The largest value is **1.5 (B)**.

In another type of equation that occasionally appears on the GRE, the variable is in the exponent. These equations are particularly easy and are basically solved by inspection.

**Example 14.**

If $2^{x+3} = 32$, what is the value of $3^{x+2}$?

(A) 5   (B) 9   (C) 27   (D) 81   (E) 125

SOLUTION. How many 2s do you have to multiply together to get 32? If you don't know that it's 5, just multiply and keep track. Count the 2s on your fingers as

you say to yourself, "2 times 2 is 4, times 2 is 8, times 2 is 16, times 2 is 32." Then

$$2^{x+3} = 32 = 2^5 \Rightarrow x + 3 = 5 \Rightarrow x = 2.$$

Therefore, $x + 2 = 4$, and $3^{x+2} = 3^4 = 3 \times 3 \times 3 \times 3 = $ **81 (D)**.

Occasionally, both sides of an equation have variables in the exponents. In that case, it is necessary to write both exponentials with the same base.

**Example 15.** If $4^{w+3} = 8^{w-1}$, what is the value of $w$?

(A) 0   (B) 1   (C) 2   (D) 3   (E) 9

SOLUTION. Since it is necessary to have the same base on each side of the equation, write $4 = 2^2$ and $8 = 2^3$. Then

$$4^{w+3} = (2^2)^{w+3} = 2^{2(w+3)} = 2^{2w+6} \text{ and}$$
$$8^{w-1} = (2^3)^{w-1} = 2^{3(w-1)} = 2^{3w-3}.$$

So, $2^{2w+6} = 2^{3w-3} \Rightarrow 2w + 6 = 3w - 3 \Rightarrow w = \textbf{9 (E)}$.

## Systems of Linear Equations

The equations $x + y = 10$ and $x - y = 2$ each have lots of solutions (infinitely many, in fact). Some of them are given in the tables below.

| $x + y = 10$ | | | | | | |
|---|---|---|---|---|---|---|
| $x$ | 5 | **6** | 4 | 1 | 1.2 | 10 | 20 |
| $y$ | 5 | **4** | 6 | 9 | 8.8 | 0 | −10 |
| $x + y$ | 10 | 10 | 10 | 10 | 10 | 10 | 10 |

| $x - y = 2$ | | | | | | |
|---|---|---|---|---|---|---|
| $x$ | 5 | **6** | 2 | 0 | 2.5 | 19 | 40 |
| $y$ | 3 | **4** | 0 | −2 | .5 | 17 | 38 |
| $x - y$ | 2 | 2 | 2 | 2 | 2 | 2 | 2 |

However, only one pair of numbers, **$x = 6$** and **$y = 4$**, satisfy both equations simultaneously: $6 + 4 = 10$ and $6 - 4 = 2$. This then is the only solution of the *system of equations*: $\begin{cases} x + y = 10 \\ x - y = 2 \end{cases}$.

A system of equations is a set of two or more equations involving two or more variables. To solve such a system, you must find values for each of the variables that will make each equation true. In an algebra course you learn several ways to solve systems of equations. On the GRE, the most useful way to solve them is to add or subtract (usually add) the equations. After demonstrating this method, we will show in Example 19 one other way to handle some systems of equations.

**Tactic**

**G4**

To solve a system of equations, add or subtract them. If there are more than two equations, add them.

| Column A | Column B |
|---|---|

**Example 16.**

$$x + y = 10$$
$$x - y = 2$$

| $x$ | $y$ |
|---|---|

SOLUTION. Add the two equations:

$$\begin{array}{r} x + y = 10 \\ + x - y = 2 \\ \hline 2x \quad = 12 \\ x = 6 \end{array}$$

Replacing $x$ with 6 in $x + y = 10$ yields $y = 4$. So, Column **A** is greater.

**Helpful Hint**

On the GRE, most problems involving systems of equations do *not* require you to solve the system. They usually ask for something other than the values of each variable. Read the questions very carefully, circle what you need, and do no more than is required.

**Example 17.**

If $3a + 5b = 10$ and $5a + 3b = 30$, what is the average (arithmetic mean) of $a$ and $b$?

(A) 2.5   (B) 4   (C) 5   (D) 20
   (E) It cannot be determined from the information given.

SOLUTION. Add the two equations:

$$\begin{array}{r} 3a + 5b = 10 \\ + 5a + 3b = 30 \\ \hline 8a + 8b = 40 \end{array}$$

Divide both sides by 8:
$$a + b = 5$$

The average of $a$ and $b$ is:
$$\frac{a+b}{2} = \frac{5}{2} = 2.5 \text{ (A)}$$

Note: It is not only unnecessary to first solve for $a$ and $b$ ($a = 7.5$ and $b = -2.5$.), but, because that procedure is so much more time-consuming, it would be foolish to do so.

| Column A | Column B |
|---|---|

**Example 18.**

$$7a - 3b = 200$$
$$7a + 3b = 100$$

| $a$ | $b$ |
|---|---|

SOLUTION. Don't actually solve the system. Add the equations: $14a = 300 \Rightarrow 7a = 150$. So, replacing $7a$ with 150 in the second equation, we get $150 + 3b = 100$; so $3b$, and hence $b$, must be negative, whereas $a$ is positive. Therefore, $a > b$, and Column **A** is greater.

**Helpful Hint**

Remember TACTIC 5, Chapter 13. On quantitative comparison questions, you don't need to know the value of the quantity in each column; you only need to know which one is greater.

Occasionally on the GRE, it is as easy, or easier, to solve the system by substitution.

**Tactic**

**G5**

If one of the equations in a system of equations consists of a single variable equal to some expression, substitute that expression for the variable in the other equation.

| Column A | Column B |
|---|---|

**Example 19.**

$$x + y = 10$$
$$y = x - 2$$

| $x$ | $y$ |
|---|---|

SOLUTION. Since the second equation states that a single variable ($y$), is equal to some expression ($x - 2$), substitute that expression for $y$ in the first equation: $x + y = 10$ becomes $x + (x - 2) = 10$. Then, $2x - 2 = 10$, $2x = 12$, and $x = 6$. As always, to find the value of the other variable ($y$), plug the value of $x$ into one of the two original equations: $y = 6 - 2 = 4$. Column **A** is greater.

# PRACTICE EXERCISES—EQUATIONS/INEQUALITIES

## Multiple-Choice Questions

1. If $4x + 12 = 36$, what is the value of $x + 3$?
   (A) 3   (B) 6   (C) 9   (D) 12   (E) 18

2. If $7x + 10 = 44$, what is the value of $7x - 10$?
   (A) $-6\frac{6}{7}$   (B) $4\frac{6}{7}$   (C) $14\frac{6}{7}$   (D) 24
   (E) 34

3. If $4x + 13 = 7 - 2x$, what is the value of $x$?
   (A) $-\frac{10}{3}$   (B) $-3$   (C) $-1$   (D) 1   (E) $\frac{10}{3}$

4. If $x - 4 = 9$, what is the value of $x^2 - 4$?
   (A) 21   (B) 77   (C) 81   (D) 165   (E) 169

5. If $ax - b = c - dx$, what is the value of $x$ in terms of $a$, $b$, $c$, and $d$?
   (A) $\frac{b+c}{a+d}$   (B) $\frac{c-b}{a-d}$   (C) $\frac{b+c-d}{a}$
   (D) $\frac{c-b}{a+d}$   (E) $\frac{c}{b} - \frac{d}{a}$

6. If $\frac{1}{3}x + \frac{1}{6}x + \frac{1}{9}x = 33$, what is the value of $x$?
   (A) 3   (B) 18   (C) 27   (D) 54   (E) 72

7. If $3x - 4 = 11$, what is the value of $(3x - 4)^2$?
   (A) 22   (B) 36   (C) 116   (D) 121   (E) 256

8. If $64^{12} = 2^{a-3}$, what is the value of $a$?
   (A) 9   (B) 15   (C) 69   (D) 72   (E) 75

9. If the average (arithmetic mean) of $3a$ and $4b$ is less than 50, and $a$ is twice $b$, what is the largest possible integer value of $a$?
   (A) 9   (B) 10   (C) 11   (D) 19   (E) 20

10. If $\frac{1}{a-b} = 5$, then $a =$
    (A) $b + 5$   (B) $b - 5$   (C) $b + \frac{1}{5}$   (D) $b - \frac{1}{5}$
    (E) $\frac{1-5b}{5}$

11. If $x = 3a + 7$ and $y = 9a^2$, what is $y$ in terms of $x$?
    (A) $(x - 7)^2$   (B) $3(x - 7)^2$   (C) $\frac{(x-7)^2}{3}$
    (D) $\frac{(x+7)^2}{3}$   (E) $(x + 7)^2$

12. If $4y - 3x = 5$, what is the smallest integer value of $x$ for which $y > 100$?
    (A) 130   (B) 131   (C) 132   (D) 395   (E) 396

## Quantitative Comparison Questions

| Column A | Column B |
|---|---|

$$a + b = 13$$
$$a - b = 13$$

| Column A | Column B |
|---|---|
| 13. $b$ | 13 |

$$\frac{2^{a-1}}{2^{b+1}} = 8$$

| Column A | Column B |
|---|---|
| 14. $a$ | $b$ |

$$4x^2 = 3x$$

| Column A | Column B |
|---|---|
| 15. $x$ | 1 |

$$a + b = 1$$
$$b + c = 2$$
$$c + a = 3$$

| Column A | Column B |
|---|---|
| 16. The average (arithmetic mean) of $a$, $b$, and $c$ | 1 |

$$3x - 4y = 5$$
$$y = 2x$$

| Column A | Column B |
|---|---|
| 17. $x$ | $y$ |

$$\frac{x}{2} - 2 > \frac{x}{3}$$

| Column A | Column B |
|---|---|
| 18. $x$ | 12 |

$$3r - 5s = 17$$
$$2r - 6s = 7$$

| Column A | Column B |
|---|---|
| 19. The average (arithmetic mean) of $r$ and $s$ | 10 |

$$\frac{1}{c} = 1 + \frac{1}{d}$$
$c$ and $d$ are positive

| Column A | Column B |
|---|---|
| 20. $c$ | $d$ |

# Answer Key

| | | | |
|---|---|---|---|
| 1. **C** | 6. **D** | 11. **A** | 16. **C** |
| 2. **D** | 7. **D** | 12. **C** | 17. **A** |
| 3. **C** | 8. **E** | 13. **B** | 18. **A** |
| 4. **D** | 9. **D** | 14. **A** | 19. **B** |
| 5. **A** | 10. **C** | 15. **B** | 20. **B** |

# Answer Explanations

1. **C.** The easiest method is to recognize that $x + 3$ is $\frac{1}{4}$ of $4x + 12$ and, therefore, equals $\frac{1}{4}$ of 36, which is 9. If you don't see that, solve normally: $4x + 12 = 36 \Rightarrow 4x = 24 \Rightarrow x = 6 \Rightarrow x + 3 = 9$.

2. **D.** Subtracting 20 from each side of $7x + 10 = 44$ gives $7x - 10 = 24$. If you don't see that, subtract 10 from each side, getting $7x = 34$. Then subtract 10 to get $7x - 10 = 24$. The worst alternative is to divide both sides of $7x = 34$ by 7 to get $x = \frac{34}{7}$; then you have to multiply by 7 to get back to 34, and then subtract 10.

3. **C.** Add $2x$ to each side: $6x + 13 = 7$. Subtract 13 from each side: $6x = -6$. Divide by 6: $x = -1$.

4. **D.** $x - 4 = 9 \Rightarrow x = 13 \Rightarrow x^2 = 169 \Rightarrow x^2 - 4 = 165$.

5. **A.** Treat $a$, $b$, $c$, and $d$ as constants, and use the six-step method to solve for $x$:

$$ax - b = c - dx \Rightarrow ax - b + dx = c \Rightarrow$$
$$ax + dx = c + b \Rightarrow x(a + d) = b + c \Rightarrow$$
$$x = \frac{b + c}{a + d}.$$

6. **D.** Multiply both sides by 18, the LCD:

$$18\left(\frac{1}{3}x + \frac{1}{6}x + \frac{1}{9}x\right) = 18(33) \Rightarrow$$
$$6x + 3x + 2x = 594 \Rightarrow 11x = 594 \Rightarrow x = 54.$$

It's actually easier not to multiply out $18 \times 33$; leave it in that form, and then divide by 11: $\frac{18 \times \cancel{33}^3}{\cancel{11}_1} = 3 \times 18 = 54$.

7. **D.** Be alert. Since you are given the value of $3x - 4$, and want the value of $(3x - 4)^2$, just square both sides: $11^2 = 121$. If you don't see that, you'll waste time solving $3x - 4 = 11$ ($x = 5$), only to use that value to calculate that $3x - 4$ is equal to 11, which you aready knew.

8. **E.** $2^{a-3} = 64^{12} = (2^6)^{12} = 2^{72} \Rightarrow a - 3 = 72 \Rightarrow a = 75$.

9. **D.** Since $a = 2b$, $2a = 4b$. Therefore, the average of $3a$ and $4b$ is the average of $3a$ and $2a$, which is $2.5a$. Therefore, $2.5a < 50 \Rightarrow a < 20$. So the largest *integer* value of $a$ is 19.

10. **C.** Taking the reciprocal of each side, we get $a - b = \frac{1}{5}$. So $a = b + \frac{1}{5}$.

11. **A.** $x = 3a + 7 \Rightarrow x - 7 = 3a \Rightarrow a = \frac{x - 7}{3}$. Therefore,

$$y = 9a^2 = 9\left(\frac{x - 7}{3}\right)^2 = 9\frac{(x - 7)^2}{3^2} = (x - 7)^2.$$

12. **C.** First, solve for $y$ in terms of $x$:

$$4y - 3x = 5 \Rightarrow 4y = 5 + 3x \Rightarrow y = \frac{5 + 3x}{4}.$$

Then, since $y > 100$:

$$\frac{5 + 3x}{4} > 100 \Rightarrow 5 + 3x > 400 \Rightarrow$$
$$3x > 395 \Rightarrow x > 131.666.$$

The smallest integer value of $x$ is 132.

13. **B.** Adding the two equations, we get that $2a = 26$. Therefore, $a = 13$ and $b = 0$.

14. **A.** Express each side of $\frac{2^{a-1}}{2^{b+1}} = 8$ as a power of 2:

$$8 = 2^3 \quad \text{and} \quad \frac{2^{a-1}}{2^{b+1}} = 2^{(a-1)-(b+1)} = 2^{a-b-2}.$$

Therefore, $a - b - 2 = 3 \Rightarrow a = b + 5$, and so $a$ is greater.

15. **B.** $4x^2 = 3x \Rightarrow 4x^2 - 3x = 0 \Rightarrow x(4x - 3) = 0 \Rightarrow$

$$x = 0 \quad \text{or} \quad 4x - 3 = 0 \Rightarrow$$
$$x = 0 \quad \text{or} \quad 4x = 3 \Rightarrow$$
$$x = 0 \quad \text{or} \quad x = \frac{3}{4}.$$

There are two possible values of $x$, both of which are less than 1.

16. **C.**   When we add all three equations, we get
$2a + 2b + 2c = 6 \Rightarrow a + b + c = 3 \Rightarrow$
$$\frac{a+b+c}{3} = 1.$$

17. **A.**   Use substitution. Replace $y$ in the first equation with $2x$: $3x - 4(2x) = 5 \Rightarrow 3x - 8x = 5 \Rightarrow$
$-5x = 5 \Rightarrow x = -1 \Rightarrow y = -2.$

18. **A.**   Multiply both sides by 6, the LCD:
$$6\left(\frac{x}{2} - 2\right) > 6\left(\frac{x}{3}\right) \Rightarrow 3x - 12 > 2x \Rightarrow$$
$-12 > -x \Rightarrow x > 12.$

19. **B.**   The first thing to try is to add the equations. That yields $5r - 11s = 24$, which does not appear to be useful. So now try to subtract the equations. That yields $r + s = 10$. So the average of $r$ and $s$ is $\dfrac{r+s}{2} = \dfrac{10}{2} = 5.$

20. **B.**   Multiply both sides by $cd$, the LCD of the fractions:
$$cd\left(\frac{1}{c}\right) = cd\left(1 + \frac{1}{d}\right) \Rightarrow$$
$$d = cd + c = c(d + 1) \Rightarrow c = \frac{d}{d+1}$$
Since $d$ is positive, $d + 1 > 1 \Rightarrow \dfrac{d}{d+1} < d.$
So $c < d.$

# 15-H. WORD PROBLEMS

On a typical GRE you will see several word problems, covering almost every math topic for which you are responsible. In this chapter you have already seen word problems on consecutive integers in Section A; fractions and percents in Sections B and C; ratios and rates in Section D; and averages in Section E. Later in this chapter you will see word problems involving probability, circles, triangles, and other geometric figures. A few of these problems can be solved with just arithmetic, but most of them require basic algebra.

To solve word problems algebraically, you must treat algebra as a foreign language and learn to translate "word for word" from English into algebra, just as you would from English into French or Spanish or any other language. When translating into algebra, we use some letter (often $x$) to represent the unknown quantity we are trying to determine. It is this translation process that causes difficulty for some students. Once translated, solving is easy using the techniques we have already reviewed. Consider the following pairs of typical GRE questions. The first ones in each pair (1a and 2a) would be considered easy, whereas the second ones (1b and 2b) would be considered harder.

**Example 1a.**

What is 4% of 4% of 40,000?

**Example 1b.**

In a lottery, 4% of the tickets printed can be redeemed for prizes, and 4% of those tickets have values in excess of $100. If the state prints 40,000 tickets, how many of them can be redeemed for more than $100?

**Example 2a.**

If $x + 7 = 2(x - 8)$, what is the value of $x$?

**Example 2b.**

In 7 years Erin will be twice as old as she was 8 years ago. How old is Erin now?

Once you translate the words into arithmetic expressions or algebraic equations, Examples 1a and 1b and 2a and 2b are identical. The problem that many students have is doing the translation. It really isn't very difficult, and we'll show you how. First, though, look over the following English to algebra "dictionary."

| English Words | Mathematical Meaning | Symbol |
|---|---|---|
| Is, was, will be, had, has, will have, is equal to, is the same as | Equals | = |
| Plus, more than, sum, increased by, added to, exceeds, received, got, older than, farther than, greater than | Addition | + |
| Minus, fewer, less than, difference, decreased by, subtracted from, younger than, gave, lost | Subtraction | − |
| Times, of, product, multiplied by | Multiplication | × |
| Divided by, quotient, per, for | Division | $\div$, $\dfrac{a}{b}$ |
| More than, greater than | Inequality | > |
| At least | Inequality | ≥ |
| Fewer than, less than | Inequality | < |
| At most | Inequality | ≤ |
| What, how many, etc. | Unknown quantity | $x$ (or some some other variable) |

Let's use our dictionary to translate some phrases and sentences.

1. The <u>sum</u> of 5 and some number <u>is</u> 13.   $5 + x = 13$

2. John <u>was</u> 2 years <u>younger than</u> Sam.   $J = S - 2$

3. Bill has <u>at most</u> $100.   $B \le 100$

4. The <u>product</u> of 2 and a number <u>exceeds</u> that number by 5 (is 5 more than).   $2N = N + 5$

In translating statements, you first must decide what quantity the variable will represent. Often it's obvious. Other times there is more than one possibility.

Let's translate and solve the two questions from the beginning of this section, and then we'll look at a few new ones.

---

**Example 1b.**

In a lottery, 4% of the tickets printed can be redeemed for prizes, and 4% of those tickets have values in excess of $100. If the state prints 40,000 tickets, how many of them can be redeemed for more than $100?

---

SOLUTION. Let $x$ = the number of tickets worth more than $100. Then

$x = 4\%$ of $4\%$ of $40,000 = .04 \times .04 \times 40,000 = \mathbf{64}$,

which is also the solution to Example 1a.

---

**Example 2b.**

In 7 years Erin will be twice as old as she was 8 years ago. How old is Erin now?

---

SOLUTION. Let $x$ = Erin's age now. Then 8 years ago she was $x - 8$, and 7 years from now she will be $x + 7$. So,

$x + 7 = 2(x - 8) \Rightarrow x + 7 = 2x - 16 \Rightarrow 7 = x - 16 \Rightarrow x = \mathbf{23}$,

which is also the solution to Example 2a.

Most algebraic word problems on the GRE are not too difficult, and if you can do the algebra, that's usually the best way. But if, after studying this section, you still get stuck on a question during the test, don't despair. Use the tactics that you learned in Chapter 12, especially TACTIC 1—backsolving.

---

**Helpful Hint**

In all word problems on the GRE, remember to write down and circle what you are looking for. Don't answer the wrong question!

---

## Age Problems

---

**Helpful Hint**

In problems involving ages, remember that "years ago" means you need to subtract, and "years from now" means you need to add.

---

**Example 3.**

In 1980, Judy was 3 times as old as Adam, but in 1984 she was only twice as old as he was. How old was Adam in 1990?

(A) 4   (B) 8   (C) 12   (D) 14   (E) 16

---

**Helpful Hint**

It is often very useful to organize the data from a word problem in a table.

---

SOLUTION. Let $x$ be Adam's age in 1980 and fill in the table below.

| Year | Judy | Adam |
|------|------|------|
| 1980 | $3x$ | $x$ |
| 1984 | $3x + 4$ | $x + 4$ |

Now translate: Judy's age in 1984 was twice Adam's age in 1984: $3x + 4 = 2(x + 4)$

$3x + 4 = 2x + 8 \Rightarrow x + 4 = 8 \Rightarrow x = 4$

So, Adam was 4 in 1980. However, 4 is *not* the answer to this question. Did you remember to circle what you're looking for? The question *could have* asked for Adam's age in 1980 (Choice A) or 1984 (Choice B) or Judy's age in any year whatsoever (Choice C is 1980 and Choice E is 1984); but it didn't. It asked for *Adam's age in 1990*. Since he was 4 in 1980, then 10 years later, in 1990, he was **14 (D)**.

## Distance Problems

Distance problems all depend on three variations of the same formula:

$$\text{distance} = \text{rate} \times \text{time} \qquad \text{rate} = \frac{\text{distance}}{\text{time}}$$

$$\text{time} = \frac{\text{distance}}{\text{rate}}$$

These are usually abbreviated, $d = rt$, $r = \dfrac{d}{t}$, and $t = \dfrac{d}{r}$.

### Example 4.

How much longer, in *seconds*, is required to drive 1 mile at 40 miles per hour than at 60 miles per hour?

SOLUTION. The time to drive 1 mile at 40 miles per hour is given by

$$t = \frac{1}{40} \text{ hour} = \frac{1}{40} \times \overset{3}{\underset{2}{60}} \text{ minutes} = 1\frac{1}{2} \text{ minutes}.$$

The time to drive 1 mile at 60 miles per hour is given by

$$t = \frac{1}{60} \text{ hour} = 1 \text{ minute}.$$

The difference is $\frac{1}{2}$ minute = **30 seconds.**

Note that this solution used the time formula given, but required only arithmetic, not algebra. Example 5 requires an algebraic solution.

### Example 5.

Avi drove from his home to college at 60 miles per hour. Returning over the same route, there was a lot of traffic, and he was only able to drive at 40 miles per hour. If the return trip took 1 hour longer, how many miles did he drive each way?
(A) 2  (B) 3  (C) 5  (D) 120  (E) 240

SOLUTION. Let $x$ = the number of hours Avi took going to college and make a table.

|  | rate | time | distance |
|---|---|---|---|
| Going | 60 | $x$ | $60x$ |
| Returning | 40 | $x + 1$ | $40(x + 1)$ |

Since he drove the same distance going and returning,

$$60x = 40(x + 1) \Rightarrow 60x = 40x + 40 \Rightarrow 20x = 40 \Rightarrow x = 2.$$

Now be sure to answer the correct question. When $x = 2$, Choices A, B, and C are the time in hours that it took going, returning, and round-trip; Choices D and E are the distances each way and round-trip. You could have been asked for any of the five. If you circled what you're looking for, you won't make a careless mistake. Avi drove **120** miles each way, and so the correct answer is **D**.

The $d$ in $d = rt$ stands for "distance," but it could really be any type of work that is performed at a certain rate, $r$, for a certain amount of time, $t$. Example 5 need not be about distance. Instead of driving 120 miles at 60 miles per hour for 2 hours, Avi could have read 120 pages at a rate of 60 pages per hour for 2 hours; or planted 120 flowers at the rate of 60 flowers per hour for 2 hours; or typed 120 words at a rate of 60 words per minute for 2 minutes.

Examples 6 and 7 illustrate two additional word problems of the type that you might find on the GRE.

### Example 6.

Lindsay is trying to collect all the cards in a special commemorative set of baseball cards. She currently has exactly $\frac{1}{4}$ of the cards in that set. When she gets 10 more cards, she will then have $\frac{1}{3}$ of the cards. How many cards are in the set?
(A) 30  (B) 60  (C) 120  (D) 180  (E) 240

SOLUTION. Let $x$ be the number cards in the set. First, translate this problem from English into algebra: $\frac{1}{4}x + 10 = \frac{1}{3}x$. Now, use the six-step method of Section 15-G to solve the equation. Multiply by 12 to get, $3x + 120 = 4x$, and then subtract $3x$ from each side: $x = \mathbf{120}$ (**D**).

### Example 7.

Jen, Ken, and Len have a total of $390. Jen has 5 times as much as Len, and Ken has $\frac{3}{4}$ as much as Jen. How much money does Ken have?
(A) $40  (B) $78  (C) $150  (D) $195
        (E) $200

**Helpful Hint**

You often have a choice as to what to let the variable represent. Don't necessarily let it represent what you're looking for; rather, choose what will make the problem easiest to solve.

Suppose, for example, that in this problem you let $x$ represent the amount of money that Ken has. Then since Ken has $\frac{3}{4}$ as much as Jen, Jen has as $\frac{4}{3}$ much as Ken: $\frac{4}{3}x$; and Jen would have $\frac{1}{5}$ of that: $\left(\frac{1}{5}\right)\left(\frac{4}{3}x\right)$. It is much easier here to let $x$ represent the amount of money Len has.

SOLUTION. Let $x$ represent the amount of money Len has. Then $5x$ is the amount that Jen has, and $\frac{3}{4}(5x)$ is the amount that Ken has. Since the total amount of money is $390,

$$x + 5x + \frac{15}{4}x = 390.$$

Multiply by 4 to get rid of the fraction: $4x + 20x + 15x = 1560$. Combine like terms and then divide: $39x = 1560 \Rightarrow x = 40$. So Len has $40, Jen has $5 \times 40 = $200$, and Ken has $\frac{3}{4}(200) = \mathbf{\$150}$ (**C**).

# PRACTICE EXERCISES—WORD PROBLEMS

## Multiple-Choice Questions

1. Howard has three times as much money as Ronald. If Howard gives Ronald $50, Ronald will then have three times as much money as Howard. How much money do the two of them have together?

   (A) $75   (B) $100   (C) $125   (D) $150
   (E) $200

2. In the afternoon, Beth read 100 pages at the rate of 60 pages per hour; in the evening, when she was tired, she read another 100 pages at the rate of 40 pages per hour. What was her average rate of reading for the day?

   (A) 45   (B) 48   (C) 50   (D) 52   (E) 55

3. If the sum of five consecutive integers is $S$, what is the largest of those integers in terms of $S$?

   (A) $\dfrac{S-10}{5}$   (B) $\dfrac{S+4}{4}$   (C) $\dfrac{S+5}{4}$   (D) $\dfrac{S-5}{2}$

   (E) $\dfrac{S+10}{5}$

4. The number of shells in Judy's collection is 80% of the number in Justin's collection. If Justin has 80 more shells than Judy, how many shells do they have altogether?

   (A) 180   (B) 320   (C) 400   (D) 720   (E) 800

5. A jar contains only red, white, and blue marbles. The number of red marbles is $\dfrac{4}{5}$ the number of

   white ones, and the number of white ones is $\dfrac{3}{4}$
   the number of blue ones. If there are 470 marbles in all, how many of them are blue?

   (A) 120   (B) 135   (C) 150   (D) 184   (E) 200

6. As a fund-raiser, the school band was selling two types of candy: lollipops for 40 cents each and chocolate bars for 75 cents each. On Monday, they sold 150 candies and raised 74 dollars. How many lollipops did they sell?

   (A) 75   (B) 90   (C) 96   (D) 110   (E) 120

7. What is the greater of two numbers whose product is 900, if the sum of the two numbers exceeds their difference by 30?

   (A) 15   (B) 60   (C) 75   (D) 90   (E) 100

8. On a certain project the only grades awarded were 75 and 100. If 85 students completed the project and the average of their grades was 85, how many earned 100?

   (A) 34   (B) 40   (C) 45   (D) 51   (E) 60

9. If $\dfrac{1}{2}x$ years ago Adam was 12, and $\dfrac{1}{2}x$ years from now he will be $2x$ years old, how old will he be $3x$ years from now?

   (A) 18   (B) 24   (C) 30   (D) 54
   (E) It cannot be determined from the information given.

10. Since 1950, when Barry was discharged from the army, he has gained 2 pounds every year. In 1980 he was 40% heavier than in 1950. What percent of his 1995 weight was his 1980 weight?

    (A) 80   (B) 85   (C) 87.5   (D) 90   (E) 95

## Quantitative Comparison Questions

| Column A | Column B |
|---|---|

Lindsay is twice as old as she was 10 years ago. Kimberly is half as old as she will be in 10 years.

11.

| Lindsay's age now | Kimberly's age now |
|---|---|

Boris spent $\dfrac{1}{4}$ of his take-home pay on Saturday

and $\dfrac{1}{3}$ of what was left on Sunday. The rest he put
in his savings account.

12.

| The amount of his take-home pay that he spent | The amount of his take-home pay that he saved |
|---|---|

In 8 years, Tiffany will be 3 times as old as she is now.

13.

| The number of years until Tiffany will be 6 times as old as she is now | 16 |
|---|---|

Rachel put exactly 50 cents worth of postage on an envelope using only 4-cent stamps and 7-cent stamps.

14.

| The number of 4-cent stamps she used | The number of 7-cent stamps she used |
|---|---|

Car A and Car B leave from the same spot at the same time.
Car A travels due north at 40 mph.
Car B travels due east at 30 mph.

15.

| Distance from Car A to Car B 9 hours after they left | 450 miles |
|---|---|

# Answer Key

| | | |
|---|---|---|
| 1. **B** | 6. **D** | 11. **A** |
| 2. **B** | 7. **B** | 12. **C** |
| 3. **E** | 8. **A** | 13. **A** |
| 4. **D** | 9. **D** | 14. **D** |
| 5. **E** | 10. **C** | 15. **C** |

# Answer Explanations

1. **B.**

| | Ronald | Howard |
|---|---|---|
| At the beginning | $x$ | $3x$ |
| After the gift | $x + 50$ | $3x - 50$ |

After the gift, Ronald will have 3 times as much money as Howard:

$$x + 50 = 3(3x - 50) \Rightarrow x + 50 = 9x - 150 \Rightarrow$$
$$8x = 200 \Rightarrow x = 25.$$

So Ronald has \$25 and Howard has \$75, for a total of \$100.

2. **B.** Beth's average rate of reading is determined by dividing the total number of pages she read (200) by the total amount of time she spent

reading. In the afternoon she read for $\dfrac{100}{60} = \dfrac{5}{3}$

hours, and in the evening for $\dfrac{100}{40} = \dfrac{5}{2}$ hours,

for a total time of $\dfrac{5}{3} + \dfrac{5}{2} = \dfrac{10}{6} + \dfrac{15}{6} = \dfrac{25}{6}$

hours. So, her average rate was

$$200 \div \dfrac{25}{6} = 200 \times \dfrac{6}{25} = 48 \text{ pages per hour.}$$

3. **E.** Let the 5 consecutive integers be $n, n + 1, n + 2, n + 3, n + 4$. Then,

$$S = n + n + 1 + n + 2 + n + 3 + n + 4 =$$
$$5n + 10 \Rightarrow 5n = S - 10 \Rightarrow n = \dfrac{S - 10}{5}.$$

Choice A, therefore, is the *smallest* of the integers; the *largest* is

$$n + 4 = \dfrac{S - 10}{5} + 4 = \dfrac{S - 10}{5} + \dfrac{20}{5} = \dfrac{S + 10}{5}.$$

4. **D.** If $x$ is the number of shells in Justin's collection, then Judy has $.80x$. Since Justin has 80 more shells than Judy,

$$x = .80x + 80 \Rightarrow .20x = 80 \Rightarrow$$
$$x = 80 \div .20 = 400.$$

So Justin has 400 and Judy has 320: a total of 720.

5. **E.** If $b$ is the number of blue marbles, then there are $\dfrac{3}{4}b$ white ones, and $\dfrac{4}{5}\left(\dfrac{3}{4}b\right) = \dfrac{3}{5}b$ red ones. Therefore,

$$470 = b + \dfrac{3}{4}b + \dfrac{3}{5}b = b\left(1 + \dfrac{3}{4} + \dfrac{3}{5}\right) = \dfrac{47}{20}b.$$

So, $b = 470 \div \dfrac{47}{20} = \overset{10}{\cancel{470}} \times \dfrac{20}{\underset{1}{\cancel{47}}} = 200.$

6. **D.** Let $x$ represent the number of chocolate bars sold; then $150 - x$ is the number of lollipops sold. We must use the same units, so we could write 75 cents as .75 dollars or 74 dollars as 7400 cents. Let's avoid the decimals: $x$ chocolates sold for $75x$ cents and $(150 - x)$ lollipops sold for $40(150 - x)$ cents. So,
$$7400 = 75x + 40(150 - x) =$$
$$75x + 6000 - 40x = 6000 + 35x \Rightarrow$$
$$1400 = 35x \Rightarrow x = 40 \text{ and } 150 - 40 = 110.$$

7. **B.** If $x$ represents the greater and $y$ the smaller of the two numbers, then $(x + y) = 30 + (x - y) \Rightarrow y = 30 - y \Rightarrow 2y = 30 \Rightarrow y = 15$; and since $xy = 900$, $x = 900 \div 15 = 60.$

8. **A.** If $x$ represents the number of students earning 100, then $85 - x$ is the number of students earning 75. So

$$85 = \dfrac{100x + 75(85 - x)}{85} \Rightarrow$$
$$85 = \dfrac{100x + 6375 - 75x}{85} = \dfrac{25x - 6375}{85} \Rightarrow$$
$$85 \times 85 = 7225 = 25x - 6375 \Rightarrow$$
$$850 = 25x \Rightarrow x = 34.$$

9. **D.** Since $\dfrac{1}{2}x$ years ago, Adam was 12, he is now $12 + \dfrac{1}{2}x$. So $\dfrac{1}{2}x$ years from now, he will be $12 + \dfrac{1}{2}x + \dfrac{1}{2}x = 12 + x$. But, we are told that at that time he will be $2x$ years old. So, $12 + x = 2x \Rightarrow x = 12$. Thus, he is now $12 + 6 = 18$, and $3x$ or 36 years from now he will be $18 + 36 = 54.$

10. C. Let $x$ be Barry's weight in 1950. By 1980, he had gained 60 pounds (2 pounds per year for 30 years) and was 40% heavier: $60 = .40x \Rightarrow x = 60 \div .4 = 150$. So in 1980, he weighed 210. Fifteen years later, in 1995, he weighed 240: $\dfrac{210}{240} = \dfrac{7}{8} = 87.5\%$.

11. A. You can do the simple algebra, but you should realize that Lindsay is as old now as Kimberly will be in 10 years. If $x$ represents Lindsay's age now, $x = 2(x - 10) \Rightarrow x = 2x - 20 \Rightarrow x = 20$. Similarly, Kimberly is now 10 and will be 20 in 10 years.

12. C. Let $x$ represent the amount of Boris's take-home pay. On Saturday, he spent $\dfrac{1}{4}x$ and still had $\dfrac{3}{4}x$; but on Sunday, he spent $\dfrac{1}{3}$ of that: $\dfrac{1}{\cancel{3}}\left(\dfrac{\cancel{3}}{4}x\right) = \dfrac{1}{4}x$. So he spent $\dfrac{1}{4}$ of his take-home pay each day. He spent $\dfrac{1}{2}$ and saved $\dfrac{1}{2}$.

13. A. If $x$ represents Tiffany's age now, then $x + 8$ is her age in 8 years, and so $x + 8 = 3x \Rightarrow 8 = 2x \Rightarrow x = 4$. Tiffany will be 6 times as old 20 years from now, when she will be 24.

14. D. If $x$ and $y$ represent the number of 4-cent stamps and 7-cent stamps that Rachel used, respectively, then $4x + 7y = 50$. There are infinitely many solutions to this equation, but there are only 2 solutions in which $x$ and $y$ are both positive integers: $y = 2$ and $x = 9$ or $y = 6$ and $x = 2$.

15. C. Draw a diagram. In 9 hours Car A drove 360 miles north and Car B drove 270 miles east. These are the legs of a right triangle, whose hypotenuse is the distance between them. You can use the Pythagorean theorem if you don't recognize that this is just a 3-4-5 right triangle: the legs are $90 \times 3$ and $90 \times 4$, and the hypotenuse is $90 \times 5 = 450$.

# GEOMETRY

Although about 30% of the math questions on the GRE have to do with geometry, there are only a relatively small number of facts you need to know—far less than you would learn in a geometry course—and, of course, there are no proofs. In the next six sections we will review all of the geometry that you need to know to do well on the GRE. We will present the material exactly as it appears on the GRE, using the same vocabulary and notation, which might be slightly different from the terminology you learned in your high school math classes. In particular, the word "congruent" and the symbol "≅" are not used—angles or line segments that have the same measure are considered "equal." The numerous multiple-choice and quantitative comparison examples will show you exactly how these topics are treated on the GRE.

## 15-I. LINES AND ANGLES

An **angle** is formed by the intersection of two line segments, rays, or lines. The point of intersection is called the **vertex**. On the GRE, angles are always measured in degrees.

**KEY FACT I1:**

**Angles are classified according to their degree measures.**

- **An acute angle measures less than 90°.**
- **A right angle measures 90°.**
- **An obtuse angle measures more than 90° but less than 180°.**
- **A straight angle measures 180°.**

NOTE: The small square in the second angle in the figure above is *always* used to mean that the angle is a right angle. On the GRE, if an angle has a square in it, it must measure exactly 90°, *whether or not you think that the figure has been drawn to scale.*

**KEY FACT I2:**

**If two or more angles form a straight angle, the sum of their measures is 180°.**

$a + b = 180$          $w + x + y + z = 180$

**Example 1.**

In the figure below, $R$, $S$, and $T$ are all on line $\ell$. What is the average of $a$, $b$, $c$, $d$, and $e$?

(A) 18   (B) 36   (C) 45   (D) 90   (E) 180

SOLUTION. Since $\angle RST$ is a straight angle, by KEY FACT 12, the sum of $a$, $b$, $c$, $d$, and $e$ is 180, and so their average is $\dfrac{180}{5} = \mathbf{36}$ **(B)**.

In the figure at the right, since $a + b + c + d = 180$ and $e + f + g = 180$, $a + b + c + d + e + f + g = 180 + 180 = 360$.

It is also true that $u + v + w + x + y + z = 360$, even though none of the angles forms a straight angle.

### KEY FACT 13:

The sum of all the measures of all the angles around a point is 360°.

Note: This fact is particularly important when the point is the center of a circle, as we shall see in Section 15-L.

$a + b + c + d = 360$

When two lines intersect, four angles are formed. The two angles in each pair of opposite angles are called **vertical angles**.

### KEY FACT 14:

**Vertical angles have equal measures.**

**Example 2.**

In the figure at the right, what is the value of $x$?

(A) 6   (B) 8
(C) 10   (D) 20
(E) 40

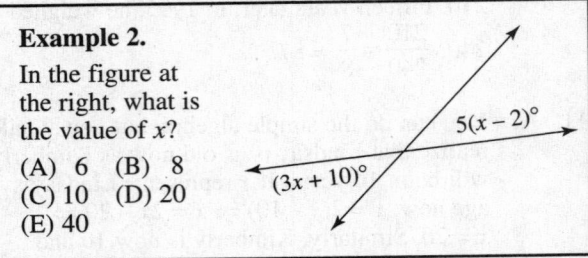

SOLUTION. Since the measures of vertical angles are equal,

$$3x + 10 = 5(x - 2) \Rightarrow 3x + 10 = 5x - 10 \Rightarrow$$
$$3x + 20 = 5x \Rightarrow 20 = 2x \Rightarrow x = \mathbf{10}\ (\mathbf{C}).$$

### KEY FACT 15:

If one of the angles formed by the intersection of two lines (or line segments) is a right angle, then all four angles are right angles.

$a = b = c = 90$

Two lines that intersect to form right angles are called **perpendicular**.

In the figures below, line $\ell$ divides $\angle ABC$ into two equal parts, and line $k$ divides line segment $DE$ into two equal parts. Line $\ell$ is said to **bisect** the angle, and line $k$ **bisects** the line segment. Point $M$ is called the **midpoint** of segment $DE$.

**Example 3.**

In the figure at the right, lines $k$, $\ell$, and $m$ intersect at $O$. If line $m$ bisects $\angle AOB$, what is the value of $x$?

(A) 25   (B) 35   (C) 45   (D) 50   (E) 60

SOLUTION. m∠AOB + 130 = 180 ⇒ m∠AOB = 50; and since *m* bisects ∠AOB, *x* = **25 (A)**.

Two lines that never intersect are said to be **parallel**. Consequently, parallel lines form no angles. However, if a third line, called a **transversal,** intersects a pair of parallel lines, eight angles are formed, and the relationships among these angles are very important.

### KEY FACT I6:

**If a pair of parallel lines is cut by a transversal that is perpendicular to the parallel lines, all eight angles are right angles.**

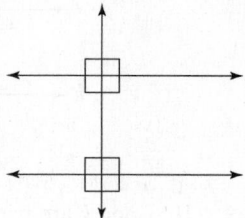

### KEY FACT I7:

**If a pair of parallel lines is cut by a transversal that is not perpendicular to the parallel lines,**

- **Four of the angles are acute and four are obtuse;**
- **The four acute angles are equal:** *a* = *c* = *e* = *g*;
- **The four obtuse angles are equal:** *b* = *d* = *f* = *h*;
- **The sum of any acute angle and any obtuse angle is 180°:** for example, *d* + *e* = 180, *c* + *f* = 180, *b* + *g* = 180, ....

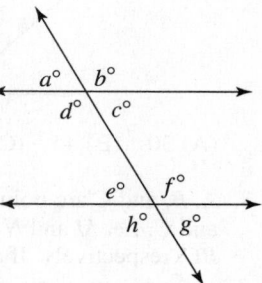

### KEY FACT I8:

**If a pair of lines that are not parallel is cut by a transversal, *none* of the properties listed in KEY FACT I7 is true.**

You must know KEY FACT I7—virtually every GRE has at least one question based on it. However, you do *not* need to know the special terms you learned in high school for these pairs of angles; those terms are not used on the GRE.

**Example 4.**
In the figure below, *AB* is parallel to *CD*. What is the value of *x*?

(A) 37   (B) 45   (C) 53   (D) 63   (E) 143

SOLUTION. Let *y* be the measure of ∠BED. Then by KEY FACT I2:

$$37 + 90 + y = 180 \Rightarrow 127 + y = 180 \Rightarrow y = 53.$$

Since *AB* is parallel to *CD*, by KEY FACT I7, *x* = *y* ⇒ *x* = **53 (C)**.

**Example 5.**
In the figure below, lines ℓ and *k* are parallel. What is the value of *a* + *b*?

(A) 45   (B) 60   (C)75   (D) 90   (E) 135

SOLUTION. It is impossible to determine the value of either *a* or *b*. We can, however, find the value of *a* + *b*. We draw a line through the vertex of the angle parallel to ℓ and *k*. Then, looking at the top two lines, we see that *a* = *x*, and looking at the bottom two lines, we see that *b* = *y*. So, *a* + *b* = *x* + *y* = **45 (A)**.

*Alternative solution.* Draw a different line and use a Key Fact from Section 15-J on triangles. Extend one of the line segments to form a triangle. Since ℓ and *k* are parallel, the measure of the third angle in the triangle equals *a*. Now, use the fact that the sum of the measures of the three angles in a triangle is 180° or, even easier, that the given 45° angle is an external angle of the triangle, and so is equal to the sum of *a* and *b*.

# PRACTICE EXERCISES—LINES AND ANGLES

## Multiple-Choice Questions

1. In the figure below, what is the average (arithmetic mean) of the measures of the five angles?

   (A) 36   (B) 45   (C) 60   (D) 72   (E) 90

2. In the figure below, what is the value of $\dfrac{b+a}{b-a}$?

   (A) 1   (B) 10   (C) 11   (D) 30   (E) 36

3. In the figure below, what is the value of $b$?

   (A) 9   (B) 18   (C) 27   (D) 36   (E) 45

4. In the figure below, what is the value of $x$ if $y:x = 3:2$?

   (A) 18   (B) 27   (C) 36   (D) 45   (E) 54

5. What is the measure of the angle formed by the minute and hour hands of a clock at 1:50?

   (A) 90°   (B) 95°   (C) 105°   (D) 115°   (E) 120°

6. Concerning the figure below, if $a = b$, which of the following statements must be true?

   I.   $c = d$
   II.  $\ell$ and $k$ are parallel
   III. $m$ and $\ell$ are perpendicular

   (A) none   (B) I only   (C) I and II only
   (D) I and III only   (E) I, II, and III

7. In the figure below, $a:b = 3:5$ and $c:b = 2:1$. What is the measure of the largest angle?

   (A) 30   (B) 45   (C) 50   (D) 90   (E) 100

8. $A$, $B$, and $C$ are points on a line with $B$ between $A$ and $C$. Let $M$ and $N$ be the midpoints of $AB$ and $BC$, respectively. If $AB:BC = 3:1$, what is $MN:BC$?

   (A) 1:2   (B) 2:3   (C) 1:1   (D) 3:2   (E) 2:1

9. In the figure below, lines $k$ and $\ell$ are parallel. What is the value of $y - x$?

   (A) 15   (B) 30   (C) 45   (D) 60   (E) 75

10. In the figure below, line $m$ bisects $\angle AOC$ and line $\ell$ bisects $\angle AOB$. What is the measure of $\angle DOE$?

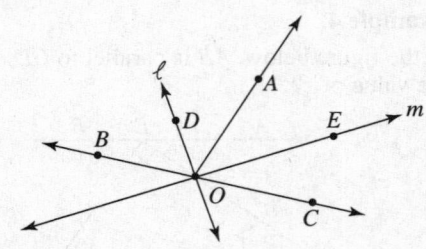

   (A) 75   (B) 90   (C) 100   (D) 105   (E) 120

## Quantitative Comparison Questions

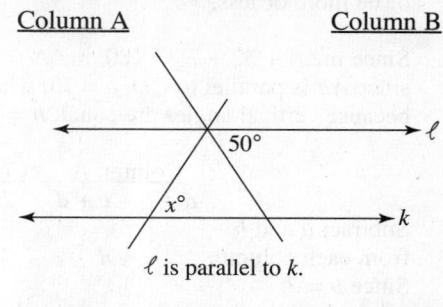

$\ell$ is parallel to $k$.

|  | Column A | Column B |
|---|---|---|
| 11. | $x$ | $50$ |

$AB$ is parallel to $CD$.

|  | Column A | Column B |
|---|---|---|
| 12. | $a$ | $b$ |

|  | Column A | Column B |
|---|---|---|
| 13. | $a + b + c + d$ | $2a + 2b$ |

|  | Column A | Column B |
|---|---|---|
| 14. | $a + b + c + d$ | $e + f + g + h$ |

$k$ and $\ell$ are parallel.

|  | Column A | Column B |
|---|---|---|
| 15. | $z$ | $x + y$ |

## Answer Key

| | | |
|---|---|---|
| 1. **D** | 6. **B** | 11. **D** |
| 2. **C** | 7. **E** | 12. **B** |
| 3. **D** | 8. **E** | 13. **D** |
| 4. **C** | 9. **C** | 14. **C** |
| 5. **D** | 10. **B** | 15. **C** |

## Answer Explanations

1.  D.   The markings in the five angles are irrelevant. The sum of the measures of the five angles is 360°, and 360 ÷ 5 = 72. If you calculated the measure of each angle you should have gotten 36, 54, 72, 90, and 108; but you wasted time.

2.  C.   From the diagram, we see that $6a = 180$, which implies that $a = 30$, and that $5b = 180$, which implies that $b = 36$. So, $\dfrac{b + a}{b - a} =$ $\dfrac{36 + 30}{36 - 30} = \dfrac{66}{6} = 11$.

3.  D.   Since vertical angles are equal, the two unmarked angles are $2b$ and $4a$. Since the sum of all six angles is 360°,

$$360 = 4a + 2b + 2a + 4a + 2b + b = 10a + 5b.$$

However, since vertical angles are equal, $b = 2a \Rightarrow 5b = 10a$. Hence,

$$360 = 10a + 5b = 10a + 10a = 20a \Rightarrow$$
$$a = 18 \Rightarrow b = 36.$$

4.  C.   Since $x + y + 90 = 180$, $x + y = 90$. Also, since
         $y:x = 3:2$, $y = 3t$ and $x = 2t$. Therefore,
$$3t + 2t = 90 \Rightarrow 5t = 90 \Rightarrow$$
$$t = 18 \Rightarrow x = 2(18) = 36.$$

5.  D.   For problems such as this, always draw a
         diagram. The measure of each of the 12
         central angles from one number to the next on
         the clock is 30°. At 1:50 the minute hand is
         pointing at 10, and the hour hand has gone
         $\dfrac{50}{60} = \dfrac{5}{6}$ of the way
         from 1 to 2. So
         from 10 to 1 on the
         clock is 90°, and
         from 1 to the hour
         hand is $\dfrac{5}{6}(30°) = 25°$,
         for a total of
         $90° + 25° = 115°$.

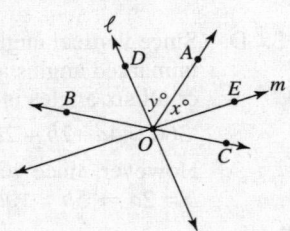

6.  B.   No conclusions can be made about the lines;
         they could form any angles whatsoever. (II
         and III are both false.) I is true:
$$c = 180 - a = 180 - b = d.$$

7.  E.   Since $a:b = 3:5$, then $a = 3x$ and $b = 5x$; and
         since $c:b = c:5x = 2:1$, $c = 10x$. Then,
$$3x + 5x + 10x = 180 \Rightarrow 18x = 180 \Rightarrow$$
$$x = 10 \Rightarrow c = 10x = 100.$$

8.  E.   If a diagram is not provided on a geometry
         question, draw one on your scrap paper.
         From the figure below, you can see that
         $MN:BC = 2:1$.

9.  C.   Since the lines are parallel, the angle marked $y$
         and the sum of the angles marked $x$ and 45 are
         equal: $y = x + 45 \Rightarrow y - x = 45$.

10. B.   Let $x = \dfrac{1}{2}\text{m}\angle AOC$, and $y = \dfrac{1}{2}\text{m}\angle AOB$. Then,
$$x + y = \dfrac{1}{2}\text{m}\angle AOC + \dfrac{1}{2}\text{m}\angle AOB =$$
$$\dfrac{1}{2}(180) = 90.$$

11. D.   No conclusion can be made: $x$ could equal 50
         or be more or less.

12. B.   Since $\text{m}\angle A + 32 + 75 = 180$, $\text{m}\angle A = 73$; and
         since $AB$ is parallel to $CD$, $a = 73$, whereas,
         because vertical angles are equal, $b = 75$.

13. D.

|  | Column A | Column B |
|---|---|---|
|  | $a + b + c + d$ | $2a + 2b$ |
| Subtract $a$ and $b$ from each column: | $c + d$ | $a + b$ |
| Since $b = d$, subtract them: | $c$ | $a$ |

There is no way to determine whether $a$ is less
than, greater than, or equal to $c$.

14. C.   Whether the lines are parallel or not,
$$a + b = c + d = e + f = g + h = 180.$$
Each column is equal to 360.

15. C.   Extend line segment $AB$ to form a transversal.
         Since $w + z = 180$ and $w + (x + y) = 180$, it
         follows that $z = x + y$.

# 15-J. TRIANGLES

More geometry questions on the GRE pertain to triangles than to any other topic. To answer them, there are
several important facts that you need to know about the
angles and sides of triangles. The KEY FACTS in this
section are extremely useful. Read them carefully, a few
times if necessary, and *make sure you learn them all.*

**KEY FACT J1:**

**In any triangle, the sum
of the measures of the
three angles is 180°:**
$x + y + z = 180.$

71 + 65 + 44 = 180        135 + 25 + 20 = 180

(a)                              (b)

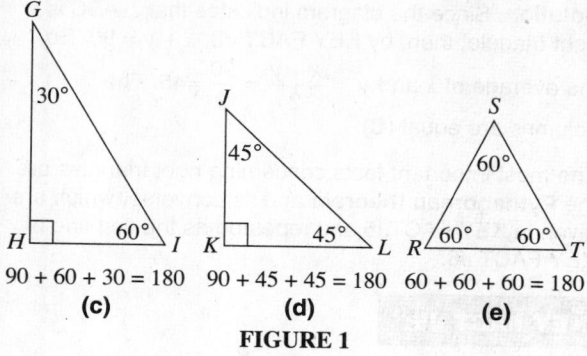

$$90 + 60 + 30 = 180 \quad 90 + 45 + 45 = 180 \quad 60 + 60 + 60 = 180$$
**(c)**           **(d)**           **(e)**
**FIGURE 1**

Figure 1 (a–e) illustrates KEY FACT J1 for five different triangles, which will be discussed below.

---

**Example 1.**

In the figure below, what is the value of $x$?

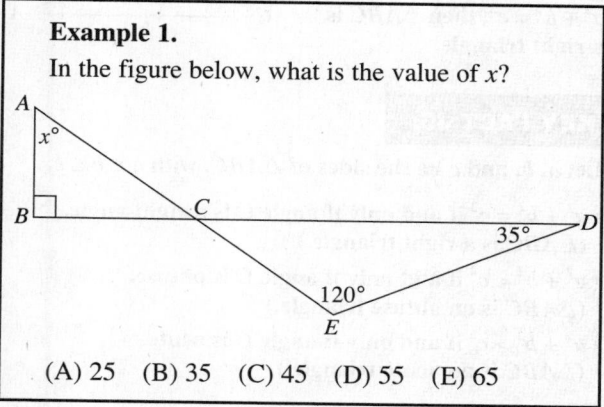

(A) 25   (B) 35   (C) 45   (D) 55   (E) 65

---

SOLUTION. Use KEY FACT J1 twice: first, for $\triangle CDE$ and then for $\triangle ABC$.

• $m\angle DCE + 120 + 35 = 180 \Rightarrow m\angle DCE + 155 = 180 \Rightarrow m\angle DCE = 25$.

• Since vertical angles are equal, $m\angle ACB = 25$ (see KEY FACT I6).

• $x + 90 + 25 = 180 \Rightarrow x + 115 = 180 \Rightarrow x = \mathbf{65}$ **(E)**.

---

**Example 2.**

In the figure at the right, what is the value of $a$?

(A) 45   (B) 60   (C) 75   (D) 120   (E) 135

---

SOLUTION. First find the value of $b$:

$$180 = 45 + 75 + b = 120 + b \Rightarrow b = 60.$$

Then, $a + b = 180 \Rightarrow a = 180 - b = 180 - 60 = \mathbf{120}$ **(D)**.

In Example 2, $\angle BCD$, which is formed by one side of $\triangle ABC$ and the extension of another side, is called an **exterior angle**. Note that to find $a$ we did not have to first find $b$; we could have just added the other two angles: $a = 75 + 45 = 120$. This is a useful fact to remember.

---

**KEY FACT J2:**

The measure of an exterior angle of a triangle is equal to the sum of the measures of the two opposite interior angles.

**KEY FACT J3:**

In any triangle:

• the longest side is opposite the largest angle;
• the shortest side is opposite the smallest angle;
• sides with the same length are opposite angles with the same measure.

---

CAUTION: In KEY FACT J3 the condition "in any triangle" is crucial. If the angles are not in the same triangle, none of the conclusions hold. For example, in the figures below, $AB$ and $DE$ are *not* equal even though they are each opposite a 90° angle, and $QS$ is not the longest side in the figure, even though it is opposite the largest angle in the figure.

---

Consider triangles $ABC$, $JKL$, and $RST$ in Figure 1.

• In $\triangle ABC$: $BC$ is the longest side since it is opposite angle $A$, the largest angle (71°). Similarly, $AB$ is the shortest side since it is opposite angle $C$, the smallest angle (54°). So $AB < AC < BC$.

• In $\triangle JKL$: angles $J$ and $L$ have the same measure (45°), so $JK = KL$.

• In $\triangle RST$: since all three angles have the same measure (60°), all three sides have the same length: $RS = ST = TR$.

---

**Example 3.**

Which of the following statements concerning the length of side $YZ$ is true?

(A) $YZ < 9$
(B) $YZ = 9$
(C) $9 < YZ < 10$
(D) $YZ = 10$
(E) $YZ > 10$

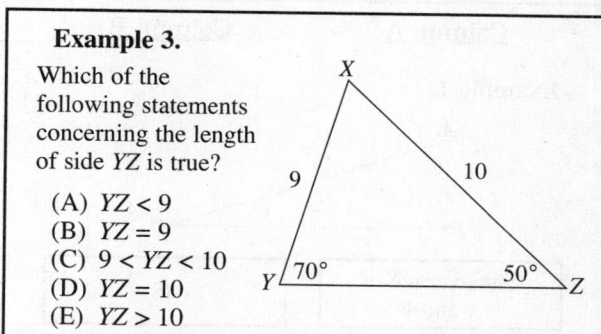

SOLUTION.

- By KEY FACT J1, $m\angle X + 70 + 50 = 180 \Rightarrow m\angle X = 60$.
- So, $Y$ is the largest angle, $Z$ is the smallest, and $X$ is in between.
- Therefore, by KEY FACT J3,
$$XY < YZ < XZ \Rightarrow 9 < YZ < 10 \text{ (C)}.$$

## Classification of Triangles

| Name | Lengths of the Sides | Measures of the Angles | Examples from Figure 1 |
|------|----------------------|------------------------|------------------------|
| *scalene* | all 3 different | all 3 different | ABC, DEF, GHI |
| *isosceles* | 2 the same | 2 the same | JKL |
| *equilateral* | all 3 the same | all 3 the same | RST |

**Acute triangles** are triangles such as *ABC* and *RST*, in which all three angles are acute. An acute triangle could be scalene, isosceles, or equilateral.

**Obtuse triangles** are triangles such as *DEF*, in which one angle is obtuse and two are acute. An obtuse triangle could be scalene or isosceles.

**Right triangles** are triangles such as *GHI* and *JKL*, which have one right angle and two acute ones. A right triangle could be scalene or isosceles. The side opposite the 90° angle is called the **hypotenuse**, and by KEY FACT J3, it is the longest side. The other two sides are called the **legs**.

If $x$ and $y$ are the measures of the acute angles of a right triangle, then by KEY FACT J1,
$$90 + x + y = 180 \Rightarrow x + y = 90.$$

### KEY FACT J4:

In any right triangle, the sum of the measures of the two acute angles is **90°**.

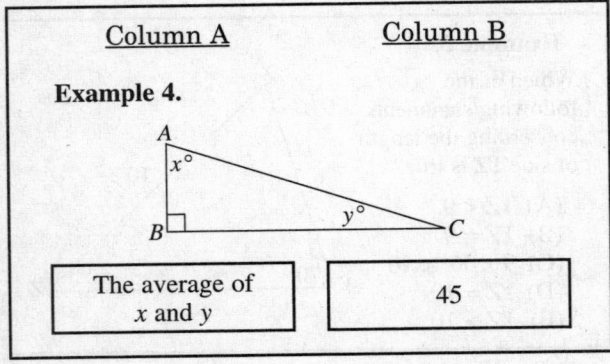

| Column A | Column B |
|----------|----------|
| **Example 4.** | |
| The average of $x$ and $y$ | 45 |

**Solution.** Since the diagram indicates that $\triangle ABC$ is a right triangle, then, by KEY FACT J3, $x + y = 90$. So the average of $x$ and $y = \dfrac{x+y}{2} = \dfrac{90}{2} = 45$. The columns are equal (**C**).

The most important facts concerning right triangles are the **Pythagorean theorem** and its converse, which are given in KEY FACT J5 and repeated as the first line of KEY FACT J6.

### KEY FACT J5:

Let $a$, $b$, and $c$ be the sides of $\triangle ABC$, with $a \le b \le c$. If $\triangle ABC$ is a right triangle, $a^2 + b^2 = c^2$; and if $a^2 + b^2 = c^2$, then $\triangle ABC$ is a right triangle.

### KEY FACT J6:

Let $a$, $b$, and $c$ be the sides of $\triangle ABC$, with $a \le b \le c$.

- $a^2 + b^2 = c^2$ if and only if angle $C$ is a right angle. ($\triangle ABC$ is a right triangle.)
- $a^2 + b^2 < c^2$ if and only if angle $C$ is obtuse. ($\triangle ABC$ is an obtuse triangle.)
- $a^2 + b^2 > c^2$ if and only if angle $C$ is acute. ($\triangle ABC$ is an acute triangle.)

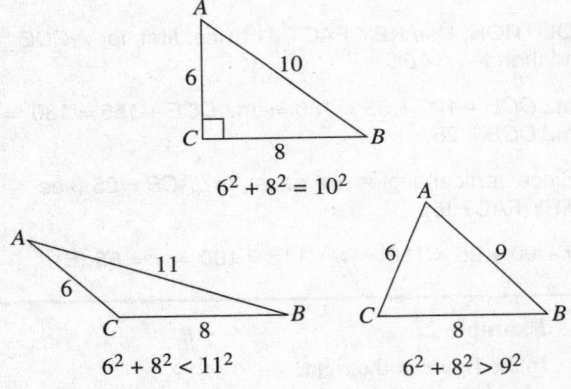

**Example 5.**
Which of the following are *not* the sides of a right triangle?
(A) 3, 4, 5   (B) 1, 1, $\sqrt{2}$   (C) 1, $\sqrt{3}$, 2
(D) $\sqrt{3}, \sqrt{4}, \sqrt{5}$   (E) 30, 40, 50

SOLUTION. Just check each choice.

A: $3^2 + 4^2 = 9 + 16 = 25 = 5^2$   These *are* the sides of a right triangle.

B: $1^2 + 1^2 = 1 + 1 = 2 = (\sqrt{2})^2$   These *are* the sides of a right triangle.

C: $1^2 + (\sqrt{3})^2 = 1 + 3 = 4 = 2^2$

These *are* the sides of a right triangle.

D: $(\sqrt{3})^2 + (\sqrt{4})^2 = 3 + 4 = 7 \neq (\sqrt{5})^2$

These *are not* the sides of a right triangle.

E: $30^2 + 40^2 = 900 + 1600 = 2500 = 50^2$

These *are* the sides of a right triangle.

The answer is **D**.

Below are the right triangles that appear most often on the GRE. You should recognize them immediately whenever they come up in questions. Carefully study each one, and memorize KEY FACTS J7–J11.

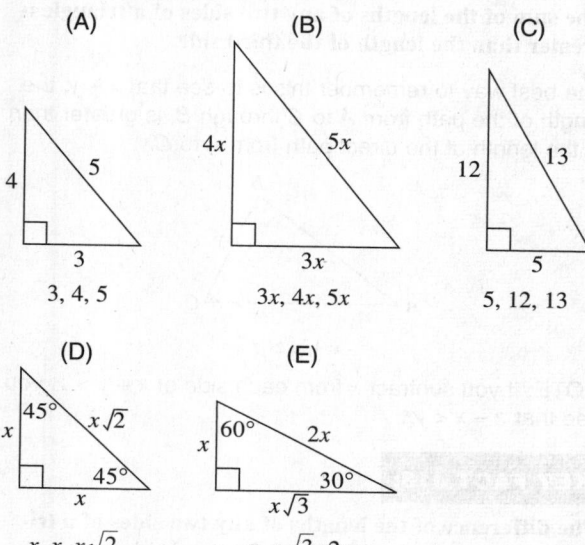

(A)

4, 5, 3

3, 4, 5

(B)

4x, 5x, 3x

3x, 4x, 5x

(C)

12, 13, 5

5, 12, 13

(D)

$45°$, $x$, $x\sqrt{2}$, $45°$, $x$

x, x, x√2

(E)

$60°$, $x$, $2x$, $30°$, $x\sqrt{3}$

x, x√3, 2x

On the GRE, the most common right triangles whose sides are integers are the 3-4-5 triangle (A) and its multiples (B).

## KEY FACT J7:

**For any positive number $x$, there is a right triangle whose sides are $3x$, $4x$, $5x$.**

For example:
| $x = 1$ | 3, 4, 5 | $x = 5$ | 15, 20, 25 |
|---|---|---|---|
| $x = 2$ | 6, 8, 10 | $x = 10$ | 30, 40, 50 |
| $x = 3$ | 9, 12, 15 | $x = 50$ | 150, 200, 250 |
| $x = 4$ | 12, 16, 20 | $x = 100$ | 300, 400, 500 |

NOTE: KEY FACT J6 applies even if $x$ is not an integer. For example:

$x = .5$   1.5, 2, 2.5   $x = \pi$   $3\pi$, $4\pi$, $5\pi$

The only other right triangle with integer sides that you should recognize immediately is the one whose sides are 5, 12, 13, (C).

Let $x$ = length of each leg, and $h$ = length of the hypotenuse, of an isosceles right triangle (D). By the Pythagorean theorem (KEY FACT J5), $x^2 + x^2 = h^2$.

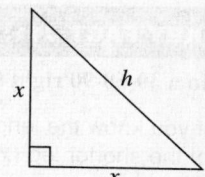

So, $2x^2 = h^2$, and $h = \sqrt{2x^2} = x\sqrt{2}$.

## KEY FACT J8:

**In a 45-45-90 right triangle, the sides are $x$, $x$, and $x\sqrt{2}$. So,**

- **by multiplying the length of a leg by $\sqrt{2}$, you get the hypotenuse.**
- **by dividing the hypotenuse by $\sqrt{2}$, you get the length of each leg.**

## KEY FACT J9:

**The diagonal of a square divides the square into two isosceles right triangles.**

The last important right triangle is the one whose angles measure 30°, 60°, and 90°. (E)

## KEY FACT J10:

**An altitude divides an equilateral triangle into two 30-60-90 right triangles.**

Let $2x$ be the length of each side of equilateral $\triangle ABC$ in which altitude $AD$ is drawn. Then $\triangle ABD$ is a 30-60-90 right triangle, and its sides are $x$, $2x$, and $h$. By the Pythagorean theorem,

$$x^2 + h^2 = (2x)^2 = 4x^2.$$

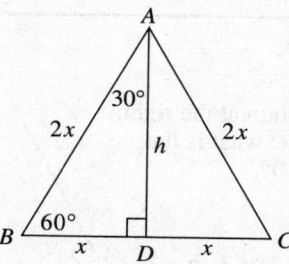

So $h^2 = 3x^2$, and $h = \sqrt{3x^2} = x\sqrt{3}$.

## KEY FACT J11:

**In a 30-60-90 right triangle the sides are $x$, $x\sqrt{3}$, and $2x$.**

If you know the length of the shorter leg ($x$),

- multiply it by $\sqrt{3}$ to get the longer leg, and
- multiply it by 2 to get the hypotenuse.

If you know the length of the longer leg ($a$),

- divide it by $\sqrt{3}$ to get the shorter leg, and
- multiply the shorter leg by 2 to get the hypotenuse.

If you know the length of the hypotenuse ($h$),

- divide it by 2 to get the shorter leg, and
- multiply the shorter leg by $\sqrt{3}$ to get the longer leg.

---

**Example 6.**

What is the area of a square whose diagonal is 10?

(A) 20    (B) 40    (C) 50    (D) 100    (E) 200

---

SOLUTION. Draw a diagonal in a square of side $s$, creating a 45-45-90 right triangle. By KEY FACT J8:

$s = \dfrac{10}{\sqrt{2}}$ and $A = s^2 = \left(\dfrac{10}{\sqrt{2}}\right)^2 =$

$\dfrac{100}{2} = 50$. The answer is **C**.

---

**Example 7.**

In the diagram at the right, if $BC = \sqrt{6}$, what is the value of $CD$?

(A) $2\sqrt{2}$    (B) $4\sqrt{2}$
(C) $2\sqrt{3}$    (D) $2\sqrt{6}$
(E) 4

---

SOLUTION. Since $\triangle ABC$ and $\triangle DAC$ are 30-60-90 and 45-45-90 right triangles, respectively, use KEY FACTS J11 and J8.

- Divide the longer leg, $BC$, by $\sqrt{3}$ to get the shorter leg, $AB$: $\dfrac{\sqrt{6}}{\sqrt{3}} = \sqrt{2}$.

- Multiply $AB$ by 2 to get the hypotenuse: $AC = 2\sqrt{2}$.

- Since $AC$ is also a leg of isosceles right $\triangle DAC$, to get hypotenuse $CD$, multiply $AC$ by $\sqrt{2}$:

$$CD = 2\sqrt{2} \times \sqrt{2} = 2 \times 2 = \mathbf{4} \ \textbf{(E)}.$$

## KEY FACT J12:

**Triangle Inequality**

**The sum of the lengths of any two sides of a triangle is greater than the length of the third side.**

The best way to remember this is to see that $x + y$, the length of the path from $A$ to $C$ through $B$, is greater than $z$, the length of the direct path from $A$ to $C$.

$$x + y > z$$

NOTE: If you subtract $x$ from each side of $x + y > z$, you see that $z - x < y$.

## KEY FACT J13:

**The difference of the lengths of any two sides of a triangle is less than the length of the third side.**

---

**Example 8.**

If the lengths of two of the sides of a triangle are 6 and 7, which of the following could be the length of the third side?

I. 1
II. 5
III. 15

(A) None    (B) I only    (C) II only
(D) I and II only    (E) I, II, and III

---

SOLUTION. Use KEY FACTS J12 and J13.

- The third side must be *less* than $6 + 7 = 13$. (III is false.)

- The third side must be *greater* than $7 - 6 = 1$. (I is false.)

- *Any* number between 1 and 13 could be the length of the third side. (I is true.)

The answer is **C**.

The following diagram illustrates several triangles, two of whose sides have lengths of 6 and 7.

On the GRE, two other terms that appear regularly in triangle problems are **perimeter** and **area** (see Section 15-K).

---

**Example 9.**

In the figure at the right, what is the perimeter of △*ABC*?

(A) $20 + 10\sqrt{2}$

(B) $20 + 10\sqrt{3}$

(C) 25

(D) 30

(E) 40

---

SOLUTION. First, use KEY FACTS J3 and J1 to find the measures of the angles.

• Since $AB = AC$, m∠$B$ = m∠$C$. Represent each of them by $x$.

• Then, $x + x + 60 = 180 \Rightarrow 2x = 120 \Rightarrow x = 60$.

• Since the measure of each angle of △*ABC* is 60, the triangle is equilateral.

• So $BC = 10$, and the perimeter is $10 + 10 + 10 = $ **30 (D)**.

**KEY FACT J14:**

The area of a triangle is given by $A = \dfrac{1}{2}bh$, where $b$ is the base and $h$ is the height.

NOTE: (1) *Any* side of the triangle can be taken as the base.

(2) The height is the altitude drawn to the base from the opposite vertex.

(3) In a right triangle, either leg can be the base and the other the height.

(4) The height may be outside the triangle. [See the figure at right.]

In the figure at the right:

• If *AC* is the base, *BD* is the height.

• If *AB* is the base, *CE* is the height.

• If *BC* is the base, *AF* is the height.

---

**Example 10.**

What is the area of an equilateral triangle whose sides are 10?

(A) 30  (B) $25\sqrt{3}$  (C) 50  (D) $50\sqrt{3}$  (E) 100

---

SOLUTION: Draw an equilateral triangle and one of its altitudes.

• By KEY FACT J10, △*ABD* is a 30-60-90 right triangle.

• By KEY FACT J11, $BD = 5$ and $AD = 5\sqrt{3}$.

• The area of △*ABC* $= \dfrac{1}{2}(10)(5\sqrt{3}) = $ **$25\sqrt{3}$ (B)**.

Replacing 10 by $s$ in Example 10 yields a very useful result.

**KEY FACT J15:**

If $A$ represents the area of an equilateral triangle with side $s$, then $A = \dfrac{s^2\sqrt{3}}{4}$.

# PRACTICE EXERCISES—TRIANGLES

## Multiple-Choice Questions

1. In the triangle above, what is the value of $x$?
   (A) 20   (B) 30   (C) 40   (D) 50   (E) 60

2. If the difference between the measures of the two smaller angles of a right triangle is 8°, what is the measure, in degrees, of the smallest angle?
   (A) 37   (B) 41   (C) 42   (D) 49   (E) 53

3. What is the area of an equilateral triangle whose altitude is 6?
   (A) 18   (B) $12\sqrt{3}$   (C) $18\sqrt{3}$   (D) 36
   (E) $24\sqrt{3}$

4. Two sides of a right triangle are 12 and 13. Which of the following *could be* the length of the third side?
   I. 5
   II. 11
   III. $\sqrt{313}$
   (A) I only   (B) II only   (C) I and II
   (D) I and III   (E) I, II, and III

5. What is the value of $PS$ in the triangle above?
   (A) $5\sqrt{2}$   (B) 10   (C) 11   (D) 13   (E) $12\sqrt{2}$

6. If the measures of the angles of a triangle are in the ratio of 1:2:3, and if the length of the smallest side of the triangle is 10, what is the length of the longest side?
   (A) $10\sqrt{2}$   (B) $10\sqrt{3}$   (C) 15   (D) 20   (E) 30

7. What is the value of $x$ in the figure above?
   (A) 80   (B) 100   (C) 115   (D) 120   (E) 130

8. In the figure above, what is the value of $w$?
   (A) 100   (B) 110   (C) 120   (D) 130   (E) 140

Questions 9–10 refer to the following figure.

ABCD is a rectangle.

9. What is the area of $\triangle BED$?
   (A) 12   (B) 24   (C) 36   (D) 48   (E) 60

10. What is the perimeter of $\triangle BED$?
    (A) $19 + 5\sqrt{2}$   (B) 28   (C) $17 + \sqrt{185}$
    (D) 32   (E) 36

Questions 11–12 refer to the following figure.

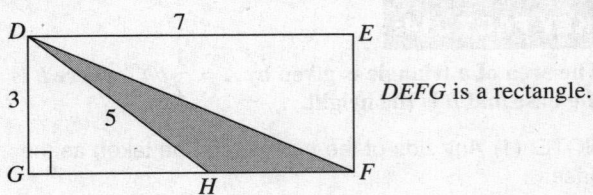

DEFG is a rectangle.

11. What is the area of $\triangle DFH$?
    (A) 3   (B) 4.5   (C) 6   (D) 7.5   (E) 10

12. What is the perimeter of $\triangle DFH$?
    (A) $8 + \sqrt{41}$   (B) $8 + \sqrt{58}$   (C) 16   (D) 17
    (E) 18

Questions 13–14 refer to the following figure.

13. What is the perimeter of $\triangle ABC$?
  (A) 48   (B) $48 + 12\sqrt{2}$   (C) $48 + 12\sqrt{3}$
      (D) 60   (E) $60 + 6\sqrt{3}$

14. What is the area of $\triangle ABC$?
  (A) 108   (B) $54 + 72\sqrt{2}$   (C) $54 + 72\sqrt{3}$
      (D) 198   (E) 216

15. Which of the following expresses a true relationship
  between $x$ and $y$ in the figure above?
  (A) $y = 60 - x$   (B) $y = x$   (C) $x + y = 90$
      (D) $y = 180 - 3x$   (E) $x = 90 - 3y$

## Quantitative Comparison Questions

|   Column A | Column B |
|---|---|

The lengths of two sides of a triangle are 7 and 11.

16.

| The length of the third side | 4 |
|---|---|

17.

| The ratio of the diagonal to a side of a square | $\sqrt{2}$ |
|---|---|

18.

| The perimeter of $\triangle ABC$ | 30 |
|---|---|

| Column A | Column B |
|---|---|

Questions 19–20 refer to the following figure.

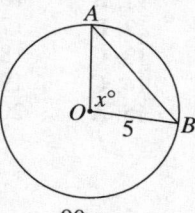

$90 < x$

19.

| The length of $AB$ | 7 |
|---|---|

20.

| The perimeter of $\triangle AOB$ | 20 |
|---|---|

21.

| The area of an equilateral triangle whose sides are 10 | The area of an equilateral triangle whose altitude is 10 |
|---|---|

Questions 22–23 refer to the following figure in which
the horizontal and vertical lines divide square $ABCD$
into 16 smaller squares.

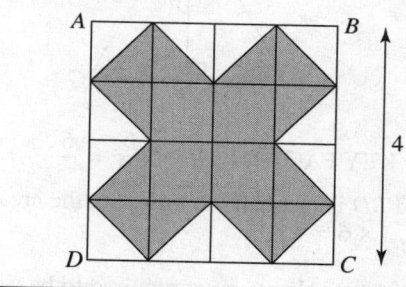

22.

| The perimeter of the shaded region | The perimeter of the square |
|---|---|

23.

| The area of the shaded region | The area of the white region |
|---|---|

24.

| $a + b$ | $c$ |
|---|---|

25.

| $PR$ | $QR$ |
|---|---|

# Answer Key

| | | | | |
|---|---|---|---|---|
| 1. **D** | 6. **D** | 11. **B** | 16. **A** | 21. **B** |
| 2. **B** | 7. **C** | 12. **B** | 17. **C** | 22. **A** |
| 3. **B** | 8. **B** | 13. **C** | 18. **D** | 23. **A** |
| 4. **D** | 9. **B** | 14. **C** | 19. **A** | 24. **C** |
| 5. **D** | 10. **D** | 15. **A** | 20. **B** | 25. **B** |

# Answer Explanations

1. **D.** $x + 2x + 30 = 180 \Rightarrow 3x + 30 = 180 \Rightarrow$ $3x = 150 \Rightarrow x = 50$.

2. **B.** Draw a diagram, label it, and then write the equations: $x + y = 90$ and $x - y = 8$.

   Adding the equations:
   $$\begin{array}{r} x + y = 90 \\ + x - y = \phantom{0}8 \\ \hline 2x = 98 \end{array}$$

   So $x = 49$ and $y = 90 - 49 = 41$.

3. **B.** Draw altitude $AD$ in equilateral $\triangle ABC$.

   By KEY FACT J11, $BD = \dfrac{6}{\sqrt{3}} = \dfrac{6\sqrt{3}}{3} = 2\sqrt{3}$,

   and $BD$ is one half the base. So, the area is $2\sqrt{3} \times 6 = 12\sqrt{3}$.

4. **D.** If the triangle were not required to be right, by KEY FACTS J11 and J12 *any* number greater than 1 and less than 25 could be the length of the third side. But for a right triangle, there are only *two* possibilities:
   - If 13 is the hypotenuse, then the legs are 12 and 5. (I is true.) (If you didn't recognize the 5-12-13 triangle, use the Pythagorean theorem: $5^2 + x^2 = 13^2$, and solve.)
   - If 12 and 13 are the two legs, then use the Pythagorean theorem to find the hypotenuse: $12^2 + 13^2 = c^2 \Rightarrow c^2 = 144 + 169 = 313 \Rightarrow$ $c = \sqrt{313}$. (III is true.)

   An 11-12-13 triangle is not a *right* triangle. So II is false.

5. **D.** Use the Pythagorean theorem twice, unless you recognize the common right triangles in this figure (*which you should*). Since $PR = 20$ and $QR = 16$, $\triangle PQR$ is a 3x-4x-5x right triangle with $x = 4$. So $PQ = 12$, and $\triangle PQS$ is a right triangle whose legs are 5 and 12. The hypotenuse, $PS$, therefore, is 13.

6. **D.** If the measures of the angles are in the ratio of 1:2:3,
   $$x + 2x + 3x = 180 \Rightarrow 6x = 180 \Rightarrow x = 30.$$

   So the triangle is a 30-60-90 right triangle, and the sides are $a$, $2a$, and $a\sqrt{3}$. Since $a = 10$, then $2a$, the length of the longest side, is 20.

7. **C.** Label the other angles in the triangle.

   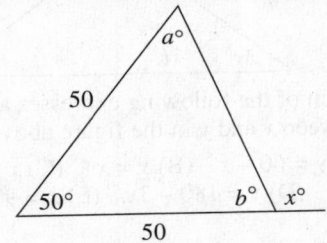

   $$50 + a + b = 180 \Rightarrow a + b = 130,$$

   and since the triangle is isosceles, $a = b$. Therefore, $a$ and $b$ are each 65, and $x = 180 - 65 = 115$.

8. **B.** Here, $50 + 90 + a = 180 \Rightarrow a = 40$, and since vertical angles are equal, $b = 40$. Then, $40 + 30 + w = 180 \Rightarrow w = 110$.

9. **B.** You *could* calculate the area of the rectangle and subtract the area of the two white right triangles, but don't. The shaded area is a triangle whose base is 4 and whose height is 12. The area is $\dfrac{1}{2}(4)(12) = 24$.

10. **D.** Since both $BD$ and $ED$ are the hypotenuses of right triangles, their lengths can be calculated by the Pythagorean theorem, but these are triangles you should recognize: the sides of $\triangle DCE$ are 5-12-13, and those of $\triangle BAD$ are 9-12-15 (3x-4x-5x, with $x = 3$). So the perimeter of $\triangle BED$ is $4 + 13 + 15 = 32$.

11. **B.** Since $\triangle DGH$ is a right triangle whose hypotenuse is 5 and one of whose legs is 3, the other leg, $GH$, is 4. Since $GF = DE$ is 7, $HF$ is 3. Now, $\triangle DFH$ has a base of 3 ($HF$) and a height of 3 ($DG$), and its area is $\frac{1}{2}(3)(3) = 4.5$.

12. **B.** In $\triangle DFH$, we already have that $DH = 5$ and $HF = 3$; we need only find $DF$, which is the hypotenuse of $\triangle DEF$. By the Pythagorean theorem, $(DF)^2 = 3^2 + 7^2 = 9 + 49 = 58 \Rightarrow DF = \sqrt{58}$. So the perimeter is
$$3 + 5 + \sqrt{58} = 8 + \sqrt{58}.$$

13. **C.** $\triangle ABD$ is a right triangle whose hypotenuse is 15 and one of whose legs is 9, so this is a $3x$-$4x$-$5x$ triangle with $x = 3$; so $AD = 12$. Now $\triangle ADC$ is a 30-60-90 triangle, whose shorter leg is 12. Hypotenuse $AC$ is 24, and leg $CD$ is $12\sqrt{3}$. So the perimeter is
$$24 + 15 + 9 + 12\sqrt{3} = 48 + 12\sqrt{3}.$$

14. **C.** From the solution to 13, we have the base $(9 + 12\sqrt{3})$ and the height (12) of $\triangle ABC$. Then, the area is $\frac{1}{2}(12)(9 + 12\sqrt{3}) = 54 + 72\sqrt{3}$.

15. **A.** $x + 2x + 3y = 180 \Rightarrow 3x + 3y = 180 \Rightarrow x + y = 60 \Rightarrow y = 60 - x$.

16. **A.** Any side of a triangle must be greater than the difference of the other two sides (KEY FACT J13), so the third side is greater than $11 - 7 = 4$.

17. **C.** Draw a diagram. A diagonal of a square is the hypotenuse of each of the two 45-45-90 right triangles formed. The ratio of the hypotenuse to a leg in such a triangle is $\sqrt{2}:1$, so the columns are equal.

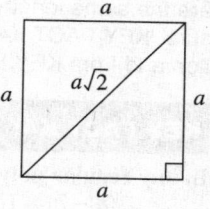

18. **D.** $BC$ can be any positive number less than 20 (by KEY FACTS J12 and J13, $BC > 10 - 10 = 0$ and $BC < 10 + 10 = 20$). So the perimeter can be *any* number greater than 20 and less than 40.

19. **A.** Since $OA$ and $OB$ are radii, they are each equal to 5. With no restrictions on $x$, $AB$ could be any positive number less than 10, and the bigger $x$ is, the bigger $AB$ is. If $x$ were 90, $AB$ would be $5\sqrt{2}$, but we are told that $x > 90$, so $AB > 5\sqrt{2} > 7$.

20. **B.** Since $AB$ must be less than 10, the perimeter is *less* than 20.

21. **B.** Don't calculate either area. The length of a side of an equilateral triangle is *greater* than the length of an altitude. So the triangle in Column B is larger (its sides are greater than 10).

22. **A.** Column A: The perimeter of the shaded region consists of 12 line segments, each of which is the hypotenuse of a 45-45-90 right triangle whose legs are 1. So each line segment is $\sqrt{2}$, and the perimeter is $12\sqrt{2}$.
Column B: The perimeter of the square is 16. To compare $12\sqrt{2}$ and 16, square them:
$(12\sqrt{2})^2 = 144 \times 2 = 288; \ 16^2 = 256.$

23. **A.** The white region consists of 12 right triangles, each of which has an area of $\frac{1}{2}$, for a total area of 6. Since the area of the large square is 16, the area of the shaded region is $16 - 6 = 10$.

24. **C.** Since $a = 180 - 145 = 35$ and $b = 180 - 125 = 55$, $a + b = 35 + 55 = 90$. Therefore, $180 = a + b + c = 90 + c \Rightarrow c = 90$.

25. **B.** Since $65 + 45 = 110$, $m\angle P = 70$. Since $\angle P$ is the largest angle, $QR$, the side opposite it, is the largest side.

# 15-K. QUADRILATERALS AND OTHER POLYGONS

A *polygon* is a closed geometric figure made up of line segments. The line segments are called *sides* and the endpoints of the line segments are called *vertices* (each one is called a *vertex*). Line segments inside the polygon drawn from one vertex to another are called *diagonals*. The simplest polygons, which have three sides, are the triangles, which you just studied in Section J. A polygon with four sides is called a *quadrilateral*. The only other terms you should be familiar with are pentagon, hexagon, octagon, and decagon, which are the names for polygons with five, six, eight, and ten sides, respectively.

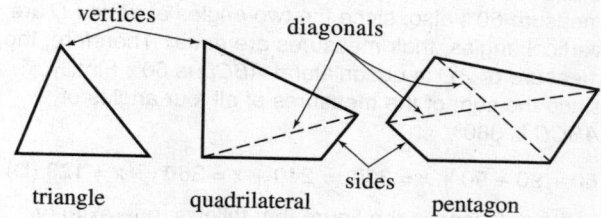

triangle          quadrilateral          pentagon

In this section we will present a few facts about polygons and quadrilaterals in general, but the emphasis will be on reviewing the key facts you need to know about four special quadrilaterals.

Every quadrilateral has two diagonals. If you draw in either one, you will divide the quadrilateral into two triangles. Since the sum of the measures of the three angles in each of the triangles is 180°, the sum of the measures of the angles in the quadrilateral is 360°.

### KEY FACT K1:

**In any quadrilateral, the sum of the measures of the four angles is 360°.**

In exactly the same way, any polygon can be divided into triangles by drawing in all of the diagonals emanating from one vertex.

Notice that the pentagon is divided into three triangles, and the hexagon is divided into four triangles. In general, an *n*-sided polygon is divided into $(n - 2)$ triangles, which leads to KEY FACT K2.

### KEY FACT K2:

**The sum of the measures of the *n* angles in a polygon with *n* sides is $(n - 2) \times 180°$.**

---

**Example 1.**

In the figure below, what is the value of *x*?

(A) 60   (B) 90   (C) 100   (D) 120   (E) 150

---

SOLUTION. Since △*DEF* is equilateral, all of its angles measure 60°; also, since the two angles at vertex *D* are vertical angles, their measures are equal. Therefore, the measure of ∠*D* in quadrilateral *ABCD* is 60°. Finally, since the sum of the measures of all four angles of *ABCD* is 360°,

$$60 + 90 + 90 + x = 360 \Rightarrow 240 + x = 360 \Rightarrow x = \textbf{120 (D)}.$$

In the polygons in the figure that follows, one exterior angle has been drawn at each vertex. Surprisingly, if you add the measures of all of the exterior angles in any of the polygons, the sums are equal.

$$100 + 120 + 140 = 360$$

$$65 + 110 + 130 + 55 = 360$$

$$60 + 60 + 60 + 60 + 60 + 60 = 360$$

### KEY FACT K3:

**In any polygon, the sum of the exterior angles, taking one at each vertex, is 360°.**

A *regular polygon* is a polygon in which all of the sides are the same length and each angle has the same measure. KEY FACT K4 follows immediately from this definition and from KEY FACTS K2 and K3.

### KEY FACT K4:

**In any regular polygon the measure of each interior angle is $\dfrac{(n - 2) \times 180°}{n}$ and the measure of each exterior angle is $\dfrac{360°}{n}$.**

---

**Example 2.**

What is the measure of each interior angle in a regular decagon?

(A) 36   (B) 72   (C) 108   (D) 144   (E) 180

---

SOLUTION 1. The measure of each of the 10 interior angles is

$$\frac{(10 - 2) \times 180}{10} = \frac{8 \times 180}{10} = \frac{1440}{10} = \textbf{144 (D)}.$$

**SOLUTION 2.** The measure of each of the 10 exterior angles is 36 (360 ÷ 10). Therefore, the measure of each interior angle is 180 − 36 = **144**.

A **parallelogram** is a quadrilateral in which both pairs of opposite sides are parallel.

### KEY FACT K5:

**Parallelograms have the following properties:**

- **Opposite sides are equal: *AB* = *CD* and *AD* = *BC*.**
- **Opposite angles are equal: *a* = *c* and *b* = *d*.**
- **Consecutive angles add up to 180°:**
  *a* + *b* = 180, *b* + *c* = 180, *c* + *d* = 180, and *a* + *d* = 180.
- **The two diagonals bisect each other:**
  *AE* = *EC* and *BE* = *ED*.
- **A diagonal divides the parallelogram into two triangles that have the exact same size and shape. (The triangles are congruent.)**

| <u>Column A</u> | <u>Column B</u> |
|---|---|
| **Example 3.** | |

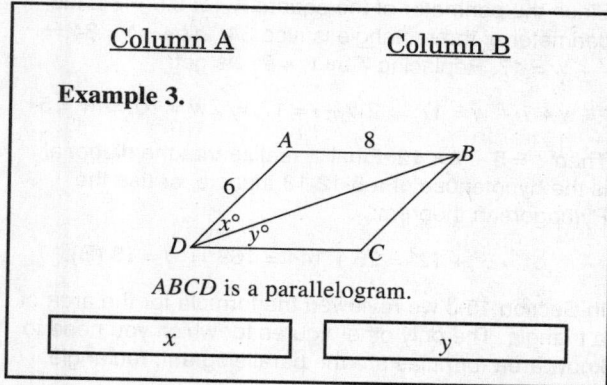

*ABCD* is a parallelogram.

| *x* | *y* |
|---|---|

**SOLUTION.** In △*ABD* the larger angle is opposite the larger side (KEY FACT J2); so *x* > m∠*ABD*. However, since *AB* and *CD* are parallel sides cut by transversal *BD*, *y* = m∠*ABD*. Therefore, *x* > *y*. Column **A** is greater.

A **rectangle** is a parallelogram in which all four angles are right angles. Two adjacent sides of a rectangle are usually called the **length** (*ℓ*) and the **width** (*w*). Note in the right-hand figure that the length is not necessarily greater than the width.

### KEY FACT K6:

**Since a rectangle is a parallelogram, all of the properties listed in KEY FACT K5 hold for rectangles. In addition:**

- **The measure of each angle in a rectangle is 90°.**
- **The diagonals of a rectangle have the same length: *AC* = *BD*.**

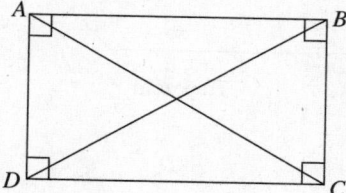

A **square** is a rectangle in which all four sides have the same length.

### KEY FACT K7:

**Since a square is a rectangle, all of the properties listed in KEY FACTS K5 and K6 hold for squares. In addition:**

- **All four sides have the same length.**
- **Each diagonal divides the square into two 45-45-90 right triangles.**
- **The diagonals are perpendicular to each other: *AC* ⊥ *BD*.**

> **Example 4.**
> What is the length of each side of a square if its diagonals are 10?
> (A) 5   (B) 7   (C) $5\sqrt{2}$   (D) $10\sqrt{2}$   (E) $10\sqrt{3}$

**SOLUTION.** Draw a diagram. In square *ABCD*, diagonal *AC* is the hypotenuse of a 45-45-90 right triangle, and side *AB* is a leg of that triangle. By KEY FACT J7,

$$AB = \frac{AC}{\sqrt{2}} = \frac{10}{\sqrt{2}} \times \frac{\sqrt{2}}{\sqrt{2}} = \frac{10\sqrt{2}}{2} = 5\sqrt{2}.$$

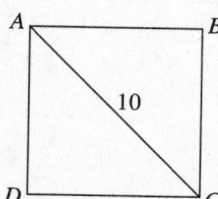

A *trapezoid* is a quadrilateral in which one pair of sides is parallel and the other pair of sides is not parallel. The parallel sides are called the *bases* of the trapezoid. The two bases are never equal. In general, the two non-parallel sides are not equal; if they are the trapezoid is called an *isosceles trapezoid*.

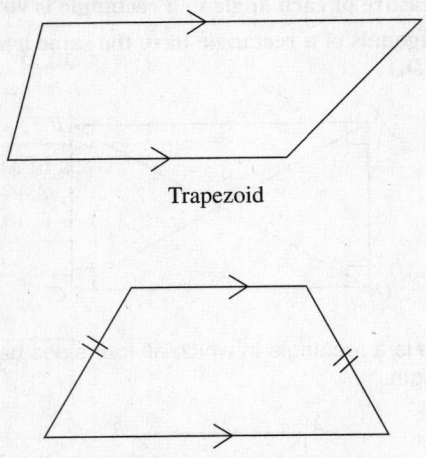

Trapezoid

Isoceles trapezoid

The *perimeter* (P) of any polygon is the sum of the lengths of all of its sides.

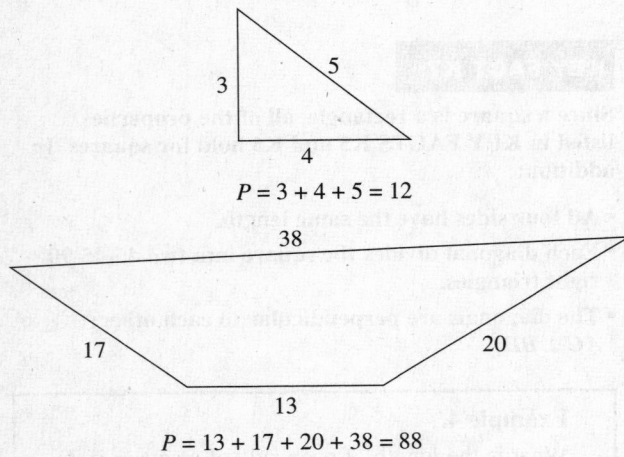

$P = 3 + 4 + 5 = 12$

$P = 13 + 17 + 20 + 38 = 88$

### KEY FACT K8:

In a rectangle, $P = 2(\ell + w)$; in a square, $P = 4s$.

$P = \ell + w + \ell + w = 2(\ell + w)$     $P = s + s + s + s = 4s$

---

### Example 5.

The length of a rectangle is 7 more than its width. If the perimeter of the rectangle is the same as the perimeter of a square of side 8.5, what is the length of a diagonal of the rectangle?

(A) 12   (B) 13   (C) 17   (D) 34   (E) 169

SOLUTION. Don't do anything until you have drawn a diagram.

$\ell = w + 7$

$P = 34$

Since the perimeter of the square = $4 \times 8.5 = 34$, the perimeter of the rectangle is also 34: $2(\ell + w) = 34 \Rightarrow \ell + w = 17$. Replacing $\ell$ by $w + 7$, we get:

$w + 7 + w = 17 \Rightarrow 2w + 7 = 17 \Rightarrow 2w = 10 \Rightarrow w = 5$

Then $\ell = 5 + 7 = 12$. Finally, realize that the diagonal is the hypotenuse of a 5-12-13 triangle, or use the Pythagorean theorem:

$$d^2 = 5^2 + 12^2 = 25 + 144 = 169 \Rightarrow d = \mathbf{13} \ \mathbf{(B)}.$$

In Section 15-J we reviewed the formula for the area of a triangle. The only other figures for which you need to know area formulas are the parallelogram, rectangle, square, and trapezoid.

### KEY FACT K9:

Here are the area formulas you need to know:

- For a parallelogram: $A = bh$.
- For a rectangle: $A = \ell w$.
- For a square: $A = s^2$ or $A = \dfrac{1}{2}d^2$.
- For a trapezoid: $A = \dfrac{1}{2}(b_1 + b_2)\,h$.

## Example 6.

In the figure below, the area of parallelogram *ABCD* is 40. What is the area of rectangle *AFCE*?

(A) 20  (B) 24  (C) 28  (D) 32  (E) 36

SOLUTION. Since the base, *CD*, is 10 and the area is 40, the height, *AE*, must be 4. Then △*AED* must be a 3-4-5 right triangle with *DE* = 3, which implies that *EC* = 7. So the area of the rectangle is 7 × 4 = **28 (C)**.

Two rectangles with the same perimeter can have different areas, and two rectangles with the same area can have different perimeters. These facts are a common source of questions on the GRE.

**RECTANGLES WHOSE PERIMETERS ARE 100**

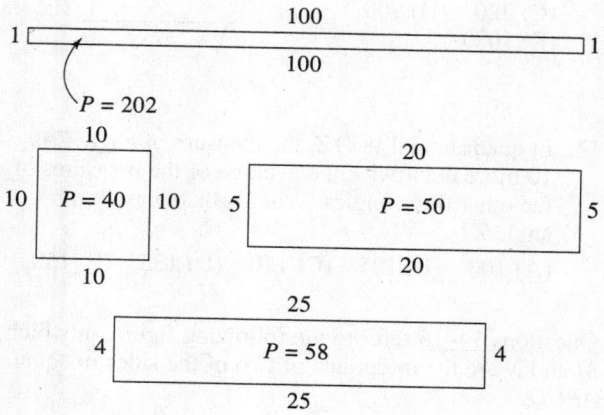

**RECTANGLES WHOSE AREAS ARE 100**

**KEY FACT K10:**

For a given perimeter, the rectangle with the largest area is a square. For a given area, the rectangle with the smallest perimeter is a square.

| Column A | Column B |
|---|---|
| **Example 7.** | |
| The area of a rectangle whose perimeter is 12 | The area of a rectangle whose perimeter is 14 |
| **Example 8.** | |
| The area of a rectangle whose perimeter is 12 | 10 |

SOLUTION 7. Draw any rectangles whose perimeters are 12 and 14 and compute their areas. As drawn below, Column A = 8 and Column B = 12.

This time Column B is greater. Is it always? Draw a different rectangle whose perimeter is also 14.

The one drawn here has an area of 6. Now Column B isn't greater. The answer is **D**.

SOLUTION 8. There are many rectangles of different areas whose perimeters are 12. But the largest area is 9, when the rectangle is a 3 × 3 square. Column **B** is greater.

# PRACTICE EXERCISES—QUADRILATERALS

## Multiple-Choice Questions

1.  If the length of a rectangle is 4 times its width, and if its area is 144, what is its perimeter?

    (A) 6    (B) 24    (C) 30    (D) 60    (E) 96

Questions 2–3 refer to the diagram below in which the diagonals of square $ABCD$ intersect at $E$.

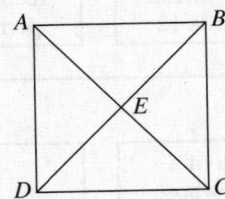

2.  What is the area of $\triangle DEC$?

    (A) $\dfrac{1}{2}$    (B) 1    (C) $\sqrt{2}$    (D) 2    (E) $2\sqrt{2}$

3.  What is the perimeter of $\triangle DEC$?

    (A) $1 + \sqrt{2}$    (B) $2 + \sqrt{2}$    (C) 4    (D) $2 + 2\sqrt{2}$
    (E) 6

4.  If the angles of a five-sided polygon are in the ratio of 2:3:3:5:5, what is the measure of the smallest angle?

    (A) 20    (B) 40    (C) 60    (D) 80    (E) 90

5.  If in the figures below, the area of rectangle $ABCD$ is 100, what is the area of rectangle $EFGH$?

    (A) 98    (B) 100    (C) 102    (D) 104    (E) 106

Questions 6–7 refer to a rectangle in which the length of each diagonal is 12, and one of the angles formed by the diagonal and a side measures 30°.

6.  What is the area of the rectangle?

    (A) 18    (B) 72    (C) $18\sqrt{3}$    (D) $36\sqrt{3}$
    (E) $36\sqrt{2}$

7.  What is the perimeter of the rectangle?

    (A) 18    (B) 24    (C) $12 + 12\sqrt{3}$    (D) $18 + 6\sqrt{3}$
    (E) $24\sqrt{2}$

8.  How many sides does a polygon have if the measure of each interior angle is 8 times the measure of each exterior angle?

    (A) 8    (B) 9    (C) 10    (D) 12    (E) 18

9.  The length of a rectangle is 5 more than the side of a square, and the width of the rectangle is 5 less than the side of the square. If the area of the square is 45, what is the area of the rectangle?

    (A) 20    (B) 25    (C) 45    (D) 50    (E) 70

Questions 10–11 refer to the following figure, in which $M, N, O,$ and $P$ are the midpoints of the sides of rectangle $ABCD$.

10.  What is the perimeter of quadrilateral $MNOP$?

    (A) 24    (B) 32    (C) 40    (D) 48    (E) 60

11.  What is the area of quadrilateral $MNOP$?

    (A) 48    (B) 60    (C) 72    (D) 96    (E) 108

12.  In the figure at the right, what is the sum of the measures of all of the marked angles?

    (A) 360    (B) 540
    (C) 720    (D) 900
    (E) 1080

13.  In quadrilateral $WXYZ$, the measure of angle $Z$ is 10 more than twice the average of the measures of the other three angles. What is the measure of angle $Z$?

    (A) 100    (B) 105    (C) 120    (D) 135    (E) 150

Questions 14–15 refer to the following figure, in which $M$ and $N$ are the midpoints of two of the sides of square $ABCD$.

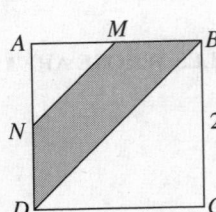

14. What is the perimeter of the shaded region?
    (A) 3   (B) $2 + 3\sqrt{2}$   (C) $3 + 2\sqrt{2}$   (D) 5   (E) 8

15. What is the area of the shaded region?
    (A) 1.5   (B) 1.75   (C) 3   (D) $2\sqrt{2}$   (E) $3\sqrt{2}$

## Quantitative Comparison Questions

Column A                                Column B

ABCD is a rectangle.

16. | The area of $\triangle AED$ | | The area of $\triangle EDC$ |

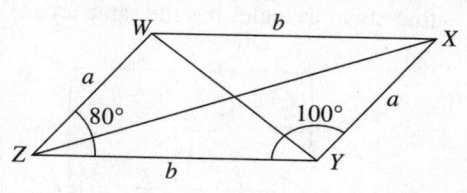

WXYZ is a parallelogram.

17. | Diagonal $WY$ | | Diagonal $XZ$ |

| Column A | Column B |
| --- | --- |

18. | The perimeter of a 30-60-90 right triangle whose shorter leg is $2x$ | The perimeter of an octagon, each of whose sides is $x$ |

19. | The perimeter of a rectangle whose area is 50 | 28 |

In parallelogram PQRS, TR bisects $\angle QRS$.

20. | $a$ | $2b$ |

## Answer Key

| | | | |
| --- | --- | --- | --- |
| 1. **D** | 6. **D** | 11. **D** | 16. **C** |
| 2. **B** | 7. **C** | 12. **C** | 17. **B** |
| 3. **D** | 8. **E** | 13. **E** | 18. **A** |
| 4. **C** | 9. **A** | 14. **B** | 19. **A** |
| 5. **C** | 10. **C** | 15. **A** | 20. **C** |

## Answer Explanations

1. **D.** Draw a diagram and label it.

   Since the area is 144, then
   $$144 = 4x^2 \Rightarrow x^2 = 36 \Rightarrow x = 6.$$
   So the width is 6, the length is 24, and the perimeter is 60.

2. **B.** The area of the square is $2^2 = 4$, and each triangle is one-fourth of the square. So the area of $\triangle DEC$ is 1.

3. **D.** $\triangle DEC$ is a 45-45-90 right triangle whose hypotenuse, $DC$, is 2. Therefore, each of the legs is $\frac{2}{\sqrt{2}} = \sqrt{2}$. So the perimeter is $2 + 2\sqrt{2}$.

4. **C.** The sum of the angles of a five-sided polygon is $(5-2) \times 180 = 3 \times 180 = 540$. Therefore,
   $$540 = 2x + 3x + 3x + 5x + 5x = 18x \Rightarrow$$
   $$x = 540 \div 18 = 30.$$
   The measure of the smallest angle is $2x = 2 \times 30 = 60$.

5. **C.** The area of rectangle $ABCD = (x+1)(x+4) = x^2 + 5x + 4$. The area of rectangle $EFGH = (x+2)(x+3) = x^2 + 5x + 6$, which is exactly 2 more than the area of rectangle $ABCD$: $100 + 2 = 102$.

6. D. Draw a picture and label it. Since $\triangle BCD$ is a 30-60-90 right triangle, $BC$ is 6 (half the hypotenuse) and $CD$ is $6\sqrt{3}$. So the area is $\ell w = 6(6\sqrt{3}) = 36\sqrt{3}$.

7. C. The perimeter of the rectangle is
$$2(\ell + w) = 2(6 + 6\sqrt{3}) = 12 + 12\sqrt{3}.$$

8. E. The sum of the degree measures of an interior and exterior angle is 180, so $180 = 8x + x = 9x \Rightarrow x = 20$. Since the sum of the measures of all the exterior angles is 360, there are $360 \div 20 = 18$ angles and 18 sides.

9. A. Let $x$ represent the side of the square. Then the dimensions of the rectangle are $(x + 5)$ and $(x - 5)$, and its area is $(x + 5)(x - 5) = x^2 - 25$. Since the area of the square is 45, $x^2 = 45 \Rightarrow x^2 - 25 = 45 - 25 = 20$.

10. C. Each triangle surrounding quadrilateral *MNOP* is a 6-8-10 right triangle. So each side of the quadrilateral is 10, and its perimeter is 40.

11. D. The area of each of the triangles is $\frac{1}{2}(6)(8) = 24$, so together the four triangles have an area of 96. The area of the rectangle is $16 \times 12 = 192$. Therefore, the area of quadrilateral *MNOP* is $192 - 96 = 96$.
*Note:* Joining the midpoints of the four sides of any quadrilateral creates a parallelogram whose area is one-half the area of the original quadrilateral.

12. C. Each of the 10 marked angles is an exterior angle of the pentagon. If we take one angle at each vertex, the sum of those five angles is 360; the sum of the other five is also 360: $360 + 360 = 720$.

13. E. Let $W, X, Y,$ and $Z$ represent the measures of the four angles. Since $W + X + Y + Z = 360$, $W + X + Y = 360 - Z$. Also,
$$Z = 10 + 2\left(\frac{W + X + Y}{3}\right) = 10 + 2\left(\frac{360 - Z}{3}\right).$$
So $Z = 10 + \frac{2}{3}(360) - \frac{2}{3}Z = 10 + 240 - \frac{2}{3}Z$
$$\Rightarrow \frac{5}{3}Z = 250 \Rightarrow Z = 150.$$

14. B. Since $M$ and $N$ are midpoints of sides of length 2, $AM, MB, AN,$ and $ND$ are all 1. $MN = \sqrt{2}$, since it's the hypotenuse of an isosceles right triangle whose legs are 1; and $BD = 2\sqrt{2}$, since it's the hypotenuse of an isosceles right triangle whose legs are 2. So the perimeter of the shaded region is $1 + \sqrt{2} + 1 + 2\sqrt{2} = 2 + 3\sqrt{2}$.

15. A. The area of $\triangle ABD = \frac{1}{2}(2)(2) = 2$, and the area of $\triangle AMN$ is $\frac{1}{2}(1)(1) = 0.5$. So the area of the shaded region is $2 - 0.5 = 1.5$.

16. C. The area of $\triangle AED$ is $\frac{1}{2}w\left(\frac{\ell}{2}\right) = \frac{\ell w}{4}$. The area of $\triangle EDC$ is $\frac{1}{2}\ell\left(\frac{w}{2}\right) = \frac{\ell w}{4}$. *Note:* Each of the four small triangles has the same area.

17. B. By KEY FACT J5, since $\angle Z$ is acute and $\angle Y$ is obtuse, $(WY)^2 < a^2 + b^2$, whereas $(XZ)^2 > a^2 + b^2$.

18. A. Since an octagon has eight sides, Column B is $8x$.
Column A: By KEY FACT J10, the hypotenuse of the triangle is $4x$, and the longer leg is $2x\sqrt{3}$. So the perimeter is $2x + 4x + 2x\sqrt{3}$. Since $\sqrt{3} > 1$, then
$$2x + 4x + 2x\sqrt{3} > 2x + 4x + 2x = 8x.$$

19. A. The perimeter of a rectangle of area 50 can be as large as we like, but the least it can be is when the rectangle is a square. In that case, each side is $\sqrt{50}$, which is greater than 7, and so the perimeter is greater than 28.

20. C. $TR$ is a transversal cutting the parallel sides $PQ$ and $RS$. So $b = x$ and $2b = 2x$. But since the opposite angles of a parallelogram are equal, $a = 2x$. So $a = 2b$.

# 15-L. CIRCLES

A *circle* consists of all the points that are the same distance from one fixed point called the *center*. That distance is called the *radius* of the circle. The figure below is a circle of radius 1 unit whose center is at the point $O$. $A$, $B$, $C$, $D$, and $E$, which are each 1 unit from $O$, are all points on circle $O$. The word *radius* is also used to represent any of the line segments joining the center and a point on the circle. The plural of *radius* is *radii*. In circle $O$, below, $OA$, $OB$, $OC$, $OD$, and $OE$ are all radii. If a circle has radius $r$, each of the radii is $r$ units long.

Any triangle, such as $\triangle COD$ in the figure above, formed by connecting the endpoints of two radii, is isosceles.

---

**Example 1.**

If $P$ and $Q$ are points on circle $O$, what is the value of $x$?

(A) 35  (B) 45  (C) 55
    (D) 65  (E) 70

---

SOLUTION. Since $\triangle POQ$ is isosceles, angles $P$ and $Q$ have the same measure. Then, $70 + x + x = 180 \Rightarrow 2x = 110 \Rightarrow x = 55$ (**C**).

A line segment, such as $CD$ in circle $O$ at the beginning of this section, both of whose endpoints are on a circle is called a *chord*. A chord such as $BE$, which passes through the center of the circle, is called a *diameter*. Since $BE$ is the sum of two radii, $OB$ and $OE$, it is twice as long as a radius.

**KEY FACT L2:**

If $d$ is the diameter and $r$ the radius of a circle, $d = 2r$.

**KEY FACT L3:**

A diameter is the longest chord that can be drawn in a circle.

---

## Column A        Column B

**Example 2.**

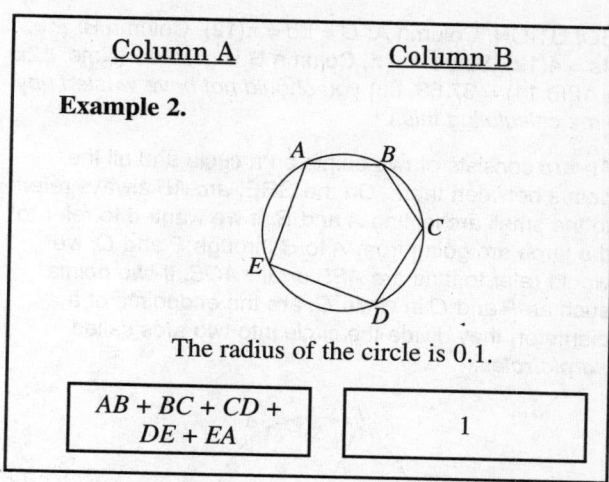

The radius of the circle is 0.1.

| $AB + BC + CD + DE + EA$ | 1 |
|---|---|

SOLUTION. Since the radius of the circle is 0.1, the diameter is 0.2. Therefore, the length of each of the five line segments is less than 0.2, and the sum of their lengths is less than $5 \times 0.2 = 1$. The answer is **B**.

The total length around a circle, from $A$ to $B$ to $C$ to $D$ to $E$ and back to $A$, is called the *circumference* of the circle. In every circle the ratio of the circumference to the diameter is exactly the same and is denoted by the symbol $\pi$ (the Greek letter "pi").

**KEY FACT L4:**

- $\pi = \dfrac{\text{circumference}}{\text{diameter}} = \dfrac{C}{d}$
- $C = \pi d$
- $C = 2\pi r$

**KEY FACT L5:**

**The value of $\pi$ is approximately 3.14.**

On GRE questions that involve circles, you are expected to leave your answer in terms of $\pi$. So *never* multiply by 3.14. If you are ever stuck on a problem whose answers involve $\pi$, try to estimate the answer, and then use 3 as an approximation of $\pi$ to test the answers. For example, assume that you think that an answer is about 50, and the answer choices are $4\pi$, $6\pi$, $12\pi$, $16\pi$, and $24\pi$. Since $\pi$ is slightly greater than 3, these choices are a little greater than 12, 18, 36, 48, and 72. The answer must be $16\pi$. (To the nearest hundredth, $16\pi$ is actually 50.27, but approximating it by 48 was close enough.)

## Column A        Column B

**Example 3.**

| The circumference of a circle whose diameter is 12 | The perimeter of a square whose side is 12 |
|---|---|

SOLUTION. Column A: $C = \pi d = \pi(12)$. Column B: $P = 4s = 4(12)$. Since $4 > \pi$, Column **B** is greater. (Note: $12\pi \approx 12(3.14) = 37.68$, but *you should not have wasted any time calculating this*.)

An *arc* consists of two points on a circle and all the points between them. On the GRE, *arc AB* always refers to the small arc joining *A* and *B*. If we wanted to refer to the large arc going from *A* to *B* through *P* and *Q*, we would refer to it as arc *APB* or arc *AQB*. If two points, such as *P* and *Q* in circle *O*, are the endpoints of a diameter, they divide the circle into two arcs called *semicircles*.

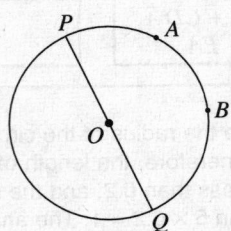

An angle whose vertex is at the center of a circle is called a *central angle*.

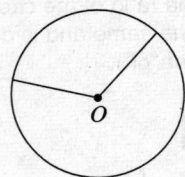

The degree measure of a complete circle is 360°.

**KEY FACT L7:**

The degree measure of an arc equals the degree measure of the central angle that intercepts it.

CAUTION: Degree measure is *not* a measure of length. In the circles above, arc *AB* and arc *CD* each measure 72°, even though arc *CD* is much longer.

How long *is* arc *CD*? Since the radius of Circle *P* is 10, its diameter is 20, and its circumference is $20\pi$. Since there are 360° in a circle, arc *CD* is $\frac{72}{360}$, or $\frac{1}{5}$, of the circumference: $\frac{1}{5}(20\pi) = 4\pi$.

**KEY FACT L8:**

The formula for the area of a circle of radius *r* is $A = \pi r^2$.

The area of Circle *P*, in KEY FACT L7, is $\pi(10)^2 = 100\pi$ square units. The area of sector *CPD* is $\frac{1}{5}$ of the area of the circle: $\frac{1}{5}(100\pi) = 20\pi$.

**KEY FACT L9:**

If an arc measures $x°$, the length of the arc is $\frac{x}{360}(2\pi r)$, and the area of the sector formed by the arc and 2 radii is $\frac{x}{360}(\pi r^2)$.

Examples 4 and 5 refer to the circle below.

**Example 4.**

What is the area of the shaded region?

(A) $144\pi - 144\sqrt{3}$    (B) $144\pi - 36\sqrt{3}$
  (C) $144 - 72\sqrt{3}$    (D) $24\pi - 36\sqrt{3}$
  (E) $24\pi - 72\sqrt{3}$

**Example 5.**

What is the perimeter of the shaded region?

(A) $12 + 4\pi$   (B) $12 + 12\pi$   (C) $12 + 24\pi$
  (D) $12\sqrt{2} + 4\pi$   (E) $12\sqrt{2} + 24\pi$

SOLUTION 4. The area of the shaded region is equal to the area of sector *COD* minus the area of △*COD*. The area of the circle is $\pi(12)^2 = 144\pi$.

Since $\frac{60}{360} = \frac{1}{6}$, the area of sector *COD* is $\frac{1}{6}(144\pi) = 24\pi$. Since m∠*O* = 60°, m∠*C* + ∠*D* = 120°; but △*COD* is isosceles, so m∠*C* = m∠*D*. Therefore, they each measure 60°, and the triangle is equilateral. By KEY FACT J15, area of $\triangle COD = \dfrac{12^2\sqrt{3}}{4} = \dfrac{144\sqrt{3}}{4} = 36\sqrt{3}$,

so the area of the shaded region is **$24\pi - 36\sqrt{3}$ (D)**.

SOLUTION 5. Since $\triangle COD$ is equilateral, $CD = 12$. Since the circumference of the circle $= 2\pi(12) = 24\pi$, arc $CD = \dfrac{1}{6}(24\pi) = 4\pi$. So the perimeter is **$12 + 4\pi$ (A)**.

Suppose that in Example 5 you see that $CD = 12$, but you don't remember how to find the length of arc $CD$. From the diagram, it is clear that it is slightly longer than $CD$, say 13. So you know that the perimeter is *about* 25. Now, approximate the value of each of the choices and see which one is closest to 25. Only Choice A is even close.

A line and a circle or two circles are ***tangent*** if they have only one point of intersection. A circle is ***inscribed*** in a triangle or square if it is tangent to each side. A polygon is ***inscribed*** in a circle if each vertex is on the circle.

Line $\ell$ is tangent to circle $O$.
Circles $O$ and $Q$ are tangent.

The circle is inscribed
in the square.

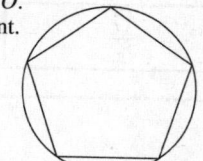

The pentagon is inscribed
in the circle.

---

### KEY FACT L10:

**If a line is tangent to a circle, a radius (or diameter) drawn to the point where the tangent touches the circle is perpendicular to the tangent line.**

Lines $\ell$ and $m$ are tangent to circle $O$.

---

**Example 6.**

*A* is the center of a circle whose radius is 8, and *B* is the center of a circle whose diameter is 8. If these two circles are tangent to one another, what is the area of the circle whose diameter is *AB*?

(A) $12\pi$   (B) $36\pi$   (C) $64\pi$   (D) $144\pi$
(E) $256\pi$

SOLUTION. Draw a diagram. Since the diameter, *AB*, of the dotted circle is 12, its radius is 6 and the area is $\pi(6)^2 = \textbf{36}\pi$ **(B)**.

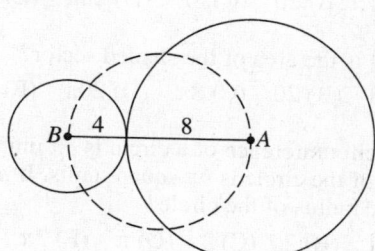

---

# PRACTICE EXERCISES—CIRCLES

## Multiple-Choice Questions

1.  What is the circumference of a circle whose area is $100\pi$?

    (A) 10   (B) 20   (C) $10\pi$   (D) $20\pi$   (E) $25\pi$

2.  What is the area of a circle whose circumference is $\pi$?

    (A) $\dfrac{\pi}{4}$   (B) $\dfrac{\pi}{2}$   (C) $\pi$   (D) $2\pi$   (E) $4\pi$

3.  What is the area of a circle that is inscribed in a square of area 2?

    (A) $\dfrac{\pi}{4}$   (B) $\dfrac{\pi}{2}$   (C) $\pi$   (D) $\pi\sqrt{2}$   (E) $2\pi$

4.  A square of area 2 is inscribed in a circle. What is the area of the circle?

    (A) $\dfrac{\pi}{4}$   (B) $\dfrac{\pi}{2}$   (C) $\pi$   (D) $\pi\sqrt{2}$   (E) $2\pi$

5. A $5 \times 12$ rectangle is inscribed in a circle. What is the radius of the circle?

   (A) 6.5   (B) 7   (C) 8.5   (D) 13   (E) 17

6. If in the figure below, the area of the shaded sector is 85% of the area of the entire circle, what is the value of $w$?

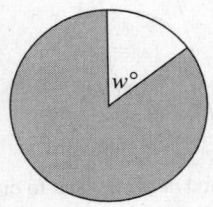

   (A) 15   (B) 30   (C) 45   (D) 54   (E) 60

Questions 7–8 refer to the following figure.

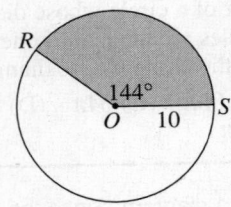

7. What is the length of arc $RS$?

   (A) 8   (B) 20   (C) $8\pi$   (D) $20\pi$   (E) $40\pi$

8. What is the area of the shaded sector?

   (A) 8   (B) 20   (C) $8\pi$   (D) $20\pi$   (E) $40\pi$

9. The circumference of a circle is $a\pi$ units, and the area of the circle is $b\pi$ square units. If $a = b$, what is the radius of the circle?

   (A) 1   (B) 2   (C) 3   (D) $\pi$   (E) $2\pi$

10. In the figure above, what is the value of $x$?

    (A) 30   (B) 36   (C) 45   (D) 54   (E) 60

11. If $A$ is the area and $C$ the circumference of a circle, which of the following is an expression for $A$ in terms of $C$?

    (A) $\dfrac{C^2}{4\pi}$   (B) $\dfrac{C^2}{4\pi^2}$   (C) $2C$   (D) $2C^2\sqrt{\pi}$

    (E) $\dfrac{C^2\sqrt{\pi}}{4}$

12. What is the area of a circle whose radius is the diagonal of a square whose area is 4?

    (A) $2\pi$   (B) $2\pi\sqrt{2}$   (C) $4\pi$   (D) $8\pi$   (E) $16\pi$

## Quantitative Comparison Questions

| Column A | Column B |
|----------|----------|

13.

| The perimeter of the pentagon | The circumference of the circle |

The circumference of a circle is $C$ inches. The area of the same circle is $A$ square inches.

14.

| $\dfrac{C}{A}$ | $\dfrac{A}{C}$ |

15.

| The area of a circle of radius 2 | The area of a semi-circle of radius 3 |

$C$ is the circumference of a circle of radius $r$

16.

| $\dfrac{C}{r}$ | 6 |

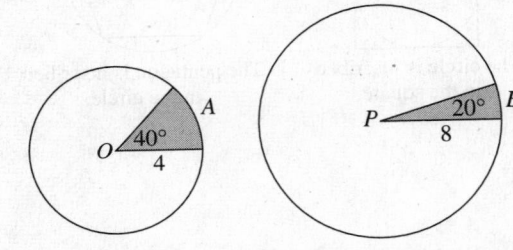

17.

| The area of sector $A$ | The area of sector $B$ |

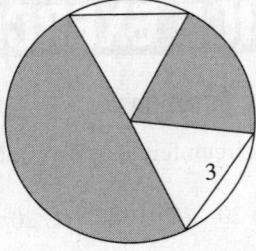

Each of the triangles is equilateral.

18.

| The area of the shaded region | $6\pi$ |

Column A

Figure 1

Column B

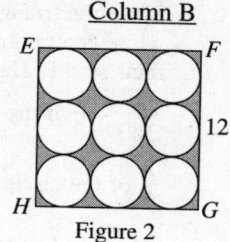

Figure 2

*ABCD* and *EFGH* are squares, and all the circles are tangent to one another and to the sides of the squares.

| Column A | Column B |
|---|---|
| 19. | The area of the shaded region in Figure 1 | The area of the shaded region in Figure 2 |

| Column A | | Column B |
|---|---|---|
| | A square and a circle have equal areas. | |
| 20. | The perimeter of the square | The circumference of the circle |

# Answer Key

| | | | |
|---|---|---|---|
| 1. **D** | 6. **D** | 11. **A** | 16. **A** |
| 2. **A** | 7. **C** | 12. **D** | 17. **B** |
| 3. **B** | 8. **E** | 13. **B** | 18. **C** |
| 4. **C** | 9. **B** | 14. **D** | 19. **C** |
| 5. **A** | 10. **D** | 15. **B** | 20. **A** |

# Answer Explanations

1. **D.** $A = \pi r^2 = 100\pi \Rightarrow r^2 = 100 \Rightarrow r = 10 \Rightarrow$
   $C = 2\pi r = 2\pi(10) = 20\pi.$

2. **A.** $C = 2\pi r = \pi \Rightarrow 2r = 1 \Rightarrow r = \frac{1}{2} \Rightarrow$

   $A = \pi r^2 = \pi\left(\frac{1}{2}\right)^2 = \frac{1}{4}\pi = \frac{\pi}{4}.$

3. **B.** Draw a diagram. Since the area of square *ABCD* is 2, $AD = \sqrt{2}$. Then diameter $EF = \sqrt{2}$
   and radius $OE = \frac{\sqrt{2}}{2}$. Then the area of the

   circle $= \pi\left(\frac{\sqrt{2}}{2}\right)^2 = \frac{2}{4}\pi = \frac{\pi}{2}.$

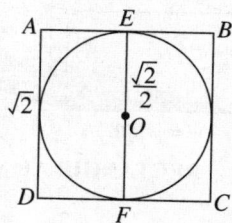

4. **C.** Draw a diagram. Since the area of square *ABCD* is 2, $AD = \sqrt{2}$. Then diagonal

$BD = \sqrt{2} \times \sqrt{2} = 2$. But *BD* is also a diameter of the circle. So the diameter is 2 and the radius is 1. Therefore, the area is $\pi(1)^2 = \pi$.

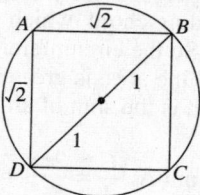

5. **A.** Draw a diagram. By the Pythagorean theorem (or by recognizing a 5-12-13 triangle), we see that diagonal *AC* is 13. But *AC* is also a diameter of the circle, so the diameter is 13 and the radius is 6.5.

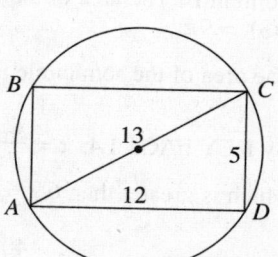

6. D.   Since the shaded area is 85% of the circle, the white area is 15% of the circle. So, $w$ is 15% of $360°$: $0.15 \times 360 = 54$.

7. C.   The length of arc $RS$ is $\frac{144}{360}$ of the circumference:
$$\left(\frac{144}{360}\right)2\pi(10) = \left(\frac{2}{5}\right)20\pi = 8\pi.$$

8. E.   The area of the shaded sector is $\left(\frac{144}{360}\right)$ of the area of the circle:
$$\left(\frac{144}{360}\right)\pi(10)^2 = \left(\frac{2}{5}\right)100\pi = 40\pi.$$

9. B.   Since $C = a\pi = b\pi = A$, we have $2\pi r = \pi r^2 \Rightarrow 2r = r^2 \Rightarrow r = 2$.

10. D.   The triangle is isosceles, so the third unmarked angle is also $x$:
$$180 = 72 + 2x \Rightarrow 2x = 108 \Rightarrow x = 54.$$

11. A.   $C = 2\pi r \Rightarrow r = \frac{C}{2\pi} \Rightarrow$
$$A = \pi\left(\frac{C}{2\pi}\right)^2 = \pi\left(\frac{C^2}{4\pi^2}\right) = \frac{C^2}{4\pi}.$$

12. D.   If the area of the square is 4, each side is 2, and the length of a diagonal is $2\sqrt{2}$. The area of a circle whose radius is $2\sqrt{2}$ is
$$\pi(2\sqrt{2})^2 = 8\pi.$$

13. B.   There's nothing to calculate here. Each arc of the circle is clearly longer than the corresponding chord, which is a side of the pentagon. So the circumference, which is the sum of all the arcs, is greater than the perimeter, which is the sum of all the chords.

14. D.   Column A: $\frac{C}{A} = \frac{2\pi r}{\pi r^2} = \frac{2}{r}$.

Column B: $\frac{A}{C} = \frac{r}{2}$. If $r = 2$, the columns are equal; otherwise, they're not.

15. B.   Column A: $A = \pi(2)^2 = 4\pi$.
Column B: The area of a circle of radius 3 is $\pi(3)^2 = 9\pi$.

The area of the semicircle is $\frac{1}{2}(9\pi) = 4.5\pi$.

16. A.   By KEY FACT L4, $\pi = \frac{C}{d} = \frac{C}{2r} \Rightarrow \frac{C}{r} = 2\pi$,

which is greater than 6.

17. B.   The area of sector $A$ is $\frac{40}{360}(16\pi) = \frac{16\pi}{9}$. The

area of sector $B$ is $\frac{20}{360}(64\pi) = \frac{64\pi}{18} = \frac{32\pi}{9}$.
So sector $B$ is twice as big as sector $A$.

18. C.   Since the triangles are equilateral, the two white central angles each measure $60°$, and their sum is $120°$. So the white area is $\frac{120}{360} = \frac{1}{3}$ of the circle, and the shaded area is $\frac{2}{3}$ of the circle. The area of the circle is $\pi(3)^2 = 9\pi$, so the shaded area is $\frac{2}{3}(9\pi) = 6\pi$.

19. C.   In Figure 1, since the radius of each circle is 3, the area of each circle is $9\pi$, and the total area of the 4 circles is $36\pi$. In Figure 2, the radius of each circle is 2, and so the area of each circle is $4\pi$, and the total area of the 9 circles is $36\pi$. In the two figures, the white areas are equal, as are the shaded areas.

20. A.   Let $A$ represent the area of the square and the circle.
Column A: $A = s^2 \Rightarrow s = \sqrt{A} \Rightarrow P = 4\sqrt{A}$.

Column B: $A = \pi r^2 \Rightarrow r = \sqrt{\frac{A}{\pi}} \Rightarrow$

$C = 2\pi\left(\frac{\sqrt{A}}{\sqrt{\pi}}\right) = 2\sqrt{\pi}\sqrt{A}$.

Since $\pi < 4$, $\sqrt{\pi} < 2 \Rightarrow 2\sqrt{\pi} < 4$.

# 15-M. SOLID GEOMETRY

There are very few solid geometry questions on the GRE, and they cover only a few elementary topics. Basically, all you need to know are the formulas for the volume and surface areas of rectangular solids (including cubes) and cylinders.

A **rectangular solid** or **box** is a solid formed by six rectangles, called **faces**. The sides of the rectangles are called **edges**. As shown in the diagram below, the edges are called the **length**, **width**, and **height**. A **cube** is a rectangular solid in which the length, width, and height are equal; so all the edges are the same length.

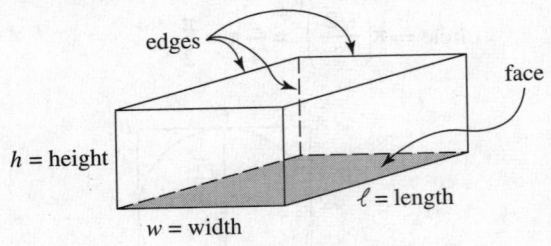

edges

face

$h$ = height

$\ell$ = length

$w$ = width

**RECTANGULAR SOLID**

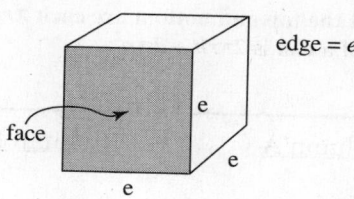

**CUBE**

The **volume** of a solid is the amount of space it takes up and is measured in **cubic units**. One cubic unit is the amount of space occupied by a cube all of whose edges are one unit long. In the figure above, if each edge of the cube is 1 inch long, then the area of each face is 1 square inch, and the volume of the cube is 1 cubic inch.

**KEY FACT M1:**

• The formula for the volume of a rectangular solid is $V = \ell wh$.

• The formula for the volume of a cube is $V = e \cdot e \cdot e = e^3$.

**Example 1.**

The base of a rectangular tank is 12 feet long and 8 feet wide; the height of the tank is 30 inches. If water is pouring into the tank at the rate of 2 cubic feet per second, how many <u>minutes</u> will be required to fill the tank?

(A) 1    (B) 2    (C) 10    (D) 120    (E) 240

SOLUTION. Draw a diagram. In order to express all of the dimensions of the tank in the same units, convert 30 inches to 2.5 feet. Then the volume of the tank is $12 \times 8 \times 2.5 = 240$ cubic feet. At 2 cubic feet per second, it will take $240 \div 2 = 120$ seconds = **2** minutes to fill the tank (**B**).

The **surface area** of a rectangular solid is the sum of the areas of the six faces. Since the top and bottom faces are equal, the front and back faces are equal, and the left and right faces are equal, we can calculate the area of one from each pair and then double the sum. In a cube, each of the six faces has the same area.

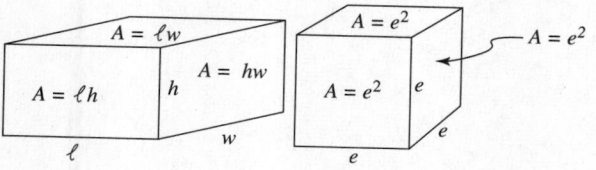

**KEY FACT M2:**

• The formula for the surface area of a rectangular solid is $A = 2(\ell w + \ell h + wh)$.

• The formula for the surface area of a cube is $A = 6e^2$.

**Example 2.**

The volume of a cube is $v$ cubic *yards*, and its surface area is $a$ square *feet*. If $v = a$, what is the length in *inches* of each edge?

(A) 12    (B) 36    (C) 144    (D) 648    (E) 1944

SOLUTION. Draw a diagram. If $e$ is the length of the edge in yards, $3e$ is the length in feet, and $36e$ the length in inches. Therefore, $v = e^3$ and $a = 6(3e)^2 = 6(9e^2) = 54e^2$. Since $v = a$, $e^3 = 54e^2 \Rightarrow e = 54$, so the length is $36(54) = $ **1944** inches (**E**).

A **diagonal** of a box is a line segment joining a vertex on the top of the box to the opposite vertex on the bottom. A box has 4 diagonals, all the same length. In the box below they are line segments *AG*, *BH*, *CE*, and *DF*.

**KEY FACT M3:**

A diagonal of a box is the longest line segment that can be drawn between two points on the box.

**KEY FACT M4:**

If the dimensions of a box are $\ell$, $w$, and $h$, and if $d$ is the length of a diagonal, then $d^2 = \ell^2 + w^2 + h^2$.

For example, in the box below:

$$d^2 = 3^2 + 4^2 + 12^2 = 9 + 16 + 144 = 169 \Rightarrow d = 13.$$

This formula is really just an extended Pythagorean theorem. *EG* is the diagonal of rectangular base *EFGH*. Since the sides of the base are 3 and 4, *EG* is 5. Now, △*CGE* is a right triangle whose legs are 12 and 5, so diagonal *CE* is 13.

---

**Example 3.**

What is the length of a diagonal of a cube whose sides are 1?

(A) 1   (B) 2   (C) 3   (D) $\sqrt{2}$   (E) $\sqrt{3}$

---

SOLUTION. Use the formula:

$$d^2 = 1^2 + 1^2 + 1^2 = 3 \Rightarrow d = \sqrt{3} \text{ (E)}.$$

Without the formula you would draw a diagram and label it. Since the base is a 1 × 1 square, its diagonal is $\sqrt{2}$. Then the diagonal of the cube is the hypotenuse of a right triangle whose legs are 1 and $\sqrt{2}$, so

$$d^2 = 1^2 + (\sqrt{2})^2 = 1 + 2 = 3, \text{ and } d = \sqrt{3}.$$

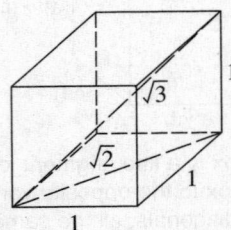

A *cylinder* is similar to a rectangular solid except that the base is a circle instead of a rectangle. The volume of a cylinder is the area of its circular base ($\pi r^2$) times its height ($h$). The surface area of a cylinder depends on whether you are envisioning a tube, such as a straw, without a top or bottom, or a can, which has both a top and a bottom.

**KEY FACT M5:**

• **The formula for the volume, $V$, of a cylinder whose circular base has radius $r$ and whose height is $h$ is $V = \pi r^2 h$.**

• **The surface area, $A$, of the side of the cylinder is the circumference of the circular base times the height: $A = 2\pi rh$.**

• The area of the top and bottom are each $\pi r^2$, so the total area of a can is $2\pi rh + 2\pi r^2$.

---

| Column A | Column B |
|---|---|

**Example 4.**

The radius of cylinder II equals the height of cylinder I.
The height of cylinder II equals the radius of cylinder I.

| The volume of cylinder I | The volume of cylinder II |
|---|---|

---

SOLUTION. Let $r$ and $h$ be the radius and height, respectively, of cylinder I. Then

| Column A | Column B |
|---|---|
| $\pi r^2 h$ | $\pi h^2 r$ |

Divide each column by $\pi rh$:

| $r$ | $h$ |
|---|---|

Either $r$ or $h$ could be greater, or the two could be equal. The answer is **D**.

These are the only formulas you need to know. Any other solid geometry questions that might appear on the GRE would require you to visualize a situation and reason it out, rather than to apply a formula.

---

**Example 5.**

How many small cubes are needed to construct the tower in the figure at the right?

(A) 25   (B) 28
(C) 35   (D) 44
(E) 67

---

SOLUTION. You need to "see" the answer. The top level consists of 1 cube, the second and third levels consist of 9 cubes each, and the bottom layer consists of 25 cubes. The total is 1 + 9 + 9 + 25 = **44 (D)**.

# PRACTICE EXERCISES—SOLID GEOMETRY

## Multiple-Choice Questions

1. The sum of the lengths of all the edges of a cube is 6 centimeters. What is the volume, in cubic centimeters, of the cube?

   (A) $\dfrac{1}{8}$  (B) $\dfrac{1}{4}$  (C) $\dfrac{1}{2}$  (D) 1  (E) 8

2. What is the volume of a cube whose surface area is 150?

   (A) 25  (B) 100  (C) 125  (D) 1000  (E) 15,625

3. What is the surface area of a cube whose volume is 64?

   (A) 16  (B) 64  (C) 96  (D) 128  (E) 384

4. What is the number of cubic inches in one cubic foot?

   (A) 12  (B) 24  (C) 144  (D) 684  (E) 1728

5. A solid metal cube of edge 3 feet is placed in a rectangular tank whose length, width, and height are 3, 4, and 5 feet, respectively. What is the volume, in cubic feet, of water that the tank can now hold?

   (A) 20  (B) 27  (C) 33  (D) 48  (E) 60

6. The height, $h$, of a cylinder is equal to the edge of a cube. If the cylinder and cube have the same volume, what is the radius of the cylinder?

   (A) $\dfrac{h}{\sqrt{\pi}}$  (B) $h\sqrt{\pi}$  (C) $\dfrac{\sqrt{\pi}}{h}$  (D) $\dfrac{h^2}{\pi}$  (E) $\pi h^2$

7. A rectangular tank has a base that is 10 centimeters by 5 centimeters and a height of 20 centimeters. If the tank is half full of water, by how many centimeters will the water level rise if 325 cubic centimeters of water are poured into the tank?

   (A) 3.25  (B) 6.5  (C) 16.25  (D) 32.5  (E) 65

8. A 5-foot-long cylindrical pipe has an inner diameter of 6 feet and an outer diameter of 8 feet. If the total surface area (inside and out, including the ends) is $k\pi$, what is the value of $k$?

   (A) 7  (B) 40  (C) 48  (D) 70  (E) 84

9. If the height of a cylinder is 4 times its circumference, what is the volume of the cylinder in terms of its circumference, $C$?

   (A) $\dfrac{C^3}{\pi}$  (B) $\dfrac{2C^3}{\pi}$  (C) $\dfrac{2C^2}{\pi^2}$  (D) $\dfrac{\pi C^2}{4}$
   (E) $4\pi C^3$

10. Three identical balls fit snugly into a cylindrical can: the radius of the spheres equals the radius of the can, and the balls just touch the bottom and the top of the can. If the formula for the volume of a sphere is $V = \dfrac{4}{3}\pi r^3$, what fraction of the volume of the can is taken up by the balls?

    (A) $\dfrac{1}{6}$  (B) $\dfrac{1}{3}$  (C) $\dfrac{1}{2}$  (D) $\dfrac{2}{3}$
    (E) $\dfrac{3}{4}$

## Quantitative Comparison Questions

| Column A | Column B |
|---|---|

Jack and Jill each roll a sheet of $9 \times 12$ paper to form a cylinder.
Jack tapes the two 9-inch edges together.
Jill tapes the two 12-inch edges together.

11.

| The volume of Jack's cylinder | The volume of Jill's cylinder |
|---|---|

12.

| The volume of a cube whose edges are 6 | The volume of a box whose dimensions are 5, 6, and 7 |
|---|---|

$A$ is the surface area of a rectangular box in square units.
$V$ is the volume of the same box in cubic units.

13.

| $A$ | $V$ |
|---|---|

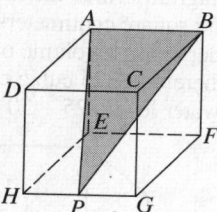

$P$ is a point on edge $GH$ of cube $ABCDEFGH$. Each edge of the cube is 1.

14.

| The area of $\triangle ABP$ | 1 |
|---|---|

15.

| The volume of a sphere whose radius is 1 | The volume of a cube whose edge is 1 |
|---|---|

# Answer Key

| | | |
|---|---|---|
| 1. **A** | 6. **A** | 11. **A** |
| 2. **C** | 7. **B** | 12. **A** |
| 3. **C** | 8. **E** | 13. **D** |
| 4. **E** | 9. **A** | 14. **B** |
| 5. **C** | 10. **D** | 15. **A** |

# Answer Explanations

1.  **A.**  Since a cube has 12 edges, we have
    $$12e = 6 \Rightarrow e = \frac{1}{2}. \text{ Therefore,}$$
    $$V = e^3 = \left(\frac{1}{2}\right)^3 = \frac{1}{8}.$$

2.  **C.**  Since the surface area is 150, each of the 6 faces is a square whose area is $150 \div 6 = 25$. So the edges are all 5, and the volume is $5^3 = 125$.

3.  **C.**  Since the volume of the cube is 64, we have $e^3 = 64 \Rightarrow e = 4$. The surface area is $6e^2 = 6 \times 16 = 96$.

4.  **E.**  The volume of a cube whose edges are 1 foot can be expressed in either of two ways:
    $$(1 \text{ foot})^3 = 1 \text{ cubic foot or}$$
    $$(12 \text{ inches})^3 = 1728 \text{ cubic inches.}$$

5.  **C.**  The volume of the tank is $3 \times 4 \times 5 = 60$ cubic units, but the solid cube is taking up $3^3 = 27$ cubic units. Therefore, the tank can hold $60 - 27 = 33$ cubic units of water.

6.  **A.**  Since the volumes are equal, $\pi r^2 h = e^3 = h^3$. Therefore,
    $$\pi r^2 = h^2 \Rightarrow r^2 = \frac{h^2}{\pi} \Rightarrow r = \frac{h}{\sqrt{\pi}}.$$

7.  **B.**  Draw a diagram. Since the area of the base is $5 \times 10 = 50$ square centimeters, each 1 centimeter of depth has a volume of 50 cubic centimeters. Therefore, 325 cubic centimeters will raise the water level $325 \div 50 = 6.5$ centimeters.

(Note that we didn't use the fact that the tank was half full, except to be sure that the tank didn't overflow. Since the tank was half full, the water was 10 centimeters deep, and the water level could rise by 6.5 centimeters. Had the tank been three-fourths full, the water would have been 15 centimeters deep and the extra water would have caused the level to rise 5 centimeters, filling the tank; the rest of the water would have spilled out.)

8.  **E.**  Draw a diagram and label it. Since the surface of a cylinder is given by $A = 2\pi rh$, the area of the exterior is $2\pi(4)(5) = 40\pi$, and the area of the interior is $2\pi(3)(5) = 30\pi$. The area of *each* shaded end is the area of the outer circle minus the area of the inner circle: $16\pi - 9\pi = 7\pi$, so total surface area =
    $$40\pi + 30\pi + 7\pi + 7\pi = 84\pi \Rightarrow k = 84.$$

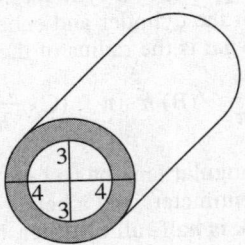

9.  **A.**  Since $V = \pi r^2 h$, we need to express $r$ and $h$ in terms of $C$. It is given that $h = 4C$; and since
    $$C = 2\pi r, \text{ then } r = \frac{C}{2\pi}. \text{ Therefore,}$$
    $$V = \pi \left(\frac{C}{2\pi}\right)^2 (4C) = \pi \left(\frac{C^2}{4\pi^2}\right)(4C) = \frac{C^3}{\pi}.$$

10. **D.**  To avoid using $r$, assume that the radii of the spheres and the can are 1. Then the volume of each ball is $\frac{4}{3}\pi(1)^3 = \frac{4}{3}\pi$, and the total volume of the 3 balls is $3\left(\frac{4}{3}\pi\right) = 4\pi$. Since the height of the can is 6 (the diameter of each

sphere is 2), the volume of the can is

$\pi(1)^2(6) = 6\pi$. So the balls take up $\dfrac{4\pi}{6\pi} = \dfrac{2}{3}$ of the can.

11. **A.** Drawing a diagram makes it easier to visualize the problem. The volume of a cylinder is $\pi r^2 h$. In each case, we know the height but have to determine the radius in order to calculate the volume.

Jack's cylinder has a circumference of 12:

$$2\pi r = 12 \Rightarrow r = \frac{12}{2\pi} = \frac{6}{\pi} \Rightarrow$$

$$V = \pi\left(\frac{6}{\pi}\right)^2(9) = \pi\left(\frac{36}{\pi^2}\right)(9) = \frac{324}{\pi}.$$

Jill's cylinder has a circumference of 9:

$$2\pi r = 9 \Rightarrow r = \frac{9}{2\pi} \Rightarrow$$

$$V = \pi\left(\frac{9}{2\pi}\right)^2(12) = \pi\left(\frac{81}{4\pi^2}\right)(12) = \frac{243}{\pi}.$$

12. **A.** Column A: $V = 6^3 = 216$.
Column B: $V = 5 \times 6 \times 7 = 210$.

13. **D.** There is no relationship between the two columns. If the box is a cube of edge 1, $A = 6$ and $V = 1$. If the box is a cube of edge 10, $A = 600$ and $V = 1000$.

14. **B.** The base, $AB$, of $\triangle ABP$ is 1. Since the diagonal is the longest line segment in the cube, the height, $h$, of the triangle is definitely less than the diagonal, which is $\sqrt{1^2 + 1^2 + 1^2} = \sqrt{3}$. So the area of the triangle is less than $\frac{1}{2}(1)\sqrt{3} \approx .87$, which is less than 1. (You could also have just calculated the area: $h = BG = \sqrt{2}$, so the area is $\frac{1}{2}\sqrt{2} \approx .71$.)

15. **A.** You probably don't know how to find the volume of a sphere; fortunately, you don't need

to. You should be able to visualize that the sphere is *much* bigger than the cube. (In fact, it is more than 4 times the size.)

# 15-N. COORDINATE GEOMETRY

The GRE has very few questions on coordinate geometry. Most often they deal with the coordinates of points and occasionally with the slope of a line. You will *never* have to draw a graph; nor will you have to provide the equation for a given graph.

The coordinate plane is formed by two perpendicular number lines called the **x-axis** and **y-axis**, which intersect at the **origin**. The axes divide the plane into four **quadrants**, labeled I, II, III, and IV.

Each point in the plane is assigned two numbers, an **x-coordinate** and a **y-coordinate**, which are written as an ordered pair, **(x, y)**.

• Points to the right of the y-axis have positive x-coordinates, and those to the left have negative x-coordinates.

• Points above the x-axis have positive y-coordinates, and those below it have negative y-coordinates.

• If a point is on the x-axis, its y-coordinate is 0.

• If a point is on the y-axis, its x-coordinate is 0.

For example, point $A$ in the following figure is labeled (2, 3), since it is 2 units to the right of the y-axis and 3 units above the x-axis. Similarly, $B(-3, -5)$ is in Quadrant III, 3 units to the left of the y-axis and 5 units below the x-axis.

- **All the points on a vertical line have the same $x$-coordinate. To find the distance between them, subtract their $y$-coordinates.**

---

### Helpful Hint

If the points have been plotted on a graph, you can find the distance between them by counting boxes.

The distance from $A$ to $C$ is $6 - 1 = 5$. The distance from $B$ to $C$ is $4 - 1 = 3$.

It is a little more difficult to find the distance between two points that are not on the same horizontal or vertical line. In this case, use the Pythagorean theorem. For example, in the figure above, if $d$ represents the distance from $A$ to $B$, $d^2 = 5^2 + 3^2 = 25 + 9 = 34 \Rightarrow d = \sqrt{34}$.

CAUTION: You *cannot* count boxes unless the points are on the same horizontal or vertical line. The distance between $A$ and $B$ is 5, not 4.

### KEY FACT N2:

**The distance, $d$, between two points, $A(x_1, y_1)$ and $B(x_2, y_2)$, can be calculated using the distance formula:**
$$d = \sqrt{(x_2 - x_1)^2 + (y_2 - y_1)^2}.$$

---

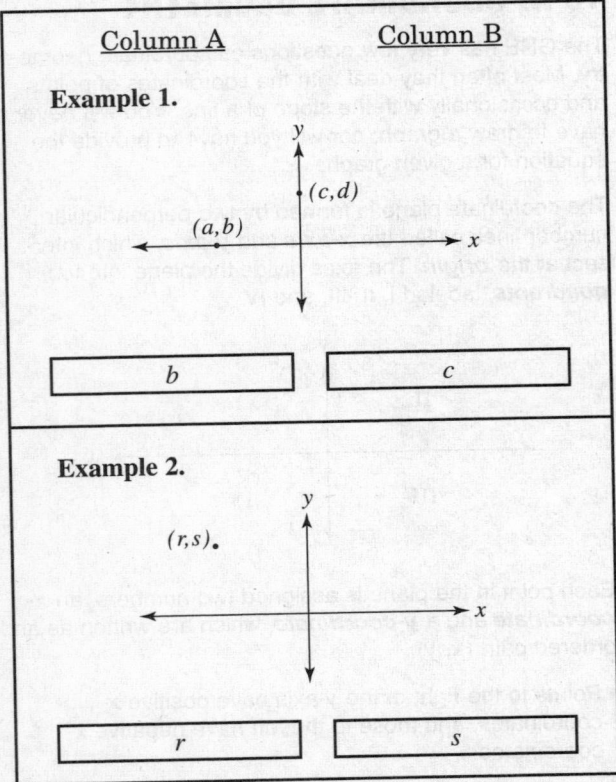

| Column A | Column B |
|---|---|

**Example 1.**

| $b$ | $c$ |
|---|---|

**Example 2.**

| $r$ | $s$ |
|---|---|

SOLUTION 1. Since $(a, b)$ lies on the $x$-axis, $b = 0$. Since $(c, d)$ lies on the $y$-axis, $c = 0$. The answer is **C**.

SOLUTION 2. Since $(r, s)$ is in Quadrant II, $r$ is negative and $s$ is positive. The answer is **B**.

Often a question requires you to calculate the distance between two points. This is easiest when the points lie on the same horizontal or vertical line.

### KEY FACT N1:

- **All the points on a horizontal line have the same $y$-coordinate. To find the distance between them, subtract their $x$-coordinates.**

**Helpful Hint**

The "distance formula" is nothing more than the Pythagorean theorem. If you ever forget the formula, and you need the distance between two points that do not lie on the same horizontal or vertical line, do as follows: create a right triangle by drawing a horizontal line through one of the points and a vertical line through the other, and then use the Pythagorean theorem.

Examples 3–4 refer to the triangle in the following figure.

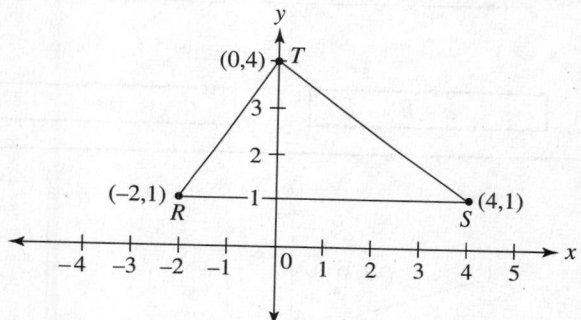

**Example 3.**

What is the area of $\triangle RST$?

(A) 6   (B) 9   (C) 12   (D) 15   (E) 18

SOLUTION. $R(-2, 1)$ and $S(4, 1)$ lie on the same horizontal line, so $RS = 4 - (-2) = 6$. Let that be the base of the triangle. Then the height is the distance along the vertical line from $T$ to $RS$: $4 - 1 = 3$. The area is

$\frac{1}{2}(6)(3) = $ **9 (B)**.

**Example 4.**

What is the perimeter of $\triangle RST$?

(A) 13   (B) 14   (C) 16   (D) $11 + \sqrt{13}$
(E) $11 + \sqrt{61}$

SOLUTION. The perimeter is $RS + ST + RT$. From the solution to Example 3, you know that $RS = 6$. Also, $ST = 5$, since it is the hypotenuse of a 3-4-5 right triangle. To calculate $RT$, either use the distance formula:

$\sqrt{(-2-0)^2 + (1-4)^2} = \sqrt{(-2)^2 + (-3)^2} = \sqrt{4+9} = \sqrt{13}$

or the Pythagorean theorem:

$RT^2 = 2^2 + 3^2 = 4 + 9 = 13 \Rightarrow RT = \sqrt{13}$.

So the perimeter is: $6 + 5 + \sqrt{13} = $ **$11 + \sqrt{13}$ (D)**.

The *slope* of a line is a number that indicates how steep the line is.

**KEY FACT N3:**

• **Vertical lines *do not have slopes*.**
• **To find the slope of any other line proceed as follows:**
   1. **Choose any two points $A(x_1, y_1)$ and $B(x_2, y_2)$ on the line.**
   2. **Take the differences of the $y$-coordinates, $y_2 - y_1$, and the $x$-coordinates, $x_2 - x_1$.**
   3. **Divide: slope $= \dfrac{y_2 - y_1}{x_2 - x_1}$.**

We will illustrate the next KEY FACT by using this formula to calculate the slopes of $RS$, $RT$, and $ST$ from Example 3: $R(-2, 1)$, $S(4, 1)$, $T(0, 4)$.

**KEY FACT N4:**

• **The slope of any horizontal line is 0:**

   slope of $RS = \dfrac{1-1}{4-(-2)} = \dfrac{0}{6} = 0$

• **The slope of any line that goes up as you move from left to right is positive:** slope of $RT = \dfrac{4-1}{0-(-2)} = \dfrac{3}{2}$

• **The slope of any line that goes down as you move from left to right is negative: slope of $ST = \dfrac{1-4}{4-0} = \dfrac{-3}{4} = -\dfrac{3}{4}$**

| Column A | Column B |
|---|---|
| **Example 5.** | |
| Line $\ell$ passes through $(1, 2)$ and $(3, 5)$ Line $m$ is perpendicular to $\ell$ | |
| The slope of $\ell$ | The slope of $m$ |

SOLUTION. First, make a quick sketch. Do not use the formula to calculate the slope of $\ell$. Simply notice that $\ell$ slopes upward, so its slope is positive, whereas $m$ slopes downward, so its slope is negative. Column **A** is greater.

# PRACTICE EXERCISES—COORDINATE GEOMETRY

## Multiple-Choice Questions

1. What is the slope of the line that passes through points (0, –2) and (3, 0)?

(A) $-\frac{3}{2}$  (B) $-\frac{2}{3}$  (C) 0  (D) $\frac{2}{3}$  (E) $\frac{3}{2}$

2. If the coordinates of $\triangle RST$ are $R(0, 0)$, $S(7, 0)$, and $T(2, 5)$, what is the sum of the slopes of the three sides of the triangle?

(A) –1.5  (B) 0  (C) 1.5  (D) 2.5  (E) 3.5

3. If $A(-1, 1)$ and $B(3, -1)$ are the endpoints of one side of square $ABCD$, what is the area of the square?

(A) 12  (B) 16  (C) 20  (D) 25  (E) 36

4. If the area of circle $O$ above is $k\pi$, what is the value of $k$?

(A) 3  (B) 6  (C) 9  (D) 18  (E) 27

5. If $P(2, 1)$ and $Q(8, 1)$ are two of the vertices of a rectangle, which of the following could *not* be another of the vertices?

(A) (2, 8)  (B) (8, 2)  (C) (2, –8)
(D) (–2, 8)  (E) (8, 8)

6. A circle whose center is at (6, 8) passes through the origin. Which of the following points is *not* on the circle?

(A) (12, 0)  (B) (6, –2)  (C) (16, 8)
(D) (–2, 12)  (E) (–4, 8)

Questions 7–8 concern parallelogram $JKLM$, whose coordinates are $J(-5, 2)$, $K(-2, 6)$, $L(5, 6)$, $M(2, 2)$.

7. What is the area of parallelogram $JKLM$?

(A) 35  (B) 28  (C) 24  (D) 20  (E) 12

8. What is the perimeter of parallelogram $JKLM$?

(A) 35  (B) 28  (C) 24  (D) 20  (E) 12

9. What is the slope of the line that passes through $(a, b)$ and $\left(\frac{1}{a}, b\right)$?

(A) 0  (B) $\frac{1}{b}$  (C) $\frac{1-a^2}{a}$  (D) $\frac{a^2-1}{a}$
(E) undefined

10. If $c \neq 0$ and the slope of the line passing through $(-c, c)$ and $(3c, a)$ is 1, which of the following is an expression for $a$ in terms of $c$?

(A) $-3c$  (B) $-\frac{c}{3}$  (C) $2c$  (D) $3c$  (E) $5c$

## Quantitative Comparison Questions

| Column A | Column B |
|---|---|

$m$ is the slope of one of the diagonals of a square.

11.

| $m^2$ | 1 |
|---|---|

12.

| $a - b$ | 0 |
|---|---|

13.

| the slope of line $k$ | the slope of line $\ell$ |
|---|---|

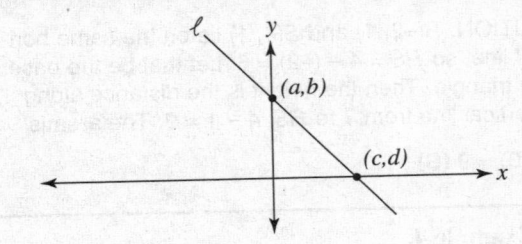

The slope of line $\ell$ is –0.8.

14.

| $c$ | $b$ |
|---|---|

The distance from $(b, 5)$ to $(c, -3)$ is 10.
$b < c$

15.

| $c - b$ | 6 |
|---|---|

# Answer Key

# Answer Explanations

1. **D.** If you sketch the line, you see immediately that the slope of the line is positive. Without even knowing the slope formula, therefore, you can eliminate Choices A, B, and C. To determine the actual slope, use the formula:
$$\frac{y_2 - y_1}{x_2 - x_1} = \frac{0 - (-2)}{3 - 0} = \frac{2}{3}.$$

2. **C.** Sketch the triangle, and then calculate the slopes.

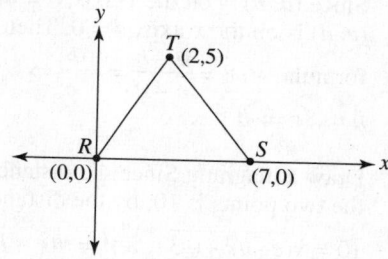

Since $RS$ is horizontal, its slope is 0. The slope of $RT = \dfrac{5 - 0}{2 - 0} = 2.5$. The slope of $ST = \dfrac{5 - 0}{2 - 7} = \dfrac{5}{-5} = -1$. Now add: $0 + 2.5 + (-1) = 1.5$

3. **C.** Draw a diagram and label it. The area of square $ABCD$ is $s^2$, where $s = AB =$ length of a side. By the Pythagorean theorem:
$$s^2 = 2^2 + 4^2 = 4 + 16 = 20.$$

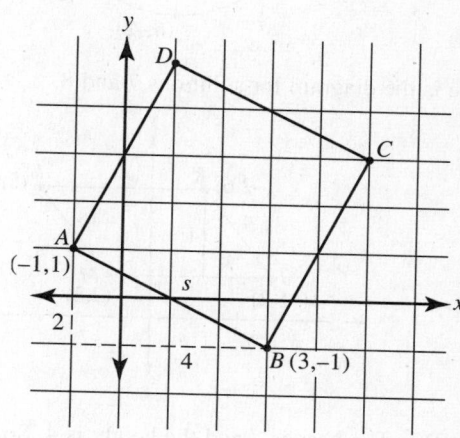

4. **D.** Since the line segment joining $(3, 3)$ and $(0, 0)$ is a radius of the circle, $r^2 = 3^2 + 3^2 = 18$. Therefore, area $= \pi r^2 = 18\pi \Rightarrow k = 18$. Note that you do not actually have to find that the value of $r$ is $3\sqrt{2}$.

5. **D.** Draw a diagram. Any point whose $x$-coordinate is 2 or 8 could be another vertex. Of the choices, only $(-2, 8)$ is *not* possible.

   • $(-2,8)$

6. **D.** Draw a diagram. The radius of the circle is 10 (since it's the hypotenuse of a 6-8-10 right triangle). Which of the choices are 10 units from $(6, 8)$? First, check the easy ones: $(-4, 8)$ and $(16, 8)$ are 10 units to the left and right of $(6, 8)$, and $(6, -2)$ is 10 units below. What

remains is to check (12, 0), which works, and
(–2, 12), which doesn't.

Here is the diagram for solutions 7 and 8.

**7. B.** The base is 7 and the height is 4. So, the area
is $7 \times 4 = 28$.

**8. C.** Sides $JM$ and $KL$ are each 7, and sides $JK$
and $LM$ are each the hypotenuse of a 3-4-5
right triangle, so they are 5. The perimeter is
$2(7 + 5) = 24$.

**9. A.** The formula for the slope is $\dfrac{y_2 - y_1}{x_2 - x_1}$, but
before using it, look. Since the y-coordinates
are equal, the numerator, and thus the fraction,
equals 0.

**10. E.** The slope is equal to
$$\frac{y_2 - y_1}{x_2 - x_1} = \frac{a - c}{3c - (-c)} = \frac{a - c}{4c} = 1 \Rightarrow$$
$$a - c = 4c \Rightarrow a = 5c.$$

**11. D.** If the sides of the square are horizontal and
vertical, then $m$ is 1 or –1, and $m^2$ is 1. But the
square could be positioned any place, and the
slope of a diagonal could be any number.

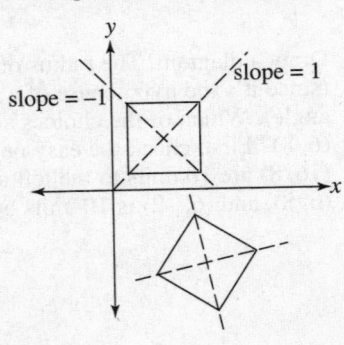

**12. A.** Line $\ell$, which goes through (0, 0) and (1, 1),
also goes through $(a, a)$, and since $(a, b)$ is
below $(a, a)$, $b < a$. Therefore, $a - b$ is
positive.

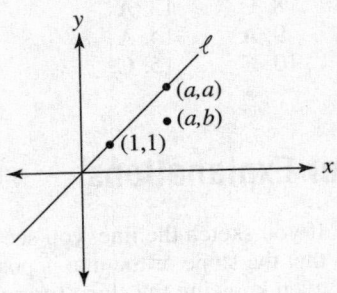

**13. A.** The line going through (–3, 3) and (0, 0) has
slope –1. Since $\ell$ is steeper, its slope is a number such as –2 or –3; since $k$ is less steep, its
slope is a number such as –0.5 or –0.3.
Therefore, the slope of $k$ is greater.

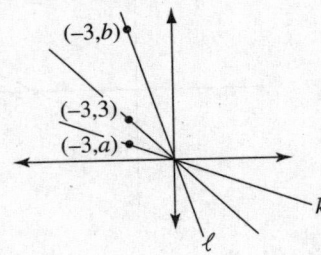

**14. A.** Since $(a, b)$ is on the y-axis, $a = 0$; and since
$(c, d)$ is on the x-axis, $d = 0$. Then by the slope
formula, $-0.8 = \dfrac{0 - b}{c - 0} = -\dfrac{b}{c} \Rightarrow$
$b = .8c \Rightarrow b < c$.

**15. C.** Draw a diagram. Since the distance between
the two points is 10, by the distance formula:
$$10 = \sqrt{(c - b)^2 + (-3 - 5)^2} = \sqrt{(c - b)^2 + (-8)^2} =$$
$$\sqrt{(c - b)^2 + 64}.$$

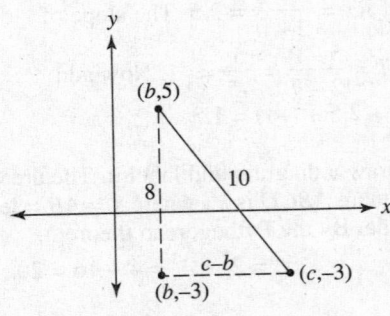

Squaring both sides gives
$$100 = (c - b)^2 + 64 \Rightarrow (c - b)^2 = 36 \Rightarrow$$
$$c - b = 6.$$

# 15-O. COUNTING AND PROBABILITY

Some questions on the GRE begin, "How many ... ." In these problems you are being asked to count something: how many apples can she buy, how many dollars did he spend, how many pages did she read, how many numbers satisfy a certain property, or how many ways are there to complete a particular task. Sometimes these problems can be handled by simple arithmetic. Other times it helps to use TACTIC 8 from Chapter 11 and systematically make a list. Occasionally it helps to know the counting principle and other strategies that we will review in this section.

## COUNTING

### Using Arithmetic to Count

The following three examples require only arithmetic. But be careful; they are not the same.

---

**Example 1.**

Brian bought some apples. If he entered the store with $113 and left with $109, how much did the apples cost?

**Example 2.**

Scott was selling tickets for the school play. One day he sold tickets numbered 109 through 113. How many tickets did he sell that day?

**Example 3.**

Brian is the 109th person in a line and Scott is the 113th person. How many people are there between Brian and Scott?

---

SOLUTIONS 1–3.

- It may seem that each of these examples requires a simple subtraction: 113 − 109 = 4. In Example 1, Brian did spend **$4** on apples; in Example 2, however, Scott sold **5** tickets; and in Example 3, only **3** people are on line between Brian and Scott!

- Assume that Brian went into the store with 113 one-dollar bills, numbered 1 through 113; he spent the 4 dollars numbered 113, 112, 111, and 110, and still had the dollars numbered 1 through 109; Scott sold the 5 tickets numbered 109, 110, 111, 112, and 113; and between Brian and Scott the 110th, 111th, and 112th persons—3 people—were on line.

In Example 1, you just needed to subtract: 113 − 109 = 4. In Example 2, you need to subtract *and then add 1*: 113 − 109 + 1 = 4 + 1 = 5. And in Example 3, you need to subtract and then *subtract 1 more*: 113 − 109 − 1 = 3. Although Example 1 is too easy for the GRE, questions such as Examples 2 and 3 do appear, because they're not as obvious and they require that little extra thought. *When do you have to add or subtract 1?*

The issue is whether or not the first and last numbers are included. In Example 1, Brian spent dollar number 113, but he still had dollar number 109 when he left the store. In Example 2, Scott sold both ticket number 109 and ticket 113. In Example 3, neither Scott (the 113th person) nor Brian (the 109th person) was to be counted.

### KEY FACT O1:

**To count how many integers there are between two integers, follow these rules:**

- **If exactly one of the endpoints is included, subtract.**
- **If both endpoints are included, subtract and add 1.**
- **If neither endpoint is included, subtract and subtract 1 more.**

---

**Example 4.**

From 1:09 to 1:13, Adam read pages 109 through 113 in his English book. What was his rate of reading, in pages per minute?

(A) $\frac{3}{5}$  (B) $\frac{3}{4}$  (C) $\frac{4}{5}$  (D) 1  (E) $\frac{5}{4}$

---

SOLUTION. Since Adam read both pages 109 and 113, he read 113 − 109 + 1 = 5 pages. He started reading during the minute that started at 1:09 (and ended at 1:10). Since he stopped reading at 1:13, he did not read during the minute that began at 1:13 (and ended at 1:14). So he read for 1:13 − 1:09 = 4 minutes. He read at the rate of $\frac{5}{4}$ pages per minute.

### Systematically Making a List

Tactic
O1

When a question asks "How many...?" and the numbers in the problem are small, just systematically list all of the possibilities.

Proper use of TACTIC O1 eliminates the risk of making an error in arithmetic. In Example 4, rather than even thinking about whether or not to add 1 or subtract 1 after subtracting the number of pages, you could have just quickly jotted down the numbers of the pages Adam read (109, 110, 111, 112, 113), and then counted them.

---

**Example 5.**

Ariel has 4 paintings in the basement. She is going to bring up 2 of them and hang 1 in her den and 1 in her bedroom. In how many ways can she choose which paintings go in each room?

(A) 4  (B) 6  (C) 12  (D) 16  (E) 24

---

SOLUTION. Label the paintings 1, 2, 3, and 4, write B for bedroom and D for den, and make a list.

| B-D | B-D | B-D | B-D |
|-----|-----|-----|-----|
| 1-2 | 2-2 | 3-1 | 4-1 |
| 1-3 | 2-3 | 3-2 | 4-2 |
| 1-4 | 2-4 | 3-4 | 4-3 |

There are **12** ways to choose (**C**).

In Example 5, making a list was feasible, but if Ariel had 10 paintings and needed to hang 4 of them, it would be impossible to list all the different ways of hanging them. In such cases, we need the *counting principle*.

## The Counting Principle

**KEY FACT O2:**

If two jobs need to be completed and there are *m* ways to do the first job and *n* ways to do the second job, then there are *m* × *n* ways to do one job followed by the other. This principle can be extended to any number of jobs.

In Example 5, the first job was to pick 1 of the 4 paintings and hang it in the bedroom. That could be done in 4 ways. The second job was to pick a second painting to hang in the den. That job could be accomplished by choosing any of the remaining 3 paintings. So there are 4 × 3 = **12** ways to hang 2 of the paintings.

Now, assume that there are 10 paintings to be hung in 4 rooms. The first job is to choose one of the 10 paintings for the bedroom. The second job is to choose one of the 9 remaining paintings to hang in the den. The third job is to choose one of the 8 remaining paintings for the living room. Finally, the fourth job is to pick one of the 7 remaining paintings for the dining room. These 4 jobs can be completed in 10 × 9 × 8 × 7 = **5040** ways.

---

**Example 6.**

How many integers are there between 100 and 1000 all of whose digits are odd?

---

SOLUTION. We're looking for three-digit numbers, such as 135, 711, 353, and 999, in which all three digits are odd. Note that we are *not* required to use three different digits. Although you certainly wouldn't want to list all of them, you could count them by listing some of them and seeing if a pattern develops. In the 100s there are 5 numbers that begin with 11: 111, 113, 115, 117, 119. Similarly, there are 5 numbers that begin with 13: 131, 133, 135, 137, 139; 5 that begin with 15; 5 that begin with 17; and 5 that begin with 19, for a total of 5 × 5 = 25 in the 100s. In the same way there are 25 in the 300s, 25 in the 500s, 25 in the 700s, and 25 in the 900s, for a grand total of 5 × 25 = **125**. You can actually do this in less time than it takes to read this paragraph.

The best way to solve Example 6, however, is to use the counting principle. Think of writing a three-digit number as three jobs that need to be done. The first job is to select one of the five odd digits and use it as the digit in the hundreds place. The second job is to select one of the five odd digits to be the digit that goes in the tens place. Finally, the third job is to select one of the five odd digits to be the digit in the units place. Each of these jobs can be done in 5 ways. So the total number of ways is 5 × 5 × 5 = **125**.

---

**Example 7.**

How many different arrangements are there of the letters *A*, *B*, *C*, and *D*?

(A) 4   (B) 6   (C) 8   (D) 12   (E) 24

---

Since from the choices given, we know that the answer is a relatively small number, we could just use TACTIC O1 and systematically list them: *ABCD*, *ABDC*, *ACBD*, .... However, this method would not be suitable if you had to arrange as few as 5 or 6 letters and would be practically impossible if you had to arrange 10 or 20 letters.

SOLUTION. Think of the act of arranging the four letters as four jobs that need to be done, and use the counting principle. The first job is to choose one of the four letters to write in the first position; there are 4 ways to complete that job. The second job is to choose one of the remaining three letters to write in the second position; there are 3 ways to complete that job. The third job is to choose one of the two remaining letters to write in the third position; there are 2 ways to complete that job. Finally, the fourth job is to choose the only remaining letter and to write it: 4 × 3 × 2 × 1 = **24**.

## Venn Diagrams

A **Venn diagram** is a figure with two or three overlapping circles, usually enclosed in a rectangle, which is used to solve certain counting problems. To illustrate this, assume that a school has 100 seniors. The following Venn diagram, which divides the rectangle into four regions, shows the distribution of those students in the band and the orchestra.

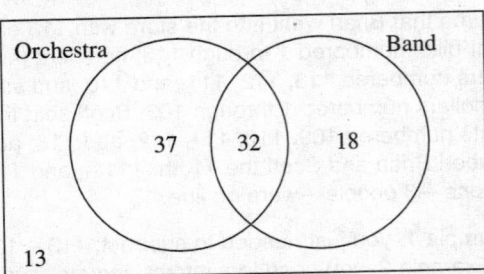

The 32 written in the part of the diagram where the two circles overlap represents the 32 seniors who are in both band and orchestra. The 18 written in the circle on the right represents the 18 seniors who are in band but not in orchestra, while the 37 written in the left circle represents the 37 seniors who are in orchestra but not in band. Finally, the 13 written in the rectangle outside of the circles represents the 13 seniors who are in neither band nor orchestra. The numbers in all four regions must add up to the total number of seniors: 32 + 18 + 37 + 13 = 100. Note that there are 50 seniors in the band—32 who are also in the orchestra and 18 who are not in the orchestra. Similarly, there are 32 + 37 = 69 seniors in the orchestra. Be careful: the 50 names on the band roster and the 69 names on the orchestra roster add up to 119 names—more than the number of seniors. That's because 32 names are on both lists and so have been counted twice. The number of seniors who are in band or orchestra is only 119 − 32 = 87. Those 87 together with the 13 seniors who are in neither make up the total of 100.

On the GRE, Venn diagrams are used in two ways. It is possible to be given a Venn diagram and asked a question about it, as in Example 7. More often, you will come across a problem, such as Example 8, that you will be able to solve more easily if you think to draw a Venn diagram.

---

**Example 7.**

If the integers from 1 through 15 are each placed in the diagram at the right, which regions are empty?

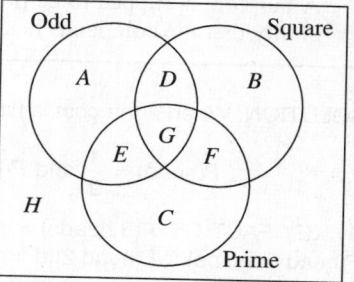

(A) D only   (B) F only   (C) G only
(D) F and G only   (E) D and G only

---

SOLUTION. The easiest way is just to put each of the numbers from 1 through 15 in the appropriate region.

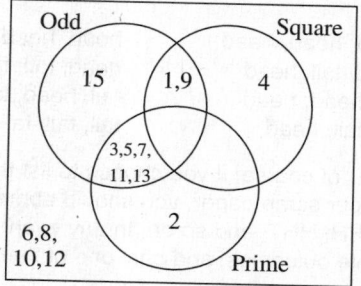

The empty regions are **F and G only (D)**.

---

**Example 8.**

Of the 410 students at H. S. Truman High School, 240 study Spanish and 180 study French. If 25 students study neither language, how many study both?

(A) 25   (B) 35   (C) 60   (D) 170   (E) 230

---

SOLUTION. Draw a Venn diagram. Let $x$ represent the number of students who study both languages, and write $x$ in the part of the diagram where the two circles overlap. Then the number who study only Spanish is $240 − x$, and the number who study only French is $180 − x$. The number who study at least one of the languages is $410 − 25 = 385$, so we have

$$385 = (240 − x) + x + (180 − x) = 420 − x \Rightarrow$$
$$x = 420 − 385 = \textbf{35} \text{ students who study both (B).}$$

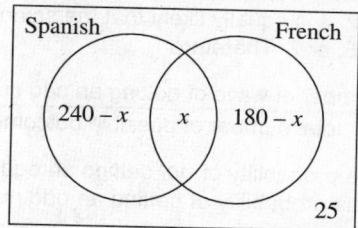

Note: No problem *requires* the use of a Venn diagram. On some problems you might even find it easier not to use one. In Example 8, you could have reasoned that if there were 410 students in the school and 25 didn't study either language, then there were 410 − 25 = 385 students who studied at least one language. There are 240 names on the Spanish class lists and 180 on the French class lists, a total of 240 + 180 = 420 names. But those 420 names belong to only 385 students. It must be that 420 − 385 = 35 names were repeated. In other words, 35 students are in both French and Spanish classes.

# PROBABILITY

The *probability* that an *event* will occur is a number between 0 and 1, usually written as a fraction, which indicates how likely it is that the event will happen. For example, if you spin the spinner below, there are 4 possible outcomes. It is equally likely that the spinner will stop in any of the 4 regions. There is 1 chance in 4 that it will stop in the region marked 2. So we say that the probability of spinning a 2 is one-fourth and write

$P(2) = \dfrac{1}{4}$. Since 2 is the only even number on the

spinner we could also say $P(\text{even}) = \dfrac{1}{4}$. There are 3 chances in 4 that the spinner will land in a region with

an odd number in it, so $P(\text{odd}) = \dfrac{3}{4}$.

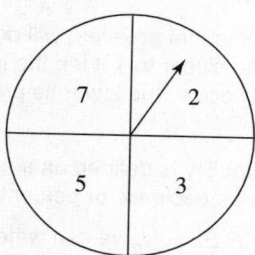

## KEY FACT O3:

If $E$ is any event, the probability that $E$ will occur is given by $P(E) = \dfrac{\text{number of favorable outcomes}}{\text{total number of possible outcomes}}$,

assuming that the possible outcomes are all equally likely.

In the preceding example, each of the 4 regions is the same size, so it is equally likely that the spinner will land on the 2, 3, 5, or 7. Therefore,

$P(\text{odd}) = \dfrac{\text{number of ways of getting an odd number}}{\text{total number of possible outcomes}} = \dfrac{3}{4}$.

Note that the probability of *not* getting an odd number is 1 minus the probability of getting an odd number: $1 - \dfrac{3}{4} = \dfrac{1}{4}$. Let's look at some other probabilities associated with spinning this spinner once.

$P(\text{number} > 10) =$
$\dfrac{\text{number of ways of getting a number} > 10}{\text{total number of possible outcomes}} = \dfrac{0}{4} = 0$.

$P(\text{prime number}) =$
$\dfrac{\text{number of ways of getting a prime number}}{\text{total number of possible outcomes}} = \dfrac{4}{4} = 1$.

$P(\text{number} < 4) =$
$\dfrac{\text{number of ways of getting a number} < 4}{\text{total number of possible outcomes}} = \dfrac{2}{4} = \dfrac{1}{2}$.

## KEY FACT O4:

Let $E$ be an event, and $P(E)$ the probability it will occur.

- If $E$ is **impossible** (such as getting a number greater than 10), **$P(E) = 0$**.

- If it is **certain** that $E$ will occur (such as getting a prime number), **$P(E) = 1$**.

- In all cases **$0 \le P(E) \le 1$**.

- The probability that event $E$ will not occur is **$1 - P(E)$**.

- If 2 or more events constitute all the outcomes, the sum of their probabilities is 1.

  [For example, $P(\text{even}) + P(\text{odd}) = \dfrac{1}{4} + \dfrac{3}{4} = 1$.]

- The more likely it is that an event will occur, the higher its probability (the closer to 1 it is); the less likely it is that an event will occur, the lower its probability (the closer to 0 it is).

Even though probability is defined as a fraction, we can write probabilities as decimals or percents, as well. Instead of writing $P(E) = \dfrac{1}{2}$, we can write $P(E) = .50$ or $P(E) = 50\%$.

### Example 9.
An integer between 100 and 999, inclusive, is chosen at random. What is the probability that all the digits of the number are odd?

SOLUTION. By KEY FACT O1, since both endpoints are included, there are $999 - 100 + 1 = 900$ integers between 100 and 999. In Example 6, we saw that there are 125 three-digit numbers all of whose digits are odd. So the probability is

$\dfrac{\text{number of favorable outcomes}}{\text{total number of possible outcomes}} = \dfrac{125}{900} = \dfrac{5}{36}$.

## KEY FACT O5:

If an experiment is done two (or more) times, the probability that first one event will occur and then a second event will occur is the product of the probabilities.

### Example 10.
A fair coin is flipped three times. What is the probability that the coin lands heads each time?

SOLUTION. When a fair coin is flipped:

$$P(\text{head}) = \dfrac{1}{2} \text{ and } P(\text{tail}) = \dfrac{1}{2}.$$

By KEY FACT O5, $P(3 \text{ heads}) =$
$P(\text{head 1st time}) \times P(\text{head 2nd time}) \times P(\text{head 3rd time})$

$$= \dfrac{1}{2} \times \dfrac{1}{2} \times \dfrac{1}{2} = \dfrac{1}{8}.$$

Another way to handle problems such as Example 10 is to make a list of all the possible outcomes. For example, if a coin is tossed three times, the possible outcomes are

| | |
|---|---|
| head, head, head | head, head, tail |
| head, tail, head | head, tail, tail |
| tail, head, head | tail, head, tail |
| tail, tail, head | tail, tail, tail |

On the GRE, of course, if you choose to list the outcomes on your scrap paper, you should abbreviate and just write HHH, HHT, and so on. In any event, there are eight possible outcomes, and only one of them (HHH) is favorable. So the probability is $\dfrac{1}{8}$.

| Column A | Column B |
|---|---|

### Example 11.
Three fair coins are flipped.

| The probability of getting more heads than tails | The probability of getting more tails than heads |
|---|---|

SOLUTION. From the list of the 8 possible outcomes mentioned, you can see that in 4 of them (HHH, HHT, HTH, THH) there are more heads than tails, and that in 4 of them (TTT, TTH, THT, HTT) there are more tails than heads. Each probability is $\frac{4}{8}$. The answer is **C**.

In Example 11, it wasn't even necessary to calculate the two probabilities. Since heads and tails are equally likely, when several coins are flipped, it is just as likely to have more heads as it is to have more tails. This is typical of quantitative comparison questions on probability; you usually can tell which of the two probabilities is greater without having to calculate either one. This is another instance where TACTIC 5 from Chapter 13 (don't calculate, compare) is useful.

| Column A | Column B |
|---|---|

**Example 12.**

The numbers from 1 to 1000 are each written on a slip of paper and placed in a box. Then 1 slip is removed.

| The probability that the number drawn is a multiple of 5 | The probability that the number drawn is a multiple of 7 |
|---|---|

SOLUTION. Since there are many more multiples of 5 than there are of 7, it is more likely that a multiple of 5 will be drawn. Column **A** is greater.

# PRACTICE EXERCISES—COUNTING AND PROBABILITY

## Multiple-Choice Questions

1. Alyssa completed exercises 6–20 on her math review sheet in 30 minutes. At this rate, how long, in minutes, will it take her to complete exercises 29–57?

   (A) 56   (B) 57   (C) 58   (D) 60   (E) 65

2. A diner serves a lunch special, consisting of soup or salad, a sandwich, coffee or tea, and a dessert. If the menu lists 3 soups, 2 salads, 7 sandwiches, and 8 desserts, how many different lunches can you choose? (*Note*: Two lunches are different if they differ in any aspect.)

   (A) 22   (B) 280   (C) 336   (D) 560   (E) 672

3. Dwight Eisenhower was born on October 14, 1890 and died on March 28, 1969. What was his age, in years, at the time of his death?

   (A) 77   (B) 78   (C) 79   (D) 80   (E) 81

4. How many four-digit numbers have only even digits?

   (A) 96   (B) 128   (C) 256   (D) 500   (E) 625

5. There are 27 students on the college debate team. What is the probability that at least 3 of them have their birthdays in the same month?

   (A) 0   (B) $\frac{3}{27}$   (C) $\frac{3}{12}$   (D) $\frac{1}{2}$   (E) 1

6. There are 100 people on a line. Aviva is the 37th person and Naomi is the 67th person. If a person on line is chosen at random, what is the probability that the person is standing between Aviva and Naomi?

   (A) $\frac{1}{100}$   (B) $\frac{29}{100}$   (C) $\frac{3}{10}$   (D) $\frac{31}{100}$   (E) $\frac{1}{2}$

7. Let $A$ be the set of primes less than 6, and $B$ be the set of positive odd numbers less than 6. How many different sums of the form $a + b$ are possible, if $a$ is in $A$ and $b$ is in $B$?

   (A) 6   (B) 7   (C) 8   (D) 9   (E) 10

8. A jar has 5 marbles, 1 of each of the colors red, white, blue, green, and yellow. If 4 marbles are removed from the jar, what is the probability that the yellow one was removed?

   (A) $\frac{1}{20}$   (B) $\frac{1}{5}$   (C) $\frac{1}{4}$   (D) $\frac{4}{5}$   (E) $\frac{5}{4}$

9. Josh works on the second floor of a building. There are 10 doors to the building and 8 staircases from the first to the second floor. Josh decided that each day he would enter by one door and leave by a different one, and go up one staircase and down another. How many days could Josh do this before he had to repeat a path he had previously taken?

   (A) 80   (B) 800   (C) 640   (D) 5040   (E) 6400

10. A jar contains 20 marbles: 4 red, 6 white, and 10 blue. If you remove marbles one at a time, randomly, what is the minimum number that must be removed to be certain that you have at least 2 marbles of each color?

    (A) 6   (B) 10   (C) 12   (D) 16   (E) 18

11. At the audition for the school play, $n$ people tried out. If $k$ people went before Judy, who went before Liz, and $m$ people went after Liz, how many people tried out between Judy and Liz?

    (A) $n - m - k - 2$   (B) $n - m - k - 1$
    (C) $n - m - k$   (D) $n - m - k + 1$
    (E) $n - m - k + 2$

12. In a group of 100 students, more students are on the fencing team than are members of the French club. If 70 are in the club and 20 are neither on the team nor in the club, what is the minimum number of students who could be both on the team and in the club?

    (A) 10   (B) 49   (C) 50   (D) 60   (E) 61

13. In a singles tennis tournament that has 125 entrants, a player is eliminated whenever he loses a match. How many matches are played in the entire tournament?

    (A) 62   (B) 63   (C) 124   (D) 125   (E) 246

Questions 14–15 refer to the following diagram. A is the set of positive integers less than 20; B is the set of positive integers that contain the digit 7; and C is the set of primes.

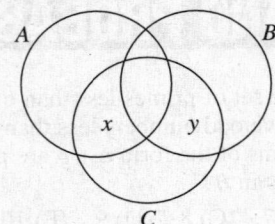

14. How many numbers are in the region labeled x?

    (A) 4   (B) 5   (C) 6   (D) 7   (E) 8

15. What is the sum of all the numbers less than 50 that are in the region labeled y?

    (A) 24   (B) 37   (C) 47   (D) 84   (E) 108

## Quantitative Comparison Questions

| Column A | Column B |
| --- | --- |

16. | The probability of getting no heads when a fair coin is flipped 7 times | The probability of getting 7 heads when a fair coin is flipped 7 times |

A jar contains 4 marbles: 2 red and 2 white. 2 marbles are chosen at random.

17. | The probability that the marbles chosen are the same color | The probability that the marbles chosen are different colors |

18. | The number of ways to assign a number from 1 to 5 to each of 4 people | The number of ways to assign a number from 1 to 5 to each of 5 people |

19. | The probability that 2 people chosen at random were born on the same day of the week | The probability that 2 people chosen at random were born in the same month |

20. | The probability that a number chosen at random from the primes between 100 and 199 is odd. | .99 |

# Answer Key

| 1. C | 6. B | 11. A | 16. C |
| 2. D | 7. B | 12. E | 17. B |
| 3. B | 8. D | 13. C | 18. C |
| 4. D | 9. D | 14. C | 19. A |
| 5. E | 10. E | 15. D | 20. A |

# Answer Explanations

1. C. Alyssa completed $20 - 6 + 1 = 15$ exercises in 30 minutes, which is a rate of 1 exercise every 2 minutes. Therefore, to complete $57 - 29 + 1 = 29$ exercises would take her 58 minutes.

2. D. You can choose your soup or salad in any of 5 ways, your beverage in any of 2 ways, your sandwich in 7 ways, and your dessert in 8 ways. The counting principle says to multiply: $5 \times 2 \times 7 \times 8 = 560$. (Note that if you got soup

and a salad, then instead of 5 choices for the first course there would have been $2 \times 3 = 6$ choices for the first two courses.)

3. B.  His last birthday was in October 1968, when he turned 78: $1968 - 1890 = 78$

4. D.  The easiest way to solve this problem is to use the counting principle. The first digit can be chosen in any of 4 ways (2, 4, 6, 8), whereas the second, third, and fourth digits can be chosen in any of 5 ways (0, 2, 4, 6, 8). Therefore, the total number of four-digit numbers all of whose digits are even is $4 \times 5 \times 5 \times 5 = 500$.

5. E.  If there were no month in which at least 3 students had a birthday, then each month would have the birthdays of at most 2 students. But that's not possible. Even if there were 2 birthdays in January, 2 in February, ..., and 2 in December, that would account for only 24 students. It is guaranteed that with more than 24 students, at least one month will have 3 or more birthdays. The probability is 1.

6. B.  There are $67 - 37 - 1 = 29$ people between Aviva and Naomi, so, the probability that one of them is chosen is $\dfrac{29}{100}$.

7. B.  $A = \{2, 3, 5\}$ and $B = \{1, 3, 5\}$. Any of the 3 numbers in $A$ could be added to any of the 3 numbers in $B$, so there are 9 sums that could be formed. However, there could be some duplication. List the sums systematically; first add 1 to each number in $A$, then 3, and then 5: 3, 4, 6; 5, 6, 10; 7, 8, 10. There are 7 different sums.

8. D.  It is equally likely that any one of the 5 marbles will be the one that is not removed. So, the probability that the yellow one is left is $\dfrac{1}{5}$ and the probability that it is removed is $\dfrac{4}{5}$.

9. D.  This is the counting principle at work. Each day Josh has four jobs to do: choose 1 of the 10 doors to enter and 1 of the 9 other doors to exit; choose 1 of the 8 staircases to go up and 1 of the other 7 to come down. This can be done in $10 \times 9 \times 8 \times 7 = 5040$ ways. So on each of 5040 days Josh could choose a different path.

10. E.  In a problem like this the easiest thing to do is to see what could go wrong in your attempt to get 2 marbles of each color. If you were really unlucky, you might remove 10 blue ones in a row, followed by all 6 white ones. At that point you would have 16 marbles, and you

still wouldn't have even 1 red one. The next 2 marbles, however, must both be red. The answer is 18.

11. A.  It may help to draw a line and label it:

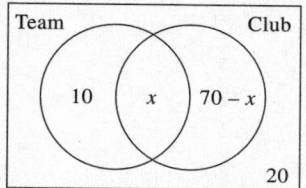

Since $k$ people went before Judy, she was number $k + 1$ to try out; and since $m$ people went after Liz, she was number $n - m$ to try out. So the number of people to try out between them was
$$(n - m) - (k + 1) - 1 = n - m - k - 2.$$

12. E.  Draw a Venn diagram, letting $x$ be the number of students both on the team and in the club. Since more students are on the team than in the club, $10 + x > 70 \Rightarrow x > 60$. Since $x$ must be an integer, the least it can be is 61.

13. C.  You could try to break it down by saying that first 124 of the 125 players would be paired off and play 62 matches. The 62 losers would be eliminated and there would still be 63 people left, the 62 winners and the 1 person who didn't play yet. Then continue until only 1 person was left. This is too time-consuming. An easier way is to observe that the winner never loses and the other 124 players each lose once. Since each match has exactly one loser, there must be 124 matches.

14. C.  The region labeled $x$ contains all of the primes less than 20 that do *not* contain the digit 7. They are 2, 3, 5, 11, 13, 19.

15. D.  Region $y$ consists of primes that contain the digit 7 and that are greater than 20. There are two of them that are less than 50: 37 and 47. Their sum is 84.

16. C.  Don't calculate the probabilities. The probability of no heads is equal to the probability of no tails; but no tails means all heads.

17. B.  The simplest solution is to notice that whatever color the first marble is, there is only 1 more marble of that color, but there are 2 of the other color, so it is twice as likely that the marbles will be of different colors.

18. C.   By the counting principle, Column A is $5\cdot4\cdot3\cdot2$ and Column B is $5\cdot4\cdot3\cdot2\cdot1$. Clearly, the columns are equal.

19. A.   Column A: the probability is $\frac{1}{7}$. Column B: the probability is $\frac{1}{12}$.

20. A.   Every prime between 100 and 199 is odd (the only even prime is 2). So the probability in Column A is 1, which is greater than .99.

# PART FIVE

## Model Tests

# 16 Model Tests

- **5 Full-Length Model Tests**
- **Answer Keys**
- **Answer Explanations**

This chapter is designed to give you further experience in what to expect on the verbal, quantitative, and analytical ability sections of the Graduate Record Examination General Test. These tests should serve as a basis for analysis, which for some may signal the need for further drill before taking the actual test, and for others, may indicate that preparation for this part of the test is adequate. For the best results, take these tests only after reviewing your weak areas, found as a result of completing our Diagnostic Test.

Remember that the actual GRE Test you take will be computer adaptive. Therefore, we strongly recommend that in addition to completing these five model tests, you take a computer-based model test on the optional CD-ROM that accompanies this book. Note that although the model tests in the book cannot be adaptive, each section has the exact same format as the test you will be taking. In each of the five model tests in this book, the order of the three sections is verbal, quantitative, and analytical. On the actual computerized GRE that you take, these sections can appear in any order (and can even be separated by an experimental section).

To best simulate actual test conditions, find a quiet place to work. Have a stopwatch or a clock handy so that you can keep perfect track of the time. Go through each section by answering the questions in the order in which they appear. If you don't know the answer to a question, guess, making an educated guess, if possible, and move on. Do not return to a question that you were unsure of, and do not go back to check your work if you have some time left over at the end of a section. (It isn't possible to do that on a real GRE.) Practice pacing yourself so that you use all your time and just finish each section in the time allowed. Do not spend too much time on any one question. If you get stuck, just guess and go on to the next question.

After you have devoted the specified time allowed for each section of a model examination, refer to the correct answers furnished, determine your raw score, judge your progress, and plan further study. You should then carefully study the explanations for the correct answers of those questions that gave you difficulty. If you find that a particular topic needs further review, refer to the earlier part of the book where this topic is treated before attempting to take the next model test. If you follow this procedure, by the time you complete the last test in this chapter you will feel confident about your success.

# 16 Model Tests

- **5 Full-Length Model Tests**
- **Answer Keys**
- **Answer Explanations**

# Answer Sheet—Model Test 1

## Section 1

1. Ⓐ Ⓑ Ⓒ Ⓓ Ⓔ
2. Ⓐ Ⓑ Ⓒ Ⓓ Ⓔ
3. Ⓐ Ⓑ Ⓒ Ⓓ Ⓔ
4. Ⓐ Ⓑ Ⓒ Ⓓ Ⓔ
5. Ⓐ Ⓑ Ⓒ Ⓓ Ⓔ
6. Ⓐ Ⓑ Ⓒ Ⓓ Ⓔ
7. Ⓐ Ⓑ Ⓒ Ⓓ Ⓔ
8. Ⓐ Ⓑ Ⓒ Ⓓ Ⓔ
9. Ⓐ Ⓑ Ⓒ Ⓓ Ⓔ
10. Ⓐ Ⓑ Ⓒ Ⓓ Ⓔ
11. Ⓐ Ⓑ Ⓒ Ⓓ Ⓔ
12. Ⓐ Ⓑ Ⓒ Ⓓ Ⓔ
13. Ⓐ Ⓑ Ⓒ Ⓓ Ⓔ
14. Ⓐ Ⓑ Ⓒ Ⓓ Ⓔ
15. Ⓐ Ⓑ Ⓒ Ⓓ Ⓔ
16. Ⓐ Ⓑ Ⓒ Ⓓ Ⓔ
17. Ⓐ Ⓑ Ⓒ Ⓓ Ⓔ
18. Ⓐ Ⓑ Ⓒ Ⓓ Ⓔ
19. Ⓐ Ⓑ Ⓒ Ⓓ Ⓔ
20. Ⓐ Ⓑ Ⓒ Ⓓ Ⓔ
21. Ⓐ Ⓑ Ⓒ Ⓓ Ⓔ
22. Ⓐ Ⓑ Ⓒ Ⓓ Ⓔ
23. Ⓐ Ⓑ Ⓒ Ⓓ Ⓔ
24. Ⓐ Ⓑ Ⓒ Ⓓ Ⓔ
25. Ⓐ Ⓑ Ⓒ Ⓓ Ⓔ
26. Ⓐ Ⓑ Ⓒ Ⓓ Ⓔ
27. Ⓐ Ⓑ Ⓒ Ⓓ Ⓔ
28. Ⓐ Ⓑ Ⓒ Ⓓ Ⓔ
29. Ⓐ Ⓑ Ⓒ Ⓓ Ⓔ
30. Ⓐ Ⓑ Ⓒ Ⓓ Ⓔ

## Section 2

1. Ⓐ Ⓑ Ⓒ Ⓓ Ⓔ
2. Ⓐ Ⓑ Ⓒ Ⓓ Ⓔ
3. Ⓐ Ⓑ Ⓒ Ⓓ Ⓔ
4. Ⓐ Ⓑ Ⓒ Ⓓ Ⓔ
5. Ⓐ Ⓑ Ⓒ Ⓓ Ⓔ
6. Ⓐ Ⓑ Ⓒ Ⓓ Ⓔ
7. Ⓐ Ⓑ Ⓒ Ⓓ Ⓔ
8. Ⓐ Ⓑ Ⓒ Ⓓ Ⓔ
9. Ⓐ Ⓑ Ⓒ Ⓓ Ⓔ
10. Ⓐ Ⓑ Ⓒ Ⓓ Ⓔ
11. Ⓐ Ⓑ Ⓒ Ⓓ Ⓔ
12. Ⓐ Ⓑ Ⓒ Ⓓ Ⓔ
13. Ⓐ Ⓑ Ⓒ Ⓓ Ⓔ
14. Ⓐ Ⓑ Ⓒ Ⓓ Ⓔ
15. Ⓐ Ⓑ Ⓒ Ⓓ Ⓔ
16. Ⓐ Ⓑ Ⓒ Ⓓ Ⓔ
17. Ⓐ Ⓑ Ⓒ Ⓓ Ⓔ
18. Ⓐ Ⓑ Ⓒ Ⓓ Ⓔ
19. Ⓐ Ⓑ Ⓒ Ⓓ Ⓔ
20. Ⓐ Ⓑ Ⓒ Ⓓ Ⓔ
21. Ⓐ Ⓑ Ⓒ Ⓓ Ⓔ
22. Ⓐ Ⓑ Ⓒ Ⓓ Ⓔ
23. Ⓐ Ⓑ Ⓒ Ⓓ Ⓔ
24. Ⓐ Ⓑ Ⓒ Ⓓ Ⓔ
25. Ⓐ Ⓑ Ⓒ Ⓓ Ⓔ
26. Ⓐ Ⓑ Ⓒ Ⓓ Ⓔ
27. Ⓐ Ⓑ Ⓒ Ⓓ Ⓔ
28. Ⓐ Ⓑ Ⓒ Ⓓ Ⓔ

## Section 3

1. Ⓐ Ⓑ Ⓒ Ⓓ Ⓔ
2. Ⓐ Ⓑ Ⓒ Ⓓ Ⓔ
3. Ⓐ Ⓑ Ⓒ Ⓓ Ⓔ
4. Ⓐ Ⓑ Ⓒ Ⓓ Ⓔ
5. Ⓐ Ⓑ Ⓒ Ⓓ Ⓔ
6. Ⓐ Ⓑ Ⓒ Ⓓ Ⓔ
7. Ⓐ Ⓑ Ⓒ Ⓓ Ⓔ
8. Ⓐ Ⓑ Ⓒ Ⓓ Ⓔ
9. Ⓐ Ⓑ Ⓒ Ⓓ Ⓔ
10. Ⓐ Ⓑ Ⓒ Ⓓ Ⓔ
11. Ⓐ Ⓑ Ⓒ Ⓓ Ⓔ
12. Ⓐ Ⓑ Ⓒ Ⓓ Ⓔ
13. Ⓐ Ⓑ Ⓒ Ⓓ Ⓔ
14. Ⓐ Ⓑ Ⓒ Ⓓ Ⓔ
15. Ⓐ Ⓑ Ⓒ Ⓓ Ⓔ
16. Ⓐ Ⓑ Ⓒ Ⓓ Ⓔ
17. Ⓐ Ⓑ Ⓒ Ⓓ Ⓔ
18. Ⓐ Ⓑ Ⓒ Ⓓ Ⓔ
19. Ⓐ Ⓑ Ⓒ Ⓓ Ⓔ
20. Ⓐ Ⓑ Ⓒ Ⓓ Ⓔ
21. Ⓐ Ⓑ Ⓒ Ⓓ Ⓔ
22. Ⓐ Ⓑ Ⓒ Ⓓ Ⓔ
23. Ⓐ Ⓑ Ⓒ Ⓓ Ⓔ
24. Ⓐ Ⓑ Ⓒ Ⓓ Ⓔ
25. Ⓐ Ⓑ Ⓒ Ⓓ Ⓔ
26. Ⓐ Ⓑ Ⓒ Ⓓ Ⓔ
27. Ⓐ Ⓑ Ⓒ Ⓓ Ⓔ
28. Ⓐ Ⓑ Ⓒ Ⓓ Ⓔ
29. Ⓐ Ⓑ Ⓒ Ⓓ Ⓔ
30. Ⓐ Ⓑ Ⓒ Ⓓ Ⓔ
31. Ⓐ Ⓑ Ⓒ Ⓓ Ⓔ
32. Ⓐ Ⓑ Ⓒ Ⓓ Ⓔ
33. Ⓐ Ⓑ Ⓒ Ⓓ Ⓔ
34. Ⓐ Ⓑ Ⓒ Ⓓ Ⓔ
35. Ⓐ Ⓑ Ⓒ Ⓓ Ⓔ

# MODEL TEST 1

1

SECTION 1—VERBAL ABILITY

**Time—30 Minutes**
**30 Questions**

**Select the best answer to the following questions, then fill in the appropriate space on your Answer Sheet.**

---

<u>Directions</u>: In each of the following antonym questions, a word printed in capital letters precedes five lettered words or phrases. From these five lettered words or phrases, pick the one most nearly <u>opposite</u> in meaning to the capitalized word.

---

1. ESTRANGE:
   (A) reconcile
   (B) feign
   (C) perplex
   (D) arbitrate
   (E) commiserate

2. PROVIDENT:
   (A) manifest
   (B) prodigal
   (C) thankful
   (D) tidy
   (E) refuted

---

<u>Directions</u>: Each of the following sentence completion questions contains one or two blanks. These blanks signify that a word or set of words has been left out. Below each sentence are five words or sets of words. For each blank, pick the word or set of words that <u>best</u> reflects the sentence's overall meaning.

---

3. Like the theory of evolution, the big-bang model of the universe's formation has undergone modification and _____, but it has _____ all serious challenges.
   (A) alteration...confirmed
   (B) refinement...resisted
   (C) transformation...ignored
   (D) evaluation...acknowledged
   (E) refutation...misdirected

4. A university training enables a graduate to see things as they are, to go right to the point, to disentangle a _____ of thought.
   (A) line
   (B) strand
   (C) mass
   (D) plethora
   (E) skein

---

<u>Directions</u>: Each of the following analogy questions presents a related pair of words linked by a colon. Five lettered pairs of words follow the linked pair. Choose the lettered pair of words whose relationship is <u>most like</u> the relationship expressed in the original linked pair.

---

5. SONG : CYCLE ::
   (A) waltz : dance
   (B) tune : arrangement
   (C) sonnet : sequence
   (D) agenda : meeting
   (E) cadenza : aria

6. OBDURATE : FLEXIBILITY ::
   (A) accurate : perception
   (B) turbid : roughness
   (C) principled : fallibility
   (D) diaphanous : transparency
   (E) adamant : submissiveness

# 1

1

Directions: Each of the following reading comprehension questions is based on the content of the following passage. Read the passage and then determine the best answer choice for each question. Base your choice on what this passage *states directly* or *implies,* not on any information you may have gained elsewhere.

*(This passage was written prior to 1950)*

In the long run a government will always encroach upon freedom to the extent to which it has the power to do so; this is almost a natural
Line law of politics, since, whatever the intentions of
(5)  the men who exercise political power, the sheer momentum of government leads to a constant pressure upon the liberties of the citizen. But in many countries society has responded by throwing up its own defenses in the shape of social
(10) classes or organized corporations which, enjoying economic power and popular support, have been able to set limits to the scope of action of the executive. Such, for example, in England was the origin of all our liberties—won from government
(15) by the stand first of the feudal nobility, then of churches and political parties, and latterly of trade unions, commercial organizations, and the societies for promoting various causes. Even in European lands which were arbitrarily ruled, the
(20) powers of the monarchy, though absolute in theory, were in their exercise checked in a similar fashion. Indeed, the fascist dictatorships of today are the first truly tyrannical governments which western Europe has known for centuries, and they
(25) have been rendered possible only because on coming to power they destroyed all forms of social organization which were in any way rivals to the state.

7. According to the passage, the natural relationship between government and individual liberty is one of

   (A) marked indifference
   (B) secret collusion
   (C) inherent opposition
   (D) moderate complicity
   (E) fundamental interdependence

8. Fascist dictatorships differ from monarchies of recent times in

   (A) setting limits to their scope of action
   (B) effecting results by sheer momentum
   (C) rivaling the state in power
   (D) exerting constant pressure on liberties
   (E) eradicating people's organizations

9. The passage suggests which of the following about fascist dictatorships?

   (A) They represent a more efficient form of the executive.
   (B) Their rise to power came about through an accident of history.
   (C) They mark a regression to earlier despotic forms of government.
   (D) Despite superficial dissimilarities, they are in essence like absolute monarchies.
   (E) They maintain their dominance by rechanneling opposing forces in new directions.

## Sentence Completion

10. We have in America a _____ speech that is neither American, Oxford English, nor colloquial English, but _____ of all three.

    (A) motley...an enhancement
    (B) hybrid...a combination
    (C) nasal...a blend
    (D) mangled...a medley
    (E) formal...a patchwork

11. Rather than portraying Joseph II as a radical reformer whose reign was strikingly enlightened, the play *Amadeus* depicts him as _____ thinker, too wedded to orthodox theories of musical composition to appreciate an artist of Mozart's genius.

    (A) a revolutionary
    (B) an idiosyncratic
    (C) a politic
    (D) a doctrinaire
    (E) an iconoclastic

# 1

# 1

## Antonyms

12. CAPITULATE:
    (A) initiate
    (B) defame
    (C) exonerate
    (D) resist
    (E) repeat

13. INDIGENOUS:
    (A) affluent
    (B) parochial
    (C) alien
    (D) serene
    (E) inimical

## Analogies

14. SCURRY : MOVE ::
    (A) chant : sing
    (B) chatter : talk
    (C) carry : lift
    (D) sleep : drowse
    (E) limp : walk

15. CHAMELEON : HERPETOLOGIST ::
    (A) fungi : ecologist
    (B) salmon : ichthyologist
    (C) mongoose : ornithologist
    (D) oriole : virologist
    (E) aphid : etymologist

## Reading Comprehension

As the works of dozens of women writers have
been rescued from what E.P. Thompson calls "the
enormous condescension of posterity," and con-
Line sidered in relation to each other, the lost continent
(5) of the female tradition has risen like Atlantis from
the sea of English literature. It is now becoming
clear that, contrary to Mill's theory, women have
had a literature of their own all along. The
woman novelist, according to Vineta Colby, was
(10) "really neither single nor anomalous," but she
was also more than a "register and spokesman for
her age." She was part of a tradition that had its
origins before her age, and has carried on through
our own.
(15)    Many literary historians have begun to reinterpret and revise the study of women writers. Ellen
Moers sees women's literature as an international
movement, "apart from, but hardly subordinate
to the mainstream: an undercurrent, rapid and
(20) powerful. This 'movement' began in the late

eighteenth century, was multinational, and produced some of the greatest literary works of two
centuries, as well as most of the lucrative pot-
boilers." Patricia Meyer Spacks, in *The Female*
(25) *Imagination*, finds that "for readily discernible
historical reasons women have characteristically
concerned themselves with matters more or less
peripheral to male concerns, or at least slightly
skewed from them. The differences between tra-
(30) ditional female preoccupations and roles and male
ones make a difference in female writing." Many
other critics are beginning to agree that when we
look at women writers collectively we can see an
imaginative continuum, the recurrence of certain
(35) patterns, themes, problems, and images from generation to generation.

16. In the second paragraph of the passage the author's
    attitude toward the literary critics cited can best be
    described as one of

    (A) irony
    (B) ambivalence
    (C) disparagement
    (D) receptiveness
    (E) awe

17. The passage supplies information for answering
    which of the following questions?

    (A) Does the author believe the female literary tra-
        dition to be richer in depth than its masculine
        counterpart?
    (B) Are women psychological as well as sociologi-
        cal chameleons?
    (C) Does Moers share Mill's concern over the
        ephemeral nature of female literary renown?
    (D) What patterns, themes, images, and problems
        recur sufficiently in the work of women
        writers to belong to the female imaginative
        continuum?
    (E) Did Mill acknowledge the existence of a sepa-
        rate female literary tradition?

18. In the first paragraph, the author makes use of all
    the following techniques EXCEPT

    (A) extended metaphor
    (B) enumeration and classification
    (C) classical allusion
    (D) direct quotation
    (E) comparison and contrast

# 1                                                    1

## Antonyms

19. CHAGRIN:

    (A) frown
    (B) disguise
    (C) make indifferent
    (D) make aware
    (E) please

20. DISINGENUOUS:

    (A) naive
    (B) accurate
    (C) hostile
    (D) witty
    (E) polite

## Sentence Completion

21. When those whom he had injured accused him of
    being a _____, he retorted curtly that he had
    never been a quack.

    (A) libertine
    (B) sycophant
    (C) charlatan
    (D) plagiarist
    (E) reprobate

22. There is an essential _____ in human ges-
    tures, and when someone raises the palms of his
    hands together, we do not know whether it is to
    bury himself in prayer or to throw himself into the
    sea.

    (A) economy
    (B) dignity
    (C) insincerity
    (D) reverence
    (E) ambiguity

## Analogies

23. ASCETIC : SELF-DENIAL ::

    (A) nomad : dissipation
    (B) miser : affluence
    (C) zealot : fanaticism
    (D) renegade : loyalty
    (E) athlete : stamina

24. CAMOUFLAGE : DISCERN ::

    (A) encipher : comprehend
    (B) adorn : admire
    (C) magnify : observe
    (D) renovate : construct
    (E) embroider : unravel

25. SEER : PROPHECY ::

    (A) mentor : reward
    (B) sage : wisdom
    (C) pilgrim : diligence
    (D) diplomat : flattery
    (E) virtuoso : penance

## Reading Comprehension

The physics of elementary particles is notorious for
the fancifulness of its terminology, abounding as
it does in names such as "quark," "flavor,"
*Line* "strangeness" and "charm." One term, however,
(5) even to the nonscientist seems most apt: "gluon."
Physicists conjecture that the gluon is the "glue"
connecting quarks into hadrons or strongly interacting particles (protons, neutrons, pions, etc.).
Initially, physicists envisaged the gluon's adhe-
(10) sive strength to be so powerful that a quark could
not be extracted from a hadron no matter how
great the force brought to bear on it. Furthermore,
the gluon itself also seemed to be permanently
bound: just as no force seemed strong enough to
(15) pry apart the quarks, none appeared strong
enough to squeeze out a single drop of the glue
that bound them. Today, however, some physicists hypothesize the existence of pure glue: glu-
ons without quarks, or gluonium, as they call it.

26. The author refers to charms and quarks (lines
    3–4) primarily in order to

    (A) demonstrate the similarity between these parti-
        cles and the gluon
    (B) make a distinction between apposite and inap-
        posite terminology
    (C) offer an objection to suggestions of similar
        frivolous names
    (D) provide illustrations of idiosyncratic nomencla-
        ture in contemporary physics
    (E) cite preliminary experimental evidence sup-
        porting the existence of gluons

27. The tone of the author's discussion of the neolo-
    gisms coined by physicists is one of

    (A) scientific detachment
    (B) moderate indignation
    (C) marked derision
    (D) amused approbation
    (E) qualified skepticism

# 1

## 1

## Antonyms

28. SPURIOUS:
    (A) cautious
    (B) fantastic
    (C) modest
    (D) genuine
    (E) pertinent

29. TANTAMOUNT:
    (A) not negotiable
    (B) not equivalent
    (C) not ambitious
    (D) not evident
    (E) not relevant

## Sentence Completion

30. It has been Virginia Woolf's peculiar destiny to be declared annoyingly feminine by male critics at the same time that she has been _____ by women interested in the sexual revolution as not really eligible to be _____ their ranks.

    (A) lauded...enlisted in
    (B) emulated...counted among
    (C) neglected...helpful to
    (D) dismissed...drafted into
    (E) excoriated...discharged from

**2**                                                                                                                    **2**

SECTION **2**—QUANTITATIVE ABILITY

**In this section solve each problem, using any available space on the page for scratchwork. Then decide which is the best of the choices given and fill in the corresponding oval on the Answer Sheet.**

Time—45 Minutes
28 Questions

Directions: In the following type of question, two quantities appear, one in Column A and one in Column B. You must compare them. The correct answer to the question is

A if the quantity in Column A is greater
B if the quantity in Column B is greater
C if the two quantities are equal
D if it is impossible to determine which quantity is greater

Notes: Sometimes information about one or both of the quantities is centered above the two columns. If the same symbol appears in both columns, it represents the same thing each time.

| Column A | Column B |
|---|---|
| The sum of the positive divisors of 19 | The product of the positive divisors of 19 |

1.

| Column A | Column B |
|---|---|
| $5(r + t)$ | $5r + t$ |

3.

2.

| $a + b$ | $c + d$ |
|---|---|

| Column A | Column B |
|---|---|
| The average (arithmetic mean) of all the positive multiples of 5 less than 26 | The average (arithmetic mean) of all the positive multiples of 7 less than 26 |

4.

Directions: In the following questions, choose the best answer from the five choices listed.

5. If it is now June, what month will it be 400 months from now?

   (A) January   (B) April   (C) June
   (D) October   (E) December

6. If $\frac{5}{9}$ of the members of the school chorus are boys, what is the ratio of girls to boys in the chorus?

   (A) $\frac{4}{9}$   (B) $\frac{4}{5}$   (C) $\frac{5}{4}$   (D) $\frac{9}{4}$
   (E) It cannot be determined from the information given.

7. What is the volume of a cube whose total surface area is 54?

   (A) 9   (B) 27   (C) 54   (D) 81   (E) 729

2                                                                    2

|   | Column A | Column B |   | Column A | Column B |
|---|----------|----------|---|----------|----------|

8. $(a + b)(a - b)$   |   $a(b + a) - b(a + b)$

Dalia put exactly 75 cents worth of postage on an envelope using only 5-cent stamps and 7-cent stamps.

9.

| The number of 5-cent stamps she used | The number of 7-cent stamps she used |

10. If $A$ is 25 kilometers east of $B$, which is 12 kilometers south of $C$, which is 9 kilometers west of $D$, how far is it, in kilometers, from $A$ to $D$?

(A) 20   (B) $5\sqrt{34}$   (C) $5\sqrt{41}$
(D) $10\sqrt{13}$   (E) 71

| Column A | Column B |

A wooden cube whose edges are 4 inches is painted red.
The cube is then cut into 64 small cubes whose edges are 1 inch.

11.

| The number of small cubes that have exactly three red faces | The number of small cubes that have no red faces |

$c$ and $d$ are positive
$$\frac{1}{c} = 1 + \frac{1}{d}$$

12. | $c$ | $d$ |

A number is a *palindrome* if it reads exactly the same from right to left as it does from left to right. For example, 959 and 24742 are palindromes.

13.

| The probability that a three-digit number chosen at random is a palindrome | $\frac{1}{10}$ |

2                                                                        2

# Total enrollment in higher education institutions, by control and type of institution: Fall 1972–95

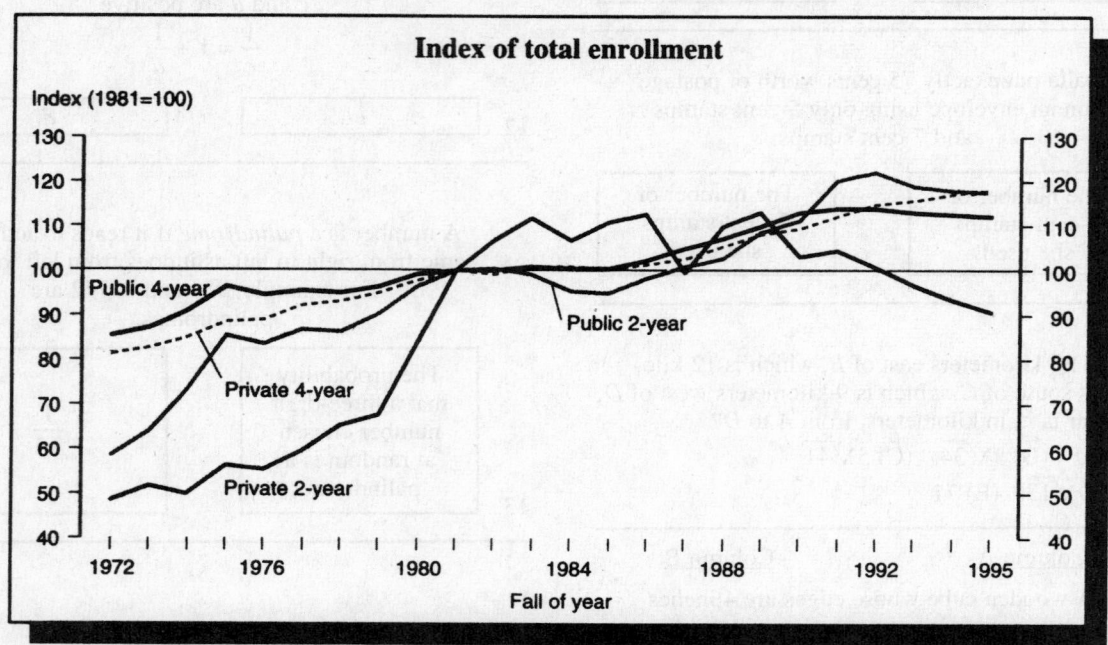

## Index of total enrollment

Index (1981=100)

Public 4-year
Private 4-year
Private 2-year
Public 2-year

Fall of year

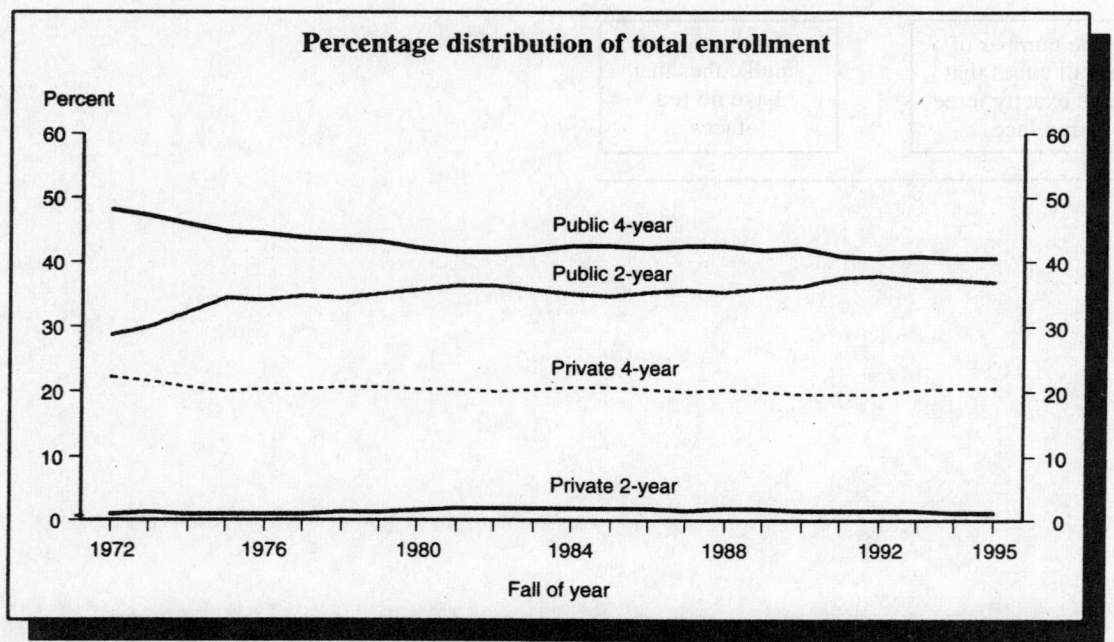

## Percentage distribution of total enrollment

Percent

Public 4-year
Public 2-year
Private 4-year
Private 2-year

Fall of year

SOURCE: U.S. Department of Education.

# 2

# 2

14. In 1995 the number of students enrolled in public institutions of higher education was approximately how many times the number of students enrolled in private institutions of higher education?

    (A) 2   (B) 2.5   (C) 3   (D) 3.5   (E) 4

15. If the total enrollment in institutions of higher education in 1972 was 5,000,000, approximately how many students were enrolled in private 4-year institutions in 1995?

    (A) 1,000,000   (B) 1,100,000   (C) 1,250,000
    (D) 1,500,000   (E) 1,650,000

---

|       Column A       |       Column B       |
| :------------------: | :------------------: |

Jack and Jill each bought the same TV set using a 10% off coupon. Jack's cashier took 10% off the price and then added 8.5% sales tax. Jill's cashier first added the tax and then took 10% off the total price.

16.

| The amount Jack paid | The amount Jill paid |

---

$$\begin{array}{r} ABA \\ \times\, A \\ \hline DCD \end{array}$$

In the multiplication problem above, each letter represents a different digit.

17.

| $B$ | 5 |

---

18. If the lengths of two of the sides of a triangle are 9 and 10, which of the following could be the length of the third side?

    I.  1
    II. 11
    III. 21

    (A) None   (B) I only   (C) II only
    (D) I and II only   (E) I, II, and III

19. Which of the following is equal to $\left(\dfrac{1}{a}+a\right)^2-\left(\dfrac{1}{a}-a\right)^2$?

    (A) 0   (B) 4   (C) $\dfrac{1}{a^2}-a^2$

    (D) $\dfrac{2}{a^2}-2a^2$   (E) $\dfrac{1}{a^2}-4-a^2$

## Percentage of students who reported spending time on homework and watching television

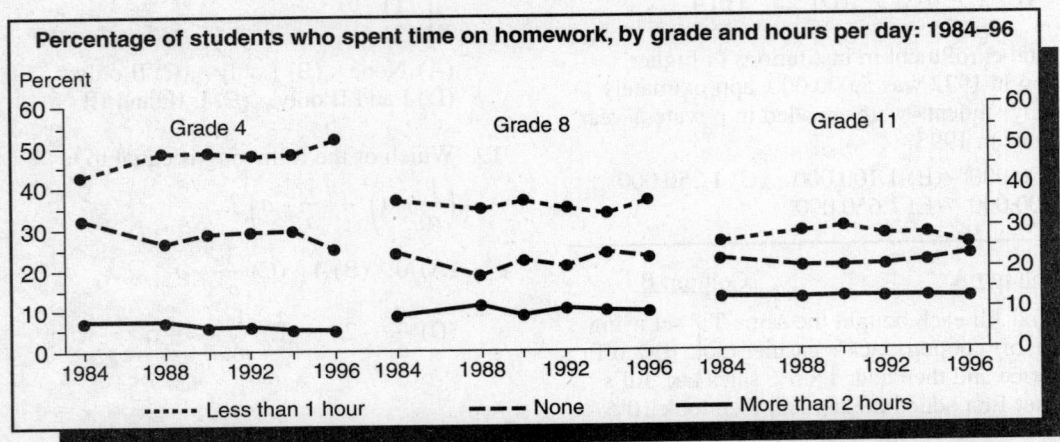

**Percentage of students who spent time on homework, by grade and hours per day: 1984–96**

Percent

Grade 4     Grade 8     Grade 11

······· Less than 1 hour      ━ ━ None      ——— More than 2 hours

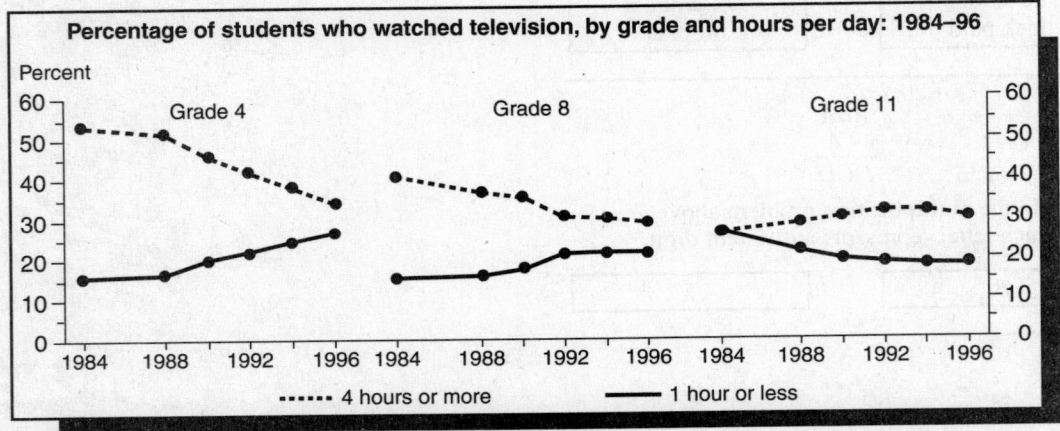

**Percentage of students who watched television, by grade and hours per day: 1984–96**

Percent

Grade 4     Grade 8     Grade 11

······· 4 hours or more      ——— 1 hour or less

SOURCE: U.S. Department of Education.

20. In 1996, what percent of fourth-graders did between 1 and 2 hours of homework per day?

    (A) 5%   (B) 15%   (C) 25%
    (D) 40%   (E) 55%

21. If in 1984 there were 2,000,000 eleventh-graders, and if between 1984 and 1996 the number of eleventh-graders increased by 10%, then approximately how many more eleventh-graders watched 1 hour or less of television in 1996 than in 1984?

    (A) 25,000   (B) 50,000   (C) 75,000
    (D) 100,000   (E) 150,000

# 2

# 2

22. Which of the following expresses the area of a circle in terms of $C$, its circumference?

(A) $\dfrac{C^2}{4\pi}$   (B) $\dfrac{C^2}{2\pi}$   (C) $\dfrac{\sqrt{C}}{2\pi}$   (D) $\dfrac{C\pi}{4}$   (E) $\dfrac{C}{4\pi}$

| Column A | Column B |
|---|---|

23. | The area of $\triangle ABC$ | The area of $\triangle DEF$ |

$A$ is the sum of the integers from 1 to 50, and $B$ is the sum of the integers from 51 to 100.

24. | $B - A$ | 2500 |

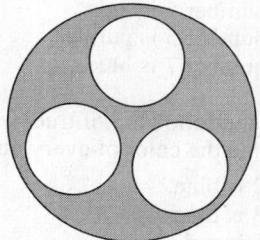

Each small circle has radius $r$, and the large circle has radius $R$.
The areas of the shaded region and the white region are equal.

25. | $\dfrac{R}{r}$ | 2 |

26. If $p$ pencils cost $c$ cents, how many can be bought for $d$ dollars?

(A) $cdp$   (B) $100\ cdp$   (C) $\dfrac{dp}{100c}$

(D) $\dfrac{100\ cd}{p}$   (E) $\dfrac{100\ dp}{c}$

27. Because her test turned out to be more difficult than she intended it to be, a teacher decided to adjust the grades by deducting only half the number of points a student missed. For example, if a student missed 10 points, she received a 95 instead of a 90. Before the grades were adjusted the class average was A. What was the average after the adjustment?

(A) $50 + \dfrac{A}{2}$   (B) $\dfrac{1}{2}(100 - A)$   (C) $100 - \dfrac{A}{2}$

(D) $\dfrac{50 + A}{2}$   (E) $A + 25$

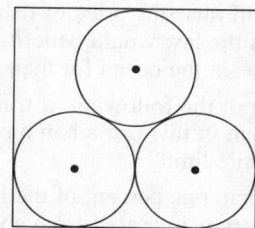

28. In the figure above, each circle is tangent to the other two circles and to the sides of the rectangle. If the diameter of each circle is 10, what is the area of the rectangle?

(A) 300   (B) 400   (C) $100 + 200\sqrt{3}$
(D) $200 + 100\sqrt{3}$   (E) $200 + 200\sqrt{3}$

# 3                                                                    3

SECTION 3—ANALYTICAL ABILITY

Time—60 Minutes
  35 Questions

Directions: In this section, each set of questions is based on a short passage or a set of conditions. Sometimes, in answering these questions, you might want to make a table or diagram. For each question, choose the best answer from the five choices listed.

1. The gill-net is used to catch halibut and sea bass, but up to 72 percent of what it ensnares is not marketable and is thrown back dead. Gill-nets are often called "walls of death" because they entangle and painfully kill mammals such as dolphins, whales, and sea otters. To use the gill-net at sea is like strip mining or clear-cutting on land.

   Powerful lobbyists representing the commercial fishing industry have prevented the legislature from passing a ban on the use of gill-nets within the three-mile limit. They claim that the banning of gill-nets will raise the price of fish. They also charge that the law would benefit rich sport fishermen who want the ocean for their yachts.

   Which one of the following, if true, would support the argument in favor of a ban on gill-nets within the three-mile limit?

   (A) Less than one percent of the fish sold in this country is imported from abroad.
   (B) Gill-net users catch all but two percent of their fish within the three-mile limit.
   (C) The halibut population has fallen to a near extinction level.
   (D) There is a serious overpopulation of the coastal sea otter.
   (E) Coastal sea otters have nearly destroyed the abalone beds along the coast.

## Questions 2–5

John purchased a toy for his young daughter. The toy included nine colorful plastic pieces in the shape of the numbers from 1 to 9. In examining these pieces he made the following observations:

   One piece is purple and two pieces each are red, green, yellow, and blue.
   The two red pieces are consecutive numbers.
   The number 4 is green.
   The two blue pieces are not consecutive numbers.
   Both the 1 and the 9 are yellow.
   The purple piece is not a number immediately greater than or less than either green piece.

2. If one of the red pieces is the number 3, what number is the other red piece?

   (A) 2   (B) 4   (C) 5   (D) 6   (E) 7

3. If the number 5 is green, each of the following could be true EXCEPT

   (A) The purple piece and one of the yellow pieces are consecutive numbers.
   (B) The number 6 is purple.
   (C) The two blue pieces and the purple piece are three consecutive numbers.
   (D) The number 2 is red.
   (E) The number 8 is red.

4. If the number 6 is green, which of the following could be true?

   (A) The number 2 is blue.
   (B) The number 3 is purple.
   (C) The number 5 is red.
   (D) The number 5 is purple.
   (E) The number 7 is blue.

5. Which of the following, if true, would enable you to determine the color of every number?

   (A) The 2 is blue.
   (B) The 3 is blue.
   (C) The 5 is red.
   (D) The 7 is blue.
   (E) The 7 is green.

# 3

# 3

## Questions 6–7

Strict gun control laws cause a decrease in violent crime; in the six months since the city council passed a gun control law, armed robberies in City X have dropped by 18 percent.

6. All of the following, if true, are valid objections to the argument above EXCEPT

   (A) A decrease in crime in one city does not mean that such a decrease would occur anywhere a gun control law was enacted.
   (B) Other factors may have caused the drop in armed robberies.
   (C) Armed robbery is only one category of violent crime that might be affected by a gun control law.
   (D) The gun control law has made it more difficult for citizens to purchase guns for legitimate purposes of self-defense.
   (E) Since the law was passed, murders involving guns in City X have increased by 22 percent.

7. Which of the following statements, if true, would weaken the argument above?

   I. In the six months since the law was passed, 40 percent more police have been hired.
   II. In the six months since the law was passed, accidental deaths by firearms have increased by 10 percent.
   III. Only 30 percent of those indicted under the new law have been convicted.

   (A) I only
   (B) III only
   (C) I and II only
   (D) I and III only
   (E) II and III only

8. Each week the forensics teams at Roslyn High School and Manhasset High School debate each other. Each team has several members, and each week three are selected to debate. Whenever Aviva debates for Roslyn, Roslyn wins; and whenever Zachary debates for Roslyn, Roslyn wins. Whenever Josh debates for Roslyn, Manhasset wins.

   If one week Roslyn lost to Manhasset, which of the following must be true?

   (A) Josh debated for Roslyn.
   (B) Either Aviva or Zachary debated for Roslyn.
   (C) Neither Aviva nor Zachary debated for Roslyn.
   (D) Josh and either Aviva or Zachary debated for Roslyn.
   (E) Josh and neither Aviva nor Zachary debated for Roslyn.

## Questions 9–13

The Fairfield Foreign Film Festival plans to show six films—one each from Belgium, Canada, Denmark, England, France, and Germany. The festival will open on a Thursday and close three days later on a Sunday. Each film will be shown once during the four days of the festival. The order in which the films will be shown must adhere to the following conditions:

   At least one film will be shown each day.
   No more than three films will be shown on any two consecutive days.
   The Belgian film must be shown on Saturday.
   The Canadian film must be shown on the same day as another film.
   The French film must be shown on a day before the German film is shown.
   The Danish film must be shown on a day after the English film is shown.

9. If only one film is shown on Thursday, it could be the entry from which of the following countries?

   (A) Belgium
   (B) Canada
   (C) Denmark
   (D) France
   (E) Germany

10. If the Belgian and French films are shown on the same day, which of the following must be true?

    (A) The film from Denmark will be shown on Thursday.
    (B) The film from Denmark will be shown on Friday.
    (C) The film from Germany will be shown on Thursday.
    (D) The film from Canada will be shown on Sunday.
    (E) The film from England will be shown on Sunday.

11. If the director of the festival decides to show two films on Thursday and two on Sunday, how many films would be eligible to be shown on Friday?

    (A) 1   (B) 2   (C) 3   (D) 4   (E) 5

# 3

# 3

12. If the English and German films are shown on the same day, which of the following must be true?

(A) The film from England will be shown on Thursday.
(B) The film from France will be shown on Friday.
(C) The film from Canada will be shown on Saturday.
(D) The film from Germany will be shown on Saturday.
(E) The film from Canada will be shown on Sunday.

13. If the film from England is shown on Saturday, which of the following films cannot be shown on the same day as any other film?

(A) The film from Belgium.
(B) The film from Canada.
(C) The film from England.
(D) The film from France.
(E) The film from Germany.

14. Excessive amounts of mercury in drinking water, which can only be caused by industrial pollution, have been shown to cause Hobson's disease. Island R. has an economy based entirely on subsistence-level agriculture; modern industry of any kind is unknown. The inhabitants of Island R. have an unusually high incidence of Hobson's disease.

Which of the following can be validly inferred from the above statements?

I. Mercury in drinking water is actually perfectly safe.
II. Mercury in drinking water can have sources other than industrial pollution.
III. Hobson's disease has causes other than mercury in drinking water.

(A) II only
(B) III only
(C) I and II only
(D) I and III only
(E) II and III only

## Questions 15–18

A group of at least three townspeople is to be chosen by the mayor to accompany her on a trip to the state capital. There are seven people who are eligible to be chosen—one man, one woman, two boys, and three girls. In choosing the group, the mayor must adhere to the following conditions:

At least one adult must be chosen.
At least one male must be chosen.
The group selected cannot include all three males.
The group selected cannot include all four females.
If the woman is chosen, at least one of the girls must be chosen.

15. If all three girls are chosen, who else must be in the group?

(A) No one else
(B) The man
(C) One of the boys
(D) The man and one of the boys
(E) The man, the woman, and one of the boys

16. Which of the following could be the complete make-up of the group?

(A) The three girls
(B) Both boys and two of the girls
(C) The woman and two of the girls
(D) The woman, a boy, and two of the girls
(E) The man, both boys, and one of the girls

17. If both adults are chosen, each of the following could be a complete list of the other members of the group EXCEPT

(A) One girl
(B) Two girls
(C) One girl and one boy
(D) Two girls and one boy
(E) Two boys and one girl

18. Each of the following statements about the composition of the group could be true EXCEPT

(A) There are more males than females.
(B) There are more females than males.
(C) There are exactly four members.
(D) There are exactly five members.
(E) There are exactly six members.

# 3

# 3

19. *Chariots of Fire* may have caught professional critics off guard in 1982 as the Motion Picture Academy's choice for an Oscar as the year's best film, but it won wide audience approval as superb entertainment.

    This award-winning film has a theme that extols traditional religious values—without a shred of offensive sex, violence, or profanity.

    Those who condemn the motion picture industry for producing many objectionable films can do their part by patronizing wholesome ones, thereby encouraging future Academy Award judges to recognize and reward decency.

    Which one of the following is a basic assumption underlying the final sentence of the passage?

    (A) Academy judges are not decent people.
    (B) The popularity of a film influences academy judges.
    (C) Future academy judges will be better than past ones.
    (D) There are those who condemn the motion picture industry.
    (E) *Chariots of Fire* is a patronizing film.

## Questions 20–23

Each of the integers from 1 to 7, inclusive, is to be assigned to one of two sets—X and Y—such that:

> No integer is a member of both sets.
> Neither set has more than four members.
> 1 and 4 must be in the same set.
> If 2 is a member of set X, then so is 7.
> If 6 is a member of set Y, then 5 is not a member of Y.

20. Which of the following could be a complete list of the integers in set X?

    (A) 1, 4
    (B) 1, 2, 7
    (C) 1, 4, 7
    (D) 1, 2, 4
    (E) 1, 4, 5, 7

21. Which of the following CANNOT be true?

    (A) 4 and 7 are in X.
    (B) 5 and 6 are in X.
    (C) 1 and 2 are in Y.
    (D) 1, 3, and 7 are in X.
    (E) 2, 3, and 6 are in Y.

22. If 5 and 7 are both members of set Y, how many different ways are there to assign the other five numbers to the two sets?

    (A) 1   (B) 2   (C) 3   (D) 5   (E) 6

23. If X has four members, none of which is 1, which of the following numbers must be in X?

    (A) 2   (B) 3   (C) 5   (D) 6   (E) 7

## Questions 24–28

A four-person congressional committee is to be formed consisting of two senators and two representatives. The senators are to be chosen from W, X, Y, and Z; the representatives are to be chosen from P, Q, R, and S. The committee will be chosen by the vice-president subject to the following conditions:

> S will not serve on the committee unless X does.
> Y will not serve on a committee with Q.
> The vice-president has decided that Y or Z must be included, but neither Y nor Z is willing to serve with the other.

24. Which of the following could be the fourth member of a committee that already consists of R, W, and Y?

    (A) P   (B) Q   (C) S   (D) X   (E) Z

25. If neither P nor R is assigned to the committee, which two senators must be on the committee?

    (A) W and Y
    (B) X and Y
    (C) W and Z
    (D) X and Z
    (E) Y and Z

26. Which of the following could be the other three members of a committee that includes Y?

    (A) P, R, Z
    (B) P, S, W
    (C) Q, R, X
    (D) R, S, X
    (E) S, W, X

27. If the vice-president chooses S to be on the committee, which of the following CANNOT be on the committee?

    (A) P   (B) Q   (C) R   (D) W   (E) X

28. If Q is chosen to be on the committee and X is not chosen, how many different committees could be formed?

    (A) 1   (B) 2   (C) 3   (D) 4   (E) 6

# 3

# 3

29. Now Mesa Electronics brings tomorrow's technology to today's home stereo. The same space-age circuitry used by the Wanderer spacecraft to send images of the most distant planets back to earth has been incorporated in the new Mesa X-2700 stereo system. If your home entertainment is important to you, why settle for an old-fashioned stereo system when the Mesa X-2700 is priced at only a few dollars more?

The most serious logical weakness of this argument is its failure to

(A) provide technical data on the manufacturing specifications of the Mesa X-2700
(B) show the relevance of space-age circuitry to the requirements of home stereo
(C) specify the exact price difference between the Mesa X-2700 and old-fashioned stereo systems
(D) acknowledge the contributions of scientists in the space program to the development of the advanced circuitry mentioned
(E) explain the precise meaning of the technical terms used

30. There are 39 members on the Central High School student government council. When a vote took place on a certain proposal, all of the seniors and none of the freshmen voted for it. Some of the juniors and some of the sophomores voted for the proposal and some voted against it.

If a simple majority of the votes cast is required for the proposal to be adopted, which of the following statements, if true, would enable you to determine whether the proposal was adopted?

(A) There are more seniors than freshmen on the council.
(B) A majority of the freshmen and a majority of the sophomores voted for the proposal.
(C) There are 18 seniors on the council.
(D) There are the same number of seniors and freshmen combined as there are sophomores and juniors combined.
(E) There are more juniors than sophomores and freshmen combined, and more than 90% of the juniors voted against the proposal.

## Questions 31–34

Seven applicants for a job—F, G, H, I, J, K, and L—are each to be interviewed on Monday or Tuesday. Each applicant is to be interviewed exactly once, and the interview schedule must conform to the following conditions:

There must be at least two interviews each day.
I cannot have the first interview on Monday.
F must have the first or last interview on either Monday or Tuesday.
H and L must interview on the same day, with no other applicant interviewing between them.
I and K cannot interview on the same day.
At least one interview must be scheduled between the interviews of G and L.

31. Which of the following is an acceptable schedule, in order, of interviews for the seven applicants?

| | Monday | Tuesday |
|---|---|---|
| (A) | H, L | F, G, I, J, K |
| (B) | K, J, G | L, H, I, F |
| (C) | H, K, L, F | I, G, J |
| (D) | L, H, I, J | K, F, G |
| (E) | L, H, K, J | I, G, F |

32. If G has the very first interview, and if exactly four people are interviewed on Tuesday, which of the following could be the schedule for the two interviews immediately following G's?

(A) First H, then L
(B) First L, then F
(C) First I, then J
(D) First F, then I
(E) First H, then F

33. If the only applicants who have interviews on Monday are F, I, and J, and if H is the first applicant to be interviewed on Tuesday, which of the following statements must be true?

(A) K has the second interview on Tuesday.
(B) G has the third interview on Tuesday.
(C) L has the third interview on Tuesday.
(D) G has the last interview on Tuesday.
(E) K has the last interview on Tuesday.

# 3                                                    3

34. If three interviews are scheduled for Monday, and if H and I have the first and last interviews, respectively, on Tuesday, which of the following must be true?

(A) F has the first interview on Monday.
(B) F has the third interview on Monday.
(C) G has an interview on Tuesday.
(D) J has the second interview on Tuesday.
(E) J has the third interview on Tuesday.

35. Sales of new homes in Arizona fell almost 20 percent in the month of February, compared to last year. Analysts attribute the decline to several factors. Record rainfalls kept both builders and buyers indoors for most of the month. The rise in the interest rates has brought mortgage rates to a ten-month high. Both the sales of new homes and housing starts have reached new lows. With every indication that mortgage rates will remain high for the rest of the year, Arizona home-builders foresee a very grim year ahead.

Which one of the following would add support to the conclusion of this passage?

(A) Last year's sales increased in the second half of the year, despite some increase in interest rates.
(B) Last year's sales were accelerated by good weather in January and February.
(C) Widespread advertising and incentives to attract buyers this February were ineffective.
(D) Rain in Arizona usually ends late in February.
(E) Home sales and building starts throughout the country are about the same this year as last year.

# Answer Key

## Section 1—Verbal Ability

| | | | | | |
|---|---|---|---|---|---|
| 1. A | 6. E | 11. D | 16. D | 21. C | 26. D |
| 2. B | 7. C | 12. D | 17. E | 22. E | 27. D |
| 3. B | 8. E | 13. C | 18. B | 23. C | 28. D |
| 4. E | 9. C | 14. B | 19. E | 24. A | 29. B |
| 5. C | 10. B | 15. B | 20. A | 25. B | 30. D |

## Section 2—Quantitative Ability

NOTE: The letters in brackets following the Quantitative Ability answers refer to the sections of Chapter 15 in which you can find the information you need to answer the questions. For example, 1. C [E] means that the answer to question 1 is C, and that the solution requires information found in Section 15-E: Averages. Also, 20. A [14] means that the answer to question 20 is based on information in Chapter 14: Data Interpretation.

| | | | | | |
|---|---|---|---|---|---|
| 1. A [A] | 6. B [B,D] | 11. C [M] | 16. C [C] | 21. E [14] | 26. E [D] |
| 2. A [N] | 7. B [M] | 12. B [B] | 17. B [A] | 22. A [L] | 27. A [E,H] |
| 3. D [A] | 8. C [F] | 13. C [O] | 18. C [J] | 23. A [J] | 28. D [K,L] |
| 4. A [A,E] | 9. D [O] | 14. D [14] | 19. B [F] | 24. C [A] | |
| 5. D [A] | 10. A [J] | 15. E [14] | 20. B [14] | 25. A [L] | |

## Section 3—Analytical Ability

| | | | | |
|---|---|---|---|---|
| 1. C | 8. C | 15. B | 22. B | 29. B |
| 2. A | 9. D | 16. D | 23. E | 30. C |
| 3. B | 10. B | 17. E | 24. A | 31. E |
| 4. E | 11. D | 18. E | 25. D | 32. C |
| 5. E | 12. E | 19. B | 26. D | 33. D |
| 6. D | 13. E | 20. E | 27. D | 34. E |
| 7. A | 14. B | 21. D | 28. B | 35. C |

# Answer Explanations

## Section 1—Verbal Ability

1.  A.  The opposite of to *estrange* or to alienate is to *reconcile*.
    Think of "estranged couples" in a divorce.

2.  B.  The opposite of *provident* or frugal is *prodigal* or extravagant.
    Think of the fable of the prodigal grasshopper and the provident ant.

3.  B.  The author concedes that the big-bang theory has been changed somewhat: it has undergone *refinement* or polishing. However, he denies that its validity has been threatened seriously by any rival theories: it has *resisted* or defied all challenges.
    The use of the support signal *and* indicates that the first missing word is similar in mean-

ing to "modification." The use of the contrast signal *but* indicates that the second missing word is contrary in meaning to "undergone modification."

4.  E.  One would have to disentangle a *skein* or coiled and twisted bundle of yarn.
    Note how the presence of the verb *disentangle*, which may be used both figuratively and literally, influences the writer's choice of words. In this case, while *line* and *strand* are possible choices, neither word possesses the connotations of twistings and tangled contortions that make *skein* the most suitable choice.

5.  C.  A *song* is part of a *cycle* or series of songs. A *sonnet* is part of a *sequence* or series of sonnets.                    (Group and Member)

6.  E.  Someone *obdurate* (unyielding, inflexible) is lacking in *flexibility*. Someone *adamant*

(unshakable in opposition) is lacking in *sub-missiveness*.                    (Antonym Variant)

7.  C.  The author says that the tendency for a government to encroach upon individual liberty to the extent to which it has the power to do so is "almost a natural law" of politics. Thus, government and individual liberty are *inherently* by their very natures in *opposition* to one another.

8.  E.  The final sentence states that the fascist dictatorships "destroyed (*eradicated*) all forms of social organization that were in any way rivals to the state."

9.  C.  If the fascist dictatorships "are the first truly tyrannical governments which western Europe has known for centuries," then it can be inferred that centuries ago there were tyrannical or *despotic* governments in western Europe. Thus, the fascist governments represent a *regression* or reversion to an earlier form of government.

10.  B.  Speech that is *hybrid* (made up of several elements) by definition combines these elements. The technical term *hybrid* best suits this context because it is a neutral term devoid of negative connotations (which *motley* and *mangled* possess).

11.  D.  A man too wedded to *orthodox* theories or doctrines can best be described as *doctrinaire* or dogmatic.

12.  D.  The opposite of to *capitulate* or yield is to *resist*.
    Think of "capitulating without a fight."

13.  C.  The opposite of *indigenous* or native is *alien* or foreign.
    Beware eye-catchers. Choice A is incorrect.
    Do not confuse *indigenous* or native with *indigent* or poor.

14.  B.  To *scurry* is to *move* in a brisk and rapid manner. To *chatter* is to *talk* in a brisk and rapid manner.                    (Manner)

15.  B.  A *chameleon*, a kind of lizard, is studied by a *herpetologist* (scientist who studies reptiles and amphibians). A *salmon*, a kind of fish, is studied by an *ichthyologist*.
                    (Defining Characteristic)

16.  D.  The author opens the paragraph by stating that many literary critics have begun reinterpreting the study of women's literature. She then goes on to cite individual comments that support her assertion. Clearly, she is *receptive* or open to the ideas of these writers, for they and she share a common sense of the need to reinterpret their common field.

Choices A and B are incorrect. The author cites the literary critics straightforwardly, presenting their statements as evidence supporting her thesis.
Choice C is incorrect. The author does not *disparage* or belittle these critics. By quoting them respectfully she implicitly acknowledges their competence.
Choice E is incorrect. The author quotes the critics as acknowledged experts in the field. However, she is quite ready to disagree with their conclusions (as she disagrees with Moers' view of women's literature as an international movement). Clearly, she does not look on these critics with *awe*.

17.  E.  Question E is answerable on the basis of the passage. According to lines 6–8, Mill disbelieved in the idea that women "have had a literature of their own all along."

18.  B.  The writer neither lists (*enumerates*) nor sorts (*classifies*) anything in the opening paragraph.
    Choice A is incorrect. The writer likens the female tradition to a lost continent and develops the metaphor by describing the continent "rising ... from the sea of English literature."
    Choice C is incorrect. The author refers or *alludes* to the classical legend of Atlantis.
    Choice D is incorrect. The author quotes Colby and Thompson.
    Choice E is incorrect. The author contrasts the revised view of women's literature with Mill's view.

19.  E.  The opposite of to *chagrin* (disappoint) is to *please*.
    Beware eye-catchers. Choice A is incorrect. *Chagrin* is unrelated to *grin*.
    Think of "being chagrined by a defeat."

20.  A.  The opposite of *disingenuous* or guileful (giving a false impression of naiveté) is *naive* or unsophisticated.
    Think of a "disingenuous appearance of candor."

21.  C.  *Charlatan* is another term for a *quack* or pretender to medical knowledge.

22.  E.  The statement that "we do not know" whether a gesture indicates devotion or despair suggests that gestures are by their nature *ambiguous* or unclear.

23.  C.  By definition, an *ascetic* (one who practices severe self-discipline) is characterized by *self-denial*. A *zealot* (extreme enthusiast) is characterized by *fanaticism*.
    Beware eye-catchers. A *miser* may hoard wealth, but he is not necessarily characterized by *affluence*. Even poor persons may be misers.                    (Defining Characteristic)

24. **A.** To *camouflage* something is to make it difficult to *discern* or perceive. To *encipher* or encode something is to make it difficult to *comprehend*.                    (Function)

25. **B.** A *seer* or prophet is by definition someone gifted in *prophecy*. A *sage* or wise person is by definition someone gifted in *wisdom*.                    (Defining Characteristic)

26. **D.** The author provides them as examples of what he means by the "fanciful ... terminology" or *idiosyncratic nomenclature* in modern particle physics.

27. **D.** Since the author considers the gluon to be *aptly* named, he clearly views this particular neologism or newly coined term with *approbation*. However, he tempers his approval with *amusement*, for he finds the terms fanciful (capricious, whimsical) as well as apt.

28. **D.** The opposite of *spurious* (false or fraudulent) is *genuine*.
Think of forgers selling "a spurious work of art."

29. **B.** The opposite of *tantamount* or equivalent in value is *not equivalent*.
Context Clue: "Failure to publish is tantamount to suppression."

30. **D.** The incongruity here is that one group finds Woolf too feminine for their tastes while another finds her not feminine (or perhaps feminist) enough for theirs.
Note that the word *peculiar* signals that Woolf's destiny is an unexpected one.

# Section 2—Quantitative Ability

Two asterisks (**) indicate an alternative method of solving.

1. **A.** The only positive divisors of 19 are 1 and 19.
Column A: $1 + 19 = 20$.
Column B: $1 \times 19 = 19$.

2. **A.** Since $(a, b)$ is on the positive portion of the *x*-axis, *a* is positive and $b = 0$; so $a + b$ is positive. Also, since $(c, d)$ is on the negative portion of the *y*-axis, *c* is negative and $d = 0$; so $c + d$ is negative. Column A is greater.

3. **D.** Column A: by the distributive law, $5(r + t) = 5r + 5t$. Subtract $5r$ from each column, and compare $5t$ and $t$. They are equal if $t = 0$ and unequal otherwise. Neither column is always greater, and the two columns are not always equal (D).

4. **A.** Column A: there are 5 positive multiples of 5 less than 26: 5, 10, 15, 20, 25; their average is 15, the middle one [KEY FACT E5].
Column B: there are 3 positive multiples of 7 less than 26: 7, 14, 21; their average is 14.
Column A is greater.

5. **D.** Since $400 = 12 \times 33 + 4$, 100 months is 4 months more than 33 years. So 33 years from now it will again be June, and 4 months later it will be October. [See Section 15-P]
**Look for a pattern. Since there are 12 months in a year, after every 12 months it will again be June; i.e., it will be June after 12, 24, 36, 48,..., 120,..., 360 months. So, 396 (33 × 12) months from now, it will again be June. Count 4 more months to October.

6. **B.** Use TACTIC 3 in Chapter 12: pick an easy-to-use number. Since $\frac{5}{9}$ of the members are boys, assume there are 9 members, 5 of whom are boys. Then the other 4 are girls, and the ratio of girls to boys is 4 to 5, or $\frac{4}{5}$.

7. **B.** Since the surface area is 54, each of the six faces of the cube is a square whose area is $54 \div 6 = 9$. Then each edge is 3, and the volume is $3^3 = 27$.

8. **C.** Column B: $a(b + a) - b(a + b) = ab + a^2 - ba - b^2 = a^2 - b^2$.
Column A: $(a + b)(a - b) = a^2 - b^2$.

9. **D.** If *x* and *y* represent the number of 5-cent stamps and 7-cent stamps, respectively, that Dalia used, then $5x + 7y = 75$. There are infinitely many solutions to this equation, but there are only two solutions in which *x* and *y* are both positive integers: $y = 10$ and $x = 1$ or $y = 5$ and $x = 8$. Neither column is always greater, and the two columns are not always equal (D).

10. **A.** Use TACTIC 1 in Chapter 11: draw a diagram. In the figure below, form rectangle *BCDE* by drawing $DE \perp AB$. Then, $BE = 9$, $AE = 16$, and $DE = 12$. Finally, $DA = 20$, because right triangle *AED* is a 3-4-5 triangle in which each side is multiplied by 4. If you don't realize that, use the Pythagorean theorem to get *DA*:
$$(DA)^2 = (AE)^2 + (DE)^2 = 256 + 144 = 400 \Rightarrow DA = 20.$$

11. C.   Draw a diagram, and on each small cube write the number of red faces it has. The cubes with three red faces are the eight corners. The cubes with no red faces are the "inside" ones that can't be seen. If you cut off the top and bottom rows, the front and back rows, and the left and right rows, you are left with a small 2-inch cube, none of whose faces is red. That 2-inch cube is made up of eight 1-inch cubes. The columns are equal (C).

12. B.   Since $\frac{1}{c} = 1 + \frac{1}{d}$, then $1 = \frac{1}{c} - \frac{1}{d} = \frac{d-c}{cd}$. Therefore, $d - c = cd$, which is positive. Then, $d - c$ is positive, and so $d > c$. Column B is greater.

13. C.   The simplest solution is to realize that there is one palindrome between 100 and 109 (101), one between 390 and 399 (393), one between 880 and 889 (888), and in general, one out of every 10 numbers. So the probability is $\frac{1}{10}$.

The answer is (C).

**The more direct solution is to count the number of palindromes. Either systematically make a list and notice that there are 10 of them between 100 and 199, and 10 in each of the hundreds from the 100s to the 900s, for a total of 90; or use the counting principle: the first digit can be chosen in any of 9 ways, the second in any of 10 ways, and the third, since it must match the first, can be chosen in only 1 way ($9 \times 10 \times 1 = 90$). Since there are 900 three-digit numbers, the probability is $\frac{90}{900} = \frac{1}{10}$.

14. D.   From the bottom graph, we can estimate the percentage distribution of total enrollment to be:

| | |
|---|---|
| Public 4-year  41% | Private 4-year  21% |
| Public 2-year  37% | Private 2-year  1% |
| Total public  78% | Total private  22% |

$78 \div 22 \approx 3.5$, so there were 3.5 times as many students enrolled in public institutions as private ones.

15. E.   In 1972, enrollment in private 4-year institutions was approximately 1,100,000 (22% of the total enrollment of 5,000,000). By 1995, the index for private 4-year institutions had increased from 80 to 120, a 50% increase. Therefore, the number of private 4-year students enrolled in 1995 was approximately 1,650,000 (50% more than the 1,100,000 students enrolled in 1972).

16. C.   Let $P$ = the price of the TV set. Then Jack paid $1.085(.90P)$, whereas Jill paid $.90(1.085P)$. The columns are equal (C). **Use TACTIC 2, Chapter 13, and choose a convenient number: assume the TV cost $100. Jack paid $90 plus $7.65 tax (8.5% of $90) for a total of $97.65. Jill's cashier rang up $100 plus $8.50 tax and then deducted $10.85 (10% of $108.50) for a final cost of $97.65.

17. B.   Since $A$ times $ABA$ is a three-digit number, $A$ has to be less than 4; but 1 times $ABA$ is $ABA$, so $A \neq 1$. Therefore, $A = 2$ or $A = 3$.

$$\begin{array}{c} 2B2 \\ \underline{\times\ 2} \\ 4C4 \end{array} \quad \text{or} \quad \begin{array}{c} 3B3 \\ \underline{\times\ 3} \\ 9C9 \end{array}$$

Since there is no carrying, either $2 \times B = C$, a one-digit number, and $B < 5$, or $3 \times B = C$, and $B < 3$. In either case, column B is greater.

18. C.   By the triangle inequality (KEY FACTS J12 and J13),
• The third side must be *less* than $9 + 10 = 19$. (III is false.)
• The third side must be *greater* than $10 - 9 = 1$. (I is false.)
• *Any* number between 1 and 19 could be the length of the third side. (II is true.)
The answer is C.

19. B.   Expand each square: $\left(\frac{1}{a} + a\right)^2 =$

$\frac{1}{a^2} + 2\left(\frac{1}{a}\right)(a) + a^2 = \frac{1}{a^2} + 2 + a^2$

Similarly, $\left(\frac{1}{a} - a\right)^2 = \frac{1}{a^2} - 2 + a^2$.

Now subtract: $\left(\frac{1}{a^2} + 2 + a^2\right) - \left(\frac{1}{a^2} - 2 + a^2\right) = 4$.

**Use TACTIC 2, Chapter 12. Let $a = 1$. Then $\left(\frac{1}{a} + a\right)^2 - \left(\frac{1}{a} - a\right)^2 = 2^2 - 0^2 = 4 - 0 = 4$.

20. B.   From the top graph, we see that among fourth-graders in 1996:

25% did no homework;
55% did less than 1 hour;
 5% did more than 2 hours.

This accounts for 85% of the fourth-graders; the other 15% did between 1 and 2 hours of homework per day.

21. E.   In 1984, approximately 540,000 eleventh-graders watched television 1 hour or less per day (27% of 2,000,000). By 1996, the number of eleventh-graders had increased by 10% to 2,200,000, but the percent of them who watched television 1 hour or less per day decreased to about 18%: 18% of 2,200,000 is 396,000. This is a decrease of 144,000 or approximately 150,000.

22. **A.** Since $C = 2\pi r$, then $r = \dfrac{C}{2\pi}$, and

    area of circle $= \pi r^2 = \pi\left(\dfrac{C}{2\pi}\right)^2 = \pi\left(\dfrac{C^2}{4\pi^2}\right) = \dfrac{C^2}{4\pi}$

23. **A.** Column A: Since the hypotenuse is 2, the

    length of each leg is $\dfrac{2}{\sqrt{2}} = \sqrt{2}$, and the area

    is $\dfrac{1}{2}(\sqrt{2})(\sqrt{2}) = \dfrac{1}{2}(2) = 1$.

    Column B: Since the hypotenuse is 2, the
    shorter leg is 1, the longer leg is $\sqrt{3}$, and the
    area is

    $$\dfrac{1}{2}(1)(\sqrt{3}) = \dfrac{\sqrt{3}}{2} \approx 0.866.$$

    Column A is greater.

24. **C.** $B - A =$
    $(51+52+53+...+99+100) - (1+2+3+...+49+50)$
    $= (51-1)+(52-2)+(53-3)+...+(99-49)+(100-50)$
    $= 50 + 50 + 50 +...+ 50 + 50 = 50 \times 50 = 2500.$

    **If you know the formula, $\dfrac{n(n+1)}{2}$, for

    adding up the first $n$ positive integers, you can

    use it: $A = \dfrac{50(51)}{2} = 25(51) = 1275$. $B$ is the

    sum of the integers from 1 to 100 minus the
    sum of the integers from 1 to 50:

    $$B = \dfrac{100(101)}{2} - 1275 = 50(101) - 1275 =$$
    $$5050 - 1275 = 3875.$$

    Finally, $B - A = 3875 - 1275 = 2500.$
    The columns are equal (C).

25. **A.** Since the area of each small circle is $\pi r^2$, the
    area of the white region is $3\pi r^2$. Also, since
    the area of the large circle is $\pi R^2$, the shaded
    area is $\pi R^2 - 3\pi r^2 = \pi(R^2 - 3r^2)$. Since the
    areas of the white region and the shaded
    region are equal:
    $$3\pi r^2 = \pi(R^2 - 3r^2) \Rightarrow 3r^2 = R^2 - 3r^2 \Rightarrow$$
    $$R^2 = 6r^2 \Rightarrow \dfrac{R^2}{r^2} = 6 \Rightarrow \dfrac{R}{r} = \sqrt{6},$$
    which is greater than 2. Column A is greater.

26. **E.** Since $p$ pencils cost $c$ cents, each pencil costs

    $\dfrac{c}{p}$ cents. By dividing the number of cents we

    have by $\dfrac{c}{p}$, we find out how many pencils we

    can buy. Since $d$ dollars equals $100d$ cents,

    we divide $100d$ by $\dfrac{c}{p}$, which is equivalent to

    multiplying $100d$ by $\dfrac{p}{c}$: $100d\left(\dfrac{p}{c}\right) = \dfrac{100dp}{c}$.

    You will probably prefer the alternate solution
    below.
    **Use TACTIC 2, Chapter 12. Assume 2 pen-
    cils cost 10 cents. So, pencils cost 5 cents each
    or 20 for one dollar. So, for 3 dollars, we can
    buy 60 pencils. Which of the choices equals 60

    when $p = 2$, $c = 10$, and $d = 3$? Only $\dfrac{100dp}{c}$.

27. **A.** If a student earned a grade of $g$, she missed
    $(100 - g)$ points. In adjusting the grades, the
    teacher decided to deduct only half that num-

    ber: $\dfrac{100 - g}{2}$. So the student's new grade was

    $$100 - \left(\dfrac{100 - g}{2}\right) = 100 - 50 + \dfrac{g}{2} = 50 + \dfrac{g}{2}.$$

    Since this was done to each student's grade,
    the effect on the average was exactly the

    same. The new average was $50 + \dfrac{A}{2}$.

28. **D.** The length of the rectangle is clearly 20, the
    length of two diameters. The width of the
    rectangle is $10 + h$, where $h$ is the height of
    the equilateral triangle formed by joining the
    centers of the three circles. Since the sides of
    that triangle are 10, the height is $5\sqrt{3}$ (KEY
    FACT J11). Then the width is $10 + 5\sqrt{3}$ and
    the area is $20(10 + 5\sqrt{3}) = 200 + 100\sqrt{3}$.

    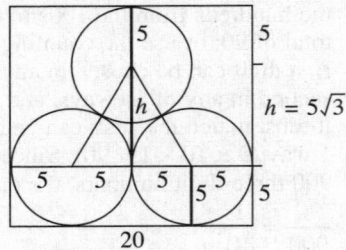

    **Use TACTIC 2, Chapter 11: trust the dia-
    gram. Clearly, the length is 20, and the width
    is much more than 10, but less than 20. You
    should even see that the width must be more
    than 15, so the area is between 300 and 400.

# Section 3—Analytical Ability

1. **C.** If the halibut population is endangered, the
    banning of gill-nets would improve the fish's
    chance for survival. If Choices A and B are
    true, the fisheries' argument about the price
    rise has more merit. If Choices D and E are
    true, the reduction of the sea otter population
    would be more defensible.

**Solutions 2–5**

$$P, R, R, G, G, Y, Y, B, B$$
$$R \ll R \quad 4 = G \quad B \lessgtr B$$
$$1 = Y \quad 9 = Y \quad P \lessgtr G \quad G \lessgtr P$$

2. A. Since the red numbers are consecutive, the other red piece must be the 2 or the 4. However, it is given that the number 4 is green; so the other red piece must be the 2.

3. B. If the number 6 were purple, then the purple piece and one of the green pieces would be consecutive numbers, which violates one of the given conditions. It is easy to show that each of the other choices is possible.

4. E. The following list shows that Choice E does not violate any of the given conditions, and so could be true:

$$\underset{1}{\underline{Y}} \quad \underset{2}{\underline{R}} \quad \underset{3}{\underline{R}} \quad \underset{4}{\underline{G}} \quad \underset{5}{\underline{B}} \quad \underset{6}{\underline{G}} \quad \underset{7}{\underline{B}} \quad \underset{8}{\underline{P}} \quad \underset{9}{\underline{Y}}$$

Each of the other choices violates at least one of the conditions.
Choice A is impossible because if 2 is blue, then the red pieces must be 7 and 8, and then the purple piece would be consecutive with one of the green pieces:

$$\underset{1}{\underline{Y}} \quad \underset{2}{\underline{B}} \quad \underset{3}{\underline{\phantom{x}}} \quad \underset{4}{\underline{G}} \quad \underset{5}{\underline{\phantom{x}}} \quad \underset{6}{\underline{G}} \quad \underset{7}{\underline{R}} \quad \underset{8}{\underline{R}} \quad \underset{9}{\underline{Y}}$$

Choices B and D are impossible because a purple and green piece cannot be consecutive numbers.
Choice C violates the condition that the two red pieces must be consecutive numbers.

5. E. Only Choice E completely determines the colors of each number. If the 7 is green, then since the purple number cannot be consecutive with either green number, the purple number must be 2. Then the red pieces must be 5 and 6 (the only consecutive numbers available), and the blue pieces must be 3 and 8.

$$\underset{1}{\underline{Y}} \quad \underset{2}{\underline{P}} \quad \underset{3}{\underline{B}} \quad \underset{4}{\underline{G}} \quad \underset{5}{\underline{R}} \quad \underset{6}{\underline{R}} \quad \underset{7}{\underline{G}} \quad \underset{8}{\underline{B}} \quad \underset{9}{\underline{Y}}$$

None of the other choices completely determines the colors of each number.

6. D. The argument states that gun control laws reduce violent crime; the evidence is a drop in armed robberies in one city. This involves unwarranted generalizations (Choices A and C), a failure to consider alternative explanations (Choice B), and a possible failure to consider contrary evidence (Choice E). Choice D, however, raises an objection to gun control laws unrelated to either the validity of the evidence or the validity of the conclusion in the argument.

7. A. Statement I weakens the argument by suggesting an alternative explanation for the drop in the crime rate. Statement II has nothing to do with the crime rate. Statement III does not, in itself, suggest that the gun control law is an ineffective *deterrent*.

8. C. Since Manhasset won, neither Aviva nor Zachary could have debated, since if either of them had debated, then Roslyn would have won. None of the other choices must be true, although some could be true.

**Solutions 9–13**

Films: B, C, D, E, F, G   Days: Th, Fri, Sat, Sun
Each day: 1 or 2 films   2 consecutive days: 2 or 3 films
$$B = Sat \quad C\!-\!x \quad F < G \quad E < D$$

9. D. Only Choice D does not violate any of the given conditions.
A violates the condition that the Belgian film will be shown on Saturday (B = Sat).
B violates the condition that the Canadian film cannot be the only film shown on a particular day (C—x).
C and E are impossible. Since the Danish film must be shown on a day after the English film is shown (E < D) and the German film must be shown on a day after the French film is shown (F < G), neither can be shown on Thursday, the first day of the festival.

10. B. The condition that the Belgian and French films are shown on the same day completely determines the schedule. They must be shown on Saturday (B = Sat). To avoid having more than three films being shown on two consecutive days, there can be only one film shown on Friday and one on Sunday, which means there will be two on Thursday. Since (F < G), the German film will be shown on Sunday. Since (E < D), the English film will be shown on Thursday and the Danish film on Friday. Finally, the Canadian film will be the second film shown on Thursday.

| C/E | D | B/F | G |
|-----|-----|-----|-----|
| Th. | Fri. | Sat. | Sun. |

Only Choice B is consistent with this schedule.

11. D. Since only one film can be shown on Friday, it cannot be the Canadian one (C—x); and, of course, it cannot be the Belgian one (B = Sat.). Any of the other four films could be shown on Friday as indicated on the following schedules:

| E/F | D | B | C/G |
|-----|-----|-----|-----|
| Th. | Fri. | Sat. | Sun. |

| C/F | E | B | D/G |
|-----|-----|-----|-----|
| Th. | Fri. | Sat. | Sun. |

| C/E | F | B | D/G |
|-----|-----|-----|-----|
| Th. | Fri. | Sat. | Sun. |

| E/F | G | B | C/D |
|-----|-----|-----|-----|
| Th. | Fri. | Sat. | Sun. |

12. **E.** The condition that the English and German films are shown on the same day completely determines the schedule. They cannot be shown on Saturday (B = Sat); they cannot be shown on Sunday since the Danish film must be shown after the English film (E < D); and they cannot be shown on Thursday since the French film must precede the German film (F < G). So the English and German films must be shown on Friday. To avoid having more than three films being shown on two consecutive days, there can be only one film shown on Thursday and one on Saturday, which means there will be two on Sunday. The complete schedule is as follows:

| F | E/G | B | C/D |
|---|---|---|---|
| Th. | Fri. | Sat. | Sun. |

Only Choice E is consistent with this schedule.

13. **E.** Since the films from England and Belgium are both being shown on Saturday, eliminate Choices A and C. Since the Canadian film may not be shown alone, eliminate Choice B. Finally, since the Danish film must be shown on Sunday (E < D), the French film must be shown on Thursday and the German film on Friday (F < G). Eliminate Choice D. The complete schedule is:

| C/F | G | B/E | D |
|---|---|---|---|
| Th. | Fri. | Sat. | Sun. |

14. **B.** I is denied by the statement that some forms of mercury cause Hobson's disease. II may be true, but it cannot be inferred from the given statement. III alludes to the fact that this island has no industrial wastes and yet has a high incidence of this disease.

## Solutions 15–18

M, W, B, B, G, G, G: at least 3

$M \vee W$    $M \vee B$    $\underline{\text{not } M, B, B}$

$\underline{\text{not } W, G, G, G}$    $W \rightarrow G$

15. **B.** The man must be chosen, because at least one adult must be chosen, and choosing the woman would violate the condition that the group cannot contain four females. Although one of the boys could also be chosen, it is not required.

16. **D.** Only Choice D does not violate any of the conditions. Since an adult must be chosen, eliminate Choices A and B; since at least one male must be chosen, eliminate Choice C; since the group cannot include all three males, eliminate Choice E.

17. **E.** Choice E violates the condition that the group cannot include all three males. None of the other choices violates a given condition.

18. **E.** Only Choice E is impossible. The mayor could choose two males and three females, but the sixth member would either be a third male or a fourth female, each of which would violate one of the given conditions. Each of the other choices is possible.

19. **B.** By urging moviegoers to patronize films *in order to* influence academy judges, the author reveals his assumption that the academy will be influenced by the number of people paying to see a movie.

## Solutions 20–23

X and Y: no # in common

Each set: at most 4 #   hence, each set: at least 3 #

$1 \leftrightarrow 4$    $2 \in X \Rightarrow 7 \in X$    $6 \in Y \Rightarrow 5 \notin Y$

20. **E.** Only Choice E does not violate any of the given conditions.
A violates the condition that each set has at least three members.
B violates the condition that 1 and 4 must be in the same set.
C violates the condition that 5 and 6 cannot both be members of set Y ($6 \in Y \Rightarrow 5 \notin Y$).
D violates the condition that if 2 is in X, then 7 is also in X ($2 \in X \Rightarrow 7 \in X$). Note that in E, 7 is in X, even though 2 is not in X; this does *not* violate the condition: $2 \in X \Rightarrow 7 \in X$.

21. **D.** Only Choice D *cannot* be true. If 1, 3, and 7 were in X, then so would 4 ($1 \leftrightarrow 4$); then Y would contain 2, 5, and 6. This, however, violates the condition: $6 \in Y \Rightarrow 5 \notin Y$. Each of the other choices *could be* true.

22. **B.** Since, $2 \in X \Rightarrow 7 \in X$, and since $7 \in Y$, 2 must also be in Y. Since 1 and 4 have to be in the same set ($1 \leftrightarrow 4$), and Y can't have five members, then 1 and 4 are in set X. Also, since $6 \in Y \Rightarrow 5 \notin Y$ and $5 \in Y$, then $6 \in X$. The only number whose position is not determined is 3, which could be in either set without violating any conditions. There are two possibilities:

X = {1, 3, 4, 6} and Y = {2, 5, 7}
X = {1, 4, 6} and Y = {2, 3, 5, 7}

23. **E.** Since 1 is in Y, 4 must also be in Y ($1 \leftrightarrow 4$). If 7 were the third member of Y, then the four members of X would be 2, 3, 5, and 6. This, however, is impossible, because $2 \in X \Rightarrow 7 \in X$. Therefore, 7 cannot be in Y, and so 7 must be in X. Each of the other choices could be the third member of Y, and hence do not have to be in X.

## Solutions 24–28

Senators: W, X, Y, Z — 2
Representatives: P, Q, R, S — 2
S ⇒ X    Y ⇒ ~Q (and equivalently Q ⇒ ~Y)
Y ∨ Z    ~(Y ∧ Z)

24. **A.** Only Choice A doesn't violate any of the given conditions.
Since Y will not serve with Q (Y ⇒ ~Q), eliminate Choice B.
Since S will not serve unless X does (S ⇒ X), eliminate Choice C.
Since the fourth member of the committee must be a second representative, eliminate Choice D.
Since Y and Z cannot both serve [~(Y ∧ Z)], eliminate Choice E.

25. **D.** Since neither P nor R is on the committee, the two representatives on the committee are Q and S. Since S won't serve unless X does (S ⇒ X), X must also be on the committee. Also, Y cannot serve on the committee (Y ⇒ ~Q). Finally, since either Y or Z must be chosen, Z is on the committee.

26. **D.** Only Choice D doesn't violate any of the given conditions.
Since Y is not willing to serve with Q or Z, eliminate Choices A and C.
Since S will not serve on the committee unless X does, eliminate Choice B.
Finally, eliminate Choice E, since it includes three senators and only one representative.

27. **D.** Since S is on the committee, so is X (S ⇒ X). Then the other senator has to be Y or Z (Y ∨ Z), so it *cannot* be W.

28. **B.** Since Q is on the committee, Y is not on the committee (Y ⇒ ~Q). Then neither X nor Y is on the committee, so the two senators on the committee are W and Z. Also, S cannot be on the committee since X isn't (S ⇒ X). The only people we don't know about are P and R, either of whom could serve. So there are two possibilities: P, Q, W, Z and Q, R, W, Z.

29. **B.** The force of the argument presented in this advertisement lies in the attractiveness of the promise of "space-age circuitry" in the X-2700 stereo system. Choice B effectively points out the fundamental weakness of this appeal. All the other choices present features of the advertisement which might be regarded as flaws, but which are very minor in comparison to the flaw indicated in Choice B.

30. **C.** At least one junior and at least one sophomore voted for the proposal, so if there are 18 seniors on the council, all of whom voted for the proposal, then there were at least 20 votes cast in favor of the proposal, and it was adopted. None of the other choices provides enough information to answer the question.

## Solutions 31–34

Mon — at least 2    Tues — at least 2
I ≠ 1st on Mon
F = 1st or last on Mon or Tues
(I = Mon) ⇒ (K = Tues)
(I = Tues) ⇒ (K = Mon)
H << L or L << H
G < x < L or L < x < G

31. **E.** Only Choice E does not violate any of the given conditions.
Choice A violates the condition that I and K cannot interview on the same day.
Choice B violates the condition that there be at least one interview scheduled between those of G and L.
Choice C violates the condition that there be no interview scheduled between those of H and L.
Choice D violates the condition that F have the first or last interview of the day.

32. **C.** Only Choice C does not violate any of the conditions.
Choice A is incorrect, because if Monday's schedule is G, H, L, then I and K both have interviews scheduled on Tuesday, which is not allowed.
Choice B violates the condition that there be an interview scheduled between those of G and L.
Choice D violates the condition that F be the first or last interview of the day.
Choice E violates the condition that H and L interview on the same day.

33. **D.** Since F, I, and J have interviews on Monday, G, H, K, and L have their interviews on Tuesday. Since it is given that H has the first interview and no interview can be scheduled between those of H and L, then L must must have the second interview. It is also required that there be at least one interview between that of G and L, so K is third and G is last. The complete Tuesday schedule is H, L, K, G, and only Choice D is true.

34. **E.** Since F does not have either the first or last interview on Tuesday, F must have the first or last interview on Monday. So either Choice A or Choice B is true, but neither one *must* be true. On Tuesday, since H is first, L must be second; but G cannot immediately follow L, so G must have an interview on Monday: eliminate Choice C. Since I has an interview

on Tuesday, K must have a Monday interview. This leaves J for the last applicant to be interviewed on Tuesday. The Tuesday schedule is H, L, J, I; Choice E is true.

35. C.  The conclusion is the prediction of a grim year for home-builders. Choices A, B, D, and E do

not point to continued bad sales, but Choice C, revealing that sales fell even with advertising and incentives, supports the prediction of a bad year ahead.

# Answer Sheet—Model Test 2

## Section 1

1. Ⓐ Ⓑ Ⓒ Ⓓ Ⓔ
2. Ⓐ Ⓑ Ⓒ Ⓓ Ⓔ
3. Ⓐ Ⓑ Ⓒ Ⓓ Ⓔ
4. Ⓐ Ⓑ Ⓒ Ⓓ Ⓔ
5. Ⓐ Ⓑ Ⓒ Ⓓ Ⓔ
6. Ⓐ Ⓑ Ⓒ Ⓓ Ⓔ
7. Ⓐ Ⓑ Ⓒ Ⓓ Ⓔ
8. Ⓐ Ⓑ Ⓒ Ⓓ Ⓔ
9. Ⓐ Ⓑ Ⓒ Ⓓ Ⓔ
10. Ⓐ Ⓑ Ⓒ Ⓓ Ⓔ

11. Ⓐ Ⓑ Ⓒ Ⓓ Ⓔ
12. Ⓐ Ⓑ Ⓒ Ⓓ Ⓔ
13. Ⓐ Ⓑ Ⓒ Ⓓ Ⓔ
14. Ⓐ Ⓑ Ⓒ Ⓓ Ⓔ
15. Ⓐ Ⓑ Ⓒ Ⓓ Ⓔ
16. Ⓐ Ⓑ Ⓒ Ⓓ Ⓔ
17. Ⓐ Ⓑ Ⓒ Ⓓ Ⓔ
18. Ⓐ Ⓑ Ⓒ Ⓓ Ⓔ
19. Ⓐ Ⓑ Ⓒ Ⓓ Ⓔ
20. Ⓐ Ⓑ Ⓒ Ⓓ Ⓔ

21. Ⓐ Ⓑ Ⓒ Ⓓ Ⓔ
22. Ⓐ Ⓑ Ⓒ Ⓓ Ⓔ
23. Ⓐ Ⓑ Ⓒ Ⓓ Ⓔ
24. Ⓐ Ⓑ Ⓒ Ⓓ Ⓔ
25. Ⓐ Ⓑ Ⓒ Ⓓ Ⓔ
26. Ⓐ Ⓑ Ⓒ Ⓓ Ⓔ
27. Ⓐ Ⓑ Ⓒ Ⓓ Ⓔ
28. Ⓐ Ⓑ Ⓒ Ⓓ Ⓔ
29. Ⓐ Ⓑ Ⓒ Ⓓ Ⓔ
30. Ⓐ Ⓑ Ⓒ Ⓓ Ⓔ

## Section 2

1. Ⓐ Ⓑ Ⓒ Ⓓ Ⓔ
2. Ⓐ Ⓑ Ⓒ Ⓓ Ⓔ
3. Ⓐ Ⓑ Ⓒ Ⓓ Ⓔ
4. Ⓐ Ⓑ Ⓒ Ⓓ Ⓔ
5. Ⓐ Ⓑ Ⓒ Ⓓ Ⓔ
6. Ⓐ Ⓑ Ⓒ Ⓓ Ⓔ
7. Ⓐ Ⓑ Ⓒ Ⓓ Ⓔ
8. Ⓐ Ⓑ Ⓒ Ⓓ Ⓔ
9. Ⓐ Ⓑ Ⓒ Ⓓ Ⓔ
10. Ⓐ Ⓑ Ⓒ Ⓓ Ⓔ

11. Ⓐ Ⓑ Ⓒ Ⓓ Ⓔ
12. Ⓐ Ⓑ Ⓒ Ⓓ Ⓔ
13. Ⓐ Ⓑ Ⓒ Ⓓ Ⓔ
14. Ⓐ Ⓑ Ⓒ Ⓓ Ⓔ
15. Ⓐ Ⓑ Ⓒ Ⓓ Ⓔ
16. Ⓐ Ⓑ Ⓒ Ⓓ Ⓔ
17. Ⓐ Ⓑ Ⓒ Ⓓ Ⓔ
18. Ⓐ Ⓑ Ⓒ Ⓓ Ⓔ
19. Ⓐ Ⓑ Ⓒ Ⓓ Ⓔ
20. Ⓐ Ⓑ Ⓒ Ⓓ Ⓔ

21. Ⓐ Ⓑ Ⓒ Ⓓ Ⓔ
22. Ⓐ Ⓑ Ⓒ Ⓓ Ⓔ
23. Ⓐ Ⓑ Ⓒ Ⓓ Ⓔ
24. Ⓐ Ⓑ Ⓒ Ⓓ Ⓔ
25. Ⓐ Ⓑ Ⓒ Ⓓ Ⓔ
26. Ⓐ Ⓑ Ⓒ Ⓓ Ⓔ
27. Ⓐ Ⓑ Ⓒ Ⓓ Ⓔ
28. Ⓐ Ⓑ Ⓒ Ⓓ Ⓔ

## Section 3

1. Ⓐ Ⓑ Ⓒ Ⓓ Ⓔ
2. Ⓐ Ⓑ Ⓒ Ⓓ Ⓔ
3. Ⓐ Ⓑ Ⓒ Ⓓ Ⓔ
4. Ⓐ Ⓑ Ⓒ Ⓓ Ⓔ
5. Ⓐ Ⓑ Ⓒ Ⓓ Ⓔ
6. Ⓐ Ⓑ Ⓒ Ⓓ Ⓔ
7. Ⓐ Ⓑ Ⓒ Ⓓ Ⓔ
8. Ⓐ Ⓑ Ⓒ Ⓓ Ⓔ
9. Ⓐ Ⓑ Ⓒ Ⓓ Ⓔ
10. Ⓐ Ⓑ Ⓒ Ⓓ Ⓔ

11. Ⓐ Ⓑ Ⓒ Ⓓ Ⓔ
12. Ⓐ Ⓑ Ⓒ Ⓓ Ⓔ
13. Ⓐ Ⓑ Ⓒ Ⓓ Ⓔ
14. Ⓐ Ⓑ Ⓒ Ⓓ Ⓔ
15. Ⓐ Ⓑ Ⓒ Ⓓ Ⓔ
16. Ⓐ Ⓑ Ⓒ Ⓓ Ⓔ
17. Ⓐ Ⓑ Ⓒ Ⓓ Ⓔ
18. Ⓐ Ⓑ Ⓒ Ⓓ Ⓔ
19. Ⓐ Ⓑ Ⓒ Ⓓ Ⓔ
20. Ⓐ Ⓑ Ⓒ Ⓓ Ⓔ

21. Ⓐ Ⓑ Ⓒ Ⓓ Ⓔ
22. Ⓐ Ⓑ Ⓒ Ⓓ Ⓔ
23. Ⓐ Ⓑ Ⓒ Ⓓ Ⓔ
24. Ⓐ Ⓑ Ⓒ Ⓓ Ⓔ
25. Ⓐ Ⓑ Ⓒ Ⓓ Ⓔ
26. Ⓐ Ⓑ Ⓒ Ⓓ Ⓔ
27. Ⓐ Ⓑ Ⓒ Ⓓ Ⓔ
28. Ⓐ Ⓑ Ⓒ Ⓓ Ⓔ
29. Ⓐ Ⓑ Ⓒ Ⓓ Ⓔ
30. Ⓐ Ⓑ Ⓒ Ⓓ Ⓔ

31. Ⓐ Ⓑ Ⓒ Ⓓ Ⓔ
32. Ⓐ Ⓑ Ⓒ Ⓓ Ⓔ
33. Ⓐ Ⓑ Ⓒ Ⓓ Ⓔ
34. Ⓐ Ⓑ Ⓒ Ⓓ Ⓔ
35. Ⓐ Ⓑ Ⓒ Ⓓ Ⓔ

# MODEL TEST 2

1

---

SECTION 1—VERBAL ABILITY

Time—30 Minutes
30 Questions

**Select the best answer to the following questions, then fill in the appropriate space on your Answer Sheet.**

---

<u>Directions</u>: In each of the following antonym questions, a word printed in capital letters precedes five lettered words or phrases. From these five lettered words or phrases, pick the one most nearly <u>opposite</u> in meaning to the capitalized word.

---

1. ELATED:
   (A) crestfallen
   (B) inebriated
   (C) punctual
   (D) insulted
   (E) lamented

2. RETICENCE:
   (A) irascibility
   (B) loquaciousness
   (C) quiescence
   (D) patience
   (E) surrender

---

<u>Directions</u>: Each of the following sentence completion questions contains one or two blanks. These blanks signify that a word or set of words has been left out. Below each sentence are five words or sets of words. For each blank, pick the word or set of words that <u>best</u> reflects the sentence's overall meaning.

---

3. You may wonder how the expert on fossil remains is able to trace descent through teeth, which seem _____ pegs upon which to hang whole ancestries.
   (A) novel
   (B) reliable
   (C) specious
   (D) inadequate
   (E) academic

4. An essential purpose of the criminal justice system is to enable purgation to take place; that is, to provide a _____ by which a community expresses its collective _____ the transgression of the criminal.
   (A) catharsis...outrage at
   (B) disclaimer...forgiveness of
   (C) means...empathy with
   (D) procedure...distaste for
   (E) document...disapprobation of

---

<u>Directions</u>: Each of the following analogy questions presents a related pair of words linked by a colon. Five lettered pairs of words follow the linked pair. Choose the lettered pair of words whose relationship is <u>most like</u> the relationship expressed in the original linked pair.

---

5. VINDICTIVE : MERCY ::
   (A) avaricious : greed
   (B) insightful : hope
   (C) modest : dignity
   (D) skeptical : trustfulness
   (E) pathetic : sympathy

6. RUFFLE : COMPOSURE ::
   (A) flounce : turmoil
   (B) flourish : prosperity
   (C) provoke : discussion
   (D) adjust : balance
   (E) upset : equilibrium

# 1                                                                    1

Given the persistent and intransigent nature of the American race system, which proved quite impervious to black attacks, Du Bois in his
*Line* speeches and writings moved from one proposed
(5) solution to another, and the salience of various parts of his philosophy changed as his perceptions of the needs and strategies of black America shifted over time. Aloof and autonomous in his personality, Du Bois did not hesitate to depart
(10) markedly from whatever was the current mainstream of black thinking when he perceived that the conventional wisdom being enunciated by black spokesmen was proving inadequate to the task of advancing the race. His willingness to
(15) seek different solutions often placed him well in advance of his contemporaries, and this, combined with a strong-willed, even arrogant personality made his career as a black leader essentially a series of stormy conflicts.
(20)     Thus Du Bois first achieved his role as a major black leader in the controversy that arose over the program of Booker T. Washington, the most prominent and influential black leader at the opening of the twentieth century. Amidst the
(25) wave of lynchings, disfranchisement, and segregation laws, Washington, seeking the good will of powerful whites, taught blacks not to protest against discrimination, but to elevate themselves through industrial education, hard work, and prop-
(30) erty accumulation; then, they would ultimately obtain recognition of their citizenship rights. At first Du Bois agreed with this gradualist strategy, but in 1903 with the publication of his most influential book, *Souls of Black Folk,* he became the
(35) chief leader of the onslaught against Washington that polarized the black community into two wings—the "conservative" supporters of Washington and his "radical" critics.

7. Which of the following statements about W.E.B. Du Bois does the passage best support?

(A) He sacrificed the proven strategies of earlier black leaders to his craving for political novelty.
(B) Preferring conflict to harmony, he followed a disruptive course that alienated him from the bulk of his followers.
(C) He proved unable to change with the times in mounting fresh attacks against white racism.

(D) He relied on the fundamental benevolence of the white population for the eventual success of his movement.
(E) Once an adherent of Washington's policies, he ultimately lost patience with them for their inefficacy.

8. It can be inferred that Booker T. Washington in comparison with W.E.B. Du Bois could be described as all of the following EXCEPT

(A) submissive to the majority
(B) concerned with financial success
(C) versatile in adopting strategies
(D) traditional in preaching industry
(E) respectful of authority

9. The author's attitude toward Du Bois' departure from conventional black policies can best be described as

(A) skeptical
(B) derisive
(C) shocked
(D) approving
(E) resigned

## Antonyms

10. REVILE:

(A) compose
(B) awake
(C) deaden
(D) praise
(E) secrete

11. PROPITIOUS:

(A) adjacent
(B) clandestine
(C) contentious
(D) unfavorable
(E) coy

# 1

## 1

## Analogies

12. OFFHAND : PREMEDITATION ::
    - (A) upright : integrity
    - (B) aboveboard : guile
    - (C) cutthroat : competition
    - (D) backward : direction
    - (E) underlying : foundation

13. LARVAL : INSECT ::
    - (A) serpentine : snake
    - (B) floral : plant
    - (C) amphibian : reptile
    - (D) embryonic : mammal
    - (E) alate : bird

## Sentence Completion

14. When facts are _____ and data hard to come by, even scientists occasionally throw aside the professional pretense of _____ and tear into each other with shameless appeals to authority and arguments that are unabashedly ad hominem.
    - (A) elusive...objectivity
    - (B) established...courtesy
    - (C) demonstrable...neutrality
    - (D) ineluctable...cooperation
    - (E) hypothetical...scholarship

15. In the tradition of scholarly _____, the poet and scholar A.E. Housman once assailed a German rival for relying on manuscripts "as a drunkard relies on lampposts, for _____ rather than illumination."
    - (A) animosity...current
    - (B) discourse...stability
    - (C) erudition...shadow
    - (D) invective...support
    - (E) competition...assistance

## Reading Comprehension

At night, schools of prey and predators are almost always spectacularly illuminated by the bioluminescence produced by the microscopic
*Line* and larger plankton. The reason for the ubiquitous
(5) production of light by the microorganisms of the sea remains obscure, and suggested explanations are controversial. It has been suggested that light is a kind of inadvertent by-product of life in transparent organisms. It has also been hypothesized
(10) that the emission of light on disturbance is advantageous to the plankton in making the predators of the plankton conspicuous to *their* predators! Unquestionably, it does act this way. Indeed, some fisheries base the detection of their prey on

(15) the bioluminescence that the fish excite. It is difficult, however, to defend the thesis that this effect was the direct factor in the original development of bioluminescence, since the effect was of no advantage to the individual microorganism
(20) that first developed it. Perhaps the luminescence of a microorganism also discourages attack by light-avoiding predators and is of initial survival benefit to the individual. As it then becomes general in the population, the effect of revealing
(25) plankton predators to their predators would also become important.

16. The primary topic of the passage is which of the following?
    - (A) The origin of bioluminescence in plankton predators
    - (B) The disadvantages of bioluminescence in microorganisms
    - (C) The varieties of marine bioluminescent life forms
    - (D) Symbiotic relationships between predators and their prey
    - (E) Hypotheses on the causes of bioluminescence in plankton

17. The author mentions the activities of fisheries in order to provide an example of
    - (A) how ubiquitous the phenomenon of bioluminescence is coastally
    - (B) how predators do make use of bioluminescence in locating their prey
    - (C) how human intervention imperils bioluminescent microorganisms
    - (D) how nocturnal fishing expeditions are becoming more and more widespread
    - (E) how limited bioluminescence is as a source of light for human use

18. The passage provides an answer to which of the following questions?
    - (A) What is the explanation for the phenomenon of bioluminescence in marine life?
    - (B) Does the phenomenon of plankton bioluminescence have any practical applications?
    - (C) Why do only certain specimens of marine life exhibit the phenomenon of bioluminescence?
    - (D) How does underwater bioluminescence differ from atmospheric bioluminescence?
    - (E) What are the steps that take place as an individual microorganism becomes bioluminescent?

# 1                                                                          1

## Antonyms

19. INCONGRUOUS:

    (A) geometric
    (B) prudent
    (C) legitimate
    (D) harmonious
    (E) efficacious

20. APOSTATE:

    (A) laggard
    (B) loyalist
    (C) martinet
    (D) predecessor
    (E) skeptic

## Analogies

21. SEXTANT : NAUTICAL ::

    (A) octet : musical
    (B) therapy : physical
    (C) forceps : surgical
    (D) comet : astronomical
    (E) blueprint : mechanical

22. REFRACTORY : MANAGE ::

    (A) redoubtable : impress
    (B) lethargic : stimulate
    (C) pedantic : convince
    (D) officious : arrange
    (E) aggrieved : distress

## Antonyms

23. ENSUE:

    (A) litigate
    (B) precede
    (C) arbitrate
    (D) accentuate
    (E) delay

## Sentence Completion

24. While the disease is in _____ state it is
    almost impossible to determine its existence by
    _____.

    (A) a dormant...postulate
    (B) a critical...examination
    (C) an acute...analysis
    (D) a suspended...estimate
    (E) a latent...observation

25. Virginia Woolf _____ conventional notions
    of truth: in her words, one cannot receive from any
    lecture "a nugget of pure truth" to wrap up between

the pages of one's notebook and keep on the
mantelpiece forever.

    (A) anticipates
    (B) articulates
    (C) neglects
    (D) mocks
    (E) rationalizes

## Reading Comprehension

The curtain rises; the Cardinal and Daniel de
Bosola enter from the right. In appearance, the
Cardinal is something between an El Greco cardinal and a Van Dyke noble lord. He has the tall,
*Line* (5) spare form—the elongated hands and features—
of the former; the trim pointed beard, the imperial
repose, the commanding authority of the latter.
But the El Greco features are not really those of
asceticism or inner mystic spirituality. They are
(10) the index to a cold, refined but ruthless cruelty in
a highly civilized controlled form. Neither is the
imperial repose an aloof mood of proud detachment. It is a refined expression of satanic pride of
place and talent.
(15) To a degree, the Cardinal's coldness is artificially cultivated. He has defined himself against
his younger brother Duke Ferdinand and is the
opposite to the overwrought emotionality of the
latter. But the Cardinal's aloof mood is not one of
(20) bland detachment. It is the deliberate detachment
of a methodical man who collects his thoughts
and emotions into the most compact and formidable shape—that when he strikes, he may strike
with the more efficient and devastating force. His
(25) easy movements are those of the slowly circling
eagle just before the swift descent with the
exposed talons. Above all else, he is a man who
never for a moment doubts his destined authority
as a governor. He derisively and sharply rebukes
(30) his brother the Duke as easily and readily as he
mocks his mistress Julia. If he has betrayed his
hireling Bosola, he uses his brother as the tool to
win back his "familiar." His court dress is a long
brilliant scarlet cardinal's gown with white cuffs
(35) and a white collar turned back over the red, both
collar and cuffs being elaborately scalloped and
embroidered. He wears a small cape, reaching
only to the elbows. His cassock is buttoned to the
ground, giving a heightened effect to his already
(40) tall presence. Richelieu would have adored his
neatly trimmed beard. A richly jeweled and
oranamented cross lies on his breast, suspended
from his neck by a gold chain.

# 1                                                     1

26. In lines 24–27 the author most likely compares the movements of the Cardinal to those of a circling eagle in order to emphasize his

   (A) flightiness
   (B) love of freedom
   (C) eminence
   (D) sense of spirituality
   (E) mercilessness

27. Which of the following best characterizes the author's attitude toward the Cardinal?

   (A) He deprecates his inability to sustain warm familial relationships.
   (B) He esteems him for his spiritual and emotional control.
   (C) He admires his grace in movement and sure sense of personal authority.
   (D) He finds him formidable both as an opponent and as a dramatic character.
   (E) He is perturbed by his inconsistencies in behavior.

## Analogies

28. AUSTERE : STYLE ::

   (A) controlled : movement
   (B) affluent : wealth
   (C) subservient : demeanor
   (D) inspirational : faith
   (E) pragmatic : speech

## Antonyms

29. RETROSPECTION:

   (A) introversion
   (B) deliberation
   (C) anticipation
   (D) gregariousness
   (E) equivocation

30. TOPICAL:

   (A) general
   (B) disinterested
   (C) chronological
   (D) fallacious
   (E) imperceptible

## SECTION 2—QUANTITATIVE ABILITY

**Time—45 Minutes
28 Questions**

In this section solve each problem, using any available space on the page for scratchwork. Then decide which is the best of the choices given and fill in the corresponding oval on the Answer Sheet.

<u>Directions</u>: In the following type of question, two quantities appear, one in Column A and one in Column B. You must compare them. The correct answer to the question is

A if the quantity in Column A is greater
B if the quantity in Column B is greater
C if the two quantities are equal
D if it is impossible to determine which quantity is greater

<u>Notes</u>: Sometimes information about one or both of the quantities is centered above the two columns. If the same symbol appears in both columns, it represents the same thing each time.

| Column A | Column B |
|---|---|
| | |

$m$ and $n$ are positive integers
$mn = 25$

1. $m$ | $n$

2. 65% of $a$ | $\dfrac{2}{3}$ of $a$

| Column A | Column B |
|---|---|

3. $c$ | 5

$ab = 0$

4. $(a + b)^2$ | $(a - b)^2$

---

<u>Directions</u>: In the following questions, choose the best answer from the five choices listed.

5. The Center City Little League is divided into $d$ divisions. Each division has $t$ teams, and each team has $p$ players. How many players are there in the entire league?

   (A) $d + t + p$   (B) $dtp$   (C) $\dfrac{pt}{d}$   (D) $\dfrac{dt}{p}$   (E) $\dfrac{d}{pt}$

6. A number $x$ is chosen at random from the set of positive integers less than 10. What is the probability that $\dfrac{9}{x} > x$ ?

   (A) $\dfrac{1}{5}$   (B) $\dfrac{2}{9}$   (C) $\dfrac{1}{3}$   (D) $\dfrac{2}{3}$   (E) $\dfrac{7}{9}$

7. If $\dfrac{1}{a} + \dfrac{1}{a} + \dfrac{1}{a} = 12$, then $a =$

   (A) $\dfrac{1}{12}$   (B) $\dfrac{1}{4}$   (C) $\dfrac{1}{3}$   (D) 3   (E) 4

2                                                                                          2

| Column A | Column B |
|----------|----------|

8.  | $y$ |        | 20 |

---

$$a + b = 24$$
$$a - b = 25$$

9.  | $b$ |        | 0 |

---

10. In 1980, the cost of $p$ pounds of potatoes was $d$ dollars. In 1990, the cost of $2p$ pounds of potatoes was $\frac{1}{2}d$ dollars. By what percent did the price of potatoes decrease from 1980 to 1990?

    (A) 25%   (B) 50%   (C) 75%   (D) 100%
    (E) 400%

| Column A | Column B |
|----------|----------|

$$a + 2b = 6d$$
$$c - b = 5d$$

11. | The average (arithmetic mean) of $a$, $b$, $c$, and $d$ | | $3d$ |

---

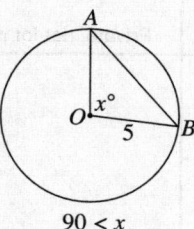

$$90 < x$$

12. | The length of $AB$ | | 7 |

---

$$x^5 = \frac{13}{17}$$

13. | $x$ | | $\left(\dfrac{13}{17}\right)^5$ |

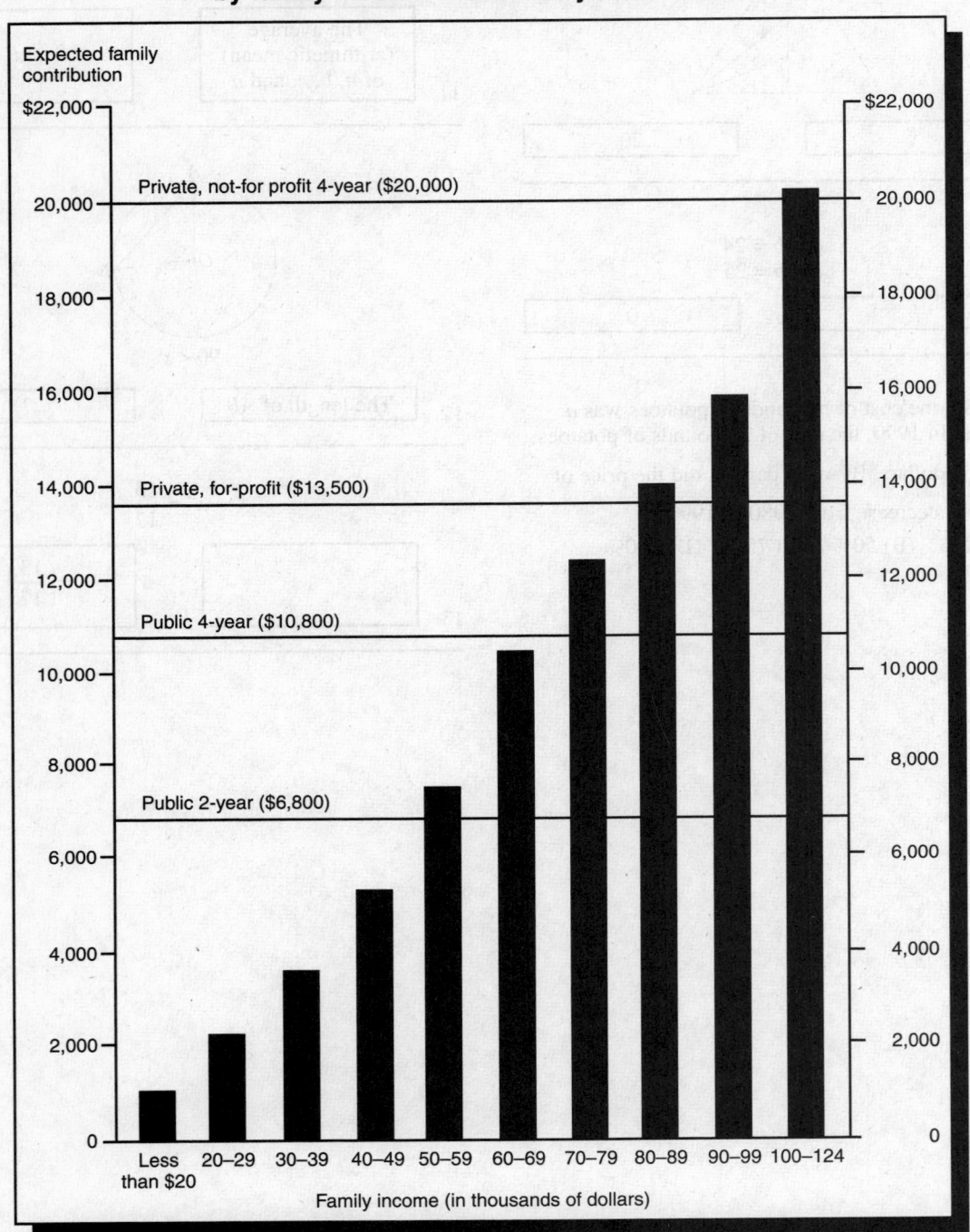

**Average expected family contribution (EFC) for dependent students, by family income: Academic year 1995–96**

NOTE: The horizontal lines on the figure represent the average student budgets for full-time, full-year students at the indicated type of institution.

SOURCE: U.S. Department of Education.

2

2

14. A family's *unmet need* (which must be covered by a financial aid package) is defined to be the total cost of attending an institution of higher education minus the expected family contribution. What is the unmet need of a family whose income is $55,000 and who has a child attending a 4-year public university?

(A) $700   (B) $3300   (C) $6800
(D) $7500   (E) $12,500

15. If family A has an income of $95,000 per year, and family B has an income of $35,000 per year, and each has a child attending a 4-year public university, to the nearest $1000, how much more would family A be expected to pay than family B?

(A) $4000   (B) $7000   (C) $10,000
(D) $12,000   (E) $15,000

---

Column A                    Column B

*a* and *b* are positive integers with $a < b$.

| The remainder when *a* is divided by *b* | The remainder when *b* is divided by *a* |

16.

Column A                                    Column B

Figure 1                                    Figure 2

*ABCD* and *EFGH* are squares, and all the circles are tangent to one another and to the sides of the squares.

| The area of the shaded region in Figure 1 | The area of the shaded region in Figure 2 |

17.

18. A bag contains 3 red, 4 white, and 5 blue marbles. Jason begins removing marbles from the bag at random, one at a time. What is the least number of marbles he must remove to be sure that he has at least one of each color?

(A) 3   (B) 6   (C) 8   (D) 10   (E) 12

19. Jordan has taken 5 math tests so far this semester. If he gets a 70 on his next test, it will lower the average (arithmetic mean) of his test scores by 4 points. What is his average now?

(A) 74   (B) 85   (C) 86   (D) 90   (E) 94

2                                                                                                    2

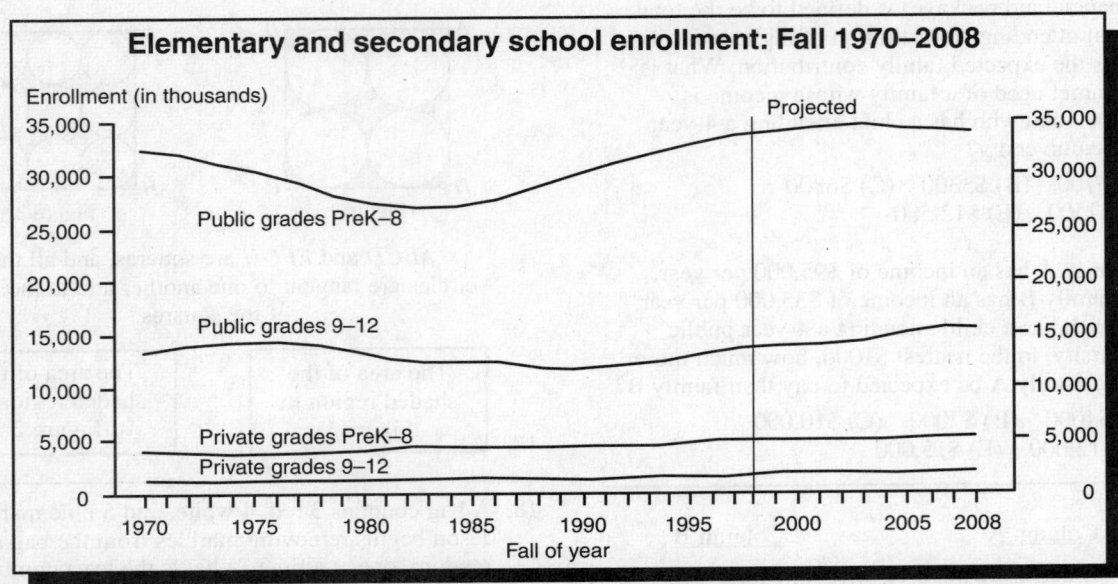

## Elementary and secondary school enrollment: Fall 1970–2008

Enrollment (in thousands)

Public grades PreK–8

Public grades 9–12

Private grades PreK–8

Private grades 9–12

Projected

Fall of year

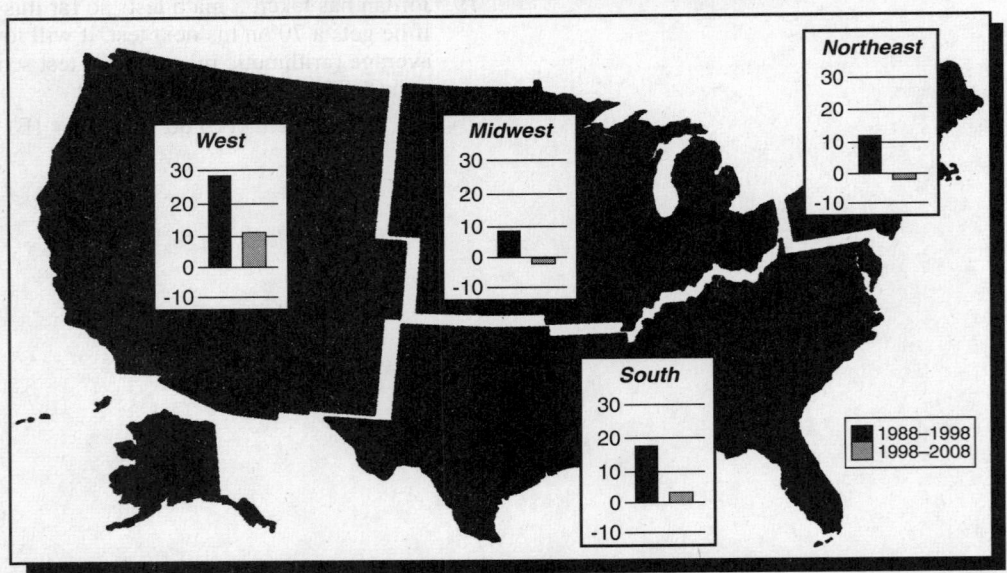

## Projected percentage change in public elementary and secondary school enrollment, by region: Fall 1988 to 2008

West

Midwest

Northeast

South

1988–1998
1998–2008

SOURCE: U.S. Department of Education, National Center for Education Statistics.

# 2

20. To the nearest million, how many more students were enrolled in school—both public and private, preK–12—in 1970 than in 1988?

(A) 3,000,000  (B) 6,000,000  (C) 10,000,000
(D) 44,000,000  (E) 51,000,000

21. In 1988 there were 40,000,000 public school students in the United States, of whom 22% lived in the West. Approximately, how many public school students are projected to be living in the West in 2008?

(A) 9,000,000  (B) 12,000,000  (C) 15,000,000
(D) 24,000,000  (E) 66,000,000

22. If $a$ and $b$ are the lengths of the legs of a right triangle whose hypotenuse is 10 and whose area is 20, what is the value of $(a + b)^2$?

(A) 100  (B) 120  (C) 140  (D) 180  (E) 200

---

| Column A | Column B |
|---|---|

The circumference of a circle is $a\pi$ inches. The area of the same circle is $b\pi$ square inches.

23.

| $a$ | $b$ |
|---|---|

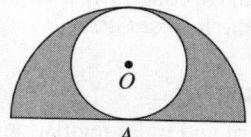

The circle with center $O$ is inscribed in the semicircle with center $A$.

24.

| The area of the shaded region | The area of the white region |
|---|---|

---

A school group charters three identical buses and occupies $\frac{4}{5}$ of the seats. After $\frac{1}{4}$ of the passengers leave, the remaining passengers use only two of the buses.

25.

| The fraction of the seats on the two buses that are now occupied | $\frac{9}{10}$ |
|---|---|

26. What is the average (arithmetic mean) of $3^{30}$, $3^{60}$, and $3^{90}$?

(A) $3^{60}$  (B) $3^{177}$  (C) $3^{10} + 3^{20} + 3^{30}$
(D) $3^{27} + 3^{57} + 3^{87}$  (E) $3^{29} + 3^{59} + 3^{89}$

27. The figure at the right consists of four semicircles in a large semicircle. If the small semicircles have radii of 1, 2, 3, and 4, what is the perimeter of the shaded region?

(A) $10\pi$  (B) $20\pi$  (C) $40\pi$  (D) $60\pi$  (E) $100\pi$

28. If the sum of all the positive even integers less than 1000 is $A$, what is the sum of all the positive odd integers less than 1000?

(A) $A - 998$  (B) $A - 499$  (C) $A + 1$
(D) $A + 500$  (E) $\frac{A}{2} + 999$

# 2

# 3                                                          3

**Time—60 Minutes**
**35 Questions**

**Directions:** In this section, each set of questions is based on a short passage or a set of conditions. Sometimes, in answering these questions, you might want to make a table or diagram. For each question, choose the best answer from the five choices listed.

1. The Census Bureau's family portrait of America may remind us of the problems we face as a nation, but it also gives us reason to take heart in our ability to solve them in an enlightened way. The 1980 census was the first in history to show that the majority of the population in every state has completed high school. And the percentage of our people with at least 4 years of college rose from 11 percent in 1970 to 16.3 percent in 1980. That's progress—where it really counts.

   Which one of the following assumptions underlies the author's conclusion in the above passage?

   (A) Greater numbers of high school and college degrees coincide with other firsts in the 1980 census.
   (B) Greater numbers of high school and college degrees coincide with greater numbers of well-educated people.
   (C) Greater numbers of high school and college degrees coincide with a great commitment to social progress.
   (D) Greater numbers of high school and college degrees coincide with a better chance to avoid national catastrophe.
   (E) Greater numbers of high school and college degrees coincide with the 1980 census.

## Questions 2–5

**Seven** students—F, G, H, I, J, K, and L—are being considered for a university fellowship. In evaluating these students, the dean has received from the registrar's office their official transcripts, including their cumulative grade point averages (GPAs). In analyzing this information, the dean made the following observations:

   None of the students has exactly the same GPA as any other student.
   K's GPA is higher than L's, but lower than H's.
   I has a higher GPA than J.
   Both F and G have higher GPAs than H.

2. Each of the following could be true EXCEPT

   (A) F has the highest GPA.
   (B) G has the highest GPA.
   (C) I has the highest GPA.
   (D) More than three students have higher GPAs than K.
   (E) More than three students have lower GPAs than K.

3. Which of the following, if true, would be sufficient to determine who has the lowest GPA?

   (A) I has the highest GPA.
   (B) I has a lower GPA than K.
   (C) K has a higher GPA than J.
   (D) J has a higher GPA than K.
   (E) Exactly five students have lower GPAs than F.

4. If J has a higher GPA than F, how many different rankings, by GPA, of the students are possible?

   (A) 1   (B) 2   (C) 4   (D) 6   (E) 8

5. If H has a higher GPA than I, which of the following CANNOT be true?

   (A) I's GPA is equal to the average of F's and G's.
   (B) I's GPA is equal to the average of K's and L's.
   (C) J's GPA is equal to the average of K's and L's.
   (D) J has the second lowest GPA.
   (E) J has the lowest GPA.

## Questions 6–7

By passing more and more regulations allegedly to protect the environment, the state is driving the manufacturing industry away. And when the employers leave, the workers will follow. The number of new no-growth or environmental rules passed each year is increasing by leaps and bounds. Rich environmentalists who think they are sympathetic to workers have no real sympathy for the blue-collar employees who are injured by their activities. One major manufacturer has been fined for failing to establish a car-pool plan. Another is accused of polluting the air with industrial emissions, although everyone knows that two thirds of the pollutants come from cars and trucks. No wonder the large manufacturers are moving to sates with fewer restrictive laws. And as the manufacturers go, unemployment and the number of workers leaving the state will rise more rapidly than ever before.

3                                                                     3

6. The author's argument that strict environmental laws will eventually lead to loss of workers in the state will be most weakened if it can be shown that

(A) so far, the number of manufacturers who have left the state is small

(B) the unemployment rate has climbed steadily in the last three years

(C) most workers who leave the state give as their reason for leaving the poor environmental quality

(D) several other manufacturing states have strict environmental laws

(E) rich environmentalists are more powerful in many other states

7. Which one of the following is NOT an argument of this passage?

(A) Environmentalists are responsible for depriving workers of their jobs.

(B) When workers leave a state, it is a sign that manufacturers will follow.

(C) A car-pool law should not be enforced, as cars and trucks are responsible for most air pollution.

(D) Large manufacturers prefer states with fewer restrictions.

(E) A rise in unemployment will lead to an increase in workers leaving the state.

8. Grades on the midterm test in Mr. Walsh's chemistry class ranged from 68 to 97. Any student who received a grade below 75 or did not hand in all of the required lab reports must complete an extra-credit project.

If the above statements are true, which of the following statements must also be true?

(A) A student who earned an 83 on the midterm and who handed in all her labs, may not do the extra-credit project.

(B) Most of the students in the class will not have to do the extra-credit project.

(C) Any student may, but is not required to, do the extra-credit project.

(D) If John's grade on the midterm was higher than the class average, and he handed in all of his labs, then he will not be required to do the extra-credit project.

(E) If John did all of his labs and earned a 72 on the midterm, he will have to do the extra-credit project.

**Questions 9–13**

The personnel director of a large computer company is scheduling interviews for six candidates for the position of Director of Marketing. The applicants—F, G, H, I, J, and K—will all be interviewed on the same day. The interviews will be scheduled at 9:00, 10:00, 11:00, 1:00, 2:00, and 3:00, with a lunch break for the interviewers at noon. In scheduling the interviews, the personnel director must adhere to the following conditions:

J must have the first interview after the lunch break.
No one can be interviewed between G and I.
H must be interviewed earlier in the day than F.

9. Which of the following candidates for the position CANNOT be scheduled for the 3:00 interview?

(A) F   (B) G   (C) H   (D) I   (E) K

10. Which of the following would be an acceptable order for the interviews?

(A) G, I, H, F, J, K
(B) G, H, F, J, K, I
(C) F, G, I, J, K, H
(D) H, I, F, J, K, G
(E) H, K, F, J, I, G

11. If H and K are both interviewed before lunch, each of the following could be true EXCEPT

(A) H has the first interview of the day.
(B) K has the first interview of the day.
(C) F has the last interview of the day.
(D) G has the last interview of the day.
(E) I has the last interview of the day.

12. If F's interview is scheduled for 2:00, which of the following must be true?

(A) H has the first interview of the day.
(B) G has the first interview of the day.
(C) I has the first interview of the day.
(D) H has the third interview of the day.
(E) K has the last interview of the day.

13. If I has the first interview of the day, which of the following must be true?

(A) J's interview is earlier in the day than F's interview.
(B) J's interview is earlier in the day than H's interview.
(C) H has an interview in the morning.
(D) K has an interview in the morning.
(E) F has the last interview of the day.

3                                                                                      3

14. Since it is possible that substances contained in certain tree roots may provide a cure for cancer, the government must provide sufficient funds to allow thorough testing of this possibility.

The argument above assumes that

(A) substances contained in certain tree roots will probably cure cancer
(B) the line of research mentioned offers at present the most promising possibility for finding a cure for cancer
(C) the possibility of finding a cure is sufficient reason for funding research into possible cancer cures
(D) a cure for cancer would be extremely valuable to society
(E) the government is the only possible source of funds for the research described

## Questions 15–18

A committee of four Republicans—Ash, Berg, Cox, and Day—and three Democrats—Ray, Sack, and Tyler—is conducting a hearing that will take place over five days, Monday through Friday. Because several committee members have other commitments and cannot attend each session, they agreed to the following guidelines:

Each day there will be the same number of Republicans and Democrats in attendance.
The three Democrats cannot all attend on the same day.
No committee member can attend on two consecutive days.
Ash and Ray will both attend at the final session on Friday.
Ray and Sack will never attend on the same day.
Neither Berg nor Tyler will attend a session unless the other does.

15. If Ash and Ray are not the only committee members in attendance on Friday, who else must be present?

(A) Berg and Tyler
(B) Berg and Sack
(C) Cox and Tyler
(D) Cox and Day
(E) Day and Tyler

16. If Ash and Ray are not the only committee members in attendance on Friday, who must be in attendance on Thursday?

(A) Berg  (B) Cox  (C) Day  (D) Sack
(E) Tyler

17. If exactly six people in total attended the sessions on Wednesday, Thursday, and Friday, and none of them attended more than one session, for which of the following could the session on Tuesday be the only one he attended all week?

(A) Tyler  (B) Sack  (C) Ray  (D) Cox
(E) Berg

18. If Ash and Berg attended Tuesday's session, who among the following could not have attended Monday's session?

(A) Cox  (B) Day  (C) Ray  (D) Sack
(E) Tyler

19. The Superintendent of Education complains that the share of the total state budget for education has decreased in each of the last four years; he blames the fall-off on the steady rise in the cost of law enforcement. Organizations opposing increased spending on education point out that the amount of money the state has spent on education has increased by at least three million dollars in each of the last four years.

Which one of the following, if true, best resolves the apparent contradiction in the passage above?

(A) The total state budget has increased more rapidly than the expenditure for education.
(B) Both the pro- and con-educational-spending spokesmen have failed to take inflation into account.
(C) Law-enforcement costs have not risen as rapidly as the superintendent claims.
(D) Some educational expenses are not included in the state budget, but are paid by local taxes.
(E) School construction is paid for by funds from bonds, not by funds from the state budget.

## Questions 20–23

At Carlo's Continental Cafe, five wines—Beaujolais, Chablis, Merlot, Pinot Grigio, and Syrah—are served by the glass on weekdays (Monday through Friday), although not each wine is available every day. In selecting the wines that will be served on a given day, Carlo adheres to the following conditions:

Exactly three wines will be served each day.
No wine can be served on three consecutive days.
On any two consecutive days, each wine must be available at least once.
Between Monday and Friday of any week, each of the wines must be available the same number of times.

3

3

20. If Merlot, Syrah, and Pinot Grigio are available on a Wednesday, which of the following could be the three wines available on Thursday of the same week?

(A) Merlot, Syrah, Pinot Grigio
(B) Chablis, Merlot, Syrah
(C) Chablis, Pinot Grigio, Syrah
(D) Beaujolais, Merlot, Pinot Grigio
(E) Beaujolais, Chablis, Pinot Grigio

21. If Beaujolais, Chablis, and Merlot are served on Monday, and if Merlot and Pinot Grigio are served on Thursday, then each of the following could be served on Wednesday EXCEPT

(A) Beaujolais
(B) Chablis
(C) Merlot
(D) Pinot Grigio
(E) Syrah

22. Which of the following could be true?

(A) The same three wines are available on Tuesday and Thursday.
(B) Merlot and Syrah are both served on Monday and Tuesday.
(C) Merlot and Syrah are both served on Monday and Thursday.
(D) Chablis and Beaujolais are never available on the same night.
(E) Neither Chablis nor Beaujolais is available on Wednesday or Friday.

23. In any week for how many of the wines is it true that that wine is available on two consecutive days?

(A) 1   (B) 2   (C) 3   (D) 4   (E) 5

## Questions 24–28

A family group consisting of two men, three women, and four children have front-row seats for a Broadway show, where they will all sit next to one another in seats 101 through 109. The decision as to who sits in which seats must conform to the following two conditions:

The four children must sit next to one another, in four consecutive seats.
The two men must sit next to each other.

24. If a man is sitting in seat 107 and a woman is sitting in seat 108, which of the following could be the seat that another woman is sitting in?

(A) 101   (B) 102   (C) 103   (D) 104   (E) 106

25. All three women will be sitting next to one another if a man is in which of the following seats?

(A) 101   (B) 104   (C) 105   (D) 107   (E) 109

26. If women are sitting in seats 103 and 109, which of the following seats could be occupied by the third woman?

(A) 101   (B) 102   (C) 104   (D) 106   (E) 107

27. If a child is in seat 101 and a woman is in seat 105, which of the following pairs of seats must be occupied by people not of the same sex?

(A) 105 and 106
(B) 105 and 107
(C) 106 and 107
(D) 106 and 108
(E) 108 and 109

28. If no woman is sitting next to another woman, which of the following must be true?

(A) A man is in seat 102.
(B) A woman is in seat 104.
(C) A child is in seat 105.
(D) A woman is in seat 106.
(E) A man is in seat 108.

29. Josh's GPA is higher than Sam's, but is lower than Dalia's. Erin's GPA is lower than Dalia's and lower than Anne's. Blayke's GPA is higher than Anne's.

Which of the following statements, if true, is sufficient to determine which of the students has the highest GPA?

(A) Erin's GPA is lower than Sam's.
(B) Dalia's GPA is higher than Anne's.
(C) Blayke's GPA is higher than Josh's.
(D) The average of Blayke's and Anne's GPAs is higher than Dalia's GPA.
(E) The average of Dalia's and Anne's GPAs is lower than Josh's GPA.

# 3

# 3

30. The traffic on the Imperial Highway has always been slowed by the dangerous curves in the road. It was built when cars were much smaller and less powerful, and very few drivers traveled between Imperial City and Fremont. All this has changed. The cost of widening and straightening the road would now be many times greater than building the proposed new toll road on the borders of the Imperial Wetlands reserve. Environmentalists fear the construction noise and waste will harm the wildlife in the reserve, and have urged that the toll road not be constructed.

Which one of the following, if true, would most strengthen the case of the environmentalists?

(A) None of the animals living in the Imperial Wetlands is on the list of endangered species.
(B) The traffic congestion on the Imperial Highway increases each year.
(C) The cost of building the new road will be amortized in ten years by the tolls collected.
(D) There are several less direct routes the toll road could take between Fremont and Imperial City.
(E) The environmentalists threaten to bring a law-suit in federal court to halt construction of the road.

## Questions 31–34

A high school principal periodically creates committees to work on special projects. Each such committee consists of three faculty members drawn from the following five departments: English, Foreign Language, Mathematics, Science, and Social Studies. The composition of a committee must conform to the following conditions:

No committee can consist entirely of teachers from the same department.
A social studies teacher can serve on a particular committee if and only if a mathematics teacher is also on the committee.
If a foreign language teacher is on a committee, an English teacher must also be on that committee.
No committee can have teachers from both the English and the Science departments.

31. Which of the following would have to be the third teacher on a committee that already has assigned to it a social studies and a science teacher?

(A) Another social studies teacher
(B) Another science teacher
(C) A mathematics teacher
(D) An English teacher
(E) A foreign language teacher

32. Which of the following would be an acceptable committee?

(A) Three foreign language teachers
(B) One teacher each from the Social Studies, Foreign Language, and English departments
(C) One teacher each from the Science, Foreign Language, and English departments
(D) Two foreign language teachers and one English teacher
(E) Two mathematics teachers and one foreign language teacher

33. Which is the only department that CANNOT have two of its teachers on a committee?

(A) Social Studies
(B) English
(C) Science
(D) Mathematics
(E) Foreign Language

34. Which of the following could be the two other teachers serving on a committee with a teacher from the Foreign Language department?

(A) Another teacher from Foreign Languages and one from Mathematics
(B) One teacher each from the Social Studies and Mathematics departments
(C) One teacher each from the Science and English departments
(D) Two mathematics teachers
(E) Two English teachers

3                                                                                      3

35. So many arrogant and ill-tempered young men
have dominated the tennis courts of late that we
had begun to fear those characteristics were prerequisites for championship tennis.

Tennis used to be a gentleman's game. What is sad
is not just that the game has changed. With so
much importance placed on success, it may be that
something has gone out of the American
character—such things as gentleness and graciousness.

Which one of the following statements, if true,
would most weaken the above argument?

(A) The American character is a result of
American goals.
(B) Tennis has only recently become a professional
sport.
(C) Some ill-tempered tennis players are
unsuccessful.
(D) The "gentlemen" of early tennis were often
arrogant and nasty off the court.
(E) Some even-tempered tennis players are
successful.

# Answer Key

## Section 1—Verbal Ability

| | | | | | | |
|---|---|---|---|---|---|---|
| 1. A | 6. E | 11. D | 16. E | 21. C | 26. E |
| 2. B | 7. E | 12. B | 17. B | 22. B | 27. D |
| 3. D | 8. C | 13. D | 18. B | 23. B | 28. A |
| 4. A | 9. D | 14. A | 19. D | 24. E | 29. C |
| 5. D | 10. D | 15. D | 20. B | 25. D | 30. A |

## Section 2—Quantitative Ability

NOTE: The letters in brackets following the Quantitative Ability answers refer to the sections of Chapter 15 in which you can find the information you need to answer the questions. For example, 1. C [E] means that the answer to question 1 is C, and that the solution requires information found in Section 15-E: Averages. Also, 20. A [14] means that the answer to question 20 is based on information in Chapter 14: Data Interpretation.

| | | | | | |
|---|---|---|---|---|---|
| 1. D [A] | 6. B [O] | 11. C [E,G] | 16. A [A] | 21. B [14] | 26. E [A] |
| 2. D [B,C] | 7. B [B,G] | 12. A [J,L] | 17. C [K,L] | 22. D [G,J] | 27. B [L] |
| 3. D [J] | 8. D [J] | 13. A [B] | 18. D [O] | 23. D [L] | 28. D [A] |
| 4. C [F] | 9. B [G] | 14. B [14] | 19. E [E] | 24. C [L] | |
| 5. B [D] | 10. C [C,D] | 15. B [14] | 20. B [14] | 25. C [B] | |

## Section 3—Analytical Ability

| | | | | |
|---|---|---|---|---|
| 1. B | 8. E | 15. A | 22. C | 29. D |
| 2. E | 9. C | 16. D | 23. D | 30. D |
| 3. D | 10. E | 17. D | 24. A | 31. C |
| 4. C | 11. C | 18. E | 25. C | 32. D |
| 5. A | 12. E | 19. A | 26. C | 33. C |
| 6. C | 13. A | 20. E | 27. D | 34. E |
| 7. B | 14. C | 21. D | 28. C | 35. D |

# Answer Explanations

## Section 1—Verbal Ability

1. A.  *Elated* (joyful, in high spirits) is the opposite of *crestfallen* (dejected).
Think of "elated by her success."

2. B.  The opposite of *reticence* (uncommunicativeness; restraint in speech) is *loquaciousness* (talkativeness).
Think of "speaking without reticence."

3. D.  If "you may wonder" how the expert reaches his conclusions, it appears that it is questionable to rely on teeth for guidance in interpreting fossils. Choice D, *inadequate*, creates the element of doubt that the clause tries to develop. Choice C, *specious*, also creates an element of doubt; however, nothing in the context justifies the idea that the reasoning is specious or false.

Note that here you are dealing with an extended metaphor. Picture yourself hanging a heavy winter coat on a slim wooden peg. Wouldn't you worry that the peg might prove inadequate or flimsy?

4. A.  Here the task is to determine the communal reaction to crime. The writer maintains that the criminal justice system of punishments allows the community to purge itself of its anger, its sense of *outrage* at the criminal's acts. Thus, it provides a *catharsis* or purgation for the community.
Remember, in double-blank sentences, go through the answers, testing the *first* word in each choice and eliminating those that don't fit. In this case, you can readily eliminate Choices B and E: it is unlikely that an *essential* purpose of the criminal justice system would be the provision of either a *disclaimer* (denial or disavowal, as in disavowing responsibility for a legal claim) or a *document*.

5. D.   Someone *vindictive* or vengeful is lacking in *mercy*. Someone *skeptical* or suspicious is lacking in *trustfulness*.    (Antonym Variant)

6. E.   To *ruffle* someone's *composure* is to disturb or trouble his self-possession. To *upset* someone's *equilibrium* is to disturb or trouble his balance.    (Function)

7. E.   The last sentence points out that Du Bois originally agreed with Washington's program. Choice A is incorrect. Nothing in the passage suggests that Du Bois sacrificed effective strategies out of a desire to try something new. Choice B is incorrect. Du Bois gained in influence, effectively winning away large numbers of blacks from Washington's policies. Choice C is incorrect. Du Bois' quickness to depart from conventional black wisdom when it proved inadequate to the task of advancing the race shows him to be well able to change with the times.
Choice D is incorrect. Washington, not Du Bois, is described as seeking the good will of powerful whites.

8. C.   The author does *not* portray Washington as versatile. Instead, he portrays Du Bois as versatile.
Choice A is incorrect. The author portrays Washington as submissive to the majority; he shows him teaching blacks not to protest.
Choice B is incorrect. The author portrays Washington as concerned with financial success; he shows him advocating property accumulation.
Choice D is incorrect. The author portrays Washington as traditional in preaching industry; he shows him advocating hard work.
Choice E is incorrect. The author portrays Washington as respectful of authority; he shows him deferring to powerful whites.

9. D.   Although the author points out that Du Bois' methods led him into conflicts, he describes Du Bois as "often...well in advance of his contemporaries" and stresses that his motives for departing from the mainstream were admirable. Thus, his attitude can best be described as *approving*.

10. D.  To *revile* (verbally abuse) something is the opposite of *praising* it.
Think of "reviled as a traitor."

11. D.  The opposite of *propitious* (favorable, advantageous) is *unfavorable*.
Think of being pleased by "propitious omens."

12. B.  An *offhand* remark is made without forethought or *premeditation*. An *aboveboard* (open) deed is done without trickery or *guile*.    (Antonym Variant)

13. D.  The *larval* (immature) stage of an *insect* best corresponds to the *embryonic* stage of a *mammal*.    (Defining Characteristic)

14. A.  Under certain circumstances scientists attack each other with *ad hominem* arguments (personal attacks) and shameless appeals. When is this likely to occur? When facts are *established* or *demonstrable* or *ineluctable* (unavoidable)? Hardly. Under such circumstances they would rely on facts to establish their case. It is when facts prove *elusive* that they lose control and, in doing so, abandon their pretense of *objectivity*.

15. D.  The key word here is *assailed*. Housman is attacking his rival. Thus he is in the tradition of scholarly *invective* (vehement verbal attack), criticizing his foe for turning to manuscripts merely for confirmation or *support* of old theories and not for enlightenment or illumination.
Again, note the use of figurative language, in this case the simile of the drunkard.

16. E.  The author first states that the reasons for bioluminescence in underwater microorganisms is obscure and then proceeds to enumerate various hypotheses.

17. B.  The author does not deny that predators make use of bioluminescence in locating their prey. Instead, he gives an example of human predators (commercial fishermen) who are drawn to their prey (the fish that prey on plankton) by the luminescence of the plankton.

18. B.  As the previous answer makes clear, the phenomenon of plankton bioluminescence does have practical applications. It is a valuable tool for fisheries interested in increasing their catch of fish that prey on plankton.

19. D.  The opposite of *incongruous* (inconsistent, not fitting) is *harmonious*.
Think of being startled by "incongruous behavior."

20. B.  An *apostate* (renegade; person faithless to an allegiance) is the opposite of a *loyalist*.
Beware eye-catchers. Do not confuse *apostate* (renegade) with *apostle* (missionary; reformer).
Think of "a faithless apostate."

21. C.  By definition, a *sextant* is a piece of equipment that is *nautical*. Similarly, a *forceps* is a piece of equipment that is *surgical*.    (Defining Characteristic)

22. B.  Someone *refractory* (stubborn; unmanageable) by definition is hard to *manage*. Likewise,

someone *lethargic* (sluggish; drowsy) by definition is hard to *stimulate*.      (Definition)

23.  B.   The opposite of to *ensue* (happen later, follow) is to *precede*.
Think of "the wedding that ensued."

24.  E.   A disease in a *latent* state has yet to manifest
itself and emerge into view. Therefore it is
impossible to *observe*.
Remember, in double-blank sentences, go
through the answers, testing the *first* word in
each choice and eliminating those that don't
fit. When a disease is in a *critical* or *acute*
state, its existence is obvious. Therefore, you
can eliminate Choices B and C.

25.  D.   The second clause presents an example of literary *mockery*. The abstract idea of preserving
a nugget of pure truth is appealing; the concrete example of setting it up on the mantel
makes fun of the whole idea.

26.  E.   The eagle is poised to strike "with exposed
talons." It, like the Cardinal, collects itself to
strike with greater force. The imagery accen-
tuates the Cardinal's *mercilessness*.
Choice A is incorrect. The Cardinal is not
*flighty* (light-headed and irresponsible); he is
cold and calculating.
Choice B is incorrect. He loves power, not
freedom.
Choice C is incorrect. An eagle poised to
strike with bare claws suggests violence, not
*eminence* (fame and high position).
Choice D is incorrect. Nothing in the passage
suggests he is spiritual.
Beware eye-catchers. "Eminence" is a title of
honor applied to cardinals in the Roman
Catholic church. Choice D may attract you for
this reason.

27.  D.   The author's depiction of the Cardinal stresses
his redoubtable qualities as a foe (calculation,
duplicity, mercilessness) and as a challenge to
an actor ("imperial repose," a commanding
presence, smooth movements suggesting latent
danger).
Choice A is incorrect. The author portrays the
Cardinal's relations with his brother and mistress as cold, but he never apologizes for the
Cardinal's lack of warmth. Indeed, the author
somewhat savors it.
Choices B and C are incorrect. Neither esteem
for a nonexistent spirituality nor admiration
for a villainous autocracy enters into the
author's depiction of the Cardinal.
Choice E is incorrect. A cause of perturbation
to others, the Cardinal is never perturbed.

28.  A.   An *austere style* is severely simple and
restrained. *Controlled movement* is restrained
as well.      (Defining Characteristic)

29.  C.   *Retrospection* (looking backward; the act of
surveying the past) is the opposite of *anticipation* (looking forward).
Word Parts Clue: *Retro-* means backward;
*spect-* means look. *Retrospection* means looking backward.
Think of "an old man lost in retrospection."

30.  A.   *Topical* (local, temporary) is the opposite of
*general*.
Remember that words may be used in several
different ways. Here *topical* does not mean
arranged according to topics (as in a topical
index).
Think of "a topical anesthetic," one applied
locally, not generally.

# Section 2—Quantitative Ability

Two asterisks (**) indicate an alternative method of
solving.

1.  D.   Use TACTIC 4, Chapter 13. Could $m$ and $n$ be
equal? Sure, if each is 5. Eliminate Choices A
and B. Must they be equal? No, not if $m = 1$
and $n = 25$. Eliminate Choice C, as well.
Neither column is always greater, and the two
columns are not always equal (D).

2.  D.   Since $\frac{2}{3} = 66\frac{2}{3}\%$, which is clearly more than
65%, it *appears* that Column B is greater. *Be
careful*! That would be true if $a$ were positive,
but no restrictions are placed on $a$. If $a = 0$,
the columns are equal; if $a$ is negative,
Column A is greater. Neither column is
always greater, and the two columns are not
always equal (D).
**Use TACTIC 1, Chapter 13. Just let $a = 0$,
and then let $a = 1$.

3.  D.   Use TACTIC 4, Chapter 13. Could the columns
be equal? Could $c = 5$? Sure, if this is a 3-4-5
right triangle. Must $c = 5$? No; if the triangle
is not a right triangle, $c$
could be less than or more
than 5. Neither column is
*always* greater, and the
columns are not *always*
equal (D). (*Note*: Since
the figure may not be
drawn to scale, do *not*
assume that the triangle
has a right angle.)

4.  C.   Column A: $(a + b)^2 = a^2 + 2ab + b^2 = a^2 + b^2$
(since $ab = 0$).
Column B: $(a - b)^2 = a^2 - 2ab + b^2 = a^2 + b^2$
(since $ab = 0$).
The columns are equal (C).
**Use TACTIC 1, Chapter 13: let $a = 0$ and
$b = 1$. Then $(a + b)^2 = (0 + 1)^2 = 1$ and $(a - b)^2 =
(0 - 1)^2 = 1$. Eliminate A and B and try other

values where either $a$ or $b$ is 0 (since $ab = 0$). The two expressions are always equal.

5.  B.   Since $d$ divisions each have $t$ teams, multiply to get $dt$ teams; and since each team has $p$ players, multiply the number of teams ($dt$) by $p$ to get the total number of players: $dtp$. **Use TACTIC 2, Chapter 12. Pick three easy-to-use numbers for $t$, $d$, and $p$. Assume that there are 2 divisions, each consisting of 4 teams, so, there are $2 \times 4 = 8$ teams. Then assume that each team has 10 players, for a total of $8 \times 10 = 80$ players. Now check the choices. Which one is equal to 80 when $d = 2$, $t = 4$, and $p = 10$? Only $dtp$.

6.  B.   There are nine positive integers less than 10: $1, 2, \ldots, 9$. For which of them is $\frac{9}{x} > x$? Only 1 and 2: $\frac{9}{1} > 1$ and $\frac{9}{2} > 2$. When $x = 3$, $\frac{9}{x} = x$, and for all the others $\frac{9}{x} < x$. The probability is $\frac{2}{9}$.

7.  B.   Solve the given equation:
$$\frac{1}{a} + \frac{1}{a} + \frac{1}{a} = 12$$
Add the fractions:
$$\frac{3}{a} = 12$$
Multiply both sides by $a$:
$$3 = 12a$$
Divide both sides by 12:
$$a = \frac{3}{12} = \frac{1}{4}.$$
**You can use TACTIC 1, Chapter 12: back-solve; try Choice C. If $a = \frac{1}{3}$, then $\frac{1}{a} = 3$, so the left-hand side equals 9. That's too small. Now, *be careful*: a fraction gets bigger when its denominator gets *smaller* [KEY FACT B4]. Eliminate Choices C, D, and E, and try a smaller value for $a$: $\frac{1}{4}$ works.

8.  D.   Use TACTIC 4, Chapter 13. Could $y = 20$? Yes, if the large triangle were equilateral, $x$ would be 30 and $y$ would be 20. Must $y = 20$? No, if $x = 45$, $y = 10$. (Note: Since the figure may not be drawn to scale, the triangle could be *any* triangle with a 60° angle.) Neither column is *always* larger, and the columns are not *always* equal (D).

9.  B.   You don't *have* to solve for $a$ and $b$. If $a - b > a + b$, then $b$ is negative and Column B is greater.

**You *could* solve. Adding the two equations yields
$$2a = 49 \Rightarrow a = 24.5 \Rightarrow b = -.5.$$

10.  C.   Since, in 1990, $2p$ pounds of potatoes cost $\frac{1}{2}d$ dollars, $p$ pounds cost half as much: $\frac{1}{2}\left(\frac{1}{2}d\right)$ $= \frac{1}{4}d$. This is $\frac{1}{4}$, or 25%, as much as the cost in 1980, which represents a decrease of 75%. **In this type of problem it is *often* easier to use TACTIC 2, Chapter 12. Assume that 1 pound of potatoes cost \$100 in 1980. Then in 1990, 2 pounds cost \$50, so 1 pound cost \$25. This is a decrease of \$75 in the cost of 1 pound of potatoes, and
$$\text{percent decrease} = \frac{\text{decrease}}{\text{original}}\,(100\%)$$
$$= \frac{75}{100}\,(100\%) = 75\%.$$

11.  C.   Adding the two given equations, we get $a + b + c = 11d$. Then $a + b + c + d = 11d + d = 12d \Rightarrow \frac{a + b + c + d}{4} = \frac{12d}{4} = 3d$. The columns are equal (C).

12.  A.   Since in the given figure $OA$ and $OB$ are radii, each is equal to 5. With no restrictions on $x$, $AB$ could be any positive number less than 10; and the larger $x$ is, the larger $AB$ is. If $x$ were 90, $AB$ would be $5\sqrt{2}$, but we are told that $x > 90$, so $AB > 5\sqrt{2} > 7$.

13.  A.   Column B $= \left(\frac{13}{17}\right)^5 = (x^5)^5 = x^{25}$. Since $0 < x < 1$, $x^{25} < x$.

14.  B.   The average expected family contribution of a family with an income between \$50,000 and \$59,000 is about \$7,500. Since the average cost of attending a 4-year public university is \$10,800, there is an unmet need of $\$10,800 - \$7,500 = \$3,300$.

15.  B.   Family A would be expected to pay \$10,800, the full annual cost for a 4-year public university. Family B would be expected to pay approximately \$3,500. Therefore, family A would pay $\$10,800 - \$3,500 = \$7,300$ more.

16. A.   Since $a < b$, when $a$ is divided by $b$, the quotient is 0 and the remainder is $a$: $a = 0 \times b + a$. When any integer is divided by $a$, the remainder must be less than $a$. Column A is greater.

17. C.   In Figure 1, since the radius of each circle is 3, the area of each circle is $9\pi$, and the total area of the four circles is $36\pi$. In Figure 2, the radius of each circle is 2, and so the area of each circle is $4\pi$, and the total area of the nine circles is $36\pi$. In the two figures, the white areas are equal, as are the shaded areas. The columns are equal (C).

18. D.   If Jason were really unlucky, what could go wrong in his attempt to get one marble of each color? Well, his first nine picks *might* yield five blue marbles and four white ones. But then the tenth marble would be red, and now he would have at least one of each color. The answer is 10.

19. E.   If $a$ represents Jordan's average after 5 tests, then he has earned a total of $5a$ points [TACTIC E1]. A grade of 70 on the sixth test will lower his average 4 points to $a - 4$. Therefore,

$$a - 4 = \frac{5a + 70}{6} \Rightarrow 6(a - 4) = 5a + 70 \Rightarrow$$
$$6a - 24 = 5a + 70 \Rightarrow 6a = 5a + 94 \Rightarrow a = 94.$$

**Assume Jordan's average is $a$ because he earned $a$ on each of his first 5 tests. Since after getting a 70 on his sixth test his average will be $a - 4$, the deviation on each of the first 5 tests is 4, for a total deviation above the average of 20 points. So, the total deviation below must also be 20 [KEY FACT E3]. Therefore, 70 is 20 less than the new average of $a - 4$:

$$70 = (a - 4) - 20 \Rightarrow a = 94.$$

**Use TACTIC 1, Chapter 12: backsolve. Start with Choice C, 86. If his 5-test average was 90, he had 450 points and a 70 on the sixth test would give him a total of 520 points, and an average of $520 \div 6 = 86.666$. So, the 70 lowered his average 3.333 points. That's not enough. Eliminate Choices A, B, and C. Try Choices D or E. Choice E, 94, works.

20. B.   Reading from the top graph, we get the following enrollment figures:

|                | 1970       | 1988       |
|----------------|------------|------------|
| Public PreK–8  | 33,000,000 | 28,000,000 |
| Public 9–12    | 13,000,000 | 12,000,000 |
| Private PreK–8 | 4,000,000  | 4,000,000  |
| Private 9–12   | 1,000,000  | 1,000,000  |
| Total          | 51,000,000 | 45,000,000 |

$51,000,000 - 45,000,000 = 6,000,000$.

21. B.   In 1988, 8,800,000 (22% of 40,000,000) students lived in the West. From 1988–1998 this figure increased by 27%—for simplicity use 25%: an additional 2,200,000 students; so the total was then 11,000,000. The projected increase from 1998–2008 is about 10%, so the number will grow by 1,100,000 to 12,100,000.

22. D.   Expand:

$$(a + b)^2 = a^2 + 2ab + b^2 = (a^2 + b^2) + 2ab.$$

By the Pythagorean theorem, $a^2 + b^2 = 10^2 = 100$; and since the area is 20,

$\frac{1}{2}ab = 20 \Rightarrow ab = 40$, and $2ab = 80$. Then

$$(a^2 + b^2) + 2ab = 100 + 80 = 180.$$

23. D.   Let $r$, $C$, and $A$ represent the radius, circumference, and area of the circle.

$$C = 2\pi r = a\pi \Rightarrow a = \frac{2\pi r}{\pi} = 2r.$$

Similarly,

$$A = \pi r^2 = b\pi \Rightarrow b = \frac{\pi r^2}{\pi} = r^2.$$

The value of Column A is $2r$, and the value of Column B is $r^2$. Which is greater? Dividing each by $r$, yields 2 in Column A and $r$ in Column B. Since there are no restrictions, $r$ could be greater than, less than, or equal to $r$. Neither column is always greater, and the two columns are not always equal (D).
**Use TACTIC 1, Chapter 13. Let $r = 1$. Then, $C = 2\pi$ and $A = \pi$; so $a = 2$ and $b = 1$. Column B is greater: eliminate A and C. Try $r = 2$. Now, $C = 4\pi$ and $A = 4\pi$; $a = b$ and the columns are equal. Eliminate Choice B. The answer is D.

24. C.   If $r$ is the radius of the white circle, $2r$ is the radius of the shaded semicircle. The area of the white circle is $\pi r^2$. The area of the semicircle is $\frac{1}{2}\pi(2r)^2 = \frac{1}{2}\pi(4r^2) = 2\pi r^2$, so the area of the shaded region is $2\pi r^2 - \pi r^2 = \pi r^2$. The columns are equal (C).

**The solution is even easier if you use TACTIC 1, Chapter 13. Let the radius of the circle be 1 instead of $r$, and proceed as above. The area of each region is $\pi$.

25. C. If there are $x$ seats on each bus, then the group is using $\frac{4}{5}(3x) = \frac{12}{5}x$ seats. After $\frac{1}{4}$ of them get off, $\frac{3}{4}$ of them, or $\frac{3}{4}\left(\frac{12}{5}x\right) = \frac{9}{5}x$ remain. What fraction of the $2x$ seats on the two buses are now being used? $\dfrac{\frac{9}{5}x}{2x} = \dfrac{\frac{9}{5}}{2} = \dfrac{9}{10}$.

**To avoid the algebra, assume there are 20 seats on each bus. At the beginning, the group is using 48 of the 60 seats on the three buses $\left[\frac{4}{5}(60) = 48\right]$. When 12 people left $\left[\frac{1}{4}(48) = 12\right]$, the 36 remaining people used $\frac{36}{40} = \frac{9}{10}$ of the 40 seats on two buses.

26. E. To find the average of three numbers, divide their sum by 3: $\dfrac{3^{30} + 3^{60} + 3^{90}}{3}$. Now use the distributive law and divide each term in the numerator by 3: $\dfrac{3^{30}}{3} + \dfrac{3^{60}}{3} + \dfrac{3^{90}}{3}$ $= 3^{29} + 3^{59} + 3^{89}$.

27. B. In the given figure, the diameters of the four small semicircles are 2, 4, 6, and 8, so the diameter of the large semicircle is $2 + 4 + 6 + 8 = 20$, and its radius is 10. The perimeter of the shaded region is the sum of the circumferences of all five semicircles. Since the circumference of a semicircle is $\pi$ times its radius, the perimeter is $\pi + 2\pi + 3\pi + 4\pi + 10\pi = 20\pi$.

28. D. Let $B$ be the sum of all the positive odd intergers less than 1000.

$A = 2 + 4 + 6 + 8 + \cdots + 996 + 998$
$\quad\downarrow\ \ \downarrow\ \ \downarrow\ \ \downarrow\qquad\ \downarrow\qquad\ \downarrow$
$B = (1 + 3 + 5 + 7 + \cdots + 995 + 997) + 999$

$A$ is the sum of 499 even integers, each of which is 1 more than the corresponding odd integer in $B$. Then $(1 + 3 + 5 + \cdots + 997) = A - 499$, and $B = (A - 499) + 999 = A + 500$.

# Section 3—Analytical Ability

1. B. To speak in positive terms about the increase in school degrees, the author must assume that the degrees indicate what they are supposed to indicate, that is, well-educated individuals. Choices A and E are empty statements; Choices C and D are altogether unsubstantiated by either expressed or implied information.

**Solutions 2–5**

$\quad$ L < K < H $\qquad$ I > J $\qquad$ F > H $\qquad$ G > H

Exhibiting this information on a line, we see:

lowest GPA $\underline{\qquad\ \ \text{L}\quad \text{K}\quad \text{H}\quad \text{F}\qquad\ }$ highest GPA
$\qquad\qquad\qquad\qquad\quad —\text{G}\rightarrow$
$\qquad\qquad\qquad \leftarrow\text{J}———\text{I}\rightarrow$

2. E. From the line we drew based on the given conditions, we see that any of F, G, or I could have the highest GPA, so any one of Choices A, B, and C could be true. F, G, and H all have GPAs higher than K's, and I (and even J) could have a higher GPA, so Choice D could be true. At most there are three students (L, J, and I) who could have a lower GPA than K, so Choice E cannot be true.

3. D. From the line we drew based on the given conditions, we know that either J or L has the lowest GPA. Clearly, if J has a higher GPA than K (Choice D), then J's GPA cannot be lowest; so L's is. None of the other choices permits us to distinguish definitively between J and L.

4. C. From the line we drew based on the given conditions, we know that the correct order of F, G, H, K, L is either:

$\qquad$ L K H G F $\quad$ or $\quad$ L K H F G

• Since J > F and it is given that I > J, in the first case, there is only one possibility: L K H G F J I.

In the second case, there are three possibilities:

• J and I could both be between F and G: L K H F J I G;

• J and I could both be greater than G: L K H F G J I;

• J could be between F and G, and I greater than G: L K H F J G I

In all, there are four possible rankings.

5. A. Since both F and G have higher GPAs than H, the average of their GPAs is higher than H's, which is higher than I's. Choice A, therefore cannot be true. None of the other choices must be true, but each of them could be true.

6. C. The passage argues that environmental restrictions will lead to losses of jobs and hence workers, but if workers are already leaving because the environmental quality is poor, the argument is seriously weakened.

7. B. The passage makes no comment on workers leaving before a manufacturer. It argues that the loss of manufacturers leads to a loss of workers (E).

8.  E.  We know who *must* do the extra-credit project; we do not know if Mr. Walsh will permit other students to do the extra-credit project, as well. Eliminate Choices A and C. Despite the fact that at least one student earned a 97, the class average could be below 75, and most of the students in the class will have to do the extra-credit project. Eliminate Choices B and D. Choice E is true: even though John did all his labs, his test grade was below 75, and so he must do the extra-credit project.

## Solutions 9–13

9, 10, 11, Lunch, 1, 2, 3

J = 1:00     G << I or I << G     H < F

9.  C.  Since H must be interviewed earlier in the day than F (H < F), H cannot have the last interview of the day.

10. E.  Only Choice E doesn't violate any of the given conditions.
Choice A violates the condition that J have the fourth interview (J = 1:00).
Choices B and D violate the condition that no one be interviewed between G and I (G << I or I << G).
Choice C violates the condition that H be interviewed earlier in the day than F (H < F).

11. C.  Since J has the 1:00 interview, and H and K both have morning interviews, the slots remaining for F, G, and I are the remaining morning slot and 2:00 and 3:00. Since G and I have interviews one after the other, they must have the last two interviews of the day. F cannot have the last interview; Choice C cannot be true.

12. E.  Given that J and F are being interviewed at 1:00 and 2:00, respectively, H cannot have the 3:00 interview (H < F). Also, since G and I must have consecutive interviews, neither of them can be interviewed at 3:00. Therefore, K must have the 3:00 interview. Each of the other choices is possible, but none *must* be true.

13. A.  Since I has the 9:00 interview, G has an interview at 10:00 (I << G). Since H's interview must precede F's interview (H < F), F cannot have the 11:00 interview, and so must have an interview at either 2:00 or 3:00, *after* J's 1:00 interview.

14. C.  Examine the structure of the argument: the only reason given for funding the research is that the possibility exists that the substances cure cancer. The unstated assumption is that this is a sufficient reason for providing funds. No probability is mentioned (Choice A), and

no comparison with other lines of research is made (Choice B). Choice D, while probably true, does not provide logical support for the argument about researching this specific possibility. The argument simply says that the government should provide the funds, not that they are definitely unavailable elsewhere (Choice E).

## Solutions 15–18

Rep: A, B, C, D   Dem: R, S, T   Days: M, T, W, Th, F

each day: 1 Rep & 1 Dem or 2 Rep & 2 Dem

no one on 2 consec. days

Fri → (A ∧ R)   R → ~S   B ↔ T

15. A.  Only Choice A doesn't violate any of the conditions.
Since neither Berg nor Tyler will attend a session unless the other does (B ↔ T), eliminate Choices B, C, and E. Since there can't be three Republicans and one Democrat, eliminate Choice D.

16. D.  In the solution to question 15, we saw that Berg and Tyler also had to be in attendance on Friday. No one attending on Friday can attend on Thursday. The only Democrat not attending Friday's session is Sack, who, therefore, must attend on Thursday.

17. D.  The three Democrats—Ray, Sack, and Tyler—each had to attend one of the sessions from Wednesday to Friday. Ash attended on Friday, and Berg attended with Tyler on either Wednesday or Thursday. Either Cox or Day attended with Sack, and the other attended on Tuesday. Day isn't one of the choices, so the answer is Choice D: Cox

18. E.  Since Berg attended on Tuesday, so did Tyler (B ↔ T). Therefore, Tyler could not have attended on Monday.

19. A.  The apparent contradiction disappears if the total state budget has increased enough so that the *expenditure* on education has been raised by three million each year while at the same time the *percentage* spent on education is a smaller part of the whole budget.

## Solutions 20–23

Wines: B, C, M, P, S   Days: M, T, W, Th, F

each day: 3 wines   no wine on 3 consec. days

no wine can skip 2 days in a row

each wine: 3 times/week

20. E.  Since neither Beaujolais nor Chablis were available on Wednesday, both must be available on Thursday. Only Choice E includes both Beaujolais and Chablis.

21. D.   Since Beaujolais, Chablis, and Merlot are served on Monday, Pinot Grigio must be served on Tuesday; and since it is given that Pinot Grigio is served on Thursday, it *cannot* be served on Wednesday, since no wine can be served on three consecutive days.

22. C.   Only Choice C doesn't violate any of the conditions.
   • If the same three wines are available on Tuesday and Thursday, none of them could be available on Wednesday (since no wine is served on three consecutive days), which would mean that only two wines (not three) would be available on Wednesday. Eliminate Choice A.
   • If Merlot and Syrah are both served on Monday and Tuesday, then of the three other wines, one could be served on Monday and one on Tuesday, but the third would could not be served on either day. Eliminate Choice B.
   • Since Chablis and Beaujolais are each available three times a week, there must be at least one day that both are available. Eliminate Choice D.
   • If neither Chablis nor Beaujolais is available on Wednesday or Friday, then the other three wines are available on both of those days. This is the same situation as in Choice A. Eliminate Choice E.

23. D.   There are only four pairs of consecutive days: Monday-Tuesday, Tuesday-Wednesday, Wednesday-Thursday, and Thursday-Friday. Since there are only five wines, and on any pair of days there are six wines available, on each pair of days there must be one wine which is available on both days. So there must be at least four wines that are available consecutively. If two different wines were available on the same two consecutive days, only two of the other three wines would be available on either of those days, which is impossible. Therefore, at most four of the wines can be available on two consecutive days. The answer is 4 (D).

## Solutions 24–28

M, M, W, W, W, C, C, C, C

C << C << C << C   M << M

24. A.   Since the two men must sit next to each other, a man is sitting in seat 106. Eliminate Choice E. Since the four children must sit in consecutive seats, they must be in seats 101–104 or 102–105; in either case, they occupy seats 102, 103, and 104. Eliminate Choices B, C, and D.

   | | C | C | C | | M | M | W | |
   |---|---|---|---|---|---|---|---|---|
   | 101 | 102 | 103 | 104 | 105 | 106 | 107 | 108 | 109 |

25. C.   If a man is in seat 105, then there are four seats on either side of him. On one side, the four seats must be used by the four children. On the other side, the seat next to the first man is reserved for the second man, and the next three seats would be for the women.

   C C C C M M W W W   or   W W W M M C C C C
   105                            105

26. C.   The four children must be in seats 104–107 or 105–108; so they must occupy seats 105, 106, and 107:

   | | W | | C | C | C | | W | |
   |---|---|---|---|---|---|---|---|---|
   | 101 | 102 | 103 | 104 | 105 | 106 | 107 | 108 | 109 |

   Since the two men must sit next to each other, they occupy seats 101 and 102. The third woman could sit in either 104 or 108, with the fourth child in the other one.

27. B.   The children occupy seats 101–104 and the adults occupy seats 105–109. The two men must be in seats 106–107, 107–108, or 108–109. In the first case, a man is in seat 106, and a woman is in seat 108; in the second and third cases, a man is in seat 108 and a woman is in seat 106.

28. C.   If no woman is next to another woman, the women must be separated by the groups of children and men. Therefore, they must be in seats 101, 109, and either 104 or 106:

   | W | C | C | C | C | W | M | M | W |
   |---|---|---|---|---|---|---|---|---|
   | 101 | 102 | 103 | 104 | 105 | 106 | 107 | 108 | 109 |

   or

   | W | M | M | W | C | C | C | C | W |
   |---|---|---|---|---|---|---|---|---|
   | 101 | 102 | 103 | 104 | 105 | 106 | 107 | 108 | 109 |

   In either case, a child is in seat 105.

29. D.   From the given statements we see that:

   S < J < D   E < D   E < A < B

   Therefore, either Dalia or Blayke has the highest GPA. If the average of Blayke's and Anne's GPAs is higher than Dalia's GPA, then either Blayke or Anne has a GPA which is higher than Dalia's and the other has a GPA which is lower than Dalia's. Since Blayke's GPA is higher than Anne's, it must be Blayke who has the highest GPA. None of the other choices allows us to determine whose GPA is the highest.

30. D.   Choices A, B, and C strengthen the case for building the toll road. The environmentalists may be able to make their case for one of the other possible routes that, if less direct, would not disturb the reserve. With the information we have, the value of Choice E is indeterminable.

## Solutions 31–34

each committee <u>exactly 3</u> from E, F, M, S, SS

2 teachers from the same department OK—but <u>not</u> 3

SS ↔ M    F → E    E → ~S (equivalently: S → ~E)

31. **C.** Any committee containing a social studies teacher, must also have a mathematics teacher [SS ↔ M].

32. **D.** Only Choice D does not violate any of the given conditions.
Choice A includes three teachers from the same department.
Choice B includes a social studies teacher, but not a mathematics teacher [SS ↔ M].
Choice C includes teachers from both the Science and English departments [E → ~S].
Choice E includes a mathematics teacher but not a social studies teacher [SS ↔ M].

33. **C.** Assume that there were two science teachers:
   - The third teacher could not be another science teacher, since all three teachers cannot be from the same department.
   - The third teacher could not be an English teacher [S → ~E].
   - Since any committee with a social studies teacher or a mathematics teacher must have teachers from both departments [SS ↔ M], and since there is room for only one more teacher, that teacher could not be from either department.
   - The third teacher could not be from the Foreign Language department since then there would have to be a teacher from the English department [F → E].
   - Each of the other departments could have two of its members on a committee.

34. **E.** Only Choice E does not violate any of the given conditions.
   - Since any committee with a foreign language teacher must also have an English teacher [F → E], eliminate Choices A, B, and D.
   - Since no committee can have teachers from both the Science and the English departments [S → ~E], eliminate Choice C.

35. **D.** The choice repudiates the suggestion that gentleness and graciousness were once part of the American character. B, another choice worth considering, is not best because it does not address the temperament of tennis players as directly as does Choice D.

# Answer Sheet—Model Test 3

## Section 1

1. Ⓐ Ⓑ Ⓒ Ⓓ Ⓔ
2. Ⓐ Ⓑ Ⓒ Ⓓ Ⓔ
3. Ⓐ Ⓑ Ⓒ Ⓓ Ⓔ
4. Ⓐ Ⓑ Ⓒ Ⓓ Ⓔ
5. Ⓐ Ⓑ Ⓒ Ⓓ Ⓔ
6. Ⓐ Ⓑ Ⓒ Ⓓ Ⓔ
7. Ⓐ Ⓑ Ⓒ Ⓓ Ⓔ
8. Ⓐ Ⓑ Ⓒ Ⓓ Ⓔ
9. Ⓐ Ⓑ Ⓒ Ⓓ Ⓔ
10. Ⓐ Ⓑ Ⓒ Ⓓ Ⓔ

11. Ⓐ Ⓑ Ⓒ Ⓓ Ⓔ
12. Ⓐ Ⓑ Ⓒ Ⓓ Ⓔ
13. Ⓐ Ⓑ Ⓒ Ⓓ Ⓔ
14. Ⓐ Ⓑ Ⓒ Ⓓ Ⓔ
15. Ⓐ Ⓑ Ⓒ Ⓓ Ⓔ
16. Ⓐ Ⓑ Ⓒ Ⓓ Ⓔ
17. Ⓐ Ⓑ Ⓒ Ⓓ Ⓔ
18. Ⓐ Ⓑ Ⓒ Ⓓ Ⓔ
19. Ⓐ Ⓑ Ⓒ Ⓓ Ⓔ
20. Ⓐ Ⓑ Ⓒ Ⓓ Ⓔ

21. Ⓐ Ⓑ Ⓒ Ⓓ Ⓔ
22. Ⓐ Ⓑ Ⓒ Ⓓ Ⓔ
23. Ⓐ Ⓑ Ⓒ Ⓓ Ⓔ
24. Ⓐ Ⓑ Ⓒ Ⓓ Ⓔ
25. Ⓐ Ⓑ Ⓒ Ⓓ Ⓔ
26. Ⓐ Ⓑ Ⓒ Ⓓ Ⓔ
27. Ⓐ Ⓑ Ⓒ Ⓓ Ⓔ
28. Ⓐ Ⓑ Ⓒ Ⓓ Ⓔ
29. Ⓐ Ⓑ Ⓒ Ⓓ Ⓔ
30. Ⓐ Ⓑ Ⓒ Ⓓ Ⓔ

## Section 2

1. Ⓐ Ⓑ Ⓒ Ⓓ Ⓔ
2. Ⓐ Ⓑ Ⓒ Ⓓ Ⓔ
3. Ⓐ Ⓑ Ⓒ Ⓓ Ⓔ
4. Ⓐ Ⓑ Ⓒ Ⓓ Ⓔ
5. Ⓐ Ⓑ Ⓒ Ⓓ Ⓔ
6. Ⓐ Ⓑ Ⓒ Ⓓ Ⓔ
7. Ⓐ Ⓑ Ⓒ Ⓓ Ⓔ
8. Ⓐ Ⓑ Ⓒ Ⓓ Ⓔ
9. Ⓐ Ⓑ Ⓒ Ⓓ Ⓔ
10. Ⓐ Ⓑ Ⓒ Ⓓ Ⓔ

11. Ⓐ Ⓑ Ⓒ Ⓓ Ⓔ
12. Ⓐ Ⓑ Ⓒ Ⓓ Ⓔ
13. Ⓐ Ⓑ Ⓒ Ⓓ Ⓔ
14. Ⓐ Ⓑ Ⓒ Ⓓ Ⓔ
15. Ⓐ Ⓑ Ⓒ Ⓓ Ⓔ
16. Ⓐ Ⓑ Ⓒ Ⓓ Ⓔ
17. Ⓐ Ⓑ Ⓒ Ⓓ Ⓔ
18. Ⓐ Ⓑ Ⓒ Ⓓ Ⓔ
19. Ⓐ Ⓑ Ⓒ Ⓓ Ⓔ
20. Ⓐ Ⓑ Ⓒ Ⓓ Ⓔ

21. Ⓐ Ⓑ Ⓒ Ⓓ Ⓔ
22. Ⓐ Ⓑ Ⓒ Ⓓ Ⓔ
23. Ⓐ Ⓑ Ⓒ Ⓓ Ⓔ
24. Ⓐ Ⓑ Ⓒ Ⓓ Ⓔ
25. Ⓐ Ⓑ Ⓒ Ⓓ Ⓔ
26. Ⓐ Ⓑ Ⓒ Ⓓ Ⓔ
27. Ⓐ Ⓑ Ⓒ Ⓓ Ⓔ
28. Ⓐ Ⓑ Ⓒ Ⓓ Ⓔ

## Section 3

1. Ⓐ Ⓑ Ⓒ Ⓓ Ⓔ
2. Ⓐ Ⓑ Ⓒ Ⓓ Ⓔ
3. Ⓐ Ⓑ Ⓒ Ⓓ Ⓔ
4. Ⓐ Ⓑ Ⓒ Ⓓ Ⓔ
5. Ⓐ Ⓑ Ⓒ Ⓓ Ⓔ
6. Ⓐ Ⓑ Ⓒ Ⓓ Ⓔ
7. Ⓐ Ⓑ Ⓒ Ⓓ Ⓔ
8. Ⓐ Ⓑ Ⓒ Ⓓ Ⓔ
9. Ⓐ Ⓑ Ⓒ Ⓓ Ⓔ
10. Ⓐ Ⓑ Ⓒ Ⓓ Ⓔ

11. Ⓐ Ⓑ Ⓒ Ⓓ Ⓔ
12. Ⓐ Ⓑ Ⓒ Ⓓ Ⓔ
13. Ⓐ Ⓑ Ⓒ Ⓓ Ⓔ
14. Ⓐ Ⓑ Ⓒ Ⓓ Ⓔ
15. Ⓐ Ⓑ Ⓒ Ⓓ Ⓔ
16. Ⓐ Ⓑ Ⓒ Ⓓ Ⓔ
17. Ⓐ Ⓑ Ⓒ Ⓓ Ⓔ
18. Ⓐ Ⓑ Ⓒ Ⓓ Ⓔ
19. Ⓐ Ⓑ Ⓒ Ⓓ Ⓔ
20. Ⓐ Ⓑ Ⓒ Ⓓ Ⓔ

21. Ⓐ Ⓑ Ⓒ Ⓓ Ⓔ
22. Ⓐ Ⓑ Ⓒ Ⓓ Ⓔ
23. Ⓐ Ⓑ Ⓒ Ⓓ Ⓔ
24. Ⓐ Ⓑ Ⓒ Ⓓ Ⓔ
25. Ⓐ Ⓑ Ⓒ Ⓓ Ⓔ
26. Ⓐ Ⓑ Ⓒ Ⓓ Ⓔ
27. Ⓐ Ⓑ Ⓒ Ⓓ Ⓔ
28. Ⓐ Ⓑ Ⓒ Ⓓ Ⓔ
29. Ⓐ Ⓑ Ⓒ Ⓓ Ⓔ
30. Ⓐ Ⓑ Ⓒ Ⓓ Ⓔ

31. Ⓐ Ⓑ Ⓒ Ⓓ Ⓔ
32. Ⓐ Ⓑ Ⓒ Ⓓ Ⓔ
33. Ⓐ Ⓑ Ⓒ Ⓓ Ⓔ
34. Ⓐ Ⓑ Ⓒ Ⓓ Ⓔ
35. Ⓐ Ⓑ Ⓒ Ⓓ Ⓔ

# MODEL TEST 3

1

SECTION **1**—VERBAL ABILITY

**Time—30 Minutes**
**30 Questions**

Select the best answer to the following questions, then
fill in the appropriate space on your Answer Sheet.

**Directions**: In each of the following antonym questions, a word printed in capital letters precedes five lettered words or phrases. From these five lettered words or phrases, pick the one most nearly <u>opposite</u> in meaning to the capitalized word.

1. PARIAH:
   (A) miser
   (B) nomad
   (C) servant
   (D) idol
   (E) renegade

2. EXACERBATE:
   (A) alleviate
   (B) bewilder
   (C) contemplate
   (D) intimidate
   (E) economize

**Directions**: Each of the following sentence completion questions contains one or two blanks. These blanks signify that a word or set of words has been left out. Below each sentence are five words or sets of words. For each blank, pick the word or set of words that <u>best</u> reflects the sentence's overall meaning.

3. Although he was generally considered an extremely _____ individual, his testimony at the trial revealed that he had been very _____.
   (A) intrepid...valiant
   (B) guileless...hypocritical
   (C) abstemious...temperate
   (D) meek...timorous
   (E) ingenuous...obtuse

4. The perpetual spinning of particles is much like that of a top, with one significant difference: unlike the top, the particles have no need to be wound up, for _____ is one of their _____ properties.
   (A) revolution...radical
   (B) motion...intangible
   (C) rotation...intrinsic
   (D) acceleration...lesser
   (E) collision...hypothetical

**Directions**: Each of the following analogy questions presents a related pair of words linked by a colon. Five lettered pairs of words follow the linked pair. Choose the lettered pair of words whose relationship is <u>most like</u> the relationship expressed in the original linked pair.

5. DEFLECT : MISSILE ::
   (A) defend : fortress
   (B) reflect : mirror
   (C) diversify : portfolio
   (D) dismantle : equipment
   (E) distract : attention

6. MULISH : PLIANCY ::
   (A) piggish : gluttony
   (B) sluggish : reluctance
   (C) kittenish : motility
   (D) apish : servility
   (E) shrewish : amiability

# 1

1

Directions: Each of the following reading comprehension questions is based on the content of the following passage. Read the passage and then determine the best answer choice for each question. Base your choice on what this passage *states directly* or *implies*, not on any information you may have gained elsewhere.

How is a newborn star formed? For the answer to this question, we must look to the familiar physical concept of gravitational instability. It is a
*Line* simple concept, long-known to scientists, having
(5) been first recognized by Isaac Newton in the late 1600s.

Let us envision a cloud of interstellar atoms and molecules, slightly admixed with dust. This cloud of interstellar gas is static and uniform.
(10) Suddenly, something occurs to disturb the gas, causing one small area within it to condense. As this small area increases in density, becoming slightly denser than the gas around it, its gravitational field likewise increases somewhat in
(15) strength. More matter now is attracted to the area, and its gravity becomes even stronger; as a result, it starts to contract, in the process increasing in density even more. This in turn further increases its gravity, so that it accumulates still more matter
(20) and contracts further still. And so the process continues, until finally the small area of gas gives birth to a gravitationally bound object, a newborn star.

7. It can be inferred from the passage that the author views the information contained within it as

(A) controversial but irrefutable
(B) speculative and unprofitable
(C) uncomplicated and traditional
(D) original but obscure
(E) sadly lacking in elaboration

8. The author provides information that answers which of the following questions?

 I. How does the small area's increasing density affect its gravitational field?
 II. What causes the disturbance that changes the cloud from its original static state?
 III. What is the end result of the gradually increasing concentration of the small area of gas?

(A) I only
(B) II only
(C) I and II only
(D) I and III only
(E) I, II and III

## Antonyms

9. CONTENTIOUS:
(A) amenable
(B) inactive
(C) dispassionate
(D) callow
(E) severe

10. DEBACLE:
(A) effort
(B) success
(C) drought
(D) transience
(E) dominance

## Sentence Completion

11. Whereas off-Broadway theater over the past several seasons has clearly _____ a talent for experimentation and improvisation, one deficiency in the commercial stage of late has been its marked incapacity for _____.

(A) manifested...spontaneity
(B) lampooned...theatricality
(C) cultivated...orthodoxy
(D) disavowed...histrionics
(E) betrayed...burlesque

## Analogies

12. CLOY : PALATE ::
(A) sniff : nose
(B) slit : tongue
(C) surfeit : appetite
(D) cling : touch
(E) refine : taste

13. PRATFALL : EMBARRASSMENT ::
(A) deadlock : mortification
(B) checkup : reluctance
(C) downfall : penitence
(D) diehard : grievance
(E) windfall : jubilation

# 1

# 1

## Reading Comprehension

With Meredith's *The Egoist* we enter into a critical problem that we have not yet before faced in these studies. That is the problem offered by a
Line writer of recognizably impressive stature, whose
(5) work is informed by a muscular intelligence, whose language has splendor, whose "view of life" wins our respect, and yet for whom we are at best able to feel only a passive appreciation which amounts, practically, to indifference. We should
(10) be unjust to Meredith and to criticism if we should, giving in to the inertia of indifference, simply avoid dealing with him and thus avoid the problem along with him. He does not "speak to us," we might say; his meaning is not a "meaning
(15) for us"; he "leaves us cold." But do not the challenge and the excitement of the critical problem as such lie in that ambivalence of attitude which allows us to recognize the intelligence and even the splendor of Meredith's work, while, at the
(20) same time, we experience a lack of sympathy, a failure of any enthusiasm of response?

14. According to the passage, the work of Meredith is noteworthy for its elements of
 (A) sensibility and artistic fervor
 (B) ambivalence and moral ambiguity
 (C) tension and sense of vitality
 (D) brilliance and linguistic grandeur
 (E) wit and whimsical frivolity

15. All of the following can be found in the author's discussion of Meredith EXCEPT
 (A) an indication of Meredith's customary effect on readers
 (B) an enumeration of the admirable qualities in his work
 (C) a selection of hypothetical comments at Meredith's expense
 (D) an analysis of the critical ramifications of Meredith's effect on readers
 (E) a refutation of the claim that Meredith evokes no sympathy

16. It can be inferred from the passage that the author finds the prospect of appraising Meredith's work critically to be
 (A) counterproductive
 (B) overly formidable
 (C) somewhat tolerable
 (D) markedly unpalatable
 (E) clearly invigorating

17. It can be inferred from the passage that the author would be most likely to agree with which of the following statements about the role of criticism?
 (A) Its prime office should be to make our enjoyment of the things that feed the mind as conscious as possible.
 (B) It should be a disinterested endeavor to learn and propagate the best that is known and thought in the world.
 (C) It should enable us to go beyond personal prejudice to appreciate the virtues of works antipathetic to our own tastes.
 (D) It should dwell upon excellencies rather than imperfections, ignoring such deficiencies as irrelevant.
 (E) It should strive both to purify literature and to elevate the literary standards of the reading public.

## Sentence Completion

18. Soap operas and situation comedies, though given to distortion, are so derivative of contemporary culture that they are inestimable _____ the attitudes and values of our society in any particular decade.
 (A) contraventions of
 (B) antidotes to
 (C) indices of
 (D) prerequisites for
 (E) determinants of

19. Perry's critics in the scientific world _____ that many of the observations he has made during more than a decade of research in Costa Rica have been reported as _____ in popular magazines rather than as carefully documented case studies in technical journals.
 (A) intimate...hypotheses
 (B) charge...anecdotes
 (C) applaud...rumors
 (D) claim...scholarship
 (E) apologize...fabrications

## Antonyms

20. GAUCHE:
 (A) grotesque
 (B) tactful
 (C) rightful
 (D) fashionable
 (E) inane

21. HAPLESS:

(A) fortuitous
(B) fortunate
(C) fortified
(D) forbidden
(E) forestalled

22. PROLIXITY:

(A) proximity
(B) disinclination
(C) circuitousness
(D) extremity
(E) terseness

## Analogies

23. CONTEMPORANEOUS : EVENTS ::

(A) adjacent : objects
(B) modern : times
(C) temporary : measures
(D) gradual : degrees
(E) repetitive : steps

24. LIMERICK : POEM ::

(A) motif : symphony
(B) prologue : play
(C) catch : song
(D) sequence : sonnet
(E) epigraph : novel

## Sentence Completion

25. Slander is like counterfeit money: many people
who would not coin it _____ it without
qualms.

(A) waste
(B) denounce
(C) circulate
(D) withdraw
(E) invest

## Antonyms

26. DIATRIBE:

(A) medley
(B) dilemma
(C) afterthought
(D) rebuttal
(E) praise

27. GAINSAY:

(A) estimate
(B) corroborate
(C) forfeit
(D) expend
(E) neglect

## Reading Comprehension

The Quechua world is submerged, so to speak,
in a cosmic magma that weighs heavily upon it. It
possesses the rare quality of being as it were
*Line* interjected into the midst of antagonistic forces,
(5) which in turn implies a whole body of social and
aesthetic structures whose innermost meaning
must be the administration of energy. This gives
rise to the social organism known as the *ayllu*, the
agrarian community that regulates the procure-
(10) ment of food. The *ayllu* formed the basic structure of the whole Inca empire.

The central idea of this organization was a
kind of closed economy, just the opposite of our
economic practices, which can be described as
(15) open. The closed economy rested on the fact that
the Inca controlled both the production and consumption of food. When one adds to this fact the
religious ideas noted in the Quechua texts cited
by the chronicler Santa Cruz Pachacuti, one
(20) comes to the conclusion that in the Andean zone
the margin of life was minimal and was made
possible only by the system of magic the Quechua
constructed through his religion. Adversities,
moreover, were numerous, for the harvest might
(25) fail at any time and bring starvation to millions.
Hence the whole purpose of the Quechua administrative and ideological system was to carry on
the arduous task of achieving *abundance* and
staving off shortages. This kind of structure pre-
(30) supposes a state of unremitting anxiety, which
could not be resolved by action. The Quechua
could not do so because his primordial response
to problems was the use of magic, that is,
recourse to the unconscious for the solution of
(35) external problems. Thus the struggle against the
world was a struggle against the dark depths of
the Quechua's own psyche, where the solution
was found. By overcoming the unconscious, the
outer world was also vanquished.

(40)    These considerations permit us to classify
Quechua culture as absolutely static or, more
accurately, as the expression of a mere state of
being. Only in this way can we understand the
refuge that it took in the germinative center of the
(45) cosmic *mandala* as revealed by Quechua art. The
Quechua empire was nothing more than a *mandala*, for it was divided into four zones, with
Cuzco in the center. Here the Quechua ensconced
himself to contemplate the decline of the world as
(50) though it were caused by an alien and
autonomous force.

1                                                                                               1

28. The term "mandala" as used in the last paragraph most likely means

   (A) an agrarian community
   (B) a kind of superstition
   (C) a closed economic pattern
   (D) a philosophy or way of regarding the world
   (E) a figure composed of four divisions

29. The author implies that the Quechua world was

   (A) uncivilized
   (B) highly introspective
   (C) vitally energetic
   (D) free of major worries
   (E) well organized

30. With which of the following statements would the author most likely agree?

   (A) Only psychological solutions can remedy economic ills.
   (B) The Quechua were renowned for equanimity and unconcern.
   (C) The Quechua limited themselves to realizable goals.
   (D) Much of Quechua existence was harsh and frustrating.
   (E) Modern Western society should adopt some Quechua economic ideas.

# 2                                                               2

**SECTION 2—QUANTITATIVE ABILITY**

**Time—45 Minutes**
**28 Questions**

**In this section solve each problem, using any available space on the page for scratchwork. Then decide which is the best of the choices given and fill in the corresponding oval on the Answer Sheet.**

Directions: In the following type of question, two quantities appear, one in Column A and one in Column B. You must compare them. The correct answer to the question is

A if the quantity in Column A is greater
B if the quantity in Column B is greater
C if the two quantities are equal
D if it is impossible to determine which quantity is greater

Notes: Sometimes information about one or both of the quantities is centered above the two columns. If the same symbol appears in both columns, it represents the same thing each time.

| Column A | Column B |
|---|---|
| The sum of the integers from −7 to 3 | The sum of the integers from −3 to 7 |

1.

$O$ is the center of the circle, and $Y$ (not shown) is a point inside the circle.

2.

| Column A | Column B |
|---|---|
| $OX$ | $OY$ |

**Column A**     **Column B**

$$x + y = 1$$

| Column A | Column B |
|---|---|
| $xy$ | 1 |

3.

| Column A | Column B |
|---|---|
| The average (arithmetic mean) of $a, b, c, d, e, f,$ and $g$ | 50 |

4.

---

Directions: In the following questions, choose the best answer from the five choices listed.

5. If 80% of the adult population of a village is registered to vote, and 60% of those registered actually voted in a particular election, what percent of the adults in the village did NOT vote in that election?

   (A) 20   (B) 40   (C) 48   (D) 50   (E) 52

6. If $\frac{3}{4}$ of a number is 7 more than $\frac{1}{6}$ of the number,

   what is $\frac{5}{3}$ of the number?

   (A) 12   (B) 15   (C) 18   (D) 20   (E) 24

7. An operation, ✱, is defined as follows: for any positive numbers $a$ and $b$, $a ✱ b = \sqrt{a} + \sqrt{b}$. Which of the following is an integer?

   (A) 11 ✱ 5   (B) 4 ✱ 9   (C) 4 ✱ 16
   (D) 7 ✱ 4   (E) 9 ✱ 9

2

2

| Column A | Column B |
|---|---|

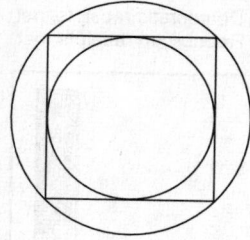

In the above figure, the small circle is inscribed in the square, which is inscribed in the large circle.

8.

| The ratio of the area of the large circle to the area of the small circle | 2:1 |
|---|---|

*x* and *y* are positive integers
$xy = 21$

9.

| $x + y$ | 15 |
|---|---|

10. Two sides of a right triangle are 5 and 6. Which of the following could be the length of the third side?

   I. $\sqrt{11}$
   II. $\sqrt{31}$
   III. $\sqrt{61}$

(A) I only  (B) III only  (C) I and II only
(D) I and III only  (E) I, II, and III

| Column A | Column B |
|---|---|

$x < y$

11.

| The average (arithmetic mean) of *x* and *y* | The average (arithmetic mean) of *x*, *y*, and *y* |
|---|---|

12.

| The sum of the areas of two equilateral triangles whose sides are 10 | The area of one equilateral triangle whose sides are 20 |
|---|---|

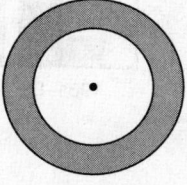

The radius of the large circle is *R*.
The radius of the small circle is *r*.
The areas of the shaded region and the white region are equal.

13.

| $\dfrac{R}{r}$ | 1.5 |
|---|---|

## Political Campaign Receipts

Millions of dollars

Democratic receipts, net
Republican receipts, net

SOURCE: U.S. Bureau of the Census.

14. In which of the following pairs of years were the ratios of Republican receipts to Democratic receipts most nearly equal?

(A) 1981–82 and 1985–86
(B) 1983–84 and 1995–96
(C) 1987–88 and 1989–90
(D) 1987–88 and 1995–96
(E) 1991–92 and 1993–94

15. Between which two consecutive two-year periods was there the greatest percent increase in the Democratic receipts?

(A) 1981–82 to 1983–84
(B) 1985–86 to 1987–88
(C) 1989–90 to 1991–92
(D) 1991–92 to 1993–94
(E) 1993–94 to 1995–96

Column A                    Column B

$$0 < a < 1$$

16.
| The area of a square whose side is $a$ | The area of a circle whose diameter is $a$ |

The distance between Ali's house and her college is exactly 135 miles. She drove $\frac{2}{3}$ of the distance in 135 minutes.

17.
| Her average speed, in miles per hour | 45 |

18. Which of the following points lies in the interior of the circle whose radius is 10 and whose center is at the origin?

(A) (–9, 4)   (B) (5, –9)   (C) (0, –10)
(D) (10, –1)   (E) (–6, 8)

19. For any numbers $a$, $b$, and $c$,

$$\boxed{\begin{matrix} a \\ b \quad c \end{matrix}} = abc - (a + b + c).$$

For which of the following equations is it true that there is exactly one positive integer that satisfies it?

I.   $\begin{matrix} a \\ 0 \quad a \end{matrix} = 0$

II.  $\begin{matrix} a \\ a \quad a \end{matrix} = 0$

III. $\begin{matrix} a \\ 2a \quad 3a \end{matrix} = 0$

(A) none   (B) I only   (C) III only
(D) I and III only   (E) I, II, and III

2

2

## Lottery Ticket Sales—Types of Game and Use of Proceeds: 1997
### Type of Game

Total ticket sales: $35.5 billion

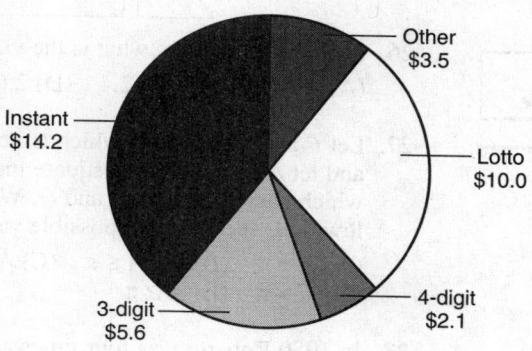

Other
$3.5

Instant
$14.2

Lotto
$10.0

3-digit
$5.6

4-digit
$2.1

### Proceeds

Total: $12.0 billion

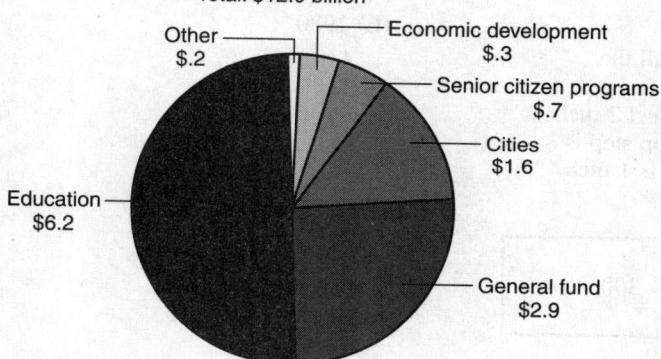

Other
$.2

Economic development
$.3

Senior citizen programs
$.7

Cities
$1.6

Education
$6.2

General fund
$2.9

SOURCE: U.S. Bureau of the Census.

20. The revenue from lottery ticket sales is divided between prize money and the various uses shown in the graph labeled "Proceeds." In 1997, what percent of the money spent on tickets was returned to the purchasers in the form of prize money?

(A) 23.5%   (B) 50%   (C) 60%   (D) 66%
(E) 74%

21. Approximately what percent of the proceeds that went to the states' General fund would have to be given to the senior citizen programs so that the proceeds for the senior citizen programs and the Cities would be equal?

(A) 0.9%   (B) 9%   (C) 31%   (D) 48%
(E) 69%

22. If $x + y = a$, $y + z = b$, and $x + z = c$, what is the average (arithmetic mean) of $x$, $y$, and $z$?

(A) $\dfrac{a + b + c}{2}$   (B) $\dfrac{a + b + c}{3}$   (C) $\dfrac{a + b + c}{4}$

(D) $\dfrac{a + b + c}{6}$   (E) $a + b + c$

# 2                                                                                                          2

<u>Column A</u>                     <u>Column B</u>

Nicole and Aviva each took pieces of wire of the
same length. Nicole bent hers into a circle, and
Aviva bent hers into a square.

23.
| The area of Nicole's circle | The area of Aviva's square |
| --- | --- |

In the stair unit in the figure above, all the
angles are right angles. The left side is
5 feet 4 inches, and the bottom is 9 feet 2 inches.
Each vertical riser is 8 inches. The top step is
10.25 inches, and each step below it is 1 inch
more than the preceding step.

24.
| The perimeter in inches of the figure above | 300 |
| --- | --- |

25.
| The number of positive three-digit numbers for which the average (arithmetic mean) of the three digits is equal to 2 | 20 |
| --- | --- |

26. In the figure above, what is the value of $h$?

(A) 2   (B) 2.2   (C) 2.4   (D) 2.6   (E) 2.8

27. Let $P$ and $Q$ be points which are two inches apart,
and let $A$ be the area, in square inches, of a circle
which passes through $P$ and $Q$. Which of the following is the set of all possible values for $A$?

(A) $0 < A$   (B) $0 < A \leq \pi$   (C) $A = \pi$
(D) $A > \pi$   (E) $A \geq \pi$

28. In 1950 Roberto was four times as old as Juan. In
1955 Roberto was three times as old as Juan. In
what year was Roberto twice as old as Juan?

(A) 1960   (B) 1965   (C) 1970   (D) 1975
(E) 1980

# 3

# 3

SECTION 3—ANALYTICAL ABILITY

Time—60 Minutes
35 Questions

Directions: In this section, each set of questions is based on a short passage or a set of conditions. Sometimes, in answering these questions, you might want to make a table or diagram. For each question, choose the best answer from the five choices listed.

1. Although there are no physical differences between the visual organs of the two groups, the inhabitants of the Bilge Islands, when shown a card displaying a spectrum of colors, perceive fewer colors than do most persons in the United States.

   Which of the following conclusions can most reliably be drawn from the information above?

   (A) Human color perception is at least partly determined by factors other than the physical structure of the visual organs.
   (B) The Bilge Islanders are probably taught in childhood to recognize fewer colors than are persons in the United States.
   (C) Differences in social structure probably affect color perception.
   (D) Color perception in humans is influenced by differences in physical environment.
   (E) Bilge Islanders may have fewer terms denoting colors in their language than do English-speaking persons.

## Questions 2–5

From among five novels—A, B, C, D, and E—and four biographies—F, G, H, and I—Ruth has to choose five books that she will assign over the summer to the participants in the book club she leads. Her selection will be made in accordance with the following requirements:

   Exactly two of the books selected will be biographies.
   If B is selected, both D and G must also be selected.
   A cannot be selected unless F is selected.
   If either C or E is selected, so must the other.
   If I is selected, neither F nor H may be selected.

2. Which of the following could be a list of the five books that Ruth selected?

   (A) D, E, F, G, H
   (B) A, B, D, F, H
   (C) B, C, D, F, G
   (D) A, C, E, F, I
   (E) A, B, D, F, G

3. If Ruth's first two selections are F and H, which of the following must she also select?

   (A) A  (B) B  (C) C  (D) D  (E) G

4. If E is not selected, then all of the following must be selected EXCEPT

   (A) A  (B) D  (C) F  (D) G  (E) H

5. If Ruth decides to select only four books—two novels and two biographies—but adheres to all the other conditions, in how many different ways can she make her selections?

   (A) 2  (B) 3  (C) 6  (D) 9  (E) 12

## Questions 6–7

*Mr. Dimple:* Mrs. Wilson's qualifications are ideal for the position. She is intelligent, forceful, determined, and trustworthy. I suggest we hire her immediately.

6. Which one of the following, if true, would most weaken Mr. Dimple's statement?

   (A) Mrs. Wilson is not interested in being hired.
   (B) There are two other applicants whose qualifications are identical to Mrs. Wilson's.
   (C) Mrs. Wilson is currently working for a rival company.
   (D) Mr. Dimple is not speaking directly to the hiring committee.
   (E) Mrs. Wilson is older than many of the other applicants.

7. Which one of the following, if true, offers the strongest support of Mr. Dimple's statement?

   (A) All the members of the hiring committee have agreed that intelligence, trustworthiness, determination, and forcefulness are important qualifications for the job.
   (B) Mr. Dimple holds exclusive responsibility for hiring new employees.
   (C) Mr. Dimple has known Mrs. Wilson longer than he has known any of the other applicants.
   (D) Mrs. Wilson is a member of Mr. Dimple's family.
   (E) Mrs. Dimple is intelligent, forceful, determined, and trustworthy.

# 3                                                              3

8. Pasquale's pizza specials always come with two toppings. Every Friday, Carlo orders a special pizza from Pasquale, even though some of the toppings give him heartburn. If either anchovies or garlic are on a pizza, Carlo gets heartburn. Carlo never gets heartburn from a pizza with mushrooms. One Friday Carlo ate a special pizza and did not get heartburn.

If all of the preceding statements are true, what must be true about the the pizza Carlo ate that Friday?

(A) Mushrooms were not on the pizza.
(B) Either anchovies or garlic, but not both were on the pizza.
(C) One of the toppings was mushrooms; the other topping was either anchovies or garlic.
(D) One of the toppings was mushrooms; the second topping was neither anchovies nor garlic.
(E) Neither anchovies nor garlic were on the pizza.

## Questions 9–13

A college has eight deans, five women—A, B, C, D, and E—and three men—F, G, and H. Each month from January to May, inclusive, two of the deans, one man and one woman, must chair the college's disciplinary committee. The president of the college will choose the deans each month in accordance with the following rules:

> No dean can chair the committee in two consecutive months.
> B must be one of the chairpeople in March.
> A and E cannot chair the committee in consecutive months.
> The only dean that C will chair the committee with is G; similarly, G will not chair the committee without C.

9. If A and F are the deans who chair the committee in January, which of the following could be the pair of deans who chair the committee in February?

(A) D and F
(B) B and G
(C) C and G
(D) E and H
(E) C and H

10. If, due to other commitments, three of the female deans are never available to chair the committee, which of the following must be true?

(A) C will chair the committee exactly once.
(B) A will chair the committee exactly twice.
(C) F will chair the committee exactly twice.
(D) G will chair the committee exactly twice.
(E) B will chair the committee exactly three times.

11. Which of the following could be the two deans who chair the committee in April?

(A) A and F
(B) A and D
(C) F and H
(D) B and H
(E) C and H

12. If February is the only month in which H is a chairperson of the committee, which of the following must be a chairperson in April?

(A) A   (B) H   (C) C   (D) D   (E) E

13. If H is a chairperson exactly twice, in January and May, each of the following could be true EXCEPT

(A) C will chair the committee exactly once.
(B) B will chair the committee more than once.
(C) Two women will each chair the committee twice.
(D) Each man will chair the committee at least once.
(E) More men than women will serve as chairpersons.

14. By spraying with pesticides like malathion, we can eradicate dangerous pests like the fruit-fly. But malathion spraying also destroys the ladybug, the best natural predator of aphids. Areas that have been sprayed with malathion are now free of the fruit-fly, but infested with aphids. This is the price we must pay to protect our citrus crop.

The argument above assumes all of the following EXCEPT

(A) pesticide spraying is the only way to eradicate the fruity-fly
(B) the aphid infestation is caused by the lack of ladybugs
(C) a pesticide that would kill fruit-flies and spare ladybugs cannot be made
(D) the use of pesticides has disadvantages
(E) the aphid infestation could be prevented by introducing a natural predator other than the ladybug

# 3                                                                    3

## Questions 15–18

Every night at Pirandello's, the owner, Carlo, chooses five dinner specials, each one from a different one of the seven categories—beef, chicken, duck, fish, pasta, seafood, and veal. In making his decision each night, Carlo always adheres to the following conditions:

> He chooses exactly one poultry dish: chicken or duck.
> Whenever there is a fish special, there is also a pasta special.
> Duck is never offered on a night when there is a beef special.

15. On a night when Carlo offers a beef special, which of the following must also be offered?
    (A) chicken   (B) duck   (C) fish
    (D) pasta   (E) veal

16. Which of the following could be a list of the five specials for one night?
    (A) beef, chicken, duck, pasta, fish
    (B) beef, fish, pasta, seafood, veal
    (C) beef, chicken, fish, seafood, veal
    (D) beef, duck, fish, pasta, veal
    (E) beef, chicken, fish, pasta, seafood

17. If there is no chicken special one night, which is the other dish that is not on special?
    (A) beef   (B) duck   (C) pasta
    (D) seafood   (E) veal

18. One night, Carlo decides to offer only four specials, one of which is beef. In how many ways can he make up the list of specials?
    (A) 2   (B) 3   (C) 4   (D) 5   (E) 6

19. A company called Popcorn Packaging is promoting the use of popcorn as a cushioning material in packing. Unlike the commonly used Styrofoam beads or chips, popcorn can be recycled as a food for birds or squirrels and can serve as a garden mulch. Used out of doors, popcorn disappears almost overnight, while the Styrofoam beads may be in the environment for centuries. Even before we became ecology conscious, popcorn was used in packing in the 1940s. Since it now costs less to produce than Styrofoam, there is every reason to return to wide-scale use of packaging by popcorn.

Which one of the following, if true, would most seriously weaken the author's argument?
(A) A package using popcorn as a cushioning material will weigh less than a package using Styrofoam beads.
(B) Popcorn may attract rodents and insects.
(C) A large number of squirrels can damage a garden by consuming flowering bulbs.
(D) Less than 1 percent of the material now used for package cushioning is recycled.
(E) Styrofoam replaced popcorn in the early 1950s because it was cheaper to produce.

## Questions 20–23

A tennis club has seven board members—P, Q, R, S, T, U, and V. Each of the board members is to be assigned to at least one of three committees: Finance, Social, and Membership. The committee assignments are subject to the following conditions:

> Each committee must have at least one and at most three members.
> No one serving on the Finance Committee can serve on any other committee.
> V is unwilling to serve on the Social Committee, and U won't serve on the Membership Committee.
> Neither P nor Q can be on a committee with V.
> If either S or T is on a committee, so is the other.
> T and U cannot be assigned to the same committee.
> If U is on the Social Committee, then V is on the Finance Committee.
> If U is on the Finance Committee, then V is on the Membership Committee.

20. If the Finance Committee has only one member, and that person is someone other than U, which of the following could be a complete list of the people on the Membership Committee?
    (A) P, Q, R
    (B) P, Q, S
    (C) R, S, T
    (D) S, T, U
    (E) P, R, V

3                                                                      3

21. If only one person serves on more than one com-
    mittee, that person could be which of the follow-
    ing?

    (A) P   (B) S   (C) T   (D) U   (E) V

22. If R is on the Membership Committee, and P is on
    the Finance Committee, which of the following
    could also be on the Finance Committee?

    (A) Q   (B) R   (C) S   (D) T   (E) V

23. If R and U are the only members of the Social
    Committee, each of the following could be true
    EXCEPT

    (A) The Finance Committee has exactly three
        members.
    (B) The Membership Committee has exactly three
        members.
    (C) No one is on two committees.
    (D) Exactly one person is on two committees.
    (E) Exactly two people are on two committees.

## Questions 24–28

On AIDS Awareness Day at Buchanan High School,
during each of the eight periods, a different student is to
discuss briefly over the PA system a famous person
who died of AIDS. The eight students chosen include
three freshmen, two sophomores, two juniors, and one
senior. The order in which they speak must conform to
the following set of conditions:

> The first or the last talk of the day must be made
> by a junior.
> A freshman must speak during fifth period.
> The three freshmen may not speak during three
> consecutive periods.
> The senior cannot speak either immediately
> before or immediately after either of the juniors.
> At least once during the day a sophomore and a
> junior must speak during two consecutive periods.

24. If the senior speaks during period 2, which of the
    following must be true?

    (A) A junior speaks during period 1.
    (B) A freshman speaks during period 1.
    (C) A freshman speaks during period 3.
    (D) A sophomore speaks during period 7.
    (E) A junior speaks during period 8.

25. Which of the following could be the grades of the
    speakers in periods 3–7?

| | Period 3 | Period 4 | Period 5 | Period 6 | Period 7 |
|---|---|---|---|---|---|
| (A) | Junior | Freshman | Freshman | Junior | Sophomore |
| (B) | Junior | Senior | Freshman | Freshman | Sophomore |
| (C) | Sophomore | Freshman | Freshman | Freshman | Junior |
| (D) | Freshman | Freshman | Senior | Freshman | Junior |
| (E) | Senior | Freshman | Freshman | Junior | Freshman |

26. If a freshman speaks during period 4, which of the
    following must be true?

    (A) The senior speaks in periods 1 or 8.
    (B) The two sophomores speak in consecutive
        periods.
    (C) The two juniors speak in consecutive periods.
    (D) A freshman must speak during the first two or
        the last two periods of the day.
    (E) One junior speaks during period 1 and the
        other junior speaks during period 8.

27. If a freshman speaks during period 1, each of the
    following could be true EXCEPT

    (A) The senior speaks during period 7.
    (B) The sophomores speak during periods 2 and 7.
    (C) Both sophomores speak before the senior.
    (D) Both juniors speak after the senior.
    (E) The speakers in two consecutive periods are
        never from the same grade.

28. If the first two talks of the day are made by sopho-
    mores, which of the following must be true?

    (A) A freshman speaks during period 6.
    (B) A freshman speaks during period 7.
    (C) A junior speaks during period 4.
    (D) A junior speaks during period 6.
    (E) The senior speaks during period 4.

29.   I. Allegra has not taken French 301.
      II. Allegra may not take French 317 this spring.

    Statement II must be true if Statement I and which
    of the following statements are true?

    (A) No student is permitted to take two 300-level
        French courses at the same time.
    (B) French 301 and 317 are taught by the same
        professor.
    (C) Freshmen are not permitted to take 300-level
        courses.
    (D) French 301 is a prerequisite for French 317.
    (E) French 317 cannot be offered unless at least
        ten people register.

3                                                                                    3

30. A recent study of cigarette smokers has shown that, of cancer patients who are heavy smokers of unfiltered cigarettes, 40 percent will die of the disease. For cancer patients who are light smokers of filter cigarettes, the percentage is 25 percent.

Which one of the following conclusions can be drawn from the information above?

(A) There are more heavy smokers of unfiltered cigarettes than light smokers of filter cigarettes.
(B) More heavy smokers of unfiltered cigarettes die of cancer than light smokers of filter cigarettes.
(C) A heavy smoker of unfiltered cigarettes who has cancer is more likely to die than a light smoker of unfiltered cigarettes.
(D) A heavy smoker of unfiltered cigarettes who has cancer may be more likely to die than a light smoker of unfiltered cigarettes.
(E) A heavy smoker of unfiltered cigarettes who has cancer is more likely to die than a light smoker of filtered cigarettes who has cancer.

**Questions 31–34**

An advertising company is creating two new logos for one of its clients. Each logo will require at least two and at most five colors chosen from the three primary colors—red, blue, and yellow—the three secondary colors—green, orange, and purple—and brown. The client has given the advertising company the following directions:

No color can be used in both logos.
Neither logo can have both red and blue in it.
If red or green is used in a logo, both colors must be used in that logo.
If yellow or brown is used in a logo, both colors must be used in that logo.
At least six of the colors must be used.

31. Which of the following could be a complete list of the colors used on a logo?

(A) Purple and yellow
(B) Blue, green, and red
(C) Brown, green, orange, red
(D) Brown, orange, purple, red
(E) Blue, brown, orange, purple, yellow

32. Each of the following is an acceptable use of the colors in the two logos EXCEPT

| First logo | Second logo |
| --- | --- |
| (A) Green, orange, purple, red | Brown, yellow |
| (B) Brown, purple, yellow | Green, orange, red |
| (C) Green, orange, red | Brown, purple, yellow |
| (D) Red, orange, purple | Blue, brown, green, yellow |
| (E) Brown, orange, purple, yellow | Green, red |

33. If the only primary color used in the first logo is blue, which of the following CANNOT be true concerning both logos?

(A) Exactly two primary colors are used.
(B) Exactly two secondary colors are used.
(C) All three primary colors are used.
(D) All three secondary colors are used.
(E) All seven colors are used.

34. All of the following statements could be true EXCEPT

(A) Blue is not used in either logo.
(B) All three secondary colors are used in the same logo.
(C) The only color not used is a primary color.
(D) The only color not used is a secondary color.
(E) Each logo uses only primary and secondary colors.

35. A new law will require labels giving consumers more nutritional information on all prepackaged foods manufactured in the United States. Food sold by restaurants or grocers with annual sales of less than $500,000 will be exempt. The required labels will reveal the number of servings, the serving size, the number of calories per serving, and the amount of fat, cholesterol, sodium, and dietary fiber.

The effectiveness of the new labels in improving overall U.S. nutrition could be seriously questioned if which one of the following were shown to be true?

(A) More than 80 percent of the food sold in this country is not prepackaged.
(B) More than 80 percent of the prepackaged food sold in this country is marketed by the eight major food corporations.
(C) The amount of money Americans spend on prepackaged foods for microwaving has more than tripled every year for the last five years, and the trend is expected to continue.
(D) An increasingly large number of consumers now read the nutritional information on food packages.
(E) Small retailers who manufacture packaged foods sell to only a tiny percentage of American food buyers.

# Answer Key

## Section 1—Verbal Ability

| | | | | |
|---|---|---|---|---|
| 1. D | 6. E | 11. A | 16. E | 21. B | 26. E |
| 2. A | 7. C | 12. C | 17. C | 22. E | 27. B |
| 3. B | 8. D | 13. E | 18. C | 23. A | 28. E |
| 4. C | 9. A | 14. D | 19. B | 24. C | 29. B |
| 5. E | 10. B | 15. E | 20. B | 25. C | 30. D |

## Section 2—Quantitative Ability

NOTE: The letters in brackets following the Quantitative Ability answers refer to the sections of Chapter 15 in which you can find the information you need to answer the questions. For example, 1. C [E] means that the answer to question 1 is C, and that the solution requires information found in Section 15-E: Averages. Also, 20. A [14] means that the answer to question 20 is based on information in Chapter 14: Data Interpretation.

| | | | | |
|---|---|---|---|---|
| 1. B [A] | 6. D [B] | 11. B [E] | 16. A [K,L] | 21. C [14] | 26. C [J] |
| 2. A [L] | 7. D [A] | 12. B [J,K] | 17. B [H] | 22. D [E,G] | 27. E [L] |
| 3. B [A] | 8. C [K,L] | 13. B [L] | 18. A [N] | 23. A [K,L] | 28. C [H] |
| 4. A [E,I] | 9. D [A] | 14. C [14] | 19. C [G] | 24. A [A] | |
| 5. E [C] | 10. D [J] | 15. A [14] | 20. D [14] | 25. A [E] | |

## Section 3—Analytical Ability

| | | | | |
|---|---|---|---|---|
| 1. A | 8. E | 15. A | 22. A | 29. D |
| 2. E | 9. C | 16. E | 23. E | 30. E |
| 3. C | 10. E | 17. A | 24. E | 31. E |
| 4. E | 11. A | 18. C | 25. E | 32. D |
| 5. D | 12. C | 19. B | 26. D | 33. A |
| 6. B | 13. A | 20. C | 27. A | 34. E |
| 7. A | 14. E | 21. A | 28. B | 35. A |

# Answer Explanations

## Section 1—Verbal Ability

1. **D.** The opposite of a *pariah* or person rejected by society is an *idol* or person greatly loved by society.
Think of being "shunned as a pariah."

2. **A.** The opposite of to *exacerbate* (to worsen or make more harsh) is to *alleviate* or lighten.
Think of "exacerbating a quarrel."

3. **B.** In reputation he was a *guileless* or undeceitful person; in real life he showed himself to have been *hypocritical* or deceptive.
Note the use of *although* to signal the contrast.

4. **C.** Particles have no need to be wound up because the property of spinning (*rotation*) is built into their makeup: it is *intrinsic*.

5. **E.** By definition, a *missile* is *deflected* when it turns aside from its original direction. Likewise, someone's *attention* is *distracted* when it turns aside from its original direction. (Definition)

6. **E.** Someone *mulish* (stubborn) is not characterized by *pliancy* (readiness to yield). Someone *shrewish* (ill-tempered) is not characterized by *amiability*. (Antonym Variant)

7. **C.** To the author the concept is both simple and traditional, dating as it does from Newton's time.

8. **D.** You can answer this question by the process of elimination.
Question I is answerable on the basis of the passage. As the area's density increases, its gravitational field increases in strength. Therefore, you can eliminate Choice B.
Question II is not answerable on the basis of the passage. The passage nowhere states what

disturbs the gas. Therefore, you can eliminate Choices C and E.

Question III is answerable on the basis of the passage. The end result of the process is the formation of a gravitationally bound object, a newborn star. Therefore, you can eliminate Choice A.

Only Choice D is left. It is the correct answer.

9.  A.   The opposite of *contentious* (quarrelsome, belligerent) is *amenable* (readily brought to yield, tractable).

Note that *contentious* derives from the verb to *contend* (to struggle or argue), not the adjective *content*.

Think of "a particularly contentious argument."

10.  B.   The opposite of a *debacle* (downfall; failure; collapse) is a *success*.

Think of "the Wall Street debacle of 1987."

11.  A.   The off-Broadway and Broadway theaters are contrasted here. The former has *manifested* or shown a talent for improvisation, extemporaneous or spontaneous performance. The latter has manifested no such talent for *spontaneity*. Note the use of *whereas* to establish the contrast.

12.  C.   By definition, an excess of once-pleasing flavors *cloys* or sates the *palate* (seat of the sense of taste). An excess of once-tempting foodstuffs *surfeits* or sates the *appetite*.

(Definition)

13.  E.   A *pratfall* is a humiliating mishap that causes you to feel *embarrassment*. A *windfall* is an unexpected piece of good fortune that causes you to feel *jubilation*.          (Cause and Effect)

14.  D.   The author cites Meredith's intelligence (*brilliance*) and his splendor of language (*linguistic grandeur*).

15.  E.   Rather than refuting the claim, the author clearly acknowledges Meredith's inability to evoke the reader's sympathy.

Choice A is incorrect. From the start the author points out how Meredith leaves readers cold.

Choice B is incorrect. The author reiterates Meredith's virtues, citing muscular intelligence and literary merit.

Choice C is incorrect. The author quotes several such imagined criticisms.

Choice D is incorrect. The author indicates that if readers choose to avoid dealing with Meredith, they shall be doing a disservice to the cause of criticism.

Only Choice E remains. It is the correct answer.

16.  E.   Speaking of the "challenge and excitement of the critical problem as such," the author clearly finds the prospect of appraising Meredith critically to be stirring and *invigorating*.

17.  C.   The author wishes us to be able to recognize the good qualities of Meredith's work while at the same time we continue to find it personally unsympathetic. Thus, she would agree that criticism should enable us to appreciate the virtues of works we dislike.

Choices A, B, and E are unsupported by the passage.

Choice D is incorrect. While the author wishes the reader to be aware of Meredith's excellences, she does not suggest that the reader should ignore those qualities in Meredith that make his work unsympathetic. Rather, she wishes the reader to come to appreciate the very ambivalence of his critical response.

18.  C.   Soap operas and situation comedies are derivative of contemporary culture: they take their elements from that culture; they serve as *indices* (signs or indications) of what is going on in that culture; they both point to and point up the social attitudes and values they portray.

Note that the soap operas and comedies here cannot be *determinants* of our society's attitudes and values: they derive from these attitudes and values; they do not determine them.

19.  B.   The critics *charge* (make the accusation) that Perry has published only *anecdotes* of his observations and not detailed analyses.

Note that *critics* would be unlikely to *applaud* the publication of *rumors* or *apologize* for Perry's publication of *fabrications* or lies. Thus, you can eliminate Choices C and E. Similarly, *popular magazines* would be unlikely to publish scientific *hypotheses* or examples of *scholarship*. You therefore can rule out Choices A and D as well.

20.  B.   The opposite of *gauche* (awkward; lacking in social grace or tact) is *tactful*.

Think of being embarrassed by "a gauche remark."

21.  B.   The opposite of *hapless* (unlucky) is *fortunate*.

Think of "hapless unfortunates."

22.  E.   The opposite of *prolixity* (wordiness) is *terseness* or brevity.

Think of "long-winded prolixity."

23.  A.   *Events* that are *contemporaneous* (occurring within the same time frame) exist in temporal reference to one another. *Objects* that are *adjacent* exist in spatial reference to one another.          (Defining Characteristic)

24. **C.** A *limerick* is a kind of *poem*. A *catch* is a kind of song.

Note how simple the relationship of the original pair of words is. Analogy questions seldom are this easy. This should alert you to be on the lookout for something particularly deceptive among the answer choices. In this case, *catch* is used in an uncommon manner.

(Class and Member)

25. **C.** Whatever word you choose here must apply equally well both to slander and to counterfeit money. People who would not make up a slanderous statement *circulate* slander by passing it on. So too people who would not coin or make counterfeit money *circulate* counterfeit money by passing it on.

Note how the extended metaphor here influences the writer's choice of words.

26. **E.** The opposite of a *diatribe* (abusive criticism) is *praise*.

Think of "a bitter diatribe."

27. **B.** The opposite of to *gainsay* or contradict is to *corroborate* or support.

Beware eye-catchers. To gainsay derives from to say *against*, not from to gain.

Think of "gainsaying an assertion."

28. **E.** The passage compare the Quechua empire to a *mandala* because "it was divided into four parts." Thus, a *mandala* is most likely a *figure composed of four divisions*.

29. **B.** The author refers to the Quechua as existing in "a state of unremitting anxiety, which could not be resolved by action" and which the Quechua could only deal with by looking into himself and struggling with the depths of his own psyche. This suggests that the Quechua world was *highly introspective*.

30. **D.** Both the unremitting anxiety of Quechua life and the recurring harvest failures that brought starvation to millions illustrate the *harshness and frustration* of Quechua existence.

# Section 2—Quantitative Ability

Two asterisks (**) indicate an alternative method of solving.

1. **B.** In each column, the sum includes the numbers from –3 to 3. Since all the other numbers in Column A are negative and those in Column B are positive, Column B is greater. (Note that we didn't have to calculate either sum. We just used TACTIC 5, Chapter 13 and compared the columns.)

2. **A.** Since $Y$ is inside the circle it is closer to the center than $X$, which is on the circle. Column A is greater.

3. **B.** Since $x + y = 1$, at least one of the numbers is positive. If either $x$ or $y$ is 0, the product $xy = 0$; and if either one is negative, then $xy$ is negative. In each case, $xy$ is less than 1. If both $x$ and $y$ are positive, then each is less than 1, and so is their product. Column B is greater.

4. **A.** There is not enough information provided to determine the values of $a, b, c, d, e, f$, and $g$, but they are irrelevant. Since the sum of the measures of the seven angles is 360°, their average is $360° \div 7 \approx 51.4°$. Column A is greater.

5. **E.** If there are $x$ adults in the village, then $.8x$ of them are registered and $.6(.8x) = .48x$ voted. Therefore, $x - .48x = .52x$ or 52% of the adults did not vote.

**You can avoid the algebra by assuming there are 100 adults. Then 80 of them are registered and 60% of 80 = 48 of them voted.

So 52 did not vote, and $\frac{52}{100} = 52\%$.

6. **D.** Let the number be $x$, and write the equation:

$$\frac{3}{4}x = 7 + \frac{1}{6}x.$$

Multiply both sides by 12:

$$9x = 84 + 2x$$

Subtract $2x$ from each side and divide by 7:

$$7x = 84$$
$$x = 12$$

*Be careful*: 12 is *not* the answer. You were asked for $\frac{5}{3}$ of the number: $\frac{5}{3}(12) = 20.$

7. **D.** There's nothing to do except check each choice until you find one that works. In questions such as this, it is often faster to start with E and work towards A.

E: $9 * 9 = \sqrt{9} + \sqrt{9} = \sqrt{9 + 3} = \sqrt{12}$, which is not an integer.

D: $7 * 4 = \sqrt{7} + \sqrt{4} = \sqrt{7 + 2} = \sqrt{9} = 3$, an integer.

Once you find the answer, do not waste any time trying the other choices—they won't work.

8. **C.** Let $r$ and $R$ be the radii of the two circles. From the figure, you can see that $\triangle OAB$ is a 45-45-90 right triangle, and so $R = r\sqrt{2}$ (KEY FACT J8). Therefore,

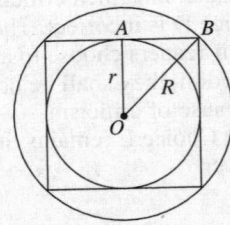

area of large circle / area of small circle $= \dfrac{\pi R^2}{\pi r^2} = \dfrac{\pi(r\sqrt{2})^2}{\pi r^2} = \dfrac{2\pi r^2}{\pi r^2} = 2$. The ratio is 2:1.

**Do exactly the same thing except use TACTIC 2, Chapter 9. Let $r = 1$; then $R = \sqrt{2}$, and the ratio is $\dfrac{\pi(\sqrt{2})^2}{\pi(1)^2} = \dfrac{2\pi}{\pi} = 2{:}1$.

9. **D.** If $x = 3$ and $y = 7$ (or vice versa), then $x + y = 10$, and Column B is greater. Eliminate Choices A and C. If $x = 1$ and $y = 21$ (or vice versa), then $x + y = 22$. This time, Column A is greater. Eliminate Choice B. Neither column is *always* greater, and the two columns are not *always* equal.

10. **D.** Either (i) 5 and 6 are the lengths of the two legs, or (ii) 5 is the length of a leg, and 6 is the hypotenuse. In either case use the Pythagorean theorem:

(i) $5^2 + 6^2 = c^2 \Rightarrow c^2 = 61 \Rightarrow c = \sqrt{61}$;

or

(ii) $a^2 + 5^2 = 6^2 \Rightarrow a^2 = 36 - 25 = 11 \Rightarrow a = \sqrt{11}$.

   (i)          (ii)

Statements I and II only are true.

11. **B.** The average of $x$ and $y$ is less than $y$, so having another $y$ raises the average [KEY FACT E4]. Column B is greater.
**Use TACTIC 1, Chapter 13. Plug in numbers. Column A: the average of 2 and 4 is 3. Column B: the average of 2, 4, and 4 is more than 3, because the extra 4 raises the average (it's 3.333). The answer is B.

12. **B.** If you draw a diagram, it is immediately clear that the area of the large triangle is *more than* twice the area of the small one. In fact, it is 4 times as great. Column B is larger.

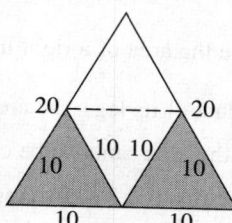

**Use the formula for the area of an equilateral triangle of side $s$:

$A = \dfrac{s^2\sqrt{3}}{4}$ (KEY FACT J15).

Column A $= 2 \times \dfrac{10^2\sqrt{3}}{4} = \dfrac{200\sqrt{3}}{4}$.

Column B $= \dfrac{20^2\sqrt{3}}{4} = \dfrac{400\sqrt{3}}{4}$.

Column B is larger.

13. **B.** The area of the large circle is $\pi R^2$ and the area of the small circle is $\pi r^2$, so the area of the shaded region is $\pi R^2 - \pi r^2 = \pi(R^2 - r^2)$. Since the shaded region and the white region have the same area,
$\pi(R^2 - r^2) = \pi r^2 \Rightarrow R^2 - r^2 = r^2 \Rightarrow$
$R^2 = 2r^2 \Rightarrow \dfrac{R^2}{r^2} = 2 \Rightarrow \dfrac{R}{r} = \sqrt{2}$,
which is *less* than 1.5. Column B is greater.

14. **C.** For each of the pairs of years in question, use the graph to approximate the ratio of Republican to Democratic receipts. For example, in 1981–82, Republican receipts were slightly over $200 million and Democratic receipts were about $40 million, a ratio of 5:1. The only two pairs of years in which the ratio was very close were 1987–88 and 1989–90; in both of those pairs of years the ratio was very nearly 2:1.

15. **A.** In 1981–82 the Democratic receipts were about $40 million and in 1983–84 they had increased to about $100 million, an increase of 150%. From 1991–92 to 1993–94 (Choice D), receipts decreased. During the periods covered by Choices B, C, and E, receipts increased, but by less than 150%.

16. **A.** Column A: the area of a square of side $a$ is $a^2$. Column B: since the diameter of the circle is $a$, the radius is $\frac{1}{2}a$, and so the area of the circle is $\pi\left(\dfrac{1}{2}a\right)^2 = \dfrac{\pi}{4}a^2$, which is less than $a^2$, since $\dfrac{\pi}{4} < 1$. Column A is greater.

17. **B.** To find the average speed, in miles per hour, divide the distance, in miles, by the time, in hours. Ali drove 90 miles $\left(\dfrac{2}{3} \text{ of } 135\right)$ in 2.25 hours (135 minutes = 2 hours and 15 minutes = $2\dfrac{1}{4}$ hours). $90 \div 2.25 = 40$. Column B is greater.

18. **A.** Find the distance from each point to (0,0), the center of the circle. We're looking for a point that is *less than* 10 units from the center. The distance from $(a,b)$ to (0,0) equals $\sqrt{(a - 0)^2 + (b - 0)^2} = \sqrt{a^2 + b^2}$. Check each point. A: $(-9,4)$ $\sqrt{(-9)^2 + 4^2} = \sqrt{81 + 16} = \sqrt{97} < 10$ (KEY FACT N2).

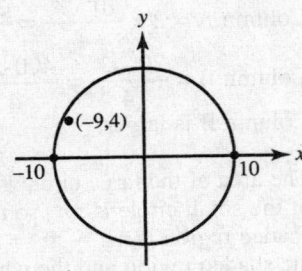

**Clearly, (0,–10) is 10 units from the origin, and so is *on* the circle. Also, since (10,0) is on the circle, (10,–1) is *outside*. The others are too close to call without knowing the formula or using the Pythagorean theorem, so if you're not sure, guess.

19. **C.** Check each choice to see which equation has *exactly one positive integer solution*.

I. For *every* number $a$: $(0)(a)(-a) = 0$ and $0 + a + (-a) = 0$, so for *every* positive integer $a$,

$$\underset{0 \quad -a}{\overset{a}{\triangle}} = 0 - 0 = 0. \text{ (I is false.)}$$

II. $\underset{a \quad a}{\overset{a}{\triangle}} = 0 \Rightarrow a^3 - 3a = 0 \Rightarrow a^3 = 3a.$ We're

looking for *positive* solutions, so assume $a \neq 0$, and divide by $a$: $a^2 = 3 \Rightarrow a = \pm \sqrt{3}$. But $\sqrt{3}$ is not an integer. (II is false.)

III. $\underset{2a \quad 3a}{\overset{a}{\triangle}} = 0 \Rightarrow 6a^3 - 6a = 0 \Rightarrow 6a^3 = 6a \Rightarrow$

$a^2 = 1$. This equation has *one* positive integer solution, $a = 1$. (III is true.)

Statement III only is true.

20. **D.** The difference between the total ticket sales ($35.5 billion) and the total distribution of the proceeds ($12.0 billion) was the amount returned to the purchasers of lottery tickets in the form of prize money:
$35.5 billion – $12.0 billion = $23.5 billion. Divide 23.5 by 35.5 (or approximate, by dividing 24 by 36) to see that 66% of the ticket sales was allocated to prize money.

21. **C.** In order for the amount received by senior citizens programs to be the same as the amount received by the Cities, an additional $0.9 billion would have to be allocated to the senior citizens programs: $0.9 billion is approximately 31% of the $2.9 billion currently going to the General fund.

22. **D.** Whenever you have three equations, add them.

$$\begin{array}{r} x + y = a \\ y + z = b \\ + \quad x + z = c \\ \hline 2x + 2y + 2z = a + b + c \end{array}$$

Divide by 2: $\qquad x + y + z = \dfrac{a + b + c}{2}$

Divide by 3: $\qquad \dfrac{x + y + z}{3} = \dfrac{a + b + c}{6}$

**Use TACTIC 2, Chapter 12: substitute for the variables. Let $x = 1$, $y = 2$, and $z = 3$. Then the average of $x$, $y$, and $z$ is 2. When $a = 1 + 2 = 3$, $b = 2 + 3 = 5$, and $c = 1 + 3 = 4$, which of the choices equals 2? Only $\dfrac{a + b + c}{6}$.

23. **A.** If $L$ represents the length of the wire, then $L$ is both the perimeter of Aviva's square and the circumference of Nicole's circle.

Column A: $L = 2\pi r \Rightarrow r = \dfrac{L}{2\pi} \Rightarrow$

$A = \pi\left(\dfrac{L}{2\pi}\right)^2 = \pi\left(\dfrac{L^2}{4\pi^2}\right) = \dfrac{L^2}{4\pi}.$

Column B: $L = 4s \Rightarrow s = \dfrac{L}{4} \Rightarrow A = \left(\dfrac{L}{4}\right)^2 = \dfrac{L^2}{16}.$

When two fractions have the same numerator, the one with the smaller denominator is greater, and $4\pi < 16$.

24. **A.** You do not need to add the lengths of the steps. Together, all the horizontal steps are equal to the bottom, and all the vertical risers are equal to the left side. The sum of the left side, 5 feet 4 inches, or 64 inches, and the bottom, 9 feet 2 inches, or 110 inches, is half the perimeter. The perimeter is $2(64 + 110) = 2(174) = 348$ inches. Column A is greater.

25. **A.** If the average of the three digits is 2, the sum of the digits is 6. The simplest thing is to list them. If there are only a few, list them all; if it seems that there will be too many to list, look for a pattern. The list starts this way: 105, 114, 123, 132, 141, 150, so there are 6 of them in the 100s. Continue: 204, 213, 222, 231, 240. There are 5 in the 200s. You can conclude, correctly, that there are 4 in the 300s, 3 in the 400s, 2 in the 500s, and 1 in the 600s. So, the total is $6 + 5 + 4 + 3 + 2 + 1 = 21$. If you don't spot the pattern, just continue the list: 303, 312, ... , 501, 510, 600.

26. **C.** Since the area of a right triangle is $\dfrac{1}{2}$ the product of its legs, the area is $\dfrac{1}{2}(3)(4) = 6$. But the area can also be calculated as $\dfrac{1}{2}bh$. Since this is a 3-4-5 triangle, the base is 5. So, $6 = \dfrac{1}{2}(5)h \Rightarrow 5h = 12 \Rightarrow h = \dfrac{12}{5}$ or 2.4.

27. **E.** If $PQ$ is a diameter of the circle, then the radius is 1 and $A$, the area, is $\pi$. This is the smallest possible value of $A$, but $A$ can be any number larger than $\pi$ if the radius is made sufficiently large, as shown by the figures

below.

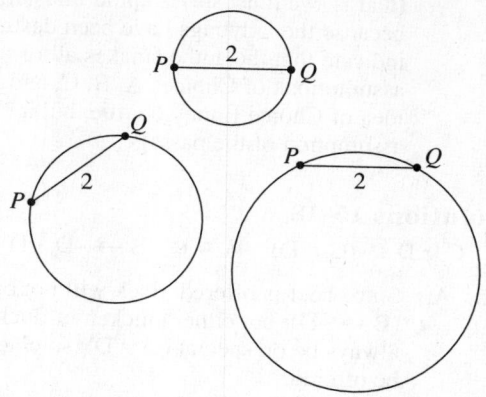

The answer is $A \geq \pi$.

28. **C.** Make tables to determine Roberto's and Juan's ages.

| **Table 1** | 1950 | 1955 |
|---|---|---|
| Roberto | $4x$ | $4x + 5$ |
| Juan | $x$ | $x + 5$ |

| **Table 2** | 1950 | $1950 + t$ |
|---|---|---|
| Roberto | 40 | $40 + t$ |
| Juan | 10 | $10 + t$ |

Let $x$ represent Juan's age in 1950, and fill in Table 1 as shown. In 1955, Roberto was 3 times as old as Juan, so

$$4x + 5 = 3(x + 5) = 3x + 15 \Rightarrow x = 10.$$

Now, make a second table in which $t$ represents the number of years since 1950 (see Table 2). Then, if Roberto is to be twice as old,

$$40 + t = 2(10 + t) = 20 + 2t \Rightarrow t = 20.$$

This occurs in $1950 + 20 = 1970$.
**This result can also be established by trial and error. Guess an age for Juan, and test it. In 1950, if Juan was 5, Roberto was 20; 5 years later they were 10 and 25 (but Roberto was *less* than 3 times as old). Try 10. Now, if in 1950 Juan and Roberto were 10 and 40, respectively, in 1960 they were 20 and 50, in 1965 they were 25 and 55, and in 1970 they were 30 and 60—that's it!

# Section 3—Analytical Ability

1. **A.** The only inference that can logically be drawn is the one in Choice A, since differences in perception exist, but since there are no physical differences, perception must depend partly on other factors. Choices B, C, and D all contain unsupported speculations about what those factors might be; Choice E is irrelevant, since the data specify that the Bilge Islanders *perceive* fewer colors, not simply that they can name fewer colors.

**Solutions 2–5**

2 of F, G, H, I    3 of A, B, C, D, E

$B \rightarrow (D \wedge G)$    $A \rightarrow F$    $C \leftrightarrow E$    $I \rightarrow \sim F$    $I \rightarrow \sim H$

2. **E.** Only Choice E doesn't violate any of the conditions.
Choice A violates the condition that there be three novels.
Choice B violates the condition that if B is selected, both D and G must be selected: $B \rightarrow (D \wedge G)$.
Choice C violates the condition that if C is selected then E must also be selected: $C \leftrightarrow E$.
Choice D violates the condition that if I is selected, F cannot be selected: $I \rightarrow \sim F$.

3. **C.** Since Ruth cannot select another biography, eliminate Choice E; also since if B is selected, G must be too, eliminate Choice B. Therefore, the other selections must be three of the four novels A, C, D, and E. If she did not select C, she could not select E either ($C \leftrightarrow E$), and then she would have only two novels. So C must be selected.

4. **E.** If E is not selected, then neither is C ($C \leftrightarrow E$), so the three novels selected are A, B, and D. Since $A \rightarrow F$ and $B \rightarrow G$, F and G must be the selected biographies; H cannot be selected.

5. **D.** • If Ruth selects A, she cannot select B (since that would force her to select D), and she cannot select either C or E (since if either one is selected, both must be). Therefore, the other novel must be D. Since $A \rightarrow F$, F must be selected, which implies that I is not selected. There are 2 possibilities: A, D, F, G and A, D, F, H.
• If Ruth does not select A, but selects B, then she must select D and G. The fourth book could be any of the other 3 biographies.
• If Ruth selects neither A nor B, she must select two of C, D, and E. But if either C or E is chosen, so is the other; so the two novels are C and E. For the two biographies there are 4 possibilities that do not violate any conditions: F–G; F–H; G–H; G–I.
• There are a total of $2 + 3 + 4 = 9$ different ways for her to make her selection.

6. **B.** Only Choice B addresses Dimple's assumption that Mrs. Wilson is the *only* applicant whose qualifications are ideal. Other choices are irrelevant to the *argument*, although some may be relevant to the implied situation.

7. **A.** Only Choice A addresses the substance of Dimple's argument.

8.  E.   The presence of either anchovies or garlic causes heartburn: $(A \lor G) \to H$, which is equivalent to $\sim H \to \sim(A \lor G)$, which is equivalent to $\sim H \to (\sim A \land \sim G)$. Therefore, since Carlo did not have heartburn ($\sim H$), there was neither anchovies ($\sim A$) nor garlic ($\sim G$). None of the other choices must be true. In particular, mushrooms need not be on the pizza; there could be several toppings that do not cause heartburn for Carlo.

## Solutions 9–13

Women: A, B, C, D, E   Men: F, G, H

Months: Jan, Feb, Mar, Apr, May

no one 2 consec. months

$B = Mar$   $C \leftrightarrow G$   $A \not\ll E$   $E \ll A$

9.  C.   Only Choice C doesn't violate any of the conditions.
Choice A violates the condition that F cannot chair the committee in consecutive months.
Choice B violates the condition that B cannot chair the committee in consecutive months (since B must be a chairperson in March).
Choice D violates the condition that A and E cannot chair the committee in consecutive months.
Choice E violates the condition that C will only cochair the committee with G.

10.  E.   Since three of the women do not serve, and no woman can serve in consecutive months, B, who is required to serve in March, must also serve in January and May.

11.  A.   Only Choice A doesn't violate any of the conditions.
Choices B and C each violate the condition that the committee always be chaired by one man and one woman.
Choice D violates the condition that B cannot chair the committee in consecutive months (since B must be a chairperson in March).
Choice E violates the condition that C will only cochair the committee with G.

12.  C.   Since B serves in March, and since G cannot serve with B (G will only serve with C), the man on the committee in March must be F. Then since F cannot serve again in April, and H serves only in February, the only man available is G. Finally, G always serves with C, so C must serve in April.

13.  A.   Since H serves as a chairperson only in January and May, and G cannot serve with B in March, F must serve in March; and since neither F nor H can serve in consecutive months, G, and hence C, must serve in both February and April.

14.  E.   The words "this is the price we must pay" (that is, we must suffer aphid infestation because the ladybugs have been destroyed) indicate that the author makes all of the assumptions of Choices A, B, C, and D. The idea of Choice E may be true, but it is not an assumption of the passage.

## Solutions 15–18

$C \lor D$   $\sim(C \land D)$   $F \to P$   $B \to \sim D$   $D \to \sim B$

15.  A.   Since beef is offered, duck will not be offered ($B \to \sim D$); but either chicken or duck must always be on special ($C \lor D$), so chicken must be offered.

16.  E.   Only Choice E doesn't violate any of the conditions.
Choice A violates the condition that there can't be a chicken special and a duck special the same night: $\sim(C \land D)$.
Choice B violates the condition that there has to be either a chicken dish or a duck dish ($C \lor D$).
Choice C violates the condition that whenever there is a fish special, there is a pasta special ($F \to P$).
Choice D violates the condition that duck is never offered when beef is on special ($B \to \sim D$).

17.  A.   Since there is no chicken special, there must be a duck special ($C \lor D$), and so there cannot be a beef special ($B \to \sim D$).

18.  C.   • Since beef is a special, duck cannot be a special ($B \to \sim D$); so chicken must be included ($C \lor D$).
• If fish is on special, so is pasta ($F \to P$), and there is only 1 possible list of specials: B, C, F, P.
• If fish is not on special, then any two of pasta, seafood, and veal could be the other specials chosen. There are three possibilities: B, C, P, S; B, C, P, V; or B, C, S, V.
• In total, there are 4 possible ways Carlo can choose the specials.

19.  B.   If popcorn attracts rodents and insects, warehouses where packages using popcorn are stored would have vermin problems.

## Solutions 20–23

members: P, Q, R, S, T, U, V

committees: Fin, Mem, Soc

each committee: 1, 2, or 3 members

Fin $\to \sim$Soc   Fin $\to \sim$Mem

$V \neq Soc$   $U \neq Mem$   $P \to \sim V$   $Q \to \sim V$   $S \leftrightarrow T$

$T \to \sim U$   $U \to \sim T$   $(U = Soc \to V = Fin)$

$(U = Fin \to V = Mem)$

20.  C.  Since U is not on the Finance Committee and can't serve on the Membership Committee, U must be on the Social Committee. Therefore, V must be on the Finance Committee. Also, since T and U cannot be on the same committee, and V is the only member of the Finance Committee, T (and hence, S) must be on the Membership Committee. The Membership Committee, therefore, consists of S, T, and either P, Q, or R. Only Choice C satisfies these conditions.

21.  A.  Only Choice A doesn't violate any of the conditions.
   • If S serves on two committees, so does T, and vice versa. Eliminate Choices B and C.
   • Since no one can serve on both the Finance Committee and another committee, if anyone is serving on more than one committee, he must be on the Membership and Social committees. Since V is unwilling to serve on the Social Committee, and U won't serve on the Membership Committee, neither can serve on both committees. Eliminate Choices D and E.

22.  A.  Only Choice A doesn't violate any of the conditions.
   • No one on the Membership Committee can also be on the Finance Committee. Eliminate Choice B.
   • Since P and V cannot serve on the same committee, eliminate Choice E.
   • If either S or T is on the Finance Committee, then so is the other, and since the committee can have at most three members, no one else can be on the committee. Therefore, U, who won't serve on the Membership Committee must be on the Social Committee; but if U is on the Social Committee, then V is on the Finance Committee, which is impossible. Therefore, neither S nor T is on the Finance Committee. Eliminate Choices C and D.

23.  E.  Since U is on the Social Committee, V is on the Finance Committee, and, therefore, both P and Q are on the Membership Committee. Since no committee can have four members, S and T must both be on the Finance Committee. The only flexibility is that R could, but does not have to, be a third member of the Membership Committee. It is impossible, however, for two people to be on more than one committee.

## Solutions 24–28

   F, F, F, S, S, J, J, Sr    J = (1 or 8)    F = 5
   3 Fs *not* in a row    Sr ≪̸ J    J ≪̸ Sr
   at least once: S ≪ J or J ≪ S

24.  E.  A junior must speak during period 1 or 8. However, since the senior is speaking during period 2, a junior *cannot* speak during period 1. Each of the other choices could be true, but none of them needs to be true.

25.  E.  Only Choice E doesn't violate any of the conditions.
   Choice A violates the condition that one of the juniors speak during period 1 or period 8.
   Choice B violates the condition that the senior cannot speak either immediately before or immediately after a junior.
   Choice C violates the condition that the three freshmen may not speak during three consecutive periods.
   Choice D violates the condition that a freshman must speak in period 5.

26.  D.  To avoid having the three freshmen speak in consecutive periods, the third freshman may *not* speak during periods 3 or 6, and, therefore, must speak in periods 1, 2, 7, or 8.

27.  A.  Since a freshman speaks during period 1, a junior must speak during period 8. Therefore, a senior cannot speak during period 7. All of the other choices are possible.

28.  B.  The condition that the first two talks of the day are made by sophomores actually determines the grade of the speaker during each period.
   • Since a junior is not speaking during period 1, a junior must speak during period 8.
   • Since at least once a junior must immediately follow or precede a sophomore, a junior must speak during period 3.
   • Since a senior and a junior cannot speak consecutively, the senior cannot speak in periods 4 or 7, and since a freshman speaks during period 5, the senior must speak during period 6.
   • The other two freshmen speak during periods 4 and 7.

   | grade | S | S | J | F | F | S | S | J |
   |---|---|---|---|---|---|---|---|---|
   | period | 1 | 2 | 3 | 4 | 5 | 6 | 7 | 8 |

29.  D.  If Choice D is true, then Allegra cannot register for French 317 unless she has already completed French 301, which she has not done. None of the other choices are even relevant.

30.  E.  The passage does not give the information that would lead to the conclusion in Choices A, B, or C. Choice E is a better answer than Choice D, the odds against the heavy smoker being 40 in 100 as opposed to 25 in 100 for the light smoker.

## Solutions 31–34

primary: R, B, Y     secondary: G, O, P     other: Br

each logo: 2, 3, 4, or 5 colors

for both logos: 6 or 7 colors

no color in both logos     $R \rightarrow \sim B$     $R \leftrightarrow G$     $Y \leftrightarrow Br$

31. **E.**  Only Choice E doesn't violate any of the conditions.
    Choices A and C violate the condition that if either yellow or brown is used in a logo, both colors must be used.
    Choice B violates the condition that blue and red cannot be used in the same logo.
    Choice D violates the condition that if either red or green is used in a logo, both colors must be used.

32. **D.**  Choice D is not acceptable because red and green are not used on the same logo. All of the others are acceptable. In particular, note that it is *not* required that all seven colors be used.

33. **A.**  If either red or yellow were not used, then green or brown, respectively, would also have to be omitted. However, because at least six colors must be used, at most one color can be left out. So red and yellow must both be used, and it is given that blue is used. All three primary colors must be used: Choice A cannot be true.

34. **E.**  If each logo uses only primary and secondary colors, then the color brown is not used. Therefore, the color yellow is also not used, and so at most five of the colors are used, which contradicts the condition that at least six colors be used. All of the other choices are possible.

35. **A.**  If the new labels will appear on less than 20 percent of the food sold, they will not be very effective.

# Answer Sheet—Model Test 4

## Section 1

1. Ⓐ Ⓑ Ⓒ Ⓓ Ⓔ
2. Ⓐ Ⓑ Ⓒ Ⓓ Ⓔ
3. Ⓐ Ⓑ Ⓒ Ⓓ Ⓔ
4. Ⓐ Ⓑ Ⓒ Ⓓ Ⓔ
5. Ⓐ Ⓑ Ⓒ Ⓓ Ⓔ
6. Ⓐ Ⓑ Ⓒ Ⓓ Ⓔ
7. Ⓐ Ⓑ Ⓒ Ⓓ Ⓔ
8. Ⓐ Ⓑ Ⓒ Ⓓ Ⓔ
9. Ⓐ Ⓑ Ⓒ Ⓓ Ⓔ
10. Ⓐ Ⓑ Ⓒ Ⓓ Ⓔ

11. Ⓐ Ⓑ Ⓒ Ⓓ Ⓔ
12. Ⓐ Ⓑ Ⓒ Ⓓ Ⓔ
13. Ⓐ Ⓑ Ⓒ Ⓓ Ⓔ
14. Ⓐ Ⓑ Ⓒ Ⓓ Ⓔ
15. Ⓐ Ⓑ Ⓒ Ⓓ Ⓔ
16. Ⓐ Ⓑ Ⓒ Ⓓ Ⓔ
17. Ⓐ Ⓑ Ⓒ Ⓓ Ⓔ
18. Ⓐ Ⓑ Ⓒ Ⓓ Ⓔ
19. Ⓐ Ⓑ Ⓒ Ⓓ Ⓔ
20. Ⓐ Ⓑ Ⓒ Ⓓ Ⓔ

21. Ⓐ Ⓑ Ⓒ Ⓓ Ⓔ
22. Ⓐ Ⓑ Ⓒ Ⓓ Ⓔ
23. Ⓐ Ⓑ Ⓒ Ⓓ Ⓔ
24. Ⓐ Ⓑ Ⓒ Ⓓ Ⓔ
25. Ⓐ Ⓑ Ⓒ Ⓓ Ⓔ
26. Ⓐ Ⓑ Ⓒ Ⓓ Ⓔ
27. Ⓐ Ⓑ Ⓒ Ⓓ Ⓔ
28. Ⓐ Ⓑ Ⓒ Ⓓ Ⓔ
29. Ⓐ Ⓑ Ⓒ Ⓓ Ⓔ
30. Ⓐ Ⓑ Ⓒ Ⓓ Ⓔ

## Section 2

1. Ⓐ Ⓑ Ⓒ Ⓓ Ⓔ
2. Ⓐ Ⓑ Ⓒ Ⓓ Ⓔ
3. Ⓐ Ⓑ Ⓒ Ⓓ Ⓔ
4. Ⓐ Ⓑ Ⓒ Ⓓ Ⓔ
5. Ⓐ Ⓑ Ⓒ Ⓓ Ⓔ
6. Ⓐ Ⓑ Ⓒ Ⓓ Ⓔ
7. Ⓐ Ⓑ Ⓒ Ⓓ Ⓔ
8. Ⓐ Ⓑ Ⓒ Ⓓ Ⓔ
9. Ⓐ Ⓑ Ⓒ Ⓓ Ⓔ
10. Ⓐ Ⓑ Ⓒ Ⓓ Ⓔ

11. Ⓐ Ⓑ Ⓒ Ⓓ Ⓔ
12. Ⓐ Ⓑ Ⓒ Ⓓ Ⓔ
13. Ⓐ Ⓑ Ⓒ Ⓓ Ⓔ
14. Ⓐ Ⓑ Ⓒ Ⓓ Ⓔ
15. Ⓐ Ⓑ Ⓒ Ⓓ Ⓔ
16. Ⓐ Ⓑ Ⓒ Ⓓ Ⓔ
17. Ⓐ Ⓑ Ⓒ Ⓓ Ⓔ
18. Ⓐ Ⓑ Ⓒ Ⓓ Ⓔ
19. Ⓐ Ⓑ Ⓒ Ⓓ Ⓔ
20. Ⓐ Ⓑ Ⓒ Ⓓ Ⓔ

21. Ⓐ Ⓑ Ⓒ Ⓓ Ⓔ
22. Ⓐ Ⓑ Ⓒ Ⓓ Ⓔ
23. Ⓐ Ⓑ Ⓒ Ⓓ Ⓔ
24. Ⓐ Ⓑ Ⓒ Ⓓ Ⓔ
25. Ⓐ Ⓑ Ⓒ Ⓓ Ⓔ
26. Ⓐ Ⓑ Ⓒ Ⓓ Ⓔ
27. Ⓐ Ⓑ Ⓒ Ⓓ Ⓔ
28. Ⓐ Ⓑ Ⓒ Ⓓ Ⓔ

## Section 3

1. Ⓐ Ⓑ Ⓒ Ⓓ Ⓔ
2. Ⓐ Ⓑ Ⓒ Ⓓ Ⓔ
3. Ⓐ Ⓑ Ⓒ Ⓓ Ⓔ
4. Ⓐ Ⓑ Ⓒ Ⓓ Ⓔ
5. Ⓐ Ⓑ Ⓒ Ⓓ Ⓔ
6. Ⓐ Ⓑ Ⓒ Ⓓ Ⓔ
7. Ⓐ Ⓑ Ⓒ Ⓓ Ⓔ
8. Ⓐ Ⓑ Ⓒ Ⓓ Ⓔ
9. Ⓐ Ⓑ Ⓒ Ⓓ Ⓔ
10. Ⓐ Ⓑ Ⓒ Ⓓ Ⓔ

11. Ⓐ Ⓑ Ⓒ Ⓓ Ⓔ
12. Ⓐ Ⓑ Ⓒ Ⓓ Ⓔ
13. Ⓐ Ⓑ Ⓒ Ⓓ Ⓔ
14. Ⓐ Ⓑ Ⓒ Ⓓ Ⓔ
15. Ⓐ Ⓑ Ⓒ Ⓓ Ⓔ
16. Ⓐ Ⓑ Ⓒ Ⓓ Ⓔ
17. Ⓐ Ⓑ Ⓒ Ⓓ Ⓔ
18. Ⓐ Ⓑ Ⓒ Ⓓ Ⓔ
19. Ⓐ Ⓑ Ⓒ Ⓓ Ⓔ
20. Ⓐ Ⓑ Ⓒ Ⓓ Ⓔ

21. Ⓐ Ⓑ Ⓒ Ⓓ Ⓔ
22. Ⓐ Ⓑ Ⓒ Ⓓ Ⓔ
23. Ⓐ Ⓑ Ⓒ Ⓓ Ⓔ
24. Ⓐ Ⓑ Ⓒ Ⓓ Ⓔ
25. Ⓐ Ⓑ Ⓒ Ⓓ Ⓔ
26. Ⓐ Ⓑ Ⓒ Ⓓ Ⓔ
27. Ⓐ Ⓑ Ⓒ Ⓓ Ⓔ
28. Ⓐ Ⓑ Ⓒ Ⓓ Ⓔ
29. Ⓐ Ⓑ Ⓒ Ⓓ Ⓔ
30. Ⓐ Ⓑ Ⓒ Ⓓ Ⓔ

31. Ⓐ Ⓑ Ⓒ Ⓓ Ⓔ
32. Ⓐ Ⓑ Ⓒ Ⓓ Ⓔ
33. Ⓐ Ⓑ Ⓒ Ⓓ Ⓔ
34. Ⓐ Ⓑ Ⓒ Ⓓ Ⓔ
35. Ⓐ Ⓑ Ⓒ Ⓓ Ⓔ

# MODEL TEST 4

### SECTION 1—VERBAL ABILITY

**Time—30 Minutes**
**30 Questions**

**Select the best answer to the following questions, then fill in the appropriate space on your Answer Sheet.**

---

<u>Directions</u>: In each of the following antonym questions, a word printed in capital letters precedes five lettered words or phrases. From these five lettered words or phrases, pick the one most nearly <u>opposite</u> in meaning to the capitalized word.

---

1. INSIPIDNESS:
   - (A) wisdom
   - (B) cowardice
   - (C) lividity
   - (D) savoriness
   - (E) tentativeness

2. SEQUESTER:
   - (A) precede in sequence
   - (B) permit to mingle
   - (C) alter in composition
   - (D) free from doubt
   - (E) attempt to better

---

<u>Directions</u>: Each of the following sentence completion questions contains one or two blanks. These blanks signify that a word or set of words has been left out. Below each sentence are five words or sets of words. For each blank, pick the word or set of words that <u>best</u> reflects the sentence's over-all meaning.

---

3. Book publishing has long been _____ profession, partly because, for younger editors, the best way to win a raise or a promotion was to move on to another publishing house.
   - (A) an innovative
   - (B) a prestigious
   - (C) an itinerant
   - (D) a rewarding
   - (E) an insular

4. For centuries, physicists have had good reason to believe in the principle of equivalence propounded by Galileo: it has _____ many rigorous tests that _____ its accuracy to extraordinary precision.
   - (A) endured...compromised
   - (B) passed...presupposed
   - (C) borne...postulated
   - (D) survived...proved
   - (E) inspired...equated

---

<u>Directions</u>: Each of the following analogy questions presents a related pair of words linked by a colon. Five lettered pairs of words follow the linked pair. Choose the lettered pair of words whose relationship is <u>most like</u> the relationship expressed in the original linked pair.

---

5. AGITATOR : FIREBRAND ::
   - (A) miser : spendthrift
   - (B) renegade : turncoat
   - (C) anarchist : backslider
   - (D) maverick : scapegoat
   - (E) reprobate : hothead

6. DISPASSIONATE : PARTISANSHIP ::
   - (A) enthusiastic : zealousness
   - (B) disconsolate : sorrow
   - (C) intemperate : moderation
   - (D) volatile : immobility
   - (E) ardent : involvement

Directions: Each of the following reading comprehension questions is based on the content of the following passage. Read the passage and then determine the best answer choice for each question. Base your choice on what this passage *states directly* or *implies,* not on any information you may have gained elsewhere.

Mary Shelley herself was the first to point to her fortuitous immersion in the literary and scientific revolutions of her day as the source of her
*Line* novel *Frankenstein*. Her extreme youth, as well as
(5) her sex, have contributed to the generally held opinion that she was not so much an author in her own right as a transparent medium through which passed the ideas of those around her. "All Mrs. Shelley did," writes Mario Praz, "was to provide
(10) a passive reflection of some of the wild fantasies which were living in the air about her."

Passive reflections, however, do not produce original works of literature, and *Frankenstein*, if not a great novel, was unquestionably an original
(15) one. The major Romantic and minor Gothic tradition to which it *should* have belonged was to the literature of the overreacher: the superman who breaks through normal human limitations to defy the rules of society and infringe upon the realm of
(20) God. In the Faust story, hypertrophy of the individual will is symbolized by a pact with the devil. Byron's and Balzac's heroes; the Wandering Jew; the chained and unchained Prometheus: all are overreachers, all are punished by their own
(25) excesses—by a surfeit of sensation, of experience, of knowledge and, most typically, by the doom of eternal life.

But Mary Shelley's overreacher is different. Frankenstein's exploration of the forbidden
(30) boundaries of human science does not cause the prolongation and extension of his own life, but the creation of a new one. He defies mortality not by living forever, but by giving birth.

7. The author quotes Mario Praz primarily in order to

(A) support her own perception of Mary Shelley's uniqueness
(B) illustrate recent changes in scholarly opinions of Shelley
(C) demonstrate Praz's unfamiliarity with Shelley's *Frankenstein*
(D) provide an example of the predominant critical view of Shelley
(E) contrast Praz's statement about Shelley with Shelley's own self-appraisal

8. The author of the passage concedes which of the following about Mary Shelley as an author?

(A) She was unaware of the literary and mythological traditions of the overreacher.
(B) She intentionally parodied the scientific and literary discoveries of her time.
(C) She was exposed to radical artistic and scientific concepts that influenced her work.
(D) She lacked the maturity to create a literary work of absolute originality.
(E) She was not so much an author in her own right as an imitator of the literary works of others.

9. According to the author, Frankenstein parts from the traditional figure of the overreacher in

(A) his exaggerated will
(B) his atypical purpose
(C) the excesses of his method
(D) the inevitability of his failure
(E) his defiance of the deity

## Antonyms

10. FLEDGLING:

(A) experienced
(B) shy
(C) cautious
(D) pedestrian
(E) fleeting

11. EQUANIMITY:

(A) clamor
(B) disparity
(C) agitation
(D) propensity
(E) indivisibility

12. ANATHEMATIZE:

(A) appraise
(B) reciprocate
(C) patronize
(D) insinuate
(E) bless

# 1

# 1

## Analogies

13. INOCULATION : IMMUNITY ::

    (A) talisman : charm
    (B) serum : antidote
    (C) exposure : weathering
    (D) indoctrination : disloyalty
    (E) invasion : fortification

14. CALLOW : MATURITY ::

    (A) incipient : fruition
    (B) eager : anxiety
    (C) youthful : senility
    (D) apathetic : disinterest
    (E) pallid : purity

## Sentence Completion

15. Although he did not consider himself _____, he felt that the inconsistencies in her story _____ a certain degree of incredulity on his part.

    (A) an apostate...justified
    (B) an optimist...intimated
    (C) a hypocrite...demonstrated
    (D) a charlatan...dignified
    (E) a skeptic...warranted

16. Among contemporary writers of fiction, Virginia Woolf is _____ figure, in some ways as radical as James Joyce, in others no more modern than Jane Austen.

    (A) a doctrinaire
    (B) an introspective
    (C) a peripheral
    (D) a disinterested
    (E) an anomalous

## Reading Comprehension
*(This passage was written prior to 1950)*

The coastlines on the two sides of the Atlantic Ocean present a notable parallelism: the eastern-
*Line* most region of Brazil, in Pernambuco, has a con-
*(5)* vexity that corresponds almost perfectly with the concavity of the African Gulf of Guinea, while the contours of the African coastline between Rio de Oro and Liberia would, by the same approximation, match those of the Caribbean Sea.
*(10)*    Similar correspondences are also observed in many other regions of the Earth. This observation began to awaken scientific interest about sixty years ago, when Alfred Wegener, a professor at the University of Hamburg, used it as a basis for
*(15)* formulating a revolutionary theory in geological

science. According to Wegener, there was originally only one continent or land mass, which he called Pangea. Inasmuch as continental masses are lighter than the base on which they rest, he
*(20)* reasoned, they must float on the substratum of igneous rock, known as sima, as ice floes float on the sea. Then why, he asked, might continents not be subject to drifting? The rotation of the globe and other forces, he thought, had caused the
*(25)* cracking and, finally, the breaking apart of the original Pangea, along an extensive line represented today by the longitudinal submerged mountain range in the center of the Atlantic. While Africa seems to have remained static, the
*(30)* Americas apparently drifted toward the west until they reached their present position after more than 100 million years. Although the phenomenon seems fantastic, accustomed as we are to the concept of the rigidity and immobility of the conti-
*(35)* nents, on the basis of the distance that separates them it is possible to calculate that the continental drift would have been no greater than two inches per year.

17. The primary purpose of the passage is to

    (A) describe the relative speed of continental movement
    (B) predict the future configuration of the continents
    (C) refute a radical theory postulating continental movement
    (D) describe the reasoning behind a geological theory
    (E) explain how to calculate the continental drift per year

18. It can be inferred from the passage that evidence for continental drift has been provided by the

    (A) correspondences between coastal contours
    (B) proof of an original solitary land mass
    (C) level of sima underlying the continents
    (D) immobility of the African continent
    (E) relative heaviness of the continental masses

19. The passage presents information that would
    answer which of the following questions?

    (A) In what ways do the coastlines of Africa and
        South America differ from one another?
    (B) How much lighter than the substratum of
        igneous rock below them are the continental
        masses?
    (C) Is the rotation of the globe affecting the stability
        of the present-day continental masses?
    (D) According to Wegener's theory, in what direc-
        tion have the Americas tended to move?
    (E) How does Wegener's theory account for
        the apparent immobility of the African
        continent?

## Antonyms

20. REPUDIATE:

    (A) mislead
    (B) minimize
    (C) ascertain
    (D) isolate
    (E) accept

21. ALOOFNESS:

    (A) exaggeration
    (B) simplicity
    (C) concern
    (D) complacency
    (E) disingenuousness

22. OBFUSCATE:

    (A) insinuate
    (B) exacerbate
    (C) protract
    (D) clarify
    (E) placate

## Sentence Completion

23. The epiphyte plants of the rain forest use trees for
    physical support but do not, like _____, sap
    nutrients from their hosts.

    (A) fauna
    (B) predators
    (C) parasites
    (D) insectivores
    (E) stumps

24. To the embittered ex-philanthropist, all the former
    recipients of his charity were _____, as
    stingy with their thanks as they were wasteful of
    his largesse.

    (A) louts
    (B) misers
    (C) ingrates
    (D) prigs
    (E) renegades

## Analogies

25. DAMPEN : ENTHUSIASM ::

    (A) moisten : throat
    (B) test : commitment
    (C) distract : attention
    (D) reverse : direction
    (E) mute : sound

26. BURST : SOUND ::

    (A) ebb : tide
    (B) tinder : fire
    (C) blast : wind
    (D) glimmer : light
    (E) shard : pottery

## Reading Comprehension

During the 1930s National Association for the
Advancement of Colored People (NAACP) attorneys Charles H. Houston, William Hastie, James
Line  M. Nabrit, Leon Ransom, and Thurgood Marshall
(5)  charted a legal strategy designed to end segregation in education. They developed a series of
legal cases challenging segregation in graduate
and professional schools. Houston believed that
the battle against segregation had to begin at the
(10) highest academic level in order to mitigate fear of
race mixing that could create even greater hostility and reluctance on the part of white judges.
After establishing a series of favorable legal
precedents in higher education, NAACP attorneys
(15) planned to launch an all-out attack on the separate-but-equal doctrine in primary and secondary
schools. The strategy proved successful. In four
major United States Supreme Court decisions
precedents were established that would enable the
(20) NAACP to construct a solid legal foundation
upon which the *Brown* case could rest: *Missouri
ex rel. Gaines* v. *Canada, Registrar of the
University of Missouri* (1938); *Sipuel* v. *Board of*

1                                                                                    1

*Regents of the University of Oklahoma* (1948);
(25)  *McLaurin* v. *Oklahoma State Regents for Higher
Education* (1950); and *Sweatt* v. *Painter* (1950).
In the Oklahoma case, the Supreme Court held
that the plaintiff was entitled to enroll in the
University. The Oklahoma Regents responded by
(30)  separating black and white students in cafeterias
and classrooms. The 1950 *McLaurin* decision
ruled that such internal separation was unconstitutional. In the *Sweatt* ruling, delivered on the same
day, the Supreme Court held that the maintenance
(35)  of separate law schools for whites and blacks was
unconstitutional. A year after Herman Sweatt
entered the University of Texas law school,
desegregation cases were filed in the states of
Kansas, South Carolina, Virginia, and Delaware,
(40)  and in the District of Columbia asking the courts
to apply the qualitative test of the *Sweatt* case to
the elementary and secondary schools and to
declare the separate-but-equal doctrine invalid in
the area of public education.
(45)     The 1954 *Brown* v. *Board of Education* decision declared that a classification based solely on
race violated the 14th Amendment to the United
States Constitution. The decision reversed the
1896 *Plessy* v. *Ferguson* ruling which had estab-
(50)  lished the separate-but-equal doctrine. The *Brown*
decision more than any other case launched the
"equalitarian revolution" in American jurisprudence and signalled the emerging primacy of
equality as a guide to constitutional decisions;
(55)  nevertheless, the decision did not end state-
sanctioned segregation. Indeed, the second *Brown*
decision, known as *Brown II* and delivered a year
later, played a decisive role in limiting the effectiveness and impact of the 1954 case by providing
(60)  southern states with the opportunity to delay the
implementation of desegregation.

27.  According to the passage, Houston aimed his legislative challenge at the graduate and professional
school level on the basis of the assumption that

(A)  the greatest inequities existed at the highest
academic and professional levels
(B)  the separate-but-equal doctrine applied solely
to the highest academic levels
(C)  there were clear precedents for reform in existence at the graduate school level
(D)  the judiciary would feel less apprehension at
desegregation on the graduate level
(E)  the consequences of desegregation would
become immediately apparent at the graduate
school level

28.  Which of the following best describes the relationship between the *McLaurin* decision and the 1954
*Brown* v. *Board of Education* decision?

(A)  The *McLaurin* decision superseded the *Brown*
decision.
(B)  The *Brown* decision provided a precedent for
the *McLaurin* decision.
(C)  The *Brown* decision reversed the *McLaurin*
decision.
(D)  The *McLaurin* decision limited the application
of the *Brown* decision.
(E)  The *McLaurin* decision provided legal
authority for the *Brown* decision.

29.  Which of the following statements is most compatible with the principles embodied in *Plessy* v.
*Ferguson* as described in the passage?

(A)  Internal separation of whites and blacks within
a given school is unconstitutional.
(B)  Whites and blacks may be educated in separate
schools so long as they offer comparable
facilities.
(C)  The maintenance of separate professional
schools for blacks and whites is unconstitutional.
(D)  The separate-but-equal doctrine is inapplicable
to the realm of private education.
(E)  Blacks may be educated in schools with whites
whenever the blacks and whites have equal
institutions.

30.  The aspect of Houston's work most extensively
discussed in the passage is its

(A)  psychological canniness
(B)  judicial complexity
(C)  fundamental efficiency
(D)  radical intellectualism
(E)  exaggerated idealism

**SECTION 2—QUANTITATIVE ABILITY**

Time—45 Minutes
28 Questions

In this section solve each problem, using any available space on the page for scratchwork. Then decide which is the best of the choices given and fill in the corresponding oval on the Answer Sheet.

Directions: In the following type of question, two quantities appear, one in Column A and one in Column B. You must compare them. The correct answer to the question is

A if the quantity in Column A is greater
B if the quantity in Column B is greater
C if the two quantities are equal
D if it is impossible to determine which quantity is greater

Notes: Sometimes information about one or both of the quantities is centered above the two columns. If the same symbol appears in both columns, it represents the same thing each time.

| Column A | Column B |
|---|---|
| 1. The product of the integers from $-7$ to 3 | The product of the integers from $-3$ to 7 |

| | |
|---|---|
| 2. $AC$ | $BC$ |

| Column A | Column B |
|---|---|
| 3. $\frac{2}{3}$ of $x$ equals $\frac{3}{4}$ of $x$ | |

| | |
|---|---|
| $\frac{4}{5}$ of $x$ | 0 |

$n$ is an odd positive integer.

| Column A | Column B |
|---|---|
| 4. The number of prime factors of $n$ | The number of prime factors of $2n$ |

Directions: In the following questions, choose the best answer from the five choices listed.

5. Camille's average on her 6 math tests this marking period is 75. Fortunately for Camille, her teacher drops each student's lowest grade, and this raises her average to 85. What was her lowest grade?

(A) 20   (B) 25   (C) 30   (D) 40   (E) 50

6. What is the surface area of a cube whose volume is 216?

(A) 36   (B) 54   (C) 216   (D) 324   (E) 1296

7. Last year Leo bought two paintings. This year he sold them for $2000 each. On one, he made a 25% profit, and on the other he had a 25% loss. What was his net loss or profit?

(A) He broke even.
(B) He lost less than $100.
(C) He lost more than $100.
(D) He earned less than $100.
(E) He earned more than $100.

| Column A | Column B |
|---|---|
| 8. The measure, in degrees, of the smaller angle formed by the hour hand and the minute hand of a clock at 11:20 | 140 |

2

2

| Column A | Column B |
|---|---|

$$x^2 - 2x - 7 = 0$$

9. | $x^2 - 7$ | | $2x$ |

10. What is the area of a circle whose radius is the diagonal of a square whose area is 4?

(A) $2\pi$    (B) $2\pi\sqrt{2}$    (C) $4\pi$    (D) $8\pi$    (E) $16\pi$

| Column A | Column B |
|---|---|

The first term of a sequence is 1. Starting with the second term, each term is 1 less than 3 times the previous term.

11. | The smallest number greater than 100 in the sequence | | 120 |

| Column A | Column B |
|---|---|

The average (arithmetic mean) of the measures of two angles of a quadrilateral is 60°.

12. | The average of the measures of the other two angles | | 120° |

Anne drove 198 kilometers between 10:00 A.M. and 1:40 P.M.

13. | Anne's average speed, in kilometers per hour | | 55 |

## Unemployed Persons 20 Years Old and Over, by Reason of Unemployment: 1997

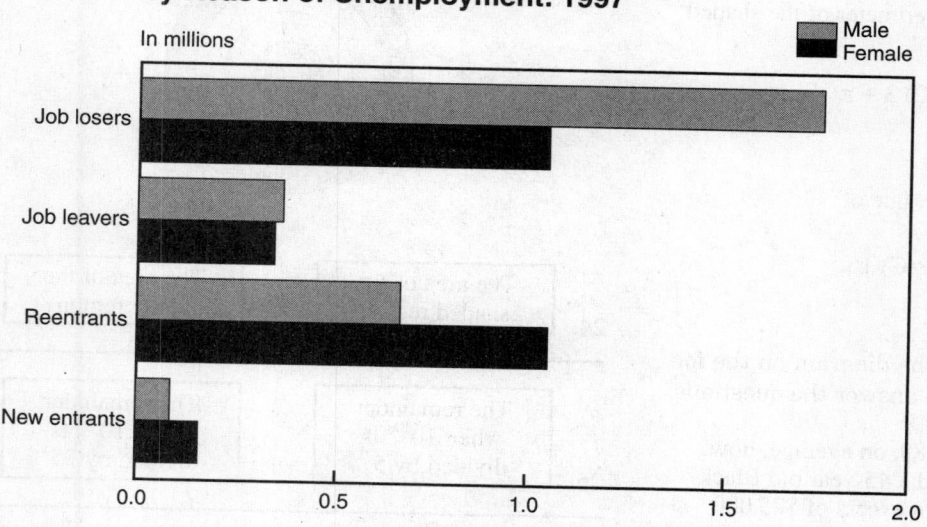

SOURCE: U.S. Bureau of the Census.

14. Of people 20 years of age or older, approximately how many more males than females were unemployed in 1997?

(A) 150,000    (B) 300,000    (C) 750,000
(D) 1,200,00    (E) 2,600,000

15. In 1997, of the unemployed males 20 years of age or older, what percent were unemployed because they had lost their jobs?

(A) 35%    (B) 50%    (C) 60%    (D) 75%
(E) 90%

Column A                    Column B

The average (arithmetic mean) amount of savings of ten students is $60. Three of the students have no savings at all, and each of the others has at least $25, including John, who has exactly $130.

16.

| The largest amount, in dollars, that any one student could have | 300 |

$$1 < a < b < 2$$

17. | $ab$ | $a + b$ |

18.

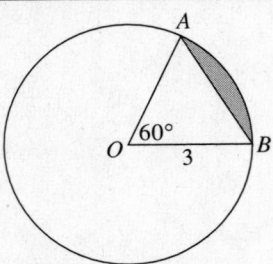

In the figure above, the radius of circle $O$ is 3, and m∠AOB = 60. What is the perimeter of the shaded region?

(A) $3 + \dfrac{\pi}{2}$   (B) $\sqrt{3} + \pi$   (C) $3 + \pi$

(D) $2\sqrt{3} + \pi$   (E) $6 + \pi$

19. If $m^2 = 17$, then what is the value of $(m + 1)(m - 1)$?
(A) $\sqrt{17} - 1$   (B) $\sqrt{17} + 1$   (C) 16
(D) 18   (E) 288

**Questions 20 and 21:** See the diagram on the following page for information to answer the questions.

20. In the period from 1979–1989, on average, how much longer, in years, could a 45-year old Black man with a family income in excess of $25,000 expect to live than a 45-year old Black man with a family income of less than $10,000?
(A) 4   (B) 6   (C) 8   (D) 10   (E) 12

21. For which of the following groups did family income have the least significance in affecting life expectancy?
(A) Black men at age 65
(B) Black women at age 65
(C) White men at age 45
(D) White women at age 45
(E) White women at age 65

22. At Tyler High School, there are twice as many girls as boys on the yearbook staff. At one staff meeting, the percentage of girls attending was twice the percentage of boys. What percent of those attending the meeting were boys?
(A) 20   (B) 25   (C) 30   (D) 33   (E) 50

Column A                    Column B

From 1970–1980 the population of Mayberry decreased 20%.
From 1980–1990 the population of Mayberry decreased 20%.
From 1990–2000 the population of Mayberry decreased 20%.

23.

| The population of Mayberry in 2000 | One-half the population of Mayberry in 1970 |

The figure below consists of four circles with the same center.
The radii of the four circles are 1, 2, 3, and 4.

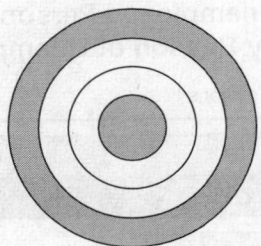

24.

| The area of the shaded region | The area of the white region |

25.

| The remainder when $10^{100}$ is divided by $5^{75}$ | The remainder when $10^{100}$ is divided by $75^5$ |

26. At Harry's Hardware, a hammer costs $d$ dollars and $c$ cents. What is the cost in dollars of $h$ hammers?

(A) $\dfrac{hd + c}{100}$   (B) $\dfrac{h(c + d)}{100}$   (C) $h(100c + d)$

(D) $\dfrac{100hd + hc}{100}$   (E) $100cdh$

2

# Life expectancy among adults 45 and 65 years of age by family income, sex, and race: United States, average annual 1979–89

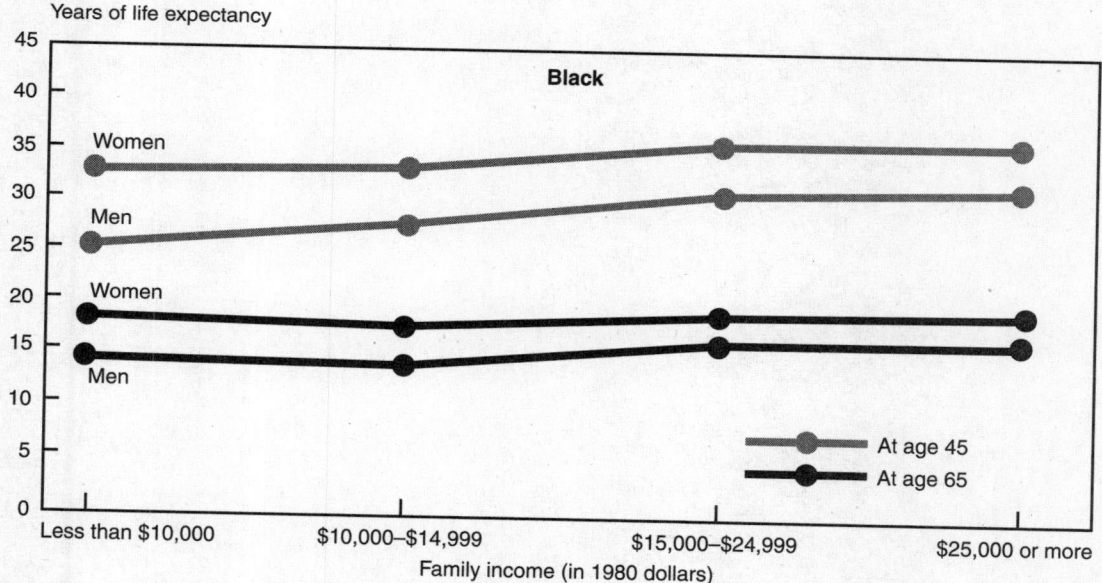

SOURCE: U.S. Bureau of the Census and National Institutes of Health.

**2**

**2**

27. A sequence of numbers begins 1, 1, 1, 2, 2, 3 and then repeats this pattern forever. What is the sum of the 135th, 136th, and 137th numbers in the sequence?

    (A) 3  (B) 4  (C) 5  (D) 6  (E) 7

28.

In the figure above, the diameter of the circle is 20 and the area of the shaded region is $80\pi$. What is the value of $a + b + c + d$?

(A) 144  (B) 216  (C) 240  (D) 270  (E) 288

# 3

# 3

3

## SECTION 3—ANALYTICAL ABILITY

**Time—60 Minutes**
**35 Questions**

<u>Directions</u>: In this section, each set of questions is based on a short passage or a set of conditions. Sometimes, in answering these questions, you might want to make a table or diagram. For each question, choose the best answer from the five choices listed.

1. But the number of flights has increased by 30% in the last ten years.

   The statement above would be a logical rebuttal to which of the following claims?

   (A) The airlines must be losing money. The cost of jet fuel has tripled in the last ten years.
   (B) Airline ticket prices have increased so fast in the last ten years that some people who could once afford to fly no longer can.
   (C) Flying is getting more unsafe. The number of airplane accidents per year has increased by over 10% in the last decade.
   (D) More air travelers are taking "short hop," commuter flights. The average number of miles traveled per flight has decreased by 20% in the last ten years.
   (E) The flight industry is being taken over by a few large airlines. There are 25% fewer airlines today than there were ten years ago.

### Questions 2–5

Of the seven members of a college chess team whose rankings qualify them to compete at the National Intercollegiate Chess Championship, four will be chosen to make the trip. The seven qualifying members consist of three juniors—Amir, Brett, and Cara—and four seniors—Rajiv, Sasha, Tomas, and Ursula. In making his selection, in addition to assessing other criteria, the coach must adhere to the following conditions:

   Rajiv and Sasha cannot both go to the Championship.
   Brett and Tomas cannot both go to the Championship.
   Neither Brett nor Cara will go to the Championship unless the other goes.

2. If Cara is selected to go to the Championship, each of the following could also be selected to go EXCEPT

   (A) Amir
   (B) Rajiv
   (C) Sasha
   (D) Tomas
   (E) Ursula

3. If Amir and Rajiv are both selected, in how many ways could the coach select the other two team members?

   (A) 1  (B) 2  (C) 3  (D) 4  (E) 6

4. If the coach decides to select two juniors and two seniors, which of the following is a pair of students neither of whom can be selected?

   (A) Amir and Tomas
   (B) Amir and Rajiv
   (C) Brett and Cara
   (D) Rajiv and Tomas
   (E) Tomas and Ursula

5. Which of the following CANNOT be true?

   (A) More juniors than seniors are selected.
   (B) More seniors than juniors are selected.
   (C) All of the juniors are selected.
   (D) None of the juniors are selected.
   (E) Amir, Ursula, and Tomas are all selected.

6. On days that both Mollie and John work, they eat dinner at home. On days that neither one goes to work, they go out to dinner.

   If the preceding statements are both true, which of the following statements must also be true?

   (A) If John did not go to work today, and they did not go out to dinner, then Mollie went to work today.
   (B) If Mollie went to work today and John didn't go to work today, then they didn't eat out.
   (C) If they ate dinner in today, then both John and Mollie went to work.
   (D) If they ate dinner in today, and John did not go to work, then Mollie did not go to work.
   (E) If they ate dinner out today, then neither John nor Mollie went to work.

**3** 3

## Questions 7–8

Statistics indicate that, on the average, women executives' salaries are about 20% lower than the salaries of men in comparable jobs. This is true in spite of the job discrimination suits filed by the U.S. government against firms such as A.T.&T. and the Bank of America in the early 1970s, as well as the passage of laws forbidding job discrimination by gender in many states and localities. In the face of this unrelenting prejudice against women, it is plain that only an amendment to the U.S. Constitution can fully remedy the iniquities under which today's women are laboring.

7. Which of the following is assumed by the author of the above argument?

   (A) All women executives are more qualified than their male counterparts.
   (B) A consitutional amendment is more likely to influence employment practices than separate state laws and court actions.
   (C) Legal remedies for discrimination can be effective only when coupled with a sincere desire for reform.
   (D) Average salaries are often misleading as indicators of the real status of a particular social group.
   (E) Discrimination against women is as serious and widespread as discrimination against members of racial and ethnic minorities.

8. All of the following are weaknesses of the above argument except that

   (A) it makes generalizations concerning the status of women based on the plight of a single group of women
   (B) it draws conclusions from statistical evidence which the data themselves may not support
   (C) it disregards efforts being made by some employers to end job discrimination within their own firms
   (D) it fails to fully consider possible remedies, other than the one proposed
   (E) it ignores other possible explanations for the cited difference in average salaries

## Questions 9–13

The six winners—K, L, M, N, O, and P—of a national science contest each won a college scholarship. The prizes for first through sixth place were $30,000, $25,000, $20,000, $15,000, $10,000, and $5,000. The following information concerning the winners was released:

   O won the $20,000 prize.
   K won less money than L did.
   The difference between the winnings of M and P was $5,000.
   The difference between the winnings of N and P was at least $10,000.

9. Which of the following could be the ranking, from sixth place through first place, of the six students?

   (A) M, P, L, O, N, K
   (B) N, P, M, O, K, L
   (C) N, M, K, O, L, P
   (D) M, P, K, O, N, L
   (E) K, L, M, P, O, N

10. If K won $10,000, how much money in total did M and P win?

    (A) $15,000
    (B) $25,000
    (C) $35,000
    (D) $45,000
    (E) $55,000

11. If L won $25,000, which of the following must be true?

    (A) N won $30,000.
    (B) K won $15,000.
    (C) P won $15,000.
    (D) M won $5,000.
    (E) K won $5,000.

12. If N won the fourth prize of $15,000, which of the following is a pair of students where the first named student won $5,000 more than the second named student?

    (A) K and L
    (B) L and K
    (C) M and O
    (D) M and P
    (E) P and M

13. If the difference in the amounts won by K and M was $5,000, which of the following pairs of students could also have won prizes that differed by $5,000?

    (A) K and N
    (B) K and P
    (C) L and O
    (D) L and P
    (E) M and O

3                                                                                     3

14. The people do not run the country; neither do elected officials. The corporations run the country. Heads of corporations routinely and imperiously hand down decisions that profoundly affect millions of people. The people affected do not vote on the decisions, or for the corporate oligarchs. Yet we are supposed to believe we live in a democracy.

Which of the following statements, if true, would support the author's views?

I. Corporate lobbies strongly influence the introduction and passage of legislation at all levels of government.

II. Growing numbers of the most talented college graduates are going to work for private corporations rather than for the government.

III. Few legal requirements are imposed on corporations as to the responsibilities they must fulfill to their employees and their communities.

(A) I only
(B) II only
(C) I and III only
(D) II and III only
(E) I, II, and III

## Questions 15–18

Whenever Cathy's Catering caters a wedding, Cathy provides a large crudites platter during the cocktail hour. The circular platter is divided into six equal wedges, with each wedge containing a different raw vegetable. The vegetables she uses are: broccoli, carrots, mushrooms, green peppers, yellow peppers, and red peppers. In making up a platter, Cathy always adheres to the following two rules:

Red peppers are always next to the yellow peppers, and never next to the green peppers. Mushrooms and carrots are never next to each other.

15. Which of the following could be the order of the vegetables, starting with red peppers, and moving clockwise around the platter?

(A) Red peppers, yellow peppers, green peppers, broccoli, carrots, mushrooms
(B) Red peppers, carrots, yellow peppers, broccoli, mushrooms, green peppers
(C) Red peppers, carrots, green peppers, broccoli, mushrooms, yellow peppers
(D) Red peppers, broccoli, carrots, mushrooms, green peppers, yellow peppers
(E) Red peppers, yellow peppers, mushrooms, broccoli, carrots, green peppers

16. If red peppers and carrots are in adjoining wedges, which of the following is a complete list of the vegetables that could be in the other wedge next to the carrots?

(A) Broccoli
(B) Green peppers
(C) Broccoli, yellow peppers
(D) Broccoli, green peppers
(E) Broccoli, mushrooms, green peppers, yellow peppers

17. If mushrooms and broccoli are in wedges directly opposite each other, which of the following is the pair of vegetables that must be on either side of the carrots?

(A) Broccoli and green peppers
(B) Broccoli and red peppers
(C) Broccoli and yellow peppers
(D) Red peppers and green peppers
(E) Broccoli and mushrooms

18. If Cathy places the mushrooms and red peppers next to each other, how many different ways are there for her to complete the platter?

(A) 1    (B) 2    (C) 3    (D) 4    (E) 6

19. Violence against racial and religious minority groups increased sharply throughout the county last year, despite a slight decline in statewide figures. Compiling incidents from police departments and private watchdog groups, the County Human Relations Committee reported almost 500 hate crimes in the year, up from only 200 last year. It was the first increase since the committee began to report a yearly figure six years ago. The lower statewide figures are probably in error due to underreporting in other counties; underreporting is the major problem that state surveyors face each year.

All of the following, if true, would support the conclusion or the explanation of the discrepancy in the state and county figures EXCEPT

(A) the number of hate crimes and those resulting in fatalities has increased in neighboring states
(B) anti-immigration sentiment was fanned this year by an anti-immigration ballot referendum
(C) funding for police departments throughout the state has decreased
(D) many law-abiding members of minority groups are fearful or distrustful of the police
(E) all of the counties in the state have active private watchdog groups that carefully monitor hate crimes

## Questions 20–23

A subcommittee of the senate Foreign Relations Committee consists of three Republicans—Ross, Shaw, and Turner—and three Democrats—Wolf, Young, and Zhang. Three of these six senators need to visit Moscow to meet with Russian leaders. The decision as to which senators will make the trip is subject to the following conditions:

> The three senators making the trip cannot be from the same party.
> Ross and Shaw cannot both make the trip.
> Neither Turner nor Young will make the trip unless the other one does.
> Wolf will not make the trip unless Zhang does.

20. Which of the following is a list of three senators who could make the trip together?

    (A) Ross, Young, Zhang
    (B) Ross, Turner, Young
    (C) Ross, Shaw, Young
    (D) Turner, Wolf, Young
    (E) Wolf, Young, Zhang

21. If Ross and Zhang are selected to make the trip, which of the following must be true?

    (A) More Democrats than Republicans make the trip.
    (B) More Republicans than Democrats make the trip.
    (C) Shaw makes the trip.
    (D) Turner makes the trip.
    (E) Young makes the trip.

22. If the Senate decides to send four of these senators, subject to the same conditions, all of the following must be true EXCEPT

    (A) Turner makes the trip.
    (B) Young makes the trip.
    (C) Zhang makes the trip.
    (D) Ross or Shaw makes the trip.
    (E) If Wolf makes the trip, then Ross doesn't make the trip.

23. If more Republicans than Democrats make the trip, which of the following must be among the senators making the trip?

    (A) Ross
    (B) Shaw
    (C) Wolf
    (D) Young
    (E) Zhang

## Questions 24–28

A university's educational policy board has nine members: three students—O, P, and Q; three professors—R, S, and T; and three deans—U, V, and W. From time to time, the board forms committees to deal with certain issues. The make-up of these committees is subject to the following three university policies and two personal preferences:

> Each committee must have at least three and at most six members.
> At least one dean must be on each committee.
> Neither students nor professors can ever constitute a majority of the members of a committee.
> U is not willing to serve on any committee with P, Q, or W.
> T is not willing to serve on any committee with P or V.

24. If a committee has exactly three members, two of whom are T and U, which of the following is a complete list of the people who could be the third member of the committee?

    (A) O
    (B) O and R
    (C) O and S
    (D) R and S
    (E) O, R, and S

25. Which of the following is an acceptable committee?

    (A) O, Q, R, T
    (B) O, P, R, S, U
    (C) P, Q, S, T, W
    (D) Q, R, S, T, W
    (E) P, R, S, V, W

26. If T and U are on a committee consisting of exactly four members, who must also be on the committee?

    (A) O   (B) Q   (C) R   (D) S   (E) W

27. How many different four-person committees can be formed that contain no professors?

    (A) 0   (B) 1   (C) 2   (D) 3   (E) 4

28. If P, Q, S, and V are four of the members of a five-person committee, each of the following could be true EXCEPT

    (A) The fifth member is O.
    (B) The fifth member is R.
    (C) The fifth member is W.
    (D) There are the same number of students as professors on the committee.
    (E) There are the same number of students as deans on the committee.

# 3

# 3

## Questions 29–30

Information that is published is part of the public record. But information that a reporter collects, and sources that he contacts, must be protected in order for our free press to function free of fear.

29. The above argument is most severely weakened by which one of the following statements?

(A) Public information is usually reliable.
(B) Undocumented evidence may be used to convict an innocent person.
(C) Members of the press act ethically in most cases.
(D) The sources that a reporter contacts are usually willing to divulge their identity.
(E) Our press has never been altogether free.

30. Which one of the following statements is consistent with the argument above?

(A) Privileged information has long been an important and necessary aspect of investigative reporting.
(B) Not all the information a reporter collects becomes part of the public record.
(C) Tape-recorded information is not always reliable.
(D) The victim of a crime must be protected at all costs.
(E) The perpetrator of a crime must be protected at all costs.

## Questions 31–34

Ramsey Road is one block long. On one side of the road there are seven houses, numbered 2, 4, 6, 8, 10, 12, and 14, in that order, from left to right. Each of these houses is owned by exactly one of the following seven homeowners: Q, R, S, T, U, V, and W. The following information is known about these homeowners:

T lives in house number 2 or house number 14.
Neither Q nor R lives next door to W.
If V lives at either end of the block, he lives next door to R.
S lives next door to either U or W, possibly both.

31. If V lives at 14 Ramsey Road, and W lives next door to T, what is the number of W's house?

(A) 2    (B) 4    (C) 8    (D) 10    (E) 12

32. If V and Q live at 2 Ramsey Road and 12 Ramsey Road, respectively, all of the following must be true EXCEPT

(A) R lives at 4 Ramsey Road.
(B) T lives at 14 Ramsey Road.
(C) W lives at 8 Ramsey Road.
(D) S lives next door to U.
(E) S lives next door to R or Q.

33. If V lives at one end of the block, which of the following could be the owners, in order, of the houses at numbers 4, 6, 8, 10, and 12?

(A) R, S, Q, U, W
(B) R, S, W, Q, U
(C) Q, U, R, S, W
(D) Q, U, S, W, R
(E) Q, U, W, S, R

34. If U and V live at 10 and 14 Ramsey Road, respectively, which of the following CANNOT be true?

(A) T lives at 2 Ramsey Road.
(B) S lives at 6 Ramsey Road.
(C) R lives at 12 Ramsey Road.
(D) Q lives next door to S.
(E) S lives next door to U.

35. If Naomi graduated from Jericho High School after 1998, then she performed community service.

The preceding statement is a logical consequence of which of the following statements?

(A) No students who graduated from Jericho High School before 1998 performed community service.
(B) Only if a student graduated from Jericho High School after 1998 could he or she have performed community service.
(C) Some students who graduated from Jericho High School after 1998 performed community service.
(D) All students who graduated from Jericho High School after 1998 performed community service.
(E) All girls at Jericho High School who performed community service graduated after 1998.

# Answer Key

## Section 1—Verbal Ability

| | | | | | |
|---|---|---|---|---|---|
| 1. D | 6. C | 11. C | 16. E | 21. C | 26. C |
| 2. B | 7. D | 12. E | 17. D | 22. D | 27. D |
| 3. C | 8. C | 13. C | 18. A | 23. C | 28. E |
| 4. D | 9. B | 14. A | 19. D | 24. C | 29. B |
| 5. B | 10. A | 15. E | 20. E | 25. E | 30. A |

## Section 2—Quantitative Ability

NOTE: The letters in brackets following the Quantitative Ability answers refer to the sections of Chapter 15 in which you can find the information you need to answer the questions. For example, 1. C [E] means that the answer to question 1 is C, and that the solution requires information found in Section 15-E: Averages. Also, 20. A [14] means that the answer to question 20 is based on information in Chapter 14: Data Interpretation.

| | | | | | |
|---|---|---|---|---|---|
| 1. C [A] | 6. C [M] | 11. A [A] | 16. A [E] | 21. E [14] | 26. D [D] |
| 2. C [J] | 7. C [C] | 12. C [E,K] | 17. B [A] | 22. A [C] | 27. C [A] |
| 3. C [G] | 8. C [I] | 13. B [H] | 18. C [J,L] | 23. A [C] | 28. E [J,L] |
| 4. B [A] | 9. C [F] | 14. B [14] | 19. C [F] | 24. C [L] | |
| 5. B [E] | 10. D [K,L] | 15. C [14] | 20. C [14] | 25. B [A] | |

## Section 3—Analytical Ability

| | | | | |
|---|---|---|---|---|
| 1. C | 8. C | 15. C | 22. D | 29. B |
| 2. D | 9. D | 16. D | 23. D | 30. A |
| 3. B | 10. E | 17. A | 24. A | 31. B |
| 4. A | 11. A | 18. D | 25. E | 32. D |
| 5. D | 12. B | 19. E | 26. A | 33. E |
| 6. A | 13. C | 20. B | 27. D | 34. E |
| 7. B | 14. C | 21. A | 28. A | 35. D |

# Answer Explanations

## Section 1—Verbal Ability

1. D. The opposite of *insipidness* or lack of flavor is *savoriness*, the quality of being flavorsome. Think of the "insipidness of overcooked boiled cabbage."

2. B. The opposite of to *sequester* or segregate is to *permit* to *mingle*.
   Word Parts Clue: *Se-* means apart. To *sequester* someone means to set him apart. Think of "sequestered jurors."

3. C. The key phrase here is "move on." If editors have to travel from firm to firm to succeed in their field, then publishing can be classified as an *itinerant* profession, a profession marked by traveling.

4. D. The physicists have had good reason to believe in the principle because it has *survived* rigorous or strict tests. These tests have *proved* that the principle is accurate.
   Note how the second clause supports the first, explaining why the physicists have had reason to be confident in the principle.

5. B. *Agitator* (troublemaker) is a synonym for *firebrand. Renegade* (traitor) is a synonym for *turncoat.*                    (Synonym)

6. C. Someone *dispassionate* or temperate in judgment is lacking in *partisanship* or bias. Someone *intemperate* or immoderate is lacking in *moderation.*           (Antonym Variant)

7. D. Immediately before quoting Praz, the author states that the general view of Shelley depicts her as "a transparent medium through which passed the ideas of those around her." The

quotation from Praz provides an excellent example of this particular point of view.
To answer this question correctly, you do not need to read the passage in its entirety. Quickly scroll through the passage, scanning for the name Praz; read only the context in which it appears.

8.  C.  The opening sentence points out that Shelley herself acknowledged the influence of her unplanned immersion in the scientific and literary revolutions of her time. Clearly, the author of the passage concedes this as true of Shelley.

9.  B.  The concluding paragraph distinguishes Frankenstein from the other overreachers in his desire not to extend his own life but to impart life to another (by creating his monster). Thus, his purpose is *atypical* of the traditional overreacher.
To say that someone *parts from* the traditional figure of the overreacher is to say that he *differs* from it. Thus, to answer this question quickly, scan the passage looking for *overreacher* and *different* (or their synonyms).

10. A.  The opposite of *fledgling* or untried is *experienced*. The image is of a young bird just capable of leaving the nest.
Think of "fledgling pilots trying their wings."

11. C.  The opposite of *equanimity* (emotional balance or composure) is *agitation*.
Word Parts Clue: *Equ-* means even. *Anim-* means mind or spirit. *Equanimity* is an evenness of mind; composure.
Think of "something shattering one's equanimity."

12. E.  The opposite of to *anathematize* or curse is to *bless*.
Think of "anathematizing one's foes."

13. C.  *Inoculation* (introduction of a serum or vaccine into a living creature) results in *immunity*. *Exposure* to the elements results in *weathering*.          (Cause and Effect)

14. A.  Someone *callow* is immature and will not reach full development till *maturity*. Something *incipient* is beginning to become apparent and will not reach full development till *fruition*.          (Antonym Variant)

15. E.  Inconsistencies in a story would *warrant* or justify disbelief or incredulity on anyone's part, whether or not he considered himself a *skeptic* (doubter).

16. E.  If Virginia Woolf combines both radical and nonradical elements in her fictions, then she presents an *anomalous* or contradictory image.

17. D.  The author takes the reader through Wegener's reasoning step by step, describing what led Wegener to reach his conclusions.

18. A.  Since the existence of the correspondences between the various coastal contours was used by Wegener as a basis for formulating his theory of continental drift, it can be inferred that the correspondences provide evidence for the theory.
Choice B is incorrect. The passage does not indicate that Pangea's existence has been proved.
Choice C is incorrect. It is the relative heaviness of sima, not the level or depth of sima, that suggested the possibility of the lighter continents drifting.
Choice D is incorrect. Mobility rather than immobility would provide evidence for continental drift.
Choice E is incorrect. The continents are lighter than the underlying sima.

19. D.  Choice D is answerable on the basis of the passage. The next-to-the-last sentence of the second paragraph states that the Americas "apparently drifted toward the west."

20. E.  The opposite of to *repudiate* (disown; refuse to acknowledge) is to *accept*.
Think of "repudiating a debt."

21. C.  The opposite of *aloofness* (remoteness, indifference) is *concern*.
Think of "haughty aloofness."

22. D.  The opposite of to *obfuscate* or confuse is to *clarify*.
Word Parts Clue: *Ob-* means completely; *fusc-* means dark; *-ate* means to make. To *obfuscate* is to becloud or make completely dark.
Think of "obfuscating the issue."

23. C.  By definition, *parasites* sap or drain nutrients from their hosts.

24. C.  The embittered benefactor thinks of them as *ingrates* (ungrateful persons) because they do not thank him sufficiently for his generosity. He does not think of them as *misers* (hoarders of wealth): although they are stingy in expressing thanks, they are extravagant in spending money. He certainly does not think of them as *louts* (clumsy oafs), *prigs* (self-righteous fussbudgets), or *renegades* (traitors): the specific attribute he resents in them is ingratitude, not cloddishness, self-satisfaction, or perfidy.

25. **E.** To *dampen enthusiasm* is to diminish it. To *mute* (muffle) *sound* is to diminish it.
Note that Choice C is incorrect: to *distract attention* is not to diminish it but to divert it in a new direction.      (Defining Characteristic)

26. **C.** A *burst* is a sudden violent outbreak of *sound*. A *blast* is a sudden violent outbreak (heavy gust) of *wind*.
Beware eye-catchers. Choice D is incorrect. A *glimmer* is a feeble or intermittent *light*, not a sudden violent flare or blast of light.
(Degree of Intensity)

27. **D.** Houston believed that the battle had to begin at the graduate level "to mitigate fear" (relieve *apprehension*) of race mixing and miscegenation that might otherwise have caused the judges to rule against the NAACP-sponsored complaints.

28. **E.** The 1950 *McLaurin* decision was one of the decisions that provided legal precedents for the 1954 *Brown* decision.
Choice A is incorrect. *McLaurin* preceded *Brown I*. Therefore, it could not have superseded a decision that had yet to be made.
Choice B is incorrect. *Brown I* followed *McLaurin*. Therefore, it could not have set a precedent for *McLaurin*.
Choice C is incorrect. *Brown I* reversed *Plessy* v. *Ferguson*. It built on *McLaurin*.
Choice D is incorrect. *McLaurin* preceded *Brown I*. Therefore, it could not have limited the application of a decision that had yet to be made.

29. **B.** The separate-but-equal doctrine established by *Plessy* v. *Ferguson* allows the existence of racially-segregated schools.

30. **A.** In assessing the possible effects on judges of race mixing in the lower grades, Houston was *psychologically canny*, shrewd in seeing potential dangers and in figuring strategies to avoid these dangers.

# Section 2—Quantitative Ability

Two asterisks (**) indicate an alternative method of solving.

1. **C.** Each column is the product of 11 integers, one of which is 0. Since 0 times any number is 0, each column is 0. The columns are equal (C).

2. **C.** Since by KEY FACT J2 the measure of an exterior angle of a triangle is equal to the sum of the measures of the two opposite interior angles,

$140 = 70 + y$, and so $y = 70$. Therefore, angles $A$ and $B$ are equal, and by KEY FACT J3 so are the sides opposite them: $AC = BC$. The columns are equal (C).
**If you don't know the theorem about the exterior angle, first find $x$: $x + 140 = 180 \Rightarrow x = 40$. Then, since the sum of the measures of the three angles of a triangle is 180, $y = 70$.

3. **C.** If $a \neq b$ and $ax = bx$, then $x$ must be 0.
So $\frac{2}{3}x = \frac{3}{4}x \Rightarrow x = 0 \Rightarrow \frac{4}{5}x = 0$.

4. **B.** Every factor of $n$ is a factor of $2n$, but 2 is a prime factor of $2n$, which is not a factor of $n$ (since $n$ is odd). So, $2n$ has more prime factors than $n$. Column B is greater.

5. **B.** On six tests combined, Camille earned a total of $6 \times 75 = 450$ points [TACTIC E1]. The total of her five best grades is $5 \times 85 = 425$ points, so her lowest grade was $450 - 425 = 25$.
**Assume that Camille's five best grades were each 85. Then each one has a deviation of 10 points above the average of 75, and the total deviation above 75 is $5 \times 10 = 50$ points. Therefore, her one bad grade must have been 50 points below 75.

6. **C.** Since the volume of the cube is 216, we have $e^3 = 216 \Rightarrow e = 6$. The area of each face is $e^2 = 36$, and since there are six faces, the total surface area is $6 \times 36 = 216$.

7. **C.** On the first painting, Leo made a 25% profit, so if he bought it for $x$, he sold it for
$$x + .25x = 1.25x = 2000 \Rightarrow$$
$$x = 2000 \div 1.25 = 1600.$$
His profit was $400. On the second painting, Leo lost 25%, so if he bought it for $y$, he sold it for
$$y - .25y = .75y = 2000 \Rightarrow$$
$$y = 2000 \div .75 = 2666.67.$$
His loss was $666.67. In all, he *lost* $266.67, which is *more than* $100.
**In these types of problems you *never* break even. Eliminate A. When you make a profit, your purchase price is less than your selling price, and when you incur a loss, your purchase price is greater than your selling price. So the first painting cost less than $2000 and the second cost more than $2000. So Leo earned 25% of a small amount and lost 25% of a large amount. He surely lost money. Eliminate D and E. If you can't solve as above, guess between B and C.

8. **C.** Draw a diagram. The minute hand, of course, is pointing right at 4. The hour hand, however, is *not* pointing at 11. It was pointing at 11 at

11:00, 20 minutes, or $\frac{1}{3}$ hour, ago. The hour hand is now one-third of the way between 11 and 12, so there are 20 degrees between the hour hand and 12 and another 120 degrees to 4, a total of 140 degrees. The columns are equal (C).

9. **C.** This one is easier than it looks. Don't try to factor. Don't solve. Just add $2x$ to both sides of the given equation to get that $x^2 - 7 = x$. The columns are equal (C).

10. **D.** If the area of the square is 4, each side is 2, and the length of a diagonal is $2\sqrt{2}$. The area of a circle whose radius is $2\sqrt{2}$ is $\pi(2\sqrt{2})^2 = 8\pi$.

11. **A.** Write out the first few terms being careful to follow the directions. The first term is 1. The second term is 1 less than 3 times the first term: $3(1) - 1 = 2$. The third term is 1 less than 3 times the second term: $3(2) - 1 = 5$. Continue: $3(5) - 1 = 14$; $3(14) - 1 = 41$; $3(41) - 1 = 122$. The smallest number greater than 100 is 122. Column A is greater.

12. **C.** The sum of the measures of the four angles in any quadrilateral is 360° [KEY FACT K1]. If the average of two of them is 60°, then they total 120° [TACTIC E1], leaving 240° for the other two angles, so their average is 120°. The columns are equal (C).

13. **B.** To find Anne's average speed, in kilometers per hour, we must divide the distance she went, in kilometers (198), by the time it took, in hours. Anne drove for 3 hours and 40 minutes, which is $3\frac{2}{3}$ hours $\left(40 \text{ minutes} = \frac{40}{60} \text{ of an hour} = \frac{2}{3} \text{ of an hour}\right)$. So her average speed was $198 \div 3\frac{2}{3} = 198 \div \frac{11}{3} = 198 \times \frac{3}{11} = 54$. Column B is greater.

14. **B.** The difference between the number of male and female job leavers was insignificant, so ignore them. Among the males, there were about 1.8 million job losers and 0.7 million reentrants, a total of 2.5 million. Among the females, there were about 1.05–1.1 million in each of those two categories, a total of 2.1–2.2 million. This represents a difference of 300–400,000—say, 350,000. Finally, there were about 50,000 more female than male new entrants, so there were approximately 300,000 more males unemployed than females. Note that your figures might be slightly different, but the answer choices are so far apart, that you should definitely choose B.

15. **C.** Adding up the number of males in each category, we see that there were approximately 3 million unemployed males of whom 1.8 million were job losers, which is 60%.

16. **A.** Since the average savings of the 10 students is $60, the total amount they have saved is $600 [TACTIC E1]. John has $130 and 3 students have none at all. If 5 other students have a total of $125 ($25 each, the least possible), then the tenth student will have $600 − $130 − $125 = $345. Column A is greater.

17. **B.** Column A: since $b < 2$, $ab < 2a$.
Column B: since $b > a$, $b + a > a + a = 2a$.
Column B is greater.
**Use TACTIC 1, Chapter 13. Plug in numbers that satisfy the condition.
Column A: $(1.1)(1.8) = 1.98$.
Column B: $1.1 + 1.8 = 2.9$.
This time, Column B is greater. Eliminate Choices A and C, and try other numbers. Each time Column B will be greater. Choose B.

18. **C.** Since each radius is 3, $OA = OB$, and by KEY FACT J3 $m\angle A = m\angle B$. Then, $60 + x + x = 180 \Rightarrow x = 60$. Therefore $\triangle AOB$ is equilateral, and $AB = 3$. The length of arc $AB$ is $\frac{60}{360} = \frac{1}{6}$ of the circumference.

$C = 2\pi(3) = 6\pi$, so the length of arc $AB = \pi$. The perimeter of the region, then, is $3 + \pi$.
**Use TACTIC 2, Chapter 11: trust the diagram. $AB$ looks about the same as $OB$, so assume it is 3, and arc $AB$ is clearly slightly bigger. Hence, the perimeter is a little more than 6. Choices A and B are both less than 5, which is definitely too small. Between C and D *guess*. C, $3 + \pi$, is the better guess, because

*AB might be* exactly 3.

19. C.   $(m + 1)(m - 1) = m^2 - 1 = 17 - 1 = 16$.
**Since $m^2 = 17$, $m$ is slightly more than 4, and $(m + 1)(m - 1)$ is the product of a number a little greater than 5 and a number a little greater than 3. The only reasonable choice is 16.

20. C.   From the lower graph, we can see that the life expectancy at age 45 for Black men with family incomes below $10,000 was 25, whereas for those whose family income was $25,000 or more, their life expectancy was 33 years: a difference of 8 years.

21. E.   The line segments constituting the graph of life expectancy for White women at age 65 are virtually horizontal. At all incomes, these women have a life expectancy of about 20 years. For none of the other categories does family income have as small an impact on life expectancy.

22. A.   Even if you can do the algebra, this type of problem is easier if you use TACTIC 2, Chapter 12. Find some easy-to-use numbers. Assume that there are 100 girls and 50 boys on staff and that 20% of the girls and 10% of the boys attended the meeting. Then, 20 girls and 5 boys were there, and 5 is 20% of 25, the total number attending.
**Of course, you *can* do this algebraically. If $x$ represents the number of boys on staff, then $2x$ is the number of girls. If $y$% of the boys attended the meeting, then $2y$% of the girls did. So, the number of boys attending was $x\left(\dfrac{y}{100}\right) = \dfrac{xy}{100}$, whereas the number of girls attending was $2x\left(\dfrac{2y}{100}\right) = \dfrac{4xy}{100}$. Therefore, there were 4 times as many girls in attendance as boys: $\dfrac{4}{5}$ of those at the meeting were girls and $\dfrac{1}{5}$ or 20% were boys.

23. A.   Note that, when a number is decreased by 20%, what remains is 80% of the original: 80% of 80% of 80% = $.8 \times .8 \times .8 = .512 = 51.2\%$, which is greater than 50%. Column A is greater.
** Use TACTIC 2, Chapter 13. *Assume* that in 1970 the population of Mayberry was 100. Then, in 1980 it was 80, in 1990 it was 64 (80% of 80), and in 2000 it was 51.2, which is greater than 50, one-half of the 1970 population.

24. C.   Since the entire region is a circle of radius 4, its area is $\pi(4)^2 = 16\pi$. The white region is a circle of radius 3 minus the small shaded circle of radius 1, so its area is $9\pi - \pi = 8\pi$. Thus, the area of the white region is one-half of the total area, and the area of the shaded region is the other half. The columns are equal (C).

25. B.   Column A: $10^{100}$ is evenly divisible by $5^{75}$. (Just imagine a fraction whose numerator is the product of 100 10s and whose denominator is the product of 75 5s. Each 5 divides into one of the 10s.) So Column A is 0.
Column B: $10^{100}$ is not evenly divisible by $75^5$, since $75^5$ is divisible by 3, but $10^{100}$ is not. Since there will be a remainder, Column B is greater than 0, and, therefore, greater than Column A.

26. D.   Since $c$ cents $= \dfrac{c}{100}$ dollars, the cost, in dollars, of 1 hammer is $d + \dfrac{c}{100}$, and the cost of $h$ hammers is
$$h\left(d + \dfrac{c}{100}\right) = h\left(\dfrac{100d + c}{100}\right) = \dfrac{100hd + hc}{100}.$$
**Use TACTIC 2, Chapter 12: plug in easy-to-use numbers. If a hammer costs 1 dollar and 50 cents, then 2 hammers cost 3 dollars. So, which of the choices equals 3 when $d = 1$, $c = 50$, and $h = 2$? Only $\dfrac{100hd + hc}{100}$.
Remember: don't waste time getting the exact value of each choice; as soon as you can see that it doesn't equal 3, eliminate it. For example, Choices C and E are gigantic.

27. C.   Since the pattern has six digits, divide 135 by 6. The quotient is 22 and the remainder is 3. Since $22 \times 6 = 132$, the 132nd number completes the pattern for the 22nd time. So the 133rd, 134th, and 135th numbers are 1s, and the 136th and 137th are 2s; and their sum is $1 + 2 + 2 = 5$.

28. E.   Since the diameter of the circle is 20, the radius is 10 and the area is $100\pi$. Since the area of the shaded region is $80\pi$, it is $\dfrac{80}{100} = \dfrac{4}{5}$ of the circle, and the white area is $\dfrac{1}{5}$ of the circle. So the sum of the measures of the two white central angles is $\dfrac{1}{5}$ of 360°, or 72°. The sum of the measures of all six angles in the triangles is 360°, so $a + b + c + d = 360 - 72 = 288$.

# Section 3—Analytical Ability

1. C.   If the number of accidents has increased by only 10%, while the number of flights has increased by 30%, then flying is actually getting safer. Thus, the original statement serves to rebut Choice C. The increase in the number of flights need not imply that the airlines must be making more money (Choice A), that all those who used to fly can still afford to fly (Choice B), or that a few large airlines are not taking over the industry (Choice E). The only way the statement in Choice D could be countered would be to dispute the figure given.

## Solutions 2–5

juniors: A, B, C    seniors: R, S, T, U    choose 4

$$R \rightarrow \sim S \quad B \rightarrow \sim T \quad B \leftrightarrow C$$

2. D.   If Cara is selected, then so is Brett (B ↔ C), which means that Tomas cannot be selected (B → ~T). Anyone else could be selected.

3. B.   If Rajiv is selected, Sasha cannot be selected (R → ~ S). If either Brett or Cara is selected, so is the other (B ↔ C). Therefore, one possibility is that the other two members selected are Brett and Cara. If they don't go, the other two spots can go only to Tomas and Ursula. There are two possibilities.

4. A.   The two juniors selected must be Brett and Cara (B ↔ C), so Amir cannot go. Since Brett is going, Tomas cannot be selected. In each of the other choices, at least one of the two people can be selected.

5. D.   If none of the juniors are selected, then all four seniors must be selected, which contradicts the condition that Rajiv and Sasha cannot both be selected. Each of the other choices is possible.

6. A.   It helps to write the given statements symbolically. Let M, J, O, and H, represent "Mollie works," "John works," "they eat out," and "they eat at home," respectively. Then the two given statements are:

$$(M \wedge J) \rightarrow H \quad \text{and} \quad (\sim M \wedge \sim J) \rightarrow O$$

which are equivalent, respectively, to

$$\sim H \rightarrow (\sim M \vee \sim J) \quad \text{and} \quad \sim O \rightarrow (M \vee J).$$

From the last symbolic statement it is clear that Choice A is true: If they didn't go out to dinner, then at least one of them went to work, and since John didn't, Molly did. None of the other choices must be true. Note in particular that we know nothing about their dining habits on days when one of them works and the other doesn't.

7. B.   This can be deduced from the fact that the author believes that a constitutional amendment will succeed where lawsuits and local statutes have failed.

8. C.   The fact that some employers do not discriminate against women does not undermine the argument as presented, since it does not imply that no problem of discrimination exists.

## Solutions 9–13

winners: K, L, M, N, O, P

prizes: $30,000, 25,000, 20,000, 15,000, 10,000, 5,000

$$O = 20 = \text{3rd place} \quad K < L \quad M << P \text{ or } P << M$$

$$N < x < P \quad \text{or} \quad P < x < N$$

9. D.   Only Choice D does not violate any of the given conditions.
Choice A violates the condition that K won less money than L did (K < L).
Choice B violates the condition that N and P can't be consecutive.
Choice C violates the condition that M and P must be consecutive.
Choice E violates the condition that O won third prize.

10. E.   Since K won fifth prize and O won third prize, M and P won two of first, second, fourth, and sixth prizes. Since the prizes won by M and P differ by only $5,000, they had to win first and second prize, with total winnings of $55,000.

$$\frac{\quad}{6} \; \frac{K}{5} \; \frac{\quad}{4} \; \frac{O}{3} \; \frac{\quad}{2} \; \frac{\quad}{1}$$

11. A.   Given that L came in second and O came in third, who could have won first prize? Not K, since K won less money than L (K < L); and neither M nor P, since they came in consecutively (either fourth and fifth or fifth and sixth, in this case). So first prize had to go to N. Each of the other choices could be true, although none of them must be true.

$$\frac{\quad}{6} \; \frac{\quad}{5} \; \frac{\quad}{4} \; \frac{O}{3} \; \frac{L}{2} \; \frac{\quad}{1}$$

12. B.   Since M and P had consecutive rankings, either they came in fifth and sixth (and K and L came in first and second) or they came in first and second (and K and L came in fifth and sixth). Either way, the prizes won by K and L differed by $5,000; and since K won less than L, the correct answer is Choice B.

$$\frac{\quad}{6} \; \frac{\quad}{5} \; \frac{N}{4} \; \frac{O}{3} \; \frac{\quad}{2} \; \frac{\quad}{1}$$

13. C.   Since the difference in the amounts won by K and M was $5,000, and the difference in the

amounts won by P and M was $5,000, these three students had to win fourth, fifth, and sixth prizes. First and second prizes, therefore, were won by L and N, in either order. Since O won third prize and L could have won second prize, the answer is Choice C.

$$\frac{K}{6} \quad \frac{M/P}{5} \quad \frac{O}{4} \quad \frac{N/L}{3 \quad 2 \quad 1}$$

or

$$\frac{M/P}{6 \quad 5} \quad \frac{K}{4} \quad \frac{O}{3} \quad \frac{N/L}{2 \quad 1}$$

14. **C.** The author asserts that the corporations, rather than people or elected officials, run the country. The author's evidence is that corporation heads make important decisions without being subject to popular controls. Statement I strengthens the conclusion by giving evidence of corporate influence in an area not dealt with in the argument. Statement III strengthens the evidence by giving additional data suggesting corporate autonomy. Statement II is unrelated to either the evidence or the conclusion.

## Solutions 15–18

vegetables: B, C, M, G, R, Y

the platter:

(↔ means next to): R ↔ Y   R ↮ G   C ↮ M

15. **C.** Only Choice C does not violate any of the given conditions.
Choices A and D violate the condition that carrots and mushrooms cannot be next to each other.
Choice B violates the condition that the red peppers and yellow peppers must be next to each other.
Choice E violates the condition that red peppers and green peppers cannot be next to each other.

16. **D.** Of the four remaining vegetables, eliminate mushrooms, which can never be placed next to the carrots. Also, eliminate yellow peppers, which must be on the other side of the red peppers. The two vegetables left, broccoli and green peppers, are both acceptable.

17. **A.** There are two wedges next to the mushrooms and two next to the broccoli. Since the carrots cannot be next to the mushrooms, they must be in one of the wedges next to the broccoli. The two wedges on the opposite side of the platter must hold the red and yellow peppers (since they must be next to each other). This leaves the green peppers to go next to the carrots.

18. **D.** Cathy must put the yellow peppers next to the red peppers, and cannot put the carrots next to the mushrooms. This leaves two possible wedges for the carrots. In each case, the other two empty wedges must have the broccoli and green peppers, in either order. There are 4 ways to do this.

19. **E.** All of the first four statements can be used to explain the underreporting. In Choice D, for example, if the size of police departments has declined, they would have less manpower available to gather and report information. Choice E is a reason against underreporting rather than an explanation for it.

## Solutions 20–23

Rep: R, S, T   Dem: W, Y, Z

2 Reps and 1 Dem   or   2 Dems and 1 Rep

R → ~ S   T ↔ Y   W → Z

20. **B.** Only Choice B doesn't violate any of the conditions.
Choice A violates the condition that neither Turner nor Young will make the trip without the other [T ↔ Y].
Choice C violates the condition that Ross and Shaw cannot both make the trip [R → ~S].
Choice D violates the condition that Wolf will not make the trip unless Zhang does [W → Z].
Choice E violates the condition that the three senators cannot all be from the same party.

21. **A.** Since three senators are making the trip, the number from each party cannot be the same, so one party must be in the majority. Choice A or Choice B must be true; eliminate Choices C, D, and E. Since two senators have already

been chosen, there is no room for both Turner and Young, so neither can go [T ↔ Y]; and since Ross is making the trip, Shaw can't [R → ~S].

Ⓡ S̶ T̶ Ⓦ X̶ Ⓩ

This leaves Wolf, a second Democrat, as the third senator going to Moscow.

22. D. If Turner and Young do not make the trip, then all four of the other senators must go; but this is impossible since Ross and Shaw cannot both go [R → ~ S]. So Turner and Young both make the trip. Choices A and B are true.

R    S    Ⓣ    W    Ⓨ    Z

If Zhang does not make the trip, then neither can Wolf [W → Z], and again this would leave Ross and Shaw; so Zhang does make the trip, and Choice C is true.

R    S    Ⓣ    W    Ⓨ Ⓩ

Any one of Ross, Shaw, and Wolf could be the fourth senator making the trip, so Choice E is true, and Choice D is false.

23. D. If more Republicans than Democrats make the trip, there are two Republicans and one Democrat going. Since the two Republicans cannot be Ross and Shaw [R → ~ S], one of them must be Turner, which means that Young also makes the trip [T ↔ Y].

**Solutions 20–24**

students: O, P, Q    profs: R, S, T    deans: U, V, W

each committee: 3, 4, 5, 6

students *not* a majority    profs *not* a majority

U ∨ V ∨ W    U →(~P ∧ ~Q ∧ ~ W)    T →(~P ∧ ~V)

24. A. Since U is on the committee and U →(~P ∧ ~Q ∧ ~ W), none of P, Q, or W can be on the committee. Also, since T is on the committee and T →(~P ∧ ~V), V cannot serve. If either R or S were the third member, the professors would constitute a majority. Only O could be the third committee member without violating any condition.

25. E. Only Choice E does not violate any condition. Choice A violates the condition that there must be a dean on every committee [U ∨ V ∨ W].
Choice B violates the condition that P and U cannot serve on the same committee [U →(~P ∧ ~ Q ∧ ~ W)].
Choice C violates the condition that P and T cannot serve on the same committee [T →(~P ∧ ~V)].
Choice D violates the condition that the professors cannot constitute a majority of the members of a committee.

26. A. Since U is on the committee and U →(~P ∧ ~Q ∧ ~ W), none of P, Q, or W can serve. Since T is on the committee and T →(~P ∧ ~V), V cannot serve.

O    P̶    Q̶    R    S    Ⓣ Ⓤ    V̶    W̶

It is not possible for both R and S to serve, since then the professors would constitute 75% of the committee (3 out of the 4 members). Therefore, only one of them can serve and the fourth member must be O.

27. D. A four-person committee that has no professors, must draw its members from the three students and three deans. If U is on a committee, then three of those people (P, Q, and W) would be ineligible to serve, and so there wouldn't be enough people left to get four members. So U cannot be on such a committee. If only one of V and W were on such a committee, the other three members would all be students, which is not permitted, since they would constitute a majority. So such a committee must include both V and W and two of the three students. There are 3 such committees: V, W, O, P; V, W, O, Q; and V, W, P, Q.

28. A. If O were the fifth member, the students would constitute a majority of the committee, which is not permissible. Each of the other choices is possible. Since P is on the committee, neither U nor T can serve. The fifth member, therefore, could be either R or W. If it is R, Choices B and E are true, whereas if it is W, Choices C and D are true.

29. B. Choices A and C strengthen the argument. Although Choices D and E partially weaken certain aspects of the argument, only Choice B introduces a situation that suggests that freedom of the press may have harmful consequences.

30. A. Choices B and C are irrelevant to the argument. Choices D and E contradict the implied assertion that a free press must be protected at all costs. Only Choice A offers a statement both favorable to the concept of a free press and directly relevant to the subject discussed: the use of privileged information.

**Solutions 31–34**

T = (2 or 14)    Q ≠ W ± 2    R ≠ W ± 2

(V = 2) → (R = 4)    (V = 14) → (R = 12)

(S = U ± 2) or (S = W ± 2)

31. B. Since V lives at 14 Ramsey Road, and T lives in house number 2 or house number 14, T must live at 2 Ramsey. Since it is given that W lives next door to T, W lives at number 4.

32. D. The given conditions *almost* determine where everyone lives. Since V lives at number 2, R lives at number 4 [(V = 2) → (R = 4)] and T lives at number 14 [T = (2 or 14)]. Since W cannot live next door to either R or Q, W must live at number 8. The only indeterminate is whether S lives at number 6 and U lives at number 10, or vice versa. In either case, S does not live next to U.

$$\underline{V}\ \underline{R}\ \_\ \underline{W}\ \_\ \underline{Q}\ \underline{T}$$
$$2\ \ 4\ \ 6\ \ 8\ \ 10\ \ 12\ \ 14$$

33. E. Only Choice E doesn't violate any of the conditions.
    Choice A violates the condition that S live next door to either U or W.
    Choice B violates the condition that Q and W do not live next door to each other.
    Choice C violates the condition that R lives at number 4 or number 12 (since V lives at one end of the block, at number 2 or 14).
    Choice D violates the condition that R and W do not live next door to each other.

34. E. The given conditions *almost* determine where everyone lives. Since V lives at number 14, R lives at number 12 [(V = 14) → (R = 12)] and T lives at number 2 [T = (2 or 14)]. Since Q and W cannot live next door to each other, S must live at number 6. The only indeterminate is whether Q lives at number 4 and W lives at number 8, or vice versa. In either case, S does not live next to U.

$$\underline{T}\ \_\ \underline{S}\ \_\ \underline{U}\ \underline{R}\ \underline{S}$$
$$2\ \ 4\ \ 6\ \ 8\ \ 10\ \ 12\ \ 14$$

35. D. Choices A and B state that if a student at Jericho High School performed community service, then he or she graduated after 1998; and Choice E states the same thing, except that it is restricted to girls. None of these statements implies that all students who graduated after 1988, including Naomi, had to perform community service. Only Choice D makes that claim; Choice C states that at least one of Naomi's classmates, but not necessarily Naomi, performed community service.

# Answer Sheet—Model Test 5

Remove answer sheet by cutting on dotted line

## Section 1

1. Ⓐ Ⓑ Ⓒ Ⓓ Ⓔ
2. Ⓐ Ⓑ Ⓒ Ⓓ Ⓔ
3. Ⓐ Ⓑ Ⓒ Ⓓ Ⓔ
4. Ⓐ Ⓑ Ⓒ Ⓓ Ⓔ
5. Ⓐ Ⓑ Ⓒ Ⓓ Ⓔ
6. Ⓐ Ⓑ Ⓒ Ⓓ Ⓔ
7. Ⓐ Ⓑ Ⓒ Ⓓ Ⓔ
8. Ⓐ Ⓑ Ⓒ Ⓓ Ⓔ
9. Ⓐ Ⓑ Ⓒ Ⓓ Ⓔ
10. Ⓐ Ⓑ Ⓒ Ⓓ Ⓔ

11. Ⓐ Ⓑ Ⓒ Ⓓ Ⓔ
12. Ⓐ Ⓑ Ⓒ Ⓓ Ⓔ
13. Ⓐ Ⓑ Ⓒ Ⓓ Ⓔ
14. Ⓐ Ⓑ Ⓒ Ⓓ Ⓔ
15. Ⓐ Ⓑ Ⓒ Ⓓ Ⓔ
16. Ⓐ Ⓑ Ⓒ Ⓓ Ⓔ
17. Ⓐ Ⓑ Ⓒ Ⓓ Ⓔ
18. Ⓐ Ⓑ Ⓒ Ⓓ Ⓔ
19. Ⓐ Ⓑ Ⓒ Ⓓ Ⓔ
20. Ⓐ Ⓑ Ⓒ Ⓓ Ⓔ

21. Ⓐ Ⓑ Ⓒ Ⓓ Ⓔ
22. Ⓐ Ⓑ Ⓒ Ⓓ Ⓔ
23. Ⓐ Ⓑ Ⓒ Ⓓ Ⓔ
24. Ⓐ Ⓑ Ⓒ Ⓓ Ⓔ
25. Ⓐ Ⓑ Ⓒ Ⓓ Ⓔ
26. Ⓐ Ⓑ Ⓒ Ⓓ Ⓔ
27. Ⓐ Ⓑ Ⓒ Ⓓ Ⓔ
28. Ⓐ Ⓑ Ⓒ Ⓓ Ⓔ
29. Ⓐ Ⓑ Ⓒ Ⓓ Ⓔ
30. Ⓐ Ⓑ Ⓒ Ⓓ Ⓔ

## Section 2

1. Ⓐ Ⓑ Ⓒ Ⓓ Ⓔ
2. Ⓐ Ⓑ Ⓒ Ⓓ Ⓔ
3. Ⓐ Ⓑ Ⓒ Ⓓ Ⓔ
4. Ⓐ Ⓑ Ⓒ Ⓓ Ⓔ
5. Ⓐ Ⓑ Ⓒ Ⓓ Ⓔ
6. Ⓐ Ⓑ Ⓒ Ⓓ Ⓔ
7. Ⓐ Ⓑ Ⓒ Ⓓ Ⓔ
8. Ⓐ Ⓑ Ⓒ Ⓓ Ⓔ
9. Ⓐ Ⓑ Ⓒ Ⓓ Ⓔ
10. Ⓐ Ⓑ Ⓒ Ⓓ Ⓔ

11. Ⓐ Ⓑ Ⓒ Ⓓ Ⓔ
12. Ⓐ Ⓑ Ⓒ Ⓓ Ⓔ
13. Ⓐ Ⓑ Ⓒ Ⓓ Ⓔ
14. Ⓐ Ⓑ Ⓒ Ⓓ Ⓔ
15. Ⓐ Ⓑ Ⓒ Ⓓ Ⓔ
16. Ⓐ Ⓑ Ⓒ Ⓓ Ⓔ
17. Ⓐ Ⓑ Ⓒ Ⓓ Ⓔ
18. Ⓐ Ⓑ Ⓒ Ⓓ Ⓔ
19. Ⓐ Ⓑ Ⓒ Ⓓ Ⓔ
20. Ⓐ Ⓑ Ⓒ Ⓓ Ⓔ

21. Ⓐ Ⓑ Ⓒ Ⓓ Ⓔ
22. Ⓐ Ⓑ Ⓒ Ⓓ Ⓔ
23. Ⓐ Ⓑ Ⓒ Ⓓ Ⓔ
24. Ⓐ Ⓑ Ⓒ Ⓓ Ⓔ
25. Ⓐ Ⓑ Ⓒ Ⓓ Ⓔ
26. Ⓐ Ⓑ Ⓒ Ⓓ Ⓔ
27. Ⓐ Ⓑ Ⓒ Ⓓ Ⓔ
28. Ⓐ Ⓑ Ⓒ Ⓓ Ⓔ

## Section 3

1. Ⓐ Ⓑ Ⓒ Ⓓ Ⓔ
2. Ⓐ Ⓑ Ⓒ Ⓓ Ⓔ
3. Ⓐ Ⓑ Ⓒ Ⓓ Ⓔ
4. Ⓐ Ⓑ Ⓒ Ⓓ Ⓔ
5. Ⓐ Ⓑ Ⓒ Ⓓ Ⓔ
6. Ⓐ Ⓑ Ⓒ Ⓓ Ⓔ
7. Ⓐ Ⓑ Ⓒ Ⓓ Ⓔ
8. Ⓐ Ⓑ Ⓒ Ⓓ Ⓔ
9. Ⓐ Ⓑ Ⓒ Ⓓ Ⓔ
10. Ⓐ Ⓑ Ⓒ Ⓓ Ⓔ

11. Ⓐ Ⓑ Ⓒ Ⓓ Ⓔ
12. Ⓐ Ⓑ Ⓒ Ⓓ Ⓔ
13. Ⓐ Ⓑ Ⓒ Ⓓ Ⓔ
14. Ⓐ Ⓑ Ⓒ Ⓓ Ⓔ
15. Ⓐ Ⓑ Ⓒ Ⓓ Ⓔ
16. Ⓐ Ⓑ Ⓒ Ⓓ Ⓔ
17. Ⓐ Ⓑ Ⓒ Ⓓ Ⓔ
18. Ⓐ Ⓑ Ⓒ Ⓓ Ⓔ
19. Ⓐ Ⓑ Ⓒ Ⓓ Ⓔ
20. Ⓐ Ⓑ Ⓒ Ⓓ Ⓔ

21. Ⓐ Ⓑ Ⓒ Ⓓ Ⓔ
22. Ⓐ Ⓑ Ⓒ Ⓓ Ⓔ
23. Ⓐ Ⓑ Ⓒ Ⓓ Ⓔ
24. Ⓐ Ⓑ Ⓒ Ⓓ Ⓔ
25. Ⓐ Ⓑ Ⓒ Ⓓ Ⓔ
26. Ⓐ Ⓑ Ⓒ Ⓓ Ⓔ
27. Ⓐ Ⓑ Ⓒ Ⓓ Ⓔ
28. Ⓐ Ⓑ Ⓒ Ⓓ Ⓔ
29. Ⓐ Ⓑ Ⓒ Ⓓ Ⓔ
30. Ⓐ Ⓑ Ⓒ Ⓓ Ⓔ

31. Ⓐ Ⓑ Ⓒ Ⓓ Ⓔ
32. Ⓐ Ⓑ Ⓒ Ⓓ Ⓔ
33. Ⓐ Ⓑ Ⓒ Ⓓ Ⓔ
34. Ⓐ Ⓑ Ⓒ Ⓓ Ⓔ
35. Ⓐ Ⓑ Ⓒ Ⓓ Ⓔ

# MODEL TEST 5

1

## SECTION 1—VERBAL ABILITY

**Time—30 Minutes**
**30 Questions**

Select the best answer to the following questions, then
fill in the appropriate space on your Answer Sheet.

---

**Directions**: In each of the following antonym questions, a word printed in capital letters precedes five lettered words or phrases. From these five lettered words or phrases, pick the one most nearly <u>opposite</u> in meaning to the capitalized word.

---

1. PANDEMONIUM:

   (A) amusement
   (B) indolence
   (C) deceleration
   (D) tranquillity
   (E) tolerance

2. ENERVATE:

   (A) aggravate
   (B) stimulate
   (C) edify
   (D) applaud
   (E) disregard

---

**Directions**: Each of the following sentence completion questions contains one or two blanks. These blanks signify that a word or set of words has been left out. Below each sentence are five words or sets of words. For each blank, pick the word or set of words that <u>best</u> reflects the sentence's over-all meaning.

---

3. Surprisingly to those who view the ocean floor as a uniformly _____ waste, each vent in the floor, where seawater is heated by the earth's interior magma, has been found to be an island-like _____ with its own distinctive fauna.

   (A) teeming...habitat
   (B) lifeless...enclave
   (C) barren...oasis
   (D) sunken...grotto
   (E) hazardous...environment

4. Rather than allowing these dramatic exchanges between her characters to develop fully, Ms. Norman unfortunately tends to _____ the discussions involving the two women.

   (A) exacerbate
   (B) protract
   (C) augment
   (D) truncate
   (E) elaborate

---

**Directions**: Each of the following analogy questions presents a related pair of words linked by a colon. Five lettered pairs of words follow the linked pair. Choose the lettered pair of words whose relationship is <u>most like</u> the relationship expressed in the original linked pair.

---

5. GLINT : LIGHT ::

   (A) blare : sound
   (B) whiff : scent
   (C) shade : color
   (D) glut : food
   (E) wave : tide

6. DOGGEREL : POET ::

   (A) symphony : composer
   (B) easel : painter
   (C) caption : cartoonist
   (D) soliloquy : playwright
   (E) potboiler : novelist

# 1                                                          1

---

Directions: Each of the following reading comprehension questions is based on the content of the following passage. Read the passage and then determine the best answer choice for each question. Base your choice on what this passage *states directly* or *implies*, not on any information you may have gained elsewhere.

---

Unlike the carefully weighted and planned compositions of Dante, Goethe's writings have always the sense of immediacy and enthusiasm.
Line He was a constant experimenter with life, with
(5) ideas, and with forms of writing. For the same reason, his works seldom have the qualities of finish or formal beauty which distinguish the masterpieces of Dante and Virgil. He came to love the beauties of classicism but these were
(10) never an essential part of his make-up. Instead, the urgency of the moment, the spirit of the thing, guided his pen. As a result, nearly all his works have serious flaws of structure, of inconsistencies, of excesses and redundancies and extraneities.
(15) In the large sense, Goethe represents the fullest development of the romanticist. It has been argued that he should not be so designated because he so clearly matured and outgrew the kind of romanticism exhibited by Wordsworth,
(20) Shelley, and Keats. Shelley and Keats died young; Wordsworth lived narrowly and abandoned his early attitudes. In contrast, Goethe lived abundantly and developed his faith in the spirit, his understanding of nature and human nature,
(25) and his reliance on feelings as man's essential motivating force. The result was an all-encompassing vision of reality and a philosophy of life broader and deeper than the partial visions and attitudes of other romanticists. Yet the spirit of
(30) youthfulness, the impatience with close reasoning or "logic-chopping," and the continued faith in nature remained his to the end, together with an occasional waywardness and impulsiveness and a disregard of artistic or logical propriety which
(35) savor strongly of romantic individualism. Since so many twentieth-century thoughts and attitudes are similarly based on the stimulus of the Romantic Movement, Goethe stands as particularly the poet of modern times as Dante stood for
(40) medieval times and as Shakespeare for the Renaissance.

7. A characteristic of romanticism NOT mentioned in this passage is its

   (A) elevation of nature
   (B) preference for spontaneity
   (C) modernity of ideas
   (D) unconcern for artistic decorum
   (E) simplicity of language

8. It can be inferred from the passage that classicism has which of the following characteristics?

   I. Sensitivity toward emotional promptings
   II. Emphasis on formal aesthetic criteria
   III. Meticulous planning of artistic works

   (A) II only
   (B) III only
   (C) I and II
   (D) II and III
   (E) I, II, and III

9. The author's attitude toward Goethe's writings is best described as

   (A) unqualified endorsement
   (B) lofty indifference
   (C) reluctant tolerance
   (D) measured admiration
   (E) undisguised contempt

## Antonyms

10. NEBULOUS:
    (A) hypothetical
    (B) querulous
    (C) lamentable
    (D) piquant
    (E) distinct

11. DECORUM:
    (A) lucidity
    (B) flexibility
    (C) impropriety
    (D) duplicity
    (E) severity

12. DENIGRATE:
    (A) emancipate
    (B) examine
    (C) desecrate
    (D) mollify
    (E) extol

# 1

# 1

## Sentence Completion

13. Neutron stars are believed to be the highly compressed remnants of exploding stars (supernovas) and thus _____ of one of the most _____ processes in nature.

    (A) causes...cataclysmic
    (B) products...violent
    (C) examples...equivocal
    (D) justifications...harsh
    (E) precursors...dynamic

14. The shortcomings of Mr. Brooks' analysis are _____ his _____ in explaining financial complexity and the sheer importance of his text.

    (A) alleviated by...ineptitude
    (B) offset by...clarity
    (C) magnified by...precision
    (D) demonstrated by...adroitness
    (E) mitigated by...incompetence

## Analogies

15. ERUDITE : SCHOLAR ::

    (A) remote : hermit
    (B) pliant : beggar
    (C) meandering : traveler
    (D) mendacious : liar
    (E) vindictive : conqueror

16. FERAL : DOMESTICATION ::

    (A) arable : cultivation
    (B) viral : infection
    (C) crude : refinement
    (D) frugal : economy
    (E) pliable : molding

## Reading Comprehension

Given the context of social change in the early 1960s, Negro history was now the object of unprecedented attention among wide segments of
*Line* the American population, black and white. In
(5) academe nothing demonstrated this growing legitimacy of black history better than the way in which certain scholars of both races, who had previously been ambivalent about being identified as specialists in the field, now reversed them-
(10) selves.

Thus Frenise Logan, returning to an academic career, decided to attempt to publish his doctoral dissertation on blacks in late nineteenth-century North Carolina. A 1960 award encouraged him to
(15) do further research, and his expanded *The Negro*

*in North Carolina, 1876–1894* appeared in 1964. It is true that as late as 1963 a white professor advised John W. Blassingame to avoid black history if he wanted to have "a future in the histori-
(20) cal profession." Yet more indicative of how things were going was that 1964–65 marked a turning point for two of Kenneth Stampp's former students—Nathan Huggins and Leon Litwack. The changing intellectual milieu seems to have
(25) permitted Huggins, whose original intention of specializing in African and Afro-American history had been overruled by practical concerns, to move into what became his long-range commitment to the field. By 1965 when his interest in
(30) intellectual history found expression in the idea of doing a book on the Harlem Renaissance, the factors that earlier would have discouraged him from such a study had dissipated. For Litwack the return to Negro history was an especially vivid
(35) experience, and he recalls the day he spoke at the University of Rochester, lecturing on Jacksonian democracy. Some students in the audience, sensing that his heart was just not in that topic, urged him to undertake research once again in the field
(40) to which he had already contributed so significantly. He settled on the study that became *Been in the Storm So Long* (1979). In short, both Huggins and Litwack now felt able to dismiss the professional considerations that had loomed so
(45) large in their earlier decision to work in other specialties and to identify themselves with what had hitherto been a marginal field of inquiry.

17. The author cites Logan, Huggins, and Litwack for their

    (A) work on curriculum reform in the public schools
    (B) participation in the Freedom Summer in Mississippi
    (C) return to the field of Afro-American history
    (D) research on blacks in nineteenth-century North Carolina
    (E) identification with nonviolent direct action

# 1                                                                                    1

18. The passage suggests that Bennett's work was similar to Logan's work in which of the following ways?

I. Both Bennett's and Logan's books recorded a then relatively unfamiliar aspect of Afro-American history.

II. Both Bennett's and Logan's work were designed to appeal to a primarily academic audience.

III. Both Bennett's and Logan's work were published in a variety of formats.

(A) I only
(B) III only
(C) I and II only
(D) I and III only
(E) II and III only

19. It can be inferred that prior to 1950, for a historian to choose to specialize in black history

(A) was encouraged by the academic establishment
(B) established his academic conventionality
(C) afforded him special opportunities for publication
(D) was detrimental to his professional career
(E) enhanced his contact with his colleagues

## Antonyms

20. DESTITUTION:
(A) civilization
(B) recompense
(C) affluence
(D) reformation
(E) parsimony

21. COGNIZANCE:
(A) ignobility
(B) disbelief
(C) impotence
(D) illegality
(E) unawareness

## Reading Comprehension

*(This passage was written prior to 1950)*

We now know that what constitutes practically all of matter is empty space; relatively enormous voids in which revolve with lightning velocity
*Line* infinitesimal particles so utterly small that they
*(5)* have never been seen or photographed. The existence of these particles has been demonstrated by mathematical physicists and their operations determined by ingenious laboratory experiments. It was not until 1911 that experiments by Sir
*(10)* Ernest Rutherford revealed the architecture of the mysterious atom. Moseley, Bohr, Fermi, Millikan, Compton, Urey, and others have also worked on the problem.

Matter is composed of molecules whose aver-
*(15)* age diameter is about 1/125 millionth of an inch. Molecules are composed of atoms so small that about 5 million could be placed in a row on the period at the end of this sentence. Long thought to be the ultimate, indivisible constituent of mat-
*(20)* ter, the atom has been found to consist roughly of a proton, the positive electrical element in the atomic nucleus, surrounded by electrons, the negative electric elements swirling about the proton.

22. According to the passage, all of the following were true of the center of the atom EXCEPT that it

(A) had not yet been seen by the naked eye
(B) contained elements that were positively charged
(C) was very little larger than a molecule
(D) followed experimentally determinable processes
(E) was smaller than 1/125 millionth of an inch

23. By referring to the period at the end of the sentence (lines 16–18), the author intends to point up the atom's

(A) density
(B) mystery
(C) velocity
(D) consistency
(E) minuteness

24. Which of the following relationships most closely parallels the relationship between the proton and the electrons described in the passage?

(A) A hawk to its prey
(B) A blueprint to a framework
(C) A planet to its satellites
(D) A magnet to iron filings
(E) A compound to its elements

## Analogies

25. GIBBER : SENSE ::
(A) jabber : noise
(B) toddle : mobility
(C) dawdle : deference
(D) vacillate : resolution
(E) disobey : order

# 1                                                    1

26. UPROARIOUS : AMUSING ::
    - (A) treacherous : steadfast
    - (B) tumultuous : windy
    - (C) menacing : aghast
    - (D) repugnant : disagreeable
    - (E) devious : clever

## Sentence Completion

27. To a person _____ natural history, his country or seaside stroll is a walk through a gallery filled with wonderful works of art, nine-tenths of which have their faces turned to the wall.
    - (A) enamored of
    - (B) uninstructed in
    - (C) responsive to
    - (D) disillusioned with
    - (E) dependent on

28. A _____ of recent cases of scientific fraud in which gross errors of fact and logic have slipped past the review panels that scrutinize submissions to journals suggests that the review system is seriously _____.
    - (A) plethora...intended
    - (B) lack...strained
    - (C) dearth...compromised
    - (D) spate...taxed
    - (E) preponderance...substantiated

## Antonyms

29. PRECIPITATE:
    - (A) intricate
    - (B) devious
    - (C) posthumous
    - (D) dilatory
    - (E) contradictory

30. TORTUOUS:
    - (A) merciful
    - (B) direct
    - (C) dangerous
    - (D) legal
    - (E) tawdry

2                                                                              2

SECTION 2—QUANTITATIVE ABILITY

Time—45 Minutes
28 Questions

In this section solve each problem, using any available space on the page for scratchwork. Then decide which is the best of the choices given and fill in the corresponding oval on the Answer Sheet.

Directions: In the following type of question, two quantities appear, one in Column A and one in Column B. You must compare them. The correct answer to the question is

A if the quantity in Column A is greater
B if the quantity in Column B is greater
C if the two quantities are equal
D if it is impossible to determine which quantity is greater

Notes: Sometimes information about one or both of the quantities is centered above the two columns. If the same symbol appears in both columns, it represents the same thing each time.

Column A                    Column B

$$a = -2$$

1.  $a^4 - a^3 + a^2 - a$          $a - a^2 + a^3 - a^4$

_____

$a$ and $b$ are primes
$a + b = 12$

2.  $b$                          $8$

Column A                    Column B

$c^\circ$
$10$
$135^\circ$        $d^\circ$
$11$

3.  $c$                          $d$

_____

On a test $\frac{4}{7}$ of the boys and $\frac{7}{11}$ of the girls earned over 90.

4.  The number of students receiving grades over 90          The number of students receiving grades of 90 or less

_____

Directions: In the following questions, choose the best answer from the five choices listed.

5.  What is the measure of the angle formed by the minute and hour hands of a clock at 1:50?

    (A) 90°   (B) 95°   (C) 105°   (D) 115°   (E) 120°

6.  Which of the following CANNOT be expressed as the sum of three consecutive integers?

    (A) 18   (B) 24   (C) 28   (D) 33   (E) 36

7.  Sandrine is now 5 times as old as Nicholas, but 7 years from now, she will be 3 times as old as he will be then. How old is Sandrine now?

    (A) 15   (B) 20   (C) 21   (D) 25   (E) 35

# 2                                                      2

| Column A | Column B |
|----------|----------|

8. | $x$ | | $y$ |

---

$ab = 48$

9. | $a + b$ | | 50 |

---

10. If $3^a = b$ and $3^c = d$, then $bd =$
(A) $3^{ac}$ (B) $3^{a+c}$ (C) $6^{a+c}$ (D) $9^{ac}$ (E) $9^{a+c}$

| Column A | Column B |
|----------|----------|

At XYZ Corp. the ratio of the number of male employees to the number of female employees is 3:2.
20% of the male and 30% of the females employees attended the company picnic.

11. | The number of males at the picnic | The number of females at the picnic |

---

At Central High School 50 girls play intramural basketball, 40 girls play intramural volleyball, and 10 girls play both sports.

12. | The ratio of the number of girls who play only basketball to the number who play only volleyball | $\dfrac{4}{3}$ |

---

$ab \neq 0$

13. | $(a + b)^2$ | $(a - b)^2$ |

---

**Questions 14–15 refer to the following graph.**

# Percentage of students who reported using a computer

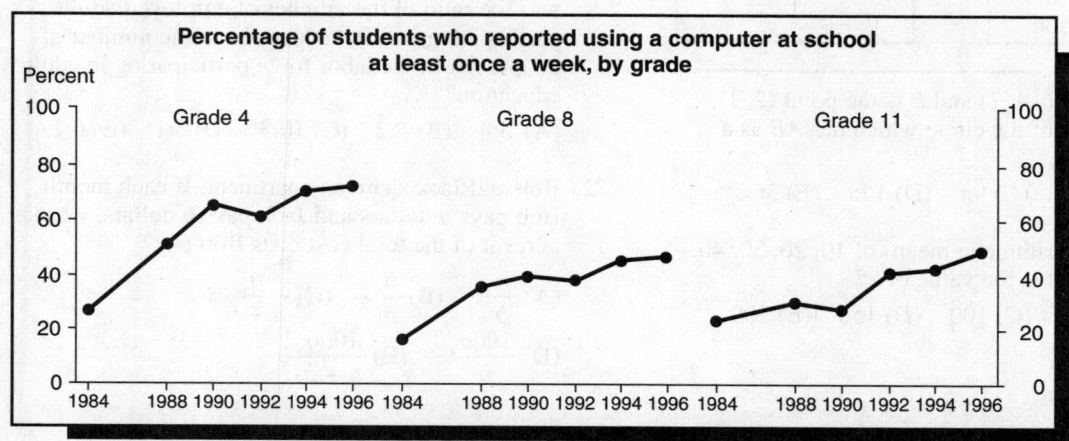

SOURCE: U.S. Department of Education.

14. If every student who was in the eleventh grade in 1996 and who used a computer in school at least once a week used a computer at least once a week in 1997, and if 20% of those students who were in the eleventh grade in 1996 and who did *not* use a computer in school at least once a week, did use a computer in school once a week in 1997, then what percent of twelfth-graders in 1997 used a computer in school at least once a week?

(A) 40% (B) 50% (C) 60% (D) 70%
(E) 80%

15. Assume that in 1990 there were 3,000,000 fourth-graders in the United States. How many fewer of those 3,000,000 students used a computer in school at least once a week in 1994 than in 1990?

    (A) 100,000   (B) 250,000   (C) 500,000
    (D) 600,000   (E) 750,000

---

| Column A | Column B |
|----------|----------|

The measures of the angles in △I are in the ratio of 1:2:3
The measures of the angles in △II are in the ratio of 2:7:9

16.

| The measure of the largest angle of △I | The measure of the largest angle of △II |
|----------|----------|

---

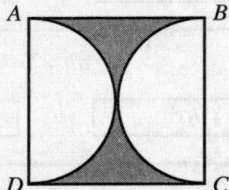

The shaded region above is bounded by two semicircles and two sides of square *ABCD*. The perimeter of the shaded region is $4 + 2\pi$.

17.

| The area of the shaded region | 1 |
|----------|----------|

18. If *A* is the point (−4, 1) and *B* is the point (2, 1), what is the area of the circle which has *AB* as a diameter?

    (A) $3\pi$   (B) $6\pi$   (C) $9\pi$   (D) $12\pi$   (E) $36\pi$

19. If the average (arithmetic mean) of 10, 20, 30, 40, and *x* is 60, what is the value of *x*?

    (A) 50   (B) 60   (C) 100   (D) 150   (E) 200

---

**Questions 20 and 21:** See the graphs on the following page for information to answer the questions.

20. Each of the following is a valid conclusion from the graphs and the fact that the population of the United States was greater in 1995 than in 1991 EXCEPT

    (A) In 1991, adults whose highest degree was at least a bachelor's degree were more than twice as likely to participate in adult education than those whose highest educational attainment was a high school diploma or GED (high school equivalency diploma).
    (B) On a percentage basis, from 1991 to 1995, the greatest increase in the adult education participation rate was among those adults whose highest educational attainment was grades 9–12, without earning a high school diploma.
    (C) In 1995, more people participated in adult education programs than in 1991.
    (D) From 1991 to 1995 the rate of participation in adult education among the groups represented in the graphs increased the least for those who had attained at least a bachelor's degree.
    (E) In 1995, more adults with at least a bachelor's degree participated in adult education than did adults who attended some college but did not earn a college degree.

21. If in the United States in 1995, there were 50 million employed adults and 20 million adults not in the the labor force, then approximately what was the ratio of the number of employed adults participating in adult education to the number of people not in the labor force participating in adult education?

    (A) 5:4   (B) 5:2   (C) 10:3   (D) 5:1   (E) 6:1

22. Bob and Jack share an apartment. If each month Bob pays *a* dollars and Jack pays *b* dollars, what percent of the total cost does Bob pay?

    (A) $\frac{a}{b}\%$   (B) $\frac{b}{a}\%$   (C) $\frac{a}{a+b}\%$

    (D) $\frac{100a}{b}\%$   (E) $\frac{100a}{a+b}\%$

2                                                                                                          2

## Adult education participation rates in the past 12 months: 1991 and 1995

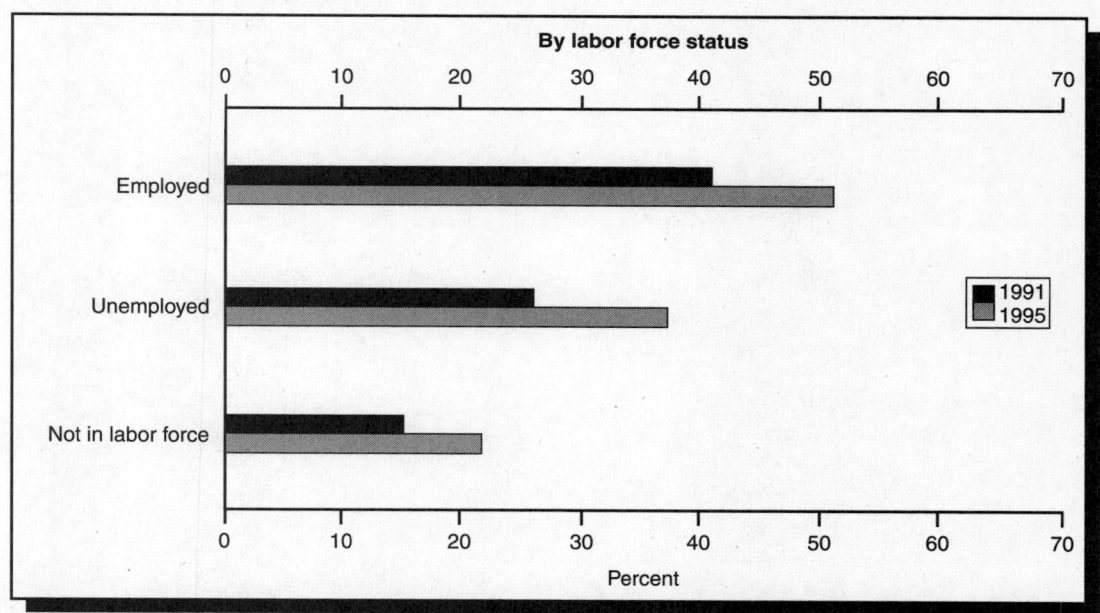

SOURCE: U.S. Department of Education.

**2**                                                                      **2**

| Column A | Column B |
|---|---|

*E* is a point on line *CD*, and *ABCD* is a rectangle.

23. | The area of $\triangle ABC$ | The area of $\triangle ABE$ |

A wooden cube whose edges are
3 inches is painted red.
The cube is then cut into 27 cubes whose
edges are 1 inch.

24. | The total surface area of all of the unpainted faces | 100 square inches |

25. | The units digit of $14^{14}$ | The units digit of $16^{16}$ |

26. If *a* is increased by 10% and *b* is decreased by 10%, the resulting numbers will be equal. What is the ratio of *a* to *b*?

(A) $\dfrac{9}{11}$    (B) $\dfrac{9}{10}$    (C) $\dfrac{1}{1}$    (D) $\dfrac{10}{9}$    (E) $\dfrac{11}{9}$

27. In the figure at the right, the legs of right triangle *ACB* are diameters of the two semicircles. If *AB* = 4, what is the sum of the areas of the semicircles?

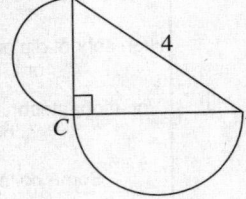

(A) $\pi$    (B) $2\pi$
(C) $4\pi$    (D) $8\pi$
(E) $16\pi$

28. A school's honor society has 100 members: 40 boys and 60 girls, of whom 30 are juniors and 70 are seniors. What is the smallest possible number of senior boys in the society?

(A) 0    (B) 5    (C) 10    (D) 15    (E) 20

# 3                                                                3

## SECTION 3—ANALYTICAL ABILITY

**Time—60 Minutes
35 Questions**

**Directions**: In this section, each set of questions is based on a short passage or a set of conditions. Sometimes, in answering these questions, you might want to make a table or diagram. For each question, choose the best answer from the five choices listed.

1. Wilbur is over six feet tall.

   The statement above can be logically deduced from which of the following statements?

   (A) The average height of the members of the basketball team is over six feet; Wilbur is the center on the basketball team.
   (B) If Wilbur was not asked to join the basketball team, then he is not six feet tall; Wilbur was asked to join the basketball team.
   (C) If Wilbur is over six feet tall, then he can see the parade; Wilbur can see the parade.
   (D) In Dr. Gray's seminar, everyone who is not over six feet tall is seated in the first row; Dr. Gray seated Wilbur in the second row.
   (E) Everyone who is over six feet tall has to help stack cartons in the stockroom; Wilbur has to help stack cartons.

## Questions 2–5

Dr. William Weinberg is a psychiatrist who has to schedule one therapy session for each of six patients—Bernstein, Cox, Dawson, Edson, Friedman, and Grant. Each session will take place on the same day. The sessions will be scheduled at 9:00, 10:00, 11:00, 1:00, 2:00, and 3:00, with a lunch break at noon. In making up the schedule for the session, Dr. Weinberg will conform to the following conditions:

   Friedman will have the first session in the afternoon.
   Dawson's session must be earlier in the day than Edson's.
   Bernstein's session must be earlier in the day than either Edson's or Friedman's.
   Cox's session must immediately precede Grant's session.

2. If Bernstein is only available at 10:00, in how many ways can the sessions be scheduled?

   (A) 1  (B) 2  (C) 3  (D) 4  (E) 6

3. If Friedman switches to a morning session, and Cox takes the 1:00 spot vacated by Friedman, which of the following must be true?

   (A) Bernstein has the first session of the day.
   (B) Bernstein or Friedman has the second session of the day.

   (C) Bernstein or Dawson has the second session of the day.
   (D) Dawson or Friedman has the third session of the day.
   (E) Dawson or Grant has the last session of the day.

4. If Grant has the last session of the day, each of the following could be true EXCEPT

   (A) Bernstein has the first session of the day.
   (B) Dawson has the first session of the day.
   (C) Dawson has his session at 10:00.
   (D) Edson has her session at 10:00.
   (E) Cox has his session at 2:00.

5. If Cox's session is earlier in the day than Friedman's, which of the following must be true?

   (A) Bernstein has the first session of the day.
   (B) Cox has the first session of the day.
   (C) Bernstein has a session at 11:00.
   (D) Grant has a session at 11:00.
   (E) Dawson has a session at 2:00.

## Questions 6 and 7

All good athletes want to win, and all athletes who want to win eat a well-balanced diet; therefore, all athletes who do not eat a well-balanced diet are bad athletes.

6. Which of the following, if true, would refute the assumptions of the argument above?

   (A) Ann wants to win, but she is not a good athlete.
   (B) Bob, the accountant, eats a well-balanced diet, but he is not a good athlete.
   (C) All the players on the Burros baseball team eat a well-balanced diet.
   (D) No athlete who does not eat a well-balanced diet wants to win.
   (E) Cindy, the basketball star, does not eat a well-balanced diet, but she is a good athlete.

# 3                                                                 3

7. If the assumptions of the preceding argument are true, then which of the following statements must be true?

   (A) No bad athlete wants to win.
   (B) No athlete who does not eat a well-balanced diet is a good athlete.
   (C) Every athlete who eats a well-balanced diet is a good athlete.
   (D) All athletes who want to win are good athletes.
   (E) Some good athletes do not eat a well-balanced diet.

8. John McCabe, an English professor, always enforces the following criteria, among others, in his freshman composition course:

   No essay with more than two spelling errors can receive an A.
   Any essay that receives an A must conform to the university's style manual.

   Which of the following statements is a logical consequence of the preceding statements?

   (A) An essay with no spelling errors will receive a higher grade than one with three spelling errors.
   (B) An essay with more than ten spelling errors that does not conform to the university's style manual will fail.
   (C) An essay that has no spelling errors and that conforms to the university's style manual will receive an A.
   (D) An essay that conforms to the university's style manual and has three spelling errors cannot receive an A.
   (E) If a student receives a B on an essay that conformed to the university's style manual but had more than two spelling errors, he can correct the spelling errors and resubmit the essay in order to get an A.

## Questions 9–13

At a ceremony at the United Nations, five diplomats—J, K, L, M, and N—are to be seated in a row on one side of rectangular table. The diplomats are to be seated in such a manner that they can converse with anyone they are sitting next to. The diplomats speak the following languages:

   J speaks only French.
   K speaks English and Chinese.
   L speaks English and German.
   M speaks French and German.
   N speaks French and Chinese.

9. Which of the following is an acceptable order, from left to right, in which the diplomats can be seated?

   (A) M, N, K, L, J
   (B) K, J, N, M, L

   (C) K, L, N, M, J
   (D) J, N, M, K, L
   (E) K, L, M, N, J

10. If N cannot attend the ceremony, and the other four diplomats are seated at the table, which of the following must be true?

    (A) J and M are not seated next to each other.
    (B) K and L are not seated next to each other.
    (C) L and M are not seated next to each other.
    (D) J and K are seated at the two ends of the table.
    (E) J and L are seated at the two ends of the table.

11. If K cannot attend the ceremony, and the other four diplomats are seated at the table, which of the following must be true?

    (A) J is seated at one end of the table.
    (B) L is seated at one end of the table.
    (C) M is seated at one end of the table.
    (D) N is seated at one end of the table.
    (E) Neither J nor M is seated at either end of the table.

12. If K must sit at the left end of the table, in how many ways can the other four diplomats be seated?

    (A) 1   (B) 2   (C) 3   (D) 4   (E) 5

13. If N is seated in the center with two diplomats on either side of him, each of the following must be true EXCEPT

    (A) J and M are seated next to each other.
    (B) K and L are seated next to each other.
    (C) K and N are seated next to each other.
    (D) J is seated at one end of the table.
    (E) L is seated at one end of the table.

14. Leafleting and speechmaking on government property should be outlawed. Radicals and fanatics have no right to use public property when peddling their unsavory views.

    The argument above is based on the assumption that

    (A) radicals and fanatics prefer using public property when disseminating their views
    (B) legal restrictions that apply to one group need not apply equally to all
    (C) the general public has a vested interest in the free exchange of varied political views
    (D) political activity that interferes with the orderly functioning of government should not be protected by law
    (E) all those who leaflet and make speeches on government property are radicals and fanatics

# 3

# 3

## Questions 15–18

On the first day of school in September, seven new students—A, B, C, D, E, F, and G—must each be assigned to a guidance counselor. There are three counselors—Rosen, Smith, and Thomas—and each student is assigned to exactly one of them. In making the assignments, the Director of Guidance must adhere to the following conditions:

No counselor can be assigned more than three of the seven students.
A and B must be assigned to the same counselor.
Neither C nor D can be assigned to the same counselor as E or F.
F is not assigned to Thomas.

15. If E is assigned to Smith and F is assigned to Rosen, which of the following CANNOT be true?

(A) A is assigned to Smith.
(B) A is assigned to Thomas.
(C) B is assigned to Rosen.
(D) B is assigned to Smith.
(E) C is assigned to Thomas.

16. If A and C are both assigned to Rosen, which of the following could be true?

(A) More students are assigned to Smith than to Rosen.
(B) More students are assigned to Thomas than to Smith.
(C) Only one student is assigned to Smith.
(D) Only one student is assigned to Thomas.
(E) Three students are assigned to Thomas.

17. If B is assigned to Smith, which of the following could be true?

(A) A is assigned to Rosen and C is assigned to Thomas.
(B) C is assigned to Rosen and D is assigned to Smith.
(C) C is assigned to Rosen and G is assigned to Smith.
(D) C is assigned to Rosen and D is assigned to Thomas.
(E) F is assigned to Rosen and E is assigned to Smith.

18. If B and F are assigned to the same counselor, and at least two students are assigned to each counselor, how many different ways are there to assign the seven students?

(A) 0   (B) 1   (C) 2   (D) 3   (E) 4

19. So far this year researchers have reported the following:

Heavy coffee consumption can increase the risk of heart attacks.
Drinking a cup of coffee in the morning increases feelings of well-being and alertness.
Boiled coffee increases blood cholesterol levels.
Coffee may protect against cancer of the colon.

If all these statements are true, which one of the following conclusions can be drawn from this information?

(A) Reducing coffee consumption will make people healthier.
(B) Reducing coffee consumption will make people feel better.
(C) People at risk for heart attack should limit their coffee drinking.
(D) Percolated coffee will not affect cholesterol levels.
(E) People at risk for cancer should reduce their coffee consumption.

## Questions 20–23

A group of six engineers are working as a team on a project which is currently well behind schedule. To catch up, they agree to work evening sessions for six days, from Monday through Saturday. Each evening they will work at the home of a different member of the team. The team consists of three men—J, K, and L—and three women—P, Q, and R. In scheduling when to meet at each team member's house, they agree to the following conditions:

The men and women will alternate hosting the sessions.
They will meet at K's house earlier in the week than they meet at R's house; and they will meet at P's house earlier in the week than they meet at L's house.

20. Which of the following is an acceptable order, from Monday to Saturday, for each team member to host a work session?

(A) Q, J, L, P, K, R
(B) J, Q, L, P, K, R
(C) P, J, Q, K, R, L
(D) L, R, J, Q, P, K
(E) R, J, P, K, Q, L

21. If L hosts the Tuesday session, on what day of the week does K host a session?

    (A) Monday
    (B) Wednesday
    (C) Thursday
    (D) Friday
    (E) Saturday

22. If J is the host on Monday and Q is the host on Tuesday, each of the following must be true EXCEPT

    (A) K is the host on Wednesday.
    (B) L is the host on Friday.
    (C) P is the host on Thursday.
    (D) R is the host on Saturday.
    (E) P hosts a session later in the week than R does.

23. In how many ways can a complete schedule be made up if J must be the host on Saturday?

    (A) 0   (B) 1   (C) 2   (D) 3   (E) 4

## Questions 24–28

The Planning Committee of the American Mathematical Society is scheduling the sites of its annual meetings for the years 2004–2009. The committee has selected the following six cities—Atlanta, Boston, Chicago, Denver, Houston, and Miami—but has not yet determined which year each city will host a meeting. The following criteria have been established so far:

> Each of the six cities will host exactly one meeting between 2004 and 2009.
> Chicago will host the meeting in 2005.
> Atlanta will host a meeting before Houston does.
> Boston and Denver will host meetings in consecutive years.

24. Which of the following cities could host the meeting in 2004?

    (A) Boston
    (B) Chicago
    (C) Denver
    (D) Houston
    (E) Miami

25. In how many ways can the Planning Committee schedule the meetings if Miami has to be the host in 2008?

    (A) 1   (B) 2   (C) 3   (D) 4   (E) 6

26. If Miami is the host in 2007, all of the following could be true EXCEPT

    (A) Atlanta is the host in 2004.
    (B) Houston is the host in 2006.
    (C) Boston is the host in 2008.
    (D) Boston is the host in 2009.
    (E) Houston is the host in 2009.

27. If Boston is the host in 2008, what is the latest year in which Atlanta could host a meeting?

    (A) 2004   (B) 2005   (C) 2006   (D) 2007
    (E) 2009

28. Which of the following CANNOT be true?

    (A) Atlanta and Miami are hosts in consecutive years.
    (B) Miami and Houston are hosts in consecutive years.
    (C) Houston and Denver are hosts in consecutive years.
    (D) Atlanta and Chicago are hosts in consecutive years.
    (E) Boston and Chicago are hosts in consecutive years.

29. A fire in May 1999 at Al's Appliance Center caused several departments in the store to be closed for over three months. As a result, total sales for June through August of 1999 were only half of what they were from June through August of 1998. Nonetheless, total sales volume for the year 1999 was actually slightly greater than for 1998.

    Which of the following, if true, is sufficient to explain this seeming contradiction?

    (A) Traditionally, very few computers are sold during the summer.
    (B) Nearly half of each year's total sales comes during the five weeks before Christmas.
    (C) There was a three month period in 1999 in which sales were more than double the sales in the same months in 1998.
    (D) In each month in 1999, other than from June to August, sales were higher than in the same month in 1998.
    (E) In 1998, 10% of the year's sales were made from June to August, and for the other nine months, sales in 1999 were 10% greater than in 1998.

3

3

30. As President of the National Association of Widget Manufacturers, I oppose government handouts to private business. But the present program of federal aid to the widget industry must continue. This is not a handout but rather a system of moderate cash subsidies to enable our beleaguered industry to withstand the shocks of rising costs and high interest rates, and so continue to provide useful employment to thousands of U.S. citizens.

The major logical weakness of the argument above is the fact that

(A) the speaker is arguing against his own personal interest

(B) it makes no attempt to explain the ultimate causes of rising costs and high interest rates

(C) it draws no meaningful distinction between handouts and subsidies

(D) it does not explain the significance of the widget industry for the U.S. economy as a whole

(E) it offers no factual evidence to substantiate the claim that the widget industry is in danger

### Questions 31–34

The marketing director of a multinational marketing firm has to send three salespeople to a conference in Stockholm and three other salespeople to a conference in Tokyo. She must select the six people who will attend the conferences from the following list of seven salespeople: J, K, L, M, N, P, and Q. In making her decisions as to who goes and where, the director is bound by the following conditions:

> J must go to Stockholm, and L must go to Tokyo. K cannot go to a conference with either L or P. Neither N nor Q can go to a conference unless the other goes, too.

31. Which of the following is a list of salespeople who could go to the conference in Stockholm?

(A) J, Q, P

(B) J, M, P

(C) J, K, P

(D) J, N, P

(E) L, N, Q

32. If Q goes to Tokyo, which of the following must be true?

(A) K goes to Stockholm.

(B) L goes to Stockholm.

(C) M goes to Stockholm.

(D) N goes to Stockholm.

(E) P goes to Stockholm.

33. If Q goes to Stockholm, which of the following must be true?

(A) K does not go to either conference.

(B) M does not go to either conference.

(C) P does not go to either conference.

(D) M and N go to Tokyo.

(E) P and N go to Tokyo.

34. If K goes to one of the conferences, all of the following must be true EXCEPT

(A) M does not go to either conference.

(B) P does not go to either conference.

(C) K goes to Stockholm.

(D) N goes to Tokyo.

(E) Q goes to Tokyo.

35. The current trend toward specialization in nearly all occupational groups is exactly the opposite of what is needed. World problems today are so diverse, complex, and interrelated that only the generalist stands a chance of understanding the broad picture. Unless our schools stress a truly broad, liberal education, the world will crumble around us as we each expertly perform our own narrow functions.

Each of the following, if true, would weaken the conclusion drawn above, EXCEPT:

(A) Many of the world's problems can be solved only by highly specialized experts working on specific problems.

(B) Relatively few generalists are needed to coordinate the work of the many specialists.

(C) Specialization does not necessarily entail losing the ability to see the broad picture.

(D) Increasingly complex problems require a growing level of technical expertise which can only be acquired through specialization.

(E) Even the traditional liberal education is becoming more highly specialized today.

# Answer Key

## Section 1—Verbal Ability

| | | | | | |
|---|---|---|---|---|---|
| 1. D | 6. E | 11. C | 16. C | 21. E | 26. D |
| 2. B | 7. E | 12. E | 17. C | 22. C | 27. B |
| 3. C | 8. D | 13. B | 18. D | 23. E | 28. D |
| 4. D | 9. D | 14. B | 19. D | 24. C | 29. D |
| 5. B | 10. E | 15. D | 20. C | 25. D | 30. B |

## Section 2—Quantitative Ability

NOTE: The letters in brackets following the Quantitative Ability answers refer to the sections of Chapter 15 in which you can find the information you need to answer the questions. For example, 1. C [E] means that the

answer to question 1 is C, and that the solution requires information found in Section 15-E: Averages. Also, 20. A [14] means that the answer to question 20 is based on information in Chapter 14: Data Interpretation.

| | | | | | |
|---|---|---|---|---|---|
| 1. A [A] | 6. C [A] | 11. C [C,D] | 16. C [D,J] | 21. E [14] | 26. A [C,D] |
| 2. B [A] | 7. E [H] | 12. C [D] | 17. B [K,L] | 22. E [C] | 27. B [J,L] |
| 3. A [J] | 8. D [J] | 13. D [F] | 18. C [L,N] | 23. C [J,K] | 28. C [O] |
| 4. A [B] | 9. D [A] | 14. C [14] | 19. E [E] | 24. A [M] | |
| 5. D [I] | 10. B [A] | 15. E [14] | 20. E [14] | 25. C [A] | |

## Section 3—Analytical Ability

| | | | | |
|---|---|---|---|---|
| 1. D | 8. D | 15. B | 22. E | 29. E |
| 2. A | 9. E | 16. D | 23. E | 30. E |
| 3. D | 10. D | 17. E | 24. E | 31. B |
| 4. D | 11. B | 18. E | 25. B | 32. C |
| 5. E | 12. C | 19. C | 26. E | 33. A |
| 6. E | 13. D | 20. C | 27. C | 34. A |
| 7. B | 14. E | 21. C | 28. A | 35. E |

# Answer Explanations

## Section 1—Verbal Ability

1. **D.** The opposite of *pandemonium* or tumultuous uproar is *tranquillity* or calm.
   Word Parts Clue: *Pan-* means all; *demon-* means evil spirit. Hell or *Pandemonium*, the place where all the evil spirits dwell, is a place of noise and uproar.
   Think of "pandemonium breaking loose."

2. **B.** To *enervate* (weaken or enfeeble) is the opposite of to *stimulate* or energize.
   Think of being "enervated by the heat."

3. **C.** Rather than being *barren* or devoid of life, the vent regions are like *oases* that support life.
   Choice A is incorrect. A *waste* by definition is not *teeming* but *barren*.

Choice B is incorrect. The vent region would not be described as an *enclave* (tract enclosed within a foreign territory).
Choice D is incorrect. A *grotto* would not be described as island-like.
Choice E is incorrect. Nothing in the sentence justifies the use of the term *hazardous*.

4. **D.** Instead of allowing the exchanges to develop fully, the playwright cuts short or *truncates* them.

5. **B.** A *glint* is a small gleam of *light*. A *whiff* is a slight puff of *scent*.          (Degree of Intensity)

6. **E.** *Doggerel* is trivial or inferior verse produced by a *poet*. A *potboiler* is a trivial or inferior literary work produced by a *novelist*.
                    (Defining Characteristic)

7. **E.** The author never mentions *simplicity of language* as a characteristic of romanticism.

Choice A is incorrect. The passage refers to a "continued faith in nature" as one aspect of Goethe's romanticism.

Choice B is incorrect. The passage refers to impulsiveness or *spontaneity* as savoring strongly of romantic individualism.

Choice C is incorrect. Since romanticism has *formed* so many modern attitudes, one finds in romanticism ideas that seem noteworthy for their modernity.

Choice D is incorrect. The passage refers to "a disregard of artistic or logical propriety" as characteristic of romanticism.

8. **D.** You can arrive at the correct answer by the process of elimination.
*Sensitivity towards emotional promptings* is characteristic of romanticism; it is an unlikely characteristic of classicism. Therefore, you can eliminate Choices C and E.
*Emphasis on formal aesthetic criteria* is a likely characteristic of classicism. The passage talks of the formal beauty that distinguishes the classical works of Dante and Virgil. Therefore, you can eliminate Choice B.
*Meticulous planning of artistic works* is a likely characteristic of classicism. The passage talks of the carefully planned compositions of the classicist Dante; it also tells of the structurally flawed compositions of the romantic Goethe. Therefore, you can eliminate Choice A.
Only Choice D is left. It is the correct answer.

9. **D.** The author both admires Goethe's writings and notes their flaws; his attitude is one of *measured admiration*.

10. **E.** The opposite of *nebulous* (vague, cloudy) is *distinct*.
Think of "a nebulous memory."

11. **C.** The opposite of *decorum* (correctness, good taste) is *impropriety* or unseemliness.
Think of "dignity and decorum."

12. **E.** The opposite of to *denigrate* (belittle or defame) is to *extol* or praise.
Think of "denigrating someone's efforts."

13. **B.** If neutron stars are the remnants or remaining traces of exploding stars, then they are the *products* or results of *violent* natural processes.
Choice A is incorrect. The neutron stars did not cause the explosions; they were *caused by* the explosions.
Choice C is incorrect. There is nothing *equivocal* or inconclusive about the explosion of a star.
Choice D is incorrect. Nothing in the statement suggests that the creation of neutron stars *justifies* or vindicates the explosion of a

star. In addition, *harsh* is far too weak a word to describe a stellar explosion.
Choice E is incorrect. Neutron stars come into existence after a supernova explodes. Thus, they are not *precursors* or forerunners of the explosion.

14. **B.** *Clarity* in explaining complicated financial matters would do a great deal to *offset* or compensate for shortcomings in a text.
Note the use of *and* linking the positive phrase "sheer importance of his text" with the second blank. This indicates that the second missing word must be a positive term.

15. **D.** A *scholar* is by definition *erudite* or learned. A *liar* is by definition *mendacious* or dishonest. Beware answer pairs that are loosely linked. While *travelers* may *meander* (stroll or wander aimlessly), they may equally as well proceed directly to their destination.
(Defining Characteristic)

16. **C.** Something *feral* or wild lacks *domestication* or taming. Something *crude* or rough lacks *refinement* or polish.    (Antonym Variant)

17. **C.** The three men are cited as examples of scholars who were encouraged to resume their earlier researches in black history.
Choices A, B, and E are incorrect. None of the three men were identified in the passage with these concerns.
Choice D is incorrect. Only Logan is identified with research on blacks in nineteenth-century North Carolina.

18. **D.** You can arrive at the correct answer by the process of elimination.
Statement I is supported by the passage. At the time Bennett and Logan wrote, both the pre-*Mayflower* period of black history and the nineteenth-century life of blacks in North Carolina were relatively unexplored. Therefore, you can eliminate Choices B and E.
Statement II is unsupported by the passage. Bennett's work was a popularization intended for a wide general audience. It was not aimed at academics. Therefore, you can eliminate Choice C.
Statement III is supported by the passage. Bennett's work appeared first as a series of magazine articles, then as a book. Logan's work first appeared as a doctoral thesis, then (with revisions) as a book. Therefore, you can eliminate Choice A.
Only Choice D is left. It is the correct answer.

19. **D.** According to the passage, prior to the early 1960s Negro history was not an object of particularly great renown in academe. In the 1950s, the advice given to Blassingame to

avoid black history if he desired "a future in the historical profession" seemed wise—graduate students of the caliber of Huggins and Litwack felt an ambivalence about entering the field because of "practical concerns." What these concerns boiled down to was the sense that to choose black history as one's specialization would be *detrimental* or harmful to one's career.

20. C. The opposite of *destitution* (privation; lack of life's necessities) is *affluence* or wealth. Think of "the poor living in destitution."

21. E. The opposite of *cognizance* (conscious knowledge, awareness) is *unawareness*.
Word Parts Clue: *Cogn-* means know. *Cognizance* means knowledge.
Context Clue: "He had no cognizance of the crime."

22. C. The passage states that molecules are made of atoms; logically, therefore, an atom is smaller, not larger, than the molecule to which it belongs.
Choice A is incorrect. Line 5 states that atoms "have never been seen or photographed."
Choice B is incorrect. Lines 21–22 mention the presence of positive electric elements.
Choice D is incorrect. Lines 5–8 note the ingenious laboratory experiments that determine its operations or processes.
Choice E is incorrect. Lines 14–15 mention the average diameter of a molecule is 1/125 millionth of an inch. Atoms are smaller yet.

23. E. The comparison emphasizes the smallness or *minuteness* of atoms.

24. C. The satellites *circle* the planet. The electrons *swirl around* the proton. As depicted, the relationships are comparable.
Choice A is incorrect. A hawk *swoops down* upon its prey. The proton does not swoop down upon the electrons.
Choice B is incorrect. A blueprint is an outline or plan. A framework is a skeletal structure, possibly constructed in accordance with a blueprint. The relationships are not comparable.
Choice D is incorrect. Iron filings are *drawn or attracted* to a magnet. Electrons *swirl around* a proton.
Choice E is incorrect. A compound is *made up* of elements. A proton is not made up of electrons.

25. D. To *gibber* (chatter foolishly) is to speak without *sense*. To *vacillate* (waver) is to act without *resolution* (firmness of resolve).
(Antonym Variant)

26. D. Something *uproarious* is by definition extremely *amusing*. Something *repugnant* is

by definition extremely *disagreeable*.
(Degree of Intensity)

27. B. If nine-tenths of the works of art in the gallery have their faces turned to the wall, then the visitor to the gallery has no clue whatsoever to what wonders they contain. Similarly, a person *uninstructed in* natural history wanders through the world with no clue whatsoever to nine-tenths of the natural wonders that surround him.

28. D. A *spate* or flood of examples of fraud suggests that the review system intended to catch such frauds is severely *taxed* or burdened.

29. D. The opposite of *precipitate* or hasty is *dilatory* or tardy.
Think of "a precipitate departure."

30. B. The opposite of *tortuous* or winding is *direct*. Beware eye-catchers. *Tortuous* has nothing to do with *torture*.
Think of "a tortuous mountain road."

# Section 2—Quantitative Ability

Two asterisks (**) indicate an alternative method of solving.

1. A. Evaluate each column. Column A = 30 and Column B = –30. Column A is greater.

2. B. The only primes whose sum is 12 are 5 and 7, both of which are less than 8. Note: 1 + 11 = 12, but 1 is not a prime [KEY FACT A26]. Column B is greater.

3. A. In any triangle, if one side is longer than a second side, the angle opposite the longer side is greater than the angle opposite the shorter side [KEY FACT J3], so $c > d$. Column A is greater. (It is irrelevant that the third angle is 135°.)

4. A. It makes no difference how many students took the test nor how many were boys and how many were girls. More than half the boys *and* more than half the girls scored over 90, so more grades were over 90 than 90 or below. Column A is greater.
**Use TACTIC 2, Chapter 13. Assume 7 boys and 11 girls took the exam. Then 11 students (4 boys and 7 girls) got over 90 and the other 7 got 90 or less.

5. D. For problems such as this, always draw a diagram. The measure of each of the 12 central angles from one number to the next on the clock is 30°. At 1:50 the minute hand is pointing at 10, and the hour hand has gone $\frac{50}{60} = \frac{5}{6}$ of the way from 1 to 2. Then, from 10 to 1 on the clock is 90°, and from 1 to the hour hand

is $\frac{5}{6}(30°) = 25°$, for a total of $90° + 25° = 115°$.

6. **C.** The sum of three consecutive integers can be expressed as

$$n + (n + 1) + (n + 2) = 3n + 3 = 3(n + 1),$$

and so must be a multiple of 3. Only 28, Choice C, is *not* a multiple of 3.
**Quickly add up sets of three consecutive integers: $4 + 5 + 6 = 15$, $5 + 6 + 7 = 18$, $6 + 7 + 8 = 21$, and so on, and see the pattern (they're all multiples of 3); or cross off the choices as you come to them.

7. **E.** Set up a table.

| Time | Nicholas | Sandrine |
|------|----------|----------|
| Now | $x$ | $5x$ |
| In 7 years | $x + 7$ | $5x + 7$ |

Then
$5x + 7 = 3(x + 7) \Rightarrow 5x + 7 = 3x + 21 \Rightarrow 2x = 14 \Rightarrow x = 7$.
Sandrine, therefore, is 35.
**Use TACTIC 1, Chapter 12, but since Sandrine is 5 times as old as Nicholas, avoid Choice C, the only answer that is not a multiple of 5. Try Choice B, 20. Then Nicholas is 4. In 7 years, he'll be 11 and Sandrine will be 27, which is less than 3 times as old. Try a larger number: 25 or 35.

8. **D.** Use TACTIC 4, Chapter 13.
Could $x$ and $y$ be equal? Yes; if $a$ and $b$ are each 90, then $x$ and $y$ are each 40. Must they be equal? No; see the figure at the right, in which $x < y$. Neither column is *always*
greater, and the columns are not *always* equal (D).

9. **D.** If $a$ and $b$ had to be integers, the greatest $a + b$ could be is 49 (when the numbers are 1 and 48). However, the variables do not have to be integers. If $a = .1$, and $b = 480$, then $ab = 48$, and $a + b = 480.1$. Neither column is always greater, and the two columns are not always equal (D).

10. **B.** $bd = (3^a)(3^c) = 3^{a+c}$. [KEY FACT A16]
**Use TACTIC 2, Chapter 12. Pick easy-to-use numbers for $a$ and $c$; $a = 1$ and $c = 2$, for example. Then, $b = 3^1 = 3$ and $d = 3^2 = 9$, so $bd = 27$. Check the choices. Only $3^{a+c}$ works.

11. **C.** Let the number of male and female employees be $3x$ and $2x$, respectively. Then Column A = $20\%(3x) = .6x$ and Column B = $30\%(2x) = .6x$. The columns are equal.
**Do the same thing, except use a number. Assume there are 300 men and 200 women and calculate.

12. **C.** Mentally, or by using a Venn diagram,

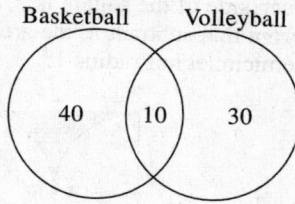

determine the number of girls who play only one sport. 40 play only basketball and 30 play only volleyball. The ratio is $40{:}30 = \frac{4}{3}$. The columns are equal (C).

13. **D.** Since $ab \neq 0$, neither $a$ nor $b$ is 0 [KEY FACT A3]. If $a$ and $b$ are each 1, then Column A = 4, and Column B = 0; if, however, $a = 1$ and $b = -1$, then Column A = 0 and Column B = 4. Neither column is always greater, and the two columns are not always equal (D).
**Column A = $a^2 + 2ab + b^2$ and Column B = $a^2 - 2ab + b^2$. After subtracting $a^2 + b^2$ from each column, we have to compare $2ab$ and $-2ab$: either one could be positive and the other negative.

14. **C.** In 1996, 50% of eleventh-graders used computers in school at least once a week, and 50% did not. Of the 50% that did not use computers in school at least once a week, 20% of them did use them the following year: 20% of 50% = $.20 \times .50 = .10 = 10\%$. So, in 1997, 60% (50% + 10%) of the twelfth-graders used computers in school at least once a week.

15. **E.** Of the 3,000,000 fourth-graders in 1990, approximately 70%, or 2,100,000, of them used a computer in school at least once a week. Four years later, in 1994, those 3,000,000 were eighth-graders, and 45%, or 1,350,000, of them used a computer in school at least once a week. This is a difference of 2,100,000 − 1,350,000 = 750,000.

16. **C.**  In each triangle the largest angle is the sum of the two smaller ones ($3 = 1 + 2$ and $9 = 2 + 7$), so each is a 90° angle. The columns are equal (C).
**Use TACTIC D2:** In ratio problems, write $x$ after each number and solve.
Column A: $x + 2x + 3x = 180 \Rightarrow 6x = 180 \Rightarrow x = 30 \Rightarrow 3x = 90$.
Column B: $2x + 7x + 9x = 180 \Rightarrow 18x = 180 \Rightarrow x = 10 \Rightarrow 9x = 90$.

17. **B.**  The perimeter of the shaded region is given as $4 + 2\pi$. You can easily prove that the lengths of the curved parts of the region are $2\pi$ and that the straight edges have a total length of 4, but you should just assume these values. Then each side of the square is 2, and its area is 4. From that subtract $\pi$, the area of a circle (two semicircles) of radius 1.

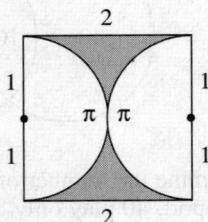

Since $\pi$ is slightly greater than 3, then $4 - \pi$ is less than 1. Column B is greater.

18. **C.**  Use TACTIC 1, Chapter 11. Draw a diagram. Since the distance between $(-4,1)$ and $(2,1)$ is 6, the diameter of the circle is 6 and the radius is 3. Then the area is $\pi(3)^2 = 9\pi$.

19. **E.**  By TACTIC E1, if the average of 5 numbers is 60, their sum is $5 \times 60 = 300$. The 4 given numbers add up to 100 ($10 + 20 + 30 + 40$), so the fifth one, $x$, is 200 ($300 - 100$).
**Use TACTIC 1, Chapter 12.** Test the choices, starting with 100. The average of 10, 20, 30, 40, and 100 is 40. That's too small. Eliminate Choices A, B, and C, and try a larger number—150 or 200: 200 works.

20. **E.**  Each of the given statements is true except Choice E.
(A) In 1991, more than 50% of the adults whose highest degree was at least a bachelor's degree participated in adult education, whereas among those whose highest educational attainment was a high school diploma or GED (high school equivalency diploma) fewer than 25% participated.

(B) From 1991 to 1995, among those adults whose highest educational attainment was grades 9–12, without earning a high school diploma, the rate of participation in adult education increased from about 15% to 23%, an increase of about 50%. None of the other groups had nearly that great an increase.
(C) Since the population of the country grew between 1991 and 1995, and the rate of participation in adult education programs increased in every category, the total number of people participating had to increase.
(D) From 1991 to 1995 the rate of participation in adult education for those who had attained at least a bachelor's degree increased from about 52% to 58%, the least increase of any group on *both* an absolute and percent basis.
(E) Without knowing how many adults have earned a college degree and how many have attended some college without earning a college degree, it is impossible to make this conclusion. For example, 50% of 100,000,000 is much more than 58% of 50,000,000.

21. **E.**  50% of 50,000,000 = 25,000,000;
20% of 20,000,000 = 4,000,000.
25,000,000:4,000,000 = 25:4 = 6.25:1.

22. **E.**  The total rent is $a + b$, so Bob's fractional share is $\dfrac{a}{a + b}$. To convert to a percent, simply multiply by 100%: $\dfrac{100a}{a + b}\%$.
**Use TACTIC 2, Chapter 12.** Pick two easy-to-use numbers. If Bob pays \$1 and Jack pays \$2, then Bob pays $\frac{1}{3}$ or $33\frac{1}{3}\%$ of the rent. Only $\dfrac{100a}{a + b}\%$ is equal to $33\frac{1}{3}\%$ when $a = 1$ and $b = 2$.

23. **C.**  Draw diagrams. The triangles in the two columns have the same base, $AB$, and the same height, $BC$, the distance between the two parallel sides. The areas of $\triangle ABC$ and $\triangle ABE$ are equal. The columns are equal (C).

24. **A.**  The area of each face of the large red cube is $(3)^2 = 9$. Therefore, the total surface area is $6 \times 9 = 54$. The surface area of each small cube is $6(1)^2 = 6$. So, the total surface area of the 27 small cubes is $27 \times 6 = 162$. Of the 162 small faces, 54 are painted red and $162 - 54 = 108$ are unpainted. Column A is greater.

25. C. You can't multiply out to look at the units digits of these numbers because they're too large ($14^{14}$ has 15 digits!). But you *can* do a little multiplication in order to see a pattern: $14^2 = 196$, $14^3 = 14 \times 196 = 2{,}744$, $14^4 = 14 \times 2{,}744 = 38{,}416$; the units digits of the powers of 14 alternate 4, 6, 4, 6, 4, ... The number 14 to an even power has a units digit of 6. *Every* power of 16 ends in 6: 16, 256, 4096, ... Therefore, Columns A and B are each equal to 6, and the answer is C. (*Note*: You don't need to do any multiplication. It is easy to reason that the product of any two numbers ending in 4 is a number ending in 6, and that the product of a number ending in 6 and a number ending in 4 is a number ending in 4, and so on.)

26. A. $a + 10\%(a) = a + .1a = 1.1a$. Also, $b - 10\%(b) = b - .1b = .9b$. Then, $1.1a = .9b$, and $\dfrac{a}{b} = \dfrac{.9}{1.1} = \dfrac{9}{11}$

    \*\*If after increasing $a$ and decreasing $b$ the results are equal, $a$ must be smaller than $b$. So, *the ratio of $a$ to $b$ must be less than 1.* Eliminate Choices C, D, and E. Now, either test Choices A and B or just guess. To test B, pick 2 numbers in the ratio of 9 to 10—90 and 100, for example: 90 increased by 10% is 99. 100 decreased by 10% is 90. They're not equal. Eliminate Choice B. The answer is Choice A. (110 decreased by 10% *is* 99.)

27. B. Let $x$ and $y$ be the radii of the two semicircles.

    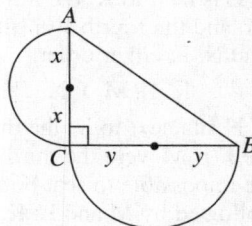

    Then the legs of right triangle $ACB$ are $2x$ and $2y$, and by the Pythagorean theorem $(2x)^2 + (2y)^2 = 4^2$. Then $4x^2 + 4y^2 = 16$, and $x^2 + y^2 = 4$. Since the area of a semicircle of radius $r$ is $\dfrac{1}{2}\pi r^2$, the sum of the areas of the semicircles is $\dfrac{1}{2}\pi x^2 + \dfrac{1}{2}\pi y^2 = \dfrac{1}{2}\pi(x^2 + y^2) = \dfrac{1}{2}\pi(4) = 2\pi$.

    \*\*Use TACTIC 2, Chapter 12. Pick numbers $a$ and $b$ for the legs of the triangle. For example, if $a$ is 2, then by the Pythagorean theorem $2^2 + b^2 = 4^2$.

28. C. Draw a Venn diagram and label each region. Let $x$ be the number of senior boys. Then $40 - x$ is the number of boys who are not seniors (i.e., are juniors), and $70 - x$ is the number of seniors who are not boys (i.e., are girls).

Then the number of junior girls =
$$100 - [(40 - x) + x + (70 - x)] =$$
$$100 - [110 - x] = x - 10.$$

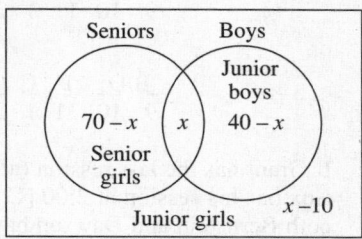

Since the number of junior girls must be at least 0, $x - 10 \geq 0 \Rightarrow x \geq 10$.

\*\*Use TACTIC 1, Chapter 12. Backsolve, but since we want the smallest number, start with Choice A. If there are no senior boys, then all 40 boys are juniors and all 70 seniors are girls; but that's 110 people. Eliminate A. If there are 5 senior boys, there will be 35 junior boys and 65 senior girls, a total of 105. Finally, check 10, which works.

# Section 3—Analytical Ability

1. D. The original statement is a conclusion. The correct answer is the argument from which it can be drawn; that is, Choice D. If Wilbur were six feet tall or less, he would be seated in the first row. He is not in the first row; therefore, he is not six feet tall or less. We can draw no conclusions from any of the other choices. They all allow the possibility that Wilbur is only 5'11" tall (or 3'11" tall, for that matter).

### Solutions 2–5

patients: B, C, D, E, F, G   times: 9, 10, 11, 1, 2, 3
F = 1:00   D < E   B < E   B < F   C << G

2. A. In conjunction with the given conditions, the requirement that Bernstein's session be at 10:00 completely determines the schedule. Since Cox and Grant need to have consecutive sessions [C << G], their sessions must be at 2:00 and 3:00, respectively. Since Bernstein's session must precede Edson's [B < E], Edson has to be scheduled for 11:00, and the first session of the day will go to Dawson. There is only 1 possible schedule:

    | D | B | E | F | C | G |
    |---|---|---|---|---|---|
    | 9 | 10 | 11 | 1 | 2 | 3 |

3. D. Friedman cannot have the first session [B < F]; so Friedman's session must be at 10:00 or 11:00. Grant has the 2:00 session [C << G]. Since both Bernstein and Dawson have their sessions before Edson has hers [B < E and D < E], Bernstein and Dawson have the other two morning slots, and Edson

has her session at 3:00. There are 2 possible schedules.

$$\underline{B}\ \underline{F}\ \underline{D}\ \underline{C}\ \underline{G}\ \underline{E}$$
$$9\ \ 10\ \ 11\ \ 1\ \ 2\ \ 3$$

or

$$\underline{B/D}\ \ \ \underline{F}\ \underline{C}\ \underline{G}\ \underline{E}$$
$$9\ \ 10\ \ 11\ \ 1\ \ 2\ \ 3$$

4. **D.** If Grant has the last session (at 3:00), then Cox has his session at 2:00 [C << G]. Since both Bernstein and Dawson have their sessions before Edson has hers, they must have their sessions at 9:00 and 10:00 (in either order), and Edson must have hers at 11:00.

$$\underline{B/D}\ \ \ \underline{E}\ \ \underline{F}\ \underline{C}\ \underline{G}$$
$$9\ \ 10\ \ 11\ \ 1\ \ 2\ \ 3$$

5. **E.** Since Cox's session is earlier in the day than Friedman's session (which is at 1:00), Cox and Grant have to have sessions at 9:00 and 10:00 or 10:00 and 11:00 [C << G]. In either case Bernstein must be the other patient to have a session in the morning [B < F]. The 2:00 and 3:00 slots must be for Dawson and Edson, in that order.

$$\underline{C}\ \underline{G}\ \underline{B}\ \underline{F}\ \underline{D}\ \underline{E}$$
$$9\ \ 10\ \ 11\ \ 1\ \ 2\ \ 3$$

or

$$\underline{B}\ \underline{C}\ \underline{G}\ \underline{F}\ \underline{D}\ \underline{E}$$
$$9\ \ 10\ \ 11\ \ 1\ \ 2\ \ 3$$

6. **E.** The conclusion of the argument states that all good athletes eat a well-balanced diet. Choice E shows that this is not true; there is at least one good athlete who does not eat a well-balanced diet. Choices B and C are both possibly true, but do not weaken the original argument. Choice D can be deduced from the argument.

7. **B.** The logic of the argument is valid, and Choice B is simply a rephrasing of the conclusion. Therefore, it must be true if the assumptions are true. It is possible for there to be some bad athletes who want to win (Choices A and D), and for some bad athletes to eat a well-balanced diet (Choice C). Choice E contradicts the argument's conclusion.

8. **D.** Regardless of how good it is and whether or not it conforms to the university's style manual, no essay that has three spelling errors can receive an A. None of the other choices must be true. Choices A, B, and E all introduce concepts that are not discussed in the given statements. Choice C is wrong because conformity to the style manual and correct spelling need not be the only criteria for an A paper; they are necessary but not sufficient conditions for earning an A.

## Solutions 9–13

J: Fr    K: Eng/Chi    L: Eng/Ger
M: Fr/Ger    N: Fr/Chi

9. **E.** Only Choice E is acceptable.
Choice A is unacceptable because J and L have no common language.
Choice B is unacceptable because J and K have no common language.
Choice C is unacceptable because L and N have no common language.
Choice D is unacceptable because K and M have no common language.

10. **D.** Since J speaks only French and there is only one other diplomat in attendance (M) who speaks French, J must be seated at one end, next to M. M, in turn must be seated next to L, the only diplomat other than J with whom he can converse. Finally, K, who can converse with L, must be at the other end. This acceptable order—J, M, L, K—shows that Choice D is true and that none of the other choices could be true.

11. **B.** When K is absent, the only diplomat with whom L can speak is M. Therefore, L *must* sit at one end of the table next to M. Choice C cannot be true; Choices A, D, and E *could* be true, but none of them must be true.

12. **C.** The diplomat sitting next to K could be L (with whom he can converse in English) or N (with whom he can converse in Chinese).
   • If L is next to K, the third diplomat must be M, and the fourth and fifth diplomats are J and N, in either order.

   K, L, M, J, N    K, L, M, N, J

   • If N sits next to K, the third diplomat must be J (if M were the third diplomat, it would be impossible to seat both J and L). J is then followed by M and L: K, N, J, M, L.
   • There are 3 ways to seat the diplomats.

13. **D.** N can converse with J and M in French and with K in Chinese. If J and M were on either side of N, there would be no other French speaker to sit next to J; so N must sit next to K, who in turn must sit next to L. On the other side of N, J and M can be seated in either order: J, M, N, K, L or M, J, N, K, L (or the reverse of these, with L on the left).

14. **E.** In this argument, the first sentence states the conclusion; the second sentence states the evidence. However, there is no real connection between the two statements unless the assumption given in Choice E is accepted as valid.

## Solutions 15–18

students: A, B, C, D, E, F, G    counselors: R, S, T

each student: 1 counselor

each counselor: 1, 2, or 3 students

A = B    C ≠ E    C ≠ F    D ≠ E    D ≠ F    F ↛ T

15. B.    Since neither C nor D can be assigned to the same counselor as E or F, each of them must be assigned to Thomas. Since Thomas can be assigned at most three of the students, he cannot have both A and B; and since A and B must have the same counselor, neither can be assigned to Thomas. Each of the other choices could be true.

```
A B C D E F G
↘ ↘ ↓ ↓ ↓ ↓ ↓
T T T T T S R
```

16. D.    The given conditions almost completely determine the assignments. Since A and C are assigned to Rosen, and since A and B must have the same counselor, B is also assigned to Rosen. Since F cannot be assigned to Thomas, and since Rosen is fully booked, F must be assigned to Smith. Since D cannot be assigned the same counselor as F (or E), D must be assigned to Thomas and E to Smith. The only flexibility is in the assignment of G. If G is assigned to Smith, then Choice D is true. None of the other choices could be true.

```
A B C D E F G
↓ ↓ ↓ ↓ ↓ ↓
R R R T S S
```

17. E.    Since A and B must have the same counselor, A must be assigned to Smith. Eliminate Choice A. If either D or G is assigned to Smith, then F must be assigned to Rosen (F is not allowed to be assigned to Thomas and Smith already has three students). But C and F cannot be assigned to the same counselor. Eliminate Choices B and C.

```
A B C D E F G
↓ ↓ ↘ ↓   ↓ ↓
S S R S   R S
```

If C is assigned to Rosen and D is assigned to Thomas, then both E and F would have to be assigned to Smith. This is not possible since Smith already has two students (A and B). Eliminate Choice D.

```
A B C D E F G
↓ ↓ ↓ ↓ ↓ ↓
S S R T S S
```

Choice E is possible as shown below:

```
A B C D E F G
↓ ↓ ↓ ↓ ↓ ↓ ↓
S S T T S R T/R
```

18. E.    Since F cannot be assigned to Thomas, B and F (and A) must be assigned to either Rosen or Smith.

•  Assume they are assigned to Rosen. Since neither C nor D can be assigned the same counselor as E, either E is assigned to Smith and C and D are assigned to Thomas, or vice versa. In either case, to assure that E's counselor not have only one student, G must be assigned to E's counselor. Therefore, there are two possibilities:

```
A B C D E F G
↓ ↓ ↓ ↓ ↓ ↓ ↓
S S T T R S R
```

or

```
A B C D E F G
↓ ↓ ↓ ↓ ↓ ↓ ↓
S S R R T S T
```

•  In the same way, there are also two possibilities if A, B, and F are assigned to Smith.

```
A B C D E F G
↓ ↓ ↓ ↓ ↓ ↓ ↓
R R T T S R S
```

or

```
A B C D E F G
↓ ↓ ↓ ↓ ↓ ↓ ↓
R R S S T R T
```

•  So there are 4 different ways to assign the students.

19. C.    Reducing coffee consumption in general will not guarantee a healthier population (A) if "heavy" consumers do not reduce their coffee intake. Reducing coffee consumption would make those who drink a morning cup of coffee feel less well (B). (C) is a logical conclusion since heavy consumption increases heart attack risk. There is no information in the passage to justify the assertion about percolated coffee (D). If coffee may protect against colon cancer, Choice E is not true.

## Solutions 20–23

men: J, K, L    women: P, Q, R

days: M, T, W, Th, F, S

M and W alternate    K < R    P < L

20. C.    Only Choice C doesn't violate any of the conditions.

Choices A and D violate the condition that the men and women alternate hosting the work sessions.

Choice B violates the condition that the session at P's house precedes the one at L's house.

Choice E violates the condition that the session at K's house precedes the one at R's house.

21. C.    Since L is the host on Tuesday, the other two men, J and K, are the hosts on Thursday and Saturday. Since K hosts a session earlier in the week than R does, K cannot host on Saturday; so K is the host on Thursday.

$$\frac{\phantom{M}}{M} \frac{L}{T} \frac{\phantom{W}}{W} \frac{K}{Th} \frac{\phantom{F}}{F} \frac{L}{S}$$

22. E.    Since J is the host on Monday, the other two men, K and L, are the hosts on Wednesday and Friday. Since L must be a host later in the week than P, L cannot be the host on Wednesday. So K is the host on Wednesday and L is the host on Friday. Since P must host a session earlier in the week than L, P must host on Thursday and R on Saturday. The schedule is

$$\frac{J}{M} \frac{Q}{T} \frac{K}{W} \frac{P}{Th} \frac{L}{F} \frac{R}{S}$$

23. E.    If J is the host on Saturday, then K and L are the hosts on Tuesday and Thursday. Consider the two cases.
   • If L is the host on Tuesday and K is the host on Thursday, then in order to satisfy both K < R and P < L, there is only 1 possibility: the order must be

$$\frac{P}{M} \frac{L}{T} \frac{Q}{W} \frac{K}{Th} \frac{R}{F} \frac{J}{S}$$

   • If K is the host on Tuesday and L is the host on Thursday, there are 3 possible schedules:

$$\frac{P}{M} \frac{K}{T} \frac{Q}{W} \frac{L}{Th} \frac{R}{F} \frac{J}{S}$$

$$\frac{P}{M} \frac{K}{T} \frac{R}{W} \frac{L}{Th} \frac{Q}{F} \frac{J}{S}$$

$$\frac{Q}{M} \frac{K}{T} \frac{P}{W} \frac{L}{Th} \frac{R}{F} \frac{J}{S}$$

   • There are 4 ways to complete the schedule.

## Solutions 24–28

cities: A, B, C, D, H, M   years: 2004–2009
C = 2005    A < H    B << D or D << B

24. E.    Only Choice E doesn't violate any of the conditions.
Since Chicago is the host in 2005, eliminate Choice B. Also, since Boston and Denver must host in consecutive years, and neither is the host in 2005, neither can be the host in 2004; eliminate Choices A and C. Finally, Houston must host a meeting sometime after Atlanta does, so Houston cannot host the first of the meetings; eliminate Choice D.

$$\frac{A}{4} \frac{C}{5} \frac{B/D}{6} \frac{M}{7} \frac{H}{8} \frac{\phantom{9}}{9}$$

25. B.    With Chicago in 2005 and Miami in 2008, the only consecutive years available for Boston and Denver are 2006 and 2007. Then, since Atlanta must be a host before Houston, Atlanta has to be the host in 2004 and Houston in 2009. There are two possible schedules, depending on the order of Boston and Denver.

26. E.    If Miami is the host in 2007, the consecutive years available for Boston and Denver are 2008 and 2009; so Choices C and D could be true. Since Atlanta must be a host before Houston, Choices A and B must be true. Only Choice E cannot be true.

$$\frac{A}{4} \frac{C}{5} \frac{H}{6} \frac{M}{7} \frac{B/D}{8 \quad 9}$$

27. C.    Since Atlanta must host a meeting before Houston does, Atlanta cannot be the host in 2009.
   • Can Atlanta be the host in 2007? No, because then Denver would be the host in 2009 (Boston and Denver need to host consecutively), and again Atlanta would not precede Houston.

$$\frac{\phantom{4}}{4} \frac{\phantom{5}}{5} \frac{\phantom{6}}{6} \frac{A}{7} \frac{B}{8} \frac{D}{9}$$

   • The latest that Atlanta could be the host is 2006, which could occur if the final order was

$$\frac{M}{4} \frac{C}{5} \frac{A}{6} \frac{D}{7} \frac{B}{8} \frac{H}{9}$$

28. A.    The only cities that are eligible to host a meeting in 2004 are Atlanta and Miami (see the solution to Question 24). So one of them must be the host in 2004 and neither is the host in 2005 (Chicago is). The other choices are all possible.

29. E.    Each of Choices A, B, C, and D *could* account for the situation described, *if* some additional sales information were known. Only Choice E is sufficient, on its own, to explain the apparent contradiction. If total sales in 1998 had been $100, $10 of which were earned from June to August, then $90 was earned during the other nine months. If in 1999, sales from June to August were only $5 (half of the 1998 figure) and sales in the other nine months were $99 (10% more than the $90 in 1998), the total sales in 1999 would be greater.

30. E.    The only difference between the "handouts" which the author deplores and the "subsidies" he favors is the words used to describe them. In one case, the words used are negatively loaded; in the other, they are positive, or at least neutral. Choice A is directly contrary to fact. Choices B and C are true, but of minor importance. Choice D is probably false; the reference in the argument to the thousands of widget industry jobs does indicate the significance of the industry for the U.S. economy.

## Solutions 31–34

salespeople: J, K, L, M, N, P, Q   cities: S, T

$$3 \Rightarrow S \quad 3 \Rightarrow T \quad J \Rightarrow S \quad L \Rightarrow T$$

$$K \rightarrow (\sim L \wedge \sim P) \quad N \leftrightarrow Q$$

31. **B.** Only Choice B doesn't violate any of the conditions.
Choices A and D violate the condition that Q and N must attend the same conference [$N \leftrightarrow Q$].
Choice C violates the condition that K and P cannot attend the same conference [$K \rightarrow \sim P$].
Choice E violates the condition that J goes to Stockholm [$J \Rightarrow S$].

32. **C.** If Q goes to Tokyo, so does N [$N \leftrightarrow Q$], and it is given that L goes to Tokyo. J goes to Stockholm with two of K, M, and P; but K and P cannot go to the same conference [$K \rightarrow \sim P$], so one of them must stay home, and the other goes to Stockholm with M.

    | J | K | L | M | N | P | Q |
    |---|---|---|---|---|---|---|
    | ↓ |   | ↓ | ↓ | ↓ |   | ↓ |
    | S |   | T | S | T |   | T |

33. **A.** If Q goes to Stockholm, then so does N [$N \leftrightarrow Q$], as well as J. So K does not go to Stockholm. Since K cannot attend a conference with L [$K \rightarrow \sim L$], who is going to Tokyo, K cannot go to Tokyo either.

34. **A.** K cannot go to Tokyo with L [$K \rightarrow \sim L$], so K goes to Stockholm with J. Since only three people can go to Stockholm, N and Q must go to Tokyo with L. This leaves M and P. Since P cannot go to Stockholm with K [$K \rightarrow \sim P$], M goes to Stockholm and P does not attend a conference.

    | J | K | L | M | N | P | Q |
    |---|---|---|---|---|---|---|
    | ↓ | ↓ | ↓ | ↓ | ↓ |   | ↓ |
    | S | S | T | S | T |   | T |

35. **E.** Choice A exposes the argument's failure to admit that many specific problems may be solved by persons who don't understand the broad picture; Choice B exposes the assumption that because generalists are needed, *all* persons should be educated as generalists; Choice C exposes the false dichotomy between specialization and seeing the broad picture; and Choice D attacks the implicit assumption that fewer specialists are needed. Choice E, however, does not weaken the argument, because the argument is simply calling for a broad, liberal education, not necessarily the traditional liberal education.

# What You Need to Know About the GRE Analytical Writing Test

## How Is the New Writing Test Organized?

The new analytical writing section is organized in two parts. In Part 1, "Present Your Perspective on an Issue," you have 45 minutes to write an essay expressing your point of view on a particular issue. You will be given your choice of two quotations, each of which states an opinion about an issue; you will probably write a better essay if you go for the quotation that "grabs" you, whose topic seems more appealing to you.

Your job is to take a stand and to support it, drawing on your own experiences and on your readings to come up with examples that reinforce your argument. It does not matter what stand you take: there is no "correct" position, no one true answer. Many different approaches can work. You can agree completely with the quotation's point of view. You can dispute it absolutely. You can disagree with some aspects of the quote, but agree with others. What matters is how you present your case.

Here are two sample quotations like the quotations you will find on Part 1 of the analytical writing test. To see the entire pool of GRE "Issues" quotations, click on the GRE web site: *www.gre.org/issuetop.html*

- "Historians and other social scientists have far less social utility than biochemists and engineers, whose discoveries benefit humanity."

- "'The heart has its reasons of which reason knows nothing': humans are incapable of living wholly rational lives."

Part 2 of the analytical writing section asks you to perform a different but complementary task. In Part 2, "Analyze an Argument," you have 30 minutes to write an essay critiquing the logical soundness of an argument. You will be given one short passage in which an author makes a claim and backs it up, giving reasons that may well be flawed. You get no choice of passages to analyze: you must work with whatever passage comes up on your screen.

This time your job is *not* to advocate a particular point of view. This is not the moment for you to agree or disagree with the author; it is the moment for you to weigh the validity of his or her reasoning. Your approach is analytical and expository, not argumentative or persuasive. Examine carefully what the author offers as evidence. Note what she or he claims explicitly. Note also what she or he assumes (not necessarily justifiably!).

Here is a brief passage like the passage you will find on Part 2 of the analytical writing test. To see the entire pool of GRE "Arguments" passages, click on the GRE web site: *www.gre.org/argutop.html*

- "If you look closely at Oakville's two leading private high schools—Collegiate Preparatory High School and Exover Academy—you must conclude that Collegiate is unmistakably superior to the Academy. Collegiate has a staff of 35 teachers, many of them with doctorates. In contrast, Exover has a staff of 22, several holding only a bachelor's degree. Moreover, Collegiate's average class size is 12, compared to Exover's average class size of 20; Collegiate's students receive much more individual attention than their peers do at the Academy. Students graduating from Collegiate High are also accepted by better universities than Exover graduates are: 40% of last year's Collegiate senior class went on to Ivy League colleges, compared to only 15% of Exover's senior class. Thus, if you want your children to get individual attention from their high school teacher and would like them to get in to good colleges, you should send them to Collegiate Prep."

## How Can You Practice for the New Writing Test?

When you sign up to take the GRE General Test, you will eventually be sent *Powerprep*, a CD-ROM containing test preparation software for the General Test and Writing Assessment. (The GRE's new analytical writing section is the same as the former Writing Assessment test, which you previously had to take separately. Don't worry about the name change; it has no significance.) However, you do not have to wait for your copy of *Powerprep* to come in the mail. You can download it *today* from the GRE web site—*for free!*

*Powerprep* is helpful because it uses the same GRE word processing software that you will have to use to write your essays during your computer-based test. It is a very basic word processor that lets you perform very basic tasks. You can insert text, delete text, and move text around using a cut-and-paste function. You can also undo an action you've just performed.

Familiarize yourself with this word processing software so that, on the test date, you'll be comfortable using it. This software simulates actual testing conditions and presents actual essay topics. Practice writing your essays while you keep one eye on the clock. You need to develop a sense of how much time to allow for thinking over your essay and how much time to set aside for the actual writing.

### A Word of Warning:
Attention, Mac users: *Powerprep* is compatible only with IBMs or PCs. If you own an Apple MacIntosh computer, you'll have to gain access to a PC in order to run *Powerprep*. Do it, even if it means making an extra trip to the campus computer lab or the nearest public library.

# Should You Sign Up to Take the Test Before October 1?

If you have already been practicing for the General Test, do well on multiple-choice examinations, enjoy analytical reasoning and logic problems, and think you may have trouble writing essays under timed conditions, you may want to register to take the GRE *before* October 1, 2002, when the new format goes into effect. You want to take the test under the conditions that show you to best advantage. However, you don't want the graduate schools to which you are applying to think you're ducking the writing test (even if you are!). Check with your schools; find out what they prefer. And if they want you to take the analytical writing test, then practice and take it. You'll be fine.

The following documentation applies if you purchased
*How to Prepare for the GRE Test, 14th Edition* book with CD-ROM.
Please disregard this information if your version does not contain the CD-ROM.

### Documentation

#### MINIMUM HARDWARD REQUIREMENTS

The program will run on a PC with
1. Intel Pentium® 166MHZ or equivalent processor
2. 16 MB RAM
3. MS Window 95/98/NT/2000
4. SVGA (256 Colors) Monitor
5. 8X CD-ROM drive
6. Keyboard, Mouse

The program will run on a Macintosh with
1. PowerPC 8600
2. Operating System 8.0 (or later)
3. 32 MB RAM
4. SVGA (256 Colors) Monitor
5. 8X CD-ROM drive
6. Keyboard, Mouse

Barron's GRE CD-ROM includes an "autorun" feature that automatically launches the application when the CD is inserted into the CD drive. In the unlikely event that the autorun features are disabled, alternate launching instructions are provided below.

#### Windows 95/98/NT/2000:

1. Put the Barron's GRE CD-ROM into the CD-ROM drive.
2. Click on the Start button and choose Run.
3. Type D:\GRE.EXE (assuming the CD is in drive D), then click OK.

#### Macintosh:

1. Put the Barron's GRE CD-ROM into the CD-ROM drive.
2. Double-click the GRE Installer icon.
3. Follow the onscreen instructions.